DATE D'

The Making of Multinational Enterprise

The Making of Multinational Enterprise

A Sourcebook of Tables Based on a Study of 187 Major
U. S. Manufacturing Corporations

JAMES W. VAUPEL
JOAN P. CURHAN

Graduate School of Business Administration
Harvard University

Division of Research
Graduate School of Business Administration
Harvard University
Boston · 1969

Library of Congress Catalog Card No. 70–94408

SBN 87584–081–7

PRINTED IN THE UNITED STATES OF AMERICA

FOREWORD

This book presents a body of data that have been drawn together over a four-year period by the Multinational Enterprise Study at the Harvard Business School. The figures are unique. They trace the development since 1900 of the 10,000 or so foreign subsidiaries of 187 U. S. parent companies. The direct investments of these 187 parent companies in manufacturing facilities outside of the United States and Canada have come to represent over 80% of all private direct investment in manufacturing by United States firms in the same areas.

A large proportion of the data in this book was obtained from public records. Indeed, our first step in the compilation of these data was to scour the companies' official reports to the Securities and Exchange Commission and their annual reports to stockholders, as well as business histories, business periodicals, and similar sources. These records were then verified and elaborated by interviews with most of the 187 companies. During the course of these interviews, commitments to preserve the confidentiality of some of the materials were undertaken.

In the ongoing research at Harvard, a considerable number of hypotheses and hunches are being tested with these materials, eventually to be described and presented in a series of forthcoming books. The systems of classification of industries and firms that are used in some of the tables offer a hint of some of the hypotheses that are being pursued. Researchers elsewhere, however, may have their own uses for the data. It seemed desirable, therefore, to make the materials available without delay.

The tabulations presented in this book have been selected from our data bank with an eye to their general utility for researchers. In some cases, our obligations to cooperating companies imposed limits on the data that could be published. We hope, however, eventually to develop a user's manual which will make it possible for other researchers to have direct access to the underlying data without violating the confidentiality constraints.

One particularly satisfying aspect of this segment of the multinational enterprise study was the discovery of the talents of its two principal authors, James W. Vaupel and Joan P. Curhan. (James Vaupel is a Research Assistant at the Harvard Business School and a doctoral candidate for a joint degree from the John F. Kennedy School of Government and the Harvard Business School. Joan P. Curhan is Visiting Associate in Research at the Harvard Business School.) Vaupel's main contribution was in designing the necessary data storage and data processing systems, and in developing the form and structure of this volume. Mrs. Curhan's contribution consisted of establishing the methods for collecting the basic data, then organizing and managing their collection.

The Multinational Enterprise Study is financed primarily by a grant from the Ford Foundation to the Harvard Business School. The large group of research assistants drawn together by Mrs. Curhan from a dozen universities during the summer months and from a few universities in the Boston area during the rest of the year, were financed primarily by the College Work-Study Program (sponsored by the United States Office of Education). To both these sources of financial support, to the staff of Baker Library at the Harvard Business School, and to the 187 co-operating companies we express our appreciation.

RAYMOND VERNON
Co-ordinator, Multinational Enterprise Study,
Harvard Business School

Soldiers Field
Boston, Massachusetts
June 1969

TABLE OF CONTENTS

Chapter 2 — The Expansion of Parent Systems (*Continued*)

Chapter 2 — The Expansion of Parent Systems *(Continued)*

Chapter 3 — The Proliferation of Foreign Subsidiaries (*Continued*)

Chapter 4 — Varieties of Entry (*Continued*)

Chapter 5 — Patterns of Ownership (*Continued*)

Section 3 — The Flow of Manufacturing by Characteristic of Parent

Chapter 5 — Patterns of Ownership *(Continued)*

CHAPTER 1
Orientation and Background

CHAPTER 1
Orientation and Background

The data tabulated in this book are based principally upon published materials such as S.E.C. Form 10-K's, annual reports, books, and magazine articles. They were gathered by over 100 part-time student researchers over a four-year period. Library research on the 187 parent systems in the study was augmented and verified through one-day or two-day interviews, conducted in the summer of 1968, with 167 of the 187 U. S. parents. Beginning in the summer of 1968 and continuing into spring of 1969, the data were prepared for computer analysis. The tables appearing in this book are photo-offset copies of output from computer programs run in June 1969.

While extensive, the data are clearly limited.

First, the 187 U. S. parents are all classified as *manufacturing* enterprises on the basis of their U. S. activities.

Second, the 187 U. S. enterprises constitute only a *sample*; although the coverage of this sample, as indicated below, is high, it does not represent a complete census of the foreign activities of U. S. manufacturing enterprises.

Third, the tables are in terms of the *number* of parent systems and the *number* of foreign subsidiaries: nowhere in these tables are data concerning sales or assets presented.

Fourth, the tables deal only with subsidiaries incorporated in a foreign country: foreign branches are not included. Although relatively little manufacturing is done through branches, this omission may be relevant in some contexts.

Fifth, most of the tables present measures of flow (e.g., the number of subsidiaries that commenced manufacture in a specified country and year), rather than measures of stock (e.g., the number of subsidiaries engaged in manufacture in a specified country and year). However, some stock figures are presented, albeit on a highly aggregated basis; and some figures on the deletion of subsidiaries for various causes also are included. Accordingly, the reader can generally estimate stock figures for disaggregated categories, with margins of error of less than 10%.

Sixth, although the response of the enterprises in the study was by and large excellent, some characteristics of the foreign subsidiaries and parent systems are unknown. The reader should be alert to the implications of these gaps in the data. For example, the "main activity" (whether manufacturing, sales, etc.) of about 22% of the subsidiaries in the study was not available. As some of these subsidiaries undoubtedly engage in manufacturing, the numbers in the tables concerning manufacturing subsidiaries are low. To give another example, subsidiaries whose liquidation or expropriation has not been reported are assumed not to have been liquidated or expropriated. Thus, according to the data, two manufacturing subsidiaries are reported in existence in Cuba in 1967.

Finally, the gathering, coding, and processing of the data file was a complex operation which involved the employment of more than 100 part-time and full-time student researchers as well as the manipulation of the equivalent of more than 100,000 computer cards. In a research effort of this magnitude, despite all precautions, checks, and double-checks, some errors will almost inevitably come to light.

SECTION 2 — ORGANIZATION OF THIS BOOK

This chapter contains the text needed to introduce the tables, while Chapters 2 through 5 contain the tables themselves. Each of the tables lists countries and regions down the page, and years or periods across the page. The tables are grouped into sections and chapters as described below.

Chapter 2 provides a record of the international spread of the 187 U. S. parent systems, breaking down the time span since 1900 into 20 periods. Chapter 3 presents a similar record in terms of the more than 10,000 foreign subsidiaries of these 187 parent systems. Chapter 4 focuses on the subsidiaries' condition on entry (whether newly formed, acquired, or "descended" from previously existing subsidiaries contained in the file); for this chapter the data are collapsed into three time periods. Chapter 5 focuses on the percentage of ownership held by a subsidiary's parent (whether wholly owned, majority interest, or minority interest), and covers the same three time periods.

There are six sections which cross Chapters 2–5 as a woof crosses a warp. Section 1 in each of the chapters presents an overview of the flow and stock of manufacturing and non-manufacturing subsidiaries. The next four sections focus on the flow of manufacturing subsidiaries. Section 2 in each of the chapters contains tables based on the principal industries of the parent systems, while Section 3 contains tables based on various other characteristics of the parent systems. Similarly, Section 4 contains tables based on the industries of the foreign subsidiaries, while Section 5 contains tables based on other characteristics of the foreign subsidiaries. In Section 6, as in Section 1, data are presented on both manufacturing and non-manufacturing subsidiaries. The tables in Section 6 deal with the number of subsidiaries undergoing changes in main activity (e.g., from non-manufacturing to manufacturing), in ownership (e.g., from joint venture to wholly owned) and in state of being (e.g., sale or liquidation). The sections in each chapter are identical, except that tables which would be meaningless in any section are omitted. For this reason Section 6 of Chapter 2 is not included.

SECTION 3 — THE SAMPLE OF 187 COMPANIES

The data relate to the foreign subsidiaries of 187 major U. S. manufacturing enterprises. These enterprises, which are listed at the end of this chapter, were chosen by two quite arbitrary rules:

(1) The enterprise appeared in *Fortune*'s "500 Largest U. S. Industrial Corporations," for the year 1964, published in 1965, or for the year 1963, published in 1964.

(2) At the end of 1963, the U. S. parent system held equity interests in manufacturing enterprises located in 6 or more foreign countries, such equity interest in each case amounting to 25% or more of the total equity.

"Manufacturing" is used here to include assembly and packaging plants. Once a U. S. parent system qualified for the study, all foreign enterprises in which it owned 5% or more of the equity, non-manufacturing as well as manufacturing, were included in the study. If a parent corporation in the study merged with a corporation outside the study after 1963, then all the foreign enterprises of the successor corporation were included in the study. Although U. S. parent systems were selected on the basis of their characteristics in 1963 and 1964, data on these corporations and their subsidiaries were gathered to the end of 1967; tables presenting data on systems should be interpreted with this in mind, therefore, for the years following 1964.

SECTION 4 — COVERAGE OF THE SAMPLE

It would be helpful for some purposes to know how closely the sample of 187 systems comes to approximating all manufacturing operations abroad controlled by U. S. parents. Unfortunately, data concerning this universe are sparse and only a few comparisons can be given.

A 1931 U. S. government study [1] states that in 1929 there were 1,057 foreign manufacturing subsidiaries of U. S. enterprises, 611 of them outside of Canada. Our sample of foreign manufacturing subsidiaries in 1929 comes to over 40% of the total number reported in this study and over 50% of the number outside Canada.

A more recent U. S. government study [2] states that in 1957 there were 3,481 foreign manufacturing subsidiaries of U. S. companies outside the petroleum industry, and of these 2,316 were outside of Canada. Our sample outside the petroleum industry in 1957 includes, as before, over 40% of the total number of foreign manufacturing subsidiaries and more than 50% of the number outside Canada.

A timely but less extensive study by Booz, Allen & Hamilton [3] states that between 1961 and 1967, 3,037 foreign manufacturing subsidiaries were established by U. S. corporations. In our sample more than 70% of this number of manufacturing subsidiaries were established during the same period. For some countries and regions, however, our sample exceeds 100% of the Booz, Allen & Hamilton sample.

As the corporations in our sample are very much larger than average, the percentage of sales or assets accounted for by the companies in our sample is probably

[1] *American Branch Factories Abroad*, Senate Document No. 258, 71st Congress, 3d Session, 1931, Table 4.

[2] *U. S. Business Investments in Foreign Countries*, U. S. Department of Commerce, Office of Business Economics, by Samuel Pizer and Frederick Cutler, U. S. Government Printing Office, Washington, D.C., 1960.

[3] "What U. S. Companies are Doing Abroad: A Statistical Summary (prepared in cooperation with Booz, Allen & Hamilton, Inc.)," *Business Abroad*, May 1969, page 13.

larger than the percentage based on number. From official U. S. data it can be calculated that if our sample included the 143 U. S. corporations with largest direct investments abroad in manufacturing, the sample would represent more than 80% of total direct investments abroad in manufacturing. As the sample of 187 includes nearly all of the U. S. corporations with large foreign manufacturing investments and as the sample has a higher coverage outside Canada than it does in the aggregate, our estimate is that the sample represents over 70% of U. S. foreign direct manufacturing investment and over 80% of U. S. foreign direct manufacturing investment outside Canada. Some rough estimates of the size of each of the 187 systems' foreign manufacturing investment produce a similar result.

SECTION 5 — THE VARIABLES FOR CLASSIFICATION

A number of different variables are used in the tables for classification purposes, some based on a characteristic of foreign subsidiaries and some based on a characteristic of parent systems. Some relevant definitions and other data relating to these variables are given below.

(1) "Country or region" means country or region of incorporation of the subsidiary. "Outside White Commonwealth" means outside the United Kingdom, Ireland, Canada, South Africa, Rhodesia, Australia, and New Zealand. "Outside Developed World" means outside of Europe, Canada, South Africa, Rhodesia, Australia, New Zealand, and Japan. "Scandinavia" includes Denmark, Norway, Sweden, and Finland, but not Iceland. "Southern Dominions" include South Africa, Rhodesia, Australia, and New Zealand.

(2) "Year of entry" of a subsidiary is the year in which it acquired subsidiary status in the parent system. If the parent system is the result of a merger, as in the case of Sperry Rand, then the year of entry is the year the subsidiary acquired such status in one of the merged companies.

(3) "Year" in the tables on stock of subsidiaries means December 31st of year.

(4) "Descendant" subsidiaries are (a) those that were formed when antecedent subsidiaries were merged or broken up, as well as (b) in the case of manufacturing subsidiaries, those that had previously been non-manufacturing subsidiaries and had commenced manufacture.

(5) "System ownership percentage" is the total percentage of ownership in a subsidiary held by that subsidiary's immediate parents in the system.

(6) "Activity" of a subsidiary is classified as manufacturing if the subsidiary does any manufacturing, assembling, or packaging. Otherwise, the subsidiary is classified by its primary activity — sales, extraction, other, or unknown.

(7) Product classifications are those given in the *Standard Industrial Classification Manual*, by the U. S. Technical Committee on Industrial Classification, published in 1967.

(8) Each firm was classified by the industry that accounted for the major share of its sales. The classification used is that provided by the Securities and Exchange Commission, *1967 Directory of Companies Filing Annual Reports with the Securities and Exchange Commission* (New York, 1967); except that Litton Industries, Inc., is classified in the electronics industry (SIC 365–367) in preference to the business machine and computer industry (SIC 357). Tables based on this classification are contained in Section 2 of each of the Chapters 2–5. The phrase "Systems in the . . . industry" means that the industry specified is the primary industry of the system.

(9) For system classifications according to sales, R & D intensity, advertising intensity, human capital intensity, physical capital intensity, growth in sales, and return on investment, "low" means less than or equal to the median of the systems for that variable, while "high" means greater than the median.

(10) System financial data, unless otherwise noted, were taken from the Standard and Poor's Compustat computer tape service, for 1966.

(11) "R & D intensity," the ratio of R & D expenditures to sales, is from *News Front*, January 1966, page 37; February 1966, page 40; and November 1965, page 16.

(12) "Advertising intensity," the ratio of advertising to sales, is from *News Front*, March 1966, pages 40–43.

(13) "Human capital intensity" is based upon the average compensation per employee.

(14) "Physical capital intensity" is the ratio of assets to sales.

(15) "Date system first manufactured outside U. S. and Canada" is the date when the system commenced operation of its first manufacturing subsidiary or *branch* outside the U. S. and Canada.

(16) "Organizational stage" is based on a classification scheme described by A. D. Chandler [4] and elaborated by John M. Stopford.[5] Basically, "Stage II" represents the centralized, functionally-departmentalized organization, while "Stage III" represents the multi-product divisional organization. "Stage III" is divided into two substages: "ID" and "Other." "ID" is an abbreviation of "international division" and denotes those enterprises which manage their foreign operations through an international division. "Other" designates those enterprises which organize their foreign operations into worldwide product divisions, area divisions, or some combination of these.

[4] A. D. Chandler, Jr., *Strategy and Structure*, Cambridge, Mass., M.I.T. Press, 1962.

[5] John M. Stopford, "Growth and Organizational Change in the Multinational Firm," unpublished D.B.A. thesis, Harvard Business School, June, 1968; and Lawrence E. Fouraker and John M. Stopford, "Organizational Structure and Multinational Strategy," *Administrative Science Quarterly*, Vol. 13, No. 1, June 1968, pages 47–64.

(17) "Product diversity" is measured by the number of different three-digit SIC industries in which the system's manufactured products appear. Systems have high "product diversity in the U. S." if they manufacture in 10 or more of these industries in the U. S. Systems have high "product diversity abroad" if they manufacture in 5 or more of these industries in foreign countries.

(18) "Geographical diversity" is measured by the number of foreign countries in which the system has manufacturing subsidiaries. Systems have high "geographical diversity" if they have manufacturing subsidiaries in more than 13 foreign countries.

(19) Subsidiaries are classified into each of the industries in which they manufacture.

(20) A "significant" change in system ownership percentage occurs if the 50% line or the 95% line in such ownership is crossed.

Section 6 — List of 187 Companies

Abbott Laboratories
ABEX Corporation
Addressograph-Multigraph Corporation
Allied Chemical Corporation
Allis-Chalmers Manufacturing Company
Aluminum Company of America
American Can Company
American Cyanamid Company
American Home Products Corporation
American Machine & Foundry Company
American Metal Climax, Incorporated
American Smelting and Refining
  Company
American Standard
Archer-Daniels-Midland Company
Armco Steel Corporation
Armour & Company
Armstrong Cork Company
Atlas Chemical Industries, Incorporated

Beatrice Foods Company
Beech-Nut Life Savers, Incorporated
Bendix Corporation
Black & Decker Manufacturing Company
Borden Company

Borg-Warner Corporation
Bristol-Myers Company
Brunswick Corporation
Budd Company
Burlington Industries, Incorporated

Cabot Corporation
Campbell Soup Company
Carborundum Company
Carnation Company
Caterpillar Tractor Company
Celanese Corporation
Champion Spark Plug Company
Chemetron Corporation
Chesebrough-Pond's Incorporated
Chicago Pneumatic Tool Company
Chrysler Corporation
Cities Service Company
Clark Equipment Company
Clevite Corporation
Coca-Cola Company
Colgate-Palmolive Company
Combustion Engineering, Incorporated
Container Corporation of America
Continental Can Company, Incorporated

Continental Oil Company
Corn Products Company
Corning Glass Works
Crane Company
Crown Cork & Seal Company,
    Incorporated

Dana Corporation
Deere & Company
Del Monte Corporation
Dow Chemical Company
Dresser Industries, Incorporated
E. I. du Pont de Nemours & Company

ESB Incorporated
Eastman Kodak Company
Eaton, Yale & Towne, Incorporated
ELTRA Corporation
Emhart Corporation
Engelhard Minerals and Chemicals
    Corporation

FMC Corporation
Federal-Mogul Corporation
Federal Pacific Electric Company
Firestone Tire & Rubber Company
Ford Motor Company
Foremost-McKesson, Incorporated
Fruehauf Corporation

General American Transportation
    Corporation
General Dynamics Corporation
General Electric Company
General Foods Corporation
General Mills, Incorporated
General Motors Corporation
General Telephone & Electronics
    Corporation
General Tire and Rubber Company
Genesco Incorporated
Gillette Company

Glen Alden Corporation
B. F. Goodrich Company
The Goodyear Tire & Rubber Company
W. R. Grace & Company
Gulf Oil Corporation

H. J. Heinz Company
Hercules, Incorporated
Hobart Manufacturing Company
Honeywell, Incorporated
Hoover Company
Hygrade Food Products Corporation

Ingersoll-Rand Company
Interchemical Corporation
International Business Machines
    Corporation
International Harvester Company
International Packers Limited
International Paper Company
International Telephone & Telegraph
    Corporation

Johns-Manville Corporation
Johnson & Johnson
Joy Manufacturing Company

Kaiser Industries Corporation
Kellogg Company
Kendall Company
Kimberly-Clark Corporation
Koppers Company, Incorporated

Libby, McNeill & Libby
Eli Lilly & Company
Litton Industries, Incorporated
Lockheed Aircraft Corporation

P. R. Mallory & Company Incorporated
Maremont Corporation
Martin Marietta Corporation
Merck & Company, Incorporated

Miles Laboratories, Incorporated
Minnesota Mining and Manufacturing
   Company
Mobil Oil Corporation
Monsanto Company

National Biscuit Company
National Cash Register Company
National Dairy Products Corporation
National Distillers & Chemical
   Corporation
National Lead Company
Norton Company

Olin Mathieson Chemical Corporation
Otis Elevator Company
Owens-Corning Fiberglas Corporation
Owens-Illinois, Incorporated

Parke, Davis & Company
Pennsalt Chemicals Corporation
PepsiCo, Incorporated
Pet Incorporated
Chas. Pfizer & Company, Incorporated
Phelps Dodge Corporation
Philip Morris Incorporated
Phillips Petroleum Company
Pillsbury Company
Pittsburgh Plate Glass Company
H. K. Porter Company, Incorporated
Procter & Gamble Company
Purex Corporation, Limited

Quaker Oats Company

Radio Corporation of America
Ralston Purina Company
Raytheon Company
Revlon, Incorporated
Reynolds Metals Company
Rheem Manufacturing Company
Richardson-Merrell, Incorporated

H. H. Robertson Company
Rockwell Manufacturing Company
Rohm & Haas Company

SCM Corporation
St. Regis Paper Company
Schering Corporation
Scott Paper Company
Scovill Manufacturing Company
Simmons Company
Singer Company
Smith Kline & French Laboratories
Sperry Rand Corporation
A. E. Staley Manufacturing Company
Standard Brands, Incorporated
Standard Oil Company of California
Standard Oil Company (Indiana)
Standard Oil Company (New Jersey)
Stauffer Chemical Company
Sterling Drug, Incorporated
Studebaker-Worthington, Incorporated
Sunbeam Corporation
Swift & Company

TRW Incorporated
Texaco Incorporated
Texas Instruments Incorporated
Time Incorporated
The Timken Roller Bearing Company

Union Carbide Corporation
UNIROYAL, Incorporated
United Merchants & Manufacturers,
   Incorporated
United Shoe Machinery Corporation
Upjohn Company

Warner-Lambert Pharmaceutical
   Company
Westinghouse Air Brake Company
Westinghouse Electric Corporation
Weyerhaeuser Company
Wm. Wrigley, Jr. Company

CHAPTER 2
The Expansion of Parent Systems

CHAPTER 2- THE EXPANSION OF PARENT SYSTEMS
SECTION 1- AN OVERVIEW OF FLOW AND STOCK, MANUFACTURING AND NON-MANUFACTURING
TABLE 1- SYSTEMS CLASSIFIED BY PERIOD SYSTEM FIRST
OPERATED A SUBSIDIARY
IN SPECIFIED COUNTRIES AND REGIONS

COUNTRY OR REGION	PRE 1968	PRE 1901	1901 -13	1914 -19	1920 -24	1925 -29	1930 -34	1935 -39	1940 -45	1946 -50	1951 -53	1954 -55	1956 -57	1958 -59	1960 -61	1962	1963	1964	1965	1966	1967	UNK
OUTSIDE U.S.	187	23	25	27	19	30	15	15	7	10	10	2	0	0	2	0	0	0	0	0	0	0
OUT. U.S. + CANADA	187	22	17	14	20	31	16	14	8	15	12	6	5	3	3	1	1	0	0	0	1	0
OUT. WEST. HEMIS.	187	22	16	12	19	31	12	13	4	12	13	9	7	9	6	2	2	0	0	0	1	0
OUT. WHITE CWEALTH	187	17	13	12	17	21	20	15	12	16	12	14	7	7	3	1	1	1	1	0	0	0
OUT. DEVLPED WORLD	187	3	8	9	10	18	16	17	17	22	15	14	10	17	8	0	1	0	0	1	2	0
CANADA	183	6	22	27	12	28	16	17	7	7	13	9	8	5	4	1	0	0	1	0	0	0
LATIN AMERICA	186	3	6	8	7	14	19	20	20	21	15	14	11	17	8	1	1	3	0	0	0	0
C. AMER.+CARIB.	184	2	3	5	3	10	15	25	14	22	15	16	13	15	13	4	5	3	0	1	0	0
CUBA	55	1	0	3	3	2	1	3	6	4	4	3	4	4	3	0	0	0	4	0	0	3
MEXICO	179	0	4	4	0	7	12	12	14	27	14	16	11	17	12	4	6	3	2	4	3	0
OTHER	128	1	0	0	0	0	3	3	6	6	11	8	11	16	28	5	3	3	4	7	3	1
S. AMERICA	175	2	4	7	6	9	8	14	11	16	16	14	17	20	10	3	3	1	0	1	0	2
ARGENTINA	112	0	3	5	2	7	7	11	6	10	4	5	8	12	10	11	3	1	2	3	1	1
BRAZIL	131	0	0	6	2	7	2	7	17	11	13	9	8	12	10	11	2	1	2	2	1	0
PERU	71	1	1	0	1	1	1	4	5	2	4	6	8	2	11	3	2	5	2	3	0	1
COLOMBIA	88	1	0	1	2	2	3	1	10	9	5	4	4	5	11	3	3	9	3	5	6	0
VENEZUELA	123	0	0	0	2	0	0	3	14	9	8	11	23	16	14	10	10	7	7	2	1	1
OTHER	85	2	1	3	4	4	2	4	4	10	5	6	2	1	8	4	3	3	5	5	4	4
EUROPE	187	22	15	8	19	31	11	13	4	11	15	8	5	13	7	3	2	0	0	0	0	0
EFTA	180	18	11	9	13	36	13	12	11	11	11	7	8	13	12	6	1	1	0	0	0	1
U.K.	180	16	13	8	12	13	13	13	11	11	10	7	7	7	6	5	3	0	0	6	1	3
SCANDINAVIA	105	2	4	5	1	9	4	4	3	2	3	5	5	7	12	6	5	8	8	4	6	1
SWITZERLAND	137	3	1	1	1	2	1	8	2	4	8	5	7	3	33	8	7	5	4	9	4	3
OTHER EFTA	64	0	4	3	3	4	1	6	4	1	1	0	4	6	3	3	3	3	5	4	1	1
EUROP. COMMUNITY	187	15	10	4	18	17	13	8	1	9	13	15	10	24	17	7	7	3	5	5	2	1
FRANCE	163	10	8	3	14	10	15	4	9	9	6	8	6	18	26	4	5	6	2	2	0	0
GERMANY	170	13	5	2	7	17	9	3	0	1	6	15	9	17	23	5	9	11	9	3	2	1
ITALY	148	3	4	4	5	8	9	4	1	4	8	8	7	24	25	12	8	11	4	4	1	1
BELGIUM + LUX	132	2	2	5	6	6	6	3	1	6	8	6	3	14	12	8	8	6	11	6	2	2
NETHERLANDS	118	1	2	4	7	8	4	7	1	7	3	6	1	15	17	7	9	5	4	5	2	1
SPAIN	121	0	2	2	0	1	3	2	2	2	5	2	3	7	7	8	14	10	15	7	1	1
GREECE + TURKEY	44	0	0	2	0	2	1	2	0	1	4	4	2	1	7	4	12	2	5	3	5	5
OTHER EUROPE	62	4	3	2	0	1	2	6	0	3	4	0	0	2	4	3	1	5	6	1	1	0
EUROPE EX. U.K.	187	16	9	6	19	17	15	8	3	9	16	14	10	24	13	3	3	0	0	0	0	0
SOUTHERN DOMINIONS	171	2	7	7	6	13	13	17	5	8	12	13	10	16	18	5	5	4	3	3	2	2
S. AFRICA +RHOD.	118	1	2	2	6	5	9	10	5	11	8	8	4	10	10	4	8	2	3	5	2	3
AUSTRALIA + N.Z.	158	2	6	6	5	12	10	12	3	4	11	12	10	16	21	7	3	3	6	3	3	3
ASIA + OTHER AFRICA	165	0	4	4	4	11	2	6	3	19	11	10	13	13	21	15	8	3	5	5	2	2
JAPAN	128	0	1	2	0	2	2	3	0	2	6	6	8	7	27	13	14	7	11	8	3	0
OTHER ASIA+AFR.	141	0	3	4	4	12	4	0	0	20	9	9	7	3	16	12	9	5	3	5	5	2
BLACK AFRICA	67	0	0	0	1	3	3	0	0	4	6	4	2	3	11	2	4	12	7	8	3	1
ARAB WORLD	48	0	2	0	1	3	0	1	1	5	2	4	2	7	6	4	3	6	2	4	2	2
INDIA	70	0	1	0	2	0	1	6	1	7	7	3	2	3	6	3	6	3	4	4	1	1
PHILIPPINES	70	0	0	0	1	3	3	2	1	3	3	8	8	7	6	9	1	1	2	3	0	0
OTHER E. ASIA	52	0	0	1	1	1	2	7	2	6	2	0	3	8	5	5	2	4	4	4	9	0
OTHER ASIA	74	0	1	3	1	4	1	6	2	2	2	3	4	6	9	2	3	3	3	7	4	1

PERIOD

CHAPTER 2— THE EXPANSION OF PARENT SYSTEMS
SECTION 1— AN OVERVIEW OF FLOW AND STOCK, MANUFACTURING AND NON-MANUFACTURING
TABLE 2— SYSTEMS CLASSIFIED BY YEAR(S) SYSTEM
OPERATED A SUBSIDIARY
IN SPECIFIED COUNTRIES AND REGIONS

YEAR

COUNTRY OR REGION	1901	1913	1919	1924	1929	1934	1939	1945	1950	1953	1955	1957	1958	1959	1960	1961	1962	1963	1964	1965	1966	1967
OUTSIDE U.S.	23	47	74	93	123	138	153	158	168	180	182	183	184	185	186	186	187	187	187	187	187	186
OUT. U.S. + CANADA	22	39	53	73	100	119	133	141	154	167	172	179	182	183	185	185	185	187	187	187	187	186
OUT. WEST. HEMIS.	22	38	50	69	100	110	123	127	137	152	159	167	171	177	182	184	184	187	187	187	187	186
OUT. WHITE CWEALTH	17	30	42	59	79	98	112	123	139	153	168	176	181	183	185	185	184	187	187	187	186	186
OUT. DEVLPED WORLD	3	11	19	29	46	61	77	95	117	131	147	157	170	175	180	182	182	185	186	186	186	184
CANADA	6	27	54	65	92	107	123	128	137	149	158	167	170	173	176	178	178	178	179	179	177	174
LATIN AMERICA	3	9	16	23	36	54	72	93	113	128	143	155	167	173	179	180	180	184	184	185	185	182
C. AMER.+CARIB.	2	5	10	13	22	37	59	73	92	108	124	137	146	155	162	167	169	175	178	181	180	176
CUBA	1	1	4	7	11	14	14	29	33	36	36	40	42	40	22	9	7	6	6	6	6	6
MEXICO	0	4	8	10	16	28	43	56	80	93	106	118	128	138	140	149	151	157	159	162	164	162
OTHER	1	1	1	1	1	4	7	18	23	34	42	59	68	75	95	102	103	107	108	110	114	112
S. AMERICA	2	6	12	18	27	34	48	71	86	102	114	132	141	154	160	162	162	167	168	167	168	165
ARGENTINA	0	3	7	9	16	22	33	39	48	52	55	61	67	73	77	84	94	97	99	99	99	99
BRAZIL	1	0	5	6	13	15	23	39	50	63	72	85	95	105	113	115	116	117	116	118	114	111
PERU	1	2	1	1	3	8	13	15	19	25	33	37	38	43	46	49	54	54	57	57	57	60
COLOMBIA	1	1	2	4	5	6	8	11	15	20	25	30	33	34	38	43	46	47	53	55	57	72
VENEZUELA	0	0	0	2	5	6	10	20	26	30	33	42	65	74	81	90	92	93	103	104	104	107
OTHER	2	3	6	9	13	15	18	23	33	37	41	42	45	45	50	52	53	56	58	65	68	71
EUROPE	22	37	45	64	95	104	116	120	129	144	154	160	163	173	180	181	184	187	187	187	187	185
EFTA	18	29	38	50	86	94	102	107	113	123	130	141	146	156	166	171	175	177	180	183	184	181
U.K.	16	29	37	49	82	92	101	104	110	118	125	135	137	143	148	150	155	159	165	169	168	167
SCANDINAVIA	3	6	11	13	22	26	29	29	31	34	38	43	42	45	51	58	64	67	75	82	86	83
SWITZERLAND	3	4	5	6	10	11	17	17	18	26	30	36	48	71	93	107	110	114	118	123	125	120
OTHER EFTA	0	3	4	7	10	11	16	17	17	16	17	22	26	30	35	36	38	40	42	47	51	51
EUROP. COMMUNITY	15	25	29	47	63	74	80	78	84	100	116	125	138	151	166	172	175	183	184	185	183	179
FRANCE	10	18	21	35	44	56	57	57	63	68	76	83	88	96	117	127	134	141	147	152	151	151
GERMANY	13	18	20	27	44	50	53	53	46	53	72	81	90	96	108	119	125	133	145	153	154	149
ITALY	2	6	8	13	21	24	26	24	26	36	43	49	54	70	85	95	102	116	120	131	132	132
BELGIUM + LUX	3	7	11	16	21	27	28	27	32	46	50	53	58	65	74	78	83	94	100	110	116	118
NETHERLANDS	1	3	4	10	17	21	26	32	41	46	50	53	47	54	57	70	78	91	96	97	101	99
SPAIN	0	2	4	11	15	18	22	23	34	29	35	36	37	41	44	48	55	67	77	91	104	109
GREECE + TURKEY	0	0	0	1	2	5	3	3	6	6	8	11	12	13	18	20	23	25	28	33	35	39
OTHER EUROPE	4	6	7	10	12	15	18	17	16	20	20	23	23	24	22	27	28	28	32	38	41	42
EUROPE EX. U.K.	16	25	31	50	66	79	86	86	94	113	128	138	149	163	172	177	181	186	187	187	186	184
SOUTHERN DOMINIONS	2	8	14	21	34	47	63	69	77	87	95	105	110	117	129	136	142	148	151	154	156	154
S. AFRICA +RHOD.	1	3	5	11	16	25	34	39	51	58	61	64	70	72	77	81	83	92	94	95	99	99
AUSTRALIA + N.Z.	2	7	12	17	29	39	50	54	58	67	77	87	93	99	109	119	126	130	133	139	139	137
ASIA + OTHER AFRICA	0	1	4	12	23	27	33	33	51	61	71	83	89	99	103	118	133	142	144	153	156	158
JAPAN	0	4	8	3	7	9	10	9	17	21	26	34	34	41	50	68	81	95	101	111	117	117
OTHER ASIA+AFK.	0	3	3	7	11	23	26	30	30	54	63	69	75	81	87	95	107	115	120	123	129	133
BLACK AFRICA	0	0	1	0	1	9	4	4	8	13	13	15	16	18	24	29	31	35	47	53	58	62
ARAB WORLD	0	2	2	2	4	4	4	3	4	13	17	19	21	24	26	29	31	35	30	32	34	37
INDIA	1	0	0	2	5	4	7	6	11	13	17	24	26	30	33	38	47	52	55	59	62	64
PHILIPPINES	0	1	1	2	5	7	12	12	13	20	24	27	32	36	42	45	47	52	55	60	62	65
OTHER E. ASIA	0	0	2	6	6	7	14	13	15	5	7	11	12	13	16	18	23	28	32	36	40	49
OTHER ASIA	0	1	4	5	9	9	14	16	24	27	27	31	35	37	43	48	53	55	58	61	66	68

CHAPTER 2- THE EXPANSION OF PARENT SYSTEMS
SECTION 1- AN OVERVIEW OF FLOW AND STOCK, MANUFACTURING AND NON-MANUFACTURING
TABLE 3- SYSTEMS CLASSIFIED BY PERIOD SYSTEM FIRST
OPERATED A MANUFACTURING SUBSIDIARY
IN SPECIFIED COUNTRIES AND REGIONS

COUNTRY OR REGION	PRE 1968	PRE 1901	1901 -13	1914 -19	1920 -24	1925 -29	1930 -34	1935 -39	1940 -45	1946 -50	1951 -53	1954 -55	1956 -57	1958 -59	1960 -61	1962	1963	1964	1965	1966	1967	UNK
OUTSIDE U.S.	187	19	22	26	15	30	13	13	8	9	8	7	4	8	5	0	0	0	0	0	0	0
OUT. U.S. + CANADA	187	18	11	13	18	29	15	11	9	14	12	10	10	10	6	0	2	0	0	0	0	0
OUT. WEST. HEMIS.	187	17	10	11	17	31	11	12	12	12	12	12	11	15	12	1	0	0	0	1	1	1
OUT. WHITE CWEALTH	187	14	8	11	16	18	16	12	10	13	13	16	14	18	7	0	2	2	0	0	2	0
OUT. DEVLPED WORLD	185	3	3	7	6	12	13	19	15	19	11	15	14	19	16	3	4	4	3	1	0	0
CANADA	178	5	20	24	7	27	15	13	7	9	11	9	7	6	7	4	4	3	0	1	1	0
LATIN AMERICA	182	3	3	5	5	9	14	20	17	18	11	14	15	18	15	5	4	3	1	0	0	0
C. AMER.+CARIB.	171	1	1	2	2	5	12	17	10	17	12	12	20	17	14	9	0	5	4	1	0	1
CUBA	36	1	0	1	1	1	3	8	7	3	9	2	6	3	1	0	0	0	0	0	0	2
MEXICO	160	0	2	0	0	4	8	9	12	20	3	11	15	20	15	6	6	5	7	3	3	0
OTHER	71	2	0	4	5	0	4	3	2	1	3	1	7	4	9	3	8	8	11	3	3	0
S. AMERICA	160	2	3	4	5	8	12	12	20	15	12	8	17	24	13	9	5	3	2	2	0	1
ARGENTINA	97	0	2	4	1	5	5	9	6	8	3	4	9	8	12	2	2	2	2	2	0	0
BRAZIL	113	0	0	4	1	6	7	7	11	14	12	7	14	18	9	2	3	3	4	2	3	0
PERU	40	1	0	0	1	0	0	1	6	2	1	3	6	0	5	0	2	1	4	2	1	0
COLOMBIA	73	0	0	0	1	0	0	1	7	8	4	4	3	4	13	3	3	3	2	2	4	0
VENEZUELA	83	0	0	1	1	0	1	1	6	8	6	6	10	12	14	2	8	8	4	4	4	1
OTHER	54	1	1	1	3	2	0	1	4	6	2	3	4	1	6	2	1	1	7	2	4	1
EUROPE	187	17	10	5	16	29	11	12	2	12	12	10	12	19	13	2	0	1	1	1	0	0
EFTA	178	16	9	5	9	28	13	15	1	10	10	9	9	10	11	8	4	4	4	2	2	0
U.K.	170	10	9	4	7	27	14	16	1	11	1	9	9	3	7	7	3	5	5	1	1	0
SCANDINAVIA	62	1	0	3	2	1	0	0	0	4	1	3	4	3	1	2	8	3	5	4	2	0
SWITZERLAND	28	0	2	0	0	0	3	4	1	2	1	0	1	3	7	5	7	3	1	1	1	1
OTHER EFTA	35	0	2	0	2	3	0	0	0	0	1	0	1	4	6	1	2	2	6	2	0	0
EUROP. COMMUNITY	184	12	4	3	14	14	11	5	1	7	15	12	13	26	28	9	4	4	1	2	1	0
FRANCE	138	7	2	1	11	8	9	4	0	7	5	5	5	16	16	6	9	6	2	4	3	0
GERMANY	137	9	3	2	5	13	8	1	0	2	5	10	11	12	22	11	2	7	6	2	2	1
ITALY	124	1	4	0	3	2	2	3	1	2	9	6	8	17	22	11	9	7	8	5	2	0
BELGIUM + LUX	76	1	1	1	1	4	4	1	2	2	2	2	1	12	13	11	7	5	7	7	2	0
NETHERLANDS	75	0	0	1	2	4	2	3	2	6	9	2	8	13	13	3	5	3	9	2	0	1
SPAIN	93	0	0	1	3	4	4	0	2	1	3	3	3	11	12	4	9	9	12	2	7	0
GREECE + TURKEY	32	0	2	1	0	1	0	0	0	0	5	5	2	4	7	8	0	4	3	3	4	0
OTHER EUROPE	37	3	2	0	1	2	1	1	2	2	3	0	1	1	5	2	2	3	1	4	0	0
EUROPE EX. U.K.	186	12	5	5	15	16	13	3	3	9	15	13	11	29	23	6	3	3	1	0	0	1
SOUTHERN DOMINIONS	154	1	2	5	3	10	11	14	5	6	10	14	11	18	14	4	5	5	6	5	5	0
S. AFRICA +RHOD.	86	1	0	5	3	2	6	6	5	7	3	5	4	9	9	5	3	2	2	1	1	1
AUSTRALIA + N.Z.	137	0	2	4	2	9	7	12	4	5	8	13	10	16	14	14	5	5	7	6	6	0
ASIA + OTHER AFRICA	145	0	1	3	9	2	1	4	0	11	10	11	12	9	24	14	4	8	8	4	1	1
JAPAN	98	0	1	1	2	2	2	1	0	1	10	3	7	3	20	12	13	8	9	5	5	2
OTHER ASIA+AFR.	118	0	3	0	0	0	1	3	0	10	2	12	6	9	19	12	10	4	4	7	1	0
BLACK AFRICA	29	0	0	0	0	0	0	0	0	0	0	1	0	0	8	2	3	4	3	4	1	1
ARAB WORLD	58	0	0	0	0	3	0	0	3	3	1	1	2	4	10	10	2	3	3	2	1	1
INDIA	29	0	0	0	1	1	1	1	0	0	3	1	1	8	8	7	1	5	5	5	2	0
PHILIPPINES	53	0	0	0	1	3	0	0	1	0	0	4	1	7	10	1	3	4	2	2	2	1
OTHER E. ASIA	28	0	0	1	1	2	0	2	0	2	0	3	8	0	3	2	4	0	3	5	1	1
OTHER ASIA	54	0	1	2	0	3	1	3	0	6	0	2	4	7	10	5	3	0	2	2	2	1

PERIOD

CHAPTER 2- THE EXPANSION OF PARENT SYSTEMS
SECTION 1- AN OVERVIEW OF FLOW AND STOCK, MANUFACTURING AND NON-MANUFACTURING
TABLE 4- SYSTEMS CLASSIFIED BY YEAR(S) SYSTEM
OPERATED A MANUFACTURING SUBSIDIARY
IN SPECIFIED COUNTRIES AND REGIONS

YEAR

COUNTRY OR REGION	1901	1913	1919	1924	1929	1934	1939	1945	1950	1953	1955	1957	1958	1959	1960	1961	1962	1963	1964	1965	1966	1967
OUTSIDE U.S.	18	39	64	80	110	122	135	138	152	162	170	174	177	182	185	186	185	187	187	187	187	185
OUT. U.S. + CANADA	17	28	40	59	88	102	113	119	135	149	158	168	173	179	182	185	185	187	187	187	187	185
OUT. WEST. HEMIS.	16	26	36	54	85	94	105	105	117	130	141	156	168	176	182	185	184	186	186	186	186	185
OUT. WHITE CWEALTH	13	21	29	46	64	79	92	96	113	129	145	159	168	176	182	185	183	186	186	186	186	184
OUT. DEVLPED WORLD	3	6	12	18	30	42	60	74	93	104	120	135	146	152	157	167	169	175	176	179	180	177
CANADA	5	24	48	54	79	91	102	107	118	128	137	142	146	148	153	156	158	161	165	165	163	161
LATIN AMERICA	3	6	10	15	24	37	56	73	90	101	114	131	141	147	152	161	165	171	172	175	176	171
C. AMER.+CARIB.	1	2	4	6	11	23	38	47	64	76	85	105	112	122	119	128	135	144	147	153	154	150
CUBA	1	2	3	4	7	7	14	15	18	19	20	28	30	30	11	4	3	2	2	2	2	2
MEXICO	0	0	2	4	8	16	24	35	55	63	71	85	92	105	107	118	122	129	131	138	140	138
OTHER	0	0	2	4	7	11	15	17	18	24	28	33	39	40	43	43	48	52	55	59	65	66
S. AMERICA	2	5	8	12	20	23	35	54	60	75	87	103	112	128	137	141	143	149	153	151	152	148
ARGENTINA	0	2	5	6	11	15	24	30	36	39	41	51	51	55	58	67	75	80	83	83	81	80
BRAZIL	0	3	3	4	10	10	17	27	41	53	60	73	79	88	94	96	96	97	96	99	98	92
PERU	1	1	1	1	1	2	9	10	9	14	20	20	23	24	24	26	29	31	33	33	33	35
COLOMBIA	0	0	1	1	2	3	8	10	14	17	21	27	31	37	37	43	43	44	52	52	60	60
VENEZUELA	0	0	0	1	1	2	8	8	15	21	25	35	39	44	56	59	59	63	64	65	70	71
OTHER	1	2	2	6	7	8	10	8	10	17	20	23	22	24	26	29	30	33	33	40	42	46
EUROPE	16	26	30	47	76	85	96	96	106	120	132	144	147	162	172	176	178	181	182	183	184	183
EFTA	11	19	24	33	61	73	83	84	92	102	110	120	122	128	135	139	146	148	155	160	163	161
U.K.	10	18	22	29	56	69	80	80	89	97	105	114	116	122	129	134	137	138	142	146	146	145
SCANDINAVIA	1	3	6	8	16	14	14	13	16	19	19	21	21	24	26	30	34	34	42	46	48	45
SWITZERLAND	0	0	0	0	1	1	4	4	6	6	5	6	7	9	13	15	15	20	22	22	22	22
OTHER EFTA	1	1	1	1	6	6	8	9	8	8	8	9	10	14	14	15	18	18	20	26	27	27
EUROP. COMMUNITY	11	15	17	32	45	54	59	54	60	75	90	103	112	129	148	159	163	171	174	174	176	171
FRANCE	7	8	9	20	27	33	36	27	39	45	51	56	59	70	87	95	96	105	110	119	121	122
GERMANY	9	12	14	19	32	37	37	23	32	38	48	59	62	71	81	93	96	108	114	118	118	113
ITALY	1	1	5	8	11	12	13	15	15	24	30	38	42	53	64	75	85	95	100	106	107	106
BELGIUM + LUX	0	1	1	4	8	10	13	14	16	18	20	21	24	34	40	45	44	53	55	61	61	64
NETHERLANDS	0	1	2	2	6	9	11	13	17	19	20	23	27	32	35	43	48	52	54	62	63	59
SPAIN	0	0	4	6	10	10	11	10	16	16	16	22	22	26	29	33	40	49	57	68	79	83
GREECE + TURKEY	0	0	0	0	0	0	0	0	0	3	3	5	6	7	10	12	16	16	20	24	26	29
OTHER EUROPE	3	5	5	6	7	9	10	10	8	12	11	12	12	13	12	15	16	17	20	21	23	23
EUROPE EX. U.K.	11	16	19	35	50	61	66	62	69	86	102	112	120	140	156	164	169	178	180	182	181	179
SOUTHERN DOMINIONS	1	3	7	10	20	31	44	50	56	64	74	85	91	102	110	117	119	125	129	133	136	135
S. AFRICA +RHOD.	1	2	2	5	7	13	14	24	21	33	35	38	44	46	49	54	56	65	68	65	69	68
AUSTRALIA + N.Z.	0	2	5	7	16	23	34	39	44	52	63	72	76	87	94	101	104	107	111	118	116	117
ASIA + OTHER AFRICA	0	1	4	6	15	18	17	17	28	37	49	61	65	70	78	93	107	119	122	131	133	134
JAPAN	0	0	1	2	4	6	6	3	15	15	17	24	24	27	33	47	59	71	79	88	91	90
OTHER ASIA+AFR.	0	3	3	5	14	13	15	15	24	26	39	45	50	54	64	73	85	93	97	102	106	108
BLACK AFRICA	0	0	0	0	0	0	0	0	0	1	2	6	4	4	4	8	11	13	19	23	24	27
ARAB WORLD	0	0	0	0	3	4	5	5	7	4	5	8	8	4	8	12	11	13	15	17	20	23
INDIA	0	0	0	0	4	4	4	4	0	10	18	21	14	16	21	26	36	43	46	51	52	53
PHILIPPINES	0	0	1	2	4	5	5	5	7	13	15	18	22	25	29	31	33	43	43	45	46	46
OTHER E. ASIA	0	0	1	2	3	3	3	4	0	1	1	2	2	2	4	5	7	10	14	17	18	23
OTHER ASIA	0	2	2	5	4	5	8	8	14	14	15	19	22	25	32	36	42	45	45	47	49	50

14

COUNTRY OR REGION	PRE 1968	PRE 1901	1901-13	1914-19	1920-24	1925-29	1930-34	1935-39	1940-45	1946-50	1951-53	1954-55	1956-57	1958-59	1960-61	1962	1963	1964	1965	1966	1967	UNK
OUTSIDE U.S.	176	12	10	9	11	16	14	9	7	14	12	8	12	15	9	3	6	2	5	2	0	0
OUT. U.S. + CANADA	174	12	10	9	8	15	9	11	7	11	10	8	10	15	16	5	7	2	4	4	1	0
OUT. WEST. HEMIS.	168	12	9	8	9	13	7	9	3	12	10	8	10	16	19	10	6	3	5	3	2	0
OUT. WHITE CWEALTH	170	9	10	7	6	8	8	9	6	9	11	10	12	20	18	5	9	1	5	5	2	0
OUT. DEVLPED WORLD	144	1	4	3	1	7	10	8	9	12	9	10	9	19	19	2	4	6	3	6	2	0
CANADA	103	1	1	2	6	6	12	4	8	7	7	4	9	5	8	7	2	5	7	3	5	3
LATIN AMERICA	132	0	2	3	0	4	10	8	9	10	7	9	11	20	20	2	5	5	3	3	0	0
C. AMER.+CARIB.	103	0	1	1	2	1	2	0	5	10	6	7	10	17	15	5	4	0	0	2	0	0
CUBA	13	0	0	0	1	1	0	0	1	2	0	1	0	0	1	0	1	3	0	1	1	1
MEXICO	59	0	1	0	0	1	3	8	4	8	6	5	4	8	5	4	2	3	1	1	0	1
OTHER	61	1	0	0	0	2	9	6	1	3	3	2	8	13	15	1	1	1	1	3	4	0
S. AMERICA	94	0	1	2	0	2	9	6	2	4	4	2	7	6	7	4	1	5	3	1	3	1
ARGENTINA	27	0	1	0	0	1	3	1	0	1	2	2	6	5	4	1	2	1	3	3	3	0
BRAZIL	38	1	1	2	0	1	1	3	0	3	2	2	0	2	7	2	2	1	3	2	3	1
PERU	23	0	0	0	0	1	0	1	0	1	1	0	1	5	0	1	1	2	3	0	2	2
COLOMBIA	19	1	0	0	0	0	1	0	1	0	2	0	1	0	4	1	2	1	2	0	1	1
VENEZUELA	45	1	0	0	0	0	0	1	2	3	1	2	1	3	0	1	5	2	0	3	1	2
OTHER	25	0	0	0	0	0	3	1	3	1	2	0	0	2	3	0	1	2	2	1	1	0
EUROPE	157	11	10	7	9	12	6	7	2	11	4	7	8	13	21	9	6	7	4	1	0	2
EFTA	127	8	6	3	6	16	6	8	2	7	3	3	5	11	15	6	7	4	1	2	4	4
U.K.	97	5	6	3	5	15	6	4	2	6	3	3	3	2	8	6	3	4	4	2	5	4
SCANDINAVIA	58	2	3	1	1	0	3	3	2	1	2	2	1	2	1	2	3	4	0	1	3	1
SWITZERLAND	71	3	2	1	0	4	1	4	1	2	3	1	3	1	7	3	3	4	2	0	3	1
OTHER EFTA	30	0	2	1	1	0	1	1	0	1	1	0	1	1	0	2	2	2	0	3	4	1
EUROP. COMMUNITY	143	6	8	4	9	4	7	3	2	7	4	7	7	14	17	10	10	13	6	2	3	1
FRANCE	75	2	7	2	4	0	6	1	0	5	0	2	3	8	10	4	7	5	5	2	4	2
GERMANY	86	4	2	1	1	5	2	0	0	2	1	1	0	8	12	9	9	14	5	5	2	0
ITALY	56	2	0	2	2	1	4	0	1	3	3	3	3	7	5	3	3	8	9	9	3	1
BELGIUM + LUX	70	1	2	4	4	4	1	5	0	5	3	1	4	3	3	6	3	7	3	3	5	0
NETHERLANDS	55	1	2	0	1	1	1	1	1	2	0	1	2	4	3	5	4	8	3	1	1	1
SPAIN	36	0	2	1	3	0	1	4	0	1	0	2	0	2	6	0	3	7	1	4	4	0
GREECE + TURKEY	13	0	0	0	0	1	1	1	2	2	1	0	0	0	0	1	1	0	4	0	1	1
OTHER EUROPE	20	1	1	2	2	2	4	4	0	1	2	2	1	1	3	0	3	0	2	1	0	0
EUROPE EX. U.K.	152	8	8	7	7	4	5	2	0	7	6	9	10	20	21	10	9	8	4	2	2	1
SOUTHERN DOMINIONS	88	1	6	2	4	4	3	7	1	5	5	3	6	8	10	8	4	2	4	1	2	2
S. AFRICA +RHOD.	46	0	1	1	2	2	2	5	1	5	3	2	1	4	2	5	4	2	1	0	1	2
AUSTRALIA + N.Z.	72	1	6	2	2	5	5	4	0	2	3	3	5	6	10	9	9	1	6	1	3	2
ASIA + OTHER AFRICA	93	0	2	0	2	1	1	4	1	5	4	4	6	6	9	6	6	10	7	7	1	1
JAPAN	48	0	0	0	0	1	1	1	0	0	3	2	2	4	10	3	6	5	3	2	0	2
OTHER ASIA+AFR.	70	0	2	0	2	4	5	5	0	6	3	3	4	2	4	1	2	6	4	9	1	0
BLACK AFRICA	24	0	0	0	0	0	0	3	0	3	0	1	1	1	1	0	1	5	6	2	0	0
ARAB WORLD	19	0	2	0	2	2	2	0	1	1	1	1	1	1	0	1	1	2	0	0	0	2
INDIA	12	0	0	0	0	0	0	4	0	0	1	0	0	1	0	0	0	0	0	2	0	1
PHILIPPINES	19	0	0	2	1	1	3	4	1	1	1	2	1	1	2	1	1	2	1	1	0	0
OTHER E. ASIA	25	0	0	0	4	4	1	0	0	1	2	0	3	1	5	1	1	2	2	2	3	0
OTHER ASIA	28	0	0	1	1	0	0	1	0	1	2	1	0	4	0	1	1	3	1	6	1	0

CHAPTER 2- THE EXPANSION OF PARENT SYSTEMS
SECTION 1- AN OVERVIEW OF FLOW AND STOCK, MANUFACTURING AND NON-MANUFACTURING
TABLE 6- SYSTEMS CLASSIFIED BY YEAR(S) SYSTEM
OPERATED A SALES SUBSIDIARY
IN SPECIFIED COUNTRIES AND REGIONS

YEAR

COUNTRY OR REGION	1901	1913	1919	1924	1929	1934	1939	1945	1950	1953	1955	1957	1958	1959	1960	1961	1962	1963	1964	1965	1966	1967
OUTSIDE U.S.	12	22	30	39	54	66	70	81	93	100	109	122	130	137	147	151	151	158	162	164	163	162
OUT. U.S. + CANADA	12	22	30	36	50	58	64	74	82	90	99	109	118	125	139	144	145	155	158	161	160	159
OUT. WEST. HEMIS.	12	21	28	35	47	53	58	61	69	76	80	92	101	109	125	138	141	149	152	153	153	151
OUT. WHITE CWEALTH	9	19	25	29	38	47	53	58	67	76	87	100	112	121	135	138	138	149	151	155	155	154
OUT. DEVLPED WORLD	1	5	7	8	15	26	31	38	47	53	62	71	85	92	100	108	104	108	112	116	117	114
CANADA	1	1	3	8	14	21	22	24	26	30	30	39	43	45	48	48	54	53	55	57	57	59
LATIN AMERICA	1	3	5	9	19	25	25	35	40	46	55	67	80	88	97	104	100	102	103	103	103	100
C. AMER.+CARIB.	1	2	2	4	5	5	7	14	17	20	27	31	36	44	54	57	67	69	67	66	67	65
CUBA	0	1	3	5	7	7	7	6	6	7	7	8	5	4	5	2	1	1	1	1	1	1
MEXICO	0	0	1	2	5	5	6	8	10	11	12	20	26	30	33	33	35	36	34	33	30	28
OTHER	0	0	0	1	3	5	6	10	11	15	16	14	16	13	14	16	17	18	16	16	17	16
S. AMERICA	1	2	3	5	10	13	15	20	26	25	33	42	45	50	54	57	55	60	63	66	65	64
ARGENTINA	0	1	2	3	6	8	8	8	10	11	12	12	12	13	13	14	15	16	17	16	17	17
BRAZIL	0	0	2	3	4	6	7	8	8	11	12	12	11	13	14	16	16	18	17	20	19	21
PERU	1	1	1	1	2	2	5	4	4	6	7	9	10	11	14	16	16	14	16	16	17	17
COLOMBIA	1	1	1	2	2	2	3	5	6	7	7	8	10	5	9	12	9	11	11	13	12	11
VENEZUELA	0	0	0	0	1	2	2	3	5	7	7	16	20	22	23	20	20	23	24	24	26	26
OTHER	1	1	1	1	4	5	5	8	9	10	11	11	12	13	14	16	15	15	17	18	17	16
EUROPE	11	21	27	34	43	48	53	54	61	65	70	77	84	94	108	115	121	131	140	139	137	136
EFTA	8	14	16	22	34	38	41	42	44	46	48	50	53	62	72	77	83	90	93	93	94	98
U.K.	5	11	12	17	27	28	30	31	32	34	34	33	33	34	37	42	46	50	55	57	57	59
SCANDINAVIA	2	5	8	13	16	16	19	19	19	21	23	26	26	27	32	36	37	40	42	46	46	48
SWITZERLAND	3	4	5	6	7	5	9	7	9	12	12	14	20	35	41	44	46	51	50	50	52	55
OTHER EFTA	0	2	3	4	5	5	6	6	5	6	6	9	11	11	16	16	15	17	19	20	22	22
EUROP. COMMUNITY	6	13	18	24	27	34	33	31	39	43	49	56	65	69	81	87	96	106	119	121	118	112
FRANCE	2	8	10	13	18	15	15	18	18	17	16	18	24	26	31	35	40	42	46	50	49	52
GERMANY	4	7	7	10	13	12	11	9	10	11	17	17	22	23	30	34	42	46	58	63	60	59
ITALY	2	2	4	7	9	7	7	8	10	10	9	18	22	23	30	36	41	44	51	54	56	53
BELGIUM + LUX	1	3	4	6	7	7	9	8	8	10	9	14	17	18	19	24	27	33	40	39	41	41
NETHERLANDS	1	1	2	4	7	8	9	8	8	10	10	12	13	12	12	12	12	15	19	19	23	22
SPAIN	0	0	0	1	1	1	2	2	2	2	2	3	3	3	3	6	6	9	9	9	10	11
GREECE + TURKEY	0	0	0	0	1	2	2	2	1	2	3	3	3	3	3	6	6	9	10	10	13	13
OTHER EUROPE	1	2	2	4	6	7	9	8	10	10	11	11	12	13	14	16	15	15	17	18	13	13
EUROPE EX. U.K.	8	16	22	27	32	37	41	38	45	50	57	66	77	88	102	108	114	126	133	133	132	133
SOUTHERN DOMINIONS	1	6	7	11	15	17	21	22	24	30	31	37	40	41	45	50	59	58	61	64	66	64
S. AFRICA +RHOD.	0	1	2	6	6	8	17	16	16	19	18	20	21	24	27	31	27	31	32	32	29	28
AUSTRALIA + N.Z.	1	6	7	10	14	16	17	16	16	19	21	26	29	27	27	32	39	41	43	46	50	50
ASIA + OTHER AFRICA	0	2	4	8	11	13	15	11	19	22	21	25	28	33	36	43	49	56	64	70	77	79
JAPAN	0	2	0	1	2	2	1	1	0	0	4	5	7	8	12	15	23	28	33	34	36	37
OTHER ASIA+AFR.	0	2	4	7	12	12	14	10	19	21	19	22	24	28	29	32	35	40	45	49	56	57
BLACK AFRICA	0	2	0	0	0	3	0	3	0	5	5	6	7	7	8	8	8	9	15	19	20	20
ARAB WORLD	0	2	2	3	2	2	6	6	7	7	7	7	8	8	8	8	8	9	10	10	10	11
INDIA	0	0	0	0	2	2	6	0	0	6	7	8	7	8	8	8	8	9	7	6	8	8
PHILIPPINES	0	0	2	2	2	2	0	4	3	7	4	4	5	5	6	6	7	7	6	9	10	8
OTHER E. ASIA	0	0	0	1	1	2	4	0	5	6	1	4	4	6	8	11	12	15	17	19	20	23
OTHER ASIA	0	0	1	4	4	4	4	5	8	4	7	7	9	11	11	11	12	12	15	16	20	20

CHAPTER 2- THE EXPANSION OF PARENT SYSTEMS
SECTION 1- AN OVERVIEW OF FLOW AND STOCK, MANUFACTURING AND NON-MANUFACTURING
TABLE 7- SYSTEMS CLASSIFIED BY PERIOD SYSTEM FIRST
OPERATED AN EXTRACTION SUBSIDIARY
IN SPECIFIED COUNTRIES AND REGIONS

COUNTRY OR REGION	PRE 1968	PRE 1901	1901 -13	1914 -19	1920 -24	1925 -29	1930 -34	1935 -39	1940 -45	1946 -50	1951 -53	1954 -55	1956 -57	1958 -59	1960 -61	1962	1963	1964	1965	1966	1967	UNK
OUTSIDE U.S.	53	2	2	6	5	5	1	1	4	5	2	6	2	2	2	2	1	3	1	2	0	0
OUT. U.S. + CANADA	44	1	3	5	4	2	0	1	2	2	3	4	3	1	4	2	1	2	1	2	1	0
OUT. WEST. HEMIS.	33	1	2	1	1	2	0	4	2	1	4	2	2	2	5	2	2	2	1	1	1	0
OUT. WHITE CWEALTH	41	1	3	5	4	2	0	1	2	1	2	4	4	2	3	3	0	2	1	2	1	0
OUT. DEVLPED WORLD	40	0	4	5	4	2	0	1	1	1	2	3	3	1	3	3	0	2	2	2	1	0
CANADA	26	1	0	2	1	4	1	1	3	3	2	2	1	1	2	3	0	2	1	1	0	1
LATIN AMERICA	35	0	2	4	4	1	0	1	2	3	2	2	4	1	3	2	0	2	2	1	0	1
C. AMER.+CARIB.	25	0	2	3	0	0	0	1	0	2	2	0	0	0	2	0	0	1	0	0	0	0
CUBA	1	0	0	0	1	0	0	0	0	0	0	0	0	0	0	0	0	0	0	0	0	0
MEXICO	14	0	2	3	0	0	0	2	0	2	1	2	0	1	3	2	0	0	1	0	0	0
OTHER	13	0	0	0	0	0	0	0	0	1	1	0	1	0	1	0	1	1	1	1	0	1
S. AMERICA	23	0	0	3	4	1	0	2	1	1	0	2	1	1	3	2	1	1	1	1	0	1
ARGENTINA	5	0	0	0	2	0	0	0	0	0	0	0	1	1	0	1	0	0	0	0	0	1
BRAZIL	3	0	0	0	0	0	0	0	0	0	0	0	1	0	0	0	1	0	0	0	0	0
PERU	5	0	0	0	1	0	0	2	0	0	0	1	2	0	0	0	0	0	0	0	0	0
COLOMBIA	4	0	0	0	0	1	0	0	0	0	0	0	0	0	1	0	1	0	1	0	0	0
VENEZUELA	6	0	0	0	2	2	0	2	1	0	0	0	0	0	1	0	0	1	0	1	0	0
OTHER	10	0	0	3	1	1	0	0	0	0	0	1	0	0	1	0	0	1	1	1	0	0
EUROPE	15	1	1	0	0	1	0	2	1	1	1	0	2	0	1	1	1	2	0	0	0	0
EFTA	8	0	0	1	1	1	1	1	1	0	0	0	0	0	1	0	0	1	0	0	0	0
U.K.	8	0	0	0	1	0	0	0	0	0	0	0	0	0	0	0	0	1	0	0	0	0
SCANDINAVIA	0	0	0	0	0	0	0	0	0	0	0	0	0	0	0	0	0	0	0	0	0	0
SWITZERLAND	0	0	0	0	0	0	0	0	0	0	0	0	0	0	0	0	0	0	0	0	0	0
OTHER EFTA	0	0	0	0	0	0	0	0	0	0	0	0	0	0	0	0	0	0	0	0	0	0
EUROP. COMMUNITY	8	1	0	0	0	0	0	0	0	1	0	0	0	1	0	0	1	2	0	0	0	0
FRANCE	4	0	0	0	0	0	0	1	1	0	1	1	0	1	0	1	0	1	0	0	0	1
GERMANY	1	0	0	0	0	0	0	0	0	0	0	0	0	0	0	0	0	0	0	0	0	1
ITALY	1	0	0	0	0	0	0	1	0	0	0	0	0	0	0	0	0	0	0	0	0	0
BELGIUM + LUX	1	1	0	0	0	0	0	0	0	0	0	0	0	0	0	0	0	0	0	0	0	0
NETHERLANDS	3	0	0	0	0	0	0	0	0	1	0	0	0	1	0	0	0	1	0	0	0	0
SPAIN	1	0	0	0	0	0	0	0	0	0	0	0	0	0	0	0	0	1	0	0	0	0
GREECE + TURKEY	2	0	0	0	0	0	0	1	0	0	0	0	0	1	0	0	0	0	0	0	0	0
OTHER EUROPE	2	0	1	0	0	0	0	0	0	0	0	0	0	0	0	1	0	0	0	0	0	0
EUROPE EX. U.K.	10	1	1	0	0	0	0	1	0	0	0	0	0	2	1	0	0	2	0	0	0	0
SOUTHERN DOMINIONS	14	0	0	0	1	1	1	1	0	1	0	0	0	0	1	3	1	0	2	1	0	0
S. AFRICA +RHOD.	5	0	0	0	1	1	0	0	1	0	0	0	0	0	0	0	0	2	0	1	0	0
AUSTRALIA + N.Z.	10	0	2	1	0	2	0	3	0	0	0	1	1	1	3	1	2	0	0	1	0	0
ASIA + OTHER AFRICA	22	0	0	0	1	0	0	3	0	0	0	0	1	0	1	0	2	1	0	0	0	0
JAPAN	0	0	2	1	0	2	0	0	0	0	0	0	0	0	0	0	0	0	0	1	0	1
OTHER ASIA+AFR.	22	0	2	2	1	1	0	3	0	0	0	2	1	1	3	0	2	2	1	2	0	0
BLACK AFRICA	13	0	0	0	0	1	0	3	0	0	0	1	0	0	1	2	2	0	0	2	0	1
ARAB WORLD	8	0	1	0	0	0	0	0	0	0	0	0	0	0	0	1	0	0	0	1	0	0
INDIA	0	0	0	0	0	0	0	0	1	0	0	0	0	0	0	0	0	1	1	0	0	1
PHILIPPINES	4	0	1	1	0	0	0	0	0	0	0	0	0	1	1	0	0	0	0	1	0	0
OTHER E. ASIA	0	0	0	0	0	0	0	0	0	0	0	0	0	0	0	0	0	1	0	0	0	1
OTHER ASIA	7	0	1	1	0	0	0	2	0	0	0	0	0	0	0	0	0	0	1	2	0	0

CHAPTER 2- THE EXPANSION OF PARENT SYSTEMS
SECTION 1- AN OVERVIEW OF FLOW AND STOCK, MANUFACTURING AND NON-MANUFACTURING
TABLE 8- SYSTEMS CLASSIFIED BY YEAR(S) SYSTEM
OPERATED AN EXTRACTION SUBSIDIARY
IN SPECIFIED COUNTRIES AND REGIONS

YEAR

COUNTRY OR REGION	1901	1913	1919	1924	1929	1934	1939	1945	1950	1953	1955	1957	1958	1959	1960	1961	1962	1963	1964	1965	1966	1967
OUTSIDE U.S.	2	4	10	14	16	17	19	22	28	30	35	35	36	37	38	39	40	41	44	46	46	45
OUT. U.S. + CANADA	1	4	9	12	13	13	15	16	19	22	25	25	26	27	29	30	32	33	35	37	37	37
OUT. WEST. HEMIS.	1	3	4	5	7	7	11	10	11	15	16	15	17	17	19	21	22	24	26	27	28	27
OUT. WHITE CWEALTH	1	4	9	12	13	13	15	16	18	20	23	25	26	27	28	27	29	30	32	34	34	34
OUT. DEVLPED WORLD	0	4	9	12	13	13	15	16	18	20	22	24	24	25	26	26	29	29	31	33	33	33
CANADA	1	1	2	3	3	4	6	9	12	13	15	15	16	16	16	17	17	17	19	19	18	17
LATIN AMERICA	0	2	5	9	9	9	11	13	14	16	18	21	21	22	23	24	26	25	27	29	28	28
C. AMER.+CARIB.	0	2	5	5	5	5	7	9	9	9	11	14	14	15	15	14	16	16	17	18	19	19
CUBA	0	2	0	1	1	1	1	0	0	0	0	0	0	0	0	0	0	0	0	0	0	0
MEXICO	0	0	5	5	5	5	6	7	6	6	8	8	8	9	9	8	8	8	8	9	10	10
OTHER	0	0	0	0	0	0	2	3	3	3	3	6	6	6	6	6	9	9	9	9	9	10
S. AMERICA	0	0	3	6	6	6	8	8	8	9	10	11	11	11	13	14	15	15	16	17	17	17
ARGENTINA	0	0	0	2	2	2	1	0	1	1	1	2	2	2	2	2	3	3	3	3	3	3
BRAZIL	0	0	0	0	0	0	1	0	0	0	0	1	1	1	2	2	3	2	2	3	3	2
PERU	0	0	0	0	0	0	0	0	0	1	2	4	4	4	4	4	4	4	4	5	5	5
COLOMBIA	0	0	0	0	1	1	0	0	0	1	1	1	1	1	1	1	1	1	1	1	1	1
VENEZUELA	0	1	0	2	2	2	2	3	3	2	2	1	2	2	3	3	4	4	4	5	4	4
OTHER	0	2	3	4	4	4	4	4	4	5	5	4	4	4	5	5	5	5	6	7	8	8
EUROPE	1	2	2	2	3	3	4	4	4	4	6	6	7	8	9	9	10	11	12	12	11	10
EFTA	0	1	1	1	3	3	4	4	4	4	4	4	4	4	5	5	6	6	6	6	5	4
U.K.	0	1	1	2	3	3	4	4	4	4	4	4	4	4	5	5	6	6	6	6	5	4
SCANDINAVIA	0	0	0	0	0	0	0	0	0	0	0	0	0	0	0	0	0	0	0	0	0	0
SWITZERLAND	0	0	0	0	0	0	0	0	0	0	0	0	0	0	0	0	0	0	0	0	0	0
OTHER EFTA	0	0	0	0	0	0	0	0	0	0	0	0	0	0	0	0	0	0	0	0	0	0
EUROP. COMMUNITY	1	1	1	1	1	1	1	1	1	2	3	3	3	3	3	3	3	4	6	5	5	5
FRANCE	1	0	0	0	0	0	1	0	0	0	1	1	1	2	2	2	3	3	4	3	3	3
GERMANY	0	0	0	0	0	0	0	0	0	0	1	1	1	1	1	1	1	1	1	1	1	1
ITALY	0	0	0	0	0	0	0	0	0	0	1	1	1	1	1	1	1	1	1	1	1	1
BELGIUM + LUX	0	1	1	1	1	1	1	1	1	1	1	1	1	1	1	1	1	1	1	1	1	1
NETHERLANDS	1	0	0	0	0	0	0	0	0	0	0	0	0	0	1	0	0	0	0	0	0	0
SPAIN	0	0	0	0	0	0	0	0	0	0	1	1	1	1	2	2	2	1	2	2	2	2
GREECE + TURKEY	0	1	1	1	1	1	1	1	1	1	1	0	0	1	2	2	2	2	2	2	2	2
OTHER EUROPE	1	0	0	0	0	0	0	0	0	0	0	1	1	1	2	2	2	2	2	2	0	0
EUROPE EX. U.K.	2	2	2	2	2	2	2	2	2	2	4	4	5	5	5	5	5	6	8	7	7	7
SOUTHERN DOMINIONS	0	0	0	1	2	3	2	4	4	6	6	5	6	6	7	8	8	8	10	11	11	11
S. AFRICA +RHOD.	0	0	0	1	2	2	2	2	2	3	3	4	2	2	2	2	2	2	4	4	4	4
AUSTRALIA + N.Z.	0	2	3	4	1	1	2	2	2	3	3	3	4	5	5	6	6	7	7	8	8	8
ASIA + OTHER AFRICA	0	0	3	6	6	6	9	8	8	10	10	11	11	12	12	13	13	15	16	17	18	18
JAPAN	0	0	0	0	0	0	0	0	0	0	0	0	0	0	0	0	0	0	0	0	0	0
OTHER ASIA+AFR.	0	2	3	4	6	6	9	8	8	10	10	11	11	12	12	13	15	15	16	17	18	18
BLACK AFRICA	0	0	1	1	2	2	2	2	2	3	3	3	3	4	4	4	7	7	8	10	10	12
ARAB WORLD	0	0	0	2	2	2	2	3	3	4	4	4	4	4	4	4	4	5	5	8	10	8
INDIA	0	1	1	0	0	0	0	0	0	0	0	0	0	0	0	0	0	0	0	0	0	0
PHILIPPINES	1	0	0	1	1	1	1	2	2	2	2	3	3	3	3	3	3	5	5	5	6	6
OTHER E. ASIA	0	2	1	0	0	1	0	0	0	2	2	3	3	3	2	3	3	3	3	3	3	3
OTHER ASIA	0	1	2	2	1	1	3	2	3	3	3	3	3	3	3	3	3	3	3	4	6	5

CHAPTER 2- THE EXPANSION OF PARENT SYSTEMS
SECTION 2- THE FLOW OF MANUFACTURING BY INDUSTRY OF PARENT SYSTEM
TABLE 1- SYSTEMS IN THE MEAT AND DAIRY INDUSTRIES (SIC 201 AND 202)
CLASSIFIED BY PERIOD SYSTEM FIRST OPERATED A MANUFACTURING SUBSIDIARY
IN SPECIFIED COUNTRIES AND REGIONS

PERIOD

COUNTRY OR REGION	PRE 1968	PRE 1901	1901 -13	1914 -19	1920 -24	1925 -29	1930 -34	1935 -39	1940 -45	1946 -50	1951 -53	1954 -55	1956 -57	1958 -59	1960 -61	1962	1963	1964	1965	1966	1967	UNK
OUTSIDE U.S.	10	2	1	2	2	1	0	0	0	1	0	0	0	0	0	0	0	0	0	0	0	0
OUT. U.S. + CANADA	10	2	0	1	3	2	0	0	1	1	0	0	0	1	1	0	0	0	0	0	0	0
OUT. WEST. HEMIS.	10	2	0	1	3	2	0	0	0	1	0	0	0	1	1	0	0	0	0	0	0	0
OUT. WHITE CWEALTH	10	0	2	1	2	2	1	0	0	0	1	0	0	1	1	0	0	0	0	0	0	0
OUT. DEVLPED WORLD	9	0	2	0	0	1	1	1	0	1	0	0	0	1	1	0	0	0	0	1	1	0
CANADA	10	0	2	1	0	2	0	1	0	0	1	0	0	0	0	1	0	0	0	0	0	0
LATIN AMERICA	9	0	2	1	0	2	1	1	1	1	0	0	0	0	1	0	0	0	0	0	0	0
C. AMER.+CARIB.	9	0	0	1	0	0	1	1	0	0	1	3	0	0	0	0	0	0	0	0	0	1
CUBA	5	0	0	1	0	0	0	0	0	0	0	0	0	0	0	0	0	0	0	0	0	1
MEXICO	8	0	0	0	0	1	0	2	0	0	1	0	0	0	1	0	0	1	0	0	0	0
OTHER	6	0	0	0	0	0	1	0	3	2	0	0	0	0	0	0	0	0	0	0	0	0
S. AMERICA	9	0	2	1	0	0	0	1	0	1	0	0	0	0	0	0	1	0	1	0	0	0
ARGENTINA	6	0	1	2	0	0	0	1	3	1	0	0	0	0	0	1	0	0	0	0	0	0
BRAZIL	6	0	0	3	0	0	0	0	0	0	0	0	0	0	0	0	0	0	1	0	0	0
PERU	4	0	0	0	0	0	0	0	0	1	0	0	0	0	1	0	0	0	0	0	0	0
COLOMBIA	4	0	0	0	0	0	0	0	3	1	0	0	0	0	0	0	1	0	0	0	0	0
VENEZUELA	4	0	0	0	0	0	0	0	1	0	0	0	0	0	1	0	0	1	0	0	0	0
OTHER	4	0	1	0	0	0	1	0	0	1	0	1	0	0	0	0	0	0	1	0	0	1
EUROPE	10	2	0	0	3	2	0	0	0	0	1	0	0	1	0	1	0	0	0	0	0	0
EFTA	10	2	0	0	1	4	0	0	0	0	1	0	0	1	0	0	0	1	0	0	0	0
U.K.	10	2	0	0	1	3	1	0	0	0	1	0	0	1	0	1	0	1	0	0	0	0
SCANDINAVIA	5	0	0	0	0	0	0	0	0	0	0	0	0	0	0	0	0	1	0	0	0	0
SWITZERLAND	0	0	0	0	0	0	0	0	0	0	0	0	0	0	0	0	0	0	0	0	0	0
OTHER EFTA	0	0	0	0	0	0	0	0	0	0	0	0	0	0	0	0	0	0	0	0	0	0
EUROP. COMMUNITY	8	0	0	0	2	2	1	0	0	0	0	2	0	0	0	1	0	1	0	0	0	0
FRANCE	6	0	0	0	2	2	0	0	0	0	0	0	0	1	1	0	0	0	0	0	0	0
GERMANY	8	0	0	0	2	3	1	0	0	0	2	0	0	2	2	2	1	1	0	0	0	0
ITALY	3	0	0	0	0	1	1	0	0	0	0	0	0	0	1	1	0	1	0	0	0	0
BELGIUM + LUX	4	0	0	0	0	0	0	0	0	0	1	0	0	0	0	1	0	1	0	0	0	0
NETHERLANDS	5	0	0	0	0	2	1	0	0	0	0	0	2	2	0	0	0	0	0	0	0	0
SPAIN	5	0	0	0	0	0	0	0	0	0	0	0	0	0	1	0	0	0	0	0	0	0
GREECE + TURKEY	0	0	0	0	0	0	0	0	0	0	0	0	0	0	0	1	0	0	0	0	0	0
OTHER EUROPE	5	0	0	0	0	0	1	0	0	1	2	0	0	0	2	0	0	0	0	0	0	0
EUROPE EX. U.K.	10	0	0	2	2	2	1	0	0	0	2	0	0	1	2	2	0	0	0	0	0	0
SOUTHERN DOMINIONS	10	0	1	1	0	1	1	2	2	1	0	0	0	2	2	0	0	1	1	1	1	0
S. AFRICA +RHOD.	2	0	0	0	0	0	0	1	1	1	0	0	0	0	0	0	0	0	0	0	0	1
AUSTRALIA + N.Z.	10	0	1	1	0	1	1	2	2	0	0	0	0	2	1	0	0	1	1	0	1	0
ASIA + OTHER AFRICA	8	0	0	0	2	2	0	0	0	0	1	0	0	2	1	2	1	0	0	0	0	0
JAPAN	3	0	0	0	0	2	0	0	0	0	0	0	0	0	1	0	0	0	0	0	0	0
OTHER ASIA+AFR.	8	0	0	0	2	0	0	0	0	0	0	0	0	2	1	0	0	0	0	0	0	0
BLACK AFRICA	1	0	0	0	0	0	0	0	0	0	0	0	0	0	1	0	0	0	0	0	0	0
ARAB WORLD	1	1	0	0	0	2	0	0	0	0	0	0	0	0	1	0	0	0	0	0	0	0
INDIA	0	0	0	0	0	0	0	0	0	0	0	0	0	0	0	0	0	0	0	0	0	0
PHILIPPINES	5	0	0	0	0	0	0	0	0	0	0	0	0	0	1	0	1	0	0	0	1	0
OTHER E. ASIA	4	0	0	0	2	0	0	0	0	0	0	0	0	0	0	0	0	0	0	0	1	0
OTHER ASIA	4	0	0	0	0	0	0	0	0	0	0	0	1	0	0	0	2	0	0	2	0	0

CHAPTER 2- THE EXPANSION OF PARENT SYSTEMS
SECTION 2- THE FLOW OF MANUFACTURING BY INDUSTRY OF PARENT SYSTEM
TABLE 2- SYSTEMS IN OTHER FOOD AND BEVERAGE INDUSTRIES (SIC 203-209)
CLASSIFIED BY PERIOD SYSTEM FIRST OPERATED A MANUFACTURING SUBSIDIARY
IN SPECIFIED COUNTRIES AND REGIONS

PERIOD

COUNTRY OR REGION	PRE 1968	PRE 1901	1901 -13	1914 -19	1920 -24	1925 -29	1930 -34	1935 -39	1940 -45	1946 -50	1951 -53	1954 -55	1956 -57	1958 -59	1960 -61	1962	1963	1964	1965	1966	1967	UNK
OUTSIDE U.S.	20	0	3	2	5	4	2	2	0	0	1	0	0	0	1	0	0	0	0	0	0	0
OUT. U.S. + CANADA	20	0	1	2	3	7	0	1	0	0	0	1	3	0	2	0	0	0	0	0	0	0
OUT. WEST. HEMIS.	20	0	1	2	2	7	2	2	0	1	1	1	2	1	2	0	0	0	0	0	0	0
OUT. WHITE CWEALTH	20	0	0	1	2	3	1	2	1	1	1	2	3	1	2	1	1	0	0	0	0	0
OUT. DEVLPED WORLD	20	0	0	0	2	2	0	4	0	2	1	1	3	1	1	1	1	1	0	0	0	0
CANADA	20	0	3	1	3	2	3	3	0	0	2	1	1	0	3	0	0	0	0	0	0	0
LATIN AMERICA	20	0	0	0	1	1	1	1	1	2	1	1	3	1	1	1	0	2	0	2	2	0
C. AMER.+CARIB.	20	0	0	0	1	0	2	4	1	1	0	1	3	0	1	2	1	2	0	0	0	0
CUBA	7	0	0	0	0	0	1	4	1	2	2	0	0	1	1	0	0	0	0	0	0	0
MEXICO	17	0	0	0	0	0	1	3	1	1	2	0	1	0	1	1	0	1	0	1	1	0
OTHER	11	0	0	0	0	1	1	0	1	1	0	1	4	0	2	3	0	1	0	0	0	0
S. AMERICA	15	0	0	0	1	1	1	0	0	0	0	1	2	1	1	2	2	0	0	0	0	0
ARGENTINA	6	0	0	0	1	1	0	0	1	1	1	1	2	0	2	2	1	1	0	0	0	1
BRAZIL	8	0	0	0	0	0	1	0	1	0	0	0	2	0	0	0	0	0	0	0	0	0
PERU	5	0	0	0	0	0	0	0	0	0	0	1	0	0	1	0	1	0	0	0	0	0
COLOMBIA	6	0	0	0	0	0	1	0	0	0	0	0	2	0	0	2	0	0	0	0	0	0
VENEZUELA	10	0	0	0	0	0	0	0	1	1	2	2	2	2	3	0	0	0	1	0	0	1
OTHER	5	0	0	0	0	0	0	0	0	0	0	0	0	0	2	1	1	0	1	1	1	0
EUROPE	20	0	1	1	1	4	0	4	0	2	0	1	1	2	3	0	0	0	0	0	0	0
EFTA	18	0	1	1	0	4	1	4	0	2	0	0	1	1	1	1	1	0	0	0	0	0
U.K.	18	0	1	1	0	4	0	6	0	2	0	0	1	1	1	0	1	1	0	0	0	0
SCANDINAVIA	7	0	1	0	0	0	1	0	1	0	0	0	1	0	0	1	0	0	0	0	0	0
SWITZERLAND	2	0	0	0	0	0	0	0	0	0	0	0	0	0	0	0	0	0	0	0	0	0
OTHER EFTA	5	0	0	0	0	0	0	0	0	0	0	0	0	1	0	1	0	1	0	1	0	0
EUROP. COMMUNITY	20	0	0	0	2	1	1	0	1	0	1	2	3	2	5	0	2	1	1	0	2	1
FRANCE	15	0	0	0	1	0	1	0	0	1	1	3	1	0	5	1	2	1	0	1	0	0
GERMANY	15	0	0	0	1	1	0	0	0	0	0	1	1	1	3	3	3	1	3	0	0	0
ITALY	12	0	0	0	0	0	0	0	2	0	0	0	0	1	3	1	1	0	1	0	1	0
BELGIUM + LUX	9	0	0	0	1	1	1	1	0	0	0	1	1	0	2	1	1	0	1	0	0	1
NETHERLANDS	7	0	0	0	0	0	0	0	0	0	0	1	0	1	0	1	1	0	1	0	0	0
SPAIN	11	0	0	0	0	0	0	0	0	0	0	1	1	0	0	1	0	2	0	2	0	0
GREECE + TURKEY	2	0	0	0	0	0	2	0	0	1	0	1	0	1	0	0	0	0	0	1	1	0
OTHER EUROPE	3	0	0	0	0	0	0	1	0	2	1	0	0	0	1	0	0	1	0	0	0	0
EUROPE EX. U.K.	20	0	0	1	1	1	2	0	1	0	1	1	1	3	5	0	1	1	0	0	0	0
SOUTHERN DOMINIONS	17	0	0	1	2	2	0	2	0	0	1	0	0	2	2	0	0	0	1	1	1	1
S. AFRICA +RHOD.	8	0	0	1	1	1	0	1	0	1	0	1	0	2	5	1	1	1	0	1	1	0
AUSTRALIA + N.Z.	14	0	0	1	1	1	0	1	0	0	1	1	3	1	5	0	0	0	1	0	0	1
ASIA + OTHER AFRICA	13	0	0	0	2	2	0	0	0	0	1	1	1	0	0	1	3	0	1	1	1	0
JAPAN	7	0	0	0	0	0	0	0	0	0	0	0	1	0	0	0	1	0	1	0	1	0
OTHER ASIA+AFR.	12	0	0	0	2	2	0	0	0	0	0	1	3	1	0	3	3	1	1	1	0	0
BLACK AFRICA	1	0	0	0	0	0	0	0	0	0	0	0	0	0	0	0	1	0	1	0	0	0
ARAB WORLD	2	0	0	0	0	0	1	0	0	0	0	1	0	0	0	1	0	0	0	1	0	0
INDIA	1	0	0	0	0	0	0	0	0	0	0	0	0	1	0	0	0	0	0	0	0	0
PHILIPPINES	6	0	0	0	2	2	0	0	0	0	0	0	0	1	0	0	2	0	0	0	0	0
OTHER E. ASIA	3	0	0	0	0	0	1	0	0	0	0	0	0	0	0	0	1	0	0	0	1	0
OTHER ASIA	2	0	0	0	0	0	0	0	0	0	1	0	1	0	0	0	0	0	0	0	0	0

CHAPTER 2- THE EXPANSION OF PARENT SYSTEMS
SECTION 2- THE FLOW OF MANUFACTURING BY INDUSTRY OF PARENT SYSTEM
TABLE 3- SYSTEMS IN THE TEXTILE AND APPAREL INDUSTRIES (SIC 22 AND 23)
CLASSIFIED BY PERIOD SYSTEM FIRST OPERATED A MANUFACTURING SUBSIDIARY
IN SPECIFIED COUNTRIES AND REGIONS

COUNTRY OR REGION	PRE 1968	PRE 1901	1901 -13	1914 -19	1920 -24	1925 -29	1930 -34	1935 -39	1940 -45	1946 -50	1951 -53	1954 -55	1956 -57	1958 -59	1960 -61	1962	1963	1964	1965	1966	1967	UNK
OUTSIDE U.S.	4	0	0	0	0	1	1	0	1	1	0	0	0	0	0	0	0	0	0	0	0	0
OUT. U.S. + CANADA	4	0	0	0	1	1	1	0	2	2	0	1	0	0	0	0	0	0	0	0	0	0
OUT. WEST. HEMIS.	4	0	0	0	0	0	0	0	2	2	0	1	1	3	1	0	0	0	0	0	0	0
OUT. WHITE CWEALTH	4	0	0	0	0	0	1	0	2	1	0	1	0	0	0	0	0	0	0	0	0	0
OUT. DEVLPED WORLD	4	0	0	0	0	0	1	0	2	2	0	1	0	0	0	0	0	0	0	0	0	0
CANADA	4	0	0	0	0	1	1	1	1	1	0	0	1	0	0	0	0	0	0	0	0	0
LATIN AMERICA	4	0	0	0	0	1	1	0	2	2	0	1	0	0	1	1	0	0	0	0	0	0
C. AMER.+CARIB.	3	0	0	0	0	0	1	0	2	0	0	1	0	0	1	1	0	0	0	0	0	0
CUBA	2	0	0	0	0	0	0	0	2	0	0	0	0	0	0	0	0	0	0	0	0	1
MEXICO	3	0	0	0	0	0	1	0	0	2	1	1	0	1	1	0	0	0	0	0	0	0
OTHER	0	0	0	0	0	0	0	0	0	0	0	0	0	0	0	0	0	0	0	0	0	0
S. AMERICA	4	0	0	0	1	1	0	0	0	1	0	0	1	1	1	2	0	0	0	0	0	1
ARGENTINA	2	0	0	0	0	0	1	0	0	0	0	1	0	0	1	0	0	0	0	0	0	0
BRAZIL	2	0	0	0	0	0	1	0	1	0	0	0	0	0	1	0	1	0	0	0	0	0
PERU	0	0	0	0	0	0	0	0	0	0	0	0	0	0	0	0	0	0	0	0	0	1
COLOMBIA	3	0	0	0	0	0	0	0	1	0	0	0	0	1	0	0	1	1	0	0	0	0
VENEZUELA	2	0	0	0	0	0	1	0	0	1	0	0	0	0	0	0	0	1	0	0	0	0
OTHER	1	0	0	0	0	0	0	0	1	0	0	0	0	0	0	0	0	0	0	0	0	0
EUROPE	4	0	0	0	0	0	0	0	0	0	0	0	0	0	0	0	0	0	0	0	0	0
EFTA	4	0	0	0	0	0	0	0	0	0	0	0	0	0	2	1	0	0	0	0	0	0
U.K.	3	0	0	0	0	0	0	0	0	0	0	0	0	0	2	1	0	0	0	0	0	0
SCANDINAVIA	0	0	0	0	0	0	0	0	0	0	0	0	0	0	0	0	0	0	0	0	0	0
SWITZERLAND	1	0	0	0	0	0	0	0	0	0	0	0	0	0	0	0	0	0	0	0	0	0
OTHER EFTA	1	0	0	0	0	0	0	0	0	0	0	0	0	0	0	0	0	0	0	0	0	0
EUROP. COMMUNITY	4	0	0	0	0	0	0	0	0	0	0	0	0	1	1	0	1	1	0	0	0	0
FRANCE	3	0	0	0	0	0	0	0	0	0	0	0	1	0	1	0	0	0	0	0	0	0
GERMANY	2	0	0	0	0	0	0	0	0	0	0	0	0	1	1	2	0	0	0	0	0	0
ITALY	3	0	0	0	0	0	0	0	0	0	0	0	0	1	1	0	1	0	0	0	0	0
BELGIUM + LUX	0	0	0	0	0	0	0	0	0	0	0	0	0	0	0	0	0	0	0	1	0	0
NETHERLANDS	1	0	0	0	0	0	0	0	0	0	0	0	0	0	0	0	0	1	1	0	0	0
SPAIN	2	0	0	0	0	0	0	0	0	0	0	0	0	0	0	0	0	1	1	0	0	0
GREECE + TURKEY	0	0	0	0	0	0	0	0	0	0	0	0	0	0	0	0	0	0	0	0	0	0
OTHER EUROPE	0	0	0	0	0	0	0	0	0	0	0	0	0	0	0	1	0	0	0	0	0	0
EUROPE EX. U.K.	4	0	0	0	0	0	0	0	0	0	0	0	0	1	1	1	0	0	0	0	0	0
SOUTHERN DOMINIONS	2	0	0	0	0	0	0	0	0	0	0	0	0	1	1	0	1	0	0	0	0	0
S. AFRICA +RHOD.	2	0	0	0	0	0	0	0	0	0	0	0	0	1	1	0	0	1	0	0	0	0
AUSTRALIA + N.Z.	1	0	0	0	0	0	0	0	0	0	0	0	0	0	0	0	1	0	1	1	0	0
ASIA + OTHER AFRICA	1	0	0	0	0	0	0	0	0	0	0	0	0	0	0	0	0	0	1	1	0	0
JAPAN	1	0	0	0	0	0	0	0	0	0	0	0	0	0	0	0	0	0	1	0	0	0
OTHER ASIA+AFR.	0	0	0	0	0	0	0	0	0	0	0	0	0	0	0	0	0	0	0	0	0	0
BLACK AFRICA	0	0	0	0	0	0	0	0	0	0	0	0	0	0	0	0	0	0	0	0	0	0
ARAB WORLD	0	0	0	0	0	0	0	0	0	0	0	0	0	0	0	0	0	0	0	0	0	0
INDIA	0	0	0	0	0	0	0	0	0	0	0	0	0	0	0	0	0	0	0	0	0	0
PHILIPPINES	0	0	0	0	0	0	0	0	0	0	0	0	0	0	0	0	0	0	0	0	0	0
OTHER E. ASIA	0	0	0	0	0	0	0	0	0	0	0	0	0	0	0	0	0	0	0	0	0	0
OTHER ASIA	0	0	0	0	0	0	0	0	0	0	0	0	0	0	0	0	0	0	0	0	0	0

PERIOD

CHAPTER 2- THE EXPANSION OF PARENT SYSTEMS
SECTION 2- THE FLOW OF MANUFACTURING BY INDUSTRY OF PARENT SYSTEM
TABLE 4- SYSTEMS IN THE LUMBER, FURNITURE, AND PAPER INDUSTRIES (SIC 24,25,26)
CLASSIFIED BY PERIOD SYSTEM FIRST OPERATED A MANUFACTURING SUBSIDIARY
IN SPECIFIED COUNTRIES AND REGIONS

PERIOD

COUNTRY OR REGION	PRE 1968	PRE 1901	1901 -13	1914 -19	1920 -24	1925 -29	1930 -36	1935 -39	1940 -45	1946 -50	1951 -53	1954 -55	1956 -57	1958 -59	1960 -61	1962	1963	1964	1965	1966	1967	UNK
OUTSIDE U.S.	6	0	0	1	0	2	0	0	1	0	0	2	1	0	1	0	0	0	0	0	0	0
OUT. U.S. + CANADA	6	0	0	0	0	1	0	0	1	1	0	2	1	1	2	0	0	0	0	0	0	0
OUT. WEST. HEMIS.	6	0	0	0	0	1	0	0	0	0	0	2	0	1	2	0	0	0	0	0	0	0
OUT. WHITE CWEALTH	6	0	0	0	0	1	0	0	1	0	0	2	0	1	2	0	0	0	0	0	0	0
OUT. DEVLPED WORLD	6	0	0	1	0	1	0	0	1	0	0	2	0	1	1	0	0	0	0	0	0	0
CANADA	5	0	0	0	0	1	1	0	0	0	0	1	0	1	1	0	0	0	0	0	0	0
LATIN AMERICA	6	0	0	1	0	1	0	0	1	0	0	2	0	1	2	0	0	0	0	0	0	0
C. AMER.+CARIB.	6	0	0	0	1	1	0	0	1	0	0	2	0	0	1	1	1	0	1	0	1	0
CUBA	1	0	0	0	0	0	0	0	0	0	0	0	0	0	0	0	0	0	0	0	0	0
MEXICO	5	0	0	0	0	1	1	0	1	0	0	2	0	1	1	0	0	0	0	0	0	0
OTHER	5	0	0	0	0	1	1	0	0	0	0	0	0	0	2	1	0	0	1	0	0	0
S. AMERICA	1	0	0	0	0	0	0	0	2	0	0	0	0	0	0	1	0	0	0	0	0	0
ARGENTINA	1	0	0	0	0	0	0	0	0	0	0	0	0	1	0	0	0	0	0	0	0	0
BRAZIL	0	0	0	0	0	0	0	0	0	0	0	0	0	0	0	0	0	0	0	0	0	0
PERU	0	0	0	0	0	0	0	0	0	0	0	0	0	1	0	0	0	0	0	0	0	0
COLOMBIA	4	0	0	0	0	0	0	0	0	0	0	0	0	1	0	0	0	0	0	0	0	0
VENEZUELA	4	0	0	0	0	0	0	0	2	0	0	1	0	1	1	0	0	0	1	1	1	0
OTHER	2	0	0	0	0	0	0	0	0	0	0	0	0	0	1	0	0	0	1	0	1	0
EUROPE	6	0	0	0	0	1	0	0	0	0	1	2	1	1	2	0	1	0	0	0	0	0
EFTA	5	0	0	0	0	0	0	0	0	0	1	1	1	0	2	1	1	0	0	0	0	0
U.K.	5	0	0	0	0	0	0	0	0	0	0	0	1	0	0	0	0	0	0	0	0	0
SCANDINAVIA	1	0	0	0	0	0	0	0	0	0	0	0	0	0	0	1	0	0	0	0	0	0
SWITZERLAND	0	0	0	0	0	0	0	0	0	0	0	0	0	0	0	0	0	0	0	0	0	0
OTHER EFTA	0	0	0	0	0	0	0	0	0	0	0	0	0	0	1	0	0	0	0	0	0	0
EUROP. COMMUNITY	6	0	0	0	0	1	0	0	0	0	0	1	1	2	0	1	0	0	0	0	0	0
FRANCE	4	0	0	0	0	0	0	0	0	0	0	1	1	0	1	0	2	0	0	0	0	0
GERMANY	5	0	0	0	0	0	1	0	0	0	0	0	1	1	1	0	1	0	0	0	0	0
ITALY	5	0	0	0	0	0	1	0	0	0	0	1	1	2	1	0	0	1	0	0	0	0
BELGIUM + LUX	3	0	0	0	0	0	1	0	0	0	0	0	0	1	1	0	0	1	1	0	0	0
NETHERLANDS	2	0	0	0	0	0	0	0	0	0	0	0	0	1	1	0	0	0	1	0	0	0
SPAIN	4	0	0	0	0	0	0	0	0	0	0	0	0	1	0	0	0	0	3	0	0	0
GREECE + TURKEY	1	0	0	0	0	0	0	0	0	0	0	0	0	0	0	1	0	1	1	0	1	0
OTHER EUROPE	1	0	0	0	0	0	0	0	0	0	1	0	0	0	0	0	0	0	0	0	0	0
EUROPE Ex. U.K.	6	0	0	0	1	1	0	0	0	0	2	1	1	1	1	0	0	0	0	0	0	0
SOUTHERN DOMINIONS	4	0	0	0	0	0	0	0	0	0	1	1	0	1	0	0	0	1	1	0	1	0
S. AFRICA +RHOD.	3	0	0	0	0	0	1	0	0	0	1	1	0	1	0	1	0	0	0	1	0	0
AUSTRALIA + N.Z.	5	0	0	0	0	1	0	0	0	0	1	1	0	1	1	0	0	1	0	0	0	0
ASIA + OTHER AFRICA	2	0	0	0	0	0	0	0	0	0	0	0	0	1	1	0	1	0	0	0	0	0
JAPAN	5	0	0	0	0	0	0	0	0	0	1	0	0	0	1	1	0	0	1	1	0	0
OTHER ASIA+AFR.	1	0	0	0	0	0	0	0	0	0	0	1	0	1	1	0	0	0	1	0	1	0
BLACK AFRICA	0	0	0	0	0	0	0	0	0	0	0	0	0	0	0	0	0	0	0	0	0	0
ARAB WORLD	1	0	0	0	0	0	0	0	0	0	1	0	0	0	0	0	0	0	0	0	0	0
INDIA	0	0	0	0	0	0	0	0	0	0	0	0	0	0	1	0	0	0	0	0	0	0
PHILIPPINES	4	0	0	0	0	0	0	0	0	0	1	0	0	0	0	0	2	0	0	1	0	0
OTHER E. ASIA	0	0	0	0	0	0	0	0	0	0	0	0	0	0	1	0	0	0	0	0	0	0
OTHER ASIA	2	0	0	0	0	0	0	0	0	0	0	0	0	1	0	0	0	0	0	0	0	0

CHAPTER 2— THE EXPANSION OF PARENT SYSTEMS
SECTION 2— THE FLOW OF MANUFACTURING BY INDUSTRY OF PARENT SYSTEM
TABLE 5— SYSTEMS IN THE CHEMICAL INDUSTRIES (SIC 281,282,285-289)
CLASSIFIED BY PERIOD SYSTEM FIRST OPERATED A MANUFACTURING SUBSIDIARY
IN SPECIFIED COUNTRIES AND REGIONS

PERIOD

COUNTRY OR REGION	PRE 1968	PRE 1901	1901-13	1914-19	1920-24	1925-29	1930-34	1935-39	1940-45	1946-50	1951-53	1954-55	1956-57	1958-59	1960-61	1962	1963	1964	1965	1966	1967	UNK
OUTSIDE U.S.	20	2	3	4	2	2	1	1	4	2	0	0	0	0	0	0	0	0	0	0	0	0
OUT. U.S. + CANADA	20	2	3	3	2	1	1	1	4	3	0	0	1	0	0	0	0	0	0	0	0	0
OUT. WEST. HEMIS.	20	1	0	1	6	3	1	0	3	3	1	0	1	1	2	0	1	0	0	0	0	0
OUT. WHITE CWEALTH	20	0	0	2	5	3	1	1	0	3	0	0	1	0	0	1	1	0	0	0	0	0
OUT. DEVLPED WORLD	20	1	0	1	4	2	1	2	4	3	1	0	1	0	1	1	1	0	0	0	0	0
CANADA	19	1	3	3	0	3	1	1	2	2	2	0	1	0	0	0	0	0	0	0	0	0
LATIN AMERICA	20	2	0	1	2	1	1	3	4	3	1	0	1	0	1	1	1	0	0	0	0	0
C. AMER.+CARIB.	19	1	0	0	0	0	0	1	3	1	1	1	3	0	1	1	0	1	1	1	0	0
CUBA	1	0	0	0	0	1	0	0	0	0	0	0	1	0	0	1	1	0	0	0	0	0
MEXICO	18	0	0	0	0	0	0	0	3	1	0	0	1	1	2	1	1	3	1	0	0	1
OTHER	13	0	0	1	0	1	1	0	0	2	1	1	1	0	1	1	1	0	0	0	0	0
S. AMERICA	18	1	0	1	2	1	2	2	1	4	3	1	1	2	0	1	3	0	1	1	0	0
ARGENTINA	16	0	0	1	0	1	2	2	1	0	1	0	1	0	0	1	1	0	1	0	0	1
BRAZIL	14	0	0	0	0	1	0	1	1	3	3	1	1	2	1	1	1	1	0	0	0	0
PERU	3	1	0	0	0	0	0	0	0	0	0	0	0	1	1	0	0	0	0	0	0	1
COLOMBIA	12	0	0	0	0	0	0	0	4	1	2	1	0	1	1	2	1	1	0	0	0	0
VENEZUELA	11	0	0	0	0	0	0	0	1	1	0	1	3	2	1	1	0	1	1	0	0	1
OTHER	10	0	0	0	3	0	0	0	1	1	0	0	2	0	0	1	1	1	0	0	0	1
EUROPE	20	0	0	1	5	3	1	0	3	3	1	2	0	1	2	0	0	2	2	0	0	0
EFTA	18	0	0	1	3	3	0	0	2	1	1	4	0	0	1	1	0	1	1	0	0	0
U.K.	17	0	0	1	3	2	1	0	0	1	1	1	0	0	1	1	1	0	0	0	0	0
SCANDINAVIA	8	0	0	1	0	1	0	0	0	0	0	1	0	0	2	0	0	2	2	0	0	0
SWITZERLAND	3	0	0	0	0	0	0	0	0	0	0	1	0	0	0	0	0	0	0	0	0	0
OTHER EFTA	3	0	0	0	0	0	0	0	0	1	0	0	0	1	1	1	1	0	0	0	0	0
EUROP. COMMUNITY	20	0	0	0	2	4	0	0	0	1	4	3	0	0	3	0	1	0	3	0	0	0
FRANCE	15	0	0	0	1	1	0	0	1	0	2	1	0	1	1	1	1	0	0	0	0	0
GERMANY	13	0	0	0	1	2	0	0	0	0	2	3	0	1	3	0	0	0	0	0	0	1
ITALY	17	0	0	0	0	1	1	0	0	1	1	0	0	1	2	0	1	1	0	0	0	0
BELGIUM + LUX	10	0	0	0	1	2	0	1	1	1	0	2	0	1	3	3	1	3	0	0	1	0
NETHERLANDS	10	0	0	0	0	0	0	0	1	1	1	0	1	2	2	1	0	1	1	0	0	1
SPAIN	14	0	0	0	0	0	0	0	1	1	2	2	3	3	3	3	1	0	0	0	0	0
GREECE + TURKEY	5	0	0	0	0	0	0	0	0	0	0	0	0	0	1	0	1	2	2	2	0	0
OTHER EUROPE	3	0	0	0	0	0	0	0	1	1	4	3	0	1	0	1	0	1	1	0	0	0
EUROPE EX. U.K.	20	0	0	1	3	3	1	0	1	1	0	3	0	1	2	0	0	1	0	0	0	0
SOUTHERN DOMINIONS	18	0	0	0	0	3	1	0	1	1	2	2	0	2	2	0	2	1	1	2	2	1
S. AFRICA +RHOD.	7	0	0	0	0	0	1	2	1	1	0	0	1	0	1	2	0	0	0	0	0	1
AUSTRALIA + N.Z.	18	0	0	0	0	3	0	1	1	2	2	2	2	2	2	1	1	1	1	2	2	0
ASIA + OTHER AFRICA	20	0	0	0	0	1	0	2	1	1	3	1	0	1	4	2	2	2	0	0	0	1
JAPAN	16	0	0	0	0	0	0	0	0	0	4	0	2	1	4	2	1	1	1	0	0	0
OTHER ASIA+AFR.	16	0	0	0	0	1	0	0	1	0	0	1	0	0	3	0	1	0	1	0	1	1
BLACK AFRICA	4	0	0	0	0	0	0	0	0	0	0	0	0	0	1	0	0	0	1	0	0	0
ARAB WORLD	1	0	0	0	0	1	0	0	0	1	0	0	0	0	0	0	0	0	0	0	0	1
INDIA	11	0	0	0	0	0	0	0	1	0	1	1	0	3	2	2	1	0	1	1	0	0
PHILIPPINES	6	0	0	0	0	0	0	0	0	0	1	0	0	1	0	0	1	1	0	0	1	1
OTHER E. ASIA	8	0	0	0	0	0	0	0	0	1	1	0	0	1	1	1	0	1	0	0	0	1
OTHER ASIA	8	0	0	0	0	0	0	0	1	1	0	0	0	0	0	0	1	0	1	1	1	2

CHAPTER 2— THE EXPANSION OF PARENT SYSTEMS
SECTION 2— THE FLOW OF MANUFACTURING BY INDUSTRY OF PARENT SYSTEM
TABLE 6— SYSTEMS IN THE DRUG INDUSTRY (SIC 283)
CLASSIFIED BY PERIOD SYSTEM FIRST OPERATED A MANUFACTURING SUBSIDIARY
IN SPECIFIED COUNTRIES AND REGIONS

COUNTRY OR REGION	PRE 1968	PRE 1901	1901 -13	1914 -19	1920 -24	1925 -29	1930 -34	1935 -39	1940 -45	1946 -50	1951 -53	1954 -55	1956 -57	1958 -59	1960 -61	1962 -63	1964	1965	1966	1967	UNK
OUTSIDE U.S.	14	0	1	0	1	3	2	2	0	1	1	2	1	0	0	0	0	0	0	0	0
OUT. U.S. + CANADA	14	0	0	1	1	2	3	1	2	2	1	1	1	1	0	0	0	0	0	0	0
OUT. WEST. HEMIS.	14	0	0	0	1	2	2	2	1	1	1	2	1	1	0	0	0	0	0	0	0
OUT. WHITE CWEALTH	14	0	1	1	2	0	1	2	1	2	1	2	1	0	0	0	0	0	0	0	0
OUT. DEVLPED WORLD	14	0	1	1	0	0	2	2	1	1	3	2	1	0	1	0	0	0	0	0	0
CANADA	12	0	1	0	0	2	2	1	1	1	1	1	1	1	0	0	0	0	0	0	0
LATIN AMERICA	14	0	0	1	2	2	1	1	1	1	2	1	1	1	0	0	0	0	0	0	0
C. AMER.+CARIB.	14	0	0	1	0	0	1	2	1	1	2	1	3	1	1	0	0	0	0	0	0
CUBA	1	0	0	0	0	0	0	0	0	1	0	0	0	0	0	0	0	0	0	0	0
MEXICO	14	0	0	1	0	0	1	0	1	1	2	0	3	1	2	1	0	1	0	0	0
OTHER	10	0	0	0	0	1	0	0	1	0	0	1	2	1	0	2	0	0	0	1	1
S. AMERICA	13	0	0	0	0	0	0	2	0	1	0	2	0	1	2	0	3	0	0	0	0
ARGENTINA	9	0	0	0	0	1	2	0	1	1	0	0	1	1	0	1	0	0	0	0	0
BRAZIL	12	0	0	0	0	1	0	0	0	0	2	2	0	2	2	1	0	0	0	0	0
PERU	6	0	0	0	0	0	0	1	1	4	0	0	0	0	0	0	0	0	0	0	0
COLOMBIA	7	0	0	0	0	0	1	1	1	0	0	0	1	0	2	0	0	0	1	0	0
VENEZUELA	8	0	0	0	0	0	0	1	1	1	0	0	0	1	6	1	0	0	1	0	0
OTHER	6	0	0	0	0	0	0	0	2	1	1	1	0	1	0	0	0	0	0	0	0
EUROPE	14	0	0	2	2	2	1	0	2	2	1	2	2	0	0	0	0	0	0	0	0
EFTA	13	0	0	1	1	2	2	2	1	1	1	1	2	0	0	0	0	0	0	0	0
U.K.	13	0	0	1	1	2	2	2	0	0	1	1	2	0	0	1	0	0	0	0	0
SCANDINAVIA	3	0	0	0	0	0	0	0	0	0	0	0	0	0	1	0	1	0	0	0	0
SWITZERLAND	2	0	0	0	0	0	1	0	0	0	0	0	0	0	0	0	0	0	0	0	0
OTHER EFTA	5	0	0	0	0	1	0	0	0	0	0	0	0	4	1	1	2	1	0	0	0
EUROP. COMMUNITY	14	0	0	1	1	0	0	1	2	2	1	3	0	3	0	0	0	0	0	0	0
FRANCE	10	0	0	1	1	0	1	0	0	0	0	1	0	1	1	1	2	0	0	1	0
GERMANY	8	0	0	0	1	0	0	0	0	1	0	1	1	1	2	1	0	0	0	0	0
ITALY	13	0	0	0	0	1	2	0	1	0	2	1	0	3	0	1	1	1	0	0	0
BELGIUM + LUX	7	0	0	0	0	0	0	0	0	0	0	1	1	2	2	0	1	0	0	0	0
NETHERLANDS	7	0	0	0	0	0	0	1	0	1	0	1	0	0	0	0	1	1	2	0	0
SPAIN	8	0	0	0	0	0	0	0	0	0	0	0	1	1	1	1	1	0	2	0	0
GREECE + TURKEY	5	0	0	0	0	0	0	0	0	1	1	0	0	0	1	0	1	1	0	0	0
OTHER EUROPE	1	0	0	0	0	0	0	0	2	0	0	0	1	0	0	0	0	0	0	0	0
EUROPE Ex. U.K.	14	0	0	1	1	0	0	0	0	2	1	3	1	4	2	1	0	0	0	0	0
SOUTHERN DOMINIONS	13	0	0	0	0	0	3	1	2	0	0	1	3	2	0	0	0	0	0	0	0
S. AFRICA +RHOD.	12	0	0	0	0	0	2	2	1	0	1	1	2	1	0	1	1	0	0	0	0
AUSTRALIA + N.Z.	11	0	0	0	0	0	1	1	2	1	1	0	3	1	0	0	0	0	0	0	0
ASIA + OTHER AFRICA	12	0	0	0	0	0	0	0	2	2	0	1	2	1	2	0	1	1	0	0	0
JAPAN	10	0	0	0	0	0	1	0	0	0	1	1	1	1	1	0	2	2	0	0	0
OTHER ASIA+AFR.	12	0	0	0	0	0	2	0	0	2	2	0	2	0	0	1	1	0	0	0	0
BLACK AFRICA	3	0	0	0	0	0	1	0	0	0	0	0	0	0	1	0	1	0	0	0	0
ARAB WORLD	2	0	0	0	0	0	1	0	0	0	0	1	0	0	0	0	0	0	0	0	0
INDIA	7	0	0	0	0	0	0	0	1	1	1	0	3	0	0	1	0	1	1	0	0
PHILIPPINES	8	0	0	0	0	0	0	0	1	0	2	1	2	1	0	1	0	0	0	0	0
OTHER E. ASIA	2	0	0	0	0	0	0	0	1	1	0	0	0	0	0	0	0	1	0	0	0
OTHER ASIA	10	0	0	0	0	0	0	0	1	1	0	0	1	2	3	2	0	0	0	0	0

CHAPTER 2- THE EXPANSION OF PARENT SYSTEMS
SECTION 2- THE FLOW OF MANUFACTURING BY INDUSTRY OF PARENT SYSTEM
TABLE 7- SYSTEMS IN THE SOAP AND COSMETICS INDUSTRY (SIC 284)
CLASSIFIED BY PERIOD SYSTEM FIRST OPERATED A MANUFACTURING SUBSIDIARY
IN SPECIFIED COUNTRIES AND REGIONS

PERIOD

COUNTRY OR REGION	PRE 1968	PRE 1901	1901 -13	1914 -19	1920 -24	1925 -29	1930 -34	1935 -39	1940 -45	1946 -50	1951 -53	1954 -55	1956 -57	1958 -59	1960 -61	1962	1963	1964	1965	1966	1967	UNK
OUTSIDE U.S.	5	0	0	2	0	1	0	0	0	0	0	0	0	0	0	0	0	0	0	0	0	0
OUT. U.S. + CANADA	5	0	0	0	1	1	0	0	2	2	0	0	0	0	0	0	0	0	0	0	0	0
OUT. WEST. HEMIS.	5	0	0	1	1	1	0	0	1	1	0	0	1	1	0	0	0	0	0	0	0	0
OUT. WHITE CWEALTH	5	0	0	0	1	1	2	0	1	1	0	0	1	1	0	0	0	0	0	0	0	0
OUT. DEVLPED WORLD	5	0	0	0	0	0	2	0	1	1	0	0	0	1	0	0	0	0	0	0	0	0
CANADA	5	0	0	2	1	1	0	0	0	0	0	0	1	0	1	0	0	0	0	0	0	0
LATIN AMERICA	5	0	0	2	1	1	2	2	1	1	0	0	1	1	0	0	0	0	0	0	0	0
C. AMER.+CARIB.	3	0	0	0	1	0	1	1	1	1	0	0	1	0	0	0	0	0	0	0	0	0
CUBA	5	0	0	0	0	1	0	2	0	0	0	0	0	0	0	0	0	0	0	0	0	0
MEXICO	2	0	0	0	1	0	1	1	1	1	0	0	1	0	0	1	0	0	1	0	0	0
OTHER	4	0	0	0	0	0	0	0	0	1	0	0	1	1	1	0	0	0	0	0	0	0
S. AMERICA	3	0	0	0	0	0	1	1	0	1	1	0	0	1	1	0	0	0	0	0	0	0
ARGENTINA	2	0	0	0	0	0	0	0	0	0	0	1	0	1	0	1	0	0	1	0	0	0
BRAZIL	3	0	0	0	0	0	1	1	0	0	1	0	1	0	1	0	0	0	0	0	0	0
PERU	3	0	0	0	0	0	0	0	0	0	0	0	0	0	0	0	0	0	0	0	0	0
COLOMBIA	3	0	0	0	0	0	0	0	0	1	1	1	1	1	0	1	0	0	0	0	0	0
VENEZUELA	3	0	0	0	0	0	0	0	1	0	0	0	0	1	1	1	0	0	1	0	1	0
OTHER	1	0	0	0	0	0	0	0	0	0	0	0	0	0	0	0	0	0	0	0	1	0
EUROPE	5	0	0	0	1	1	0	1	1	1	0	0	0	1	0	0	0	0	0	0	0	0
EFTA	4	0	0	0	1	1	1	1	1	1	0	0	1	0	0	0	1	1	1	0	0	0
U.K.	4	0	0	0	0	0	0	0	0	0	0	0	0	0	0	0	0	0	0	0	0	0
SCANDINAVIA	3	0	0	0	0	0	0	0	0	0	0	0	0	0	1	0	0	1	1	0	0	0
SWITZERLAND	0	0	0	0	0	0	0	0	0	0	0	0	0	0	0	0	0	0	0	0	0	0
OTHER EFTA	1	0	0	0	0	0	0	0	0	0	0	0	0	0	0	0	0	0	0	0	0	0
EUROP. COMMUNITY	5	0	0	1	1	0	0	0	0	0	1	1	1	1	0	1	0	0	0	0	0	0
FRANCE	5	0	0	1	0	1	0	0	0	0	1	1	1	1	0	1	0	0	0	0	1	0
GERMANY	4	0	0	0	0	0	0	0	0	0	0	0	1	1	2	0	0	0	0	0	0	0
ITALY	4	0	0	0	0	1	0	0	0	0	1	1	1	1	0	0	0	0	0	0	0	0
BELGIUM + LUX	3	0	0	0	1	1	0	0	0	0	0	0	0	1	0	0	0	0	0	0	0	0
NETHERLANDS	0	0	0	0	0	0	0	0	0	0	0	0	0	0	0	0	0	0	0	0	0	0
SPAIN	2	0	0	0	0	0	0	0	0	0	0	0	0	0	1	0	0	0	0	2	0	0
GREECE + TURKEY	2	0	0	0	0	0	0	0	0	0	0	0	0	0	0	0	0	0	0	0	0	0
OTHER EUROPE	2	0	0	0	0	0	0	0	0	0	0	0	0	0	0	0	0	0	0	0	0	0
EUROPE EX. U.K.	5	0	0	1	1	0	0	0	0	0	1	1	1	1	0	1	0	0	0	0	0	0
SOUTHERN DOMINIONS	4	0	0	0	0	0	1	0	0	0	1	0	0	1	0	1	0	0	0	0	0	0
S. AFRICA +RHOD.	4	0	0	0	0	0	0	1	0	0	2	1	0	2	1	1	0	0	0	0	0	0
AUSTRALIA + N.Z.	3	0	0	0	0	0	1	1	0	1	1	0	0	0	3	0	0	0	0	0	0	0
ASIA + OTHER AFRICA	5	0	0	0	0	0	1	1	0	0	0	0	0	0	2	0	1	0	0	0	0	0
JAPAN	3	0	0	0	1	0	0	0	1	1	0	0	0	0	1	0	0	0	0	0	0	0
OTHER ASIA+AFR.	4	0	0	0	0	0	1	1	0	0	1	0	1	1	0	0	0	1	0	0	0	0
BLACK AFRICA	2	0	0	0	0	0	0	0	0	0	0	0	0	0	0	0	0	0	0	0	0	0
ARAB WORLD	2	0	0	0	0	0	0	0	0	0	0	0	0	0	0	0	0	0	2	0	0	0
INDIA	2	0	0	0	0	0	1	1	1	1	0	0	1	1	1	0	0	0	0	0	0	0
PHILIPPINES	2	0	0	0	0	0	0	0	0	0	0	0	0	0	0	0	0	0	0	0	0	0
OTHER E. ASIA	2	0	0	0	0	0	0	0	0	1	1	0	0	1	1	1	0	1	0	0	0	0
OTHER ASIA	4	0	0	0	0	0	0	0	0	0	0	0	0	1	1	2	0	0	0	0	0	0

CHAPTER 2- THE EXPANSION OF PARENT SYSTEMS
SECTION 2- THE FLOW OF MANUFACTURING BY INDUSTRY OF PARENT SYSTEM
TABLE 8- SYSTEMS IN THE PETROLEUM INDUSTRY (SIC 291)
CLASSIFIED BY PERIOD SYSTEM FIRST OPERATED A MANUFACTURING SUBSIDIARY
IN SPECIFIED COUNTRIES AND REGIONS

PERIOD

COUNTRY OR REGION	PRE 1968	PRE 1901	1901 -13	1914 -19	1920 -24	1925 -29	1930 -34	1935 -39	1940 -45	1946 -50	1951 -53	1954 -55	1956 -57	1958 -59	1960 -61	1962	1963	1964	1965	1966	1967	UNK
OUTSIDE U.S.	9	2	0	0	1	0	0	0	1	0	0	0	0	3	1	0	0	0	0	0	0	0
OUT. U.S. + CANADA	9	2	0	0	1	0	0	1	1	0	0	0	1	3	1	0	0	0	0	0	0	0
OUT. WEST. HEMIS.	9	2	0	0	1	0	0	1	1	1	0	0	1	3	1	0	0	0	0	0	0	0
OUT. WHITE CWEALTH	9	2	1	0	1	0	0	1	0	1	0	0	1	3	1	0	0	0	0	0	0	0
OUT. DEVLPED WORLD	9	1	0	0	1	1	1	1	0	1	0	0	0	0	4	0	0	0	0	0	0	0
CANADA	8	0	0	1	0	0	0	1	1	0	0	0	1	1	1	0	0	0	0	0	0	0
LATIN AMERICA	9	0	0	0	1	2	0	1	0	1	0	0	1	3	3	1	0	1	0	1	0	0
C. AMER.+CARIB.	8	1	0	0	1	0	0	1	0	0	2	0	1	3	2	1	1	0	0	0	0	0
CUBA	2	1	1	0	0	0	0	2	0	0	0	0	0	0	0	0	0	0	0	0	0	0
MEXICO	5	0	0	0	0	0	1	0	0	0	0	0	0	2	2	2	0	1	0	1	0	0
OTHER	7	0	1	0	0	0	0	0	0	0	2	0	1	0	2	0	0	0	1	0	0	0
S. AMERICA	8	0	0	1	1	1	0	2	0	0	0	0	0	0	4	0	0	0	0	0	0	0
ARGENTINA	5	0	1	0	1	0	0	0	0	1	0	1	0	1	3	0	1	1	1	0	0	0
BRAZIL	3	0	0	0	1	0	0	0	0	0	0	0	0	0	0	0	1	0	1	0	0	0
PERU	2	0	0	0	0	0	0	0	0	0	0	0	1	0	1	0	0	0	0	0	0	0
COLOMBIA	3	0	0	0	0	0	0	0	0	0	0	0	0	0	0	0	1	0	0	0	0	0
VENEZUELA	4	0	0	0	1	0	0	0	0	1	0	0	0	0	0	1	0	1	1	1	0	0
OTHER	2	0	0	0	1	0	0	0	0	0	0	1	1	0	0	0	0	0	0	0	0	0
EUROPE	9	2	0	0	0	0	1	1	1	0	0	0	3	3	1	0	0	0	0	0	0	0
EFTA	8	1	0	0	1	0	0	2	1	0	0	0	0	0	0	1	1	1	1	1	0	0
U.K.	8	0	1	0	0	0	0	2	0	1	0	0	0	0	1	1	0	1	0	0	0	0
SCANDINAVIA	3	1	0	0	0	0	0	0	0	0	0	0	0	0	0	0	0	0	0	0	0	0
SWITZERLAND	2	0	0	0	0	0	0	0	0	0	0	0	0	1	0	2	0	0	0	0	0	0
OTHER EFTA	1	0	0	0	0	0	0	0	0	1	0	0	0	0	0	0	0	0	0	0	0	0
EUROP. COMMUNITY	9	2	0	0	1	0	1	0	0	1	0	0	2	3	2	0	0	0	1	0	0	0
FRANCE	7	1	0	0	0	0	0	0	0	1	0	0	0	2	0	1	0	0	0	0	0	0
GERMANY	7	2	0	0	0	0	0	1	0	0	0	0	0	1	1	0	1	0	0	1	0	0
ITALY	9	1	0	0	0	0	0	0	0	0	0	0	1	1	3	0	1	1	1	1	0	0
BELGIUM + LUX	6	0	0	0	0	0	1	1	0	0	0	0	0	3	1	1	1	1	0	0	0	0
NETHERLANDS	7	0	0	0	0	0	0	0	0	0	0	0	0	1	3	0	1	0	1	0	0	0
SPAIN	6	0	0	0	0	0	0	0	0	0	2	0	1	0	0	0	0	1	0	0	0	0
GREECE + TURKEY	2	0	0	0	1	0	0	0	0	0	0	0	0	0	0	1	0	1	1	0	0	0
OTHER EUROPE	3	1	1	0	0	0	0	0	0	0	2	0	0	0	2	0	0	0	1	0	0	0
EUROPE EX. U.K.	9	2	0	0	0	1	1	0	0	1	0	0	0	3	2	0	0	0	0	0	0	0
SOUTHERN DOMINIONS	7	0	0	0	0	1	0	0	0	0	2	1	0	1	0	0	0	0	0	2	0	0
S. AFRICA +RHOD.	2	0	0	0	0	0	0	0	0	0	2	1	0	1	0	0	0	1	1	0	0	0
AUSTRALIA + N.Z.	7	0	0	0	1	1	1	1	0	0	2	1	0	0	3	0	0	0	0	2	2	0
ASIA + OTHER AFRICA	9	0	0	0	0	0	0	0	0	0	0	0	0	0	2	0	0	0	0	1	0	1
JAPAN	6	0	0	0	0	1	0	1	0	0	0	0	0	0	2	0	0	0	0	1	0	0
OTHER ASIA+AFR.	9	0	0	0	1	0	1	0	0	0	2	0	0	0	3	1	2	0	0	0	0	0
BLACK AFRICA	3	0	0	0	0	0	0	0	0	0	0	1	0	1	2	0	1	0	1	0	0	1
ARAB WORLD	8	0	0	0	0	0	0	0	0	0	0	0	0	0	3	1	0	0	0	0	0	0
INDIA	4	0	0	0	1	0	0	0	1	0	0	0	0	1	1	2	0	0	0	1	0	1
PHILIPPINES	4	0	0	0	0	0	0	0	0	0	0	0	1	0	0	0	1	1	1	1	0	0
OTHER E. ASIA	2	0	0	0	0	0	0	0	0	0	0	0	0	0	1	0	0	0	0	0	0	0
OTHER ASIA	7	0	0	0	0	1	1	2	0	1	0	1	0	0	1	1	0	1	0	0	0	1

CHAPTER 2— THE EXPANSION OF PARENT SYSTEMS
SECTION 2— THE FLOW OF MANUFACTURING BY INDUSTRY OF PARENT SYSTEM
TABLE 9— SYSTEMS IN THE RUBBER AND TIRE INDUSTRY (SIC 30)
CLASSIFIED BY PERIOD SYSTEM FIRST OPERATED A MANUFACTURING SUBSIDIARY
IN SPECIFIED COUNTRIES AND REGIONS

PERIOD

COUNTRY OR REGION	PRE 1968	PRE 1901	1901 -13	1914 -19	1920 -24	1925 -29	1930 -34	1935 -39	1940 -45	1946 -50	1951 -53	1954 -55	1956 -57	1958 -59	1960 -61	1962	1963	1964	1965	1966	1967	UNK
OUTSIDE U.S.	5	0	1	2	1	0	0	0	0	0	0	0	0	0	0	0	0	0	0	0	0	0
OUT. U.S. + CANADA	5	0	1	1	1	1	0	0	0	0	0	0	0	0	0	0	0	0	0	0	0	0
OUT. WEST. HEMIS.	5	0	0	3	1	0	1	0	1	0	0	0	0	0	0	0	0	0	0	0	0	0
OUT. WHITE CWEALTH	5	0	0	3	1	1	0	0	0	0	0	0	0	0	0	0	0	0	0	0	0	0
OUT. DEVLPED WORLD	5	0	0	2	0	2	1	1	0	0	0	0	0	0	0	0	0	0	0	0	0	0
CANADA	5	0	1	1	1	0	0	0	0	0	0	0	0	0	0	0	0	0	0	0	0	0
LATIN AMERICA	5	0	0	0	0	1	1	0	0	0	0	0	0	0	0	0	0	0	0	0	0	0
C. AMER.+CARIB.	5	0	0	0	0	0	1	1	0	1	0	0	0	0	0	0	0	0	0	0	0	0
CUBA	4	0	0	0	0	0	1	1	2	2	0	0	0	0	0	0	0	0	0	0	0	0
MEXICO	5	0	0	0	3	0	2	0	0	0	3	0	1	0	0	0	1	1	0	0	0	0
OTHER	3	0	0	0	0	0	0	1	0	0	0	0	0	0	0	0	0	0	0	0	0	0
S. AMERICA	5	0	0	0	2	0	0	0	2	2	0	0	0	0	0	0	0	0	0	0	0	0
ARGENTINA	4	0	0	0	0	0	0	0	2	0	0	0	0	0	0	0	0	0	0	0	0	0
BRAZIL	5	0	0	0	0	0	1	1	0	0	0	0	0	0	0	0	0	0	0	0	0	0
PERU	2	0	0	0	0	0	0	0	0	0	0	0	0	0	0	0	0	0	0	0	0	0
COLOMBIA	3	0	0	0	0	0	1	3	0	0	0	0	0	0	0	0	0	0	0	0	0	0
VENEZUELA	5	0	0	0	0	0	2	2	2	2	0	0	0	0	1	0	0	0	0	1	0	0
OTHER	2	0	0	0	0	0	0	1	0	0	0	0	0	0	0	0	0	0	0	0	0	0
EUROPE																						
EFTA	5	0	0	0	2	1	0	0	1	0	0	0	0	0	0	0	0	0	0	0	0	0
U.K.	5	0	0	0	2	1	1	0	0	0	0	0	0	0	0	0	0	0	0	0	0	0
SCANDINAVIA	4	0	0	0	1	2	0	0	0	1	0	0	0	0	0	0	0	0	0	0	0	0
SWITZERLAND	2	0	0	0	1	1	1	0	0	0	0	0	0	0	1	0	0	0	0	0	0	0
OTHER EFTA	2	0	0	0	0	0	1	1	0	1	0	0	0	1	0	1	0	0	0	0	0	0
EUROP. COMMUNITY	5	0	0	0	0	0	0	0	0	1	2	0	0	2	0	0	1	0	0	0	0	0
FRANCE	4	0	0	0	1	1	0	0	1	0	0	1	1	0	1	1	1	0	0	0	0	0
GERMANY	5	0	0	0	0	0	0	0	0	0	1	1	0	1	0	1	1	0	0	0	0	0
ITALY	4	0	0	0	0	0	0	0	0	1	0	1	0	0	1	0	0	1	0	0	0	0
BELGIUM + LUX	2	0	0	0	0	0	0	0	0	1	1	1	0	0	0	1	1	0	0	0	0	0
NETHERLANDS	2	0	0	0	0	1	0	0	0	1	1	0	0	1	1	0	0	0	0	0	0	0
SPAIN	3	0	0	0	0	0	0	0	0	0	1	0	0	0	0	0	0	0	0	0	0	0
GREECE + TURKEY	2	0	0	0	1	1	0	0	0	1	1	0	0	1	1	0	0	0	0	0	0	0
OTHER EUROPE	1	0	0	0	0	0	0	0	0	0	0	0	0	0	0	0	0	0	0	0	0	0
EUROPE EX. U.K.	5	0	0	2	0	0	1	0	1	0	0	0	0	0	0	0	0	0	0	0	0	0
SOUTHERN DOMINIONS	5	0	0	0	0	1	1	1	1	1	0	0	0	0	0	1	0	0	0	0	0	0
S. AFRICA +RHOD.	4	0	0	0	1	0	1	1	1	0	0	0	0	0	0	1	0	0	0	0	0	0
AUSTRALIA + N.Z.	4	0	0	3	0	1	1	1	0	1	0	0	0	0	0	0	0	0	0	0	0	0
ASIA + OTHER AFRICA	5	0	0	1	0	0	0	0	1	1	0	0	0	0	1	0	0	0	0	0	0	0
JAPAN	3	0	0	2	0	0	1	1	0	0	0	0	0	0	0	0	0	0	0	1	0	0
OTHER ASIA+AFR.	5	0	0	0	0	0	0	0	0	1	0	1	0	1	1	1	1	1	1	0	0	0
BLACK AFRICA	3	0	0	0	0	0	0	0	0	0	0	0	0	0	1	0	0	0	1	0	0	0
ARAB WORLD	2	0	0	0	0	0	0	0	0	1	0	0	0	0	0	0	0	0	0	0	0	0
INDIA	3	0	0	0	0	0	1	0	1	1	1	0	0	1	1	0	1	1	0	0	0	0
PHILIPPINES	3	0	0	0	0	0	0	1	0	0	0	0	0	0	0	0	0	0	0	0	0	0
OTHER E. ASIA	0	0	0	0	0	0	0	0	0	0	0	0	0	0	0	0	0	0	0	0	0	0
OTHER ASIA	5	0	0	2	0	0	0	0	0	1	0	1	0	1	0	0	0	0	0	0	0	0

CHAPTER 2— THE EXPANSION OF PARENT SYSTEMS
SECTION 2— THE FLOW OF MANUFACTURING BY INDUSTRY OF PARENT SYSTEM
TABLE 10— SYSTEMS IN THE STONE, CLAY, AND GLASS INDUSTRY (SIC 32)
CLASSIFIED BY PERIOD SYSTEM FIRST OPERATED A MANUFACTURING SUBSIDIARY
IN SPECIFIED COUNTRIES AND REGIONS

COUNTRY OR REGION	PRE 1968	PRE 1901	1901 -13	1914 -19	1920 -24	1925 -29	1930 -34	1935 -39	1940 -45	1946 -50	1951 -53	1954 -55	1956 -57	1958 -59	1960 -61	1962	1963	1964	1965	1966	1967	UNK
OUTSIDE U.S.	7	0	3	0	1	1	0	2	0	0	0	0	0	0	0	0	0	0	0	0	0	0
OUT. U.S. + CANADA	7	0	3	1	1	1	0	1	0	0	0	1	1	0	0	0	1	1	0	0	0	0
OUT. WEST. HEMIS.	7	0	3	1	1	1	0	1	0	0	0	1	1	0	0	1	1	1	0	0	0	0
OUT. WHITE CWEALTH	7	0	3	1	1	1	0	1	0	0	0	1	1	0	0	0	1	1	0	0	0	0
OUT. DEVLPED WORLD	7	0	0	0	1	1	0	2	0	1	1	3	0	0	0	0	0	0	0	0	0	0
CANADA	7	0	0	2	0	2	0	1	1	0	0	0	0	1	0	0	0	0	0	0	0	0
LATIN AMERICA	7	0	0	0	1	1	0	2	0	0	1	1	3	1	0	0	1	1	0	0	0	0
C. AMER.+CARIB.	7	0	0	0	1	0	0	1	0	0	2	1	2	0	0	1	0	1	0	0	0	0
CUBA	1	0	0	0	0	0	0	0	0	0	0	0	1	0	1	0	0	0	0	0	0	0
MEXICO	7	0	0	0	0	0	0	1	0	0	2	1	1	1	1	1	0	0	0	0	0	0
OTHER	0	0	0	0	0	0	0	0	0	0	0	0	0	0	0	0	0	0	0	0	0	0
S. AMERICA	7	0	0	0	0	1	0	2	0	0	0	1	2	1	0	0	1	0	0	0	0	0
ARGENTINA	5	0	2	0	1	0	0	2	0	0	0	0	1	0	0	0	0	0	0	0	0	0
BRAZIL	6	0	0	0	1	0	0	2	0	0	1	0	1	0	0	0	0	0	0	0	0	0
PERU	1	0	0	0	0	0	0	0	0	0	0	0	0	1	0	0	0	0	0	0	0	0
COLOMBIA	4	0	0	0	0	1	0	0	0	0	0	1	1	0	0	1	1	0	0	0	0	0
VENEZUELA	3	0	0	0	0	0	0	0	1	0	1	0	1	0	0	1	0	0	1	0	1	0
OTHER	3	0	0	0	0	0	0	2	1	1	0	0	0	0	0	0	0	0	0	0	0	0
EUROPE	7	0	3	0	1	1	0	1	0	0	0	0	0	0	0	1	0	0	0	0	0	0
EFTA	7	0	1	0	1	1	1	0	0	0	0	1	0	0	0	1	1	1	0	0	0	0
U.K.	6	0	1	0	1	1	0	0	0	0	0	1	0	0	0	1	1	1	0	0	0	0
SCANDINAVIA	3	0	0	0	0	0	0	0	0	0	0	0	0	0	0	1	1	1	0	0	0	0
SWITZERLAND	0	0	0	0	0	0	0	0	0	0	0	0	0	0	0	0	0	0	0	0	0	0
OTHER EFTA	0	0	0	0	0	0	0	0	0	0	0	0	0	0	0	0	0	0	0	0	0	0
EUROP. COMMUNITY	7	0	3	0	0	0	0	1	0	0	0	0	0	0	0	0	1	0	0	0	0	0
FRANCE	5	0	0	0	1	0	0	0	0	1	0	0	0	2	0	0	0	0	0	0	0	0
GERMANY	4	0	2	1	0	0	0	0	0	0	0	0	0	1	1	0	1	0	0	0	0	0
ITALY	6	0	0	0	0	0	0	1	0	0	1	1	0	0	2	0	1	0	1	0	0	0
BELGIUM + LUX	5	0	1	0	1	1	0	1	0	0	0	0	0	0	0	0	1	0	1	1	0	0
NETHERLANDS	2	0	0	0	0	0	0	0	0	0	0	0	0	0	1	0	1	0	0	2	0	0
SPAIN	4	0	0	0	0	0	0	0	0	0	0	0	0	0	0	0	0	0	1	0	0	0
GREECE + TURKEY	0	0	0	0	0	0	0	0	0	0	0	0	0	0	0	0	0	0	0	1	0	0
OTHER EUROPE	2	0	0	0	0	0	0	0	0	0	1	0	0	0	0	0	0	0	1	0	0	0
EUROPE EX. U.K.	7	0	3	0	1	1	0	1	0	0	0	0	0	0	0	1	0	0	0	0	0	0
SOUTHERN DOMINIONS	4	0	0	0	0	0	0	2	0	0	0	0	0	1	0	0	0	0	1	1	0	0
S. AFRICA +RHOD.	4	0	0	0	0	0	0	2	0	1	0	0	0	0	1	0	0	1	0	1	0	0
AUSTRALIA + N.Z.	3	0	0	0	0	0	0	2	0	0	0	1	0	1	0	1	1	1	1	0	0	0
ASIA + OTHER AFRICA	7	0	0	0	0	0	0	0	0	0	0	1	0	0	2	1	0	0	1	1	0	0
JAPAN	6	0	0	0	0	0	0	0	0	0	0	1	0	1	2	1	1	1	0	1	0	0
OTHER ASIA+AFR.	3	0	0	0	0	0	0	0	0	0	0	0	0	0	0	0	0	0	1	0	1	1
BLACK AFRICA	1	0	0	0	0	0	0	0	0	0	0	0	0	0	0	0	0	0	0	0	0	0
ARAB WORLD	0	0	0	0	0	0	0	0	0	0	0	0	0	0	0	0	0	0	0	0	0	0
INDIA	3	0	0	0	0	0	0	0	0	0	0	1	0	0	0	1	0	0	0	0	0	1
PHILIPPINES	0	0	0	0	0	0	0	0	0	0	0	0	0	0	0	0	0	0	0	0	0	0
OTHER E. ASIA	1	0	0	0	0	0	0	0	0	0	0	0	0	0	0	1	0	0	1	0	0	0
OTHER ASIA	0	0	0	0	0	0	0	0	0	0	0	0	0	0	0	0	0	0	0	0	0	0

PERIOD

CHAPTER 2— THE EXPANSION OF PARENT SYSTEMS
SECTION 2— THE FLOW OF MANUFACTURING BY INDUSTRY OF PARENT SYSTEM
TABLE 11— SYSTEMS IN THE PRIMARY METAL INDUSTRY (SIC 33)
CLASSIFIED BY PERIOD SYSTEM FIRST OPERATED A MANUFACTURING SUBSIDIARY
IN SPECIFIED COUNTRIES AND REGIONS

PERIOD

COUNTRY OR REGION	PRE 1968	PRE 1901	1901 -13	1914 -19	1920 -24	1925 -29	1930 -34	1935 -39	1940 -45	1946 -50	1951 -53	1954 -55	1956 -57	1958 -59	1960 -61	1962	1963	1964	1965	1966	1967	UNK
OUTSIDE U.S.	8	1	2	0	0	0	1	1	0	0	0	2	0	0	1	0	0	0	0	0	0	0
OUT. U.S. + CANADA	8	1	1	0	0	1	1	0	1	1	0	1	0	1	1	0	0	0	0	0	0	0
OUT. WEST. HEMIS.	8	1	1	0	0	1	0	2	0	1	1	2	0	2	1	0	0	0	0	0	0	0
OUT. WHITE CWEALTH	8	1	0	0	0	1	0	2	0	1	0	1	0	1	1	0	0	0	0	0	0	0
OUT. DEVLPED WORLD	8	0	1	0	0	1	2	2	1	1	0	1	0	1	1	0	0	0	0	0	0	0
CANADA	7	0	1	0	0	0	2	0	0	0	1	1	1	1	1	0	0	0	0	0	0	0
LATIN AMERICA	8	0	1	0	0	1	2	0	1	1	0	0	1	1	1	0	0	0	0	0	0	0
C. AMER.+CARIB.	7	0	1	0	0	1	1	1	1	1	0	0	1	1	1	0	1	0	0	0	0	0
CUBA	2	0	1	0	0	0	1	0	0	0	0	0	0	0	0	0	0	0	0	0	0	0
MEXICO	7	0	0	0	0	1	1	1	0	0	0	0	1	1	1	0	1	0	0	0	0	0
OTHER	2	0	1	0	0	0	1	0	0	0	0	0	0	0	0	0	0	0	0	0	0	0
S. AMERICA	7	0	0	0	1	0	1	1	0	0	0	0	0	2	1	0	0	1	1	0	0	0
ARGENTINA	2	0	0	0	0	0	0	0	0	0	0	0	0	1	1	0	0	0	0	0	0	0
BRAZIL	3	0	0	0	0	0	1	1	0	0	0	0	0	0	0	0	1	0	0	0	0	0
PERU	1	0	0	0	0	0	0	0	0	0	0	0	0	0	1	0	0	0	0	0	0	0
COLOMBIA	6	0	0	0	0	0	0	0	0	0	1	2	2	0	2	0	0	1	0	0	0	0
VENEZUELA	4	0	0	1	0	0	1	0	0	1	0	0	1	0	1	0	0	0	0	0	0	0
OTHER	2	0	0	0	0	0	0	0	1	0	0	0	0	1	0	0	0	0	1	0	0	0
EUROPE	8	1	0	0	0	1	0	0	0	0	1	0	1	2	2	0	1	1	0	0	0	0
EFTA	8	1	0	0	0	2	0	0	0	0	1	0	1	1	1	1	1	1	1	0	0	0
U.K.	8	0	0	0	0	2	0	0	0	0	1	0	0	2	1	0	0	0	1	0	0	0
SCANDINAVIA	3	0	0	0	0	0	0	0	0	0	0	0	0	1	1	0	0	0	0	0	0	0
SWITZERLAND	2	0	0	0	0	0	0	0	0	0	0	0	0	0	1	0	0	0	1	0	0	0
OTHER EFTA	0	0	0	0	0	0	0	0	0	0	0	0	0	0	0	0	0	0	0	0	0	0
EUROP. COMMUNITY	8	1	0	0	0	0	1	1	0	0	0	0	1	2	2	1	1	1	0	0	0	0
FRANCE	3	1	0	0	0	0	0	0	0	0	0	0	0	1	1	0	0	0	0	0	0	0
GERMANY	6	0	0	0	0	0	1	0	0	0	1	0	1	1	1	1	0	1	0	0	0	0
ITALY	4	0	0	0	0	0	1	0	0	0	0	0	0	1	1	0	1	1	0	0	0	0
BELGIUM + LUX	3	1	0	0	0	0	0	0	0	0	0	0	0	1	1	0	0	0	0	0	0	0
NETHERLANDS	3	0	0	0	0	0	0	0	0	0	1	0	0	0	0	1	1	0	1	0	0	0
SPAIN	3	0	0	0	0	0	0	0	0	0	0	0	0	0	0	0	1	1	1	0	0	0
GREECE + TURKEY	2	0	0	0	0	0	0	0	0	0	0	0	0	0	1	0	0	0	1	0	0	0
OTHER EUROPE	0	0	0	0	0	0	0	0	0	0	0	0	0	0	0	0	0	0	0	0	0	0
EUROPE EX. U.K.	8	1	0	0	0	1	1	0	0	0	0	0	0	3	2	0	1	0	0	0	0	0
SOUTHERN DOMINIONS	6	0	0	0	0	0	1	0	0	1	0	0	0	2	2	0	0	0	1	0	0	0
S. AFRICA +RHOD.	1	0	0	0	0	0	0	0	0	1	0	0	0	0	0	0	0	0	0	0	0	0
AUSTRALIA + N.Z.	6	0	0	0	0	1	1	0	0	0	3	0	0	2	2	0	1	1	1	0	0	0
ASIA + OTHER AFRICA	6	0	0	0	0	0	0	0	0	0	0	0	0	1	1	0	1	1	0	0	0	0
JAPAN	4	0	0	0	0	0	0	0	0	0	3	0	0	1	1	0	0	1	0	0	0	0
OTHER ASIA+AFR.	5	0	0	0	0	0	1	0	0	0	0	0	0	1	1	0	1	0	0	0	0	0
BLACK AFRICA	2	0	0	0	0	0	0	0	0	0	1	0	0	0	0	0	0	1	0	0	0	0
ARAB WORLD	2	0	0	0	0	0	0	0	0	0	0	0	0	1	1	0	0	0	0	0	0	0
INDIA	3	0	0	0	0	0	0	0	0	0	0	0	0	0	0	1	1	0	1	0	0	0
PHILIPPINES	2	0	0	0	0	0	0	0	0	0	2	0	0	0	0	0	0	0	0	0	0	0
OTHER E. ASIA	0	0	0	0	0	0	0	0	0	0	0	0	0	0	0	0	0	0	0	0	0	0
OTHER ASIA	1	0	0	0	0	1	0	0	0	0	0	0	1	0	0	0	0	0	0	0	0	0

CHAPTER 2- THE EXPANSION OF PARENT SYSTEMS
SECTION 2- THE FLOW OF MANUFACTURING BY INDUSTRY OF PARENT SYSTEM
TABLE 12- SYSTEMS IN THE FABRICATED METAL INDUSTRY (SIC 34)
CLASSIFIED BY PERIOD SYSTEM FIRST OPERATED A MANUFACTURING SUBSIDIARY
IN SPECIFIED COUNTRIES AND REGIONS

COUNTRY OR REGION	PRE 1968	PRE 1901	1901 -13	1914 -19	1920 -24	1925 -29	1930 -34	1935 -39	1940 -45	1946 -50	1951 -53	1954 -55	1956 -57	1958 -59	1960 -61	1962	1963	1964	1965	1966	1967	UNK
OUTSIDE U.S.	10	1	0	3	1	1	2	1	0	0	1	0	0	0	0	0	0	0	0	0	0	0
OUT. U.S. + CANADA	10	1	0	1	1	1	2	1	0	0	3	0	0	0	0	0	0	0	0	0	0	0
OUT. WEST. HEMIS.	10	1	0	1	1	1	2	0	0	0	2	0	1	0	1	1	0	0	0	0	0	0
OUT. WHITE CWEALTH	10	1	0	2	2	1	2	0	1	1	2	0	0	0	1	0	0	0	0	0	0	0
OUT. DEVLPED WORLD	9	0	0	1	1	0	1	0	1	2	1	0	1	1	1	0	0	0	1	1	0	0
CANADA	10	0	1	3	1	1	1	1	0	1	0	1	0	0	0	0	0	0	0	0	0	0
LATIN AMERICA	9	0	0	1	0	1	1	0	1	2	0	0	1	1	1	0	0	0	1	1	0	0
C. AMER.+CARIB.	9	0	0	1	0	1	1	0	1	2	1	0	1	0	2	0	1	0	1	1	0	0
CUBA	1	0	0	0	0	0	0	0	0	0	0	0	1	0	0	0	0	0	0	0	0	0
MEXICO	9	0	0	0	0	1	0	0	1	2	0	1	0	1	2	0	0	1	1	1	0	0
OTHER	2	0	0	0	0	0	0	0	0	1	0	0	0	0	0	0	0	0	1	0	0	0
S. AMERICA	7	0	0	0	1	0	0	0	2	2	2	0	1	0	0	1	0	1	0	1	0	0
ARGENTINA	4	0	0	1	0	0	0	0	2	1	2	0	0	1	1	0	0	0	1	0	0	0
BRAZIL	6	0	0	0	0	0	0	0	2	1	1	0	1	0	2	0	0	0	0	1	1	0
PERU	3	0	0	0	0	0	0	0	1	1	1	0	0	0	0	0	0	1	0	0	0	0
COLOMBIA	4	0	0	0	0	0	0	0	0	0	1	0	0	2	1	0	0	0	0	1	0	0
VENEZUELA	4	0	0	0	0	0	0	0	0	0	2	0	1	1	0	0	1	0	1	0	1	0
OTHER	3	0	0	0	0	0	0	0	1	1	0	0	0	1	1	1	0	0	0	0	0	0
EUROPE	10	1	1	1	1	2	2	0	1	1	2	0	0	0	0	1	0	0	0	0	0	0
EFTA	10	0	1	1	1	1	2	0	1	1	2	0	0	0	0	0	0	0	0	1	0	0
U.K.	5	0	1	1	0	0	0	0	1	1	1	0	1	1	1	1	0	1	0	0	1	0
SCANDINAVIA	4	0	1	1	0	0	0	0	1	1	1	0	0	0	0	0	0	1	0	0	0	0
SWITZERLAND	3	0	0	0	0	0	0	0	0	1	0	0	1	1	1	0	0	1	0	0	0	0
OTHER EFTA	3	0	1	0	1	1	0	0	1	0	0	0	0	1	1	0	1	1	0	0	0	0
EUROP. COMMUNITY	10	1	1	2	1	2	2	0	0	1	0	0	0	1	0	1	1	0	0	0	0	0
FRANCE	7	1	0	0	1	1	0	0	1	0	1	1	1	1	1	1	0	0	0	0	0	0
GERMANY	8	1	1	1	1	0	0	0	0	0	0	0	0	1	2	1	0	0	1	1	0	0
ITALY	6	0	0	0	0	2	0	0	0	0	1	0	0	0	1	1	0	0	0	0	0	0
BELGIUM + LUX	4	1	1	1	0	0	1	1	0	0	0	0	0	0	0	0	0	0	0	0	0	0
NETHERLANDS	8	0	0	0	0	1	2	0	0	2	1	1	0	1	1	0	0	0	0	0	0	0
SPAIN	7	0	0	0	0	0	0	0	0	0	0	0	0	1	0	2	0	0	2	1	0	0
GREECE + TURKEY	3	0	0	0	0	0	0	0	0	0	0	1	0	0	1	1	0	1	1	1	1	0
OTHER EUROPE	1	1	0	0	0	0	0	0	0	0	0	0	0	0	0	0	0	0	0	0	0	0
EUROPE EX. U.K.	10	1	0	2	1	2	0	0	1	1	1	1	1	0	0	1	1	1	0	0	0	0
SOUTHERN DOMINIONS	10	0	0	0	0	2	1	1	0	0	0	0	1	1	1	1	0	1	2	0	0	0
S. AFRICA +RHOD.	6	0	0	0	0	2	0	0	0	0	0	0	1	1	1	0	0	0	0	2	0	0
AUSTRALIA + N.Z.	8	0	0	0	0	0	2	2	0	3	0	2	0	0	0	1	1	1	2	0	0	0
ASIA + OTHER AFRICA	5	0	0	0	0	0	0	0	0	3	0	0	0	0	0	0	1	0	0	0	0	0
JAPAN	3	0	0	0	0	0	0	0	0	3	0	0	0	0	0	1	0	1	0	0	0	0
OTHER ASIA+AFR.	5	0	0	0	0	0	0	0	0	2	0	0	0	0	0	0	0	0	0	0	0	0
BLACK AFRICA	2	0	0	0	0	0	0	0	0	0	1	0	0	0	0	0	0	0	0	0	0	0
ARAB WORLD	2	0	0	0	0	0	0	0	0	2	0	0	0	0	0	0	0	0	0	0	0	0
INDIA	0	0	0	0	0	0	0	0	0	0	0	0	0	0	0	0	0	0	0	0	0	0
PHILIPPINES	3	0	0	0	0	0	0	0	0	0	1	0	0	0	0	1	0	0	0	1	0	0
OTHER E. ASIA	0	0	0	0	0	0	0	0	0	0	0	0	0	0	0	0	0	0	0	0	0	0
OTHER ASIA	3	0	0	0	0	0	0	0	0	1	1	0	0	0	0	1	1	0	0	0	0	0

CHAPTER 2- THE EXPANSION OF PARENT SYSTEMS
SECTION 2- THE FLOW OF MANUFACTURING BY INDUSTRY OF PARENT SYSTEM
TABLE 13- SYSTEMS IN THE FARM MACHINERY INDUSTRY (SIC 352)
CLASSIFIED BY PERIOD SYSTEM FIRST OPERATED A MANUFACTURING SUBSIDIARY
IN SPECIFIED COUNTRIES AND REGIONS

COUNTRY OR REGION	PRE 1968	PRE 1901	1901 -13	1914 -19	1920 -24	1925 -29	1930 -34	1935 -39	1940 -45	1946 -50	1951 -53	1954 -55	1956 -57	1958 -59	1960 -61	1962	1963	1964	1965	1966	1967	UNK
OUTSIDE U.S.	3	0	2	0	0	0	0	0	0	1	1	0	0	0	0	0	0	0	0	0	0	0
OUT. U.S. + CANADA	3	0	1	0	0	0	0	0	0	0	1	1	0	1	1	0	0	0	0	0	0	0
OUT. WEST. HEMIS.	3	0	1	0	0	0	0	0	0	0	1	1	1	1	0	0	0	0	0	0	0	0
OUT. WHITE CWEALTH	3	0	1	0	0	0	0	0	0	1	0	1	1	0	0	0	0	0	0	0	0	0
OUT. DEVLPED WORLD	3	0	0	0	0	0	0	0	0	1	0	1	1	0	0	0	0	0	0	0	0	0
CANADA	3	0	2	0	0	0	0	0	0	1	0	0	0	0	0	0	0	0	0	0	0	0
LATIN AMERICA	3	0	0	0	0	0	0	0	0	1	0	1	1	0	0	0	0	0	0	0	0	0
C. AMER.+CARIB.	3	0	0	0	0	0	0	0	0	1	0	1	1	0	1	0	0	0	0	0	0	0
CUBA	0	0	0	0	0	0	0	0	0	0	0	0	0	0	0	0	0	0	0	0	0	0
MEXICO	3	0	0	0	0	0	0	0	0	1	0	1	0	0	0	0	0	0	0	0	0	0
OTHER	1	0	0	0	0	0	0	0	0	0	0	0	1	1	1	0	0	0	0	0	0	0
S. AMERICA	2	0	0	0	0	0	0	0	0	1	0	0	0	0	0	0	0	0	0	0	0	0
ARGENTINA	1	0	0	0	0	0	0	0	0	1	0	1	1	1	0	0	0	0	0	0	0	0
BRAZIL	1	0	0	0	0	0	0	0	0	0	0	0	0	0	0	0	0	0	0	0	0	0
PERU	0	0	0	0	0	0	0	0	0	0	0	0	0	0	0	0	0	0	0	0	0	0
COLOMBIA	0	0	0	0	0	0	0	0	0	0	0	0	0	0	0	0	0	0	0	0	0	0
VENEZUELA	0	0	0	0	0	0	0	0	0	0	0	0	0	0	0	0	0	0	0	0	0	0
OTHER	0	0	0	0	0	0	0	0	0	0	0	0	0	0	0	0	0	0	0	0	0	0
EUROPE	3	0	1	0	0	0	0	0	0	0	1	1	0	1	1	0	0	0	0	0	0	0
EFTA	3	0	1	0	0	0	0	0	0	0	1	0	0	1	1	0	0	0	0	0	0	0
U.K.	3	0	0	0	0	0	0	0	0	1	0	0	1	0	0	0	0	0	0	0	0	0
SCANDINAVIA	1	0	1	0	0	0	0	0	0	0	0	0	0	0	0	0	0	0	0	0	0	0
SWITZERLAND	0	0	0	0	0	0	0	0	0	0	0	0	0	0	0	0	0	0	0	0	0	0
OTHER EFTA	0	0	0	0	0	0	0	0	0	1	0	0	0	0	0	0	0	0	0	0	0	0
EUROP. COMMUNITY	3	0	1	0	0	0	0	0	0	0	0	1	1	0	0	0	0	0	0	0	0	0
FRANCE	3	0	1	0	0	0	0	0	0	0	0	0	0	0	0	0	0	0	0	0	0	0
GERMANY	2	0	1	0	0	0	0	0	0	0	0	1	1	2	2	0	0	0	0	0	0	0
ITALY	1	0	0	0	0	0	0	0	0	0	0	0	1	1	0	0	0	0	0	0	0	0
BELGIUM + LUX	0	0	0	0	0	0	0	0	0	0	0	0	0	0	0	0	0	0	0	0	0	0
NETHERLANDS	0	0	0	0	0	0	0	0	0	0	0	0	0	0	0	0	0	0	0	0	0	0
SPAIN	2	0	0	0	0	0	0	0	0	0	0	0	0	0	0	0	0	0	0	0	0	0
GREECE + TURKEY	1	0	0	0	0	0	0	0	0	0	0	1	0	0	0	0	0	1	0	1	0	0
OTHER EUROPE	0	0	0	0	0	0	0	0	0	0	0	0	0	0	0	0	0	1	0	0	0	0
EUROPE EX. U.K.	3	0	1	0	0	0	0	0	0	0	0	1	1	1	0	0	0	0	0	0	0	0
SOUTHERN DOMINIONS	3	0	0	0	0	0	1	0	0	0	0	0	1	0	0	1	0	0	0	0	0	0
S. AFRICA +RHOD.	2	0	0	0	0	0	0	0	0	0	0	0	0	0	0	2	0	0	0	0	0	0
AUSTRALIA + N.Z.	2	0	0	0	0	0	1	0	0	0	0	1	1	0	0	0	0	0	0	0	0	0
ASIA + OTHER AFRICA	1	0	0	0	0	0	0	0	0	0	0	0	0	0	0	0	0	1	1	0	0	0
JAPAN	1	0	0	0	0	0	0	0	0	0	0	1	0	0	0	0	0	0	1	1	0	0
OTHER ASIA+AFR.	1	0	0	0	0	0	0	0	0	0	0	0	0	0	0	0	0	0	0	0	0	0
BLACK AFRICA	0	0	0	0	0	0	0	0	0	0	0	0	0	0	0	0	0	1	0	0	0	0
ARAB WORLD	1	0	0	0	0	0	0	0	0	0	0	1	0	0	0	0	0	1	0	0	0	0
INDIA	1	0	0	0	0	0	0	0	0	0	0	0	0	0	0	0	0	1	0	0	0	0
PHILIPPINES	1	0	0	0	0	0	0	0	0	0	0	0	0	0	0	0	0	0	0	0	0	0
OTHER E. ASIA	0	0	0	0	0	0	0	0	0	0	0	0	0	0	0	0	0	0	0	0	0	0
OTHER ASIA	0	0	0	0	0	0	0	0	0	0	0	0	0	0	0	0	0	0	0	0	0	0

CHAPTER 2- THE EXPANSION OF PARENT SYSTEMS
SECTION 2- THE FLOW OF MANUFACTURING BY INDUSTRY OF PARENT SYSTEM
TABLE 14- SYSTEMS IN THE OFFICE AND COMPUTING MACHINE INDUSTRY (SIC 357)
CLASSIFIED BY PERIOD SYSTEM FIRST OPERATED A MANUFACTURING SUBSIDIARY
IN SPECIFIED COUNTRIES AND REGIONS

PERIOD

COUNTRY OR REGION	PRE 1968	PRE 1901	1901 -13	1914 -19	1920 -24	1925 -29	1930 -34	1935 -39	1940 -45	1946 -50	1951 -53	1954 -55	1956 -57	1958 -59	1960 -61	1962	1963	1964	1965	1966	1967	UNK
OUTSIDE U.S.	4	1	1	1	0	1	0	0	0	0	0	0	0	0	0	0	0	0	0	0	0	0
OUT. U.S. + CANADA	4	1	1	0	0	1	1	1	0	0	0	0	0	0	0	0	0	0	0	0	0	0
OUT. WEST. HEMIS.	4	1	1	0	1	1	1	1	0	0	0	0	0	0	0	0	0	0	0	0	0	0
OUT. WHITE CWEALTH	4	1	0	1	1	1	1	1	1	0	0	0	0	0	0	0	0	0	0	0	0	0
OUT. DEVLPED WORLD	4	0	0	0	0	0	1	1	0	0	0	1	1	0	0	0	0	0	0	0	0	0
CANADA	4	0	0	3	0	0	0	0	0	0	0	0	0	0	0	0	0	0	0	0	0	0
LATIN AMERICA	4	0	0	0	1	0	0	1	1	0	0	1	1	3	0	0	0	0	0	0	0	0
C. AMER.+CARIB.	4	0	0	0	0	0	0	0	0	0	0	1	0	0	0	0	0	0	0	0	0	0
CUBA	1	0	0	0	0	0	0	0	0	0	0	1	0	3	0	0	0	0	0	0	0	0
MEXICO	4	0	0	0	0	0	0	0	0	0	0	1	1	1	0	0	0	0	0	0	0	0
OTHER	1	0	0	0	0	0	0	1	0	0	0	0	2	0	0	0	0	0	0	0	0	0
S. AMERICA	4	0	0	0	0	0	0	0	1	0	0	0	1	1	0	0	0	0	0	0	0	0
ARGENTINA	1	0	0	0	0	0	0	0	0	0	0	0	2	0	0	0	1	0	0	0	0	0
BRAZIL	4	0	0	0	0	0	0	1	1	0	0	0	0	0	0	0	0	0	0	0	0	0
PERU	0	0	0	0	0	0	0	0	0	0	0	0	0	1	0	0	0	0	0	0	0	0
COLOMBIA	1	0	0	0	0	0	0	1	0	0	0	0	0	0	0	0	0	0	0	0	0	0
VENEZUELA	0	0	0	0	0	0	0	0	0	0	0	0	0	0	0	0	0	0	0	0	0	0
OTHER	1	0	0	0	0	0	0	0	0	0	0	1	0	0	0	0	0	0	0	0	0	0
EUROPE	4	1	1	0	0	0	1	1	0	1	0	0	0	0	0	0	0	0	0	0	0	0
EFTA	4	1	1	0	0	0	1	1	0	1	0	0	0	0	0	0	0	0	0	0	0	0
U.K.	4	1	1	0	0	0	1	1	0	1	0	0	0	0	0	0	0	0	0	0	0	0
SCANDINAVIA	3	0	0	0	0	0	0	1	0	1	0	0	0	0	0	0	0	0	0	0	0	0
SWITZERLAND	2	0	0	0	1	0	0	0	0	1	0	0	0	0	0	0	0	0	0	0	0	0
OTHER EFTA	1	0	0	0	1	0	0	0	0	1	0	0	0	0	0	0	0	0	0	0	0	0
EUROP. COMMUNITY	4	1	1	0	0	1	1	1	0	0	0	0	0	0	0	0	0	0	0	0	0	0
FRANCE	3	0	0	1	0	1	1	0	0	0	0	0	0	0	0	0	0	0	0	0	0	0
GERMANY	4	1	1	0	1	1	1	1	1	0	0	0	0	0	0	1	0	0	0	0	0	0
ITALY	3	0	0	1	0	1	1	1	0	0	0	0	0	0	0	0	0	0	0	0	0	0
BELGIUM + LUX	2	0	0	0	0	1	1	0	1	0	1	0	0	0	0	0	0	0	0	0	0	0
NETHERLANDS	1	0	0	0	0	0	0	0	1	0	1	0	0	0	0	0	0	0	0	0	0	0
SPAIN	0	0	0	0	0	0	0	0	0	0	0	0	0	0	0	0	0	0	0	0	0	0
GREECE + TURKEY	0	0	0	0	0	0	0	0	0	0	0	0	0	0	0	0	0	0	0	0	0	0
OTHER EUROPE	0	0	0	0	0	0	0	0	0	0	0	0	0	0	0	0	0	0	0	0	0	0
EUROPE EX. U.K.	4	1	0	1	1	1	1	1	0	0	0	0	0	0	0	0	0	0	0	0	0	0
SOUTHERN DOMINIONS	3	0	0	0	0	0	0	0	1	0	1	0	0	0	0	0	1	1	0	0	0	0
S. AFRICA +RHOD.	2	0	0	0	0	0	0	0	0	1	0	0	0	0	0	0	1	1	0	0	0	0
AUSTRALIA + N.Z.	2	0	0	0	0	0	1	1	1	0	1	0	0	0	0	0	1	1	0	0	0	0
ASIA + OTHER AFRICA	4	0	0	0	0	0	1	1	0	0	1	0	0	0	0	0	1	0	0	0	0	0
JAPAN	1	0	0	0	0	0	0	0	0	0	0	0	0	0	0	0	1	0	0	0	0	0
OTHER ASIA+AFR.	0	0	0	0	0	0	1	1	0	0	1	0	0	0	0	0	1	0	0	0	0	0
BLACK AFRICA	0	0	0	0	0	0	0	0	0	0	0	0	0	0	0	0	0	0	0	0	0	0
ARAB WORLD	0	0	0	0	0	0	0	0	0	0	0	0	0	0	0	0	0	0	0	0	0	0
INDIA	1	0	0	0	0	0	0	0	0	0	0	0	0	0	0	1	0	0	0	0	0	0
PHILIPPINES	0	0	0	0	0	0	0	0	0	0	0	0	0	0	0	0	0	0	0	0	0	0
OTHER E. ASIA	0	0	0	0	0	0	0	0	0	0	0	0	0	0	0	1	0	0	0	0	0	0
OTHER ASIA	0	0	0	0	0	0	0	0	0	0	0	0	0	0	0	0	0	0	0	0	0	0

CHAPTER 2- THE EXPANSION OF PARENT SYSTEMS
SECTION 2- THE FLOW OF MANUFACTURING BY INDUSTRY OF PARENT SYSTEM
TABLE 15- SYSTEMS IN OTHER NON-ELECTRICAL MACHINERY INDUSTRIES (OTHER SIC 35)
CLASSIFIED BY PERIOD SYSTEM FIRST OPERATED A MANUFACTURING SUBSIDIARY
IN SPECIFIED COUNTRIES AND REGIONS

PERIOD

COUNTRY OR REGION	PRE 1968	PRE 1901	1901 -13	1914 -19	1920 -24	1925 -29	1930 -34	1935 -39	1940 -45	1946 -50	1951 -53	1954 -55	1956 -57	1958 -59	1960 -61	1962	1963	1964	1965	1966	1967	UNK
OUTSIDE U.S.	13	5	0	2	0	2	1	0	0	0	1	1	0	1	0	0	0	0	0	0	0	0
OUT. U.S. + CANADA	13	5	0	1	0	2	0	0	1	0	2	1	0	1	0	0	0	0	0	0	0	0
OUT. WEST. HEMIS.	13	5	0	1	1	2	0	0	0	0	1	2	1	2	0	0	0	0	0	0	0	0
OUT. WHITE CWEALTH	13	4	0	0	1	0	0	0	1	0	1	1	1	2	1	0	0	0	0	0	0	0
OUT. DEVLPED WORLD	13	0	0	1	0	0	0	2	0	2	1	1	3	3	1	1	1	1	1	0	0	0
CANADA	13	1	3	1	0	1	1	2	0	1	1	1	1	3	0	1	1	1	0	0	0	0
LATIN AMERICA	12	0	0	1	0	1	0	2	1	2	1	1	0	2	1	0	1	1	2	0	0	0
C. AMER.+CARIB.	10	0	0	0	1	0	1	0	1	2	1	0	0	2	0	0	1	0	1	0	1	0
CUBA	0	0	0	0	0	0	0	0	0	0	0	0	0	0	0	0	0	0	0	0	0	0
MEXICO	10	0	0	0	1	0	1	2	2	2	1	0	0	2	0	1	2	1	1	0	0	1
OTHER	1	0	0	0	0	0	0	0	0	0	0	0	0	0	0	0	0	0	0	0	0	0
S. AMERICA	11	0	0	1	0	0	0	2	0	2	1	1	1	3	1	1	2	2	1	1	0	0
ARGENTINA	4	0	0	0	0	0	0	0	0	1	0	0	0	1	1	0	0	0	0	0	0	1
BRAZIL	8	0	1	1	0	0	2	1	1	1	0	1	1	1	1	1	1	2	0	1	0	0
PERU	1	0	0	0	0	0	0	0	0	0	0	1	0	0	0	0	0	0	0	0	0	0
COLOMBIA	1	0	0	0	0	0	0	0	0	0	0	0	1	0	0	0	0	0	0	0	0	0
VENEZUELA	3	0	0	0	0	0	0	0	0	0	0	1	0	1	0	0	1	0	0	0	0	0
OTHER	2	0	0	1	0	0	0	0	0	0	0	0	0	0	0	0	0	0	0	0	0	0
EUROPE	13	5	0	1	0	2	0	0	0	1	1	2	1	1	0	0	0	0	0	0	0	0
EFTA	12	4	0	1	0	2	1	0	0	1	1	2	0	0	0	0	1	0	0	0	0	0
U.K.	12	4	1	1	0	2	1	0	0	0	0	0	0	0	1	1	1	1	0	0	0	0
SCANDINAVIA	2	0	0	0	0	0	0	0	0	0	0	0	0	0	0	0	0	0	0	0	0	0
SWITZERLAND	0	0	1	0	0	0	0	0	0	0	0	0	0	0	0	0	0	1	1	1	0	0
OTHER EFTA	3	0	0	0	1	0	0	0	0	0	0	0	1	0	4	0	0	0	0	0	0	0
EUROP. COMMUNITY	13	4	0	1	1	2	0	0	0	0	1	1	1	1	3	0	0	0	0	0	0	0
FRANCE	13	3	0	0	1	2	0	0	0	0	0	0	0	0	0	0	0	0	0	0	0	0
GERMANY	9	3	1	0	1	2	1	1	0	0	0	0	1	1	1	1	1	1	1	0	0	0
ITALY	7	0	0	0	2	0	0	0	0	0	0	0	0	1	0	0	0	0	0	0	0	0
BELGIUM + LUX	4	0	1	1	0	0	0	1	1	1	0	0	0	0	1	2	2	2	1	1	0	0
NETHERLANDS	5	0	0	0	2	0	0	0	0	0	0	0	0	0	0	0	1	1	1	1	0	0
SPAIN	4	0	0	0	0	0	1	0	0	1	0	0	0	1	1	1	2	0	2	1	0	0
GREECE + TURKEY	0	1	0	0	0	1	0	0	0	0	0	0	0	0	0	0	0	1	1	0	0	0
OTHER EUROPE	1	1	0	0	1	0	1	0	0	0	0	1	1	1	0	1	0	0	0	0	0	0
EUROPE EX. U.K.	13	4	0	0	2	2	1	0	0	0	1	1	1	1	3	0	0	0	0	0	0	0
SOUTHERN DOMINIONS	12	0	0	2	1	0	0	2	1	1	1	1	0	0	1	0	1	0	0	0	1	0
S. AFRICA +RHOD.	8	0	0	1	2	0	0	2	1	1	1	0	1	1	0	1	1	1	1	1	0	0
AUSTRALIA + N.Z.	12	0	0	1	1	1	1	2	0	1	0	1	1	1	3	1	1	1	0	1	1	0
ASIA + OTHER AFRICA	9	0	0	0	0	0	0	0	0	0	0	0	1	0	1	0	1	0	0	0	0	0
JAPAN	6	0	0	0	0	0	1	0	0	0	0	0	1	1	3	1	2	1	1	1	0	0
OTHER ASIA+AFR.	6	0	0	0	0	0	0	0	0	0	0	0	0	0	2	2	0	0	0	0	0	0
BLACK AFRICA	0	0	0	0	0	0	0	0	0	0	0	0	0	0	1	0	0	0	0	0	0	0
ARAB WORLD	1	0	0	0	0	0	0	0	0	0	0	1	0	0	0	0	1	0	1	0	0	0
INDIA	5	0	0	0	0	1	1	1	0	0	0	0	1	0	1	1	0	1	0	0	0	0
PHILIPPINES	0	0	0	0	0	0	0	0	0	0	0	0	0	0	0	0	0	0	0	0	0	0
OTHER E. ASIA	0	0	0	0	0	0	0	0	0	0	0	0	0	0	0	0	0	0	0	0	0	0
OTHER ASIA	1	0	0	0	0	0	1	0	0	0	0	0	0	0	1	0	0	0	0	0	0	0

CHAPTER 2- THE EXPANSION OF PARENT SYSTEMS
SECTION 2- THE FLOW OF MANUFACTURING BY INDUSTRY OF PARENT SYSTEM
TABLE 16- SYSTEMS IN THE HOUSEHOLD APPLIANCE INDUSTRY (SIC 363)
CLASSIFIED BY PERIOD SYSTEM FIRST OPERATED A MANUFACTURING SUBSIDIARY
IN SPECIFIED COUNTRIES AND REGIONS

PERIOD

COUNTRY OR REGION	PRE 1968	PRE 1901	1901 -13	1914 -19	1920 -24	1925 -29	1930 -34	1935 -39	1940 -45	1946 -50	1951 -53	1954 -55	1956 -57	1958 -59	1960 -61	1962	1963	1964	1965	1966	1967	UNK
OUTSIDE U.S.	3	0	1	1	0	0	1	0	0	0	0	0	0	0	0	0	0	0	0	0	0	0
OUT. U.S. + CANADA	3	0	1	1	0	1	2	0	0	0	0	0	0	0	0	0	0	0	0	0	0	0
OUT. WEST. HEMIS.	3	0	1	0	0	2	0	0	0	0	1	1	1	1	0	0	0	0	0	0	0	0
OUT. WHITE CWEALTH	3	0	1	0	0	0	0	0	0	0	1	1	1	1	0	0	0	0	0	0	0	0
OUT. DEVLPED WORLD	3	0	0	0	0	0	1	0	1	0	1	1	1	1	0	0	0	0	0	0	0	0
CANADA	3	0	0	0	0	0	1	0	0	0	0	0	0	0	0	0	0	0	0	0	0	0
LATIN AMERICA	3	0	0	0	0	0	0	0	0	0	1	1	1	1	0	0	0	0	0	0	0	0
C. AMER.+CARIB.	3	0	0	0	0	0	0	0	0	0	1	1	1	0	1	1	0	0	0	0	1	0
CUBA	0	0	0	0	0	0	0	0	0	0	0	0	0	0	0	0	0	0	0	0	0	0
MEXICO	3	0	0	0	0	0	0	0	0	0	1	1	1	1	1	1	1	0	0	0	1	0
OTHER	1	0	0	0	0	0	0	0	0	0	0	0	0	0	0	0	0	0	0	0	0	0
S. AMERICA	3	0	0	0	0	0	0	1	1	0	1	1	1	1	1	1	1	0	0	0	1	0
ARGENTINA	2	0	0	0	0	0	0	1	0	0	0	0	1	1	1	0	0	0	1	0	0	0
BRAZIL	3	0	0	0	0	0	0	1	0	0	0	1	1	0	1	1	1	0	0	0	0	0
PERU	1	0	0	0	0	0	0	0	0	0	0	0	0	0	0	0	0	0	0	0	0	0
COLOMBIA	1	0	0	0	0	0	0	0	0	0	0	0	0	1	1	0	0	0	0	0	0	0
VENEZUELA	2	0	0	0	0	0	0	0	0	0	0	0	1	1	1	0	0	0	0	1	1	0
OTHER	2	0	0	0	0	0	0	0	0	0	0	0	0	0	1	1	0	0	0	0	0	0
EUROPE	3	0	0	0	0	1	0	0	0	0	0	1	1	0	0	0	0	0	0	0	0	0
EFTA	3	0	0	0	0	1	0	0	0	0	0	1	1	0	0	0	0	0	0	0	0	0
U.K.	3	0	1	0	0	1	0	0	0	0	0	0	0	0	0	0	0	0	0	0	0	0
SCANDINAVIA	1	0	0	0	0	0	0	0	0	0	0	0	0	0	0	0	0	0	0	0	0	0
SWITZERLAND	0	0	0	0	0	0	0	0	0	0	0	0	0	0	0	0	0	0	0	0	0	0
OTHER EFTA	0	0	0	0	0	0	0	0	0	0	0	0	0	0	0	0	0	0	0	0	0	0
EUROP. COMMUNITY	3	0	0	0	0	0	0	1	0	0	0	1	1	1	0	0	0	0	0	0	0	0
FRANCE	3	0	0	0	0	0	0	1	0	0	0	0	0	0	1	0	1	0	0	0	0	0
GERMANY	2	0	0	0	0	0	0	0	1	0	0	0	0	0	0	1	0	1	0	0	0	0
ITALY	2	0	0	0	0	0	0	0	0	1	0	1	1	0	0	0	0	0	0	0	0	0
BELGIUM + LUX	1	0	0	0	0	0	0	0	0	0	0	0	0	0	0	0	1	0	0	0	0	0
NETHERLANDS	1	0	0	0	0	0	0	0	0	0	0	0	0	0	0	0	0	0	0	0	0	0
SPAIN	0	0	0	0	0	0	0	0	0	0	0	0	0	0	0	0	0	0	0	0	0	0
GREECE + TURKEY	1	0	0	0	0	0	0	0	0	0	0	0	0	0	0	0	0	0	0	0	0	0
OTHER EUROPE	1	0	1	0	0	0	0	0	0	0	1	0	0	0	0	0	0	0	0	0	0	0
EUROPE EX. U.K.	3	0	0	0	0	0	0	0	0	0	0	1	1	0	0	0	0	0	0	0	1	0
SOUTHERN DOMINIONS	3	0	0	0	0	0	1	0	0	0	1	0	0	0	0	0	0	1	0	0	0	0
S. AFRICA +RHOD.	2	0	0	0	0	0	0	0	0	0	0	0	0	0	0	0	1	1	0	0	0	0
AUSTRALIA + N.Z.	3	0	0	0	0	0	1	0	0	0	1	0	0	0	0	0	0	1	0	0	0	0
ASIA + OTHER AFRICA	1	0	0	0	0	0	0	0	0	0	0	0	0	0	0	0	0	0	0	0	0	0
JAPAN	1	0	0	0	0	0	0	0	0	0	0	0	1	1	1	0	0	0	0	0	0	0
OTHER ASIA+AFR.	1	0	0	0	0	0	0	0	0	0	0	0	1	1	1	0	0	0	0	0	0	0
BLACK AFRICA	1	0	0	0	0	0	0	0	0	0	0	0	0	0	0	0	0	0	1	0	0	0
ARAB WORLD	1	0	0	0	0	0	0	0	0	0	0	0	0	1	0	0	0	0	0	0	0	0
INDIA	1	0	0	0	0	0	0	0	0	0	0	0	0	0	1	0	0	0	0	0	0	0
PHILIPPINES	1	0	0	0	0	0	0	0	0	0	0	0	0	0	0	0	0	0	0	0	0	0
OTHER E. ASIA	1	0	0	0	0	0	0	0	0	0	0	0	0	1	0	0	0	1	0	0	1	0
OTHER ASIA	1	0	0	0	0	0	0	0	0	0	0	0	1	0	1	0	0	0	0	0	0	0

CHAPTER 2- THE EXPANSION OF PARENT SYSTEMS
SECTION 2- THE FLOW OF MANUFACTURING BY INDUSTRY OF PARENT SYSTEM
TABLE 17- SYSTEMS IN THE ELECTRONICS INDUSTRY (SIC 365-367)
CLASSIFIED BY PERIOD SYSTEM FIRST OPERATED A MANUFACTURING SUBSIDIARY
IN SPECIFIED COUNTRIES AND REGIONS

PERIOD

COUNTRY OR REGION	PRE 1968	PRE 1901	1901 -13	1914 -19	1920 -24	1925 -29	1930 -34	1935 -39	1940 -45	1946 -50	1951 -53	1954 -55	1956 -57	1958 -59	1960 -61	1962	1963	1964	1965	1966	1967	UNK
OUTSIDE U.S.	8	0	1	0	1	1	0	1	0	0	1	0	2	1	0	0	0	0	0	0	0	0
OUT. U.S. + CANADA	8	0	1	0	0	2	0	1	0	0	1	0	2	1	0	0	0	0	0	0	0	0
OUT. WEST. HEMIS.	8	0	1	1	0	2	1	1	0	0	1	0	2	1	0	0	0	0	0	0	0	0
OUT. WHITE CWEALTH	8	0	1	0	0	2	0	0	1	0	1	0	1	3	2	0	0	0	0	0	0	0
OUT. DEVLPED WORLD	8	0	0	0	0	2	0	0	1	0	0	0	0	2	2	0	0	0	1	0	0	0
CANADA	7	0	0	0	2	0	0	0	2	2	0	1	1	1	0	0	0	0	0	0	0	0
LATIN AMERICA	7	0	0	0	0	2	0	1	1	0	0	0	0	1	1	0	0	1	1	0	0	0
C. AMER.+CARIB.	7	0	0	0	0	0	0	1	0	0	0	0	1	2	0	0	1	2	1	1	0	0
CUBA	1	0	0	0	0	2	0	0	1	0	0	0	0	2	0	1	0	0	0	0	0	0
MEXICO	7	0	0	0	0	0	0	1	0	1	0	0	1	1	1	1	1	0	2	0	0	0
OTHER	1	0	0	0	0	2	0	0	0	0	0	0	0	0	0	0	0	0	0	0	0	0
S. AMERICA	6	0	0	0	0	2	0	1	0	1	0	0	0	2	1	1	1	0	0	1	0	0
ARGENTINA	5	0	0	0	0	1	0	0	1	0	0	0	1	1	0	1	0	0	0	0	0	0
BRAZIL	6	0	0	0	0	0	0	1	0	1	0	0	0	2	1	0	0	0	0	0	0	0
PERU	0	0	0	0	0	1	0	0	0	0	0	0	1	0	0	0	0	0	0	0	0	0
COLOMBIA	1	0	0	0	0	0	0	0	0	0	0	0	0	0	0	0	0	0	1	0	0	0
VENEZUELA	3	0	0	0	0	0	0	0	0	0	1	0	1	0	1	0	0	1	1	0	1	0
OTHER	3	0	0	0	1	1	0	0	0	0	1	0	0	0	0	0	0	1	1	0	0	0
EUROPE	8	0	1	0	0	2	0	1	0	0	1	0	2	1	0	0	0	0	0	0	0	0
EFTA	8	0	1	0	0	2	0	1	0	0	0	0	1	3	1	0	0	0	0	0	0	0
U.K.	8	0	1	0	0	2	1	1	0	1	0	0	1	3	1	0	0	0	0	0	0	0
SCANDINAVIA	3	0	0	0	0	0	0	0	0	0	0	0	0	0	1	0	0	0	0	0	0	1
SWITZERLAND	2	0	0	0	0	1	1	0	1	1	0	0	0	0	0	0	1	0	0	0	0	0
OTHER EFTA	1	0	0	0	0	1	0	0	0	0	0	0	1	3	1	0	0	0	0	0	0	0
EUROP. COMMUNITY	8	0	0	0	0	1	0	0	1	0	2	0	1	3	0	0	0	0	0	0	0	0
FRANCE	4	0	1	0	0	1	0	0	0	1	0	1	0	2	1	1	0	0	0	0	0	0
GERMANY	6	0	1	1	0	1	0	0	1	0	0	0	0	1	0	1	1	1	1	0	0	0
ITALY	7	0	0	0	0	0	0	0	0	1	1	0	1	1	1	1	1	0	0	0	0	0
BELGIUM + LUX	3	0	0	1	0	1	0	0	0	0	0	1	0	0	0	0	0	1	0	0	0	0
NETHERLANDS	4	0	0	0	0	0	0	0	1	1	1	0	1	2	0	0	1	0	0	1	0	0
SPAIN	1	0	0	0	0	1	0	0	0	0	0	0	0	0	0	0	0	0	1	0	0	0
GREECE + TURKEY	2	0	0	0	0	0	0	0	1	0	1	0	1	0	1	0	0	1	0	0	0	0
OTHER EUROPE	8	0	0	1	0	1	0	0	0	0	0	0	0	0	0	0	0	0	0	0	0	0
EUROPE EX. U.K.	8	0	1	0	0	1	0	0	0	0	2	0	1	3	0	0	0	0	0	0	0	0
SOUTHERN DOMINIONS	5	0	0	0	0	1	0	0	0	0	0	2	1	1	0	0	0	0	0	0	0	0
S. AFRICA +RHOD.	1	0	0	0	0	0	0	0	0	1	0	0	1	0	0	0	0	0	2	0	0	0
AUSTRALIA + N.Z.	5	0	0	0	0	1	0	0	0	1	0	2	1	1	0	0	0	0	1	0	0	0
ASIA + OTHER AFRICA	7	0	0	0	0	1	0	0	0	0	0	0	0	0	0	0	0	0	0	0	0	0
JAPAN	5	0	0	0	0	0	0	0	0	0	0	0	0	1	1	0	0	1	1	0	0	0
OTHER ASIA+AFR.	6	0	0	0	0	1	0	0	0	1	0	0	1	0	3	0	0	0	2	1	1	1
BLACK AFRICA	1	0	0	0	0	0	0	0	0	1	0	0	1	1	0	0	0	0	1	0	0	0
ARAB WORLD	0	0	0	0	0	0	0	0	0	0	0	0	0	0	0	0	0	0	0	0	0	0
INDIA	4	0	0	0	0	1	0	0	0	0	0	0	0	0	0	0	0	1	1	0	1	0
PHILIPPINES	3	0	0	0	0	0	0	0	0	0	0	0	0	0	1	0	0	0	1	0	0	0
OTHER E. ASIA	2	0	0	0	0	1	0	0	0	0	0	0	0	0	0	0	0	0	1	0	1	0
OTHER ASIA	0	0	0	0	0	0	0	0	0	0	0	0	0	0	0	0	0	0	0	0	0	0

CHAPTER 2- THE EXPANSION OF PARENT SYSTEMS
SECTION 2- THE FLOW OF MANUFACTURING BY INDUSTRY OF PARENT SYSTEM
TABLE 18- SYSTEMS IN OTHER ELECTRICAL MACHINERY INDUSTRIES (OTHER SIC 36)
CLASSIFIED BY PERIOD SYSTEM FIRST OPERATED A MANUFACTURING SUBSIDIARY
IN SPECIFIED COUNTRIES AND REGIONS

PERIOD

COUNTRY OR REGION	PRE 1968	PRE 1901	1901 -13	1914 -19	1920 -24	1925 -29	1930 -34	1935 -39	1940 -45	1946 -50	1951 -53	1954 -55	1956 -57	1958 -59	1960 -61	1962	1963	1964	1965	1966	1967	UNK
OUTSIDE U.S.	8	3	0	2	0	1	0	0	0	0	0	1	0	1	0	0	0	0	0	0	0	0
OUT. U.S. + CANADA	8	3	0	1	1	1	0	1	0	0	0	1	0	1	0	0	0	0	0	0	0	0
OUT. WEST. HEMIS.	8	3	0	1	0	0	2	1	0	1	0	1	0	3	0	0	0	0	0	0	0	0
OUT. WHITE CWEALTH	8	2	0	0	0	0	0	0	0	0	0	1	0	3	1	0	0	1	0	0	0	0
OUT. DEVLPED WORLD	8	1	0	0	0	0	0	1	1	1	0	1	0	3	0	1	1	0	0	0	0	0
CANADA	8	2	0	1	1	1	0	1	0	0	0	1	0	1	0	0	1	1	0	0	0	0
LATIN AMERICA	8	1	0	0	0	0	0	1	1	1	0	1	0	3	1	0	1	1	1	0	0	0
C. AMER.+CARIB.	8	0	0	0	0	0	0	1	1	1	0	0	1	2	0	0	0	1	0	0	0	0
CUBA	2	0	0	0	0	0	0	0	0	1	0	1	0	2	1	0	0	0	0	0	0	0
MEXICO	8	0	0	0	0	0	0	0	1	0	0	1	1	3	1	0	0	1	0	0	0	0
OTHER	1	0	0	0	0	0	0	1	0	0	0	0	0	0	0	0	0	0	0	0	0	0
S. AMERICA	6	1	0	0	0	0	0	1	1	0	0	0	1	2	1	0	0	1	1	0	0	0
ARGENTINA	3	0	0	0	0	0	0	0	0	0	0	0	0	1	0	0	0	0	0	0	0	0
BRAZIL	6	0	0	0	0	0	0	1	0	0	0	1	0	2	1	1	0	1	1	0	0	0
PERU	1	0	0	0	0	0	0	0	0	0	0	0	0	0	0	1	0	0	0	0	0	0
COLOMBIA	4	0	0	0	0	0	0	1	0	0	0	1	0	1	1	2	0	1	0	0	0	0
VENEZUELA	4	0	0	0	0	0	0	0	0	0	0	0	0	0	1	0	0	1	0	0	0	0
OTHER	1	1	0	0	0	0	0	0	0	0	0	0	0	0	0	0	0	0	0	0	0	0
EUROPE	8	3	0	0	0	0	0	1	0	0	0	0	0	2	0	0	0	1	0	1	0	0
EFTA	8	3	0	0	0	0	0	1	0	0	0	0	0	1	1	0	0	1	0	1	0	0
U.K.	0	3	0	0	0	0	0	0	0	0	0	0	0	0	0	0	0	0	0	0	0	0
SCANDINAVIA	1	0	0	0	0	0	0	0	0	0	0	0	0	0	1	1	0	0	0	0	0	0
SWITZERLAND	3	0	1	0	0	0	0	0	0	0	0	0	0	0	0	0	0	1	1	0	0	0
OTHER EFTA	7	1	0	1	0	0	2	0	0	0	0	0	0	0	1	0	0	0	1	1	1	0
EUROP. COMMUNITY	6	1	0	0	0	1	1	0	0	0	0	0	0	1	2	0	0	1	1	1	0	0
FRANCE	6	1	0	0	0	1	1	0	0	0	0	0	0	2	1	0	1	1	0	1	0	0
GERMANY	4	0	0	1	0	0	0	0	0	0	0	0	0	1	0	0	1	1	1	0	0	0
ITALY	1	0	0	0	0	0	0	0	0	0	0	0	0	0	1	1	0	0	0	0	0	0
BELGIUM + LUX	2	0	1	0	0	0	0	0	0	0	0	0	0	1	0	0	0	0	0	0	0	0
NETHERLANDS	4	0	0	0	0	0	0	0	0	0	0	0	0	1	2	0	0	0	0	0	0	0
SPAIN	2	0	0	0	0	0	0	0	0	0	1	0	0	0	0	1	0	0	1	0	0	0
GREECE + TURKEY	3	1	0	0	1	0	1	0	0	0	1	0	0	0	0	0	0	0	0	0	0	0
OTHER EUROPE	7	1	0	0	0	2	0	0	0	0	1	0	0	2	0	0	0	0	0	0	0	0
EUROPE EX. U.K.	6	1	0	1	0	0	0	0	0	0	1	2	0	0	0	0	0	0	0	0	0	0
SOUTHERN DOMINIONS	3	0	0	0	0	0	0	0	0	0	1	2	0	0	0	0	0	0	1	0	0	0
S. AFRICA +RHOD.	6	0	1	1	0	0	0	0	0	0	1	0	0	0	1	1	0	1	0	1	0	0
AUSTRALIA + N.Z.	5	0	0	1	0	0	0	0	0	0	0	0	0	2	0	0	0	0	0	0	0	0
ASIA + OTHER AFRICA	3	1	1	0	0	0	0	0	0	0	0	0	0	2	0	3	0	0	1	0	1	0
JAPAN	4	0	0	0	0	0	0	0	0	0	0	0	0	2	0	0	0	0	0	1	0	0
OTHER ASIA+AFR.	0	0	0	0	0	0	0	0	0	0	0	0	0	2	0	0	0	0	1	0	1	0
BLACK AFRICA	0	0	0	0	0	0	0	0	0	0	0	0	0	0	0	0	0	0	0	0	0	0
ARAB WORLD	2	0	0	0	0	0	0	0	0	0	0	0	0	0	1	0	0	0	0	0	1	0
INDIA	1	0	0	0	0	0	0	0	0	0	1	0	0	0	0	0	0	0	0	0	0	0
PHILIPPINES	1	0	0	1	0	0	0	0	0	0	1	0	0	0	0	0	0	0	0	0	0	0
OTHER E. ASIA	2	0	0	1	0	0	0	0	0	0	0	0	0	0	0	0	0	0	0	0	1	0
OTHER ASIA	1	0	0	0	0	0	0	0	0	0	0	0	0	1	0	0	0	0	0	0	0	0

CHAPTER 2- THE EXPANSION OF PARENT SYSTEMS
SECTION 2- THE FLOW OF MANUFACTURING BY INDUSTRY OF PARENT SYSTEM
TABLE 19- SYSTEMS IN THE MOTOR VEHICLES INDUSTRY (SIC 371)
CLASSIFIED BY PERIOD SYSTEM FIRST OPERATED A MANUFACTURING SUBSIDIARY
IN SPECIFIED COUNTRIES AND REGIONS

PERIOD

COUNTRY OR REGION	PRE 1968	PRE 1901	1901 -13	1914 -19	1920 -24	1925 -29	1930 -34	1935 -39	1940 -45	1946 -50	1951 -53	1954 -55	1956 -57	1958 -59	1960 -61	1962	1963	1964	1965	1966	1967	UNK
OUTSIDE U.S.	11	0	0	0	0	6	0	1	0	1	0	0	0	1	1	0	0	0	0	0	0	0
OUT. U.S. + CANADA	11	2	2	0	0	4	0	0	0	2	2	0	0	0	0	0	1	0	0	0	0	0
OUT. WEST. HEMIS.	11	2	2	0	0	4	0	0	0	2	2	0	0	0	0	0	1	1	0	1	0	0
OUT. WHITE CWEALTH	11	0	0	1	1	1	1	0	0	1	1	1	0	2	0	1	1	1	1	0	0	0
OUT. DEVLPED WORLD	11	0	0	1	0	1	0	0	0	1	1	1	0	3	1	1	1	0	0	0	0	0
CANADA	11	0	2	0	0	4	1	0	0	0	2	1	0	1	0	0	0	0	0	0	0	0
LATIN AMERICA	11	0	0	1	0	1	0	1	0	0	1	1	0	3	1	1	0	0	0	0	0	0
C. AMER.+CARIB.	11	0	0	0	0	0	0	0	0	0	0	0	0	1	1	1	3	1	1	1	0	0
CUBA	0	0	0	0	0	1	0	1	0	0	2	1	0	1	0	0	0	1	1	0	0	0
MEXICO	11	0	0	0	0	0	0	0	0	0	1	0	0	1	0	1	3	0	0	1	0	0
OTHER	1	0	0	1	0	1	1	1	0	1	0	1	1	0	0	1	0	1	0	0	1	0
S. AMERICA	10	0	0	1	0	1	0	0	0	0	0	0	1	3	0	2	2	0	0	1	0	0
ARGENTINA	9	0	0	0	0	1	0	0	1	0	2	0	1	1	0	0	0	0	0	0	0	0
BRAZIL	8	0	0	1	0	1	0	0	0	0	2	0	1	3	0	0	0	2	0	0	0	0
PERU	4	0	0	0	0	0	0	0	1	0	0	0	0	0	0	0	0	0	1	0	0	0
COLOMBIA	5	0	0	0	0	0	0	0	0	1	0	0	0	1	1	2	0	2	0	1	0	0
VENEZUELA	6	0	0	0	0	0	0	0	0	1	0	0	0	0	0	0	0	0	1	0	0	0
OTHER	2	0	0	0	0	1	0	0	0	0	1	0	0	0	0	2	0	0	1	0	0	0
EUROPE	11	0	0	0	0	4	0	0	0	2	2	0	0	0	0	0	1	0	0	0	0	0
EFTA	11	0	0	0	0	4	0	0	0	1	1	0	0	1	1	0	2	0	0	0	0	0
U.K.	11	2	2	0	0	0	0	0	0	1	2	0	0	1	0	0	2	0	0	0	0	0
SCANDINAVIA	4	0	0	0	0	0	0	1	0	0	0	0	0	0	0	1	0	0	0	0	0	0
SWITZERLAND	2	0	0	1	1	0	0	1	0	1	1	0	0	1	0	0	1	0	0	0	0	0
OTHER EFTA	2	0	0	0	0	0	0	1	0	0	1	0	0	0	1	0	0	0	0	0	0	0
EUROP. COMMUNITY	11	0	0	1	1	1	1	0	0	1	1	0	0	2	1	0	1	0	0	0	0	0
FRANCE	8	0	0	1	0	3	1	0	0	0	0	0	0	1	0	1	0	0	0	0	0	0
GERMANY	9	0	0	1	1	0	0	0	0	0	1	0	0	0	1	3	0	0	0	1	0	0
ITALY	4	0	0	0	0	0	0	0	0	0	0	0	0	1	0	0	1	0	0	0	0	0
BELGIUM + LUX	3	0	0	0	0	0	0	0	0	1	0	0	0	0	1	0	0	1	1	0	1	0
NETHERLANDS	3	0	0	0	0	1	0	0	0	0	0	1	0	1	1	1	1	0	0	0	0	0
SPAIN	7	0	0	1	1	0	0	0	0	1	1	0	0	1	0	2	2	2	0	0	0	0
GREECE + TURKEY	2	0	0	0	0	1	0	0	0	0	0	1	0	0	1	0	0	0	0	0	0	0
OTHER EUROPE	4	0	0	1	1	1	0	0	0	1	0	0	1	1	0	0	1	0	1	0	0	0
EUROPE EX. U.K.	11	0	1	1	1	1	0	0	0	1	0	1	0	2	1	0	1	0	0	0	1	0
SOUTHERN DOMINIONS	9	0	0	0	0	2	0	0	0	0	1	4	0	2	2	0	1	1	0	0	0	0
S. AFRICA +RHOD.	7	0	0	0	0	1	0	0	0	0	0	0	0	2	0	0	1	0	0	1	1	0
AUSTRALIA + N.Z.	8	0	0	0	0	2	0	0	0	1	1	4	0	2	0	0	1	0	0	0	0	0
ASIA + OTHER AFRICA	9	0	0	0	0	2	0	0	0	0	0	0	0	2	0	1	2	2	0	0	0	0
JAPAN	6	0	0	0	0	2	0	0	0	1	0	0	0	0	0	1	1	0	0	0	0	0
OTHER ASIA+AFR.	8	0	0	0	0	0	0	0	0	0	1	3	0	2	0	1	1	0	0	0	0	0
BLACK AFRICA	2	0	0	0	0	2	0	0	1	1	0	0	0	0	0	1	1	0	0	0	0	0
ARAB WORLD	3	0	0	0	0	0	0	0	3	0	0	0	0	2	0	1	0	0	1	0	0	0
INDIA	7	0	0	0	0	0	0	0	0	1	0	0	0	1	0	1	1	0	0	1	0	0
PHILIPPINES	2	0	0	0	0	0	0	0	0	0	0	0	0	1	0	2	0	0	0	0	0	0
OTHER E. ASIA	0	0	0	0	0	0	0	0	0	0	0	0	0	0	0	0	0	0	0	0	0	0
OTHER ASIA	3	0	0	0	0	2	0	0	0	1	0	0	0	0	0	0	0	0	0	0	0	0

CHAPTER 2- THE EXPANSION OF PARENT SYSTEMS
SECTION 2- THE FLOW OF MANUFACTURING BY INDUSTRY OF PARENT SYSTEM
TABLE 20- SYSTEMS IN OTHER TRANSPORTATION EQUIPMENT INDUSTRIES (SIC 372-379)
CLASSIFIED BY PERIOD SYSTEM FIRST OPERATED A MANUFACTURING SUBSIDIARY
IN SPECIFIED COUNTRIES AND REGIONS

PERIOD

COUNTRY OR REGION	PRE 1968	PRE 1901	1901 -13	1914 -19	1920 -24	1925 -29	1930 -34	1935 -39	1940 -45	1946 -50	1951 -53	1954 -55	1956 -57	1958 -59	1960 -61	1962	1963	1964	1965	1966	1967	UNK
OUTSIDE U.S.	7	1	0	1	0	1	1	1	0	0	0	0	1	1	0	0	0	0	0	0	0	0
OUT. U.S. + CANADA	7	1	0	0	1	1	1	0	1	0	0	1	1	2	0	0	1	1	0	0	0	1
OUT. WEST. HEMIS.	7	1	0	0	1	1	0	0	0	1	0	1	1	2	1	0	1	1	0	0	0	1
OUT. WHITE CWEALTH	7	1	0	0	1	1	0	0	1	0	0	1	1	2	1	0	1	0	0	0	0	0
OUT. DEVLPED WORLD	7	0	0	0	0	0	0	0	1	0	0	1	1	2	0	0	1	1	0	0	0	1
CANADA	6	0	0	1	0	1	1	1	0	0	0	0	0	1	1	0	0	0	0	0	0	0
LATIN AMERICA	7	0	0	0	0	1	1	0	1	0	0	1	2	2	1	0	1	0	0	0	0	1
C. AMER.+CARIB.	5	0	0	0	0	0	0	0	1	0	0	1	2	2	0	0	0	0	0	0	0	1
CUBA	5	0	0	0	0	0	0	0	0	0	0	0	0	2	0	0	0	0	0	0	0	0
MEXICO	5	0	0	0	0	0	0	0	1	0	0	1	1	2	1	0	0	0	0	0	0	0
OTHER	1	0	0	0	0	0	0	0	0	0	0	0	0	3	0	0	1	0	0	0	0	0
S. AMERICA	6	0	0	0	0	0	1	0	1	1	1	0	1	2	0	0	0	0	0	0	0	0
ARGENTINA	4	0	0	0	0	0	0	0	0	0	0	1	0	2	0	1	1	0	0	0	0	0
BRAZIL	4	0	0	0	0	0	0	0	0	1	0	0	1	0	0	0	0	1	0	0	0	0
PERU	1	0	0	0	0	0	0	0	0	0	0	0	0	0	0	0	0	0	0	0	0	0
COLOMBIA	2	0	0	0	0	0	0	0	1	1	0	0	0	0	0	0	1	0	0	0	0	0
VENEZUELA	1	0	0	0	0	0	0	0	0	0	0	0	0	0	0	0	0	0	0	0	0	0
OTHER	1	0	0	0	0	0	0	0	0	0	0	0	0	0	1	0	0	0	0	0	0	0
EUROPE	7	1	0	0	0	1	0	1	0	0	0	0	2	1	1	0	1	1	0	0	0	0
EFTA	6	1	0	0	0	0	0	0	0	0	0	2	2	1	1	0	2	2	0	0	0	0
U.K.	4	0	0	0	0	0	0	0	0	0	0	2	2	0	1	0	1	1	0	0	0	0
SCANDINAVIA	0	0	0	0	0	0	0	0	0	0	0	0	0	0	0	0	0	0	0	0	0	0
SWITZERLAND	4	0	0	0	0	1	0	1	0	0	0	0	0	1	0	0	1	1	0	0	0	0
OTHER EFTA	1	0	0	0	0	0	0	0	0	0	0	0	0	0	1	0	1	0	0	0	0	0
EUROP. COMMUNITY	7	1	1	0	0	1	1	1	0	0	0	0	1	1	2	1	1	0	0	0	0	0
FRANCE	5	1	1	0	0	0	1	0	0	0	0	0	0	0	1	1	0	1	0	0	0	0
GERMANY	5	1	0	0	0	1	0	1	0	0	0	0	1	0	1	0	1	0	0	0	0	0
ITALY	3	0	0	0	0	0	0	0	0	0	0	0	0	1	0	0	1	1	1	0	0	0
BELGIUM + LUX	1	1	0	0	0	0	0	0	0	0	0	0	0	0	0	0	0	0	0	0	0	0
NETHERLANDS	1	0	0	0	0	0	0	0	0	0	0	0	1	0	0	0	0	0	0	0	0	0
SPAIN	1	0	0	0	0	0	0	0	0	0	0	1	0	0	0	0	0	0	1	0	0	0
GREECE + TURKEY	1	0	0	0	0	1	0	0	0	0	0	0	0	0	1	0	0	1	0	0	0	0
OTHER EUROPE	1	0	0	0	0	1	0	0	0	0	0	0	0	1	0	0	0	0	0	0	0	0
EUROPE EX. U.K.	7	1	0	0	1	1	0	0	0	0	0	1	1	1	2	1	1	0	0	0	0	0
SOUTHERN DOMINIONS	4	0	0	0	0	0	0	0	0	1	1	0	0	0	0	0	0	0	2	0	0	0
S. AFRICA +RHOD.	4	0	0	0	0	0	0	0	0	1	0	0	0	0	1	0	0	1	1	1	1	0
AUSTRALIA + N.Z.	3	0	0	0	0	0	0	0	0	0	1	0	0	0	0	0	0	1	0	0	0	1
ASIA + OTHER AFRICA	4	0	0	0	0	0	0	0	0	0	0	0	0	0	2	2	1	0	0	0	0	1
JAPAN	4	0	0	0	0	0	0	0	0	0	0	0	0	0	0	2	1	0	0	0	0	1
OTHER ASIA+AFR.	1	0	0	0	0	0	0	0	0	0	0	0	0	0	0	0	0	0	0	0	1	0
BLACK AFRICA	0	0	0	0	0	0	0	0	0	0	0	0	0	0	0	0	0	0	0	0	0	0
ARAB WORLD	0	0	0	0	0	0	0	0	0	0	0	0	0	0	0	0	0	0	0	0	0	0
INDIA	0	0	0	0	0	0	0	0	0	0	0	0	0	0	0	0	0	0	0	0	0	0
PHILIPPINES	0	0	0	0	0	0	0	0	0	0	0	0	0	0	0	0	0	0	0	0	0	0
OTHER E. ASIA	1	0	0	0	0	0	0	0	0	0	0	0	0	0	0	0	0	0	0	1	1	0
OTHER ASIA	0	0	0	0	0	0	0	0	0	0	0	0	0	0	0	0	0	0	0	0	0	0

CHAPTER 2- THE EXPANSION OF PARENT SYSTEMS
SECTION 2- THE FLOW OF MANUFACTURING BY INDUSTRY OF PARENT SYSTEM
TABLE 21- SYSTEMS IN THE INSTRUMENTS AND PRECISION GOODS INDUSTRIES (SIC 38)
CLASSIFIED BY PERIOD SYSTEM FIRST OPERATED A MANUFACTURING SUBSIDIARY
IN SPECIFIED COUNTRIES AND REGIONS

PERIOD

COUNTRY OR REGION	PRE 1968	PRE 1901	1901 -13	1914 -19	1920 -24	1925 -29	1930 -34	1935 -39	1940 -45	1946 -50	1951 -53	1954 -55	1956 -57	1958 -59	1960 -61	1962	1963	1964	1965	1966	1967	UNK
OUTSIDE U.S.	5	1	0	1	0	0	0	0	0	1	2	0	0	0	0	0	0	0	0	0	0	0
OUT. U.S. + CANADA	5	1	0	0	1	1	0	0	1	1	1	0	1	0	0	0	0	0	0	0	0	0
OUT. WEST. HEMIS.	5	1	0	0	1	0	0	0	1	0	1	0	1	0	0	0	0	0	0	0	0	0
OUT. WHITE CWEALTH	5	1	0	0	1	1	1	0	0	2	0	0	1	0	1	0	0	0	1	1	0	0
OUT. DEVLPED WORLD	5	0	0	0	0	0	0	0	0	1	1	0	0	1	1	0	1	0	1	1	0	0
CANADA	5	1	0	1	0	0	0	0	0	0	2	0	1	0	0	0	0	0	0	0	0	0
LATIN AMERICA	5	0	0	0	0	0	0	0	0	0	2	0	0	0	1	0	1	0	1	1	0	0
C. AMER.+CARIB.	4	0	0	0	0	1	1	0	0	1	1	0	0	1	0	0	1	0	0	0	0	0
CUBA	1	0	0	0	0	0	0	0	0	0	0	0	0	0	0	0	1	0	1	0	0	0
MEXICO	4	0	0	0	0	1	0	0	0	0	1	0	0	0	1	0	0	0	0	0	0	0
OTHER	1	0	0	0	0	0	0	0	0	1	0	0	0	1	1	0	0	0	1	0	0	0
S. AMERICA	4	0	0	0	0	1	1	1	0	0	1	0	0	1	1	0	0	0	1	0	0	0
ARGENTINA	3	0	0	0	0	0	1	1	0	0	0	0	1	1	0	0	0	0	0	1	0	0
BRAZIL	3	0	0	0	0	0	1	1	0	0	0	0	0	0	1	0	0	0	1	0	0	0
PERU	1	0	0	0	0	0	0	0	0	0	0	0	0	0	0	0	0	0	1	0	0	0
COLOMBIA	2	0	0	0	0	0	0	0	0	0	1	0	0	0	1	0	0	0	0	1	0	0
VENEZUELA	1	0	0	0	0	0	0	0	0	0	0	1	0	0	0	0	0	0	0	0	0	0
OTHER	1	0	0	0	0	0	0	0	0	0	0	0	0	0	0	0	0	0	1	0	0	0
EUROPE	5	1	0	0	0	1	0	0	1	1	1	0	1	0	0	0	0	0	0	0	0	0
EFTA	5	1	0	0	0	1	0	0	1	1	1	0	0	0	0	0	0	0	0	0	0	0
U.K.	5	1	0	0	0	1	0	0	1	0	1	0	0	1	0	0	0	0	0	0	0	0
SCANDINAVIA	1	0	0	0	0	0	0	0	0	0	0	0	1	0	0	0	0	0	0	0	0	0
SWITZERLAND	1	0	0	0	0	0	0	0	0	0	0	0	0	0	0	1	0	0	0	0	0	0
OTHER EFTA	2	0	0	0	0	0	0	0	0	0	0	0	0	1	1	1	0	0	0	0	0	0
EUROP. COMMUNITY	5	1	0	0	0	0	0	0	0	0	2	0	2	1	0	1	0	0	0	0	0	0
FRANCE	5	0	0	0	0	1	0	0	0	0	1	0	1	0	1	0	0	0	0	0	0	0
GERMANY	5	1	0	0	0	1	0	0	0	0	1	0	3	1	2	0	0	0	0	0	0	0
ITALY	3	0	0	0	0	0	0	0	0	0	0	0	0	0	0	0	0	0	0	0	0	0
BELGIUM + LUX	2	0	0	0	0	0	0	0	0	0	1	0	1	0	2	0	0	0	0	0	0	0
NETHERLANDS	2	0	0	0	0	0	0	0	0	0	0	0	0	1	1	1	0	0	0	0	0	0
SPAIN	1	0	0	0	0	0	0	0	0	0	1	0	0	0	0	0	0	0	0	0	0	0
GREECE + TURKEY	0	0	0	0	0	0	0	0	0	0	0	0	0	0	0	0	0	0	0	0	0	0
OTHER EUROPE	1	0	0	0	0	0	0	0	0	1	0	0	0	0	0	0	0	0	0	0	0	0
EUROPE EX. U.K.	5	1	0	0	0	0	0	0	1	1	2	0	1	0	0	0	0	0	0	0	0	0
SOUTHERN DOMINIONS	4	0	1	0	0	1	1	0	0	0	1	0	0	0	0	0	1	0	1	0	0	0
S. AFRICA +RHOD.	2	0	0	0	0	1	0	0	0	0	0	1	0	0	0	0	0	0	1	0	0	0
AUSTRALIA + N.Z.	4	0	1	0	0	0	1	0	0	0	1	0	1	0	1	0	1	0	0	0	0	0
ASIA + OTHER AFRICA	4	0	0	0	0	1	0	0	0	0	1	0	1	0	1	0	1	0	0	0	0	0
JAPAN	3	0	0	0	0	0	0	0	0	0	0	0	0	0	1	0	1	0	0	0	0	0
OTHER ASIA+AFR.	2	0	0	0	0	0	0	0	0	0	1	0	0	0	0	0	1	0	1	0	0	0
BLACK AFRICA	1	0	0	0	0	0	0	0	0	0	0	0	1	0	0	0	0	0	0	0	0	0
ARAB WORLD	0	0	0	0	0	0	0	0	0	0	0	0	0	0	0	0	0	0	0	0	0	0
INDIA	2	0	0	0	0	0	0	0	0	0	0	0	0	1	0	0	0	0	0	0	0	0
PHILIPPINES	1	0	0	0	0	0	0	0	0	0	0	0	0	0	0	0	0	0	0	0	0	0
OTHER E. ASIA	0	0	0	0	0	0	0	0	0	0	0	0	0	0	0	0	0	0	0	0	0	0
OTHER ASIA	1	0	0	0	0	0	0	0	0	0	0	0	0	0	1	0	0	0	0	0	0	0

CHAPTER 2- THE EXPANSION OF PARENT SYSTEMS
SECTION 2- THE FLOW OF MANUFACTURING BY INDUSTRY OF PARENT SYSTEM
TABLE 22- SYSTEMS IN OTHER INDUSTRIES (SIC 21,27, AND 39)
CLASSIFIED BY PERIOD SYSTEM FIRST OPERATED A MANUFACTURING SUBSIDIARY
IN SPECIFIED COUNTRIES AND REGIONS

COUNTRY OR REGION	PRE 1968	PRE 1901	1901 -13	1914 -19	1920 -24	1925 -29	1930 -34	1935 -39	1940 -45	1946 -50	1951 -53	1954 -55	1956 -57	1958 -59	1960 -61	1962	1963	1964	1965	1966	1967	UNK
OUTSIDE U.S.	7	0	1	2	0	1	0	1	1	0	1	0	0	0	0	0	0	0	0	0	0	0
OUT. U.S. + CANADA	7	0	0	1	0	2	1	1	1	1	0	0	1	0	0	0	0	0	0	0	0	0
OUT. WEST. HEMIS.	7	0	0	1	0	2	1	1	0	1	0	1	1	1	0	0	0	0	0	0	0	0
OUT. WHITE CWEALTH	7	0	0	0	0	2	1	0	1	0	1	1	1	0	0	0	0	0	0	0	0	0
OUT. DEVLPED WORLD	7	0	0	0	0	1	1	0	1	0	1	1	1	1	0	0	0	0	0	0	0	0
CANADA	6	0	1	1	0	1	1	0	1	0	1	0	0	1	1	0	0	0	0	0	0	0
LATIN AMERICA	6	0	0	0	0	1	1	1	1	0	1	1	0	0	0	0	0	0	0	0	0	0
C. AMER.+CARIB.	5	0	0	0	0	1	1	0	1	0	0	1	0	0	0	0	0	1	0	1	0	0
CUBA	1	0	0	0	0	0	0	0	0	0	1	0	0	0	0	0	0	0	0	0	0	0
MEXICO	4	0	0	0	0	1	1	0	1	0	1	0	1	0	0	0	1	1	1	0	0	0
OTHER	2	0	0	0	0	0	0	0	0	0	0	0	0	0	0	0	1	0	0	0	0	0
S. AMERICA	6	0	0	0	0	0	0	0	0	1	1	0	2	0	1	0	0	0	1	1	0	0
ARGENTINA	4	0	0	0	0	0	0	0	0	0	0	1	2	0	1	1	1	0	0	0	0	0
BRAZIL	2	0	0	0	0	0	0	0	0	1	0	1	0	0	0	1	1	0	1	0	1	0
PERU	1	0	0	0	0	0	0	0	0	0	0	0	0	1	0	0	0	0	0	0	0	0
COLOMBIA	1	0	0	0	0	0	0	0	0	1	0	0	0	0	0	0	1	0	0	1	0	0
VENEZUELA	2	0	0	0	0	0	0	0	0	0	0	1	0	1	0	0	0	0	0	0	0	0
OTHER	0	0	0	0	0	0	0	0	0	0	0	0	0	0	0	0	0	0	0	0	0	0
EUROPE	7	0	0	1	0	2	1	1	0	0	0	1	1	2	0	0	0	0	0	0	0	0
EFTA	7	0	0	1	0	1	2	0	0	0	0	0	0	2	1	1	0	0	0	0	0	0
U.K.	7	0	0	1	0	1	2	0	0	0	0	0	0	2	0	0	0	0	0	0	0	0
SCANDINAVIA	4	0	0	0	0	0	0	0	0	0	0	0	0	0	2	0	1	1	0	0	1	0
SWITZERLAND	1	0	0	0	0	0	0	0	0	1	0	0	0	0	1	0	1	0	1	0	0	0
OTHER EFTA	1	0	0	0	0	0	0	0	0	0	0	0	0	0	3	0	0	0	1	0	0	0
EUROP. COMMUNITY	7	0	0	0	0	0	0	0	0	0	0	0	2	0	3	0	0	0	0	0	0	0
FRANCE	4	0	0	0	0	0	0	0	0	0	0	0	0	0	1	1	1	0	0	0	0	0
GERMANY	4	0	0	0	0	0	0	0	0	0	0	0	0	0	0	1	0	1	1	0	1	0
ITALY	4	0	0	0	0	0	0	0	0	0	0	0	1	0	1	0	1	0	0	0	0	0
BELGIUM + LUX	3	0	0	0	0	1	0	0	0	0	0	0	0	0	0	1	0	1	0	0	0	0
NETHERLANDS	2	0	0	0	0	0	0	0	0	0	0	0	1	1	1	0	0	0	0	0	0	0
SPAIN	1	0	0	0	0	0	0	0	0	0	0	0	0	0	0	0	0	1	0	0	0	0
GREECE + TURKEY	0	0	0	0	0	0	0	0	0	0	0	0	0	0	0	0	0	0	0	0	0	0
OTHER EUROPE	1	0	0	0	0	1	0	0	0	0	0	0	0	0	0	0	0	0	0	0	0	0
EUROPE EX. U.K.	7	0	0	0	0	1	0	0	0	1	0	2	0	1	1	1	1	0	0	0	0	0
SOUTHERN DOMINIONS	5	0	0	0	0	0	0	0	0	0	0	1	0	4	0	0	0	0	0	0	0	0
S. AFRICA +RHOD.	5	0	0	0	0	0	0	0	0	0	0	0	0	0	0	0	0	0	0	0	0	0
AUSTRALIA + N.Z.	5	0	0	0	0	0	0	0	0	1	0	0	0	4	0	0	1	0	0	1	0	0
ASIA + OTHER AFRICA	6	0	0	0	0	0	0	0	0	0	0	0	0	1	0	1	1	0	1	1	1	0
JAPAN	2	0	0	0	0	0	0	0	0	1	0	0	0	0	0	2	1	0	0	0	0	0
OTHER ASIA+AFR.	4	0	0	0	0	0	0	0	0	0	0	0	0	1	0	1	1	0	0	0	0	0
BLACK AFRICA	1	0	0	0	0	0	0	0	0	1	0	0	0	0	0	0	0	0	0	1	0	0
ARAB WORLD	1	0	0	0	0	0	0	0	0	0	0	0	0	0	0	0	0	0	0	1	0	0
INDIA	1	0	0	0	0	0	0	0	0	0	0	0	0	1	0	0	0	0	0	0	0	0
PHILIPPINES	0	0	0	0	0	0	0	0	0	0	0	0	0	0	0	0	0	0	0	0	0	0
OTHER E. ASIA	0	0	0	0	0	0	0	0	0	0	0	0	0	0	0	0	0	0	0	0	0	0
OTHER ASIA	2	0	0	0	0	0	0	0	0	1	0	0	0	0	0	1	0	0	0	0	0	0

PERIOD

CHAPTER 2- THE EXPANSION OF PARENT SYSTEMS
SECTION 3- THE FLOW OF MANUFACTURING BY CHARACTERISTIC OF PARENT SYSTEM
TABLE A1- SYSTEMS WITH LOW SALES IN 1966
CLASSIFIED BY PERIOD SYSTEM FIRST OPERATED A MANUFACTURING SUBSIDIARY
IN SPECIFIED COUNTRIES AND REGIONS

PERIOD

COUNTRY OR REGION	PRE 1968	PRE 1901	1901 -13	1914 -19	1920 -24	1925 -29	1930 -34	1935 -39	1940 -45	1946 -50	1951 -53	1954 -55	1956 -57	1958 -59	1960 -61	1962	1963	1964	1965	1966	1967	UNK
OUTSIDE U.S.	94	7	6	16	7	17	8	7	2	6	4	6	3	3	2	0	0	0	0	0	0	0
OUT. U.S. + CANADA	94	7	3	7	9	14	10	7	2	9	7	7	5	3	5	0	1	0	0	0	0	0
OUT. WEST. HEMIS.	94	7	3	6	9	14	8	8	1	5	6	7	7	7	5	0	1	0	0	0	0	0
OUT. WHITE CWEALTH	94	5	2	2	9	12	8	5	2	7	11	8	8	9	4	1	2	0	0	0	1	1
OUT. DEVLPED WORLD	92	0	0	3	3	4	6	9	5	9	9	9	8	11	9	1	2	2	1	0	1	1
CANADA	86	2	8	14	3	14	8	5	4	4	6	5	4	3	3	0	2	1	0	0	1	0
LATIN AMERICA	90	0	0	3	1	3	0	9	5	9	8	8	10	11	11	1	6	0	1	0	1	1
C. AMER.+CARIB.	86	0	0	1	2	1	5	4	2	8	6	2	11	9	11	3	0	4	2	1	1	1
CUBA	12	0	0	0	1	1	0	1	0	1	1	7	2	1	1	0	0	0	0	0	0	0
MEXICO	82	0	0	1	1	4	4	3	0	9	1	10	10	11	7	3	5	4	2	2	1	1
OTHER	29	0	0	0	1	0	1	8	2	1	1	4	2	2	4	1	3	5	3	1	0	0
S. AMERICA	78	0	0	2	2	3	0	1	1	6	2	9	14	7	4	5	3	5	2	1	2	0
ARGENTINA	46	0	0	1	0	2	1	6	6	1	7	4	9	4	4	1	5	2	0	0	0	0
BRAZIL	52	0	0	2	1	1	5	5	1	5	3	3	5	5	6	5	5	3	3	2	2	0
PERU	16	0	0	0	0	0	1	1	1	1	1	1	1	3	0	1	1	0	0	0	0	0
COLOMBIA	30	0	0	0	0	0	0	4	0	3	0	2	1	0	2	2	0	3	3	1	0	0
VENEZUELA	34	0	0	0	0	0	1	0	1	1	1	3	4	6	9	0	4	4	2	1	1	1
OTHER	20	0	0	1	1	0	0	0	2	2	0	0	1	1	1	2	1	0	0	0	3	0
EUROPE	94	7	3	3	8	14	6	8	0	6	7	5	8	9	5	2	1	0	1	1	0	0
EFTA	88	4	3	3	2	13	10	9	0	5	5	5	6	3	6	6	2	1	2	1	0	0
U.K.	84	4	3	1	0	12	2	10	0	0	4	1	1	3	5	1	4	0	1	2	1	0
SCANDINAVIA	24	1	1	0	0	1	1	0	0	1	2	2	0	1	3	3	5	1	3	2	0	0
SWITZERLAND	11	0	0	0	0	0	0	1	0	1	1	0	0	1	1	2	1	1	3	1	0	0
OTHER EFTA	16	1	1	1	0	1	0	1	0	3	1	1	1	1	1	0	2	2	1	0	0	0
EUROP. COMMUNITY	91	5	2	0	9	6	5	2	0	3	4	6	9	13	16	6	5	5	2	2	0	0
FRANCE	64	3	1	0	6	3	2	1	0	3	4	2	2	8	10	2	4	3	1	2	1	0
GERMANY	64	3	1	0	4	5	5	1	0	0	2	3	5	7	8	7	6	2	2	4	1	0
ITALY	57	0	2	1	1	0	0	1	1	1	2	2	1	9	12	8	8	3	4	1	1	1
BELGIUM + LUX	30	1	2	1	0	1	0	2	0	0	1	1	1	8	6	2	7	2	1	1	2	0
NETHERLANDS	31	0	0	0	1	1	1	2	1	3	1	2	2	5	5	1	3	2	1	1	5	0
SPAIN	33	0	0	0	1	0	0	0	0	0	0	1	1	1	6	3	3	3	8	5	0	0
GREECE + TURKEY	7	0	1	0	0	0	0	0	0	1	0	0	2	0	0	0	1	2	5	2	0	0
OTHER EUROPE	14	1	0	0	0	1	0	1	0	1	3	0	1	2	2	2	3	0	1	2	0	0
EUROPE EX. U.K.	93	5	2	0	9	9	5	1	0	4	6	8	8	16	11	3	4	4	1	0	0	0
SOUTHERN DOMINIONS	77	0	0	5	2	1	1	7	3	2	2	7	5	12	10	2	3	3	1	3	3	0
S. AFRICA +RHOD.	43	0	0	1	2	0	5	7	2	3	2	1	1	4	4	1	5	2	1	2	3	1
AUSTRALIA + N.Z.	68	0	0	2	2	1	4	5	2	3	3	4	6	12	8	1	8	1	3	2	3	0
ASIA + OTHER AFRICA	69	0	0	0	0	1	1	0	0	4	3	5	3	3	13	8	6	3	6	2	2	0
JAPAN	43	0	0	0	0	0	1	0	0	0	2	1	4	0	6	11	6	6	3	2	1	0
OTHER ASIA+AFR.	51	0	0	0	0	0	0	0	0	4	1	1	0	0	10	10	6	2	0	3	1	0
BLACK AFRICA	11	0	0	0	0	0	0	0	0	0	1	1	0	0	0	1	1	2	0	1	0	0
ARAB WORLD	7	0	0	0	0	0	0	0	0	1	1	1	1	5	3	3	1	1	2	1	1	0
INDIA	25	0	0	0	0	0	1	0	0	1	0	3	1	0	1	1	3	0	1	1	0	0
PHILIPPINES	18	0	0	0	0	0	0	0	0	1	0	0	0	5	1	1	5	5	2	1	0	0
OTHER E. ASIA	9	0	0	0	0	0	0	0	0	0	3	2	1	1	1	1	1	2	1	1	0	0
OTHER ASIA	18	0	0	0	0	0	0	0	0	2	0	0	2	1	6	4	0	1	0	0	0	0

CHAPTER 2- THE EXPANSION OF PARENT SYSTEMS
SECTION 3- THE FLOW OF MANUFACTURING BY CHARACTERISTIC OF PARENT SYSTEM
TABLE A2- SYSTEMS WITH HIGH SALES IN 1966
CLASSIFIED BY PERIOD SYSTEM FIRST OPERATED A MANUFACTURING SUBSIDIARY
IN SPECIFIED COUNTRIES AND REGIONS

PERIOD

COUNTRY OR REGION	PRE 1968	PRE 1901	1901 -13	1914 -19	1920 -24	1925 -29	1930 -34	1935 -39	1940 -45	1946 -50	1951 -53	1954 -55	1956 -57	1958 -59	1960 -61	1962	1963	1964	1965	1966	1967	UNK
OUTSIDE U.S.	93	12	16	10	8	13	5	6	6	3	5	3	1	1	5	3	0	1	0	0	0	0
OUT. U.S. + CANADA	93	11	8	6	9	15	4	4	7	5	3	5	5	7	7	3	1	1	2	0	0	0
OUT. WEST. HEMIS.	93	10	7	5	8	17	2	3	2	7	6	5	6	8	8	0	1	0	0	0	0	0
OUT. WHITE CWEALTH	93	9	6	9	7	6	7	7	8	6	4	6	6	9	9	1	0	1	0	0	0	0
OUT. DEVLPED WORLD	93	3	3	4	3	8	7	10	10	10	2	6	6	8	7	2	1	1	2	1	0	0
CANADA	92	3	12	10	6	13	7	8	3	5	5	4	3	3	4	3	1	2	0	1	0	0
LATIN AMERICA	92	3	3	1	2	6	8	11	12	9	3	3	7	8	4	4	1	3	2	0	0	1
C. AMER.+CARIB.	86	1	1	1	0	4	7	13	8	9	6	0	9	9	4	6	1	2	0	0	0	2
CUBA	24	1	0	1	0	1	2	7	2	2	0	5	4	2	0	3	2	1	0	0	1	3
MEXICO	80	0	2	0	0	3	2	6	10	11	5	0	5	11	5	5	3	1	1	1	0	0
OTHER	43	2	0	2	0	0	3	6	1	0	2	5	3	2	6	0	2	0	0	3	0	1
S. AMERICA	82	0	3	3	3	5	4	4	14	9	5	0	8	10	8	4	6	3	5	2	1	0
ARGENTINA	53	2	2	1	1	3	4	2	5	7	1	4	8	4	6	0	3	3	3	1	0	1
BRAZIL	61	0	0	0	1	3	3	3	7	9	2	1	9	7	3	0	5	4	4	4	0	0
PERU	24	0	2	2	0	5	0	0	1	1	1	3	7	3	3	1	3	6	6	0	0	1
COLOMBIA	43	0	0	1	0	0	0	0	4	5	3	2	2	3	5	2	5	4	5	1	1	0
VENEZUELA	50	0	0	0	1	1	1	1	5	6	5	2	2	5	5	2	6	2	2	0	3	1
OTHER	34	1	1	0	2	2	0	1	1	4	1	3	6	0	5	0	1	1	4	3	1	2
EUROPE	93	10	7	2	8	15	4	4	2	7	5	4	4	10	7	1	4	0	2	0	0	0
EFTA	90	7	6	7	7	15	6	4	2	6	5	3	3	7	5	4	3	2	2	0	0	0
U.K.	86	6	6	1	5	15	3	6	1	7	5	3	3	7	6	2	4	3	3	2	1	1
SCANDINAVIA	38	1	1	3	2	2	1	6	4	4	0	1	1	2	6	4	2	0	1	1	2	2
SWITZERLAND	20	0	0	0	0	2	0	0	1	7	0	0	1	3	3	0	4	2	3	2	1	1
OTHER EFTA	19	1	1	1	1	2	6	4	0	1	0	1	0	2	2	3	2	0	0	1	0	0
EUROP. COMMUNITY	93	7	2	3	5	8	3	3	1	4	11	6	4	13	12	3	0	2	0	0	0	0
FRANCE	74	4	1	1	8	5	7	2	0	0	3	3	3	8	15	3	5	6	5	3	1	0
GERMANY	73	6	1	1	2	5	3	2	0	1	3	7	4	8	14	3	3	3	4	1	0	0
ITALY	67	1	2	0	2	8	1	0	1	2	0	4	4	5	10	4	4	6	6	4	0	1
BELGIUM + LUX	48	2	0	1	1	3	3	3	1	2	7	2	0	8	4	2	5	5	1	2	0	0
NETHERLANDS	44	0	1	0	3	1	2	3	1	3	1	1	2	4	7	3	1	2	5	1	1	1
SPAIN	60	0	0	0	2	3	4	0	2	3	5	5	1	2	6	5	5	7	5	8	2	0
GREECE + TURKEY	25	2	0	0	1	1	1	2	0	0	3	1	1	5	7	0	0	2	2	2	2	0
OTHER EUROPE	22	2	2	0	1	1	0	2	2	1	0	3	3	2	5	1	1	3	2	0	4	1
EUROPE EX. U.K.	93	7	3	5	6	7	8	2	5	5	0	3	3	0	12	3	1	2	0	0	0	0
SOUTHERN DOMINIONS	77	1	2	0	1	9	4	7	2	4	8	5	5	6	4	2	2	4	3	3	2	1
S. AFRICA +RHOD.	43	2	0	0	2	2	1	3	3	4	0	2	4	5	4	4	3	2	1	2	1	1
AUSTRALIA + N.Z.	70	0	2	1	0	8	3	7	2	2	8	8	5	5	6	1	3	3	2	2	1	0
ASIA + OTHER AFRICA	71	1	1	3	1	2	1	2	7	7	5	7	7	6	11	1	2	5	3	3	2	1
JAPAN	56	0	0	0	2	0	0	4	1	1	8	2	5	3	14	1	5	7	3	3	0	0
OTHER ASIA+AFR.	67	1	0	1	2	8	3	3	0	6	1	8	3	5	9	2	4	3	3	4	2	1
BLACK AFRICA	18	0	0	0	0	0	1	0	0	0	0	1	1	0	5	1	0	4	4	0	1	1
ARAB WORLD	22	0	0	0	0	0	0	0	0	2	0	0	1	4	4	0	2	6	0	1	0	1
INDIA	33	0	0	0	1	3	1	1	1	1	1	6	0	3	3	2	2	5	3	1	1	1
PHILIPPINES	35	0	0	1	1	2	2	0	2	1	1	0	2	7	7	1	0	1	2	1	0	1
OTHER E. ASIA	19	0	0	1	0	2	0	1	1	0	0	2	2	5	2	1	2	2	1	3	1	1
OTHER ASIA	37	0	2	0	2	3	1	3	0	4	0	2	2	6	4	1	0	0	0	1	1	3

CHAPTER 2— THE EXPANSION OF PARENT SYSTEMS
SECTION 3— THE FLOW OF MANUFACTURING BY CHARACTERISTIC OF PARENT SYSTEM
TABLE B1— SYSTEMS WITH LOW "R&D INTENSITY" IN 1964
CLASSIFIED BY PERIOD SYSTEM FIRST OPERATED A MANUFACTURING SUBSIDIARY
IN SPECIFIED COUNTRIES AND REGIONS

PERIOD

COUNTRY OR REGION	PRE 1968	PRE 1901	1901 -13	1914 -19	1920 -24	1925 -29	1930 -34	1935 -39	1940 -45	1946 -50	1951 -53	1954 -55	1956 -57	1958 -59	1960 -61	1962	1963	1964	1965	1966	1967	UNK
OUTSIDE U.S.	46	6	7	6	0	5	6	4	6	0	2	1	2	3	3	0	0	0	0	0	0	0
OUT. U.S. + CANADA	46	6	4	2	0	5	3	2	5	4	4	2	2	3	3	0	0	0	0	0	0	0
OUT. WEST. HEMIS.	46	5	3	2	2	6	3	1	3	3	5	5	3	4	2	2	1	0	0	0	0	0
OUT. WHITE CWEALTH	46	6	3	3	3	4	4	3	5	4	2	4	4	5	3	1	1	0	0	0	0	0
OUT. DEVLPED WORLD	45	2	1	1	2	3	2	4	6	7	0	1	4	6	3	1	1	1	0	0	0	0
CANADA	44	0	5	7	1	3	5	7	4	2	2	4	1	0	2	0	1	0	0	0	0	0
LATIN AMERICA	45	2	1	0	1	4	5	4	6	7	0	1	5	6	2	2	1	0	1	1	0	0
C. AMER.+CARIB.	42	1	1	0	0	3	3	4	5	1	2	1	5	5	0	4	0	0	0	0	1	1
CUBA	8	0	0	0	0	1	1	2	1	0	1	0	0	1	1	0	1	0	0	0	0	0
MEXICO	41	2	0	0	0	2	2	2	6	5	2	1	0	2	4	3	1	2	0	1	1	1
OTHER	17	1	2	0	0	3	1	1	0	0	0	0	4	5	2	0	1	1	0	0	0	0
S. AMERICA	42	1	1	0	2	3	2	1	7	8	0	1	1	5	5	2	0	1	0	0	0	0
ARGENTINA	24	0	1	0	0	1	1	1	2	3	2	2	3	2	2	1	0	0	0	0	0	2
BRAZIL	28	0	0	0	0	3	2	1	5	1	1	1	2	4	2	1	1	0	0	0	1	0
PERU	10	1	0	0	1	0	1	0	1	3	1	2	1	0	2	0	0	0	0	0	1	1
COLOMBIA	23	0	0	0	1	0	0	0	0	4	2	2	1	4	3	3	3	2	0	0	0	0
VENEZUELA	22	0	0	1	1	1	1	0	0	4	3	2	1	3	3	0	0	0	2	2	0	1
OTHER	13	0	0	2	0	0	0	0	0	3	1	0	1	0	1	0	0	2	0	0	1	1
EUROPE	46	5	3	1	2	6	4	1	1	2	5	3	2	7	2	1	1	0	0	0	0	0
EFTA	44	3	3	1	1	4	5	2	1	1	5	1	3	3	3	2	3	2	2	0	0	0
U.K.	41	2	4	0	0	4	4	1	1	1	4	1	3	3	4	1	1	2	2	1	1	0
SCANDINAVIA	20	1	0	1	0	0	0	0	0	0	1	0	0	2	2	3	0	1	1	2	1	0
SWITZERLAND	9	0	0	0	0	1	1	0	0	2	0	1	1	1	1	0	1	0	0	0	0	0
OTHER EFTA	8	5	1	0	2	0	2	3	1	0	0	1	2	2	0	2	2	2	1	0	0	0
EUROP. COMMUNITY	46	4	1	1	3	4	2	3	0	2	3	3	0	6	6	1	0	2	1	1	0	0
FRANCE	32	4	0	0	2	2	2	0	1	4	1	1	5	6	6	1	1	2	2	2	0	0
GERMANY	34	4	1	1	1	3	3	2	1	2	4	3	5	3	3	4	3	2	1	1	1	1
ITALY	34	1	1	0	2	1	1	0	0	1	0	1	1	2	7	2	1	3	0	0	0	0
BELGIUM + LUX	28	0	0	1	2	3	2	2	1	2	2	3	1	4	4	3	3	1	1	1	1	1
NETHERLANDS	23	0	0	1	1	0	1	0	1	0	1	0	1	4	4	2	2	2	0	1	0	0
SPAIN	25	0	0	0	0	1	1	0	0	0	2	2	1	0	4	3	3	3	4	3	0	0
GREECE + TURKEY	9	0	2	0	0	1	1	0	0	0	0	0	0	1	1	2	0	2	2	2	0	0
OTHER EUROPE	12	1	1	2	0	1	0	0	1	1	0	0	0	0	0	0	1	1	2	3	0	0
EUROPE EX. U.K.	46	5	2	2	2	5	2	1	2	2	4	3	3	6	5	0	2	2	2	0	0	0
SOUTHERN DOMINIONS	38	0	0	1	1	2	3	0	0	1	1	5	0	4	6	0	2	0	1	2	1	1
S. AFRICA +RHOD.	20	0	0	0	1	0	0	0	3	0	0	0	2	2	2	1	4	1	1	1	1	1
AUSTRALIA + N.Z.	36	0	0	0	1	2	2	4	1	4	1	5	3	3	7	2	2	1	1	0	2	1
ASIA + OTHER AFRICA	31	0	0	1	1	1	1	1	0	0	0	1	1	1	2	2	1	2	2	0	1	0
JAPAN	25	0	0	0	0	1	1	0	1	3	0	3	2	1	9	3	3	0	1	1	0	1
OTHER ASIA+AFR.	24	0	0	0	1	1	1	1	0	0	1	0	1	1	3	2	0	1	3	1	1	1
BLACK AFRICA	8	0	0	0	0	0	0	0	0	1	0	1	0	0	3	0	1	2	1	0	0	1
ARAB WORLD	11	0	0	0	0	0	1	0	1	0	0	0	1	1	1	2	1	0	1	0	1	0
INDIA	12	0	0	0	0	0	0	1	0	1	1	1	0	2	1	1	1	1	0	1	2	2
PHILIPPINES	9	0	0	0	1	0	0	0	0	0	0	0	1	2	1	1	0	0	0	0	0	0
OTHER E. ASIA	6	0	0	0	0	0	0	0	0	0	1	1	0	2	0	0	2	2	2	1	1	1
OTHER ASIA	15	0	0	1	0	1	0	1	0	1	1	2	2	2	2	0	1	0	1	0	1	1

CHAPTER 2- THE EXPANSION OF PARENT SYSTEMS
SECTION 3- THE FLOW OF MANUFACTURING BY CHARACTERISTIC OF PARENT SYSTEM
TABLE B2- SYSTEMS WITH HIGH "R&D INTENSITY" IN 1964
CLASSIFIED BY PERIOD SYSTEM FIRST OPERATED A MANUFACTURING SUBSIDIARY
IN SPECIFIED COUNTRIES AND REGIONS

COUNTRY OR REGION	PRE 1968	PRE 1901	1901-13	1914-19	1920-24	1925-29	1930-34	1935-39	1940-45	1946-50	1951-53	1954-55	1956-57	1958-59	1960-61	1962	1963	1964	1965	1966	1967	UNK
OUTSIDE U.S.	46	5	7	5	3	6	2	5	1	3	3	3	3	3	0	0	0	0	0	0	0	0	0
OUT. U.S. + CANADA	46	4	3	3	6	3	3	5	1	3	4	4	6	0	0	0	0	0	0	0	0	0
OUT. WEST. HEMIS.	46	4	3	2	7	3	4	3	0	3	5	4	5	2	1	0	0	0	0	0	0	0
OUT. WHITE CWEALTH	46	4	3	2	4	2	3	3	2	3	4	6	7	1	1	2	0	0	0	0	0	0
OUT. DEVLPED WORLD	46	0	0	1	1	2	3	2	5	4	5	7	7	1	5	2	0	1	1	1	1	0
CANADA	42	2	5	6	0	6	3	2	3	4	5	0	1	2	0	0	0	2	0	0	1	0
LATIN AMERICA	45	0	0	1	1	1	3	3	5	4	4	7	7	1	5	2	3	0	1	1	0	0
C. AMER.+CARIB.	43	0	0	1	0	0	2	2	1	6	5	4	7	3	3	2	3	1	1	1	0	0
CUBA	5	0	0	0	0	0	0	0	0	0	0	2	3	0	0	0	0	0	0	0	0	0
MEXICO	43	0	0	1	0	0	2	2	1	6	4	0	6	4	4	2	3	1	3	0	1	0
OTHER	18	0	0	0	1	0	1	0	0	0	1	3	2	1	2	1	1	0	3	0	1	0
S. AMERICA	38	0	0	0	0	2	1	2	4	3	7	5	6	1	3	2	1	1	0	1	0	0
ARGENTINA	24	0	0	0	0	0	0	2	2	1	2	1	5	1	2	2	2	6	1	1	0	0
BRAZIL	30	0	0	0	0	0	0	0	4	4	4	5	5	3	2	1	0	0	2	0	1	0
PERU	6	0	0	0	0	0	0	0	1	0	0	0	1	2	2	0	4	0	0	0	0	0
COLOMBIA	20	0	0	0	0	0	0	0	1	3	2	0	0	2	2	1	4	0	1	1	1	0
VENEZUELA	14	0	0	0	0	0	0	0	1	0	1	1	2	2	5	0	1	2	1	1	1	0
OTHER	10	0	0	0	1	0	0	0	3	0	1	1	1	1	0	0	1	0	0	0	0	0
EUROPE	46	4	3	2	7	3	3	5	0	3	4	5	5	0	1	1	1	0	0	0	0	0
EFTA	43	1	2	2	3	3	5	5	3	3	4	5	3	1	1	3	2	1	0	0	0	0
U.K.	41	1	1	2	3	3	5	4	4	4	4	5	3	1	1	1	2	1	1	0	0	0
SCANDINAVIA	11	0	1	1	0	0	1	0	1	1	0	1	0	0	2	1	0	1	0	0	0	0
SWITZERLAND	7	0	0	0	0	1	0	1	0	2	1	0	0	0	2	1	0	0	1	0	0	0
OTHER EFTA	9	0	0	0	4	1	0	1	0	0	0	0	0	0	2	0	1	0	0	1	1	0
EUROP. COMMUNITY	46	4	3	0	3	3	2	2	0	2	4	5	4	0	2	1	1	1	2	0	0	0
FRANCE	34	1	1	0	3	2	2	1	0	2	3	1	0	7	7	1	3	1	0	0	0	0
GERMANY	33	3	2	0	2	1	2	1	0	0	3	2	2	7	4	2	5	3	0	1	0	0
ITALY	34	0	1	0	0	1	2	0	0	0	1	1	4	3	3	0	0	3	0	2	1	0
BELGIUM + LUX	20	1	1	0	0	1	0	1	0	1	0	1	0	6	3	3	3	2	3	1	1	0
NETHERLANDS	18	0	0	0	0	1	0	1	0	0	1	2	1	4	1	0	1	3	2	1	2	0
SPAIN	23	0	0	0	0	1	0	0	0	1	0	1	0	2	3	0	0	0	2	6	0	0
GREECE + TURKEY	8	0	0	0	1	0	0	0	0	0	0	0	1	1	1	0	0	1	1	2	2	0
OTHER EUROPE	2	0	0	0	0	0	2	0	0	2	3	6	3	0	0	0	0	2	0	0	0	0
EUROPE EX. U.K.	46	4	3	1	5	2	3	2	0	2	3	3	3	7	4	2	0	0	0	0	0	0
SOUTHERN DOMINIONS	39	0	1	0	0	3	4	2	1	0	4	5	6	7	1	1	0	0	2	2	0	0
S. AFRICA +RHOD.	24	0	0	0	0	0	2	2	1	0	2	3	3	1	3	3	0	1	2	2	1	0
AUSTRALIA + N.Z.	34	0	1	0	0	3	3	1	0	1	4	3	4	8	5	0	1	0	2	1	0	0
ASIA + OTHER AFRICA	37	0	0	0	0	1	0	1	0	3	5	4	2	2	5	5	4	1	3	1	0	0
JAPAN	34	0	0	0	0	0	0	0	0	0	1	1	1	0	6	5	4	2	6	3	0	0
OTHER ASIA+AFR.	28	0	0	0	0	1	0	1	0	3	0	1	1	2	5	5	4	1	1	1	0	0
BLACK AFRICA	5	0	0	0	0	0	0	0	0	0	0	0	0	0	0	0	0	1	1	0	1	0
ARAB WORLD	3	0	0	0	0	0	0	0	0	0	0	0	0	0	0	0	0	2	1	0	1	0
INDIA	21	0	0	0	0	1	0	0	0	2	3	2	0	3	3	4	3	0	0	1	0	0
PHILIPPINES	13	0	0	0	0	0	0	0	0	1	1	0	0	2	1	0	0	1	1	1	1	0
OTHER E. ASIA	8	0	0	0	0	0	0	0	0	0	1	0	0	0	2	1	0	0	1	1	1	0
OTHER ASIA	11	0	0	0	0	0	0	0	0	2	0	1	1	3	2	2	0	0	1	0	0	0

PERIOD

CHAPTER 2— THE EXPANSION OF PARENT SYSTEMS
SECTION 3— THE FLOW OF MANUFACTURING BY CHARACTERISTIC OF PARENT SYSTEM
TABLE C1— SYSTEMS WITH LOW "ADVERTISING INTENSITY" IN 1965
CLASSIFIED BY PERIOD SYSTEM FIRST OPERATED A MANUFACTURING SUBSIDIARY
IN SPECIFIED COUNTRIES AND REGIONS

PERIOD

COUNTRY OR REGION	PRE 1968	PRE 1901	1901-13	1914-19	1920-24	1925-29	1930-34	1935-39	1940-45	1946-50	1951-53	1954-55	1956-57	1958-59	1960-61	1962	1963	1964	1965	1966	1967	UNK
OUTSIDE U.S.	51	9	7	7	4	6	1	5	5	1	2	0	2	2	0	0	0	0	0	0	0	0
OUT. U.S. + CANADA	51	8	5	3	6	7	1	3	4	5	3	0	4	2	2	0	0	0	0	0	0	0
OUT. WEST. HEMIS.	51	8	5	5	5	5	1	2	1	3	3	1	3	4	3	0	1	0	0	0	0	0
OUT. WHITE CMEALTH	51	6	4	4	6	5	0	3	3	6	4	1	1	5	0	0	1	0	0	0	0	0
OUT. DEVLPED WORLD	51	2	2	1	3	5	3	2	5	8	3	2	5	2	4	0	1	1	2	1	0	1
CANADA	48	2	6	7	2	7	3	4	2	2	2	2	3	3	2	1	1	1	0	0	0	0
LATIN AMERICA	50	2	2	1	3	4	2	5	5	8	3	6	2	2	2	1	1	2	2	0	0	2
C. AMER.+CARIB.	45	1	0	1	0	3	1	5	4	8	3	3	1	2	0	0	0	0	3	0	2	1
CUBA	12	0	0	1	0	1	1	1	1	1	0	0	0	1	0	0	0	1	1	0	0	0
MEXICO	41	0	1	1	0	2	1	3	4	9	3	4	4	2	3	2	2	2	0	3	2	0
OTHER	15	1	3	0	0	3	2	1	0	0	0	2	2	3	2	1	1	2	1	1	0	0
S. AMERICA	45	0	1	1	3	3	3	5	5	6	4	3	4	4	2	2	0	0	0	0	0	0
ARGENTINA	27	0	2	2	1	2	0	1	1	1	1	0	5	2	3	1	1	0	2	1	0	0
BRAZIL	35	0	0	1	0	3	3	2	3	2	2	4	0	4	3	0	0	0	1	0	0	0
PERU	7	0	0	0	0	0	0	0	0	0	0	1	1	0	4	0	2	2	1	1	0	0
COLOMBIA	25	0	0	0	1	1	0	1	2	3	1	2	2	2	1	0	1	0	0	1	1	0
VENEZUELA	22	0	0	0	1	0	1	0	1	3	1	0	4	4	0	1	2	2	1	1	1	0
OTHER	17	1	1	0	2	1	0	0	2	2	1	2	2	0	0	1	1	0	2	0	0	1
EUROPE	51	8	5	2	5	7	2	2	1	3	2	1	3	4	2	2	1	0	1	0	0	0
EFTA	48	6	4	2	4	6	1	3	1	2	2	1	3	3	3	0	3	1	1	0	1	0
U.K.	42	5	5	2	2	5	1	2	1	1	1	2	0	3	3	2	0	1	0	1	0	0
SCANDINAVIA	20	1	0	0	2	1	0	1	0	0	0	0	0	2	2	0	1	2	1	0	0	0
SWITZERLAND	10	0	0	2	0	0	0	2	0	0	1	0	1	0	2	0	0	0	0	0	0	0
OTHER EFTA	9	0	1	0	1	1	0	1	0	0	0	0	2	1	0	0	0	0	0	0	0	0
EUROP. COMMUNITY	51	5	2	1	2	7	1	2	0	2	2	2	1	0	2	2	1	1	0	2	2	0
FRANCE	37	4	1	2	4	2	1	0	0	3	1	1	1	7	6	2	1	1	2	2	1	0
GERMANY	36	3	1	1	2	3	1	0	0	0	2	1	2	1	6	2	2	1	3	2	0	0
ITALY	36	1	0	0	3	5	1	1	0	1	1	1	2	2	9	2	3	3	2	0	1	0
BELGIUM + LUX	25	0	2	1	1	2	1	1	0	0	1	0	2	5	3	4	1	4	2	0	0	0
NETHERLANDS	23	0	1	1	0	0	0	0	0	2	0	1	0	0	7	0	1	4	2	1	1	0
SPAIN	29	0	1	0	2	0	1	1	0	1	1	2	1	3	4	1	1	4	3	0	2	0
GREECE + TURKEY	11	0	0	1	0	1	0	1	0	0	0	0	1	0	1	1	0	0	1	2	0	1
OTHER EUROPE	13	2	1	0	1	1	1	1	1	0	1	1	1	0	4	2	0	1	0	0	0	0
EUROPE EX. U.K.	51	5	3	2	5	7	1	1	0	1	0	3	2	8	4	2	1	0	1	0	0	0
SOUTHERN DOMINIONS	40	1	1	1	0	7	2	1	1	1	0	1	1	3	3	0	2	1	2	2	0	0
S. AFRICA +RHOD.	20	0	0	1	0	1	0	2	1	1	1	0	0	4	1	1	0	0	2	2	0	0
AUSTRALIA + N.Z.	38	0	1	1	1	7	2	2	1	1	1	2	2	3	2	2	2	3	2	1	1	1
ASIA + OTHER AFRICA	43	0	0	1	1	5	2	1	0	0	3	1	1	7	3	3	2	3	1	1	0	1
JAPAN	33	0	1	1	0	2	1	0	0	0	0	1	1	2	8	2	3	4	2	0	0	0
OTHER ASIA+AFR.	32	0	1	1	1	5	1	1	0	0	4	0	0	0	5	2	1	4	2	0	0	0
BLACK AFRICA	9	0	0	0	0	0	0	0	0	0	0	0	0	1	4	1	0	1	0	1	1	1
ARAB WORLD	9	0	0	0	0	0	0	0	0	0	0	0	0	0	0	0	0	0	0	1	1	1
INDIA	20	0	1	0	1	3	0	2	1	0	2	0	2	2	4	2	2	1	2	0	1	0
PHILIPPINES	11	0	0	0	0	0	0	0	0	0	1	1	1	0	0	1	1	1	0	1	1	1
OTHER E. ASIA	11	0	0	1	0	1	1	0	0	0	1	0	1	1	1	1	1	0	1	1	1	0
OTHER ASIA	15	0	0	0	0	3	1	2	0	1	0	1	1	1	0	1	0	0	1	0	1	1

CHAPTER 2- THE EXPANSION OF PARENT SYSTEMS
SECTION 3- THE FLOW OF MANUFACTURING BY CHARACTERISTIC OF PARENT SYSTEM
TABLE C2- SYSTEMS WITH HIGH "ADVERTISING INTENSITY" IN 1965
CLASSIFIED BY PERIOD SYSTEM FIRST OPERATED A MANUFACTURING SUBSIDIARY
IN SPECIFIED COUNTRIES AND REGIONS

PERIOD

COUNTRY OR REGION	PRE 1968	PRE 1901	1901 -13	1914 -19	1920 -24	1925 -29	1930 -34	1935 -39	1940 -45	1946 -50	1951 -53	1954 -55	1956 -57	1958 -59	1960 -61	1962	1963	1964	1965	1966	1967	UNK
OUTSIDE U.S.	51	2	6	5	9	9	4	5	1	4	2	2	0	1	1	0	1	0	0	0	0	0
OUT. U.S. + CANADA	51	2	6	4	8	12	5	3	1	6	1	3	3	2	2	0	1	0	0	0	0	0
OUT. WEST. HEMIS.	51	2	0	3	8	12	5	4	0	5	2	5	5	1	3	0	1	0	0	0	0	0
OUT. WHITE CMEALTH	51	2	0	3	5	5	5	4	4	6	3	2	5	2	2	1	1	1	0	0	0	0
OUT. DEVLPED WORLD	51	0	0	2	2	4	4	8	3	7	4	5	4	3	2	1	1	1	1	0	0	0
CANADA	50	1	6	4	4	7	6	5	1	1	4	2	2	2	1	0	0	0	0	0	0	0
LATIN AMERICA	50	0	0	1	1	2	5	8	5	6	4	5	4	2	4	1	1	1	1	0	0	0
C. AMER.+CARIB.	13	0	0	0	1	0	1	3	1	5	6	4	7	1	3	1	1	0	1	0	0	0
CUBA	47	0	0	1	0	0	1	1	1	8	4	0	1	1	1	2	0	2	0	0	0	1
MEXICO	30	0	0	0	0	0	2	2	1	1	2	5	7	3	4	1	1	5	0	1	1	0
OTHER	42	0	0	0	0	3	0	4	7	3	5	2	2	3	3	1	1	1	1	1	0	1
S. AMERICA	27	0	0	0	0	2	0	4	2	3	1	3	2	2	2	1	1	1	0	1	0	0
ARGENTINA	29	0	0	0	0	2	0	1	2	1	0	2	5	4	4	2	2	2	0	2	0	0
BRAZIL	14	0	0	0	0	0	1	3	1	1	1	0	0	0	1	3	1	3	0	0	0	1
PERU	19	0	0	0	0	1	0	1	1	1	1	2	1	1	0	1	2	0	0	2	0	0
COLOMBIA	28	0	0	0	0	0	0	0	2	2	0	2	3	3	3	3	3	0	3	1	1	1
VENEZUELA	16	0	0	0	0	1	0	1	1	1	0	1	4	4	10	1	0	0	0	2	2	0
OTHER	—	0	0	0	1	0	0	0	2	1	0	1	0	1	2	0	1	3	3	1	2	1
EUROPE	51	2	0	1	7	9	4	6	0	6	1	2	4	4	3	1	1	0	0	0	0	0
EFTA	49	1	0	1	3	10	7	7	0	4	1	2	4	3	0	3	2	0	1	0	0	0
U.K.	48	0	0	0	3	10	6	9	0	4	0	2	4	3	0	2	2	0	0	0	0	0
SCANDINAVIA	17	0	0	0	0	0	1	0	0	1	1	1	0	1	2	2	0	2	0	0	0	0
SWITZERLAND	9	0	0	0	0	0	0	0	0	0	0	0	1	0	2	2	3	0	1	0	0	0
OTHER EFTA	11	0	0	1	0	0	0	1	0	2	0	0	0	3	0	3	0	0	4	0	0	1
EUROP. COMMUNITY	51	2	0	0	5	0	0	0	1	0	5	5	5	3	8	1	6	4	0	0	0	0
FRANCE	37	0	0	0	4	1	2	0	0	2	2	2	3	9	8	4	4	0	0	1	0	1
GERMANY	36	1	0	0	2	2	3	0	0	2	1	1	2	4	7	3	6	3	3	2	0	0
ITALY	35	0	0	0	0	2	0	0	0	0	2	5	5	3	5	1	3	3	2	0	0	1
BELGIUM + LUX	22	1	0	0	0	1	0	0	1	0	1	1	3	2	5	2	1	1	4	0	0	0
NETHERLANDS	21	0	0	0	0	0	2	2	0	0	1	1	0	6	5	0	3	4	5	0	0	0
SPAIN	28	0	0	0	3	0	0	0	1	1	1	0	1	1	1	2	3	2	1	0	4	0
GREECE + TURKEY	10	0	0	0	0	0	0	0	2	0	1	0	1	0	2	0	1	1	5	2	2	1
OTHER EUROPE	9	0	0	0	0	0	1	1	1	2	0	0	1	3	3	1	0	0	1	0	0	0
EUROPE EX. U.K.	51	2	0	1	5	1	5	0	1	5	4	1	4	9	7	4	4	1	0	0	0	0
SOUTHERN DOMINIONS	48	0	1	1	2	2	6	4	2	0	2	3	6	6	6	1	3	2	2	1	1	0
S. AFRICA +RHOD.	30	0	0	1	1	1	3	3	2	1	0	2	2	4	5	0	3	1	1	0	0	1
AUSTRALIA + N.Z.	40	0	1	1	1	1	5	3	3	3	2	3	5	6	5	2	2	0	2	1	1	0
ASIA + OTHER AFRICA	41	0	0	1	1	4	0	2	0	3	1	4	2	3	6	4	6	2	1	1	2	0
JAPAN	23	0	0	1	0	0	0	0	0	0	1	6	2	1	4	4	4	3	3	1	1	0
OTHER ASIA+AFR.	39	0	0	1	1	4	0	0	0	3	1	2	5	4	5	6	0	1	0	1	0	0
BLACK AFRICA	9	0	0	0	0	0	1	0	0	0	0	0	2	0	2	0	0	0	1	2	0	0
ARAB WORLD	3	0	0	0	0	0	0	0	0	0	0	0	0	1	1	1	0	1	0	0	0	0
INDIA	12	0	0	0	0	1	1	0	0	1	1	0	0	4	1	2	0	0	0	0	0	0
PHILIPPINES	21	0	0	0	0	0	0	0	0	1	0	2	0	1	3	6	1	0	1	0	1	0
OTHER E. ASIA	8	0	0	0	0	0	0	0	0	0	0	0	0	1	4	1	2	2	0	2	1	0
OTHER ASIA	19	0	0	1	0	0	0	0	0	2	0	1	2	0	3	1	1	0	1	2	0	0

CHAPTER 2— THE EXPANSION OF PARENT SYSTEMS
SECTION 3— THE FLOW OF MANUFACTURING BY CHARACTERISTIC OF PARENT SYSTEM
TABLE D1— SYSTEMS WITH LOW "HUMAN CAPITAL INTENSITY" IN 1966
CLASSIFIED BY PERIOD SYSTEM FIRST OPERATED A MANUFACTURING SUBSIDIARY
IN SPECIFIED COUNTRIES AND REGIONS

PERIOD

COUNTRY OR REGION	PRE 1968	PRE 1901	1901 -13	1914 -19	1920 -24	1925 -29	1930 -34	1935 -39	1940 -45	1946 -50	1951 -53	1954 -55	1956 -57	1958 -59	1960 -61	1962	1963	1964	1965	1966	1967	UNK
OUTSIDE U.S.	42	5	4	6	6	4	3	1	3	2	2	1	2	2	1	0	0	0	0	0	0	0
OUT. U.S. + CANADA	42	5	2	5	6	6	0	1	2	2	3	3	4	2	1	0	0	0	0	0	0	0
OUT. WEST. HEMIS.	42	5	2	5	6	6	0	1	2	3	3	3	4	2	2	0	0	0	0	1	0	0
OUT. WHITE CMEALTH	42	4	3	5	6	4	2	1	3	4	1	3	4	2	2	1	0	0	1	1	0	0
OUT. DEVLPED WORLD	42	1	1	2	3	4	3	1	4	4	1	3	5	2	5	1	0	2	2	1	1	0
CANADA	41	0	5	6	3	5	6	1	5	4	2	1	3	3	2	0	1	1	2	2	0	0
LATIN AMERICA	41	1	1	0	2	2	5	2	4	4	1	3	5	2	4	1	2	2	2	1	2	1
C. AMER.+CARIB.	13	1	0	0	1	1	1	1	5	5	2	1	4	2	3	3	1	0	2	0	1	1
CUBA	35	0	1	0	0	1	1	1	2	2	0	0	3	0	3	0	1	1	2	0	0	2
MEXICO	18	1	0	0	0	3	3	1	2	6	1	0	3	3	3	3	1	0	2	0	0	0
OTHER	36	0	1	0	0	1	1	1	5	5	0	1	3	4	3	2	1	1	2	2	0	0
S. AMERICA	20	0	2	0	1	1	0	2	3	3	0	2	4	2	1	0	0	0	0	0	0	0
ARGENTINA	25	0	0	1	1	1	0	1	4	4	3	2	4	2	2	0	0	0	1	1	1	0
BRAZIL	10	0	1	0	0	0	0	0	3	3	0	0	1	2	3	1	0	1	0	0	0	0
PERU	13	0	0	1	1	0	0	1	1	2	3	1	2	1	2	0	0	1	1	1	0	0
COLOMBIA	17	0	0	0	0	0	0	0	2	3	0	0	2	0	2	1	1	2	1	0	2	1
VENEZUELA	10	0	0	0	0	0	1	1	1	1	0	1	1	1	1	0	1	1	1	1	0	1
OTHER	42	5	2	2	6	6	2	1	1	2	3	3	3	3	2	0	2	0	1	0	0	0
EUROPE	41	3	2	2	5	5	2	2	1	2	3	3	3	3	1	3	1	0	1	0	0	0
EFTA	38	2	3	1	4	5	2	2	1	2	2	1	3	0	1	2	2	1	2	1	0	0
U.K.	15	1	0	2	0	0	2	2	0	0	1	0	1	0	3	0	1	1	0	1	1	0
SCANDINAVIA	9	0	0	0	1	1	0	1	0	0	0	0	1	2	0	1	0	0	0	0	0	0
SWITZERLAND	7	0	1	0	0	0	0	0	0	1	0	1	1	0	0	1	1	1	0	0	0	0
OTHER EFTA	42	4	1	0	0	4	4	3	0	0	6	3	4	2	6	1	0	1	0	0	0	0
EUROP. COMMUNITY	34	4	0	2	2	3	7	0	0	1	9	3	3	4	6	1	1	2	1	1	0	0
FRANCE	34	3	1	0	2	2	3	0	0	1	2	4	5	2	6	1	1	2	2	3	1	1
GERMANY	32	1	1	0	2	2	0	1	1	1	3	2	2	2	5	2	2	2	2	1	0	0
ITALY	25	0	2	0	1	1	1	1	1	2	0	0	1	4	5	3	0	0	2	3	1	1
BELGIUM + LUX	20	0	0	1	1	2	2	0	2	0	2	1	2	1	0	2	1	4	5	1	0	0
NETHERLANDS	25	0	0	1	1	0	1	0	0	2	2	1	2	2	2	2	2	0	5	1	0	0
SPAIN	9	0	0	1	1	1	0	2	1	0	0	0	0	3	2	0	0	1	1	1	2	0
GREECE + TURKEY	10	0	2	0	0	0	0	0	0	1	1	1	2	1	1	0	0	0	0	0	0	0
OTHER EUROPE	42	4	2	2	3	5	5	2	1	1	0	2	4	3	5	0	1	0	0	1	0	1
EUROPE EX. U.K.	36	0	1	1	1	3	3	3	2	0	3	1	1	4	3	1	1	2	3	2	0	0
SOUTHERN DOMINIONS	19	0	0	1	1	0	0	3	3	1	0	0	1	1	2	2	2	1	1	1	0	0
S. AFRICA +RHOD.	32	0	1	0	1	3	3	1	2	1	3	2	2	2	5	3	1	2	3	1	1	0
AUSTRALIA + N.Z.	34	0	3	3	2	4	1	2	0	1	3	2	2	0	10	2	1	0	1	1	1	0
ASIA + OTHER AFRICA	24	0	1	1	2	0	1	0	0	0	0	0	0	4	3	0	1	0	0	0	0	0
JAPAN	28	0	0	2	2	4	0	0	0	1	3	2	2	0	3	3	3	3	3	3	0	0
OTHER ASIA+AFR.	8	0	0	0	0	0	0	0	0	0	0	0	1	1	1	1	1	1	3	1	1	0
BLACK AFRICA	7	0	0	0	0	0	1	0	1	0	0	0	0	0	2	1	1	1	1	0	0	0
ARAB WORLD	15	0	0	1	1	1	1	0	1	1	1	0	0	2	1	0	1	1	1	1	0	0
INDIA	17	0	0	1	1	1	0	0	1	0	1	2	0	5	1	2	1	0	0	1	0	0
PHILIPPINES	6	0	0	0	0	1	0	2	0	0	0	0	0	0	0	1	1	1	0	0	1	0
OTHER E. ASIA	16	0	2	2	1	0	2	2	0	2	2	0	0	2	3	1	1	1	0	1	0	0

CHAPTER 2— THE EXPANSION OF PARENT SYSTEMS
SECTION 3— THE FLOW OF MANUFACTURING BY CHARACTERISTIC OF PARENT SYSTEM
TABLE D2— SYSTEMS WITH HIGH "HUMAN CAPITAL INTENSITY" IN 1966
CLASSIFIED BY PERIOD SYSTEM FIRST OPERATED A MANUFACTURING SUBSIDIARY
IN SPECIFIED COUNTRIES AND REGIONS

PERIOD

COUNTRY OR REGION	PRE 1968	PRE 1901	1901 -13	1914 -19	1920 -24	1925 -29	1930 -34	1935 -39	1940 -45	1946 -50	1951 -53	1954 -55	1956 -57	1958 -59	1960 -61	1962	1963	1964	1965	1966	1967	UNK
OUTSIDE U.S.	41	5	7	4	1	7	3	4	2	0	2	1	0	4	1	0	0	0	0	0	0	0
OUT. U.S. + CANADA	41	5	7	3	3	7	3	2	2	3	3	3	3	5	1	0	0	0	0	0	0	0
OUT. WEST. HEMIS.	41	4	3	1	2	8	2	2	0	1	4	2	2	7	3	1	0	0	0	0	0	0
OUT. WHITE CWEALTH	41	3	2	1	3	5	3	0	2	3	1	5	5	6	1	0	0	0	0	0	0	0
OUT. DEVLPED WORLD	41	1	1	1	2	3	2	3	3	4	2	2	4	7	3	2	1	0	0	0	0	0
CANADA	40	3	6	3	1	6	2	2	2	0	1	0	0	0	0	2	2	2	0	0	3	0
LATIN AMERICA	40	1	1	1	2	3	2	3	4	4	1	4	4	6	2	3	1	0	1	1	0	0
C. AMER.+CARIB.	39	0	0	1	0	2	1	1	5	2	1	0	1	1	1	3	2	1	1	0	0	0
CUBA	6	0	0	0	0	0	1	1	0	1	0	1	0	1	0	0	0	0	0	0	0	0
MEXICO	36	0	0	1	0	2	1	0	4	3	0	1	1	3	5	4	2	2	2	2	0	0
OTHER	14	0	1	0	0	3	0	3	0	2	1	0	2	2	2	1	1	1	1	0	0	0
S. AMERICA	33	1	1	1	2	3	0	3	1	2	1	0	3	6	3	2	4	0	1	2	0	0
ARGENTINA	22	0	0	2	0	1	0	4	3	2	2	2	2	3	0	0	1	2	1	2	0	0
BRAZIL	23	1	1	0	0	4	0	2	1	1	1	1	1	4	3	2	1	2	0	1	0	0
PERU	7	0	0	1	0	0	1	0	1	2	1	2	2	0	1	0	0	0	0	1	0	0
COLOMBIA	19	0	0	0	0	0	0	0	0	1	1	1	1	1	4	2	0	2	0	1	0	0
VENEZUELA	21	0	0	0	0	0	0	1	1	2	3	1	1	1	1	3	2	2	2	2	1	0
OTHER	17	1	1	0	0	2	0	0	1	4	0	1	0	2	2	0	0	0	1	1	0	1
EUROPE	41	4	3	1	2	8	2	0	0	0	3	2	2	8	2	2	0	2	1	1	0	0
EFTA	38	4	2	1	1	7	2	1	0	0	2	2	2	2	4	2	2	2	1	0	0	0
U.K.	36	0	0	1	1	7	2	0	0	1	2	0	1	2	4	0	1	1	1	0	1	0
SCANDINAVIA	14	0	0	0	0	0	0	1	0	0	0	0	0	2	4	0	2	2	2	2	3	0
SWITZERLAND	6	0	1	1	0	0	0	1	0	1	1	0	0	2	1	0	0	2	0	0	0	0
OTHER EFTA	9	0	1	0	0	0	1	0	0	0	1	0	0	3	1	0	0	0	0	0	0	0
EUROP. COMMUNITY	41	2	1	1	1	5	2	0	0	1	2	2	4	7	3	0	0	2	2	2	0	0
FRANCE	29	1	0	1	2	2	1	0	0	0	1	2	0	4	8	1	1	4	0	2	0	0
GERMANY	25	1	1	0	2	4	0	0	0	0	2	4	4	3	5	1	2	1	3	1	1	0
ITALY	23	0	1	0	1	0	0	0	1	1	0	0	2	3	6	1	2	2	2	1	1	0
BELGIUM + LUX	19	0	0	1	1	1	1	0	0	0	2	0	0	4	3	0	4	4	2	2	1	0
NETHERLANDS	15	0	1	0	2	2	2	0	0	0	0	1	0	4	6	3	0	1	2	1	1	0
SPAIN	24	0	0	0	0	2	0	0	0	0	2	1	2	0	4	4	0	1	1	2	1	0
GREECE + TURKEY	7	0	0	0	1	0	1	0	0	1	0	1	0	0	1	0	0	1	0	0	1	0
OTHER EUROPE	9	1	0	0	1	1	1	0	0	1	2	0	0	0	0	2	0	1	1	0	1	0
EUROPE EX. U.K.	41	2	1	1	2	6	2	1	0	1	2	3	2	5	2	2	1	1	1	0	1	0
SOUTHERN DOMINIONS	29	1	1	0	0	3	2	1	0	1	1	2	2	4	1	1	0	0	2	1	3	0
S. AFRICA +RHOD.	15	1	0	1	0	1	1	0	0	2	0	0	0	2	2	0	1	3	1	0	0	0
AUSTRALIA + N.Z.	28	1	1	1	0	3	1	0	0	1	1	3	2	5	5	3	3	3	3	3	3	0
ASIA + OTHER AFRICA	33	0	1	0	0	4	0	0	0	1	1	0	4	4	4	5	3	3	3	1	0	0
JAPAN	23	0	0	1	0	2	0	0	0	0	0	1	2	1	2	3	0	1	1	1	0	0
OTHER ASIA+AFR.	27	0	1	1	0	4	0	0	0	1	0	0	0	3	3	0	0	0	2	1	0	0
BLACK AFRICA	6	0	0	0	0	0	0	0	1	0	0	0	0	1	2	2	1	2	1	1	1	0
ARAB WORLD	16	0	0	1	0	2	0	0	0	2	0	0	0	3	0	0	2	1	1	1	0	0
INDIA	8	0	0	0	0	0	0	0	0	0	0	0	0	1	2	1	0	0	1	1	1	0
PHILIPPINES	8	0	0	0	0	1	0	1	0	0	0	1	1	0	0	1	0	0	1	1	0	0
OTHER E. ASIA	5	0	0	1	0	1	0	0	0	0	0	0	0	0	0	0	0	0	1	0	0	1
OTHER ASIA	9	0	0	0	0	2	0	0	0	0	0	2	2	1	2	1	1	0	0	0	1	1

CHAPTER 2— THE EXPANSION OF PARENT SYSTEMS
SECTION 3— THE FLOW OF MANUFACTURING BY CHARACTERISTIC OF PARENT SYSTEM
TABLE E1— SYSTEMS WITH LOW "PHYSICAL CAPITAL INTENSITY" IN 1966
CLASSIFIED BY PERIOD SYSTEM FIRST OPERATED A MANUFACTURING SUBSIDIARY
IN SPECIFIED COUNTRIES AND REGIONS

PERIOD

COUNTRY OR REGION	PRE 1968	PRE 1901	1901 -13	1914 -19	1920 -24	1925 -29	1930 -34	1935 -39	1940 -45	1946 -50	1951 -53	1954 -55	1956 -57	1958 -59	1960 -61	1962	1963	1964	1965	1966	1967	UNK
OUTSIDE U.S.	93	8	10	15	9	16	8	6	2	4	3	2	2	5	5	3	0	2	0	0	0	0
OUT. U.S. + CANADA	93	8	5	7	10	19	7	4	4	5	5	3	5	6	7	0	2	2	0	0	0	0
OUT. WEST. HEMIS.	93	8	5	5	10	20	5	4	1	6	3	4	5	8	7	0	2	2	0	0	0	0
OUT. WHITE CMEALTH	93	5	3	7	8	10	12	6	6	4	4	3	6	12	12	4	0	1	2	0	0	0
OUT. DEVLPED WORLD	91	1	2	5	2	7	8	10	7	9	3	4	5	14	14	7	1	3	2	0	0	0
CANADA	90	2	11	12	5	16	9	7	0	3	3	5	2	4	5	5	2	1	0	0	0	0
LATIN AMERICA	90	1	2	4	2	3	9	10	9	9	3	4	5	14	12	3	2	1	2	0	0	1
C. AMER.+CARIB.	84	0	0	2	0	3	9	10	6	6	7	1	5	12	6	3	2	2	2	0	1	1
CUBA	21	0	0	1	0	3	5	7	1	2	2	1	1	0	0	0	0	0	0	0	0	1
MEXICO	80	0	0	0	0	3	5	5	8	9	4	5	6	13	5	3	3	3	5	2	0	0
OTHER	30	0	1	1	0	2	2	1	2	0	3	2	2	2	5	2	2	0	0	2	0	0
S. AMERICA	81	1	2	3	1	6	2	6	13	7	1	3	9	16	5	4	4	0	1	0	1	1
ARGENTINA	52	0	1	4	0	4	0	5	3	6	1	1	3	6	5	3	3	0	0	2	0	0
BRAZIL	58	0	0	0	1	5	0	4	5	9	2	2	7	12	5	6	1	2	2	2	1	0
PERU	24	0	0	0	0	0	1	1	0	2	1	4	1	0	1	1	0	2	2	1	0	0
COLOMBIA	32	0	0	0	2	0	0	0	4	1	2	1	2	6	7	2	2	5	1	2	2	0
VENEZUELA	42	0	0	0	1	0	1	0	5	1	2	2	1	6	5	4	4	0	1	0	1	1
OTHER	27	1	1	0	0	2	0	0	1	3	1	1	2	1	5	0	0	1	3	1	3	1
EUROPE	93	8	5	3	9	18	6	5	1	5	4	3	5	11	6	2	2	2	0	0	0	0
EFTA	90	5	6	3	4	19	8	7	1	6	1	1	7	7	6	2	4	1	1	0	0	0
U.K.	85	5	5	2	1	18	9	8	0	6	1	1	1	1	3	1	3	2	2	0	1	0
SCANDINAVIA	36	0	1	2	2	2	1	0	0	4	0	0	4	2	3	3	2	4	0	2	0	0
SWITZERLAND	19	0	0	0	0	2	0	2	0	2	0	0	1	1	1	2	1	3	2	0	1	1
OTHER EFTA	20	2	2	0	0	0	0	2	1	0	0	0	0	2	1	2	1	2	0	2	0	0
EUROP. COMMUNITY	91	4	1	2	9	6	9	2	1	3	2	2	2	3	3	2	2	2	3	4	2	1
FRANCE	71	3	1	1	7	3	6	1	1	3	0	2	7	14	4	2	2	4	2	2	1	0
GERMANY	71	3	1	2	2	9	6	2	0	0	2	2	4	8	8	3	3	3	4	3	3	1
ITALY	58	0	1	2	0	3	6	2	0	1	6	1	3	6	12	5	5	5	2	1	0	0
BELGIUM + LUX	35	0	3	0	2	2	0	1	1	2	2	2	1	10	10	2	8	2	3	4	1	1
NETHERLANDS	35	0	0	1	1	1	1	1	0	2	1	1	0	7	6	1	2	1	3	0	1	0
SPAIN	47	0	0	0	1	3	3	2	1	3	2	2	2	5	7	1	6	5	5	2	4	0
GREECE + TURKEY	17	0	0	0	1	0	0	2	0	0	2	1	1	0	4	4	0	2	6	1	0	0
OTHER EUROPE	21	1	1	1	1	1	2	1	1	2	3	0	0	3	2	2	1	0	3	1	0	1
EUROPE EX. U.K.	93	4	3	3	9	8	10	2	2	5	6	4	6	14	11	3	4	2	0	0	0	0
SOUTHERN DOMINIONS	77	1	1	2	1	4	5	9	2	4	3	6	8	8	10	3	4	4	2	1	3	0
S. AFRICA +RHOD.	44	0	0	1	1	2	3	4	3	5	6	5	7	7	5	1	4	1	1	3	3	1
AUSTRALIA + N.Z.	68	0	1	1	1	3	4	7	3	6	4	5	6	5	11	6	8	4	3	1	1	0
ASIA + OTHER AFRICA	68	0	1	1	0	2	0	3	0	1	2	5	1	5	10	6	8	3	2	0	3	0
JAPAN	42	0	0	0	1	0	0	0	0	5	1	2	2	2	7	3	3	1	0	4	3	0
OTHER ASIA+AFR.	54	0	2	0	1	0	0	1	1	0	0	1	5	5	7	1	5	3	1	1	3	0
BLACK AFRICA	11	0	0	0	0	0	0	2	0	2	0	1	0	0	3	1	3	1	1	0	3	0
ARAB WORLD	15	0	0	0	0	0	0	0	1	0	1	0	1	4	0	2	1	2	0	0	1	0
INDIA	19	0	0	0	0	1	1	0	0	2	0	2	2	0	5	1	0	1	3	1	0	0
PHILIPPINES	24	0	1	1	0	2	1	1	1	0	1	2	5	5	0	2	2	0	2	0	0	0
OTHER E. ASIA	12	0	1	1	1	2	0	0	0	1	0	1	0	0	1	1	0	1	1	1	3	0
OTHER ASIA	25	0	0	0	0	2	1	1	0	3	0	2	2	2	5	2	2	0	3	3	1	0

CHAPTER 2- THE EXPANSION OF PARENT SYSTEMS
SECTION 3- THE FLOW OF MANUFACTURING BY CHARACTERISTIC OF PARENT SYSTEM
TABLE E2- SYSTEMS WITH HIGH "PHYSICAL CAPITAL INTENSITY" IN 1966
CLASSIFIED BY PERIOD SYSTEM FIRST OPERATED A MANUFACTURING SUBSIDIARY
IN SPECIFIED COUNTRIES AND REGIONS

PERIOD

COUNTRY OR REGION	PRE 1968	PRE 1901	1901 -13	1914 -19	1920 -24	1925 -29	1930 -34	1935 -39	1940 -45	1946 -50	1951 -53	1954 -55	1956 -57	1958 -59	1960 -61	1962	1963	1964	1965	1966	1967	UNK
OUTSIDE U.S.	94	11	12	11	6	14	7	7	6	5	5	7	2	3	2	0	0	0	0	0	0	0
OUT. U.S. + CANADA	94	10	12	6	9	10	7	7	5	9	5	7	5	4	2	0	0	0	0	0	0	0
OUT. WEST. HEMIS.	94	9	5	6	7	11	5	7	2	6	9	8	8	7	5	1	0	0	0	0	0	0
OUT. WHITE CWEALTH	94	9	5	4	8	8	6	3	4	9	8	13	8	6	3	0	0	0	0	0	1	1
OUT. DEVLPED WORLD	94	2	1	2	4	5	5	9	8	10	8	11	9	5	9	2	1	1	1	0	1	1
CANADA	88	3	9	12	2	11	6	6	7	6	8	4	5	2	2	1	1	0	0	1	0	0
LATIN AMERICA	92	2	1	1	4	3	5	10	8	9	8	10	10	6	10	3	2	1	1	0	1	1
C. AMER.+CARIB.	88	1	1	0	2	2	1	7	4	11	5	8	15	1	8	0	2	0	2	0	1	1
CUBA	15	0	2	0	1	1	3	1	1	1	0	1	1	1	1	3	0	2	1	1	1	1
MEXICO	82	0	0	0	0	1	1	4	4	11	5	7	9	8	10	3	2	6	5	2	1	1
OTHER	42	0	1	0	0	0	3	3	1	1	0	1	9	2	1	4	6	6	6	2	3	3
S. AMERICA ARGENTINA	79	1	1	1	4	2	1	2	0	1	11	5	5	8	8	1	1	3	0	1	0	0
BRAZIL	47	1	1	0	1	1	4	6	7	8	3	3	8	2	8	3	3	2	2	2	2	2
PERU	55	0	0	1	0	0	3	3	3	2	2	5	6	6	4	2	2	1	2	0	1	1
COLOMBIA	16	1	0	0	1	1	0	0	1	5	10	2	7	3	4	5	2	2	2	0	1	0
VENEZUELA	41	0	0	0	0	0	0	1	3	7	3	2	2	3	6	1	3	3	1	1	3	1
OTHER	42	0	0	1	1	0	0	1	1	3	4	1	4	6	9	2	2	4	2	4	3	1
	27	0	1	3	3	0	0	1	3	3	1	2	2	0	1	2	2	1	4	1	0	1
EUROPE	94	9	5	2	7	11	4	7	1	8	8	7	7	8	6	2	0	2	1	1	0	0
EFTA	88	6	3	2	1	9	5	8	1	6	5	8	5	3	6	4	3	3	1	1	0	0
U.K.	85	5	4	2	4	9	5	8	1	6	5	8	5	3	5	4	7	2	2	1	2	0
SCANDINAVIA	26	1	1	1	0	0	1	0	1	0	0	0	0	2	5	4	4	3	1	2	2	1
SWITZERLAND	12	0	0	0	0	0	0	2	1	0	0	0	0	1	1	3	0	1	1	1	1	0
OTHER EFTA	15	0	0	0	0	3	2	1	0	0	0	0	1	1	2	1	2	0	1	2	0	1
EUROP. COMMUNITY	93	8	3	1	5	8	3	3	0	4	9	8	6	12	14	3	2	5	3	2	0	0
FRANCE	67	4	1	0	4	5	3	2	0	0	5	3	3	8	9	5	3	1	1	1	2	1
GERMANY	66	6	2	1	3	4	2	0	0	0	4	4	7	6	10	6	6	3	0	2	0	0
ITALY	66	1	1	1	2	1	1	3	1	1	6	4	5	5	12	1	3	5	3	1	1	0
BELGIUM + LUX	43	1	1	0	0	3	1	3	0	1	1	1	0	7	7	3	5	4	4	5	1	0
NETHERLANDS	40	0	0	1	0	1	1	3	0	2	1	2	1	1	8	1	5	4	6	2	1	0
SPAIN	46	0	0	2	2	2	2	0	0	3	1	1	1	4	5	4	5	3	6	2	6	3
GREECE + TURKEY	15	0	2	0	0	1	0	1	2	1	2	2	1	1	2	3	0	4	1	6	4	0
OTHER EUROPE	15	2	2	0	0	0	0	1	0	0	0	0	0	2	1	0	1	0	1	0	0	0
EUROPE EX. U.K.	93	8	4	2	6	8	3	2	0	4	9	9	5	15	12	3	1	1	0	0	0	0
SOUTHERN DOMINIONS	77	0	1	4	1	6	6	5	3	2	7	8	6	10	4	1	4	1	4	2	1	1
S. AFRICA +RHOD.	42	0	0	1	2	0	3	2	2	3	3	7	3	2	2	4	1	2	1	0	1	1
AUSTRALIA + N.Z.	70	0	1	3	1	6	3	5	1	3	7	7	5	11	3	1	8	1	4	3	2	1
ASIA + OTHER AFRICA	78	0	0	2	2	3	2	1	0	5	6	8	8	4	14	8	5	3	3	1	1	1
JAPAN	57	0	0	1	1	0	1	0	0	0	8	2	6	13	13	6	5	5	3	1	2	2
OTHER ASIA+AFR.	64	0	0	1	0	3	1	1	0	5	1	1	2	4	12	9	1	2	3	2	1	1
BLACK AFRICA	18	0	0	0	0	0	0	0	0	0	1	8	1	0	9	0	1	2	0	3	1	1
ARAB WORLD	14	0	0	0	0	0	0	0	1	1	0	0	1	0	5	1	1	1	1	1	1	2
INDIA	39	0	0	0	1	1	1	1	0	2	0	1	1	7	5	8	5	2	0	2	2	1
PHILIPPINES	29	0	0	0	0	0	0	0	1	1	3	0	0	2	3	0	3	3	2	3	1	1
OTHER E. ASIA	16	0	0	1	1	1	1	0	0	0	1	0	0	0	2	1	5	1	1	1	1	1
OTHER ASIA	30	0	0	0	0	1	0	2	0	3	0	2	2	5	5	3	1	0	0	3	0	3

CHAPTER 2- THE EXPANSION OF PARENT SYSTEMS
SECTION 3- THE FLOW OF MANUFACTURING BY CHARACTERISTIC OF PARENT SYSTEM
TABLE F1- SYSTEMS WITH LOW GROWTH IN SALES 1950-1966
CLASSIFIED BY PERIOD SYSTEM FIRST OPERATED A MANUFACTURING SUBSIDIARY
IN SPECIFIED COUNTRIES AND REGIONS

PERIOD

COUNTRY OR REGION	PRE 1968	PRE 1901	1901-13	1914-19	1920-24	1925-29	1930-34	1935-39	1940-45	1946-50	1951-53	1954-55	1956-57	1958-59	1960-61	1962	1963	1964	1965	1966	1967	UNK
OUTSIDE U.S.	83	8	13	15	7	15	5	6	2	2	3	3	0	2	2	0	0	0	0	0	0	0
OUT. U.S. + CANADA	83	7	13	9	12	16	5	6	2	3	4	5	4	4	3	1	0	0	0	0	0	0
OUT. WEST. HEMIS.	83	7	4	8	10	18	2	7	1	0	4	5	5	6	7	0	1	0	0	0	0	0
OUT. WHITE CWEALTH	83	5	5	6	12	12	4	5	5	5	3	10	6	3	3	1	1	0	0	0	0	0
OUT. DEVLPED WORLD	83	1	3	5	4	9	8	8	3	8	3	8	6	5	9	2	2	0	0	0	0	0
CANADA	79	3	13	11	2	16	6	5	1	5	3	3	2	2	2	3	1	0	0	0	0	0
LATIN AMERICA	82	1	3	3	4	5	10	9	5	8	3	7	7	4	9	5	4	1	0	0	0	0
C. AMER.+CARIB.	78	0	1	1	2	3	8	11	3	8	3	1	11	3	6	5	4	1	2	0	0	1
CUBA	24	0	0	1	1	0	8	4	2	8	1	1	1	2	1	0	0	0	0	1	1	1
MEXICO	70	0	1	0	1	3	4	7	3	10	2	8	4	5	7	3	3	3	3	0	0	0
OTHER	34	1	0	0	0	0	1	3	2	1	1	1	7	3	3	4	1	2	7	3	2	0
S. AMERICA	71	1	2	3	4	4	3	5	9	5	4	9	9	8	6	3	1	1	1	1	0	0
ARGENTINA	43	0	1	3	1	2	6	6	2	4	0	3	3	3	2	1	2	2	2	1	2	2
BRAZIL	50	0	2	4	4	4	4	4	4	7	5	5	7	5	4	0	1	0	1	1	0	2
PERU	22	0	0	1	0	0	0	0	1	1	1	4	1	0	2	0	2	1	1	1	0	0
COLOMBIA	28	0	0	0	0	0	0	1	5	1	3	3	3	3	4	0	5	2	1	3	1	0
VENEZUELA	45	0	0	0	0	0	0	1	3	3	3	5	1	9	4	0	0	5	1	3	1	0
OTHER	26	1	1	1	2	1	0	1	2	5	0	1	1	0	2	1	0	0	4	1	1	1
EUROPE	83	7	4	2	10	17	4	7	1	2	4	4	2	8	7	2	0	3	1	1	0	0
EFTA	78	5	4	2	5	17	5	9	1	2	3	1	2	5	5	5	4	1	1	0	0	0
U.K.	77	5	3	2	4	17	5	10	1	3	3	1	2	3	5	2	3	1	1	1	1	0
SCANDINAVIA	25	0	2	1	2	1	1	2	0	2	0	1	4	1	2	0	2	0	1	0	1	0
SWITZERLAND	13	0	0	0	0	1	0	0	0	0	1	0	0	2	1	2	2	2	1	0	2	0
OTHER EFTA	17	0	2	0	8	1	4	3	1	0	1	0	0	2	1	0	0	2	1	1	1	0
EUROP. COMMUNITY	81	4	2	0	8	10	4	3	0	3	4	5	4	10	12	2	4	2	0	2	0	0
FRANCE	60	3	1	0	6	4	4	2	1	2	1	1	0	5	14	5	5	5	0	2	0	0
GERMANY	61	2	1	0	2	10	2	0	0	0	2	5	7	5	6	3	2	2	5	2	1	0
ITALY	51	0	3	0	2	2	1	0	1	1	2	2	1	10	11	5	3	2	2	1	0	0
BELGIUM + LUX	34	1	1	0	0	2	0	0	3	4	1	2	0	7	6	1	1	4	1	1	0	0
NETHERLANDS	33	0	0	1	2	2	1	0	2	0	1	1	1	6	6	3	1	4	5	3	0	0
SPAIN	44	0	0	0	0	2	3	3	0	0	1	0	0	5	3	6	6	4	4	2	3	0
GREECE + TURKEY	13	0	0	0	0	0	0	0	0	2	0	0	1	2	1	0	2	2	1	2	2	0
OTHER EUROPE	17	2	0	0	0	2	1	1	0	2	1	0	0	0	2	2	0	2	4	0	1	1
EUROPE EX. U.K.	82	4	2	1	10	11	5	2	1	5	2	6	2	12	10	3	2	3	1	0	0	0
SOUTHERN DOMINIONS	66	1	1	4	0	4	6	7	3	0	4	3	4	7	9	2	2	1	4	2	2	0
S. AFRICA +RHOD.	35	1	0	0	1	0	4	4	2	1	1	1	0	5	3	2	1	1	0	3	1	1
AUSTRALIA + N.Z.	59	0	1	4	0	3	3	6	4	0	4	2	6	8	9	7	1	2	5	1	2	0
ASIA + OTHER AFRICA	66	0	3	3	1	6	3	2	0	5	4	6	3	1	7	7	6	2	3	3	2	0
JAPAN	41	0	1	1	0	1	0	0	0	0	0	1	1	0	8	5	7	3	2	2	1	0
OTHER ASIA+AFR.	58	0	0	0	3	0	0	2	0	5	4	7	2	7	6	5	5	4	3	2	2	0
BLACK AFRICA	16	0	0	0	1	0	0	0	0	0	0	1	0	0	3	0	1	4	0	3	0	0
ARAB WORLD	17	0	0	0	0	0	0	0	1	2	1	0	1	3	3	0	2	2	3	0	1	1
INDIA	23	0	0	0	0	2	1	1	0	1	2	5	0	4	4	4	2	2	0	1	0	0
PHILIPPINES	29	0	0	1	0	0	0	1	1	1	1	0	1	0	0	2	6	0	1	1	1	1
OTHER E. ASIA	13	0	1	0	0	2	0	0	0	0	0	1	0	1	1	1	2	2	1	1	0	1
OTHER ASIA	25	0	2	2	2	1	0	3	0	2	0	1	1	4	4	2	1	0	0	2	1	1

CHAPTER 2- THE EXPANSION OF PARENT SYSTEMS
SECTION 3- THE FLOW OF MANUFACTURING BY CHARACTERISTIC OF PARENT SYSTEM
TABLE F2- SYSTEMS WITH HIGH GROWTH IN SALES 1950-1966
CLASSIFIED BY PERIOD SYSTEM FIRST OPERATED A MANUFACTURING SUBSIDIARY
IN SPECIFIED COUNTRIES AND REGIONS

PERIOD

COUNTRY OR REGION	PRE 1968	PRE 1901	1901 -13	1914 -19	1920 -24	1925 -29	1930 -34	1935 -39	1940 -45	1946 -50	1951 -53	1954 -55	1956 -57	1958 -59	1960 -61	1962	1963	1964	1965	1966	1967	UNK
OUTSIDE U.S.	82	8	5	9	7	14	7	6	5	4	5	3	3	4	2	0	1	0	0	0	0	0
OUT. U.S. + CANADA	82	8	3	1	6	12	10	5	5	8	8	8	5	7	4	0	1	0	0	0	0	0
OUT. WEST. HEMIS.	82	7	3	1	6	12	7	4	2	7	8	6	7	8	4	0	1	0	0	0	0	0
OUT. WHITE CWEALTH	82	7	1	2	4	5	6	6	6	6	8	6	9	8	3	0	1	0	0	0	0	0
OUT. DEVLPED WORLD	81	2	0	0	1	3	10	8	9	8	8	6	7	12	5	1	1	1	2	1	1	1
CANADA	78	1	5	12	4	9	8	6	6	2	5	4	5	1	1	1	2	2	0	1	0	0
LATIN AMERICA	79	2	0	0	1	3	4	8	9	8	7	6	7	12	4	1	1	2	2	1	1	1
C. AMER.+CARIB.	77	1	0	0	0	1	3	6	5	7	8	5	8	12	4	2	3	3	3	0	1	1
CUBA	12	1	0	0	0	1	1	4	7	0	1	1	2	1	0	3	0	0	0	0	1	1
MEXICO	75	0	1	0	0	0	3	2	5	8	6	4	7	13	7	4	1	2	6	2	1	2
OTHER	31	0	0	0	0	2	1	0	7	0	1	0	5	0	6	2	1	4	2	1	1	0
S. AMERICA	71	1	1	0	1	1	2	4	9	9	6	3	7	16	4	4	2	1	2	2	1	0
ARGENTINA	44	0	1	0	0	2	1	1	4	3	2	1	4	5	7	5	3	1	2	0	1	0
BRAZIL	48	0	0	0	1	1	0	2	6	5	6	2	5	12	2	2	2	0	3	2	0	1
PERU	15	1	0	0	1	1	0	1	1	1	0	0	2	2	2	1	2	0	2	1	1	0
COLOMBIA	35	0	0	0	0	0	0	0	2	6	1	1	2	0	6	6	2	1	1	1	0	1
VENEZUELA	31	0	0	0	1	1	0	1	6	3	2	0	2	2	9	3	3	1	3	1	0	0
OTHER	22	0	0	0	1	1	0	0	2	1	2	1	2	0	2	2	2	1	3	1	1	1
EUROPE	82	7	3	1	5	12	5	5	1	7	7	6	8	8	4	2	1	0	0	0	0	0
EFTA	78	4	3	1	4	11	5	5	1	6	6	8	5	4	4	3	3	3	3	0	0	0
U.K.	73	3	4	1	3	10	6	5	0	6	5	8	5	4	4	2	2	4	3	3	1	0
SCANDINAVIA	31	1	0	0	0	0	0	0	0	2	1	0	0	2	4	0	1	0	0	0	1	1
SWITZERLAND	11	0	0	0	0	0	0	1	1	2	0	0	0	1	3	0	0	1	4	0	0	0
OTHER EFTA	13	0	0	0	1	2	6	0	0	2	0	0	1	2	0	2	0	1	0	0	1	0
EUROP. COMMUNITY	81	6	1	2	4	3	0	1	1	3	9	6	8	11	14	3	3	1	1	0	0	0
FRANCE	63	4	2	0	3	3	5	1	0	5	5	4	4	9	10	2	2	3	1	1	0	0
GERMANY	54	5	1	2	2	3	5	1	0	0	1	3	7	3	12	8	1	2	1	2	1	0
ITALY	57	1	1	0	1	2	6	2	0	1	5	2	0	5	9	1	4	3	4	1	2	0
BELGIUM + LUX	35	0	0	0	0	0	1	1	2	2	2	2	3	5	6	8	3	3	4	2	0	0
NETHERLANDS	32	0	0	0	1	2	0	0	0	1	2	2	6	1	6	1	3	2	4	2	0	0
SPAIN	38	0	0	0	0	1	2	0	2	1	2	2	3	2	3	3	7	2	6	3	1	0
GREECE + TURKEY	12	0	0	1	0	1	0	0	0	0	1	0	0	1	4	2	1	1	1	1	0	1
OTHER EUROPE	12	1	1	1	0	1	0	0	2	0	0	0	0	0	0	2	0	0	2	0	0	0
EUROPE EX. U.K.	82	6	1	2	4	4	7	1	1	3	10	7	8	12	11	3	2	0	0	0	0	0
SOUTHERN DOMINIONS	68	0	1	1	2	4	4	5	2	4	4	10	5	9	4	1	1	2	2	3	1	1
S. AFRICA +RHOD.	40	0	0	1	0	4	3	2	3	4	2	3	3	4	4	5	3	1	2	3	1	1
AUSTRALIA + N.Z.	60	0	1	0	2	4	3	4	0	4	9	9	3	10	3	1	2	1	4	3	1	1
ASIA + OTHER AFRICA	65	0	0	0	0	2	2	2	0	5	6	5	6	1	12	6	6	1	4	2	1	2
JAPAN	47	0	0	0	0	0	1	1	0	4	5	2	4	2	8	5	5	3	4	3	1	2
OTHER ASIA+AFR.	50	0	0	0	2	2	0	1	1	0	2	0	2	0	10	5	1	0	3	4	1	1
BLACK AFRICA	9	0	0	0	0	0	0	0	0	0	0	0	0	3	2	1	1	1	0	0	0	1
ARAB WORLD	9	0	0	0	0	0	0	0	0	1	1	1	2	0	0	4	1	0	1	0	0	1
INDIA	27	0	0	0	0	1	0	0	1	1	2	3	1	4	5	1	0	1	2	2	1	1
PHILIPPINES	21	0	0	0	0	0	0	0	0	0	0	0	2	0	2	4	1	1	2	2	0	1
OTHER E. ASIA	11	0	0	0	0	1	0	0	0	0	1	1	1	1	2	0	2	0	2	1	1	1
OTHER ASIA	23	0	0	2	0	1	1	0	0	3	0	1	3	2	5	1	1	0	2	0	1	1

CHAPTER 2— THE EXPANSION OF PARENT SYSTEMS
SECTION 3— THE FLOW OF MANUFACTURING BY CHARACTERISTIC OF PARENT SYSTEM
TABLE G1— SYSTEMS WITH LOW RETURN ON INVESTED CAPITAL IN 1966
CLASSIFIED BY PERIOD SYSTEM FIRST OPERATED A MANUFACTURING SUBSIDIARY
IN SPECIFIED COUNTRIES AND REGIONS

COUNTRY OR REGION	PRE 1968	PRE 1901	1901-13	1914-19	1920-24	1925-29	1930-34	1935-39	1940-45	1946-50	1951-53	1954-55	1956-57	1958-59	1960-61	1962	1963	1964	1965	1966	1967	UNK
OUTSIDE U.S.	92	11	12	12	3	14	6	6	6	6	3	2	2	6	3	0	0	0	0	0	0	0
OUT. U.S. + CANADA	92	10	7	7	7	10	6	4	5	10	4	4	4	7	4	2	0	0	0	0	0	1
OUT. WEST. HEMIS.	92	9	7	7	6	10	5	4	1	8	7	6	5	7	10	1	2	0	0	0	0	2
OUT. WHITE CWEALTH	92	8	7	5	7	8	5	4	8	7	7	8	7	10	4	0	2	1	1	2	0	2
OUT. DEVLPED WORLD	91	2	2	3	2	7	6	5	10	10	5	7	9	8	11	0	2	1	1	1	1	1
CANADA																						
LATIN AMERICA	90	2	9	13	2	10	7	7	3	5	6	7	5	5	5	2	2	1	0	1	0	0
C. AMER.+CARIB.	90	2	2	1	2	4	6	6	9	9	6	7	10	8	10	1	4	1	1	1	1	1
CUBA	84	1	0	1	2	3	5	3	5	10	4	7	11	8	8	2	0	3	0	1	0	2
MEXICO	21	0	0	0	1	1	3	3	2	10	1	0	1	1	1	0	0	3	3	1	1	2
OTHER	77	1	1	0	1	2	3	3	6	11	3	6	6	8	8	3	3	3	3	0	0	1
S. AMERICA	37	0	3	0	0	2	1	1	0	8	1	4	0	3	5	1	1	1	6	3	3	2
ARGENTINA	79	1	2	3	2	2	3	2	10	8	7	10	4	10	9	3	3	3	1	2	2	0
BRAZIL	48	0	2	1	0	3	2	0	3	6	4	5	3	3	6	4	3	2	2	2	1	0
PERU	54	0	0	0	0	0	2	3	0	5	8	2	0	8	3	0	0	1	1	2	1	3
COLOMBIA	19	1	0	0	0	0	0	6	3	6	1	1	1	0	2	1	1	2	2	2	1	0
VENEZUELA	41	0	0	1	1	0	1	5	5	4	2	1	7	2	5	2	3	2	2	3	3	1
OTHER	42	0	1	1	2	0	1	3	3	3	6	0	0	5	7	1	2	1	3	1	0	2
EUROPE	92	9	7	3	7	10	5	4	1	6	4	5	5	9	10	3	2	2	1	1	0	0
EFTA	88	6	6	3	4	10	6	1	1	6	2	4	3	7	7	3	6	2	1	1	0	0
U.K.	84	5	6	3	2	11	5	1	1	7	3	3	1	7	8	4	4	5	3	1	1	0
SCANDINAVIA	33	1	2	1	1	1	2	0	0	3	2	1	1	2	2	4	0	3	3	3	0	1
SWITZERLAND	18	0	0	0	0	1	0	1	0	1	0	0	0	1	4	0	5	1	2	3	1	0
OTHER EFTA	16	0	2	1	0	1	0	1	0	0	1	0	6	1	1	5	2	1	3	1	1	1
EUROP. COMMUNITY	91	7	4	0	2	3	3	2	0	3	8	6	6	14	13	2	2	2	3	2	1	0
FRANCE	69	5	1	1	7	4	2	1	0	3	2	3	3	10	12	6	7	6	6	4	0	0
GERMANY	68	6	1	0	4	2	2	1	0	2	3	1	1	5	11	4	4	4	5	2	0	0
ITALY	62	1	3	1	2	2	2	1	1	2	5	6	6	5	12	7	2	2	2	1	2	0
BELGIUM + LUX	37	0	1	0	1	1	2	1	0	1	2	1	1	7	7	5	5	2	2	1	1	0
NETHERLANDS	40	0	0	1	0	3	2	1	1	3	1	1	1	6	5	2	2	3	3	3	0	0
SPAIN	48	0	0	0	1	1	1	0	0	0	2	0	0	5	5	4	5	5	5	2	2	0
GREECE + TURKEY	19	0	2	0	0	0	0	1	2	0	6	1	1	1	3	6	1	3	3	0	0	1
OTHER EUROPE	20	3	2	0	7	5	1	0	0	0	1	0	0	3	2	2	2	2	2	3	0	0
EUROPE EX. U.K.	91	7	5	2	7	5	2	2	3	2	8	5	5	2	13	3	5	1	1	0	0	3
SOUTHERN DOMINIONS	74	0	1	2	0	4	5	7	2	1	3	5	5	9	9	3	5	4	3	1	1	1
S. AFRICA +RHOD.	38	0	0	0	1	0	2	2	2	2	2	1	1	5	5	5	1	1	1	1	1	1
AUSTRALIA + N.Z.	66	0	1	2	0	4	3	8	2	4	3	3	4	7	7	3	3	3	3	1	1	1
ASIA + OTHER AFRICA	74	0	2	3	1	5	1	3	0	6	5	4	5	5	14	2	2	3	2	1	1	1
JAPAN	53	0	0	1	0	0	0	1	0	1	1	4	4	4	14	6	6	5	1	2	2	2
OTHER ASIA+AFR.	60	0	0	0	0	1	2	2	0	5	0	0	0	2	13	9	0	2	1	1	1	1
BLACK AFRICA	16	0	0	2	0	0	0	0	0	2	1	1	0	3	6	4	3	4	1	1	1	1
ARAB WORLD	16	0	0	1	0	1	1	0	1	0	1	0	2	2	1	0	0	0	1	2	1	1
INDIA	29	0	0	0	0	0	2	1	1	1	1	1	2	3	2	1	1	1	1	1	1	1
PHILIPPINES	28	0	0	2	0	1	0	0	0	0	1	0	0	6	6	4	3	2	2	1	1	1
OTHER E. ASIA	17	0	0	1	0	2	1	0	0	0	1	0	1	3	3	3	2	2	1	3	3	1
OTHER ASIA	27	0	0	2	0	1	2	2	0	3	0	1	0	3	4	1	1	1	1	0	0	3

PERIOD

CHAPTER 2- THE EXPANSION OF PARENT SYSTEMS
SECTION 3- THE FLOW OF MANUFACTURING BY CHARACTERISTIC OF PARENT SYSTEM
TABLE G2- SYSTEMS WITH HIGH RETURN ON INVESTED CAPITAL IN 1966
CLASSIFIED BY PERIOD SYSTEM FIRST OPERATED A MANUFACTURING SUBSIDIARY
IN SPECIFIED COUNTRIES AND REGIONS

PERIOD

COUNTRY OR REGION	PRE 1968	PRE 1901	1901 -13	1914 -19	1920 -24	1925 -29	1930 -34	1935 -39	1940 -45	1946 -50	1951 -53	1954 -55	1956 -57	1958 -59	1960 -61	1962	1963	1964	1965	1966	1967	UNK
OUTSIDE U.S.	92	8	9	13	11	16	7	7	2	3	5	5	2	2	2	0	0	0	0	0	0	0
OUT. U.S. + CANADA	92	8	4	5	11	18	7	7	4	4	8	5	6	3	2	2	0	0	0	0	0	0
OUT. WEST. HEMIS.	92	8	3	11	11	20	5	7	2	4	8	6	7	7	2	2	0	0	0	0	0	0
OUT. WHITE CWEALTH	92	6	1	5	9	10	10	7	6	5	6	8	8	8	3	2	0	0	0	0	0	0
OUT. DEVLPED WORLD	91	1	1	3	4	5	6	14	7	8	6	8	5	11	5	5	1	1	0	0	0	0
CANADA	85	3	10	11	4	17	8	6	4	4	5	2	2	1	2	1	1	2	3	2	1	0
LATIN AMERICA	89	1	1	3	3	5	6	14	8	8	5	5	5	10	5	4	4	2	3	3	0	0
C. AMER.+CARIB.	85	0	0	1	0	2	1	12	5	6	8	4	9	10	6	5	5	3	0	0	0	0
CUBA	15	0	1	0	0	0	6	2	1	1	1	1	2	1	0	4	0	2	4	1	1	0
MEXICO	82	0	1	0	0	2	5	6	8	8	6	4	3	11	7	5	4	4	4	2	1	1
OTHER	34	0	0	0	0	0	1	2	0	2	2	0	1	1	1	4	2	5	0	1	0	0
S. AMERICA	79	1	0	2	4	6	11	10	10	7	5	4	4	14	4	2	2	2	1	2	0	1
ARGENTINA	49	0	2	2	1	4	2	7	3	3	3	1	6	5	4	2	2	1	0	1	0	0
BRAZIL	58	0	0	0	1	1	5	5	5	8	4	5	2	10	3	1	5	2	3	2	0	0
PERU	21	0	0	0	1	1	1	1	1	1	0	1	1	0	1	2	2	1	3	0	1	0
COLOMBIA	32	0	1	0	0	5	1	2	3	4	2	1	2	3	8	0	1	3	0	2	1	0
VENEZUELA	42	0	0	0	0	0	0	0	5	5	0	1	9	7	5	6	4	2	2	0	1	1
OTHER	28	1	0	0	1	2	0	0	2	2	1	3	2	1	1	0	0	0	1	1	3	0
EUROPE	92	8	3	2	9	19	5	8	1	6	8	5	7	8	2	0	0	0	0	0	0	0
EFTA	87	5	3	2	5	18	8	11	1	4	8	5	6	2	3	2	2	1	1	0	0	0
U.K.	83	5	3	1	1	16	9	11	0	4	7	5	3	2	1	3	3	2	1	0	1	0
SCANDINAVIA	28	0	0	2	0	3	0	0	0	0	1	0	1	1	1	0	2	2	2	0	1	0
SWITZERLAND	13	0	0	0	0	1	0	3	1	1	1	2	2	1	2	1	1	0	1	0	1	0
OTHER EFTA	19	0	0	0	0	1	0	0	1	0	0	0	1	3	2	1	1	3	3	0	1	0
EUROP. COMMUNITY	91	5	0	2	8	7	8	2	1	4	7	8	7	11	14	1	2	2	1	2	1	0
FRANCE	69	2	1	1	8	7	5	2	0	5	4	3	2	6	13	3	3	3	2	3	1	0
GERMANY	68	3	0	1	7	5	6	1	0	0	2	6	5	6	11	4	3	3	3	1	0	1
ITALY	61	0	1	0	3	7	1	1	0	2	4	6	5	12	9	8	4	4	5	1	2	0
BELGIUM + LUX	41	1	0	1	1	1	2	2	1	1	1	2	2	7	6	2	3	3	6	2	2	0
NETHERLANDS	35	0	0	0	1	3	1	0	1	3	3	1	5	5	1	3	0	3	7	5	0	0
SPAIN	45	0	0	0	1	2	0	0	0	0	0	1	2	2	2	4	2	3	5	5	0	0
GREECE + TURKEY	12	0	0	0	2	2	1	0	1	2	2	1	1	3	1	0	1	1	1	1	0	0
OTHER EUROPE	14	0	0	0	1	4	0	1	2	1	1	1	1	0	1	0	2	1	2	0	0	0
EUROPE EX. U.K.	92	5	0	3	8	10	8	1	2	7	7	8	6	13	10	2	0	2	0	5	0	0
SOUTHERN DOMINIONS	77	1	1	2	3	5	6	7	3	5	7	6	5	9	5	1	2	3	3	1	4	0
S. AFRICA +RHOD.	47	1	0	1	2	2	4	4	3	5	1	3	2	5	4	2	3	1	1	2	0	1
AUSTRALIA + N.Z.	69	0	1	1	2	4	4	4	2	4	7	5	5	9	7	7	7	2	6	2	4	0
ASIA + OTHER AFRICA	71	0	1	0	2	4	1	2	0	5	3	6	9	4	10	7	4	2	2	1	2	0
JAPAN	46	0	0	0	0	2	1	1	0	0	4	4	6	4	2	6	6	2	8	1	1	0
OTHER ASIA+AFR.	57	0	1	0	2	4	0	0	0	5	1	6	2	5	6	6	2	3	1	1	1	0
BLACK AFRICA	13	0	0	0	0	0	0	0	1	0	0	1	2	0	0	2	1	0	0	1	1	0
ARAB WORLD	13	0	0	0	0	0	0	0	0	2	0	0	1	2	2	1	3	1	2	2	2	0
INDIA	29	0	0	0	1	2	0	0	1	1	3	0	1	6	4	1	0	1	0	0	0	1
PHILIPPINES	25	0	0	0	0	0	0	0	0	0	0	1	2	2	0	1	1	1	1	2	1	0
OTHER E. ASIA	11	0	0	1	1	0	1	1	0	3	0	0	1	0	3	0	0	1	0	0	1	0
OTHER ASIA	27	0	0	0	0	2	8	1	0	3	0	0	3	4	6	2	0	2	1	2	0	0

CHAPTER 2— THE EXPANSION OF PARENT SYSTEMS
SECTION 3— THE FLOW OF MANUFACTURING BY CHARACTERISTIC OF PARENT SYSTEM
TABLE H1— SYSTEMS WHICH FIRST MANUFACTURED OUTSIDE U.S. AND CANADA BEFORE 1901
CLASSIFIED BY PERIOD SYSTEM FIRST OPERATED A MANUFACTURING SUBSIDIARY
IN SPECIFIED COUNTRIES AND REGIONS

COUNTRY OR REGION	PRE 1968	PRE 1901	1901 -13	1914 -19	1920 -24	1925 -29	1930 -34	1935 -39	1940 -45	1946 -50	1951 -53	1954 -55	1956 -57	1958 -59	1960 -61	1962	1963	1964	1965	1966	1967	UNK
OUTSIDE U.S.	21	18	2	0	1	0	0	0	0	0	0	0	0	0	0	0	0	0	0	0	0	0
OUT. U.S. + CANADA	21	18	1	0	2	0	0	0	0	0	0	0	0	0	0	0	0	0	0	0	0	0
OUT. WEST. HEMIS.	21	17	1	0	3	0	0	0	0	0	0	1	0	0	0	0	0	0	0	0	0	0
OUT. WHITE CWEALTH	21	14	3	1	3	1	0	0	0	0	0	0	0	0	0	0	0	0	0	0	0	0
OUT. DEVLPED WORLD	21	3	2	1	1	0	3	3	1	3	0	2	2	1	0	0	1	0	1	0	0	0
CANADA	21	4	6	2	1	1	0	0	1	1	1	1	0	1	0	0	0	1	0	0	0	0
LATIN AMERICA	20	3	2	1	0	0	3	3	3	3	0	1	2	1	0	1	0	0	1	0	0	0
C. AMER.+CARIB.	19	1	0	1	0	1	2	2	0	3	0	0	1	3	1	0	0	0	2	0	0	1
CUBA	4	1	0	1	0	1	0	0	0	0	0	0	0	1	0	0	0	0	0	0	0	1
MEXICO	18	0	1	0	1	0	2	2	3	3	0	0	0	1	2	0	0	0	3	0	0	0
OTHER	5	0	3	0	1	1	2	0	0	0	0	0	1	1	0	0	0	0	1	0	0	0
S. AMERICA	17	2	3	1	1	0	1	2	1	2	0	2	1	1	1	1	0	0	0	0	0	0
ARGENTINA	11	0	2	1	0	0	1	1	1	1	0	1	2	1	2	1	0	0	1	0	0	1
BRAZIL	17	0	0	0	1	0	2	0	2	2	0	2	0	2	1	0	0	2	0	0	0	0
PERU	1	1	0	0	0	0	0	0	0	0	0	0	0	0	0	1	0	0	1	0	0	0
COLOMBIA	8	0	0	0	1	0	1	0	1	0	0	1	0	1	2	1	0	0	0	0	0	0
VENEZUELA	6	0	0	0	1	0	0	0	0	0	0	0	0	0	0	0	0	0	0	1	0	0
OTHER	7	1	1	1	1	0	0	0	0	0	0	0	1	2	1	0	1	0	1	0	0	1
EUROPE	21	17	1	0	2	0	0	0	0	0	0	1	0	0	0	0	0	0	0	0	0	0
EFTA	21	11	2	0	2	3	1	1	1	1	0	1	0	0	0	0	0	0	0	0	0	0
U.K.	20	10	3	0	1	2	1	1	1	1	0	0	0	1	1	0	0	0	1	0	0	0
SCANDINAVIA	6	0	1	0	1	1	0	0	1	0	0	0	0	1	0	1	0	0	0	0	0	0
SWITZERLAND	5	0	0	0	0	0	0	0	1	1	0	1	1	1	0	0	0	0	1	1	0	0
OTHER EFTA	9	0	2	0	1	1	1	1	1	1	0	0	0	0	1	0	0	0	0	0	0	0
EUROP. COMMUNITY	21	12	0	0	2	2	0	0	0	0	0	2	0	1	0	0	0	2	0	0	0	0
FRANCE	20	7	1	0	3	3	0	1	0	1	0	0	1	1	0	1	0	0	1	0	0	0
GERMANY	9	1	0	0	1	2	0	0	0	0	0	1	1	1	0	0	0	0	1	0	0	0
ITALY	17	4	4	0	2	0	0	0	0	0	0	2	0	1	2	0	0	0	2	0	0	0
BELGIUM + LUX	12	1	0	1	0	1	1	0	1	0	0	0	0	0	0	0	0	1	2	1	0	0
NETHERLANDS	11	0	0	0	0	0	0	0	0	0	0	1	1	0	3	2	1	0	1	1	0	0
SPAIN	7	0	0	0	0	2	1	0	1	1	0	0	0	0	0	1	0	0	1	1	0	0
GREECE + TURKEY	8	3	2	0	0	0	0	0	1	0	1	0	1	0	0	0	0	1	2	0	0	0
OTHER EUROPE	21	12	1	0	3	1	1	0	0	0	0	0	1	0	1	0	0	0	0	0	0	0
EUROPE EX. U.K.	18	1	2	2	1	1	0	0	1	1	0	2	0	1	1	0	1	2	3	0	0	0
SOUTHERN DOMINIONS	18	1	2	2	1	1	0	0	1	1	0	2	0	1	1	0	1	2	3	0	0	0
S. AFRICA +RHOD.	9	1	0	1	2	0	0	1	1	0	0	1	1	2	2	0	0	1	0	1	0	0
AUSTRALIA + N.Z.	18	0	2	2	1	2	1	0	0	0	1	1	1	3	3	1	1	0	3	1	0	0
ASIA + OTHER AFRICA	16	0	1	0	0	0	1	0	0	0	1	1	1	1	1	2	0	0	0	0	0	0
JAPAN	11	0	0	0	0	0	0	1	0	0	1	0	1	1	3	1	0	0	2	0	0	0
OTHER ASIA+AFR.	14	0	1	0	0	0	0	0	0	0	1	1	1	0	2	1	0	0	1	0	0	0
BLACK AFRICA	3	0	0	0	0	0	0	0	0	0	0	0	0	0	0	0	0	0	1	0	0	0
ARAB WORLD	9	0	0	0	0	1	1	0	0	0	0	0	0	0	3	1	1	0	1	0	0	1
INDIA	9	0	0	1	0	0	0	0	0	0	1	1	1	1	0	0	0	0	1	0	0	0
PHILIPPINES	5	0	0	0	0	0	0	0	0	0	0	0	1	0	0	0	0	0	1	0	0	0
OTHER E. ASIA	5	0	0	0	0	0	0	0	0	0	0	0	0	0	0	2	0	2	0	0	1	0
OTHER ASIA	4	0	0	0	0	1	0	0	0	0	1	0	0	1	1	0	0	0	0	0	0	0

CHAPTER 2- THE EXPANSION OF PARENT SYSTEMS
SECTION 3- THE FLOW OF MANUFACTURING BY CHARACTERISTIC OF PARENT SYSTEM
TABLE H2- SYSTEMS WHICH FIRST MANUFACTURED OUTSIDE U.S. AND CANADA 1901-1919
CLASSIFIED BY PERIOD SYSTEM FIRST OPERATED A MANUFACTURING SUBSIDIARY
IN SPECIFIED COUNTRIES AND REGIONS

PERIOD

COUNTRY OR REGION	PRE 1968	PRE 1901	1901 -13	1914 -19	1920 -24	1925 -29	1930 -34	1935 -39	1940 -45	1946 -50	1951 -53	1954 -55	1956 -57	1958 -59	1960 -61	1962	1963	1964	1965	1966	1967	UNK
OUTSIDE U.S.	28	0	13	11	1	1	2	0	0	0	0	0	0	0	0	0	0	0	0	0	0	0
OUT. U.S. + CANADA	28	0	10	13	2	1	2	0	0	0	0	0	0	0	0	0	0	0	0	0	0	0
OUT. WEST. HEMIS.	28	0	9	11	2	3	2	1	0	0	0	0	0	0	0	0	0	0	0	0	0	0
OUT. WHITE CMWEALTH	28	0	5	11	4	2	1	1	0	0	2	2	2	0	0	0	0	0	0	0	0	0
OUT. DEVLPED WORLD	28	0	1	6	3	2	1	4	2	1	1	3	3	1	1	0	0	0	0	0	0	0
CANADA	28	0	7	7	2	4	1	3	0	0	2	1	0	0	0	0	0	0	0	0	0	0
LATIN AMERICA	28	0	1	4	2	2	3	5	2	1	1	2	3	1	1	0	0	0	0	0	0	0
C. AMER.+CARIB.	25	0	1	1	0	0	3	4	2	3	1	2	1	1	1	1	0	0	0	0	1	0
CUBA	6	0	0	0	0	2	2	0	2	1	1	1	1	1	0	0	0	0	0	0	0	0
MEXICO	23	0	1	1	0	2	1	3	1	1	1	2	2	1	0	0	0	1	0	0	0	0
OTHER	7	0	0	0	0	0	1	1	0	0	0	0	1	0	1	0	0	0	0	0	0	0
S. AMERICA	25	0	0	3	3	3	1	4	4	2	1	2	3	2	2	0	1	0	1	3	0	1
ARGENTINA	17	0	0	1	0	3	2	2	1	1	3	1	2	3	0	1	0	1	0	0	0	0
BRAZIL	22	0	0	2	1	2	2	3	3	3	0	2	2	1	3	1	1	1	0	0	0	0
PERU	9	0	0	0	0	0	0	0	1	0	1	0	0	0	1	0	0	0	0	0	0	1
COLOMBIA	12	0	0	1	1	0	0	3	1	3	3	1	2	0	2	0	1	1	2	0	0	0
VENEZUELA	17	0	0	0	0	0	1	1	0	1	2	0	1	2	1	1	1	0	1	0	1	1
OTHER	12	0	0	0	1	1	0	1	2	3	1	2	1	3	1	1	0	0	0	0	0	0
EUROPE	28	0	9	5	2	5	3	1	0	0	1	1	1	1	0	0	0	0	0	0	0	0
EFTA	28	0	7	5	1	4	4	1	0	0	1	1	1	1	0	1	1	1	1	0	0	0
U.K.	14	0	6	4	1	3	5	2	1	1	1	1	1	0	2	1	1	1	1	1	0	0
SCANDINAVIA	8	0	1	3	1	0	0	0	1	1	0	0	1	0	2	1	0	0	1	0	0	0
SWITZERLAND	8	0	0	0	0	1	0	3	0	0	0	0	0	1	1	0	0	0	1	1	1	0
OTHER EFTA	26	0	4	3	5	5	0	3	0	1	1	2	1	2	1	0	1	1	1	1	1	0
EUROP. COMMUNITY	24	0	4	1	1	2	2	1	1	0	1	2	2	2	2	0	1	2	1	0	0	0
FRANCE	22	0	3	2	5	3	1	1	0	1	2	4	2	3	2	0	2	0	1	1	1	0
GERMANY	19	0	1	0	2	2	3	0	1	0	0	0	2	1	2	1	2	1	0	2	1	0
ITALY	16	0	0	0	2	2	1	1	1	1	2	1	2	1	2	2	2	3	2	0	0	1
BELGIUM + LUX	13	0	1	1	1	0	2	0	1	3	0	0	0	3	2	0	0	3	1	0	0	0
NETHERLANDS	17	0	0	0	0	1	0	2	1	1	1	2	1	2	2	1	2	1	1	2	1	1
SPAIN	4	0	0	0	1	0	0	0	0	0	0	0	0	0	0	1	0	0	0	0	0	0
GREECE + TURKEY	8	0	0	0	1	0	0	1	1	0	1	1	1	0	0	1	0	1	0	2	2	0
OTHER EUROPE	27	0	4	5	4	4	4	1	0	1	0	0	2	1	1	1	0	1	0	0	0	0
EUROPE EX. U.K.	25	0	0	3	1	3	3	7	1	1	1	1	0	2	0	1	1	0	0	0	0	0
SOUTHERN DOMINIONS	13	0	0	3	1	1	1	2	0	2	2	0	0	2	1	1	0	1	0	1	0	0
S. AFRICA +RHOD.	25	0	0	3	0	3	3	7	1	1	0	1	2	0	3	1	1	0	0	1	0	0
AUSTRALIA + N.Z.	19	0	0	3	2	3	0	0	1	1	3	3	0	6	1	1	1	0	1	1	1	0
ASIA + OTHER AFRICA	17	0	0	1	0	2	0	0	1	0	4	0	0	1	1	0	1	0	0	0	0	0
JAPAN	15	0	0	2	2	2	0	0	0	0	0	0	0	0	0	0	0	0	2	0	1	0
OTHER ASIA+AFR.	6	0	0	0	2	0	0	0	1	1	1	1	1	1	1	0	0	1	2	0	1	0
BLACK AFRICA	7	0	0	0	0	3	0	0	1	0	0	0	0	0	0	0	1	0	0	0	0	0
ARAB WORLD	10	0	0	0	0	0	1	1	0	0	1	1	0	1	0	1	0	1	0	0	0	0
INDIA	8	0	0	0	1	0	1	0	1	0	3	3	0	0	0	1	1	2	0	0	0	0
PHILIPPINES	2	0	0	0	0	0	0	0	0	0	0	0	0	0	0	0	0	0	0	0	0	0
OTHER E. ASIA	11	0	0	2	0	2	1	1	1	1	0	0	2	1	1	1	0	0	0	1	1	0
OTHER ASIA	11	0	0	2	0	2	0	1	0	1	0	0	0	2	1	0	0	0	0	0	1	0

CHAPTER 2— THE EXPANSION OF PARENT SYSTEMS
SECTION 3— THE FLOW OF MANUFACTURING BY CHARACTERISTIC OF PARENT SYSTEM
TABLE H3— SYSTEMS WHICH FIRST MANUFACTURED OUTSIDE U.S. AND CANADA 1920–1929
CLASSIFIED BY PERIOD SYSTEM FIRST OPERATED A MANUFACTURING SUBSIDIARY
IN SPECIFIED COUNTRIES AND REGIONS

PERIOD

COUNTRY OR REGION	PRE 1968	PRE 1901	1901 -13	1914 -19	1920 -24	1925 -29	1930 -34	1935 -39	1940 -45	1946 -50	1951 -53	1954 -55	1956 -57	1958 -59	1960 -61	1962	1963	1964	1965	1966	1967	UNK
OUTSIDE U.S.	49	0	5	8	12	21	1	2	0	0	0	0	0	0	0	0	0	0	0	0	0	0
OUT. U.S. + CANADA	49	0	5	0	13	22	5	3	0	1	0	0	0	0	0	0	0	0	0	0	0	0
OUT. WEST. HEMIS.	49	0	0	0	12	28	3	3	0	1	2	0	0	0	0	0	0	0	0	0	0	0
OUT. WHITE CWEALTH	49	0	0	0	8	16	9	3	1	2	1	1	1	1	0	1	0	1	0	0	0	0
OUT. DEVLPED WORLD	49	0	0	0	2	10	7	9	4	5	1	1	1	5	2	1	0	1	0	0	0	0
CANADA	48	0	5	8	4	14	7	3	2	1	1	1	2	0	0	1	0	0	0	0	0	0
LATIN AMERICA	48	0	5	0	2	7	7	9	6	5	4	1	3	4	3	1	1	1	2	0	0	0
C. AMER.+CARIB.	47	0	0	0	1	3	3	8	3	6	4	4	2	4	4	0	3	0	2	2	2	0
CUBA	12	0	0	0	1	1	6	5	1	2	3	1	1	1	1	0	1	1	0	1	0	0
MEXICO	46	0	0	0	0	2	4	4	2	8	3	1	3	5	5	2	3	3	3	3	1	0
OTHER	22	0	0	0	0	0	1	1	1	1	0	0	0	1	1	1	1	2	2	2	1	0
S. AMERICA	45	0	0	0	1	5	5	6	4	3	3	1	3	3	3	2	1	2	3	1	0	0
ARGENTINA	33	0	0	0	0	2	2	2	4	4	2	1	5	2	1	2	1	0	2	0	0	0
BRAZIL	32	0	0	0	0	3	2	1	4	0	4	2	4	3	4	0	3	1	1	1	0	0
PERU	15	0	0	0	0	0	0	0	4	0	1	1	0	0	1	0	1	1	1	1	1	0
COLOMBIA	21	0	0	0	0	0	0	1	4	1	1	2	1	1	4	0	2	2	1	0	0	0
VENEZUELA	25	0	0	0	0	0	0	0	3	3	0	1	0	3	3	2	2	1	1	2	1	0
OTHER	12	0	0	0	1	1	0	0	2	2	1	0	2	0	0	1	1	0	0	0	0	0
EUROPE	49	0	0	0	11	24	3	5	0	3	1	0	0	1	1	0	0	0	0	0	0	0
EFTA	47	0	0	0	6	22	3	7	0	3	0	3	1	0	2	0	0	0	0	0	0	0
U.K.	47	0	0	0	5	22	4	7	0	1	0	3	4	0	1	0	0	1	1	1	1	1
SCANDINAVIA	17	0	0	0	1	1	1	0	0	1	0	1	0	1	2	1	2	1	1	1	1	0
SWITZERLAND	4	0	0	0	0	0	0	0	0	0	0	0	0	0	1	0	0	0	0	0	1	0
OTHER EFTA	9	0	0	0	0	2	0	0	0	0	0	0	0	2	1	1	1	1	0	1	1	0
EUROP. COMMUNITY	48	0	0	0	5	7	6	4	1	3	1	1	2	2	1	2	1	1	0	0	0	0
FRANCE	37	0	0	0	4	3	4	2	0	4	3	3	2	2	7	3	3	2	0	1	0	0
GERMANY	35	0	0	0	1	5	5	0	0	0	1	3	2	3	7	2	1	0	4	0	0	0
ITALY	29	0	0	0	0	1	0	1	0	2	6	1	2	3	8	1	3	1	2	1	0	0
BELGIUM + LUX	18	0	0	0	0	4	0	0	1	0	0	1	0	2	2	2	2	0	1	1	1	0
NETHERLANDS	16	0	0	0	1	2	2	1	1	2	2	2	1	1	2	1	2	2	1	1	0	0
SPAIN	23	0	0	0	2	1	1	0	0	0	1	0	0	1	0	3	2	2	3	3	3	1
GREECE + TURKEY	9	0	0	0	0	0	0	0	1	2	2	0	0	0	3	3	2	0	0	1	0	0
OTHER EUROPE	12	0	0	0	0	1	0	0	0	1	0	0	1	1	3	1	0	1	0	0	1	1
EUROPE EX. U.K.	49	0	0	0	7	10	6	0	1	5	5	4	1	5	4	0	0	1	0	0	0	0
SOUTHERN DOMINIONS	41	0	0	1	1	6	5	6	2	0	4	2	4	3	5	0	1	1	0	1	0	0
S. AFRICA +RHOD.	26	0	0	0	0	1	3	3	4	1	1	1	1	2	2	0	3	0	0	0	0	0
AUSTRALIA + N.Z.	35	0	0	1	1	5	3	3	1	1	4	6	6	4	5	6	5	1	1	0	1	0
ASIA + OTHER AFRICA	42	0	0	0	0	4	0	3	2	5	3	4	4	4	1	4	4	3	3	1	1	0
JAPAN	26	0	0	0	0	0	0	3	0	0	5	3	2	5	3	4	4	3	3	1	1	0
OTHER ASIA+AFR.	36	0	0	0	0	4	0	0	0	0	1	1	2	1	2	5	3	2	1	1	0	0
BLACK AFRICA	12	0	0	0	0	0	0	0	0	2	0	1	0	2	1	3	1	4	0	0	0	0
ARAB WORLD	8	0	0	0	0	0	0	0	0	0	1	0	1	0	0	1	1	1	1	1	1	0
INDIA	17	0	0	0	0	3	0	1	1	2	2	1	1	3	2	2	1	1	0	0	0	0
PHILIPPINES	19	0	0	0	0	1	0	0	0	0	0	0	0	2	2	4	4	1	1	0	1	0
OTHER E. ASIA	9	0	0	0	0	0	0	2	0	1	1	1	1	1	1	0	1	2	0	1	0	0
OTHER ASIA	16	0	0	0	0	0	0	0	0	1	5	0	1	3	2	4	2	0	1	0	0	0

CHAPTER 2- THE EXPANSION OF PARENT SYSTEMS
SECTION 3- THE FLOW OF MANUFACTURING BY CHARACTERISTIC OF PARENT SYSTEM
TABLE H4- SYSTEMS WHICH FIRST MANUFACTURED OUTSIDE U.S. AND CANADA 1930-1945
CLASSIFIED BY PERIOD SYSTEM FIRST OPERATED A MANUFACTURING SUBSIDIARY
IN SPECIFIED COUNTRIES AND REGIONS

COUNTRY OR REGION	PRE 1968	PRE 1901	1901 -13	1914 -19	1920 -24	1925 -29	1930 -34	1935 -39	1940 -45	1946 -50	1951 -53	1954 -55	1956 -57	1958 -59	1960 -61	1962	1963	1964	1965	1966	1967	UNK
OUTSIDE U.S.	31	0	0	5	0	2	6	7	7	2	1	0	0	0	1	0	0	0	0	0	0	0
OUT. U.S. + CANADA	31	0	0	0	0	0	7	9	9	3	2	0	1	1	1	1	0	0	0	0	0	0
OUT. WEST. HEMIS.	31	0	0	0	0	0	5	8	3	6	2	2	2	1	2	3	0	0	1	0	1	0
OUT. WHITE CWEALTH	31	0	0	0	0	0	4	4	8	6	2	1	1	4	4	3	2	0	0	0	1	0
OUT. DEVLPED WORLD	31	0	0	0	0	0	2	2	8	5	4	3	3	2	2	2	0	0	0	0	0	1
CANADA	28	0	0	5	0	2	3	3	3	6	0	0	0	2	2	1	0	0	0	0	0	0
LATIN AMERICA	31	0	0	0	0	0	3	2	8	5	3	3	3	3	2	2	0	0	0	0	0	0
C. AMER.+CARIB.	29	0	0	0	0	0	2	2	6	3	3	1	1	4	4	2	1	1	2	1	1	1
CUBA	8	0	0	0	0	0	1	2	0	0	1	1	1	1	0	1	0	0	0	1	0	0
MEXICO	28	0	0	0	0	0	1	2	8	4	2	2	4	4	1	0	2	0	0	0	0	1
OTHER	14	0	0	0	0	0	0	0	0	6	1	1	1	3	5	1	0	1	1	0	2	2
S. AMERICA	30	0	0	0	0	1	1	0	6	3	3	1	1	1	5	3	1	0	1	0	0	0
ARGENTINA	18	0	0	0	0	0	1	1	0	5	1	0	3	1	2	1	0	1	1	0	1	1
BRAZIL	22	0	0	0	0	0	0	0	0	2	4	0	1	1	5	2	1	2	2	1	0	0
PERU	6	0	0	0	0	0	3	0	0	0	1	0	0	1	0	1	0	0	0	0	0	0
COLUMBIA	15	0	0	0	0	0	0	1	1	2	2	1	1	1	2	2	0	1	0	1	1	1
VENEZUELA	18	0	0	0	0	0	1	1	3	4	1	0	0	0	4	3	1	0	1	0	1	0
OTHER	12	0	0	0	0	0	1	3	1	2	0	2	2	2	0	4	0	0	0	1	0	2
EUROPE	31	0	0	0	0	4	3	7	2	5	1	2	2	4	2	3	0	2	0	2	0	0
EFTA	30	0	0	0	0	3	3	6	2	3	2	1	3	3	2	1	2	1	3	2	0	0
U.K.	28	0	0	0	0	3	3	6	1	3	2	2	3	1	1	2	1	0	1	1	0	0
SCANDINAVIA	10	0	0	0	0	0	0	0	0	1	1	0	0	0	1	1	1	1	2	1	1	0
SWITZERLAND	5	0	0	0	0	0	0	2	0	0	0	0	0	0	1	0	0	0	0	0	0	0
OTHER EFTA	5	0	0	0	0	0	0	0	1	0	0	0	0	1	2	3	3	1	2	1	1	0
EUROP. COMMUNITY	31	0	0	0	0	2	2	2	0	3	2	0	0	1	5	3	1	1	1	1	0	1
FRANCE	21	0	0	0	0	0	1	1	1	2	1	1	0	0	4	5	2	2	1	1	0	1
GERMANY	21	0	0	0	0	1	0	0	0	0	0	3	3	3	5	6	1	1	1	1	1	0
ITALY	24	0	0	0	0	0	1	1	0	1	1	1	3	1	0	1	4	2	2	2	0	1
BELGIUM + LUX	13	0	0	0	0	1	0	0	0	1	1	1	1	1	1	3	1	1	0	0	0	1
NETHERLANDS	13	0	0	0	0	0	1	1	0	1	1	0	1	1	1	1	2	2	0	1	0	0
SPAIN	16	0	0	0	0	1	1	0	0	0	0	2	0	1	1	3	1	2	2	0	1	0
GREECE + TURKEY	6	0	0	0	0	0	1	1	1	0	2	0	1	0	2	0	1	0	1	0	1	1
OTHER EUROPE	3	0	0	0	0	0	0	0	0	0	0	0	0	0	0	2	0	0	1	0	0	0
EUROPE EX. U.K.	31	0	0	0	0	2	1	2	1	3	3	3	1	2	7	5	2	2	2	0	0	2
SOUTHERN DOMINIONS	25	0	0	0	0	3	1	1	3	3	3	4	2	3	3	1	0	0	0	0	3	1
S. AFRICA +RHOD.	17	0	0	0	0	2	1	1	3	0	3	1	2	2	1	0	1	0	0	2	2	1
AUSTRALIA + N.Z.	22	0	0	0	0	1	0	2	2	2	4	4	2	3	3	3	0	0	0	3	0	1
ASIA + OTHER AFRICA	21	0	0	0	0	0	0	0	0	4	0	2	2	2	4	1	2	1	0	0	2	0
JAPAN	14	0	0	0	0	0	0	0	0	0	4	0	2	0	2	3	1	3	0	2	0	1
OTHER ASIA+AFR.	18	0	0	0	0	0	0	0	0	1	0	0	0	1	1	0	2	0	0	0	0	1
BLACK AFRICA	4	0	0	0	0	0	0	0	0	0	1	0	0	0	2	2	0	0	1	0	1	1
ARAB WORLD	5	0	0	0	0	0	0	0	0	1	0	0	0	1	1	0	0	0	0	0	0	0
INDIA	6	0	0	0	0	0	0	0	0	0	1	2	1	1	0	1	1	0	1	0	1	0
PHILIPPINES	8	0	0	0	0	0	0	0	1	0	0	0	0	0	0	2	1	1	0	1	1	1
OTHER E. ASIA	4	0	0	0	0	0	1	0	1	0	0	1	0	1	0	0	0	0	0	0	0	1
OTHER ASIA	9	0	0	0	0	0	0	0	0	3	0	1	1	0	0	0	2	0	1	0	0	2

CHAPTER 2— THE EXPANSION OF PARENT SYSTEMS
SECTION 3— THE FLOW OF MANUFACTURING BY CHARACTERISTIC OF PARENT SYSTEM
TABLE H5— SYSTEMS WHICH FIRST MANUFACTURED OUTSIDE U.S. AND CANADA AFTER 1946
CLASSIFIED BY PERIOD SYSTEM FIRST OPERATED A MANUFACTURING SUBSIDIARY
IN SPECIFIED COUNTRIES AND REGIONS

PERIOD

COUNTRY OR REGION	PRE 1998	PRE 1901	1901 -13	1914 -19	1920 -24	1925 -29	1930 -34	1935 -39	1940 -45	1946 -50	1951 -53	1954 -55	1956 -57	1958 -59	1960 -61	1962	1963	1964	1965	1966	1967	UNK
OUTSIDE U.S.	58	1	2	2	1	6	4	4	1	7	7	7	4	7	5	0	0	0	0	0	0	0
OUT. U.S. + CANADA	58	1	2	0	1	0	0	1	0	10	10	10	10	9	6	2	0	0	1	0	0	0
OUT. WEST. HEMIS.	58	0	0	0	1	0	0	0	0	6	8	9	11	13	9	1	2	2	1	2	0	0
OUT. WHITE CWEALTH	58	0	0	0	1	0	0	0	1	5	10	10	11	12	7	2	3	3	2	2	0	1
OUT. DEVLPED WORLD	56	0	0	0	0	0	0	1	0	5	5	8	6	10	11	3	1	3	2	1	1	1
CANADA	53	1	2	2	1	6	4	4	1	4	6	3	3	3	6	3	2	2	2	1	1	0
LATIN AMERICA	55	0	0	0	0	0	1	1	0	4	7	7	6	10	9	4	3	1	2	2	0	1
C. AMER.+CARIB.	52	0	0	0	0	0	1	1	0	2	4	5	10	8	5	0	1	4	1	1	0	1
CUBA	6	0	0	0	0	0	0	0	0	0	0	1	3	1	0	3	0	0	0	0	0	0
MEXICO	47	0	0	0	0	0	1	1	0	3	4	5	7	8	6	2	5	3	2	2	0	1
OTHER	24	0	0	0	0	0	0	0	0	2	0	2	2	0	3	5	1	1	0	1	0	1
S. AMERICA	43	0	0	0	0	0	0	0	0	2	5	3	2	11	4	4	2	1	4	4	0	0
ARGENTINA	20	0	0	0	0	0	1	0	1	0	0	2	2	4	4	1	5	2	1	1	0	0
BRAZIL	20	0	0	0	0	0	0	0	0	0	5	0	4	4	2	0	2	2	0	1	0	0
PERU	9	0	0	0	0	0	0	0	0	0	0	1	2	1	2	0	2	0	2	2	1	0
COLOMBIA	17	0	0	0	0	0	0	0	1	1	1	0	1	0	4	1	0	0	1	0	0	0
VENEZUELA	18	0	0	0	0	0	0	0	0	1	0	0	2	3	3	2	4	4	0	2	1	0
OTHER	11	0	0	0	0	0	0	0	0	1	1	1	0	1	1	0	1	1	3	1	3	0
EUROPE	58	0	0	0	1	0	0	0	0	5	9	7	7	15	8	3	2	3	1	0	0	0
EFTA	52	0	0	0	0	1	0	0	0	4	7	4	4	7	8	6	6	3	2	0	0	0
U.K.	47	0	0	0	1	1	0	0	0	0	6	4	4	7	8	2	3	2	1	1	1	0
SCANDINAVIA	15	0	0	0	0	1	0	0	0	1	1	1	0	2	1	6	3	1	1	0	0	0
SWITZERLAND	9	0	0	0	0	0	0	0	0	1	0	0	0	2	4	0	0	0	2	1	0	0
OTHER EFTA	4	0	0	0	0	0	0	0	0	0	0	0	0	0	0	0	0	0	0	0	0	0
EUROP. COMMUNITY	58	0	0	0	1	0	0	0	0	1	2	0	8	16	13	2	2	2	1	1	0	0
FRANCE	36	0	0	0	1	0	0	0	0	0	6	3	3	7	9	4	5	5	2	2	1	0
GERMANY	39	0	0	0	1	0	0	0	0	2	2	7	7	4	6	3	2	2	1	4	1	0
ITALY	35	0	0	0	0	0	0	0	0	3	3	1	3	8	7	4	3	2	5	0	0	1
BELGIUM + LUX	23	0	0	0	0	1	0	0	0	0	0	1	1	7	5	3	1	2	2	2	0	0
NETHERLANDS	21	0	0	0	0	0	0	0	0	1	1	1	2	5	3	1	2	2	5	0	0	0
SPAIN	26	0	0	0	0	0	0	0	0	1	0	2	1	2	3	4	2	2	6	2	0	0
GREECE + TURKEY	6	0	0	0	0	0	0	0	0	1	1	1	0	1	0	0	0	0	1	1	1	0
OTHER EUROPE	5	0	0	0	0	0	0	0	0	0	0	0	1	0	0	0	1	1	2	0	0	0
EUROPE EX. U.K.	58	0	0	0	1	0	0	0	0	1	7	5	7	18	11	3	3	1	2	0	0	0
SOUTHERN DOMINIONS	45	0	0	0	0	0	0	0	1	1	1	5	4	10	7	3	2	2	3	5	5	0
S. AFRICA +RHOD.	21	0	0	0	0	0	0	0	0	0	0	3	2	3	4	2	0	1	2	1	0	1
AUSTRALIA + N.Z.	38	0	0	0	0	0	0	0	1	1	1	4	2	9	7	6	2	2	3	3	5	0
ASIA + OTHER AFRICA	48	0	0	0	0	0	0	0	0	1	1	3	3	4	14	6	3	2	3	2	2	1
JAPAN	31	0	0	0	0	0	0	0	0	0	1	1	1	1	4	4	0	4	4	2	2	2
OTHER ASIA+AFR.	35	0	0	0	0	0	0	0	0	1	0	3	2	3	7	4	2	0	1	2	2	0
BLACK AFRICA	4	0	0	0	0	0	0	0	0	0	0	0	0	0	2	0	0	1	1	0	0	0
ARAB WORLD	6	0	0	0	0	0	0	0	0	0	0	0	0	3	1	0	1	0	0	2	0	0
INDIA	16	0	0	0	0	0	0	0	0	1	0	2	0	2	4	3	0	1	3	0	0	0
PHILIPPINES	13	0	0	0	0	0	0	0	0	0	0	0	0	0	2	3	1	0	0	1	1	0
OTHER E. ASIA	8	0	0	0	0	0	0	0	0	0	0	0	0	2	2	0	0	0	1	3	3	0
OTHER ASIA	15	0	0	0	0	0	0	0	0	1	0	2	2	2	6	1	0	0	0	0	0	1

CHAPTER 2- THE EXPANSION OF PARENT SYSTEMS
SECTION 3- THE FLOW OF MANUFACTURING BY CHARACTERISTIC OF PARENT SYSTEM
TABLE 11- SYSTEMS IN "ORGANIZATIONAL STAGE II" IN 1966
CLASSIFIED BY PERIOD SYSTEM FIRST OPERATED A MANUFACTURING SUBSIDIARY
IN SPECIFIED COUNTRIES AND REGIONS

PERIOD

COUNTRY OR REGION	PRE 1968	PRE 1901	1901 -13	1914 -19	1920 -24	1925 -29	1930 -34	1935 -39	1940 -45	1946 -50	1951 -53	1954 -55	1956 -57	1958 -59	1960 -61	1962	1963	1964	1965	1966	1967	UNK
OUTSIDE U.S.	16	0	4	1	1	4	1	2	0	0	0	3	2	0	0	0	0	0	0	0	0	0
OUT. U.S. + CANADA	16	0	2	1	1	4	1	1	1	1	1	4	2	1	2	1	0	0	0	0	0	0
OUT. WEST. HEMIS.	16	0	1	1	0	4	1	0	0	1	1	5	2	1	1	2	0	0	0	0	0	0
OUT. WHITE CWEALTH	16	0	1	0	0	4	0	0	0	1	1	6	2	0	2	2	0	0	0	0	0	0
OUT. DEVLPED WORLD	16	0	1	0	0	1	1	1	1	1	1	5	1	0	1	1	1	0	0	0	0	0
CANADA	14	0	3	1	0	1	1	2	1	0	0	0	2	2	0	0	1	1	0	0	0	0
LATIN AMERICA	16	0	1	0	0	1	1	1	1	1	2	4	2	0	2	1	1	0	0	1	0	0
C. AMER.+CARIB.	15	0	0	0	0	0	1	1	0	2	1	3	2	0	1	1	0	1	1	1	0	0
CUBA	5	0	0	0	0	0	1	1	0	0	1	1	1	1	0	0	0	0	0	0	0	0
MEXICO	14	0	1	0	0	1	1	0	0	3	0	3	1	0	1	1	1	0	0	1	0	0
OTHER	2	0	0	0	0	0	0	0	1	0	0	0	0	1	0	0	0	0	0	0	0	0
S. AMERICA	12	0	0	0	1	3	0	0	0	0	0	2	3	2	1	0	0	0	0	1	0	0
ARGENTINA	3	0	0	0	0	2	0	1	1	0	0	0	0	0	1	0	0	0	0	0	0	0
BRAZIL	6	0	0	0	1	2	0	0	0	0	0	2	1	1	0	1	0	1	1	1	0	0
PERU	3	0	0	0	0	0	1	0	0	0	0	0	0	0	1	0	1	0	0	1	0	0
COLOMBIA	7	0	0	0	1	0	1	0	0	0	0	2	1	1	0	0	0	0	0	1	0	0
VENEZUELA	6	0	0	0	0	0	0	0	0	0	0	2	1	2	1	0	1	0	1	1	0	0
OTHER	2	0	0	0	0	0	0	0	0	0	0	0	0	0	1	1	0	1	1	0	0	0
EUROPE	16	0	1	0	0	4	0	1	0	0	1	3	2	2	1	0	0	0	0	0	0	0
EFTA	14	0	1	0	0	4	0	1	0	0	1	1	2	1	1	1	1	0	0	0	0	0
U.K.	13	0	1	0	0	4	0	1	0	0	0	1	0	1	0	1	1	0	1	1	0	0
SCANDINAVIA	4	0	0	0	0	0	0	0	0	0	0	0	2	1	0	0	0	0	0	0	0	0
SWITZERLAND	1	0	0	0	0	1	0	0	0	0	0	0	0	1	1	0	0	0	0	0	0	0
OTHER EFTA	2	0	0	0	0	1	0	0	0	0	0	0	1	1	0	0	0	0	0	0	0	0
EUROP. COMMUNITY	16	0	0	0	3	0	0	0	0	0	0	2	2	0	3	0	0	2	0	1	0	0
FRANCE	9	0	0	0	2	0	0	0	0	0	0	0	0	0	3	1	1	1	1	1	0	0
GERMANY	9	0	0	0	2	0	0	0	0	0	0	1	1	1	2	0	1	0	1	1	0	0
ITALY	7	0	0	0	0	0	1	1	0	1	1	0	0	1	2	1	0	1	0	1	0	0
BELGIUM + LUX	7	0	0	0	0	0	0	0	1	0	0	1	0	0	0	0	0	0	1	0	0	0
NETHERLANDS	3	0	0	0	0	0	1	0	0	0	0	0	1	1	0	1	1	0	0	1	0	0
SPAIN	5	0	0	0	0	0	0	0	0	0	0	0	0	0	1	0	0	2	0	1	0	0
GREECE + TURKEY	2	0	0	0	0	0	0	0	0	0	0	0	0	0	0	0	0	0	1	1	0	0
OTHER EUROPE	0	0	0	0	0	0	0	0	0	0	0	0	0	0	0	0	0	0	0	0	0	0
EUROPE EX. U.K.	16.	0	0	0	0	3	0	0	0	0	0	3	1	4	3	1	0	1	0	0	0	0
SOUTHERN DOMINIONS	13	0	0	0	1	0	2	1	0	0	0	2	0	3	2	1	0	0	0	0	0	0
S. AFRICA +RHOD.	8	0	0	0	0	0	2	0	0	1	0	1	0	0	1	0	0	0	0	0	0	0
AUSTRALIA + N.Z.	9	0	0	1	1	0	0	1	0	0	0	1	1	3	1	3	0	0	0	0	0	0
ASIA + OTHER AFRICA	10	0	0	0	0	1	0	0	0	0	0	2	2	2	0	2	2	0	0	0	0	0
JAPAN	6	0	0	0	0	0	0	0	0	0	0	0	0	1	2	2	0	0	0	0	0	0
OTHER ASIA+AFR.	8	0	0	0	0	0	0	0	0	1	0	0	1	1	0	0	0	0	0	0	0	0
BLACK AFRICA	3	0	0	0	0	0	0	0	0	0	0	0	0	0	2	2	0	1	0	0	0	0
ARAB WORLD	2	0	0	0	0	0	0	0	0	1	0	0	0	2	0	0	0	0	0	0	0	0
INDIA	4	0	0	0	0	0	0	0	0	0	0	2	2	1	2	2	1	1	0	1	0	0
PHILIPPINES	5	0	0	0	1	0	0	0	0	0	0	0	0	0	0	0	0	0	0	0	0	0
OTHER E. ASIA	0	0	0	0	0	0	0	0	0	0	0	0	0	1	1	1	1	0	1	1	0	0
OTHER ASIA	3	0	0	0	0	0	0	0	0	0	0	0	1	0	0	0	0	0	0	0	0	0

CHAPTER 2- THE EXPANSION OF PARENT SYSTEMS
SECTION 3- THE FLOW OF MANUFACTURING BY CHARACTERISTIC OF PARENT SYSTEM
TABLE I2- SYSTEMS IN "ORGANIZATIONAL STAGE III-ID" IN 1966
CLASSIFIED BY PERIOD SYSTEM FIRST OPERATED A MANUFACTURING SUBSIDIARY
IN SPECIFIED COUNTRIES AND REGIONS

COUNTRY OR REGION	PRE 1968	PRE 1901	1901-13	1914-19	1920-24	1925-29	1930-34	1935-39	1940-45	1946-50	1951-53	1954-55	1956-57	1958-59	1960-61	1962	1963	1964	1965	1966	1967	UNK
OUTSIDE U.S.	91	6	12	10	9	15	8	9	2	4	7	4	2	2	1	0	0	0	0	0	0	0
OUT. U.S. + CANADA	91	5	10	6	12	16	9	8	2	4	8	3	6	4	2	0	0	0	0	0	0	0
OUT. WEST. HEMIS.	91	5	5	5	11	17	9	9	1	4	8	3	6	6	5	0	0	0	0	0	0	0
OUT. WHITE CMEALTH	91	4	5	5	11	10	9	9	4	8	8	4	8	8	3	1	0	0	0	0	0	0
OUT. DEVLPED WORLD	90	0	1	3	4	7	8	15	5	8	6	4	9	9	8	1	0	1	1	1	1	0
CANADA	87	1	12	11	5	16	8	6	2	5	5	5	4	2	2	1	0	1	0	0	1	0
LATIN AMERICA	88	0	1	1	4	6	10	15	6	8	6	4	8	8	9	3	4	1	1	1	0	1
C. AMER.+CARIB.	85	0	0	0	1	3	7	12	2	3	2	3	10	9	0	4	0	1	0	4	0	1
CUBA	21	0	0	0	1	1	1	1	2	3	2	1	3	2	9	1	4	0	2	0	3	0
MEXICO	81	0	0	1	0	2	5	7	5	10	7	3	8	11	9	2	3	2	0	4	3	1
OTHER	42	0	1	0	3	5	1	1	1	1	0	1	4	2	6	4	3	1	0	1	1	0
S. AMERICA	82	0	1	0	3	5	4	9	8	8	7	4	8	11	6	1	2	3	2	1	1	1
ARGENTINA	51	0	1	0	0	3	5	6	2	5	1	2	4	4	6	6	3	2	2	2	1	0
BRAZIL	63	0	0	0	1	3	0	6	5	5	8	2	6	9	4	1	2	3	3	1	0	0
PERU	21	0	0	0	1	3	0	0	2	2	0	2	3	0	7	0	1	1	0	2	0	0
COLOMBIA	39	0	0	0	0	0	0	1	4	6	3	2	1	5	3	3	5	4	4	1	0	0
VENEZUELA	44	0	0	0	0	0	1	1	6	2	1	4	5	6	9	0	1	1	2	2	1	0
OTHER	27	0	0	0	2	2	0	1	2	3	1	1	5	1	4	1	1	1	4	1	1	1
EUROPE	91	5	5	1	12	16	5	9	1	4	9	2	7	8	4	2	2	0	0	1	0	0
EFTA	86	3	4	1	6	15	8	9	5	5	6	4	4	5	4	3	3	1	1	1	0	0
U.K.	83	3	3	1	5	15	8	10	0	1	5	4	4	5	4	2	4	1	1	1	1	0
SCANDINAVIA	28	0	1	0	2	3	0	0	1	2	1	2	3	0	4	2	2	2	0	2	1	0
SWITZERLAND	13	0	0	0	0	1	0	3	0	0	1	0	0	1	1	0	1	1	0	0	1	0
OTHER EFTA	14	0	0	1	1	0	0	0	1	4	0	0	1	3	1	0	3	2	2	0	1	0
EUROP- COMMUNITY	89	4	3	0	9	6	6	3	4	4	11	5	7	11	11	3	3	2	0	0	1	1
FRANCE	69	2	3	1	6	1	6	2	0	0	5	2	2	10	13	4	2	0	1	1	1	0
GERMANY	67	3	2	0	5	4	6	2	1	4	4	6	6	5	9	3	5	2	2	1	1	0
ITALY	62	0	3	1	2	0	0	2	1	0	2	0	3	9	9	7	6	2	1	1	2	0
BELGIUM + LUX	36	0	0	0	2	2	1	2	1	2	5	2	3	7	4	3	3	2	2	1	1	0
NETHERLANDS	45	0	0	0	2	2	3	0	1	3	1	2	1	1	6	5	3	5	2	2	1	0
SPAIN	45	0	0	0	2	3	0	0	1	1	2	1	4	5	7	5	7	5	7	0	4	0
GREECE + TURKEY	12	0	0	0	0	1	0	1	0	0	2	0	1	2	2	2	0	1	1	2	1	1
OTHER EUROPE	16	0	0	0	0	2	0	2	0	2	2	1	1	2	2	3	2	3	2	0	0	0
EUROPE EX. U.K.	90	4	3	0	11	8	7	2	2	6	9	5	6	11	8	3	2	2	0	0	1	1
SOUTHERN DOMINIONS	77	0	1	2	1	5	6	9	3	3	6	5	5	9	9	1	3	1	2	4	2	0
S. AFRICA +RHOD.	40	0	0	1	1	2	5	3	3	3	3	1	2	5	3	1	4	1	1	3	0	0
AUSTRALIA + N.Z.	68	0	1	1	4	4	5	7	2	3	5	5	4	9	8	1	3	3	1	2	2	1
ASIA + OTHER AFRICA	75	0	3	3	3	3	1	4	0	6	3	5	8	4	15	6	6	6	3	0	2	1
JAPAN	49	0	0	1	1	1	1	1	0	0	5	0	4	1	10	7	7	1	1	1	3	0
OTHER ASIA+AFR.	59	0	2	0	0	3	3	3	0	6	0	6	5	5	10	6	4	3	1	1	3	1
BLACK AFRICA	14	0	0	0	0	0	0	0	1	0	0	0	0	4	3	5	3	3	1	3	3	1
ARAB WORLD	14	0	0	0	0	0	0	0	0	0	2	1	2	2	2	0	1	1	1	1	1	0
INDIA	29	0	0	0	1	1	1	1	0	2	0	1	1	4	2	3	2	3	2	0	0	1
PHILIPPINES	23	0	0	0	0	2	0	2	1	1	1	1	4	5	4	6	5	1	0	0	1	0
OTHER E. ASIA	14	0	0	2	0	0	0	0	0	1	2	1	2	1	3	1	2	1	1	1	3	1
OTHER ASIA	27	0	0	0	0	1	0	2	0	4	0	3	1	5	2	1	0	0	3	0	0	1

CHAPTER 2— THE EXPANSION OF PARENT SYSTEMS
SECTION 3— THE FLOW OF MANUFACTURING BY CHARACTERISTIC OF PARENT SYSTEM
TABLE 13— SYSTEMS IN "ORGANIZATIONAL STAGE III-OTHER" IN 1966
CLASSIFIED BY PERIOD SYSTEM FIRST OPERATED A MANUFACTURING SUBSIDIARY
IN SPECIFIED COUNTRIES AND REGIONS

COUNTRY OR REGION	PRE 1968	PRE 1901	1901 -13	1914 -19	1920 -24	1925 -29	1930 -34	1935 -39	1940 -45	1946 -50	1951 -53	1954 -55	1956 -57	1958 -59	1960 -61	1962	1963	1964	1965	1966	1967	UNK
OUTSIDE U.S.	58	10	5	12	4	7	3	1	5	5	0	0	1	4	1	0	0	0	0	0	0	0
OUT. U.S. + CANADA	58	10	4	5	5	6	3	0	7	6	2	3	1	4	1	0	0	0	0	0	0	0
OUT. WEST. HEMIS.	58	9	4	5	5	6	3	1	6	6	2	4	2	5	2	0	0	0	0	0	0	0
OUT. WHITE CWEALTH	58	8	3	5	4	3	1	3	9	6	3	5	2	7	1	0	0	0	0	0	0	0
OUT. DEVLPED WORLD	57	3	1	3	2	4	1	3	9	6	3	5	3	6	4	0	0	1	2	0	0	0
CANADA	56	4	3	10	1	5	6	3	3	4	4	2	1	4	3	2	2	0	0	0	0	0
LATIN AMERICA	57	3	1	3	1	3	0	3	10	5	3	5	5	6	4	1	2	1	2	0	0	0
C. AMER.+CARIB.	53	1	0	1	1	2	1	4	6	3	7	5	2	1	3	0	2	2	2	0	0	2
CUBA	7	0	1	0	0	1	0	2	0	0	0	0	0	1	0	0	0	0	0	0	1	0
MEXICO	52	0	1	0	1	2	1	2	3	4	5	6	4	7	3	1	2	3	4	0	0	0
OTHER	22	2	2	3	0	3	2	3	1	0	3	0	5	3	3	0	1	1	3	0	0	0
S. AMERICA	51	0	0	1	1	1	0	1	8	5	4	6	5	4	4	2	1	0	0	0	0	0
ARGENTINA	35	0	2	3	0	2	0	2	4	2	2	2	2	2	7	2	1	0	1	0	1	0
BRAZIL	37	0	1	0	1	2	0	1	7	7	3	2	6	6	4	3	0	0	0	0	0	1
PERU	15	1	0	0	0	0	0	0	0	0	0	1	0	0	1	1	1	1	1	1	1	1
COLOMBIA	22	0	0	0	0	1	1	0	1	5	0	1	2	2	1	1	2	3	1	2	0	1
VENEZUELA	29	0	0	1	1	0	0	0	2	2	0	2	3	4	5	1	3	0	2	1	1	1
OTHER	21	1	1	1	1	0	0	2	2	1	3	1	2	0	2	0	1	1	1	2	1	1
EUROPE	58	9	4	4	4	6	4	0	1	8	1	5	2	6	3	0	2	0	2	0	0	0
EFTA	58	6	4	4	3	6	3	3	1	5	2	4	3	4	4	2	1	1	3	0	0	0
U.K.	57	5	5	3	2	6	3	3	1	5	2	4	1	4	5	1	1	1	4	1	1	0
SCANDINAVIA	24	1	1	0	0	1	0	0	1	1	0	1	0	1	1	3	1	4	0	1	1	0
SWITZERLAND	13	0	0	1	0	0	1	0	0	0	0	0	3	0	3	2	1	2	0	0	0	0
OTHER EFTA	16	0	1	0	1	1	1	0	0	1	0	0	0	3	2	1	2	0	0	1	1	1
EUROP. COMMUNITY	57	6	0	2	4	3	3	0	0	3	4	4	3	11	8	3	2	2	1	0	0	0
FRANCE	47	6	2	1	4	4	2	2	0	3	2	1	2	4	7	2	1	3	1	0	1	0
GERMANY	46	4	1	1	0	2	2	1	0	2	1	4	4	5	9	2	3	2	1	1	0	0
ITALY	44	1	0	0	1	0	1	0	0	1	3	3	1	5	10	2	2	3	1	1	1	0
BELGIUM + LUX	27	0	3	1	1	2	1	0	1	2	0	0	1	4	4	0	4	2	3	1	1	1
NETHERLANDS	32	0	0	0	0	1	0	0	0	0	1	2	1	6	6	2	2	3	2	0	0	0
SPAIN	35	0	0	1	2	1	1	1	0	2	2	0	2	2	4	2	1	2	3	5	3	0
GREECE + TURKEY	15	0	2	2	0	0	0	0	2	0	2	2	1	2	6	1	0	3	0	0	1	0
OTHER EUROPE	15	2	2	0	1	1	1	0	0	0	0	1	0	2	1	0	2	0	0	1	0	0
EUROPE EX. U.K.	58	6	4	4	3	3	4	0	3	3	5	4	3	10	8	1	2	0	0	0	0	0
SOUTHERN DOMINIONS	52	1	1	0	1	2	2	4	2	2	3	4	3	5	3	2	2	3	1	1	2	1
S. AFRICA +RHOD.	30	1	0	2	2	0	0	2	2	2	0	1	1	3	4	1	4	2	0	1	2	2
AUSTRALIA + N.Z.	50	0	1	2	0	5	2	3	0	2	3	4	4	3	5	5	2	2	2	1	1	1
ASIA + OTHER AFRICA	45	0	1	0	2	1	1	0	0	3	4	7	3	8	8	4	2	6	2	1	0	0
JAPAN	36	0	0	1	0	0	0	0	0	1	2	2	3	8	8	1	2	0	2	2	2	1
OTHER ASIA+AFR.	38	0	0	0	2	5	0	0	0	0	0	0	0	3	3	1	1	3	2	2	0	0
BLACK AFRICA	10	0	0	1	0	0	1	0	1	1	0	0	0	0	1	1	1	0	1	1	0	1
ARAB WORLD	9	0	0	0	0	0	0	0	0	2	1	1	1	0	3	1	2	1	2	1	0	1
INDIA	22	0	0	0	0	2	0	0	0	0	2	0	0	1	6	2	1	4	1	2	1	1
PHILIPPINES	13	0	0	1	1	0	0	0	0	1	1	0	1	2	2	2	2	2	1	0	1	1
OTHER E. ASIA	13	0	1	1	1	2	1	0	0	0	0	0	0	0	0	0	0	0	1	1	1	1
OTHER ASIA	22	0	0	0	0	1	1	1	0	2	0	2	0	2	1	2	0	0	2	2	2	2

PERIOD

CHAPTER 2- THE EXPANSION OF PARENT SYSTEMS
SECTION 3- THE FLOW OF MANUFACTURING BY CHARACTERISTIC OF PARENT SYSTEM
TABLE J1- SYSTEMS WITH LOW "PRODUCT DIVERSITY IN THE U.S." IN 1966
CLASSIFIED BY PERIOD SYSTEM FIRST OPERATED A MANUFACTURING SUBSIDIARY
IN SPECIFIED COUNTRIES AND REGIONS

COUNTRY OR REGION	PRE 1968	PRE 1901	1901-13	1914-19	1920-24	1925-29	1930-34	1935-39	1940-45	1946-50	1951-53	1954-55	1956-57	1958-59	1960-61	1962	1963	1964	1965	1966	1967	UNK
OUTSIDE U.S.	94	8	9	17	7	16	7	7	3	6	3	4	2	3	3	2	0	0	0	0	0	0
OUT. U.S. + CANADA	94	8	8	6	10	15	9	8	4	7	5	8	5	5	3	3	0	0	0	0	0	0
OUT. WEST. HEMIS.	94	8	3	5	11	15	7	8	2	5	5	7	7	6	5	3	0	0	0	0	0	0
OUT. WHITE CWEALTH	94	3	3	5	9	10	6	11	4	7	5	10	7	6	4	4	1	1	0	0	0	0
OUT. DEVLPED WORLD	92	1	2	2	4	4	5	15	4	10	8	9	8	4	10	2	1	2	2	0	0	0
CANADA	89	1	10	18	3	14	7	7	3	4	6	3	6	2	2	2	1	2	0	1	1	0
LATIN AMERICA	90	1	2	2	3	4	4	15	4	9	8	9	8	4	9	4	4	2	1	0	0	1
C. AMER.+CARIB.	86	1	1	1	0	2	1	11	2	8	2	2	3	4	10	5	4	0	0	1	0	1
CUBA	19	0	0	0	0	0	2	1	0	0	1	0	1	1	1	0	0	2	1	0	1	0
MEXICO	80	0	2	1	0	2	1	7	4	8	6	9	8	6	9	3	3	0	3	1	0	1
OTHER	38	0	0	0	0	0	3	3	1	0	1	0	2	1	5	2	2	4	1	2	1	0
S. AMERICA	77	0	2	1	4	4	8	8	6	7	8	4	4	2	7	5	3	5	7	1	0	1
ARGENTINA	41	0	2	1	1	3	5	5	2	0	1	3	8	1	5	3	3	1	0	1	0	0
BRAZIL	52	0	2	1	1	1	2	2	4	6	2	2	2	2	7	5	3	0	1	0	0	2
PERU	21	0	0	0	1	0	0	2	0	0	0	1	4	6	5	6	2	3	3	0	0	1
COLOMBIA	34	0	0	0	1	0	1	1	3	2	2	1	1	2	4	1	2	2	0	2	0	0
VENEZUELA	38	0	0	0	1	0	1	1	2	4	2	3	3	5	7	2	5	1	1	1	1	1
OTHER	20	0	0	0	1	0	0	0	2	2	1	1	2	1	2	2	0	1	0	2	2	2
EUROPE	94	8	3	3	9	13	7	10	1	6	6	7	6	7	5	3	0	2	2	0	0	0
EFTA	89	5	3	3	4	14	8	11	1	5	4	5	5	5	4	5	3	1	3	0	0	0
U.K.	87	4	4	2	3	13	8	13	1	5	4	5	5	5	5	3	3	1	0	1	2	0
SCANDINAVIA	28	1	0	1	0	3	1	0	1	2	1	2	0	1	3	0	1	0	1	1	1	1
SWITZERLAND	11	0	0	0	0	0	0	1	0	2	0	0	1	0	2	2	2	2	1	1	1	0
OTHER EFTA	16	0	1	0	1	0	0	0	0	0	1	0	1	3	1	0	0	1	1	1	2	1
EUROP. COMMUNITY	92	2	1	1	10	6	4	4	1	4	5	6	8	14	11	4	3	3	1	2	1	0
FRANCE	68	2	1	0	9	5	3	2	0	0	4	2	2	9	9	6	2	2	0	3	0	1
GERMANY	67	5	1	1	3	7	4	1	0	6	2	4	8	7	7	8	4	3	2	3	1	0
ITALY	63	1	0	0	1	2	1	2	1	0	6	1	5	8	8	8	6	8	8	1	2	1
BELGIUM + LUX	39	0	0	1	0	1	1	3	2	1	1	1	1	8	5	1	1	3	5	2	0	0
NETHERLANDS	34	0	0	0	1	1	2	0	0	3	0	2	2	9	4	4	5	3	2	6	0	0
SPAIN	42	0	0	0	1	2	0	0	0	0	2	2	2	3	4	2	5	4	6	8	4	1
GREECE + TURKEY	11	0	0	0	0	0	0	1	0	0	0	0	1	0	1	1	0	2	3	1	1	0
OTHER EUROPE	14	1	0	0	0	1	0	0	1	5	2	3	1	0	1	2	1	2	1	0	0	0
EUROPE EX. U.K.	94	6	1	2	9	8	5	3	1	5	6	9	7	14	10	5	1	2	0	0	0	2
SOUTHERN DOMINIONS	82	0	2	3	3	3	5	9	4	3	5	8	5	11	9	4	2	0	1	3	1	1
S. AFRICA +RHOD.	49	0	0	1	2	1	4	6	3	3	2	4	1	6	4	4	4	1	1	2	0	2
AUSTRALIA + N.Z.	72	0	2	2	2	4	2	3	3	5	5	5	6	10	8	4	4	0	1	3	1	1
ASIA + OTHER AFRICA	66	0	0	0	2	2	2	3	0	5	3	5	8	1	11	6	8	4	1	1	3	0
JAPAN	45	0	0	0	0	2	1	0	0	0	5	1	5	1	9	8	8	4	1	1	0	0
OTHER ASIA+AFR.	53	0	0	0	2	1	2	0	0	5	4	5	4	4	8	5	6	4	1	2	3	1
BLACK AFRICA	12	0	0	0	0	0	0	0	1	0	0	0	1	0	0	0	2	2	1	0	1	1
ARAB WORLD	15	0	0	0	0	0	0	0	0	1	0	1	1	4	3	2	2	1	0	1	1	1
INDIA	25	0	0	0	0	0	1	1	0	1	2	1	2	0	2	3	5	1	3	1	1	1
PHILIPPINES	23	0	0	0	1	0	0	0	0	2	0	0	1	4	1	3	6	0	0	1	0	1
OTHER E. ASIA	13	0	0	1	1	1	0	2	2	0	0	0	1	5	1	1	1	2	1	2	3	1
OTHER ASIA	28	0	0	2	0	1	1	0	0	2	0	2	2	3	5	3	2	0	0	2	0	2

CHAPTER 2- THE EXPANSION OF PARENT SYSTEMS
SECTION 3- THE FLOW OF MANUFACTURING BY CHARACTERISTIC OF PARENT SYSTEM
TABLE J2- SYSTEMS WITH HIGH "PRODUCT DIVERSITY IN THE U.S." IN 1966
CLASSIFIED BY PERIOD SYSTEM FIRST OPERATED A MANUFACTURING SUBSIDIARY
IN SPECIFIED COUNTRIES AND REGIONS

PERIOD

COUNTRY OR REGION	PRE 1968	PRE 1901	1901 -13	1914 -19	1920 -24	1925 -29	1930 -34	1935 -39	1940 -45	1946 -50	1951 -53	1954 -55	1956 -57	1958 -59	1960 -61	1962	1963	1964	1965	1966	1967	UNK
OUTSIDE U.S.	93	11	13	9	8	14	6	6	5	3	5	3	2	5	3	3	0	0	0	0	0	0
OUT. U.S. + CANADA	93	10	7	7	8	14	5	5	5	7	8	5	5	7	7	0	2	1	0	0	0	0
OUT. WEST. HEMIS.	93	9	7	6	6	16	3	3	1	7	7	6	4	9	7	1	2	0	0	0	0	0
OUT. WHITE CWEALTH	93	8	5	7	7	8	9	1	6	6	6	6	7	12	3	1	2	0	0	0	0	0
OUT. DEVLPED WORLD	93	2	1	5	2	8	8	4	11	9	3	6	6	15	6	1	2	1	2	1	1	1
CANADA	89	4	10	6	4	13	11	6	4	5	5	6	1	4	5	2	2	1	1	2	0	0
LATIN AMERICA	92	2	1	3	2	5	10	5	13	9	3	5	7	14	6	1	2	2	0	1	0	1
C. AMER.+CARIB.	86	0	0	1	1	3	8	6	8	9	6	2	11	14	4	0	0	0	1	0	1	1
CUBA	17	0	0	1	1	2	1	1	2	0	0	3	0	2	0	3	2	1	0	0	1	1
MEXICO	82	0	0	0	0	0	6	5	8	10	5	3	7	15	6	4	4	1	3	1	1	2
OTHER	34	0	0	3	0	6	0	4	1	2	1	1	3	2	0	4	2	3	4	2	0	0
S. AMERICA	83	2	1	3	1	4	3	4	14	8	4	1	9	13	6	2	2	3	1	1	1	0
ARGENTINA	58	0	0	3	0	2	0	5	8	8	1	3	7	5	7	2	2	1	2	2	0	1
BRAZIL	61	0	0	2	0	2	0	7	7	8	6	2	8	10	3	2	2	1	1	1	0	0
PERU	19	1	0	0	0	1	0	3	3	2	1	2	2	0	1	0	1	0	1	0	0	0
COLOMBIA	39	0	0	0	0	0	0	5	5	6	2	2	2	2	6	1	0	1	2	2	2	0
VENEZUELA	46	0	0	0	0	2	0	5	4	4	4	3	7	7	7	1	1	1	2	1	3	0
OTHER	34	1	1	1	2	2	0	1	2	4	1	2	2	0	4	2	2	2	6	2	1	0
EUROPE	93	9	7	2	7	16	3	2	1	7	6	3	6	12	7	1	2	2	1	1	1	0
EFTA	89	6	6	2	5	14	5	2	0	6	5	4	4	5	7	4	5	1	2	1	1	0
U.K.	83	6	5	2	4	14	6	3	0	7	5	4	4	5	6	2	2	3	1	1	3	0
SCANDINAVIA	34	0	0	0	2	1	1	0	0	2	1	0	0	2	4	2	4	4	2	3	2	1
SWITZERLAND	20	2	2	0	0	1	0	3	0	0	0	0	0	3	4	0	3	3	1	1	1	0
OTHER EFTA	19	0	0	0	1	1	0	2	1	0	1	0	0	1	1	1	1	1	4	0	1	0
EUROP. COMMUNITY	92	6	2	4	8	8	7	6	0	3	10	6	5	12	5	2	2	7	2	2	2	1
FRANCE	70	5	3	2	3	4	2	4	0	3	3	3	3	7	7	1	3	3	2	2	0	0
GERMANY	70	4	1	1	6	3	6	2	0	3	3	3	0	3	16	3	3	3	4	4	0	0
ITALY	61	2	1	2	1	1	0	1	1	2	1	5	3	9	14	3	5	4	0	2	0	0
BELGIUM + LUX	39	0	0	2	2	3	3	1	0	0	1	1	0	3	8	6	6	2	2	1	2	0
NETHERLANDS	41	1	1	2	1	3	2	1	1	2	3	3	1	8	8	4	4	5	3	2	3	0
SPAIN	51	0	0	0	0	0	0	0	0	3	1	2	2	2	8	4	4	5	1	1	4	0
GREECE + TURKEY	21	0	0	1	1	1	1	0	0	1	3	1	4	1	6	2	0	1	1	1	3	1
OTHER EUROPE	22	2	1	0	0	4	8	1	2	1	1	0	0	1	2	1	2	1	2	2	0	0
EUROPE EX. U.K.	92	6	4	6	8	8	8	0	1	4	9	4	4	15	13	1	4	1	1	0	0	1
SOUTHERN DOMINIONS	72	1	0	2	0	7	6	5	1	3	5	5	5	7	7	3	5	5	5	2	2	0
S. AFRICA +RHOD.	37	1	0	1	1	1	2	2	2	4	1	2	2	3	5	4	2	2	1	3	1	0
AUSTRALIA + N.Z.	66	0	0	2	0	7	5	6	1	6	5	5	5	7	6	4	5	4	4	1	4	1
ASIA + OTHER AFRICA	80	0	0	3	0	7	0	1	0	1	5	6	5	6	13	8	5	4	4	4	2	2
JAPAN	54	0	0	1	0	2	0	0	0	1	6	2	3	2	11	7	4	3	5	2	1	1
OTHER ASIA+AFR.	65	0	1	3	0	7	4	0	0	5	0	7	2	5	11	6	3	3	3	1	1	1
BLACK AFRICA	17	0	0	0	0	0	0	1	1	0	1	1	1	0	5	1	1	2	1	2	2	2
ARAB WORLD	14	0	0	0	0	0	0	0	0	2	2	0	0	3	0	7	0	1	2	2	0	0
INDIA	33	0	0	0	0	3	0	1	1	1	2	0	2	4	8	4	2	2	2	1	1	1
PHILIPPINES	30	0	0	1	0	2	0	1	0	0	1	7	1	2	2	2	2	0	2	1	1	0
OTHER E. ASIA	15	0	0	0	0	2	0	1	1	0	0	0	0	0	5	1	2	2	3	1	1	1
OTHER ASIA	27	0	0	2	0	2	0	1	0	4	0	2	2	5	0	1	0	2	1	1	1	1

CHAPTER 2- THE EXPANSION OF PARENT SYSTEMS
SECTION 3- THE FLOW OF MANUFACTURING BY CHARACTERISTIC OF PARENT SYSTEM
TABLE K1- SYSTEMS WITH LOW "PRODUCT DIVERSITY ABROAD" IN 1966
CLASSIFIED BY PERIOD SYSTEM FIRST OPERATED A MANUFACTURING SUBSIDIARY
IN SPECIFIED COUNTRIES AND REGIONS

COUNTRY OR REGION	PRE 1968	PRE 1901	1901 -13	1914 -19	1920 -24	1925 -29	1930 -34	1935 -39	1940 -45	1946 -50	1951 -53	1954 -55	1956 -57	1958 -59	1960 -61	1962	1963	1964	1965	1966	1967	UNK
OUTSIDE U.S.	89	4	9	13	9	14	6	5	4	7	4	6	3	4	1	0	0	0	0	0	0	0
OUT. U.S. + CANADA	89	3	6	5	11	12	8	5	7	7	3	8	8	4	2	0	0	0	0	0	0	0
OUT. WEST. HEMIS.	89	3	5	5	11	12	5	6	6	6	4	11	8	8	4	0	0	0	0	0	0	0
OUT. WHITE CWEALTH	89	2	3	3	10	9	6	8	4	4	7	11	8	8	3	0	0	0	0	0	0	0
OUT. DEVLPED WORLD	88	0	1	1	3	5	8	12	5	5	5	10	8	9	8	1	2	2	0	1	0	1
CANADA	80	1	8	13	4	14	3	6	3	2	6	3	5	3	2	1	2	2	0	0	1	0
LATIN AMERICA	86	0	1	1	3	4	6	12	6	5	4	9	8	8	9	2	2	2	0	1	0	1
C. AMER.+CARIB.	81	0	0	0	0	0	7	11	8	8	2	7	5	6	6	5	4	4	0	1	0	1
CUBA	20	0	1	0	0	3	1	1	1	1	1	1	1	1	1	0	0	0	0	0	0	0
MEXICO	76	0	0	0	0	3	4	6	9	9	3	8	4	7	7	3	4	4	3	3	1	1
OTHER	29	0	0	0	4	3	1	1	0	5	1	0	4	1	6	3	4	1	1	2	1	0
S. AMERICA	74	0	1	1	4	3	2	7	8	5	3	6	7	12	2	2	4	1	1	1	0	1
ARGENTINA	38	0	0	1	1	2	2	2	2	2	1	3	2	7	1	3	1	0	2	1	0	0
BRAZIL	46	0	0	0	1	1	0	5	5	4	5	3	3	3	6	0	2	2	2	0	0	1
PERU	18	0	0	0	1	2	1	1	1	1	2	2	2	9	6	1	0	1	1	1	0	0
COLOMBIA	28	0	0	1	2	0	1	1	1	1	0	5	3	0	2	1	2	0	2	2	0	0
VENEZUELA	33	0	0	0	0	0	1	1	2	2	2	2	2	2	5	1	1	1	1	1	2	0
OTHER	16	0	0	0	0	1	0	0	1	1	1	0	0	3	7	1	0	1	3	0	1	0
EUROPE	89	3	5	2	10	12	5	7	5	5	4	7	8	9	5	2	2	0	0	1	0	0
EFTA	80	2	4	2	5	12	5	9	5	5	3	5	5	3	3	3	1	1	1	1	0	0
U.K.	76	2	3	2	4	13	5	10	6	6	3	5	5	3	2	3	1	1	0	1	1	0
SCANDINAVIA	20	0	1	1	1	1	1	1	1	1	0	1	1	0	2	1	2	2	1	2	0	0
SWITZERLAND	6	0	0	0	0	1	0	0	1	0	0	0	0	0	2	3	0	0	0	0	2	0
OTHER EFTA	11	0	2	0	2	2	0	2	0	1	0	1	1	2	0	3	1	1	1	2	0	0
EUROP. COMMUNITY	88	2	2	2	4	4	5	2	4	4	7	8	8	10	16	3	5	3	1	3	0	0
FRANCE	66	1	2	1	3	3	5	2	4	4	3	2	4	4	12	2	3	4	2	4	1	1
GERMANY	61	1	1	1	6	6	4	5	0	0	2	3	8	9	4	6	5	3	2	0	1	0
ITALY	52	2	2	0	3	1	1	1	0	2	7	1	3	7	10	1	3	3	2	1	2	0
BELGIUM + LUX	29	0	1	1	1	1	1	3	2	3	1	1	1	1	1	1	2	2	4	1	1	0
NETHERLANDS	30	0	2	0	1	1	3	1	3	1	2	0	0	4	4	4	3	3	4	1	0	0
SPAIN	33	0	0	0	0	1	1	0	1	1	4	3	3	3	3	1	2	1	3	2	0	0
GREECE + TURKEY	12	0	0	0	0	0	0	1	0	2	1	0	0	0	4	1	0	1	0	1	4	0
OTHER EUROPE	9	0	0	0	0	0	0	2	3	3	1	0	0	1	3	2	2	2	0	0	1	0
EUROPE EX. U.K.	88	2	2	2	10	5	5	2	1	3	0	7	7	13	12	2	4	2	0	1	0	0
SOUTHERN DOMINIONS	75	0	3	3	3	3	4	9	4	4	5	5	4	14	6	4	3	1	2	3	0	0
S. AFRICA +RHOD.	44	0	1	1	1	0	3	3	5	5	2	2	1	4	5	4	4	1	1	4	0	0
AUSTRALIA + N.Z.	63	0	2	2	0	3	6	6	4	4	5	4	5	14	4	10	1	2	2	4	0	0
ASIA + OTHER AFRICA	69	0	1	1	2	3	1	4	6	6	4	4	7	9	9	7	2	1	3	2	2	1
JAPAN	43	0	0	0	1	1	1	1	0	0	5	4	4	8	7	4	1	2	3	1	0	1
OTHER ASIA+AFR.	50	0	0	0	0	3	0	3	6	6	1	5	4	4	2	4	5	2	0	3	2	1
BLACK AFRICA	9	0	0	0	0	0	0	0	0	0	1	0	1	0	2	1	1	2	0	0	1	0
ARAB WORLD	13	0	0	0	0	0	0	0	2	2	0	0	1	4	1	0	4	2	3	1	2	0
INDIA	24	0	0	0	1	1	0	1	1	1	2	3	1	3	2	3	3	3	3	3	1	0
PHILIPPINES	22	0	0	0	0	2	1	0	2	2	0	0	1	2	1	2	4	4	0	1	2	0
OTHER E. ASIA	9	0	0	0	0	0	0	0	0	0	0	3	3	5	1	3	1	1	0	0	1	0
OTHER ASIA	23	0	0	0	0	1	0	3	2	2	0	2	1	3	4	0	3	2	0	1	0	0

CHAPTER 2- THE EXPANSION OF PARENT SYSTEMS
SECTION 3- THE FLOW OF MANUFACTURING BY CHARACTERISTIC OF PARENT SYSTEM
TABLE K2- SYSTEMS WITH HIGH "PRODUCT DIVERSITY ABROAD" IN 1966
CLASSIFIED BY PERIOD SYSTEM FIRST OPERATED A MANUFACTURING SUBSIDIARY
IN SPECIFIED COUNTRIES AND REGIONS

COUNTRY OR REGION	PRE 1968	PRE 1901	1901 -13	1914 -19	1920 -24	1925 -29	1930 -34	1935 -39	1940 -42	1946 -50	1951 -53	1954 -55	1956 -57	1958 -59	1960 -61	1962	1963	1964	1965	1966	1967	UNK
OUTSIDE U.S.	98	15	13	13	6	16	7	8	4	2	4	1	1	4	4	0	0	0	0	0	0	0
OUT. U.S. + CANADA	98	15	13	8	7	17	6	5	4	7	9	2	2	6	4	0	0	0	0	0	0	0
OUT. WEST. HEMIS.	98	14	5	6	6	19	5	5	0	6	8	5	3	7	8	1	0	0	0	0	0	1
OUT. WHITE CWEALTH	98	12	5	8	6	9	8	4	0	9	6	5	6	10	4	1	0	0	0	0	0	0
OUT. DEVLPED WORLD	97	3	2	6	3	7	5	7	9	14	6	5	6	10	8	2	1	0	3	0	3	3
CANADA	98	4	12	11	3	13	10	7	4	7	5	6	2	3	5	3	2	1	0	0	0	0
LATIN AMERICA	96	3	2	4	2	5	6	8	11	13	7	5	7	10	6	3	1	0	3	0	0	0
C. AMER.+CARIB.	10	1	0	2	2	2	5	3	7	9	10	5	11	9	8	4	0	1	0	0	0	1
CUBA	80	0	1	1	1	1	1	1	1	2	0	4	1	1	0	0	3	0	7	1	2	2
MEXICO	43	0	0	1	1	0	4	3	7	11	8	4	9	11	8	3	4	4	8	3	1	3
OTHER	86	2	3	0	0	5	2	5	1	10	9	3	3	3	3	2	1	2	0	0	0	0
S. AMERICA	61	0	2	3	2	5	3	4	12	4	2	2	10	6	6	1	1	1	1	1	0	2
ARGENTINA	67	0	0	3	5	3	0	5	4	6	8	3	7	3	3	1	1	0	1	1	0	0
BRAZIL	22	2	0	4	1	4	0	5	6	10	1	2	11	9	3	0	1	1	2	2	0	1
PERU	45	1	0	0	0	0	1	0	3	1	2	1	3	0	8	2	6	1	2	2	2	1
COLOMBIA	51	0	0	0	1	0	0	0	3	7	1	6	1	2	7	1	3	7	1	3	1	0
VENEZUELA	38	1	1	1	2	0	0	1	2	6	1	1	4	9	4	1	2	0	4	2	1	1
EUROPE	98	14	5	3	6	17	5	5	0	8	8	3	4	10	7	2	0	0	1	0	0	0
EFTA	98	9	5	3	4	16	7	6	0	6	7	4	4	7	8	4	2	3	3	0	1	0
U.K.	94	8	6	2	3	14	9	6	0	6	1	4	4	7	9	2	1	2	4	2	1	0
SCANDINAVIA	25	1	1	0	1	3	1	0	0	3	1	0	3	3	5	1	1	3	1	1	0	1
SWITZERLAND	24	0	0	0	0	1	0	3	0	1	1	0	1	3	6	3	0	1	6	1	0	1
OTHER EFTA	96	10	2	1	2	10	6	3	0	3	8	6	5	16	12	3	2	1	0	2	0	0
EUROP. COMMUNITY	72	6	1	0	5	5	4	2	1	3	4	3	3	10	13	3	1	5	2	2	0	0
FRANCE	76	8	1	1	5	7	4	1	0	0	3	7	3	8	13	3	1	3	4	0	2	0
GERMANY	72	1	1	0	1	2	0	2	1	2	2	5	5	8	12	4	6	3	6	5	1	0
ITALY	49	1	1	0	1	3	7	1	1	1	2	2	1	5	10	2	2	3	3	2	1	1
BELGIUM + LUX	45	0	0	0	2	3	2	2	1	3	2	5	3	8	8	3	6	3	5	2	2	0
NETHERLANDS	60	0	0	1	0	2	3	1	1	0	1	1	1	5	5	3	2	6	8	10	0	0
SPAIN	20	0	0	0	0	1	0	0	0	0	1	4	2	2	2	6	5	0	3	2	3	0
GREECE + TURKEY	27	2	2	1	0	2	1	0	2	2	1	1	1	0	2	2	3	3	1	3	0	1
OTHER EUROPE	98	3	2	2	0	1	8	1	1	6	8	0	4	2	11	4	1	1	4	0	0	0
EUROPE EX. U.K.	98	10	3	3	5	11	8	1	1	6	8	4	4	16	11	4	1	1	4	2	1	3
SOUTHERN DOMINIONS	79	1	2	2	2	7	7	5	1	2	9	6	6	4	8	0	2	4	4	2	5	1
S. AFRICA +RHOD.	42	1	0	2	3	2	3	3	1	2	3	2	2	5	4	1	2	2	1	1	1	2
AUSTRALIA + N.Z.	75	1	2	2	0	6	6	6	1	5	9	5	5	3	10	0	4	3	5	3	3	1
ASIA + OTHER AFRICA	77	0	1	2	1	6	1	0	0	1	7	6	6	6	15	7	3	7	5	2	5	0
JAPAN	56	0	0	0	0	1	0	0	0	4	2	4	2	5	12	8	4	2	5	4	2	1
OTHER ASIA+AFR.	68	0	0	3	0	6	1	0	0	0	5	2	5	0	6	0	1	3	4	1	1	1
BLACK AFRICA	20	0	0	0	0	0	0	0	2	1	1	1	1	1	1	1	3	1	4	3	2	1
ARAB WORLD	16	0	0	0	0	1	1	1	0	0	1	0	0	0	8	7	1	3	1	1	1	2
INDIA	34	0	0	0	0	0	1	1	0	0	1	1	0	1	2	2	6	0	1	2	1	1
PHILIPPINES	31	0	0	0	0	1	0	1	0	1	5	5	2	4	2	0	2	2	2	2	1	2
OTHER E. ASIA	19	0	0	1	1	2	1	0	0	0	0	0	1	0	2	2	1	0	2	2	0	1
OTHER ASIA	32	0	0	2	0	2	1	0	0	3	0	0	3	4	6	2	1	0	2	2	1	3

CHAPTER 2- THE EXPANSION OF PARENT SYSTEMS
SECTION 3- THE FLOW OF MANUFACTURING BY CHARACTERISTIC OF PARENT SYSTEM
TABLE LI- SYSTEMS WITH LOW "GEOGRAPHICAL DIVERSITY" IN 1966
CLASSIFIED BY PERIOD SYSTEM FIRST OPERATED A MANUFACTURING SUBSIDIARY
IN SPECIFIED COUNTRIES AND REGIONS

COUNTRY OR REGION	PRE 1968	PRE 1901	1901 -12	1914 -19	1920 -24	1925 -29	1930 -34	1935 -39	1940 -45	1946 -50	1951 -53	1954 -55	1956 -57	1958 -59	1960 -61	1962	1963	1964	1965	1966	1967	UNK
OUTSIDE U.S.	99	11	6	15	6	15	7	6	5	6	2	5	4	7	4	0	0	0	0	0	0	0
OUT. U.S. + CANADA	99	10	3	5	7	11	8	4	5	10	6	6	9	9	4	0	2	0	0	0	0	0
OUT. WEST. HEMIS.	99	10	2	5	7	11	5	4	3	8	8	6	10	10	10	0	2	0	0	0	0	0
OUT. WHITE CWEALTH	99	7	3	1	8	9	9	1	4	6	7	9	12	16	5	0	2	0	0	0	0	0
OUT. DEVLPED WORLD	97	0	2	1	2	3	6	6	7	8	4	7	11	15	13	2	3	2	3	1	1	1
CANADA	92	3	7	13	2	12	7	4	7	3	6	5	5	5	6	2	3	3	3	3	1	0
LATIN AMERICA	94	0	1	1	2	2	6	6	7	8	5	8	10	14	13	3	3	2	3	1	0	1
C. AMER.+CARIB.	85	0	0	0	0	1	4	4	2	7	5	6	10	12	9	3	8	4	4	1	0	2
CUBA	8	0	1	0	0	0	1	1	0	0	2	0	1	1	1	0	0	0	0	1	0	2
MEXICO	77	0	0	0	0	1	3	2	2	8	4	5	8	13	10	5	7	3	4	0	0	1
OTHER	18	0	1	1	3	0	0	3	0	0	0	1	2	1	1	3	4	1	1	2	0	0
S. AMERICA	75	0	0	1	0	1	2	3	8	6	2	4	6	18	10	3	4	3	0	1	0	1
ARGENTINA	37	0	1	1	1	0	3	3	5	3	1	1	4	3	5	6	4	1	1	1	0	0
BRAZIL	42	0	0	2	1	0	0	0	1	2	3	1	4	11	4	3	4	0	0	1	0	1
PERU	7	0	0	0	0	0	0	0	1	1	0	3	1	0	1	1	1	0	1	0	0	0
COLOMBIA	25	0	0	0	1	0	0	0	0	4	1	0	0	1	8	0	3	4	0	1	0	0
VENEZUELA	22	0	0	0	0	0	0	0	2	2	0	2	1	5	5	0	2	0	0	0	0	0
OTHER	13	0	0	0	1	1	0	0	3	2	0	0	0	0	2	0	1	0	0	1	1	1
EUROPE	99	10	2	3	6	11	3	5	2	7	7	5	10	13	10	2	2	2	1	0	0	0
EFTA	92	6	1	3	1	10	6	5	2	6	7	4	7	7	9	7	5	2	2	0	0	0
U.K.	85	6	1	3	1	10	5	7	1	1	6	4	7	7	8	4	4	2	2	0	1	0
SCANDINAVIA	16	0	0	0	0	0	1	1	0	1	1	1	0	1	3	3	1	1	2	1	0	0
SWITZERLAND	12	0	0	0	0	0	0	0	1	1	0	0	0	0	1	0	3	1	1	0	1	0
OTHER EFTA	12	0	1	0	1	0	0	1	0	0	1	0	0	1	1	3	1	1	1	1	0	0
EUROP. COMMUNITY	98	7	1	0	8	5	5	2	1	3	6	4	9	14	20	3	6	4	1	1	0	0
FRANCE	68	3	1	0	5	3	5	1	0	0	2	2	2	6	12	6	3	8	2	1	2	0
GERMANY	62	5	0	0	2	0	4	0	0	0	2	3	6	5	12	5	5	2	2	4	1	0
ITALY	56	0	2	0	2	0	0	1	0	1	3	0	4	7	14	1	7	4	2	3	0	0
BELGIUM + LUX	23	2	0	0	1	0	0	0	1	1	0	1	1	0	5	1	1	1	3	0	1	0
NETHERLANDS	29	0	1	0	0	1	0	1	0	0	2	0	1	6	7	3	3	6	1	1	0	0
SPAIN	35	0	0	0	0	0	1	0	0	0	1	2	2	1	2	0	0	0	2	2	1	0
GREECE + TURKEY	5	0	0	0	0	0	2	0	0	3	1	0	0	0	0	1	1	1	0	0	0	0
OTHER EUROPE	10	0	0	0	0	2	0	0	1	0	2	0	1	2	0	0	0	3	1	1	2	0
EUROPE EX. U.K.	99	7	1	0	8	7	6	0	1	3	7	6	8	16	16	4	5	5	1	0	0	0
SOUTHERN DOMINIONS	74	0	2	2	2	1	3	3	2	4	3	7	7	13	7	3	2	3	4	3	3	3
S. AFRICA +RHOD.	29	0	0	2	1	0	2	0	1	4	3	0	1	3	6	3	2	1	1	3	3	0
AUSTRALIA + N.Z.	64	0	2	2	1	1	1	3	1	3	3	7	7	13	8	2	2	3	3	2	3	1
ASIA + OTHER AFRICA	62	0	0	0	0	2	0	1	0	2	3	2	4	4	8	8	8	2	5	5	3	1
JAPAN	35	0	0	0	0	0	0	0	0	0	1	0	1	1	7	7	10	8	5	2	0	1
OTHER ASIA+AFR.	41	0	0	0	0	2	0	1	0	2	0	2	3	3	6	0	7	2	2	6	3	0
BLACK AFRICA	3	0	0	0	0	0	0	0	0	0	0	0	0	0	1	1	6	0	6	0	1	0
ARAB WORLD	7	0	0	0	0	0	0	0	0	0	0	0	0	2	1	3	0	0	0	1	1	0
INDIA	17	0	0	0	0	2	0	0	0	0	0	0	0	1	3	1	1	1	0	3	0	0
PHILIPPINES	10	0	0	0	0	0	0	0	0	0	1	0	0	0	1	1	3	0	3	0	2	0
OTHER E. ASIA	8	0	0	0	0	0	0	0	0	2	0	0	0	0	0	1	1	1	2	1	0	0
OTHER ASIA	11	0	0	0	0	0	0	1	1	0	0	1	2	1	1	1	0	0	0	2	0	0

CHAPTER 2- THE EXPANSION OF PARENT SYSTEMS
SECTION 3- THE FLOW OF MANUFACTURING BY CHARACTERISTIC OF PARENT SYSTEM
TABLE L2- SYSTEMS WITH HIGH "GEOGRAPHICAL DIVERSITY" IN 1966
CLASSIFIED BY PERIOD SYSTEM FIRST OPERATED A MANUFACTURING SUBSIDIARY
IN SPECIFIED COUNTRIES AND REGIONS

PERIOD

COUNTRY OR REGION	PRE 1908	PRE 1901	1901 -13	1914 -19	1920 -24	1925 -29	1930 -34	1935 -39	1940 -45	1946 -50	1951 -53	1954 -55	1956 -57	1958 -59	1960 -61	1962	1963	1964	1965	1966	1967	UNK
OUTSIDE U.S.	88	8	16	11	9	15	6	7	3	3	6	2	0	1	1	0	0	0	0	0	0	0
OUT. U.S. + CANADA	88	8	8	8	11	18	6	7	4	4	6	4	1	1	2	1	0	0	0	0	0	0
OUT. WEST. HEMIS.	88	7	8	6	10	20	5	7	0	4	6	6	5	5	2	2	1	0	0	0	0	0
OUT. WHITE CWEALTH	88	7	5	10	8	9	6	11	6	7	6	7	2	2	2	1	1	0	0	0	0	0
OUT. DEVLPED WORLD	88	3	1	6	4	9	7	13	8	11	7	8	3	4	3	1	1	0	0	3	0	0
CANADA	86	2	13	11	5	15	8	9	2	6	5	4	2	1	1	1	0	0	0	0	0	0
LATIN AMERICA	88	3	1	4	3	7	8	14	10	10	8	7	5	4	2	2	0	0	0	0	0	0
C. AMER.+CARIB.	87	1	0	2	2	4	8	13	8	10	7	6	10	6	5	4	0	1	0	0	0	0
CUBA	28	1	0	1	1	1	2	7	2	3	5	0	5	3	3	0	3	2	2	2	3	1
MEXICO	85	0	1	0	1	3	5	7	10	3	0	2	7	8	5	3	2	5	3	3	0	0
OTHER	54	2	0	2	0	0	3	1	2	0	9	0	5	3	8	3	1	2	10	3	2	3
S. AMERICA	85	2	2	3	1	7	5	9	1	4	9	4	6	5	7	3	1	1	0	0	0	0
ARGENTINA	62	0	1	1	0	5	3	7	2	5	2	3	5	7	5	3	1	0	1	0	0	0
BRAZIL	71	0	0	0	1	5	0	4	4	5	9	4	7	0	5	1	1	3	3	1	2	1
PERU	33	0	0	0	0	0	0	1	6	5	1	3	0	3	4	1	4	4	3	3	0	0
COLOMBIA	48	0	0	1	1	0	1	1	5	4	4	2	5	1	5	1	1	1	2	2	1	1
VENEZUELA	62	0	0	1	2	0	0	1	0	6	5	3	3	9	9	4	6	3	2	2	4	1
OTHER	41	1	1	1	0	1	0	1	1	4	2	3	4	1	4	2	1	1	7	1	2	1
EUROPE	88	7	8	2	10	18	7	7	0	6	5	5	2	6	2	2	0	3	0	1	0	0
EFTA	86	5	8	2	8	18	7	8	0	5	3	5	2	3	2	2	1	1	2	1	0	0
U.K.	85	4	3	3	6	17	9	9	0	6	0	2	2	4	3	2	3	1	2	1	1	0
SCANDINAVIA	46	1	2	0	2	4	0	3	0	3	1	0	4	3	4	1	1	1	3	2	1	1
SWITZERLAND	19	0	0	0	0	1	0	0	0	0	0	0	1	3	3	3	2	7	0	1	0	0
OTHER EFTA	23	0	1	0	1	3	0	3	0	0	1	0	1	2	2	0	0	2	1	0	1	0
EUROP. COMMUNITY	86	5	1	3	6	9	6	3	1	4	9	8	4	12	8	2	1	1	0	1	0	1
FRANCE	70	4	1	1	0	5	5	2	0	0	5	3	5	10	13	3	6	0	1	1	0	0
GERMANY	75	4	1	2	1	7	4	1	0	2	3	7	1	7	10	3	4	4	4	4	1	1
ITALY	68	1	3	0	2	3	1	2	1	2	6	5	0	10	8	6	4	3	6	0	1	0
BELGIUM + LUX	55	0	2	1	2	3	4	4	1	5	2	2	5	6	8	2	2	2	4	2	0	1
NETHERLANDS	46	0	0	0	0	1	1	1	2	0	1	2	0	5	8	3	3	7	7	3	0	0
SPAIN	58	0	0	0	3	2	4	2	0	2	2	2	6	8	5	5	0	2	6	10	6	1
GREECE + TURKEY	27	2	2	1	0	1	2	4	0	0	2	3	3	5	5	4	6	1	3	3	2	1
OTHER EUROPE	26	2	2	0	1	1	1	0	0	2	1	0	1	2	4	1	1	0	0	0	0	1
EUROPE EX. U.K.	87	5	4	5	7	9	7	3	1	6	8	7	3	13	7	2	0	0	0	0	0	3
SOUTHERN DOMINIONS	80	1	0	3	1	9	8	11	3	2	7	7	3	5	7	1	3	3	2	2	2	2
S. AFRICA +RHOD.	57	1	0	1	2	2	4	6	4	3	3	5	2	6	3	2	6	1	1	2	1	1
AUSTRALIA + N.Z.	74	0	0	2	1	8	6	9	3	2	7	6	3	4	9	1	1	3	4	4	2	0
ASIA + OTHER AFRICA	84	0	1	1	2	7	2	7	1	9	5	9	9	16	5	4	5	1	3	2	1	1
JAPAN	64	0	0	0	0	1	1	2	0	1	7	7	7	15	3	5	6	6	6	0	1	1
OTHER ASIA+AFR.	77	0	1	3	2	0	1	0	0	8	3	3	1	13	7	6	7	3	3	1	1	1
BLACK AFRICA	26	0	0	0	0	0	0	2	2	0	1	0	6	7	7	2	1	5	4	2	2	2
ARAB WORLD	22	0	0	0	0	0	0	0	0	3	1	2	0	2	2	1	4	5	3	2	0	1
INDIA	41	0	0	0	1	3	1	1	2	2	0	1	7	7	7	7	2	2	3	4	2	2
PHILIPPINES	43	0	0	0	1	1	0	2	1	2	3	8	2	2	2	4	8	0	1	1	2	1
OTHER E. ASIA	20	0	0	1	1	2	0	0	0	0	1	0	3	5	3	3	2	3	1	1	1	1
OTHER ASIA	44	0	0	2	0	3	1	2	0	4	0	1	2	6	9	4	3	0	2	1	1	3

CHAPTER 2- THE EXPANSION OF PARENT SYSTEMS
SECTION 4- THE FLOW OF MANUFACTURING BY INDUSTRY OF SUBSIDIARY
TABLE 1- SYSTEMS CLASSIFIED BY PERIOD SYSTEM FIRST OPERATED
IN SPECIFIED COUNTRIES AND REGIONS A SUBSIDIARY MANUFACTURING
MEAT PRODUCTS (SIC 201)

PERIOD

COUNTRY OR REGION	PRE 1968	PRE 1901	1901 -13	1914 -19	1920 -24	1925 -29	1930 -34	1935 -39	1940 -45	1946 -50	1951 -53	1954 -55	1956 -57	1958 -59	1960 -61	1962	1963	1964	1965	1966	1967	UNK
OUTSIDE U.S.	10	1	1	1	0	0	0	0	1	1	0	0	0	0	1	0	0	0	1	2	1	0
OUT. U.S. + CANADA	10	1	1	1	0	0	0	0	1	1	0	0	0	0	1	0	0	0	1	2	1	0
OUT. WEST. HEMIS.	9	0	0	1	0	1	0	0	1	1	0	0	0	0	0	1	0	0	1	2	1	0
OUT. WHITE CWEALTH	7	0	2	1	0	0	0	0	0	0	1	0	0	0	1	0	0	0	1	0	0	1
OUT. DEVLPED WORLD	5	0	2	1	0	0	0	0	0	0	0	0	0	0	1	0	0	0	0	0	1	0
CANADA	5	0	1	0	0	0	0	0	1	1	1	0	0	0	1	0	0	0	0	0	0	0
LATIN AMERICA	5	0	2	1	0	0	0	0	0	0	0	0	0	0	0	1	0	1	0	0	0	0
C. AMER.+CARIB.	4	0	0	0	0	0	0	0	0	0	0	0	0	0	0	0	0	1	0	2	0	1
CUBA	1	0	0	0	0	0	0	0	0	0	0	0	0	0	0	0	0	0	0	0	0	1
MEXICO	3	0	0	0	0	0	0	0	0	0	0	0	0	0	0	0	0	1	0	2	0	0
OTHER	1	0	0	0	0	0	0	0	0	0	0	0	0	0	0	0	0	0	0	0	1	0
S. AMERICA	4	0	2	1	0	0	0	0	0	0	0	0	0	0	0	1	0	0	0	0	0	0
ARGENTINA	4	0	2	2	0	0	0	0	0	0	0	0	0	0	0	0	0	0	0	0	0	0
BRAZIL	3	0	1	0	0	0	0	0	0	0	0	0	0	0	1	0	0	0	0	0	1	0
PERU	0	0	0	0	0	0	0	0	0	0	0	0	0	0	0	0	0	0	0	0	0	0
COLOMBIA	0	0	0	0	0	0	0	0	0	0	0	0	0	0	0	0	0	0	0	0	0	0
VENEZUELA	1	0	0	0	0	0	0	0	0	0	0	0	0	0	1	0	0	0	0	0	0	0
OTHER	2	0	1	0	0	0	0	0	0	0	0	0	0	0	0	0	0	0	0	0	0	1
EUROPE	8	1	0	0	0	0	0	0	1	1	1	0	0	1	1	0	0	0	2	0	0	0
EFTA	6	1	0	0	0	0	0	0	0	1	1	0	0	1	0	0	0	0	2	0	0	0
U.K.	6	1	0	0	0	0	0	0	0	1	1	0	0	1	0	0	0	0	2	0	0	0
SCANDINAVIA	0	0	0	0	0	0	0	0	0	0	0	0	0	0	0	0	0	0	0	0	0	0
SWITZERLAND	0	0	0	0	0	0	0	0	0	0	0	0	0	0	0	0	0	0	0	0	0	0
OTHER EFTA	0	0	0	0	0	0	0	0	0	0	0	0	0	0	0	0	0	0	0	0	0	0
EUROP. COMMUNITY	4	0	0	0	0	0	0	0	1	0	0	0	0	0	1	1	0	0	0	0	0	1
FRANCE	1	0	0	0	0	0	0	0	1	0	0	0	0	0	0	0	0	0	0	0	0	0
GERMANY	1	0	0	0	0	0	0	0	0	0	0	0	0	0	0	1	0	0	0	0	0	0
ITALY	1	0	0	0	0	0	0	0	0	0	0	0	0	0	1	0	0	0	0	0	0	0
BELGIUM + LUX	0	0	0	0	0	0	0	0	0	0	0	0	0	0	0	0	0	0	0	0	0	0
NETHERLANDS	1	0	0	0	0	0	0	0	0	0	0	0	0	0	0	0	0	0	0	0	0	1
SPAIN	2	0	0	0	0	0	0	0	0	0	0	0	0	0	1	1	0	0	0	0	0	0
GREECE + TURKEY	0	0	0	0	0	0	0	0	0	0	0	0	0	0	0	0	0	0	0	0	0	0
OTHER EUROPE	3	0	0	0	0	0	0	0	0	1	0	0	0	0	0	0	0	1	1	0	0	0
EUROPE EX. U.K.	5	0	0	0	0	0	0	0	1	0	0	0	0	0	1	2	0	0	1	0	0	0
SOUTHERN DOMINIONS	4	0	0	1	0	0	0	0	1	0	0	0	0	0	0	0	0	1	1	0	0	0
S. AFRICA +RHOD.	0	0	0	0	0	0	0	0	0	0	0	0	0	0	0	0	0	0	0	0	0	0
AUSTRALIA + N.Z.	4	0	0	1	0	0	0	0	1	0	0	0	0	0	0	0	0	1	1	0	0	0
ASIA + OTHER AFRICA	1	0	0	0	0	1	0	0	0	0	0	0	0	0	0	0	0	0	0	0	0	0
JAPAN	1	0	0	0	0	0	0	0	0	0	0	0	0	0	0	0	0	0	1	0	0	0
OTHER ASIA+AFR.	1	0	0	0	0	1	0	0	0	0	0	0	0	0	0	0	0	0	0	0	0	0
BLACK AFRICA	0	0	0	0	0	0	0	0	0	0	0	0	0	0	0	0	0	0	0	0	0	0
ARAB WORLD	0	0	0	0	0	0	0	0	0	0	0	0	0	0	0	0	0	0	0	0	0	0
INDIA	0	0	0	0	0	0	0	0	0	0	0	0	0	0	0	0	0	0	0	0	0	0
PHILIPPINES	0	0	0	0	0	0	0	0	0	0	0	0	0	0	0	0	0	0	0	0	0	0
OTHER E. ASIA	1	0	0	0	0	1	0	0	0	0	0	0	0	0	0	0	0	0	0	0	0	0
OTHER ASIA	0	0	0	0	0	0	0	0	0	0	0	0	0	0	0	0	0	0	0	0	0	0

CHAPTER 2- THE EXPANSION OF PARENT SYSTEMS
SECTION 4- THE FLOW OF MANUFACTURING BY INDUSTRY OF SUBSIDIARY
TABLE 2- SYSTEMS CLASSIFIED BY PERIOD SYSTEM FIRST OPERATED
IN SPECIFIED COUNTRIES AND REGIONS A SUBSIDIARY MANUFACTURING
DAIRY PRODUCTS (SIC 202)

PERIOD

COUNTRY OR REGION	PRE 1968	PRE 1901	1901 -13	1914 -19	1920 -24	1925 -29	1930 -34	1935 -39	1940 -45	1946 -50	1951 -53	1954 -55	1956 -57	1958 -59	1960 -61	1962	1963	1964	1965	1966	1967	UNK
OUTSIDE U.S.	14	0	2	0	1	4	0	0	1	1	0	0	0	1	1	0	0	1	0	0	0	0
OUT. U.S. + CANADA	13	0	1	0	1	2	1	0	1	1	1	1	0	0	1	1	0	1	1	0	1	0
OUT. WEST. HEMIS.	12	1	1	0	1	2	1	1	0	0	0	1	1	0	1	0	1	0	0	1	0	0
OUT. WHITE CWEALTH	13	0	0	0	1	3	1	0	1	1	0	1	0	0	1	0	0	1	1	0	0	0
OUT. DEVLPED WORLD	8	0	0	0	0	0	3	1	1	1	0	0	0	0	0	0	0	0	1	1	0	0
CANADA	7	1	0	0	0	2	0	0	1	0	1	0	0	1	1	0	0	0	1	1	1	0
LATIN AMERICA	8	0	0	0	0	3	1	1	0	0	1	0	0	1	0	1	1	1	1	1	0	0
C. AMER.+CARIB.	4	0	0	0	0	3	1	1	0	0	1	0	1	0	1	0	1	1	1	1	0	0
CUBA	5	0	0	0	0	0	2	2	0	2	0	0	0	0	0	0	0	0	0	0	0	0
MEXICO	7	0	0	0	0	0	0	1	1	1	1	1	1	0	0	0	0	0	1	1	0	0
OTHER	5	0	0	0	0	1	1	0	0	0	0	0	0	0	1	0	0	0	0	1	1	0
S. AMERICA	2	0	0	0	0	0	0	0	0	0	0	0	0	0	0	0	0	0	0	0	0	0
ARGENTINA	2	0	0	0	0	0	1	0	3	1	1	1	0	0	0	0	0	0	1	0	1	0
BRAZIL	3	0	0	0	0	0	0	0	0	0	0	0	0	2	0	0	0	0	0	0	0	0
PERU	1	0	0	0	0	0	0	0	0	1	0	0	0	0	0	0	0	0	1	0	0	0
COLOMBIA	3	0	0	0	0	0	0	0	3	0	1	0	0	0	0	0	0	0	0	0	0	0
VENEZUELA	3	0	0	0	0	0	0	0	1	1	0	1	0	1	1	0	0	0	0	0	0	0
OTHER	0	0	0	0	0	0	0	0	0	0	0	1	1	0	0	0	0	0	0	0	0	0
EUROPE	11	0	0	0	1	3	1	0	0	0	0	0	0	0	0	0	0	0	0	1	0	0
EFTA	5	0	0	0	0	2	1	0	0	0	0	1	0	0	0	0	0	1	1	0	0	0
U.K.	3	0	0	0	0	0	1	0	0	0	0	2	0	0	1	1	1	0	0	0	0	0
SCANDINAVIA	3	0	0	0	1	0	1	0	0	0	0	0	0	0	0	0	0	0	1	0	0	0
SWITZERLAND	0	0	0	0	0	0	0	0	0	0	0	0	0	0	1	0	0	0	0	0	0	0
OTHER EFTA	0	0	0	0	1	3	0	0	0	0	0	0	0	0	0	0	0	0	0	0	0	0
EUROP. COMMUNITY	11	0	0	0	1	0	1	0	0	0	0	0	0	0	0	1	0	0	0	1	0	0
FRANCE	3	0	0	0	1	4	1	0	1	0	0	0	0	0	0	0	0	0	0	1	0	0
GERMANY	6	0	0	0	0	0	1	0	1	0	0	0	0	0	1	0	0	0	0	1	1	0
ITALY	1	0	0	0	0	0	0	0	0	0	0	0	0	0	0	0	0	0	0	0	0	0
BELGIUM + LUX	5	0	0	0	0	2	0	0	0	1	0	0	0	2	0	0	0	0	0	2	2	0
NETHERLANDS	5	0	0	0	0	0	0	0	0	0	1	0	0	0	0	0	0	1	0	0	0	0
SPAIN	2	0	0	0	0	0	0	0	0	0	0	0	0	0	1	0	0	0	0	0	0	0
GREECE + TURKEY	0	0	0	0	0	0	0	0	0	0	0	0	0	0	0	0	0	1	0	1	1	0
OTHER EUROPE	2	0	0	0	0	0	1	0	0	0	0	0	1	0	0	0	0	1	0	0	0	0
EUROPE Ex. U.K.	11	0	0	1	3	1	1	0	0	0	1	1	1	0	1	0	0	1	0	0	1	0
SOUTHERN DOMINIONS	6	0	1	0	0	0	2	1	0	0	0	0	0	1	1	0	0	0	0	0	0	0
S. AFRICA +RHOD.	3	0	0	0	0	0	1	1	0	0	0	0	0	1	0	0	0	0	0	0	0	0
AUSTRALIA + N.Z.	6	0	1	0	0	0	2	2	0	0	0	0	1	0	2	0	0	0	0	0	1	0
ASIA + OTHER AFRICA	5	0	0	0	0	0	0	0	0	0	0	0	0	0	0	0	0	0	0	0	0	0
JAPAN	1	0	0	0	0	0	0	0	0	0	0	0	0	1	0	0	0	0	0	0	0	0
OTHER ASIA+AFR.	5	0	0	0	0	0	0	0	0	0	0	1	1	0	1	0	0	0	0	0	0	0
BLACK AFRICA	1	0	0	0	0	0	0	0	0	0	0	0	0	2	0	0	0	0	0	1	0	0
ARAB WORLD	1	0	0	0	0	0	0	0	0	0	0	0	0	0	0	0	0	0	0	0	0	0
INDIA	0	0	0	0	0	0	0	0	0	0	0	0	0	2	0	1	0	0	0	0	0	0
PHILIPPINES	3	0	0	0	0	0	0	0	0	0	0	0	0	0	0	0	0	0	0	0	0	0
OTHER E. ASIA	1	0	0	0	0	0	0	0	0	0	0	0	1	0	0	0	0	0	0	0	1	0
OTHER ASIA	4	0	0	0	0	0	0	0	0	0	0	0	1	0	0	0	2	0	0	0	1	0

CHAPTER 2- THE EXPANSION OF PARENT SYSTEMS
SECTION 4- THE FLOW OF MANUFACTURING BY INDUSTRY OF SUBSIDIARY
TABLE 3- SYSTEMS CLASSIFIED BY PERIOD SYSTEM FIRST OPERATED
IN SPECIFIED COUNTRIES AND REGIONS A SUBSIDIARY MANUFACTURING
CANNED FOODS (SIC 203)

PERIOD

COUNTRY OR REGION	PRE 1968	PRE 1901	1901 -13	1914 -19	1920 -24	1925 -29	1930 -34	1935 -39	1940 -45	1946 -50	1951 -53	1954 -55	1956 -57	1958 -59	1960 -61	1962	1963	1964	1965	1966	1967	UNK
OUTSIDE U.S.	22	1	1	0	1	2	0	1	0	1	0	1	3	2	4	2	2	1	0	0	0	0
OUT. U.S. + CANADA	22	1	0	0	1	2	0	0	1	0	0	1	3	2	5	1	2	1	0	1	1	0
OUT. WEST. HEMIS.	21	0	0	0	1	2	0	1	1	0	0	1	1	2	6	1	2	1	0	1	2	0
OUT. WHITE CWEALTH	19	0	0	0	0	1	0	1	0	0	0	1	3	1	4	0	3	2	0	1	1	0
OUT. DEVLPED WORLD	11	0	0	0	0	1	1	0	0	0	0	1	3	1	1	0	1	0	1	0	0	0
CANADA	10	1	1	0	0	1	0	0	1	0	0	1	1	1	0	0	0	0	0	1	1	0
LATIN AMERICA	9	0	0	0	0	0	0	0	1	1	0	1	1	1	0	1	0	2	0	1	0	0
C. AMER.+CARIB.	9	0	0	0	0	0	0	0	0	0	0	0	3	1	1	2	3	3	1	0	0	0
CUBA	3	0	0	0	0	0	0	0	0	0	0	0	0	0	1	0	0	0	0	0	0	0
MEXICO	4	0	0	0	0	0	0	0	1	0	0	0	0	1	1	0	1	0	1	0	0	0
OTHER	3	0	0	0	0	0	0	0	0	0	0	0	1	1	1	1	0	2	1	1	0	0
S. AMERICA	5	0	0	0	0	0	0	0	0	0	0	0	0	0	0	0	0	0	0	0	0	0
ARGENTINA	0	0	0	0	0	0	0	0	0	0	0	0	1	0	0	1	1	1	0	1	1	0
BRAZIL	1	0	0	0	0	0	0	0	0	0	0	0	0	0	0	0	0	0	0	0	0	0
PERU	3	0	0	0	0	0	0	0	0	0	0	0	0	0	0	0	1	0	0	0	0	0
COLOMBIA	1	0	0	0	0	0	0	0	0	0	0	0	0	1	0	0	0	0	1	0	0	0
VENEZUELA	2	0	0	0	0	0	0	0	0	0	0	0	0	0	0	0	0	0	0	0	0	0
OTHER	2	0	0	0	0	0	0	0	0	0	0	0	0	0	0	2	0	1	1	0	2	0
EUROPE	18	1	0	0	1	1	0	1	1	1	0	0	1	2	5	0	2	0	0	1	0	0
EFTA	7	1	0	0	1	1	0	1	1	1	0	0	0	1	1	0	1	0	0	0	0	0
U.K.	7	1	0	0	1	1	0	1	1	1	0	0	0	1	1	0	1	0	0	0	0	0
SCANDINAVIA	0	0	0	0	0	0	0	0	0	0	0	0	0	0	0	0	0	0	0	0	0	0
SWITZERLAND	1	0	0	0	0	0	0	0	0	0	0	0	0	0	0	0	0	0	0	0	0	0
OTHER EFTA	0	0	0	0	0	0	0	0	0	0	0	0	0	0	0	0	0	0	0	0	0	0
EUROP. COMMUNITY	13	0	0	0	0	0	0	0	0	0	0	0	1	1	5	0	3	0	0	0	2	0
FRANCE	3	0	0	0	0	0	0	0	1	0	0	0	0	0	0	0	1	0	0	0	1	0
GERMANY	4	0	0	0	0	0	0	0	0	0	0	0	1	1	2	0	1	0	0	1	0	0
ITALY	4	0	0	0	0	0	0	0	0	0	0	0	0	0	2	0	1	1	0	0	0	0
BELGIUM + LUX	1	0	0	0	0	0	0	0	0	0	0	0	0	0	1	0	0	0	0	0	2	0
NETHERLANDS	1	0	0	0	0	0	0	0	0	0	0	0	0	0	0	0	1	0	1	0	0	0
SPAIN	3	0	0	0	0	0	0	0	0	0	0	0	0	0	0	0	0	0	0	0	0	0
GREECE + TURKEY	0	0	0	0	0	1	0	0	1	0	0	0	0	0	0	1	0	1	0	1	0	0
OTHER EUROPE	2	0	0	0	0	0	0	0	1	1	0	0	0	0	0	0	0	0	0	0	0	0
EUROPE EX. U.K.	15	0	0	0	0	0	0	0	0	1	0	0	1	1	4	0	2	0	0	1	2	0
SOUTHERN DOMINIONS	9	0	0	0	0	0	0	1	0	0	0	0	0	1	4	1	0	1	0	0	0	0
S. AFRICA +RHOD.	3	0	0	0	0	0	0	0	0	0	0	0	0	0	2	0	0	0	0	0	0	0
AUSTRALIA + N.Z.	6	0	0	0	0	0	1	1	0	0	0	1	0	1	2	1	0	1	0	0	0	0
ASIA + OTHER AFRICA	3	0	0	0	0	1	0	1	0	0	0	0	0	0	0	0	0	0	0	0	0	0
JAPAN	0	0	0	0	0	0	0	0	0	0	0	0	0	0	0	0	0	1	0	0	0	0
OTHER ASIA+AFR.	3	0	0	0	0	0	1	0	0	0	0	1	0	0	0	0	0	0	0	0	0	0
BLACK AFRICA	0	0	0	0	0	0	0	0	0	0	0	0	0	0	0	0	0	1	0	0	0	0
ARAB WORLD	1	0	0	0	0	1	0	0	0	0	0	1	0	0	0	0	0	0	0	0	0	0
INDIA	1	0	0	0	0	0	0	0	0	0	0	0	0	0	0	0	0	0	0	0	0	0
PHILIPPINES	1	0	0	0	0	0	1	0	0	0	0	0	0	0	0	0	0	0	0	0	0	0
OTHER E. ASIA	0	0	0	0	0	0	0	0	0	0	0	0	0	0	0	0	0	0	0	0	0	0
OTHER ASIA	0	0	0	0	0	0	0	0	0	0	0	0	0	0	0	0	0	0	0	0	0	0

CHAPTER 2- THE EXPANSION OF PARENT SYSTEMS
SECTION 4- THE FLOW OF MANUFACTURING BY INDUSTRY OF SUBSIDIARY
TABLE 4- SYSTEMS CLASSIFIED BY PERIOD SYSTEM FIRST OPERATED
IN SPECIFIED COUNTRIES AND REGIONS A SUBSIDIARY MANUFACTURING
GRAIN MILL PRODUCTS (SIC 204)

COUNTRY OR REGION	PRE 1908	PRE 1901	1901 -13	1914 -19	1920 -24	1925 -29	1930 -34	1935 -39	1940 -45	1946 -50	1951 -53	1954 -55	1956 -57	1958 -59	1960 -61	1962	1963	1964	1965	1966	1967	UNK
OUTSIDE U.S.	23	0	0	1	1	1	0	3	1	1	1	1	0	2	0	3	1	2	1	0	2	0
OUT. U.S. + CANADA	21	0	1	1	1	1	0	2	1	1	0	0	2	1	4	1	2	1	1	2	2	0
OUT. WEST. HEMIS.	16	0	1	1	1	1	0	1	1	0	0	0	2	2	3	1	2	1	1	2	1	0
OUT. WHITE CWEALTH	19	0	1	1	0	0	0	1	1	0	1	1	2	1	4	0	2	1	1	2	0	0
OUT. DEVLPED WORLD	16	0	0	0	0	0	0	2	1	0	1	0	3	1	2	0	1	1	1	2	0	0
CANADA	9	0	0	0	0	0	0	2	0	0	1	1	0	0	0	0	0	0	0	0	2	0
LATIN AMERICA	16	0	0	0	0	2	0	2	1	0	2	0	3	1	2	0	0	1	1	2	0	0
C. AMER.+CARIB.	11	0	0	0	0	1	1	1	0	0	1	0	2	0	1	0	1	0	1	1	1	0
CUBA	1	0	0	0	0	0	0	0	0	0	0	0	0	0	0	1	0	0	0	0	0	0
MEXICO	9	0	0	0	0	0	0	1	0	0	0	0	2	0	2	1	1	1	1	1	0	0
OTHER	6	0	0	0	0	1	0	0	1	0	0	0	0	0	0	0	0	0	0	1	0	0
S. AMERICA	12	0	0	0	0	1	0	1	1	0	2	0	2	0	2	0	0	0	1	0	0	0
ARGENTINA	4	0	0	0	0	1	0	0	1	0	1	1	0	1	0	0	0	0	1	1	1	0
BRAZIL	5	0	0	0	0	1	0	1	0	0	1	0	2	0	0	0	0	0	1	0	0	0
PERU	3	0	0	0	0	0	0	0	0	0	0	1	0	1	0	0	0	0	0	0	0	0
COLOMBIA	5	0	0	0	0	0	1	1	1	0	1	0	1	0	1	0	1	0	1	1	1	0
VENEZUELA	5	0	0	0	0	0	0	0	0	0	1	1	1	0	1	0	0	0	1	1	0	0
OTHER	6	0	1	0	0	0	0	1	0	0	0	0	0	1	1	0	0	1	1	1	1	0
EUROPE	14	0	1	1	1	1	0	1	1	1	1	0	2	1	2	1	3	0	0	0	1	0
EFTA	10	0	0	0	1	1	1	1	1	1	1	0	1	1	1	1	1	0	0	0	1	0
U.K.	10	0	1	0	1	1	0	3	0	0	0	0	0	1	1	0	1	0	0	0	0	0
SCANDINAVIA	3	0	0	0	0	0	1	0	0	0	0	0	0	0	0	0	0	0	0	0	0	0
SWITZERLAND	1	0	1	0	0	0	0	0	0	0	1	0	0	0	0	0	1	0	0	0	1	0
OTHER EFTA	2	0	0	0	0	1	0	0	0	0	0	0	1	0	3	0	0	1	0	0	0	0
EUROP. COMMUNITY	10	0	0	2	2	0	0	0	0	1	0	0	0	0	3	0	2	0	1	0	0	0
FRANCE	3	0	0	0	1	0	0	0	0	0	1	0	0	1	4	1	0	0	0	0	1	0
GERMANY	7	0	0	1	1	1	0	0	0	0	0	0	0	0	4	0	0	0	0	0	0	0
ITALY	6	0	0	0	0	0	0	0	0	1	1	0	1	1	1	0	2	0	0	1	0	0
BELGIUM + LUX	2	0	0	0	0	1	0	0	0	0	0	0	0	0	1	0	0	0	0	0	0	0
NETHERLANDS	2	0	0	1	0	1	0	1	0	0	1	0	0	0	0	0	2	1	0	1	1	0
SPAIN	3	0	0	0	0	0	0	1	0	0	0	0	0	0	0	0	0	0	0	0	1	0
GREECE + TURKEY	0	0	0	0	0	0	0	0	0	0	0	0	0	0	0	0	0	0	0	0	0	0
OTHER EUROPE	1	0	0	0	0	0	1	0	0	0	1	0	0	0	0	0	0	0	0	0	0	0
EUROPE EX. U.K.	10	0	1	1	0	0	0	1	0	0	1	1	0	1	3	0	2	0	1	0	1	0
SOUTHERN DOMINIONS	7	0	0	0	0	0	0	0	0	1	0	0	0	0	4	0	0	0	0	0	0	0
S. AFRICA +RHOD.	2	0	0	1	1	0	0	0	0	1	0	0	0	0	0	1	0	2	0	2	0	0
AUSTRALIA + N.Z.	6	0	0	0	0	0	0	0	0	0	0	0	0	0	4	0	2	1	0	0	1	0
ASIA + OTHER AFRICA	7	0	0	0	0	0	0	0	0	0	0	0	0	0	0	1	1	0	0	1	0	0
JAPAN	1	0	0	0	0	0	0	0	0	0	0	0	0	0	0	0	0	0	0	0	1	0
OTHER ASIA+AFR.	6	0	0	0	0	0	0	0	0	0	0	0	0	0	0	0	1	1	0	0	0	0
BLACK AFRICA	1	0	0	0	0	0	0	0	0	0	0	0	0	0	0	0	1	1	0	1	0	0
ARAB WORLD	1	0	0	0	0	0	0	0	0	0	0	0	0	0	0	0	0	0	0	0	0	0
INDIA	1	0	0	0	0	0	0	0	0	0	1	0	0	0	0	0	0	0	0	1	0	0
PHILIPPINES	3	0	0	0	0	0	0	0	0	0	0	0	0	0	0	0	1	1	0	1	1	0
OTHER E. ASIA	1	0	0	0	0	0	0	0	0	0	0	0	0	0	0	0	0	0	0	0	0	0
OTHER ASIA	0	0	0	0	0	0	0	0	0	0	0	0	0	0	0	0	0	0	0	1	0	0

CHAPTER 2— THE EXPANSION OF PARENT SYSTEMS
SECTION 4— THE FLOW OF MANUFACTURING BY INDUSTRY OF SUBSIDIARY
TABLE 5— SYSTEMS CLASSIFIED BY PERIOD SYSTEM FIRST OPERATED
IN SPECIFIED COUNTRIES AND REGIONS A SUBSIDIARY MANUFACTURING
BAKERY PRODUCTS (SIC 205)

PERIOD

COUNTRY OR REGION	PRE 1968	PRE 1901	1901 -13	1914 -19	1920 -24	1925 -29	1930 -34	1935 -39	1940 -45	1946 -50	1951 -53	1954 -55	1956 -57	1958 -59	1960 -61	1962	1963	1964	1965	1966	1967	UNK
OUTSIDE U.S.	11	0	1	0	0	1	0	0	0	2	2	0	0	0	1	0	1	2	1	0	0	0
OUT. U.S. + CANADA	10	0	0	0	0	1	0	1	1	2	2	0	0	0	2	0	1	2	1	0	0	0
OUT. WEST. HEMIS.	9	0	0	0	0	1	0	1	1	1	0	0	0	0	3	0	1	2	1	0	0	0
OUT. WHITE CWEALTH	10	0	0	0	0	0	0	1	1	1	0	0	0	0	0	0	1	0	1	1	1	0
OUT. DEVLPED WORLD	5	0	0	0	0	0	0	1	0	2	0	0	0	0	0	0	0	0	0	1	1	0
CANADA	4	0	1	0	0	1	0	1	0	0	0	0	0	0	0	0	0	0	0	1	0	0
LATIN AMERICA	5	0	0	0	0	0	0	1	0	2	0	1	0	1	0	0	0	0	0	0	1	0
C. AMER.+CARIB.	5	0	1	0	0	1	1	1	0	0	1	1	1	0	1	1	0	1	0	1	1	0
CUBA	1	0	0	0	0	0	0	0	0	0	0	0	0	0	0	0	0	0	0	0	0	0
MEXICO	4	0	1	0	0	1	0	1	0	0	1	0	1	0	1	1	0	0	0	1	0	0
OTHER	2	0	0	0	0	0	0	0	0	2	0	0	0	0	0	0	0	0	0	0	0	0
S. AMERICA	4	0	0	0	0	0	0	0	0	2	0	1	0	1	0	0	0	0	0	0	0	0
ARGENTINA	0	0	0	0	0	0	0	0	0	0	0	0	0	0	0	0	0	0	0	1	0	0
BRAZIL	1	0	0	0	0	0	0	0	0	0	1	0	1	0	0	0	0	1	1	0	0	0
PERU	1	0	0	0	0	0	0	0	0	1	0	1	0	1	0	0	0	0	0	0	0	0
COLOMBIA	2	0	0	0	0	0	0	0	0	1	0	0	0	0	0	0	1	0	1	0	0	0
VENEZUELA	2	0	0	0	0	0	0	0	0	1	0	0	0	0	0	0	0	0	1	1	0	0
OTHER	0	0	0	0	0	0	0	0	0	0	0	0	0	0	0	0	0	0	0	0	0	0
EUROPE	9	0	0	0	0	0	1	1	1	1	0	0	0	0	2	0	1	2	1	0	0	0
EFTA	5	0	0	0	0	0	1	1	0	0	0	0	0	0	1	0	1	0	1	0	0	0
U.K.	2	0	0	0	0	0	0	0	0	0	0	0	0	0	0	0	0	0	0	0	0	0
SCANDINAVIA	4	0	0	0	0	0	1	1	1	0	0	1	0	0	1	0	0	0	0	0	0	0
SWITZERLAND	1	0	0	0	0	0	0	0	1	0	0	0	0	0	0	0	0	0	0	0	0	0
OTHER EFTA	0	0	0	0	0	0	0	0	0	0	0	0	0	0	0	0	0	0	0	0	0	0
EUROP. COMMUNITY	7	0	0	0	0	0	0	0	0	1	0	0	0	0	2	0	1	2	1	0	0	0
FRANCE	4	0	0	0	0	0	0	0	0	0	0	0	0	0	3	0	0	1	0	0	0	0
GERMANY	2	0	0	0	0	0	0	0	0	0	0	0	0	0	0	0	0	2	0	0	0	0
ITALY	3	0	0	0	0	0	0	0	0	0	0	0	0	0	1	0	0	0	2	0	0	0
BELGIUM + LUX	2	0	0	0	0	0	0	0	0	0	1	0	1	0	0	0	0	0	0	0	0	0
NETHERLANDS	0	0	0	0	0	0	0	0	0	0	0	0	0	0	0	0	0	0	0	0	0	0
SPAIN	3	0	0	0	0	0	0	0	0	0	0	0	0	0	2	0	0	0	1	0	0	0
GREECE + TURKEY	0	0	0	0	0	0	0	0	0	1	0	0	0	0	0	0	0	0	0	0	0	0
OTHER EUROPE	1	0	0	0	0	0	0	0	0	2	0	0	0	0	0	0	1	0	1	2	0	0
EUROPE EX. U.K.	9	0	0	0	0	0	0	0	0	0	0	0	0	0	2	0	1	2	1	0	0	0
SOUTHERN DOMINIONS	2	0	0	0	0	1	0	0	0	0	0	0	0	0	0	0	0	0	0	0	0	0
S. AFRICA +RHOD.	1	0	0	0	0	1	0	0	0	0	0	0	0	0	0	0	0	0	0	0	0	0
AUSTRALIA + N.Z.	1	0	0	0	0	0	0	0	0	0	0	0	0	0	0	0	0	0	0	0	0	0
ASIA + OTHER AFRICA	0	0	0	0	0	0	0	0	0	0	0	0	0	0	0	0	0	0	0	0	0	0
JAPAN	0	0	0	0	0	0	0	0	0	0	0	0	0	0	0	0	0	0	0	0	0	0
OTHER ASIA+AFR.	0	0	0	0	0	0	0	0	0	0	0	0	0	0	0	0	0	0	0	0	0	0
BLACK AFRICA	0	0	0	0	0	0	0	0	0	0	0	0	0	0	0	0	0	0	0	0	0	0
ARAB WORLD	0	0	0	0	0	0	0	0	0	0	0	0	0	0	0	0	0	0	0	0	0	0
INDIA	0	0	0	0	0	0	0	0	0	0	0	0	0	0	0	0	0	0	0	0	0	0
PHILIPPINES	0	0	0	0	0	0	0	0	0	0	0	0	0	0	0	0	0	0	0	0	0	0
OTHER E. ASIA	0	0	0	0	0	0	0	0	0	0	0	0	0	0	0	0	0	0	0	0	0	0
OTHER ASIA	0	0	0	0	0	0	0	0	0	0	0	0	0	0	0	0	0	0	0	0	0	0

CHAPTER 2- THE EXPANSION OF PARENT SYSTEMS
SECTION 4- THE FLOW OF MANUFACTURING BY INDUSTRY OF SUBSIDIARY
TABLE 6- SYSTEMS CLASSIFIED BY PERIOD SYSTEM FIRST OPERATED
IN SPECIFIED COUNTRIES AND REGIONS A SUBSIDIARY MANUFACTURING
CONFECTIONERY AND RELATED PRODUCTS (SIC 207)

PERIOD

COUNTRY OR REGION	PRE 1968	PRE 1901	1901 -13	1914 -19	1920 -24	1925 -29	1930 -34	1935 -39	1940 -42	1946 -50	1951 -53	1954 -55	1956 -57	1958 -59	1960 -61	1962	1963	1964	1965	1966	1967	UNK
OUTSIDE U.S.	13	0	0	1	0	2	0	0	0	1	0	0	1	0	2	2	3	1	1	1	0	0
OUT. U.S. + CANADA	13	0	0	1	1	1	0	0	0	2	0	0	0	0	1	1	3	2	1	0	1	0
OUT. WEST. HEMIS.	11	0	0	1	1	1	0	0	0	3	0	0	0	0	2	2	2	1	2	0	1	0
OUT. WHITE CWEALTH	13	0	0	0	0	0	0	0	0	3	1	0	0	0	1	0	3	1	2	0	3	0
OUT. DEVLPED WORLD	10	0	0	0	0	0	0	0	0	3	1	0	0	0	0	1	1	1	0	0	3	0
CANADA	5	0	0	0	0	1	0	0	0	0	0	0	1	0	1	0	0	1	0	0	0	0
LATIN AMERICA	10	0	0	1	1	0	0	0	0	3	0	1	0	0	1	1	1	1	0	2	0	0
C. AMER.+CARIB.	9	0	0	1	0	0	0	0	0	3	0	1	0	0	0	0	0	0	2	1	3	0
CUBA	0	0	0	0	0	0	0	0	0	0	0	0	0	0	0	1	1	1	0	1	0	0
MEXICO	6	0	0	1	0	0	0	0	0	2	0	0	1	0	1	0	0	0	1	2	2	0
OTHER	4	0	0	0	0	0	0	0	0	0	0	1	0	0	0	0	0	0	2	2	0	0
S. AMERICA	4	0	0	0	0	0	0	0	0	1	0	0	0	0	0	1	0	0	0	0	0	0
ARGENTINA	0	0	0	0	0	0	0	0	0	0	0	0	1	0	0	0	0	0	0	0	0	0
BRAZIL	2	0	0	0	0	0	0	0	0	1	0	0	0	0	0	1	0	0	0	0	0	0
PERU	2	0	0	0	0	0	0	0	0	1	0	0	0	0	0	1	0	0	0	0	2	0
COLOMBIA	3	0	0	0	0	0	0	0	0	1	0	1	0	0	1	1	0	0	0	0	0	0
VENEZUELA	2	0	0	0	0	0	0	0	0	0	0	0	1	0	0	1	0	0	1	0	0	0
OTHER	2	0	0	0	0	0	0	0	0	0	0	1	0	0	0	1	0	0	0	0	0	0
EUROPE	11	0	0	0	1	1	0	0	0	1	0	0	0	0	1	2	2	1	2	1	1	0
EFTA	5	0	0	0	1	1	0	0	0	1	0	0	0	0	0	1	0	0	0	1	1	0
U.K.	4	0	0	0	1	1	0	0	0	0	0	0	0	0	0	0	0	0	0	1	0	0
SCANDINAVIA	0	0	0	0	0	0	0	0	0	0	0	0	0	0	0	0	0	0	0	0	0	0
SWITZERLAND	0	0	0	0	0	0	0	0	0	0	0	0	0	1	0	0	0	0	0	0	0	0
OTHER EFTA	2	0	0	0	0	0	0	0	0	0	0	0	0	0	0	0	0	0	0	0	0	0
EUROP. COMMUNITY	9	0	0	0	0	0	0	0	0	0	0	0	0	0	2	2	3	0	2	1	1	0
FRANCE	3	0	0	0	0	0	0	0	0	0	0	0	0	0	1	0	1	1	1	1	0	0
GERMANY	5	0	0	0	0	0	0	0	0	0	0	0	0	0	1	1	1	1	1	0	1	0
ITALY	3	0	0	0	0	0	0	0	0	0	0	0	0	0	0	0	0	1	0	0	0	0
BELGIUM + LUX	2	0	0	0	0	0	0	0	0	0	0	0	0	0	0	0	2	0	1	0	1	0
NETHERLANDS	1	0	0	0	0	0	0	0	0	0	0	0	0	0	0	0	0	0	0	0	0	0
SPAIN	1	0	0	0	0	0	0	0	0	0	0	0	0	0	0	0	0	1	0	0	0	0
GREECE + TURKEY	1	0	0	0	0	0	0	0	0	0	0	0	0	0	1	0	0	0	1	0	1	0
OTHER EUROPE	1	0	0	0	0	0	0	0	0	0	0	0	0	0	0	0	0	0	0	0	0	0
EUROPE EX. U.K.	9	0	0	0	0	0	0	0	0	1	0	0	0	1	1	2	2	1	2	0	0	0
SOUTHERN DOMINIONS	7	0	0	1	1	1	0	0	0	0	0	0	0	0	1	2	0	0	1	0	1	0
S. AFRICA +RHOD.	3	0	0	0	0	0	0	0	0	0	0	0	0	0	0	1	0	0	1	0	0	0
AUSTRALIA + N.Z.	5	0	0	1	0	1	0	0	0	0	0	0	0	0	1	1	0	0	0	0	1	0
ASIA + OTHER AFRICA	4	0	0	1	0	0	0	0	0	0	0	0	0	0	1	0	1	0	2	0	0	0
JAPAN	3	0	0	0	0	0	0	0	0	0	0	0	0	0	1	1	0	1	1	0	0	0
OTHER ASIA+AFR.	3	0	0	1	0	0	0	0	0	0	0	0	0	0	1	1	0	1	1	0	0	0
BLACK AFRICA	0	0	0	0	0	0	0	0	0	0	0	0	0	0	0	0	0	0	0	0	0	0
ARAB WORLD	1	0	0	0	0	0	0	0	0	0	0	0	0	0	0	0	0	0	0	0	0	0
INDIA	0	0	0	0	0	0	0	0	0	0	0	0	0	0	0	0	0	0	0	0	0	0
PHILIPPINES	1	0	0	0	0	0	0	0	0	0	0	0	0	0	0	0	0	0	0	0	0	0
OTHER E. ASIA	0	0	0	0	0	0	0	0	0	0	0	0	0	0	0	0	0	0	0	0	0	0
OTHER ASIA	2	0	0	0	0	0	0	0	0	0	0	0	0	0	0	1	0	0	1	0	0	0

CHAPTER 2— THE EXPANSION OF PARENT SYSTEMS
SECTION 4— THE FLOW OF MANUFACTURING BY INDUSTRY OF SUBSIDIARY
TABLE 7— SYSTEMS CLASSIFIED BY PERIOD SYSTEM FIRST OPERATED
IN SPECIFIED COUNTRIES AND REGIONS A SUBSIDIARY MANUFACTURING
BEVERAGES (SIC 208)

PERIOD

COUNTRY OR REGION	PRE 1968	PRE 1901	1901 -13	1914 -19	1920 -24	1925 -29	1930 -34	1935 -39	1940 -45	1946 -50	1951 -53	1954 -55	1956 -57	1958 -59	1960 -61	1962	1963	1964	1965	1966	1967	UNK
OUTSIDE U.S.	11	0	0	0	2	1	1	1	0	0	0	1	1	0	0	0	2	0	1	1	0	0
OUT. U.S. + CANADA	8	0	0	0	1	2	0	2	0	0	0	0	0	0	0	0	1	1	0	1	0	0
OUT. WEST. HEMIS.	8	0	0	0	1	1	0	1	0	1	0	0	0	0	1	1	1	0	0	1	0	0
OUT. WHITE CWEALTH	8	0	0	0	0	2	1	1	1	1	0	0	0	0	0	0	1	0	0	1	0	0
OUT. DEVLPED WORLD	7	0	0	0	0	2	0	2	0	1	0	1	1	0	1	0	1	0	0	1	0	0
CANADA	7	0	0	0	1	0	0	1	0	0	0	0	0	0	0	0	1	0	1	0	1	0
LATIN AMERICA	7	0	0	0	0	2	0	2	1	1	0	1	1	0	1	0	0	0	0	1	0	0
C. AMER.+CARIB.	5	0	0	0	1	0	0	2	0	1	0	0	0	0	1	1	1	0	0	1	1	0
CUBA	2	0	0	0	0	0	0	2	0	1	0	1	1	0	1	0	0	0	0	1	0	0
MEXICO	4	0	0	0	0	0	0	0	0	0	0	0	0	0	0	0	1	0	0	2	0	0
OTHER	2	0	0	0	0	2	0	0	1	0	0	1	0	0	0	0	0	1	0	1	1	0
S. AMERICA	6	0	0	0	2	2	0	0	0	0	0	1	0	1	0	0	0	1	1	0	0	0
ARGENTINA	3	0	0	0	0	1	1	0	1	0	0	1	0	0	1	0	0	0	1	0	0	0
BRAZIL	3	0	0	0	0	0	0	0	1	0	0	1	1	1	1	0	0	0	1	0	0	0
PERU	2	0	0	0	0	1	0	0	1	0	0	0	0	0	0	0	1	0	0	1	0	0
COLOMBIA	2	0	0	0	0	0	0	0	0	0	0	0	0	0	0	0	0	0	0	1	0	0
VENEZUELA	0	0	0	0	0	0	0	0	0	0	0	0	0	0	0	0	0	0	0	1	0	0
OTHER	1	0	0	0	0	0	1	0	0	0	0	0	1	1	1	0	1	0	0	0	0	0
EUROPE	5	0	0	0	0	1	0	2	0	0	0	0	0	0	0	0	1	1	0	0	0	0
EFTA	3	0	0	0	0	1	0	2	0	0	0	0	0	0	0	0	0	0	0	0	0	0
U.K.	0	0	0	0	0	1	1	0	0	0	0	0	0	0	0	0	0	0	0	0	0	0
SCANDINAVIA	0	0	0	0	0	0	0	0	0	0	0	0	0	0	0	0	1	0	0	0	0	0
SWITZERLAND	0	0	0	0	0	0	1	0	1	0	1	0	0	0	0	0	0	1	0	0	0	0
OTHER EFTA	4	0	0	0	0	0	0	0	0	0	0	0	0	0	0	0	1	0	0	0	0	0
EUROP. COMMUNITY	3	0	0	0	0	0	1	0	0	1	1	0	0	0	0	0	0	0	0	0	0	0
FRANCE	3	0	0	0	0	0	0	0	0	0	1	0	0	0	0	0	1	0	0	0	0	0
GERMANY	2	0	0	0	0	0	0	0	0	0	0	0	0	0	0	0	0	0	2	0	0	0
ITALY	2	0	0	0	0	0	0	0	0	0	0	0	0	1	0	0	1	1	1	0	0	0
BELGIUM + LUX	1	0	0	0	0	0	0	0	0	0	0	0	0	0	0	0	0	0	0	0	0	0
NETHERLANDS	1	0	0	0	0	0	0	0	0	0	0	0	0	0	0	0	0	1	0	0	0	0
SPAIN	2	0	0	0	0	0	0	0	0	0	0	0	0	0	0	0	0	0	0	0	0	0
GREECE + TURKEY	1	0	0	0	0	0	0	0	0	0	0	0	0	0	0	0	1	1	0	0	0	0
OTHER EUROPE	0	0	0	0	0	0	0	0	0	0	0	0	0	0	0	0	0	0	0	0	0	0
EUROPE EX. U.K.	4	0	0	0	0	0	0	0	0	0	0	0	0	0	0	0	1	1	0	0	0	0
SOUTHERN DOMINIONS	4	0	0	0	1	0	0	1	0	0	1	0	0	0	1	0	0	1	0	0	0	0
S. AFRICA +RHOD.	3	0	0	0	0	0	0	1	0	0	0	0	0	1	0	0	0	0	0	1	0	0
AUSTRALIA + N.Z.	2	0	0	0	0	0	1	0	0	0	1	2	0	0	1	0	0	0	0	1	0	0
ASIA + OTHER AFRICA	5	0	0	0	0	0	0	0	0	0	0	1	0	0	0	0	0	0	0	0	0	0
JAPAN	3	0	0	0	0	0	1	0	0	0	0	2	1	0	0	0	0	0	0	0	0	0
OTHER ASIA+AFR.	4	0	0	0	0	0	0	0	0	0	0	1	0	1	0	0	0	0	0	1	0	0
BLACK AFRICA	1	0	0	0	0	0	1	0	0	0	0	0	0	0	0	0	0	0	0	0	0	0
ARAB WORLD	0	0	0	0	0	0	0	0	0	0	0	0	0	0	0	0	0	0	0	0	0	0
INDIA	1	0	0	0	0	0	0	0	0	0	0	0	0	0	0	0	0	0	0	1	0	0
PHILIPPINES	3	0	0	0	0	1	1	0	0	0	0	0	0	0	0	0	0	0	0	0	0	0
OTHER E. ASIA	0	0	0	0	0	0	0	0	0	0	0	0	0	0	0	0	0	0	0	0	0	0
OTHER ASIA	1	0	0	0	0	0	0	0	0	0	0	0	0	0	0	1	0	0	0	0	0	0

CHAPTER 2- THE EXPANSION OF PARENT SYSTEMS
SECTION 4- THE FLOW OF MANUFACTURING BY INDUSTRY OF SUBSIDIARY
TABLE 8- SYSTEMS CLASSIFIED BY PERIOD SYSTEM FIRST OPERATED
IN SPECIFIED COUNTRIES AND REGIONS A SUBSIDIARY MANUFACTURING
OTHER FOOD PRODUCTS (SIC 206 AND 209)

PERIOD

COUNTRY OR REGION	PRE 1968	PRE 1901	1914 -19	1920 -24	1925 -29	1930 -34	1935 -39	1940 -45	1946 -50	1951 -53	1954 -55	1956 -57	1958 -59	1960 -61	1962	1963	1964	1965	1966	1967	UNK
OUTSIDE U.S.	30	1	3	0	0	0	0	0	1	1	4	1	6	1	2	3	0	1	0	0	0
OUT: U.S. + CANADA	29	1	2	0	0	0	2	1	2	1	4	1	6	1	2	2	1	1	0	0	0
OUT: WEST. HEMIS.	22	0	0	0	0	1	1	1	1	1	3	1	6	0	3	2	0	1	1	0	0
OUT: WHITE CWEALTH	27	1	2	0	1	1	1	1	1	2	4	0	5	0	2	1	1	1	1	0	0
OUT: DEVLPED WORLD	18	1	2	0	1	1	1	1	1	1	2	0	2	1	1	1	1	2	2	0	0
CANADA	9	0	1	0	0	1	1	0	0	0	0	0	0	0	0	1	0	0	3	1	0
LATIN AMERICA	15	1	2	0	1	1	1	1	1	1	2	0	1	1	1	1	1	0	2	0	0
C. AMER.+CARIB.	8	0	0	0	1	1	1	1	0	0	0	0	1	0	0	0	0	1	1	0	0
CUBA	2	0	0	0	1	0	0	0	0	0	0	0	0	0	0	0	0	0	0	0	0
MEXICO	6	0	0	0	0	1	1	0	1	0	1	1	1	0	0	1	0	1	1	1	0
OTHER	2	1	0	0	1	0	0	0	0	0	0	0	0	0	0	0	0	0	0	0	0
S. AMERICA	9	0	2	0	1	0	0	0	0	0	2	1	0	0	0	0	0	1	1	0	0
ARGENTINA	1	1	0	0	0	0	0	0	0	0	0	0	1	0	0	0	0	0	1	0	0
BRAZIL	2	0	2	0	1	0	0	0	0	0	1	0	0	0	0	0	0	0	0	0	0
PERU	3	1	0	0	0	0	0	0	0	1	0	0	1	0	0	0	0	0	0	0	0
COLOMBIA	2	0	0	0	0	0	0	0	0	0	0	0	0	0	0	1	0	0	1	0	0
VENEZUELA	0	0	0	0	1	0	0	0	0	0	1	0	1	0	0	0	0	1	0	0	0
OTHER	3	0	0	1	0	0	0	0	0	0	0	0	0	1	1	1	1	1	0	0	0
EUROPE	19	0	0	0	0	1	1	1	1	0	2	2	6	0	2	2	0	0	1	0	0
EFTA	11	0	0	0	0	2	2	1	1	0	2	1	1	0	0	0	1	1	1	1	0
U.K.	9	0	0	0	1	0	0	1	1	0	1	1	1	0	0	0	0	0	0	0	0
SCANDINAVIA	4	0	0	0	1	0	0	0	0	0	0	0	0	0	0	0	0	0	0	0	0
SWITZERLAND	1	0	0	0	0	0	0	0	0	0	0	0	1	0	0	0	0	0	0	0	0
OTHER EFTA	1	0	0	0	1	0	0	0	0	0	1	1	0	0	0	0	0	0	0	0	0
EUROP. COMMUNITY	14	0	0	0	0	0	0	0	0	0	2	2	4	0	2	2	0	1	0	0	0
FRANCE	3	0	0	0	0	0	0	0	0	0	1	0	2	0	0	0	0	1	0	0	0
GERMANY	5	0	0	0	0	0	0	0	0	0	1	1	1	0	0	0	1	0	0	0	0
ITALY	6	0	0	0	0	0	0	0	0	0	1	1	1	0	1	1	1	0	0	0	0
BELGIUM + LUX	0	0	0	0	0	0	0	0	0	0	0	0	0	0	0	0	0	0	0	0	0
NETHERLANDS	0	0	0	0	0	0	0	0	0	0	0	0	0	0	0	0	0	0	0	0	0
SPAIN	3	0	0	0	0	0	0	0	0	0	0	0	1	0	1	0	1	1	0	0	0
GREECE + TURKEY	1	0	0	0	0	0	0	0	1	0	0	0	0	0	0	0	0	1	1	0	0
CTHER EUROPE	3	0	0	0	1	0	0	0	1	0	0	0	1	0	0	0	0	0	0	0	0
EUROPE EX. U.K.	16	0	0	0	2	1	1	1	1	1	2	2	5	0	2	1	1	1	0	0	0
SOUTHERN DOMINIONS	7	0	0	0	1	0	0	0	0	0	0	0	1	2	0	0	0	1	0	0	0
S. AFRICA +RHOD.	1	0	0	0	1	0	0	0	0	0	0	1	0	2	0	0	0	0	0	0	0
AUSTRALIA + N.Z.	6	0	0	0	0	0	1	0	0	0	1	1	1	0	0	0	0	0	0	0	0
ASIA + OTHER AFRICA	7	0	0	0	1	1	0	0	0	0	1	0	0	0	0	0	0	0	0	0	0
JAPAN	5	0	0	0	0	0	0	0	0	0	1	1	1	0	0	0	0	0	0	0	0
OTHER ASIA+AFR.	0	0	0	0	0	0	0	0	0	0	0	0	0	0	0	0	0	0	0	0	0
BLACK AFRICA	0	0	0	0	0	0	0	0	0	0	0	0	0	0	0	0	0	0	0	0	0
ARAB WORLD	0	0	0	0	0	0	0	0	0	0	0	0	0	0	0	0	0	0	0	0	0
INDIA	2	0	0	0	0	1	0	0	0	1	0	0	0	0	0	0	0	0	0	0	0
PHILIPPINES	1	0	0	0	1	0	1	0	0	1	0	0	0	0	0	0	0	0	0	0	0
OTHER E. ASIA	1	0	0	0	1	0	0	0	0	0	0	0	0	0	0	0	0	1	0	0	0
OTHER ASIA	1	0	0	0	0	0	0	0	0	0	0	0	1	0	0	0	0	0	0	0	0

CHAPTER 2— THE EXPANSION OF PARENT SYSTEMS
SECTION 4— THE FLOW OF MANUFACTURING BY INDUSTRY OF SUBSIDIARY
TABLE 9— SYSTEMS CLASSIFIED BY PERIOD SYSTEM FIRST OPERATED
IN SPECIFIED COUNTRIES AND REGIONS A SUBSIDIARY MANUFACTURING
TEXTILES AND APPAREL (SIC 22 AND 23)

PERIOD

COUNTRY OR REGION	PRE 1968	PRE 1901	1901-13	1914-19	1920-24	1925-29	1930-34	1935-39	1940-45	1946-50	1951-53	1954-55	1956-57	1958-59	1960-61	1962	1963	1964	1965	1966	1967	UNK
OUTSIDE U.S.	28	0	1	1	1	2	2	2	2	0	2	2	0	4	3	0	1	0	2	3	0	0
OUT. U.S. + CANADA	23	0	1	0	1	0	0	0	1	1	1	2	1	4	3	1	0	0	2	2	0	0
OUT. WEST. HEMIS.	18	0	0	0	0	1	1	1	1	1	2	2	1	4	4	2	0	0	2	1	0	0
OUT. WHITE CWEALTH	20	0	1	0	1	1	1	1	1	1	1	2	1	4	7	1	0	0	1	1	0	1
OUT. DEVLPED WORLD	14	0	1	0	1	1	1	1	1	1	1	2	1	3	3	0	0	0	0	1	0	0
CANADA	13	0	0	0	0	0	1	2	1	0	0	0	0	0	1	1	0	1	0	2	0	0
LATIN AMERICA	13	0	1	1	1	0	1	1	1	1	1	2	1	2	0	0	0	1	0	1	0	0
C. AMER.+CARIB.	9	0	0	0	0	0	1	0	0	1	1	0	1	1	0	0	1	0	1	1	0	0
CUBA	2	0	0	0	0	0	0	0	0	1	0	0	0	0	0	0	0	0	0	1	0	1
MEXICO	8	0	1	1	1	0	0	0	1	0	0	0	0	0	0	0	0	0	1	0	0	0
OTHER	1	0	0	0	0	0	0	0	0	0	1	0	0	1	0	0	0	0	1	2	0	0
S. AMERICA	10	0	0	1	0	1	1	1	1	2	0	2	0	2	0	0	0	0	1	0	0	0
ARGENTINA	4	0	1	0	0	0	0	0	0	2	0	1	0	1	0	0	0	0	0	0	0	1
BRAZIL	2	0	0	0	0	0	0	0	0	0	1	0	0	0	0	0	0	0	0	0	0	0
PERU	2	0	1	0	0	0	1	0	1	0	0	0	0	0	0	0	0	0	0	0	0	1
COLOMBIA	5	0	0	1	1	0	0	0	0	1	0	0	0	0	0	0	0	0	0	0	0	0
VENEZUELA	4	0	0	0	0	0	0	0	0	0	0	0	0	2	0	1	0	0	0	0	0	1
OTHER	2	0	0	0	0	0	0	0	1	1	0	0	0	0	0	0	1	0	0	0	0	0
EUROPE	16	0	0	0	0	0	0	0	0	0	1	0	0	3	7	2	0	0	2	1	0	0
EFTA	12	0	0	0	0	0	0	0	0	0	1	0	0	1	5	2	1	0	1	1	0	0
U.K.	9	0	0	0	0	0	0	0	0	0	0	0	0	1	4	2	0	1	1	1	0	0
SCANDINAVIA	2	0	0	0	0	0	0	0	0	0	1	0	0	0	0	0	0	0	0	0	0	0
SWITZERLAND	2	0	0	0	0	0	0	0	0	0	0	0	0	0	1	1	1	0	2	0	0	1
OTHER EFTA	1	0	0	0	0	0	0	0	0	0	0	0	0	0	0	0	0	0	0	0	0	0
EUROP. COMMUNITY	12	0	0	0	0	0	0	0	0	0	1	0	0	2	5	1	1	1	0	0	0	1
FRANCE	6	0	0	0	0	0	0	0	0	0	1	0	0	2	3	0	0	0	1	0	0	0
GERMANY	4	0	0	0	0	0	0	0	0	0	0	0	0	0	1	1	1	1	1	0	0	0
ITALY	4	0	0	0	0	0	0	0	0	0	0	0	0	0	1	0	0	0	1	0	0	1
BELGIUM + LUX	4	0	0	0	0	0	0	0	0	0	0	0	0	1	1	0	1	0	1	1	0	0
NETHERLANDS	1	0	0	0	0	0	0	0	0	0	0	0	0	0	0	0	0	1	0	0	0	0
SPAIN	2	0	0	0	0	0	0	0	0	0	0	0	0	1	0	1	0	0	1	0	0	0
GREECE + TURKEY	0	0	0	0	0	0	0	0	0	0	0	0	0	0	0	0	0	0	0	0	0	0
OTHER EUROPE	0	0	0	0	0	0	0	0	0	0	0	0	0	0	0	0	0	0	0	0	0	0
EUROPE EX. U.K.	13	0	0	0	0	0	0	0	0	0	1	0	0	2	6	2	1	0	1	0	0	0
SOUTHERN DOMINIONS	5	0	0	0	0	0	0	0	0	0	0	0	0	1	1	0	0	0	0	0	0	1
S. AFRICA +RHOD.	3	0	0	0	0	0	0	0	0	0	0	0	0	0	1	0	0	1	0	0	0	1
AUSTRALIA + N.Z.	3	0	0	0	0	0	0	0	0	0	0	0	0	1	1	0	1	0	1	0	0	0
ASIA + OTHER AFRICA	5	0	0	0	0	0	0	0	0	0	0	1	0	2	0	0	0	0	0	0	0	1
JAPAN	3	0	0	0	0	0	0	0	0	0	0	0	0	2	0	0	0	0	0	0	0	1
OTHER ASIA+AFR.	3	0	0	0	0	0	0	0	0	0	0	1	0	0	0	0	0	0	0	0	0	0
BLACK AFRICA	0	0	0	0	0	0	0	0	0	0	0	0	0	1	0	0	0	0	0	0	0	0
ARAB WORLD	1	0	0	0	0	0	0	0	0	0	0	0	0	0	0	0	0	0	0	0	0	0
INDIA	1	0	0	0	0	0	0	0	0	0	0	1	0	0	0	0	0	0	0	0	0	0
PHILIPPINES	0	0	0	0	0	0	0	0	0	0	0	0	0	0	0	0	0	0	0	0	0	0
OTHER E. ASIA	1	0	0	0	0	0	0	0	0	0	0	0	0	0	0	0	0	0	0	0	0	1
OTHER ASIA	0	0	0	0	0	0	0	0	0	0	0	0	0	0	0	0	0	0	0	0	0	0

CHAPTER 2- THE EXPANSION OF PARENT SYSTEMS
SECTION 4- THE FLOW OF MANUFACTURING BY INDUSTRY OF SUBSIDIARY
TABLE 10- SYSTEMS CLASSIFIED BY PERIOD SYSTEM FIRST OPERATED
IN SPECIFIED COUNTRIES AND REGIONS A SUBSIDIARY MANUFACTURING
PAPER AND PAPERBOARD PRODUCTS, EXCEPT CONTAINERS (SIC 264)

PERIOD

COUNTRY OR REGION	PRE 1968	PRE 1901	1901 -13	1914 -19	1920 -24	1925 -29	1930 -34	1935 -39	1940 -45	1946 -50	1951 -53	1954 -55	1956 -57	1958 -59	1960 -61	1962 -63	1964	1965	1966	1967	UNK
OUTSIDE U.S.	11	1	0	1	0	0	0	0	1	1	0	3	1	0	1	0	0	1	1	0	0
OUT. U.S. + CANADA	11	1	0	0	0	0	0	0	0	0	0	3	2	0	1	0	0	1	1	1	0
OUT. WEST. HEMIS.	7	1	0	0	0	0	0	0	1	0	0	1	1	0	0	1	1	0	1	1	0
OUT. WHITE CWEALTH	10	0	0	0	0	0	0	0	0	0	0	3	1	1	1	0	1	0	1	0	0
OUT. DEVLPED WORLD	10	0	0	0	0	0	0	0	1	0	0	3	1	1	1	0	1	0	1	0	0
CANADA	4	0	0	1	0	0	1	0	1	0	0	1	0	0	0	0	0	0	0	0	0
LATIN AMERICA	10	0	0	0	0	0	1	1	1	0	0	3	1	0	0	1	1	0	1	1	0
C. AMER.+CARIB.	6	0	0	0	0	1	1	0	0	0	0	2	0	0	0	0	1	1	1	0	0
CUBA	1	0	0	0	0	1	0	1	0	0	0	0	0	0	1	0	0	0	0	0	0
MEXICO	3	0	0	0	0	0	1	0	0	0	0	1	1	0	0	1	0	0	0	0	0
OTHER	4	0	0	0	0	0	0	0	1	0	0	1	0	0	1	0	0	1	0	0	0
S. AMERICA	8	0	0	0	0	0	0	0	0	0	0	0	2	2	2	0	0	1	0	0	0
ARGENTINA	1	0	0	0	0	0	0	0	0	0	0	0	0	0	1	0	0	0	0	0	0
BRAZIL	2	0	0	0	0	0	0	0	0	0	0	0	2	0	1	0	0	0	0	0	0
PERU	1	0	0	0	0	0	0	0	0	0	0	0	0	0	0	0	0	1	0	0	0
COLOMBIA	3	0	0	0	0	0	1	0	0	0	0	0	0	0	0	1	1	1	0	0	0
VENEZUELA	3	0	0	0	0	0	0	0	1	0	0	1	0	1	0	1	0	0	0	1	0
OTHER	0	0	0	0	0	0	0	0	0	0	0	0	0	0	1	0	0	0	0	0	0
EUROPE	6	1	0	0	1	0	1	0	1	0	0	1	1	0	0	1	0	1	0	0	0
EFTA	6	1	0	0	0	0	0	0	0	0	0	1	1	1	1	1	0	1	0	0	0
U.K.	5	1	0	0	0	0	0	0	0	0	0	1	1	1	0	0	0	0	0	0	0
SCANDINAVIA	0	0	0	0	0	0	0	0	0	0	0	0	0	0	1	0	0	0	0	0	0
SWITZERLAND	0	0	0	0	0	0	0	0	0	0	0	0	0	0	0	1	0	0	0	0	0
OTHER EFTA	1	0	0	0	0	0	0	0	0	0	0	0	1	0	0	0	0	1	0	0	0
EUROP. COMMUNITY	5	0	0	0	0	1	1	0	0	0	0	0	1	1	0	1	0	0	0	0	0
FRANCE	4	0	0	0	0	1	1	0	0	0	0	0	0	0	0	0	0	0	0	0	0
GERMANY	2	0	0	0	0	0	0	0	0	0	0	2	0	2	0	0	2	0	0	0	0
ITALY	3	0	0	0	0	0	1	0	0	0	0	0	1	0	1	0	0	0	0	0	0
BELGIUM + LUX	0	0	0	0	0	0	0	0	0	0	0	0	0	0	0	0	0	0	0	0	0
NETHERLANDS	2	0	0	0	0	0	1	0	0	0	0	0	0	1	0	1	0	1	0	0	0
SPAIN	1	0	0	0	0	0	0	0	0	0	0	0	0	0	0	0	0	1	0	0	0
GREECE + TURKEY	1	0	0	0	0	0	0	0	0	1	0	0	0	0	0	0	0	0	0	0	0
OTHER EUROPE	1	0	0	0	0	0	0	0	0	1	0	1	0	1	1	1	0	0	0	0	0
EUROPE EX. U.K.	5	0	0	0	0	0	0	0	0	0	0	1	0	1	1	0	0	0	0	1	0
SOUTHERN DOMINIONS	4	0	0	0	0	0	0	0	1	0	0	1	1	1	1	0	0	0	0	0	0
S. AFRICA +RHOD.	2	0	0	0	0	0	0	0	0	0	0	0	0	0	1	0	0	0	0	0	0
AUSTRALIA + N.Z.	4	0	0	0	0	0	0	0	1	0	0	1	0	1	0	1	0	0	0	0	0
ASIA + OTHER AFRICA	4	0	0	0	0	0	0	0	0	0	0	1	1	1	0	0	0	0	0	1	0
JAPAN	2	0	0	0	0	0	0	0	0	0	0	0	0	0	0	0	0	0	0	0	0
OTHER ASIA+AFR.	3	0	0	0	0	0	0	0	0	0	0	1	1	1	0	0	0	0	0	1	0
BLACK AFRICA	0	0	0	0	0	0	0	0	0	0	0	0	0	0	0	0	0	0	0	0	0
ARAB WORLD	0	0	0	0	0	0	0	0	0	0	0	0	0	0	0	0	0	0	0	0	0
INDIA	1	0	0	0	0	0	0	0	0	0	0	0	0	0	0	0	0	0	0	0	0
PHILIPPINES	3	0	0	0	0	0	0	0	0	0	0	1	1	1	0	0	0	0	0	1	0
OTHER E. ASIA	0	0	0	0	0	0	0	0	0	0	0	0	0	0	0	0	0	0	0	1	0
OTHER ASIA	2	0	0	0	0	0	0	0	0	0	0	0	0	0	0	0	0	0	0	0	0

CHAPTER 2— THE EXPANSION OF PARENT SYSTEMS
SECTION 4— THE FLOW OF MANUFACTURING BY INDUSTRY OF SUBSIDIARY
TABLE 11— SYSTEMS CLASSIFIED BY PERIOD SYSTEM FIRST OPERATED
IN SPECIFIED COUNTRIES AND REGIONS A SUBSIDIARY MANUFACTURING
PAPERBOARD CONTAINERS AND BOXES (SIC 265)

COUNTRY OR REGION	PRE 1968	PRE 1901	1901 -13	1914 -19	1920 -24	1925 -29	1930 -34	1935 -39	1940 -42	1946 -50	1951 -53	1954 -55	1956 -57	1958 -59	1960 -61	1962	1963	1964	1965	1966	1967	UNK
OUTSIDE U.S.	12	0	0	0	0	1	1	1	2	0	0	2	2	2	2	0	0	1	0	1	0	0
OUT. U.S. + CANADA	11	0	0	0	1	1	1	0	2	0	0	1	1	2	2	1	0	1	0	1	0	0
OUT. WEST. HEMIS.	10	0	0	0	1	0	1	0	0	0	0	2	0	1	3	0	0	1	0	1	0	0
OUT. WHITE CWEALTH	10	0	0	0	1	1	1	0	2	1	0	1	0	2	1	1	1	1	0	1	0	0
OUT. DEVLPED WORLD	8	0	0	0	0	1	0	0	2	1	0	1	0	1	0	0	1	1	0	0	0	0
CANADA	6	0	0	0	0	0	0	0	0	0	0	0	0	0	0	0	0	0	0	1	0	0
LATIN AMERICA	7	0	0	0	1	0	0	2	2	0	0	0	0	2	0	0	0	0	0	1	0	0
C. AMER.+CARIB.	5	0	0	0	1	0	0	1	1	1	0	1	0	0	0	0	0	0	0	0	0	0
CUBA	1	0	0	0	0	0	0	0	0	1	0	0	0	0	0	0	0	0	0	0	0	0
MEXICO	4	0	0	0	1	0	0	1	0	0	1	0	0	1	1	0	1	0	0	0	0	0
OTHER	3	0	0	0	0	0	0	0	1	0	0	0	0	0	1	0	0	0	1	0	0	0
S. AMERICA	7	0	0	0	0	0	0	2	0	1	1	0	1	0	1	0	0	0	0	0	0	0
ARGENTINA	1	0	0	0	0	0	0	0	0	1	0	1	0	0	0	0	0	0	0	0	0	0
BRAZIL	3	0	0	0	0	0	0	0	1	1	1	0	1	0	0	0	0	0	1	0	0	0
PERU	2	0	0	0	0	0	0	0	1	0	0	0	0	0	0	0	0	0	0	0	0	0
COLOMBIA	2	0	0	0	0	0	0	1	1	1	1	0	0	0	0	0	0	0	0	1	0	0
VENEZUELA	5	0	0	0	0	0	0	0	0	1	1	0	0	2	2	1	1	0	0	1	0	0
OTHER	3	0	0	0	0	0	0	0	0	0	0	0	0	0	2	1	0	0	1	0	0	0
EUROPE	7	0	0	0	0	0	1	0	0	0	0	1	0	1	1	1	0	0	1	2	1	0
EFTA	4	0	0	0	0	0	0	0	0	0	0	0	0	1	1	1	0	0	0	2	1	0
U.K.	2	0	0	0	0	0	0	0	0	0	0	0	0	1	1	1	0	0	0	1	1	0
SCANDINAVIA	2	0	0	0	0	0	0	0	0	0	0	0	0	0	0	1	0	0	0	1	0	0
SWITZERLAND	0	0	0	0	0	0	0	0	0	0	0	0	0	0	0	1	0	0	0	0	0	0
OTHER EFTA	0	0	0	0	0	0	0	0	0	0	0	0	0	0	0	0	0	0	0	1	0	0
EUROP. COMMUNITY	6	0	0	0	0	0	1	0	0	0	0	1	0	0	0	0	0	1	0	0	0	0
FRANCE	1	0	0	0	0	0	0	0	0	0	0	0	0	0	0	0	0	0	0	0	0	0
GERMANY	5	0	0	0	0	0	1	0	0	0	0	0	0	1	1	1	0	0	0	1	0	0
ITALY	1	0	0	0	0	0	0	0	0	0	0	1	0	2	0	0	0	0	0	0	0	0
BELGIUM + LUX	2	0	0	0	0	1	0	0	1	1	0	0	0	1	1	0	0	0	1	1	0	0
NETHERLANDS	3	0	0	0	0	0	0	0	0	0	0	0	0	0	0	0	0	0	1	0	0	0
SPAIN	4	0	0	0	0	0	0	0	0	0	0	0	0	2	2	0	0	0	2	0	0	0
GREECE + TURKEY	0	0	0	0	0	0	0	0	0	0	0	0	0	0	0	0	0	1	0	0	0	0
OTHER EUROPE	1	0	0	0	0	0	0	0	0	0	0	1	0	1	1	0	0	0	1	0	0	0
EUROPE EX. U.K.	7	0	0	0	0	1	0	0	0	0	0	1	0	1	1	1	0	0	1	1	0	0
SOUTHERN DOMINIONS	5	0	0	0	0	0	1	0	0	0	0	1	0	0	2	0	0	0	1	0	0	0
S. AFRICA +RHOD.	3	0	0	0	0	0	0	0	0	0	1	1	0	0	2	0	0	2	1	0	0	0
AUSTRALIA + N.Z.	4	0	0	0	0	0	1	0	0	1	0	0	0	0	0	0	0	1	0	0	0	0
ASIA + OTHER AFRICA	5	0	0	0	0	0	0	0	0	0	0	0	0	0	0	0	0	1	1	1	0	0
JAPAN	2	0	0	0	0	0	0	0	1	0	0	0	0	0	0	0	0	0	1	0	0	0
OTHER ASIA+AFR.	4	0	0	0	0	0	0	0	0	1	0	0	0	1	0	0	0	0	0	1	0	0
BLACK AFRICA	1	0	0	0	0	0	0	0	1	0	0	0	0	0	0	0	0	0	0	1	0	0
ARAB WORLD	1	0	0	0	0	0	0	0	0	0	0	0	0	0	0	0	0	0	0	0	0	0
INDIA	0	0	0	0	0	0	0	0	0	0	0	0	0	0	0	0	0	0	0	0	0	0
PHILIPPINES	0	0	0	0	0	0	0	0	0	0	0	0	0	0	0	0	0	0	0	0	0	0
OTHER E. ASIA	1	0	0	0	0	0	0	0	0	0	0	0	0	0	0	0	0	1	0	0	0	0
OTHER ASIA	1	0	0	0	0	0	0	0	0	0	0	0	0	1	0	0	0	1	0	0	0	0

PERIOD

CHAPTER 2- THE EXPANSION OF PARENT SYSTEMS
SECTION 4- THE FLOW OF MANUFACTURING BY INDUSTRY OF SUBSIDIARY
TABLE 12- SYSTEMS CLASSIFIED BY PERIOD SYSTEM FIRST OPERATED
IN SPECIFIED COUNTRIES AND REGIONS A SUBSIDIARY MANUFACTURING
OTHER WOOD, FURNITURE, AND PAPER PRODUCTS (SIC 24,25,261-263, AND 266)

COUNTRY OR REGION	PRE 1968	PRE 1901	1901 -13	1914 -19	1920 -24	1925 -29	1930 -34	1935 -39	1940 -45	1946 -50	1951 -53	1954 -55	1956 -57	1958 -59	1960 -61	1962	1963	1964	1965	1966	1967	UNK
OUTSIDE U.S.	24	1	1	1	0	4	0	0	1	2	0	2	2	3	1	1	0	0	3	1	1	0
OUT. U.S. + CANADA	20	1	1	0	0	2	0	0	1	0	0	1	3	5	1	1	0	0	3	0	1	0
OUT. WEST. HEMIS.	14	1	1	0	0	2	0	0	0	0	0	0	1	3	3	0	0	0	3	0	0	0
OUT. WHITE CWEALTH	19	1	0	0	0	2	0	0	1	0	0	1	3	4	1	1	0	1	2	0	2	0
OUT. DEVLPED WORLD	11	0	0	0	0	1	0	0	1	0	0	1	2	2	0	2	1	0	0	0	1	0
CANADA	13	1	0	0	1	2	0	0	0	2	0	2	0	1	1	0	0	0	2	1	0	0
LATIN AMERICA	10	0	0	0	0	1	0	1	1	0	0	1	2	2	0	2	0	0	0	0	1	0
C. AMER.+CARIB.	7	0	0	0	0	1	0	1	1	0	0	1	1	0	0	1	0	1	0	0	0	0
CUBA	0	0	0	0	0	0	0	0	0	0	0	0	0	0	0	0	0	0	0	0	0	0
MEXICO	3	0	0	0	0	0	0	0	1	0	0	0	0	0	0	0	0	1	0	0	0	0
OTHER	4	0	0	0	0	1	0	1	0	0	0	1	0	0	1	1	0	0	0	0	0	0
S. AMERICA	7	0	0	0	0	1	0	0	0	0	0	0	1	2	0	1	0	0	1	0	1	0
ARGENTINA	2	0	0	0	0	0	0	0	0	0	0	1	0	1	0	0	0	0	0	0	0	0
BRAZIL	1	0	0	0	0	0	0	0	0	0	0	0	0	0	0	0	0	0	0	0	0	0
PERU	1	0	0	0	0	1	0	0	0	0	0	0	0	0	0	0	0	0	1	0	0	0
COLOMBIA	1	0	0	0	0	0	0	0	0	0	0	0	1	1	0	0	0	0	0	1	0	0
VENEZUELA	3	0	0	0	0	1	0	0	0	0	0	0	0	0	1	1	0	0	0	1	0	0
OTHER	0	0	0	0	0	0	0	0	0	0	0	0	0	0	0	0	0	0	0	0	0	0
EUROPE	14	1	1	0	0	2	0	0	0	0	0	0	1	3	2	0	0	0	4	0	0	0
EFTA	7	1	1	0	0	1	0	0	0	0	0	0	0	2	1	0	0	1	1	0	0	0
U.K.	6	1	1	0	0	1	0	0	0	0	0	0	0	1	1	0	0	2	1	0	0	0
SCANDINAVIA	0	0	0	0	0	1	0	0	0	0	0	0	0	1	0	0	0	0	1	0	0	0
SWITZERLAND	0	0	0	0	0	0	0	0	0	0	0	0	0	0	0	0	0	0	1	0	0	0
OTHER EFTA	0	0	0	0	0	0	0	0	0	0	0	0	0	0	0	0	0	0	0	0	0	0
EUROP. COMMUNITY	7	1	0	0	0	1	0	0	0	0	0	0	0	1	0	0	0	0	2	0	0	0
FRANCE	4	1	0	0	0	0	0	0	0	0	0	0	0	1	1	0	0	1	0	0	0	0
GERMANY	3	0	0	0	0	0	0	0	0	0	0	0	0	0	0	0	0	0	1	0	0	0
ITALY	2	0	0	0	0	1	0	0	0	0	0	0	0	1	0	0	0	1	1	0	1	0
BELGIUM + LUX	1	0	0	0	0	1	0	0	0	0	0	0	0	0	0	0	0	0	0	1	0	0
NETHERLANDS	0	0	0	0	0	0	0	0	0	0	0	0	0	1	1	0	0	0	1	0	0	0
SPAIN	0	0	0	1	0	0	0	0	0	0	0	0	0	0	0	0	0	0	1	0	0	0
GREECE + TURKEY	0	0	0	0	0	0	0	0	0	0	0	0	0	0	0	0	0	0	0	0	0	0
OTHER EUROPE	0	0	0	0	0	1	0	0	0	0	0	0	0	0	1	0	0	1	0	0	1	0
EUROPE EX. U.K.	12	1	0	0	1	1	0	0	0	0	0	0	0	2	1	0	0	0	3	0	1	0
SOUTHERN DOMINIONS	2	0	0	1	0	0	0	0	0	0	0	0	0	1	0	0	0	0	0	0	0	0
S. AFRICA +RHOD.	1	0	0	0	0	0	0	0	0	0	0	0	0	0	0	0	0	0	0	0	0	0
AUSTRALIA + N.Z.	2	0	0	1	0	0	0	0	0	0	0	0	0	1	0	0	0	0	0	0	0	0
ASIA + OTHER AFRICA	5	0	0	0	0	0	0	0	0	0	0	0	0	0	2	2	2	1	0	0	0	0
JAPAN	2	0	0	0	0	0	0	0	0	0	0	0	0	1	1	1	1	1	0	1	0	0
OTHER ASIA+AFR.	3	0	0	0	0	0	0	0	0	0	0	0	0	0	1	0	1	0	0	0	0	0
BLACK AFRICA	0	0	0	0	0	0	0	0	0	0	0	0	0	0	0	0	0	0	0	0	0	0
ARAB WORLD	0	0	0	0	0	0	0	0	0	0	0	0	0	0	0	0	0	0	0	0	0	0
INDIA	3	0	0	0	0	0	0	0	0	0	0	0	0	0	1	0	0	0	0	1	0	0
PHILIPPINES	0	0	0	0	0	0	0	0	0	0	0	0	0	0	0	0	0	0	0	0	0	0
OTHER E. ASIA	0	0	0	0	0	0	0	0	0	0	0	0	0	0	0	0	0	0	0	0	0	0
OTHER ASIA	0	0	0	0	0	0	0	0	0	0	0	0	0	0	0	0	0	0	0	0	0	0

PERIOD

CHAPTER 2— THE EXPANSION OF PARENT SYSTEMS
SECTION 4— THE FLOW OF MANUFACTURING BY INDUSTRY OF SUBSIDIARY
TABLE 13— SYSTEMS CLASSIFIED BY PERIOD SYSTEM FIRST OPERATED
IN SPECIFIED COUNTRIES AND REGIONS A SUBSIDIARY MANUFACTURING
PRINTED MATTER (SIC 27)

PERIOD

COUNTRY OR REGION	PRE 1968	PRE 1901	1914 -13	1920 -19	1925 -24	1930 -29	1935 -34	1940 -39	1946 -45	1951 -50	1954 -53	1956 -55	1958 -57	1960 -59	1962 -61	1963	1964	1965	1966	1967	UNK
OUTSIDE U.S.	6	1	0	0	0	0	0	0	0	0	1	1	0	0	1	1	1	0	1	1	0
OUI. U.S. + CANADA	5	0	0	0	0	0	1	1	0	0	0	1	0	0	1	0	0	0	1	1	0
OUI. WEST. HEMIS.	5	0	0	0	0	0	0	0	1	0	0	1	0	0	1	0	1	0	1	1	0
OUI. WHITE CWEALTh	4	0	0	0	0	0	0	1	0	0	0	1	0	0	0	1	1	0	1	0	0
OUI. DEVLPED WORLD	2	0	0	0	0	0	0	1	0	0	0	0	0	0	1	0	0	0	0	0	0
CANADA	2	1	0	0	0	0	0	0	0	0	0	0	0	0	0	0	0	0	0	0	0
LATIN AMERICA	2	0	0	0	0	0	0	1	0	0	1	0	0	0	0	1	0	0	0	0	0
C. AMER.+CARIB.	1	0	0	0	0	0	0	0	0	0	0	0	0	0	0	0	0	0	0	0	0
CUBA	0	0	0	0	0	0	0	0	0	0	0	0	0	0	0	0	0	0	0	0	0
MEXICO	1	0	0	0	0	0	0	1	0	0	0	0	0	0	0	1	0	0	0	0	0
OTHER	0	0	0	0	0	0	0	0	0	0	0	0	0	0	0	0	0	0	0	0	0
S. AMERICA	2	0	0	0	0	0	0	1	0	0	1	0	0	0	0	0	0	0	0	0	0
ARGENTINA	2	0	0	0	0	0	0	0	0	0	0	0	0	0	0	0	0	0	0	0	0
BRAZIL	1	0	0	0	0	0	0	1	0	0	0	0	0	0	0	0	0	0	0	0	0
PERU	0	0	0	0	0	0	0	0	0	0	0	0	0	0	0	0	0	0	0	0	0
COLOMBIA	0	0	0	0	0	0	0	0	0	0	0	0	0	0	0	0	0	0	0	0	0
VENEZUELA	0	0	0	0	0	0	0	0	0	0	0	0	0	0	0	0	0	0	0	0	0
OTHER	0	0	0	0	0	0	0	0	0	0	0	0	0	0	0	0	0	0	0	0	0
EUROPE	4	0	0	0	0	0	0	0	1	0	0	1	0	0	0	0	1	0	1	1	0
EFTA	3	0	0	0	0	0	0	0	0	0	0	0	1	0	0	0	1	0	1	0	1
U.K.	2	0	0	0	0	0	0	0	0	0	0	0	0	0	0	0	0	0	0	0	0
SCANDINAVIA	1	0	0	0	0	0	0	0	0	0	0	0	1	0	0	0	1	0	1	0	1
SWITZERLAND	1	0	0	0	0	0	0	0	1	0	0	0	0	0	0	0	0	0	0	0	0
OTHER EFTA	0	0	0	0	0	0	0	0	0	0	0	0	0	0	0	0	1	0	0	0	0
EUROP. COMMUNITY	4	0	0	0	0	0	0	0	1	0	0	1	0	0	0	0	0	0	1	1	0
FRANCE	2	0	0	0	0	0	0	0	0	0	0	0	0	0	0	0	0	0	1	0	0
GERMANY	3	0	0	0	0	0	0	0	1	0	0	1	0	0	0	0	0	0	0	0	0
ITALY	3	0	0	0	0	0	0	0	0	0	0	0	0	0	0	0	1	0	1	0	0
BELGIUM + LUX	0	0	0	0	0	0	0	0	0	0	0	0	0	0	0	0	0	0	0	0	0
NETHERLANDS	1	0	0	0	0	0	0	0	0	0	1	0	1	0	0	0	0	0	0	0	0
SPAIN	1	0	0	0	0	0	0	0	0	0	0	0	0	0	0	0	0	0	0	0	0
GREECE + TURKEY	0	0	0	0	0	0	0	0	0	0	0	0	0	0	0	0	0	0	0	0	0
OTHER EUROPE	0	0	0	0	0	0	0	0	0	0	0	0	0	0	0	0	0	0	0	0	0
EUROPE EX. U.K.	4	0	0	0	0	0	0	0	1	0	0	1	0	0	0	0	0	0	1	1	0
SOUTHERN DOMINIONS	1	0	0	0	0	0	0	0	0	0	0	0	0	0	0	1	1	0	0	0	0
S. AFRICA +RHOD.	1	0	0	0	0	0	0	0	0	0	0	0	0	0	0	1	1	0	0	0	0
AUSTRALIA + N.Z.	0	0	0	0	0	0	0	0	0	0	0	0	0	0	0	0	0	0	0	0	0
ASIA + OTHER AFRICA	1	0	0	0	0	0	0	0	0	0	0	0	0	0	0	0	0	0	0	0	0
JAPAN	1	0	0	0	0	0	0	0	0	0	0	0	0	0	0	0	0	0	0	0	0
OTHER ASIA+AFR.	0	0	0	0	0	0	0	0	0	0	0	0	0	0	0	0	0	0	0	0	0
BLACK AFRICA	0	0	0	0	0	0	0	0	0	0	0	0	0	0	0	0	0	0	0	0	0
ARAB WORLD	0	0	0	0	0	0	0	0	0	0	0	0	0	0	0	0	0	0	0	0	0
INDIA	0	0	0	0	0	0	0	0	0	0	0	0	0	0	0	0	0	0	0	0	0
PHILIPPINES	0	0	0	0	0	0	0	0	0	0	0	0	0	0	0	0	0	0	0	0	0
OTHER E. ASIA	0	0	0	0	0	0	0	0	0	0	0	0	0	0	0	0	0	0	0	0	0
OTHER ASIA	0	0	0	0	0	0	0	0	0	0	0	0	0	0	0	0	0	0	0	0	0

CHAPTER 2- THE EXPANSION OF PARENT SYSTEMS
SECTION 4- THE FLOW OF MANUFACTURING BY INDUSTRY OF SUBSIDIARY
TABLE 14- SYSTEMS CLASSIFIED BY PERIOD SYSTEM FIRST OPERATED
IN SPECIFIED COUNTRIES AND REGIONS A SUBSIDIARY MANUFACTURING
INDUSTRIAL CHEMICALS (SIC 281)

PERIOD

COUNTRY OR REGION	PRE 1968	PRE 1901	1901 -13	1914 -19	1920 -24	1925 -29	1930 -34	1935 -39	1940 -45	1946 -50	1951 -53	1954 -55	1956 -57	1958 -59	1960 -61	1962	1963	1964	1965	1966	1967	UNK
OUTSIDE U.S.	61	2	3	0	3	5	1	3	2	7	5	5	2	4	3	3	2	4	0	5	0	0
OUT. U.S. + CANADA	55	1	1	0	2	3	1	1	3	4	6	5	4	7	6	2	3	1	1	5	0	0
OUT. WEST. HEMIS.	51	1	1	0	2	2	2	0	2	1	2	6	4	7	7	2	2	3	2	3	0	0
OUT. WHITE CWEALTH	52	1	1	0	0	3	1	0	2	7	4	5	4	3	7	1	1	4	1	5	0	0
OUT. DEVLPED WORLD	39	0	0	0	1	1	1	0	2	7	4	2	4	2	5	1	1	1	0	4	0	0
CANADA	31	1	2	0	1	1	1	2	2	4	3	3	1	2	2	2	0	4	0	0	1	0
LATIN AMERICA	33	0	0	0	1	2	2	0	2	7	4	2	3	3	3	0	1	1	0	4	0	0
C. AMER.+CARIB.	25	0	0	0	1	1	1	0	1	5	2	2	5	1	1	0	1	1	0	2	0	0
CUBA	1	0	0	0	0	0	0	0	0	0	0	0	0	0	0	0	0	0	0	0	0	1
MEXICO	24	0	0	0	1	1	1	0	1	5	2	2	3	2	2	0	0	1	0	2	0	0
OTHER	6	0	0	0	0	0	0	0	2	0	1	0	1	1	4	1	1	1	0	0	0	0
S. AMERICA	22	0	0	0	0	0	1	2	0	2	3	0	1	2	2	3	0	0	0	0	0	0
ARGENTINA	9	0	0	0	0	1	1	0	0	2	1	0	2	1	1	0	0	0	0	0	0	0
BRAZIL	9	0	0	0	0	0	0	0	0	3	1	0	0	1	1	1	0	0	0	0	1	0
PERU	3	0	0	0	0	1	1	1	0	0	0	0	0	1	2	0	1	0	0	0	0	0
COLOMBIA	9	0	0	0	0	0	0	0	0	2	0	0	0	1	1	1	0	1	0	2	0	0
VENEZUELA	7	0	0	0	0	0	0	0	1	1	0	0	0	0	2	0	0	1	0	2	1	0
OTHER	3	0	0	0	0	0	0	0	0	0	0	0	0	0	2	1	0	0	0	0	0	0
EUROPE	47	1	1	0	2	1	1	1	1	0	1	5	4	4	7	4	4	3	4	3	1	0
EFTA	22	0	0	0	2	1	1	1	0	0	1	3	2	2	2	1	2	2	3	0	0	0
U.K.	19	0	0	0	2	1	1	1	0	0	0	3	3	1	1	1	1	1	2	0	0	0
SCANDINAVIA	5	0	0	0	0	0	0	0	0	0	1	1	0	0	0	0	0	0	1	0	0	0
SWITZERLAND	0	0	0	0	0	0	0	0	0	0	0	0	0	1	1	0	0	0	0	0	0	0
OTHER EFTA	3	0	1	0	0	0	0	0	0	0	1	0	0	0	0	0	1	0	1	0	0	0
EUROP. COMMUNITY	39	1	0	0	0	2	1	0	0	0	2	4	3	4	7	5	3	3	2	0	1	0
FRANCE	15	0	1	0	0	1	1	1	0	0	1	1	0	1	3	2	1	2	0	0	0	0
GERMANY	15	1	0	0	0	1	0	0	0	0	0	1	1	0	2	4	1	1	2	0	1	0
ITALY	19	0	1	0	0	0	0	0	0	0	1	1	2	1	3	0	2	2	2	0	0	0
BELGIUM + LUX	6	0	1	0	0	0	0	0	0	0	0	0	0	0	1	1	0	2	0	0	1	0
NETHERLANDS	9	0	1	0	0	0	0	0	0	1	1	1	1	1	4	0	2	0	2	0	0	0
SPAIN	11	0	0	0	0	0	0	0	0	0	0	0	0	2	0	1	0	0	2	0	1	0
GREECE + TURKEY	2	0	0	0	0	0	0	0	0	0	0	0	0	0	0	0	1	0	0	0	0	0
OTHER EUROPE	1	0	1	0	0	0	0	0	0	0	0	0	0	0	0	0	0	0	0	0	1	0
EUROPE EX. U.K.	43	1	0	0	0	2	1	0	1	0	3	5	2	4	8	5	3	3	3	3	1	0
SOUTHERN DOMINIONS	14	0	0	0	2	2	0	0	1	1	0	1	0	2	2	0	0	0	0	2	1	0
S. AFRICA +RHOD.	3	0	0	0	0	0	0	0	0	0	0	0	0	0	2	0	0	0	0	1	1	0
AUSTRALIA + N.Z.	13	0	0	0	2	2	0	0	1	1	2	2	2	2	0	2	1	1	1	5	1	1
ASIA + OTHER AFRICA	24	0	0	0	0	0	0	0	0	0	0	0	1	0	1	0	0	2	2	4	1	1
JAPAN	17	0	0	0	0	0	0	0	0	0	0	1	1	1	0	1	2	1	1	1	0	0
OTHER ASIA+AFR.	11	0	0	0	0	0	0	0	0	0	0	0	0	0	0	0	0	0	0	0	0	1
BLACK AFRICA	0	0	0	0	0	0	0	0	0	0	0	0	0	0	0	0	0	0	0	0	0	1
ARAB WORLD	4	0	0	0	0	0	0	0	0	0	1	1	1	1	0	1	0	0	1	0	0	0
INDIA	1	0	0	0	0	0	0	0	0	0	0	0	0	0	0	0	0	1	0	0	0	0
PHILIPPINES	3	0	0	0	0	0	0	0	0	0	0	1	0	0	0	0	0	0	1	0	0	0
OTHER E. ASIA	2	0	0	0	0	0	0	0	0	0	0	0	0	0	0	0	0	0	0	0	0	0
OTHER ASIA	3	0	0	0	0	0	0	0	0	0	0	0	1	1	1	0	0	0	0	1	0	0

CHAPTER 2- THE EXPANSION OF PARENT SYSTEMS
SECTION 4- THE FLOW OF MANUFACTURING BY INDUSTRY OF SUBSIDIARY
TABLE 15- SYSTEMS CLASSIFIED BY PERIOD SYSTEM FIRST OPERATED
IN SPECIFIED COUNTRIES AND REGIONS A SUBSIDIARY MANUFACTURING
PLASTICS AND SYNTHETICS (SIC 282)

COUNTRY OR REGION	PRE 1998	PRE 1901	1901 -13	1914 -19	1920 -24	1925 -29	1930 -34	1935 -39	1940 -45	1946 -50	1951 -53	1954 -55	1956 -57	1958 -59	1960 -61	1962	1963	1964	1965	1966	1967	UNK
OUTSIDE U.S.	51	0	1	1	2	2	1	4	2	1	4	4	7	2	6	2	5	1	4	2	0	0
OUT. U.S. + CANADA	49	0	0	0	1	1	1	3	2	3	5	4	6	2	7	2	6	1	4	2	0	0
OUT. WEST. HEMIS.	45	0	0	0	1	1	1	2	2	2	5	4	4	5	7	3	4	2	4	2	0	1
OUT. WHITE CWEALTH	38	0	0	0	0	1	0	1	2	3	4	2	5	1	2	0	4	2	3	2	0	0
OUT. DEVLPED WORLD	27	0	0	0	0	0	1	1	2	3	4	2	4	1	2	0	3	1	2	2	0	0
CANADA	19	0	1	1	1	1	1	1	1	0	1	1	2	1	2	1	2	2	0	1	1	0
LATIN AMERICA	24	0	0	0	0	0	0	1	2	3	0	3	3	1	2	1	2	1	3	2	0	0
C. AMER.+CARIB.	17	0	0	0	0	0	1	1	1	2	4	2	3	0	1	0	3	2	3	1	0	0
CUBA	0	0	0	0	0	0	0	0	0	0	0	0	0	0	0	0	0	0	0	0	0	0
MEXICO	14	0	0	0	0	0	0	1	0	2	2	0	2	0	2	1	1	1	2	0	0	0
OTHER	4	0	0	0	0	0	1	0	1	0	0	2	0	0	0	0	1	0	0	0	0	0
S. AMERICA	17	0	0	0	0	0	0	1	1	2	4	2	1	1	1	1	2	0	1	2	0	0
ARGENTINA	7	0	0	0	0	0	1	1	0	2	1	1	0	1	0	0	1	1	1	0	0	0
BRAZIL	7	0	0	0	0	0	0	0	0	1	3	1	1	0	1	3	1	0	1	1	0	0
PERU	1	0	0	0	0	0	0	0	0	0	0	0	0	0	0	0	0	0	0	0	0	0
COLOMBIA	6	0	0	0	0	0	0	1	0	1	0	0	1	0	1	1	0	1	0	0	0	0
VENEZUELA	7	0	0	0	0	0	0	0	0	0	0	0	1	1	1	0	1	0	2	1	1	0
OTHER	1	0	0	0	0	0	0	0	0	0	0	0	0	0	0	0	0	0	0	1	1	0
EUROPE	37	0	0	1	1	1	1	1	0	1	3	4	2	3	7	2	3	1	5	2	0	0
EFTA	22	0	0	1	1	1	1	1	0	1	1	3	1	0	4	2	3	0	4	0	0	0
U.K.	19	0	0	1	1	0	1	1	0	1	1	3	1	0	4	1	2	0	3	0	0	0
SCANDINAVIA	5	0	0	0	0	0	0	0	0	0	0	0	0	0	1	1	2	0	1	0	0	0
SWITZERLAND	1	0	0	0	0	0	0	0	0	0	0	0	0	0	0	0	0	0	1	0	0	0
OTHER EFTA	1	0	0	0	0	0	0	0	0	0	0	0	0	0	0	0	0	0	1	0	0	0
EUROP. COMMUNITY	24	0	0	0	0	0	0	0	0	0	2	3	1	4	5	2	2	0	2	0	0	0
FRANCE	9	0	0	0	0	0	0	0	0	0	1	2	0	1	1	1	2	0	0	0	0	0
GERMANY	9	0	0	0	0	1	0	0	0	0	0	0	1	1	2	1	1	1	0	0	0	0
ITALY	8	0	0	0	0	0	0	0	0	0	1	0	0	0	2	3	1	0	1	0	0	0
BELGIUM + LUX	5	0	0	0	0	0	0	0	0	0	0	0	1	0	1	0	1	0	0	0	0	0
NETHERLANDS	8	0	0	0	0	0	0	0	0	0	1	1	2	1	1	3	0	1	1	0	0	1
SPAIN	6	0	0	0	0	0	0	0	0	0	0	0	0	1	1	1	1	0	1	0	0	0
GREECE + TURKEY	3	0	0	0	0	0	0	0	0	0	0	0	0	0	1	0	0	0	0	2	0	0
OTHER EUROPE	0	0	0	0	0	0	0	0	0	0	2	0	0	0	0	0	0	0	0	0	0	0
EUROPE EX. U.K.	28	0	0	0	0	1	0	0	0	0	2	3	1	4	5	4	2	1	2	3	0	0
SOUTHERN DOMINIONS	17	0	0	0	0	0	0	1	0	0	0	1	0	4	5	0	1	0	1	1	2	1
S. AFRICA +RHOD.	5	0	0	0	0	0	0	1	0	0	0	0	0	0	0	0	2	0	0	0	0	1
AUSTRALIA + N.Z.	14	0	0	0	0	0	0	0	0	0	0	1	4	4	5	2	3	1	1	1	2	0
ASIA + OTHER AFRICA	20	0	0	0	0	0	0	0	0	0	2	0	1	1	3	2	2	3	2	1	0	0
JAPAN	16	0	0	0	0	0	0	0	0	0	0	1	1	0	4	0	1	2	2	1	0	0
OTHER ASIA+AFR.	10	0	0	0	0	0	0	0	0	0	0	0	1	0	1	1	0	1	1	0	0	0
BLACK AFRICA	2	0	0	0	0	0	0	0	0	0	0	0	1	0	0	0	0	0	1	0	0	0
ARAB WORLD	0	0	0	0	0	0	0	0	0	0	0	0	0	0	0	0	0	0	1	0	0	0
INDIA	5	0	0	0	0	0	0	0	0	0	0	0	0	1	1	0	0	1	0	0	0	0
PHILIPPINES	2	0	0	0	0	0	0	0	0	0	0	0	0	0	0	0	1	0	0	0	0	0
OTHER E. ASIA	1	0	0	0	0	0	0	0	0	0	0	0	0	0	0	0	0	0	0	0	0	0
OTHER ASIA	1	0	0	0	0	0	0	0	0	0	0	0	0	0	0	1	0	0	0	0	0	0

CHAPTER 2- THE EXPANSION OF PARENT SYSTEMS
SECTION 4- THE FLOW OF MANUFACTURING BY INDUSTRY OF SUBSIDIARY
TABLE 16- SYSTEMS CLASSIFIED BY PERIOD SYSTEM FIRST OPERATED
IN SPECIFIED COUNTRIES AND REGIONS A SUBSIDIARY MANUFACTURING
DRUGS (SIC 283)

PERIOD

COUNTRY OR REGION	PRE 1968	PRE 1901	1901 -13	1914 -19	1920 -24	1925 -29	1930 -34	1935 -39	1940 -45	1946 -50	1951 -53	1954 -55	1956 -57	1958 -59	1960 -61	1962	1963	1964	1965	1966	1967	UNK
OUTSIDE U.S.	27	0	0	1	0	3	3	1	1	4	2	1	2	2	5	2	0	1	0	0	1	0
OUT. U.S. + CANADA	27	0	0	1	1	3	3	1	1	2	3	1	1	1	5	1	0	1	0	0	1	0
OUT. WEST. HEMIS.	27	0	0	0	0	3	2	2	0	2	2	2	2	3	6	2	1	1	1	0	1	0
OUT. WHITE CWEALTH	26	0	0	1	1	0	1	3	2	3	3	1	1	1	3	3	1	1	1	0	1	0
OUT. DEVLPED WORLD	22	0	0	1	0	0	1	3	2	3	3	1	2	0	0	3	0	1	1	0	1	0
CANADA	14	0	0	0	1	0	0	2	3	2	1	1	1	0	0	0	0	0	0	0	0	0
LATIN AMERICA	22	0	0	1	0	0	1	3	2	2	1	1	2	0	0	0	1	0	0	0	2	1
C. AMER.+CARIB.	20	0	0	1	1	0	1	2	1	2	3	1	2	0	0	1	0	0	0	0	2	0
CUBA	2	0	0	0	0	0	0	0	0	1	0	0	1	0	0	0	0	0	0	0	0	0
MEXICO	17	0	0	1	0	0	1	0	1	1	1	1	3	0	4	2	1	0	1	0	2	1
OTHER	10	0	0	0	0	1	0	2	1	0	0	0	1	1	0	1	0	1	1	0	1	0
S. AMERICA	20	0	0	1	0	0	0	0	1	2	4	2	1	1	4	1	2	0	0	0	1	0
ARGENTINA	12	0	0	1	0	0	0	3	1	1	2	0	1	1	1	1	0	0	0	0	1	0
BRAZIL	12	0	0	0	0	1	0	1	1	0	2	0	1	1	1	0	0	1	0	0	1	0
PERU	5	0	0	0	0	1	0	1	1	1	0	0	0	0	1	0	0	0	0	1	0	0
COLOMBIA	9	0	0	0	0	0	0	0	0	1	2	0	0	0	2	1	1	0	0	0	0	0
VENEZUELA	11	0	0	0	0	0	0	0	0	0	0	1	0	0	1	0	1	1	2	1	0	0
OTHER	9	0	0	0	0	0	0	0	0	1	1	0	0	1	8	3	0	0	2	0	1	0
EUROPE	25	0	0	1	0	3	2	1	1	2	1	1	2	2	3	0	0	1	0	0	1	0
EFTA	18	0	0	0	0	3	3	1	1	2	1	0	2	1	2	0	0	1	0	0	0	0
U.K.	16	0	0	0	0	3	3	1	0	2	1	0	2	1	1	1	0	1	0	0	0	0
SCANDINAVIA	5	0	0	0	0	0	0	0	0	0	1	1	1	4	0	1	1	2	0	0	1	0
SWITZERLAND	3	0	0	0	0	0	0	0	0	0	0	0	0	1	1	2	1	0	2	0	0	0
OTHER EFTA	5	0	0	0	0	0	0	0	1	0	2	0	0	3	0	0	1	0	0	0	0	0
EUROP. COMMUNITY	21	0	0	0	0	0	0	0	0	0	1	0	1	3	4	1	1	2	0	0	1	0
FRANCE	10	0	0	1	0	0	0	0	0	1	0	0	0	1	2	2	1	0	1	0	1	0
GERMANY	12	0	0	0	0	0	0	0	0	0	1	2	2	3	3	1	2	2	0	0	1	0
ITALY	17	0	0	0	0	0	0	0	0	0	2	1	1	3	3	0	0	0	0	0	1	0
BELGIUM + LUX	9	0	0	0	0	0	0	0	0	0	0	0	0	0	0	0	0	0	0	0	0	0
NETHERLANDS	3	0	0	0	0	0	0	0	0	0	1	0	0	1	1	1	2	0	0	0	2	0
SPAIN	7	0	0	0	0	0	0	0	0	0	0	0	0	0	1	0	0	2	0	0	0	0
GREECE + TURKEY	6	0	0	0	0	0	0	0	0	0	0	0	0	1	3	2	0	0	0	0	0	0
OTHER EUROPE	2	0	0	0	0	0	0	0	0	0	0	0	0	0	0	0	0	0	0	0	1	0
EUROPE EX. U.K.	24	0	0	1	1	0	0	0	0	1	3	3	1	7	3	2	0	0	0	0	1	0
SOUTHERN DOMINIONS	16	0	0	0	0	3	3	2	1	0	0	2	2	3	1	0	1	0	0	0	0	0
S. AFRICA +RHOD.	13	0	0	0	0	1	1	2	2	0	1	1	1	3	1	0	0	0	0	0	0	0
AUSTRALIA + N.Z.	14	0	0	0	0	3	3	1	1	2	3	0	2	2	1	1	0	0	0	0	1	0
ASIA + OTHER AFRICA	18	0	0	0	0	0	0	1	1	4	1	1	2	0	1	1	0	0	2	0	0	0
JAPAN	7	0	0	0	0	0	0	0	2	0	0	2	0	3	3	0	1	2	0	0	0	0
OTHER ASIA+AFR.	18	0	0	0	0	0	0	0	1	3	0	0	3	1	1	0	2	0	0	1	1	0
BLACK AFRICA	2	0	0	0	0	0	0	0	1	0	0	0	1	0	0	0	1	0	0	1	0	0
ARAB WORLD	2	0	0	0	0	0	0	0	0	0	0	0	0	0	0	0	0	0	0	0	0	0
INDIA	12	0	0	0	0	0	0	0	0	2	2	0	0	0	2	1	1	1	0	1	0	0
PHILIPPINES	7	0	0	0	0	0	0	0	0	0	0	0	0	0	1	1	0	0	0	0	0	0
OTHER E. ASIA	3	0	0	0	0	0	0	0	0	1	0	0	0	0	2	0	0	0	1	1	0	0
OTHER ASIA	12	0	0	0	0	0	0	0	0	1	1	0	1	3	3	2	0	0	1	0	1	0

CHAPTER 2— THE EXPANSION OF PARENT SYSTEMS
SECTION 4— THE FLOW OF MANUFACTURING BY INDUSTRY OF SUBSIDIARY
TABLE 17— SYSTEMS CLASSIFIED BY PERIOD SYSTEM FIRST OPERATED
IN SPECIFIED COUNTRIES AND REGIONS A SUBSIDIARY MANUFACTURING
SOAP AND COSMETICS (SIC 284)

PERIOD

COUNTRY OR REGION	PRE 1968	PRE 1901	1901 -13	1914 -19	1920 -24	1925 -29	1930 -34	1935 -39	1940 -45	1946 -50	1951 -53	1954 -55	1956 -57	1958 -59	1960 -61	1962	1963	1964	1965	1966	1967	UNK
OUTSIDE U.S.	31	1	2	2	1	4	3	1	1	1	1	2	2	2	2	2	1	2	1	1	0	0
OUI. U.S. + CANADA	28	1	2	1	1	3	4	1	0	1	1	2	2	1	1	2	2	1	1	1	0	0
OUI. WEST. HEMIS.	25	1	1	2	2	3	4	0	0	1	2	2	3	2	2	1	1	2	1	1	0	0
OUI. WHITE CWEALTH	25	0	1	1	0	0	1	3	1	0	1	2	2	3	2	2	2	1	0	1	1	0
OUI. DEVLPED WORLD	21	0	0	0	1	1	0	3	1	1	1	2	2	3	2	1	0	0	0	1	0	0
CANADA	13	0	0	0	0	1	3	3	1	0	0	2	2	1	2	0	1	2	0	0	0	0
LATIN AMERICA	21	1	1	2	1	1	0	3	1	1	1	2	2	3	2	1	0	1	1	1	0	0
C. AMER.+CARIB.	12	0	0	1	0	1	1	1	0	1	0	0	1	2	0	0	0	0	1	1	0	0
CUBA	2	0	0	0	0	0	0	1	0	1	0	0	0	0	0	0	0	0	0	0	0	0
MEXICO	10	0	0	0	0	1	0	0	1	0	1	0	1	2	0	0	0	1	0	1	0	0
OTHER	5	0	1	1	1	0	1	1	0	0	0	0	1	0	0	1	0	0	0	0	0	0
S. AMERICA	18	1	0	1	0	1	0	1	1	0	1	2	1	2	4	1	1	0	2	0	0	0
ARGENTINA	7	1	0	0	1	0	0	1	0	0	0	0	0	0	0	0	0	0	0	0	0	0
BRAZIL	7	0	0	1	0	1	0	1	0	0	0	2	1	0	1	1	0	0	0	0	1	0
PERU	6	0	0	2	0	0	0	0	0	0	0	0	0	1	2	0	1	0	0	0	0	0
COLOMBIA	2	0	0	0	0	0	0	0	0	0	0	0	0	0	0	0	0	0	0	0	0	0
VENEZUELA	6	0	0	0	0	0	1	0	0	0	0	1	1	2	1	0	0	2	0	0	0	0
OTHER	1	0	0	0	0	0	0	0	0	0	0	0	0	0	0	1	0	0	0	0	0	0
EUROPE	23	1	1	0	2	2	3	0	0	1	1	2	2	2	1	1	3	1	0	1	0	0
EFTA	17	1	1	0	2	2	4	0	0	1	0	1	1	0	0	0	3	2	0	0	0	0
U.K.	13	1	0	0	0	0	0	0	0	0	0	0	0	0	0	0	3	2	1	0	0	0
SCANDINAVIA	6	0	0	0	0	0	0	0	0	0	0	1	0	0	0	0	0	0	0	0	0	0
SWITZERLAND	2	0	1	0	0	0	0	0	0	0	0	0	0	0	1	1	0	0	1	0	0	0
OTHER EFTA	2	0	0	0	0	0	0	0	0	0	0	0	0	0	1	1	0	0	0	0	0	0
EUROP. COMMUNITY	18	0	0	0	2	0	0	0	0	1	0	0	2	2	1	0	0	0	0	1	1	1
FRANCE	11	0	1	2	0	0	0	0	0	0	0	2	2	3	1	0	0	0	0	0	0	0
GERMANY	10	0	1	1	0	1	0	0	0	0	1	0	0	3	3	2	0	1	0	1	0	0
ITALY	11	0	1	0	2	0	0	0	0	0	0	0	1	1	1	0	0	0	0	0	0	1
BELGIUM + LUX	6	0	0	0	1	0	0	0	0	0	0	0	0	3	1	0	0	0	0	0	0	1
NETHERLANDS	2	0	0	0	0	0	0	0	0	0	0	1	0	0	0	0	0	0	0	0	0	0
SPAIN	8	0	0	0	0	0	0	0	0	0	0	0	0	0	1	1	1	1	0	1	0	0
GREECE + TURKEY	1	0	0	0	0	0	0	0	0	0	0	0	0	0	1	0	0	0	0	0	0	0
OTHER EUROPE	3	0	0	0	0	0	0	0	0	0	0	0	0	1	1	1	1	0	0	0	0	0
EUROPE EX. U.K.	20	1	1	2	0	1	1	0	0	0	1	0	4	4	1	1	1	0	0	0	0	0
SOUTHERN DOMINIONS	12	0	0	0	0	0	0	2	1	0	0	1	1	1	0	0	1	0	0	1	0	0
S. AFRICA +RHOD.	10	0	0	0	0	0	0	1	1	0	0	0	0	2	1	0	0	2	0	0	0	0
AUSTRALIA + N.Z.	9	0	0	0	0	0	0	2	1	0	0	2	0	0	3	1	0	2	0	0	0	0
ASIA + OTHER AFRICA	9	0	0	0	0	0	0	1	0	0	0	1	0	1	1	0	1	0	0	1	0	0
JAPAN	4	0	0	0	0	0	0	1	0	0	0	0	1	1	0	0	0	0	0	0	0	0
OTHER ASIA+AFR.	7	0	0	0	0	0	1	0	0	0	0	0	0	3	1	0	1	0	0	0	0	0
BLACK AFRICA	2	0	0	0	0	0	0	1	0	0	0	0	0	0	0	0	0	0	0	0	0	0
ARAB WORLD	2	0	0	0	0	0	0	0	0	0	0	0	0	0	0	1	0	0	0	0	0	0
INDIA	2	0	0	0	0	0	0	0	0	0	0	0	0	1	0	0	0	0	0	0	0	0
PHILIPPINES	2	0	0	0	0	0	0	0	0	0	0	0	1	0	0	0	0	0	0	0	0	0
OTHER E. ASIA	2	0	0	0	0	0	0	0	0	0	0	0	0	0	0	2	0	0	0	1	0	0
OTHER ASIA	7	0	0	0	0	0	0	0	0	0	1	0	0	0	3	1	2	0	0	0	0	0

CHAPTER 2- THE EXPANSION OF PARENT SYSTEMS
SECTION 4- THE FLOW OF MANUFACTURING BY INDUSTRY OF SUBSIDIARY
TABLE 18- SYSTEMS CLASSIFIED BY PERIOD SYSTEM FIRST OPERATED
IN SPECIFIED COUNTRIES AND REGIONS A SUBSIDIARY MANUFACTURING
PAINTS (SIC 285)

COUNTRY OR REGION	PRE 1968	PRE 1901	1901 -13	1914 -19	1920 -24	1925 -29	1930 -34	1935 -39	1940 -45	1946 -50	1951 -53	1954 -55	1956 -57	1958 -59	1960 -61	1962	1963	1964	1965	1966	1967	UNK
OUTSIDE U.S.	21	0	0	1	0	0	0	0	1	0	1	5	1	1	2	0	0	0	5	1	2	1
OUT. U.S. + CANADA	16	0	0	0	0	1	0	0	0	0	1	4	0	1	2	0	0	0	4	0	2	1
OUT. WEST. HEMIS.	14	0	0	0	0	1	0	0	0	0	0	2	0	1	3	0	0	1	3	0	2	1
OUT. WHITE CMEALTH	13	0	0	0	0	1	0	0	0	0	1	4	0	1	1	0	0	0	3	0	1	1
OUT. DEVLPED WORLD	10	0	0	0	0	0	0	0	0	0	2	3	0	1	0	0	0	0	1	1	1	1
CANADA	10	0	0	1	0	0	0	0	1	0	0	2	0	0	1	0	0	0	2	1	1	1
LATIN AMERICA	9	0	0	0	0	0	0	0	0	0	0	2	2	0	0	1	0	0	2	0	1	1
C. AMER.+CARIB.	6	0	0	0	0	1	0	0	0	0	0	1	1	0	0	0	0	0	2	0	1	0
CUBA	5	0	0	0	0	1	0	0	0	0	0	2	2	0	0	0	0	0	0	0	0	0
MEXICO	3	0	0	0	0	0	0	0	0	0	0	1	0	0	0	0	0	0	1	0	1	0
OTHER	0	0	0	0	0	0	0	0	0	0	0	0	0	0	0	0	0	0	0	0	0	0
S. AMERICA	8	0	0	0	0	0	0	0	0	0	0	1	1	0	0	1	0	0	2	0	2	1
ARGENTINA	3	0	0	0	0	0	0	0	0	0	0	1	0	0	0	0	0	0	1	0	1	0
BRAZIL	3	0	0	0	0	0	0	0	0	0	0	0	0	0	0	1	0	0	1	0	0	1
PERU	0	0	0	0	0	0	0	0	0	0	0	0	0	0	0	0	0	0	0	0	0	0
COLOMBIA	2	0	0	0	0	0	0	0	0	0	0	0	1	0	0	0	0	0	1	0	0	0
VENEZUELA	2	0	0	0	0	0	0	0	0	0	0	1	0	0	0	0	0	0	0	0	1	0
OTHER	3	0	0	0	0	0	0	0	0	0	0	1	0	0	0	1	0	0	0	0	0	1
EUROPE	9	0	0	0	0	1	0	0	0	0	0	1	0	0	0	1	0	0	3	0	1	2
EFTA	5	0	0	0	0	1	0	0	0	0	0	1	0	0	0	0	0	0	2	0	0	1
U.K.	4	0	0	0	0	1	0	0	0	0	0	0	0	0	0	1	0	0	1	0	0	1
SCANDINAVIA	2	0	0	0	0	0	0	0	0	0	0	0	0	0	0	1	0	0	0	0	0	1
SWITZERLAND	1	0	0	0	0	0	0	0	0	0	0	1	0	0	0	0	0	0	0	0	0	0
OTHER EFTA	0	0	0	0	0	0	0	0	0	0	0	0	0	0	0	0	0	0	0	0	0	0
EUROP. COMMUNITY	8	0	0	0	0	0	0	0	0	0	0	1	1	0	1	1	0	1	1	0	1	1
FRANCE	3	0	0	0	0	0	0	0	0	0	0	0	0	0	0	1	0	1	0	0	0	1
GERMANY	3	0	0	0	0	0	0	0	0	0	0	0	0	0	0	0	0	0	1	0	1	1
ITALY	2	0	0	0	0	0	0	0	0	0	0	0	0	0	0	0	1	1	0	0	0	0
BELGIUM + LUX	4	0	0	0	0	0	0	0	0	0	0	1	0	0	2	0	0	1	0	0	0	0
NETHERLANDS	3	0	0	0	0	0	0	0	0	0	0	0	0	0	0	1	1	1	0	0	0	0
SPAIN	1	0	0	0	0	0	0	0	0	0	0	0	0	0	0	0	0	0	0	0	0	1
GREECE + TURKEY	0	0	0	0	0	0	0	0	0	0	0	0	0	0	0	0	0	0	0	0	0	0
OTHER EUROPE	1	0	0	0	0	0	0	0	0	0	0	0	0	0	0	0	0	0	1	0	0	0
EUROPE EX. U.K.	9	0	0	0	0	1	0	0	0	0	0	1	0	0	1	1	0	1	2	0	1	1
SOUTHERN DOMINIONS	4	0	0	0	0	0	0	0	0	0	0	0	0	0	0	1	1	0	0	0	0	2
S. AFRICA +RHOD.	1	0	0	0	0	0	0	0	0	0	0	0	0	0	0	0	0	0	0	0	0	1
AUSTRALIA + N.Z.	4	0	0	0	0	0	0	0	0	0	0	0	0	0	0	1	1	0	0	0	0	2
ASIA + OTHER AFRICA	4	0	0	0	0	0	0	0	0	0	0	1	0	0	0	1	0	0	0	0	1	1
JAPAN	3	0	0	0	0	0	0	0	0	0	0	0	0	0	0	1	0	0	0	0	1	1
OTHER ASIA+AFR.	2	0	0	0	0	0	0	0	0	0	0	1	0	0	0	0	0	0	0	0	0	1
BLACK AFRICA	1	0	0	0	0	0	0	0	0	0	0	1	0	0	0	0	0	0	0	0	0	0
ARAB WORLD	0	0	0	0	0	0	0	0	0	0	0	0	0	0	0	0	0	0	0	0	0	0
INDIA	1	0	0	0	0	0	0	0	0	0	0	0	0	0	0	1	0	0	0	0	0	0
PHILIPPINES	1	0	0	0	0	0	0	0	0	0	0	0	0	0	0	0	0	0	0	0	0	1
OTHER E. ASIA	0	0	0	0	0	0	0	0	0	0	0	0	0	0	0	0	0	0	0	0	0	0
OTHER ASIA	2	0	0	0	0	0	0	0	0	0	0	1	0	0	0	0	0	0	0	0	0	1

CHAPTER 2- THE EXPANSION OF PARENT SYSTEMS
SECTION 4- THE FLOW OF MANUFACTURING BY INDUSTRY OF SUBSIDIARY
TABLE 19- SYSTEMS CLASSIFIED BY PERIOD SYSTEM FIRST OPERATED
IN SPECIFIED COUNTRIES AND REGIONS A SUBSIDIARY MANUFACTURING
AGRICULTURAL CHEMICALS (SIC 287)

COUNTRY OR REGION	PRE 1968	PRE 1901	1901 -13	1914 -19	1920 -24	1925 -29	1930 -34	1935 -39	1940 -45	1946 -50	1951 -53	1954 -55	1956 -57	1958 -59	1960 -61	1962	1963	1964	1965	1966	1967	UNK
OUTSIDE U.S.	25	0	0	1	2	1	1	0	0	2	1	1	1	3	4	0	1	2	2	2	1	1
OUT. U.S. + CANADA	24	0	0	1	1	1	1	0	0	1	2	1	1	3	4	1	0	2	1	1	3	1
OUT. WEST. HEMIS.	21	0	0	0	1	0	0	0	0	1	0	1	0	2	2	1	2	2	3	1	3	0
OUT. WHITE CWEALTH	22	0	0	1	1	0	1	0	0	1	2	1	1	2	2	1	0	1	1	2	3	1
OUT. DEVLPED WORLD	19	0	0	1	0	0	1	1	0	0	2	1	1	2	2	0	1	1	1	2	2	1
CANADA	6	0	0	0	1	0	0	0	0	1	0	0	0	2	1	1	1	1	2	1	1	0
LATIN AMERICA	15	0	0	1	1	1	1	0	0	1	2	0	1	2	2	1	1	1	0	2	0	0
C. AMER.+CARIB.	9	0	0	1	0	0	1	1	0	0	2	0	0	2	0	1	1	0	1	2	0	1
CUBA	1	0	0	1	0	0	0	0	0	0	0	0	0	0	0	0	0	0	0	0	0	0
MEXICO	4	0	0	1	0	0	1	0	0	0	0	0	0	1	2	0	1	0	1	0	0	0
OTHER	5	0	0	0	0	0	0	1	0	0	2	0	1	0	0	1	0	0	1	1	0	1
S. AMERICA	10	0	0	0	0	0	0	0	0	0	0	0	0	2	2	0	1	0	0	0	0	0
ARGENTINA	3	0	0	0	0	0	0	0	0	0	0	0	0	0	1	1	0	1	1	1	0	0
BRAZIL	3	0	0	0	0	0	0	0	0	0	0	0	0	1	0	0	1	0	1	0	0	0
PERU	1	0	0	0	0	0	0	0	0	0	0	0	0	0	0	0	0	0	0	0	0	0
COLOMBIA	4	0	0	0	0	0	0	0	0	1	1	0	1	2	2	1	1	1	0	0	0	1
VENEZUELA	2	0	0	0	0	0	0	0	0	0	1	0	0	0	0	0	1	0	0	0	0	0
OTHER	0	0	0	0	0	0	0	0	0	0	0	0	0	0	0	0	0	0	0	0	0	0
EUROPE	16	0	0	1	0	0	0	0	0	1	0	0	0	3	3	1	2	2	2	2	1	0
EFTA	4	0	0	0	0	0	0	0	0	1	0	0	0	1	1	0	0	1	1	0	0	0
U.K.	3	0	0	0	0	0	0	0	0	1	0	0	0	1	1	0	0	0	1	0	0	0
SCANDINAVIA	1	0	0	0	0	0	0	0	0	0	0	0	0	0	0	0	0	1	0	0	0	0
SWITZERLAND	0	0	0	0	0	0	0	0	0	0	0	0	0	0	0	0	0	0	0	0	0	0
OTHER EFTA	0	0	0	0	0	0	0	0	0	0	0	0	0	0	0	0	0	0	0	0	0	0
EUROP. COMMUNITY	8	0	0	0	0	0	0	0	0	0	0	0	0	2	2	0	2	0	0	0	0	0
FRANCE	4	0	0	0	0	0	0	0	0	1	0	0	0	0	0	0	2	0	0	0	0	0
GERMANY	1	0	0	0	0	0	0	0	0	0	0	0	0	0	0	0	0	0	0	0	0	0
ITALY	2	0	0	0	0	0	0	0	0	1	1	0	0	1	1	0	0	0	0	0	0	0
BELGIUM + LUX	1	0	0	0	0	0	0	0	0	0	0	0	0	0	0	0	0	0	0	0	0	0
NETHERLANDS	1	0	0	0	0	0	0	0	0	0	0	0	0	0	0	0	0	0	0	0	0	0
SPAIN	6	0	0	0	0	0	0	0	0	1	1	0	1	1	1	1	0	1	0	2	0	0
GREECE + TURKEY	0	0	0	0	0	0	0	0	0	0	0	0	0	0	0	0	0	0	0	0	0	0
OTHER EUROPE	0	0	0	0	0	0	0	0	0	0	0	0	0	0	0	0	0	0	0	0	1	0
EUROPE EX. U.K.	14	0	0	1	0	0	0	0	0	1	1	0	1	2	2	1	2	2	1	2	1	0
SOUTHERN DOMINIONS	8	0	0	0	0	0	0	0	0	0	0	0	1	1	1	0	1	0	1	1	2	0
S. AFRICA +RHOD.	3	0	0	0	0	0	0	0	0	0	0	1	1	0	0	0	1	0	1	1	0	0
AUSTRALIA + N.Z.	5	0	0	0	0	0	0	0	0	1	0	0	0	1	1	0	0	1	2	0	2	0
ASIA + OTHER AFRICA	7	0	0	0	0	0	0	0	0	0	1	1	0	0	0	0	1	2	2	0	2	0
JAPAN	1	0	0	0	0	0	0	0	0	0	0	0	0	0	0	0	0	0	0	0	1	0
OTHER ASIA+AFR.	7	0	0	0	0	0	0	0	0	1	0	1	0	1	0	1	2	1	1	0	2	0
BLACK AFRICA	1	0	0	0	0	0	0	0	0	0	0	0	0	0	0	0	0	0	0	0	0	0
ARAB WORLD	1	0	0	0	0	0	0	0	0	0	0	0	0	0	0	0	1	0	0	0	0	0
INDIA	2	0	0	0	0	0	0	0	0	1	0	1	0	1	1	0	0	0	0	0	0	0
PHILIPPINES	1	0	0	0	0	0	0	0	0	0	0	0	0	0	0	0	1	1	0	0	0	0
OTHER E. ASIA	4	0	0	0	0	0	0	0	0	0	0	0	0	1	0	1	0	0	1	0	2	0
OTHER ASIA	1	0	0	0	0	0	0	0	0	0	0	0	0	0	0	0	0	0	1	0	0	0

CHAPTER 2- THE EXPANSION OF PARENT SYSTEMS
SECTION 4- THE FLOW OF MANUFACTURING BY INDUSTRY OF SUBSIDIARY
TABLE 20- SYSTEMS CLASSIFIED BY PERIOD SYSTEM FIRST OPERATED
IN SPECIFIED COUNTRIES AND REGIONS A SUBSIDIARY MANUFACTURING
MISCELLANEOUS CHEMICAL PRODUCTS (SIC 289)

PERIOD

COUNTRY OR REGION	PRE 1968	PRE 1901	1901 -13	1914 -19	1920 -24	1925 -29	1930 -34	1935 -39	1940 -45	1946 -50	1951 -53	1954 -55	1956 -57	1958 -59	1960 -61	1962	1963	1964	1965	1966	1967	UNK
OUTSIDE U.S.	24	1	0	1	3	1	0	0	1	0	3	1	3	2	3	2	1	2	1	0	1	0
OUT. U.S. + CANADA	21	1	1	1	3	1	1	1	0	0	3	2	0	3	2	0	1	2	0	0	1	0
OUT. WEST. HEMIS.	15	1	1	0	1	0	1	1	0	0	2	1	0	2	2	2	1	2	0	0	0	1
OUT. WHITE CWEALTH	20	0	1	1	2	1	0	0	0	1	3	2	0	2	3	0	1	1	0	0	1	0
OUT. DEVLPED WORLD	17	0	0	0	2	0	0	0	0	1	2	1	0	1	4	0	1	0	0	0	0	0
CANADA	13	0	0	1	1	2	2	2	1	0	0	0	3	0	0	1	0	0	1	0	0	0
LATIN AMERICA	16	0	0	1	2	2	0	0	0	1	1	1	0	1	4	0	0	0	1	0	1	0
C. AMER.+CARIB.	10	0	0	0	0	0	0	0	0	1	2	0	0	1	0	1	0	0	1	1	1	1
CUBA	0	0	0	0	0	0	0	0	0	0	1	0	0	0	0	0	0	0	0	0	0	0
MEXICO	7	0	0	0	0	0	1	0	0	1	0	0	0	1	0	0	0	0	0	1	0	1
OTHER	4	0	0	1	2	0	0	0	0	0	1	1	0	0	0	1	0	0	1	0	1	0
S. AMERICA	14	0	0	0	0	0	2	0	0	1	0	0	0	2	4	0	0	0	1	0	0	0
ARGENTINA	5	0	0	1	0	0	0	0	0	0	0	1	0	0	3	0	0	0	0	1	0	0
BRAZIL	7	0	0	0	0	0	0	0	0	0	2	0	0	1	1	0	0	1	0	0	0	0
PERU	0	0	0	0	0	0	0	0	0	0	0	1	0	0	0	1	0	0	0	0	0	0
COLUMBIA	4	0	0	0	0	0	0	0	0	1	2	0	0	0	2	1	0	0	0	0	0	0
VENEZUELA	1	0	0	0	0	0	0	0	0	0	0	0	0	1	0	0	0	0	0	0	0	0
OTHER	3	0	0	1	2	0	0	0	0	0	0	0	0	0	0	0	0	0	0	0	0	0
EUROPE	11	1	1	0	0	1	0	0	0	0	2	1	0	1	3	1	0	0	0	1	0	0
EFTA	9	1	0	0	0	0	0	1	0	0	1	1	0	0	0	1	0	2	0	1	1	0
U.K.	9	1	0	0	0	0	0	1	0	0	1	1	0	0	0	1	0	2	0	1	1	0
SCANDINAVIA	0	0	0	0	0	0	0	0	0	0	0	0	0	0	0	0	0	0	0	0	0	0
SWITZERLAND	1	0	0	0	0	0	0	0	0	0	0	0	0	0	0	0	0	0	0	1	0	0
OTHER EFTA	1	0	0	0	0	0	0	0	0	0	0	0	0	0	0	0	0	0	1	1	0	0
EUROP. COMMUNITY	10	0	1	0	0	0	0	0	0	0	2	1	0	1	3	1	0	0	0	0	0	0
FRANCE	5	0	1	0	0	0	0	0	0	0	0	0	0	1	2	1	0	0	1	0	0	0
GERMANY	5	0	1	0	0	0	0	0	0	0	2	0	0	0	1	0	0	0	0	0	0	0
ITALY	7	0	1	0	0	1	0	0	0	0	0	1	0	1	1	0	0	0	0	0	0	0
BELGIUM + LUX	0	0	1	0	0	0	0	0	0	0	0	0	0	0	0	0	0	0	0	0	0	0
NETHERLANDS	3	0	0	0	0	0	0	0	0	0	0	1	0	1	1	2	0	0	0	0	0	0
SPAIN	5	0	0	0	0	0	0	0	0	0	0	0	0	0	0	0	0	0	0	3	0	0
GREECE + TURKEY	0	0	0	0	0	0	0	0	0	0	0	0	0	1	1	1	0	0	0	0	0	0
OTHER EUROPE	1	0	0	0	0	0	0	0	0	0	0	0	0	0	0	1	0	0	0	0	0	0
EUROPE EX. U.K.	11	0	1	0	1	1	0	0	0	0	2	1	0	1	3	1	0	0	0	0	0	0
SOUTHERN DOMINIONS	7	0	0	1	1	0	0	1	0	0	0	1	0	2	0	0	0	0	0	1	0	0
S. AFRICA +RHOD.	4	0	0	1	1	0	1	1	0	1	0	1	0	0	0	0	0	0	0	0	0	0
AUSTRALIA + N.Z.	6	0	0	0	0	0	0	0	0	0	0	0	1	2	0	0	0	0	1	1	0	0
ASIA + OTHER AFRICA	9	0	0	0	0	0	1	0	0	0	1	0	0	0	1	2	1	2	0	1	0	0
JAPAN	4	0	0	0	0	0	0	0	0	0	1	0	0	0	1	1	0	0	0	1	0	0
OTHER ASIA+AFR.	6	0	0	0	0	0	1	0	0	0	0	0	0	0	0	1	1	2	0	0	0	0
BLACK AFRICA	0	0	0	0	0	0	0	0	0	0	0	0	0	0	0	0	0	0	0	1	0	0
ARAB WORLD	0	0	0	0	0	0	0	0	0	0	0	0	0	0	0	0	0	0	0	0	0	0
INDIA	3	0	0	0	0	0	1	0	0	0	0	0	0	0	0	0	1	0	1	1	1	0
PHILIPPINES	2	0	0	0	0	0	0	0	0	0	0	0	0	1	0	0	0	0	0	0	0	0
OTHER E. ASIA	3	0	0	0	0	0	0	0	0	0	0	0	0	0	0	1	0	0	0	0	0	0
OTHER ASIA	0	0	0	0	0	0	0	0	0	0	0	0	0	0	0	0	0	2	0	0	0	0

CHAPTER 2- THE EXPANSION OF PARENT SYSTEMS
SECTION 4- THE FLOW OF MANUFACTURING BY INDUSTRY OF SUBSIDIARY
TABLE 21- SYSTEMS CLASSIFIED BY PERIOD SYSTEM FIRST OPERATED
IN SPECIFIED COUNTRIES AND REGIONS A SUBSIDIARY MANUFACTURING
REFINED PETROLEUM (SIC 2911)

PERIOD

COUNTRY OR REGION	PRE 1908	PRE 1901	1901 -13	1914 -19	1920 -24	1925 -29	1930 -34	1935 -39	1940 -45	1946 -50	1951 -53	1954 -55	1956 -57	1958 -59	1960 -61	1962	1963	1964	1965	1966	1967	UNK
OUTSIDE U.S.	10	1	0	0	1	2	0	1	1	1	0	0	0	0	3	0	0	0	0	0	1	0
OUT. U.S. + CANADA	10	1	0	0	1	1	1	1	1	1	0	0	0	0	2	1	1	0	0	0	1	0
OUT. WEST. HEMIS.	10	1	0	0	1	1	1	1	1	1	0	0	0	0	2	1	1	1	0	0	1	0
OUT. WHITE CWEALTH	9	1	0	0	1	1	1	1	1	1	0	0	0	0	2	1	1	1	0	0	0	0
OUT. DEVLPED WORLD	7	1	0	0	0	1	2	2	1	1	0	0	0	1	0	1	1	1	0	0	0	0
CANADA	6	0	0	1	0	1	1	1	0	0	0	0	1	0	1	0	0	1	0	0	0	0
LATIN AMERICA	6	1	0	0	0	0	0	2	1	1	0	0	1	1	0	0	0	1	0	0	0	0
C. AMER.+CARIB.	5	1	1	0	0	0	0	2	0	0	0	0	1	0	0	1	0	0	0	0	0	0
CUBA	2	1	0	0	0	0	0	0	0	0	0	0	0	0	0	0	0	0	0	0	0	0
MEXICO	1	0	1	0	0	0	0	0	1	0	0	0	0	0	0	0	0	0	0	0	0	0
OTHER	5	0	1	0	0	0	0	2	0	0	0	0	1	0	2	1	1	0	0	0	0	0
S. AMERICA	5	0	0	0	0	0	0	0	0	1	0	0	0	0	0	0	0	0	0	0	0	0
ARGENTINA	2	0	0	0	0	0	0	0	0	0	1	0	0	0	1	1	0	0	0	0	0	0
BRAZIL	0	0	0	0	0	0	0	0	0	0	0	0	0	0	0	0	0	0	0	0	0	0
PERU	1	0	0	1	1	0	0	0	0	0	0	0	0	0	0	0	1	0	0	0	0	0
COLOMBIA	2	0	0	0	0	0	0	0	1	0	0	0	0	0	1	0	0	0	0	0	0	0
VENEZUELA	2	0	0	0	1	0	0	0	0	1	0	0	0	0	0	0	0	0	1	0	0	0
OTHER	1	0	0	0	0	0	0	0	0	0	0	1	0	0	0	1	0	1	0	0	0	0
EUROPE	9	1	0	0	1	1	1	0	0	1	1	0	0	0	2	0	0	1	0	0	0	0
EFTA	6	0	1	0	1	0	0	0	0	1	2	0	0	0	0	0	0	1	0	0	0	0
U.K.	5	0	0	0	1	0	0	0	0	1	2	0	0	0	0	0	0	1	0	0	0	0
SCANDINAVIA	1	0	0	0	0	0	0	0	0	0	0	0	0	0	0	0	0	0	0	0	0	0
SWITZERLAND	0	0	0	0	0	0	0	0	0	0	0	0	0	0	0	0	0	0	0	0	0	0
OTHER EFTA	1	0	1	0	0	0	0	0	0	0	0	0	0	0	0	0	0	0	0	0	0	0
EUROP. COMMUNITY	8	1	0	0	1	0	1	1	0	0	0	2	0	0	3	0	0	0	0	0	0	0
FRANCE	3	1	0	0	0	0	0	0	0	0	0	0	0	0	0	1	0	0	0	0	0	0
GERMANY	5	1	0	0	0	0	0	1	0	1	0	0	1	0	1	1	0	1	0	1	0	0
ITALY	7	1	0	0	0	0	0	0	1	0	2	0	0	0	1	1	0	0	0	0	0	0
BELGIUM + LUX	1	0	0	0	0	0	0	0	0	0	0	0	0	0	0	1	0	0	0	0	0	0
NETHERLANDS	4	0	0	0	0	0	0	0	0	1	2	0	0	0	1	0	1	0	1	0	0	0
SPAIN	2	0	0	0	0	0	0	0	0	0	0	0	0	0	0	1	0	1	0	0	0	0
GREECE + TURKEY	2	0	0	0	0	0	1	0	0	0	0	0	0	0	0	0	0	0	1	0	0	0
OTHER EUROPE	3	0	1	0	0	0	0	1	0	0	1	0	0	0	0	1	0	0	0	0	0	0
EUROPE EX. U.K.	9	1	0	0	1	1	1	0	0	1	1	0	0	0	3	0	0	1	0	0	0	0
SOUTHERN DOMINIONS	7	0	0	0	0	1	0	0	0	0	2	1	0	0	0	0	0	1	1	1	0	1
S. AFRICA +RHOD.	2	0	0	0	0	0	0	0	0	0	0	0	0	0	0	0	0	1	0	0	1	0
AUSTRALIA + N.Z.	6	0	0	0	1	1	0	2	0	0	2	1	0	0	1	0	1	1	1	0	1	0
ASIA + OTHER AFRICA	3	0	0	0	1	0	1	2	0	0	2	1	0	0	1	0	0	0	0	0	0	0
JAPAN	6	0	0	0	0	0	0	0	0	0	0	0	0	0	0	0	0	0	0	0	0	0
OTHER ASIA+AFR.	2	0	0	0	1	1	0	2	0	0	0	1	0	1	0	1	1	0	0	0	0	0
BLACK AFRICA	4	0	0	0	0	0	0	0	0	0	0	0	0	0	1	0	0	0	0	0	0	1
ARAB WORLD	1	0	0	0	0	0	0	0	0	0	0	0	0	0	2	0	1	0	0	0	0	0
INDIA	1	0	0	0	0	0	0	0	0	0	0	0	0	0	0	0	0	0	0	0	0	0
PHILIPPINES	2	0	0	0	0	0	0	0	0	0	0	0	0	0	0	0	1	0	0	0	0	0
OTHER E. ASIA	1	0	0	0	0	0	0	0	0	0	0	0	0	0	0	1	0	0	0	0	0	0
OTHER ASIA	6	0	0	0	1	1	2	2	0	0	0	0	0	0	0	1	0	0	0	0	0	1

CHAPTER 2- THE EXPANSION OF PARENT SYSTEMS
SECTION 4- THE FLOW OF MANUFACTURING BY INDUSTRY OF SUBSIDIARY
TABLE 22- SYSTEMS CLASSIFIED BY PERIOD SYSTEM FIRST OPERATED
IN SPECIFIED COUNTRIES AND REGIONS A SUBSIDIARY MANUFACTURING
OTHER PRODUCTS OF PETROLEUM AND COAL (SIC 295 AND 299)

PERIOD

COUNTRY OR REGION	PRE 1908	PRE 1901-13	1914-19	1920-24	1925-29	1930-34	1935-39	1940-45	1946-50	1951-53	1954-55	1956-57	1958-59	1960-61	1962	1963	1964	1965	1966	1967	UNK
OUTSIDE U.S.	16	2	0	0	0	2	2	0	1	0	0	1	1	3	2	1	0	0	0	0	0
OUT. U.S. + CANADA	15	2	0	0	0	1	2	1	1	0	0	0	1	3	2	1	0	0	1	1	0
OUT. WEST. HEMIS.	15	2	0	0	0	1	2	0	0	0	0	0	2	2	2	1	0	0	2	2	0
OUT. WHITE CWEALTH	13	2	0	0	1	0	0	1	1	0	0	2	1	4	2	1	0	0	0	0	0
OUT. DEVLPED WORLD	8	0	0	0	0	0	0	1	1	0	0	1	1	3	0	1	0	0	0	0	0
CANADA	5	0	1	0	0	1	1	0	0	0	0	1	0	0	1	0	1	0	1	0	0
LATIN AMERICA	6	0	0	1	1	0	0	1	0	1	1	1	1	0	0	0	0	0	0	0	0
C. AMER.+CARIB.	5	0	0	0	1	0	0	0	0	0	1	1	0	2	0	0	0	0	0	0	0
CUBA	1	0	0	0	0	0	0	0	0	0	0	0	1	0	0	0	0	0	0	0	0
MEXICO	4	0	0	0	1	0	0	0	0	0	0	0	0	2	0	0	0	0	0	0	0
OTHER	0	0	0	0	0	0	0	1	0	0	0	1	0	0	0	0	0	0	0	0	0
S. AMERICA	4	0	0	0	0	1	0	0	0	1	1	0	0	0	0	0	0	0	0	0	0
ARGENTINA	1	0	0	0	0	1	0	0	0	0	0	0	0	0	1	0	0	0	0	0	0
BRAZIL	2	0	0	0	0	0	0	0	0	0	0	0	0	0	1	0	0	0	0	0	0
PERU	1	0	0	0	0	0	0	0	0	0	0	0	0	0	0	0	0	0	0	0	0
COLOMBIA	1	0	0	0	0	0	0	0	0	1	0	0	0	0	0	1	0	1	0	0	0
VENEZUELA	1	0	0	0	0	0	0	1	0	0	0	0	0	0	0	1	0	0	0	0	0
OTHER	1	0	0	0	0	0	0	0	0	0	0	0	0	0	1	0	0	0	0	0	0
EUROPE	12	2	0	0	1	1	2	0	0	0	0	0	1	2	1	2	0	0	0	0	0
EFTA	9	2	1	0	1	1	2	0	0	1	0	0	0	0	1	2	0	0	0	0	0
U.K.	6	0	0	0	1	1	2	0	0	0	0	0	0	0	0	2	0	0	0	0	0
SCANDINAVIA	4	0	1	0	0	0	0	0	0	1	0	0	0	0	2	0	0	0	0	0	0
SWITZERLAND	0	0	0	0	0	0	0	0	0	0	0	0	0	0	0	0	0	0	0	0	0
OTHER EFTA	0	0	0	0	0	0	0	0	0	0	0	0	0	0	0	0	0	0	0	0	0
EUROP. COMMUNITY	8	0	0	0	0	0	0	0	0	0	0	1	0	3	0	0	0	0	0	0	0
FRANCE	6	2	0	0	1	1	1	1	0	0	0	1	0	1	1	0	0	0	0	0	0
GERMANY	5	2	0	0	1	0	0	0	0	0	0	1	0	1	1	0	0	2	2	0	0
ITALY	1	0	0	0	0	0	0	0	0	0	0	0	0	0	0	0	0	0	0	0	0
BELGIUM + LUX	3	0	0	0	1	0	0	0	0	0	0	0	0	0	1	1	0	0	0	0	0
NETHERLANDS	1	0	0	0	0	0	0	0	0	0	0	0	0	1	1	0	0	0	0	0	0
SPAIN	2	0	0	0	0	0	0	0	0	0	0	0	0	0	0	0	0	0	0	0	0
GREECE + TURKEY	1	0	0	0	1	0	0	0	0	1	0	0	0	1	1	1	0	1	0	0	0
OTHER EUROPE	1	0	0	0	0	0	0	1	0	0	0	0	0	0	0	0	0	0	0	0	0
EUROPE EX. U.K.	10	2	0	0	0	0	0	0	0	1	1	1	1	3	0	0	1	0	1	0	0
SOUTHERN DOMINIONS	5	0	0	0	0	0	0	0	0	0	0	0	1	1	0	0	0	0	1	0	0
S. AFRICA +RHOD.	1	0	0	0	0	0	0	0	0	0	0	0	1	0	1	0	1	0	0	1	1
AUSTRALIA + N.Z.	5	0	0	0	0	0	0	0	0	0	0	0	0	1	1	0	0	1	0	0	0
ASIA + OTHER AFRICA	9	0	0	0	0	0	0	0	0	0	0	0	1	3	1	0	0	0	0	1	1
JAPAN	5	0	0	0	0	0	0	0	0	0	0	0	0	2	0	1	0	0	0	0	1
OTHER ASIA+AFR.	5	0	0	0	0	0	0	0	0	0	0	0	1	1	1	0	0	1	0	0	0
BLACK AFRICA	1	0	0	0	0	0	0	0	0	0	0	0	0	0	0	0	0	0	0	0	0
ARAB WORLD	0	0	0	0	0	0	0	0	0	0	0	0	0	1	0	1	0	0	0	0	0
INDIA	3	0	0	0	0	0	0	0	0	0	0	0	1	0	1	0	1	0	1	0	0
PHILIPPINES	1	0	0	0	0	0	0	0	0	0	0	0	0	1	0	0	0	0	0	0	1
OTHER E. ASIA	1	0	0	0	0	0	0	0	0	0	0	0	0	0	1	1	0	0	0	0	0
OTHER ASIA	0	0	0	0	0	0	0	0	0	0	0	0	0	0	0	0	0	0	0	0	0

CHAPTER 2- THE EXPANSION OF PARENT SYSTEMS
SECTION 4- THE FLOW OF MANUFACTURING BY INDUSTRY OF SUBSIDIARY
TABLE 23- SYSTEMS CLASSIFIED BY PERIOD SYSTEM FIRST OPERATED
IN SPECIFIED COUNTRIES AND REGIONS A SUBSIDIARY MANUFACTURING
TIRES (SIC 301)

PERIOD

COUNTRY OR REGION	PRE 1968	PRE 1901	1901 -13	1914 -19	1920 -24	1925 -29	1930 -34	1935 -39	1940 -45	1946 -50	1951 -53	1954 -55	1956 -57	1958 -59	1960 -61	1962	1963	1964	1965	1966	1967	UNK
OUTSIDE U.S.	6	0	1	0	1	1	1	0	0	0	0	0	0	1	0	0	0	0	0	0	0	0
OUT. U.S. + CANADA	6	0	0	0	1	1	3	1	0	1	0	0	0	1	0	0	0	0	0	0	0	0
OUT. WEST. HEMIS.	6	0	0	0	1	1	2	1	1	2	0	0	0	1	0	0	0	0	0	0	0	0
OUT. WHITE CMWEALTH	5	0	0	0	1	0	4	0	0	0	0	0	0	0	0	0	0	0	0	0	0	0
OUT. DEVLPED WORLD	5	0	0	0	0	0	4	1	0	0	0	0	0	0	0	0	0	0	0	0	0	0
CANADA	5	0	1	1	1	1	1	0	0	0	0	0	0	0	0	0	0	0	0	0	0	0
LATIN AMERICA	5	0	0	0	0	0	1	1	0	1	0	0	0	1	0	0	0	0	0	0	0	0
C. AMER.+CARIB.	5	0	0	0	0	0	1	1	1	2	0	0	0	1	0	0	0	0	0	0	0	0
CUBA	3	0	0	0	0	0	0	0	0	0	0	0	0	0	0	0	0	0	0	0	0	0
MEXICO	5	0	0	0	0	0	3	1	1	2	0	0	0	1	0	0	0	0	0	0	0	0
OTHER	3	0	0	0	0	0	0	0	0	0	0	0	0	0	0	0	0	0	0	0	0	0
S. AMERICA	5	0	0	0	0	0	2	0	3	2	2	1	0	1	0	0	0	0	0	0	0	0
ARGENTINA	4	0	0	0	0	0	2	0	0	0	0	0	0	0	0	0	0	0	0	0	0	0
BRAZIL	5	0	0	0	0	0	0	0	1	0	0	0	0	1	0	0	0	0	0	0	0	0
PERU	2	0	0	0	0	0	0	0	3	1	0	0	0	0	0	0	0	0	0	0	0	0
COLOMBIA	3	0	0	0	0	0	0	0	2	2	0	0	0	0	0	0	0	0	0	0	0	0
VENEZUELA	4	0	0	0	0	0	0	0	0	2	0	0	0	0	0	0	0	0	0	0	0	0
OTHER	2	0	0	0	0	0	0	1	0	0	0	0	0	1	0	0	0	0	0	0	0	0
EUROPE	6	0	0	0	1	1	2	0	1	0	0	0	0	1	0	0	0	0	0	0	0	0
EFTA	6	0	0	0	1	1	0	1	1	1	0	0	0	1	0	0	0	0	0	0	0	0
U.K.	4	0	0	0	1	1	0	0	1	1	0	0	0	1	0	0	0	0	0	0	0	0
SCANDINAVIA	1	0	0	0	0	0	0	0	0	0	0	0	0	0	0	0	0	0	0	0	0	0
SWITZERLAND	2	0	0	0	0	0	1	0	1	0	0	0	0	0	0	0	0	0	0	0	0	0
OTHER EFTA	5	0	0	0	0	0	1	1	1	1	0	0	0	0	0	0	0	0	0	0	0	0
EUROP. COMMUNITY	3	0	0	0	1	0	0	0	0	0	0	0	0	0	0	0	0	0	0	0	0	0
FRANCE	4	0	0	0	0	0	0	0	0	0	2	0	0	2	0	0	0	0	0	0	0	0
GERMANY	2	0	0	0	0	0	0	0	0	1	1	1	0	0	0	0	0	0	1	0	0	0
ITALY	2	0	0	0	0	0	0	0	0	0	0	0	0	0	0	0	0	0	0	0	0	0
BELGIUM + LUX	2	0	0	0	1	0	0	0	1	1	1	0	0	0	1	0	0	0	0	0	0	0
NETHERLANDS	2	0	0	0	0	0	0	0	0	1	1	0	0	0	0	0	0	0	0	0	0	0
SPAIN	2	0	0	0	0	1	0	0	0	0	0	0	0	0	1	0	0	0	0	0	0	0
GREECE + TURKEY	1	0	0	0	0	0	1	0	0	0	0	0	0	0	0	0	0	0	0	0	0	0
OTHER EUROPE	0	0	0	0	0	0	0	0	0	0	0	0	0	0	0	0	0	0	0	0	0	0
EUROPE EX. U.K.	5	0	0	1	0	2	0	1	1	1	0	0	0	0	0	0	0	0	0	0	0	1
SOUTHERN DOMINIONS	5	0	0	0	0	0	1	1	1	1	0	0	0	0	0	0	1	0	0	0	0	0
S. AFRICA +RHOD.	3	0	0	0	0	0	1	1	1	1	0	0	0	0	0	0	1	0	1	0	0	0
AUSTRALIA + N.Z.	4	0	0	0	1	0	1	1	1	0	0	1	0	0	0	0	1	0	0	0	0	0
ASIA + OTHER AFRICA	5	0	0	0	0	0	0	2	0	0	0	0	0	0	0	0	1	0	0	0	0	0
JAPAN	2	0	0	0	0	0	0	0	0	0	0	0	0	0	0	0	0	0	0	0	0	0
OTHER ASIA+AFR.	4	0	0	0	0	0	0	0	1	1	0	0	0	0	0	0	1	0	1	0	0	0
BLACK AFRICA	2	0	0	0	0	0	0	0	0	0	0	0	0	0	0	0	0	0	0	0	0	0
ARAB WORLD	2	0	0	0	0	0	0	1	1	0	1	0	0	0	0	0	1	0	0	0	0	0
INDIA	2	0	0	0	0	0	1	1	0	1	0	0	0	0	0	0	1	0	0	0	0	0
PHILIPPINES	3	0	0	0	0	0	0	0	0	0	0	0	0	0	1	0	0	0	0	0	0	0
OTHER E. ASIA	0	0	0	0	0	0	0	0	0	0	0	0	0	0	0	0	0	0	0	0	0	0
OTHER ASIA	4	0	0	0	0	0	1	1	0	1	0	0	0	1	1	0	0	0	0	0	0	0

CHAPTER 2- THE EXPANSION OF PARENT SYSTEMS
SECTION 4- THE FLOW OF MANUFACTURING BY INDUSTRY OF SUBSIDIARY
TABLE 24- SYSTEMS CLASSIFIED BY PERIOD SYSTEM FIRST OPERATED
IN SPECIFIED COUNTRIES AND REGIONS A SUBSIDIARY MANUFACTURING
OTHER RUBBER PRODUCTS (OTHER SIC 30)

PERIOD

COUNTRY OR REGION	PRE 1968	PRE 1901	1901 -13	1914 -19	1920 -24	1925 -29	1930 -34	1935 -39	1940 -45	1946 -50	1951 -53	1954 -55	1956 -57	1958 -59	1960 -61	1962	1963	1964	1965	1966	1967	UNK
OUTSIDE U.S.	23	1	1	2	0	1	0	0	1	1	1	1	0	2	4	0	3	2	1	1	0	1
OUT. U.S. + CANADA	18	1	0	1	0	2	1	0	1	0	1	0	0	2	3	0	2	1	1	1	0	1
OUT. WEST. HEMIS.	15	1	0	1	1	2	1	0	0	0	1	0	0	1	4	0	2	0	1	1	0	0
OUT. WHITE CMEALTH	14	0	0	1	0	0	1	0	2	0	1	0	0	1	1	0	3	1	1	0	0	1
OUT. DEVLPED WORLD	10	0	0	0	0	0	1	1	2	0	1	0	0	1	0	0	0	2	1	0	0	1
CANADA	11	0	1	1	0	1	0	0	0	1	0	2	0	0	1	0	1	2	0	1	0	0
LATIN AMERICA	9	0	1	0	0	1	1	1	2	0	0	0	0	1	0	0	0	2	1	0	0	1
C. AMER.+CARIB.	7	0	0	0	0	0	1	1	1	0	0	1	0	0	0	0	0	2	1	0	0	0
CUBA	2	0	0	0	0	0	0	0	1	0	0	0	1	0	0	0	0	0	0	0	0	0
MEXICO	6	0	0	0	0	0	1	1	1	0	1	1	0	0	0	0	0	2	1	0	1	0
OTHER	2	0	0	0	0	0	0	0	1	0	0	0	0	0	0	0	0	0	0	0	0	1
S. AMERICA	7	0	0	0	0	0	1	1	0	0	1	1	0	1	0	0	0	0	0	0	0	1
ARGENTINA	2	0	0	0	0	0	1	0	0	0	0	0	0	0	0	0	0	0	0	0	0	1
BRAZIL	4	0	0	0	0	0	0	0	1	0	1	0	0	2	0	0	0	0	0	0	0	0
PERU	2	0	0	0	0	0	0	0	1	0	0	1	0	0	0	0	0	0	0	0	0	0
COLOMBIA	1	0	0	0	0	0	0	1	1	0	1	0	0	0	0	0	0	0	0	0	0	0
VENEZUELA	3	0	0	0	0	0	1	0	2	0	0	0	0	0	0	0	0	0	0	1	0	0
OTHER	0	0	0	0	0	0	0	0	0	0	0	0	0	0	0	0	0	0	0	0	0	0
EUROPE	10	1	0	0	0	1	1	0	0	0	1	0	0	0	2	0	3	0	0	0	0	0
EFTA	7	0	0	1	1	1	1	0	0	0	0	0	0	0	1	0	1	1	1	0	0	0
U.K.	5	0	0	1	1	1	1	0	0	0	0	0	0	0	1	0	0	1	0	0	0	0
SCANDINAVIA	2	0	0	0	0	0	0	0	0	0	0	0	0	0	0	0	1	0	1	0	0	0
SWITZERLAND	0	0	0	0	0	0	0	0	0	0	0	0	0	0	0	0	0	0	0	0	0	0
OTHER EFTA	0	0	0	0	0	0	0	0	0	0	0	0	0	0	0	0	0	0	0	0	0	0
EUROP. COMMUNITY	7	0	0	2	2	1	1	0	0	0	1	0	0	0	0	0	2	0	1	1	0	0
FRANCE	2	0	0	1	1	1	0	0	0	0	0	0	0	0	1	0	0	0	1	0	0	0
GERMANY	3	0	0	1	1	1	0	0	0	0	0	1	0	0	1	0	1	0	1	0	0	0
ITALY	2	0	0	0	0	0	0	0	0	0	0	0	0	0	0	0	1	0	0	0	0	0
BELGIUM + LUX	0	0	0	0	0	0	0	0	0	0	0	0	0	0	0	0	0	0	0	0	0	0
NETHERLANDS	2	0	0	0	0	0	0	0	0	1	1	1	0	0	1	0	1	0	1	1	0	0
SPAIN	3	0	0	0	0	0	0	0	0	0	0	0	0	0	0	0	2	0	0	0	0	0
GREECE + TURKEY	0	0	0	0	0	0	0	0	0	0	0	0	0	0	0	0	0	0	1	0	0	0
OTHER EUROPE	2	1	0	0	0	0	0	0	0	0	0	0	0	0	0	0	0	0	0	0	0	0
EUROPE EX. U.K.	9	0	0	1	1	0	0	0	0	0	1	1	0	0	2	0	3	0	0	0	0	0
SOUTHERN DOMINIONS	8	0	0	0	0	2	0	0	1	0	0	0	0	1	2	0	1	0	0	1	0	0
S. AFRICA +RHOD.	3	0	0	0	0	0	0	0	1	0	0	0	0	0	1	0	1	0	0	0	0	0
AUSTRALIA + N.Z.	6	0	0	1	0	2	0	0	1	0	0	0	0	1	1	0	0	0	1	1	0	0
ASIA + OTHER AFRICA	5	0	0	1	0	0	0	1	1	0	0	0	0	1	1	0	0	0	2	0	0	0
JAPAN	2	0	0	1	0	0	0	0	1	0	0	0	0	0	0	0	0	0	1	1	0	0
OTHER ASIA+AFR.	4	0	0	0	0	0	0	1	0	0	0	0	0	1	0	0	0	0	2	0	0	0
BLACK AFRICA	1	0	0	0	0	0	0	0	0	0	0	0	0	0	0	0	0	0	1	0	0	0
ARAB WORLD	2	0	0	0	0	0	0	1	0	0	0	0	0	1	0	0	0	0	1	1	0	0
INDIA	1	0	0	0	0	0	0	0	0	0	0	0	0	0	0	0	0	0	0	0	0	0
PHILIPPINES	0	0	0	0	0	0	0	0	0	0	0	0	0	1	0	0	0	0	0	1	0	0
OTHER E. ASIA	1	0	0	0	0	0	0	0	0	0	0	0	0	0	0	0	0	0	1	0	0	0
OTHER ASIA	1	0	0	0	0	0	0	1	0	0	0	0	0	0	0	0	0	0	0	0	0	0

CHAPTER 2- THE EXPANSION OF PARENT SYSTEMS
SECTION 4- THE FLOW OF MANUFACTURING BY INDUSTRY OF SUBSIDIARY
TABLE 25- SYSTEMS CLASSIFIED BY PERIOD SYSTEM FIRST OPERATED
IN SPECIFIED COUNTRIES AND REGIONS A SUBSIDIARY MANUFACTURING
GLASS PRODUCTS (SIC 321-323)

PERIOD

COUNTRY OR REGION	PRE 1968	PRE 1901	1901 -13	1914 -19	1920 -24	1925 -29	1930 -34	1935 -39	1940 -45	1946 -50	1951 -53	1954 -55	1956 -57	1958 -59	1960 -61	1962	1963	1964	1965	1966	1967	UNK
OUTSIDE U.S.	7	0	0	1	0	1	0	1	1	1	0	0	0	0	1	0	1	0	0	0	0	0
OUT. U.S. + CANADA	7	0	1	1	0	1	0	1	1	1	0	0	1	1	1	0	1	0	0	0	0	0
OUT. WEST. HEMIS.	6	0	1	1	0	0	0	1	2	1	1	1	1	0	2	0	0	0	0	0	0	0
OUT. WHITE CWEALTH	6	0	1	1	0	0	0	0	2	1	0	0	1	0	0	0	1	0	0	1	0	0
OUT. DEVLPED WORLD	5	0	1	1	0	0	0	0	2	0	0	1	0	0	0	0	1	0	0	0	0	0
CANADA	3	0	0	0	0	0	0	0	1	0	0	0	0	1	0	0	0	0	0	0	0	0
LATIN AMERICA	4	0	0	0	0	1	0	0	2	0	1	1	1	1	1	0	0	0	0	1	0	0
C. AMER.+CARIB.	2	0	0	0	0	1	0	0	0	0	1	1	1	1	0	0	0	0	0	1	0	0
CUBA	1	0	0	0	0	0	0	0	0	0	0	0	0	0	0	0	0	0	0	0	0	0
MEXICO	2	0	0	0	1	0	0	0	0	0	1	1	1	0	2	0	0	0	0	1	0	0
OTHER	0	0	0	0	0	0	0	0	0	0	0	0	0	0	0	0	0	0	0	0	0	0
S. AMERICA	4	0	0	0	0	0	0	0	2	0	0	1	1	1	1	0	0	0	0	0	0	0
ARGENTINA	2	0	0	0	0	0	0	0	2	0	0	0	0	0	0	0	0	0	0	0	0	0
BRAZIL	3	0	0	0	0	0	0	0	2	0	0	0	0	1	0	0	0	0	0	0	0	0
PERU	0	0	0	0	0	0	0	0	0	0	0	0	0	0	0	0	0	0	0	0	0	0
COLOMBIA	2	0	0	0	0	0	0	0	0	1	0	0	1	0	0	0	0	0	1	0	0	0
VENEZUELA	3	0	0	0	0	0	0	0	0	0	0	1	0	1	1	0	0	1	1	0	0	0
OTHER	2	0	0	0	0	0	0	0	2	0	0	0	0	0	0	0	0	0	0	0	0	0
EUROPE	4	0	0	0	0	0	1	0	0	1	0	1	1	1	1	0	0	0	0	0	0	0
EFTA	2	0	0	0	0	0	0	0	0	1	0	1	0	0	0	0	0	0	0	0	0	0
U.K.	2	0	0	0	0	0	0	0	0	1	0	1	0	0	0	0	0	0	0	0	0	0
SCANDINAVIA	0	0	0	0	0	0	0	0	0	0	0	0	0	0	0	0	0	0	0	0	0	0
SWITZERLAND	0	0	0	0	0	0	0	0	0	0	0	0	0	0	0	0	0	0	0	0	0	0
OTHER EFTA	0	0	0	0	0	0	0	0	0	0	0	0	0	0	0	0	0	0	0	0	0	0
EUROP. COMMUNITY	4	0	0	0	0	0	1	0	0	1	0	0	0	0	1	0	0	1	0	0	1	0
FRANCE	1	0	0	0	0	0	0	0	1	1	0	0	0	1	0	0	0	0	0	0	0	0
GERMANY	1	0	0	0	0	0	0	0	0	1	0	0	0	0	0	0	0	1	0	0	0	0
ITALY	3	0	0	0	0	0	1	0	0	0	0	0	0	0	1	0	0	0	0	0	1	0
BELGIUM + LUX	1	0	0	0	0	0	0	1	0	0	0	0	0	0	0	0	0	0	0	0	0	0
NETHERLANDS	0	0	0	0	0	0	0	0	0	0	0	0	0	0	0	0	0	0	0	1	0	0
SPAIN	1	0	0	0	0	0	0	0	0	0	0	0	0	0	1	0	0	0	0	0	0	0
GREECE + TURKEY	0	0	0	0	0	0	0	0	0	0	0	0	0	0	0	0	0	0	0	0	0	0
OTHER EUROPE	0	0	0	0	0	0	0	1	0	0	0	0	0	0	0	0	0	0	0	1	0	0
EUROPE EX. U.K.	4	0	0	0	0	0	1	0	0	1	0	0	0	0	1	0	1	0	0	0	0	0
SOUTHERN DOMINIONS	2	0	0	0	0	0	0	0	0	0	0	1	0	0	1	0	0	0	1	1	0	0
S. AFRICA +RHOD.	1	0	0	0	0	0	0	0	0	0	0	0	0	0	1	0	0	0	0	0	0	0
AUSTRALIA + N.Z.	1	0	0	0	0	0	0	0	0	0	0	1	0	0	0	0	0	0	1	0	0	0
ASIA + OTHER AFRICA	3	0	0	1	0	0	0	0	0	0	0	0	0	0	1	0	0	0	0	0	0	0
JAPAN	2	0	0	0	0	0	0	0	0	0	0	0	0	0	1	1	0	1	0	0	0	0
OTHER ASIA+AFR.	2	0	0	1	0	0	0	0	0	0	0	0	0	0	0	0	0	0	0	0	0	0
BLACK AFRICA	0	0	0	0	0	0	0	0	0	0	0	0	0	0	0	0	0	0	0	0	0	0
ARAB WORLD	0	0	0	0	0	0	0	0	0	0	0	0	0	0	0	0	0	0	0	0	0	0
INDIA	1	0	0	0	0	0	0	0	0	0	0	0	0	0	0	0	0	0	1	0	0	0
PHILIPPINES	0	0	0	0	0	0	0	0	0	0	0	0	0	0	0	0	0	0	0	0	0	0
OTHER E. ASIA	1	0	0	1	0	0	0	0	0	0	0	0	0	0	0	0	0	0	0	0	0	0
OTHER ASIA	0	0	0	0	0	0	0	0	0	0	0	0	0	0	0	0	0	0	0	0	0	0

CHAPTER 2- THE EXPANSION OF PARENT SYSTEMS
SECTION 4- THE FLOW OF MANUFACTURING BY INDUSTRY OF SUBSIDIARY
TABLE 26- SYSTEMS CLASSIFIED BY PERIOD SYSTEM FIRST OPERATED
IN SPECIFIED COUNTRIES AND REGIONS A SUBSIDIARY MANUFACTURING
STONE, CLAY, AND CONCRETE PRODUCTS (SIC 324-329)

PERIOD

COUNTRY OR REGION	PRE 1968	PRE 1901	1901 -13	1914 -19	1920 -24	1925 -29	1930 -34	1935 -39	1940 -45	1946 -50	1951 -53	1954 -55	1956 -57	1958 -59	1960 -61	1962	1963	1964	1965	1966	1967	UNK
OUTSIDE U.S.	19	0	2	0	1	2	1	2	0	0	3	1	1	1	2	1	0	0	0	0	2	0
OUT. U.S. + CANADA	18	0	2	0	1	2	1	2	0	0	3	0	1	1	2	1	0	1	0	0	1	0
OUT. WEST. HEMIS.	15	0	2	0	1	1	1	2	0	0	1	0	0	1	4	1	1	0	0	0	1	0
OUT. WHITE CWEALTH	16	0	2	0	1	4	1	1	0	0	4	0	2	1	1	1	0	0	0	0	1	0
OUT. DEVLPED WORLD	15	0	0	0	0	1	0	0	2	0	4	0	4	2	1	1	0	0	0	0	0	0
CANADA	9	0	0	1	0	0	0	0	1	1	2	1	0	0	1	0	1	0	0	2	0	0
LATIN AMERICA	14	0	0	0	0	1	0	1	2	0	4	0	4	2	1	1	1	0	0	0	2	0
C. AMER.+CARIB.	7	0	0	0	0	0	0	1	1	1	2	0	1	0	0	1	0	0	0	1	0	0
CUBA	7	0	0	0	0	0	0	0	0	0	0	0	0	0	0	0	0	0	0	0	0	0
MEXICO	0	0	0	0	0	0	0	0	1	0	2	0	1	1	1	1	0	0	0	0	0	0
OTHER	0	0	0	0	0	0	0	0	0	0	0	0	0	0	0	0	0	0	0	0	0	0
S. AMERICA	13	0	0	0	0	1	0	0	1	1	2	1	4	3	0	1	0	0	0	0	0	0
ARGENTINA	4	0	0	0	0	0	0	0	0	0	0	0	1	1	0	0	0	0	0	0	0	0
BRAZIL	5	0	0	0	0	0	0	0	0	0	2	0	2	1	0	0	0	0	0	0	0	0
PERU	1	0	0	0	0	0	0	0	0	0	0	0	0	0	0	0	0	0	0	0	0	0
COLOMBIA	1	0	0	0	0	0	0	0	0	0	0	0	0	0	0	1	0	0	0	1	0	0
VENEZUELA	2	0	0	0	0	0	0	0	0	0	0	0	0	0	1	0	0	0	0	0	0	0
OTHER	5	0	0	0	0	1	0	0	1	1	0	0	1	1	0	0	0	0	0	0	0	0
EUROPE	10	0	2	0	1	1	1	2	0	0	1	0	0	0	0	1	0	1	1	0	0	0
EFTA	8	0	2	0	0	1	1	1	0	0	1	0	0	0	0	0	0	1	1	0	1	0
U.K.	7	0	2	0	0	1	1	1	0	0	1	0	0	0	0	0	0	0	0	0	1	0
SCANDINAVIA	3	0	0	0	0	1	0	0	0	0	0	0	0	0	0	0	0	1	1	0	0	0
SWITZERLAND	0	0	0	0	0	0	0	0	0	0	0	0	0	0	0	0	0	0	0	0	0	0
OTHER EFTA	0	0	0	0	1	0	0	0	0	0	0	0	0	0	0	0	0	0	0	0	0	0
EUROP. COMMUNITY	9	0	0	0	1	2	0	1	0	1	3	0	1	1	0	1	0	1	0	0	0	0
FRANCE	6	0	0	0	1	0	0	0	0	0	1	1	0	1	0	0	0	0	0	0	0	0
GERMANY	4	0	0	0	1	1	0	0	0	0	1	0	1	0	0	0	0	0	0	0	0	0
ITALY	2	0	0	0	0	0	0	0	0	0	2	0	1	0	0	0	0	0	0	0	0	0
BELGIUM + LUX	1	0	0	0	0	1	0	0	0	0	0	0	1	0	0	0	0	0	0	0	0	0
NETHERLANDS	3	0	0	0	0	0	0	0	0	0	0	0	1	0	0	1	0	0	1	0	2	0
SPAIN	3	0	0	0	0	0	0	0	0	0	0	0	0	0	0	0	0	0	1	1	0	0
GREECE + TURKEY	1	0	0	0	0	0	0	0	0	0	1	0	0	0	0	0	0	0	1	0	0	0
OTHER EUROPE	2	0	0	0	0	3	0	0	0	0	2	0	0	0	0	1	0	0	1	0	0	0
EUROPE EX. U.K.	10	0	0	0	1	0	0	1	0	0	0	0	0	0	0	1	0	1	1	0	0	0
SOUTHERN DOMINIONS	7	0	0	0	0	0	0	3	0	0	0	1	0	0	1	0	0	1	0	0	0	0
S. AFRICA +RHOD.	4	0	0	0	0	0	0	3	0	0	0	1	0	0	0	0	0	1	1	0	0	0
AUSTRALIA + N.Z.	6	0	0	0	0	0	0	3	0	0	1	0	0	0	1	1	0	1	1	0	0	0
ASIA + OTHER AFRICA	7	0	0	0	0	0	0	0	0	0	0	0	0	0	3	1	0	1	0	0	0	1
JAPAN	3	0	0	0	0	0	0	0	0	0	0	0	0	0	0	1	0	1	0	0	0	0
OTHER ASIA+AFR.	6	0	0	0	0	0	0	0	0	0	0	1	0	0	3	1	0	1	0	0	0	0
BLACK AFRICA	1	0	0	0	0	0	0	0	0	0	0	0	0	0	0	0	0	0	1	0	0	0
ARAB WORLD	1	0	0	0	0	0	0	0	0	0	0	0	0	0	2	1	0	1	0	0	0	0
INDIA	4	0	0	0	0	0	0	0	0	0	0	1	0	0	0	0	1	0	0	0	0	1
PHILIPPINES	1	0	0	0	0	0	0	0	0	0	0	0	0	0	0	0	0	0	0	0	0	0
OTHER E. ASIA	0	0	0	0	0	0	0	0	0	0	0	0	0	0	0	1	0	0	0	0	0	0
OTHER ASIA	2	0	0	0	0	0	0	0	0	0	0	0	0	0	1	0	0	0	1	0	0	0

CHAPTER 2- THE EXPANSION OF PARENT SYSTEMS
SECTION 4- THE FLOW OF MANUFACTURING BY INDUSTRY OF SUBSIDIARY
TABLE 27- SYSTEMS CLASSIFIED BY PERIOD SYSTEM FIRST OPERATED
IN SPECIFIED COUNTRIES AND REGIONS A SUBSIDIARY MANUFACTURING
SMELTED AND REFINED NONFERROUS METALS (SIC 333)

PERIOD

COUNTRY OR REGION	PRE 1968	PRE 1901	1901 -13	1914 -19	1920 -24	1925 -29	1930 -34	1935 -39	1940 -45	1946 -50	1951 -53	1954 -55	1956 -57	1958 -59	1960 -61	1962	1963	1964	1965	1966	1967	UNK
OUTSIDE U.S.	13	0	0	0	2	1	1	1	0	0	0	0	2	3	1	0	1	0	0	0	1	0
OUT. U.S. + CANADA	11	0	0	0	2	1	2	1	0	0	0	0	2	2	0	0	1	0	0	0	1	0
OUT. WEST. HEMIS.	9	0	0	0	0	0	0	0	0	0	1	0	1	1	0	0	2	0	0	1	1	0
OUT. WHITE CWEALTH	10	0	0	0	2	0	2	1	0	0	0	0	1	3	0	0	2	0	0	0	0	0
OUT. DEVLPED WORLD	9	0	0	0	2	0	1	1	0	0	0	0	2	1	0	0	1	0	1	0	0	0
CANADA	7	0	0	0	0	2	0	0	0	0	1	0	0	2	1	0	0	1	0	0	0	0
LATIN AMERICA	8	0	0	2	0	1	1	1	0	0	0	0	2	1	1	0	0	1	1	0	0	0
C. AMER.+CARIB.	2	0	0	0	0	1	1	0	0	0	1	0	0	0	0	0	0	0	0	0	0	0
CUBA	0	0	0	0	0	1	0	0	0	0	0	0	0	0	0	0	0	0	0	0	0	0
MEXICO	2	0	0	0	0	0	1	1	0	0	0	0	0	0	0	0	0	0	0	0	0	0
OTHER	0	0	0	0	0	0	0	0	0	0	1	0	0	0	0	0	0	0	0	0	0	0
S. AMERICA	7	0	0	2	0	0	1	1	0	0	1	0	2	0	0	0	0	0	1	0	1	0
ARGENTINA	2	0	0	1	0	0	0	0	0	0	0	0	0	1	1	0	0	0	0	0	0	0
BRAZIL	2	0	0	0	0	0	1	0	0	0	0	0	0	0	0	0	0	0	1	0	0	0
PERU	1	0	0	1	0	0	0	1	0	0	0	0	0	0	0	0	0	0	0	0	0	0
COLOMBIA	1	0	0	0	0	0	0	0	0	0	0	0	1	0	0	0	0	0	0	0	0	0
VENEZUELA	1	0	0	0	0	0	0	0	0	0	0	0	0	0	1	0	0	0	0	0	0	0
OTHER	1	0	0	0	0	0	0	0	0	0	0	1	0	0	0	0	0	0	0	0	0	0
EUROPE	7	0	0	0	0	0	1	1	0	0	1	0	1	3	0	0	0	0	0	0	1	0
EFTA	7	0	0	0	0	0	1	1	0	0	1	0	1	3	0	0	0	0	0	0	1	0
U.K.	6	0	0	0	0	0	1	1	0	0	1	0	1	1	1	0	0	0	0	0	1	0
SCANDINAVIA	2	0	0	0	0	0	0	0	0	0	0	0	0	2	0	0	0	0	0	0	0	0
SWITZERLAND	2	0	0	0	0	0	0	0	0	0	0	0	0	1	1	1	0	0	0	1	0	0
OTHER EFTA	0	0	0	0	0	0	0	0	0	0	0	0	0	0	0	0	0	0	0	0	0	0
EUROP. COMMUNITY	2	0	0	0	0	0	0	0	0	0	0	0	0	1	0	0	1	0	1	0	0	0
FRANCE	0	0	0	0	0	0	0	0	0	0	0	0	0	0	0	0	0	0	0	0	0	0
GERMANY	2	0	0	0	0	0	0	0	0	0	0	0	0	1	0	0	0	0	1	0	0	0
ITALY	0	0	0	0	0	0	0	0	0	0	0	0	0	0	0	0	0	0	0	0	0	0
BELGIUM + LUX	1	0	0	0	0	0	0	0	0	0	0	0	0	0	0	0	1	0	0	0	0	0
NETHERLANDS	0	0	0	0	0	0	0	0	0	0	0	0	0	0	0	0	0	0	0	0	0	0
SPAIN	1	0	0	0	0	0	0	0	0	0	0	0	0	0	1	0	0	0	0	1	0	0
GREECE + TURKEY	0	0	0	0	0	0	0	0	0	0	0	0	0	0	0	0	0	0	0	0	0	0
OTHER EUROPE	0	0	0	0	0	0	0	0	0	0	0	0	0	0	1	0	0	0	0	0	0	0
EUROPE EX. U.K.	4	0	0	0	0	0	0	0	0	0	0	0	0	3	1	0	2	1	0	0	0	0
SOUTHERN DOMINIONS	4	0	0	0	0	0	1	0	0	0	0	0	0	1	1	0	0	1	1	0	0	0
S. AFRICA +RHOD.	2	0	0	0	0	0	0	1	0	0	1	0	0	0	0	0	0	0	1	0	0	0
AUSTRALIA + N.Z.	4	0	0	0	0	0	1	0	0	0	0	0	0	1	1	0	0	1	0	0	0	0
ASIA + OTHER AFRICA	5	0	0	0	0	0	0	0	0	0	0	0	0	1	0	0	2	2	1	1	0	0
JAPAN	2	0	0	0	0	0	0	0	0	0	0	0	0	0	0	0	1	1	0	0	0	0
OTHER ASIA+AFR.	4	0	0	0	0	0	1	0	0	0	0	0	0	1	2	0	1	1	1	0	0	0
BLACK AFRICA	3	0	0	0	0	0	0	0	0	0	0	0	0	0	0	0	0	1	0	0	0	0
ARAB WORLD	0	0	0	0	0	0	0	0	0	0	0	0	0	0	0	0	0	0	0	0	0	0
INDIA	1	0	0	0	0	0	0	0	0	0	0	0	0	1	0	0	0	0	0	0	0	0
PHILIPPINES	0	0	0	0	0	0	0	0	0	0	0	0	0	0	0	0	0	0	0	0	0	1
OTHER E. ASIA	0	0	0	0	0	0	0	0	0	0	0	0	0	0	0	0	0	0	0	0	0	0
OTHER ASIA	3	0	0	0	0	0	0	0	0	0	0	0	0	0	0	0	2	0	0	0	1	1

CHAPTER 2- THE EXPANSION OF PARENT SYSTEMS
SECTION 4- THE FLOW OF MANUFACTURING BY INDUSTRY OF SUBSIDIARY
TABLE 28- SYSTEMS CLASSIFIED BY PERIOD SYSTEM FIRST OPERATED
IN SPECIFIED COUNTRIES AND REGIONS A SUBSIDIARY MANUFACTURING
OTHER NONFERROUS METAL PRODUCTS (SIC 334-336)

PERIOD

COUNTRY OR REGION	PRE 1968	PRE 1901	1901 -13	1914 -19	1920 -24	1925 -29	1930 -34	1935 -39	1940 -45	1946 -50	1951 -53	1954 -55	1956 -57	1958 -59	1960 -61	1962	1963	1964	1965	1966	1967	UNK
OUTSIDE U.S.	13	0	0	0	1	1	0	0	0	2	0	1	2	1	2	0	1	0	0	1	1	1
OUT. U.S. + CANADA	11	0	0	0	0	0	0	0	0	0	0	1	2	2	2	0	1	1	1	1	1	1
OUT. WEST. HEMIS.	10	0	0	0	1	0	0	0	0	1	0	1	2	3	1	0	1	1	0	1	1	1
OUT. WHITE CWEALTH	8	0	0	0	0	0	0	0	1	0	0	0	2	2	1	0	0	1	1	1	1	0
OUT. DEVLPED WORLD	6	0	0	0	0	0	0	0	1	0	0	0	0	2	1	0	0	0	1	1	0	0
CANADA	6	0	0	0	0	0	0	0	1	1	0	1	1	1	1	0	0	1	0	0	1	1
LATIN AMERICA	6	0	0	0	1	1	0	0	1	1	0	0	0	2	2	0	1	1	1	1	0	1
C. AMER.+CARIB.	3	0	0	0	0	0	0	0	1	1	0	0	0	0	1	0	0	0	1	0	1	1
CUBA	0	0	0	0	0	0	0	0	0	0	0	0	0	0	0	0	0	0	0	0	0	0
MEXICO	3	0	0	0	0	0	0	0	1	1	0	0	0	0	1	0	1	0	1	1	0	0
OTHER	1	0	0	0	0	0	0	0	0	0	0	0	0	0	0	0	0	0	0	0	0	0
S. AMERICA	4	0	0	0	0	0	0	0	0	0	0	0	0	2	1	0	1	0	1	1	0	0
ARGENTINA	2	0	0	0	0	0	0	0	0	0	0	0	0	1	1	0	0	1	0	1	0	0
BRAZIL	1	0	0	0	0	0	0	0	0	0	0	0	0	0	0	1	0	0	0	0	0	0
PERU	0	0	0	0	0	0	0	0	0	0	0	0	0	0	0	0	0	0	0	0	0	0
COLOMBIA	1	0	0	0	0	0	0	0	0	0	0	0	0	0	1	0	0	0	0	0	0	0
VENEZUELA	2	0	0	0	0	0	0	0	0	1	0	0	0	1	0	0	0	0	0	0	0	0
OTHER	0	0	0	0	0	0	0	0	0	0	0	0	0	0	0	0	0	0	0	0	0	0
EUROPE	8	0	0	0	0	0	0	0	0	0	0	0	2	2	1	0	1	1	2	0	0	1
EFTA	6	0	0	0	0	0	0	0	0	0	0	1	1	2	1	0	1	1	0	0	0	1
U.K.	6	0	0	0	0	0	0	0	0	0	0	1	1	1	1	0	2	1	0	0	0	1
SCANDINAVIA	2	0	0	0	0	0	0	0	0	0	0	0	0	0	0	0	0	0	0	0	0	0
SWITZERLAND	0	0	0	0	0	0	0	0	0	0	0	0	0	0	0	0	0	0	0	0	0	0
OTHER EFTA	2	0	0	0	0	0	0	0	0	0	0	0	0	0	0	0	0	0	1	0	0	0
EUROP. COMMUNITY	4	0	0	0	0	0	0	0	0	1	0	0	0	0	1	1	0	1	1	1	1	0
FRANCE	0	0	0	0	0	0	0	0	0	0	0	0	0	0	0	0	0	0	0	0	0	0
GERMANY	1	0	0	0	0	0	0	0	0	1	0	0	0	0	0	1	1	0	0	0	1	0
ITALY	1	0	0	0	0	0	0	0	0	0	0	0	0	0	1	0	0	1	0	0	0	0
BELGIUM + LUX	2	0	0	0	0	0	0	0	0	0	0	0	0	1	0	0	0	0	1	1	0	1
NETHERLANDS	0	0	0	0	0	0	0	0	0	0	0	0	0	0	0	0	0	0	0	0	0	0
SPAIN	1	0	0	0	0	0	0	0	0	0	0	0	0	0	0	0	0	0	0	0	0	0
GREECE + TURKEY	0	0	0	0	0	0	0	0	0	0	0	0	0	0	0	0	0	0	0	0	0	1
OTHER EUROPE	0	0	0	0	0	0	0	0	0	0	0	0	1	0	0	0	0	0	0	0	0	0
EUROPE EX. U.K.	6	0	0	0	0	0	0	0	0	0	0	1	1	2	0	1	1	0	1	1	1	0
SOUTHERN DOMINIONS	4	0	0	0	0	0	0	0	0	0	0	0	0	0	3	0	0	0	0	0	1	0
S. AFRICA +RHOD.	4	0	0	0	0	0	0	0	0	0	0	0	0	0	3	0	0	0	0	0	1	0
AUSTRALIA + N.Z.	2	0	0	0	0	0	0	0	0	0	0	0	0	1	0	1	0	0	0	0	0	0
ASIA + OTHER AFRICA	2	0	0	0	0	0	0	0	0	0	0	0	0	2	1	0	1	1	0	0	0	0
JAPAN	2	0	0	0	0	0	0	0	0	0	0	0	0	2	0	0	0	0	0	0	0	0
OTHER ASIA+AFR.	0	0	0	0	0	0	0	0	0	0	0	0	0	1	1	0	1	1	0	0	0	0
BLACK AFRICA	1	0	0	0	0	0	0	0	0	0	0	0	0	0	0	0	0	0	0	0	0	0
ARAB WORLD	0	0	0	0	0	0	0	0	0	0	0	0	0	0	0	0	0	0	0	0	0	0
INDIA	1	0	0	0	0	0	0	0	0	0	0	0	0	1	1	0	1	0	0	0	0	0
PHILIPPINES	0	0	0	0	0	0	0	0	0	0	0	0	0	0	0	0	0	0	0	0	0	0
OTHER E. ASIA	0	0	0	0	0	0	0	0	0	0	0	0	0	0	0	0	0	0	0	0	0	0
OTHER ASIA	0	0	0	0	0	0	0	0	0	0	0	0	0	0	0	0	0	0	0	0	0	0

96

CHAPTER 2- THE EXPANSION OF PARENT SYSTEMS
SECTION 4- THE FLOW OF MANUFACTURING BY INDUSTRY OF SUBSIDIARY
TABLE 29- SYSTEMS CLASSIFIED BY PERIOD SYSTEM FIRST OPERATED
IN SPECIFIED COUNTRIES AND REGIONS A SUBSIDIARY MANUFACTURING
IRON, STEEL, AND MISCELLANEOUS NONFERROUS PRODUCTS (SIC 331,332,AND 339)

PERIOD

COUNTRY OR REGION	PRE 1968	PRE 1901	1901-13	1914-19	1920-24	1925-29	1930-34	1935-39	1940-45	1946-50	1951-53	1954-55	1956-57	1958-59	1960-61	1962	1963	1964	1965	1966	1967	UNK
OUTSIDE U.S.	26	1	0	0	2	2	1	1	0	3	1	1	0	0	2	2	1	0	6	1	1	1
OUT. U.S. + CANADA	23	1	0	0	1	1	1	1	0	2	1	0	0	1	3	2	1	0	6	0	1	1
OUT. WEST. HEMIS.	20	1	0	0	0	1	1	1	0	2	0	0	0	0	6	1	1	0	6	0	1	1
OUT. WHITE CWEALTH	18	1	0	0	1	1	1	1	0	2	2	0	0	1	3	2	0	0	3	0	1	0
OUT. DEVLPED WORLD	10	0	0	0	1	0	0	0	0	2	2	0	0	1	1	2	0	0	1	0	0	0
CANADA	8	0	0	0	0	0	0	0	0	2	2	1	0	0	2	0	0	0	0	1	1	0
LATIN AMERICA	9	0	0	0	0	0	0	1	0	2	2	0	0	1	1	1	0	0	1	0	1	0
C. AMER.+CARIB.	3	0	0	0	0	0	0	0	0	0	0	0	0	0	1	1	0	0	0	0	0	0
CUBA	0	0	0	0	0	0	0	0	0	0	0	0	0	0	0	0	0	0	0	0	0	0
MEXICO	3	0	0	0	0	0	0	0	0	0	0	0	0	0	1	1	0	0	0	0	0	0
OTHER	0	0	0	0	0	0	0	0	0	0	0	0	0	0	0	0	0	0	0	0	0	0
S. AMERICA	6	0	0	0	0	0	0	0	0	2	0	0	0	1	0	1	0	0	1	0	1	0
ARGENTINA	1	0	0	0	0	0	0	0	0	0	0	0	0	0	1	0	0	0	0	0	0	0
BRAZIL	4	0	0	0	0	0	0	0	0	1	0	0	0	1	0	0	0	0	1	0	1	0
PERU	0	0	0	0	0	0	0	0	0	0	0	0	0	0	0	0	0	0	0	0	0	0
COLOMBIA	1	0	0	0	0	0	0	0	0	1	0	0	0	0	0	0	0	0	0	0	0	0
VENEZUELA	0	0	0	0	0	0	0	0	0	0	0	0	0	0	0	0	0	0	0	0	0	0
OTHER	1	0	0	0	0	0	0	0	0	0	0	0	0	0	1	0	0	0	0	0	0	0
EUROPE	17	1	0	0	1	1	1	1	0	0	0	0	0	0	4	0	1	1	5	0	0	1
EFTA	10	0	0	0	0	0	1	1	0	0	0	0	0	0	3	0	1	0	2	0	0	2
U.K.	10	0	0	0	0	0	1	1	0	0	0	0	0	0	3	0	1	0	2	0	0	2
SCANDINAVIA	0	0	0	0	0	0	0	0	0	0	0	0	0	0	0	0	0	0	0	0	0	0
SWITZERLAND	0	0	0	0	0	0	0	0	0	0	0	0	0	0	0	0	0	0	0	0	0	0
OTHER EFTA	0	0	0	0	0	0	0	0	0	0	0	0	0	0	0	0	0	0	0	0	0	0
EUROP. COMMUNITY	10	1	0	1	1	1	0	1	0	0	0	0	0	0	2	0	0	1	0	0	1	0
FRANCE	5	1	0	1	0	0	0	0	0	0	1	0	0	0	0	0	0	1	0	0	1	0
GERMANY	2	0	0	0	0	0	0	1	0	0	0	0	0	0	1	0	0	0	0	0	0	0
ITALY	2	0	0	0	0	1	0	0	0	0	0	0	0	0	0	0	0	0	1	0	0	0
BELGIUM + LUX	1	0	0	0	0	0	0	0	0	0	0	0	0	0	1	0	0	0	0	0	0	0
NETHERLANDS	3	0	0	0	0	0	0	0	0	1	0	0	0	0	0	0	0	0	2	0	0	0
SPAIN	0	0	0	0	0	0	0	0	0	0	0	0	0	0	0	0	0	0	0	0	0	0
GREECE + TURKEY	1	0	0	0	0	0	0	0	0	0	0	0	0	0	0	0	0	0	0	0	1	0
OTHER EUROPE	0	0	0	0	0	0	0	0	0	0	0	0	0	0	1	0	0	0	0	0	0	0
EUROPE EX. U.K.	11	1	0	0	0	1	1	1	0	0	0	0	0	0	3	0	0	1	3	0	1	0
SOUTHERN DOMINIONS	4	0	0	0	0	0	1	1	0	0	0	0	0	0	1	0	0	0	1	0	0	0
S. AFRICA +RHOD.	1	0	0	0	0	0	0	1	0	0	0	0	0	0	0	0	0	0	0	0	0	0
AUSTRALIA + N.Z.	3	0	0	0	0	0	1	0	0	0	0	0	0	0	1	0	0	0	1	0	0	0
ASIA + OTHER AFRICA	3	0	0	0	0	0	0	0	0	0	0	0	0	0	1	1	0	0	1	0	0	0
JAPAN	1	0	0	0	0	0	0	0	0	0	0	0	0	0	0	0	0	0	1	0	0	0
OTHER ASIA+AFR.	3	0	0	0	0	0	1	0	0	0	0	0	0	0	1	1	0	0	0	0	0	0
BLACK AFRICA	1	0	0	0	0	0	0	0	0	0	0	0	0	0	0	1	0	0	0	0	0	0
ARAB WORLD	0	0	0	0	0	0	0	0	0	0	0	0	0	0	0	0	0	0	0	0	0	0
INDIA	1	0	0	0	0	0	0	0	0	0	0	0	0	0	1	0	0	0	0	0	0	0
PHILIPPINES	0	0	0	0	0	0	0	0	0	0	0	0	0	0	0	0	0	0	0	0	0	0
OTHER E. ASIA	0	0	0	0	0	0	0	0	0	0	0	0	0	0	0	0	0	0	0	0	0	0
OTHER ASIA	1	0	0	0	0	1	0	0	0	0	0	0	0	0	0	0	0	0	1	0	0	0

CHAPTER 2- THE EXPANSION OF PARENT SYSTEMS
SECTION 4- THE FLOW OF MANUFACTURING BY INDUSTRY OF SUBSIDIARY
TABLE 30- SYSTEMS CLASSIFIED BY PERIOD SYSTEM FIRST OPERATED
IN SPECIFIED COUNTRIES AND REGIONS A SUBSIDIARY MANUFACTURING
METAL CANS (SIC 341)

PERIOD

COUNTRY OR REGION	PRE 1968	PRE 1901	1901 -13	1914 -19	1920 -24	1925 -29	1930 -34	1935 -39	1940 -45	1946 -50	1951 -53	1954 -55	1956 -57	1958 -59	1960 -61	1962	1963	1964	1965	1966	1967	UNK
OUTSIDE U.S.	11	0	0	0	1	0	1	0	0	0	0	2	3	0	1	1	0	1	1	0	0	0
OUT. U.S. + CANADA	10	0	0	0	1	1	1	0	0	0	0	4	4	0	1	1	1	0	0	0	0	0
OUT. WEST. HEMIS.	6	0	0	0	1	0	1	0	0	0	1	1	0	0	1	1	1	1	0	0	0	0
OUT. WHITE CWEALTH	10	0	0	0	1	0	1	0	0	0	0	0	5	0	1	1	0	0	0	0	0	0
OUT. DEVLPED WORLD	10	0	0	0	1	0	1	0	0	0	0	0	5	0	1	1	0	0	0	0	0	0
CANADA	6	0	0	0	0	0	0	1	0	0	0	1	1	0	1	0	0	0	1	1	0	0
LATIN AMERICA	8	0	0	0	0	0	0	0	0	0	0	0	5	0	0	0	1	0	0	1	0	0
C. AMER.+CARIB.	7	0	0	0	0	1	1	0	0	0	0	0	4	0	1	1	1	1	1	0	1	0
CUBA	4	0	0	0	0	1	1	0	0	0	0	0	3	0	0	0	0	0	0	0	0	0
MEXICO	3	0	0	0	1	0	1	0	0	0	0	0	1	0	1	0	1	1	0	0	0	0
OTHER	1	0	0	0	0	0	0	1	1	0	0	0	0	0	0	0	0	0	0	0	0	0
S. AMERICA	3	0	0	0	0	0	0	0	0	0	0	0	2	0	0	0	0	0	0	0	0	0
ARGENTINA	0	0	0	0	0	0	0	1	1	0	0	0	1	0	0	0	1	0	0	0	0	0
BRAZIL	2	0	0	0	0	0	0	0	0	0	0	0	0	0	0	0	0	0	0	0	0	0
PERU	2	0	0	0	0	0	0	0	1	0	0	0	1	0	0	0	0	0	0	0	0	0
COLOMBIA	2	0	0	0	0	0	0	0	0	1	0	0	0	0	1	1	0	0	0	0	0	0
VENEZUELA	1	0	0	0	1	0	0	0	0	0	0	0	0	0	0	0	0	0	0	0	0	0
OTHER	1	0	0	0	0	0	0	0	0	1	0	0	0	0	0	0	0	0	0	0	0	0
EUROPE	2	0	0	0	0	1	0	0	0	0	1	0	0	0	0	0	0	0	1	0	0	0
EFTA	2	0	0	0	0	0	0	0	0	1	0	0	0	0	0	0	0	0	0	1	1	0
U.K.	1	0	0	0	0	0	0	0	0	0	0	0	0	0	0	1	0	0	0	0	1	0
SCANDINAVIA	1	0	0	0	0	0	0	0	0	1	0	0	0	0	0	0	0	0	0	0	0	0
SWITZERLAND	0	0	0	0	0	0	0	0	0	0	0	0	0	0	0	0	0	0	0	0	0	0
OTHER EFTA	0	0	0	0	0	0	0	0	0	0	0	0	0	0	0	0	0	0	0	0	0	0
EUROP. COMMUNITY	1	0	0	0	0	1	0	0	0	0	0	0	0	0	0	0	0	0	0	0	0	0
FRANCE	0	0	0	0	0	0	0	0	0	0	0	0	0	0	0	0	0	0	0	0	0	0
GERMANY	1	0	0	0	0	0	0	0	0	0	0	0	0	0	0	1	0	0	0	0	0	0
ITALY	0	0	0	0	0	0	0	0	0	0	0	0	0	0	0	0	0	0	0	0	0	0
BELGIUM + LUX	0	0	0	0	0	0	0	0	0	0	0	0	0	0	0	0	0	0	0	0	0	0
NETHERLANDS	1	0	0	0	0	1	0	0	0	0	0	0	0	0	0	1	0	0	0	0	0	0
SPAIN	2	0	0	0	0	0	1	0	0	0	0	0	0	0	0	0	0	0	1	0	0	0
GREECE + TURKEY	1	0	0	0	0	0	0	0	0	0	0	0	0	0	0	0	0	0	1	0	0	0
OTHER EUROPE	0	0	0	0	0	0	0	0	0	0	0	0	0	0	0	1	0	0	0	0	0	0
EUROPE EX. U.K.	2	0	0	0	0	1	0	0	0	0	0	0	0	0	0	0	0	0	1	0	0	0
SOUTHERN DOMINIONS	3	0	0	0	0	1	1	0	0	0	0	1	0	0	0	0	0	0	1	0	0	0
S. AFRICA +RHOD.	2	0	0	0	0	1	0	0	0	0	0	1	0	0	0	0	0	0	0	0	0	0
AUSTRALIA + N.Z.	1	0	0	0	0	0	1	0	0	0	0	0	0	0	1	0	0	0	1	0	0	0
ASIA + OTHER AFRICA	5	0	0	0	0	0	0	0	0	0	0	0	0	0	0	2	0	0	0	0	0	0
JAPAN	2	0	0	0	1	0	0	0	0	0	0	0	0	0	1	1	0	0	0	0	0	0
OTHER ASIA+AFR.	3	0	0	0	0	0	0	0	0	0	0	0	0	0	0	1	0	0	0	0	0	0
BLACK AFRICA	0	0	0	0	0	0	0	0	0	0	0	0	0	0	0	0	0	0	0	0	0	0
ARAB WORLD	0	0	0	0	0	0	0	0	0	0	0	0	0	0	0	0	0	0	0	0	0	0
INDIA	0	0	0	0	0	0	0	0	0	0	0	0	0	0	0	0	0	0	0	0	0	0
PHILIPPINES	1	0	0	0	1	0	0	0	0	0	0	0	0	0	0	0	0	0	0	0	0	0
OTHER E. ASIA	0	0	0	0	0	0	0	0	0	0	0	0	0	0	0	0	0	0	0	0	0	0
OTHER ASIA	2	0	0	0	0	0	0	0	0	0	0	0	0	0	1	1	0	0	0	0	0	0

CHAPTER 2- THE EXPANSION OF PARENT SYSTEMS
SECTION 4- THE FLOW OF MANUFACTURING BY INDUSTRY OF SUBSIDIARY
TABLE 31- SYSTEMS CLASSIFIED BY PERIOD SYSTEM FIRST OPERATED
IN SPECIFIED COUNTRIES AND REGIONS A SUBSIDIARY MANUFACTURING
HEATING APPARATUS AND PLUMBING FIXTURES (SIC 343)

COUNTRY OR REGION	PRE 1968	PRE 1901	1901 -13	1914 -19	1920 -24	1925 -29	1930 -34	1935 -39	1940 -45	1946 -50	1951 -53	1954 -55	1956 -57	1958 -59	1960 -61	1962 -63	1964	1965	1966	1967	UNK
OUTSIDE U.S.	9	1	0	1	0	0	0	0	0	1	2	0	2	0	0	0	0	0	1	1	0
OUT. U.S. + CANADA	5	1	0	1	0	0	0	0	0	1	0	0	2	0	0	0	0	0	0	1	0
OUT. WEST. HEMIS.	4	1	0	1	0	0	0	0	0	1	0	0	1	0	0	0	0	0	0	0	0
OUT. WHITE CWEALTH	5	1	0	0	0	0	0	0	0	1	0	0	2	1	1	0	0	0	0	1	0
OUT. DEVLPED WORLD	3	0	0	0	0	0	0	0	0	1	0	0	1	0	1	0	0	0	0	1	0
CANADA	7	0	1	0	0	0	0	0	0	0	2	0	0	0	0	0	0	0	1	1	0
LATIN AMERICA	3	0	0	0	0	1	0	0	0	1	0	0	1	0	0	0	0	0	0	1	0
C. AMER.+CARIB.	1	0	0	0	0	0	0	0	0	0	0	0	0	0	0	0	0	0	0	1	0
CUBA	0	0	0	0	0	0	0	0	0	1	0	0	0	0	0	0	0	0	0	0	0
MEXICO	1	0	0	0	0	0	0	0	0	0	0	0	0	0	0	0	0	0	0	1	0
OTHER	0	0	0	0	0	0	0	0	0	0	0	0	0	0	0	0	0	0	0	0	0
S. AMERICA	2	0	0	0	0	1	0	0	0	1	0	0	1	0	0	0	0	0	0	0	0
ARGENTINA	1	0	0	0	0	0	0	0	0	1	0	0	1	0	0	0	0	0	0	0	0
BRAZIL	1	0	0	0	0	1	0	0	0	0	0	0	0	0	0	0	0	0	0	0	0
PERU	0	0	0	0	0	0	0	0	0	0	0	0	0	0	0	0	0	0	0	0	0
COLOMBIA	1	0	0	0	0	0	0	0	0	0	0	0	0	0	0	0	0	0	0	0	0
VENEZUELA	0	0	0	0	0	0	0	0	0	0	0	0	0	0	0	0	0	0	0	0	0
OTHER	0	0	0	0	0	0	0	0	0	0	0	0	0	0	0	0	0	0	0	0	0
EUROPE	4	1	0	1	0	0	0	0	0	0	0	0	1	0	0	0	0	0	0	0	0
EFTA	2	0	1	1	0	0	0	0	0	0	0	0	0	0	0	0	0	0	0	0	0
U.K.	2	0	1	1	0	0	0	0	0	0	0	0	0	0	0	0	0	0	0	0	0
SCANDINAVIA	0	0	0	0	0	0	0	0	0	0	0	0	0	0	0	0	0	0	0	0	0
SWITZERLAND	1	0	1	0	0	0	0	0	0	0	0	0	0	0	0	0	0	0	0	0	0
OTHER EFTA	1	0	0	0	0	0	0	0	0	0	0	0	0	1	0	0	0	0	0	0	0
EUROP. COMMUNITY	4	1	1	0	0	0	0	0	0	0	0	0	1	1	1	0	0	0	0	0	0
FRANCE	3	0	0	0	0	0	0	0	0	0	0	0	1	0	0	0	0	0	0	0	0
GERMANY	3	1	1	0	0	0	0	0	0	0	0	0	1	1	2	0	0	0	0	0	0
ITALY	2	0	1	0	0	0	0	0	0	0	0	0	1	0	0	0	0	0	0	0	0
BELGIUM + LUX	1	0	0	0	0	0	0	0	0	0	0	0	0	1	0	0	0	0	0	0	0
NETHERLANDS	2	0	1	0	0	0	0	0	0	0	0	0	0	0	1	0	0	0	1	0	0
SPAIN	1	0	0	0	0	0	0	0	0	0	0	0	0	1	0	0	1	0	0	0	0
GREECE + TURKEY	1	0	0	0	0	0	0	0	0	0	0	0	0	0	0	0	0	1	0	0	0
OTHER EUROPE	0	0	0	0	0	0	0	0	0	0	0	0	0	0	1	0	0	0	0	0	0
EUROPE EX. U.K.	4	1	0	0	0	0	0	0	0	0	0	0	1	1	0	0	0	0	0	0	0
SOUTHERN DOMINIONS	1	0	0	0	0	0	0	0	0	0	0	0	0	0	0	0	0	0	0	0	0
S. AFRICA +RHOD.	0	0	0	0	0	0	0	0	0	0	0	0	0	0	0	0	0	0	0	0	0
AUSTRALIA + N.Z.	1	0	0	0	0	0	0	0	0	1	0	0	0	0	0	0	0	0	0	0	0
ASIA + OTHER AFRICA	1	0	0	0	0	0	0	0	0	0	0	0	0	0	0	0	0	0	0	0	0
JAPAN	0	0	0	0	0	0	0	0	0	1	0	0	0	0	0	0	0	0	0	0	0
OTHER ASIA+AFR.	1	0	0	0	0	0	0	0	0	0	0	0	0	1	0	0	0	0	0	0	0
BLACK AFRICA	1	0	0	0	0	0	0	0	0	0	0	0	0	0	0	0	0	0	0	0	0
ARAB WORLD	0	0	0	0	0	0	0	0	0	0	0	0	0	1	0	0	0	0	0	0	0
INDIA	0	0	0	0	0	0	0	0	0	0	0	0	0	0	0	0	0	0	0	0	0
PHILIPPINES	0	0	0	0	0	0	0	0	0	0	0	0	0	0	0	0	0	0	0	0	0
OTHER E. ASIA	0	0	0	0	0	0	0	0	0	0	0	0	0	0	0	0	0	0	0	0	0
OTHER ASIA	1	0	0	0	0	0	0	0	0	1	0	0	0	0	0	0	0	0	0	0	0

PERIOD

CHAPTER 2- THE EXPANSION OF PARENT SYSTEMS
SECTION 4- THE FLOW OF MANUFACTURING BY INDUSTRY OF SUBSIDIARY
TABLE 32- SYSTEMS CLASSIFIED BY PERIOD SYSTEM FIRST OPERATED
IN SPECIFIED COUNTRIES AND REGIONS A SUBSIDIARY MANUFACTURING
OTHER FABRICATED METAL PRODUCTS (SIC 342,344-349)

PERIOD

COUNTRY OR REGION	PRE 1968	PRE 1901	1901 -13	1914 -19	1920 -24	1925 -29	1930 -34	1935 -39	1940 -45	1946 -50	1951 -53	1954 -55	1956 -57	1958 -59	1960 -61	1962	1963	1964	1965	1966	1967	UNK
OUTSIDE U.S.	49	1	0	2	0	3	3	3	1	6	1	2	3	3	8	0	2	5	2	3	3	1
OUT. U.S. + CANADA	44	1	0	0	1	2	3	1	1	3	1	2	3	3	10	1	2	4	2	3	2	1
OUT. WEST. HEMIS.	36	1	0	1	1	1	0	1	0	2	0	2	1	3	7	2	1	4	4	1	2	1
OUT. WHITE CWEALTH	39	0	0	1	1	2	0	2	0	2	0	1	4	2	8	2	1	2	3	3	1	2
OUT. DEVLPED WORLD	25	0	0	0	0	1	0	1	0	2	0	1	2	1	7	0	0	2	3	2	1	0
CANADA	20	0	0	2	0	1	0	1	0	4	1	1	2	0	1	0	0	1	1	0	1	0
LATIN AMERICA	23	0	0	0	0	1	0	1	0	2	1	0	2	1	6	1	1	2	3	2	1	0
C. AMER.+CARIB.	15	0	0	0	0	0	0	1	0	1	0	0	1	2	4	2	0	0	1	1	1	0
CUBA	1	0	0	0	0	0	0	0	0	0	0	0	0	0	0	0	1	0	0	0	0	0
MEXICO	14	0	0	0	0	0	0	1	0	1	0	0	1	2	4	2	0	0	1	0	1	0
OTHER	2	0	0	0	0	1	0	0	0	0	0	0	0	0	0	0	0	0	0	1	0	0
S. AMERICA	13	0	0	0	0	1	0	0	0	1	0	0	2	0	4	0	0	2	0	0	0	0
ARGENTINA	5	0	0	0	1	0	0	1	0	0	0	0	0	0	2	0	2	0	2	2	0	1
BRAZIL	4	0	0	0	0	0	0	0	1	1	0	0	0	0	1	0	0	0	0	0	0	0
PERU	2	0	0	0	0	0	0	0	0	1	0	0	0	0	1	0	0	0	0	0	0	0
COLOMBIA	3	0	0	0	0	0	0	0	0	1	0	1	0	1	0	0	0	1	0	0	0	0
VENEZUELA	6	0	0	0	0	0	0	1	0	0	0	0	1	1	1	1	0	0	0	2	0	0
OTHER	2	0	0	0	0	0	0	0	0	1	0	0	0	0	1	0	0	0	0	0	0	0
EUROPE	32	1	0	1	1	1	0	3	0	2	1	0	2	3	6	1	1	5	2	2	2	1
EFTA	21	0	0	0	0	0	0	3	0	3	1	0	1	2	2	2	2	2	0	0	2	1
U.K.	20	0	0	0	0	0	0	3	0	3	1	0	1	1	2	1	0	2	0	0	2	1
SCANDINAVIA	0	0	0	0	0	0	0	0	0	0	0	0	0	0	0	0	0	0	0	0	0	0
SWITZERLAND	2	0	0	0	0	0	0	0	0	0	0	0	0	0	0	0	0	0	0	0	0	0
OTHER EFTA	0	0	0	0	0	0	0	0	0	0	0	0	0	0	0	0	0	0	0	0	0	0
EUROP. COMMUNITY	22	0	0	0	1	1	0	2	0	0	0	0	2	1	4	0	1	2	1	1	0	0
FRANCE	7	0	0	0	1	1	0	1	0	0	0	1	0	0	4	0	0	0	0	1	1	0
GERMANY	15	0	0	0	1	1	0	0	0	0	0	0	2	0	4	2	2	4	1	0	0	0
ITALY	10	0	0	0	0	0	0	1	0	0	0	1	0	0	1	0	0	0	0	1	1	0
BELGIUM + LUX	4	0	0	0	0	0	0	0	0	0	0	0	0	0	2	2	1	0	0	1	0	0
NETHERLANDS	7	0	0	0	0	0	0	0	0	2	0	0	1	1	1	0	0	0	1	1	1	0
SPAIN	2	0	1	0	0	0	0	0	0	0	0	0	0	0	0	0	1	0	0	0	0	0
GREECE + TURKEY	2	0	0	0	0	0	0	0	0	0	0	0	0	0	1	0	0	0	1	0	0	0
OTHER EUROPE	25	1	0	1	1	0	0	2	0	1	0	1	1	3	4	1	1	3	1	2	1	0
EUROPE EX. U.K.	12	0	0	0	0	0	1	1	0	0	0	1	0	0	2	0	0	0	0	2	0	0
SOUTHERN DOMINIONS	7	0	0	0	0	1	0	0	0	1	0	0	0	2	1	0	0	0	2	1	0	0
S. AFRICA +RHOD.	9	0	0	0	0	0	0	0	0	0	0	0	0	1	1	1	2	2	2	1	0	0
AUSTRALIA +N.Z.	9	0	0	0	0	0	0	0	0	0	0	0	0	0	1	1	1	0	1	0	0	0
ASIA + OTHER AFRICA	5	0	0	0	0	0	0	0	0	0	0	0	0	0	1	0	1	2	0	0	0	1
JAPAN	5	0	0	0	0	0	0	0	0	0	0	0	0	1	1	1	1	0	1	0	0	0
OTHER ASIA+AFR.	1	0	0	0	0	0	0	0	0	0	0	0	0	0	0	0	0	0	0	0	0	0
BLACK AFRICA	1	0	0	0	0	0	0	0	0	0	0	0	0	0	1	0	0	0	0	0	0	0
ARAB WORLD	3	0	0	0	0	0	0	0	0	0	0	1	0	0	0	0	1	0	0	0	0	0
INDIA	2	0	0	0	0	0	0	0	0	1	0	0	1	0	0	0	0	0	0	0	0	0
PHILIPPINES	0	0	0	0	0	0	0	0	0	0	0	0	0	0	0	0	0	0	0	0	0	0
OTHER E. ASIA	2	0	0	0	0	0	0	0	0	0	0	0	1	0	0	0	0	0	0	0	0	0
OTHER ASIA	2	0	0	0	0	0	0	0	0	0	0	0	0	0	0	0	0	0	0	0	0	0

CHAPTER 2— THE EXPANSION OF PARENT SYSTEMS
SECTION 4— THE FLOW OF MANUFACTURING BY INDUSTRY OF SUBSIDIARY
TABLE 33— SYSTEMS CLASSIFIED BY PERIOD SYSTEM FIRST OPERATED
IN SPECIFIED COUNTRIES AND REGIONS A SUBSIDIARY MANUFACTURING
FARM MACHINERY (SIC 352)

PERIOD

COUNTRY OR REGION	PRE 1968	PRE 1901	1901 -13	1914 -19	1920 -24	1925 -29	1930 -34	1935 -39	1940 -45	1946 -50	1951 -53	1954 -55	1956 -57	1958 -59	1960 -61	1962	1963	1964	1965	1966	1967	UNK
OUTSIDE U.S.	12	0	1	0	0	0	1	1	0	2	1	1	0	1	2	1	1	0	0	0	1	0
OUT. U.S. + CANADA	10	0	1	0	0	0	0	0	0	2	1	1	0	1	2	1	0	0	1	0	0	0
OUT. WEST. HEMIS.	10	0	1	0	0	0	0	0	0	2	1	1	0	1	2	1	0	1	0	0	0	0
OUT. WHITE CWEALTH	9	0	1	0	0	0	0	0	0	1	0	1	0	0	2	0	1	1	0	0	0	0
OUT. DEVLPED WORLD	4	0	0	0	0	0	0	0	0	1	0	1	0	0	0	0	1	1	0	0	0	0
CANADA	4	0	0	0	0	0	0	0	0	0	0	0	0	0	0	1	0	0	0	0	1	0
LATIN AMERICA	4	0	0	0	0	0	1	1	0	1	1	1	0	0	0	0	0	0	0	0	0	0
C. AMER.+CARIB.	2	0	0	0	0	0	0	0	0	1	1	1	0	0	0	0	0	0	0	0	0	0
CUBA	2	0	0	0	0	0	0	0	0	1	0	0	0	0	0	0	0	0	0	0	0	0
MEXICO	1	0	0	0	0	0	0	0	0	0	0	1	0	0	0	0	0	0	1	0	0	0
OTHER	1	0	0	0	0	0	0	0	0	1	0	0	0	0	0	0	0	0	0	0	0	0
S. AMERICA	4	0	0	0	0	0	0	0	0	1	0	0	1	0	0	0	0	1	1	0	0	0
ARGENTINA	2	0	0	0	0	0	0	0	0	0	0	0	1	0	0	0	0	0	0	0	0	0
BRAZIL	1	0	0	0	0	0	0	0	0	1	0	0	0	0	0	0	0	0	0	0	0	0
PERU	0	0	0	0	0	0	0	0	0	0	0	0	0	0	0	0	0	0	0	0	0	0
COLOMBIA	1	0	0	0	0	0	0	0	0	1	0	0	0	0	0	0	1	0	0	1	0	0
VENEZUELA	0	0	0	0	0	0	0	0	0	0	0	0	0	0	0	0	0	0	0	0	0	0
OTHER	1	0	0	0	0	0	0	0	0	0	0	0	0	0	0	1	0	0	0	0	0	0
EUROPE	8	0	1	0	0	0	0	0	0	1	1	2	0	1	1	1	0	0	0	0	0	0
EFTA	5	0	1	0	0	0	0	0	0	0	1	1	0	1	1	1	0	0	0	0	0	0
U.K.	5	0	0	0	0	0	0	0	0	1	1	1	0	0	1	1	0	0	0	0	0	0
SCANDINAVIA	1	0	1	0	0	0	0	0	0	0	0	0	0	0	0	0	0	0	0	0	0	0
SWITZERLAND	0	0	0	0	0	0	0	0	0	0	0	0	0	0	0	0	0	0	0	0	0	0
OTHER EFTA	0	0	0	0	0	0	0	0	0	0	0	0	0	0	0	0	0	0	0	0	0	0
EUROP. COMMUNITY	7	0	1	0	0	0	0	0	0	1	0	1	0	1	2	0	0	1	0	0	0	0
FRANCE	6	0	1	0	0	0	0	0	0	1	0	0	1	1	3	0	0	0	0	0	0	0
GERMANY	2	0	1	0	0	0	0	0	0	0	0	0	0	0	0	1	0	0	0	0	0	0
ITALY	1	0	0	0	0	0	0	0	0	1	0	0	0	1	0	0	0	0	0	0	0	0
BELGIUM + LUX	1	0	0	0	0	0	0	0	0	0	0	0	0	0	0	0	1	0	0	0	0	0
NETHERLANDS	0	0	0	0	0	0	0	0	0	0	0	0	0	0	0	0	0	0	0	0	0	0
SPAIN	3	0	0	0	0	0	0	0	0	0	0	0	0	0	0	1	0	1	0	0	0	0
GREECE + TURKEY	1	0	0	0	0	0	0	0	0	0	0	1	0	0	0	0	0	0	0	0	0	0
OTHER EUROPE	0	0	0	0	0	0	0	0	0	0	0	0	0	0	0	0	0	0	0	0	0	0
EUROPE EX. U.K.	7	0	1	0	0	0	0	0	0	1	0	1	0	1	2	0	1	0	0	0	0	0
SOUTHERN DOMINIONS	6	0	0	0	0	0	0	0	0	0	1	1	0	0	1	1	0	0	0	1	0	0
S. AFRICA +RHOD.	3	0	0	0	0	0	1	0	0	0	1	0	0	0	0	2	0	0	0	0	0	0
AUSTRALIA + N.Z.	4	0	0	0	0	0	0	1	0	1	0	1	0	1	1	0	0	0	0	1	0	0
ASIA + OTHER AFRICA	2	0	0	0	0	0	0	0	0	1	0	1	0	0	0	0	0	0	0	1	0	0
JAPAN	1	0	0	0	0	0	0	0	0	0	0	0	0	0	0	0	0	0	1	0	0	0
OTHER ASIA+AFR.	1	0	0	0	0	0	0	0	0	1	0	1	0	0	0	0	0	0	1	0	0	0
BLACK AFRICA	0	0	0	0	0	0	0	0	0	0	0	0	0	0	0	0	0	0	0	0	0	0
ARAB WORLD	1	0	0	0	0	0	0	0	0	0	0	1	0	0	0	0	0	0	1	0	0	0
INDIA	1	0	0	0	0	0	0	0	0	0	0	0	0	0	0	0	0	1	0	0	0	0
PHILIPPINES	1	0	0	0	0	0	0	0	0	0	0	1	0	0	0	0	0	0	0	0	0	0
OTHER E. ASIA	0	0	0	0	0	0	0	0	0	0	0	0	0	0	0	0	0	0	0	0	0	0
OTHER ASIA	0	0	0	0	0	0	0	0	0	0	0	0	0	0	0	0	0	0	0	0	0	0

CHAPTER 2- THE EXPANSION OF PARENT SYSTEMS
SECTION 4- THE FLOW OF MANUFACTURING BY INDUSTRY OF SUBSIDIARY
TABLE 34- SYSTEMS CLASSIFIED BY PERIOD SYSTEM FIRST OPERATED
IN SPECIFIED COUNTRIES AND REGIONS A SUBSIDIARY MANUFACTURING
CONSTRUCTION MACHINERY (SIC 353)

PERIOD

COUNTRY OR REGION	PRE 1968	PRE 1901	1901 -13	1914 -19	1920 -24	1925 -29	1930 -34	1935 -39	1940 -45	1946 -50	1951 -53	1954 -55	1956 -57	1958 -59	1960 -61	1962	1963	1964	1965	1966	1967	UNK
OUTSIDE U.S.	22	2	3	0	0	0	0	0	2	4	4	4	2	2	1	0	1	0	1	0	0	0
OUT. U.S. + CANADA	18	2	1	0	0	0	0	0	1	4	0	4	2	2	2	0	1	0	1	0	0	0
OUT. WEST. HEMIS.	17	2	1	0	0	0	0	0	1	2	0	3	1	4	0	0	0	2	1	0	0	0
OUT. WHITE CWEALTH	13	2	1	0	0	0	0	0	0	3	1	1	1	2	2	1	1	0	0	1	0	0
OUT. DEVLPED WORLD	11	0	0	0	0	0	0	0	0	3	1	2	0	2	0	1	0	2	0	0	0	0
CANADA	18	1	3	0	0	0	0	0	1	1	3	1	0	3	1	1	1	1	1	0	0	0
LATIN AMERICA	11	0	0	0	0	0	0	0	0	3	1	2	0	2	0	1	0	2	0	0	0	0
C. AMER.+CARIB.	8	0	0	0	0	0	0	0	0	1	1	1	0	1	0	0	1	2	1	0	0	0
CUBA	0	0	0	0	0	0	0	0	0	0	0	0	0	0	0	0	0	0	0	0	0	0
MEXICO	8	0	0	0	0	0	0	0	0	1	0	1	0	1	0	0	0	2	0	1	0	0
OTHER	0	0	0	0	0	0	0	0	0	0	1	0	0	0	0	0	1	0	0	0	0	0
S. AMERICA	9	0	0	0	0	0	0	0	0	3	0	1	0	2	0	1	0	0	0	0	0	0
ARGENTINA	3	0	0	0	0	0	0	0	0	0	0	0	0	1	2	0	0	0	0	0	0	0
BRAZIL	6	0	0	0	0	0	0	0	0	3	0	1	0	0	0	2	0	0	0	0	0	0
PERU	1	0	0	0	0	0	0	0	0	0	0	0	0	1	0	0	0	0	0	0	0	0
COLOMBIA	0	0	0	0	0	0	0	0	0	0	0	0	0	0	0	0	0	0	0	0	0	0
VENEZUELA	3	0	0	0	0	0	0	0	0	0	0	0	0	0	0	0	0	0	0	0	0	0
OTHER	1	0	0	0	0	0	0	0	0	0	0	0	0	1	0	0	1	0	0	1	1	0
EUROPE	13	2	1	0	0	0	0	0	0	2	0	4	1	2	2	0	1	0	0	0	0	0
EFTA	8	1	0	0	0	0	0	0	0	2	0	3	1	1	1	0	0	0	0	0	0	0
U.K.	7	1	0	0	0	0	0	0	0	2	0	3	1	1	0	0	0	0	0	0	0	0
SCANDINAVIA	0	0	0	0	0	0	0	0	0	0	0	0	0	0	1	0	0	0	0	0	0	0
SWITZERLAND	0	0	0	0	0	0	0	0	0	0	0	0	0	0	0	0	0	0	0	0	0	0
OTHER EFTA	1	0	1	0	0	0	0	0	0	0	0	0	0	0	0	0	0	0	0	0	0	0
EUROP. COMMUNITY	11	2	1	0	0	0	0	0	0	0	0	0	1	2	4	0	1	0	0	1	0	0
FRANCE	7	2	0	0	0	0	0	0	0	0	0	0	1	2	3	0	0	0	1	0	0	0
GERMANY	3	0	0	0	0	0	0	0	0	0	0	0	0	1	0	0	1	0	0	0	0	0
ITALY	4	0	1	0	0	1	0	0	0	0	0	1	1	1	1	0	0	0	2	0	1	0
BELGIUM + LUX	5	0	0	0	1	0	0	0	0	1	0	0	0	1	0	0	0	0	0	0	0	0
NETHERLANDS	3	0	1	0	1	0	0	0	0	0	0	0	0	1	1	0	0	0	1	0	0	0
SPAIN	3	0	0	0	0	0	0	0	0	0	0	1	0	0	0	0	0	0	0	0	0	0
GREECE + TURKEY	0	0	0	0	0	0	0	0	0	0	0	0	0	0	1	0	0	0	0	0	0	0
OTHER EUROPE	0	0	0	0	0	0	0	0	0	0	0	0	0	0	0	0	0	0	0	0	0	0
EUROPE EX. U.K.	11	2	1	0	0	0	0	0	0	0	0	1	1	2	3	1	0	0	0	0	0	0
SOUTHERN DOMINIONS	14	0	0	2	0	0	0	0	1	1	1	1	1	3	1	1	0	1	1	1	0	0
S. AFRICA +RHOD.	5	0	0	1	1	1	0	0	1	1	0	0	0	3	1	1	0	0	0	0	1	0
AUSTRALIA + N.Z.	14	0	0	1	1	1	1	0	0	2	1	0	1	0	1	1	0	1	1	1	0	0
ASIA + OTHER AFRICA	4	0	0	0	0	0	0	0	0	0	0	0	0	0	1	1	1	0	0	0	0	0
JAPAN	4	0	0	0	0	0	1	0	0	0	0	0	0	1	1	0	0	0	0	0	0	0
OTHER ASIA+AFR.	2	0	0	0	0	0	0	0	0	0	0	0	0	0	0	0	0	0	0	0	0	0
BLACK AFRICA	0	0	0	0	0	0	0	0	0	0	0	0	0	0	0	0	0	0	0	0	0	0
ARAB WORLD	0	0	0	0	0	0	0	0	0	0	0	0	0	0	0	0	0	0	0	0	0	0
INDIA	2	0	0	0	0	0	0	0	0	0	0	0	0	1	0	0	1	0	0	0	0	0
PHILIPPINES	0	0	0	0	0	0	0	0	0	0	0	0	0	0	0	0	0	0	0	0	0	0
OTHER E. ASIA	0	0	0	0	0	0	0	0	0	0	0	0	0	0	0	1	0	0	0	0	0	0
OTHER ASIA	0	0	0	0	0	0	0	0	0	0	0	0	0	0	0	0	0	0	0	0	0	0

CHAPTER 2- THE EXPANSION OF PARENT SYSTEMS
SECTION 4- THE FLOW OF MANUFACTURING BY INDUSTRY OF SUBSIDIARY
TABLE 35- SYSTEMS CLASSIFIED BY PERIOD SYSTEM FIRST OPERATED
IN SPECIFIED COUNTRIES AND REGIONS A SUBSIDIARY MANUFACTURING
SPECIAL INDUSTRY MACHINERY (SIC 354 AND 355)

COUNTRY OR REGION	PRE 1968	PRE 1901	1901-13	1914-19	1920-24	1925-29	1930-34	1935-39	1940-45	1946-50	1951-53	1954-55	1956-57	1958-59	1960-61	1962	1963	1964	1965	1966	1967	UNK
OUTSIDE U.S.	34	1	1	0	0	0	1	2	1	1	3	0	3	0	3	3	4	4	2	5	0	0
OUT. U.S. + CANADA	26	1	0	0	1	0	0	1	1	1	1	0	2	0	3	2	4	1	2	6	0	0
OUT. WEST. HEMIS.	26	1	0	0	1	0	0	0	0	1	1	1	1	0	4	2	4	3	3	6	0	0
OUT. WHITE CWEALTH	19	1	0	0	1	0	0	0	1	1	0	0	2	0	2	2	4	1	1	2	0	0
OUT. DEVLPED WORLD	7	0	0	0	1	0	0	0	1	1	0	1	3	0	0	0	0	1	0	0	0	0
CANADA																						
LATIN AMERICA	12	0	1	0	0	0	1	1	0	0	2	0	2	0	0	1	3	0	0	0	0	0
C. AMER.+CARIB.	6	0	0	0	1	0	0	0	1	1	0	0	2	0	0	0	1	1	0	0	0	0
CUBA	4	0	0	0	1	0	0	0	1	1	0	0	1	0	1	0	1	0	0	0	0	0
MEXICO	1	0	0	0	0	0	0	0	0	0	0	0	0	0	1	0	0	0	0	0	0	0
OTHER	4	0	0	0	1	0	0	0	0	0	0	0	1	0	1	0	0	1	0	0	0	0
S. AMERICA	3	0	0	0	0	0	0	0	1	0	2	0	0	0	1	1	0	0	0	0	0	0
ARGENTINA	0	0	0	0	0	0	0	0	1	0	0	0	0	0	2	0	0	0	0	0	0	0
BRAZIL	2	0	0	0	0	0	0	0	0	0	0	0	1	0	0	1	0	0	0	0	0	0
PERU	0	0	0	0	0	0	0	0	0	0	0	0	0	0	0	0	0	0	0	0	0	0
COLOMBIA	1	0	0	0	0	0	0	0	0	0	0	0	1	0	0	0	0	0	0	0	0	0
VENEZUELA	1	0	0	0	0	0	0	0	0	0	0	0	1	0	0	0	0	0	0	0	0	0
OTHER	1	0	0	0	0	0	0	0	0	0	0	0	0	0	0	0	0	1	0	1	0	0
EUROPE	20	1	0	1	1	0	0	0	1	1	1	1	1	0	3	2	4	2	2	3	0	0
EFTA	9	1	0	1	0	0	0	0	0	0	3	0	0	0	2	0	0	1	1	3	0	0
U.K.	8	1	0	0	0	0	0	0	0	0	3	0	0	0	1	0	0	0	0	2	0	0
SCANDINAVIA	1	0	1	0	0	0	0	0	0	0	0	0	0	0	0	0	0	0	0	0	0	0
SWITZERLAND	1	0	0	0	0	0	0	0	0	0	0	0	0	0	1	0	0	1	0	0	0	0
OTHER EFTA	0	0	0	0	0	0	0	0	0	0	0	0	0	0	1	0	0	0	0	0	0	0
EUROP. COMMUNITY	16	1	0	1	1	0	0	0	1	1	0	0	1	0	2	2	4	2	2	2	0	0
FRANCE	6	1	0	0	0	0	0	0	0	0	0	0	0	0	0	1	1	0	1	2	0	0
GERMANY	9	1	0	0	1	0	0	0	1	1	0	0	1	0	2	0	2	1	1	1	0	0
ITALY	8	0	0	0	1	1	0	0	0	0	0	0	0	0	3	2	1	1	0	1	0	0
BELGIUM + LUX	2	0	1	0	0	0	0	0	0	0	0	0	0	0	0	0	0	0	0	0	0	0
NETHERLANDS	1	0	0	0	0	0	0	0	0	0	0	0	0	0	1	0	0	0	0	1	0	0
SPAIN	3	0	0	0	0	0	0	0	0	0	0	0	0	0	0	0	1	0	0	1	0	0
GREECE + TURKEY	1	0	0	0	0	0	0	0	0	0	0	0	0	0	0	0	0	0	0	0	0	0
OTHER EUROPE	0	0	0	0	0	0	0	0	0	0	0	0	1	0	1	1	0	0	0	1	0	0
EUROPE EX. U.K.	17	1	0	1	1	0	0	0	1	1	0	1	1	0	3	4	4	2	2	3	0	0
SOUTHERN DOMINIONS	10	0	0	1	1	0	0	1	0	2	0	0	0	1	1	0	0	1	1	3	0	0
S. AFRICA +RHOD.	4	0	0	0	0	0	0	0	0	1	0	0	0	0	0	0	0	0	1	1	2	0
AUSTRALIA + N.Z.	8	0	0	1	1	0	0	1	0	1	1	0	1	1	1	0	0	0	0	2	0	0
ASIA + OTHER AFRICA	6	0	0	1	0	0	0	0	0	0	0	0	1	0	1	1	0	0	0	1	2	0
JAPAN	4	0	0	0	0	0	0	0	0	0	0	0	0	0	1	0	0	0	1	1	1	0
OTHER ASIA+AFR.	2	0	0	1	0	0	0	0	0	0	0	0	1	0	0	0	0	0	1	1	0	0
BLACK AFRICA	0	0	0	0	0	0	0	0	0	0	0	0	0	0	0	0	0	0	0	0	1	0
ARAB WORLD	1	0	0	0	0	0	0	0	0	0	0	0	1	0	1	0	0	0	0	0	0	0
INDIA	1	0	0	0	0	0	0	0	0	0	0	0	0	0	1	0	0	0	0	1	0	0
PHILIPPINES	0	0	0	0	0	0	0	0	0	0	0	0	0	0	0	0	0	0	0	0	0	0
OTHER E. ASIA	0	0	0	0	0	0	0	0	0	0	0	0	0	0	0	0	0	0	0	0	0	0
OTHER ASIA	0	0	0	0	0	0	0	0	0	0	0	0	0	0	0	0	0	0	0	0	0	0

PERIOD

CHAPTER 2- THE EXPANSION OF PARENT SYSTEMS
SECTION 4- THE FLOW OF MANUFACTURING BY INDUSTRY OF SUBSIDIARY.
TABLE 36- SYSTEMS CLASSIFIED BY PERIOD SYSTEM FIRST OPERATED
IN SPECIFIED COUNTRIES AND REGIONS A SUBSIDIARY MANUFACTURING
GENERAL INDUSTRIAL MACHINES (SIC 356)

PERIOD

COUNTRY OR REGION	PRE 1968	PRE 1901	1901 -13	1914 -19	1920 -24	1925 -29	1930 -34	1935 -39	1940 -45	1946 -50	1951 -53	1954 -55	1956 -57	1958 -59	1960 -61	1962	1963	1964	1965	1966	1967	UNK
OUTSIDE U.S.	25	3	1	1	2	2	0	0	0	2	2	2	1	2	2	0	3	0	0	0	1	1
OUT. U.S. + CANADA	19	3	0	1	2	1	0	0	0	2	1	1	0	2	2	0	3	0	0	0	1	0
OUT. WEST. HEMIS.	19	3	0	1	2	1	0	0	0	2	1	1	0	2	2	0	3	0	0	0	1	0
OUT. WHITE CWEALTH	18	3	0	0	2	1	0	0	0	1	1	1	2	2	2	0	3	0	0	0	1	0
OUT. DEVLPED WORLD	11	0	0	0	1	0	0	1	0	1	1	0	1	3	1	0	1	0	0	0	1	0
CANADA	16	0	1	0	1	1	0	1	1	1	2	3	1	1	0	0	1	1	0	0	1	1
LATIN AMERICA	10	0	0	0	1	0	0	0	0	1	1	0	0	2	1	0	1	0	1	0	1	0
C. AMER.+CARIB.	9	0	0	0	1	0	0	1	0	1	1	0	0	1	2	0	1	0	1	1	0	0
CUBA	0	0	0	0	0	0	0	0	0	0	0	0	0	0	0	0	0	0	0	0	0	0
MEXICO	9	0	0	0	0	0	0	0	1	1	0	0	1	0	0	0	1	0	1	1	1	0
OTHER	1	0	0	0	0	0	0	1	0	0	1	0	0	1	1	0	0	0	1	0	0	0
S. AMERICA	6	0	0	1	0	1	0	0	0	1	0	0	0	0	2	0	0	0	1	0	1	0
ARGENTINA	2	0	0	0	1	0	0	0	1	1	0	0	1	1	0	0	0	0	1	0	0	0
BRAZIL	5	0	0	0	1	1	0	1	0	1	0	0	0	0	0	0	0	0	1	0	1	0
PERU	1	0	0	0	0	0	0	0	0	0	0	1	0	0	0	0	0	0	0	0	0	0
COLOMBIA	1	0	0	0	0	0	0	0	0	0	0	0	0	0	0	0	0	0	1	0	1	0
VENEZUELA	0	0	0	0	0	0	0	0	0	0	0	0	0	0	0	0	0	0	0	0	0	0
OTHER	0	0	0	0	0	0	0	0	0	0	0	0	0	0	0	0	0	0	0	0	0	0
EUROPE	15	3	0	1	2	1	0	0	0	0	2	0	0	0	1	0	4	0	0	0	1	0
EFTA	8	0	0	2	0	1	0	0	0	0	2	0	0	0	1	0	1	0	0	0	1	0
U.K.	7	0	0	2	0	1	0	0	0	0	2	0	0	0	1	0	0	0	0	0	1	0
SCANDINAVIA	1	0	0	0	0	0	0	0	0	0	0	0	0	1	0	0	0	0	0	0	1	0
SWITZERLAND	1	0	0	0	1	0	0	0	0	0	0	0	0	0	0	0	1	0	0	0	0	0
OTHER EFTA	1	0	0	0	1	0	0	0	0	0	0	0	0	1	0	0	0	0	0	0	0	0
EUROP. COMMUNITY	13	3	0	0	2	0	1	0	0	0	0	0	0	1	1	0	3	0	0	1	1	0
FRANCE	3	0	0	0	1	0	1	0	0	0	0	0	1	0	1	0	0	0	1	0	1	0
GERMANY	8	2	0	0	1	1	0	0	0	0	0	0	0	1	1	0	2	0	0	0	0	0
ITALY	7	2	0	0	0	1	0	0	0	0	0	0	0	0	0	0	2	0	0	0	1	0
BELGIUM + LUX	4	0	0	0	1	0	0	1	0	0	0	0	1	0	0	0	2	0	0	0	0	0
NETHERLANDS	2	0	0	0	0	0	1	0	0	0	0	0	0	0	0	0	0	0	0	1	1	0
SPAIN	4	0	0	0	1	0	0	0	0	0	0	0	0	0	0	0	0	0	1	0	0	0
GREECE + TURKEY	0	0	0	0	0	0	1	0	0	0	0	0	0	0	1	1	0	0	0	0	1	0
OTHER EUROPE	0	0	0	0	0	0	0	0	0	0	0	0	0	0	0	0	0	0	0	0	0	0
EUROPE EX. U.K.	14	3	0	0	2	1	0	0	0	0	0	0	1	1	1	0	4	0	0	0	1	0
SOUTHERN DOMINIONS	10	0	0	0	1	0	0	0	0	2	0	1	2	0	0	1	1	0	0	1	1	0
S. AFRICA +RHOD.	3	0	0	0	1	0	0	0	0	1	0	0	1	0	0	0	0	0	0	0	1	0
AUSTRALIA + N.Z.	10	0	0	0	0	0	0	0	0	1	1	1	2	1	1	2	1	0	1	1	0	0
ASIA + OTHER AFRICA	7	0	0	0	0	0	0	0	0	1	0	0	1	1	1	0	0	0	0	0	1	0
JAPAN	3	0	0	0	0	0	0	0	0	0	0	1	0	0	0	0	1	0	1	0	0	0
OTHER ASIA+AFR.	4	0	0	0	0	0	0	0	0	0	0	0	1	0	0	0	0	0	0	1	0	0
BLACK AFRICA	0	0	0	0	0	0	0	0	0	0	0	0	0	0	0	0	0	0	1	0	0	0
ARAB WORLD	0	0	0	0	0	0	0	0	0	0	0	0	0	0	0	0	0	0	0	0	0	0
INDIA	2	0	0	0	0	0	0	0	0	0	0	0	1	0	0	0	0	0	1	1	0	0
PHILIPPINES	1	0	0	0	0	0	0	0	0	0	0	0	0	1	0	0	0	0	0	0	0	0
OTHER E. ASIA	0	0	0	0	0	0	0	0	0	0	0	0	0	0	0	0	0	0	0	0	0	0
OTHER ASIA	1	0	0	0	0	0	0	0	0	0	0	0	0	0	0	0	0	0	0	1	1	0

CHAPTER 2- THE EXPANSION OF PARENT SYSTEMS
SECTION 4- THE FLOW OF MANUFACTURING BY INDUSTRY OF SUBSIDIARY
TABLE 37- SYSTEMS CLASSIFIED BY PERIOD SYSTEM FIRST OPERATED
IN SPECIFIED COUNTRIES AND REGIONS A SUBSIDIARY MANUFACTURING
OFFICE AND COMPUTING MACHINES (SIC 357)

PERIOD

COUNTRY OR REGION	PRE 1968	PRE 1901	1901 -13	1914 -19	1920 -24	1925 -29	1930 -34	1935 -39	1940 -45	1946 -50	1951 -53	1954 -55	1956 -57	1958 -59	1960 -61	1962	1963	1964	1965	1966	1967	UNK
OUTSIDE U.S.	10	0	1	2	0	1	1	1	0	0	0	0	0	2	1	0	0	1	0	0	0	0
OUT. U.S. + CANADA	10	0	1	1	0	1	2	1	1	1	0	0	0	1	2	0	0	1	1	1	0	0
OUT. WEST. HEMIS.	10	0	1	1	0	1	2	1	2	1	0	0	0	1	2	0	0	1	1	0	0	0
OUT. WHITE CWEALTH	10	0	0	2	0	1	2	1	0	2	0	0	2	1	2	0	0	0	1	0	0	0
OUT. DEVLPED WORLD	6	0	0	0	0	0	0	1	2	0	0	0	0	0	0	0	0	0	1	0	0	0
CANADA	5	0	0	2	1	0	0	0	1	0	0	0	0	1	2	0	0	0	0	0	0	0
LATIN AMERICA	6	0	0	0	0	0	0	1	2	0	0	0	2	0	1	0	0	0	1	1	0	0
C. AMER.+CARIB.	5	0	0	0	0	0	0	0	1	1	0	0	0	3	1	0	0	0	1	1	0	0
CUBA	0	0	0	0	0	0	0	1	1	1	0	0	0	3	0	0	0	0	0	0	0	0
MEXICO	5	0	0	0	0	0	0	0	0	2	0	0	0	3	1	0	0	0	1	1	0	0
OTHER	5	0	0	0	0	0	0	0	1	1	0	0	0	0	0	0	0	0	0	0	0	0
S. AMERICA	5	0	0	0	0	0	0	1	2	0	0	0	2	0	0	0	0	0	0	1	0	0
ARGENTINA	0	0	0	0	0	0	0	0	0	0	0	0	0	0	0	0	0	0	0	0	0	0
BRAZIL	4	0	0	0	0	0	0	1	2	0	0	0	0	0	1	0	0	0	0	0	0	0
PERU	0	0	0	0	0	0	0	0	0	0	0	0	0	0	1	0	0	0	0	0	0	0
COLOMBIA	1	0	0	0	0	0	0	1	0	0	1	0	0	0	1	0	0	0	0	0	0	0
VENEZUELA	1	0	0	0	0	0	0	0	0	0	1	0	0	1	0	0	0	0	0	0	0	0
OTHER	1	0	0	0	0	1	0	0	0	0	1	0	0	0	0	0	0	0	0	0	0	0
EUROPE	10	0	1	1	0	1	2	1	0	0	0	0	0	1	2	0	0	1	0	0	0	0
EFTA	6	0	1	0	0	1	1	1	0	1	0	0	0	0	1	0	0	0	0	0	0	0
U.K.	4	0	1	0	0	0	1	0	0	1	0	0	0	0	0	0	0	0	0	0	0	0
SCANDINAVIA	2	0	0	0	0	1	0	1	0	2	0	0	0	0	1	0	0	0	1	0	0	0
SWITZERLAND	1	0	0	0	0	0	0	0	0	1	0	0	0	1	0	0	0	0	0	0	0	0
OTHER EFTA	1	0	0	0	0	0	0	1	0	0	0	0	0	0	0	0	0	0	0	0	0	0
EUROP. COMMUNITY	10	0	0	2	0	1	2	1	0	0	0	0	0	0	1	0	0	1	1	0	0	0
FRANCE	6	0	0	1	0	1	1	1	0	1	1	0	0	1	0	0	0	1	0	0	0	0
GERMANY	6	0	0	2	0	0	2	1	0	0	1	0	0	0	1	0	0	1	0	0	0	0
ITALY	3	0	0	0	0	0	1	0	0	0	1	0	0	1	1	0	0	0	0	0	0	0
BELGIUM + LUX	3	0	0	0	0	0	0	1	0	0	0	0	0	0	0	0	0	0	1	0	0	0
NETHERLANDS	4	0	1	0	0	0	0	0	0	0	0	0	0	1	0	0	0	0	1	0	0	0
SPAIN	0	0	0	0	0	0	0	0	0	0	0	0	0	0	0	0	0	0	0	0	0	0
GREECE + TURKEY	0	0	0	0	0	0	0	0	0	0	0	0	0	0	0	0	0	0	0	0	0	0
OTHER EUROPE	1	0	0	0	0	1	0	1	1	0	1	0	0	0	0	0	1	0	0	0	0	0
EUROPE EX. U.K.	10	0	0	2	0	1	2	1	0	0	0	0	0	1	2	0	1	1	0	0	0	0
SOUTHERN DOMINIONS	2	0	0	0	0	0	0	0	0	1	0	1	0	0	0	0	0	0	0	0	0	0
S. AFRICA +RHOD.	1	0	0	0	0	0	0	0	0	0	0	1	0	0	0	0	0	0	0	0	0	0
AUSTRALIA + N.Z.	1	0	0	0	0	0	0	0	0	1	0	0	0	0	0	0	0	0	1	0	0	0
ASIA + OTHER AFRICA	6	0	0	0	0	0	0	1	0	0	1	0	1	0	0	0	0	0	1	0	0	0
JAPAN	5	0	0	0	0	0	0	1	0	0	1	0	1	1	0	0	0	0	1	0	0	0
OTHER ASIA+AFR.	2	0	0	0	0	0	0	0	0	0	0	0	0	0	0	0	0	0	0	0	0	0
BLACK AFRICA	0	0	0	0	0	0	0	0	0	0	1	0	0	0	0	0	0	0	1	0	0	0
ARAB WORLD	0	0	0	0	0	0	0	0	0	0	0	0	0	0	0	0	0	0	0	0	0	0
INDIA	2	0	0	0	0	0	0	0	0	0	1	0	0	0	0	0	0	0	0	1	0	0
PHILIPPINES	0	0	0	0	0	0	0	0	0	0	0	0	0	0	0	0	0	0	0	0	0	0
OTHER E. ASIA	0	0	0	0	0	0	0	0	0	0	0	0	0	0	0	0	0	0	0	0	0	0
OTHER ASIA	0	0	0	0	0	0	0	0	0	0	0	0	0	0	0	0	0	0	0	0	0	0

CHAPTER 2- THE EXPANSION OF PARENT SYSTEMS
SECTION 4- THE FLOW OF MANUFACTURING BY INDUSTRY OF SUBSIDIARY
TABLE 38- SYSTEMS CLASSIFIED BY PERIOD SYSTEM FIRST OPERATED
IN SPECIFIED COUNTRIES AND REGIONS A SUBSIDIARY MANUFACTURING
SERVICE INDUSTRY MACHINES (SIC 358)

COUNTRY OR REGION	PRE 1968	PRE 1901	1901 -13	1914 -19	1920 -24	1925 -29	1930 -34	1935 -39	1940 -45	1946 -50	1951 -53	1954 -55	1956 -57	1958 -59	1960 -61	1962	1963	1964	1965	1966	1967	UNK
OUTSIDE U.S.	14	0	0	0	0	1	1	1	0	0	0	0	2	0	1	1	3	1	0	1	0	1
OUT. U.S. + CANADA	10	0	0	0	0	1	1	1	0	0	0	0	1	0	1	1	1	1	0	1	0	1
OUT. WEST. HEMIS.	9	0	0	0	0	1	0	1	0	0	0	0	1	0	1	1	1	1	0	0	0	1
OUT. WHITE CWEALTH	8	0	0	0	0	1	0	0	0	0	0	0	1	0	1	1	1	0	1	1	0	0
OUT. DEVLPED WORLD	6	0	0	0	0	0	0	1	0	0	0	0	1	0	0	1	1	0	1	1	0	0
CANADA	8	0	0	0	0	1	1	0	0	0	0	0	1	0	0	0	3	0	1	1	0	0
LATIN AMERICA	6	0	0	0	0	0	0	1	0	0	0	0	1	0	0	0	1	0	1	2	0	0
C. AMER.+CARIB.	4	0	0	0	0	0	0	0	0	0	0	0	0	0	0	0	0	1	0	1	0	0
CUBA	0	0	0	0	0	0	0	0	0	0	0	0	0	0	0	0	0	0	0	0	0	0
MEXICO	2	0	0	0	0	0	0	0	0	0	0	0	0	0	0	0	0	1	0	2	0	0
OTHER	3	0	0	0	0	0	0	1	0	0	0	0	0	0	0	0	0	0	1	0	1	0
S. AMERICA	4	0	0	0	0	0	0	0	0	0	0	0	1	0	0	0	0	1	1	1	1	0
ARGENTINA	0	0	0	0	0	0	0	1	0	0	0	0	0	0	0	0	0	0	0	0	0	0
BRAZIL	2	0	0	0	0	0	0	0	0	0	0	0	1	0	0	0	0	1	0	0	1	0
PERU	0	0	0	0	0	0	0	1	0	0	0	0	0	0	0	0	0	0	0	0	0	0
COLOMBIA	0	0	0	0	0	0	0	0	0	0	0	0	0	0	0	0	0	0	0	0	0	0
VENEZUELA	1	0	0	0	0	0	0	0	0	0	0	0	0	0	0	0	1	0	0	0	0	0
OTHER	1	0	0	0	0	0	0	0	0	0	0	0	0	0	0	0	0	0	0	0	1	0
EUROPE	8	0	0	0	0	1	0	0	0	0	0	0	1	0	1	1	1	1	0	0	1	1
EFTA	5	0	0	0	0	0	0	0	0	0	0	0	1	0	1	0	0	1	0	1	1	1
U.K.	4	0	0	0	0	1	0	0	0	0	0	1	0	0	1	0	0	0	0	1	0	1
SCANDINAVIA	1	0	0	0	0	0	0	0	0	0	0	0	0	0	1	0	0	1	0	0	0	0
SWITZERLAND	1	0	0	0	0	0	0	0	0	0	0	0	0	0	0	0	0	1	0	1	0	1
OTHER EFTA	1	0	0	0	0	0	0	0	0	0	0	0	0	0	0	0	0	1	0	0	0	0
EUROP. COMMUNITY	6	0	0	0	1	1	0	0	0	0	0	1	0	0	1	1	0	1	0	0	0	0
FRANCE	6	0	0	0	1	1	0	0	0	0	0	0	0	0	1	2	0	1	0	0	0	0
GERMANY	4	0	0	0	0	0	0	0	0	0	0	0	0	0	0	1	1	1	0	0	0	0
ITALY	1	0	0	0	0	0	0	0	0	0	0	0	0	0	0	1	1	0	0	0	0	0
BELGIUM + LUX	1	0	0	0	0	0	0	0	0	0	0	1	0	0	0	1	1	0	1	0	0	0
NETHERLANDS	2	0	0	0	0	0	0	0	0	0	0	0	0	0	0	0	0	0	0	1	0	0
SPAIN	0	0	0	0	0	0	0	0	0	0	0	0	0	0	0	0	0	0	0	0	0	0
GREECE + TURKEY	0	0	0	0	0	0	0	0	0	0	0	0	0	0	0	0	0	1	0	0	0	0
OTHER EUROPE	0	0	0	0	0	0	0	0	0	0	0	0	0	0	0	0	0	0	0	0	0	0
EUROPE EX. U.K.	6	0	0	0	0	1	0	0	0	0	0	0	0	0	1	1	1	1	0	0	1	1
SOUTHERN DOMINIONS	6	0	0	0	0	0	0	2	0	0	0	0	0	1	0	1	0	2	0	0	0	0
S. AFRICA +RHOD.	0	0	0	0	0	0	0	0	0	0	0	0	0	0	0	0	0	0	0	0	0	0
AUSTRALIA + N.Z.	6	0	0	0	0	0	0	2	0	0	0	0	0	1	0	1	0	2	0	0	0	0
ASIA + OTHER AFRICA	1	0	0	0	0	0	0	0	0	0	0	0	0	0	0	1	0	1	0	0	0	0
JAPAN	1	0	0	0	0	0	0	0	0	0	0	0	0	1	0	1	0	0	0	0	0	0
OTHER ASIA+AFR.	0	0	0	0	0	0	0	0	0	0	0	0	0	0	0	0	0	0	0	0	0	0
BLACK AFRICA	0	0	0	0	0	0	0	0	0	0	0	0	0	1	0	1	0	0	0	0	0	0
ARAB WORLD	1	0	0	0	0	0	0	0	0	0	0	0	0	0	0	0	0	0	0	0	0	0
INDIA	1	0	0	0	0	0	0	0	0	0	0	0	0	1	0	1	0	1	0	0	0	0
PHILIPPINES	0	0	0	0	0	0	0	0	0	0	0	0	0	0	0	0	0	0	0	0	0	0
OTHER E. ASIA	0	0	0	0	0	0	0	0	0	0	0	0	0	0	0	0	0	0	0	0	0	0
OTHER ASIA	0	0	0	0	0	0	0	0	0	0	0	0	0	0	0	0	0	0	0	0	0	0

PERIOD

CHAPTER 2- THE EXPANSION OF PARENT SYSTEMS
SECTION 4- THE FLOW OF MANUFACTURING BY INDUSTRY OF SUBSIDIARY
TABLE 39- SYSTEMS CLASSIFIED BY PERIOD SYSTEM FIRST OPERATED
IN SPECIFIED COUNTRIES AND REGIONS A SUBSIDIARY MANUFACTURING
OTHER NON-ELECTRICAL MACHINERY (SIC 351 AND 359)

PERIOD

COUNTRY OR REGION	PRE 1968	PRE 1901	1901 -13	1914 -19	1920 -24	1925 -29	1930 -34	1935 -39	1940 -45	1946 -50	1951 -53	1954 -55	1956 -57	1958 -59	1960 -61	1962	1963	1964	1965	1966	1967	UNK
OUTSIDE U.S.	25	2	0	1	0	1	1	1	1	0	2	1	1	3	4	3	1	1	2	0	0	1
OUT. U.S. + CANADA	22	2	0	0	0	1	1	1	1	0	1	1	1	3	3	2	1	1	2	0	0	1
OUT. WEST. HEMIS.	19	2	0	0	0	0	1	1	1	1	1	1	1	2	3	1	1	1	2	0	0	0
OUT. WHITE CWEALTH	16	1	0	0	0	1	0	2	0	0	1	0	1	2	1	1	1	1	2	0	0	0
OUT. DEVLPED WORLD	5	0	0	0	0	1	0	0	1	0	0	0	1	1	0	0	0	0	0	0	0	0
CANADA	6	0	0	1	0	0	0	0	0	0	0	0	0	1	1	0	0	1	1	0	0	1
LATIN AMERICA	5	0	0	0	0	0	0	0	1	0	0	0	1	1	0	1	0	1	0	0	0	0
C. AMER.+CARIB.	1	0	0	0	0	0	0	0	0	0	0	0	1	0	0	0	0	0	0	0	0	0
CUBA	0	0	0	0	0	0	0	0	0	0	0	0	0	0	0	0	0	0	0	0	0	0
MEXICO	0	0	0	0	0	0	0	0	0	0	0	0	0	0	0	0	0	0	0	0	0	0
OTHER	0	0	0	0	0	0	0	0	0	0	0	0	0	0	0	0	0	0	0	0	0	0
S. AMERICA	5	0	0	0	0	0	0	0	1	0	0	0	1	1	0	0	1	1	0	0	0	0
ARGENTINA	2	0	0	0	0	0	0	0	1	0	0	0	0	1	0	0	0	0	0	0	0	0
BRAZIL	4	0	0	0	0	0	0	0	0	0	0	0	1	0	1	0	1	1	0	0	0	0
PERU	0	0	0	0	0	0	0	0	0	0	0	0	0	0	0	0	0	0	0	0	0	0
COLOMBIA	0	0	0	0	0	0	0	0	0	0	0	0	0	0	0	0	0	0	0	0	0	0
VENEZUELA	0	0	0	0	0	0	0	0	0	0	0	0	0	0	0	0	0	0	0	0	0	0
OTHER	0	0	0	0	0	0	0	0	0	0	0	0	0	0	0	0	0	0	0	0	0	0
EUROPE	16	2	0	0	0	1	1	2	0	0	1	0	1	2	2	1	1	0	2	0	0	0
EFTA	8	1	0	0	0	1	0	1	0	0	0	0	0	1	1	1	0	0	1	0	0	1
U.K.	7	2	0	0	0	0	0	1	0	0	0	1	0	0	2	0	1	0	0	0	0	0
SCANDINAVIA	1	0	0	0	0	0	0	0	0	0	0	0	0	0	1	0	0	0	0	0	0	0
SWITZERLAND	0	0	0	0	0	0	0	0	0	0	0	0	0	0	0	0	0	0	0	0	0	0
OTHER EFTA	0	0	0	0	0	0	0	0	0	0	0	0	0	0	0	0	0	0	0	0	0	0
EUROP. COMMUNITY	10	1	0	0	0	2	1	0	1	0	0	0	1	0	1	0	2	0	0	0	0	1
FRANCE	6	1	0	0	0	0	1	0	1	0	0	0	0	0	1	0	1	0	0	0	0	1
GERMANY	4	0	0	0	0	1	0	0	0	0	0	0	0	0	0	0	1	0	1	0	0	1
ITALY	1	0	0	0	0	0	0	0	0	0	0	0	0	0	0	0	1	0	0	0	0	0
BELGIUM + LUX	2	0	0	0	0	0	0	1	0	0	0	0	0	1	0	0	0	0	0	0	0	0
NETHERLANDS	2	0	0	0	0	0	0	0	1	0	0	0	0	1	0	0	0	0	0	0	0	0
SPAIN	2	0	0	0	0	0	0	0	0	0	0	0	0	0	0	0	1	0	1	0	0	0
GREECE + TURKEY	0	0	0	0	0	0	0	0	0	0	0	0	0	0	0	0	0	0	0	0	0	0
OTHER EUROPE	1	0	0	0	0	0	0	0	0	0	0	0	0	0	0	0	0	1	0	0	0	0
EUROPE EX. U.K.	12	2	0	0	0	1	1	2	0	0	1	0	1	1	1	1	0	1	0	0	0	0
SOUTHERN DOMINIONS	3	0	0	0	0	0	0	0	0	0	0	0	0	1	1	0	0	0	1	0	0	0
S. AFRICA +RHOD.	0	0	0	0	0	0	0	0	0	0	0	0	0	0	0	0	0	0	0	0	0	0
AUSTRALIA + N.Z.	3	0	0	0	0	0	0	0	0	0	0	0	0	1	1	0	0	0	1	0	0	0
ASIA + OTHER AFRICA	1	0	0	0	0	0	0	0	0	0	1	0	0	0	0	0	0	0	0	0	0	0
JAPAN	1	0	0	0	0	0	0	0	0	0	1	0	0	0	0	0	0	0	0	0	0	0
OTHER ASIA+AFR.	0	0	0	0	0	0	0	0	0	0	0	0	0	0	0	0	0	0	0	0	0	0
BLACK AFRICA	0	0	0	0	0	0	0	0	0	0	0	0	0	0	0	0	0	0	0	0	0	0
ARAB WORLD	0	0	0	0	0	0	0	0	0	0	0	0	0	0	0	0	0	0	0	0	0	0
INDIA	0	0	0	0	0	0	0	0	0	0	0	0	0	0	0	0	0	0	0	0	0	0
PHILIPPINES	0	0	0	0	0	0	0	0	0	0	0	0	0	0	0	0	0	0	0	0	0	0
OTHER E. ASIA	0	0	0	0	0	0	0	0	0	0	0	0	0	0	0	0	0	0	0	0	0	0
OTHER ASIA	0	0	0	0	0	0	0	0	0	0	0	0	0	0	0	0	0	0	0	0	0	0

CHAPTER 2- THE EXPANSION OF PARENT SYSTEMS
SECTION 4- THE FLOW OF MANUFACTURING BY INDUSTRY OF SUBSIDIARY
TABLE 40- SYSTEMS CLASSIFIED BY PERIOD SYSTEM FIRST OPERATED
IN SPECIFIED COUNTRIES AND REGIONS A SUBSIDIARY MANUFACTURING
HOUSEHOLD APPLIANCES (SIC 363)

PERIOD

COUNTRY OR REGION	PRE 1968	PRE 1901	1901 -13	1914 -19	1920 -24	1925 -29	1930 -34	1935 -39	1940 -45	1946 -50	1951 -53	1954 -55	1956 -57	1958 -59	1960 -61	1962	1963	1964	1965	1966	1967	UNK
OUTSIDE U.S.	24	0	1	0	2	2	1	1	0	2	1	1	1	2	4	1	1	1	0	1	2	0
OUT. U.S. + CANADA	22	0	1	0	1	3	1	1	0	0	1	1	2	2	4	1	1	1	0	1	1	0
OUT. WEST. HEMIS.	20	0	1	0	1	3	1	0	0	1	1	1	2	2	4	2	0	1	0	0	1	1
OUT. WHITE CWEALTH	18	0	1	0	0	1	0	2	0	1	1	2	1	0	2	1	0	2	0	1	1	0
OUT. DEVLPED WORLD	9	0	0	0	0	0	2	2	1	1	1	1	1	1	0	0	0	0	0	1	0	0
CANADA	5	0	0	0	0	0	0	0	0	1	0	0	0	1	0	0	0	0	0	0	1	0
LATIN AMERICA	8	0	0	0	1	0	0	2	1	1	0	1	1	1	4	0	2	0	0	1	0	0
C. AMER.+CARIB.	6	0	0	0	0	0	0	1	1	1	0	1	1	1	2	0	0	0	1	1	1	0
CUBA	0	0	0	0	0	0	0	0	0	1	0	1	0	0	2	0	0	0	1	0	0	0
MEXICO	6	0	0	0	0	0	0	0	0	0	0	0	1	1	2	0	0	0	0	1	1	0
OTHER	1	0	0	0	0	0	0	1	0	1	0	0	0	0	0	0	0	0	0	0	0	0
S. AMERICA	5	0	0	0	0	0	0	0	1	0	0	0	1	0	1	1	0	0	1	0	0	0
ARGENTINA	4	0	0	0	0	0	0	1	0	0	0	0	0	1	1	0	1	0	0	0	0	0
BRAZIL	2	0	0	0	0	0	0	0	1	0	0	0	0	1	1	1	0	0	0	0	0	0
PERU	1	0	0	0	0	0	0	0	0	0	0	0	0	1	0	0	0	0	0	0	0	0
COLOMBIA	2	0	0	0	0	0	0	0	1	0	0	0	0	0	1	0	0	0	0	0	0	0
VENEZUELA	2	0	0	0	0	0	0	0	0	0	0	0	0	1	1	0	0	0	0	0	1	0
OTHER	2	0	0	0	0	0	0	0	0	0	0	0	0	0	0	1	1	1	1	1	0	0
EUROPE	20	0	1	0	1	2	1	0	0	1	0	1	2	2	4	1	1	1	2	0	1	0
EFTA	10	0	0	0	1	1	1	0	0	1	0	0	1	2	2	0	1	0	0	0	0	0
U.K.	10	0	0	0	1	1	1	0	0	1	0	1	1	2	2	0	1	0	0	0	0	0
SCANDINAVIA	1	0	0	0	0	0	0	0	0	0	0	0	0	0	0	0	0	0	0	0	0	0
SWITZERLAND	0	0	0	0	0	0	0	0	0	0	0	0	0	0	0	0	0	0	0	0	0	0
OTHER EFTA	0	0	0	0	0	0	0	0	0	0	0	0	0	0	0	0	0	0	0	0	0	0
EUROP. COMMUNITY	13	0	0	0	0	1	0	1	0	0	0	1	2	0	1	2	0	3	3	0	1	0
FRANCE	6	0	0	0	0	0	0	0	0	0	0	0	0	1	1	1	1	3	1	0	1	0
GERMANY	6	0	0	0	0	0	0	0	0	0	0	0	1	0	0	0	2	0	0	0	0	0
ITALY	5	0	0	0	0	0	0	0	0	0	0	1	1	0	1	1	0	0	0	0	1	0
BELGIUM + LUX	1	0	0	0	0	1	0	0	0	1	0	0	0	0	0	0	0	0	0	0	0	0
NETHERLANDS	0	0	0	0	0	0	0	0	0	0	0	0	0	0	0	0	0	0	0	0	0	0
SPAIN	0	0	0	0	0	0	0	0	0	0	0	0	0	0	0	0	0	0	0	0	0	0
GREECE + TURKEY	2	0	0	0	0	0	0	0	0	0	0	0	0	1	1	0	0	0	0	0	0	0
OTHER EUROPE	1	0	0	0	0	0	0	0	0	0	0	0	0	0	0	0	0	0	0	0	1	0
EUROPE EX. U.K.	14	0	1	0	0	1	0	0	0	0	0	2	2	2	2	1	1	3	3	0	1	0
SOUTHERN DOMINIONS	4	0	0	0	0	1	0	0	0	0	0	1	0	0	0	1	0	1	0	0	0	0
S. AFRICA +RHOD.	2	0	0	0	0	0	0	0	0	0	0	0	0	0	2	0	1	1	0	0	0	1
AUSTRALIA + N.Z.	4	0	0	0	0	1	0	0	0	0	1	1	1	0	1	1	0	0	0	0	0	1
ASIA + OTHER AFRICA	4	0	0	0	0	0	0	0	0	0	0	0	0	0	0	0	0	0	0	0	0	1
JAPAN	2	0	0	0	0	0	0	0	0	0	1	0	0	0	0	0	0	0	0	0	0	0
OTHER ASIA+AFR.	3	0	0	0	0	0	0	0	0	0	0	0	0	0	1	0	0	0	0	0	0	0
BLACK AFRICA	1	0	0	0	0	0	0	0	0	0	1	0	0	0	1	0	0	0	1	0	0	0
ARAB WORLD	1	0	0	0	0	0	0	0	0	0	0	0	0	0	0	0	0	0	0	0	0	0
INDIA	0	0	0	0	0	0	0	0	0	0	0	0	0	0	1	0	0	0	0	0	0	0
PHILIPPINES	2	0	0	0	0	0	0	0	0	0	0	0	0	0	0	1	0	0	0	0	0	0
OTHER E. ASIA	2	0	0	0	0	0	0	0	0	0	1	0	0	0	0	0	0	0	0	0	1	0
OTHER ASIA	1	0	0	0	0	0	0	0	0	0	0	0	0	0	1	0	0	0	0	0	0	0

CHAPTER 2- THE EXPANSION OF PARENT SYSTEMS
SECTION 4- THE FLOW OF MANUFACTURING BY INDUSTRY OF SUBSIDIARY
TABLE 41- SYSTEMS CLASSIFIED BY PERIOD SYSTEM FIRST OPERATED
IN SPECIFIED COUNTRIES AND REGIONS A SUBSIDIARY MANUFACTURING
COMMUNICATION EQUIPMENT (SIC 366)

PERIOD

COUNTRY OR REGION	PRE 1968	PRE 1901	1901 -13	1914 -19	1920 -24	1925 -29	1930 -34	1935 -39	1940 -45	1946 -50	1951 -53	1954 -55	1956 -57	1958 -59	1960 -61	1962	1963	1964	1965	1966	1967	UNK
OUTSIDE U.S.	11	0	0	0	2	1	0	0	0	0	1	2	1	1	2	0	0	0	0	0	1	0
OUT. U.S. + CANADA	10	0	0	0	1	1	0	0	0	0	1	2	0	1	3	0	0	0	0	0	1	0
OUT. WEST. HEMIS.	9	0	0	0	1	1	0	0	0	0	1	2	0	1	2	0	0	1	0	0	1	0
OUT. WHITE CWEALTH	9	0	0	0	1	1	0	0	0	0	0	2	0	1	2	0	1	1	0	0	1	0
OUT. DEVLPED WORLD	3	0	0	0	0	1	0	0	0	0	0	0	0	0	1	0	0	1	0	0	0	0
CANADA	5	0	0	0	1	0	0	0	0	1	0	1	1	0	1	0	0	0	0	0	0	0
LATIN AMERICA	2	0	0	0	1	1	0	0	0	0	0	0	0	0	0	0	0	0	0	0	0	0
C. AMER.+CARIB.	2	0	0	0	0	1	0	0	0	1	0	0	0	0	0	0	0	0	0	0	0	0
CUBA	0	0	0	0	0	0	0	0	0	0	0	0	0	0	0	0	0	0	0	0	0	0
MEXICO	2	0	0	0	0	0	0	0	0	1	0	0	0	1	0	0	0	0	0	0	0	0
OTHER	0	0	0	0	0	0	0	0	0	0	0	0	0	0	0	0	0	0	0	0	0	0
S. AMERICA	1	0	0	0	0	1	0	0	0	0	0	0	0	0	0	0	0	0	0	0	0	0
ARGENTINA	1	0	0	0	0	1	0	0	0	0	0	0	0	0	0	0	0	0	0	0	0	0
BRAZIL	0	0	0	0	0	0	0	0	0	0	0	0	0	0	0	0	0	0	0	0	0	0
PERU	0	0	0	0	0	0	0	0	0	0	0	0	0	0	0	0	0	0	0	0	0	0
COLOMBIA	0	0	0	0	0	0	0	0	0	0	0	0	0	0	0	0	0	0	0	0	0	0
VENEZUELA	0	0	0	0	0	0	0	0	0	0	0	0	0	0	0	0	0	0	0	0	0	0
OTHER	0	0	0	0	0	0	0	0	0	0	0	0	0	0	0	0	0	0	0	0	0	0
EUROPE	9	0	0	0	1	1	0	0	0	1	0	2	0	1	2	0	0	0	0	0	1	0
EFTA	3	0	0	0	1	1	0	0	0	0	0	1	0	1	1	0	0	0	0	0	0	0
U.K.	3	0	0	0	0	1	1	0	0	0	0	0	0	1	0	0	0	0	0	0	0	0
SCANDINAVIA	1	0	0	0	0	0	0	0	0	0	0	1	0	0	0	0	0	0	0	0	0	0
SWITZERLAND	0	0	0	0	0	1	0	0	0	0	0	0	0	0	0	0	0	0	0	0	0	0
OTHER EFTA	1	0	0	0	0	0	0	0	0	0	0	0	0	0	0	0	0	0	0	0	0	0
EUROP. COMMUNITY	5	0	0	0	1	1	0	0	0	0	0	1	0	0	0	1	0	0	0	0	0	0
FRANCE	2	0	0	0	1	1	0	0	0	0	0	0	0	0	0	0	0	0	0	0	0	0
GERMANY	3	0	0	0	0	1	0	0	0	0	0	1	0	0	1	0	0	0	0	0	0	0
ITALY	1	0	0	0	0	1	0	0	0	0	0	0	0	0	0	0	0	0	0	0	0	0
BELGIUM + LUX	1	0	0	0	0	0	0	0	1	0	0	0	0	0	1	0	0	0	0	0	0	0
NETHERLANDS	1	0	0	0	0	0	0	0	0	0	1	0	0	0	0	0	0	0	0	0	0	0
SPAIN	2	0	0	0	0	0	0	0	0	0	1	0	0	0	1	0	0	0	0	0	0	0
GREECE + TURKEY	1	0	0	0	0	0	0	0	0	0	0	0	0	0	0	0	0	0	1	0	0	0
OTHER EUROPE	1	0	0	0	0	0	0	0	1	0	0	0	0	0	0	0	0	0	0	0	0	0
EUROPE EX. U.K.	7	0	0	0	1	0	0	0	0	0	1	2	0	1	1	0	0	0	0	0	1	0
SOUTHERN DOMINIONS	1	0	0	0	0	0	0	0	0	0	0	0	0	0	0	0	0	1	0	0	0	0
S. AFRICA +RHOD.	1	0	0	0	0	1	0	0	0	0	0	0	0	0	0	0	0	0	0	0	0	0
AUSTRALIA + N.Z.	1	0	0	0	0	0	0	0	0	0	0	0	1	0	0	0	0	0	0	0	0	0
ASIA + OTHER AFRICA	3	0	0	0	0	0	0	0	0	0	0	0	0	0	0	0	1	1	1	0	0	0
JAPAN	1	0	0	0	0	0	0	0	0	0	0	0	0	0	0	0	0	1	0	0	0	0
OTHER ASIA+AFR.	2	0	0	0	0	0	0	0	0	0	0	1	0	0	0	0	0	1	0	0	0	0
BLACK AFRICA	0	0	0	0	0	0	0	0	0	0	0	0	0	0	0	0	0	0	0	0	0	0
ARAB WORLD	0	0	0	0	0	0	0	0	0	0	0	0	0	0	0	0	0	0	0	0	0	0
INDIA	2	0	0	0	0	0	0	0	0	0	0	0	0	1	0	0	0	0	1	0	0	0
PHILIPPINES	0	0	0	0	0	0	0	0	0	0	0	0	0	0	0	0	0	0	0	0	0	0
OTHER E. ASIA	1	0	0	0	0	0	0	0	0	0	0	0	0	0	1	0	0	0	0	0	0	0
OTHER ASIA	0	0	0	0	0	0	0	0	0	0	0	0	0	0	0	0	0	0	0	0	0	0

CHAPTER 2- THE EXPANSION OF PARENT SYSTEMS
SECTION 4- THE FLOW OF MANUFACTURING BY INDUSTRY OF SUBSIDIARY
TABLE 42- SYSTEMS CLASSIFIED BY PERIOD SYSTEM FIRST OPERATED
IN SPECIFIED COUNTRIES AND REGIONS A SUBSIDIARY MANUFACTURING
OTHER ELECTRONIC EQUIPMENT (SIC 365 AND 367)

PERIOD

COUNTRY OR REGION	PRE 1968	PRE 1901	1901-13	1914-19	1920-24	1925-29	1930-34	1935-39	1940-45	1946-50	1951-53	1954-55	1956-57	1958-59	1960-61	1962	1963	1964	1965	1966	1967	UNK
OUTSIDE U.S.	19	0	0	1	1	1	1	0	0	1	1	1	0	2	7	0	1	1	2	0	1	0
OUT. U.S. + CANADA	17	0	0	0	0	1	1	0	0	0	1	2	0	2	6	1	1	1	1	0	2	0
OUT. WEST. HEMIS.	16	0	0	0	0	1	1	0	0	0	1	1	0	2	4	0	1	0	1	0	2	0
OUT. WHITE CWEALTH	15	0	0	0	0	1	0	0	0	0	1	1	0	3	5	1	0	1	1	0	2	0
OUT. DEVLPED WORLD	10	0	0	0	0	1	0	0	0	0	0	1	0	1	5	0	0	1	1	0	1	0
CANADA	8	0	0	1	1	0	0	0	2	0	0	0	1	1	2	0	0	0	1	0	1	0
LATIN AMERICA	8	0	0	1	1	0	0	0	0	0	0	0	0	1	4	1	0	1	1	0	1	0
C. AMER.+CARIB.	5	0	0	0	0	1	0	0	0	0	0	0	0	1	2	1	0	0	1	0	0	0
CUBA	0	0	0	0	0	1	0	0	0	0	0	0	0	0	0	0	0	0	0	0	0	0
MEXICO	5	0	0	0	0	0	0	0	0	0	0	1	0	1	2	1	0	0	0	0	0	0
OTHER	1	0	0	0	0	1	0	0	0	0	0	0	0	0	0	0	0	1	0	0	0	0
S. AMERICA	7	0	0	0	0	0	0	0	0	0	0	1	0	1	2	0	1	1	0	0	1	0
ARGENTINA	3	0	0	0	0	1	0	0	0	0	0	0	0	1	0	0	0	0	0	0	0	0
BRAZIL	5	0	0	0	0	0	0	0	0	0	0	1	0	0	2	1	0	0	1	0	0	0
PERU	0	0	0	0	0	0	0	0	0	0	0	0	0	0	0	0	0	0	0	0	0	0
COLOMBIA	0	0	0	0	0	1	0	0	0	0	0	0	0	0	0	0	0	0	0	0	0	0
VENEZUELA	2	0	0	0	0	0	0	0	0	0	0	0	0	0	1	0	0	0	0	0	1	0
OTHER	2	0	0	0	0	1	0	0	0	0	0	0	0	1	0	1	0	1	1	0	0	0
EUROPE	13	0	0	0	0	1	1	0	0	0	1	0	0	3	4	0	1	0	1	0	1	0
EFTA	8	0	0	0	0	1	1	0	0	0	1	0	0	1	2	0	1	1	0	0	0	0
U.K.	6	0	0	0	0	1	1	0	0	0	1	0	0	1	1	0	1	0	0	0	0	0
SCANDINAVIA	0	0	0	0	0	0	0	0	0	0	0	0	0	0	0	0	0	0	0	0	0	0
SWITZERLAND	2	0	0	0	0	0	0	0	0	0	0	0	0	0	1	1	0	0	1	0	0	0
OTHER EFTA	0	0	0	0	0	0	0	0	0	0	0	0	0	0	0	0	0	0	0	0	0	0
EUROP. COMMUNITY	11	0	0	0	0	0	0	0	0	0	0	0	0	3	1	1	1	0	1	0	1	0
FRANCE	4	0	0	0	0	0	0	0	0	0	0	0	0	0	0	1	0	0	0	0	0	0
GERMANY	6	0	0	0	0	0	0	0	0	0	0	1	0	1	2	1	0	1	0	0	0	0
ITALY	5	0	0	0	0	0	0	0	0	0	0	0	0	2	1	0	0	0	0	0	1	0
BELGIUM + LUX	1	0	0	0	0	0	0	0	0	0	0	0	0	0	1	0	0	0	0	0	0	0
NETHERLANDS	0	0	0	0	0	0	0	0	0	0	0	0	0	0	0	0	0	0	0	1	0	0
SPAIN	2	0	0	0	0	0	0	0	0	0	0	0	0	0	0	0	0	0	0	0	0	0
GREECE + TURKEY	1	0	0	0	0	0	0	0	0	0	0	0	0	0	0	0	0	0	0	0	0	1
OTHER EUROPE	0	0	0	0	0	0	0	0	0	0	0	0	0	0	0	0	0	0	0	0	0	0
EUROPE EX. U.K.	12	0	0	0	0	0	0	0	0	0	1	1	0	3	3	1	1	0	1	0	1	0
SOUTHERN DOMINIONS	4	0	0	0	0	0	0	0	0	0	0	0	1	0	1	0	0	0	0	0	0	0
S. AFRICA +RHOD.	0	0	0	0	0	0	0	0	0	0	0	0	0	0	0	0	0	0	0	0	0	0
AUSTRALIA + N.Z.	4	0	0	0	0	0	0	0	0	0	0	0	1	0	1	0	0	0	1	1	0	0
ASIA + OTHER AFRICA	7	0	0	0	0	1	0	0	0	0	1	0	0	0	1	1	0	1	0	0	2	0
JAPAN	5	0	0	0	0	0	0	0	0	0	0	0	0	0	1	1	0	1	0	0	0	1
OTHER ASIA+AFR.	6	0	0	0	0	1	0	0	0	0	1	0	0	0	1	0	0	0	0	0	2	0
BLACK AFRICA	1	0	0	0	0	0	0	0	0	0	0	0	0	0	0	1	1	0	0	0	0	0
ARAB WORLD	0	0	0	0	0	0	0	0	0	0	0	0	0	0	0	0	0	0	0	0	0	0
INDIA	1	0	0	0	1	0	0	0	0	0	0	0	0	0	1	0	0	1	0	0	0	0
PHILIPPINES	1	0	0	0	0	1	0	0	0	0	0	0	0	0	0	0	0	0	0	1	0	0
OTHER E. ASIA	3	0	0	0	0	0	0	0	0	0	0	0	0	0	0	0	0	0	0	0	1	0
OTHER ASIA	0	0	0	0	0	0	0	0	0	0	0	0	0	0	0	0	0	0	0	0	0	0

CHAPTER 2- THE EXPANSION OF PARENT SYSTEMS
SECTION 4- THE FLOW OF MANUFACTURING BY INDUSTRY OF SUBSIDIARY
TABLE 43- SYSTEMS CLASSIFIED BY PERIOD SYSTEM FIRST OPERATED
IN SPECIFIED COUNTRIES AND REGIONS A SUBSIDIARY MANUFACTURING
OTHER ELECTRICAL MACHINERY (OTHER SIC 36)

PERIOD

COUNTRY OR REGION	PRE 1968	PRE 1901	1901 -13	1914 -19	1920 -24	1925 -29	1930 -34	1935 -39	1940 -45	1946 -50	1951 -53	1954 -55	1956 -57	1958 -59	1960 -61	1962	1963	1964	1965	1966	1967	UNK
OUTSIDE U.S.	47	2	2	2	1	1	1	4	0	3	3	2	2	6	3	5	3	1	0	3	3	1
OUT. U.S. + CANADA	41	2	2	2	1	1	1	3	0	2	2	1	1	5	3	3	3	2	0	2	3	0
OUT. WEST. HEMIS.	33	1	3	2	1	1	1	2	0	1	1	1	0	5	2	6	2	2	0	1	2	0
OUT. WHITE CWEALTH	37	2	1	0	2	2	0	2	0	3	2	2	1	4	4	7	1	2	1	2	2	0
OUT. DEVLPED WORLD	23	1	0	0	1	1	0	2	0	3	0	1	1	2	2	2	3	1	1	2	2	0
CANADA	22	0	1	1	1	0	1	2	0	3	2	2	1	3	1	0	0	0	0	2	2	1
LATIN AMERICA	20	1	0	0	0	0	0	3	0	3	0	1	1	2	1	1	1	1	0	2	2	0
C. AMER.+CARIB.	13	0	0	0	0	0	1	1	0	2	0	0	1	2	2	0	1	1	0	1	1	0
CUBA	2	0	0	0	0	0	0	0	0	0	0	0	0	2	1	0	0	0	0	0	0	0
MEXICO	13	0	0	0	0	0	0	0	0	0	0	0	0	2	1	1	0	1	0	1	1	0
OTHER	3	0	0	0	0	0	0	0	0	0	0	0	0	0	0	0	1	0	0	1	1	0
S. AMERICA	13	1	0	0	0	0	0	3	0	2	0	0	0	1	2	1	0	0	1	0	0	0
ARGENTINA	5	0	0	0	0	0	0	1	0	1	0	1	0	1	0	0	1	0	0	1	1	0
BRAZIL	9	0	0	0	0	0	0	2	0	1	0	0	0	0	0	0	1	0	0	1	1	0
PERU	1	0	0	0	0	0	0	0	0	0	0	0	0	0	0	0	0	1	0	0	0	0
COLOMBIA	3	0	0	0	0	0	0	0	0	1	0	1	0	1	1	0	1	0	0	0	0	0
VENEZUELA	5	0	0	0	0	0	0	0	0	1	0	0	0	1	0	0	0	0	0	0	0	0
OTHER	1	1	0	0	0	0	0	0	0	0	0	0	0	0	0	0	0	0	0	0	0	0
EUROPE	30	1	2	2	0	1	0	1	0	1	1	1	0	5	1	4	4	2	0	2	2	0
EFTA	15	1	1	2	0	0	0	1	0	0	0	0	0	4	0	1	2	0	0	1	2	0
U.K.	14	1	1	2	0	0	0	1	0	0	0	0	0	4	0	0	2	0	0	1	2	0
SCANDINAVIA	2	0	0	0	0	0	0	0	0	0	0	0	0	0	0	1	0	0	0	0	0	0
SWITZERLAND	1	0	0	0	0	0	0	0	0	0	0	0	0	0	1	0	0	0	0	0	0	0
OTHER EFTA	2	0	1	0	1	0	0	0	0	0	0	0	0	0	0	0	0	1	0	0	0	0
EUROP. COMMUNITY	22	1	1	1	1	2	0	0	0	2	0	0	0	3	2	4	1	1	0	0	1	1
FRANCE	13	1	0	1	1	0	0	0	0	1	0	1	0	0	1	1	2	1	1	0	0	0
GERMANY	6	0	0	0	0	1	0	0	0	0	0	0	0	1	0	3	1	0	0	0	0	0
ITALY	10	0	2	0	0	0	0	0	0	1	0	0	0	2	2	0	0	0	0	0	1	0
BELGIUM + LUX	0	0	0	0	0	0	0	0	0	0	0	0	0	0	0	0	0	0	0	0	0	0
NETHERLANDS	1	0	0	0	1	1	0	0	0	0	0	0	0	0	0	0	0	0	0	0	0	0
SPAIN	2	0	0	0	0	0	0	0	0	0	0	0	0	0	0	0	1	1	0	1	1	0
GREECE + TURKEY	3	0	0	0	0	0	0	0	0	0	0	0	0	0	0	0	0	0	0	1	0	0
OTHER EUROPE	1	0	0	0	0	0	0	0	0	0	0	0	0	0	0	1	0	1	0	0	0	0
EUROPE EX. U.K.	25	1	0	0	1	2	0	0	0	2	1	1	0	3	2	5	3	2	1	1	1	0
SOUTHERN DOMINIONS	8	0	0	0	0	0	2	0	0	0	1	0	0	2	0	1	0	0	1	0	0	0
S. AFRICA +RHOD.	1	0	0	0	0	0	0	0	0	0	1	0	0	0	1	0	0	0	0	0	0	0
AUSTRALIA + N.Z.	7	0	0	0	0	0	2	0	0	0	0	0	0	2	1	1	2	0	1	0	0	0
ASIA + OTHER AFRICA	11	0	1	0	0	0	0	0	0	0	1	0	1	0	2	2	0	1	2	0	0	1
JAPAN	6	0	0	0	0	0	0	0	0	0	1	0	0	0	0	1	1	0	1	1	1	0
OTHER ASIA+AFR.	8	0	0	0	0	0	0	0	0	1	1	0	1	0	3	3	0	0	1	0	0	0
BLACK AFRICA	1	0	0	0	0	0	0	0	0	0	0	0	0	0	0	0	0	0	0	0	0	0
ARAB WORLD	0	0	0	0	0	0	0	0	0	0	0	0	0	0	0	0	0	0	0	0	0	0
INDIA	5	0	0	0	0	0	0	0	0	1	0	0	0	0	3	1	0	0	0	0	0	0
PHILIPPINES	2	0	0	0	1	0	0	0	0	0	0	0	0	0	0	0	1	0	0	1	0	0
OTHER E. ASIA	4	0	0	0	0	0	0	0	0	1	0	1	0	0	0	1	0	1	0	0	0	0
OTHER ASIA	2	0	1	0	0	0	0	0	0	0	0	0	0	0	1	0	0	0	0	0	0	0

CHAPTER 2— THE EXPANSION OF PARENT SYSTEMS
SECTION 4— THE FLOW OF MANUFACTURING BY INDUSTRY OF SUBSIDIARY
TABLE 44— SYSTEMS CLASSIFIED BY PERIOD SYSTEM FIRST OPERATED
IN SPECIFIED COUNTRIES AND REGIONS A SUBSIDIARY MANUFACTURING
MOTOR VEHICLES AND MOTOR VEHICLES EQUIPMENT (SIC 371)

COUNTRY OR REGION	PRE 1968	PRE 1901	1901 -13	1914 -19	1920 -24	1925 -29	1930 -34	1935 -39	1940 -45	1946 -50	1951 -53	1954 -55	1956 -57	1958 -59	1960 -61	1962	1963	1964	1965	1966	1967	UNK
OUTSIDE U.S.	34	1	2	1	0	4	2	3	0	3	3	0	0	7	3	1	2	2	1	1	1	0
OUT. U.S. + CANADA	34	1	1	0	1	2	2	1	1	3	3	1	2	7	0	2	2	0	0	3	1	0
OUT. WEST. HEMIS.	29	1	0	1	1	2	2	1	0	3	3	1	1	5	0	2	2	0	0	3	0	0
OUT. WHITE CWEALTH	30	0	0	1	1	0	2	0	1	2	1	2	2	10	3	2	2	1	0	2	1	0
OUT. DEVLPED WORLD	26	0	0	1	0	1	0	0	1	2	1	1	2	10	2	1	2	1	0	0	1	0
CANADA	17	1	1	1	0	3	1	2	0	1	2	0	0	1	0	0	2	0	3	0	0	0
LATIN AMERICA	26	0	0	1	0	1	1	0	1	1	2	0	2	1	0	1	2	0	3	0	1	0
C. AMER.+CARIB.	18	0	0	0	0	1	0	0	1	1	2	0	0	0	1	0	3	0	0	1	1	0
CUBA	10	0	0	0	0	1	0	0	1	0	0	0	0	7	0	0	3	0	0	1	0	0
MEXICO	18	0	0	0	0	1	0	0	0	1	0	0	0	0	1	0	0	0	1	0	1	0
OTHER	2	0	0	0	0	0	0	0	0	0	0	0	0	0	0	0	0	0	0	0	0	0
S. AMERICA	24	0	0	1	0	1	0	0	0	1	2	0	2	7	2	3	1	1	0	0	0	0
ARGENTINA	15	0	0	1	0	1	0	0	1	0	2	0	2	2	4	1	1	2	0	0	1	0
BRAZIL	16	0	0	0	0	1	0	0	0	0	0	0	0	6	1	1	1	1	0	0	0	0
PERU	2	0	0	0	0	0	0	0	1	0	0	0	2	0	0	0	0	0	0	1	0	0
COLOMBIA	5	0	0	0	0	0	0	0	0	0	2	0	0	0	2	0	2	0	1	0	0	0
VENEZUELA	6	0	0	0	0	0	0	0	0	0	0	0	0	1	0	0	3	0	0	0	0	0
OTHER	1	0	0	0	0	0	0	0	0	0	1	0	0	0	0	0	0	0	0	0	0	0
EUROPE	25	1	1	1	1	2	1	0	0	2	2	0	1	6	3	1	0	1	0	3	0	0
EFTA	14	0	1	0	0	3	0	0	0	2	0	0	0	0	0	0	2	2	0	3	0	1
U.K.	12	1	1	0	0	3	0	0	0	2	0	0	0	0	0	1	1	0	0	1	0	2
SCANDINAVIA	3	0	0	1	0	0	0	0	0	0	0	0	0	0	0	0	0	1	0	2	0	0
SWITZERLAND	1	0	0	0	0	0	0	0	0	0	0	0	0	0	0	0	0	0	0	0	0	0
OTHER EFTA	1	0	0	1	1	0	0	0	0	0	0	0	0	0	0	0	0	0	0	0	0	0
EUROP. COMMUNITY	20	0	0	1	1	0	2	0	0	1	0	0	0	4	5	0	1	1	1	1	1	0
FRANCE	14	1	0	1	0	2	2	0	0	1	1	0	0	1	2	1	0	0	1	1	1	0
GERMANY	10	0	0	0	0	0	0	0	0	0	0	0	0	0	2	1	0	1	1	0	1	0
ITALY	8	1	1	1	0	2	0	0	0	1	0	0	0	2	1	1	1	0	0	2	0	0
BELGIUM + LUX	3	0	0	0	0	0	0	0	0	0	0	0	0	0	0	0	0	0	1	0	1	0
NETHERLANDS	2	1	0	1	0	0	1	0	1	0	0	0	0	0	0	0	0	0	0	0	0	0
SPAIN	6	0	0	0	0	0	0	0	0	0	0	0	0	2	0	0	2	1	0	0	0	0
GREECE + TURKEY	2	0	0	0	0	0	0	0	0	0	0	0	0	0	1	1	0	0	0	0	0	0
OTHER EUROPE	3	0	0	0	0	0	0	0	0	0	1	0	1	0	0	0	0	0	0	0	0	1
EUROPE EX. U.K.	22	1	0	1	1	2	2	0	0	0	2	0	1	6	4	1	1	1	1	2	0	0
SOUTHERN DOMINIONS	17	0	0	0	0	2	1	1	0	0	2	0	4	1	2	1	1	2	1	1	1	0
S. AFRICA +RHOD.	11	0	0	0	0	1	1	0	0	0	0	0	0	1	0	2	0	1	1	0	0	0
AUSTRALIA + N.Z.	12	0	0	0	0	1	1	1	0	1	2	0	4	1	0	0	1	1	1	1	1	0
ASIA + OTHER AFRICA	13	0	0	0	0	2	0	0	0	1	0	0	0	1	2	1	2	1	0	1	0	0
JAPAN	4	0	0	0	0	0	0	0	0	0	0	0	0	0	0	0	1	0	0	0	0	0
OTHER ASIA+AFR.	9	0	0	0	0	2	0	0	0	1	0	0	0	1	2	0	1	0	0	1	0	0
BLACK AFRICA	2	0	0	0	0	0	0	0	0	0	0	0	0	1	0	0	0	0	0	0	0	0
ARAB WORLD	2	0	0	0	0	0	0	0	0	1	0	0	0	1	0	0	0	0	0	1	0	0
INDIA	7	0	0	0	0	2	0	0	0	0	0	0	0	0	2	0	0	1	0	0	1	0
PHILIPPINES	2	0	0	0	0	0	0	0	0	0	0	0	0	0	0	0	0	0	0	0	0	0
OTHER E. ASIA	0	0	0	0	0	0	0	0	0	0	0	0	0	0	0	0	0	0	0	0	0	0
OTHER ASIA	2	0	0	0	0	1	0	0	1	1	0	0	0	0	0	0	0	0	0	0	0	0

PERIOD

CHAPTER 2- THE EXPANSION OF PARENT SYSTEMS
SECTION 4- THE FLOW OF MANUFACTURING BY INDUSTRY OF SUBSIDIARY
TABLE 45- SYSTEMS CLASSIFIED BY PERIOD SYSTEM FIRST OPERATED
IN SPECIFIED COUNTRIES AND REGIONS A SUBSIDIARY MANUFACTURING
OTHER TRANSPORTATION EQUIPMENT (SIC 372-379)

PERIOD

COUNTRY OR REGION	PRE 1968	PRE 1901	1901 -13	1914 -19	1920 -24	1925 -29	1930 -34	1935 -39	1940 -45	1946 -50	1951 -53	1954 -55	1956 -57	1958 -59	1960 -61	1962	1963	1964	1965	1966	1967	UNK
OUTSIDE U.S.	15	1	0	1	0	0	0	0	0	2	1	1	0	1	3	1	0	1	1	1	0	1
OUT. U.S. + CANADA	11	1	0	1	0	0	0	0	0	0	1	0	0	2	3	1	0	0	1	0	0	1
OUT. WEST. HEMIS.	10	1	0	1	0	0	0	0	0	0	1	0	0	2	3	1	0	0	1	0	0	1
OUT. WHITE CWEALTH	8	1	0	0	0	0	0	0	0	0	1	0	0	2	3	1	0	0	0	0	0	0
OUT. DEVLPED WORLD	2	0	0	0	0	0	0	0	0	0	0	0	1	0	0	0	0	0	1	0	0	0
CANADA	6	0	0	0	0	0	0	0	2	0	0	0	0	0	0	1	0	1	0	1	0	1
LATIN AMERICA	2	0	0	0	0	0	0	0	0	0	0	0	0	0	0	1	0	1	0	0	0	1
C. AMER.+CARIB.	1	0	0	0	0	0	0	0	0	0	0	0	1	0	0	0	0	0	1	0	0	1
CUBA	0	0	0	0	0	0	0	0	0	0	0	0	0	0	0	0	0	0	0	0	0	0
MEXICO	1	0	0	0	0	0	0	0	0	0	0	0	1	0	0	0	0	0	1	0	0	1
OTHER	0	0	0	0	0	0	0	0	0	0	0	0	0	0	0	0	0	0	0	0	0	0
S. AMERICA	1	0	0	0	0	0	0	0	0	0	0	0	0	0	0	1	0	0	0	0	0	0
ARGENTINA	0	0	0	0	0	0	0	0	0	0	0	0	0	0	0	0	0	0	0	0	0	0
BRAZIL	1	0	0	0	0	0	0	0	0	0	0	0	0	0	0	1	0	0	0	0	0	0
PERU	0	0	0	0	0	0	0	0	0	0	0	0	0	0	0	0	0	0	0	0	0	0
COLOMBIA	0	0	0	0	0	0	0	0	0	0	0	0	0	0	0	0	0	0	0	0	0	0
VENEZUELA	0	0	0	0	0	0	0	0	0	0	0	0	0	0	0	0	0	0	0	0	0	0
OTHER	0	0	0	0	0	0	0	0	0	0	0	0	0	0	0	0	0	0	0	0	0	0
EUROPE	9	1	0	1	0	0	0	0	0	0	1	0	0	2	3	0	0	0	0	0	0	1
EFTA	4	0	0	1	0	0	0	0	0	0	1	0	0	0	1	0	0	0	0	0	0	1
U.K.	3	0	0	1	0	0	0	0	0	0	0	0	0	0	1	0	0	0	0	0	0	1
SCANDINAVIA	0	0	0	0	0	0	0	0	0	0	0	0	0	0	0	0	0	0	0	0	0	0
SWITZERLAND	0	0	0	0	0	0	0	0	0	0	0	0	0	0	0	0	0	0	0	0	0	0
OTHER EFTA	1	0	0	0	0	0	0	0	0	0	1	0	0	0	0	0	0	0	0	0	0	0
EUROP. COMMUNITY	6	1	0	0	0	0	0	0	0	0	0	0	0	2	3	0	0	0	0	0	0	0
FRANCE	3	1	0	0	0	0	0	0	0	0	0	0	0	1	1	0	0	0	0	0	0	0
GERMANY	3	1	0	0	0	0	0	0	0	0	0	0	0	0	2	0	0	0	0	0	0	0
ITALY	3	0	1	0	0	0	0	0	0	0	0	0	0	1	1	0	0	0	0	0	0	0
BELGIUM + LUX	0	0	0	0	0	0	0	0	0	0	0	0	0	0	0	0	0	0	0	0	0	0
NETHERLANDS	0	0	0	0	0	0	0	0	0	0	0	0	0	0	0	0	0	0	0	0	0	0
SPAIN	0	0	0	0	0	0	0	0	0	0	0	0	0	0	0	0	0	0	0	0	0	0
GREECE + TURKEY	0	0	0	0	0	0	0	0	0	0	0	0	0	0	0	0	0	0	0	0	0	0
OTHER EUROPE	0	0	0	0	0	0	0	0	0	0	0	0	0	0	0	0	0	0	0	0	0	0
EUROPE EX. U.K.	7	1	0	0	0	0	0	0	0	0	1	0	0	2	3	0	0	0	0	0	0	0
SOUTHERN DOMINIONS	2	0	0	0	0	0	0	0	0	0	0	0	1	0	0	1	0	0	0	0	0	0
S. AFRICA +RHOD.	1	0	0	0	0	0	0	0	0	0	0	0	0	1	0	0	0	0	0	0	0	0
AUSTRALIA + N.Z.	2	0	0	0	0	0	0	0	0	0	0	0	1	0	0	1	0	0	0	0	0	0
ASIA + OTHER AFRICA	0	0	0	0	0	0	0	0	0	0	0	0	0	0	0	0	0	0	0	0	0	0
JAPAN	0	0	0	0	0	0	0	0	0	0	0	0	0	0	0	0	0	0	0	0	0	0
OTHER ASIA+AFR.	0	0	0	0	0	0	0	0	0	0	0	0	0	0	0	0	0	0	0	0	0	0
BLACK AFRICA	0	0	0	0	0	0	0	0	0	0	0	0	0	0	0	0	0	0	0	0	0	0
ARAB WORLD	0	0	0	0	0	0	0	0	0	0	0	0	0	0	0	0	0	0	0	0	0	0
INDIA	0	0	0	0	0	0	0	0	0	0	0	0	0	0	0	0	0	0	0	0	0	0
PHILIPPINES	0	0	0	0	0	0	0	0	0	0	0	0	0	0	0	0	0	0	0	0	0	0
OTHER E. ASIA	0	0	0	0	0	0	0	0	0	0	0	0	0	0	0	0	0	0	0	0	0	0
OTHER ASIA	0	0	0	0	0	0	0	0	0	0	0	0	0	0	0	0	0	0	0	0	0	0

CHAPTER 2- THE EXPANSION OF PARENT SYSTEMS
SECTION 4- THE FLOW OF MANUFACTURING BY INDUSTRY OF SUBSIDIARY
TABLE 46- SYSTEMS CLASSIFIED BY PERIOD SYSTEM FIRST OPERATED
IN SPECIFIED COUNTRIES AND REGIONS A SUBSIDIARY MANUFACTURING
MEDICAL INSTRUMENTS AND SUPPLIES (SIC 384)

PERIOD

COUNTRY OR REGION	PRE 1968	PRE 1901	1901 -13	1914 -19	1920 -24	1925 -29	1930 -34	1935 -39	1940 -45	1946 -50	1951 -53	1954 -55	1956 -57	1958 -59	1960 -61	1962	1963	1964	1965	1966	1967	UNK
OUTSIDE U.S.	12	0	0	1	0	0	0	0	0	1	0	0	1	1	2	1	0	1	1	1	2	0
OUT. U.S. + CANADA	11	0	0	0	0	1	0	0	0	1	0	0	1	1	2	1	0	1	1	1	1	0
OUT. WEST. HEMIS.	10	0	0	0	0	1	1	0	0	1	0	0	0	0	3	1	0	1	1	1	1	0
OUT. WHITE CWEALTH	8	0	0	0	0	0	1	0	0	0	0	0	1	1	1	0	0	1	1	1	1	0
OUT. DEVLPED WORLD	5	0	0	0	0	0	1	0	0	0	0	0	1	1	0	0	1	0	0	1	1	0
CANADA	6	0	0	1	0	0	0	0	0	0	0	0	1	0	1	1	0	1	1	1	2	0
LATIN AMERICA	6	0	0	0	0	0	0	0	0	0	0	0	1	0	1	1	0	1	1	1	2	0
C. AMER.+CARIB.	5	0	0	0	0	0	1	0	0	0	0	0	1	0	1	0	0	1	0	0	1	0
CUBA	1	0	0	0	0	0	1	0	0	1	0	0	0	0	0	0	0	0	0	0	0	0
MEXICO	1	0	0	0	0	0	0	0	0	0	0	0	1	0	0	0	0	0	1	1	0	0
OTHER	1	0	0	0	0	0	1	0	0	0	0	0	0	0	0	0	0	0	0	0	0	0
S. AMERICA	5	0	0	0	0	0	0	0	0	0	0	0	0	0	0	0	0	0	0	0	1	0
ARGENTINA	2	0	0	0	0	0	0	0	0	0	0	0	1	0	0	0	0	0	0	1	1	0
BRAZIL	4	0	0	0	0	0	0	1	0	0	0	1	1	0	0	0	0	2	0	0	0	0
PERU	0	0	0	0	0	0	0	0	0	0	0	1	0	0	0	0	0	0	0	0	0	0
COLOMBIA	1	0	0	0	0	0	0	1	0	0	0	0	0	1	0	0	0	1	0	0	0	0
VENEZUELA	1	0	0	0	0	0	0	0	0	0	0	0	0	0	0	0	0	0	0	0	0	0
OTHER	0	0	0	0	0	0	0	0	0	0	0	0	0	0	0	0	0	0	0	0	0	0
EUROPE	10	0	0	0	0	1	0	0	0	1	0	0	0	0	2	2	0	1	1	1	1	0
EFTA	7	0	0	0	0	1	0	0	0	1	0	0	0	0	1	1	0	1	1	1	1	0
U.K.	7	0	0	0	0	1	0	0	0	1	0	0	1	0	1	1	0	0	0	0	1	0
SCANDINAVIA	1	0	0	0	0	0	0	0	0	0	0	0	0	0	0	0	0	0	0	0	0	0
SWITZERLAND	0	0	0	0	0	0	0	0	0	0	0	0	0	0	0	0	0	0	1	0	0	0
OTHER EFTA	1	0	0	0	0	0	0	0	0	0	0	0	1	0	0	0	1	1	0	0	0	0
EUROP. COMMUNITY	6	0	0	0	0	0	0	0	0	0	0	0	0	0	0	0	0	0	1	2	1	0
FRANCE	3	0	0	0	0	0	0	0	0	0	0	0	1	0	1	0	0	1	0	0	0	0
GERMANY	4	0	0	0	0	0	0	0	0	0	0	0	0	0	1	0	0	0	1	0	0	0
ITALY	3	0	0	0	0	0	0	0	0	0	0	0	0	0	1	1	0	2	0	0	0	0
BELGIUM + LUX	0	0	0	0	0	0	0	0	0	0	0	0	0	0	0	0	0	0	0	0	0	0
NETHERLANDS	2	0	0	0	0	0	0	0	0	0	0	0	0	0	0	0	1	0	0	0	0	0
SPAIN	0	0	0	0	0	0	0	0	0	0	0	0	0	0	0	0	0	0	0	0	0	0
GREECE + TURKEY	0	0	0	0	0	0	0	0	0	0	0	0	0	0	0	0	0	0	0	0	0	0
OTHER EUROPE	1	0	0	0	0	0	0	0	0	1	0	0	0	0	0	0	1	0	0	0	0	0
EUROPE EX. U.K.	6	0	0	0	0	0	0	0	0	1	0	0	0	1	0	1	1	1	1	1	1	0
SOUTHERN DOMINIONS	3	0	0	0	0	0	1	0	0	0	0	0	0	0	1	1	0	1	0	1	1	0
S. AFRICA +RHOD.	1	0	0	0	0	0	0	0	0	0	0	0	0	0	1	0	0	0	1	0	1	0
AUSTRALIA + N.Z.	2	0	0	0	0	0	1	0	0	0	0	0	0	0	0	0	0	1	0	0	0	0
ASIA + OTHER AFRICA	1	0	0	0	0	0	0	0	0	0	0	0	0	0	0	0	0	0	0	1	0	0
JAPAN	0	0	0	0	0	0	0	0	0	0	0	0	0	1	0	0	0	0	0	0	0	0
OTHER ASIA+AFR.	1	0	0	0	0	0	0	0	0	0	0	0	1	0	1	0	0	0	0	0	0	0
BLACK AFRICA	0	0	0	0	0	0	0	0	0	0	0	0	0	1	0	0	0	0	0	0	0	0
ARAB WORLD	0	0	0	0	0	0	0	0	0	0	0	0	0	0	0	0	0	0	0	0	0	0
INDIA	1	0	0	0	0	0	0	0	0	0	0	0	0	0	0	0	0	0	0	0	0	0
PHILIPPINES	0	0	0	0	0	0	0	0	0	0	0	0	0	0	0	0	0	0	0	0	0	0
OTHER E. ASIA	0	0	0	0	0	0	0	0	0	0	0	0	0	0	0	0	0	0	0	0	0	0
OTHER ASIA	1	0	0	0	0	0	0	0	0	0	0	0	0	0	0	0	0	0	0	0	1	0

CHAPTER 2- THE EXPANSION OF PARENT SYSTEMS
SECTION 4- THE FLOW OF MANUFACTURING BY INDUSTRY OF SUBSIDIARY
TABLE 47- SYSTEMS CLASSIFIED BY PERIOD SYSTEM FIRST OPERATED
IN SPECIFIED COUNTRIES AND REGIONS A SUBSIDIARY MANUFACTURING
OTHER INSTRUMENTS AND PRECISION GOODS (OTHER SIC 38)

PERIOD

COUNTRY OR REGION	PRE 1968	PRE 1901	1901-13	1914-19	1920-24	1925-29	1930-34	1935-39	1940-45	1946-50	1951-53	1954-55	1956-57	1958-59	1960-61	1962	1963	1964	1965	1966	1967	UNK
OUTSIDE U.S.	21	1	0	0	0	0	1	1	0	1	1	0	1	1	1	3	3	3	2	1	1	0
OUT. U.S. + CANADA	20	1	0	0	0	1	1	0	1	1	1	0	1	0	1	3	4	4	2	1	1	0
OUT. WEST. HEMIS.	19	0	0	0	0	1	1	0	0	1	1	0	1	0	1	2	3	4	1	1	1	0
OUT. WHITE CWEALTH	14	0	0	0	0	0	1	0	0	0	1	0	1	0	0	3	1	3	1	0	0	0
OUT. DEVLPED WORLD	6	0	0	0	0	0	0	0	0	0	1	0	0	0	0	2	1	1	1	0	0	0
CANADA	3	1	0	0	0	0	1	1	0	0	1	0	1	1	0	2	1	1	0	1	1	0
LATIN AMERICA	6	0	0	0	0	0	0	0	0	0	1	0	2	0	0	1	0	1	1	1	0	0
C. AMER.+CARIB.	4	0	0	0	0	0	0	0	0	0	0	0	1	1	0	0	0	0	0	0	0	0
CUBA	0	0	0	0	0	0	0	0	0	0	0	0	0	0	0	0	0	0	0	0	0	0
MEXICO	3	0	0	0	0	0	0	0	0	0	1	0	1	0	0	0	1	0	1	0	0	0
OTHER	1	0	0	0	0	0	0	0	0	0	0	0	1	1	0	1	1	0	1	0	0	0
S. AMERICA	4	0	0	0	0	0	0	0	0	0	0	1	2	0	0	0	0	0	0	0	0	0
ARGENTINA	3	0	0	0	0	0	0	0	0	0	1	1	1	1	0	1	1	1	0	1	0	0
BRAZIL	3	0	0	0	0	0	0	0	0	0	1	0	2	0	0	0	0	0	0	1	0	0
PERU	1	0	0	0	0	0	0	0	0	0	1	0	1	0	0	0	0	0	0	0	0	0
COLOMBIA	1	0	0	0	0	0	0	0	0	0	1	0	1	0	0	0	0	0	0	0	0	0
VENEZUELA	0	0	0	0	0	0	0	0	0	0	0	0	1	0	0	0	0	0	0	0	0	0
OTHER	1	0	0	0	0	0	0	0	0	0	0	0	1	0	0	0	0	0	0	0	0	0
EUROPE	17	1	0	0	1	0	1	0	0	0	2	0	1	0	1	2	4	3	2	1	1	0
EFTA	9	1	0	0	0	0	0	0	0	0	1	0	1	0	0	1	4	1	1	1	0	1
U.K.	9	1	0	0	0	0	0	0	0	0	1	0	1	0	0	1	4	1	1	1	0	0
SCANDINAVIA	0	0	0	0	0	0	0	0	0	0	0	0	0	0	0	0	3	0	0	0	0	0
SWITZERLAND	0	0	0	0	1	0	1	0	0	0	0	0	0	0	1	0	0	0	0	0	0	0
OTHER EFTA	1	0	0	0	0	0	0	0	0	0	2	0	0	1	0	0	1	0	0	0	0	0
EUROP. COMMUNITY	12	0	0	0	1	1	0	0	0	0	2	0	0	1	1	1	3	2	1	0	0	0
FRANCE	6	0	0	0	1	1	0	0	0	0	1	0	1	0	0	1	0	0	1	0	1	0
GERMANY	6	0	0	0	1	1	0	0	0	0	2	0	0	1	1	0	3	1	0	0	0	0
ITALY	2	0	0	0	0	1	0	0	0	0	1	0	1	0	0	1	0	1	1	0	0	0
BELGIUM + LUX	3	0	0	0	0	1	0	0	0	0	1	0	1	1	0	0	1	1	0	0	0	0
NETHERLANDS	1	0	0	0	0	0	0	0	0	0	0	0	1	0	1	0	0	0	0	0	1	0
SPAIN	1	0	0	0	0	0	0	0	0	0	0	0	0	0	0	0	0	0	0	0	0	0
GREECE + TURKEY	0	0	0	0	0	0	0	0	0	0	0	0	0	0	0	0	0	0	0	0	0	0
OTHER EUROPE	0	0	0	0	0	0	0	0	0	0	0	0	0	0	1	0	0	0	0	0	0	0
EUROPE EX. U.K.	13	0	0	0	1	1	0	0	0	0	2	0	0	1	1	2	3	3	1	0	0	0
SOUTHERN DOMINIONS	4	0	1	0	0	0	0	0	0	1	0	0	1	0	0	0	1	0	0	0	0	0
S. AFRICA +RHOD.	1	0	0	0	0	0	0	0	0	1	0	0	0	0	0	0	0	0	0	0	0	0
AUSTRALIA + N.Z.	3	0	1	0	0	0	0	0	0	0	0	0	1	0	0	0	1	0	0	0	0	0
ASIA + OTHER AFRICA	1	0	0	0	0	0	0	0	0	0	0	0	0	0	0	0	0	0	0	0	0	0
JAPAN	0	0	0	0	0	0	0	0	0	0	0	0	0	0	0	0	0	0	0	0	0	0
OTHER ASIA+AFR.	1	0	0	0	0	0	0	0	0	0	0	0	0	0	0	0	0	0	0	0	0	0
BLACK AFRICA	0	0	0	0	0	0	0	0	0	0	0	0	0	0	0	0	0	0	0	0	0	0
ARAB WORLD	0	0	0	0	0	0	0	0	0	0	0	0	0	0	0	0	0	0	0	0	0	0
INDIA	1	0	0	0	0	0	0	0	0	0	0	0	0	0	0	0	0	0	0	0	0	0
PHILIPPINES	0	0	0	0	0	0	0	0	0	0	0	0	0	0	0	0	0	0	0	0	0	0
OTHER E. ASIA	0	0	0	0	0	0	0	0	0	0	0	0	0	0	0	0	0	0	0	0	0	0
OTHER ASIA	0	0	0	0	0	0	0	0	0	0	0	0	0	0	0	0	0	0	0	0	0	0

CHAPTER 2- THE EXPANSION OF PARENT SYSTEMS
SECTION 4- THE FLOW OF MANUFACTURING BY INDUSTRY OF SUBSIDIARY
TABLE 48- SYSTEMS CLASSIFIED BY PERIOD SYSTEM FIRST OPERATED
IN SPECIFIED COUNTRIES AND REGIONS A SUBSIDIARY MANUFACTURING
OTHER PRODUCTS (SIC 19,21,31,AND 39) OR UNKNOWN PRODUCT

PERIOD

COUNTRY OR REGION	PRE 1968	PRE 1901	1901 -13	1914 -19	1920 -24	1925 -29	1930 -34	1935 -39	1940 -45	1946 -50	1951 -53	1954 -55	1956 -57	1958 -59	1960 -61	1962	1963	1964	1965	1966	1967	UNK
OUTSIDE U.S.	105	3	4	3	5	9	4	7	2	5	8	4	4	5	13	6	2	4	4	3	7	3
OUT. U.S. + CANADA	97	3	2	2	5	8	3	8	1	3	6	4	2	6	16	6	5	2	4	2	7	2
OUT. WEST. HEMIS.	87	3	2	2	5	7	2	7	1	3	6	3	3	6	13	7	5	1	4	1	7	2
OUT. WHITE CWEALTH	82	2	1	2	6	4	2	3	1	2	4	2	3	7	16	3	4	2	4	3	7	2
OUT. DEVLPED WORLD	50	0	0	3	2	2	1	3	2	1	1	1	3	4	9	1	4	2	0	4	3	3
CANADA	51	1	2	1	1	1	2	5	1	3	4	3	5	2	4	1	3	6	2	2	1	4
LATIN AMERICA	42	0	0	1	1	2	2	3	3	3	1	1	3	4	8	0	1	1	0	4	1	3
C. AMER.+CARIB.	23	0	0	0	0	0	0	2	0	2	1	0	1	3	2	1	0	0	0	4	0	0
CUBA	2	0	0	0	0	0	0	1	0	2	0	0	0	0	0	0	0	0	0	4	0	1
MEXICO	16	0	0	0	0	0	1	1	0	0	1	0	0	1	1	1	0	1	0	0	0	2
OTHER	6	0	0	0	1	0	0	1	0	0	0	0	1	0	0	1	0	0	0	0	0	2
S. AMERICA	32	0	0	1	0	0	1	2	4	2	0	0	2	0	8	1	1	1	0	0	0	2
ARGENTINA	8	0	0	0	1	0	0	0	3	0	0	0	0	1	0	1	0	0	0	1	0	0
BRAZIL	11	0	0	1	0	0	0	2	1	1	0	1	1	0	2	1	1	1	0	1	0	0
PERU	3	0	0	0	0	0	0	0	1	1	0	0	0	0	0	0	0	0	0	1	0	0
COLOMBIA	9	0	0	1	0	0	0	0	1	1	0	1	1	2	4	1	1	0	0	1	0	0
VENEZUELA	10	0	0	0	1	1	0	0	1	1	0	1	0	0	1	0	0	1	0	0	1	0
OTHER	7	0	0	1	0	1	0	1	0	0	0	1	1	1	1	1	0	0	0	0	0	0
EUROPE	80	3	2	0	4	8	3	6	0	1	4	3	1	5	13	5	8	0	4	2	6	2
EFTA	50	2	2	0	1	6	3	6	0	1	0	2	0	1	7	2	4	1	3	2	5	2
U.K.	36	1	1	0	0	6	4	6	0	1	0	2	0	0	4	1	1	1	1	1	2	0
SCANDINAVIA	9	1	1	0	1	0	0	0	0	0	0	0	0	0	1	2	1	0	1	1	0	1
SWITZERLAND	10	0	0	0	0	0	0	2	0	0	2	0	0	0	2	0	0	0	2	2	2	1
OTHER EFTA	4	0	0	0	0	0	1	0	0	0	0	0	0	1	2	1	0	1	0	0	0	1
EUROP. COMMUNITY	44	1	1	0	3	4	0	1	0	0	2	0	2	4	8	4	5	0	1	4	3	1
FRANCE	19	1	1	0	2	2	1	0	0	0	1	1	2	0	3	3	3	1	0	2	2	1
GERMANY	20	0	0	0	0	1	0	0	0	0	1	0	1	2	5	0	1	1	0	4	2	1
ITALY	12	0	0	0	0	1	1	0	0	0	0	1	1	1	3	0	3	1	0	0	0	1
BELGIUM + LUX	6	0	0	0	0	0	0	0	0	0	0	0	0	0	0	1	0	1	0	0	0	1
NETHERLANDS	10	0	0	0	0	1	1	0	0	0	1	0	2	1	2	2	2	2	2	0	1	1
SPAIN	11	0	0	0	0	0	0	0	0	0	1	0	0	1	1	1	0	0	1	0	1	0
GREECE + TURKEY	3	0	0	0	1	1	0	0	0	0	0	0	0	0	0	0	0	2	0	0	0	0
OTHER EUROPE	8	0	0	0	0	1	1	0	0	0	1	0	0	2	0	1	0	2	2	2	1	1
EUROPE EX. U.K.	63	2	1	1	4	2	0	1	0	0	4	1	2	5	10	5	8	2	4	2	6	1
SOUTHERN DOMINIONS	18	1	0	0	0	2	1	1	0	1	3	1	0	3	3	1	0	1	0	0	0	0
S. AFRICA +RHOD.	6	0	0	0	0	0	1	0	0	1	0	0	0	1	1	0	0	0	0	0	0	0
AUSTRALIA + N.Z.	14	1	0	2	2	2	1	1	0	0	3	1	0	2	3	1	2	0	1	3	3	2
ASIA + OTHER AFRICA	27	0	0	2	1	2	0	0	0	3	0	0	0	1	4	2	3	3	0	3	3	2
JAPAN	11	0	0	0	1	2	0	0	0	3	0	0	0	0	3	0	1	2	1	0	3	0
OTHER ASIA+AFR.	19	0	0	2	0	1	0	0	1	0	0	1	0	0	1	0	0	0	0	3	1	1
BLACK AFRICA	7	0	0	0	0	0	0	0	0	1	0	0	0	0	0	0	1	0	1	0	0	0
ARAB WORLD	3	0	0	0	0	0	0	1	0	0	0	0	0	0	0	0	0	0	1	0	0	0
INDIA	2	0	0	0	0	0	0	0	0	0	0	0	0	1	0	1	1	1	1	0	0	0
PHILIPPINES	3	0	0	0	0	0	0	0	0	0	0	0	0	0	0	0	0	0	1	1	1	0
OTHER E. ASIA	2	0	0	2	1	0	0	0	0	1	0	0	0	0	1	0	0	0	0	0	0	1
OTHER ASIA	12	0	0	0	0	1	0	0	0	1	0	0	0	0	0	0	1	1	0	1	1	1

CHAPTER 2- THE EXPANSION OF PARENT SYSTEMS
SECTION 5- THE FLOW OF MANUFACTURING BY CHARACTERISTIC OF SUBSIDIARY
TABLE A1- SYSTEMS CLASSIFIED BY PERIOD SYSTEM FIRST OPERATED
IN SPECIFIED COUNTRIES AND REGIONS A MANUFACTURING SUBSIDIARY
WHICH WAS NEWLY FORMED

COUNTRY OR REGION	PERIOD																					
	PRE 1968	PRE 1901	1901-13	1914-19	1920-24	1925-29	1930-34	1935-39	1940-45	1946-50	1951-53	1954-55	1956-57	1958-59	1960-61	1962	1963	1964	1965	1966	1967	UNK
OUTSIDE U.S.	182	10	10	11	11	24	13	15	11	13	11	8	14	13	10	3	0	2	0	1	0	1
OUT. U.S. + CANADA	182	10	10	6	11	19	16	13	10	14	13	8	16	15	14	2	2	2	2	0	0	1
OUT. WEST. HEMIS.	176	10	6	6	9	18	11	11	3	13	12	13	11	19	24	7	3	3	1	0	0	1
OUT. WHITE CWEALTH	179	8	3	8	8	14	11	10	12	17	14	7	15	18	19	3	1	2	6	1	2	1
OUT. DEVLPED WORLD	160	1	1	5	5	8	10	14	13	18	12	11	15	13	12	9	1	3	5	4	2	0
CANADA	104	1	5	8	5	11	5	10	9	13	10	5	3	3	2	5	2	1	3	1	2	0
LATIN AMERICA	155	1	5	3	4	7	10	16	13	11	12	9	15	14	11	7	5	2	7	5	2	0
C. AMER.+CARIB.	130	1	1	2	2	3	7	13	6	11	7	6	20	9	10	5	0	4	9	8	0	1
CUBA	18	0	0	1	1	0	0	0	0	1	1	1	1	0	1	0	3	0	0	4	0	1
MEXICO	100	0	1	1	0	3	5	3	5	14	6	5	12	11	10	2	0	2	4	4	2	2
OTHER	53	0	0	0	0	0	2	9	1	0	2	0	6	1	4	6	3	6	9	4	0	0
S. AMERICA	131	0	2	2	4	6	3	3	0	13	13	7	16	15	13	4	3	6	2	4	2	0
ARGENTINA	59	0	2	1	0	3	0	7	0	1	2	4	4	3	10	2	1	0	2	4	0	0
BRAZIL	74	0	0	3	1	3	0	0	0	4	10	0	10	13	5	5	6	1	6	1	0	3
PERU	25	0	0	1	1	4	0	1	0	1	0	3	4	0	3	1	2	0	3	2	0	1
COLOMBIA	46	0	0	0	0	0	0	0	1	5	3	3	2	3	9	0	0	1	3	2	3	0
VENEZUELA	58	0	0	0	1	2	1	1	5	5	4	1	7	8	12	2	2	5	2	2	0	0
OTHER	32	0	0	1	2	2	5	2	1	3	1	2	2	2	4	2	1	1	2	3	3	0
EUROPE	165	9	5	2	7	16	11	8	2	10	11	10	9	19	27	9	3	1	2	3	0	0
EFTA	113	3	4	1	4	11	7	12	1	7	6	4	6	7	14	8	1	2	3	4	1	1
U.K.	93	1	1	1	3	10	7	9	0	7	0	0	5	5	9	4	2	2	3	3	2	3
SCANDINAVIA	35	1	0	1	1	1	0	1	0	2	1	4	3	1	4	0	0	9	3	3	3	0
SWITZERLAND	13	0	0	0	0	0	0	2	0	0	0	0	0	1	5	2	1	1	0	0	0	0
OTHER EFTA	24	0	2	0	2	2	0	3	1	7	0	0	0	2	2	0	0	2	0	2	0	0
EUROP. COMMUNITY	147	8	1	4	5	10	5	1	0	7	12	10	6	23	31	9	2	1	3	3	1	1
FRANCE	82	5	1	1	3	4	3	1	0	4	5	2	3	11	18	7	5	2	1	2	0	0
GERMANY	80	6	1	2	7	7	4	0	0	2	3	5	6	17	20	4	7	4	4	2	2	1
ITALY	76	1	4	0	3	1	1	2	0	2	7	3	1	10	6	6	8	4	3	1	0	0
BELGIUM + LUX	39	0	0	1	1	1	0	2	0	1	1	1	1	6	6	2	3	1	1	1	1	0
NETHERLANDS	42	0	0	2	3	3	3	2	0	3	2	0	2	5	9	2	0	6	3	1	0	0
SPAIN	44	0	0	1	1	0	0	0	0	4	4	3	2	3	4	0	3	3	7	2	3	0
GREECE + TURKEY	25	0	1	0	0	1	0	1	1	0	1	1	2	2	4	2	0	1	1	4	3	0
OTHER EUROPE	16	1	2	0	0	0	1	0	1	1	3	0	1	1	3	3	1	0	1	2	0	1
EUROPE EX. U.K.	158	8	2	4	5	11	5	1	2	10	14	10	7	23	28	11	5	3	5	3	1	1
SOUTHERN DOMINIONS	108	1	2	3	2	7	6	11	4	5	7	4	4	18	13	3	3	6	2	2	1	1
S. AFRICA +RHOD.	59	1	0	1	3	1	4	5	4	6	2	3	2	6	15	2	4	2	3	1	1	3
AUSTRALIA + N.Z.	85	0	2	2	1	7	4	9	2	1	6	6	11	14	11	9	1	6	6	3	1	0
ASIA + OTHER AFRICA	109	0	0	0	1	4	3	1	1	7	5	8	11	10	20	8	9	5	5	4	5	2
JAPAN	65	0	0	0	0	2	1	0	0	0	4	2	5	3	14	7	7	6	2	9	2	1
OTHER ASIA+AFR.	89	0	0	2	0	1	0	1	0	7	3	7	7	8	9	9	6	1	2	4	5	1
BLACK AFRICA	19	0	0	0	0	0	0	0	0	0	0	0	2	0	6	1	1	2	2	4	3	1
ARAB WORLD	20	0	0	0	0	0	0	0	0	1	1	1	1	4	7	6	2	4	1	3	0	2
INDIA	36	0	0	0	3	1	1	1	1	2	3	0	4	4	1	6	1	1	2	1	1	0
PHILIPPINES	31	0	0	0	1	0	0	0	0	1	0	1	2	5	6	1	6	4	1	0	1	0
OTHER E. ASIA	19	0	0	1	0	1	1	1	0	1	3	1	2	0	2	3	1	2	2	3	3	1
OTHER ASIA	40	0	0	1	5	1	2	2	0	4	0	0	7	3	9	4	1	3	3	2	2	1

CHAPTER 2- THE EXPANSION OF PARENT SYSTEMS
SECTION 5- THE FLOW OF MANUFACTURING BY CHARACTERISTIC OF SUBSIDIARY
TABLE A2- SYSTEMS CLASSIFIED BY PERIOD SYSTEM FIRST OPERATED
IN SPECIFIED COUNTRIES AND REGIONS A MANUFACTURING SUBSIDIARY
WHICH WAS ACQUIRED

COUNTRY OR REGION	PRE 1968	PRE 1901	1901-13	1914-19	1920-24	1925-29	1930-34	1935-39	1940-45	1946-50	1951-53	1954-55	1956-57	1958-59	1960-61	1962	1963	1964	1965	1966	1967	UNK
OUTSIDE U.S.	182	6	8	3	10	25	10	9	9	16	13	21	17	12	12	4	4	2	2	0	1	0
OUT. U.S. + CANADA	178	6	4	2	8	21	8	4	4	14	14	23	19	16	14	5	6	2	2	1	1	0
OUT. WEST. HEMIS.	173	6	3	2	9	20	9	6	4	8	15	19	12	17	24	5	9	3	4	0	1	0
OUT. WHITE CWEALTH	171	3	3	1	9	16	10	7	7	11	11	21	21	19	11	5	7	3	1	3	3	0
OUT. DEVLPED WORLD	139	1	1	1	3	7	2	5	8	10	3	13	19	20	13	7	7	4	7	4	4	0
CANADA	133	1	0	1	1	10	8	7	7	9	8	7	11	5	14	7	9	7	7	1	3	1
LATIN AMERICA	132	1	1	1	3	2	2	5	9	8	4	13	17	18	15	8	5	3	6	4	5	0
C. AMER.+CARIB.	103	0	0	0	0	2	1	1	4	3	6	8	9	17	11	5	8	6	8	5	6	0
CUBA	7	0	0	0	0	1	1	1	1	1	0	1	0	1	0	0	0	0	0	0	0	0
MEXICO	87	0	1	0	0	1	0	1	4	1	5	7	9	13	11	4	7	5	6	4	5	0
OTHER	28	1	1	0	3	1	1	1	0	1	1	1	0	3	1	1	1	1	3	2	1	0
S. AMERICA	102	1	1	1	1	2	3	3	7	8	3	9	13	15	12	6	5	4	3	2	2	0
ARGENTINA	51	0	1	1	0	1	2	2	3	3	1	4	6	5	7	1	3	3	1	3	1	0
BRAZIL	47	0	1	0	3	2	1	0	3	1	3	3	4	8	5	3	2	1	3	2	2	0
PERU	13	0	1	0	0	1	0	1	0	1	1	0	0	0	0	1	0	2	1	2	1	0
COLOMBIA	25	1	0	0	0	1	0	0	2	4	0	3	1	1	2	1	3	0	2	2	1	0
VENEZUELA	27	0	0	0	1	1	0	0	0	1	1	3	3	4	4	2	3	3	0	2	2	0
OTHER	26	1	1	0	1	0	2	2	2	3	0	1	1	0	1	2	2	1	1	0	3	0
EUROPE	169	6	3	1	8	16	9	7	1	4	12	17	9	9	22	22	10	6	3	5	3	1	0
EFTA	127	4	2	1	1	11	3	6	1	4	7	6	9	8	16	15	11	9	4	5	4	5	0
U.K.	111	4	2	1	10	10	2	3	1	3	6	5	9	8	15	15	9	7	2	2	3	1	0
SCANDINAVIA	28	0	0	0	0	1	0	1	1	0	0	2	1	1	2	3	1	4	3	3	2	0	0
SWITZERLAND	12	2	0	0	0	1	2	1	0	0	0	0	0	0	1	1	3	2	2	1	2	1	0
OTHER EFTA	11	0	0	0	0	0	0	1	0	1	0	0	1	1	2	1	1	1	1	1	0	1	0
EUROP. COMMUNITY	143	2	2	0	6	8	10	3	1	1	9	10	6	6	16	32	9	7	7	4	3	4	0
FRANCE	86	1	2	0	5	4	5	2	0	1	5	5	2	2	6	21	6	7	2	2	5	5	0
GERMANY	83	1	2	0	1	7	6	0	0	0	1	8	4	4	8	12	7	6	6	6	3	1	0
ITALY	73	0	0	0	0	1	1	0	1	0	5	3	1	1	7	14	5	8	8	8	3	0	0
BELGIUM + LUX	37	0	0	0	0	1	1	1	0	2	4	0	1	1	5	6	5	3	3	5	2	3	0
NETHERLANDS	33	0	0	0	2	2	2	0	0	1	0	1	1	0	2	3	2	4	1	8	0	3	0
SPAIN	54	0	0	0	0	1	1	1	0	0	1	0	1	0	5	3	5	5	5	5	2	3	0
GREECE + TURKEY	6	0	0	0	0	0	0	0	0	2	0	0	0	0	0	1	2	1	1	0	2	1	0
OTHER EUROPE	16	0	0	0	0	0	1	1	1	0	1	1	0	0	2	3	2	2	2	2	1	0	0
EUROPE EX. U.K.	157	2	2	0	8	12	11	4	1	2	9	15	5	5	17	29	11	6	4	6	4	4	0
SOUTHERN DOMINIONS	87	0	0	1	0	3	5	1	1	0	3	7	7	9	9	16	3	4	7	7	3	1	0
S. AFRICA +RHOD.	31	0	0	0	0	5	1	0	0	1	1	2	2	4	4	4	5	3	3	1	3	1	0
AUSTRALIA + N.Z.	73	0	0	1	0	2	4	2	1	2	2	6	5	6	6	15	10	2	8	8	5	7	0
ASIA + OTHER AFRICA	85	1	1	0	0	0	0	1	0	4	8	8	6	2	4	11	10	5	5	5	8	6	1
JAPAN	39	1	0	0	0	3	0	1	0	3	8	0	2	4	0	7	5	8	3	2	2	2	0
OTHER ASIA+AFR.	59	0	0	0	3	3	2	1	0	3	0	0	4	4	0	6	8	3	7	7	5	5	0
BLACK AFRICA	10	0	0	0	0	0	0	0	0	1	0	0	0	0	0	2	1	3	0	1	0	1	0
ARAB WORLD	7	0	0	0	0	0	1	0	0	0	0	0	0	0	0	0	1	1	1	2	1	0	1
INDIA	17	0	0	0	0	1	0	0	0	0	0	1	1	1	3	3	4	4	1	1	3	0	0
PHILIPPINES	15	0	0	0	0	0	1	1	0	1	1	0	1	2	1	1	5	5	0	1	0	1	0
OTHER E. ASIA	7	0	0	0	0	2	0	0	0	0	0	0	1	0	0	0	1	1	0	0	1	0	0
OTHER ASIA	16	0	0	0	0	0	0	0	0	2	0	0	2	2	2	2	1	0	0	2	3	3	1

CHAPTER 2- THE EXPANSION OF PARENT SYSTEMS
SECTION 5- THE FLOW OF MANUFACTURING BY CHARACTERISTIC OF SUBSIDIARY
TABLE B1- SYSTEMS CLASSIFIED BY PERIOD SYSTEM FIRST OPERATED
IN SPECIFIED COUNTRIES AND REGIONS A MANUFACTURING SUBSIDIARY
WHICH WAS WHOLLY OWNED WHEN MANUFACTURE COMMENCED

COUNTRY OR REGION	PRE 1968	PRE 1901	1901-12	1914-19	1920-24	1925-29	1930-34	1935-39	1940-45	1946-50	1951-53	1954-55	1956-57	1958-59	1960-61	1962	1963	1964	1965	1966	1967	UNK
OUTSIDE U.S.	186	10	13	11	13	24	18	13	10	17	12	13	8	9	8	4	1	1	0	0	0	0
OUT. U.S. + CANADA	185	10	7	6	12	22	20	9	7	13	16	13	16	10	12	5	2	2	1	2	1	0
OUT. WEST. HEMIS.	182	10	7	5	11	21	15	10	2	11	15	12	8	24	18	3	4	2	3	1	2	1
OUT. WHITE CWEALTH	183	7	5	6	11	14	16	14	8	11	17	15	19	12	13	6	2	2	1	2	0	0
OUT. DEVLPED WORLD	163	0	3	5	4	10	9	15	8	17	12	15	18	14	10	7	4	1	3	4	4	0
CANADA	156	2	11	9	7	12	11	17	14	15	10	8	6	4	12	7	4	4	1	1	2	2
LATIN AMERICA	158	0	3	4	2	9	9	7	9	17	11	12	18	15	11	7	4	1	3	3	3	0
C. AMER.+CARIB.	129	0	0	2	1	4	7	5	3	15	9	13	18	13	12	7	4	0	4	0	1	1
CUBA	22	0	0	1	0	0	2	2	1	2	1	1	1	2	1	0	0	0	0	0	0	0
MEXICO	113	0	0	0	1	4	5	4	4	14	7	13	14	14	8	6	3	1	4	2	2	2
OTHER	38	0	3	1	0	0	1	9	1	0	1	1	1	0	2	2	1	4	0	3	2	0
S. AMERICA	123	0	2	3	0	8	5	7	9	11	10	9	5	7	7	3	2	2	5	3	2	0
ARGENTINA	63	0	0	3	3	3	0	5	5	3	2	3	5	7	7	3	1	2	2	1	2	0
BRAZIL	83	0	0	0	1	4	8	5	5	8	8	6	4	13	9	3	2	1	2	3	2	0
PERU	22	0	0	4	1	1	1	1	3	1	1	1	1	0	1	1	0	1	3	1	2	0
COLOMBIA	38	0	0	0	0	0	0	1	1	4	4	2	4	2	2	1	3	0	2	3	1	0
VENEZUELA	49	0	0	0	0	0	0	1	2	4	4	6	5	2	8	3	3	2	1	0	0	1
OTHER	33	0	1	1	0	1	0	1	3	5	2	2	1	1	3	3	1	3	4	1	3	1
EUROPE	178	9	6	2	9	20	13	11	1	8	15	10	10	25	17	6	5	4	3	3	0	1
EFTA	145	4	5	1	5	21	10	12	0	6	12	5	8	12	16	6	5	6	3	4	2	1
U.K.	131	4	4	4	4	18	12	11	0	5	10	5	8	12	13	4	5	6	3	3	5	2
SCANDINAVIA	41	0	2	1	1	3	2	0	0	4	1	2	3	2	3	0	1	1	0	3	1	0
SWITZERLAND	23	0	0	0	0	1	0	3	0	2	1	0	0	2	6	1	1	5	2	2	2	1
OTHER EFTA	22	0	1	0	2	1	1	3	0	0	1	0	0	3	5	8	11	5	0	1	2	0
EUROP. COMMUNITY	158	7	2	3	7	6	8	5	2	5	12	10	11	23	21	7	5	3	3	6	2	1
FRANCE	92	5	1	3	6	3	8	3	0	4	5	2	2	14	13	8	8	3	5	6	2	0
GERMANY	82	5	2	1	3	5	5	1	0	2	5	7	4	7	10	4	6	4	2	2	1	1
ITALY	80	1	1	2	2	2	1	1	0	2	6	7	9	9	11	8	6	5	4	4	3	2
BELGIUM + LUX	54	0	0	0	0	2	0	2	2	1	1	4	6	8	6	3	2	4	7	3	5	0
NETHERLANDS	49	0	0	0	0	1	2	2	0	1	2	4	2	8	6	2	0	4	9	2	5	0
SPAIN	33	0	0	0	0	0	2	2	2	2	1	2	2	2	2	1	1	3	5	3	3	0
GREECE + TURKEY	13	0	0	0	0	1	0	0	0	2	2	3	1	2	3	1	3	0	0	1	3	0
OTHER EUROPE	23	1	2	0	1	2	0	0	0	0	2	1	0	2	3	1	9	0	0	4	0	1
EUROPE EX. U.K.	167	7	3	3	8	8	9	7	2	10	14	12	9	24	18	8	8	5	3	2	3	1
SOUTHERN DOMINIONS	121	1	1	4	2	7	7	11	4	7	8	10	7	14	12	4	5	5	3	5	4	1
S. AFRICA +RHOD.	67	1	0	1	3	2	3	4	5	7	2	3	3	7	4	3	3	3	1	3	3	2
AUSTRALIA + N.Z.	101	0	1	3	2	6	5	10	2	4	7	9	8	13	11	4	6	5	3	6	3	0
ASIA + OTHER AFRICA	74	0	0	0	0	0	1	0	0	0	1	1	3	3	1	2	1	1	0	1	1	0
JAPAN	24	0	0	0	2	2	3	3	0	6	1	1	6	1	7	2	1	1	4	1	1	0
OTHER ASIA+AFR.	64	0	0	1	0	6	1	0	0	6	1	5	3	3	7	2	0	3	2	0	0	0
BLACK AFRICA	15	0	0	0	0	0	0	1	0	0	0	0	1	0	4	0	1	0	2	1	0	0
ARAB WORLD	14	0	0	0	0	0	0	0	1	2	0	1	1	2	3	2	0	1	2	0	0	0
INDIA	15	0	0	0	1	3	1	1	0	2	0	0	3	3	2	0	2	0	2	2	0	0
PHILIPPINES	31	0	0	0	1	2	0	2	0	2	2	5	0	1	2	2	0	0	2	0	0	1
OTHER E. ASIA	14	0	0	1	0	0	0	0	0	0	1	0	1	0	2	1	3	3	1	3	1	0
OTHER ASIA	28	0	0	0	1	3	3	3	0	3	0	0	1	3	4	3	2	1	0	2	0	2

CHAPTER 2- THE EXPANSION OF PARENT SYSTEMS
SECTION 5- THE FLOW OF MANUFACTURING BY CHARACTERISTIC OF SUBSIDIARY
TABLE B2- SYSTEMS CLASSIFIED BY PERIOD SYSTEM FIRST OPERATED
IN SPECIFIED COUNTRIES AND REGIONS A MANUFACTURING SUBSIDIARY
WHICH WAS A JOINT VENTURE WHEN MANUFACTURE COMMENCED

PERIOD

COUNTRY OR REGION	PRE 1968	PRE 1901	1901 -13	1914 -19	1920 -24	1925 -29	1930 -34	1935 -39	1940 -45	1946 -50	1951 -53	1954 -55	1956 -57	1958 -59	1960 -61	1962	1963	1964	1965	1966	1967	UNK
OUTSIDE U.S.	176	3	8	2	6	19	15	8	13	15	16	10	13	18	15	4	8	1	1	1	1	0
OUT. U.S. + CANADA	174	3	7	2	7	19	14	9	12	13	15	10	13	19	21	5	7	1	1	1	0	0
OUT. WEST. HEMIS.	172	3	6	2	5	16	14	7	10	8	13	10	12	23	30	5	11	2	3	1	1	0
OUT. WHITE CWEALTH	169	2	6	0	6	14	10	6	13	17	11	8	15	21	23	5	8	1	1	1	0	0
OUT. DEVLPED WORLD	147	1	1	0	3	0	4	7	17	16	9	8	13	20	20	7	6	5	6	3	1	1
CANADA	65	0	1	1	3	6	3	3	3	6	5	7	3	1	4	3	4	4	4	1	3	1
LATIN AMERICA	132	1	1	0	3	0	3	7	17	15	9	7	12	16	15	3	5	3	6	3	3	1
C. AMER.+CARIB.	98	1	0	0	0	0	3	1	6	7	5	3	9	14	12	6	7	5	5	6	3	0
CUBA	10	1	0	0	0	1	1	0	1	1	0	1	2	0	0	3	0	4	5	0	4	0
MEXICO	81	0	0	0	0	0	1	3	5	5	4	2	6	12	13	3	5	4	7	6	1	0
OTHER	44	0	1	0	3	1	1	2	1	1	2	0	3	2	0	3	6	1	4	3	2	1
S. AMERICA	111	0	1	0	3	0	3	3	17	11	7	8	13	12	12	5	5	1	4	3	3	1
ARGENTINA	41	0	0	0	1	0	1	2	5	5	1	5	5	2	4	7	6	0	0	4	2	0
BRAZIL	51	0	1	0	0	0	0	0	2	7	1	2	5	8	8	3	4	0	3	2	1	0
PERU	20	0	0	1	0	0	1	1	3	1	1	0	2	0	3	4	1	0	2	2	2	0
COLOMBIA	42	0	1	0	0	0	0	0	6	5	5	3	3	2	5	0	1	5	2	2	2	1
VENEZUELA	46	0	0	0	0	0	0	0	4	3	2	1	1	6	7	1	8	1	2	4	2	0
OTHER	27	0	0	0	3	0	0	1	1	1	0	1	3	0	6	2	4	1	4	1	4	0
EUROPE	161	3	5	2	5	15	9	6	0	5	9	7	11	22	33	6	10	7	3	2	1	0
EFTA	101	2	3	2	1	6	2	3	1	5	4	6	11	9	10	6	12	5	5	5	3	1
U.K.	78	1	1	2	1	2	3	2	1	5	4	1	9	8	8	3	8	3	1	2	0	0
SCANDINAVIA	25	1	0	0	0	2	1	0	1	1	0	1	1	2	2	3	4	4	1	3	0	1
SWITZERLAND	8	0	0	0	0	0	1	0	0	0	0	0	1	1	1	0	0	0	1	0	0	0
OTHER EFTA	13	0	1	0	0	2	1	1	0	0	0	0	1	1	1	0	0	0	1	1	1	1
EUROP. COMMUNITY	144	1	3	0	4	13	6	4	0	3	6	6	5	21	43	7	9	6	3	2	1	0
FRANCE	85	1	1	0	2	5	3	2	1	2	2	5	1	4	24	5	7	10	2	3	5	1
GERMANY	74	1	1	0	1	8	4	1	1	0	2	2	5	8	16	3	7	3	6	3	2	0
ITALY	68	1	1	0	1	1	3	0	0	0	5	2	3	11	14	7	9	5	4	3	1	1
BELGIUM + LUX	29	0	0	0	0	1	0	1	0	1	0	2	1	5	6	1	3	1	2	1	1	0
NETHERLANDS	29	0	0	1	1	1	3	1	0	3	5	0	2	1	7	4	2	1	0	0	5	1
SPAIN	95	0	0	0	0	0	0	0	0	1	0	0	2	2	6	6	11	6	8	10	5	0
GREECE + TURKEY	20	0	0	0	1	2	2	0	0	0	2	3	2	2	2	2	2	3	3	3	2	0
OTHER EUROPE	12	0	0	0	0	0	1	0	1	0	1	0	0	0	0	1	0	3	1	1	0	1
EUROPE EX. U.K.	158	2	4	0	4	15	7	4	0	4	0	5	6	24	39	8	11	9	3	4	1	0
SOUTHERN DOMINIONS	86	0	1	0	1	3	5	4	3	5	5	5	3	9	14	3	5	4	10	3	3	0
S. AFRICA +RHOD.	30	0	0	0	0	0	2	1	0	2	2	1	0	2	7	2	4	1	3	2	1	0
AUSTRALIA + N.Z.	67	0	1	1	1	3	3	3	4	3	5	5	3	7	10	1	2	3	9	1	1	0
ASIA + OTHER AFRICA	111	1	1	0	0	0	2	1	1	5	9	7	6	16	17	12	12	5	9	4	3	1
JAPAN	74	1	0	0	0	0	0	1	0	1	2	4	2	12	13	8	8	7	5	3	3	0
OTHER ASIA+AFR.	84	0	0	0	0	0	0	0	1	4	1	2	0	16	16	0	9	2	4	1	1	1
BLACK AFRICA	14	0	0	0	0	0	0	0	0	0	0	0	0	2	5	1	1	2	2	2	0	0
ARAB WORLD	15	0	0	0	0	0	0	0	1	0	1	0	0	6	0	8	2	2	1	1	1	0
INDIA	42	0	0	0	0	0	0	0	0	0	2	3	0	0	10	7	8	7	3	3	3	0
PHILIPPINES	21	0	0	0	0	0	0	0	0	0	0	0	0	6	2	1	2	0	1	2	1	1
OTHER E. ASIA	10	0	0	0	0	0	1	0	0	0	0	1	0	0	1	3	1	1	2	1	1	0
OTHER ASIA	36	0	0	0	0	0	0	0	0	0	0	0	3	4	8	3	3	2	2	3	3	0

CHAPTER 3
The Proliferation of Foreign Subsidiaries

CHAPTER 3— THE PROLIFERATION OF FOREIGN SUBSIDIARIES
SECTION 1— AN OVERVIEW OF FLOW AND STOCK, MANUFACTURING AND NON-MANUFACTURING
TABLE 1— SUBSIDIARIES CLASSIFIED BY COUNTRY OR REGION,
AND BY PERIOD ACTIVITY BEGAN

COUNTRY OR REGION	PRE 1968	PRE 1901	1901 -13	1914 -19	1920 -24	1925 -29	1930 -34	1935 -39	1940 -45	1946 -50	1951 -53	1954 -55	1956 -57	1958 -59	1960 -61	1962	1963	1964	1965	1966	1967	UNK
OUTSIDE U.S.	11152	107	163	154	228	451	391	623	305	536	580	498	632	829	1224	596	696	714	714	622	503	586
OUT. U.S. + CANADA	9455	98	132	98	182	335	294	508	238	427	476	409	520	739	1106	535	635	619	627	546	456	475
OUT. WEST. HEMIS.	6755	86	117	69	141	280	234	360	90	230	308	265	294	501	807	410	504	486	481	443	347	327
OUT. WHITE CWEALTH	7294	71	97	71	145	234	207	347	194	337	358	319	414	591	857	400	487	492	513	443	380	337
OUT. DEVLPED WORLD	3522	12	20	36	47	79	73	185	159	242	227	185	257	384	384	171	186	204	208	189	162	200
CANADA	1697	9	31	56	46	116	97	115	67	109	104	89	112	90	118	61	61	95	87	76	47	111
LATIN AMERICA	2700	12	15	29	41	55	60	148	148	197	168	144	226	238	299	125	131	133	146	128	109	148
C. AMER.+CARIB.	1251	2	6	12	18	20	28	82	48	86	79	61	121	118	127	54	54	66	80	67	53	69
CUBA	92	1	0	1	1	7	5	19	8	5	5	5	14	3	4	5	3	6	2	1	0	4
MEXICO	625	0	6	5	7	13	19	50	24	44	37	37	38	57	56	23	31	34	39	36	27	36
OTHER	534	1	0	6	10	0	4	13	16	37	37	19	69	58	67	26	20	26	39	30	26	29
S. AMERICA	1449	10	9	17	23	35	32	66	100	111	89	83	105	120	172	71	77	67	66	61	56	79
ARGENTINA	283	0	3	5	5	10	8	21	14	22	10	20	14	24	31	19	8	10	7	31	26	26
BRAZIL	346	0	0	3	3	10	6	16	22	23	30	19	28	40	36	12	15	14	17	18	56	11
PERU	127	4	5	7	1	2	1	4	4	4	5	6	13	9	17	6	11	8	5	8	10	10
COLOMBIA	196	1	0	1	2	2	2	5	9	23	22	8	7	3	23	11	14	11	13	4	17	8
VENEZUELA	292	0	0	2	5	5	1	7	20	20	13	20	35	15	45	6	21	15	15	8	2	9
OTHER	205	5	1	4	7	9	7	13	12	19	9	10	8	5	20	9	8	9	15	9	11	15
EUROPE	4755	83	100	49	123	230	187	272	61	139	173	168	213	356	558	280	343	329	344	300	244	203
EFTA	2004	36	48	26	37	110	77	151	36	64	89	64	102	152	242	115	121	122	116	116	77	103
U.K.	1189	23	24	15	25	77	56	112	26	44	58	39	63	70	120	72	66	62	55	61	41	80
SCANDINAVIA	384	7	18	7	6	18	16	19	5	14	18	13	18	22	33	20	21	33	34	29	21	12
SWITZERLAND	317	6	2	3	3	6	9	9	1	3	10	10	15	46	77	20	28	20	18	15	10	10
OTHER EFTA	114	0	4	1	3	9	11	11	4	3	3	2	6	14	12	3	6	7	10	11	5	1
EUROP. COMMUNITY	2300	43	45	19	62	97	88	91	19	68	64	89	99	186	280	142	186	176	185	144	135	82
FRANCE	670	12	12	4	6	26	38	29	8	18	12	26	33	57	93	44	45	54	33	36	52	22
GERMANY	632	18	20	5	7	41	24	22	8	9	16	32	33	45	76	31	48	45	54	52	36	21
ITALY	434	5	5	3	7	14	11	13	2	18	18	16	17	40	58	29	40	41	38	49	29	19
BELGIUM + LUX	288	4	3	6	14	11	9	13	3	9	11	8	11	17	30	17	26	16	33	22	17	11
NETHERLANDS	276	4	5	1	2	10	8	14	3	14	7	7	16	23	23	21	27	20	27	19	21	9
SPAIN	221	0	2	2	11	9	8	7	2	2	5	10	4	11	15	6	20	18	27	18	16	6
GREECE + TURKEY	80	0	0	2	0	1	2	1	0	4	9	3	3	5	14	6	7	7	7	28	20	3
OTHER EUROPE	150	4	5	4	13	13	12	22	4	4	6	2	5	2	20	10	10	18	9	7	3	9
EUROPE EX. U.K.	3566	60	76	34	98	153	131	160	35	95	115	129	150	286	438	208	277	267	289	239	203	123
SOUTHERN DOMINIONS	902	3	11	11	11	22	31	46	17	43	52	50	40	76	122	58	73	59	53	38	32	54
S. AFRICA +RHOD.	280	1	2	2	6	6	11	14	6	24	17	15	9	19	19	20	40	25	10	9	6	19
AUSTRALIA + N.Z.	622	2	9	9	5	16	20	32	11	19	35	35	31	57	103	38	33	34	43	29	26	35
ASIA + OTHER AFRICA	1098	0	6	9	7	28	16	42	12	48	83	47	41	69	127	72	88	98	84	80	71	70
JAPAN	276	0	1	2	1	4	3	5	1	3	24	6	10	11	42	26	33	27	22	19	18	18
OTHER ASIA+AFR.	822	0	5	7	6	24	13	37	11	45	59	41	31	58	85	46	55	71	62	61	53	52
BLACK AFRICA	197	0	0	3	1	5	0	0	4	12	23	15	17	6	26	10	9	29	16	12	13	20
ARAB WORLD	121	0	3	0	0	4	7	7	2	7	11	6	6	12	13	5	6	13	9	7	8	9
INDIA	95	0	0	0	2	3	1	8	2	7	5	3	2	13	7	1	6	3	9	4	8	4
PHILIPPINES	107	0	1	1	1	4	3	8	0	4	7	12	6	13	9	3	3	7	7	5	5	4
OTHER E. ASIA	96	0	0	1	4	5	3	3	2	2	4	0	6	9	11	14	10	10	9	8	13	4
OTHER ASIA	206	1	1	6	5	5	3	11	2	16	9	5	5	21	17	17	11	14	16	25	12	11

CHAPTER 3- THE PROLIFERATION OF FOREIGN SUBSIDIARIES
SECTION 1- AN OVERVIEW OF FLOW AND STOCK, MANUFACTURING AND NON-MANUFACTURING
TABLE 2- SUBSIDIARIES CLASSIFIED BY COUNTRY OR REGION,
AND BY YEAR(S) SUBSIDIARY WAS ACTIVE

YEAR

COUNTRY OR REGION	1901	1913	1919	1924	1929	1934	1939	1945	1950	1953	1955	1957	1958	1959	1960	1961	1962	1963	1964	1965	1966	1967
OUTSIDE U.S.	107	255	390	591	987	1302	1763	1965	2289	2785	3114	3669	3946	4315	4796	5304	5736	6287	6834	7379	7725	7927
OUT. U.S. + CANADA	98	219	304	468	772	1016	1410	1568	1816	2230	2514	2978	3224	3564	4004	4476	4876	5392	5871	6362	6659	6879
OUT. WEST. HEMIS.	86	192	255	382	633	828	1095	1116	1210	1487	1658	1921	2087	2317	2663	3024	3339	3764	4172	4549	4783	4955
OUT. WHITE CMWEALTH	71	161	223	352	560	734	999	1126	1327	1641	1873	2241	2433	2716	3054	3420	3726	4128	4502	4919	5172	5378
OUT. DEVLPED WORLD	12	32	61	104	181	281	396	537	729	922	1062	1291	1396	1532	1665	1816	1941	2080	2219	2386	2504	2597
CANADA	9	36	86	123	215	286	353	397	473	555	600	691	722	751	792	828	860	895	963	1017	1066	1048
LATIN AMERICA	12	27	49	86	139	188	315	452	606	743	856	1057	1137	1247	1341	1452	1537	1628	1699	1813	1876	1924
C. AMER.+CARIB.	2	8	19	36	55	81	146	188	256	321	370	478	513	571	585	629	662	701	723	786	820	855
CUBA	1	1	5	8	15	24	35	40	47	53	55	65	66	63	29	15	13	12	12	12	12	12
MEXICO	0	1	13	27	39	56	93	113	147	177	205	234	249	278	291	324	342	358	356	382	397	412
OTHER	1	6	1	1	1	1	18	35	62	91	110	179	198	230	265	290	307	331	355	392	411	431
S. AMERICA	10	19	30	50	84	107	169	264	350	422	486	579	624	676	756	823	875	927	976	1027	1056	1069
ARGENTINA	3	7	12	22	35	56	69	85	91	103	112	112	120	127	133	151	166	170	176	177	180	187
BRAZIL	0	0	6	8	22	23	58	61	82	109	126	151	168	184	202	213	222	230	239	252	262	267
PERU	4	9	5	8	9	9	13	22	24	28	33	46	46	48	57	63	69	78	86	91	92	98
COLUMBIA	1	1	2	4	5	7	12	31	48	68	71	78	86	93	105	115	121	133	142	154	155	150
VENEZUELA	0	0	0	5	5	3	9	30	47	56	74	108	120	140	165	178	187	199	208	213	222	213
OTHER	5	6	10	16	25	30	41	51	64	70	79	84	84	84	94	103	110	117	125	140	145	154
EUROPE	83	173	218	327	530	683	883	884	904	1055	1165	1355	1471	1633	1872	2112	2325	2605	2871	3140	3282	3401
EFTA	36	80	104	136	242	304	419	435	449	523	562	653	703	772	881	981	1062	1153	1256	1335	1378	1405
U.K.	23	44	57	80	155	196	284	297	307	352	373	431	460	480	530	577	630	672	724	756	779	800
SCANDINAVIA	7	25	32	38	56	72	85	87	94	112	121	137	140	154	163	184	198	217	247	273	280	287
SWITZERLAND	6	8	11	11	19	21	26	26	23	33	40	52	65	93	137	166	178	205	220	233	239	235
OTHER EFTA	0	3	4	7	12	15	24	25	25	26	28	33	38	45	51	54	56	59	65	73	80	83
EUROP. COMMUNITY	43	83	101	156	238	310	370	361	397	454	513	601	666	748	869	986	1099	1257	1391	1540	1605	1675
FRANCE	12	23	26	52	84	102	117	122	131	140	160	180	198	220	255	293	332	369	410	434	448	456
GERMANY	5	10	13	20	32	43	53	46	54	72	84	120	154	215	250	281	303	341	374	419	455	493
ITALY	22	35	40	46	72	101	117	109	111	125	145	153	150	150	162	185	209	243	274	305	311	310
BELGIUM + LUX	4	9	15	22	26	35	47	48	54	64	68	76	84	94	111	122	132	149	166	197	205	219
NETHERLANDS	0	6	7	16	24	29	36	36	47	53	56	72	80	69	91	105	123	155	167	185	186	197
SPAIN	0	2	4	13	20	27	36	36	35	41	50	53	54	60	66	75	85	103	120	147	174	185
GREECE + TURKEY	0	4	0	0	1	2	3	3	2	7	9	14	15	18	23	31	36	42	49	56	58	66
OTHER EUROPE	0	0	0	22	29	40	57	51	21	30	31	34	33	35	39	43	50	55	49	56	67	70
EUROPE EX. U.K.	60	129	161	247	375	487	599	587	597	703	792	924	1011	1153	1342	1535	1695	1933	2147	2384	2503	2601
SOUTHERN DOMINIONS	3	13	22	33	53	82	120	137	172	219	250	285	310	345	399	452	490	555	603	639	658	648
S. AFRICA +RHOD.	1	3	5	11	17	28	40	46	69	85	92	99	107	114	125	129	142	179	202	203	208	209
AUSTRALIA + N.Z.	2	10	17	22	36	54	80	91	103	134	158	186	203	231	274	323	348	376	401	436	450	439
ASIA + OTHER AFRICA	0	6	15	22	50	63	92	95	134	213	243	281	306	339	392	460	524	604	698	770	843	906
JAPAN	0	0	3	4	8	8	11	10	11	34	37	47	47	54	68	96	120	152	178	197	215	233
OTHER ASIA+AFR.	0	6	12	18	42	55	81	85	123	179	206	234	259	285	324	364	404	452	520	573	628	673
BLACK AFRICA	0	0	0	1	6	6	11	5	9	31	42	49	52	55	65	80	90	99	128	142	155	166
ARAB WORLD	0	3	3	7	10	10	16	17	29	39	43	48	50	52	56	54	63	70	74	77	83	88
INDIA	0	0	0	2	6	7	14	15	22	27	28	30	35	41	48	54	55	63	74	80	84	86
PHILIPPINES	0	1	1	2	5	5	7	15	17	23	34	39	45	52	54	59	60	74	76	81	84	87
OTHER E. ASIA	0	1	2	6	7	8	8	8	14	9	8	13	17	18	29	34	40	49	49	57	65	76
OTHER ASIA	0	1	6	2	8	19	25	25	32	50	51	55	60	67	72	83	96	97	119	136	157	170

CHAPTER 3— THE PROLIFERATION OF FOREIGN SUBSIDIARIES
SECTION 1— AN OVERVIEW OF FLOW AND STOCK, MANUFACTURING AND NON-MANUFACTURING
TABLE 3— MANUFACTURING SUBSIDIARIES CLASSIFIED BY COUNTRY OR REGION,
AND BY PERIOD MANUFACTURE BEGAN

PERIOD

COUNTRY OR REGION	PRE 1968	PRE 1901	1901-13	1914-19	1920-24	1925-29	1930-34	1935-39	1940-45	1946-50	1951-53	1954-55	1956-57	1958-59	1960-61	1962	1963	1964	1965	1966	1967	UNK
OUTSIDE U.S.	5209	47	78	74	93	220	155	215	149	261	235	227	301	420	683	320	345	339	365	327	231	124
OUT. U.S. + CANADA	4404	41	50	41	72	153	123	170	113	206	189	172	252	381	616	294	317	291	320	292	206	105
OUT. WEST. HEMIS.	3079	38	43	28	59	128	100	120	41	118	119	110	132	247	449	220	247	222	232	207	143	76
OUT. WHITE CWEALTH	3326	26	36	29	52	101	73	100	91	151	142	129	201	296	469	230	239	233	262	231	165	70
OUT. DEVLPED WORLD	1685	3	7	18	15	36	26	56	75	106	78	76	135	165	222	105	106	101	118	87		41
CANADA	805	6	28	33	21	67	32	45	36	55	46	55	49	39	67	26	28	48	45	35	25	19
LATIN AMERICA	1325	3	7	13	13	25	23	50	72	88	70	62	120	134	167	74	70	69	88	85	63	29
C. AMER.+CARIB.	563	1	3	3	2	8	14	25	22	33	26	19	52	60	62	27	27	39	45	46	32	17
CUBA	46				1	2	3	2	4	4	3	2	2	3	2	0	0	0	0	0	0	2
MEXICO	363	0	3	1	1	6	8	8	15	25	20	16	29	45	40	16	16	26	23	30	20	11
OTHER	154	0	0	2	0	0	3	5	5	4	3	1	11	12	21	11	11	13	22	16	12	4
S. AMERICA	762	2	4	10	11	17	9	25	50	55	44	43	68	74	105	47	43	30	43	39	31	12
ARGENTINA	160	0	2	4	2	6	8	11	12	8	4	10	12	14	20	14	8	6	5	7	5	2
BRAZIL	200	0	0	5	1	7	0	8	13	19	19	10	22	31	19	9	7	6	7	13	6	2
PERU	57	1	1	0	1	0	1	1	7	3	1	4	7	1	5	2	2	4	5	2	4	3
COLOMBIA	116	0	0	0	1	0	0	4	7	9	8	6	6	9	24	6	4	6	9	7	2	1
VENEZUELA	143	0	0	1	2	3	0	1	7	9	8	9	16	17	27	10	11	8	7	7	6	3
OTHER	86	1	1	1	4	3	0	3	4	7	3	4	5	2	10	6	9	4	10	3	8	3
EUROPE	2002	37	40	16	51	102	76	84	22	78	76	69	89	164	295	145	151	138	160	142	90	37
EFTA	753	14	21	9	18	49	34	54	7	41	27	21	37	48	90	48	46	44	47	50	25	21
U.K.	555	13	12	6	14	39	30	41	7	32	22	18	29	34	68	36	33	18	30	34	19	20
SCANDINAVIA	113	1	7	3	2	6	1	3	0	6	2	3	6	5	11	9	6	18	9	10	3	1
SWITZERLAND	36	0	0	0	0	1	0	4	0	2	1	0	1	3	8	0	5	6	2	2	1	0
OTHER EFTA	49	0	2	0	2	3	3	6	0	1	2	0	0	6	8	3	2	3	6	4	2	0
EUROP. COMMUNITY	1077	20	17	6	25	45	37	26	10	34	35	40	46	105	182	81	86	74	84	63	46	15
FRANCE	324	8	5	1	13	12	13	12	2	9	8	12	9	20	61	28	20	28	8	18	20	6
GERMANY	304	10	6	3	5	21	15	9	3	10	10	16	17	20	44	19	24	17	27	24	9	3
ITALY	223	2	5	0	3	4	2	3	1	3	12	13	13	25	44	21	23	18	19	8	9	3
BELGIUM + LUX	117	0	1	1	4	4	3	5	2	5	2	2	2	15	18	6	18	15	12	7	5	3
NETHERLANDS	109	0	0	1	3	4	4	5	2	7	2	3	5	14	15	13	6	6	18	11	1	0
SPAIN	137	0	0	0	1	6	1	0	3	0	6	3	3	6	12	6	13	11	21	5	12	0
GREECE + TURKEY	42	0	0	0	6	4	0	0	0	0	3	1	1	3	7	2	2	4	5	1	1	0
OTHER EUROPE	53	3	2	0	2	3	1	4	3	0	5	2	4	2	4	4	4	5	3	4	6	1
EUROPE Ex. U.K.	1507	24	28	10	37	63	46	43	15	46	54	51	60	130	227	109	118	120	130	108	71	17
SOUTHERN DOMINIONS	488	1	2	6	5	13	20	28	14	21	20	24	21	49	75	27	41	35	26	25	21	14
S. AFRICA +RHOD.	158	1	0	1	3	2	7	6	6	11	6	6	5	12	13	10	31	14	5	8	4	7
AUSTRALIA + N.Z.	330	0	2	5	2	11	13	22	8	10	14	18	16	37	62	17	10	21	21	17	17	7
ASIA + OTHER AFRICA	529	0	1	6	3	13	4	8	5	19	23	17	22	34	79	48	55	49	46	40	32	25
JAPAN	169	0	1	1	2	4	1	2	2	1	15	3	7	7	24	17	19	17	16	16	8	13
OTHER ASIA+AFR.	360	0	0	5	1	11	3	6	3	18	8	14	15	31	55	31	36	32	30	24	24	12
BLACK AFRICA	46	0	0	0	0	0	0	0	0	0	1	1	3	0	10	3	2	11	5	8	6	2
ARAB WORLD	39	0	0	0	0	0	0	0	2	4	2	1	7	5	4	1	2	2	4	2	4	1
INDIA	68	0	1	0	1	3	1	1	0	3	1	1	1	1	14	10	8	3	6	4	2	1
PHILIPPINES	59	0	0	1	1	2	0	2	1	4	2	9	4	7	12	2	3	0	2	3	1	2
OTHER E. ASIA	39	0	0	1	2	3	0	3	0	0	5	0	2	0	4	3	0	8	4	1	6	1
OTHER ASIA	109	0	0	4	3	3	2	3	2	9	0	2	4	8	19	12	8	8	7	9	6	5

CHAPTER 3- THE PROLIFERATION OF FOREIGN SUBSIDIARIES
SECTION 1- AN OVERVIEW OF FLOW AND STOCK, MANUFACTURING AND NON-MANUFACTURING
TABLE 4- MANUFACTURING SUBSIDIARIES CLASSIFIED BY COUNTRY OR REGION,
AND BY YEAR(S) SUBSIDIARY ENGAGED IN MANUFACTURE

YEAR

COUNTRY OR REGION	1901	1913	1919	1924	1929	1934	1939	1945	1950	1953	1955	1957	1958	1959	1960	1961	1962	1963	1964	1965	1966	1967
OUTSIDE U.S.	47	116	180	263	467	573	715	807	988	1179	1311	1568	1691	1891	2144	2437	2647	2912	3155	3403	3585	3646
OUT. U.S. + CANADA	41	86	119	187	330	424	546	615	763	923	1033	1257	1370	1561	1789	2060	2272	2519	2733	2963	3127	3203
OUT. WEST. HEMIS.	38	76	99	155	274	350	432	433	504	610	676	793	868	989	1177	1375	1537	1736	1910	2075	2193	2253
OUT. WHITE CWEALTH	26	59	82	131	226	279	347	400	513	633	722	902	989	1143	1306	1517	1693	1891	2060	2267	2398	2461
OUT. DEVLPED WORLD	3	10	25	39	74	93	136	205	297	358	413	534	587	672	740	836	915	997	1067	1155	1221	1260
CANADA	6	30	61	76	137	149	169	192	225	256	278	311	321	330	355	377	375	393	422	440	458	443
LATIN AMERICA	3	10	20	32	56	74	114	182	259	313	357	464	502	572	612	685	735	783	823	888	934	950
C. AMER.+CARIB.	1	4	8	8	16	30	48	68	98	116	128	174	192	225	219	245	263	284	305	344	372	383
CUBA	1	2	6	5	8	13	14	17	18	20	20	31	33	32	11	4	3	2	2	2	2	2
MEXICO	0	3	4	5	11	19	27	41	65	80	90	114	127	153	161	184	193	205	215	231	247	255
OTHER	0	0	2	0	0	8	8	14	16	17	18	29	32	40	47	57	67	77	88	111	123	126
S. AMERICA	2	6	14	24	40	44	66	114	161	197	229	290	310	347	393	440	472	499	518	544	562	567
ARGENTINA	0	0	5	7	12	17	27	32	43	45	49	58	61	65	69	84	96	101	103	103	105	108
BRAZIL	0	2	5	5	12	12	20	47	51	61	77	96	106	119	128	134	139	140	141	145	154	149
PERU	1	0	2	2	3	3	3	11	13	14	18	25	25	26	29	30	32	34	38	43	43	47
COLOMBIA	0	2	0	1	2	1	3	10	18	26	30	36	39	45	58	67	70	79	86	90	91	90
VENEZUELA	0	0	0	2	2	2	2	9	17	23	30	46	51	62	76	86	92	98	100	103	106	101
OTHER	1	2	3	7	10	9	10	13	19	21	25	29	28	30	33	39	43	47	50	60	63	72
EUROPE	37	72	84	132	226	282	335	324	363	430	472	549	596	677	792	920	1024	1138	1238	1350	1423	1438
EFTA	14	32	40	57	104	131	167	167	189	211	221	250	265	288	324	361	394	417	452	471	498	494
U.K.	13	23	28	41	78	101	128	129	146	164	173	197	210	221	250	276	300	313	326	334	354	356
SCANDINAVIA	1	8	11	13	19	22	24	23	27	29	31	34	34	39	41	48	54	58	73	77	81	76
SWITZERLAND	0	0	1	1	1	1	4	5	5	6	5	6	7	9	14	17	17	22	26	27	28	27
OTHER EFTA	0	1	0	3	6	7	11	13	11	12	12	13	14	19	19	20	23	24	27	33	35	35
EUROP. COMMUNITY	20	35	39	64	106	131	146	133	153	184	211	254	285	334	405	483	541	615	662	729	751	759
FRANCE	8	12	12	25	36	44	52	47	54	61	72	80	87	98	121	141	165	181	199	205	214	223
GERMANY	10	15	18	23	43	52	50	40	47	55	65	81	88	97	114	136	147	168	179	199	213	211
ITALY	1	7	7	10	13	15	18	17	16	28	34	47	54	69	87	106	123	143	155	169	167	161
BELGIUM + LUX	0	1	1	4	8	11	14	15	18	20	20	21	26	35	44	51	51	63	65	76	78	87
NETHERLANDS	0	1	1	2	6	9	12	14	18	20	20	25	30	35	39	49	55	60	64	80	79	77
SPAIN	0	0	0	0	8	12	12	12	13	19	24	26	26	31	36	43	52	65	75	94	114	119
GREECE + TURKEY	3	5	4	0	1	0	10	10	8	13	3	5	6	8	12	15	18	20	24	29	30	35
OTHER EUROPE	0	4	0	6	0	8	10	10	8	13	13	14	14	16	15	18	19	21	25	27	30	31
EUROPE EX. U.K.	24	49	56	91	148	181	207	195	217	266	299	352	386	456	542	644	724	825	912	1016	1069	1082
SOUTHERN DOMINIONS	1	3	8	13	25	43	69	83	99	116	128	147	160	184	221	252	264	298	326	340	351	361
S. AFRICA +RHOD.	1	1	2	5	7	14	20	26	35	40	41	46	52	55	60	66	73	102	115	115	121	123
AUSTRALIA + N.Z.	0	2	6	8	18	29	49	57	64	76	87	101	108	129	161	186	191	196	211	225	230	238
ASIA + OTHER AFRICA	0	1	0	10	23	25	28	26	42	64	76	97	112	128	164	203	249	300	346	385	419	454
JAPAN	0	1	7	3	5	6	6	3	4	6	20	27	27	28	36	52	69	86	102	118	132	144
OTHER ASIA+AFR.	0	0	2	5	18	19	22	23	38	45	56	70	85	100	128	151	180	214	244	267	287	310
BLACK AFRICA	0	0	5	7	0	0	0	0	0	0	1	2	5	5	10	15	18	19	30	34	36	43
ARAB WORLD	0	0	0	0	0	0	0	0	5	1	5	5	5	9	13	13	14	16	19	23	27	30
INDIA	0	0	0	0	3	4	5	5	7	9	6	9	15	12	28	34	44	52	55	60	61	62
PHILIPPINES	0	0	1	1	4	4	4	3	7	10	8	8	9	20	31	34	35	47	49	60	50	50
OTHER E. ASIA	0	1	2	2	4	3	3	3	7	11	1	23	26	30	31	34	10	14	14	19	25	30
OTHER ASIA	0	4	4	4	7	8	10	10	19	19	20	23	27	30	40	48	59	66	74	79	88	95

CHAPTER 3- THE PROLIFERATION OF FOREIGN SUBSIDIARIES
SECTION 1- AN OVERVIEW OF FLOW AND STOCK, MANUFACTURING AND NON-MANUFACTURING
TABLE 5- SALES SUBSIDIARIES CLASSIFIED BY COUNTRY OR REGION,
AND BY PERIOD SALES BEGAN

PERIOD

COUNTRY OR REGION	PRE 1968	PRE 1901	1901 -13	1914 -19	1920 -24	1925 -29	1930 -34	1935 -39	1940 -45	1946 -50	1951 -53	1954 -55	1956 -57	1958 -59	1960 -61	1962	1963	1964	1965	1966	1967	UNK
OUTSIDE U.S.	2217	36	59	34	73	93	94	110	52	119	96	94	101	179	225	115	148	153	128	103	138	67
OUT. U.S. + CANADA	1989	35	58	32	59	82	72	97	49	109	83	82	87	163	207	103	142	136	111	97	127	58
OUT. WEST. HEMIS.	1575	31	56	28	58	77	59	74	22	74	57	56	59	113	160	85	120	114	95	83	109	45
OUT. WHITE CWEALTH	1586	29	43	23	46	48	53	69	44	88	65	68	68	145	162	76	113	115	93	85	114	39
OUT. DEVLPED WORLD	610	4	5	4	4	12	19	33	33	48	42	38	34	66	59	25	34	39	29	31	31	20
CANADA	228	1	1	2	14	11	22	13	3	10	13	12	14	16	18	12	6	17	17	6	11	9
LATIN AMERICA	414	4	2	4	1	5	13	23	27	35	26	26	28	50	47	18	22	16	17	14	18	13
C. AMER.+CARIB.	186	0	0	2	1	2	3	11	9	17	12	8	18	27	23	13	9	10	7	5	0	4
CUBA	14	0	0	0	0	1	0	0	4	1	2	1	0	0	0	0	0	0	0	0	1	1
MEXICO	77	0	1	0	1	0	3	9	4	8	7	5	5	9	5	7	5	5	2	4	0	3
OTHER	95	0	0	0	0	0	2	4	7	8	4	5	6	9	17	5	4	5	0	1	1	0
S. AMERICA	228	4	1	2	0	3	10	12	18	18	14	18	10	23	24	5	13	9	9	14	4	9
ARGENTINA	36	0	2	2	3	1	3	2	2	6	6	3	6	2	2	2	1	3	0	3	2	1
BRAZIL	46	0	1	0	0	1	2	4	4	7	3	6	0	5	2	2	3	3	3	6	3	3
PERU	27	1	0	0	0	0	1	4	4	2	2	1	1	2	4	1	1	1	1	3	0	0
COLOMBIA	25	0	0	0	0	1	0	0	0	3	1	0	1	0	7	1	2	1	0	1	1	1
VENEZUELA	52	2	0	0	0	0	1	0	6	3	4	9	10	5	0	1	2	6	0	1	3	1
OTHER	42	2	0	0	0	0	0	1	2	5	4	3	0	0	2	6	3	1	3	3	1	2
EUROPE	1143	30	45	24	50	63	45	53	14	50	28	34	40	80	113	61	88	80	72	56	88	29
EFTA	515	17	20	11	12	38	22	29	9	20	17	15	20	38	61	26	37	28	26	23	31	15
U.K.	205	5	7	4	7	26	12	17	3	9	8	6	6	7	21	11	14	11	13	3	8	11
SCANDINAVIA	156	6	10	4	3	8	8	8	3	5	5	5	4	7	15	9	8	10	9	9	12	1
SWITZERLAND	110	6	6	2	1	3	1	2	1	3	3	2	3	22	19	6	13	4	3	6	5	2
OTHER EFTA	44	0	2	1	1	1	2	2	2	25	1	2	3	2	6	0	2	3	2	6	3	1
EUROP. COMMUNITY	522	12	22	10	26	18	18	10	0	25	7	16	17	39	49	33	41	47	42	27	48	13
FRANCE	125	2	6	2	8	4	7	4	0	7	0	4	3	11	12	10	6	6	5	10	12	4
GERMANY	148	4	11	1	3	6	3	0	1	2	1	7	2	11	18	4	10	15	12	16	16	6
ITALY	81	2	1	2	3	3	2	0	1	7	3	1	1	7	5	12	15	11	11	5	6	2
BELGIUM + LUX	92	1	2	2	5	1	5	5	0	6	3	3	5	5	18	6	5	9	6	5	7	0
NETHERLANDS	76	3	3	5	7	4	1	5	0	7	0	1	1	5	8	5	9	4	4	4	6	1
SPAIN	43	0	0	0	3	2	1	1	2	2	2	2	1	2	6	0	5	5	1	0	0	0
GREECE + TURKEY	17	1	0	0	0	0	0	0	0	1	1	0	2	0	3	2	0	0	1	2	3	1
OTHER EUROPE	46	1	2	2	9	5	3	8	1	3	6	3	1	0	0	2	2	0	2	1	0	1
EUROPE EX. U.K.	938	25	38	20	43	37	33	36	11	41	20	28	34	73	92	50	74	69	63	53	80	18
SOUTHERN DOMINIONS	182	1	8	4	5	6	7	10	2	11	9	8	11	11	24	14	10	7	8	5	7	7
S. AFRICA +RHOD.	62	0	1	1	2	4	2	5	1	7	3	3	2	5	5	7	5	1	1	1	3	3
AUSTRALIA + N.Z.	120	1	7	3	3	4	5	5	1	4	6	5	9	6	19	9	5	6	16	4	4	4
ASIA + OTHER AFRICA	250	0	3	0	3	8	7	11	6	13	20	14	8	22	23	10	18	24	16	19	16	9
JAPAN	54	0	0	0	0	1	1	0	0	4	4	2	2	6	11	3	6	3	3	2	3	2
OTHER ASIA+AFR.	196	0	3	0	3	7	6	10	6	13	16	12	6	16	12	7	12	17	13	17	13	7
BLACK AFRICA	45	0	0	0	0	0	1	0	3	1	6	3	3	1	3	2	5	6	5	3	1	4
ARAB WORLD	36	3	0	0	0	2	0	4	2	4	3	1	1	3	1	2	0	1	0	1	1	2
INDIA	13	0	0	0	0	0	0	1	0	1	0	1	0	1	0	0	2	0	4	0	3	0
PHILIPPINES	25	0	0	0	0	2	3	4	0	2	1	0	1	0	2	1	2	2	1	0	1	0
OTHER E. ASIA	30	0	0	0	1	3	1	0	0	1	1	3	0	2	5	3	3	5	2	2	5	0
OTHER ASIA	47	0	0	0	1	4	0	1	2	2	6	1	0	8	1	1	3	3	4	8	3	1

CHAPTER 3- THE PROLIFERATION OF FOREIGN SUBSIDIARIES
SECTION 1- AN OVERVIEW OF FLOW AND STOCK, MANUFACTURING AND NON-MANUFACTURING
TABLE 6- SALES SUBSIDIARIES CLASSIFIED BY COUNTRY OR REGION,
AND BY YEAR(S) SUBSIDIARY ENGAGED IN SALES

YEAR

COUNTRY OR REGION	1901	1913	1919	1924	1929	1934	1939	1945	1950	1953	1955	1957	1958	1959	1960	1961	1962	1963	1964	1965	1966	1967
OUTSIDE U.S.	36	89	118	176	248	317	369	377	416	485	530	603	683	743	836	920	989	1090	1199	1287	1319	1358
OUT. U.S. + CANADA	35	88	115	160	222	277	324	331	368	429	466	527	598	653	740	818	876	980	1077	1153	1186	1230
OUT. WEST. HEMIS.	31	82	106	150	207	250	276	258	282	330	347	388	435	474	542	611	668	761	849	915	949	997
OUT. WHITE CWEALTH	29	69	91	123	157	203	237	245	275	320	356	405	470	520	592	650	691	776	859	926	960	1005
OUT. DEVLPED WORLD	4	9	12	16	27	44	71	94	117	144	165	190	219	240	262	278	283	302	327	348	361	367
CANADA	1	1	3	16	26	40	45	46	48	56	64	76	85	90	96	102	113	110	122	134	133	128
LATIN AMERICA	4	6	9	10	15	27	48	73	86	99	119	139	163	179	198	207	208	219	228	238	237	233
C. AMER.+CARIB.	0	1	2	3	6	6	28	36	36	46	52	64	78	86	97	101	105	107	110	109	108	104
CUBA	0	0	0	0	0	0	7	8	8	10	8	5	5	5	5	2	1	1	1	1	1	1
MEXICO	0	0	0	0	0	0	18	8	10	14	17	27	30	35	35	37	42	43	42	42	36	31
OTHER	0	1	2	3	6	6	10	28	26	32	35	48	55	57	62	62	62	63	67	69	72	72
S. AMERICA	4	5	7	7	9	18	20	37	50	53	67	75	85	93	101	106	103	112	118	126	128	129
ARGENTINA	0	1	2	2	3	3	6	6	8	12	18	18	18	19	16	18	17	18	19	19	20	20
BRAZIL	0	2	0	1	2	2	5	5	6	8	12	11	13	15	16	18	18	20	19	22	22	25
PERU	0	0	0	1	1	2	2	2	4	8	4	11	5	5	9	10	12	13	14	16	18	25
COLOMBIA	1	1	1	1	2	2	2	8	9	8	8	5	5	9	10	12	13	13	16	17	18	18
VENEZUELA	0	0	0	0	2	2	8	9	3	3	7	16	20	24	26	22	21	24	26	26	28	14
OTHER	2	2	2	2	6	9	13	16	15	15	18	17	18	19	22	25	23	23	25	26	25	28
EUROPE	30	71	92	128	173	204	223	208	215	236	250	275	312	340	397	441	482	554	613	663	681	722
EFTA	17	35	44	53	84	97	115	114	113	126	129	142	154	175	206	229	242	273	291	306	316	336
U.K.	5	11	13	20	41	44	54	53	53	59	59	60	62	65	75	84	90	100	107	110	108	112
SCANDINAVIA	6	15	19	22	29	37	40	39	39	44	46	52	54	58	64	72	78	86	94	103	107	116
SWITZERLAND	6	7	9	7	10	10	12	12	11	14	14	17	23	38	48	54	56	67	67	69	73	78
OTHER EFTA	0	2	3	4	5	6	8	8	11	9	10	13	15	14	19	19	18	20	23	24	28	30
EUROP. COMMUNITY	12	33	43	58	68	82	76	65	82	86	94	103	127	135	161	179	206	238	274	306	309	327
FRANCE	2	7	9	14	17	22	20	19	22	21	22	24	33	35	41	45	53	57	67	75	74	81
GERMANY	2	15	16	13	16	18	16	14	22	16	22	21	28	29	41	45	54	61	71	80	84	91
ITALY	4	2	4	7	11	11	9	4	10	12	10	9	11	16	20	20	22	32	34	44	43	44
BELGIUM + LUX	1	3	8	11	16	16	21	20	24	27	29	33	35	35	40	43	48	51	58	63	61	61
NETHERLANDS	3	6	6	13	15	15	10	8	11	11	11	16	20	20	21	29	37	44	44	47	50	50
SPAIN	0	0	0	1	2	3	6	6	6	8	6	6	7	8	8	13	13	17	22	22	26	26
GREECE + TURKEY	1	0	0	0	1	1	2	2	2	3	3	4	4	4	4	7	7	10	10	11	11	14
OTHER EUROPE	0	2	2	2	13	16	20	16	8	10	11	13	13	13	13	13	14	16	16	18	19	19
EUROPE EX. U.K.	25	60	79	108	132	160	169	155	162	177	191	215	250	275	322	357	392	454	506	553	573	610
SOUTHERN DOMINIONS	1	8	11	16	21	27	29	29	36	45	46	55	59	61	66	77	87	95	102	106	106	101
S. AFRICA +RHOD.	1	2	2	4	6	8	11	11	17	20	20	22	23	27	31	31	34	37	40	40	36	34
AUSTRALIA + N.Z.	0	7	9	12	15	19	18	18	19	25	26	33	36	34	35	46	53	58	62	66	70	67
ASIA + OTHER AFRICA	0	7	9	6	13	19	24	21	31	49	51	58	64	73	79	93	99	112	134	146	162	174
JAPAN	0	3	3	0	1	2	0	0	4	4	5	7	8	12	15	22	24	29	35	36	38	40
OTHER ASIA+AFR.	0	3	6	6	9	17	23	21	31	45	46	51	56	61	64	71	75	83	99	110	124	134
BLACK AFRICA	0	3	3	3	5	5	7	7	10	8	9	10	12	13	14	16	18	22	28	33	36	37
ARAB WORLD	0	0	3	2	7	7	7	7	11	11	14	14	14	12	12	12	12	14	14	15	16	18
INDIA	0	0	0	0	2	5	7	6	7	7	7	8	8	8	8	8	8	7	7	6	8	8
PHILIPPINES	0	0	0	0	2	7	6	6	5	8	6	6	6	7	6	8	8	10	12	13	14	15
OTHER E. ASIA	0	0	0	1	2	4	7	4	5	7	6	6	5	6	8	11	12	15	18	20	22	26
OTHER ASIA	0	0	0	4	4	0	0	0	5	11	9	9	11	15	16	16	18	17	20	23	28	30

CHAPTER 3- THE PROLIFERATION OF FOREIGN SUBSIDIARIES
SECTION 1- AN OVERVIEW OF FLOW AND STOCK, MANUFACTURING AND NON-MANUFACTURING
TABLE 7- EXTRACTION SUBSIDIARIES CLASSIFIED BY COUNTRY OR REGION,
AND BY PERIOD EXTRACTION BEGAN

PERIOD

COUNTRY OR REGION	PRE 1968	PRE 1901	1901 -13	1914 -19	1920 -24	1925 -29	1930 -34	1935 -39	1940 -45	1946 -50	1951 -53	1954 -55	1956 -57	1958 -59	1960 -61	1962	1963	1964	1965	1966	1967	UNK
OUTSIDE U.S.	320	2	5	13	20	15	13	42	10	19	25	21	22	16	22	8	14	12	17	12	6	6
OUT. U.S. + CANADA	248	1	5	10	19	10	11	40	6	13	19	15	14	9	18	7	7	10	14	10	6	4
OUT. WEST. HEMIS.	118	1	3	2	2	8	6	15	1	6	16	10	2	7	10	2	6	5	11	4	5	4
OUT. WHITE CWEALTH	202	1	5	9	18	7	7	33	6	10	15	13	13	7	14	5	4	7	11	8	5	4
OUT. DEVLPED WORLD	187	0	4	9	18	6	7	32	6	8	15	10	13	4	14	5	3	5	11	8	5	4
CANADA	72	1	0	3	1	5	2	2	4	6	6	6	8	7	4	1	7	2	3	3	0	2
LATIN AMERICA	130	0	2	8	17	2	5	25	5	7	3	5	12	2	8	5	1	4	9	6	1	3
C. AMER.+CARIB.	81	0	2	5	10	1	4	20	3	3	1	4	5	0	3	2	1	3	5	3	1	1
CUBA	1	0	0	0	0	0	0	0	0	0	0	0	0	0	0	0	0	0	0	0	0	1
MEXICO	63	0	2	5	9	1	4	18	2	5	1	4	5	0	3	2	0	2	5	3	1	0
OTHER	17	0	0	0	0	0	0	2	0	0	0	0	0	0	0	0	1	1	0	0	0	1
S. AMERICA	49	0	0	3	7	2	1	5	2	5	2	1	7	2	5	3	0	1	4	3	0	2
ARGENTINA	7	0	0	0	2	1	0	0	0	1	0	1	1	1	0	1	1	0	0	0	0	0
BRAZIL	3	0	0	0	1	0	0	0	0	0	0	0	1	0	0	0	0	0	0	0	0	0
PERU	6	0	0	0	0	0	0	0	0	1	1	0	0	0	1	0	0	0	0	1	0	0
COLOMBIA	4	0	0	0	1	0	0	2	0	0	0	0	1	0	1	1	0	0	0	0	0	0
VENEZUELA	13	1	0	0	2	0	0	1	2	0	1	0	0	0	2	0	1	1	0	1	0	0
OTHER	16	0	0	3	1	1	1	2	0	0	1	1	1	0	1	0	0	3	3	1	0	1
EUROPE	27	1	1	1	0	2	2	4	0	3	0	3	1	3	1	1	1	3	3	3	0	0
EFTA	12	0	0	1	0	1	2	3	0	1	0	1	1	0	1	1	0	1	1	0	0	0
U.K.	12	0	0	1	0	1	2	3	0	1	0	1	1	0	1	1	0	1	1	0	0	0
SCANDINAVIA	0	0	0	0	0	0	0	0	0	0	0	0	0	0	0	0	0	0	0	0	0	0
SWITZERLAND	0	0	0	0	0	0	0	0	0	0	0	0	0	0	0	0	0	0	0	0	0	0
OTHER EFTA	0	0	0	0	0	0	0	0	0	0	0	0	0	0	0	0	0	0	0	0	0	0
EUROP. COMMUNITY	10	1	0	1	0	0	0	1	2	2	0	2	0	1	0	0	1	2	0	0	0	2
FRANCE	4	0	0	1	0	0	0	0	0	0	0	1	0	0	0	1	0	0	0	1	0	1
GERMANY	1	0	0	0	0	0	0	0	0	0	0	0	0	0	0	0	0	0	0	0	0	0
ITALY	1	0	0	0	0	0	0	0	0	0	0	0	0	0	0	0	0	0	0	0	0	0
BELGIUM + LUX	3	1	0	0	0	0	0	1	1	0	1	1	1	1	1	0	0	0	0	0	0	0
NETHERLANDS	1	1	0	0	0	0	0	0	0	0	0	0	0	0	0	0	0	0	0	0	0	1
SPAIN	2	0	0	0	0	0	0	0	0	0	0	0	0	1	1	0	0	1	0	1	1	0
GREECE + TURKEY	2	0	0	0	0	0	0	0	0	0	0	0	0	0	0	0	0	0	1	0	0	0
OTHER EUROPE	2	1	1	0	0	0	0	1	0	0	1	0	0	1	2	0	1	0	1	0	0	0
EUROPE EX. U.K.	15	1	0	0	0	1	0	1	0	2	1	0	0	3	0	1	1	2	1	0	0	1
SOUTHERN DOMINIONS	34	0	0	1	1	2	2	4	0	2	4	2	0	2	3	1	3	2	3	2	1	0
S. AFRICA +RHOD.	13	0	0	1	1	1	1	4	0	1	3	1	0	2	0	0	1	2	1	0	0	3
AUSTRALIA + N.Z.	21	0	2	0	0	1	1	3	1	1	1	1	2	2	3	1	0	0	2	2	1	1
ASIA + OTHER AFRICA	57	2	0	1	1	4	2	7	1	1	12	5	0	2	4	0	3	1	2	2	4	0
JAPAN	0	0	0	0	0	0	0	0	0	0	0	0	0	0	0	0	0	0	0	0	0	0
OTHER ASIA+AFR.	57	2	0	1	1	0	0	7	1	1	12	5	2	2	6	2	2	1	2	0	3	0
BLACK AFRICA	26	0	0	0	0	2	2	0	0	0	2	5	1	1	0	1	1	1	0	2	1	1
ARAB WORLD	15	0	0	1	0	0	0	4	1	0	7	4	1	1	5	1	0	0	0	0	0	0
INDIA	0	0	0	0	0	0	0	0	0	0	0	0	0	0	0	0	0	0	0	0	0	0
PHILIPPINES	5	1	1	1	0	1	1	0	1	1	0	0	1	1	1	0	1	1	1	0	0	0
OTHER E. ASIA	0	0	0	0	0	0	0	0	0	0	0	0	0	0	0	0	0	0	0	0	0	0
OTHER ASIA	11	0	1	1	0	1	0	3	0	1	0	1	0	0	0	0	0	1	1	0	0	0

CHAPTER 3- THE PROLIFERATION OF FOREIGN SUBSIDIARIES
SECTION I- AN OVERVIEW OF FLOW AND STOCK, MANUFACTURING AND NON-MANUFACTURING
TABLE 8- EXTRACTION SUBSIDIARIES CLASSIFIED BY COUNTRY OR REGION,
AND BY YEAR(S) SUBSIDIARY ENGAGED IN EXTRACTION

YEAR

COUNTRY OR REGION	1901	1913	1919	1924	1929	1934	1939	1945	1950	1953	1955	1957	1958	1959	1960	1961	1962	1963	1964	1965	1966	1967
OUTSIDE U.S.	2	7	19	34	41	51	74	74	81	103	121	135	138	142	147	158	163	168	162	169	177	172
OUT. U.S. + CANADA	1	6	16	30	38	46	67	64	66	83	96	105	107	111	116	123	129	131	125	132	139	136
OUT. WEST. HEMIS.	1	4	6	8	15	19	31	29	28	44	53	53	54	58	59	64	65	69	74	78	81	80
OUT. WHITE CWEALTH	1	6	15	28	33	38	53	50	51	64	75	85	87	90	94	100	105	105	97	101	107	105
OUT. DEVLPED WORLD	0	4	13	26	30	35	50	47	48	61	69	79	80	82	86	92	97	96	86	91	97	95
CANADA	1	1	3	4	3	5	7	10	15	20	25	30	31	31	31	35	34	37	37	37	38	36
LATIN AMERICA	0	2	10	22	23	27	36	35	38	39	43	52	53	53	57	59	64	62	51	54	58	56
C. AMER.+CARIB.	0	2	7	15	16	19	24	24	27	28	31	34	35	35	36	36	38	38	26	25	27	28
CUBA	0	0	0	1	1	1	2	2	2	2	1	1	1	0	0	0	0	0	0	0	0	0
MEXICO	0	2	7	14	15	18	21	21	24	25	28	27	27	28	28	28	28	28	15	12	14	14
OTHER	0	0	0	0	0	0	3	3	3	3	0	7	8	8	8	8	10	10	11	13	13	14
S. AMERICA	0	0	3	7	7	8	12	11	11	11	12	18	18	18	21	23	26	24	25	29	31	28
ARGENTINA	0	0	2	1	1	0	1	0	0	1	0	3	3	3	3	3	4	4	2	4	4	4
BRAZIL	0	0	0	0	0	0	0	0	0	0	1	1	1	1	1	2	2	2	5	4	6	2
PERU	0	1	0	0	0	0	0	0	0	1	1	4	4	4	5	5	5	5	5	5	6	6
COLUMBIA	0	0	0	0	0	0	1	1	1	1	1	1	1	1	1	1	1	1	7	8	8	1
VENEZUELA	0	0	0	2	2	2	2	1	3	2	2	3	3	4	5	5	7	6	7	8	8	5
OTHER	0	0	3	3	5	5	7	6	6	6	6	6	6	7	7	7	6	6	6	9	10	10
EUROPE	1	2	3	3	5	6	9	9	9	9	12	13	13	14	15	15	16	16	18	17	16	15
EFTA	0	0	1	1	1	3	6	8	6	6	6	7	6	6	7	7	8	7	7	7	6	5
U.K.	0	0	1	1	2	3	6	6	6	6	6	7	6	7	7	7	8	7	7	7	6	5
SCANDINAVIA	0	0	0	0	0	0	0	0	0	0	0	0	0	0	0	0	0	0	0	0	0	0
SWITZERLAND	0	0	0	0	0	0	0	0	0	0	0	0	0	0	0	0	0	0	0	0	0	0
OTHER EFTA	0	1	0	1	1	1	1	1	0	0	0	0	0	0	0	0	0	0	0	0	0	0
EUROP. COMMUNITY	0	0	0	0	0	0	0	0	3	3	5	5	5	5	5	5	6	6	8	7	7	7
FRANCE	0	0	0	0	0	0	0	0	0	0	1	1	1	2	2	2	3	3	4	3	3	3
GERMANY	0	0	0	0	0	0	0	0	0	0	1	1	1	1	1	1	1	1	1	1	1	1
ITALY	0	1	1	1	1	1	1	1	1	1	1	1	1	1	1	1	1	1	1	1	1	1
BELGIUM + LUX	0	0	0	0	0	0	0	0	0	0	0	0	0	0	0	0	0	0	0	0	0	0
NETHERLANDS	1	1	1	1	1	1	1	1	1	1	1	1	1	1	1	1	1	1	2	2	2	2
SPAIN	0	0	0	0	0	0	0	0	0	0	0	0	0	0	1	1	1	1	1	1	1	1
GREECE + TURKEY	0	0	0	0	2	2	2	2	2	2	1	1	1	2	2	2	2	2	2	2	2	2
OTHER EUROPE	1	1	1	1	2	3	3	3	3	3	6	6	7	8	8	8	8	9	11	10	10	10
EUROPE EX. U.K.	1	2	2	2	3	3	3	3	3	3	6	6	7	8	8	8	8	9	11	10	10	10
SOUTHERN DOMINIONS	0	0	1	1	3	5	8	8	9	13	15	13	14	15	15	16	16	19	21	24	26	26
S. AFRICA +RHOD.	0	0	1	1	3	4	4	4	5	8	9	7	7	7	7	7	7	7	9	10	10	10
AUSTRALIA + N.Z.	0	0	0	0	0	1	4	4	5	5	6	6	7	8	8	9	9	12	12	14	16	16
ASIA + OTHER AFRICA	0	2	3	3	7	8	14	12	10	22	26	27	27	29	29	33	33	34	35	37	39	39
JAPAN	0	0	0	0	0	0	0	0	0	0	0	0	0	0	0	0	0	0	0	0	0	0
OTHER ASIA+AFR.	0	2	3	3	7	8	14	12	10	22	26	27	27	29	29	33	33	34	35	37	39	39
BLACK AFRICA	0	0	1	1	3	3	4	3	3	10	13	13	13	14	15	18	18	18	19	20	20	20
ARAB WORLD	0	0	2	2	2	2	6	6	7	7	7	7	7	8	8	8	8	8	9	9	9	10
INDIA	0	0	0	0	0	0	0	0	0	0	0	0	0	0	0	0	0	0	0	0	0	0
PHILIPPINES	0	0	1	1	1	1	1	1	2	2	2	3	3	3	3	3	3	3	3	3	3	3
OTHER E. ASIA	0	1	0	0	1	0	0	0	0	0	0	0	0	0	0	0	0	0	0	0	0	0
OTHER ASIA	0	2	2	2	2	2	4	3	3	3	4	4	4	4	4	4	4	4	4	5	7	6

CHAPTER 3- THE PROLIFERATION OF FOREIGN SUBSIDIARIES
SECTION 1- AN OVERVIEW OF FLOW AND STOCK, MANUFACTURING AND NON-MANUFACTURING
TABLE 9- SUBSIDIARIES WITH OTHER MAIN ACTIVITY CLASSIFIED BY COUNTRY OR REGION,
AND BY PERIOD ACTIVITY BEGAN

COUNTRY OR REGION	PRE 1968	PRE 1901	1901 -13	1914 -19	1920 -24	1925 -29	1930 -34	1935 -39	1940 -45	1946 -50	1951 -53	1954 -55	1956 -57	1958 -59	1960 -61	1962	1963	1964	1965	1966	1967	UNK
OUTSIDE U.S.	1805	9	7	14	28	41	46	94	78	110	121	96	103	146	189	92	123	92	111	116	122	67
OUT. U.S. + CANADA	1543	9	7	8	24	34	32	76	70	73	97	83	88	130	177	80	108	79	95	102	112	59
OUT. WEST. HEMIS.	1043	4	3	6	15	25	24	45	52	35	52	52	43	87	126	59	77	58	78	82	84	36
OUT. WHITE CWEALTH	1226	8	6	7	21	27	25	57	60	63	77	70	75	104	146	56	86	60	78	78	84	38
OUT. DEVLPED WORLD	629	5	4	2	9	12	10	35	35	50	61	41	48	51	60	26	41	26	24	31	39	30
CANADA	262	0	0	6	4	7	14	18	24	37	24	13	15	16	12	12	15	13	16	14	10	8
LATIN AMERICA	500	5	4	2	9	9	8	31	18	38	45	31	45	43	51	21	31	17	17	20	28	23
C. AMER.+CARIB.	260	1	0	2	4	1	3	25	6	17	17	17	31	25	24	6	18	9	10	13	18	13
CUBA	17	0	0	1	1	1	1	6	1	1	3	1	3	0	2	0	0	0	0	0	0	0
MEXICO	78	0	0	1	3	0	1	19	3	4	3	4	3	7	7	2	4	1	4	4	5	7
OTHER	165	0	0	0	3	0	1	2	0	4	12	12	26	22	15	4	14	8	6	9	13	6
S. AMERICA	240	4	4	0	5	8	5	6	12	21	28	14	14	18	27	15	13	12	7	7	10	10
ARGENTINA	43	0	0	0	1	3	3	1	1	7	2	3	1	5	7	3	0	1	1	2	2	0
BRAZIL	58	0	0	0	0	1	1	1	3	2	5	4	1	7	7	3	5	5	3	3	5	4
PERU	25	2	4	0	0	1	0	0	0	0	2	2	1	1	3	3	0	0	0	3	1	1
COLOMBIA	23	0	0	0	1	0	1	0	0	2	5	5	0	0	0	2	4	3	1	0	0	2
VENEZUELA	58	0	0	0	0	1	0	1	6	8	15	2	6	4	9	2	2	2	2	1	2	2
OTHER	33	2	0	0	2	3	0	3	0	2	3	2	2	1	1	1	2	1	2	1	0	3
EUROPE	772	4	3	5	15	21	21	38	41	19	26	37	38	64	103	38	52	46	62	56	63	20
EFTA	382	1	2	1	4	11	8	17	15	11	16	22	23	38	67	18	19	29	24	22	22	12
U.K.	197	1	1	1	3	6	16	16	10	7	12	10	12	12	19	8	15	15	7	13	17	12
SCANDINAVIA	47	0	0	0	0	1	0	1	0	2	1	4	3	5	5	2	3	3	3	5	3	0
SWITZERLAND	123	0	1	0	1	3	1	0	4	2	2	6	8	5	9	8	3	4	13	5	3	0
OTHER EFTA	15	0	0	0	0	0	0	0	1	0	1	0	0	1	1	0	1	1	1	0	2	0
EUROP. COMMUNITY	343	3	1	4	8	10	11	16	21	8	10	13	14	25	32	17	31	15	31	30	35	8
FRANCE	125	1	1	1	4	2	8	5	8	3	4	3	2	10	14	6	12	6	6	12	17	2
GERMANY	89	3	0	1	0	6	3	10	3	0	3	5	6	7	15	5	15	3	9	3	6	3
ITALY	44	0	0	1	1	0	0	0	7	0	1	1	1	3	8	1	2	3	2	3	4	2
BELGIUM + LUX	44	0	0	0	0	0	0	0	0	4	2	2	3	3	4	4	4	2	11	7	4	3
NETHERLANDS	41	0	0	1	0	1	0	0	2	0	0	2	1	2	3	0	4	2	3	4	4	1
SPAIN	15	0	0	0	0	0	0	3	0	0	0	1	1	1	2	1	0	1	1	1	4	0
GREECE + TURKEY	8	0	0	0	0	1	1	0	0	0	0	0	0	0	0	2	0	1	0	0	0	0
OTHER EUROPE	24	0	0	2	2	0	2	0	5	0	2	0	0	0	2	1	2	0	3	3	2	0
EUROPE EX. U.K.	575	3	2	4	12	15	15	22	31	12	14	27	26	52	84	30	43	31	55	43	46	8
SOUTHERN DOMINIONS	108	0	0	0	0	1	1	3	0	3	8	3	1	14	10	14	11	4	7	10	9	9
S. AFRICA +RHOD.	20	0	0	0	0	0	0	1	0	1	3	0	0	1	1	2	1	0	0	3	4	3
AUSTRALIA + N.Z.	88	0	0	0	0	1	1	2	0	2	5	3	1	13	9	12	10	4	7	7	5	6
ASIA + OTHER AFRICA	163	0	0	1	0	3	2	4	11	13	18	12	4	9	13	7	10	8	9	16	12	7
JAPAN	34	0	0	0	1	0	2	0	5	1	2	2	1	1	4	2	4	3	2	5	6	1
OTHER ASIA+AFR.	129	0	0	1	0	3	2	4	6	12	16	10	3	8	9	5	10	5	7	11	11	7
BLACK AFRICA	46	0	0	0	0	3	0	0	0	1	6	7	4	2	2	3	3	3	3	4	4	5
ARAB WORLD	20	0	0	0	0	2	2	0	2	1	1	3	1	0	0	0	3	0	0	1	1	0
INDIA	7	0	0	0	0	0	0	0	0	0	0	1	1	0	3	0	0	0	0	0	1	0
PHILIPPINES	15	0	0	1	1	2	2	1	1	0	2	2	2	3	1	1	3	1	1	1	1	1
OTHER E. ASIA	22	0	0	1	0	2	2	2	0	1	2	1	0	1	1	2	0	3	3	2	2	2
OTHER ASIA	19	0	0	0	2	0	0	1	1	2	2	1	0	2	1	0	2	0	0	3	3	1

CHAPTER 3- THE PROLIFERATION OF FOREIGN SUBSIDIARIES
SECTION 1- AN OVERVIEW OF FLOW AND STOCK, MANUFACTURING AND NON-MANUFACTURING
TABLE 10- SUBSIDIARIES WITH OTHER MAIN ACTIVITY CLASSIFIED BY COUNTRY OR REGION,
AND BY YEAR(S) SUBSIDIARY WAS ACTIVE

YEAR

COUNTRY OR REGION	1901	1913	1919	1924	1929	1934	1939	1945	1950	1953	1955	1957	1958	1959	1960	1961	1962	1963	1964	1965	1966	1967
OUTSIDE U.S.	9	14	24	46	85	125	193	251	300	408	484	574	599	665	732	795	863	956	1022	1103	1169	1247
OUT. U.S. + CANADA	9	14	18	37	70	97	154	206	222	308	377	455	474	535	602	664	724	804	861	932	988	1062
OUT. WEST. HEMIS.	4	5	11	22	46	69	100	136	124	169	211	250	259	305	356	404	450	513	562	624	676	724
OUT. WHITE CWEALTH	8	12	15	32	59	80	123	166	180	249	309		384	435	493	541	581	642	681	737	781	841
OUT. DEVLPED WORLD	5	9	7	15	27	33	61	82	116	173	208	249	259	278	300	314	332	356	368	383	398	431
CANADA	0	0	6	9	15	28	39	45	78	100	107	119	125	130	130	131	139	152	161	171	181	185
LATIN AMERICA	5	9	7	15	24	28	54	70	98	139	166	205	215	230	246	260	274	291	299	308	312	338
C. AMER.+CARIB.	1	1	3	7	8	10	31	36	50	66	83	111	116	128	131	138	139	147	147	153	155	177
CUBA	0	0	1	2	4	4	7	7	8	10	11	12	11	11	5	4	4	4	4	4	4	4
MEXICO	0	0	1	4	4	7	20	22	25	28	32	33	33	35	36	40	40	43	41	44	46	56
OTHER	1	1	1	1	2	2	7	7	17	28	40	66	72	82	90	94	95	100	102	105	105	117
S. AMERICA	4	8	4	8	16	18	23	34	48	73	83	94	99	102	115	122	135	144	152	155	157	161
ARGENTINA	0	0	0	1	2	3	4	7	10	11	14	16	16	17	18	20	21	22	22	23	23	23
BRAZIL	0	0	2	3	4	4	7	7	9	11	14	17	22	27	28	30	33	36	36	37	37	42
PERU	2	2	1	2	3	3	3	3	3	4	6	7	7	7	9	12	14	16	16	16	16	16
COLOMBIA	0	0	0	0	0	0	1	2	3	17	14	14	14	14	14	15	16	17	16	16	17	17
VENEZUELA	0	0	1	1	0	1	5	7	14	16	21	25	25	29	33	38	39	42	43	44	45	43
OTHER	2	2	0	1	3	5	7	8	9	12	14	16	13	14	14	13	18	18	19	21	20	20
EUROPE	4	5	10	21	41	61	87	114	95	116	145	180	185	219	260	300	328	372	411	459	489	529
EFTA	1	3	4	7	17	24	35	46	44	57	74	94	103	119	149	171	183	200	227	242	246	250
U.K.	1	2	3	5	10	15	26	35	36	45	51	63	67	70	77	83	89	98	113	118	121	131
SCANDINAVIA	0	0	1	2	2	3	5	5	6	4	10	13	13	12	12	14	15	18	22	24	26	28
SWITZERLAND	0	1	0	2	5	5	5	5	2	5	10	16	21	31	54	68	73	78	85	92	91	83
OTHER EFTA	0	0	0	0	0	0	0	0	1	2	3	2	2	6	6	6	6	6	7	8	8	8
EUROP. COMMUNITY	3	6	6	11	21	32	42	57	46	54	64	78	76	93	105	119	132	157	167	193	215	245
FRANCE	0	1	2	6	8	16	17	26	24	27	29	31	30	36	40	48	52	63	65	69	78	95
GERMANY	3	2	4	10	13	13	22	26	18	20	23	30	30	36	35	38	38	40	42	50	52	53
ITALY	0	1	1	2	2	6	7	7	8	8	11	13	13	13	13	15	18	18	20	21	25	29
BELGIUM + LUX	3	1	1	2	0	1	2	2	2	2	4	8	9	8	9	8	12	15	17	28	34	37
NETHERLANDS	0	0	0	0	1	1	2	2	0	0	1	0	0	9	4	10	12	18	20	25	26	31
SPAIN	0	0	0	1	1	1	1	3	0	2	4	4	3	4	4	8	4	4	5	8	7	13
GREECE + TURKEY	0	0	0	0	1	1	4	3	2	2	2	3	3	4	4	10	5	5	6	7	7	7
OTHER EUROPE	0	0	2	2	3	5	5	7	1	1	1	0	0	0	0	2	4	5	6	6	12	14
EUROPE EX. U.K.	3	3	7	16	31	46	61	79	59	71	94	117	118	149	183	217	239	274	298	341	368	398
SOUTHERN DOMINIONS	0	0	0	0	1	2	5	5	6	14	17	18	23	30	32	38	50	58	61	68	76	78
S. AFRICA +RHOD.	0	0	0	1	0	2	1	2	2	5	5	5	6	5	5	6	8	9	9	9	12	16
AUSTRALIA + N.Z.	0	0	1	1	2	2	4	4	4	9	12	13	17	25	26	32	42	49	52	59	64	62
ASIA + OTHER AFRICA	0	1	1	4	6	6	8	17	23	39	49	52	51	56	64	66	72	83	90	97	111	117
JAPAN	0	0	0	1	1	1	1	1	3	5	7	8	7	8	10	12	14	18	21	22	25	24
OTHER ASIA+AFR.	0	1	0	1	3	5	5	7	12	18	34	44	44	48	54	54	58	65	69	75	86	93
BLACK AFRICA	0	0	0	0	0	0	2	7	8	8	11	13	12	15	16	17	20	24	27	29	33	36
ARAB WORLD	0	0	0	0	0	0	0	2	8	8	11	12	12	12	13	13	13	15	15	15	15	15
INDIA	0	0	0	0	0	1	1	2	2	3	3	3	4	3	3	3	3	3	3	3	4	4
PHILIPPINES	0	0	0	0	1	1	3	3	8	2	4	4	5	6	8	7	5	8	8	9	10	9
OTHER E. ASIA	0	0	0	3	5	5	7	4	3	2	5	6	6	7	7	7	9	8	9	12	14	16
OTHER ASIA	0	0	0	0	1	1	2	3	5	5	6	5	6	6	7	6	5	7	7	7	10	13

CHAPTER 3- THE PROLIFERATION OF FOREIGN SUBSIDIARIES
SECTION I- AN OVERVIEW OF FLOW AND STOCK, MANUFACTURING AND NON-MANUFACTURING
TABLE II- SUBSIDIARIES WITH UNKNOWN ACTIVITY CLASSIFIED BY COUNTRY OR REGION,
AND BY PERIOD ACTIVITY BEGAN

PERIOD

COUNTRY OR REGION	PRE 1968	PRE 1901	1901 -13	1914 -19	1920 -24	1925 -29	1930 -34	1935 -39	1940 -45	1946 -50	1951 -53	1954 -55	1956 -57	1958 -59	1960 -61	1962	1963	1964	1965	1966	1967	UNK
OUTSIDE U.S.	2407	13	19	25	27	100	106	222	81	118	150	84	137	114	174	102	114	158	148	123	70	322
OUT. U.S. + CANADA	1954	12	19	12	19	71	69	179	60	95	128	75	75	96	150	83	103	135	130	100	66	249
OUT. WEST. HEMIS.	1413	12	16	8	16	55	57	143	28	50	75	52	73	72	102	65	80	107	101	84	48	169
OUT. WHITE CWEALTH	1459	7	9	6	18	59	55	122	45	78	98	51	76	69	115	55	74	102	100	79	55	186
OUT. DEVLPED WORLD	683	0	0	5	3	15	13	48	35	57	60	27	39	30	58	23	24	45	42	27	25	105
CANADA	453	1	3	13	8	29	37	43	21	23	22	9	31	18	24	19	11	23	18	23	4	73
LATIN AMERICA	541	0	0	4	3	16	12	36	32	45	53	23	33	24	48	18	23	28	29	16	18	80
C. AMER.+CARIB.	254	0	0	1	1	8	8	15	10	17	25	15	22	9	26	9	11	12	19	7	9	34
CUBA	23	0	0	0	0	3	4	1	1	2	1	2	1	1	0	0	1	0	0	0	0	1
MEXICO	100	0	0	1	0	5	3	9	2	5	9	10	3	2	8	5	2	5	10	3	5	14
OTHER	131	0	0	0	0	0	0	4	5	10	15	3	18	6	18	4	9	7	8	4	4	19
S. AMERICA	287	0	0	3	2	8	8	21	22	28	28	8	11	15	22	9	12	16	10	9	9	46
ARGENTINA	64	0	0	0	0	2	2	9	4	4	4	3	3	4	3	2	1	2	1	0	3	22
BRAZIL	66	0	0	2	0	2	2	4	1	5	5	0	3	3	7	1	2	6	7	3	1	5
PERU	16	0	0	0	0	1	1	0	1	1	1	1	1	1	1	0	1	2	1	1	0	3
COLOMBIA	52	0	0	1	1	0	0	2	3	9	13	2	1	3	1	3	3	0	0	0	1	6
VENEZUELA	45	0	0	0	0	0	0	5	5	3	2	2	4	4	5	1	1	4	3	1	0	3
OTHER	44	0	0	0	0	2	3	3	4	6	4	3	1	0	3	0	4	2	0	4	1	7
EUROPE	1077	11	15	6	16	53	53	123	22	26	52	34	58	57	71	49	61	77	76	69	31	117
EFTA	507	4	8	5	3	19	17	64	14	12	32	13	29	31	38	29	26	28	35	30	15	55
U.K.	328	4	6	4	1	12	12	50	12	6	17	10	21	19	17	21	15	20	19	17	8	37
SCANDINAVIA	96	0	2	0	1	3	4	8	1	6	11	1	4	4	6	2	4	3	11	8	5	10
SWITZERLAND	68	0	0	1	1	2	1	3	0	0	4	2	2	6	6	6	6	5	5	4	1	8
OTHER EFTA	15	0	0	0	0	2	0	3	0	0	0	0	2	7	2	0	1	0	0	0	1	0
EUROP. COMMUNITY	483	7	6	0	11	26	26	46	6	14	18	20	27	25	27	17	30	45	36	36	14	46
FRANCE	128	2	1	0	4	8	10	12	3	3	8	6	9	7	10	6	6	11	11	5	4	10
GERMANY	141	1	3	0	3	9	6	11	1	5	2	5	11	10	11	3	10	13	17	9	2	10
ITALY	103	2	0	0	1	7	7	10	1	0	4	2	2	1	3	2	6	16	7	7	2	11
BELGIUM + LUX	51	2	2	0	2	1	1	4	0	3	5	5	3	6	2	1	5	7	4	2	1	11
NETHERLANDS	60	1	2	0	1	4	2	9	0	3	0	2	3	2	2	8	5	4	4	5	5	11
SPAIN	35	0	0	0	0	3	3	2	0	0	0	1	1	1	1	1	4	2	1	2	2	4
GREECE + TURKEY	12	0	0	0	1	0	0	0	0	0	2	0	1	0	3	2	2	1	1	0	0	6
OTHER EUROPE	40	0	1	1	1	4	7	11	2	0	2	0	0	0	2	0	1	2	0	1	0	3
EUROPE EX. U.K.	749	7	9	2	15	41	41	73	10	20	35	24	37	38	54	28	46	57	57	52	23	80
SOUTHERN DOMINIONS	157	1	1	1	0	0	2	6	3	11	11	14	9	8	17	7	12	12	11	4	3	24
S. AFRICA +RHOD.	44	0	1	0	0	0	1	2	0	6	2	5	2	2	2	3	4	5	3	0	0	6
AUSTRALIA + N.Z.	113	1	0	1	0	0	1	4	3	5	9	9	7	6	15	4	8	7	8	4	3	18
ASIA + OTHER AFRICA	179	0	0	0	0	2	2	14	13	13	12	4	6	7	14	9	8	18	14	11	14	28
JAPAN	37	0	0	0	0	1	1	2	0	1	5	0	0	1	0	4	6	1	1	1	7	3
OTHER ASIA+AFR.	142	0	0	1	0	1	1	12	12	12	7	4	6	6	10	5	1	17	13	11	7	25
BLACK AFRICA	42	0	0	0	0	0	0	3	3	1	1	1	1	0	6	3	0	8	3	4	1	5
ARAB WORLD	26	0	0	0	1	0	1	0	0	2	2	0	0	0	0	0	0	6	2	2	0	2
INDIA	16	0	0	0	0	0	0	2	1	0	1	0	2	2	1	3	0	0	0	0	1	5
PHILIPPINES	15	0	0	0	0	0	0	3	0	2	2	0	1	0	0	1	1	0	3	3	0	2
OTHER E. ASIA	8	0	0	0	0	0	0	1	0	0	1	0	0	2	1	0	0	1	1	0	3	3
OTHER ASIA	35	0	0	1	0	0	0	4	2	5	1	0	1	0	2	2	0	3	4	4	2	4

CHAPTER 3- THE PROLIFERATION OF FOREIGN SUBSIDIARIES
SECTION 1- AN OVERVIEW OF FLOW AND STOCK, MANUFACTURING AND NON-MANUFACTURING
TABLE 12- SUBSIDIARIES WITH UNKNOWN ACTIVITY CLASSIFIED BY COUNTRY OR REGION,
AND BY YEAR(S) SUBSIDIARY WAS ACTIVE

YEAR

COUNTRY OR REGION	1901	1913	1919	1924	1929	1934	1939	1945	1950	1953	1955	1957	1958	1959	1960	1961	1962	1963	1964	1965	1966	1967
OUTSIDE U.S.	13	29	49	72	146	236	412	456	504	610	668	789	835	874	937	994	1074	1161	1296	1417	1475	1504
OUT: U.S. + CANADA	12	25	36	54	112	172	319	352	397	487	542	634	675	704	757	811	875	958	1075	1182	1219	1248
OUT: WEST. HEMIS.	12	25	33	47	91	140	256	260	272	334	371	437	471	491	529	570	619	685	777	857	884	901
OUT: WHITE CWEALTH	7	15	20	38	85	134	239	265	308	375	411	475	503	528	569	612	656	714	805	888	926	966
OUT: DEVLPED WORLD	0	0	4	8	23	35	78	109	151	186	207	239	251	260	277	296	314	329	371	409	427	444
CANADA	1	4	13	18	34	64	93	104	107	123	126	155	160	170	180	183	199	203	221	235	256	256
LATIN AMERICA	0	0	3	7	21	32	63	92	125	153	171	197	204	213	228	241	256	273	298	325	335	347
C. AMER.+CARIB.	0	0	0	2	9	13	11	32	45	65	76	95	92	97	102	109	117	125	135	152	157	163
CUBA	0	0	0	0	3	4	4	12	14	14	16	17	17	16	8	5	5	5	5	5	5	5
MEXICO	0	0	0	2	0	9	10	14	15	22	28	31	27	28	31	35	39	39	43	53	54	56
OTHER	0	0	0	0	0	0	0	6	16	29	32	47	48	53	63	69	73	81	87	94	98	102
S. AMERICA	0	0	3	5	12	19	40	60	80	88	95	102	112	116	126	132	139	148	163	173	178	184
ARGENTINA	0	0	0	1	3	5	15	15	19	20	20	19	22	23	25	25	27	27	29	30	29	32
BRAZIL	0	0	2	2	4	6	9	13	16	20	23	25	26	27	30	31	33	35	41	47	47	49
PERU	0	0	0	0	0	0	3	4	4	4	4	5	6	6	7	7	7	8	10	10	9	11
COLOMBIA	0	0	0	2	2	3	5	10	17	16	18	19	21	22	22	23	25	26	26	30	31	28
VENEZUELA	0	0	0	0	0	0	0	8	10	12	14	18	21	22	26	27	28	29	32	32	35	36
OTHER	0	0	0	0	0	4	7	10	14	16	16	16	16	16	18	18	19	23	25	24	27	28
EUROPE	11	23	29	43	85	130	229	229	222	264	286	338	365	383	408	436	475	525	591	651	673	697
EFTA	4	10	15	18	35	49	96	100	97	123	132	160	184	184	195	213	235	256	279	309	312	320
U.K.	4	8	12	13	24	33	70	74	66	78	84	104	115	118	121	127	143	154	171	187	190	196
SCANDINAVIA	0	2	2	3	6	10	17	18	23	33	34	38	39	44	46	50	51	55	58	69	66	67
SWITZERLAND	0	0	0	2	4	5	5	5	5	9	11	13	14	15	21	27	32	38	42	45	47	47
OTHER EFTA	0	0	0	0	1	1	5	3	3	3	3	5	7	7	7	9	9	9	8	8	9	10
EUROP. COMMUNITY	7	12	12	22	42	64	105	105	113	127	139	161	173	181	193	200	215	241	280	305	323	337
FRANCE	2	3	3	11	11	19	28	30	31	31	36	44	47	49	51	57	60	65	75	82	86	91
GERMANY	1	4	4	6	15	19	29	29	30	33	34	43	50	53	61	61	63	71	81	89	98	100
ITALY	1	1	1	2	6	8	24	24	26	29	34	35	37	39	41	43	49	49	64	70	75	75
BELGIUM + LUX	2	2	4	6	6	7	11	11	11	14	15	17	18	19	19	20	21	26	26	30	32	34
NETHERLANDS	0	0	0	1	3	2	13	12	15	20	20	22	21	21	21	26	26	30	34	34	32	37
SPAIN	0	0	0	0	0	3	8	8	8	8	9	10	10	11	12	14	15	16	17	22	24	26
GREECE + TURKEY	0	1	0	0	0	0	0	0	0	0	0	0	1	1	1	3	4	5	5	7	8	8
OTHER EUROPE	0	2	2	2	5	11	20	16	16	13	11	6	7	6	5	6	6	7	7	8	6	6
EUROPE Ex. U.K.	7	15	17	30	61	97	159	155	156	186	202	234	250	265	287	309	332	371	420	464	483	501
SOUTHERN DOMINIONS	1	2	3	3	3	5	9	12	22	31	44	52	54	55	65	69	73	85	93	101	99	82
S. AFRICA +RHOD.	0	1	1	1	1	2	4	4	10	12	17	19	19	20	21	19	20	24	29	29	29	26
AUSTRALIA + N.Z.	1	1	2	2	3	3	5	8	12	19	27	33	35	35	44	50	53	61	64	72	70	56
ASIA + OTHER AFRICA	0	0	1	1	1	2	8	19	28	39	41	47	52	53	56	65	71	75	93	105	112	122
JAPAN	0	0	0	0	1	2	2	3	6	6	5	5	6	6	7	10	13	19	20	21	20	25
OTHER ASIA+AFR.	0	1	2	1	3	3	15	17	26	33	36	42	47	47	49	55	58	56	73	84	92	97
BLACK AFRICA	0	0	0	0	0	1	2	2	4	4	7	8	8	8	9	14	16	16	24	26	30	30
ARAB WORLD	0	0	0	0	0	0	3	3	5	8	7	8	8	8	8	10	8	8	13	15	16	15
INDIA	0	0	0	0	0	0	3	3	8	8	8	8	9	10	9	8	8	9	9	11	11	12
PHILIPPINES	0	0	1	1	2	2	2	3	2	3	3	4	6	6	6	9	9	8	6	7	7	10
OTHER E. ASIA	0	0	0	0	0	0	1	1	1	1	1	1	3	3	4	3	3	7	6	3	4	4
OTHER ASIA	0	1	1	1	2	4	5	7	11	12	12	13	13	12	12	14	16	15	18	22	24	26

CHAPTER 3— THE PROLIFERATION OF FOREIGN SUBSIDIARIES
SECTION 2— THE FLOW OF MANUFACTURING BY INDUSTRY OF PARENT SYSTEM
TABLE 1— MANUFACTURING SUBSIDIARIES IN A SYSTEM IN THE
MEAT AND DAIRY INDUSTRIES (SIC 201 AND 202)
CLASSIFIED BY COUNTRY OR REGION AND BY PERIOD MANUFACTURE BEGAN

PERIOD

COUNTRY OR REGION	PRE 1968	PRE 1901	1901 -12	1914 -19	1920 -24	1925 -29	1930 -34	1935 -39	1940 -45	1946 -50	1951 -53	1954 -55	1956 -57	1958 -59	1960 -61	1962	1963	1964	1965	1966	1967	UNK
OUTSIDE U.S.	291	3	6	9	3	20	14	10	9	8	16	8	12	16	47	11	14	19	24	23	11	8
OUT. U.S. + CANADA	239	3	3	8	3	13	13	10	9	8	12	8	11	16	39	7	12	16	19	19	8	5
OUT. WEST. HEMIS.	137	3	1	1	3	10	10	5	3	3	8	4	5	10	19	4	8	10	16	7	5	2
OUT. WHITE CWEALTH	180	0	2	7	2	7	8	8	6	5	7	7	11	10	29	6	10	14	13	18	7	3
OUT. DEVLPED WORLD	120	0	2	7	0	2	3	5	6	5	4	6	8	8	23	3	7	8	12	12	5	3
CANADA	52	3	3	1	3	10	1	0	0	0	4	0	1	0	8	4	2	3	5	4	3	3
LATIN AMERICA	102	2	2	7	0	0	3	5	6	5	4	4	6	6	20	3	4	6	3	12	3	3
C. AMER.+CARIB.	48	0	0	1	0	0	3	4	0	2	1	3	4	2	9	2	0	0	2	8	1	2
CUBA	9	0	0	1	0	0	2	2	0	0	0	0	1	0	0	0	0	4	2	0	0	1
MEXICO	18	0	0	0	0	0	0	0	2	2	1	1	1	2	7	1	0	2	2	3	0	1
OTHER	21	0	0	0	0	1	1	1	0	0	1	0	2	0	2	1	0	2	0	5	2	0
S. AMERICA	54	0	2	6	0	0	0	2	3	3	3	2	0	4	11	1	4	2	1	4	1	1
ARGENTINA	9	0	1	2	0	0	1	1	1	1	0	1	2	2	1	1	0	2	0	0	0	0
BRAZIL	12	0	0	0	0	0	0	1	0	1	0	0	1	0	0	0	1	0	0	1	0	1
PERU	4	0	0	0	0	0	0	0	3	0	1	0	0	0	0	0	0	0	0	1	0	0
COLUMBIA	15	0	0	4	0	0	0	1	1	1	2	0	1	2	8	1	1	1	0	1	0	0
VENEZUELA	9	0	0	0	0	0	0	0	0	0	0	0	0	0	2	0	1	1	0	1	0	0
OTHER	5	0	1	0	0	0	0	0	1	0	0	1	0	0	0	0	1	0	1	0	1	1
EUROPE	88	3	0	0	3	8	7	5	0	0	6	1	3	8	9	3	3	8	12	7	2	0
EFTA	36	3	0	0	1	4	2	2	0	0	1	0	3	6	3	0	0	4	3	3	0	0
U.K.	26	3	0	0	1	3	2	2	0	0	1	0	3	6	3	0	1	3	1	1	0	0
SCANDINAVIA	10	0	0	0	0	1	0	0	0	0	0	0	0	0	3	0	0	3	1	2	0	0
SWITZERLAND	0	0	0	0	0	0	0	0	0	0	0	0	0	0	0	0	0	0	0	0	0	0
OTHER EFTA	0	0	0	0	0	0	0	0	0	0	0	0	0	0	0	0	0	0	0	0	0	0
EUROP. COMMUNITY	38	0	0	0	0	4	5	3	0	0	3	0	0	2	5	2	2	2	6	0	1	0
FRANCE	6	0	0	0	0	0	1	0	0	0	0	0	0	0	2	0	0	0	0	0	1	0
GERMANY	15	0	0	0	0	2	3	2	0	0	2	0	0	0	2	0	0	1	2	0	0	0
ITALY	4	0	0	0	0	0	1	0	0	0	0	1	0	0	1	0	0	0	1	0	0	0
BELGIUM + LUX	5	0	0	0	0	2	0	0	0	0	0	0	0	2	0	1	1	1	1	0	1	0
NETHERLANDS	8	0	0	0	0	0	0	1	0	0	1	0	0	0	0	1	1	1	0	0	1	0
SPAIN	7	0	0	0	0	2	0	0	0	0	0	0	0	0	0	0	0	0	2	3	0	0
GREECE + TURKEY	0	0	0	0	0	0	0	0	0	0	0	0	0	0	0	0	0	0	0	0	0	0
OTHER EUROPE	7	0	0	0	0	0	0	0	0	0	2	0	0	0	0	1	1	1	1	0	0	1
EUROPE EX. U.K.	62	0	0	0	2	5	5	3	0	0	5	3	0	2	6	3	2	8	9	6	2	0
SOUTHERN DOMINIONS	26	0	1	1	0	3	0	0	0	3	2	1	2	0	6	0	1	0	2	0	1	2
S. AFRICA +RHOD.	3	0	0	0	0	0	0	0	3	3	0	1	0	0	0	0	1	0	0	0	0	1
AUSTRALIA + N.Z.	23	0	1	1	0	3	0	0	0	3	2	0	2	0	6	1	4	2	2	0	2	1
ASIA + OTHER AFRICA	23	0	0	0	0	0	0	0	0	0	2	2	0	4	4	4	3	2	2	0	0	0
JAPAN	5	0	0	0	0	0	0	0	0	0	0	0	0	0	3	1	1	2	0	0	0	0
OTHER ASIA+AFR.	18	0	0	0	0	2	0	0	0	0	2	2	2	3	0	1	3	1	0	0	2	0
BLACK AFRICA	1	0	0	0	0	0	0	0	0	0	0	0	0	0	0	0	1	0	0	0	0	0
ARAB WORLD	2	0	0	0	0	0	0	0	0	0	0	0	0	0	0	0	1	1	0	0	0	0
INDIA	0	0	0	0	0	0	0	0	0	0	0	0	0	0	0	0	0	0	0	0	0	0
PHILIPPINES	5	0	0	0	0	0	0	0	0	0	2	0	1	2	0	0	0	0	0	0	0	0
OTHER E. ASIA	4	0	0	0	0	2	0	0	0	0	0	1	0	0	0	1	0	0	0	0	0	1
OTHER ASIA	6	0	0	0	0	0	3	0	0	0	0	0	0	3	3	2	1	1	0	0	1	0

CHAPTER 3- THE PROLIFERATION OF FOREIGN SUBSIDIARIES
SECTION 2- THE FLOW OF MANUFACTURING BY INDUSTRY OF PARENT SYSTEM
TABLE 2-- MANUFACTURING SUBSIDIARIES IN A SYSTEM IN THE
OTHER FOOD AND BEVERAGE INDUSTRIES (SIC 203-209)
CLASSIFIED BY COUNTRY OR REGION AND BY PERIOD MANUFACTURE BEGAN

COUNTRY OR REGION	PRE 1908	PRE 1901	1901-13	1914-19	1920-24	1925-29	1930-34	1935-39	1940-42	1946-20	1951-53	1954-55	1956-57	1958-59	1960-61	1962	1963	1964	1965	1966	1967	UNK
OUTSIDE U.S.	503	0	4	3	10	27	14	35	12	16	12	23	35	29	65	29	38	33	36	41	33	8
OUT. U.S. + CANADA	402	0	1	2	6	13	8	26	8	14	6	15	28	26	59	23	38	27	33	34	29	6
OUT. WEST. HEMIS.	260	0	1	2	5	11	5	22	7	7	4	10	16	20	41	13	14	14	23	17	14	5
OUT. WHITE CMEALTH	311	0	0	1	4	7	8	5	7	10	4	13	27	18	40	19	35	23	27	32	27	5
OUT. DEVLPED WORLD	163	0	0	0	2	4	4	4	4	7	2	6	16	8	18	11	15	14	10	20	17	1
CANADA	101	0	3	1	4	14	6	9	4	2	6	8	7	3	6	6	12	6	3	7	4	2
LATIN AMERICA	142	0	0	0	1	2	3	4	4	7	2	5	12	6	18	10	13	13	10	17	15	1
C. AMER.+CARIB.	82	0	0	0	1	0	2	4	2	5	2	1	6	3	7	5	4	10	6	14	10	0
CUBA	8	0	0	0	1	0	2	3	0	5	2	0	1	1	1	0	0	0	0	0	0	0
MEXICO	50	0	0	0	0	0	1	1	1	3	2	1	4	2	3	3	2	9	2	9	7	0
OTHER	24	0	0	0	0	0	1	0	1	1	0	0	1	0	1	1	1	1	4	5	3	1
S. AMERICA	60	0	0	0	0	2	1	0	2	2	0	4	6	3	11	5	8	5	4	5	5	0
ARGENTINA	10	0	0	0	0	1	1	0	1	0	0	1	1	1	1	1	2	3	0	3	2	1
BRAZIL	10	0	0	0	0	0	0	0	0	0	0	1	0	0	2	0	2	1	2	0	0	0
PERU	8	0	0	0	0	1	1	0	0	1	0	0	2	0	1	0	4	0	0	0	0	0
COLOMBIA	9	0	0	0	0	0	0	0	1	1	0	2	1	1	1	1	0	1	1	0	2	1
VENEZUELA	14	0	0	0	0	0	0	0	0	0	0	0	2	2	3	2	0	0	0	2	1	1
OTHER	9	0	0	0	0	0	1	0	0	0	0	0	0	0	3	0	1	1	1	2	2	0
EUROPE	188	0	1	1	2	7	4	19	4	6	3	6	11	12	26	9	21	10	19	11	11	5
EFTA	70	0	1	1	0	4	1	17	1	3	2	0	3	6	6	3	8	3	5	2	3	1
U.K.	48	0	1	0	0	4	0	17	0	2	2	0	1	3	5	2	3	1	3	1	1	1
SCANDINAVIA	14	0	0	1	0	0	1	0	0	1	0	0	1	1	1	1	4	1	1	0	1	0
SWITZERLAND	2	0	0	0	0	0	0	0	0	0	0	0	0	0	0	0	0	0	0	0	1	0
OTHER EFTA	6	0	0	0	0	0	0	0	0	0	0	0	1	2	0	0	1	1	1	1	1	0
EUROP. COMMUNITY	98	0	0	0	2	3	3	1	3	2	1	4	7	5	19	4	11	5	13	6	7	4
FRANCE	26	0	0	0	1	0	0	0	0	1	1	0	0	1	8	2	5	2	1	3	3	0
GERMANY	29	0	0	0	1	3	1	1	3	1	0	3	2	1	3	0	3	2	4	3	1	3
ITALY	15	0	0	0	1	1	0	0	0	1	0	1	1	1	1	1	1	1	4	1	1	0
BELGIUM + LUX	13	0	0	0	0	0	0	1	0	0	0	0	2	0	4	1	0	0	2	1	1	1
NETHERLANDS	15	0	0	0	0	1	2	0	2	0	0	1	1	0	3	0	1	0	3	1	1	0
SPAIN	15	0	0	0	1	0	0	1	1	0	0	2	1	3	4	2	2	1	1	3	3	0
GREECE + TURKEY	3	0	0	0	0	0	0	0	0	1	0	0	0	0	1	0	0	1	0	0	1	0
OTHER EUROPE	2	0	0	0	0	0	0	0	0	0	1	0	0	0	0	0	0	0	0	0	0	0
EUROPE EX. U.K.	140	0	0	1	2	3	4	2	3	4	1	6	10	9	21	7	18	9	16	10	10	4
SOUTHERN DOMINIONS	40	0	0	0	2	2	0	3	0	1	1	2	0	5	13	2	0	3	3	3	1	0
S. AFRICA +RHOD.	15	0	0	1	1	1	0	3	0	1	0	1	0	3	3	0	0	2	2	1	0	0
AUSTRALIA + N.Z.	25	0	0	0	1	1	0	2	0	0	1	1	0	3	10	2	0	1	1	1	1	0
ASIA + OTHER AFRICA	32	0	0	0	2	2	1	0	0	0	0	2	5	1	2	2	5	1	1	5	2	0
JAPAN	11	0	0	0	0	0	0	0	0	0	0	1	1	0	0	1	2	0	1	2	0	0
OTHER ASIA+AFR.	21	0	0	0	1	2	1	0	0	0	0	1	4	2	0	3	3	1	0	3	2	0
BLACK AFRICA	2	0	0	0	0	0	0	0	0	0	0	0	1	0	0	1	0	0	0	1	0	0
ARAB WORLD	2	0	0	0	0	0	0	0	0	0	0	1	0	0	0	0	0	0	0	0	0	0
INDIA	1	0	0	0	0	1	1	0	0	1	0	0	0	1	0	0	0	0	0	0	0	0
PHILIPPINES	7	0	0	0	0	0	0	0	0	0	0	2	2	0	2	2	2	0	1	2	2	0
OTHER E. ASIA	6	0	0	0	1	0	1	0	0	1	0	0	0	1	0	0	1	0	0	0	0	0
OTHER ASIA	3	0	0	1	0	0	0	0	0	0	1	0	1	0	0	0	0	0	0	0	0	0

CHAPTER 3- THE PROLIFERATION OF FOREIGN SUBSIDIARIES
SECTION 2- THE FLOW OF MANUFACTURING BY INDUSTRY OF PARENT SYSTEM
TABLE 3- MANUFACTURING SUBSIDIARIES IN A SYSTEM IN THE
TEXTILE AND APPAREL INDUSTRIES (SIC 22 AND 23)
CLASSIFIED BY COUNTRY OR REGION AND BY PERIOD MANUFACTURE BEGAN

COUNTRY OR REGION	PRE 1968	PRE 1901	1901 -13	1914 -19	1920 -24	1925 -29	1930 -34	1935 -39	1940 -45	1946 -50	1951 -53	1954 -55	1956 -57	1958 -59	1960 -61	1962	1963	1964	1965	1966	1967	UNK
OUTSIDE U.S.	76	0	0	0	0	1	2	0	3	11	3	2	3	4	15	4	5	6	5	5	3	4
OUT. U.S. + CANADA	58	0	0	0	0	2	1	0	1	5	2	2	3	3	15	4	5	6	2	4	2	3
OUT. WEST. HEMIS.	33	0	0	0	0	0	1	0	0	5	2	0	3	1	11	4	4	5	2	3	2	1
OUT. WHITE CWEALTH	44	0	0	0	0	1	1	0	1	5	2	2	3	2	7	2	4	5	4	4	1	3
OUT. DEVLPED WORLD	25	0	0	0	0	1	1	0	1	5	2	2	3	2	4	0	1	1	0	1	0	2
CANADA	18	0	0	0	0	1	1	0	2	6	1	0	0	1	0	0	0	3	0	1	0	2
LATIN AMERICA	25	0	0	0	0	1	1	0	1	5	2	2	3	2	4	0	1	1	0	1	1	0
C. AMER.+CARIB.	8	0	0	0	0	1	0	0	0	2	1	1	0	1	1	0	1	0	0	1	0	1
CUBA	2	0	0	0	0	0	0	0	0	0	1	0	0	0	0	0	0	0	0	0	0	1
MEXICO	6	0	0	0	0	1	0	0	0	2	0	1	0	1	1	0	1	0	0	0	0	0
OTHER	0	0	0	0	0	0	0	0	0	0	0	0	0	0	0	0	0	0	0	0	0	0
S. AMERICA	17	0	0	0	0	1	1	0	1	3	1	1	3	1	3	0	0	1	0	0	1	1
ARGENTINA	2	0	0	0	0	1	0	0	0	0	0	0	0	0	0	0	0	0	0	0	0	1
BRAZIL	3	0	0	0	0	0	0	0	0	1	0	1	0	1	0	0	0	0	0	0	0	0
PERU	0	0	0	0	0	0	0	0	0	0	0	0	0	0	0	0	0	0	0	0	0	0
COLOMBIA	4	0	0	0	0	0	1	0	1	0	1	0	0	0	1	0	0	0	0	0	0	0
VENEZUELA	6	0	0	0	0	0	0	0	0	1	1	1	2	0	1	0	0	1	0	1	0	0
OTHER	2	0	0	0	0	0	0	0	0	1	0	0	0	0	0	0	0	0	0	0	1	0
EUROPE	28	0	0	0	0	0	0	0	0	0	0	0	0	1	10	4	3	4	1	2	2	1
EFTA	14	0	0	0	0	0	0	0	0	0	0	0	0	0	7	2	1	2	0	0	2	0
U.K.	11	0	0	0	0	0	0	0	0	0	0	0	0	0	7	2	0	0	0	0	2	0
SCANDINAVIA	0	0	0	0	0	0	0	0	0	0	0	0	0	0	0	0	0	0	0	0	0	0
SWITZERLAND	2	0	0	0	0	0	0	0	0	0	0	0	0	0	0	0	1	1	0	0	0	0
OTHER EFTA	1	0	0	0	0	0	0	0	0	0	0	0	0	0	0	0	0	1	0	0	0	0
EUROP. COMMUNITY	11	0	0	0	0	0	0	0	0	0	0	0	0	1	3	2	2	1	1	2	0	1
FRANCE	4	0	0	0	0	0	0	0	0	0	0	0	0	0	1	2	0	0	0	0	0	1
GERMANY	3	0	0	0	0	0	0	0	0	0	0	0	0	1	1	0	1	0	0	0	0	0
ITALY	3	0	0	0	0	0	0	0	0	0	0	0	0	0	1	0	1	1	1	1	0	0
BELGIUM + LUX	0	0	0	0	0	0	0	0	0	0	0	0	0	0	0	0	0	0	0	0	0	0
NETHERLANDS	1	0	0	0	0	0	0	0	0	0	0	0	0	0	0	0	0	0	0	1	0	0
SPAIN	3	0	0	0	0	0	0	0	0	0	0	0	0	0	0	0	0	1	0	0	0	0
GREECE + TURKEY	0	0	0	0	0	0	0	0	0	0	0	0	0	0	0	0	0	0	0	0	0	0
OTHER EUROPE	0	0	0	0	0	0	0	0	0	0	0	0	0	0	0	0	0	0	1	2	0	0
EUROPE EX. U.K.	17	0	0	0	0	0	0	0	0	0	0	0	0	1	3	2	3	4	1	2	0	1
SOUTHERN DOMINIONS	3	0	0	0	0	0	0	0	0	0	0	0	0	1	1	0	1	0	0	0	0	0
S. AFRICA +RHOD.	2	0	0	0	0	0	0	0	0	0	0	0	0	1	1	0	0	0	0	0	0	0
AUSTRALIA + N.Z.	1	0	0	0	0	0	0	0	0	0	0	0	0	0	0	0	1	0	0	0	0	0
ASIA + OTHER AFRICA	2	0	0	0	0	0	0	0	0	0	0	0	0	0	0	0	0	0	0	2	0	0
JAPAN	2	0	0	0	0	0	0	0	0	0	0	0	0	0	0	0	0	0	0	2	0	0
OTHER ASIA+AFR.	0	0	0	0	0	0	0	0	0	0	0	0	0	0	0	0	0	0	0	0	0	0
BLACK AFRICA	0	0	0	0	0	0	0	0	0	0	0	0	0	0	0	0	0	0	0	0	0	0
ARAB WORLD	0	0	0	0	0	0	0	0	0	0	0	0	0	0	0	0	0	0	0	0	0	0
INDIA	0	0	0	0	0	0	0	0	0	0	0	0	0	0	0	0	0	0	0	0	0	0
PHILIPPINES	0	0	0	0	0	0	0	0	0	0	0	0	0	0	0	0	0	0	0	0	0	0
OTHER E. ASIA	0	0	0	0	0	0	0	0	0	0	0	0	0	0	0	0	0	0	0	0	0	0
OTHER ASIA	0	0	0	0	0	0	0	0	0	0	0	0	0	0	0	0	0	0	0	0	0	0

CHAPTER 3- THE PROLIFERATION OF FOREIGN SUBSIDIARIES
SECTION 2- THE FLOW OF MANUFACTURING BY INDUSTRY OF PARENT SYSTEM
TABLE 4- MANUFACTURING SUBSIDIARIES IN A SYSTEM IN THE
LUMBER, FURNITURE, AND PAPER INDUSTRIES (SIC 24,25,26)
CLASSIFIED BY COUNTRY OR REGION AND BY PERIOD MANUFACTURE BEGAN

COUNTRY OR REGION	PRE 1968	PRE 1901	1901 -13	1914 -19	1920 -24	1925 -29	1930 -34	1935 -39	1940 -45	1946 -50	1951 -53	1954 -55	1956 -57	1958 -59	1960 -61	1962	1963	1964	1965	1966	1967	UNK
OUTSIDE U.S.	182	0	0	1	0	3	5	2	6	2	0	18	15	15	24	5	32	12	18	12	9	3
OUT. U.S. + CANADA	149	0	0	0	0	2	3	0	3	1	0	10	11	15	19	5	31	11	16	12	9	1
OUT. WEST. HEMIS.	110	0	0	0	0	1	3	0	3	1	0	5	6	11	15	4	26	10	11	9	7	1
OUT. WHITE CWEALTH	94	0	0	0	0	2	2	0	0	0	0	7	8	14	11	4	9	9	14	11	4	1
OUT. DEVLPED WORLD	49	0	0	0	0	1	0	0	3	0	0	6	5	5	5	2	7	4	6	6	2	0
CANADA	33	0	0	1	0	1	2	2	3	1	0	8	4	0	5	0	1	1	2	2	0	1
LATIN AMERICA	39	0	0	0	0	1	0	3	3	0	0	5	5	4	4	1	5	1	5	3	2	0
C. AMER.+CARIB.	21	0	0	0	0	1	0	0	1	0	0	2	4	0	3	0	4	1	3	1	1	0
CUBA	10	0	0	0	0	1	0	0	0	0	0	2	0	0	0	0	0	0	0	1	0	0
MEXICO	10	0	0	0	0	0	0	0	1	0	0	0	0	0	1	0	1	0	0	0	1	0
OTHER	18	0	0	0	0	0	0	0	0	0	0	3	0	0	2	0	3	1	3	2	1	0
S. AMERICA	2	0	0	0	0	0	0	0	0	0	0	0	0	0	0	0	0	0	0	0	0	0
ARGENTINA	2	0	0	0	0	0	0	0	0	0	0	0	0	1	1	1	1	0	0	2	1	0
BRAZIL	1	0	0	0	0	0	0	0	1	0	0	0	0	0	0	0	0	0	0	0	1	0
PERU	0	0	0	0	0	0	0	0	0	0	0	0	0	0	0	0	0	0	0	0	0	0
COLOMBIA	4	0	0	0	0	0	0	0	0	0	0	0	0	1	1	0	1	0	1	0	0	0
VENEZUELA	9	0	0	0	0	0	0	0	2	0	0	0	0	2	1	1	1	0	1	0	1	0
OTHER	2	0	0	0	0	0	0	0	0	0	0	0	0	0	0	0	0	0	1	1	0	1
EUROPE	52	0	0	0	0	2	2	0	0	0	0	2	6	9	8	3	1	3	8	6	2	1
EFTA	10	0	0	0	0	0	0	0	0	0	0	1	3	0	3	1	0	0	0	2	0	0
U.K.	9	0	0	0	0	0	0	0	0	0	0	1	3	0	3	1	0	0	0	1	0	0
SCANDINAVIA	1	0	0	0	0	0	0	0	0	0	0	0	0	0	0	0	0	0	0	1	0	0
SWITZERLAND	0	0	0	0	0	0	0	0	0	0	0	0	0	0	0	0	0	0	0	0	0	0
OTHER EFTA	0	0	0	0	0	0	0	0	0	0	0	0	0	0	0	0	0	0	0	0	0	0
EUROP. COMMUNITY	33	0	0	0	0	2	2	0	0	0	0	1	3	9	5	3	1	3	2	3	0	0
FRANCE	10	0	0	0	0	1	1	0	0	0	0	0	2	2	0	1	1	2	0	0	1	0
GERMANY	6	0	0	0	0	1	1	0	0	0	0	1	1	3	1	0	0	0	0	2	1	0
ITALY	10	0	0	0	0	0	0	0	0	0	0	1	0	1	3	0	0	1	1	2	1	1
BELGIUM + LUX	5	0	0	0	0	0	1	0	0	0	0	0	0	1	0	1	0	0	5	0	0	0
NETHERLANDS	2	0	0	0	0	0	1	0	0	0	0	0	0	1	1	0	0	0	1	0	0	0
SPAIN	7	0	0	0	0	0	0	0	0	0	0	0	0	0	0	0	0	0	5	1	1	0
GREECE + TURKEY	1	0	0	0	0	0	0	0	0	0	0	0	0	0	0	0	0	0	0	0	0	0
OTHER EUROPE	1	0	0	0	0	0	0	0	0	0	0	0	0	0	0	0	0	0	0	0	1	0
EUROPE EX. U.K.	43	0	0	0	0	1	2	0	0	0	0	1	3	9	5	2	1	3	8	5	2	1
SOUTHERN DOMINIONS	46	0	0	0	0	1	0	0	0	1	0	2	0	1	5	0	22	7	2	0	5	0
S. AFRICA +RHOD.	33	0	0	0	0	0	0	0	0	0	0	1	0	0	1	0	22	5	1	0	3	0
AUSTRALIA + N.Z.	13	0	0	0	0	1	0	0	0	1	0	1	0	1	4	0	0	2	1	3	2	0
ASIA + OTHER AFRICA	12	0	0	0	0	1	0	0	0	0	0	1	0	0	2	1	3	0	1	0	0	0
JAPAN	2	0	0	0	0	0	0	0	0	0	0	1	0	1	1	0	1	0	0	0	0	0
OTHER ASIA+AFR.	10	0	0	0	0	1	0	0	0	0	0	0	0	0	1	0	2	0	1	3	0	0
BLACK AFRICA	2	0	0	0	0	0	0	0	0	0	0	0	0	0	0	0	0	0	1	0	0	0
ARAB WORLD	0	0	0	0	0	0	0	0	0	0	0	0	0	0	0	0	0	0	0	0	0	0
INDIA	1	0	0	0	0	0	0	0	0	0	0	0	0	0	1	0	0	0	0	0	0	0
PHILIPPINES	4	0	0	0	0	1	0	0	0	0	0	0	0	1	0	1	0	0	0	1	1	0
OTHER E. ASIA	0	0	0	0	0	0	0	0	0	0	0	0	0	0	0	0	0	0	0	0	0	0
OTHER ASIA	3	0	0	0	0	0	0	0	0	0	0	0	0	1	0	0	0	0	0	1	0	0

CHAPTER 3- THE PROLIFERATION OF FOREIGN SUBSIDIARIES
SECTION 2- THE FLOW OF MANUFACTURING BY INDUSTRY OF PARENT SYSTEM
TABLE 5- MANUFACTURING SUBSIDIARIES IN A SYSTEM IN THE
CHEMICAL INDUSTRIES (SIC 281(282,285-289)
CLASSIFIED BY COUNTRY OR REGION AND BY PERIOD MANUFACTURE BEGAN

COUNTRY OR REGION	PRE 1908	PRE 1901	1901 -13	1914 -19	1920 -24	1925 -29	1930 -34	1935 -39	1940 -45	1946 -50	1951 -53	1954 -55	1956 -57	1958 -59	1960 -61	1962	1963	1964	1965	1966	1967	UNK
OUTSIDE U.S.	813	2	6	11	16	31	15	18	18	44	45	38	42	60	102	57	37	51	66	59	34	61
OUT. U.S. + CANADA	682	1	1	3	11	18	12	14	10	33	35	33	34	55	94	56	32	41	61	52	32	54
OUT. WEST. HEMIS.	436	0	0	2	6	14	8	7	2	12	19	24	12	29	64	39	24	30	43	39	26	33
OUT. WHITE CMEALTH	540	1	1	2	8	12	7	9	9	26	30	21	29	44	74	48	25	30	51	40	28	45
OUT. DEVLPED WORLD	300	1	1	1	5	5	4	7	8	23	19	11	23	27	34	22	13	13	26	15	11	31
CANADA	131	1	5	8	5	13	3	4	8	11	10	5	8	5	8	1	5	10	5	7	2	7
LATIN AMERICA	246	1	1	1	5	4	1	7	8	21	16	9	22	26	30	17	8	8	18	13	6	21
C. AMER.+CARIB.	95	0	0	0	0	1	0	1	4	6	6	6	7	11	13	7	4	5	6	6	1	12
CUBA	1	0	0	0	0	0	0	0	0	0	0	0	1	0	0	0	0	0	0	0	0	0
MEXICO	72	0	1	0	0	0	0	0	4	6	6	5	5	8	11	5	3	5	5	4	0	9
OTHER	22	0	0	0	0	1	0	1	0	0	0	1	1	2	2	2	1	0	0	2	1	3
S. AMERICA	151	1	0	1	5	3	4	6	4	15	10	7	15	15	17	10	4	3	9	7	5	9
ARGENTINA	33	1	1	1	1	1	0	4	2	1	1	2	4	2	5	3	1	1	3	3	1	1
BRAZIL	41	0	0	0	0	1	0	0	1	6	5	2	3	4	5	3	0	0	0	6	1	2
PERU	14	1	1	0	0	0	0	0	0	1	0	0	0	1	1	1	1	1	4	0	2	3
COLOMBIA	25	0	0	0	0	0	0	0	0	4	2	1	5	5	2	2	2	2	1	0	1	1
VENEZUELA	16	0	0	0	0	1	0	0	0	2	2	2	1	2	2	1	0	0	0	0	1	0
OTHER	22	0	0	0	4	1	0	1	0	1	0	0	4	1	2	3	1	0	2	0	1	2
EUROPE	268	0	0	2	6	10	7	4	1	8	9	20	8	18	40	28	13	17	27	30	15	5
EFTA	83	0	0	2	3	5	4	2	0	5	2	11	3	3	6	6	9	5	8	9	1	1
U.K.	63	0	0	1	3	3	4	2	0	5	2	10	4	2	4	6	2	3	4	6	0	0
SCANDINAVIA	14	0	0	0	0	2	0	0	0	0	0	1	0	1	0	0	0	0	2	0	0	1
SWITZERLAND	3	0	0	0	0	0	0	0	0	0	0	0	0	0	0	0	0	0	1	1	1	0
OTHER EFTA	3	0	0	0	0	0	0	0	0	0	0	0	0	0	1	0	1	1	1	0	0	0
EUROP. COMMUNITY	146	0	0	0	2	5	3	2	0	2	5	7	4	15	22	18	8	10	15	13	10	4
FRANCE	35	0	0	1	1	1	1	1	0	1	2	1	1	2	5	3	2	2	5	8	3	1
GERMANY	34	0	0	0	1	2	1	1	0	0	2	3	1	4	3	6	2	3	5	2	1	0
ITALY	38	0	0	0	0	1	1	0	0	0	1	2	2	3	7	2	2	3	7	1	6	0
BELGIUM + LUX	20	0	0	0	0	1	1	1	0	1	0	0	0	1	3	1	0	0	1	1	0	3
NETHERLANDS	19	0	0	0	0	0	0	0	1	0	0	1	0	3	3	2	1	3	2	1	2	0
SPAIN	27	0	0	0	0	0	0	0	0	1	1	2	0	0	6	3	1	0	4	6	2	0
GREECE + TURKEY	6	0	0	0	0	0	0	0	0	1	0	0	0	0	1	0	0	1	0	1	2	0
OTHER EUROPE	6	0	0	0	0	0	0	0	1	0	1	0	0	0	0	1	2	1	0	1	1	0
EUROPE EX. U.K.	205	0	0	1	3	7	3	2	1	3	7	10	4	16	34	22	11	14	23	24	15	5
SOUTHERN DOMINIONS	74	0	0	0	0	3	1	3	1	2	3	2	1	9	14	2	3	7	6	5	3	9
S. AFRICA +RHOD.	13	0	0	0	0	0	0	2	0	1	1	0	0	0	1	0	1	2	1	1	0	4
AUSTRALIA + N.Z.	61	0	0	0	0	3	1	1	1	1	2	2	1	9	13	2	2	7	5	4	3	5
ASIA + OTHER AFRICA	94	0	0	0	0	1	0	0	0	2	7	2	3	2	10	9	8	9	4	10	4	19
JAPAN	40	0	0	0	0	1	0	1	0	2	2	1	1	2	6	4	5	5	1	5	2	9
OTHER ASIA+AFR.	54	0	0	0	0	1	0	0	0	2	5	1	2	1	4	5	5	3	0	8	0	10
BLACK AFRICA	7	0	0	0	0	0	0	0	0	0	0	0	0	0	0	1	0	0	1	0	0	2
ARAB WORLD	1	0	0	0	0	0	0	0	0	0	0	0	0	0	0	0	0	0	0	0	0	1
INDIA	12	0	0	0	0	1	0	0	0	0	1	1	2	0	2	2	1	1	0	1	1	1
PHILIPPINES	7	0	0	0	0	0	0	0	0	0	1	1	0	1	0	1	1	0	0	0	1	1
OTHER E. ASIA	9	0	0	0	0	0	0	0	0	0	0	0	1	0	1	1	1	1	0	1	0	1
OTHER ASIA	18	0	0	1	3	0	2	0	1	3	0	0	4	1	0	5	2	2	1	2	1	5

CHAPTER 3- THE PROLIFERATION OF FOREIGN SUBSIDIARIES
SECTION 2- THE FLOW OF MANUFACTURING BY INDUSTRY OF PARENT SYSTEM
TABLE 6- MANUFACTURING SUBSIDIARIES IN A SYSTEM IN THE
DRUG INDUSTRY (SIC 283)
CLASSIFIED BY COUNTRY OR REGION AND BY PERIOD MANUFACTURE BEGAN

COUNTRY OR REGION	PRE 1968	PRE 1901	1901-13	1914-19	1920-24	1925-29	1930-34	1935-39	1940-42	1946-50	1951-53	1954-55	1956-57	1958-59	1960-61	1962	1963	1964	1965	1966	1967	UNK
OUTSIDE U.S.	473	0	1	1	5	11	19	24	23	30	27	25	39	49	56	26	31	34	29	17	23	3
OUT. U.S. + CANADA	425	0	0	1	3	9	15	19	16	25	24	22	37	47	56	26	30	32	25	16	19	3
OUT. WEST. HEMIS.	296	0	0	0	3	8	14	14	4	14	12	14	25	33	41	20	23	24	18	11	16	2
OUT. WHITE CWEALTH	305	0	1	1	2	3	1	7	12	17	18	18	22	39	44	18	23	28	24	13	16	1
OUT. DEVLPED WORLD	175	0	0	1	0	1	1	5	12	14	14	9	15	22	22	10	10	15	10	8	5	1
CANADA	48	0	1	0	2	2	4	5	7	5	3	3	2	2	0	0	1	2	4	1	4	0
LATIN AMERICA	129	0	1	1	0	0	1	2	12	11	12	8	12	14	15	6	7	8	7	5	3	1
C. AMER.+CARIB.	57	0	0	1	0	0	1	2	4	4	1	2	8	8	4	0	3	7	4	2	0	1
CUBA	1	0	0	0	0	0	0	0	0	0	0	0	0	0	0	0	0	0	0	0	0	0
MEXICO	33	0	0	0	0	0	1	0	1	3	4	1	3	5	3	0	2	4	2	2	1	1
OTHER	23	0	0	0	0	0	0	2	1	1	7	0	5	3	1	0	1	3	0	2	0	0
S. AMERICA	72	0	0	0	0	1	0	0	10	7	7	6	5	6	11	6	4	1	3	3	3	0
ARGENTINA	15	0	0	0	0	0	0	3	4	0	1	1	4	1	1	2	1	3	0	0	0	0
BRAZIL	21	0	0	0	0	0	0	2	1	5	3	3	1	3	10	4	0	0	1	0	0	0
PERU	7	0	0	0	0	0	0	0	1	0	1	2	1	0	2	2	2	0	1	1	0	0
COLOMBIA	9	0	0	0	0	0	0	0	1	1	0	0	1	0	2	1	2	0	1	2	0	0
VENEZUELA	10	0	0	0	0	0	0	0	1	0	1	0	0	1	7	1	2	0	1	0	0	0
OTHER	10	0	0	0	0	0	0	0	2	1	2	1	0	1	0	1	0	1	0	0	0	0
EUROPE	181	0	0	0	3	8	7	6	0	9	7	8	14	19	25	13	17	13	13	4	13	2
EFTA	72	0	0	0	1	6	7	5	0	6	4	2	7	3	6	7	5	2	1	0	3	2
U.K.	60	0	0	0	1	6	7	4	0	6	3	1	7	2	5	5	5	1	1	0	3	2
SCANDINAVIA	4	0	0	0	0	0	0	0	0	0	0	1	0	0	1	1	1	0	1	0	0	0
SWITZERLAND	2	0	0	0	0	0	0	0	0	0	0	0	0	0	0	0	0	0	0	0	0	0
OTHER EFTA	6	0	0	0	0	0	0	1	0	0	3	0	0	0	1	0	1	0	0	2	0	0
EUROP. COMMUNITY	92	0	0	0	2	2	0	0	0	3	3	6	6	12	16	5	9	9	8	2	0	0
FRANCE	29	0	0	0	1	1	0	0	0	2	0	1	1	4	4	1	3	2	1	2	2	0
GERMANY	21	0	0	0	1	1	0	0	0	0	0	2	0	2	5	1	1	3	1	1	1	0
ITALY	24	0	0	0	0	0	0	0	0	1	3	4	4	4	3	2	2	3	4	1	0	0
BELGIUM + LUX	10	0	0	0	0	1	0	0	0	0	0	0	0	2	1	1	1	1	1	0	1	0
NETHERLANDS	8	0	0	0	0	0	0	1	0	1	3	1	1	1	1	0	2	0	1	0	0	0
SPAIN	10	0	0	0	0	0	0	0	0	0	0	0	0	0	2	1	1	1	0	2	2	0
GREECE + TURKEY	6	0	0	0	0	0	0	0	0	0	0	0	0	0	2	0	0	0	1	0	0	0
OTHER EUROPE	1	0	0	0	0	0	0	0	0	0	0	0	0	0	0	0	0	0	0	0	0	0
EUROPE EX. U.K.	121	0	0	0	2	2	0	2	0	3	4	7	7	17	20	7	12	12	12	4	10	0
SOUTHERN DOMINIONS	59	0	0	0	0	0	7	8	4	2	3	3	7	6	7	2	3	3	0	3	1	0
S. AFRICA +RHOD.	22	0	0	0	0	0	3	2	1	1	2	1	3	2	0	1	1	1	0	1	0	0
AUSTRALIA + N.Z.	37	0	0	0	0	0	4	6	3	1	1	2	4	4	7	1	2	2	0	2	1	0
ASIA + OTHER AFRICA	56	0	0	0	0	0	0	0	1	3	2	3	4	8	9	5	3	8	5	4	2	0
JAPAN	10	0	0	0	0	0	0	0	0	0	0	1	0	0	2	1	0	1	3	3	0	0
OTHER ASIA+AFR.	46	0	0	0	0	0	0	0	0	3	2	2	3	8	7	4	3	7	2	0	2	0
BLACK AFRICA	8	0	0	0	0	0	0	0	0	0	0	0	0	0	0	0	1	0	2	0	1	0
ARAB WORLD	3	0	0	0	0	0	0	0	0	0	0	0	0	0	0	0	0	1	0	0	0	0
INDIA	7	0	0	0	0	0	0	0	1	1	2	0	0	3	1	1	1	1	0	0	0	0
PHILIPPINES	8	0	0	0	0	0	0	0	1	0	0	0	0	2	0	1	0	0	1	1	0	0
OTHER E. ASIA	2	0	0	0	0	0	0	0	0	0	0	0	0	0	1	0	0	0	1	1	0	0
OTHER ASIA	18	0	0	0	0	0	0	0	0	1	0	1	1	3	5	3	1	1	1	1	1	0

PERIOD

CHAPTER 3- THE PROLIFERATION OF FOREIGN SUBSIDIARIES
SECTION 2- THE FLOW OF MANUFACTURING BY INDUSTRY OF PARENT SYSTEM
TABLE 7- MANUFACTURING SUBSIDIARIES IN A SYSTEM IN THE
SOAP AND COSMETICS INDUSTRY (SIC 284)
CLASSIFIED BY COUNTRY OR REGION AND BY PERIOD MANUFACTURE BEGAN

COUNTRY OR REGION	PRE 1898	PRE 1901 -13	1914 -19	1920 -24	1925 -29	1930 -34	1935 -39	1940 -45	1946 -50	1951 -53	1954 -55	1956 -57	1958 -59	1960 -61	1962	1963	1964	1965	1966	1967	UNK
OUTSIDE U.S.	129	0	2	2	7	1	8	2	6	1	7	9	14	24	9	10	7	8	2	8	2
OUT. U.S. + CANADA	112	0	0	1	6	1	7	2	6	1	5	7	14	19	8	10	6	7	2	8	2
OUT. WEST. HEMIS.	82	0	0	1	4	1	4	0	4	0	3	3	11	16	8	9	6	4	2	4	2
OUT. WHITE CWEALTH	91	0	0	1	5	0	4	2	3	1	4	7	11	14	7	8	6	7	2	8	1
OUT. DEVLPED WORLD	56	0	0	0	2	0	4	2	3	1	2	5	6	8	3	4	4	6	1	5	0
CANADA	17	0	2	1	1	0	1	0	0	0	2	2	0	5	1	0	1	1	0	0	1
LATIN AMERICA	30	0	0	0	2	0	3	2	2	0	2	4	3	3	1	1	3	3	0	4	0
C. AMER.+CARIB.	16	0	0	0	1	0	2	1	1	0	1	4	2	1	1	0	2	2	0	1	0
CUBA	5	0	0	0	1	0	2	1	0	0	0	0	0	0	0	0	0	0	0	0	0
MEXICO	7	0	0	0	0	0	0	0	1	1	0	3	1	1	0	1	0	2	0	1	0
OTHER	4	0	0	0	1	0	1	0	0	0	1	1	1	0	1	0	0	0	0	0	0
S. AMERICA	14	0	0	0	1	0	1	1	1	0	2	0	1	2	1	1	1	1	0	3	0
ARGENTINA	5	0	0	0	0	0	1	1	0	0	0	0	0	1	1	0	0	0	0	0	0
BRAZIL	2	0	0	0	1	0	0	0	0	0	0	1	0	1	1	0	1	1	0	3	0
PERU	3	0	0	0	0	0	1	1	0	0	0	0	1	0	0	0	0	0	0	0	0
COLOMBIA	0	0	0	0	1	0	1	0	0	0	1	0	0	0	0	0	0	1	0	0	0
VENEZUELA	3	0	0	0	0	0	0	0	0	0	0	0	0	0	0	0	0	0	0	1	0
OTHER	1	0	0	0	0	0	0	0	0	0	0	0	0	0	0	0	0	0	0	1	0
EUROPE	44	0	0	1	4	1	2	0	3	0	2	2	5	7	5	4	2	1	1	3	1
EFTA	16	0	0	0	1	1	2	0	3	0	2	0	2	2	2	0	1	1	0	1	0
U.K.	10	0	0	0	1	1	2	0	3	0	2	0	0	2	1	0	0	0	0	1	0
SCANDINAVIA	4	0	0	0	0	0	0	0	0	0	0	0	0	0	1	0	1	0	0	0	0
SWITZERLAND	0	0	0	0	0	0	0	0	0	0	0	0	0	2	0	0	0	0	0	0	0
OTHER EFTA	2	0	0	0	0	0	0	0	0	0	0	0	0	0	0	0	0	0	0	0	0
EUROP. COMMUNITY	22	0	0	0	3	0	0	0	0	0	2	0	3	3	2	3	0	0	0	0	0
FRANCE	9	0	0	1	1	0	0	0	0	0	1	0	1	1	2	2	0	0	0	2	0
GERMANY	4	0	0	0	0	0	0	0	0	0	0	0	0	2	0	0	0	0	0	0	1
ITALY	6	0	0	0	1	0	0	0	0	0	0	0	1	0	1	1	1	0	0	0	0
BELGIUM + LUX	3	0	0	0	1	0	0	0	0	0	0	1	1	0	0	0	0	0	0	0	0
NETHERLANDS	0	0	0	0	0	0	0	0	0	0	0	0	0	0	0	0	0	0	0	0	0
SPAIN	2	0	0	0	0	0	0	0	0	0	0	0	1	0	1	0	0	0	0	2	0
GREECE + TURKEY	2	0	0	0	0	0	0	0	0	0	0	0	1	1	0	0	0	0	0	0	0
OTHER EUROPE	2	0	0	0	0	0	0	0	0	0	2	0	0	1	4	1	0	1	1	3	1
EUROPE EX. U.K.	34	0	0	1	3	0	0	0	0	0	2	2	5	5	4	4	2	1	1	3	1
SOUTHERN DOMINIONS	9	0	0	0	0	0	1	0	0	0	1	0	3	2	0	1	0	0	0	0	0
S. AFRICA +RHOD.	4	0	0	0	0	0	0	0	0	0	0	0	2	1	0	1	0	0	0	0	0
AUSTRALIA + N.Z.	5	0	0	0	0	0	1	0	0	0	1	0	1	1	0	0	0	0	0	0	0
ASIA + OTHER AFRICA	29	0	0	0	0	0	1	0	1	0	0	0	3	7	3	4	4	3	1	1	0
JAPAN	3	0	0	0	0	0	0	0	0	0	0	0	0	2	0	0	0	0	0	1	0
OTHER ASIA+AFR.	26	0	0	0	0	0	1	0	1	0	0	0	3	5	3	4	3	3	1	1	0
BLACK AFRICA	4	0	0	0	0	0	0	0	0	0	0	0	0	1	0	0	0	0	0	0	0
ARAB WORLD	3	0	0	0	0	0	0	0	0	0	0	0	2	0	0	0	0	0	0	0	0
INDIA	2	0	0	0	0	0	0	0	1	0	0	1	0	0	0	2	0	2	0	0	0
PHILIPPINES	2	0	0	0	0	0	1	0	0	0	0	0	0	0	0	0	0	0	0	0	0
OTHER E. ASIA	6	0	0	0	0	0	0	0	0	0	0	0	0	2	1	0	2	0	1	0	0
OTHER ASIA	9	0	0	0	0	0	0	0	0	0	2	0	1	2	1	2	1	1	1	3	0

CHAPTER 3- THE PROLIFERATION OF FOREIGN SUBSIDIARIES
SECTION 2- THE FLOW OF MANUFACTURING BY INDUSTRY OF PARENT SYSTEM
TABLE 8- THE FLOW OF MANUFACTURING SUBSIDIARIES IN A SYSTEM IN THE
PETROLEUM INDUSTRY (SIC 291)
CLASSIFIED BY COUNTRY OR REGION AND BY PERIOD MANUFACTURE BEGAN

COUNTRY OR REGION	PRE 1968	PRE 1901	1901-13	1914-19	1920-24	1925-29	1930-34	1935-39	1940-45	1946-50	1951-53	1954-55	1956-57	1958-59	1960-61	1962-63	1964	1965	1966	1967	UNK
OUTSIDE U.S.	367	8	4	15	14	8	17	12	7	7	23	6	15	18	20	21	29	31	25	18	10
OUT. U.S. + CANADA	336	8	1	14	12	6	14	10	6	5	23	6	13	17	18	19	27	30	25	18	7
OUT. WEST. HEMIS.	257	5	0	10	9	4	11	5	5	5	20	4	8	10	14	16	23	23	18	16	7
OUT. WHITE CWEALTH	270	7	1	10	10	5	12	9	5	5	16	3	12	14	12	17	20	27	22	15	5
OUT. DEVLPED WORLD	124	3	1	5	4	3	5	6	2	2	3	3	6	8	6	10	6	12	9	5	2
CANADA	31	0	3	1	2	2	3	2	2	1	0	0	2	1	1	2	2	1	0	0	3
LATIN AMERICA	79	3	1	4	3	2	3	3	5	0	3	2	5	7	4	3	4	7	7	2	0
C. AMER.+CARIB.	32	2	2	3	1	1	3	1	3	0	0	0	1	2	2	1	1	2	1	1	0
CUBA	4	0	1	0	0	0	0	0	0	0	0	0	0	1	0	0	0	0	0	0	0
MEXICO	9	2	0	0	1	1	3	1	0	0	0	0	1	0	0	0	1	0	0	0	0
OTHER	19	0	1	0	0	1	0	0	1	0	0	0	0	1	2	1	0	1	1	1	0
S. AMERICA	47	1	0	4	1	1	3	2	1	0	3	2	3	2	2	3	3	5	6	1	0
ARGENTINA	7	0	0	1	0	0	0	0	0	0	0	0	0	1	0	0	0	2	0	1	0
BRAZIL	8	0	0	0	0	1	1	1	0	0	0	0	1	0	0	1	1	0	4	1	0
PERU	2	0	0	0	1	0	0	0	0	0	0	0	0	0	0	0	0	1	0	0	0
COLOMBIA	8	0	0	1	0	0	0	0	0	1	1	0	0	0	1	1	1	1	0	0	0
VENEZUELA	18	0	0	2	0	0	1	0	1	0	2	1	0	2	1	1	1	0	2	0	0
OTHER	4	0	0	0	0	0	0	0	0	0	0	0	1	0	1	0	1	0	0	0	0
EUROPE	168	5	0	9	7	3	9	4	4	4	12	3	7	6	10	8	15	15	14	9	1
EFTA	52	4	0	5	1	1	6	2	1	1	3	2	1	2	4	2	9	4	0	4	0
U.K.	30	1	0	4	1	1	2	1	1	0	2	1	1	1	3	2	5	1	0	2	0
SCANDINAVIA	16	3	0	0	0	0	1	1	0	0	0	0	0	0	1	0	0	0	0	2	0
SWITZERLAND	2	0	0	0	0	0	0	0	0	0	0	0	0	0	0	0	0	0	0	0	0
OTHER EFTA	4	0	0	1	0	0	0	0	0	0	0	0	0	0	1	0	0	0	0	0	1
EUROP. COMMUNITY	89	0	0	0	4	2	2	2	3	3	6	2	5	4	16	5	4	9	11	11	1
FRANCE	19	0	0	0	1	1	2	2	1	1	1	1	1	1	2	2	0	2	1	1	0
GERMANY	28	0	0	0	2	0	3	2	0	0	1	1	3	0	3	0	2	5	6	1	0
ITALY	23	0	0	0	0	1	1	0	0	1	4	0	0	1	7	0	2	0	1	1	1
BELGIUM + LUX	11	0	0	0	1	0	0	0	1	0	0	0	0	2	1	3	2	1	2	1	0
NETHERLANDS	16	0	0	0	0	0	0	0	1	1	2	0	1	0	3	1	1	1	1	1	0
SPAIN	3	0	0	0	0	0	0	0	0	0	0	0	0	0	0	0	0	0	2	2	0
GREECE + TURKEY	8	1	0	3	1	1	1	0	0	0	2	0	0	0	0	1	0	1	0	0	0
OTHER EUROPE	8	0	1	1	1	0	1	1	1	0	0	0	0	0	0	0	0	1	0	1	1
EUROPE EX. U.K.	138	4	0	5	6	2	7	3	3	3	10	2	6	6	17	6	11	14	14	7	1
SOUTHERN DOMINIONS	27	0	0	0	1	0	0	0	0	0	0	1	0	3	7	2	3	1	2	1	2
S. AFRICA +RHOD.	4	0	0	0	0	0	0	0	0	0	0	0	0	1	0	1	1	0	2	0	1
AUSTRALIA + N.Z.	23	0	0	1	1	1	2	0	0	0	4	1	1	1	7	1	2	1	2	1	1
ASIA + OTHER AFRICA	62	0	0	0	0	1	1	2	1	1	4	2	5	1	14	8	5	7	2	6	4
JAPAN	17	0	0	0	0	0	2	0	0	0	0	0	1	0	12	1	3	2	3	0	2
OTHER ASIA+AFR.	45	0	0	0	2	0	2	2	1	1	4	1	3	1	4	7	2	5	2	3	2
BLACK AFRICA	4	0	0	0	0	0	0	0	0	0	0	0	0	0	2	1	1	0	0	1	0
ARAB WORLD	12	0	0	0	0	0	0	0	1	0	0	1	0	1	1	0	3	1	1	0	1
INDIA	6	0	0	0	0	0	0	0	0	0	2	0	0	0	0	1	0	0	0	0	0
PHILIPPINES	5	0	0	0	0	0	0	0	0	1	1	0	1	1	1	1	0	1	1	1	0
OTHER E. ASIA	5	0	0	0	1	1	0	0	0	0	0	0	0	0	0	0	0	0	0	0	1
OTHER ASIA	13	0	0	1	2	0	0	2	1	0	1	0	0	0	4	1	1	0	0	1	1

CHAPTER 3- THE PROLIFERATION OF FOREIGN SUBSIDIARIES
SECTION 2- THE FLOW OF MANUFACTURING BY INDUSTRY OF PARENT SYSTEM
TABLE 9- MANUFACTURING SUBSIDIARIES IN A SYSTEM IN THE
RUBBER AND TIRE INDUSTRY (SIC 30)
CLASSIFIED BY COUNTRY OR REGION AND BY PERIOD MANUFACTURE BEGAN

PERIOD

COUNTRY OR REGION	PRE 1908	PRE 1901	1901 -13	1914 -19	1920 -24	1925 -29	1930 -34	1935 -39	1940 -45	1946 -50	1951 -53	1954 -55	1956 -57	1958 -59	1960 -61	1962	1963	1964	1965	1966	1967	UNK
OUTSIDE U.S.	163	0	2	6	4	5	13	13	15	13	11	10	3	13	11	11	10	5	8	6	3	1
OUT. U.S. + CANADA	145	0	0	5	3	3	10	12	15	13	10	8	3	13	11	10	10	4	6	5	3	1
OUT. WEST. HEMIS.	100	0	0	5	3	3	5	8	15	7	6	8	1	11	9	8	9	4	4	4	3	1
OUT. WHITE CWEALTH	120	0	0	5	2	0	8	10	12	11	10	8	2	12	9	7	8	4	5	4	3	0
OUT. DEVLPED WORLD	71	0	0	4	0	0	6	7	11	7	4	5	2	5	3	5	2	3	3	2	2	0
CANADA	18	0	2	1	1	1	3	1	0	0	0	1	0	0	2	1	0	1	2	1	0	0
LATIN AMERICA	45	0	0	1	0	2	5	4	10	6	4	2	2	2	2	1	2	0	2	0	1	0
C. AMER.+CARIB.	18	0	0	0	0	0	3	1	4	2	1	2	0	1	0	0	0	0	0	0	0	0
CUBA	4	0	0	0	0	0	0	0	2	2	1	0	1	1	0	0	0	0	0	0	0	0
MEXICO	10	0	0	0	0	0	3	1	4	2	1	2	0	1	0	0	0	0	0	0	0	0
OTHER	4	0	0	0	0	0	0	0	2	0	0	0	1	0	0	0	0	0	0	0	0	0
S. AMERICA	27	0	0	0	0	0	2	3	6	4	3	2	0	1	2	2	2	0	2	0	0	0
ARGENTINA	6	0	0	0	0	0	2	2	0	2	0	1	0	1	0	0	0	0	0	0	0	0
BRAZIL	6	0	0	0	0	0	2	2	1	0	3	0	1	0	0	0	0	0	0	0	0	0
PERU	2	0	0	0	0	0	0	0	3	0	0	0	0	0	0	0	0	0	0	0	0	0
COLUMBIA	4	0	0	0	0	0	0	0	1	1	0	0	1	0	0	0	0	0	0	0	0	0
VENEZUELA	7	0	0	0	0	0	0	1	2	2	0	0	0	0	0	0	0	0	0	1	1	0
OTHER	2	0	0	0	0	0	0	1	0	0	0	0	0	1	1	0	0	0	0	0	0	0
EUROPE	56	0	0	0	3	2	4	3	2	5	5	3	1	7	6	5	4	2	2	2	1	0
EFTA	22	0	0	0	2	2	2	2	1	1	1	0	1	1	3	3	0	1	1	0	0	0
U.K.	12	0	0	0	1	2	2	0	0	1	0	0	1	0	1	0	0	0	0	0	0	0
SCANDINAVIA	3	0	0	0	0	0	0	0	0	0	0	0	0	0	1	0	0	0	0	0	0	0
SWITZERLAND	3	0	0	0	0	0	1	1	1	0	0	0	0	0	1	0	1	0	1	2	0	0
OTHER EFTA	4	0	0	0	1	0	1	0	0	0	1	0	0	1	0	0	0	0	0	0	0	0
EUROP. COMMUNITY	26	0	0	0	1	1	1	1	0	4	2	3	0	6	2	1	3	1	0	0	0	0
FRANCE	6	0	0	0	0	0	0	0	0	0	1	1	0	2	0	0	0	0	0	0	0	0
GERMANY	7	0	0	0	0	1	1	0	0	1	0	1	0	0	1	0	3	1	0	0	0	0
ITALY	6	0	0	0	1	0	0	0	0	0	1	1	1	2	0	1	0	1	2	0	0	0
BELGIUM + LUX	3	0	0	0	0	0	0	0	0	1	0	0	0	0	0	0	1	0	0	0	0	0
NETHERLANDS	4	0	0	0	0	0	0	0	0	2	0	0	0	1	1	0	0	0	0	0	1	0
SPAIN	4	0	0	0	0	0	0	0	0	0	2	1	0	1	1	1	1	0	0	0	0	0
GREECE + TURKEY	3	0	0	0	0	0	0	0	0	0	0	0	0	0	0	0	0	1	0	0	0	0
OTHER EUROPE	1	0	0	0	0	0	1	1	0	1	0	0	0	0	1	0	0	0	0	0	0	0
EUROPE EX. U.K.	44	0	0	0	2	2	2	3	1	4	5	3	0	7	5	2	4	2	2	2	1	0
SOUTHERN DOMINIONS	15	0	0	0	0	0	0	2	2	1	1	0	0	1	1	0	0	0	1	1	0	1
S. AFRICA +RHOD.	5	0	0	0	0	0	1	1	1	1	1	0	0	0	1	0	0	0	0	1	0	1
AUSTRALIA + N.Z.	8	0	0	5	0	0	3	1	1	0	0	0	1	3	2	3	3	0	1	0	0	0
ASIA + OTHER AFRICA	31	0	0	1	0	1	0	1	1	1	1	1	0	2	2	3	3	3	2	2	1	0
JAPAN	5	0	0	0	0	0	0	0	0	0	0	0	0	0	1	0	0	0	0	0	0	0
OTHER ASIA+AFR.	26	0	0	0	0	0	3	0	1	1	0	1	0	3	3	3	3	2	2	2	1	0
BLACK AFRICA	3	0	0	0	0	0	0	0	0	0	0	1	0	0	1	1	2	0	0	0	0	0
ARAB WORLD	2	0	0	0	0	0	0	0	0	0	0	0	0	1	1	0	0	0	0	0	0	0
INDIA	4	0	0	0	0	0	1	1	1	1	1	0	0	1	0	0	0	1	1	0	0	0
PHILIPPINES	3	0	0	0	0	0	0	0	0	0	0	0	0	0	0	0	0	1	0	1	0	0
OTHER E. ASIA	0	0	0	0	0	0	0	0	0	0	0	0	0	0	0	0	0	0	0	0	0	0
OTHER ASIA	14	0	0	4	0	1	1	1	0	1	0	1	0	1	2	2	0	0	0	0	0	0

CHAPTER 3- THE PROLIFERATION OF FOREIGN SUBSIDIARIES
SECTION 2- THE FLOW OF MANUFACTURING BY INDUSTRY OF PARENT SYSTEM
TABLE 10- MANUFACTURING SUBSIDIARIES IN A SYSTEM IN THE
STONE, CLAY, AND GLASS INDUSTRY (SIC 32)
CLASSIFIED BY COUNTRY OR REGION AND BY PERIOD MANUFACTURE BEGAN

PERIOD

COUNTRY OR REGION	PRE 1968	PRE 1901	1901 -13	1914 -19	1920 -24	1925 -29	1930 -34	1935 -39	1940 -45	1946 -50	1951 -53	1954 -55	1956 -57	1958 -59	1960 -61	1962	1963	1964	1965	1966	1967	UNK
OUTSIDE U.S.	175	0	4	2	1	7	1	5	9	8	14	7	8	13	15	9	16	6	19	15	12	4
OUT. U.S. + CANADA	157	0	4	0	1	5	1	4	7	6	11	6	8	12	15	9	16	6	19	13	11	3
OUT. WEST. HEMIS.	108	0	4	0	1	4	1	4	0	3	3	3	1	10	12	7	6	5	16	13	7	2
OUT. WHITE CWEALTH	119	0	3	0	1	4	0	2	2	5	8	4	8	7	12	8	13	5	12	9	8	3
OUT. DEVLPED WORLD	54	0	0	0	0	1	0	0	7	3	6	4	7	2	3	3	6	2	4	0	4	2
CANADA	18	0	0	2	0	2	0	1	2	2	3	1	0	1	0	0	0	0	0	0	1	1
LATIN AMERICA	49	0	0	0	0	1	0	7	7	3	6	3	7	2	3	6	6	1	3	2	4	1
C. AMER.+CARIB.	14	0	0	0	0	0	0	1	1	1	3	0	2	0	1	0	0	0	1	0	3	0
CUBA	1	0	0	0	0	0	0	0	0	0	0	0	1	0	0	0	0	0	0	0	0	0
MEXICO	13	0	0	0	0	0	0	0	0	1	3	0	1	0	1	0	0	0	1	0	3	0
OTHER	0	0	0	0	0	0	0	0	1	0	0	0	0	0	0	0	0	0	0	0	0	0
S. AMERICA	35	0	0	0	0	1	0	6	6	2	3	3	5	2	2	6	6	1	2	0	3	1
ARGENTINA	6	0	0	0	0	0	0	1	1	0	1	3	1	1	1	1	1	0	1	0	0	0
BRAZIL	13	0	0	0	0	1	0	3	3	0	3	1	1	0	1	1	0	3	0	0	3	1
PERU	1	0	0	0	0	0	0	0	0	0	0	0	0	0	0	0	0	0	1	0	0	0
COLOMBIA	6	0	0	0	0	0	0	0	0	1	1	0	2	1	0	0	3	0	0	0	0	0
VENEZUELA	6	0	0	0	0	1	0	0	1	0	0	1	0	0	1	3	0	0	1	0	1	0
OTHER	3	0	0	0	0	0	0	2	0	1	0	0	0	0	0	1	0	0	0	0	0	0
EUROPE	78	0	4	2	1	4	1	2	0	2	4	2	0	7	8	4	10	4	14	5	5	1
EFTA	26	0	1	0	1	2	1	0	0	0	1	2	0	2	1	2	2	2	7	2	1	0
U.K.	23	0	1	0	1	2	1	0	0	0	1	2	0	2	1	1	2	1	7	2	1	0
SCANDINAVIA	3	0	1	0	0	1	0	0	0	0	0	0	0	0	0	1	0	0	0	0	0	0
SWITZERLAND	0	0	0	0	0	0	0	0	0	0	0	0	0	0	0	0	0	1	0	0	0	0
OTHER EFTA	0	0	0	0	0	0	0	0	0	0	0	0	0	0	0	0	0	0	0	0	0	0
EUROP. COMMUNITY	45	0	3	0	1	2	0	2	2	2	2	0	0	5	7	2	7	2	6	1	2	1
FRANCE	15	0	0	0	1	1	0	0	1	1	1	0	0	2	2	1	3	0	1	1	1	1
GERMANY	9	0	2	0	0	0	0	0	0	0	0	0	0	2	1	0	2	1	1	1	0	0
ITALY	10	0	0	0	0	2	1	1	1	1	1	0	0	1	2	1	2	1	4	0	1	0
BELGIUM + LUX	9	0	1	0	1	0	0	0	0	0	0	0	0	0	1	0	1	1	0	0	0	0
NETHERLANDS	2	0	0	0	0	0	0	0	0	0	0	0	0	1	0	0	1	0	0	1	1	0
SPAIN	4	0	0	0	0	0	0	0	0	0	0	0	0	0	0	0	0	0	1	0	2	1
GREECE + TURKEY	0	0	0	0	0	0	0	0	0	0	0	0	0	0	0	0	0	0	0	1	0	0
OTHER EUROPE	3	0	0	0	0	0	0	0	0	1	0	0	0	0	0	0	0	0	0	1	0	0
EUROPE EX. U.K.	55	0	3	0	3	2	0	2	0	2	3	0	0	5	7	3	8	3	7	3	4	1
SOUTHERN DOMINIONS	13	0	0	0	0	2	0	2	1	1	1	0	0	3	2	0	0	0	0	2	2	0
S. AFRICA +RHOD.	6	0	0	0	0	0	0	0	1	1	1	0	0	1	1	1	0	1	2	0	0	0
AUSTRALIA + N.Z.	7	0	0	0	0	2	0	2	0	0	0	0	1	2	2	1	0	1	1	0	2	0
ASIA + OTHER AFRICA	17	0	0	0	0	0	0	0	0	0	0	0	0	0	0	0	0	0	2	6	2	0
JAPAN	12	0	0	0	0	0	0	0	0	0	0	0	1	0	0	0	0	1	1	6	0	0
OTHER ASIA+AFR.	5	0	0	0	0	0	0	0	0	0	0	0	0	0	0	0	0	0	1	0	0	0
BLACK AFRICA	1	0	0	0	0	0	0	0	0	0	0	0	0	0	0	0	0	0	0	0	0	0
ARAB WORLD	0	0	0	0	0	0	0	0	0	0	0	0	0	0	0	0	0	0	0	0	0	0
INDIA	3	0	0	0	0	0	0	0	0	0	0	0	0	0	1	0	0	0	0	0	1	0
PHILIPPINES	0	0	0	0	0	0	0	0	0	0	0	0	0	0	0	0	0	0	0	0	0	0
OTHER E. ASIA	1	0	0	0	0	0	0	0	0	0	0	0	0	0	0	0	1	0	1	0	0	0
OTHER ASIA	0	0	0	0	0	0	0	0	0	0	0	0	0	0	0	0	0	0	0	0	0	0

CHAPTER 3- THE PROLIFERATION OF FOREIGN SUBSIDIARIES
SECTION 2- THE FLOW OF MANUFACTURING BY INDUSTRY OF PARENT SYSTEM
TABLE 11- MANUFACTURING SUBSIDIARIES IN A SYSTEM IN THE
PRIMARY METAL INDUSTRY (SIC 33)
CLASSIFIED BY COUNTRY OR REGION AND BY PERIOD MANUFACTURE BEGAN

COUNTRY OR REGION	PRE 1968	PRE 1901	1901 -13	1914 -19	1920 -24	1925 -29	1930 -34	1935 -39	1940 -45	1946 -50	1951 -53	1954 -55	1956 -57	1958 -59	1960 -61	1962	1963	1964	1965	1966	1967	UNK
OUTSIDE U.S.	176	1	2	0	1	1	3	15	1	5	4	8	12	24	31	11	13	12	13	8	11	0
OUT. U.S. + CANADA	148	1	1	0	1	0	3	10	1	5	3	4	11	21	25	9	12	10	12	8	11	0
OUT. WEST. HEMIS.	96	1	0	0	0	0	2	5	0	3	2	3	4	13	17	6	11	8	8	7	8	0
OUT. WHITE CWEALTH	106	1	1	0	1	0	1	6	1	4	2	4	10	15	18	8	6	9	7	7	5	0
OUT. DEVLPED WORLD	65	0	1	0	1	0	1	5	1	4	1	4	8	9	10	3	2	3	5	2	5	0
CANADA	28	0	1	0	0	1	0	5	0	5	1	4	1	3	6	2	1	2	1	0	0	0
LATIN AMERICA	52	0	1	0	1	1	1	5	1	4	1	1	7	8	8	3	1	2	4	1	3	0
C. AMER.+CARIB.	23	0	1	0	0	0	0	3	0	3	0	0	2	5	2	2	0	0	1	0	0	0
CUBA	3	0	0	0	0	0	0	1	0	0	0	0	0	0	0	0	0	0	0	0	0	0
MEXICO	17	0	1	0	0	0	1	2	0	3	0	0	2	5	2	1	0	0	1	0	1	0
OTHER	3	0	0	0	0	0	0	0	0	0	0	0	0	0	0	1	0	0	0	1	0	0
S. AMERICA	29	0	0	0	1	1	1	2	1	1	1	1	5	3	6	1	1	2	3	1	3	0
ARGENTINA	2	0	0	0	0	0	0	1	0	0	0	0	0	0	0	0	0	0	0	0	0	0
BRAZIL	3	0	0	0	0	0	0	0	1	0	0	0	0	1	0	0	0	0	1	0	0	0
PERU	3	0	0	0	0	0	0	0	0	0	1	1	1	0	0	0	0	0	0	0	0	0
COLOMBIA	9	0	0	0	1	0	1	0	0	0	0	0	0	1	3	1	1	1	0	0	0	0
VENEZUELA	8	0	0	0	0	0	0	1	0	0	0	0	3	1	2	1	0	0	1	0	1	0
OTHER	4	0	0	0	0	0	0	0	0	1	0	1	0	0	1	0	0	0	0	0	0	0
EUROPE	66	1	0	0	0	0	2	3	0	0	2	0	3	9	12	5	10	6	4	5	0	0
EFTA	35	0	0	0	0	0	2	2	0	0	1	0	1	7	6	1	6	2	2	1	3	0
U.K.	29	0	0	0	0	0	2	2	0	0	1	0	1	4	5	1	4	1	1	0	4	0
SCANDINAVIA	4	0	0	0	0	0	0	0	0	0	0	0	0	1	1	0	0	1	1	1	0	0
SWITZERLAND	2	0	0	0	0	0	0	0	0	0	0	0	0	0	0	1	0	0	0	0	0	0
OTHER EFTA	0	1	0	0	0	0	0	0	0	0	0	0	0	0	1	0	0	0	0	0	0	0
EUROP. COMMUNITY	26	0	0	0	0	0	0	1	0	0	0	0	2	2	5	3	3	3	2	3	0	0
FRANCE	4	0	0	0	0	0	0	1	0	0	0	0	1	0	1	0	0	0	0	0	0	0
GERMANY	7	0	0	0	0	0	0	0	0	0	0	0	1	1	1	0	1	2	0	1	0	0
ITALY	7	1	0	0	0	0	0	1	0	0	0	0	0	1	2	1	1	0	0	0	0	0
BELGIUM + LUX	5	0	0	0	0	0	0	0	0	0	0	0	0	0	1	1	1	1	1	1	0	0
NETHERLANDS	3	0	0	0	0	0	0	0	0	0	0	0	0	0	0	0	1	0	1	0	1	0
SPAIN	3	0	0	0	0	0	0	0	0	0	0	0	0	0	0	1	0	0	0	0	0	0
GREECE + TURKEY	2	0	0	0	0	0	0	1	0	0	0	1	0	0	1	0	0	0	0	0	0	0
OTHER EUROPE	0	0	0	0	0	0	0	0	0	0	0	0	0	0	0	0	0	0	0	0	0	0
EUROPE EX. U.K.	37	1	0	0	0	0	0	1	0	0	1	1	2	4	7	4	4	5	5	5	0	0
SOUTHERN DOMINIONS	13	0	0	0	0	0	2	2	0	1	0	0	0	2	2	0	0	0	3	1	2	0
S. AFRICA +RHOD.	1	0	0	0	0	0	0	0	0	1	0	0	0	0	0	0	0	0	1	1	1	0
AUSTRALIA + N.Z.	12	0	0	0	0	0	2	2	0	0	0	1	1	2	3	1	1	2	1	0	1	0
ASIA + OTHER AFRICA	17	0	0	0	0	0	0	0	0	0	0	0	1	1	3	1	0	1	1	0	2	0
JAPAN	13	0	0	0	0	0	0	0	0	0	0	1	0	2	2	0	0	1	0	1	2	0
OTHER ASIA+AFR.	4	0	0	0	0	0	0	0	0	0	0	0	1	0	2	0	1	0	1	0	0	0
BLACK AFRICA	1	0	0	0	0	0	0	0	0	0	0	0	0	1	0	0	0	0	0	0	0	0
ARAB WORLD	4	0	0	0	0	0	0	0	0	0	0	0	0	0	2	0	1	0	1	0	1	0
INDIA	4	0	0	0	0	0	0	0	0	0	1	0	1	1	0	0	0	0	0	0	0	0
PHILIPPINES	2	0	0	0	0	0	0	0	0	0	0	0	0	0	0	0	0	0	0	0	0	0
OTHER E. ASIA	0	0	0	0	0	0	0	0	0	0	0	0	0	0	0	0	0	0	0	0	0	0
OTHER ASIA	2	0	0	0	0	0	0	0	0	0	0	1	1	0	0	0	0	0	0	0	1	0

PERIOD

CHAPTER 3- THE PROLIFERATION OF FOREIGN SUBSIDIARIES
SECTION 2- THE FLOW OF MANUFACTURING BY INDUSTRY OF PARENT SYSTEM
TABLE 12- MANUFACTURING SUBSIDIARIES IN A SYSTEM IN THE
FABRICATED METAL INDUSTRY (SIC 34)
CLASSIFIED BY COUNTRY OR REGION AND BY PERIOD MANUFACTURE BEGAN

PERIOD

COUNTRY OR REGION	PRE 1968	PRE 1901	1901 -13	1914 -19	1920 -24	1925 -29	1930 -34	1935 -39	1940 -45	1946 -50	1951 -53	1954 -55	1956 -57	1958 -59	1960 -61	1962 -63	1964	1965	1966	1967	UNK
OUTSIDE U.S.	268	2	4	7	9	18	7	5	24	19	4	18	14	34	25	13	13	22	13	13	0
OUT. U.S. + CANADA	223	2	3	5	6	14	5	3	17	16	2	11	13	31	23	12	12	21	13	13	0
OUT. WEST. HEMIS.	164	2	3	4	6	13	5	3	10	9	2	4	6	25	18	11	10	15	10	10	0
OUT. WHITE CWEALTH	175	2	1	2	4	8	3	0	15	12	2	10	11	23	20	9	9	16	9	12	0
OUT. DEVLPED WORLD	73	0	0	0	1	1	0	3	11	9	0	7	7	8	8	3	1	6	4	4	0
CANADA	45	0	1	3	2	4	2	2	7	3	2	7	1	3	3	1	1	1	0	0	0
LATIN AMERICA	59	0	0	0	3	1	0	3	7	7	0	7	7	6	6	2	3	6	3	3	0
C. AMER.+CARIB.	21	0	0	1	0	1	0	1	2	1	0	2	2	2	5	1	2	0	2	1	0
CUBA	1	0	0	0	0	1	0	0	0	0	0	0	0	0	1	0	0	0	0	0	0
MEXICO	18	0	0	0	1	1	0	0	2	2	0	4	2	2	1	1	1	2	1	1	0
OTHER	2	0	0	0	0	0	0	0	0	0	0	0	0	0	1	0	0	0	1	0	0
S. AMERICA	38	0	0	0	0	0	0	0	5	6	0	3	5	2	4	0	0	3	0	0	0
ARGENTINA	4	0	0	1	1	0	0	0	2	1	0	0	0	0	1	0	0	0	0	1	0
BRAZIL	12	0	0	0	0	0	0	0	1	1	0	2	2	2	2	1	0	0	0	2	0
PERU	3	0	0	0	0	0	0	0	1	1	0	1	0	0	1	0	0	0	1	0	0
COLOMBIA	5	0	0	0	0	0	0	0	0	1	0	0	2	3	2	0	1	1	0	0	0
VENEZUELA	8	0	0	0	0	0	0	0	0	2	0	0	0	0	0	1	1	1	0	0	0
OTHER	6	0	0	0	0	0	0	0	1	0	0	0	0	1	1	1	0	0	0	1	0
EUROPE	128	2	3	4	4	11	3	3	5	6	2	3	3	4	20	13	8	9	12	9	0
EFTA	41	2	2	1	1	4	0	0	3	4	0	0	0	1	6	3	3	1	7	2	0
U.K.	28	0	1	1	2	4	0	0	1	3	0	0	0	1	5	2	0	2	2	1	0
SCANDINAVIA	6	0	0	0	0	0	0	0	1	1	0	0	0	1	1	1	1	2	2	1	0
SWITZERLAND	4	0	1	0	1	0	0	0	1	0	0	0	0	0	0	0	0	0	0	0	0
OTHER EFTA	3	0	0	0	0	0	0	0	0	0	0	0	0	0	0	0	1	1	1	0	0
EUROP. COMMUNITY	69	0	2	3	2	7	3	0	2	2	0	2	3	12	8	3	4	5	3	6	0
FRANCE	18	2	1	1	1	1	2	0	0	1	1	0	1	5	4	1	1	2	0	0	0
GERMANY	21	1	1	0	0	3	2	0	0	4	0	1	0	2	2	1	2	1	2	4	0
ITALY	13	0	1	0	1	0	0	1	2	1	1	0	1	3	3	0	0	1	0	2	0
BELGIUM + LUX	6	0	0	1	0	1	0	0	0	0	0	0	0	1	1	1	1	0	0	0	0
NETHERLANDS	11	0	0	0	2	2	1	0	2	0	0	1	0	1	1	0	0	2	1	2	0
SPAIN	9	0	0	0	0	0	0	0	0	0	0	0	0	0	0	0	0	3	0	0	0
GREECE + TURKEY	0	0	0	0	0	0	0	0	0	0	0	0	0	0	2	1	1	2	2	1	0
OTHER EUROPE	1	0	0	0	0	0	0	0	1	0	0	0	0	0	0	0	0	0	0	0	0
EUROPE EX. U.K.	100	2	2	3	4	7	3	3	4	3	2	3	4	15	11	5	9	10	5	8	0
SOUTHERN DOMINIONS	19	0	0	0	0	2	2	2	1	1	0	2	1	3	3	0	2	3	2	0	0
S. AFRICA +RHOD.	8	0	0	0	2	2	2	0	1	1	0	1	1	1	2	1	0	2	2	0	0
AUSTRALIA + N.Z.	11	0	0	0	0	0	0	0	0	0	0	1	0	2	1	1	1	1	0	1	0
ASIA + OTHER AFRICA	17	0	0	0	0	0	0	0	1	2	0	0	0	0	0	1	0	0	1	1	0
JAPAN	3	0	0	0	0	0	0	0	0	1	0	1	0	0	0	0	0	0	0	0	0
OTHER ASIA+AFR.	14	0	0	0	0	2	0	0	4	4	0	0	3	2	2	0	0	0	0	0	0
BLACK AFRICA	4	0	0	0	0	0	0	0	0	0	0	1	0	1	0	0	0	0	0	0	0
ARAB WORLD	2	0	0	0	0	0	0	0	2	0	0	0	1	2	0	0	0	0	0	0	0
INDIA	0	0	0	0	0	0	0	0	0	0	0	0	0	0	0	0	0	0	0	0	0
PHILIPPINES	3	0	0	0	0	0	0	0	0	0	0	0	1	0	0	0	0	0	0	1	0
OTHER E. ASIA	0	0	0	0	0	0	0	0	0	0	0	0	0	0	0	0	0	0	0	0	0
OTHER ASIA	5	0	0	0	0	0	0	0	2	0	0	0	0	0	1	0	0	0	0	0	0

CHAPTER 3- THE PROLIFERATION OF FOREIGN SUBSIDIARIES
SECTION 2- THE FLOW OF MANUFACTURING BY INDUSTRY OF PARENT SYSTEM
TABLE 13- MANUFACTURING SUBSIDIARIES IN A SYSTEM IN THE
FARM MACHINERY INDUSTRY (SIC 352)
CLASSIFIED BY COUNTRY OR REGION AND BY PERIOD MANUFACTURE BEGAN

PERIOD

COUNTRY OR REGION	PRE 1968	PRE 1901	1901 -13	1914 -19	1920 -24	1925 -29	1930 -34	1935 -39	1940 -45	1946 -50	1951 -53	1954 -55	1956 -57	1958 -59	1960 -61	1962	1963	1964	1965	1966	1967	UNK
OUTSIDE U.S.	45	0	6	0	2	1	0	1	2	4	3	1	1	1	8	3	3	4	3	1	1	0
OUT. U.S. + CANADA	38	0	3	0	1	0	0	1	1	3	3	1	1	1	8	3	3	4	3	1	1	0
OUT. WEST. HEMIS.	30	0	3	0	1	0	0	1	0	2	2	0	0	1	8	2	2	3	3	1	1	0
OUT. WHITE CWEALTH	27	0	3	0	0	0	0	0	1	2	3	1	1	1	6	1	3	2	1	1	1	0
OUT. DEVLPED WORLD	11	0	0	0	0	0	0	0	1	1	2	1	1	1	0	1	1	1	0	0	1	0
CANADA	7	0	3	0	1	1	0	0	1	1	0	0	0	0	0	0	0	0	0	0	0	0
LATIN AMERICA	8	0	0	0	0	0	0	0	1	1	1	1	1	0	0	1	1	1	0	0	0	0
C. AMER.+CARIB.	5	0	0	0	0	0	0	0	1	1	0	0	1	0	0	1	0	1	0	0	0	0
CUBA	0	0	0	0	0	0	0	0	0	0	0	0	0	0	0	0	0	0	0	0	0	0
MEXICO	4	0	0	0	0	0	0	0	1	1	0	0	1	0	0	0	0	1	0	0	0	0
OTHER	1	0	0	0	0	0	0	0	0	0	0	0	0	0	0	1	0	0	0	0	0	0
S. AMERICA	3	0	0	0	0	0	0	0	0	0	1	1	0	0	0	0	1	0	0	0	0	0
ARGENTINA	2	0	0	0	0	0	0	0	0	0	1	0	0	0	0	0	1	0	0	0	0	0
BRAZIL	1	0	0	0	0	0	0	0	0	0	0	1	0	0	0	0	0	0	0	0	0	0
PERU	0	0	0	0	0	0	0	0	0	0	0	0	0	0	0	0	0	0	0	0	0	0
COLOMBIA	0	0	0	0	0	0	0	0	0	0	0	0	0	0	0	0	0	0	0	0	0	0
VENEZUELA	0	0	0	0	0	0	0	0	0	0	0	0	0	0	0	0	0	0	0	0	0	0
OTHER	0	0	0	0	0	0	0	0	0	0	0	0	0	0	0	0	0	0	0	0	0	0
EUROPE	19	0	3	0	1	0	0	0	0	1	1	0	0	0	8	0	1	2	1	1	0	0
EFTA	5	0	1	0	1	0	0	0	0	0	0	0	0	0	2	0	0	1	0	0	0	0
U.K.	4	0	0	0	1	0	0	0	0	0	0	0	0	0	2	0	0	1	0	0	0	0
SCANDINAVIA	1	0	1	0	0	0	0	0	0	0	0	0	0	0	0	0	0	0	0	0	0	0
SWITZERLAND	0	0	0	0	0	0	0	0	0	0	0	0	0	0	0	0	0	0	0	0	0	0
OTHER EFTA	0	0	0	0	0	0	0	0	0	0	0	0	0	0	0	0	0	0	0	0	0	0
EUROP. COMMUNITY	11	0	2	0	0	0	0	0	0	1	0	0	0	0	6	0	0	1	1	0	0	0
FRANCE	8	0	1	0	0	0	0	0	0	1	0	0	0	0	6	0	0	0	0	0	0	0
GERMANY	2	0	1	0	0	0	0	0	0	0	0	0	0	0	0	0	0	1	0	0	0	0
ITALY	1	0	0	0	0	0	0	0	0	0	0	0	0	0	0	0	0	0	1	0	0	0
BELGIUM + LUX	0	0	0	0	0	0	0	0	0	0	0	0	0	0	0	0	0	0	0	0	0	0
NETHERLANDS	0	0	0	0	0	0	0	0	0	0	0	0	0	0	0	0	0	0	0	0	0	0
SPAIN	2	0	0	0	0	0	0	0	0	0	1	0	0	0	0	0	1	0	0	0	0	0
GREECE + TURKEY	1	0	0	0	0	0	0	0	0	0	0	0	0	0	0	0	0	0	0	1	0	0
OTHER EUROPE	0	0	0	0	0	0	0	0	0	0	0	0	0	0	0	0	0	0	0	0	0	0
EUROPE EX. U.K.	15	0	3	0	0	0	0	0	0	1	1	0	0	0	6	0	1	1	1	1	0	0
SOUTHERN DOMINIONS	7	0	0	0	0	0	0	1	0	1	0	0	0	0	0	2	0	1	2	0	0	0
S. AFRICA +RHOD.	3	0	0	0	0	0	0	1	0	0	0	0	0	0	0	1	0	0	1	0	0	0
AUSTRALIA + N.Z.	4	0	0	0	0	0	0	0	0	1	0	0	0	0	0	1	0	1	1	0	0	0
ASIA + OTHER AFRICA	4	0	0	0	0	0	0	0	0	0	1	0	0	1	0	0	1	0	0	0	1	0
JAPAN	1	0	0	0	0	0	0	0	0	0	0	0	0	0	0	0	1	0	0	0	0	0
OTHER ASIA+AFR.	3	0	0	0	0	0	0	0	0	0	1	0	0	1	0	0	0	0	0	0	1	0
BLACK AFRICA	0	0	0	0	0	0	0	0	0	0	0	0	0	0	0	0	0	0	0	0	0	0
ARAB WORLD	1	0	0	0	0	0	0	0	0	0	1	0	0	0	0	0	0	0	0	0	0	0
INDIA	1	0	0	0	0	0	0	0	0	0	0	0	0	1	0	0	0	0	0	0	0	0
PHILIPPINES	1	0	0	0	0	0	0	0	0	0	0	0	0	0	0	0	0	0	0	0	1	0
OTHER E. ASIA	0	0	0	0	0	0	0	0	0	0	0	0	0	0	0	0	0	0	0	0	0	0
OTHER ASIA	0	0	0	0	0	0	0	0	0	0	0	0	0	0	0	0	0	0	0	0	0	0

CHAPTER 3- THE PROLIFERATION OF FOREIGN SUBSIDIARIES
SECTION 2- THE FLOW OF MANUFACTURING BY INDUSTRY OF PARENT SYSTEM
TABLE 14- MANUFACTURING SUBSIDIARIES IN A SYSTEM IN THE
OFFICE AND COMPUTING MACHINE INDUSTRY (SIC 357)
CLASSIFIED BY COUNTRY OR REGION AND BY PERIOD MANUFACTURE BEGAN

COUNTRY OR REGION	PRE 1968	PRE 1901	1901 -13	1914 -19	1920 -24	1925 -29	1930 -34	1935 -39	1940 -42	1946 -50	1951 -53	1954 -55	1956 -57	1958 -59	1960 -61	1962	1963	1964	1965	1966	1967	UNK
OUTSIDE U.S.	73	1	1	4	1	3	5	9	3	6	5	2	5	6	7	1	4	3	0	5	2	0
OUT. U.S. + CANADA	65	1	1	4	1	2	5	9	1	6	4	2	5	6	7	1	4	2	0	4	2	0
OUT. WEST. HEMIS.	48	1	1	1	1	2	5	8	2	6	4	1	1	2	4	1	4	2	0	3	2	0
OUT. WHITE CWEALTH	54	1	1	1	1	2	4	8	1	6	4	1	5	5	6	1	4	2	0	3	1	0
OUT. DEVLPED WORLD	18	0	0	0	0	0	0	1	1	0	0	1	4	4	3	0	1	2	0	1	0	0
CANADA	8	0	0	3	0	0	0	0	1	0	1	0	0	0	0	0	1	1	0	1	0	0
LATIN AMERICA	17	0	0	0	0	1	0	1	1	0	0	1	4	4	3	0	2	2	0	1	1	0
C. AMER.+CARIB.	11	0	0	0	0	0	0	0	1	0	0	1	1	0	2	0	2	0	0	1	0	0
CUBA	1	0	0	0	0	0	0	0	0	0	0	0	1	0	0	0	0	0	0	0	0	0
MEXICO	6	0	0	0	0	0	0	0	1	0	0	1	0	0	1	0	2	0	0	1	0	0
OTHER	4	0	0	0	0	0	0	1	0	0	0	0	0	1	1	0	0	0	0	0	1	0
S. AMERICA	6	0	0	0	0	1	0	1	0	0	0	0	0	1	1	1	0	0	0	0	0	0
ARGENTINA	1	0	0	0	0	0	0	0	1	0	0	0	0	0	0	0	0	0	0	0	0	0
BRAZIL	4	0	0	0	0	1	0	0	0	0	0	0	0	1	1	0	0	0	0	0	0	0
PERU	0	0	0	0	0	0	0	0	0	0	0	0	0	0	0	0	0	0	0	0	0	0
COLOMBIA	1	0	0	0	0	0	0	1	0	0	0	0	0	0	0	0	0	0	0	0	0	0
VENEZUELA	0	0	0	0	0	0	0	0	0	0	0	0	0	0	0	0	0	0	0	0	0	0
OTHER	0	0	0	0	0	0	0	0	0	0	0	0	0	0	0	0	0	0	0	0	0	0
EUROPE	38	1	1	1	1	2	5	7	1	5	3	0	0	2	4	0	2	0	0	1	2	0
EFTA	15	1	1	0	0	2	1	3	0	3	0	0	1	1	2	0	0	0	0	1	1	0
U.K.	7	0	1	0	0	1	1	1	0	1	0	0	0	0	1	0	0	0	0	1	0	0
SCANDINAVIA	5	0	0	0	0	1	0	1	0	1	0	0	0	0	1	0	0	0	0	1	1	0
SWITZERLAND	2	0	0	0	0	0	0	1	0	1	0	0	0	0	0	0	0	0	0	0	0	0
OTHER EFTA	1	0	0	0	0	0	0	0	0	0	0	0	1	0	0	0	0	0	0	0	0	0
EUROP. COMMUNITY	23	1	0	1	1	0	4	4	1	2	3	0	0	1	2	0	2	0	0	0	1	0
FRANCE	6	0	0	1	1	0	1	2	0	1	0	0	0	1	1	0	0	0	0	0	1	0
GERMANY	10	1	0	0	0	0	2	1	0	1	1	0	0	0	1	0	1	0	0	0	0	0
ITALY	3	0	0	0	0	0	1	0	0	0	1	0	0	0	0	0	1	0	0	0	0	0
BELGIUM + LUX	1	0	0	0	0	0	0	1	0	0	0	0	0	0	0	0	0	0	0	0	0	0
NETHERLANDS	0	0	0	0	0	0	0	0	0	0	0	0	0	0	0	0	0	0	0	0	0	0
SPAIN	0	0	0	0	0	0	0	0	0	0	0	0	0	0	0	0	0	0	0	0	0	0
GREECE + TURKEY	0	0	0	0	0	0	0	0	0	0	0	0	0	0	0	0	0	0	0	0	0	0
OTHER EUROPE	0	0	0	0	0	0	0	0	0	0	0	0	0	0	0	0	0	0	0	0	0	0
EUROPE EX. U.K.	31	1	0	1	1	2	4	6	1	4	3	0	0	2	3	0	2	0	0	0	2	0
SOUTHERN DOMINIONS	4	0	0	0	0	0	0	0	0	1	0	1	0	0	0	0	0	0	0	2	0	0
S. AFRICA +RHOD.	2	0	0	0	0	0	0	0	0	0	0	0	0	0	0	0	0	1	0	1	1	0
AUSTRALIA + N.Z.	2	0	0	0	0	0	0	1	0	1	0	1	0	0	0	0	2	1	0	1	0	0
ASIA + OTHER AFRICA	6	0	0	0	0	0	0	1	0	0	1	1	1	0	0	0	1	0	0	0	0	0
JAPAN	5	0	0	0	0	0	0	1	0	0	1	1	1	0	0	1	1	0	0	0	0	0
OTHER ASIA+AFR.	1	0	0	0	0	0	0	0	0	0	0	0	0	0	0	0	0	0	0	0	0	0
BLACK AFRICA	0	0	0	0	0	0	0	0	0	0	0	0	0	0	0	0	0	0	0	0	0	0
ARAB WORLD	0	0	0	0	0	0	0	0	0	0	0	0	0	0	0	0	0	0	0	0	0	0
INDIA	1	0	0	0	0	0	0	0	0	0	0	0	0	0	0	0	1	0	0	0	0	0
PHILIPPINES	0	0	0	0	0	0	0	0	0	0	0	0	0	0	0	0	0	0	0	0	0	0
OTHER E. ASIA	0	0	0	0	0	0	0	0	0	0	0	0	0	0	0	0	0	0	0	0	0	0
OTHER ASIA	0	0	0	0	0	0	0	0	0	0	0	0	0	0	0	0	0	0	0	0	0	0

PERIOD

CHAPTER 3— THE PROLIFERATION OF FOREIGN SUBSIDIARIES

SECTION 2— THE FLOW OF MANUFACTURING BY INDUSTRY OF PARENT SYSTEM

TABLE 15— MANUFACTURING SUBSIDIARIES IN A SYSTEM IN THE
OTHER NON-ELECTRICAL MACHINERY INDUSTRIES (OTHER SIC 35)
CLASSIFIED BY COUNTRY OR REGION AND BY PERIOD MANUFACTURE BEGAN

PERIOD

COUNTRY OR REGION	PRE 1908	PRE 1901	1901-13	1914-19	1920-24	1925-29	1930-34	1935-39	1940-45	1946-50	1951-53	1954-55	1956-57	1958-59	1960-61	1962	1963	1964	1965	1966	1967	UNK
OUTSIDE U.S.	271	16	14	10	12	8	5	13	6	15	8	11	12	21	24	10	15	16	14	22	16	3
OUT. U.S. + CANADA	216	14	11	9	12	6	4	10	4	12	6	9	10	17	21	9	9	8	13	19	11	2
OUT. WEST. HEMIS.	174	14	11	7	11	6	4	8	4	7	5	6	9	10	17	8	8	4	12	16	6	1
OUT. WHITE CWEALTH	138	7	11	4	8	4	2	4	1	6	3	4	5	13	17	5	8	6	9	13	7	1
OUT. DEVLPED WORLD	49	0	0	2	1	0	0	2	0	5	1	3	2	8	6	1	2	4	2	4	5	1
CANADA	55	2	3	1	0	2	1	3	3	3	2	4	2	4	3	3	6	8	1	3	5	1
LATIN AMERICA	42	0	0	2	0	0	0	2	0	5	1	3	1	7	4	1	1	4	1	3	5	1
C. AMER.+CARIB.	18	0	0	0	1	0	0	0	0	2	1	1	0	3	0	1	0	4	1	2	2	0
CUBA	0	0	0	0	1	0	0	0	0	0	0	0	0	0	0	0	0	0	0	0	0	0
MEXICO	17	0	0	0	0	0	0	0	0	2	1	1	0	3	4	1	0	3	1	2	2	0
OTHER	1	0	0	0	0	0	0	0	0	0	0	0	0	0	0	0	0	1	0	0	0	1
S. AMERICA	24	0	0	2	0	0	0	2	0	3	0	2	1	4	4	0	1	0	0	1	3	0
ARGENTINA	6	0	0	1	0	0	0	0	0	1	0	0	0	2	2	0	0	0	0	0	0	1
BRAZIL	9	0	0	0	0	0	0	2	0	2	0	1	0	1	2	0	0	0	0	0	3	0
PERU	1	0	0	1	0	0	0	0	0	0	0	0	0	0	0	0	0	0	0	0	0	0
COLOMBIA	1	0	0	0	0	0	0	0	0	0	0	1	1	0	0	0	1	0	0	0	1	0
VENEZUELA	5	0	0	0	0	0	0	0	0	0	0	0	0	0	0	0	0	0	0	0	1	0
OTHER	2	0	0	1	0	0	0	0	0	0	0	0	0	1	0	0	1	0	0	0	1	0
EUROPE	127	14	11	4	8	6	2	6	2	3	4	4	6	8	12	4	5	3	8	14	2	1
EFTA	52	6	3	2	2	2	1	4	2	2	3	2	4	2	1	1	0	1	2	9	2	1
U.K.	42	6	3	2	1	2	1	4	2	2	3	2	3	0	1	1	0	0	0	5	2	1
SCANDINAVIA	6	0	0	0	1	0	0	0	0	0	0	0	0	0	0	0	0	0	1	3	0	0
SWITZERLAND	0	0	3	0	0	0	0	0	0	0	0	0	0	0	0	0	0	0	0	1	0	0
OTHER EFTA	4	0	0	0	1	0	0	0	0	1	0	0	1	0	0	0	0	1	1	0	0	0
EUROP. COMMUNITY	65	7	8	1	0	4	0	2	0	1	0	0	1	4	10	3	5	0	5	5	0	0
FRANCE	25	4	3	0	0	2	0	1	0	0	0	0	2	1	6	1	2	0	1	3	0	0
GERMANY	19	3	3	0	0	1	0	0	0	1	0	0	0	1	1	3	1	0	5	0	0	0
ITALY	11	0	2	0	0	2	1	0	0	0	1	0	2	1	2	1	1	0	1	3	0	0
BELGIUM + LUX	4	0	0	0	0	0	0	1	0	0	0	0	0	1	0	0	2	0	0	0	0	0
NETHERLANDS	6	0	0	1	0	0	1	0	0	1	0	0	0	1	1	1	0	0	1	1	0	0
SPAIN	0	0	0	0	0	0	0	0	0	0	0	0	0	0	0	0	0	0	0	0	0	0
GREECE + TURKEY	0	0	0	0	0	1	1	0	0	1	0	0	0	1	1	0	1	0	0	0	0	0
OTHER EUROPE	4	1	0	0	0	0	0	0	0	0	0	0	1	0	0	0	0	0	0	0	0	0
EUROPE EX. U.K.	85	8	11	2	7	4	1	2	0	1	1	2	3	6	11	3	5	2	7	9	0	0
SOUTHERN DOMINIONS	32	0	0	3	3	0	1	2	1	4	0	2	2	1	2	3	3	1	3	1	2	0
S. AFRICA +RHOD.	12	0	0	1	2	0	0	0	1	3	0	0	0	0	1	2	0	0	1	0	0	0
AUSTRALIA + N.Z.	20	0	0	2	1	0	1	2	0	1	0	2	2	1	1	1	1	1	2	1	2	0
ASIA + OTHER AFRICA	15	0	0	0	0	1	1	0	1	1	1	0	1	3	3	1	2	1	0	1	2	0
JAPAN	8	0	0	0	0	1	0	0	1	0	0	0	1	1	1	1	1	0	1	0	0	0
OTHER ASIA+AFR.	7	0	0	0	0	0	0	0	0	1	1	0	0	2	2	0	1	1	0	1	2	0
BLACK AFRICA	0	0	0	0	0	0	0	0	0	0	0	0	0	0	0	0	0	0	0	0	0	0
ARAB WORLD	1	0	0	0	0	0	0	0	0	1	0	0	0	1	1	0	0	0	0	0	0	0
INDIA	5	0	0	0	0	1	0	0	0	1	1	0	1	0	0	0	1	0	0	1	0	0
PHILIPPINES	0	0	0	0	0	0	0	0	0	0	0	0	0	1	1	0	0	0	0	0	0	0
OTHER E. ASIA	0	0	0	0	0	0	0	0	0	0	0	0	0	0	0	0	1	0	0	0	0	0
OTHER ASIA	1	0	0	0	0	0	0	0	0	0	0	0	0	1	1	0	0	0	0	0	0	0

CHAPTER 3- THE PROLIFERATION OF FOREIGN SUBSIDIARIES
SECTION 2- THE FLOW OF MANUFACTURING BY INDUSTRY OF PARENT SYSTEM
TABLE 16- MANUFACTURING SUBSIDIARIES IN A SYSTEM IN THE
HOUSEHOLD APPLIANCE INDUSTRY (SIC 363)
CLASSIFIED BY COUNTRY OR REGION AND BY PERIOD MANUFACTURE BEGAN

COUNTRY OR REGION	PRE 1968	PRE 1901	1901 -13	1914 -19	1920 -24	1925 -29	1930 -34	1935 -39	1940 -45	1946 -50	1951 -53	1954 -55	1956 -57	1958 -59	1960 -61	1962	1963	1964	1965	1966	1967	UNK
OUTSIDE U.S.	76	0	1	1	0	0	3	1	1	2	0	4	7	5	15	10	8	6	4	3	4	0
OUT. U.S. + CANADA	67	0	2	0	0	0	3	1	1	1	0	3	7	5	14	9	6	6	3	3	4	0
OUT. WEST. HEMIS.	51	0	2	0	0	0	2	1	1	1	0	2	5	3	9	9	5	6	2	2	2	0
OUT. WHITE CWEALTH	49	0	1	0	0	0	2	1	0	1	0	2	2	2	12	5	4	4	3	1	4	0
OUT. DEVLPED WORLD	29	0	0	0	0	0	0	1	0	0	0	1	2	2	10	2	1	2	3	1	4	0
CANADA	9	0	0	1	0	0	1	0	0	1	1	1	0	0	1	1	2	1	1	0	0	0
LATIN AMERICA	16	0	0	0	0	0	0	0	1	1	2	1	2	2	5	1	1	1	1	1	2	0
C. AMER.+CARIB.	5	0	0	0	0	0	0	0	0	0	1	1	1	1	1	0	0	0	0	0	1	0
CUBA	0	0	0	0	0	0	0	0	0	0	0	0	0	0	0	0	0	0	0	0	0	0
MEXICO	4	0	0	0	0	0	0	0	0	0	0	0	1	1	1	0	0	0	0	0	1	0
OTHER	1	0	0	0	0	0	0	0	0	1	0	0	0	0	0	0	0	0	0	0	0	0
S. AMERICA	11	0	0	0	0	0	0	1	1	0	1	1	1	1	4	1	1	1	1	1	0	0
ARGENTINA	2	0	0	0	0	0	0	1	0	0	0	0	0	1	1	0	0	0	0	0	0	0
BRAZIL	3	0	0	0	0	0	0	0	1	0	0	1	1	1	1	0	1	0	0	0	0	0
PERU	1	0	0	0	0	0	0	0	0	0	0	0	0	0	0	0	0	0	0	0	0	0
COLOMBIA	1	0	0	0	0	0	0	0	0	0	0	0	0	0	1	0	0	1	0	0	0	0
VENEZUELA	2	0	0	0	0	0	0	0	0	0	0	1	0	0	0	0	0	0	0	0	1	0
OTHER	2	0	0	0	0	0	0	0	0	0	0	0	0	0	0	0	0	0	1	1	0	0
EUROPE	24	2	1	0	0	0	1	1	0	1	1	1	3	3	2	3	4	2	0	1	0	0
EFTA	7	1	1	0	0	0	1	0	0	0	1	1	1	0	1	0	1	0	0	1	0	0
U.K.	6	1	1	0	0	0	1	0	0	0	0	0	0	0	0	0	0	0	0	1	0	0
SCANDINAVIA	1	0	0	0	0	0	0	0	0	0	1	0	0	0	0	0	0	0	0	0	0	0
SWITZERLAND	0	0	0	0	0	0	0	0	0	0	0	0	0	0	0	0	0	0	0	0	0	0
OTHER EFTA	0	0	0	0	0	0	0	0	0	0	0	0	0	0	0	0	0	0	0	0	0	0
EUROP. COMMUNITY	15	0	0	0	0	0	1	1	1	1	0	0	2	2	4	3	3	2	1	0	1	0
FRANCE	5	0	0	0	0	0	0	0	0	0	0	0	1	0	1	0	1	0	0	0	0	0
GERMANY	4	0	0	0	0	0	1	0	0	0	0	0	0	1	1	2	0	1	0	0	0	0
ITALY	4	0	0	0	0	0	0	1	1	1	0	0	0	0	0	0	1	0	1	0	0	0
BELGIUM + LUX	1	0	0	0	0	0	0	0	0	0	0	0	0	0	1	0	0	0	0	0	0	0
NETHERLANDS	1	0	0	0	0	0	0	0	0	0	0	0	0	0	0	1	0	0	0	0	0	0
SPAIN	0	0	0	0	0	0	0	0	0	0	0	0	0	0	0	0	0	0	0	0	0	0
GREECE + TURKEY	1	0	0	0	0	0	0	0	0	0	0	0	0	0	0	0	0	0	0	0	0	0
OTHER EUROPE	1	1	1	0	0	0	0	0	0	1	1	0	2	0	1	0	0	0	0	0	0	0
EUROPE EX. U.K.	18	1	0	0	0	0	0	1	0	1	1	1	2	3	1	3	3	2	0	0	0	0
SOUTHERN DOMINIONS	12	0	0	0	0	0	1	0	0	0	1	1	1	0	1	4	1	2	0	1	0	0
S. AFRICA +RHOD.	2	0	0	0	0	0	0	0	0	0	0	0	0	0	1	0	1	1	0	0	1	0
AUSTRALIA + N.Z.	10	0	0	0	0	0	1	0	1	0	1	1	1	0	6	4	1	1	0	1	0	0
ASIA + OTHER AFRICA	15	0	0	0	0	0	0	0	0	0	1	1	0	0	5	2	0	2	2	0	2	0
JAPAN	13	0	0	0	0	0	0	0	0	0	0	0	2	1	5	2	2	0	1	0	0	0
OTHER ASIA+AFR.	3	0	0	0	0	0	0	0	0	0	1	0	0	0	2	0	0	1	0	0	0	0
BLACK AFRICA	2	0	0	0	0	0	0	0	0	0	0	0	0	0	0	0	0	0	0	0	0	0
ARAB WORLD	1	0	0	0	0	0	0	0	0	0	0	0	0	0	1	0	0	1	0	0	0	0
INDIA	1	0	0	0	0	0	0	0	0	0	1	0	0	0	0	0	0	0	0	0	0	0
PHILIPPINES	1	0	0	0	0	0	0	0	0	0	0	0	0	0	0	0	0	0	0	0	0	0
OTHER E. ASIA	1	0	0	0	0	0	0	0	0	0	0	0	0	0	2	0	0	0	1	1	0	0
OTHER ASIA	5	0	0	0	0	0	1	0	0	0	0	0	0	0	0	0	0	0	0	0	1	0

PERIOD

CHAPTER 3- THE PROLIFERATION OF FOREIGN SUBSIDIARIES
SECTION 2- THE FLOW OF MANUFACTURING BY INDUSTRY OF PARENT SYSTEM
TABLE 17- MANUFACTURING SUBSIDIARIES IN A SYSTEM IN THE
ELECTRONICS INDUSTRY (SIC 365-367)
CLASSIFIED BY COUNTRY OR REGION AND BY PERIOD MANUFACTURE BEGAN

COUNTRY OR REGION	PRE 1968	PRE 1901	1901-13	1914-19	1920-24	1925-29	1930-34	1935-39	1940-45	1946-50	1951-53	1954-55	1956-57	1958-59	1960-61	1962	1963	1964	1965	1966	1967	UNK
OUTSIDE U.S.	203	0	2	4	2	18	10	3	9	11	11	13	8	26	24	10	7	11	14	10	5	5
OUT. U.S. + CANADA	177	0	2	4	0	17	10	3	9	7	10	7	6	23	22	10	6	10	11	10	5	5
OUT. WEST. HEMIS.	138	0	2	4	0	14	10	2	7	5	7	6	4	15	20	7	5	8	7	8	2	5
OUT. WHITE CWEALTH	140	0	0	3	0	13	8	2	5	6	10	3	3	19	18	8	4	9	11	9	5	4
OUT. DEVLPED WORLD	49	0	0	0	0	4	0	1	2	2	4	1	2	8	5	3	1	3	7	2	4	0
CANADA	26	0	0	0	2	1	0	0	0	4	1	6	2	3	2	0	1	5	3	0	0	0
LATIN AMERICA	39	0	0	0	0	3	0	1	2	2	3	1	1	8	2	3	1	1	4	2	3	0
C. AMER.+CARIB.	15	0	0	0	0	0	0	1	1	0	0	0	1	4	1	0	1	0	2	2	2	0
CUBA	1	0	0	0	0	0	0	0	0	0	0	0	0	0	0	0	0	0	0	0	0	0
MEXICO	12	0	0	0	0	0	0	1	1	0	0	0	0	4	1	0	1	0	2	1	1	0
OTHER	2	0	0	0	0	0	0	0	0	0	0	0	1	0	0	0	0	0	0	1	1	0
S. AMERICA	24	0	0	0	0	3	0	0	1	2	3	1	0	4	1	3	0	1	2	0	1	0
ARGENTINA	8	0	0	0	0	1	0	0	0	1	0	1	0	2	0	2	0	0	0	0	0	0
BRAZIL	10	0	0	0	0	1	0	1	1	1	1	0	0	2	1	1	0	1	2	0	0	0
PERU	0	0	0	0	0	0	0	0	0	0	0	0	0	0	0	0	0	0	0	0	0	0
COLOMBIA	0	0	0	0	0	0	0	0	0	0	0	0	0	0	0	0	0	0	0	0	0	0
VENEZUELA	3	0	0	0	0	0	0	0	0	0	1	0	0	0	0	0	0	0	0	0	1	0
OTHER	3	0	0	0	0	1	0	0	0	0	1	0	0	0	0	0	0	0	0	0	0	0
EUROPE	107	0	2	3	0	12	0	2	6	3	4	3	2	13	16	7	4	5	3	6	0	4
EFTA	40	0	2	1	0	4	0	2	3	1	4	1	1	2	8	3	2	1	0	2	0	2
U.K.	25	0	2	1	0	3	0	1	2	1	0	1	1	2	4	2	2	1	0	1	0	1
SCANDINAVIA	7	0	0	0	0	0	0	1	1	0	0	0	0	0	4	1	0	0	0	1	0	0
SWITZERLAND	4	0	0	0	0	0	0	0	0	0	0	0	0	0	1	0	0	0	0	0	0	1
OTHER EFTA	4	0	0	0	0	1	0	0	0	0	0	0	0	0	3	0	0	0	0	0	0	0
EUROP. COMMUNITY	59	0	0	3	0	7	0	0	1	2	0	0	1	11	7	4	2	3	3	3	1	2
FRANCE	13	0	0	3	0	1	0	0	0	2	2	0	0	3	1	1	2	0	3	0	0	0
GERMANY	20	0	0	0	0	5	0	0	0	0	0	0	0	4	4	2	0	2	0	2	1	0
ITALY	13	0	0	0	0	1	0	0	1	0	1	0	1	2	0	1	0	0	0	2	0	2
BELGIUM + LUX	6	0	0	0	0	0	0	0	0	0	0	0	0	0	2	0	1	0	1	0	0	0
NETHERLANDS	7	0	0	0	0	0	0	0	0	0	0	0	0	2	0	0	1	1	0	0	1	0
SPAIN	5	0	0	0	0	0	0	0	0	0	1	0	0	0	0	0	0	0	1	0	1	0
GREECE + TURKEY	1	0	0	0	0	0	0	0	0	1	0	0	0	0	1	0	0	0	0	0	0	0
OTHER EUROPE	2	0	0	0	0	1	0	0	0	0	0	0	0	0	0	0	1	0	0	0	0	0
EUROPE EX. U.K.	82	0	0	2	0	9	0	1	4	2	4	2	1	11	12	5	2	4	3	5	0	3
SOUTHERN DOMINIONS	11	0	0	3	0	0	0	0	1	1	0	3	2	2	0	0	0	1	0	0	0	0
S. AFRICA +RHOD.	2	0	0	0	0	0	0	0	0	1	0	0	0	0	0	0	0	0	0	0	0	0
AUSTRALIA + N.Z.	9	0	0	3	0	0	0	0	1	0	0	3	2	2	4	0	0	1	0	1	0	0
ASIA + OTHER AFRICA	20	0	0	0	0	0	0	1	1	0	1	0	0	2	4	0	1	2	3	0	1	0
JAPAN	10	0	0	0	0	0	0	0	0	0	1	0	0	0	3	0	1	1	3	0	0	0
OTHER ASIA+AFR.	10	0	0	0	0	0	0	1	1	0	0	0	0	2	1	0	0	2	0	0	1	0
BLACK AFRICA	1	0	0	0	0	0	0	0	0	0	0	0	0	0	1	0	0	0	0	0	0	0
ARAB WORLD	0	0	0	0	0	0	0	0	0	0	0	0	0	0	0	0	0	0	0	0	0	0
INDIA	4	0	0	0	0	0	0	1	1	0	0	0	0	0	0	0	0	2	0	0	0	0
PHILIPPINES	3	0	0	0	0	0	0	0	0	0	0	0	0	1	1	0	0	0	0	1	0	0
OTHER E. ASIA	2	0	0	0	0	0	0	0	0	0	0	0	0	1	0	0	0	0	0	0	1	0
OTHER ASIA	0	0	0	0	0	0	0	0	0	0	0	0	0	0	0	0	0	0	0	0	0	0

CHAPTER 3- THE PROLIFERATION OF FOREIGN SUBSIDIARIES
SECTION 2- THE FLOW OF MANUFACTURING BY INDUSTRY OF PARENT SYSTEM
TABLE 18- MANUFACTURING SUBSIDIARIES IN A SYSTEM IN THE
OTHER ELECTRICAL MACHINERY INDUSTRIES (OTHER SIC 36)
CLASSIFIED BY COUNTRY OR REGION AND BY PERIOD MANUFACTURE BEGAN

PERIOD

COUNTRY OR REGION	PRE 1908	PRE 1901	1901 -13	1914 -19	1920 -24	1925 -29	1930 -34	1935 -39	1940 -42	1946 -50	1951 -53	1954 -55	1956 -57	1958 -59	1960 -61	1962	1963	1964	1965	1966	1967	UNK
OUTSIDE U.S.	223	9	7	3	2	9	4	15	2	3	5	11	21	22	30	16	7	18	15	3	15	6
OUT. U.S. + CANADA	180	7	7	2	1	7	4	10	2	3	5	4	15	16	26	15	6	17	12	3	14	4
OUT. WEST. HEMIS.	125	6	4	2	1	5	4	4	3	2	5	4	8	8	20	10	4	14	10	3	9	3
OUT. WHITE CWEALTH	138	3	4	1	1	3	4	9	2	3	1	5	11	12	23	10	5	16	9	2	11	3
OUT. DEVLPED WORLD	65	1	0	1	0	2	0	7	2	1	0	3	7	8	10	6	3	4	3	0	6	1
CANADA	43	2	3	1	1	2	0	5	0	0	0	4	6	6	4	1	1	1	3	0	1	2
LATIN AMERICA	55	1	0	0	0	2	0	7	2	1	0	3	7	8	6	5	2	3	2	0	5	1
C. AMER.+CARIB.	22	0	0	0	0	0	0	3	0	1	0	0	4	5	2	2	0	0	1	0	2	1
CUBA	2	0	0	0	0	0	0	0	1	0	0	0	0	2	0	0	0	0	0	0	0	0
MEXICO	15	0	0	0	0	0	0	3	1	1	0	0	2	2	1	1	0	1	0	0	2	1
OTHER	5	0	0	0	0	0	0	0	0	0	0	0	2	1	1	1	0	0	1	0	0	0
S. AMERICA	33	1	0	0	0	2	0	4	0	0	0	3	3	3	4	3	2	2	1	0	3	0
ARGENTINA	16	0	0	0	0	2	1	1	1	0	0	0	1	0	1	1	0	0	0	0	1	0
BRAZIL	6	0	0	0	0	0	0	2	0	0	0	3	1	3	4	3	2	2	0	0	2	0
PERU	1	0	0	0	0	0	0	0	1	0	0	0	1	0	1	0	0	1	1	0	0	0
COLOMBIA	4	0	0	0	0	0	0	0	0	0	0	2	0	1	1	0	0	1	0	0	0	0
VENEZUELA	4	0	0	0	0	0	0	0	0	0	0	0	0	1	1	0	0	0	0	0	0	0
OTHER	2	1	0	0	0	0	0	1	0	0	0	0	0	0	0	0	2	0	0	0	0	0
EUROPE	90	5	3	0	0	5	4	2	0	2	3	2	5	6	15	5	2	12	6	3	7	3
EFTA	27	3	1	0	0	4	0	1	0	0	1	0	2	2	3	2	0	2	2	1	2	1
U.K.	22	3	0	0	0	4	0	1	0	0	1	0	2	2	2	1	0	2	2	1	2	0
SCANDINAVIA	2	0	0	0	0	0	0	0	0	0	0	0	0	0	0	0	0	0	0	0	0	0
SWITZERLAND	0	0	1	0	0	0	0	0	0	0	0	0	0	0	0	1	0	0	0	0	0	0
OTHER EFTA	3	0	0	0	0	0	0	0	0	0	0	0	0	0	1	0	0	0	0	0	0	0
EUROP. COMMUNITY	52	1	2	0	0	1	3	1	2	2	0	2	2	4	10	3	4	10	2	2	4	2
FRANCE	27	1	1	0	1	1	2	1	0	0	0	1	2	2	4	3	1	6	2	2	3	1
GERMANY	16	0	2	0	1	0	1	0	2	2	0	1	0	1	3	0	0	3	0	0	3	0
ITALY	5	0	1	0	0	0	0	0	0	0	0	0	0	0	1	0	0	1	0	0	1	1
BELGIUM + LUX	1	0	0	0	0	0	0	0	0	0	0	0	2	0	0	0	0	0	0	0	0	0
NETHERLANDS	3	0	0	0	0	1	1	0	0	0	0	0	0	0	2	0	1	0	1	0	0	0
SPAIN	6	0	0	0	0	0	0	0	0	0	0	0	0	1	2	1	0	0	0	0	0	1
GREECE + TURKEY	2	1	0	0	0	0	0	0	0	1	1	0	0	0	0	0	0	0	1	0	0	0
OTHER EUROPE	3	0	0	0	0	0	1	1	0	1	2	2	0	0	0	0	2	0	1	0	0	0
EUROPE EX. U.K.	68	2	3	0	0	1	4	1	0	2	2	2	3	4	13	4	2	12	4	2	5	2
SOUTHERN DOMINIONS	19	1	0	1	0	0	0	0	0	0	2	2	2	2	1	4	1	1	1	0	1	0
S. AFRICA +RHOD.	6	0	0	1	0	0	0	0	0	0	1	1	1	0	0	2	0	1	0	0	0	0
AUSTRALIA + N.Z.	13	1	0	1	0	0	0	1	0	0	1	1	1	0	1	2	1	0	3	0	1	0
ASIA + OTHER AFRICA	16	0	1	0	0	0	0	1	0	0	0	0	1	0	4	2	1	0	2	0	0	1
JAPAN	10	0	1	1	1	0	0	1	0	0	0	2	0	0	0	3	0	1	1	0	0	0
OTHER ASIA+AFR.	6	0	0	0	0	0	0	0	0	0	0	0	0	0	4	0	0	0	1	0	0	0
BLACK AFRICA	0	0	0	0	0	0	0	0	0	0	0	0	0	0	0	3	0	0	0	0	0	0
ARAB WORLD	0	0	0	0	0	0	0	0	0	0	0	0	0	0	0	0	0	0	0	0	0	0
INDIA	4	0	0	0	0	0	0	0	0	0	0	0	0	0	3	0	0	1	1	0	0	0
PHILIPPINES	0	0	0	0	0	0	0	0	0	0	0	0	0	0	0	0	0	0	0	0	0	0
OTHER E. ASIA	2	0	0	0	0	0	0	0	0	0	0	0	0	0	0	0	0	0	0	0	1	0
OTHER ASIA	2	0	0	0	0	0	0	0	0	0	0	0	0	0	1	0	0	0	0	0	0	0

CHAPTER 3- THE PROLIFERATION OF FOREIGN SUBSIDIARIES
SECTION 2- THE FLOW OF MANUFACTURING BY INDUSTRY OF PARENT SYSTEM
TABLE 19- MANUFACTURING SUBSIDIARIES IN A SYSTEM IN THE
MOTOR VEHICLES INDUSTRY (SIC 371)
CLASSIFIED BY COUNTRY OR REGION AND BY PERIOD MANUFACTURE BEGAN

PERIOD

COUNTRY OR REGION	PRE 1968	PRE 1901	1901 -13	1914 -19	1920 -24	1925 -29	1930 -34	1935 -39	1940 -45	1946 -50	1951 -53	1954 -55	1956 -57	1958 -59	1960 -61	1962	1963	1964	1965	1966	1967	UNK
OUTSIDE U.S.	328	0	5	5	9	34	8	8	3	17	12	8	10	33	31	18	36	23	20	22	8	18
OUT. U.S. + CANADA	271	0	3	3	8	27	6	5	3	13	8	4	9	28	27	18	32	20	13	18	5	18
OUT. WEST. HEMIS.	197	0	3	2	8	23	6	4	2	12	5	6	6	18	21	13	21	13	7	8	4	17
OUT. WHITE CWEALTH	188	0	0	3	5	17	3	3	3	8	5	6	4	23	17	15	26	17	11	17	3	3
OUT. DEVLPED WORLD	98	0	0	1	0	8	0	1	2	5	3	3	3	14	9	8	14	7	6	12	1	1
CANADA	57	0	2	2	1	7	2	3	0	4	4	1	1	5	4	0	4	3	7	4	3	0
LATIN AMERICA	74	0	0	1	0	4	1	1	1	1	3	3	3	10	6	5	11	7	6	10	1	1
C. AMER.+CARIB.	23	0	0	0	0	1	1	1	0	0	0	1	0	1	3	1	4	2	3	5	0	0
CUBA	0	0	0	0	0	0	0	0	0	0	1	1	0	1	0	0	0	0	0	0	0	0
MEXICO	22	0	0	0	0	1	0	0	0	0	1	1	0	1	3	2	4	2	2	5	0	0
OTHER	1	0	0	0	0	0	0	0	0	0	0	0	0	0	0	0	0	0	1	0	0	0
S. AMERICA	51	0	0	1	0	3	0	0	1	1	2	0	3	9	3	4	7	5	3	5	1	0
ARGENTINA	19	0	0	1	0	1	0	1	0	0	2	2	2	3	1	2	3	1	3	3	0	1
BRAZIL	13	0	0	0	0	1	0	0	0	0	0	1	1	5	1	0	2	0	0	3	0	0
PERU	4	0	0	0	0	0	0	0	0	0	0	0	0	0	0	1	2	2	1	0	1	0
COLOMBIA	5	0	0	0	0	0	0	0	0	1	0	0	0	0	1	0	0	0	0	1	0	1
VENEZUELA	7	0	0	0	0	1	0	0	0	0	0	0	0	1	0	1	2	1	0	0	0	0
OTHER	3	0	0	0	0	1	0	0	0	1	0	1	0	0	0	1	0	0	1	0	0	0
EUROPE	130	0	3	2	8	12	4	3	1	7	4	4	2	11	12	8	14	6	6	5	2	16
EFTA	61	0	0	1	3	6	1	2	0	6	3	1	1	2	2	3	4	1	3	2	0	15
U.K.	48	0	3	0	2	5	1	0	4	4	2	1	1	2	4	2	3	2	2	0	0	15
SCANDINAVIA	3	0	0	0	1	1	0	0	2	2	0	0	0	0	0	1	0	1	1	1	0	0
SWITZERLAND	2	0	0	0	1	1	0	1	0	0	0	0	0	0	0	0	1	0	0	0	0	0
OTHER EFTA	3	0	0	0	0	0	0	0	0	0	0	0	0	0	0	1	0	0	0	1	1	0
EUROP. COMMUNITY	53	0	0	0	3	4	3	1	0	0	1	3	3	8	7	1	7	4	3	2	2	0
FRANCE	21	0	0	1	1	4	1	0	0	0	1	0	0	7	2	0	2	2	0	2	1	0
GERMANY	18	0	0	0	0	0	2	0	0	0	1	1	0	0	2	3	5	1	3	2	1	0
ITALY	7	0	0	0	1	4	0	0	0	1	0	0	0	0	2	1	0	1	0	1	0	0
BELGIUM + LUX	3	0	0	0	0	0	1	0	0	0	0	0	0	0	3	0	1	0	0	0	1	0
NETHERLANDS	4	0	0	0	1	0	0	1	0	0	1	0	1	1	0	1	0	0	0	0	0	0
SPAIN	7	0	0	0	0	1	0	0	0	0	0	0	0	1	1	0	2	0	1	0	0	0
GREECE + TURKEY	3	0	0	0	0	1	0	0	1	1	0	0	1	0	0	0	0	0	0	0	0	1
OTHER EUROPE	6	0	0	0	1	1	1	0	0	0	0	0	0	0	0	1	0	1	1	0	0	1
EUROPE EX. U.K.	82	0	2	2	6	7	3	3	1	3	2	3	1	9	8	6	11	5	4	5	2	1
SOUTHERN DOMINIONS	33	0	0	0	0	5	2	1	0	1	1	0	4	3	6	1	3	2	0	1	2	1
S. AFRICA +RHOD.	9	0	0	0	0	1	0	0	0	0	0	0	0	2	2	0	1	0	0	0	1	1
AUSTRALIA + N.Z.	24	0	0	0	2	4	2	0	0	1	1	0	4	4	4	1	2	2	0	1	1	0
ASIA + OTHER AFRICA	34	0	0	0	6	2	0	1	4	4	0	0	0	4	3	4	4	5	2	2	1	0
JAPAN	10	0	0	0	0	0	0	0	0	0	0	0	0	0	3	1	3	5	1	2	0	0
OTHER ASIA+AFR.	24	0	0	0	4	4	0	1	4	4	0	0	0	4	0	2	0	0	2	0	0	0
BLACK AFRICA	3	0	0	0	0	0	0	0	0	0	0	0	0	1	1	0	0	1	0	0	0	0
ARAB WORLD	9	0	0	0	0	2	0	0	0	0	0	0	0	2	2	1	2	0	2	0	0	0
INDIA	3	0	0	0	0	0	0	0	0	0	0	0	0	1	0	0	1	0	0	0	0	0
PHILIPPINES	9	0	0	0	2	2	0	0	0	1	0	0	0	0	0	0	0	0	1	2	0	0
OTHER E. ASIA	2	0	0	0	0	0	0	0	0	0	0	0	0	0	0	0	0	0	0	0	0	0
OTHER ASIA	7	0	0	0	2	2	0	0	3	3	0	0	0	0	0	0	1	0	1	0	0	0

CHAPTER 3- THE PROLIFERATION OF FOREIGN SUBSIDIARIES
SECTION 2- THE FLOW OF MANUFACTURING BY INDUSTRY OF PARENT SYSTEM
TABLE 20- MANUFACTURING SUBSIDIARIES IN A SYSTEM IN THE.
OTHER TRANSPORTATION EQUIPMENT INDUSTRIES (SIC 372-379)
CLASSIFIED BY COUNTRY OR REGION AND BY PERIOD MANUFACTURE BEGAN

COUNTRY OR REGION	PRE 1968	PRE 1901	1901 -13	1914 -19	1920 -24	1925 -29	1930 -34	1935 -39	1940 -45	1946 -50	1951 -53	1954 -55	1956 -57	1958 -59	1960 -61	1962	1963	1964	1965	1966	1967	UNK
OUTSIDE U.S.	125	2	1	1	1	2	1	3	4	6	2	4	8	11	23	7	10	17	4	14	0	4
OUT. U.S. + CANADA	102	2	1	0	1	1	0	2	2	3	1	3	6	9	19	7	10	14	4	13	0	4
OUT. WEST. HEMIS.	71	2	1	0	1	1	0	2	1	1	1	2	3	4	10	5	9	11	3	13	0	3
OUT. WHITE CWEALTH	74	2	1	0	1	0	2	2	2	2	2	4	7	17	11	7	9	11	3	2	0	4
OUT. DEVLPED WORLD	32	0	0	0	0	0	0	2	2	2	1	3	5	9	2	1	3	1	1	0	1
CANADA	23	0	0	1	1	1	1	2	3	3	1	2	2	4	2	1	3	1	1	0	0
LATIN AMERICA	31	0	0	0	0	0	2	2	2	2	1	3	5	9	6	1	3	1	1	0	1
C. AMER.+CARIB.	14	0	0	0	0	0	1	0	0	1	1	0	1	1	6	1	1	0	0	0	1
CUBA	0	0	0	0	0	0	0	0	0	0	0	0	0	0	0	0	0	0	0	0	0
MEXICO	12	0	0	0	1	0	0	1	0	0	0	0	1	2	5	0	0	0	0	0	0
OTHER	2	0	0	0	0	0	0	0	0	1	0	0	0	0	1	0	0	0	0	0	0
S. AMERICA	17	0	0	0	0	0	1	1	2	0	0	1	3	3	1	2	0	2	0	0	0
ARGENTINA	5	0	0	0	0	0	1	1	0	0	0	0	3	1	0	0	1	0	0	0	0
BRAZIL	6	0	0	0	0	1	0	0	1	0	0	1	0	1	0	1	1	0	0	0	0
PERU	1	0	0	0	0	0	0	0	0	1	0	0	0	0	0	0	0	0	0	0	0
COLOMBIA	2	0	0	0	0	0	0	0	0	0	0	0	0	0	0	0	1	1	0	0	0
VENEZUELA	1	0	0	0	0	0	0	0	0	0	0	0	0	0	0	0	0	0	0	0	0
OTHER	2	0	0	0	0	0	0	0	1	0	0	0	0	2	0	0	0	0	0	0	0
EUROPE	58	2	1	0	1	0	0	0	0	0	0	3	3	4	9	3	7	9	3	11	0	2
EFTA	26	0	0	0	0	0	0	0	0	0	0	2	2	2	2	0	3	5	1	1	0	0
U.K.	21	0	0	0	0	0	0	0	0	0	0	2	2	2	1	0	1	4	1	10	0	0
SCANDINAVIA	4	0	0	0	0	0	0	0	0	0	0	0	0	0	0	0	0	0	1	0	0	0
SWITZERLAND	1	0	0	0	0	0	0	0	0	0	0	0	0	0	1	0	1	1	0	0	0	0
OTHER EFTA	0	0	0	0	0	0	0	0	0	0	0	0	0	0	0	0	0	0	0	0	0	0
EUROP. COMMUNITY	29	2	1	0	0	0	1	0	0	0	1	2	2	2	7	3	4	4	1	0	0	2
FRANCE	14	1	0	0	0	0	0	0	0	0	0	0	0	0	5	2	0	3	0	1	0	1
GERMANY	6	0	1	0	0	0	1	0	0	0	1	1	1	0	2	1	1	0	1	0	0	0
ITALY	5	0	0	0	0	0	0	0	0	0	0	0	0	1	0	0	1	0	0	0	0	1
BELGIUM + LUX	3	0	1	0	0	0	0	0	0	0	0	0	0	0	0	0	1	0	0	0	0	0
NETHERLANDS	1	0	0	0	0	0	0	0	0	0	0	0	0	0	0	0	1	0	0	0	0	0
SPAIN	1	0	0	0	0	0	0	0	0	0	0	0	0	0	0	1	0	0	0	0	0	0
GREECE + TURKEY	1	0	0	0	0	0	0	0	0	0	0	0	0	0	0	0	0	0	0	0	0	0
OTHER EUROPE	1	0	0	0	0	1	0	0	0	0	0	0	0	0	0	0	0	0	0	0	0	0
EUROPE EX. U.K.	37	2	1	0	1	0	2	0	0	0	1	1	0	2	8	3	6	5	2	1	0	2
SOUTHERN DOMINIONS	7	0	0	0	0	0	0	0	0	1	1	0	0	0	1	0	0	2	1	1	0	0
S. AFRICA +RHOD.	4	0	0	0	0	0	0	0	0	1	0	1	0	0	1	0	0	1	1	1	0	0
AUSTRALIA + N.Z.	3	0	0	0	0	0	0	0	0	0	1	0	0	0	0	0	0	1	0	0	0	0
ASIA + OTHER AFRICA	6	0	0	0	0	0	0	0	0	0	0	0	0	0	0	2	0	0	0	1	0	1
JAPAN	5	0	0	0	0	0	0	0	0	0	0	0	0	0	0	2	2	0	0	0	0	1
OTHER ASIA+AFK.	1	0	0	0	0	0	0	0	0	1	1	0	0	0	0	0	0	0	0	1	1	0
BLACK AFRICA	0	0	0	0	0	0	0	0	0	0	0	0	0	0	0	0	0	0	0	0	0	0
ARAB WORLD	0	0	0	0	0	0	0	0	0	0	0	0	0	0	0	0	0	0	0	0	0	0
INDIA	0	0	0	0	0	0	0	0	0	1	0	0	0	0	0	0	0	0	0	0	0	0
PHILIPPINES	1	0	0	0	0	0	0	0	0	1	1	0	0	0	0	0	0	0	0	1	0	0
OTHER E. ASIA	0	0	0	0	0	0	0	0	0	0	0	0	0	0	0	0	0	0	0	0	0	0
OTHER ASIA	0	0	0	0	0	0	0	0	0	0	0	0	0	0	0	0	0	0	0	0	0	0

CHAPTER 3- THE PROLIFERATION OF FOREIGN SUBSIDIARIES
SECTION 2- THE FLOW OF MANUFACTURING BY INDUSTRY OF PARENT SYSTEM
TABLE 21- MANUFACTURING SUBSIDIARIES IN A SYSTEM IN THE
INSTRUMENTS AND PRECISION GOODS INDUSTRIES (SIC 38)
CLASSIFIED BY COUNTRY OR REGION AND BY PERIOD MANUFACTURE BEGAN

PERIOD

COUNTRY OR REGION	PRE 1908	PRE 1901	1901 -13	1914 -19	1920 -24	1925 -29	1930 -34	1935 -39	1940 -45	1946 -50	1951 -53	1954 -55	1956 -57	1958 -59	1960 -61	1962	1963	1964	1965	1966	1967	UNK
OUTSIDE U.S.	116	3	2	1	0	4	4	3	2	9	12	8	11	5	15	6	9	5	8	9	0	0
OUT. U.S. + CANADA	99	2	2	0	0	4	4	3	1	7	8	7	9	4	14	6	8	5	8	7	0	0
OUT. WEST. HEMIS.	79	2	2	0	0	4	3	1	1	6	8	6	7	4	11	6	7	4	5	5	0	0
OUT. WHITE CWEALTH	73	1	0	0	0	3	2	2	0	1	6	6	9	3	12	5	7	5	6	5	0	0
OUT. DEVLPED WORLD	28	0	0	0	0	1	2	2	0	2	2	2	3	2	4	1	2	1	3	4	0	0
CANADA	17	1	1	1	0	0	0	0	1	2	2	1	2	1	1	0	1	1	0	2	0	0
LATIN AMERICA	20	0	0	0	0	1	1	2	0	1	2	2	2	0	3	1	3	0	3	2	0	0
C. AMER.+CARIB.	7	0	0	0	0	1	0	0	1	1	1	1	0	1	1	0	1	0	1	0	0	0
CUBA	5	0	0	0	0	1	0	0	1	1	0	0	0	0	0	0	0	0	0	0	0	0
MEXICO	1	0	0	0	0	0	0	0	0	0	1	1	0	1	2	0	1	1	1	2	0	0
OTHER	1	0	0	0	0	0	2	1	0	0	0	0	0	0	0	0	0	0	0	0	0	0
S. AMERICA	13	0	0	0	0	0	2	0	0	0	1	1	2	0	2	0	2	0	2	2	0	0
ARGENTINA	4	0	0	0	0	0	0	0	0	0	1	0	1	0	1	0	0	0	0	0	0	0
BRAZIL	3	0	0	0	0	0	1	0	0	0	0	0	1	0	0	0	0	0	1	0	0	0
PERU	1	0	0	0	0	0	0	0	0	0	0	0	0	0	0	0	1	0	0	0	0	0
COLUMBIA	2	0	0	0	0	0	0	0	0	0	0	0	0	0	1	0	0	1	0	1	0	0
VENEZUELA	2	0	0	0	0	0	0	0	0	0	0	1	0	0	0	0	1	0	0	1	0	0
OTHER	1	0	0	0	0	0	0	0	0	0	0	0	0	0	0	0	0	0	1	0	0	0
EUROPE	57	2	1	0	0	4	1	0	0	5	4	4	6	2	8	4	6	4	4	4	1	0
EFTA	18	1	1	0	0	1	1	0	5	5	1	0	1	2	1	1	1	0	2	1	1	0
U.K.	14	1	1	0	0	1	0	0	5	5	1	0	0	1	1	1	1	0	0	1	1	0
SCANDINAVIA	1	0	0	0	0	0	0	0	0	0	0	0	0	0	0	0	0	0	0	0	0	0
SWITZERLAND	1	0	0	0	0	0	0	0	0	0	0	0	0	1	0	0	0	0	1	0	0	0
OTHER EFTA	2	0	0	0	0	1	1	0	0	0	0	0	1	0	0	1	0	1	1	0	0	0
EUROP. COMMUNITY	37	1	0	0	0	3	0	0	0	0	3	4	4	0	7	3	5	4	2	0	0	0
FRANCE	13	1	0	0	0	1	0	0	0	0	1	3	1	0	2	2	2	0	0	0	0	0
GERMANY	12	0	0	0	0	1	0	0	0	0	1	0	3	0	2	2	1	1	1	0	0	0
ITALY	7	1	0	0	0	2	0	0	0	0	1	0	0	0	1	0	2	2	1	0	0	0
BELGIUM + LUX	2	0	0	0	0	0	0	0	0	0	0	0	0	0	1	0	0	0	0	0	0	0
NETHERLANDS	3	0	0	0	0	0	0	0	0	0	0	0	0	0	1	0	0	1	0	0	0	0
SPAIN	1	0	0	0	0	0	0	0	0	0	0	0	0	0	0	0	0	0	0	0	0	0
GREECE + TURKEY	0	0	0	0	0	0	0	0	0	0	0	0	0	0	0	0	0	0	0	0	0	0
OTHER EUROPE	0	0	0	0	0	0	0	0	0	0	0	0	0	0	1	0	0	0	0	0	0	0
EUROPE EX. U.K.	43	1	0	0	0	3	0	0	0	1	3	4	6	1	7	4	5	4	3	3	0	0
SOUTHERN DOMINIONS	11	0	1	0	0	0	1	0	0	0	1	1	0	0	1	1	0	1	1	1	0	0
S. AFRICA +RHOD.	3	0	0	0	0	0	0	0	0	0	0	1	0	0	0	1	0	0	0	0	0	0
AUSTRALIA + N.Z.	8	0	1	0	0	2	1	1	0	0	1	0	1	0	2	0	0	1	1	1	0	0
ASIA + OTHER AFRICA	11	0	0	0	0	0	0	0	0	0	1	0	1	0	2	1	3	0	0	3	0	0
JAPAN	3	0	0	0	0	0	0	0	0	0	0	0	0	0	0	0	1	0	0	1	0	0
OTHER ASIA+AFR.	8	0	0	0	0	0	0	0	0	0	1	0	1	2	2	1	2	0	0	2	0	0
BLACK AFRICA	1	0	0	0	0	0	0	0	0	0	0	0	0	0	0	0	0	0	1	0	0	0
ARAB WORLD	0	0	0	0	0	0	0	0	0	0	0	0	0	0	0	0	0	0	0	0	0	0
INDIA	3	0	0	0	0	0	0	0	0	0	0	0	1	0	1	0	0	0	0	1	0	0
PHILIPPINES	2	0	0	0	0	0	0	0	0	0	0	0	0	0	0	1	0	0	0	1	0	0
OTHER E. ASIA	0	0	0	0	0	0	0	0	0	0	0	0	0	0	0	0	0	0	0	0	0	0
OTHER ASIA	2	0	0	0	0	0	0	0	0	1	0	0	0	0	1	0	0	0	0	1	0	0

CHAPTER 3- THE PROLIFERATION OF FOREIGN SUBSIDIARIES
SECTION 2- THE FLOW OF MANUFACTURING BY INDUSTRY OF PARENT SYSTEM
TABLE 22- MANUFACTURING SUBSIDIARIES IN A SYSTEM IN THE
OTHER INDUSTRIES (SIC 21,27, AND 39)
CLASSIFIED BY COUNTRY OR REGION AND BY PERIOD MANUFACTURE BEGAN

PERIOD

COUNTRY OR REGION	PRE 1968	PRE 1901	1901-13	1914-19	1920-24	1925-29	1930-34	1935-39	1940-45	1946-50	1951-53	1954-55	1956-57	1958-59	1960-61	1962	1963	1964	1965	1966	1967	UNK
OUTSIDE U.S.	103	0	1	2	0	4	2	2	1	2	2	3	4	16	22	15	5	5	3	9	3	1
OUT. U.S. + CANADA	87	0	0	1	0	4	1	2	1	2	1	4	4	15	19	12	4	4	2	8	3	0
OUT. WEST. HEMIS.	61	0	0	1	0	3	0	0	1	1	0	1	2	12	16	9	3	3	1	4	2	0
OUT. WHITE CWEALTH	66	0	0	0	0	3	1	0	0	2	0	2	4	7	14	11	5	2	2	8	2	0
OUT. DEVLPED WORLD	31	0	0	0	0	1	1	0	1	2	1	2	2	5	3	4	1	1	1	4	2	0
CANADA	16	0	1	1	0	0	1	0	0	0	1	1	0	1	3	3	1	1	1	1	0	1
LATIN AMERICA	26	0	0	0	0	1	1	0	1	1	1	2	2	3	3	3	1	1	1	4	1	0
C. AMER.+CARIB.	11	0	0	0	0	1	1	0	1	0	1	0	0	1	0	2	1	1	0	2	1	0
CUBA	1	0	0	0	0	1	0	0	0	1	1	0	0	0	0	0	0	0	0	0	1	0
MEXICO	5	0	0	0	0	0	0	0	0	0	0	0	0	1	2	2	1	0	0	2	0	0
OTHER	5	0	0	0	0	1	1	0	1	0	0	2	2	1	0	0	0	1	0	0	0	0
S. AMERICA	15	0	0	0	0	1	0	0	0	1	0	1	0	2	3	3	1	1	1	2	0	0
ARGENTINA	5	0	0	0	0	0	0	0	0	0	0	0	0	0	0	0	1	0	1	0	0	0
BRAZIL	2	0	0	0	0	0	0	0	0	1	0	0	0	2	3	2	1	1	0	2	0	0
PERU	1	0	0	0	0	1	0	0	0	1	0	0	0	0	0	0	0	0	0	0	0	0
COLOMBIA	1	0	0	0	0	0	0	0	1	0	0	1	0	1	3	0	0	0	0	0	0	0
VENEZUELA	6	0	0	0	0	1	0	0	0	0	0	0	0	0	0	0	0	0	0	0	0	0
OTHER	0	0	0	0	0	0	0	0	0	0	0	0	0	0	0	0	0	0	0	0	0	0
EUROPE	47	0	0	1	0	3	0	2	0	0	0	0	2	5	16	6	3	3	1	4	1	0
EFTA	20	0	0	1	0	1	0	2	0	0	0	0	0	2	8	2	1	1	1	0	1	0
U.K.	13	0	0	1	0	1	0	2	0	0	0	0	0	2	5	5	0	1	0	0	1	0
SCANDINAVIA	5	0	0	0	0	1	0	0	0	0	0	0	0	0	2	2	1	0	1	0	0	0
SWITZERLAND	1	0	0	0	0	1	0	0	0	0	0	0	0	0	0	0	0	0	0	0	0	0
OTHER EFTA	1	0	0	0	0	0	0	0	0	0	0	0	0	0	0	0	0	0	0	0	0	0
EUROP. COMMUNITY	24	0	0	0	0	0	0	0	0	0	0	0	2	2	0	4	2	2	0	4	0	0
FRANCE	7	0	0	0	0	0	0	0	0	0	0	0	0	2	8	4	0	1	0	1	0	1
GERMANY	6	0	0	0	0	0	0	0	0	0	0	0	0	1	3	3	0	0	0	3	0	0
ITALY	6	0	0	0	0	0	0	0	0	1	0	1	0	1	1	1	1	0	0	0	0	0
BELGIUM + LUX	3	0	0	0	0	0	0	0	0	0	0	0	0	1	1	1	1	1	0	0	0	0
NETHERLANDS	2	0	0	0	0	2	0	0	0	0	0	0	1	0	0	0	0	0	0	0	0	0
SPAIN	2	0	0	0	0	2	0	0	0	0	0	0	0	0	0	0	0	0	0	0	0	0
GREECE + TURKEY	0	0	0	0	0	0	0	0	0	0	0	0	0	0	0	0	0	0	0	0	0	0
OTHER EUROPE	1	0	0	0	0	0	0	0	0	0	0	0	0	1	1	0	0	0	0	0	0	0
EUROPE EX. U.K.	34	0	0	0	0	2	0	0	0	0	0	0	2	3	11	6	3	2	1	4	0	0
SOUTHERN DOMINIONS	7	0	0	0	0	0	0	0	0	0	0	1	0	5	0	0	0	0	0	0	0	0
S. AFRICA +RHOD.	0	0	0	0	0	0	0	0	0	0	0	0	0	5	0	0	0	0	0	0	0	0
AUSTRALIA + N.Z.	7	0	0	0	0	0	0	0	0	0	0	1	0	2	0	0	0	0	0	0	0	0
ASIA + OTHER AFRICA	7	0	0	0	0	0	0	0	0	0	0	1	0	2	0	0	0	0	0	0	0	0
JAPAN	2	0	0	0	0	0	0	0	0	0	0	0	0	0	0	0	0	0	0	0	0	0
OTHER ASIA+AFR.	5	0	0	0	0	0	0	0	0	1	0	0	0	2	0	0	0	0	0	0	0	0
BLACK AFRICA	1	0	0	0	0	0	0	0	0	0	0	0	0	0	0	1	0	0	0	0	0	0
ARAB WORLD	1	0	0	0	0	0	0	0	0	1	0	1	0	1	0	1	1	0	0	0	0	0
INDIA	1	0	0	0	0	0	0	0	0	0	0	0	0	1	0	0	0	0	0	0	0	0
PHILIPPINES	0	0	0	0	0	0	0	0	0	0	0	0	0	0	0	0	0	0	0	0	0	0
OTHER E. ASIA	0	0	0	0	0	0	0	0	0	0	0	0	0	0	0	0	0	0	0	0	0	0
OTHER ASIA	2	0	0	0	0	0	0	0	0	1	0	0	0	0	1	1	0	0	0	0	0	0

CHAPTER 3- THE PROLIFERATION OF FOREIGN SUBSIDIARIES
SECTION 3- THE FLOW OF MANUFACTURING BY CHARACTERISTIC OF PARENT SYSTEM
TABLE A1- MANUFACTURING SUBSIDIARIES IN A SYSTEM
WITH LOW SALES IN 1966
CLASSIFIED BY COUNTRY OR REGION AND BY PERIOD MANUFACTURE BEGAN

PERIOD

COUNTRY OR REGION	PRE 1968	PRE 1901	1901 -13	1914 -19	1920 -24	1925 -29	1930 -34	1935 -39	1940 -45	1946 -50	1951 -53	1954 -55	1956 -57	1958 -59	1960 -61	1962	1963	1964	1965	1966	1967	UNK
OUTSIDE U.S.	2082	18	26	30	35	60	58	83	47	102	95	82	131	182	289	139	146	115	135	161	113	35
OUT. U.S. + CANADA	1753	15	17	16	27	40	45	65	35	78	71	66	110	167	255	130	131	96	122	141	97	29
OUT. WEST. HEMIS.	1216	15	17	11	22	36	40	50	13	47	47	36	57	104	178	105	102	67	91	94	59	25
OUT. WHITE CWEALTH	1284	8	14	11	20	26	16	27	25	50	45	49	84	126	200	104	106	82	96	113	75	11
OUT. DEVLPED WORLD	659	0	0	6	5	15	15	22	22	37	28	34	34	73	101	40	43	41	39	58	45	5
CANADA	329	3	9	14	8	20	13	18	12	24	24	16	21	15	34	9	15	19	13	20	16	6
LATIN AMERICA	537	0	0	5	5	4	5	15	22	31	24	30	53	63	77	25	29	29	31	47	38	4
C. AMER.+CARIB.	245	0	0	1	2	1	1	5	3	16	11	11	30	30	28	10	11	21	15	27	17	2
CUBA	15	0	0	0	1	1	0	1	1	0	1	1	2	0	1	0	0	1	0	0	0	0
MEXICO	159	0	0	0	0	1	0	3	1	11	8	8	16	23	15	6	7	10	9	20	17	0
OTHER	71	0	0	0	1	0	1	1	1	4	2	2	11	7	12	4	4	0	6	7	0	7
S. AMERICA	292	0	0	3	3	1	10	19	15	15	13	19	23	33	49	15	18	8	16	20	21	2
ARGENTINA	68	0	0	4	3	2	1	5	6	5	5	6	7	8	8	2	6	2	5	4	4	1
BRAZIL	81	0	0	2	1	1	0	5	5	6	7	6	6	15	8	6	4	5	2	5	4	1
PERU	19	0	0	0	0	0	0	0	2	1	1	2	1	3	0	3	0	2	0	1	1	1
COLOMBIA	39	0	0	0	0	0	0	1	0	3	5	1	3	1	2	2	2	1	5	5	3	1
VENEZUELA	55	0	0	0	2	1	0	2	1	3	1	5	5	8	14	2	5	2	2	5	3	2
OTHER	30	0	0	0	0	0	0	0	0	2	1	2	1	2	2	1	1	1	5	0	7	0
EUROPE	839	15	17	5	18	34	25	36	6	29	33	22	36	67	125	62	71	45	68	63	42	20
EFTA	319	6	7	3	3	17	16	25	4	16	17	7	14	15	36	17	17	16	27	23	16	15
U.K.	253	6	7	3	3	13	15	24	4	15	14	7	12	12	29	11	13	7	17	14	14	15
SCANDINAVIA	37	0	3	0	0	2	1	0	0	0	1	2	1	1	3	3	1	6	5	6	2	0
SWITZERLAND	11	0	0	0	0	1	0	0	0	1	1	0	1	1	3	0	2	1	0	0	0	0
OTHER EFTA	18	0	1	0	0	1	0	1	0	1	1	0	1	1	1	2	1	2	3	2	0	0
EUROP. COMMUNITY	445	8	10	14	14	14	11	11	2	11	12	11	18	47	83	39	48	26	26	31	19	5
FRANCE	143	4	3	7	7	5	5	2	0	3	4	2	8	11	32	16	12	8	7	9	5	2
GERMANY	128	3	4	4	4	7	1	5	0	3	5	4	8	10	18	7	12	8	12	13	9	3
ITALY	87	1	3	1	1	5	2	1	0	2	2	2	4	12	19	11	12	6	6	7	4	3
BELGIUM + LUX	43	0	0	1	1	1	0	0	0	1	1	1	2	2	7	4	5	2	2	3	2	0
NETHERLANDS	44	0	0	1	1	1	2	2	1	3	1	2	2	4	7	3	5	2	3	2	1	1
SPAIN	44	0	0	1	1	0	0	0	1	1	0	1	1	3	7	1	4	1	12	5	6	0
GREECE + TURKEY	12	0	0	0	0	1	0	0	0	1	0	1	1	0	2	0	2	0	0	3	1	0
OTHER EUROPE	19	1	0	1	0	2	0	0	2	3	4	1	1	2	3	2	2	0	0	1	0	5
EUROPE EX. U.K.	586	9	14	2	15	21	10	12	2	14	19	15	24	55	96	51	58	38	51	47	28	5
SOUTHERN DOMINIONS	200	0	0	0	6	4	1	14	6	12	8	9	13	27	23	14	10	7	9	12	8	3
S. AFRICA +RHOD.	61	0	0	0	1	2	0	3	4	7	4	2	2	7	6	4	6	5	4	4	0	2
AUSTRALIA + N.Z.	139	0	0	5	2	0	1	11	1	5	4	7	11	20	17	10	4	8	8	19	8	1
ASIA + OTHER AFRICA	177	0	0	0	2	1	1	1	1	6	6	5	8	10	30	29	21	15	14	8	9	2
JAPAN	55	0	0	0	0	0	0	0	0	6	4	2	3	10	6	14	17	3	8	8	7	1
OTHER ASIA+AFR.	122	0	0	0	0	1	0	0	0	6	2	4	5	10	24	15	14	12	8	11	2	1
BLACK AFRICA	13	0	0	0	0	0	0	0	0	0	0	1	0	0	4	1	1	0	1	1	2	0
ARAB WORLD	9	0	0	0	0	0	0	0	0	1	1	0	1	0	4	0	1	2	0	1	0	0
INDIA	28	0	0	0	1	1	0	1	0	1	0	1	1	6	4	5	3	3	3	2	1	0
PHILIPPINES	20	0	0	0	1	0	0	0	0	0	3	0	1	3	1	1	6	1	1	1	2	0
OTHER E. ASIA	21	0	0	0	0	0	0	0	0	0	0	0	1	0	4	3	1	5	2	3	3	0
OTHER ASIA	31	0	0	0	2	1	0	0	0	3	0	0	2	1	11	5	2	2	1	3	1	0

CHAPTER 3- THE PROLIFERATION OF FOREIGN SUBSIDIARIES
SECTION 3- THE FLOW OF MANUFACTURING BY CHARACTERISTIC OF PARENT SYSTEM
TABLE A2- MANUFACTURING SUBSIDIARIES IN A SYSTEM
WITH HIGH SALES IN 1966
CLASSIFIED BY COUNTRY OR REGION AND BY PERIOD MANUFACTURE BEGAN

COUNTRY OR REGION	PRE 1968	PRE 1921	1901 -13	1914 -19	1920 -24	1925 -29	1930 -34	1935 -39	1940 -45	1946 -50	1951 -53	1954 -55	1956 -57	1958 -59	1960 -61	1962	1963	1964	1965	1966	1967	UNK
OUTSIDE U.S.	3150	30	52	44	57	159	97	129	100	148	139	142	173	242	401	177	198	225	235	169	125	108
OUT. U.S. + CANADA	2666	27	33	25	44	112	78	102	76	119	117	106	144	218	362	159	185	195	203	153	117	91
OUT. WEST. HEMIS.	1862	24	26	17	36	92	60	67	26	62	72	73	75	146	273	111	144	154	144	111	87	62
OUT. WHITE CWEALTH	2062	19	22	23	31	74	57	71	64	92	95	80	120	173	270	124	134	153	171	122	98	70
OUT. DEVLPED WORLD	1050	3	7	13	10	30	21	41	53	68	49	43	79	94	123	65	63	63	82	55	47	41
CANADA	484	3	19	19	13	47	19	27	24	29	22	36	29	24	39	18	13	30	32	16	8	17
LATIN AMERICA	804	3	7	8	8	20	18	35	50	57	45	33	69	72	89	48	41	41	59	42	30	29
C. AMER.+CARIB.	331	1	3	2	0	7	10	20	19	18	15	9	24	31	34	17	16	19	31	22	17	16
CUBA	33	1	0	2	0	2	3	7	2	3	1	0	8	3	0	0	0	0	2	0	2	2
MEXICO	211	0	3	0	0	2	4	9	13	15	12	9	13	23	25	10	9	14	14	12	11	10
OTHER	87	0	0	0	0	5	3	4	4	0	2	0	3	6	0	7	7	5	17	10	6	4
S. AMERICA	473	2	4	6	8	13	8	15	31	39	30	24	45	41	55	31	25	22	28	20	13	13
ARGENTINA	93	0	2	3	2	7	7	6	7	7	1	5	6	8	12	6	3	4	4	3	2	2
BRAZIL	118	0	0	3	0	6	0	4	14	14	12	4	15	15	10	14	11	3	5	8	2	2
PERU	39	1	1	0	1	1	0	0	7	7	1	1	6	1	1	0	6	3	2	1	3	3
COLOMBIA	76	0	0	0	1	0	1	1	5	2	2	4	4	8	3	1	4	6	8	2	0	1
VENEZUELA	90	0	0	2	1	0	0	1	6	6	7	4	11	9	9	9	4	4	5	3	3	2
OTHER	57	1	1	0	2	3	0	3	1	4	8	4	5	0	13	4	3	3	5	3	3	3
EUROPE	1216	23	23	11	32	68	51	45	15	41	44	46	52	97	169	80	79	92	94	79	51	24
EFTA	432	8	14	6	15	32	18	28	5	24	11	12	22	32	54	30	28	27	22	26	10	8
U.K.	298	7	9	3	11	26	15	16	3	17	9	11	16	21	39	24	19	11	13	17	5	6
SCANDINAVIA	79	1	4	3	2	4	2	4	0	6	1	1	5	4	8	6	5	11	5	5	2	1
SWITZERLAND	26	0	0	0	0	0	1	5	0	1	0	0	1	2	5	0	1	4	1	2	2	1
OTHER EFTA	29	0	1	0	2	2	0	3	2	0	1	0	0	5	2	0	3	1	3	2	1	0
EUROP. COMMUNITY	626	13	7	5	10	31	28	13	7	16	23	28	28	59	98	40	38	49	57	33	28	15
FRANCE	180	4	7	1	6	7	11	6	2	5	4	10	7	19	29	11	8	20	17	7	12	5
GERMANY	170	7	2	3	1	14	9	2	1	2	5	5	9	10	26	11	11	10	19	11	5	3
ITALY	135	2	2	0	2	4	3	1	1	3	10	0	4	14	24	10	9	12	13	7	2	3
BELGIUM + LUX	75	0	1	0	1	3	3	3	1	4	1	1	0	1	7	5	8	3	10	4	9	1
NETHERLANDS	66	0	0	1	0	2	3	1	2	2	3	2	3	4	11	3	9	4	11	4	0	4
SPAIN	95	0	0	0	5	2	4	0	2	4	6	5	1	9	8	7	8	9	10	16	7	0
GREECE + TURKEY	30	2	2	0	2	2	0	0	0	0	3	1	0	3	11	2	2	3	2	1	5	1
OTHER EUROPE	33	2	2	0	2	1	1	4	3	1	1	1	0	0	5	0	3	4	1	3	1	0
EUROPE EX. U.K.	918	16	14	8	21	42	36	29	12	24	35	35	36	76	130	56	60	81	81	62	46	18
SOUTHERN DOMINIONS	288	1	2	0	1	12	6	14	8	9	12	15	8	24	52	11	30	27	17	12	13	14
S. AFRICA +RHOD.	100	1	0	0	0	2	1	3	4	4	2	1	5	6	5	6	25	12	4	4	4	7
AUSTRALIA + N.Z.	188	0	2	0	1	10	5	11	4	5	10	11	3	18	45	5	5	15	13	8	9	7
ASIA + OTHER AFRICA	358	0	1	6	3	12	3	8	3	12	16	12	15	25	52	20	35	35	33	20	23	24
JAPAN	112	0	1	0	0	2	0	2	0	1	2	2	5	3	18	3	13	13	10	17	6	12
OTHER ASIA+AFR.	246	0	0	5	2	10	3	6	3	11	14	10	10	22	34	17	22	22	23	17	12	12
BLACK AFRICA	33	0	0	0	0	0	0	0	0	1	0	0	1	0	6	1	1	2	5	2	3	2
ARAB WORLD	30	0	0	0	0	3	0	0	0	5	0	1	0	5	4	0	1	9	4	3	0	1
INDIA	41	0	0	0	0	3	1	1	2	2	0	0	1	4	10	1	1	2	4	2	1	1
PHILIPPINES	39	0	0	1	0	0	2	2	1	3	0	7	0	1	5	5	5	5	2	2	1	1
OTHER E. ASIA	23	0	0	1	0	2	0	0	0	1	1	0	3	0	3	1	6	0	2	2	4	1
OTHER ASIA	80	0	0	4	0	3	0	3	0	6	2	2	2	7	9	7	6	3	6	5	6	6

CHAPTER 3- THE PROLIFERATION OF FOREIGN SUBSIDIARIES
SECTION 3- THE FLOW OF MANUFACTURING BY CHARACTERISTIC OF PARENT SYSTEM
TABLE 81- MANUFACTURING SUBSIDIARIES IN A SYSTEM
WITH LOW "R&D INTENSITY" IN 1964
CLASSIFIED BY COUNTRY OR REGION AND BY PERIOD MANUFACTURE BEGAN

PERIOD

COUNTRY OR REGION	PRE 1968	PRE 1901	1901 -13	1914 -19	1920 -24	1925 -29	1930 -34	1935 -39	1940 -45	1946 -50	1951 -53	1954 -55	1956 -57	1958 -59	1960 -61	1962	1963	1964	1965	1966	1967	UNK
OUTSIDE U.S.	1462	17	27	23	31	55	46	55	49	76	65	66	74	131	182	87	106	96	91	66	55	64
OUT. U.S. + CANADA	1227	17	20	12	26	40	34	40	35	57	53	49	60	117	164	83	97	77	79	61	51	55
OUT. WEST. HEMIS.	849	15	15	11	20	28	24	28	11	26	28	30	34	69	122	63	82	57	57	44	40	36
OUT. WHITE CWEALTH	968	15	15	9	20	33	23	26	32	49	41	40	54	95	125	69	60	65	53	43	43	47
OUT. DEVLPED WORLD	475	2	5	4	7	13	13	13	25	35	26	22	30	55	58	27	20	34	22	19	19	28
CANADA	235	0	7	11	5	15	12	15	14	19	12	17	14	14	18	4	9	19	5	4	9	9
LATIN AMERICA	378	2	5	6	6	12	10	12	24	31	25	19	26	48	42	20	15	11	22	17	11	19
C. AMER.+CARIB.	161	1	3	1	0	6	5	6	11	8	10	2	1	2	0	2	0	7	5	4	6	9
CUBA	12	1	1	0	0	2	1	2	1	0	2	0	0	1	0	1	0	0	0	0	0	1
MEXICO	109	0	3	0	0	4	2	1	8	8	8	7	10	17	9	7	4	3	5	4	3	7
OTHER	40	0	0	0	0	0	1	2	0	0	0	2	1	0	3	4	3	2	7	8	3	1
S. AMERICA	217	1	2	0	6	6	5	6	13	23	15	17	14	25	30	9	8	8	8	8	5	10
ARGENTINA	35	0	1	0	0	1	4	3	1	3	3	3	1	4	7	3	0	6	0	1	0	2
BRAZIL	45	0	0	0	0	3	0	1	5	5	4	4	2	2	1	1	0	2	0	2	1	3
PERU	22	1	1	0	0	1	1	2	1	2	1	1	2	1	1	1	0	0	1	1	1	1
COLOMBIA	45	0	1	0	0	0	0	0	1	5	1	4	4	5	6	1	4	0	3	2	2	3
VENEZUELA	44	0	0	0	1	1	1	1	3	5	5	5	2	7	7	1	3	2	1	2	0	1
OTHER	26	0	0	0	2	1	2	1	0	3	1	0	3	4	4	2	1	0	2	3	2	2
EUROPE	567	15	15	7	17	25	17	22	9	16	19	21	26	51	73	49	42	38	39	34	25	7
EFTA	180	3	9	3	6	6	9	12	2	5	8	4	7	20	23	14	10	11	16	7	4	1
U.K.	118	2	5	2	4	5	8	8	2	3	2	1	1	4	19	10	7	10	10	3	2	0
SCANDINAVIA	38	1	3	1	0	0	1	1	0	2	2	1	1	4	2	1	1	5	4	3	1	1
SWITZERLAND	11	0	0	0	0	1	0	0	0	0	0	0	1	1	2	0	2	1	1	0	0	0
OTHER EFTA	13	0	1	0	2	0	0	3	0	0	0	0	3	0	0	2	0	0	0	0	1	0
EUROP. COMMUNITY	316	11	4	4	7	16	7	8	6	11	8	14	18	29	48	28	26	19	16	14	16	6
FRANCE	77	4	2	0	2	2	2	1	2	4	2	6	8	4	15	6	6	4	5	4	1	3
GERMANY	85	5	2	2	2	7	2	1	1	1	3	8	8	8	18	6	6	5	4	5	4	0
ITALY	71	2	1	0	2	3	2	2	1	3	3	4	3	9	14	11	8	4	3	2	1	1
BELGIUM + LUX	47	0	0	1	2	1	0	0	1	2	1	0	2	5	6	5	5	5	2	1	9	2
NETHERLANDS	36	0	1	1	2	1	2	0	1	1	3	2	3	4	5	3	1	3	2	2	1	1
SPAIN	40	0	0	0	3	0	1	1	0	1	1	1	1	1	1	5	2	2	2	2	4	2
GREECE + TURKEY	11	0	2	0	0	1	0	0	0	0	0	0	0	0	0	2	0	2	0	3	0	0
OTHER EUROPE	20	1	1	1	2	2	2	2	1	0	2	0	0	2	0	2	3	2	2	3	1	0
EUROPE EX. U.K.	449	13	10	5	13	20	9	14	7	13	13	18	22	39	54	39	35	35	29	31	23	7
SOUTHERN DOMINIONS	130	0	0	1	2	2	3	5	0	5	4	6	2	10	20	4	27	18	4	4	5	8
S. AFRICA +RHOD.	53	0	0	0	1	2	2	5	0	3	2	0	0	2	2	1	25	7	1	1	0	5
AUSTRALIA + N.Z.	77	0	0	1	1	1	2	0	0	2	2	6	2	8	18	3	13	11	3	3	5	3
ASIA + OTHER AFRICA	152	0	0	3	1	4	4	1	2	5	5	6	6	8	29	10	13	10	14	6	10	21
JAPAN	55	0	0	0	0	1	1	0	1	1	4	4	4	7	13	3	8	4	2	1	2	12
OTHER ASIA+AFR.	97	0	0	3	3	3	3	1	1	4	2	2	2	1	16	7	5	6	12	5	8	9
BLACK AFRICA	13	0	0	0	0	0	0	0	0	0	0	0	1	0	3	0	0	3	5	3	1	2
ARAB WORLD	15	0	0	0	3	1	1	0	1	2	1	1	0	2	2	1	1	0	3	0	2	1
INDIA	13	0	0	0	0	0	0	0	0	0	0	0	1	2	2	1	2	0	2	2	0	2
PHILIPPINES	10	0	0	0	1	0	1	0	0	1	0	1	1	2	2	1	0	0	1	1	2	0
OTHER E. ASIA	9	0	0	1	0	1	0	0	0	0	0	0	0	0	2	0	2	2	0	0	1	1
OTHER ASIA	37	0	0	3	3	2	1	1	0	1	3	2	2	2	7	4	3	1	3	3	3	3

CHAPTER 3- THE PROLIFERATION OF FOREIGN SUBSIDIARIES
SECTION 3- THE FLOW OF MANUFACTURING BY CHARACTERISTIC OF PARENT SYSTEM
TABLE B2- MANUFACTURING SUBSIDIARIES IN A SYSTEM
WITH HIGH "R&D INTENSITY" IN 1964
CLASSIFIED BY COUNTRY OR REGION AND BY PERIOD MANUFACTURE BEGAN

PERIOD

COUNTRY OR REGION	PRE 1968	PRE 1900	1901-13	1914-19	1920-24	1925-29	1930-34	1935-39	1940-45	1946-50	1951-53	1954-55	1956-57	1958-59	1960-61	1962	1963	1964	1965	1966	1967	UNK
OUTSIDE U.S.	1216	8	16	13	19	37	45	32	30	56	78	65	75	102	162	69	74	79	108	73	51	24
OUT. U.S. + CANADA	1771	6	9	4	12	29	38	28	22	42	61	58	67	95	154	66	73	74	103	66	44	20
OUT. WEST. HEMIS.	778	6	9	3	10	27	35	24	8	25	39	39	35	71	119	50	53	54	74	49	34	14
OUT. WHITE CWEALTH	801	5	6	2	9	21	18	13	17	31	46	41	46	69	121	50	53	65	85	49	34	13
OUT. DEVLPED WORLD	379	0	0	1	2	3	3	4	14	22	27	24	36	33	45	25	27	32	39	22	15	7
CANADA	145	2	7	9	7	8	7	4	8	14	17	7	8	7	8	3	1	5	5	7	7	4
LATIN AMERICA	293	2	7	1	7	8	7	4	14	17	17	19	12	24	35	16	20	14	14	7	10	6
C. AMER.+CARIB.	127	0	0	1	2	2	2	2	14	17	8	6	7	11	14	8	8	14	14	10	7	4
CUBA	5	0	0	0	0	0	0	0	0	1	0	1	1	0	1	0	0	0	0	0	0	0
MEXICO	92	0	0	0	0	2	2	2	10	7	7	3	7	11	9	5	7	6	8	9	5	2
OTHER	30	0	0	0	2	0	0	0	1	1	6	2	4	5	6	2	0	2	1	1	2	2
S. AMERICA	166	2	7	0	2	2	2	2	13	14	14	13	20	7	21	15	11	15	29	4	5	2
ARGENTINA	42	2	2	0	2	2	2	2	2	5	5	7	2	13	9	4	4	4	1	1	3	2
BRAZIL	56	0	0	0	0	1	1	0	5	6	7	2	7	6	6	2	6	1	4	2	2	1
PERU	7	0	0	0	0	0	0	0	1	0	0	0	0	0	2	1	1	1	1	0	0	1
COLOMBIA	25	0	0	0	0	0	0	0	1	0	2	1	1	6	2	0	5	2	4	2	2	0
VENEZUELA	21	0	0	0	0	0	0	0	1	0	1	1	3	2	7	5	1	1	3	0	1	0
OTHER	15	0	2	0	0	0	0	0	3	0	2	1	0	1	0	1	1	1	2	0	1	0
EUROPE	502	6	8	3	10	23	27	14	4	18	22	25	21	41	84	26	39	30	48	23	21	9
EFTA	173	1	3	3	3	8	15	9	2	12	9	11	11	5	24	12	11	14	14	8	4	3
U.K.	132	1	2	3	3	5	12	6	1	9	8	10	11	0	14	9	9	10	10	6	4	3
SCANDINAVIA	19	0	1	0	0	2	0	1	1	1	0	0	0	0	2	0	0	2	0	0	0	1
SWITZERLAND	9	0	0	0	0	0	1	1	0	1	0	1	0	0	4	0	0	0	2	0	0	0
OTHER EFTA	13	0	0	0	0	1	1	1	0	2	1	0	0	0	2	1	0	2	0	0	0	1
EUROP. COMMUNITY	282	5	5	1	6	14	12	5	1	5	12	11	8	31	51	14	26	23	29	12	7	5
FRANCE	85	1	1	0	4	6	4	2	0	3	3	4	1	9	17	7	7	6	7	5	5	2
GERMANY	78	3	2	0	2	5	6	1	0	1	5	3	2	6	12	1	4	8	9	5	5	1
ITALY	63	0	1	0	0	1	1	0	0	1	3	1	5	7	12	5	8	6	10	3	2	0
BELGIUM + LUX	30	1	1	0	0	1	1	1	0	1	1	2	0	5	5	1	3	0	4	1	2	0
NETHERLANDS	26	1	1	1	0	1	0	0	1	0	1	1	0	4	5	0	3	0	5	1	0	2
SPAIN	36	0	0	0	1	0	0	0	0	1	1	2	1	3	8	0	2	1	4	8	3	0
GREECE + TURKEY	9	0	0	0	0	0	0	0	0	0	0	0	1	0	1	0	0	0	0	0	2	0
OTHER EUROPE	2	0	0	0	0	0	0	0	0	0	0	1	0	0	0	0	0	0	0	0	0	0
EUROPE EX. U.K.	370	5	6	7	7	18	15	8	3	9	14	15	10	36	70	17	30	28	38	17	17	6
SOUTHERN DOMINIONS	137	0	1	0	0	3	8	9	4	2	7	7	9	21	19	7	4	8	8	11	6	4
S. AFRICA +RHOD.	37	0	0	0	0	3	3	2	0	0	3	3	3	5	3	4	2	7	7	5	1	0
AUSTRALIA + N.Z.	100	0	1	0	0	3	5	7	3	5	4	4	6	18	16	3	2	1	18	15	5	4
ASIA + OTHER AFRICA	139	0	0	0	0	1	1	1	0	2	10	5	5	9	16	17	10	17	8	15	7	1
JAPAN	53	0	0	0	0	0	1	0	0	5	5	2	4	9	9	3	7	3	10	8	5	0
OTHER ASIA+AFR.	86	0	0	0	0	0	0	0	0	0	5	5	2	0	10	7	0	12	0	12	5	1
BLACK AFRICA	12	0	0	0	0	0	0	0	0	2	0	1	0	0	3	0	0	4	1	3	3	0
ARAB WORLD	4	0	0	0	0	0	0	0	0	0	1	1	0	3	1	3	3	2	1	0	0	0
INDIA	22	0	0	0	0	0	1	0	0	1	3	1	2	2	2	1	1	2	1	1	1	0
PHILIPPINES	14	0	0	0	1	0	0	0	0	0	1	3	0	0	2	3	3	0	0	0	0	0
OTHER E. ASIA	9	0	0	0	0	0	0	0	0	1	1	0	1	4	4	0	1	1	2	0	0	0
OTHER ASIA	25	0	0	0	0	0	0	0	0	2	0	0	1	1	4	1	3	1	4	1	1	1

CHAPTER 3— THE PROLIFERATION OF FOREIGN SUBSIDIARIES
SECTION 3— THE FLOW OF MANUFACTURING BY CHARACTERISTIC OF PARENT SYSTEM
TABLE C1— MANUFACTURING SUBSIDIARIES IN A SYSTEM
WITH LOW "ADVERTISING INTENSITY" IN 1965
CLASSIFIED BY COUNTRY OR REGION AND BY PERIOD MANUFACTURE BEGAN

PERIOD

COUNTRY OR REGION	PRE 1968	PRE 1901	1901-13	1914-19	1920-24	1925-29	1930-34	1935-39	1940-45	1946-50	1951-53	1954-55	1956-57	1958-59	1960-61	1962	1963	1964	1965	1966	1967	UNK
OUTSIDE U.S.	1555	24	35	36	46	82	38	50	51	78	81	65	85	130	214	80	97	94	112	71	48	38
OUT. U.S. + CANADA	1325	22	25	20	35	65	29	42	39	60	67	49	65	119	196	73	93	83	99	66	46	32
OUT. WEST. HEMIS.	942	20	20	13	28	52	21	26	17	32	43	37	27	77	152	54	69	71	74	50	38	21
OUT. WHITE CWEALTH	1023	15	17	16	25	44	20	33	31	49	53	34	55	90	151	64	60	69	81	57	35	24
OUT. DEVLPED WORLD	491	2	5	8	20	20	9	18	25	32	27	17	41	47	59	26	34	21	38	21	17	16
CANADA	230	2	10	16	11	17	9	8	12	18	14	16	20	11	18	7	4	11	13	5	8	6
LATIN AMERICA	383	2	5	1	7	13	8	16	22	28	24	12	16	42	44	19	24	12	25	16	8	11
C. AMER.+CARIB.	150	1	2	2	0	6	2	1	8	12	8	2	6	17	20	6	9	3	9	6	5	7
CUBA	15	0	0	0	0	2	1	1	1	1	0	0	1	1	1	0	0	0	0	0	0	2
MEXICO	103	0	2	0	4	4	5	5	11	11	8	2	10	12	16	5	5	1	5	4	4	3
OTHER	32	0	0	2	1	0	1	2	0	0	0	0	1	4	4	1	4	2	4	3	1	2
S. AMERICA	233	1	3	0	7	7	6	8	14	16	16	10	10	25	24	13	15	9	16	9	3	4
ARGENTINA	45	0	2	0	2	2	1	4	3	1	1	2	4	4	6	3	1	0	1	1	3	1
BRAZIL	69	0	0	0	1	4	6	4	3	6	8	1	0	4	6	3	2	1	3	5	0	0
PERU	7	0	0	0	0	0	0	0	0	0	0	0	1	0	0	0	0	0	1	0	0	1
COLOMBIA	37	0	0	0	1	0	0	0	2	3	0	2	0	0	6	0	6	2	1	0	1	0
VENEZUELA	48	1	0	0	2	0	0	0	4	4	5	1	2	4	5	1	4	3	4	1	1	1
OTHER	27	1	1	0	3	1	1	1	2	2	1	2	2	1	1	2	2	1	3	1	1	1
EUROPE	627	19	18	10	25	33	15	18	10	23	24	26	20	54	104	40	31	47	48	33	18	11
EFTA	214	7	11	5	11	14	5	11	4	10	8	11	9	17	32	9	13	12	14	6	2	3
U.K.	148	6	7	3	8	11	5	4	4	7	5	2	7	13	22	6	10	3	10	4	1	3
SCANDINAVIA	40	1	3	2	2	3	0	1	0	3	2	1	1	3	4	3	0	6	3	1	0	0
SWITZERLAND	14	0	0	0	1	0	0	2	0	0	0	0	1	0	4	0	2	3	1	0	1	0
OTHER EFTA	12	0	1	0	0	0	0	4	0	0	0	0	0	0	2	0	1	0	0	1	0	0
EUROP. COMMUNITY	333	10	6	5	8	14	9	4	2	12	11	12	10	36	62	25	15	28	25	20	10	7
FRANCE	99	4	2	1	2	4	4	2	3	3	3	5	4	15	17	8	3	11	1	3	2	4
GERMANY	87	2	1	2	3	8	2	0	1	1	4	4	3	8	9	6	8	6	9	10	5	2
ITALY	77	2	1	2	2	2	1	1	1	4	4	2	0	2	5	3	5	4	8	3	2	0
BELGIUM + LUX	37	0	1	0	1	1	1	0	0	3	0	1	1	7	9	2	3	1	6	3	2	2
NETHERLANDS	33	0	0	1	0	2	1	1	0	1	0	1	0	5	5	2	1	5	4	4	6	0
SPAIN	46	0	0	0	4	1	0	0	0	0	2	0	0	2	9	1	1	1	8	6	3	1
GREECE + TURKEY	15	0	0	0	0	1	0	0	0	0	2	0	0	1	7	4	2	2	1	1	0	0
OTHER EUROPE	19	2	0	2	2	3	3	3	2	2	1	0	0	1	3	2	0	1	0	3	3	1
EUROPE EX. U.K.	479	13	11	7	17	22	10	14	6	16	19	17	13	41	82	34	21	44	38	29	17	8
SOUTHERN DOMINIONS	149	1	1	1	1	10	4	5	3	4	8	6	3	16	23	3	23	10	8	5	10	4
S. AFRICA +RHOD.	54	1	0	1	0	1	2	2	1	1	1	3	0	3	2	2	23	6	1	3	0	2
AUSTRALIA + N.Z.	95	0	1	0	1	9	2	3	2	3	6	5	4	13	19	11	0	4	18	2	10	2
ASIA + OTHER AFRICA	166	0	1	2	2	9	4	3	5	5	11	5	1	7	25	5	15	14	18	12	10	6
JAPAN	58	0	0	1	1	2	1	1	1	0	5	0	3	2	10	4	5	5	9	2	0	1
OTHER ASIA+AFR.	108	0	1	1	7	7	0	0	4	12	8	5	1	5	15	7	10	9	13	5	9	5
BLACK AFRICA	12	0	0	0	0	0	0	0	0	3	0	0	0	1	7	0	1	1	3	1	2	0
ARAB WORLD	14	0	0	0	0	3	2	2	1	1	0	0	0	2	5	1	2	2	1	1	1	1
INDIA	22	0	0	0	0	0	0	0	0	2	2	1	1	5	2	2	1	1	2	0	1	1
PHILIPPINES	14	0	0	1	0	1	0	0	0	0	0	0	1	1	2	1	3	0	0	3	1	2
OTHER E. ASIA	15	0	0	0	0	3	2	0	0	0	3	3	0	1	4	3	3	3	2	2	1	2
OTHER ASIA	31	0	0	0	0	3	1	2	1	2	1	0	1	1	4	2	2	2	4	2	2	2

CHAPTER 3- THE PROLIFERATION OF FOREIGN SUBSIDIARIES
SECTION 3- THE FLOW OF MANUFACTURING BY CHARACTERISTIC OF PARENT SYSTEM
TABLE C2- MANUFACTURING SUBSIDIARIES IN A SYSTEM
WITH HIGH "ADVERTISING INTENSITY" IN 1965
CLASSIFIED BY COUNTRY OR REGION AND BY PERIOD MANUFACTURE BEGAN

PERIOD

COUNTRY OR REGION	PRE 1968	PRE 1901	1901 -13	1914 -19	1920 -24	1925 -29	1930 -34	1935 -39	1940 -45	1946 -50	1951 -53	1954 -55	1956 -57	1958 -59	1960 -61	1962	1963	1964	1965	1966	1967	UNK
OUTSIDE U.S.	1471	4	10	10	21	65	64	73	46	71	55	66	99	116	205	88	111	87	102	83	75	20
OUT. U.S. + CANADA	1222	3	2	6	14	38	49	60	32	60	43	50	85	106	176	76	107	75	91	69	66	14
OUT. WEST. HEMIS.	823	3	2	5	13	33	40	43	10	31	23	31	53	74	123	53	81	50	64	38	42	11
OUT. WHITE CWEALTH	903	2	0	5	6	24	24	23	24	39	34	39	64	85	125	55	87	65	77	59	57	8
OUT. DEVLPED WORLD	505	0	0	4	2	9	11	17	22	33	22	24	40	47	67	30	39	36	31	40	28	3
CANADA	249	1	8	4	7	27	15	13	14	11	12	16	14	10	29	12	4	12	11	14	9	6
LATIN AMERICA	399	0	0	1	1	5	9	17	22	29	20	19	32	32	53	23	26	25	27	31	24	3
C. AMER.+CARIB.	198	0	0	1	1	0	8	11	15	15	10	7	18	16	16	9	9	20	14	21	14	1
CUBA	19	0	0	0	1	0	2	5	1	2	1	0	1	1	0	0	0	0	0	0	0	0
MEXICO	112	0	0	0	0	0	4	5	2	9	7	6	9	7	7	4	5	13	6	13	9	0
OTHER	68	0	0	0	0	0	2	2	4	4	2	0	5	4	8	5	4	7	8	8	5	1
S. AMERICA	201	0	0	0	0	5	1	6	14	14	10	12	14	16	37	14	17	5	13	10	10	2
ARGENTINA	46	0	0	0	0	2	0	4	5	3	1	5	2	3	3	2	4	5	3	4	4	1
BRAZIL	44	0	0	0	0	2	0	1	2	5	6	2	5	5	8	2	3	2	2	1	2	1
PERU	17	0	0	0	0	0	0	0	1	0	0	0	1	0	8	2	4	0	3	1	1	0
COLOMBIA	28	0	0	0	0	0	1	0	3	1	3	2	1	1	2	0	3	1	1	3	0	0
VENEZUELA	43	0	0	0	0	0	0	0	1	2	0	2	1	5	5	4	3	0	0	3	2	1
OTHER	23	0	0	0	0	1	0	0	2	1	0	1	0	1	16	3	1	2	4	1	4	0
EUROPE	537	3	1	1	10	27	27	31	3	25	17	15	34	44	72	35	53	28	49	21	32	9
EFTA	213	2	1	1	3	14	15	25	1	19	7	3	17	12	20	15	19	7	15	7	7	4
U.K.	161	1	1	0	3	14	14	24	1	17	6	2	11	11	17	12	10	2	6	5	4	4
SCANDINAVIA	28	0	0	1	0	0	0	0	0	1	1	1	5	1	1	2	5	3	4	1	2	0
SWITZERLAND	11	0	0	0	0	0	0	0	0	0	0	0	0	1	2	0	3	0	1	1	0	0
OTHER EFTA	13	0	0	0	0	0	1	1	0	0	0	0	1	1	0	1	1	2	4	0	1	0
EUROP. COMMUNITY	268	2	0	0	6	11	10	5	2	4	8	10	15	29	46	16	28	18	25	9	19	5
FRANCE	77	2	0	0	4	2	3	0	0	2	2	0	4	8	15	5	8	6	9	4	10	0
GERMANY	74	0	0	0	0	5	6	2	0	2	3	2	3	4	15	5	10	4	6	4	4	4
ITALY	55	1	0	0	0	1	0	0	1	0	1	6	1	8	7	5	1	1	3	3	3	0
BELGIUM + LUX	28	0	0	0	0	3	0	2	1	0	3	0	0	8	2	2	5	6	8	4	1	1
NETHERLANDS	34	0	0	0	0	0	1	0	1	0	1	1	6	7	7	2	1	1	6	0	4	0
SPAIN	35	0	0	0	0	2	2	3	0	2	1	0	2	4	2	2	5	2	6	5	2	0
GREECE + TURKEY	11	0	0	0	0	0	0	0	0	0	1	0	0	1	2	2	0	1	1	1	0	0
OTHER EUROPE	10	0	0	0	0	0	0	1	0	2	0	0	1	0	3	0	1	0	2	0	2	0
EUROPE EX. U.K.	376	2	0	1	7	13	13	7	2	8	11	13	23	37	55	23	43	26	43	16	28	5
SOUTHERN DOMINIONS	149	0	1	1	2	2	11	12	7	2	3	9	9	14	31	9	9	8	7	5	5	2
S. AFRICA +RHOD.	55	0	0	1	1	1	7	3	3	2	1	3	3	6	8	3	4	4	3	2	3	1
AUSTRALIA + N.Z.	94	0	1	1	1	1	4	9	4	0	2	6	6	8	23	6	5	4	4	12	5	1
ASIA + OTHER AFRICA	137	0	0	3	4	4	7	0	0	4	3	7	10	16	20	9	19	14	8	12	5	0
JAPAN	31	0	0	0	1	0	2	0	0	0	1	1	2	2	6	2	6	3	4	3	1	0
OTHER ASIA+AFR.	106	0	0	3	3	4	2	0	0	4	2	5	8	15	14	7	13	11	4	9	4	0
BLACK AFRICA	16	0	0	0	0	0	0	0	0	0	0	1	3	1	3	1	0	1	1	1	1	0
ARAB WORLD	4	0	0	0	0	0	0	0	0	0	0	0	0	0	0	0	0	0	1	0	0	0
INDIA	16	0	0	0	1	0	1	0	1	1	0	2	0	1	2	1	2	1	0	0	0	0
PHILIPPINES	23	0	0	0	0	3	0	0	0	0	0	0	3	0	1	0	1	1	0	3	2	0
OTHER E. ASIA	15	0	0	0	1	1	1	1	0	2	1	1	0	4	4	1	3	2	0	0	2	0
OTHER ASIA	32	0	0	3	0	0	1	0	0	3	0	0	2	4	4	3	3	2	1	3	1	0

CHAPTER 3- THE PROLIFERATION OF FOREIGN SUBSIDIARIES
SECTION 3- THE FLOW OF MANUFACTURING BY CHARACTERISTIC OF PARENT SYSTEM
TABLE 01- MANUFACTURING SUBSIDIARIES IN A SYSTEM
WITH LOW "HUMAN CAPITAL INTENSITY" IN 1966
CLASSIFIED BY COUNTRY OR REGION AND BY PERIOD MANUFACTURE BEGAN

COUNTRY OR REGION	PRE 1968	PRE 1901	1901 -13	1914 -19	1920 -24	1925 -29	1930 -34	1935 -39	1940 -45	1946 -50	1951 -53	1954 -55	1956 -57	1958 -59	1960 -61	1962	1963	1964	1965	1966	1967	UNK
OUTSIDE U.S.	1316	15	25	22	37	66	60	53	47	58	63	56	88	100	187	69	93	63	95	60	44	15
OUT. U.S. + CANADA	1126	15	18	12	29	42	45	44	37	48	51	48	75	92	168	66	88	57	82	56	43	10
OUT. WEST. HEMIS.	837	14	14	10	24	36	33	34	13	21	36	35	51	69	129	51	76	46	66	40	33	6
OUT. WHITE CMFEALTH	861	12	14	10	19	25	32	29	29	38	42	38	60	72	131	54	52	44	67	47	37	9
OUT. DEVLPED WORLD	396	1	4	6	7	10	14	14	26	30	17	18	25	34	55	27	19	17	28	23	16	5
CANADA	190	0	7	10	8	24	15	9	10	10	12	8	13	8	19	3	5	6	13	4	1	5
LATIN AMERICA	289	1	4	2	5	6	12	10	24	27	15	13	24	23	39	15	12	11	16	16	10	4
C. AMER.+CARIB.	132	1	2	1	0	4	8	5	9	9	4	6	8	11	16	7	7	7	11	7	7	2
CUBA	18	1	0	1	0	2	2	1	2	2	0	1	4	0	0	0	0	0	0	0	0	2
MEXICO	73	0	2	0	0	2	3	1	4	7	3	5	0	9	11	5	4	3	3	2	5	2
OTHER	41	0	0	0	0	1	1	1	3	0	1	0	4	2	5	2	3	4	8	5	2	0
S. AMERICA	157	0	2	0	5	2	4	5	15	18	11	7	16	12	23	8	5	5	9	9	3	2
ARGENTINA	28	0	2	1	1	1	3	3	3	3	1	1	2	2	8	2	0	4	5	5	1	0
BRAZIL	42	0	2	1	1	1	0	2	1	7	6	2	7	5	4	2	0	1	0	6	1	0
PERU	10	0	0	0	0	0	0	0	1	3	0	1	0	0	2	0	0	0	1	5	1	0
COLOMBIA	27	0	0	1	0	0	1	0	3	1	3	2	2	5	5	3	2	0	0	1	0	0
VENEZUELA	35	0	0	0	2	0	0	0	5	3	1	1	0	2	6	2	1	0	2	2	2	1
OTHER	15	0	0	0	0	0	0	1	3	1	0	1	4	3	2	1	2	1	2	2	0	1
EUROPE	564	14	13	4	20	29	27	23	4	16	25	22	45	47	79	36	40	27	44	25	20	4
EFTA	187	4	7	3	9	16	10	11	2	7	6	3	19	14	24	16	16	4	8	6	2	0
U.K.	129	3	3	1	8	14	10	7	7	7	4	3	12	9	14	13	10	2	6	3	1	0
SCANDINAVIA	36	1	3	2	1	1	0	1	0	0	2	0	1	0	1	0	0	1	1	0	1	0
SWITZERLAND	13	0	0	0	0	0	0	2	0	0	0	0	1	2	5	1	1	1	1	0	0	0
OTHER EFTA	9	0	1	0	0	1	0	1	0	0	0	0	1	3	0	1	0	0	0	0	0	0
EUROP. COMMUNITY	306	10	4	1	7	10	16	10	4	8	16	15	24	29	49	16	20	17	26	13	9	4
FRANCE	88	4	1	0	2	4	8	5	2	0	4	5	6	10	14	5	5	6	2	1	6	2
GERMANY	90	2	2	0	2	3	5	2	0	1	5	7	6	4	15	4	5	4	11	7	1	0
ITALY	63	2	2	0	1	1	1	1	2	2	5	2	6	6	10	4	5	5	3	5	1	1
BELGIUM + LUX	37	0	0	1	1	0	1	1	0	2	0	0	2	4	7	1	5	2	6	0	1	1
NETHERLANDS	28	0	0	0	1	3	1	1	0	2	2	1	4	5	10	2	5	0	4	0	0	0
SPAIN	45	0	2	1	3	1	1	1	0	3	2	3	2	4	3	2	0	5	8	4	6	0
GREECE + TURKEY	12	0	0	0	0	0	0	0	0	0	1	1	0	3	1	1	0	1	0	2	3	0
OTHER EUROPE	14	0	2	0	1	2	0	2	0	1	1	0	0	1	2	0	1	1	2	0	0	0
EUROPE EX. U.K.	435	11	10	3	12	15	17	16	2	9	21	19	33	38	65	24	30	27	38	22	19	4
SOUTHERN DOMINIONS	129	0	1	1	2	3	3	3	6	2	4	7	3	11	22	5	25	12	8	6	5	1
S. AFRICA +RHOD.	55	0	0	1	1	0	0	2	4	1	0	4	1	1	3	2	2	2	2	2	3	0
AUSTRALIA + N.Z.	74	0	1	0	1	3	3	5	2	1	4	3	2	10	19	3	23	5	6	4	2	1
ASIA + OTHER AFRICA	144	0	0	5	2	4	3	4	1	3	7	6	3	11	28	2	11	5	14	9	8	1
JAPAN	37	0	0	4	0	0	1	0	2	0	5	1	2	1	12	3	4	7	2	2	2	1
OTHER ASIA+AFR.	107	0	0	4	2	4	2	4	1	3	2	5	1	11	16	4	7	6	12	7	6	0
BLACK AFRICA	14	0	0	0	0	0	0	0	0	0	0	0	0	0	2	1	1	1	4	1	3	0
ARAB WORLD	11	0	0	0	2	0	0	0	0	1	2	0	1	1	2	0	0	4	2	1	0	0
INDIA	16	0	0	1	0	0	1	0	0	1	0	0	0	3	3	1	1	0	1	1	1	0
PHILIPPINES	18	0	0	1	0	1	1	1	1	1	1	3	0	1	1	0	0	1	0	1	0	1
OTHER E. ASIA	9	0	0	0	0	1	0	1	1	0	1	0	0	0	0	1	2	0	1	0	0	0
OTHER ASIA	39	0	0	4	2	1	1	2	0	0	0	0	1	6	6	3	2	3	4	3	1	1

CHAPTER 3- THE PROLIFERATION OF FOREIGN SUBSIDIARIES
SECTION 3- THE FLOW OF MANUFACTURING BY CHARACTERISTIC OF PARENT SYSTEM
TABLE D2- MANUFACTURING SUBSIDIARIES IN A SYSTEM
WITH HIGH "HUMAN CAPITAL INTENSITY" IN 1966
CLASSIFIED BY COUNTRY OR REGION AND BY PERIOD MANUFACTURE BEGAN

COUNTRY OR REGION	PRE 1968	PRE 1901	1901-13	1914-19	1920-24	1925-29	1930-34	1935-39	1940-45	1946-50	1951-53	1954-55	1956-57	1958-59	1960-61	1962	1963	1964	1965	1966	1967	UNK
OUTSIDE U.S.	1070	12	21	17	20	66	26	44	27	48	38	35	53	87	158	58	70	72	79	68	32	39
OUT. U.S. + CANADA	889	9	11	9	14	50	22	31	15	37	30	24	44	81	146	50	62	60	71	62	28	33
OUT. WEST. HEMIS.	608	8	10	4	11	40	17	13	4	19	15	16	19	54	108	35	44	48	52	41	24	26
OUT. WHITE CWEALTH	680	4	6	8	10	34	12	23	14	26	23	15	39	61	115	43	54	49	55	54	21	14
OUT. DEVLPED WORLD	346	1	1	6	3	16	5	18	12	21	15	9	28	33	47	20	27	27	25	26	9	9
CANADA	181	3	10	8	16	16	4	13	12	11	8	11	9	6	12	8	8	12	8	6	4	6
LATIN AMERICA	281	1	1	5	3	10	5	18	11	18	15	8	25	27	38	15	18	12	19	21	4	7
C. AMER.+CARIB.	110	0	0	1	0	2	2	7	4	5	5	2	12	12	17	8	7	5	7	8	2	4
CUBA	7	0	0	1	0	2	1	2	4	1	1	0	2	1	0	0	0	0	0	0	0	0
MEXICO	81	0	0	0	0	2	1	6	0	4	4	2	9	10	14	4	3	2	5	6	2	3
OTHER	22	0	0	0	0	1	0	0	0	0	0	0	1	1	3	0	3	2	2	2	0	1
S. AMERICA	171	1	1	4	3	8	6	11	7	13	10	6	13	15	21	7	11	7	12	13	2	3
ARGENTINA	34	0	0	2	0	1	3	3	1	2	1	1	2	2	7	2	2	5	2	2	0	1
BRAZIL	47	0	0	2	0	5	0	6	3	2	2	5	5	5	5	2	4	6	5	5	1	1
PERU	7	0	0	0	0	1	0	0	1	0	0	1	1	0	0	2	2	1	1	2	1	0
COLOMBIA	23	0	0	0	0	1	0	3	0	2	2	1	1	2	3	0	0	2	5	2	0	0
VENEZUELA	35	1	0	0	0	0	0	0	1	3	3	2	2	5	2	3	4	3	2	3	0	1
OTHER	25	1	1	0	3	2	0	1	1	4	0	0	0	1	4	0	1	0	3	1	1	0
EUROPE	418	7	8	3	10	26	12	7	2	13	12	12	12	38	79	21	27	35	33	30	11	20
EFTA	155	4	5	2	4	11	5	5	0	10	6	6	4	15	23	3	7	10	11	9	1	14
U.K.	118	4	4	1	3	10	5	3	0	7	5	6	3	11	16	1	6	6	7	5	1	14
SCANDINAVIA	21	0	0	1	1	1	0	0	0	3	0	1	1	2	3	2	1	2	2	5	1	0
SWITZERLAND	7	0	1	0	0	0	0	0	1	0	1	0	0	2	1	0	0	0	1	2	0	0
OTHER EFTA	9	0	0	0	0	0	0	1	1	0	0	0	0	2	3	0	0	2	1	2	0	0
EUROP. COMMUNITY	210	2	3	1	4	11	6	1	1	2	3	5	8	22	49	13	13	23	15	15	8	5
FRANCE	69	1	1	1	2	2	3	1	0	1	1	2	0	9	17	5	5	11	3	6	3	2
GERMANY	47	1	1	1	0	7	0	1	0	1	0	1	5	4	8	2	2	5	3	6	3	0
ITALY	43	0	1	1	1	1	1	0	1	0	2	5	0	5	11	2	2	4	6	2	0	2
BELGIUM + LUX	31	1	1	0	1	1	1	0	0	1	0	1	0	1	8	2	3	1	1	5	3	0
NETHERLANDS	20	0	0	0	1	2	0	0	1	0	0	0	0	8	5	2	0	0	2	2	0	0
SPAIN	33	0	0	0	0	3	0	0	0	0	2	0	0	5	5	4	6	0	5	4	0	1
GREECE + TURKEY	8	0	0	1	1	0	1	1	1	0	1	0	0	1	2	1	1	1	1	2	1	0
OTHER EUROPE	12	1	0	1	0	1	1	4	2	1	2	2	0	0	0	0	0	0	1	0	0	1
EUROPE EX. U.K.	300	3	4	2	7	16	7	4	2	6	7	6	9	27	63	20	21	29	26	25	10	6
SOUTHERN DOMINIONS	85	1	1	0	0	6	5	5	2	3	2	3	2	9	15	6	4	2	8	8	6	4
S. AFRICA +RHOD.	21	1	0	0	1	1	0	0	0	1	1	0	2	3	13	4	1	1	1	2	0	1
AUSTRALIA + N.Z.	64	0	1	1	1	5	5	5	1	2	1	3	0	6	14	2	2	15	11	9	7	3
ASIA + OTHER AFRICA	105	0	1	1	1	8	3	1	0	3	1	0	2	7	14	8	6	6	5	4	5	2
JAPAN	40	0	1	1	1	2	0	1	0	3	1	0	5	1	9	3	3	9	6	5	6	2
OTHER ASIA+AFR.	65	0	0	0	0	6	3	1	1	0	1	0	0	6	11	5	3	3	1	1	1	0
BLACK AFRICA	5	0	0	0	0	0	0	0	0	0	0	0	0	1	1	1	1	0	1	2	0	0
ARAB WORLD	11	0	0	0	1	2	0	0	0	2	0	1	2	4	5	2	0	1	2	2	1	0
INDIA	21	0	0	1	1	1	1	0	0	0	0	0	0	0	0	1	0	1	0	1	1	1
PHILIPPINES	10	0	0	0	0	2	0	0	0	0	2	1	0	0	0	1	0	0	1	0	1	0
OTHER E. ASIA	5	0	0	1	0	1	0	0	0	0	0	0	1	2	0	0	1	0	0	0	0	0
OTHER ASIA	13	0	0	0	2	2	0	0	0	1	0	2	2	2	2	0	1	0	2	1	2	1

PERIOD

CHAPTER 3- THE PROLIFERATION OF FOREIGN SUBSIDIARIES
SECTION 3- THE FLOW OF MANUFACTURING BY CHARACTERISTIC OF PARENT SYSTEM
TABLE E1- MANUFACTURING SUBSIDIARIES IN A SYSTEM
WITH LOW "PHYSICAL CAPITAL INTENSITY" IN 1966
CLASSIFIED BY COUNTRY OR REGION AND BY PERIOD MANUFACTURE BEGAN

PERIOD

COUNTRY OR REGION	PRE 1968	PRE 1901	1901 -13	1914 -19	1920 -24	1925 -29	1930 -34	1935 -39	1940 -45	1946 -50	1951 -53	1954 -55	1956 -57	1958 -59	1960 -61	1962	1963	1964	1965	1966	1967	UNK
OUTSIDE U.S.	2548	17	37	38	42	136	95	109	77	136	98	99	136	225	353	148	166	163	161	150	110	52
OUT. U.S. + CANADA	2109	15	20	24	29	88	75	85	61	108	75	73	118	204	313	132	149	143	133	127	94	43
OUT. WEST. HEMIS.	1446	14	18	14	27	73	62	57	19	62	55	46	61	137	226	111	111	107	96	81	57	36
OUT. WHITE CWEALTH	1599	8	12	20	21	54	42	51	49	76	55	58	98	157	237	107	128	118	111	100	79	18
OUT. DEVLPED WORLD	814	1	2	14	3	23	15	30	44	54	31	32	65	82	110	49	54	53	46	55	44	7
CANADA	439	2	17	14	13	48	20	24	16	16	26	26	18	21	40	16	17	20	28	28	16	9
LATIN AMERICA	663	1	2	10	10	15	13	28	42	46	23	27	57	67	87	36	38	37	37	46	37	7
C. AMER.+CARIB.	296	0	0	2	0	3	10	16	13	17	14	9	26	30	32	12	15	24	21	31	18	3
CUBA	30	0	0	0	0	0	3	1	1	3	1	1	8	2	0	0	2	1	0	0	0	1
MEXICO	184	0	0	1	0	3	5	7	10	11	8	8	13	23	17	8	10	17	11	19	12	1
OTHER	82	0	0	1	0	0	2	2	2	3	3	0	5	5	15	4	5	7	10	12	6	1
S. AMERICA	367	1	2	8	2	12	3	12	29	29	15	18	31	37	55	24	23	12	16	15	19	4
ARGENTINA	86	0	1	4	1	4	2	5	8	6	1	4	4	9	11	8	6	1	2	4	4	1
BRAZIL	97	0	2	1	6	2	0	5	6	11	6	2	10	19	11	7	2	3	2	2	2	0
PERU	28	0	0	0	0	0	0	1	5	2	1	2	4	1	1	2	4	5	3	1	2	0
COLOMBIA	49	0	0	0	1	0	0	0	5	5	3	3	2	0	15	5	4	3	5	3	0	2
VENEZUELA	68	0	1	0	0	0	1	0	1	2	1	2	2	7	10	5	5	1	3	1	8	2
OTHER	39	1	1	0	0	2	1	1	3	3	1	2	1	1	7	0	2	1	5	1	8	1
EUROPE	1023	13	16	9	23	56	46	35	8	43	33	29	43	94	159	67	73	73	69	60	44	30
EFTA	391	6	10	5	7	31	20	19	3	28	14	5	17	29	51	21	21	26	23	24	13	18
U.K.	285	6	7	3	5	27	19	15	2	20	10	1	11	21	39	15	11	13	11	19	9	18
SCANDINAVIA	59	0	1	0	2	3	1	1	0	6	1	4	5	2	4	5	6	8	6	4	3	0
SWITZERLAND	23	0	0	2	2	1	0	0	2	1	1	0	1	2	7	0	2	4	1	1	1	0
OTHER EFTA	24	0	2	0	0	0	0	2	1	0	2	0	0	2	1	0	2	3	1	0	0	0
EUROP. COMMUNITY	523	6	6	4	14	22	23	14	3	13	12	9	22	62	99	34	43	37	33	24	22	11
FRANCE	173	3	2	2	8	4	8	7	0	4	2	5	8	20	40	14	8	16	8	9	11	4
GERMANY	150	3	1	1	2	12	11	3	0	4	3	3	8	12	25	8	14	9	10	8	5	4
ITALY	98	3	0	0	2	2	1	0	0	1	1	1	1	6	20	3	14	8	8	7	3	2
BELGIUM + LUX	47	0	0	0	1	1	0	1	0	2	4	3	6	4	8	8	4	2	7	2	3	1
NETHERLANDS	55	0	0	1	1	3	2	1	2	1	2	1	2	8	6	3	7	5	8	8	1	0
SPAIN	60	0	0	0	1	0	0	3	1	0	0	2	4	3	2	6	5	8	4	2	0	1
GREECE + TURKEY	24	0	0	0	0	2	0	0	0	0	2	1	1	1	0	6	5	2	2	1	2	0
OTHER EUROPE	25	1	0	0	0	0	1	2	2	0	2	0	0	0	2	4	1	2	4	2	0	1
EUROPE EX. U.K.	738	7	9	6	18	29	27	20	6	23	23	25	32	73	120	52	62	62	56	41	35	12
SOUTHERN DOMINIONS	208	1	1	1	2	7	14	18	9	10	8	11	8	26	35	9	9	11	8	8	6	6
S. AFRICA +RHOD.	69	1	0	0	1	2	4	4	4	5	3	2	1	10	7	4	5	4	3	4	4	4
AUSTRALIA + N.Z.	139	1	1	1	1	5	10	14	5	9	5	9	7	16	28	5	5	7	5	4	5	2
ASIA + OTHER AFRICA	215	0	1	4	2	10	2	4	2	1	3	6	10	17	32	20	29	23	19	13	7	0
JAPAN	64	0	1	1	2	2	2	2	0	0	1	1	2	2	9	7	13	6	10	4	0	0
OTHER ASIA+AFR.	151	0	0	4	1	8	0	2	2	1	2	5	8	15	23	13	16	17	9	9	7	0
BLACK AFRICA	18	0	0	0	0	0	0	0	0	0	2	0	1	1	0	1	1	5	1	2	1	0
ARAB WORLD	15	0	0	0	0	0	0	0	1	0	0	0	5	5	4	3	1	3	1	1	1	0
INDIA	23	0	0	0	1	2	1	1	0	1	0	1	2	6	6	2	3	1	5	2	0	0
PHILIPPINES	28	0	0	0	1	2	0	0	1	1	0	0	2	2	2	7	2	1	0	1	3	0
OTHER E. ASIA	21	0	0	1	0	0	0	1	0	1	0	0	3	6	4	0	5	0	1	0	3	0
OTHER ASIA	46	0	0	3	0	2	1	1	0	5	0	3	2	5	9	5	3	2	3	2	2	0

CHAPTER 3- THE PROLIFERATION OF FOREIGN SUBSIDIARIES
SECTION 3- THE FLOW OF MANUFACTURING BY CHARACTERISTIC OF PARENT SYSTEM
TABLE E2- MANUFACTURING SUBSIDIARIES IN A SYSTEM
WITH HIGH "PHYSICAL CAPITAL INTENSITY" IN 1966
CLASSIFIED BY COUNTRY OR REGION AND BY PERIOD MANUFACTURE BEGAN

COUNTRY OR REGION	PRE 1968	PRE 1901	1901 -13	1914 -19	1920 -24	1925 -29	1930 -34	1935 -39	1940 -45	1946 -50	1951 -53	1954 -55	1956 -57	1958 -59	1960 -61	1962	1963	1964	1965	1966	1967	UNK
OUTSIDE U.S.	2684	31	41	36	50	83	60	103	70	114	136	125	168	199	337	168	178	177	209	180	128	91
OUT. U.S. + CANADA	2319	27	30	17	42	64	48	82	50	89	113	99	136	181	304	157	167	148	192	167	120	77
OUT. WEST. HEMIS.	1632	25	25	14	31	55	38	60	20	47	73	63	71	106	225	120	135	114	139	124	89	51
OUT. WHITE CWEALTH	1747	19	24	9	30	46	31	47	40	66	85	71	106	142	233	121	112	117	156	135	94	63
OUT. DEVLPED WORLD	895	2	5	4	12	12	11	26	31	51	46	45	72	85	114	56	52	51	75	58	48	39
CANADA	374	4	11	19	8	19	12	21	20	25	23	26	32	18	33	11	11	29	17	13	8	14
LATIN AMERICA	678	2	5	3	11	9	10	22	30	42	40	36	65	68	79	37	32	34	53	43	31	26
C. AMER.+CARIB.	280	1	3	1	2	5	4	9	9	17	12	11	28	31	30	15	12	16	25	18	16	15
CUBA	18	1	1		1	2		1	1	1	1			1	1							1
MEXICO	186		3		1	2	3	5	3	13	6	6	16	23	23	8	6	10	13	13	9	10
OTHER	76			1		1	1	3	5	3	5	5	12	7	6	7	6	6	12	5	7	4
S. AMERICA	398	1	2	2	9	4	6	13	21	25	28	25	37	37	49	22	20	18	28	25	15	11
ARGENTINA	75		2		1	1		6	4	9	5	6	8	6	9	5	5	5	11	4	3	3
BRAZIL	102		1	1	1	3		3	7	8	13	8	4	11	8	2	5	1	3	2	2	2
PERU	30	1			1	1				1	3		3	1	4	5		7	3	4	2	3
COLOMBIA	66		1		1	1	3		3	2	4	2	4	8	8	2			4	2	2	1
VENEZUELA	77				2	1	1	1	7	4	6	2	6	10	8	5	4	4	4	3	3	2
OTHER	48			1	4	1	2	2	3	3	2	2	4	3	3	6	3	2	3	5	2	2
EUROPE	1032	25	24	7	27	46	30	46	13	27	44	39	45	70	135	75	77	64	93	82	49	14
EFTA	360	8	11	4	11	18	14	34	6	12	14	16	19	18	39	26	24	17	26	25	13	5
U.K.	266	7	6	3	9	12	11	25	5	12	13	14	17	12	29	20	21	7	17	14	10	3
SCANDINAVIA	57	1				2		4			1	2	1	3	7	5	3	9	5	6	2	1
SWITZERLAND	14													1	1	1		1	1	2		1
OTHER EFTA	23				2	3		2						2	1		3		3	3		
EUROP. COMMUNITY	548	15	11	2	10	23	14	10	6	14	23	20	24	44	82	45	43	38	50	40	25	9
FRANCE	150	5	3	1	5	8	5	4	2	4	6	7	7	10	21	13	12	12	3	10	10	3
GERMANY	148	7	5	1	3	9	5	3	1	1	6	6	9	8	19	13	9	12	18	14	4	1
ITALY	124	2	2		2	2	2	3	1	2	7	4	7	12	23	13	9	10	12	7	2	1
BELGIUM + LUX	71	1	1			1	1	1	1	3	2	3			10	3	9	3	7	5	4	
NETHERLANDS	55			1		5	3			4	4	1	1	5	10	3	4	4	10	9	6	4
SPAIN	79				5	3	1		2	1	3	2	1	5	9	3	6	6	14	12	6	
GREECE + TURKEY	18					1					1			1	1			1	1	2	4	
OTHER EUROPE	27	2	2		1	1		2	1		3	2		2	2	3	3	2	2	3	1	
EUROPE EX. U.K.	766	18	19	4	18	34	19	21	8	15	31	25	28	58	106	55	56	57	76	68	39	11
SOUTHERN DOMINIONS	280		1	5	3	6	6	10	5	11	12	13	13	25	40	16	31	23	18	16	15	11
S. AFRICA +RHOD.	92			1	2	6	3	2	2	5	9	4	4	3	6	2	5	10	2	4	3	5
AUSTRALIA + N.Z.	188		1	4	1	6	3	8	3	2	17	9	9	22	34	10	26	13	16	12	12	6
ASIA + OTHER AFRICA	320			2		3	2	4	2	9	11	11	13	18	50	29	27	27	28	26	25	26
JAPAN	103			1		1	1		1		2	6	1	1	15	7	7	10	6	11	8	13
OTHER ASIA+AFR.	217			1		3	1	4	1	9	9	7	6	17	35	19	20	17	22	15	17	13
BLACK AFRICA	31					1					1	2	2		6	2	1	6	4	1	5	3
ARAB WORLD	21						1		1	1				4	4	2	1	2	1	2	2	1
INDIA	46				1	1	1	2		2	1	1	1	1	8	8	6	3	2	3	3	2
PHILIPPINES	31			1						1	3		2	9	4		5		1	1	1	1
OTHER E. ASIA	23					1	1	2	1		1	1		1	2	1	4	3	4	3	3	1
OTHER ASIA	65			1		2	1			4		2	2	6	11	7	3	5	5	4	4	6

PERIOD

CHAPTER 3- THE PROLIFERATION OF FOREIGN SUBSIDIARIES
SECTION 3- THE FLOW OF MANUFACTURING BY CHARACTERISTIC OF PARENT SYSTEM
TABLE F1- MANUFACTURING SUBSIDIARIES IN A SYSTEM
WITH LOW GROWTH IN SALES 1950-1966
CLASSIFIED BY COUNTRY OR REGION AND BY PERIOD MANUFACTURE BEGAN

COUNTRY OR REGION	PRE 1968	PRE 1901	1901 -13	1914 -19	1920 -24	1925 -29	1930 -34	1935 -39	1940 -45	1946 -50	1951 -53	1954 -55	1956 -57	1958 -59	1960 -61	1962	1963	1964	1965	1966	1967	UNK
OUTSIDE U.S.	2314	23	46	43	46	128	68	132	67	118	95	84	138	180	280	130	127	137	173	157	103	39
OUT. U.S. + CANADA	1925	19	26	25	34	76	52	104	55	91	76	67	110	168	246	116	119	122	159	138	95	27
OUT. WEST. HEMIS.	1316	18	23	15	26	65	38	20	20	44	44	33	45	86	185	97	101	118	93	63	20	
OUT. WHITE CWEALTH	1490	21	21	18	26	50	30	57	41	68	60	59	92	133	181	96	100	101	132	115	83	18
OUT. DEVLPED WORLD	789	3	3	15	9	18	15	41	37	55	37	43	69	70	82	44	41	39	56	58	46	10
CANADA	389	4	20	18	12	52	16	28	12	27	19	17	28	12	34	34	15	22	15	14	19	8
LATIN AMERICA	609	4	26	10	8	12	14	36	35	47	32	34	65	54	61	30	22	21	41	45	32	7
C. AMER.+CARIB.	266	0	1	1	2	3	8	19	11	21	9	12	33	20	24	16	12	10	17	26	19	2
CUBA	31	0	0	0	1	0	3	4	5	3	0	1	2	0	0	0	0	0	0	0	0	1
MEXICO	158	1	1	0	1	3	4	10	5	14	6	10	10	15	15	7	6	5	6	17	12	1
OTHER	77	0	0	0	0	0	3	1	4	4	1	1	17	8	8	5	0	4	12	9	7	1
S. AMERICA	343	1	2	9	6	8	6	17	24	26	23	22	32	34	37	14	10	14	24	19	13	5
ARGENTINA	69	0	1	3	2	2	5	8	5	4	2	2	4	7	6	5	0	1	5	3	2	3
BRAZIL	93	0	0	3	0	5	5	8	5	10	11	5	10	12	10	3	1	1	5	7	3	3
PERU	25	0	0	0	1	0	0	1	1	1	1	4	2	0	2	0	2	0	2	1	0	0
COLOMBIA	38	0	0	0	0	0	0	0	1	1	5	2	2	5	5	2	4	2	3	3	0	0
VENEZUELA	79	0	0	0	1	0	0	0	5	1	6	7	11	11	11	2	4	6	6	6	2	1
OTHER	39	1	1	3	3	1	2	2	2	5	0	2	1	3	2	1	1	5	1	1	5	1
EUROPE	886	17	21	4	23	51	26	48	10	30	24	18	31	77	126	60	63	66	79	64	36	12
EFTA	323	8	10	3	9	25	12	37	6	17	9	9	14	21	39	17	20	20	20	19	10	4
U.K.	241	8	4	2	7	20	11	33	6	15	8	8	9	14	33	12	14	12	12	12	5	4
SCANDINAVIA	47	0	4	1	2	3	0	0	0	2	0	0	5	2	1	2	0	2	5	2	2	0
SWITZERLAND	15	0	4	0	0	0	2	2	0	0	0	1	0	1	1	2	0	3	2	2	1	0
OTHER EFTA	20	0	2	0	0	1	2	2	0	0	1	0	0	4	3	0	2	2	2	1	1	0
EUROP. COMMUNITY	457	7	11	12	21	4	10	3	2	11	11	12	15	52	77	31	32	38	45	32	17	7
FRANCE	134	4	3	8	4	4	3	2	0	3	1	2	2	11	34	11	7	18	3	3	6	3
GERMANY	125	2	3	2	11	3	1	3	1	2	3	6	3	12	12	9	9	10	16	16	5	2
ITALY	90	0	4	2	3	2	2	1	2	6	6	4	4	14	14	7	4	7	11	3	3	2
BELGIUM + LUX	55	1	1	0	2	1	0	0	1	0	0	2	1	9	9	1	3	1	4	4	2	0
NETHERLANDS	53	0	1	0	2	3	3	3	1	5	1	3	1	6	8	4	1	2	4	2	3	0
SPAIN	64	0	0	0	2	0	1	2	1	0	3	1	1	8	8	3	2	5	10	8	4	0
GREECE + TURKEY	20	2	0	0	0	0	1	0	0	0	1	1	0	4	4	10	5	1	1	3	0	1
OTHER EUROPE	22	2	0	0	0	1	0	0	0	2	2	0	1	3	3	1	2	2	2	2	2	1
EUROPE EX. U.K.	645	9	17	16	31	15	15	4	4	15	16	16	22	63	93	48	49	56	67	52	31	8
SOUTHERN DOMINIONS	179	1	1	5	1	6	11	14	8	6	8	5	9	20	29	7	5	9	13	10	7	4
S. AFRICA +RHOD.	55	1	0	0	1	2	4	3	2	4	2	1	1	6	4	5	3	3	3	3	1	2
AUSTRALIA + N.Z.	124	0	1	5	0	4	7	10	6	2	6	3	8	14	25	19	6	26	10	5	6	2
ASIA + OTHER AFRICA	251	0	1	6	2	8	6	6	2	8	12	10	5	17	30	9	29	26	19	20	6	4
JAPAN	180	0	1	0	0	0	0	0	1	0	0	0	0	16	21	30	19	8	11	6	13	14
OTHER ASIA+AFR.	180	0	1	1	5	1	1	0	2	8	7	4	9	21	21	18	19	15	13	14	7	3
BLACK AFRICA	23	0	0	0	1	0	0	0	0	0	1	1	1	3	3	7	3	3	1	3	1	0
ARAB WORLD	20	0	0	0	0	0	0	0	2	2	0	0	0	4	4	9	2	2	3	1	0	0
INDIA	30	0	0	0	0	0	2	1	1	1	1	0	1	5	5	1	2	4	2	0	1	0
PHILIPPINES	33	0	0	0	0	2	0	0	1	1	2	6	0	5	9	3	8	4	0	3	2	0
OTHER E. ASIA	24	0	0	1	1	2	0	1	0	1	1	0	1	3	3	8	4	2	3	3	2	0
OTHER ASIA	50	0	0	4	0	2	1	3	0	4	0	1	1	4	6	3	3	4	4	5	2	2

CHAPTER 3- THE PROLIFERATION OF FOREIGN SUBSIDIARIES
SECTION 3- THE FLOW OF MANUFACTURING BY CHARACTERISTIC OF PARENT SYSTEM
TABLE F2- MANUFACTURING SUBSIDIARIES IN A SYSTEM
WITH HIGH GROWTH IN SALES 1950-1966
CLASSIFIED BY COUNTRY OR REGION AND BY PERIOD MANUFACTURE BEGAN

COUNTRY OR REGION	PRE 1968	PRE 1901	1901 -13	1914 -19	1920 -24	1925 -29	1930 -34	1935 -39	1940 -45	1946 -50	1951 -53	1954 -55	1956 -57	1958 -59	1960 -61	1962	1963	1964	1965	1966	1967	UNK
OUTSIDE U.S.	2351	18	23	23	33	73	64	53	72	102	110	108	132	197	317	148	183	160	164	162	122	87
OUT. U.S. + CANADA	2019	17	18	9	27	60	51	44	50	80	89	83	115	179	289	135	166	135	139	147	106	80
OUT. WEST. HEMIS.	1402	15	14	8	22	51	45	33	18	46	57	61	71	107	207	100	122	95	97	104	73	56
OUT. WHITE CWEALTH	1507	14	11	6	17	37	35	31	42	58	69	54	87	135	226	101	116	105	112	114	82	55
OUT. DEVLPED WORLD	759	2	4	1	5	11	7	12	33	40	35	27	55	84	108	46	57	53	54	53	40	32
CANADA	332	1	5	14	6	13	13	9	22	22	21	25	17	18	28	13	17	25	25	16	16	7
LATIN AMERICA	617	2	4	1	5	9	6	11	32	34	32	27	44	72	82	35	44	40	42	43	33	24
C. AMER.+CARIB.	274	1	2	1	0	4	4	3	9	11	14	7	19	38	34	9	14	25	24	23	14	15
CUBA	17	1	0	1	0	2	2	2	0	1	1	1	4	1	9	0	0	0	0	0	0	1
MEXICO	185	0	2	0	0	2	3	0	8	10	12	6	10	27	22	6	8	18	15	15	9	10
OTHER	72	1	0	0	0	2	1	2	1	0	1	0	5	1	0	3	6	7	9	8	0	4
S. AMERICA	343	1	2	0	5	5	2	5	23	23	18	15	25	34	48	26	30	15	18	20	19	9
ARGENTINA	71	0	1	0	0	1	1	1	2	3	2	1	5	9	9	8	8	4	0	4	4	1
BRAZIL	83	0	1	0	1	2	0	2	7	7	7	4	7	8	5	4	5	5	5	6	3	2
PERU	30	1	0	0	1	1	0	1	7	3	0	0	1	1	1	2	2	2	3	3	3	3
COLOMBIA	65	0	0	0	0	0	0	0	2	2	3	3	4	6	2	4	4	1	6	6	2	1
VENEZUELA	57	0	0	0	2	0	0	1	2	6	3	2	4	7	14	3	6	4	1	5	2	0
OTHER	37	0	0	0	1	2	0	1	3	1	3	1	3	5	15	5	2	3	4	2	5	2
EUROPE	934	15	13	7	19	45	39	24	10	28	41	40	43	65	136	64	71	56	70	74	50	24
EFTA	349	4	9	2	8	24	15	13	3	15	14	17	19	20	40	25	20	19	27	29	11	15
U.K.	256	3	6	2	7	19	12	6	1	11	11	15	17	15	27	20	17	17	17	21	9	13
SCANDINAVIA	59	1	0	0	0	3	3	3	0	2	1	0	1	3	6	5	2	6	6	5	2	1
SWITZERLAND	14	0	3	0	0	2	1	1	1	2	1	0	0	1	5	5	2	0	0	1	2	3
OTHER EFTA	20	0	0	0	1	2	1	3	1	0	0	0	0	1	2	0	2	0	4	2	0	1
EUROP. COMMUNITY	492	10	3	5	7	18	22	10	2	12	21	21	23	39	85	37	44	30	31	30	30	9
FRANCE	157	2	2	0	3	6	8	6	5	6	6	8	5	16	23	12	13	9	1	12	15	2
GERMANY	133	6	1	3	2	8	11	1	2	1	5	6	6	7	23	12	13	6	10	7	4	3
ITALY	104	2	0	0	1	2	1	1	1	2	6	3	9	8	24	10	13	8	8	5	3	0
BELGIUM + LUX	54	0	0	1	0	2	2	2	0	2	2	2	0	8	8	5	3	4	5	3	8	0
NETHERLANDS	44	0	0	1	1	1	0	0	2	2	2	2	3	6	7	3	3	4	6	3	0	4
SPAIN	60	0	0	0	0	0	2	0	0	1	3	2	1	2	8	3	1	3	10	12	7	0
GREECE + TURKEY	14	0	0	0	3	1	1	0	0	2	1	0	0	2	7	1	1	1	1	1	1	0
OTHER EUROPE	19	1	1	0	1	1	1	1	2	0	0	0	0	0	4	0	3	2	2	2	1	0
EUROPE EX. U.K.	678	12	7	5	12	26	27	18	9	17	30	25	26	50	109	44	54	49	53	53	41	11
SOUTHERN DOMINIONS	245	0	0	1	3	4	4	7	6	11	7	14	11	28	36	14	30	21	10	11	14	12
S. AFRICA +RHOD.	89	0	0	0	1	0	1	2	4	5	3	3	4	7	6	3	27	2	2	2	3	6
AUSTRALIA + N.Z.	156	0	1	1	2	4	3	5	2	6	4	11	7	21	30	11	21	12	8	9	11	6
ASIA + OTHER AFRICA	223	0	1	0	2	2	2	2	2	7	9	7	17	14	35	22	8	18	17	9	9	20
JAPAN	81	0	0	0	0	0	1	1	1	1	6	2	6	2	9	11	1	15	5	9	2	20
OTHER ASIA+AFR.	142	0	0	0	0	2	1	1	1	6	3	5	11	12	26	11	13	13	12	7	1	2
BLACK AFRICA	16	0	0	0	0	0	0	0	0	1	0	2	2	2	9	1	1	2	2	4	1	2
ARAB WORLD	14	0	0	0	0	0	0	1	0	1	1	0	0	0	1	1	1	1	1	1	1	1
INDIA	28	0	0	0	0	0	0	0	0	1	2	1	1	3	3	1	4	3	2	3	0	1
PHILIPPINES	23	0	0	0	0	0	0	0	0	0	0	3	3	1	1	1	4	3	2	2	0	1
OTHER E. ASIA	16	0	0	0	0	1	1	0	0	1	2	0	1	0	3	4	0	3	2	2	0	1
OTHER ASIA	45	0	0	0	0	1	1	0	0	3	0	1	3	3	12	3	3	3	3	3	3	3

CHAPTER 3— THE PROLIFERATION OF FOREIGN SUBSIDIARIES
SECTION 3— THE FLOW OF MANUFACTURING BY CHARACTERISTIC OF PARENT SYSTEM
TABLE G1— MANUFACTURING SUBSIDIARIES IN A SYSTEM
WITH LOW RETURN ON INVESTED CAPITAL IN 1966
CLASSIFIED BY COUNTRY OR REGION AND BY PERIOD MANUFACTURE BEGAN

PERIOD

COUNTRY OR REGION	PRE 1968	PRE 1901	1901-13	1914-19	1920-24	1925-29	1930-34	1935-39	1940-45	1946-50	1951-53	1954-55	1956-57	1958-59	1960-61	1962	1963	1964	1965	1966	1967	UNK
OUTSIDE U.S.	2711	32	52	44	44	87	66	96	71	118	119	113	154	211	360	169	188	193	193	196	108	97
OUT. U.S.+ CANADA	2305	29	39	26	34	63	52	73	58	92	96	85	119	186	321	157	175	165	169	178	105	83
OUT. WEST. HEMIS.	1613	27	33	18	26	53	43	58	22	49	54	52	113	113	241	123	139	125	142	126	79	54
OUT. WHITE CWEALTH	1750	20	31	18	26	45	35	38	46	71	78	62	98	148	239	122	120	126	142	140	79	66
OUT. DEVLPED WORLD	892	2	6	12	8	15	11	19	38	51	46	41	66	85	112	51	52	54	71	67	44	41
CANADA	406	3	13	18	10	24	14	23	13	26	23	28	35	25	39	12	13	28	24	18	3	14
LATIN AMERICA	692	2	6	8	8	10	9	15	36	43	42	33	62	73	80	34	36	40	48	52	26	29
C. AMER.+CARIB.	286	1	2	2	2	6	5	8	13	16	10	10	25	31	33	11	16	19	24	25	12	15
CUBA	26	1	0	0	1	2	1	3	2	2	2	0	6	1	1	0	0	0	0	0	2	2
MEXICO	181	0	2	2	4	4	2	3	9	13	7	9	14	22	22	5	9	15	10	16	8	10
OTHER	79	0	1	0	1	0	2	2	2	1	1	1	5	8	10	6	7	4	14	9	4	3
S. AMERICA	406	1	4	6	6	4	4	7	23	27	32	23	37	42	47	23	20	21	24	27	14	14
ARGENTINA	72	0	2	1	0	1	4	2	3	5	1	6	16	14	9	6	3	4	2	3	2	4
BRAZIL	103	0	2	4	0	1	4	2	6	9	14	5	16	9	6	2	3	2	4	12	2	3
PERU	31	1	1	1	0	1	0	0	4	2	1	1	2	1	2	2	2	7	1	3	2	3
COLOMBIA	73	1	0	0	0	1	0	0	5	4	6	2	5	8	10	4	6	7	4	4	2	1
VENEZUELA	83	0	0	0	2	0	0	1	4	3	9	4	3	11	17	4	5	4	4	5	4	1
OTHER	44	0	1	1	3	0	0	2	1	4	1	1	4	11	17	3	3	2	6	1	1	3
EUROPE	1068	27	32	10	25	44	36	41	14	32	32	32	40	77	158	85	79	76	79	90	39	20
EFTA	396	9	16	6	10	19	16	30	6	17	7	11	14	21	54	31	26	26	22	35	11	9
U.K.	285	8	7	5	7	14	12	23	5	13	5	10	12	14	43	22	20	13	12	23	10	7
SCANDINAVIA	63	1	1	1	1	1	3	1	0	1	1	0	0	3	6	8	1	10	5	7	1	1
SWITZERLAND	23	0	0	0	2	2	0	1	1	0	1	0	0	1	1	0	1	2	2	2	0	1
OTHER EFTA	25	0	2	0	2	1	2	4	0	1	0	0	0	3	6	0	5	1	3	3	0	0
EUROP. COMMUNITY	539	15	14	3	10	22	17	9	6	15	18	18	24	52	89	45	39	37	40	38	18	10
FRANCE	157	6	3	2	2	5	6	4	2	3	4	4	7	19	28	13	9	12	4	14	5	4
GERMANY	142	7	6	2	2	10	1	5	1	3	5	5	8	8	21	12	10	11	13	9	4	1
ITALY	117	2	4	0	1	3	1	2	0	3	1	2	5	10	23	12	9	11	11	7	4	1
BELGIUM + LUX	62	0	1	0	1	1	3	1	1	3	1	2	2	7	12	9	10	9	6	4	1	0
NETHERLANDS	61	0	0	1	0	3	2	1	2	4	2	2	2	8	8	5	2	5	6	4	7	4
SPAIN	75	0	0	0	1	1	0	0	0	2	2	2	2	8	9	5	8	8	6	4	5	4
GREECE + TURKEY	24	0	0	0	1	1	0	0	0	0	1	0	1	1	3	3	2	2	2	3	0	1
OTHER EUROPE	34	3	2	0	0	1	0	2	2	0	4	2	1	3	3	4	4	3	3	2	1	0
EUROPE EX. U.K.	783	19	25	5	18	30	24	18	9	19	27	22	28	63	115	63	59	63	67	67	29	13
SOUTHERN DOMINIONS	246	0	1	3	1	4	5	12	6	8	9	12	9	23	36	13	31	23	13	13	15	9
S. AFRICA +RHOD.	86	0	0	0	2	2	2	2	4	4	3	2	2	5	7	7	27	14	9	7	4	5
AUSTRALIA + N.Z.	160	0	1	3	0	4	3	10	4	4	6	10	7	18	29	8	4	14	11	11	4	4
ASIA + OTHER AFRICA	299	0	1	5	0	5	2	5	2	9	13	8	8	13	47	25	29	26	29	23	25	25
JAPAN	99	0	0	0	0	2	2	5	2	1	9	8	4	13	15	8	13	12	6	8	7	13
OTHER ASIA+AFR.	200	0	0	0	0	4	4	4	0	8	9	8	4	12	32	17	16	14	23	15	18	12
BLACK AFRICA	25	0	0	0	0	0	0	0	1	0	3	0	0	1	7	1	1	3	5	1	5	2
ARAB WORLD	23	0	0	0	0	0	0	0	1	3	1	1	1	2	3	1	4	0	4	2	2	1
INDIA	35	0	0	0	1	1	2	0	0	3	0	0	0	3	4	6	1	2	3	1	1	1
PHILIPPINES	30	0	0	0	0	0	0	1	1	1	1	1	1	3	4	1	4	0	2	3	1	1
OTHER E. ASIA	24	0	0	4	2	1	2	0	1	1	1	1	0	3	0	1	3	3	3	3	5	1
OTHER ASIA	63	0	0	5	0	2	2	2	0	4	0	2	1	3	9	7	3	4	6	5	4	6

CHAPTER 3- THE PROLIFERATION OF FOREIGN SUBSIDIARIES
SECTION 3- THE FLOW OF MANUFACTURING BY CHARACTERISTIC OF PARENT SYSTEM
TABLE G2- MANUFACTURING SUBSIDIARIES IN A SYSTEM
WITH HIGH RETURN ON INVESTED CAPITAL IN 1966
CLASSIFIED BY COUNTRY OR REGION AND BY PERIOD MANUFACTURE BEGAN

COUNTRY OR REGION	PRE 1968	PRE 1901	1901 -13	1914 -19	1920 -24	1925 -29	1930 -34	1935 -39	1940 -45	1946 -50	1951 -53	1954 -55	1956 -57	1958 -59	1960 -61	1962	1963	1964	1965	1966	1967	UNK
OUTSIDE U.S.	2477	16	25	27	47	131	85	116	75	129	115	108	150	204	324	143	154	145	176	134	127	46
OUT. U.S. + CANADA	2076	13	11	12	37	88	68	94	52	102	92	84	135	190	290	129	140	125	155	116	106	37
OUT. WEST. HEMIS.	1440	12	10	9	32	74	55	59	17	58	65	55	75	132	204	90	106	96	114	79	65	33
OUT. WHITE CWEALTH	1579	7	5	9	25	55	37	60	42	70	62	66	106	147	229	105	120	108	124	95	92	15
OUT. DEVLPED WORLD	803	1	1	4	7	20	14	37	36	53	31	35	71	78	112	53	54	49	49	46	47	5
CANADA	401	3	14	15	10	43	17	22	23	27	23	24	15	14	34	14	14	20	21	18	21	9
LATIN AMERICA	636	1	1	3	5	14	13	35	35	44	27	29	60	58	86	39	34	29	41	37	41	4
C. AMER.+CARIB.	286	0	1	1	0	2	8	17	9	17	16	9	29	30	29	16	11	21	21	24	22	3
CUBA	22	0	0	0	0	2	5	5	0	2	1	0	0	0	0	0	0	0	0	0	0	0
MEXICO	186	0	1	1	0	2	1	9	6	12	13	7	15	24	18	11	7	12	13	16	13	1
OTHER	78	0	0	0	0	0	0	3	3	3	2	0	6	4	11	7	4	9	8	8	9	2
S. AMFRICA	350	0	0	2	5	12	5	18	26	27	11	20	31	28	57	23	23	8	20	13	19	1
ARGENTINA	84	0	2	2	2	4	1	8	8	3	2	4	5	6	11	7	5	1	3	4	4	0
BRAZIL	92	0	0	1	1	6	4	9	7	10	5	5	6	14	13	7	5	2	3	1	3	1
PERU	27	0	0	0	1	0	0	6	1	1	1	0	1	0	1	0	2	0	3	1	1	1
COLOMBIA	42	0	0	2	0	0	1	1	2	5	2	2	3	1	13	2	5	2	2	4	2	0
VENEZUELA	62	0	0	2	0	0	1	0	3	6	0	5	11	6	10	5	5	1	3	3	2	1
OTHER	43	1	0	0	1	2	0	1	3	2	2	3	2	1	7	2	1	2	4	3	9	0
EUROPE	974	11	8	6	25	58	40	40	7	37	45	36	48	83	131	56	71	61	83	52	52	24
EFTA	346	5	5	3	8	30	18	23	3	22	21	10	22	23	32	16	19	17	27	14	14	14
U.K.	258	5	5	1	7	25	18	17	2	18	18	8	16	16	22	13	12	5	18	10	8	14
SCANDINAVIA	52	0	0	2	1	4	0	0	0	1	1	0	4	2	6	1	2	5	6	3	4	0
SWITZERLAND	14	0	0	0	0	0	0	3	0	1	1	0	1	3	2	2	0	3	0	1	1	0
OTHER EFTA	22	6	3	0	0	1	0	2	1	0	1	0	1	2	2	0	2	3	3	3	1	0
EUROP. COMMUNITY	531	6	3	3	14	23	20	15	3	12	17	21	22	54	91	34	47	38	43	26	29	10
FRANCE	166	2	2	1	7	17	9	7	0	5	4	8	2	11	33	6	11	16	4	5	5	3
GERMANY	156	2	2	3	3	11	8	3	0	2	5	8	9	12	23	13	13	11	13	15	5	4
ITALY	104	3	0	1	2	1	1	1	1	2	6	2	8	16	19	9	14	7	8	2	4	2
BELGIUM + LUX	56	1	1	2	1	1	1	1	1	0	1	1	0	10	10	3	5	1	6	3	4	1
NETHERLANDS	49	0	0	1	1	3	2	2	1	3	1	1	3	5	6	2	1	1	2	0	0	0
SPAIN	64	0	0	1	2	0	1	0	0	1	4	4	2	4	3	2	0	3	11	8	8	0
GREECE + TURKEY	17	0	0	1	0	3	0	2	1	2	1	1	1	2	4	1	0	1	0	2	1	0
OTHER EUROPE	16	0	0	0	0	2	0	2	0	2	1	0	1	1	1	1	0	1	0	1	0	0
EUROPE EX. U.K.	716	6	3	5	18	33	22	23	5	19	27	28	32	67	109	43	59	56	65	42	44	10
SOUTHERN DOMINIONS	231	1	1	2	4	8	13	16	8	12	11	10	12	27	38	11	8	11	13	11	6	8
S. AFRICA +RHOD.	74	1	1	1	2	2	8	4	4	7	3	3	3	9	6	6	4	5	3	3	4	4
AUSTRALIA + N.Z.	157	0	0	1	2	6	5	12	4	5	8	7	9	19	32	6	4	6	10	7	6	4
ASIA + OTHER AFRICA	235	0	1	1	3	8	8	3	2	5	9	9	15	22	35	23	27	24	18	16	17	1
JAPAN	68	0	0	1	1	2	2	1	1	1	5	3	4	2	2	14	20	24	10	16	6	1
OTHER ASIA+AFR.	167	0	1	0	2	6	6	2	1	9	4	6	11	20	26	12	20	20	8	9	11	0
BLACK AFRICA	21	0	0	0	2	0	1	0	0	0	0	1	3	1	3	0	1	0	2	1	1	1
ARAB WORLD	16	0	0	0	0	0	0	0	1	1	0	1	0	1	1	0	1	2	2	2	2	0
INDIA	34	0	0	1	1	2	1	1	1	1	0	1	1	5	5	4	4	8	4	4	1	0
PHILIPPINES	29	0	0	0	1	0	0	0	0	5	1	3	3	0	6	1	1	0	0	1	0	1
OTHER E. ASIA	20	0	0	1	1	2	0	1	0	0	0	4	1	6	11	3	0	5	1	4	1	0
OTHER ASIA	47	0	0	0	0	2	0	1	0	5	0	0	3	0	11	4	5	4	1	4	2	0

CHAPTER 3- THE PROLIFERATION OF FOREIGN SUBSIDIARIES
SECTION 3- THE FLOW OF MANUFACTURING BY CHARACTERISTIC OF PARENT SYSTEM
TABLE HI- MANUFACTURING SUBSIDIARIES IN A SYSTEM
WHICH FIRST MANUFACTURED OUTSIDE U.S. AND CANADA BEFORE 1901
CLASSIFIED BY COUNTRY OR REGION AND BY PERIOD MANUFACTURE BEGAN

COUNTRY OR REGION	PRE 1968	PRE 1901	1901 -13	1914 -19	1920 -24	1925 -29	1930 -34	1935 -39	1940 -45	1946 -50	1951 -53	1954 -55	1956 -57	1958 -59	1960 -61	1962	1963	1964	1965	1966	1967	UNK
OUTSIDE U.S.	749	47	44	19	35	31	20	37	21	26	19	29	30	40	68	41	35	59	64	34	31	19
OUT. U.S. + CANADA	655	42	35	15	31	27	19	30	16	24	15	23	28	38	64	38	29	47	58	31	30	15
OUT. WEST. HEMIS.	481	39	29	7	25	20	16	20	8	16	13	13	16	18	48	27	22	43	42	25	24	10
OUT. WHITE CWEALTH	511	27	29	11	22	22	15	26	14	20	9	18	24	28	51	30	22	34	47	26	25	10
OUT. DEVLPED WORLD	224	3	6	9	6	9	4	10	9	9	2	11	14	21	31	16	9	7	24	8	10	6
CANADA	94	5	9	4	4	4	1	7	5	2	2	6	2	2	4	3	3	12	6	3	1	4
LATIN AMERICA	174	3	6	8	6	7	3	10	8	8	4	10	12	20	16	11	7	4	16	6	6	5
C. AMER.+CARIB.	62	1	2	2	1	3	2	4	1	3	2	1	1	1	3	3	1	2	12	4	3	2
CUBA	6	0	0	0	0	1	0	0	0	0	0	0	0	0	0	0	0	0	0	0	0	1
MEXICO	41	0	2	0	1	2	1	4	0	3	0	1	0	1	3	1	1	1	9	3	1	0
OTHER	15	0	0	0	0	0	1	0	0	0	0	0	0	0	2	1	1	0	3	1	2	1
S. AMERICA	112	2	4	6	5	4	1	6	7	5	2	9	11	9	13	8	5	3	4	3	2	3
ARGENTINA	17	0	2	1	0	1	1	1	3	1	0	2	1	1	3	0	1	0	2	2	0	1
BRAZIL	31	1	0	4	1	0	0	3	2	2	1	3	4	1	0	4	5	0	2	1	0	0
PERU	10	0	1	0	1	2	0	0	1	1	0	0	0	0	0	1	0	0	0	0	2	1
COLOMBIA	20	1	0	0	0	1	0	0	0	1	1	4	1	1	4	1	1	1	2	0	1	0
VENEZUELA	17	0	0	0	2	0	0	0	1	0	0	0	2	2	5	0	2	1	0	0	0	0
OTHER	17	1	1	1	1	1	0	2	0	0	0	3	3	0	1	2	1	1	0	0	1	1
EUROPE	353	38	26	3	21	17	14	18	6	13	11	9	12	13	24	15	16	29	25	22	15	6
EFTA	123	14	12	1	8	5	5	9	2	4	5	1	5	6	7	4	4	8	10	9	2	2
U.K.	79	13	4	1	6	4	4	4	2	2	1	1	3	5	5	3	3	2	5	4	2	2
SCANDINAVIA	25	1	6	1	0	0	1	1	0	1	1	0	1	1	1	1	0	4	3	1	0	0
SWITZERLAND	6	0	0	0	0	1	0	0	0	0	0	0	0	0	0	0	0	2	1	1	0	0
OTHER EFTA	13	0	2	0	2	0	0	3	0	0	0	0	1	0	1	0	1	0	2	0	0	0
EUROP. COMMUNITY	184	21	12	2	8	10	7	8	4	9	4	6	6	4	13	10	9	17	13	8	10	4
FRANCE	50	8	4	1	2	3	0	5	1	1	1	1	1	0	1	2	1	7	1	1	3	2
GERMANY	60	10	3	0	2	6	7	0	4	2	2	3	3	1	4	5	5	5	8	2	0	0
ITALY	36	2	5	0	2	1	3	2	2	4	1	0	0	1	5	2	2	2	4	4	0	2
BELGIUM + LUX	17	1	0	1	1	1	0	0	0	1	1	0	1	1	3	0	1	2	2	0	1	0
NETHERLANDS	21	0	0	0	1	0	1	1	0	1	0	0	1	1	0	0	0	2	3	0	5	0
SPAIN	19	0	0	0	4	0	0	0	1	0	0	0	0	1	3	0	1	0	1	2	1	0
GREECE + TURKEY	9	0	2	0	0	1	1	0	0	0	0	0	1	0	0	0	2	2	0	2	0	0
OTHER EUROPE	18	3	2	0	1	1	0	0	0	0	1	0	2	0	1	0	2	2	0	3	0	0
EUROPE EX. U.K.	274	25	22	2	15	13	10	14	4	11	7	8	9	8	19	12	13	27	20	18	13	4
SOUTHERN DOMINIONS	55	1	2	3	3	1	0	0	0	2	0	3	1	4	7	5	2	9	6	1	2	2
S. AFRICA +RHOD.	15	1	0	1	2	0	0	0	0	2	1	0	0	0	2	3	1	2	0	0	0	1
AUSTRALIA + N.Z.	40	0	2	2	1	1	0	0	0	0	1	3	1	4	5	2	1	7	6	1	2	1
ASIA + OTHER AFRICA	73	0	1	1	1	2	2	2	2	1	1	1	3	1	17	7	4	5	11	2	1	2
JAPAN	23	0	1	0	0	2	2	0	1	0	0	0	2	1	2	2	2	2	3	2	2	1
OTHER ASIA+AFR.	50	0	0	1	0	0	0	0	1	1	1	0	1	0	15	5	0	3	8	0	0	1
BLACK AFRICA	5	0	0	0	0	0	0	0	0	0	1	0	0	0	3	1	0	1	1	0	1	0
ARAB WORLD	7	0	0	0	0	0	0	0	0	0	0	0	0	1	1	1	2	2	2	1	0	1
INDIA	11	0	0	1	0	0	0	0	0	1	0	1	1	0	4	2	1	0	0	0	0	0
PHILIPPINES	7	0	0	0	0	1	0	0	0	0	0	0	0	0	2	1	1	2	2	1	2	0
OTHER E. ASIA	6	0	0	0	0	0	0	0	0	0	0	0	0	0	0	0	0	1	1	0	0	0
OTHER ASIA	14	0	0	0	0	1	0	0	0	0	1	0	0	2	5	2	0	2	1	0	0	0

CHAPTER 3- THE PROLIFERATION OF FOREIGN SUBSIDIARIES
SECTION 3- THE FLOW OF MANUFACTURING BY CHARACTERISTIC OF PARENT SYSTEM
TABLE H2- MANUFACTURING SUBSIDIARIES IN A SYSTEM
WHICH FIRST MANUFACTURED OUTSIDE U.S. AND CANADA 1901-1919
CLASSIFIED BY COUNTRY OR REGION AND BY PERIOD MANUFACTURE BEGAN

PERIOD

COUNTRY OR REGION	PRE 1968	PRE 1901	1901 -13	1914 -19	1920 -24	1925 -29	1930 -34	1935 -39	1940 -45	1946 -50	1951 -53	1954 -55	1956 -57	1958 -59	1960 -61	1962	1963	1964	1965	1966	1967	UNK
OUTSIDE U.S.	905	0	25	39	30	65	51	72	30	55	50	39	44	61	83	48	42	41	60	34	21	15
OUT. U.S. + CANADA	767	0	15	26	23	48	43	58	24	45	41	30	37	60	77	46	41	38	56	29	20	10
OUT. WEST. HEMIS.	552	0	14	21	19	40	35	42	11	26	26	17	19	41	53	36	31	28	42	27	16	8
OUT. WHITE CWEALTH	569	0	7	18	18	37	20	34	18	33	31	26	32	49	59	31	31	34	45	21	17	6
OUT. DEVLPED WORLD	282	0	1	9	6	13	10	19	14	22	18	18	19	23	26	16	14	18	20	4	9	3
CANADA	138	0	10	13	7	17	8	14	6	10	9	9	7	1	6	2	1	3	4	5	1	5
LATIN AMERICA	215	0	1	5	4	8	8	16	13	19	15	13	18	19	24	10	10	10	14	2	4	2
C. AMER.+CARIB.	74	0	1	1	0	2	3	6	5	5	4	3	7	5	9	4	2	8	6	0	0	0
CUBA	6	0	0	0	0	0	0	0	2	1	1	0	1	1	0	0	0	0	0	0	0	0
MEXICO	53	0	1	1	0	2	2	4	1	0	4	3	2	4	8	3	4	6	2	0	0	0
OTHER	15	0	0	0	0	0	1	0	2	0	0	0	1	0	1	1	0	2	4	0	1	2
S. AMERICA	141	0	0	4	4	6	5	10	8	14	11	10	11	14	15	6	6	2	8	2	3	1
ARGENTINA	30	0	0	3	2	3	4	4	1	1	2	2	2	4	2	1	1	2	1	0	0	1
BRAZIL	46	0	0	1	1	1	3	3	3	7	2	3	4	7	4	3	2	2	0	2	3	0
PERU	12	0	0	0	0	2	0	0	1	1	0	1	1	0	1	0	1	0	1	2	0	0
COLOMBIA	14	0	0	0	1	0	0	1	2	0	1	0	0	2	2	2	0	2	2	0	1	0
VENEZUELA	21	0	0	0	0	0	1	1	0	2	1	2	3	2	3	2	2	0	0	3	1	1
OTHER	18	0	0	0	1	1	0	1	1	3	2	0	1	1	3	1	2	0	2	0	0	0
EUROPE	365	0	14	13	16	27	22	22	8	17	14	9	15	31	37	21	17	17	32	19	8	6
EFTA	147	0	9	8	6	11	12	13	3	10	5	1	4	10	17	7	3	5	12	7	3	3
U.K.	102	0	8	5	3	5	12	6	3	7	4	1	3	5	12	7	2	2	8	5	1	3
SCANDINAVIA	25	0	1	3	1	5	0	1	0	3	0	0	0	1	3	0	0	2	2	2	1	0
SWITZERLAND	9	0	0	0	1	0	0	0	0	0	1	0	1	1	1	0	0	1	1	0	1	0
OTHER EFTA	11	0	0	0	0	1	0	3	3	0	0	0	0	3	1	0	1	0	1	0	1	0
EUROP. COMMUNITY	180	0	5	5	10	14	8	6	3	7	6	6	10	21	20	8	10	8	17	10	3	3
FRANCE	54	0	1	1	0	3	4	6	3	1	1	2	1	5	9	2	3	4	3	1	3	2
GERMANY	49	0	3	3	6	8	8	2	0	2	2	3	3	5	4	1	3	0	5	6	3	0
ITALY	36	0	0	0	2	2	4	0	0	1	2	2	0	5	4	2	2	1	6	1	0	1
BELGIUM + LUX	22	0	1	0	1	1	2	1	1	1	3	2	1	5	2	2	2	1	2	1	0	0
NETHERLANDS	19	0	0	0	0	2	0	2	1	0	0	0	2	5	4	1	3	3	1	1	0	1
SPAIN	23	0	0	0	1	1	1	0	1	4	2	2	1	4	2	4	0	3	2	2	2	0
GREECE + TURKEY	4	0	0	0	0	0	0	0	0	0	0	0	0	0	0	1	0	1	0	0	0	0
OTHER EUROPE	11	0	0	0	1	1	0	3	2	0	1	0	0	0	0	1	1	0	0	0	1	0
EUROPE EX. U.K.	263	0	6	8	13	22	10	16	5	10	10	8	12	26	25	14	15	15	24	14	7	3
SOUTHERN DOMINIONS	89	0	0	3	3	6	11	17	8	5	5	3	1	6	6	7	5	2	3	3	2	1
S. AFRICA +RHOD.	22	0	0	0	1	1	2	2	3	2	3	0	1	1	1	2	2	1	1	1	1	1
AUSTRALIA + N.Z.	67	0	0	3	2	5	9	15	2	3	3	3	3	5	5	5	3	2	2	2	2	0
ASIA + OTHER AFRICA	98	0	0	5	7	7	2	3	4	7	2	7	3	8	8	8	9	7	7	5	6	1
JAPAN	31	0	0	1	2	2	2	0	1	1	4	5	2	2	2	2	1	1	3	2	1	0
OTHER ASIA+AFR.	67	0	0	4	5	5	2	3	3	6	3	5	1	6	6	6	4	8	6	5	5	1
BLACK AFRICA	9	0	0	0	0	0	0	0	0	1	0	0	0	2	2	1	1	2	2	3	3	0
ARAB WORLD	8	0	0	0	0	3	1	1	0	1	1	0	0	1	0	0	0	2	1	1	0	0
INDIA	11	0	0	0	0	0	0	0	1	0	1	1	1	0	1	0	1	2	0	1	0	1
PHILIPPINES	9	0	0	0	1	0	0	1	0	0	1	0	0	1	0	0	1	0	0	0	0	0
OTHER E. ASIA	3	0	0	0	1	1	1	0	0	0	0	0	0	0	0	0	0	0	0	0	0	0
OTHER ASIA	27	0	0	4	0	2	0	1	0	2	0	0	1	2	1	5	1	2	3	1	1	1

CHAPTER 3— THE PROLIFERATION OF FOREIGN SUBSIDIARIES
SECTION 3— THE FLOW OF MANUFACTURING BY CHARACTERISTIC OF PARENT SYSTEM
TABLE H3— MANUFACTURING SUBSIDIARIES IN A SYSTEM
WHICH FIRST MANUFACTURED OUTSIDE U.S. AND CANADA 1920-1929
CLASSIFIED BY COUNTRY OR REGION AND BY PERIOD MANUFACTURE BEGAN

COUNTRY OR REGION	PRE 1968	PRE 1901	1901-13	1914-19	1920-24	1925-29	1930-34	1935-39	1940-45	1946-50	1951-53	1954-55	1956-57	1958-59	1960-61	1962	1963	1964	1965	1966	1967	UNK
OUTSIDE U.S.	1524	0	6	8	27	114	63	79	59	81	67	61	87	107	217	80	111	82	100	85	53	37
OUT. U.S. + CANADA	1274	0	0	0	17	77	49	66	50	67	58	48	73	94	193	74	103	70	84	72	48	31
OUT. WEST. HEMIS.	900	0	0	0	14	68	40	44	16	37	39	32	45	66	139	53	53	53	54	40	34	29
OUT. WHITE CWEALTH	895	0	0	0	11	41	32	34	39	46	46	34	52	71	133	54	67	55	70	60	42	8
OUT. DEVLPED WORLD	482	0	0	0	3	13	9	25	35	36	22	19	33	42	68	23	30	28	36	39	18	3
CANADA	250	0	6	8	10	37	14	13	9	14	9	13	14	13	24	6	8	12	16	13	5	6
LATIN AMERICA	374	0	0	0	3	9	9	22	34	30	19	16	28	28	54	11	16	17	30	32	14	2
C. AMER.+CARIB.	169	0	0	0	1	3	7	13	7	16	8	4	12	12	24	4	6	8	14	20	9	1
CUBA	19	0	0	0	0	1	2	6	1	2	1	0	5	0	1	0	0	0	0	0	0	0
MEXICO	93	0	0	0	1	2	4	4	4	10	6	4	5	11	11	2	4	3	5	14	6	0
OTHER	57	0	0	0	0	0	1	3	3	4	1	0	1	1	12	2	2	5	9	6	3	1
S. AMERICA	205	0	0	0	2	6	2	9	27	14	11	12	16	16	30	7	10	9	16	12	5	1
ARGENTINA	54	0	0	0	0	2	2	6	8	3	2	3	3	3	4	4	2	2	5	3	2	0
BRAZIL	50	0	0	0	0	3	0	2	5	5	3	0	5	9	8	1	3	1	2	3	0	0
PERU	17	0	0	0	0	0	0	1	0	1	0	2	0	0	0	0	0	1	1	2	1	0
COLOMBIA	32	0	0	0	0	0	0	0	4	5	4	1	4	1	11	1	3	1	3	3	0	0
VENEZUELA	34	0	0	0	0	1	0	0	1	0	0	4	4	3	6	0	1	2	1	1	1	1
OTHER	18	0	0	0	2	1	0	0	2	2	2	3	0	0	0	1	3	1	4	1	3	0
EUROPE	574	0	0	0	13	58	34	33	4	25	24	21	26	37	85	39	43	27	36	24	25	20
EFTA	241	0	0	0	6	33	14	25	1	15	7	9	15	11	24	17	15	9	8	11	5	16
U.K.	191	0	0	0	5	30	11	24	0	13	6	8	10	7	19	14	10	5	6	6	2	15
SCANDINAVIA	33	0	0	0	1	0	1	0	0	1	0	1	0	0	4	2	5	4	1	4	1	1
SWITZERLAND	4	0	0	0	0	1	0	0	1	1	0	0	0	1	0	0	0	0	0	0	1	0
OTHER EFTA	13	0	0	0	0	2	1	0	0	0	1	0	0	3	1	0	0	0	1	1	1	0
EUROP. COMMUNITY	274	0	0	0	6	21	19	8	2	7	14	11	11	24	52	17	24	15	20	6	14	3
FRANCE	94	0	0	0	5	6	6	4	0	1	3	4	3	11	20	5	6	5	3	2	5	1
GERMANY	76	0	0	0	1	7	10	2	0	0	2	5	2	5	15	5	9	3	8	3	3	1
ITALY	52	0	0	0	0	1	0	0	0	3	8	0	5	11	11	1	4	3	1	0	2	0
BELGIUM + LUX	26	0	0	0	0	4	1	1	1	0	0	1	0	4	4	1	3	0	8	2	0	0
NETHERLANDS	26	0	0	0	0	3	2	1	1	3	1	1	0	2	2	1	3	0	2	0	2	0
SPAIN	35	0	0	0	0	2	2	1	1	3	0	1	0	3	7	3	3	0	6	5	0	0
GREECE + TURKEY	11	0	0	0	0	0	1	0	0	1	1	1	0	0	0	1	1	1	0	0	2	0
OTHER EUROPE	13	0	0	0	0	1	0	0	1	2	0	0	0	1	3	1	3	0	1	2	0	1
EUROPE EX. U.K.	383	0	0	0	8	28	23	9	4	12	18	13	16	30	66	25	33	22	30	18	23	5
SOUTHERN DOMINIONS	180	0	0	0	1	6	6	8	11	25	6	6	11	15	38	3	26	10	7	6	4	7
S. AFRICA +RHOD.	64	0	0	0	0	1	3	3	5	3	1	2	2	4	24	1	4	2	2	2	1	1
AUSTRALIA + N.Z.	116	0	0	0	1	5	3	5	6	3	5	4	9	11	35	2	2	4	5	4	3	6
ASIA + OTHER AFRICA	146	0	0	0	0	4	0	3	1	6	9	5	8	14	16	18	18	16	11	10	5	2
JAPAN	38	0	0	0	0	0	0	0	0	0	6	2	3	1	6	6	4	8	5	3	1	1
OTHER ASIA+AFR.	108	0	0	0	0	4	3	3	1	6	3	3	5	14	14	12	14	11	6	7	4	1
BLACK AFRICA	17	0	0	0	0	0	0	0	0	0	1	0	1	0	2	1	2	1	2	2	2	0
ARAB WORLD	10	0	0	0	0	0	0	0	1	2	0	1	0	3	2	0	0	0	0	0	0	0
INDIA	19	0	0	0	0	0	0	0	0	0	1	1	1	4	1	4	2	1	1	1	1	0
PHILIPPINES	21	0	0	0	0	3	1	1	1	2	0	2	0	2	1	0	5	0	0	0	0	1
OTHER E. ASIA	12	0	0	0	0	1	0	0	0	1	1	0	1	0	3	2	1	1	2	2	2	0
OTHER ASIA	29	0	0	0	0	0	2	2	0	1	0	0	0	0	7	5	4	3	3	1	0	0

CHAPTER 3- THE PROLIFERATION OF FOREIGN SUBSIDIARIES
SECTION 3- THE FLOW OF MANUFACTURING BY CHARACTERISTIC OF PARENT SYSTEM
TABLE H4- MANUFACTURING SUBSIDIARIES IN A SYSTEM
WHICH FIRST MANUFACTURED OUTSIDE U.S. AND CANADA 1930-1945
CLASSIFIED BY COUNTRY OR REGION AND BY PERIOD MANUFACTURE BEGAN

PERIOD

COUNTRY OR REGION	PRE 1968	PRE 1901	1901 -13	1914 -19	1920 -24	1925 -29	1930 -34	1935 -39	1940 -45	1946 -50	1951 -53	1954 -55	1956 -57	1958 -59	1960 -61	1962	1963	1964	1965	1966	1967	UNK
OUTSIDE U.S.	890	0	0	5	0	2	16	16	32	61	52	39	56	89	135	65	59	55	43	63	45	57
OUT. U.S. + CANADA	753	0	0	0	0	0	12	13	21	43	44	32	46	76	120	60	54	46	36	56	41	53
OUT. WEST. HEMIS.	469	0	0	0	0	0	9	11	4	19	21	19	14	45	82	44	41	34	27	42	26	31
OUT. WHITE CWEALTH	605	0	0	0	0	0	6	4	18	33	35	23	39	61	100	53	41	41	30	40	32	47
OUT. DEVLPED WORLD	332	0	0	0	0	0	3	2	17	29	25	15	35	35	42	19	20	14	11	17	17	31
CANADA	137	0	0	5	0	2	4	3	11	18	8	7	10	13	15	5	5	9	7	7	4	4
LATIN AMERICA	284	0	0	0	0	0	3	2	17	24	23	13	32	31	38	16	13	12	9	14	15	22
C. AMER. +CARIB.	122	0	0	0	0	0	2	2	7	7	10	6	16	12	10	6	4	9	2	7	7	13
CUBA	10	0	0	0	0	0	1	2	1	1	2	1	2	0	0	0	0	0	0	0	1	0
MEXICO	82	0	0	0	0	0	1	0	6	6	6	4	12	6	7	5	5	5	1	5	5	9
OTHER	30	0	0	0	0	0	1	0	0	0	2	1	2	6	3	1	1	4	1	2	2	3
S. AMERICA	162	0	0	0	0	0	1	0	8	17	13	7	16	19	28	10	9	3	7	7	8	9
ARGENTINA	26	0	0	0	0	0	1	0	0	2	1	1	1	2	6	4	1	0	0	3	0	2
BRAZIL	43	0	0	0	0	0	1	0	5	5	3	1	6	1	4	2	1	0	1	3	4	2
PERU	8	0	0	0	0	0	0	0	0	0	0	0	1	0	1	1	0	1	0	1	0	2
COLOMBIA	29	0	0	0	0	0	1	0	1	1	2	2	3	3	2	1	4	0	4	0	1	0
VENEZUELA	39	0	0	0	0	0	0	0	1	4	6	5	3	6	10	2	2	1	1	0	0	1
OTHER	17	0	0	0	0	0	0	0	1	2	0	1	1	0	5	1	1	0	1	0	3	2
EUROPE	319	0	0	0	0	0	6	8	3	8	12	12	6	30	68	37	31	28	19	24	20	7
EFTA	101	0	0	0	0	0	3	6	5	5	4	5	3	8	18	12	12	7	6	6	6	1
U.K.	76	0	0	0	0	0	3	6	4	4	3	4	3	6	15	9	9	3	4	5	6	0
SCANDINAVIA	13	0	0	0	0	0	0	0	2	1	0	1	0	1	2	2	1	0	0	0	0	1
SWITZERLAND	6	0	0	0	0	0	0	0	0	0	0	0	0	1	1	0	2	0	1	0	0	0
OTHER EFTA	6	0	0	0	0	0	0	0	0	0	1	0	0	0	0	1	0	2	1	0	0	0
EUROP. COMMUNITY	181	0	0	0	0	0	3	2	3	3	4	5	2	21	44	26	18	16	9	12	10	6
FRANCE	48	0	0	0	0	0	0	0	2	2	1	0	0	5	11	9	2	2	0	8	7	1
GERMANY	51	0	0	0	0	0	1	1	0	3	1	3	1	8	12	4	9	7	4	8	3	2
ITALY	48	0	0	0	0	0	0	1	0	0	0	1	0	7	12	4	9	4	3	3	1	0
BELGIUM + LUX	15	0	0	0	0	0	1	0	0	0	1	1	0	0	5	2	1	4	1	1	1	0
NETHERLANDS	19	0	0	0	0	0	1	0	0	0	1	1	1	1	4	2	1	3	1	0	0	3
SPAIN	23	0	0	0	0	0	0	0	0	0	2	2	1	1	2	3	1	2	2	5	0	0
GREECE + TURKEY	11	0	0	0	0	0	0	0	0	0	1	0	0	0	4	0	0	0	0	1	1	0
OTHER EUROPE	3	0	0	0	0	0	0	0	0	0	1	0	0	0	0	0	0	0	0	0	0	0
EUROPE EX. U.K.	243	0	0	0	0	0	3	2	1	4	9	8	3	24	53	31	22	28	15	19	14	7
SOUTHERN DOMINIONS	69	0	0	0	0	0	2	3	1	6	5	5	4	9	5	1	1	4	2	10	3	6
S. AFRICA +RHOD.	31	0	0	0	0	0	2	3	1	4	2	1	0	4	2	1	1	3	0	3	0	5
AUSTRALIA + N.Z.	38	0	0	0	0	0	1	2	0	2	3	4	4	5	3	0	1	1	2	6	3	1
ASIA + OTHER AFRICA	81	0	0	0	0	0	2	1	0	5	4	2	4	6	9	6	8	2	6	8	6	18
JAPAN	33	0	0	0	0	0	0	0	0	5	2	2	1	2	5	3	1	4	5	5	1	9
OTHER ASIA+AFR.	48	0	0	0	0	0	2	0	0	5	2	2	3	4	4	3	7	2	3	3	2	9
BLACK AFRICA	5	0	0	0	0	0	0	0	0	1	0	0	0	0	2	0	1	0	0	0	0	2
ARAB WORLD	5	0	0	0	0	0	0	0	0	0	0	0	0	2	2	1	0	0	0	0	0	0
INDIA	7	0	0	0	0	0	0	0	0	1	2	1	2	1	2	2	2	1	0	0	1	0
PHILIPPINES	9	0	0	0	0	0	0	0	0	0	0	0	0	1	0	0	3	0	0	1	0	1
OTHER E. ASIA	6	0	0	0	0	0	0	0	0	0	0	0	1	0	0	2	0	1	1	1	1	1
OTHER ASIA	16	0	0	0	0	0	0	0	0	4	0	1	0	0	0	3	1	1	1	2	1	4

CHAPTER 3- THE PROLIFERATION OF FOREIGN SUBSIDIARIES
SECTION 3- THE FLOW OF MANUFACTURING BY CHARACTERISTIC OF PARENT SYSTEM
TABLE H5- MANUFACTURING SUBSIDIARIES IN A SYSTEM
WHICH FIRST MANUFACTURED OUTSIDE U.S. AND CANADA AFTER 1946
CLASSIFIED BY COUNTRY OR REGION AND BY PERIOD MANUFACTURE BEGAN

COUNTRY OR REGION	PRE 1968	PRE 1901	1901 -13	1914 -19	1920 -24	1925 -29	1930 -34	1935 -39	1940 -45	1946 -50	1951 -53	1954 -55	1956 -57	1958 -59	1960 -61	1962	1963	1964	1965	1966	1967	UNK
OUTSIDE U.S.	1111	1	3	3	0	7	5	8	5	26	46	56	84	119	177	80	95	98	96	108	81	13
OUT. U.S. + CANADA	929	0	0	0	0	0	0	0	0	17	30	39	68	109	159	70	87	87	85	101	68	9
OUT. WEST. HEMIS.	651	0	0	0	0	0	0	0	0	11	20	28	38	73	125	45	63	61	66	70	44	7
OUT. WHITE CWEALTH	728	0	0	0	0	0	0	0	0	9	19	28	55	84	123	59	73	68	69	83	50	8
OUT. DEVLPED WORLD	365	0	0	0	0	0	0	0	0	8	10	14	34	44	54	30	33	34	27	41	33	3
CANADA	182	1	3	3	0	7	5	8	5	9	16	17	16	10	18	10	8	11	11	7	13	4
LATIN AMERICA	278	0	0	0	0	0	0	0	0	6	10	11	30	36	34	25	24	26	19	31	24	2
C. AMER.+CARIB.	139	0	0	0	0	0	0	0	0	2	4	6	16	21	16	10	11	13	11	15	12	2
CUBA	5	0	0	0	0	0	0	0	0	0	0	1	1	1	0	0	0	0	0	0	0	0
MEXICO	96	0	0	0	0	0	0	0	0	2	4	5	11	19	12	5	4	11	6	8	8	1
OTHER	38	0	0	0	0	0	0	0	0	0	0	0	2	1	4	5	10	2	5	7	4	1
S. AMERICA	139	0	0	0	0	0	0	0	0	4	6	5	14	15	18	15	13	13	8	16	12	0
ARGENTINA	32	0	0	0	0	0	0	0	0	0	0	2	4	5	5	6	2	4	0	1	3	0
BRAZIL	29	0	0	0	0	0	0	0	0	0	5	2	3	4	3	1	2	1	2	5	1	0
PERU	10	0	0	0	0	0	0	0	0	1	0	0	1	1	0	1	2	1	1	1	1	0
COLOMBIA	20	0	0	0	0	0	0	0	0	2	1	0	2	0	4	2	2	4	2	3	0	0
VENEZUELA	33	0	0	0	0	0	0	0	0	1	0	1	4	4	3	6	4	4	2	4	3	0
OTHER	15	0	0	0	0	0	0	0	0	1	0	1	0	1	1	1	0	2	3	1	4	0
EUROPE	431	0	0	0	0	0	0	0	0	7	16	17	29	49	79	30	42	36	47	52	23	4
EFTA	136	0	0	0	0	0	0	0	0	6	7	5	9	12	24	11	11	14	11	16	9	1
U.K.	103	0	0	0	0	0	0	0	0	6	6	4	9	21	17	5	8	9	7	13	8	1
SCANDINAVIA	17	0	0	0	0	0	0	0	0	0	1	1	0	0	0	4	0	4	2	1	1	0
SWITZERLAND	12	0	0	0	0	0	0	0	0	0	0	0	0	0	6	2	3	0	1	1	0	0
OTHER EFTA	4	0	0	0	0	0	0	0	0	0	0	0	0	0	0	0	0	0	1	1	0	0
EUROP. COMMUNITY	244	0	0	0	0	0	0	0	0	1	7	11	17	32	51	18	24	19	24	27	10	3
FRANCE	74	0	0	0	0	0	0	0	0	0	2	3	8	8	19	10	7	8	9	8	3	1
GERMANY	61	0	0	0	0	0	0	0	0	0	1	4	8	4	9	3	3	4	6	5	6	1
ITALY	49	0	0	0	0	0	0	0	0	0	3	3	3	10	11	7	6	5	0	7	1	1
BELGIUM + LUX	36	0	0	0	0	0	0	0	0	1	0	2	1	1	8	3	2	2	5	5	4	0
NETHERLANDS	24	0	0	0	0	0	0	0	0	0	1	1	1	0	4	1	2	2	7	5	2	0
SPAIN	37	0	0	0	0	0	0	0	0	0	1	1	2	3	4	2	2	0	9	7	7	0
GREECE + TURKEY	7	0	0	0	0	0	0	0	0	0	0	0	0	2	0	0	0	1	1	2	1	0
OTHER EUROPE	7	0	0	0	0	0	0	0	0	0	0	0	0	2	0	0	1	0	0	1	0	0
EUROPE EX. U.K.	328	0	0	0	0	0	0	0	0	1	10	13	20	39	62	25	34	27	40	39	15	3
SOUTHERN DOMINIONS	92	0	0	0	0	0	0	0	0	2	3	7	4	15	19	6	5	9	8	4	10	0
S. AFRICA +RHOD.	27	0	0	0	0	0	0	0	0	2	3	3	2	3	5	3	3	2	2	1	3	0
AUSTRALIA + N.Z.	65	0	0	0	0	0	0	0	0	2	1	4	2	12	14	3	2	7	6	3	7	0
ASIA + OTHER AFRICA	128	0	0	0	0	0	0	0	0	2	1	4	5	9	27	9	16	16	11	14	11	3
JAPAN	41	0	0	0	0	0	0	0	0	2	0	1	1	1	7	4	7	8	3	4	2	3
OTHER ASIA+AFR.	87	0	0	0	0	0	0	0	0	0	1	3	4	8	20	5	9	8	8	10	9	2
BLACK AFRICA	10	0	0	0	0	0	0	0	0	0	0	0	0	0	0	1	0	1	1	3	1	1
ARAB WORLD	9	0	0	0	0	0	0	0	0	0	0	0	0	0	3	1	0	1	2	0	2	0
INDIA	20	0	0	0	0	0	0	0	0	2	0	2	0	4	1	0	4	0	3	0	1	0
PHILIPPINES	12	0	0	0	0	0	0	0	0	0	0	1	0	1	6	1	0	1	0	1	3	0
OTHER E. ASIA	12	0	0	0	0	0	0	0	0	2	0	1	0	0	1	0	4	0	1	1	1	0
OTHER ASIA	24	0	0	0	0	0	0	0	0	0	0	1	2	3	6	0	2	3	0	3	3	1

CHAPTER 3— THE PROLIFERATION OF FOREIGN SUBSIDIARIES
SECTION 3— THE FLOW OF MANUFACTURING BY CHARACTERISTIC OF PARENT SYSTEM
TABLE II— MANUFACTURING SUBSIDIARIES IN A SYSTEM
IN "ORGANIZATIONAL STAGE II" IN 1966
CLASSIFIED BY COUNTRY OR REGION AND BY PERIOD MANUFACTURE BEGAN

PERIOD

COUNTRY OR REGION	PRE 1968	PRE 1901	1901-13	1914-19	1920-24	1925-29	1930-34	1935-39	1940-45	1946-50	1951-53	1954-55	1956-57	1958-59	1960-61	1962	1963	1964	1965	1966	1967	UNK
OUTSIDE U.S.	269	0	5	2	2	11	5	10	4	8	7	18	26	33	43	20	21	16	14	16	8	0
OUT. U.S. + CANADA	225	0	2	1	2	10	4	7	3	7	4	15	19	29	39	18	20	12	13	13	7	0
OUT. WEST. HEMIS.	153	0	1	1	1	10	4	5	2	3	3	8	8	22	28	11	18	8	9	7	4	0
OUT. WHITE CWEALTH	170	0	1	1	1	6	1	3	2	5	3	12	15	20	32	11	13	12	11	13	5	0
OUT. DEVLPED WORLD	94	0	1	0	1	1	0	2	1	5	2	9	12	10	13	9	5	5	5	8	5	0
CANADA	44	0	3	1	0	1	1	3	1	1	3	3	7	4	4	2	1	4	1	3	1	0
LATIN AMERICA	72	0	1	0	1	0	0	2	0	4	1	7	11	7	11	7	2	4	4	6	3	0
C. AMER.+CARIB.	33	0	1	0	0	0	0	1	0	4	1	4	4	3	4	3	1	1	0	3	2	0
CUBA	6	0	0	0	0	0	0	1	0	0	0	1	1	0	1	0	0	0	0	3	0	0
MEXICO	24	0	0	1	0	0	0	1	1	4	0	1	3	3	3	2	0	1	0	3	2	0
OTHER	3	0	0	0	0	0	0	0	0	0	0	0	0	0	1	1	1	0	0	1	1	0
S. AMERICA	39	0	0	0	0	0	0	0	1	0	0	3	7	4	7	4	1	3	4	3	1	0
ARGENTINA	4	0	0	0	0	0	0	0	1	0	0	0	0	0	0	0	0	0	0	1	0	0
BRAZIL	6	0	0	0	1	0	0	0	0	0	0	2	1	1	1	2	0	0	1	1	0	0
PERU	5	0	0	0	0	0	0	0	0	0	0	1	0	1	1	0	1	0	0	1	0	0
COLOMBIA	9	0	0	0	0	0	0	0	0	0	0	0	2	1	2	0	1	1	0	1	0	0
VENEZUELA	10	0	0	0	0	0	0	0	0	0	0	0	3	2	3	1	0	1	1	1	0	0
OTHER	5	0	0	0	0	0	0	0	0	0	0	0	1	0	0	1	0	1	2	0	1	0
EUROPE	101	0	1	0	0	9	2	3	2	0	2	4	5	13	21	7	13	7	7	5	0	0
EFTA	39	0	1	0	0	5	1	2	1	0	1	1	3	8	4	2	8	1	1	0	0	0
U.K.	31	0	1	0	0	4	1	2	1	0	1	1	3	4	4	1	7	0	1	0	0	0
SCANDINAVIA	5	0	0	0	0	0	0	0	0	0	0	0	0	2	0	1	1	1	0	0	0	0
SWITZERLAND	1	0	0	0	0	0	0	0	0	0	0	0	0	1	0	0	0	0	0	0	0	0
OTHER EFTA	2	0	0	0	0	1	0	0	0	0	0	0	0	1	0	1	0	0	0	0	0	0
EUROP. COMMUNITY	53	0	0	0	0	4	1	1	0	0	0	2	0	1	15	4	5	4	6	4	2	0
FRANCE	13	0	0	0	0	2	0	0	1	0	0	1	2	1	7	1	1	1	0	0	2	0
GERMANY	16	0	0	0	0	2	0	1	0	0	0	1	0	1	2	0	1	2	4	3	0	0
ITALY	10	0	0	0	0	1	0	0	0	0	1	0	1	1	3	1	1	0	1	0	0	0
BELGIUM + LUX	11	0	0	0	0	0	1	0	1	0	0	0	0	1	0	1	2	1	1	0	0	0
NETHERLANDS	3	0	0	0	0	1	0	0	0	0	0	0	0	0	1	1	0	0	0	1	0	0
SPAIN	7	0	0	0	0	0	0	0	0	0	0	0	0	2	1	1	0	2	0	0	2	0
GREECE + TURKEY	2	0	0	0	0	0	0	0	0	0	0	1	0	0	1	0	0	0	0	1	0	0
OTHER EUROPE	0	0	0	0	0	0	0	0	0	0	0	0	0	0	0	0	0	0	0	0	0	0
EUROPE EX. U.K.	70	0	0	0	0	5	1	1	1	0	1	3	2	9	17	6	6	7	6	5	0	0
SOUTHERN DOMINIONS	24	0	0	1	1	0	2	2	0	2	0	2	1	5	3	2	0	0	1	0	2	0
S. AFRICA +RHOD.	9	0	0	0	0	0	0	2	0	2	0	0	0	2	2	2	0	0	0	0	0	0
AUSTRALIA + N.Z.	15	0	0	1	1	0	2	2	0	1	0	1	1	5	1	1	0	1	1	0	2	0
ASIA + OTHER AFRICA	28	0	0	0	0	1	0	0	0	1	1	2	2	4	4	2	5	1	1	2	2	0
JAPAN	6	0	0	0	0	0	0	0	0	0	0	0	1	1	2	2	2	0	0	2	0	0
OTHER ASIA+AFR.	22	0	0	0	0	1	0	0	0	1	1	2	1	3	2	2	3	1	1	2	2	0
BLACK AFRICA	2	0	0	0	0	0	0	0	0	0	0	0	0	0	0	0	0	0	0	1	0	0
ARAB WORLD	5	0	0	0	0	0	0	0	0	1	0	0	1	1	1	0	0	1	1	0	1	0
INDIA	5	0	0	0	0	1	0	0	0	0	0	0	0	0	0	1	2	1	0	0	0	0
PHILIPPINES	5	0	0	0	0	0	0	0	0	0	0	0	0	1	0	0	1	0	0	0	0	0
OTHER E. ASIA	0	0	0	0	0	0	0	0	0	0	0	0	0	0	0	0	0	0	0	0	0	0
OTHER ASIA	5	0	0	0	0	0	0	0	0	0	0	1	1	0	1	0	0	0	0	1	1	0

CHAPTER 3- THE PROLIFERATION OF FOREIGN SUBSIDIARIES
SECTION 3- THE FLOW OF MANUFACTURING BY CHARACTERISTIC OF PARENT SYSTEM
TABLE 12- MANUFACTURING SUBSIDIARIES IN A SYSTEM
IN "ORGANIZATIONAL STAGE III-ID" IN 1966
CLASSIFIED BY COUNTRY OR REGION AND BY PERIOD MANUFACTURE BEGAN

COUNTRY OR REGION	PRE 1968	PRE 1901	1901-13	1914-19	1920-24	1925-29	1930-34	1935-39	1940-45	1946-50	1951-53	1954-55	1956-57	1958-59	1960-61	1962	1963	1964	1965	1966	1967	UNK
OUTSIDE U.S.	2409	10	30	29	46	103	86	122	67	114	115	113	132	186	311	154	172	157	165	158	96	43
OUT. U.S. + CANADA	2028	9	14	13	34	62	67	101	54	99	94	80	111	172	285	139	163	132	144	140	87	28
OUT. WEST. HEMIS.	1407	9	13	11	29	51	52	70	18	57	67	47	61	119	203	100	131	102	99	93	53	22
OUT. WHITE CWEALTH	1519	5	9	9	25	37	39	61	44	70	66	65	89	133	209	109	118	104	120	111	79	17
OUT. DEVLPED WORLD	793	0	1	6	5	15	16	36	38	51	30	39	60	72	107	52	50	50	56	56	45	8
CANADA	381	1	16	16	12	41	19	21	13	15	21	33	21	14	26	19	9	25	21	18	9	15
LATIN AMERICA	621	2	1	2	5	11	11	31	36	42	27	33	50	53	82	35	32	30	45	47	34	6
C. AMER.+CARIB.	267	0	0	1	1	3	8	14	11	17	11	8	26	25	29	16	11	15	24	27	17	3
CUBA	26	0	0	0	0	1	1	5	4	4	2	0	6	2	0	0	0	0	0	0	0	1
MEXICO	162	0	0	1	0	2	2	7	7	12	9	7	15	20	16	7	7	8	11	16	12	0
OTHER	79	0	0	0	0	0	5	2	0	1	0	1	5	3	13	0	4	7	13	11	5	2
S. AMERICA	354	0	1	1	4	8	7	17	25	25	16	25	24	28	53	23	21	15	21	20	17	3
ARGENTINA	80	0	1	0	0	0	3	8	3	5	1	5	5	5	8	8	5	3	4	3	5	1
BRAZIL	89	0	0	1	1	3	7	6	5	7	8	6	6	12	13	8	3	3	4	7	5	0
PERU	25	0	0	0	0	0	0	0	4	2	0	0	3	0	3	3	4	3	4	1	2	0
COLOMBIA	51	0	0	0	1	0	0	1	6	2	3	2	2	2	9	1	2	4	3	2	0	0
VENEZUELA	72	0	0	0	0	0	3	1	4	6	2	6	8	8	16	5	6	3	1	2	2	1
OTHER	37	0	0	0	3	2	0	1	2	3	2	2	0	1	4	2	1	2	5	2	4	1
EUROPE	905	9	12	4	27	39	37	48	7	39	44	30	38	72	123	67	71	62	68	62	33	13
EFTA	319	4	5	2	10	23	16	31	3	21	15	9	17	14	42	20	17	21	18	19	7	5
U.K.	240	4	4	2	7	18	15	24	2	18	12	7	12	12	30	17	11	11	12	15	5	5
SCANDINAVIA	46	0	1	0	2	4	1	1	0	2	1	1	4	0	6	0	3	7	3	4	2	0
SWITZERLAND	16	0	0	0	0	0	0	1	0	1	1	2	0	1	5	2	1	1	2	0	1	0
OTHER EFTA	17	0	0	0	1	1	0	3	1	0	1	0	0	1	1	1	2	2	2	0	0	0
EUROP. COMMUNITY	486	5	7	2	16	12	18	16	4	15	21	20	18	55	73	39	42	33	36	30	17	7
FRANCE	155	2	3	0	7	3	7	7	0	5	5	8	3	16	29	12	11	13	12	12	5	2
GERMANY	127	3	4	1	5	5	9	2	0	3	7	7	7	10	15	8	13	9	5	7	3	4
ITALY	104	0	0	0	2	2	0	2	1	3	6	2	7	16	16	13	12	7	11	4	5	1
BELGIUM + LUX	49	0	0	1	1	2	0	2	0	0	2	1	0	7	6	1	2	2	4	5	1	0
NETHERLANDS	51	0	0	0	2	3	2	3	2	4	1	1	1	6	7	5	3	2	11	2	0	0
SPAIN	62	0	0	0	1	3	1	0	2	3	4	2	6	1	2	2	5	3	11	10	6	0
GREECE + TURKEY	19	0	0	0	0	0	0	0	0	0	1	1	0	2	4	1	1	3	1	0	3	0
OTHER EUROPE	19	0	0	0	0	1	3	1	0	2	1	0	1	0	2	1	0	1	2	3	0	1
EUROPE EX. U.K.	665	5	8	2	20	21	22	24	5	21	32	23	26	60	93	50	60	51	56	47	31	8
SOUTHERN DOMINIONS	255	0	0	2	2	7	13	16	8	9	13	8	9	27	44	13	33	15	11	13	6	5
S. AFRICA +RHOD.	86	0	1	1	1	2	4	3	3	3	4	2	3	7	5	3	27	9	3	5	0	1
AUSTRALIA + N.Z.	169	0	1	1	1	5	9	13	5	6	9	6	6	20	39	10	6	6	8	8	6	4
ASIA + OTHER AFRICA	247	0	0	5	0	5	2	6	3	6	10	9	14	36	36	20	27	25	20	18	14	4
JAPAN	75	0	0	0	0	1	1	1	1	9	7	3	4	11	11	7	9	5	9	9	3	2
OTHER ASIA+AFR.	172	0	4	5	1	4	1	5	2	0	3	6	10	19	25	13	18	20	11	9	11	2
BLACK AFRICA	22	0	0	0	0	0	0	0	0	0	0	0	3	0	4	0	1	5	3	2	0	0
ARAB WORLD	18	0	0	0	0	0	0	1	1	0	1	1	0	5	2	5	1	3	3	1	0	1
INDIA	34	0	0	0	0	1	0	1	0	2	2	1	0	2	5	0	4	3	0	0	1	0
PHILIPPINES	25	0	0	0	0	2	0	2	1	1	1	4	0	5	1	3	7	0	1	3	0	0
OTHER E. ASIA	21	0	0	0	0	1	0	0	0	1	0	0	3	1	4	0	1	4	1	3	4	0
OTHER ASIA	52	0	0	4	0	1	1	2	0	6	0	0	3	6	9	4	6	6	0	3	2	1

CHAPTER 3- THE PROLIFERATION OF FOREIGN SUBSIDIARIES
SECTION 3- THE FLOW OF MANUFACTURING BY CHARACTERISTIC OF PARENT SYSTEM
TABLE I3- MANUFACTURING SUBSIDIARIES IN A SYSTEM
IN "ORGANIZATIONAL STAGE III-OTHER" IN 1966
CLASSIFIED BY COUNTRY OR REGION AND BY PERIOD MANUFACTURE BEGAN

PERIOD

COUNTRY OR REGION	PRE 1968	PRE 1901	1901 -13	1914 -19	1920 -24	1925 -29	1930 -34	1935 -39	1940 -45	1946 -50	1951 -53	1954 -55	1956 -57	1958 -59	1960 -61	1962	1963	1964	1965	1966	1967	UNK
OUTSIDE U.S.	2097	33	38	40	41	87	53	70	69	102	89	81	115	169	286	111	118	145	147	122	97	84
OUT. U.S. + CANADA	1805	28	31	26	33	72	42	53	52	76	73	69	104	150	253	106	104	130	131	110	86	76
OUT. WEST. HEMIS.	1275	25	26	16	27	59	37	36	19	43	39	47	59	89	193	85	77	99	98	85	65	51
OUT. WHITE CWEALTH	1380	19	23	19	23	52	27	31	41	55	60	47	82	120	195	83	82	104	109	83	65	60
OUT. DEVLPED WORLD	678	3	5	11	8	19	7	18	34	39	38	26	48	70	87	35	40	41	50	34	29	36
CANADA	292	5	7	14	8	15	11	17	17	26	16	12	11	19	33	5	14	15	16	12	11	8
LATIN AMERICA	530	3	5	10	6	13	5	17	33	33	34	22	45	61	60	21	27	31	33	25	21	25
C. AMER.+CARIB.	220	1	2	2	2	3	3	2	10	9	13	7	16	24	24	9	12	20	17	14	10	13
CUBA	11	1	1	0	1	1	0	0	0	0	1	0	3	1	2	0	0	0	0	0	0	0
MEXICO	148	0	0	2	0	4	1	2	7	6	9	7	8	19	17	5	7	17	10	9	5	10
OTHER	61	2	3	0	0	0	1	0	3	3	3	0	5	4	5	4	5	3	7	5	5	3
S. AMERICA	310	2	3	8	5	8	2	3	23	24	21	15	29	34	36	16	15	11	16	11	11	12
ARGENTINA	60	0	0	3	1	2	1	0	9	4	9	5	4	7	9	1	2	2	2	2	0	3
BRAZIL	86	0	1	4	2	4	2	2	5	11	9	2	12	14	11	9	6	5	2	4	2	2
PERU	26	0	0	0	0	1	1	0	1	0	0	1	1	1	3	1	1	1	1	1	0	3
COLOMBIA	48	0	0	1	1	0	0	1	1	6	4	2	0	6	11	1	2	3	5	2	2	1
VENEZUELA	52	0	0	0	0	1	1	0	3	3	5	3	6	6	7	1	3	3	4	1	1	1
OTHER	38	1	1	1	1	1	0	2	2	1	1	2	4	0	5	3	3	2	3	1	3	2
EUROPE	875	24	24	12	22	47	31	25	12	27	24	32	43	64	128	58	51	61	66	61	44	19
EFTA	326	8	14	7	8	18	14	18	5	16	8	11	15	21	37	22	15	19	23	27	13	7
U.K.	232	7	7	4	7	15	11	12	4	12	7	10	12	14	29	15	12	7	13	17	12	5
SCANDINAVIA	54	1	6	3	0	2	1	2	0	3	1	1	2	3	3	2	3	8	6	5	0	1
SWITZERLAND	15	0	0	0	0	1	0	1	0	1	0	0	1	0	3	0	1	3	0	2	1	1
OTHER EFTA	25	1	1	0	1	1	1	3	1	0	0	0	0	4	2	0	1	3	4	3	0	0
EUROP. COMMUNITY	446	14	8	4	7	25	15	4	4	11	11	15	25	39	79	30	30	36	33	21	23	12
FRANCE	131	5	1	1	5	6	5	3	2	3	3	2	5	12	22	12	7	13	3	5	11	5
GERMANY	129	7	8	2	1	11	6	0	2	7	5	7	9	8	21	9	6	7	13	12	4	0
ITALY	95	2	4	0	0	4	1	1	0	3	5	4	5	6	23	6	8	10	7	1	2	2
BELGIUM + LUX	42	0	0	0	1	2	1	1	0	3	0	0	2	6	5	3	5	2	5	1	6	1
NETHERLANDS	49	0	0	1	0	2	2	0	0	1	1	0	4	7	8	2	7	4	7	1	0	4
SPAIN	57	0	0	0	5	1	1	0	1	2	2	2	4	7	8	3	6	4	7	9	6	0
GREECE + TURKEY	18	2	2	1	2	2	0	3	0	0	1	3	2	1	2	2	1	1	2	3	1	0
OTHER EUROPE	28	2	2	0	2	2	1	1	2	1	1	1	1	1	2	1	3	1	1	1	1	0
EUROPE EX. U.K.	643	17	17	8	15	32	20	13	8	15	17	22	31	50	99	43	39	54	53	44	32	14
SOUTHERN DOMINIONS	176	1	1	3	3	5	4	9	6	9	5	11	10	15	27	7	7	18	8	9	8	11
S. AFRICA +RHOD.	52	1	0	0	2	0	0	3	3	5	1	1	4	4	6	4	4	5	1	1	1	7
AUSTRALIA + N.Z.	124	0	1	3	0	5	4	6	3	4	4	10	6	11	21	3	3	13	7	7	7	4
ASIA + OTHER AFRICA	224	0	1	1	3	7	4	2	3	7	6	4	8	10	38	19	19	20	24	15	13	21
JAPAN	76	0	0	0	1	1	0	1	1	1	0	1	6	1	11	2	0	10	7	6	5	10
OTHER ASIA+AFR.	148	0	0	1	2	6	2	1	0	6	6	4	3	9	27	14	16	10	17	9	8	11
BLACK AFRICA	19	0	0	0	0	0	0	0	0	0	0	0	0	0	0	5	2	5	2	0	3	2
ARAB WORLD	13	0	0	0	0	2	2	0	1	2	1	0	3	0	2	1	1	0	1	1	1	1
INDIA	26	0	0	0	1	0	0	0	0	0	1	2	1	2	8	4	1	0	3	1	0	1
PHILIPPINES	23	0	0	0	0	0	0	0	0	1	0	0	0	5	3	2	0	2	2	1	0	1
OTHER E. ASIA	17	0	1	1	1	2	2	0	0	3	2	2	1	0	9	3	3	2	2	1	2	1
OTHER ASIA	50	0	0	0	0	2	1	1	0	3	0	2	0	2	9	6	3	2	7	5	2	5

CHAPTER 3- THE PROLIFERATION OF FOREIGN SUBSIDIARIES
SECTION 3- THE FLOW OF MANUFACTURING BY CHARACTERISTIC OF PARENT SYSTEM
TABLE J1- MANUFACTURING SUBSIDIARIES IN A SYSTEM
WITH LOW "PRODUCT DIVERSITY IN THE U.S." IN 1966
CLASSIFIED BY COUNTRY OR REGION AND BY PERIOD MANUFACTURE BEGAN

PERIOD

COUNTRY OR REGION	PRE 1968	PRE 1901	1901-13	1914-19	1920-24	1925-29	1930-34	1935-39	1940-45	1946-50	1951-53	1954-55	1956-57	1958-59	1960-61	1962	1963	1964	1965	1966	1967	UNK
OUTSIDE U.S.	2350	19	29	33	52	82	63	112	63	99	111	98	139	176	310	149	147	154	160	163	112	79
OUT. U.S. + CANADA	2010	18	19	13	40	63	52	89	47	80	94	77	118	160	279	137	140	131	144	144	100	65
OUT. WEST. HEMIS.	1395	17	14	8	32	53	44	62	18	48	62	43	70	109	201	108	104	88	108	97	64	45
OUT. WHITE CWEALTH	1528	13	12	8	29	45	27	52	38	57	65	58	94	122	207	106	116	108	117	119	86	49
OUT. DEVLPED WORLD	784	5	5	5	10	12	10	30	30	40	35	39	57	66	107	43	59	56	48	55	47	29
CANADA	340	1	10	20	12	19	11	23	16	19	17	21	21	16	31	12	7	23	16	19	12	14
LATIN AMERICA	615	1	5	5	8	10	8	27	29	32	32	34	48	51	78	29	36	43	36	47	36	20
C. AMER.+CARIB.	284	1	3	2	0	5	5	17	17	17	12	11	27	20	28	8	12	30	20	27	20	10
CUBA	26	1	0	1	0	1	0	7	0	1	1	1	1	1	0	0	0	0	0	0	0	1
MEXICO	165	0	3	1	0	1	0	5	0	13	8	9	13	10	13	0	5	21	9	19	13	7
OTHER	93	0	0	0	0	3	3	5	4	3	1	0	7	9	14	5	7	0	11	8	0	2
S. AMERICA	331	0	2	3	8	5	3	10	20	15	20	23	21	31	50	21	24	13	16	20	16	10
ARGENTINA	62	0	2	1	1	3	2	5	6	0	7	5	2	7	6	7	5	0	4	1	3	2
BRAZIL	76	0	2	1	2	2	0	2	4	6	5	5	6	12	8	2	2	1	3	5	1	1
PERU	29	0	0	0	1	0	0	1	0	0	0	2	5	0	4	7	2	0	4	2	0	2
COLOMBIA	58	0	0	0	1	0	1	1	3	3	4	3	3	3	14	3	4	1	3	2	2	1
VENEZUELA	73	0	0	0	2	0	0	1	3	4	5	6	5	8	14	5	8	5	2	6	2	1
OTHER	33	0	0	0	2	0	0	0	2	2	2	2	1	1	4	3	1	3	3	0	4	3
EUROPE	912	17	12	5	26	48	30	42	10	28	41	24	45	66	123	69	61	55	81	71	45	13
EFTA	321	6	8	3	8	20	15	27	3	15	15	8	15	18	42	23	17	20	23	16	14	5
U.K.	233	5	5	2	7	15	14	20	3	11	13	6	12	11	32	15	13	9	16	12	8	4
SCANDINAVIA	52	1	3	1	0	0	1	1	0	2	1	2	1	3	5	6	1	0	5	2	3	1
SWITZERLAND	14	0	0	0	0	0	0	2	0	2	1	0	1	0	4	0	2	0	2	1	1	0
OTHER EFTA	22	0	0	0	1	2	0	4	0	0	0	0	1	1	1	0	0	1	1	1	2	0
EUROP. COMMUNITY	498	10	3	2	14	25	13	13	7	13	20	13	27	44	77	36	35	26	45	42	25	8
FRANCE	151	2	2	1	9	6	4	5	2	5	5	3	4	12	28	15	9	5	16	16	13	2
GERMANY	148	6	1	1	3	11	6	2	1	2	6	6	11	18	18	10	10	7	13	15	7	3
ITALY	99	2	0	0	1	3	1	1	0	2	1	1	1	8	19	9	11	8	13	7	2	0
BELGIUM + LUX	52	0	0	0	1	1	1	2	1	2	8	1	7	1	7	1	3	3	6	3	2	1
NETHERLANDS	48	0	0	0	0	4	1	3	2	2	1	2	4	10	9	1	1	8	6	2	1	2
SPAIN	61	0	0	0	3	0	2	0	0	3	2	0	3	4	5	6	3	5	9	11	5	0
GREECE + TURKEY	12	0	1	0	1	0	0	2	0	0	1	0	1	0	2	1	0	2	3	0	1	0
OTHER EUROPE	20	1	1	0	2	2	0	2	0	0	4	0	1	1	1	2	0	2	1	0	2	0
EUROPE Ex. U.K.	679	12	7	3	19	33	16	22	7	17	28	18	33	55	91	54	48	46	65	59	37	9
SOUTHERN DOMINIONS	236	0	2	3	4	3	11	16	6	12	12	13	11	27	39	15	11	12	10	11	6	12
S. AFRICA +RHOD.	76	0	0	1	2	1	5	4	3	6	3	5	1	9	7	6	5	5	3	4	0	6
AUSTRALIA + N.Z.	160	0	2	2	2	2	6	12	3	6	9	8	10	18	32	9	6	7	7	7	6	6
ASIA + OTHER AFRICA	247	0	0	2	2	2	3	12	2	8	9	6	14	16	39	24	32	21	17	15	13	20
JAPAN	78	0	0	0	2	2	2	1	1	0	6	1	5	1	10	10	9	8	5	7	2	11
OTHER ASIA+AFR.	169	0	0	0	2	2	3	3	1	8	3	5	9	15	29	14	23	13	12	8	11	9
BLACK AFRICA	19	0	0	0	0	0	0	0	0	1	0	1	1	0	4	1	4	1	1	0	2	1
ARAB WORLD	22	0	0	0	0	0	0	1	0	1	0	1	2	2	4	2	2	2	4	2	1	1
INDIA	29	0	0	0	1	0	1	0	0	2	0	1	1	4	4	4	3	5	1	1	1	1
PHILIPPINES	25	0	0	0	0	1	0	1	0	0	0	1	3	0	5	3	6	2	0	0	0	0
OTHER E. ASIA	20	0	1	1	1	0	1	0	0	2	2	2	1	2	2	0	2	1	1	1	4	1
OTHER ASIA	54	0	0	3	0	1	1	2	0	3	0	2	2	3	13	7	5	4	3	4	3	4

CHAPTER 3- THE PROLIFERATION OF FOREIGN SUBSIDIARIES
SECTION 3- THE FLOW OF MANUFACTURING BY CHARACTERISTIC OF PARENT SYSTEM
TABLE J2- MANUFACTURING SUBSIDIARIES IN A SYSTEM
WITH HIGH "PRODUCT DIVERSITY IN THE U.S." IN 1966
CLASSIFIED BY COUNTRY OR REGION AND BY PERIOD MANUFACTURE BEGAN

PERIOD

COUNTRY OR REGION	PRE 1968	PRE 1901	1901 -13	1914 -19	1920 -24	1925 -29	1930 -34	1935 -39	1940 -45	1946 -50	1951 -53	1954 -55	1956 -57	1958 -59	1960 -61	1962	1963	1964	1965	1966	1967	UNK
OUTSIDE U.S.	2829	29	49	41	40	137	92	100	84	150	123	126	162	240	370	165	195	181	203	161	119	62
OUT. U.S. + CANADA	2368	24	31	28	31	89	71	78	64	116	94	95	134	217	334	151	174	157	175	145	107	53
OUT. WEST. HEMIS.	1658	22	29	20	26	75	56	55	21	61	57	66	62	134	246	107	140	131	123	107	80	40
OUT. WHITE CWEALTH	1780	14	24	21	22	55	46	46	51	84	75	71	108	171	259	121	122	124	144	111	80	31
OUT. DEVLPED WORLD	901	2	2	13	5	23	16	26	45	64	42	38	78	99	114	61	47	45	70	54	40	17
CANADA	461	5	18	13	9	48	21	22	20	34	29	31	28	23	36	14	21	24	28	16	12	9
LATIN AMERICA	710	2	2	8	5	14	15	23	43	55	37	29	72	83	88	44	34	26	52	38	27	13
C. AMER.+CARIB.	282	0	0	1	2	3	9	8	13	16	14	9	25	41	34	19	15	9	25	19	12	8
CUBA	20	0	0	1	1	1	3	1	2	1	0	0	0	3	0	1	1	0	0	0	1	1
MEXICO	200	0	0	1	1	2	6	7	10	12	12	8	16	36	27	11	11	5	14	11	10	4
OTHER	62	0	0	0	0	0	0	1	1	2	2	1	4	4	7	8	4	4	11	8	5	3
S. AMERICA	428	2	2	7	3	11	6	15	30	39	23	20	47	42	54	25	19	17	27	19	15	5
ARGENTINA	97	0	0	3	0	2	0	6	9	8	1	5	10	7	14	6	6	5	4	6	5	2
BRAZIL	123	1	2	3	3	5	6	6	6	13	12	5	16	18	11	7	5	2	3	1	2	1
PERU	28	1	0	0	0	2	0	0	4	8	1	1	2	11	7	1	3	3	2	6	1	1
COLOMBIA	57	0	1	0	0	5	0	0	5	3	1	2	4	4	9	1	3	5	4	0	4	0
VENEZUELA	71	0	0	1	0	0	0	0	4	6	4	3	11	6	13	5	5	1	5	5	4	1
OTHER	52	1	1	0	2	3	0	3	2	4	1	2	4	1	6	3	3	1	7	3	4	0
EUROPE	1130	21	28	11	24	54	46	39	11	42	36	44	43	94	170	73	88	82	78	70	46	30
EFTA	427	13	13	6	10	29	19	26	6	25	13	13	21	29	48	24	28	23	24	33	11	18
U.K.	318	8	8	4	7	24	16	20	5	21	10	12	16	22	36	20	19	9	14	21	11	17
SCANDINAVIA	61	0	4	2	2	1	1	1	4	4	1	1	5	3	6	5	5	8	4	8	0	1
SWITZERLAND	23	0	0	0	0	1	0	3	0	0	0	0	0	3	4	0	3	5	2	1	0	0
OTHER EFTA	25	2	2	0	1	2	1	2	0	0	2	0	0	1	2	1	1	1	4	3	0	0
EUROP. COMMUNITY	565	11	14	4	10	20	24	11	14	14	15	26	19	58	103	43	50	49	38	21	22	11
FRANCE	169	6	3	1	4	6	9	6	3	3	3	9	5	17	32	11	11	23	13	6	8	5
GERMANY	149	4	5	2	2	10	9	2	3	3	4	9	6	10	26	8	13	11	9	9	8	1
ITALY	122	0	5	0	2	1	1	1	1	2	4	6	1	17	24	12	12	10	6	6	2	3
BELGIUM + LUX	64	1	1	1	2	3	2	1	0	2	1	1	1	15	11	8	13	2	6	3	2	0
NETHERLANDS	61	0	0	1	0	4	3	1	1	4	3	1	6	9	10	4	4	3	6	1	0	2
SPAIN	76	0	0	1	3	4	2	0	0	1	4	1	2	2	10	5	5	6	12	10	7	0
GREECE + TURKEY	30	0	1	0	1	1	1	0	0	3	1	1	2	2	6	2	1	2	2	2	5	0
OTHER EUROPE	32	2	1	0	0	1	1	2	3	0	1	1	0	2	3	0	4	2	2	2	1	1
EUROPE EX. U.K.	812	13	21	7	17	30	30	19	7	21	26	32	27	72	134	53	69	73	64	49	35	13
SOUTHERN DOMINIONS	249	1	0	3	1	10	9	12	8	9	8	11	10	22	36	10	29	22	16	13	15	4
S. AFRICA +RHOD.	83	1	0	0	1	1	2	2	3	5	3	4	4	19	6	6	26	9	2	4	4	2
AUSTRALIA + N.Z.	166	0	0	3	0	9	7	10	5	4	5	10	6	18	30	24	23	13	14	9	11	2
ASIA + OTHER AFRICA	279	1	1	6	1	11	7	4	2	10	13	11	9	18	40	24	23	27	29	24	19	6
JAPAN	88	0	1	1	1	1	1	1	2	1	8	2	3	16	14	17	10	8	11	8	6	2
OTHER ASIA+AFR.	191	0	0	5	5	9	6	3	0	9	5	2	6	16	26	7	13	19	18	16	13	4
BLACK AFRICA	27	0	0	0	0	2	1	0	1	0	0	1	0	0	6	2	0	6	4	2	4	0
ARAB WORLD	17	0	0	0	0	0	0	0	0	0	0	0	0	3	0	1	0	2	2	3	0	1
INDIA	39	0	0	0	1	3	0	1	1	1	2	0	1	6	10	7	0	2	3	1	1	1
PHILIPPINES	33	0	0	0	0	2	0	1	0	0	2	0	1	2	2	2	2	2	2	2	2	0
OTHER E. ASIA	19	0	0	1	0	2	2	0	0	0	1	0	0	0	2	0	6	0	3	1	0	0
OTHER ASIA	56	0	0	4	0	2	1	1	0	6	1	0	2	5	6	3	5	3	4	3	3	2

CHAPTER 3- THE PROLIFERATION OF FOREIGN SUBSIDIARIES
SECTION 3- THE FLOW OF MANUFACTURING BY CHARACTERISTIC OF PARENT SYSTEM
TABLE K1- MANUFACTURING SUBSIDIARIES IN A SYSTEM
WITH LOW "PRODUCT DIVERSITY ABROAD" IN 1966
CLASSIFIED BY COUNTRY OR REGION AND BY PERIOD MANUFACTURE BEGAN

COUNTRY OR REGION	PRE 1968	PRE 1901	1901-13	1914-19	1920-24	1925-29	1930-34	1935-39	1940-45	1946-50	1951-53	1954-55	1956-57	1958-59	1960-61	1962	1963	1964	1965	1966	1967	UNK
OUTSIDE U.S.	1766	5	19	25	38	70	50	92	62	86	97	84	124	143	226	112	124	100	97	108	69	35
OUT. U.S. + CANADA	1510	4	9	11	29	47	42	76	51	76	79	70	103	131	201	99	117	91	84	95	64	31
OUT. WEST. HEMIS.	1041	4	8	10	24	40	33	50	19	49	60	36	56	90	145	74	89	69	56	66	38	25
OUT. WHITE CWEALTH	1147	2	6	6	22	29	29	48	39	54	55	55	80	98	158	79	94	73	74	75	55	16
OUT. DEVLPED WORLD	597	0	1	1	6	11	29	30	33	35	22	39	53	55	72	37	45	38	34	36	34	6
CANADA	256	1	10	14	9	23	8	16	11	10	18	14	21	12	25	13	7	9	13	13	5	4
LATIN AMERICA	469	0	1	1	5	7	9	26	32	27	19	34	47	41	56	25	28	22	28	29	26	6
C. AMER.+CARIB.	220	0	1	0	0	3	7	16	10	16	7	11	29	21	22	10	9	14	9	18	13	4
CUBA	26	0	0	0	0	0	1	5	1	1	3	1	2	2	0	0	0	0	0	0	0	0
MEXICO	134	0	1	0	0	3	4	7	6	11	4	10	12	17	11	4	4	10	3	15	9	3
OTHER	60	0	0	0	0	0	2	4	3	3	0	0	8	2	10	4	5	0	6	3	4	1
S. AMERICA	249	0	1	1	5	4	2	10	22	11	12	23	18	20	34	15	19	8	19	11	13	2
ARGENTINA	56	0	0	0	1	2	0	5	5	2	2	2	3	3	9	4	7	1	1	4	3	1
BRAZIL	60	0	0	0	1	0	2	2	5	5	1	6	3	11	8	4	6	8	3	2	3	1
PERU	23	0	0	0	2	0	0	1	3	2	0	3	1	0	2	0	2	0	3	0	2	0
COLOMBIA	35	0	0	0	0	0	0	1	4	1	2	4	4	2	5	3	2	3	4	2	0	0
VENEZUELA	48	0	0	0	0	0	1	1	3	1	2	7	3	2	7	3	4	1	1	2	3	0
OTHER	27	0	0	2	1	1	0	0	2	1	2	2	0	0	3	2	0	3	5	0	5	0
EUROPE	680	4	8	6	21	31	28	33	8	28	38	23	35	49	97	48	56	39	39	42	28	19
EFTA	222	2	4	3	4	17	10	18	4	13	10	10	15	9	20	17	17	8	6	12	11	11
U.K.	174	2	3	2	4	14	9	16	3	9	9	8	12	6	18	10	14	5	3	9	7	11
SCANDINAVIA	29	2	0	1	1	1	1	1	0	3	0	0	0	0	2	4	1	2	3	2	1	0
SWITZERLAND	6	0	0	0	0	0	0	0	0	0	0	0	0	0	0	0	1	0	0	0	0	0
OTHER EFTA	13	0	3	0	0	2	0	1	1	1	1	2	3	3	0	3	2	1	0	1	2	0
EUROP. COMMUNITY	388	2	4	5	14	12	17	13	3	14	18	12	20	35	69	26	32	25	24	26	11	8
FRANCE	129	1	2	3	7	6	6	0	5	3	4	9	8	7	9	8	9	8	11	6	4	4
GERMANY	110	1	2	1	4	7	2	0	3	4	4	1	9	11	2	9	9	7	11	14	6	3
ITALY	76	0	0	1	1	6	1	0	0	0	1	1	4	19	8	9	8	3	3	1	2	0
BELGIUM + LUX	33	0	0	0	0	3	2	0	2	2	0	0	7	1	2	1	3	7	4	1	1	0
NETHERLANDS	40	0	0	0	1	1	0	3	0	4	2	1	0	4	6	8	2	1	5	2	2	1
SPAIN	44	0	0	0	2	0	3	2	2	0	5	0	0	6	4	5	5	3	8	3	1	0
GREECE + TURKEY	13	0	0	1	0	0	0	0	1	4	1	0	0	3	1	2	3	0	1	0	2	0
OTHER EUROPE	13	0	0	0	0	0	0	2	0	0	4	0	1	1	2	1	2	0	3	0	0	0
EUROPE EX. U.K.	506	2	5	4	17	17	19	17	5	19	29	15	23	43	79	38	42	34	36	33	21	8
SOUTHERN DOMINIONS	180	0	3	3	2	4	4	12	9	13	11	7	11	26	24	10	7	13	7	11	2	4
S. AFRICA +RHOD.	61	0	1	1	0	4	3	3	4	8	2	3	2	5	8	4	6	3	1	6	2	2
AUSTRALIA + N.Z.	119	0	2	2	2	0	1	9	5	5	9	4	9	21	16	6	6	10	6	5	2	2
ASIA + OTHER AFRICA	181	0	1	1	1	1	1	9	2	8	11	6	10	24	16	16	26	17	10	13	8	2
JAPAN	128	0	0	0	1	0	1	2	1	0	3	1	6	15	14	14	9	1	4	6	0	2
OTHER ASIA+AFR.	53	0	0	0	0	1	0	4	1	8	1	5	1	8	16	2	17	16	6	7	8	0
BLACK AFRICA	14	0	0	0	0	0	1	1	0	1	0	1	1	4	2	2	2	1	0	2	1	0
ARAB WORLD	14	0	0	0	0	0	0	0	2	0	1	1	0	2	0	2	3	5	0	7	2	0
INDIA	24	0	0	0	1	0	1	0	0	2	0	4	2	1	2	0	4	1	3	0	1	0
PHILIPPINES	24	0	0	0	1	0	0	0	2	2	0	2	3	3	5	3	4	3	1	1	1	0
OTHER E. ASIA	15	0	0	1	2	0	0	1	0	1	2	3	0	0	1	0	2	0	4	1	2	0
OTHER ASIA	38	0	5	0	1	3	3	0	0	3	0	2	1	7	3	3	5	3	3	4	1	0

CHAPTER 3- THE PROLIFERATION OF FOREIGN SUBSIDIARIES
SECTION 3- THE FLOW OF MANUFACTURING BY CHARACTERISTIC OF PARENT SYSTEM
TABLE K2- MANUFACTURING SUBSIDIARIES IN A SYSTEM
WITH HIGH "PRODUCT DIVERSITY ABROAD" IN 1966
CLASSIFIED BY COUNTRY OR REGION AND BY PERIOD MANUFACTURE BEGAN

PERIOD

COUNTRY OR REGION	PRE 1968	PRE 1901	1901-13	1914-19	1920-24	1925-29	1930-34	1935-39	1940-45	1946-50	1951-53	1954-55	1956-57	1958-59	1960-61	1962	1963	1964	1965	1966	1967	UNK
OUTSIDE U.S.	3613	43	59	49	54	149	105	120	85	163	137	140	177	273	454	202	218	235	266	216	162	106
OUT. U.S. + CANADA	2868	38	41	30	42	105	81	91	60	120	109	102	149	246	412	189	197	197	235	194	143	87
OUT. WEST. HEMIS.	2012	35	35	18	34	88	67	67	20	60	59	73	76	153	302	141	155	150	175	138	106	60
OUT. WHITE CWEALTH	2161	25	30	23	29	71	44	50	50	87	85	74	122	195	308	148	144	159	187	155	111	64
OUT. DEVLPED WORLD	1088	3	6	17	9	24	17	26	42	69	55	38	82	110	149	67	61	63	84	73	53	40
CANADA	545	5	18	19	12	44	24	29	25	43	28	38	28	27	42	13	21	38	31	22	19	19
LATIN AMERICA	856	3	6	12	8	17	14	24	40	60	50	29	73	93	110	48	42	47	60	56	37	27
C. AMER.+CARIB.	346	1	2	2	2	5	7	9	12	17	19	1	23	40	40	17	18	25	36	28	19	14
CUBA	20	1	0	1	1	2	1	3	1	2	0	1	3	1	0	0	0	0	0	0	0	2
MEXICO	231	0	2	2	1	3	4	5	2	14	16	7	17	29	29	12	12	16	20	15	11	8
OTHER	95	0	0	1	0	0	2	1	9	1	3	1	3	10	11	5	6	9	16	13	8	4
S. AMERICA	510	2	4	9	6	12	7	15	28	43	31	20	50	53	70	31	24	22	24	28	18	13
ARGENTINA	103	0	2	3	1	4	6	6	8	6	8	2	11	11	11	9	1	5	4	11	4	3
BRAZIL	139	0	1	5	1	5	0	6	1	15	14	8	19	19	11	7	4	2	4	3	2	1
PERU	34	1	1	0	0	1	0	4	0	2	1	1	3	1	3	1	2	1	2	1	4	3
COLOMBIA	80	0	0	0	1	1	1	0	3	8	6	3	3	7	18	3	2	7	5	2	2	1
VENEZUELA	96	0	0	1	2	0	0	0	4	7	7	2	11	13	20	6	6	5	4	4	3	2
OTHER	58	1	1	1	2	2	0	3	2	5	1	2	5	2	7	4	4	5	5	3	3	3
EUROPE	1362	34	32	10	29	71	48	48	13	42	39	45	53	111	196	94	93	98	120	99	63	24
EFTA	526	12	17	6	13	32	24	35	4	27	18	11	21	38	70	28	28	35	41	37	14	12
U.K.	377	11	9	4	10	25	21	24	2	23	14	10	16	27	50	30	18	13	27	24	12	10
SCANDINAVIA	84	0	6	2	2	5	2	2	4	3	2	1	4	5	9	5	5	5	6	8	2	1
SWITZERLAND	31	0	0	0	1	1	0	3	0	1	1	0	1	3	8	0	3	2	2	3	1	0
OTHER EFTA	34	0	2	0	0	1	0	6	0	0	1	0	0	3	3	0	0	2	6	3	1	1
EUROP. COMMUNITY	675	19	13	3	10	33	20	11	6	13	17	27	26	67	111	53	53	50	59	37	36	11
FRANCE	191	7	3	3	6	9	7	6	2	3	5	8	3	21	31	13	11	21	7	10	15	3
GERMANY	187	9	4	2	1	15	8	1	1	3	6	11	6	13	33	16	14	10	15	10	7	1
ITALY	145	2	5	1	1	3	3	2	1	2	3	3	9	16	24	13	14	11	16	10	4	3
BELGIUM + LUX	83	1	1	0	0	3	1	1	1	2	2	6	2	8	14	5	10	3	8	5	4	1
NETHERLANDS	69	0	0	0	2	2	1	1	1	2	1	1	1	4	9	6	4	5	8	4	10	3
SPAIN	93	0	0	0	0	3	3	0	0	0	1	5	3	9	8	8	8	8	13	18	8	0
GREECE + TURKEY	29	0	2	0	1	2	0	2	2	0	1	1	1	2	4	8	2	8	4	3	4	0
OTHER EUROPE	39	3	0	1	1	3	0	2	2	2	1	2	1	3	3	1	2	4	4	3	1	1
EUROPE Ex. U.K.	985	23	23	6	19	46	27	24	9	19	25	35	37	84	146	69	75	85	93	75	51	14
SOUTHERN DOMINIONS	305	1	2	3	3	9	16	16	5	8	9	17	10	23	51	15	33	21	19	13	19	12
S. AFRICA +RHOD.	98	1	0	0	3	2	4	6	3	5	4	3	3	7	5	6	25	11	4	2	4	6
AUSTRALIA + N.Z.	207	0	2	3	0	7	12	13	2	3	5	14	7	16	46	9	10	10	15	11	15	6
ASIA + OTHER AFRICA	345	0	1	5	2	8	3	3	2	10	11	11	13	19	55	32	29	31	36	26	24	24
JAPAN	113	0	0	1	1	1	0	1	0	1	6	2	1	2	16	13	20	15	12	17	8	11
OTHER ASIA+AFR.	232	0	0	5	1	7	3	2	2	9	5	9	9	17	39	19	19	16	24	17	16	13
BLACK AFRICA	32	0	0	0	0	0	0	0	2	0	0	2	2	0	1	1	1	6	5	2	4	2
ARAB WORLD	25	0	0	0	0	0	0	0	2	2	0	1	1	0	2	1	1	5	5	1	2	1
INDIA	44	0	0	0	0	2	1	1	0	1	0	1	1	7	12	7	4	6	3	1	0	1
PHILIPPINES	35	0	0	1	0	2	0	0	0	2	2	2	0	2	3	2	8	0	2	2	2	2
OTHER E. ASIA	24	0	0	1	1	2	2	1	2	0	1	6	2	4	2	0	2	2	3	3	4	1
OTHER ASIA	72	0	0	4	0	2	2	0	0	6	0	0	3	5	12	8	3	5	6	5	5	6

CHAPTER 3- THE PROLIFERATION OF FOREIGN SUBSIDIARIES
SECTION 3- THE FLOW OF MANUFACTURING BY CHARACTERISTIC OF PARENT SYSTEM
TABLE L1- MANUFACTURING SUBSIDIARIES IN A SYSTEM
WITH LOW "GEOGRAPHICAL DIVERSITY" IN 1966
CLASSIFIED BY COUNTRY OR REGION AND BY PERIOD MANUFACTURE BEGAN

PERIOD

COUNTRY OR REGION	PRE 1968	PRE 1901	1901 -13	1914 -19	1920 -24	1925 -29	1930 -34	1935 -39	1940 -45	1946 -50	1951 -53	1954 -55	1956 -57	1958 -59	1960 -61	1962	1963	1964	1965	1966	1967	UNK
OUTSIDE U.S.	1685	20	22	23	51	42	45	40	40	80	82	71	109	164	243	117	121	104	107	113	69	39
OUT. U.S. + CANADA	1375	17	13	9	17	33	31	33	29	56	63	51	87	146	211	106	111	84	87	102	61	28
OUT. WEST. HEMIS.	965	17	11	6	13	30	26	24	24	32	45	29	48	88	159	78	80	56	70	73	49	22
OUT. WHITE CWEALTH	1003	10	9	3	14	20	20	21	10	39	41	38	63	107	163	81	93	68	64	73	41	12
OUT. DEVLPED WORLD	471	2	2	3	4	5	5	10	3	26	19	24	42	64	60	34	40	31	23	35	18	6
CANADA	310	3	9	14	6	18	11	12	11	24	19	20	20	18	32	11	10	20	20	11	8	11
LATIN AMERICA	410	0	2	3	4	3	5	9	20	24	18	22	39	58	52	28	31	28	17	29	12	6
C. AMER.+CARIB.	195	0	2	0	0	1	3	6	9	24	18	19	28	19	14	15	21	12	17	17	6	3
CUBA	9	0	0	0	0	0	1	0	3	0	9	0	2	0	0	0	0	0	0	0	0	0
MEXICO	155	0	1	0	0	1	0	2	9	7	2	8	14	25	17	8	11	18	10	14	6	2
OTHER	31	0	0	0	0	0	0	1	0	0	7	0	4	2	1	0	11	3	3	3	0	1
S. AMERICA	215	0	1	3	4	2	2	3	17	15	9	13	20	30	33	14	16	7	5	12	6	3
ARGENTINA	55	0	1	1	0	2	0	3	3	3	2	2	5	5	7	9	5	2	1	4	2	2
BRAZIL	66	0	0	2	1	0	3	7	2	3	4	2	8	16	5	2	4	5	2	3	2	0
PERU	10	0	0	1	1	0	0	1	0	0	0	0	1	2	0	1	2	1	1	0	0	0
COLOMBIA	26	0	0	0	1	0	1	1	4	0	1	1	1	1	5	2	2	4	1	2	0	0
VENEZUELA	42	0	0	0	0	0	1	0	4	3	4	4	4	7	10	1	2	0	0	2	1	0
OTHER	16	2	0	0	2	1	0	0	2	3	2	1	1	1	2	0	1	0	0	1	1	1
EUROPE	707	17	9	4	11	27	21	18	6	20	33	20	33	57	127	53	56	44	49	50	35	17
EFTA	260	7	3	4	2	12	7	9	4	10	15	7	13	16	39	18	15	13	19	20	14	13
U.K.	214	7	2	4	1	12	6	8	3	10	12	6	13	14	30	12	10	9	14	18	13	13
SCANDINAVIA	18	0	0	0	0	0	1	0	0	1	1	1	0	1	3	4	3	2	1	3	1	0
SWITZERLAND	15	0	0	0	0	0	1	0	1	0	2	0	0	0	5	0	1	1	3	1	0	0
OTHER EFTA	13	0	0	0	1	0	0	1	0	0	0	0	0	1	1	2	1	2	1	1	0	0
EUROP. COMMUNITY	379	9	6	3	9	12	9	7	2	9	18	10	18	39	86	31	36	23	16	22	16	4
FRANCE	128	3	2	0	5	4	7	2	0	4	8	3	9	9	31	15	7	11	5	8	5	2
GERMANY	100	5	1	0	2	7	6	0	0	2	4	4	8	7	19	4	11	5	3	8	4	0
ITALY	84	2	1	1	0	6	0	0	1	4	4	1	1	9	21	10	13	5	5	6	2	2
BELGIUM + LUX	30	1	0	0	1	0	0	0	0	1	2	0	1	7	7	1	4	1	1	2	2	0
NETHERLANDS	37	0	2	2	1	2	0	1	1	0	4	2	2	7	8	4	1	1	7	1	1	0
SPAIN	52	0	0	0	0	2	2	0	1	1	2	2	1	2	8	3	4	7	12	2	2	0
GREECE + TURKEY	5	0	0	0	0	0	0	0	0	1	0	1	0	1	2	0	1	1	1	0	0	0
OTHER EUROPE	11	1	0	0	1	0	0	0	0	0	3	0	0	1	0	1	0	0	1	0	2	0
EUROPE EX. U.K.	493	10	7	0	10	15	15	10	3	13	21	14	20	43	97	41	46	35	35	32	22	4
SOUTHERN DOMINIONS	151	0	2	2	2	1	3	3	10	7	7	11	24	18	12	7	6	9	11	7	3	3
S. AFRICA +RHOD.	38	0	0	0	1	1	1	1	5	1	0	1	3	6	3	4	3	4	4	3	2	2
AUSTRALIA + N.Z.	113	0	2	2	1	3	4	2	5	6	7	10	21	12	9	4	3	8	7	4	1	1
ASIA + OTHER AFRICA	107	0	0	1	0	0	2	0	2	5	2	4	7	14	13	17	6	12	12	4	2	2
JAPAN	46	0	0	0	0	0	1	0	0	4	1	1	6	6	7	8	3	3	6	1	2	2
OTHER ASIA+AFR.	61	0	2	0	0	0	1	0	2	0	3	0	6	8	6	9	0	6	6	6	1	0
BLACK AFRICA	3	0	0	0	0	0	0	0	0	0	0	0	0	1	1	0	0	0	0	0	1	0
ARAB WORLD	7	0	0	0	0	0	0	0	0	0	0	2	1	1	1	0	3	0	0	0	1	0
INDIA	18	0	0	0	0	0	1	0	0	1	1	1	1	4	1	3	1	0	3	1	1	0
PHILIPPINES	10	0	0	0	0	0	0	1	0	0	0	0	0	1	1	0	1	1	1	1	0	0
OTHER E. ASIA	10	0	0	0	0	0	1	0	2	0	0	0	2	1	2	2	2	0	1	2	2	0
OTHER ASIA	13	0	0	0	0	1	0	0	0	2	0	1	2	1	1	1	1	1	0	1	1	0

CHAPTER 3- THE PROLIFERATION OF FOREIGN SUBSIDIARIES
SECTION 3- THE FLOW OF MANUFACTURING BY CHARACTERISTIC OF PARENT SYSTEM
TABLE L2- MANUFACTURING SUBSIDIARIES IN A SYSTEM
WITH HIGH "GEOGRAPHICAL DIVERSITY" IN 1966
CLASSIFIED BY COUNTRY OR REGION AND BY PERIOD MANUFACTURE BEGAN

PERIOD

COUNTRY OR REGION	PRE 1968	PRE 1901	1901-13	1914-19	1920-24	1925-29	1930-34	1935-39	1940-45	1946-50	1951-53	1954-55	1956-57	1958-59	1960-61	1962	1963	1964	1965	1966	1967	UNK
OUTSIDE U.S.	3494	28	56	51	69	168	113	167	107	169	152	153	192	252	437	197	221	231	256	211	162	102
OUT. U.S. + CANADA	3003	25	37	32	54	119	92	134	82	140	125	121	165	231	402	182	203	204	232	187	146	90
OUT. WEST. HEMIS.	2088	22	32	22	45	98	74	93	30	77	74	80	84	155	288	137	164	163	161	131	95	63
OUT. WHITE CWEALTH	2305	17	27	26	37	80	53	77	66	102	99	91	139	186	303	146	145	164	197	157	125	68
OUT. DEVLPED WORLD	1214	3	25	15	11	30	21	46	55	78	58	53	101	161	161	70	66	70	95	74	69	40
CANADA	491	3	19	19	15	49	21	33	25	29	27	32	27	21	35	15	18	27	24	24	16	12
LATIN AMERICA	915	3	5	10	9	21	18	41	52	63	51	41	81	76	114	45	39	41	71	56	51	27
C. AMER.+CARIB.	371	1	2	3	2	7	11	19	12	24	17	11	33	33	43	13	12	18	33	29	26	15
CUBA	37	1	0	2	1	2	1	7	2	4	1	2	2	1	0	0	0	2	0	0	0	0
MEXICO	210	0	2	1	1	5	5	9	13	16	13	9	15	21	23	8	5	8	13	16	17	10
OTHER	124	0	0	0	0	0	5	3	4	4	3	0	20	11	20	5	7	8	20	13	9	5
S. AMERICA	544	2	3	7	7	14	7	22	33	39	34	30	48	43	71	32	27	23	38	27	25	12
ARGENTINA	104	0	1	3	2	5	6	11	9	5	2	8	7	9	13	4	3	4	4	3	3	2
BRAZIL	133	0	3	0	0	5	0	0	9	17	15	7	14	14	14	7	3	1	6	10	3	2
PERU	47	1	0	1	1	6	0	1	6	2	1	3	1	1	4	2	2	4	4	2	4	3
COLOMBIA	89	0	1	0	0	0	0	1	5	5	8	4	5	8	15	5	9	4	9	5	2	1
VENEZUELA	102	0	0	0	2	0	0	1	5	6	1	5	12	10	17	8	7	6	10	5	6	2
OTHER	69	1	1	1	2	2	0	3	1	4	3	3	5	1	8	6	3	4	2	2	7	2
EUROPE	1335	21	31	12	39	75	55	63	15	50	44	48	55	103	166	89	93	93	110	91	56	26
EFTA	488	7	18	5	16	37	27	44	5	30	13	14	23	31	51	29	30	30	28	29	11	10
U.K.	337	6	10	2	13	27	24	32	4	25	11	12	15	19	38	22	20	16	16	15	6	8
SCANDINAVIA	95	1	0	3	2	6	2	3	0	5	1	1	6	4	8	9	5	9	6	9	6	1
SWITZERLAND	22	0	7	0	0	1	0	3	1	0	1	0	1	3	3	0	2	1	1	1	3	1
OTHER EFTA	34	0	1	0	1	3	1	6	0	0	0	1	1	5	2	1	2	2	5	3	1	0
EUROP. COMMUNITY	684	12	11	6	15	33	25	15	7	18	25	29	28	63	94	48	49	52	67	41	31	15
FRANCE	192	5	3	1	8	8	7	4	4	4	6	8	6	20	29	12	13	17	13	13	14	5
GERMANY	197	5	5	3	3	14	9	9	2	1	8	11	9	13	25	14	12	13	23	16	5	4
ITALY	137	3	3	0	2	4	4	3	1	3	8	4	9	16	22	11	10	13	15	7	5	1
BELGIUM + LUX	86	0	0	1	2	4	3	4	1	4	2	6	1	8	11	5	12	4	7	5	3	1
NETHERLANDS	72	0	0	1	0	2	2	4	1	4	1	2	1	6	7	6	2	5	3	0	0	4
SPAIN	85	0	0	0	1	1	2	0	0	6	2	2	3	6	10	7	6	9	15	14	9	0
GREECE + TURKEY	37	0	0	0	0	1	0	0	2	0	1	4	1	5	7	4	9	4	4	4	4	0
OTHER EUROPE	41	2	2	0	2	2	2	4	0	0	2	0	2	1	4	1	3	4	2	3	4	0
EUROPE EX. U.K.	998	15	21	10	26	48	31	31	11	25	33	36	40	84	128	66	71	84	94	76	50	18
SOUTHERN DOMINIONS	334	1	0	4	3	12	15	24	11	11	13	17	10	25	57	13	33	28	17	13	14	13
S. AFRICA +RHOD.	121	1	0	1	2	2	5	6	5	6	5	6	4	9	7	7	28	12	4	4	1	6
AUSTRALIA + N.Z.	213	0	0	3	1	10	10	18	6	5	8	11	6	16	50	6	5	16	13	9	13	7
ASIA + OTHER AFRICA	419	0	1	6	3	11	4	6	4	16	17	15	19	27	65	35	38	42	34	27	25	24
JAPAN	120	0	1	1	1	2	3	1	1	1	0	3	7	2	18	10	11	13	10	9	7	11
OTHER ASIA+AFR.	299	0	0	5	2	9	3	5	3	15	10	12	12	25	47	25	27	29	24	18	18	13
BLACK AFRICA	43	0	0	0	0	0	0	0	0	1	1	0	3	0	9	4	2	11	5	2	5	3
ARAB WORLD	32	0	0	0	0	3	0	0	0	4	0	3	1	3	3	9	3	4	6	3	3	1
INDIA	50	0	0	0	1	0	1	1	2	2	2	1	0	1	10	0	5	1	3	3	0	0
PHILIPPINES	48	0	0	0	1	3	0	0	0	0	3	1	4	0	3	7	2	4	2	1	1	2
OTHER E. ASIA	29	0	1	1	1	2	2	1	1	2	3	0	2	0	4	2	2	0	1	1	4	1
OTHER ASIA	97	0	0	0	4	3	2	2	0	7	0	1	2	7	18	11	7	7	5	8	5	6

CHAPTER 3- THE PROLIFERATION OF FOREIGN SUBSIDIARIES
SECTION 4- THE FLOW OF MANUFACTURING BY INDUSTRY OF SUBSIDIARY
TABLE 1- SUBSIDIARIES MANUFACTURING
MEAT PRODUCTS (SIC 201)
CLASSIFIED BY COUNTRY OR REGION AND BY PERIOD MANUFACTURE BEGAN

PERIOD

COUNTRY OR REGION	PRE 1968	PRE 1901	1901-13	1914-19	1920-24	1925-29	1930-34	1935-39	1940-45	1946-50	1951-53	1954-55	1956-57	1958-59	1960-61	1962	1963	1964	1965	1966	1967	UNK
OUTSIDE U.S.	72	3	4	7	0	1	2	0	1	3	8	2	1	5	5	7	2	3	3	8	4	3
OUT. U.S. + CANADA	58	3	3	7	0	1	2	0	1	3	5	5	0	5	5	3	2	2	3	4	4	2
OUT. WEST. HEMIS.	34	3	1	1	0	1	2	0	1	3	5	1	0	1	4	3	2	1	3	2	0	2
OUT. WHITE CWEALTH	32	0	2	1	0	1	2	0	1	0	1	2	0	4	1	3	1	1	1	2	4	2
OUT. DEVLPED WORLD	25	0	2	6	0	1	0	0	0	0	0	1	0	1	1	1	0	1	0	2	2	2
CANADA	14	0	1	0	0	0	0	0	1	0	3	0	1	0	0	4	0	0	0	4	0	1
LATIN AMERICA	24	0	2	6	0	1	2	0	1	0	0	1	0	4	4	1	1	1	0	2	4	2
C. AMER.+CARIB.	8	0	0	0	0	1	2	0	1	0	0	1	0	0	1	0	0	0	0	2	2	1
CUBA	1	0	0	0	1	1	0	0	0	0	0	1	0	1	1	0	1	0	2	2	0	1
MEXICO	6	0	0	0	0	0	0	0	0	0	0	0	0	0	0	0	0	1	0	0	2	0
OTHER	1	0	0	0	0	0	0	0	0	0	0	0	0	0	0	0	0	0	0	0	0	0
S. AMERICA	16	0	2	6	0	0	0	0	0	0	0	0	0	4	0	1	1	0	0	0	2	1
ARGENTINA	6	0	1	2	0	0	0	0	0	0	0	0	0	2	0	0	0	0	0	0	1	0
BRAZIL	7	0	1	4	0	0	0	0	0	0	0	0	0	0	0	0	0	0	0	0	1	0
PERU	0	0	0	0	0	0	0	0	0	0	0	0	0	0	0	0	0	0	0	0	0	0
COLOMBIA	0	0	0	0	0	0	0	0	0	0	0	0	0	0	0	0	0	0	0	0	0	0
VENEZUELA	1	0	0	0	0	0	0	0	0	0	0	0	0	0	0	1	0	0	0	0	0	0
OTHER	2	1	0	0	0	0	0	0	0	0	0	0	0	0	0	0	0	0	0	0	0	1
EUROPE	20	3	0	0	0	0	0	0	1	0	3	1	0	1	2	2	1	2	2	2	0	0
EFTA	10	3	0	0	0	0	0	0	0	0	1	1	0	1	2	0	1	1	0	2	0	0
U.K.	10	3	0	0	0	0	0	0	0	0	1	1	0	1	2	0	1	1	0	2	0	0
SCANDINAVIA	0	0	0	0	0	0	0	0	0	0	0	0	0	0	0	0	0	0	0	0	0	0
SWITZERLAND	0	0	0	0	0	0	0	0	0	0	0	0	0	0	0	0	0	0	0	0	0	0
OTHER EFTA	0	0	0	0	0	0	0	0	0	0	0	0	0	0	0	0	0	0	0	0	0	0
EUROP. COMMUNITY	5	0	0	0	0	0	0	0	1	0	0	1	0	1	0	0	1	0	0	0	0	0
FRANCE	1	0	0	0	0	0	0	0	0	0	0	0	0	0	0	1	0	0	1	0	0	0
GERMANY	2	0	0	0	0	0	0	0	0	0	1	0	0	0	0	0	0	0	0	0	0	0
ITALY	1	0	0	0	0	0	0	0	1	0	1	1	0	1	0	0	0	0	1	0	0	0
BELGIUM + LUX	0	0	0	0	0	0	0	0	0	0	0	0	0	0	0	0	0	0	0	0	0	0
NETHERLANDS	1	0	0	0	0	0	0	0	1	0	0	0	0	0	0	1	1	0	0	0	0	0
SPAIN	2	0	0	0	0	0	0	0	0	1	0	0	0	0	0	1	0	0	0	0	0	0
GREECE + TURKEY	0	0	0	0	0	0	0	0	1	0	1	1	0	1	0	0	1	1	1	0	0	0
OTHER EUROPE	3	0	0	0	0	0	0	0	0	0	1	0	0	0	2	2	0	1	0	0	0	0
EUROPE EX. U.K.	10	0	0	0	0	0	0	0	1	0	2	1	0	0	2	2	1	1	2	0	0	0
SOUTHERN DOMINIONS	13	0	1	1	0	0	2	0	0	3	2	0	0	2	2	1	1	0	1	0	0	0
S. AFRICA +RHOD.	0	0	0	0	0	0	0	0	0	0	0	0	0	0	0	0	0	0	0	0	0	0
AUSTRALIA + N.Z.	13	0	1	1	0	0	2	0	0	3	2	0	0	2	2	1	1	0	1	0	0	0
ASIA + OTHER AFRICA	1	0	0	0	0	0	0	0	0	0	0	0	0	0	0	0	0	0	0	0	0	0
JAPAN	1	0	0	0	0	0	0	0	0	0	0	0	0	0	0	0	0	0	0	0	0	0
OTHER ASIA+AFR.	0	0	0	0	0	0	0	0	0	0	0	0	0	0	0	0	0	0	0	0	0	0
BLACK AFRICA	0	0	0	0	0	0	0	0	0	0	0	0	0	0	0	0	0	0	0	0	0	0
ARAB WORLD	0	0	0	0	0	0	0	0	0	0	0	0	0	0	0	0	0	0	0	0	0	0
INDIA	0	0	0	0	0	0	0	0	0	0	0	0	0	0	0	0	0	0	0	0	0	0
PHILIPPINES	1	0	0	0	0	0	0	0	0	0	0	0	0	0	0	0	0	0	0	0	0	0
OTHER E. ASIA	1	0	1	0	0	1	0	0	0	0	0	0	0	0	0	0	0	0	0	0	0	0
OTHER ASIA	0	0	0	0	0	0	0	0	0	0	0	0	0	0	0	0	0	0	0	0	0	0

CHAPTER 3- THE PROLIFERATION OF FOREIGN SUBSIDIARIES
SECTION 4- THE FLOW OF MANUFACTURING BY INDUSTRY OF SUBSIDIARY
TABLE 2- SUBSIDIARIES MANUFACTURING
DAIRY PRODUCTS (SIC 202)
CLASSIFIED BY COUNTRY OR REGION AND BY PERIOD MANUFACTURE BEGAN

PERIOD

COUNTRY OR REGION	PRE 1968	PRE 1901	1901 -13	1914 -19	1920 -24	1925 -29	1930 -34	1935 -39	1940 -45	1946 -50	1951 -53	1954 -55	1956 -57	1958 -59	1960 -61	1962	1963	1964	1965	1966	1967	UNK
OUTSIDE U.S.	134	0	4	2	3	17	11	9	10	3	6	3	7	8	22	6	2	5	4	3	7	2
OUT. U.S. + CANADA	107	0	2	1	3	7	10	9	9	3	5	3	7	7	17	5	2	5	3	2	6	1
OUT. WEST. HEMIS.	65	0	2	1	3	7	7	4	4	0	2	1	5	5	17	5	2	3	2	1	6	1
OUT. WHITE CWEALTH	88	0	2	0	2	5	8	8	6	3	5	3	7	6	14	5	4	2	2	2	6	0
OUT. DEVLPED WORLD	54	0	0	0	0	0	3	5	5	3	3	2	4	4	13	3	2	4	1	1	1	0
CANADA	27	0	2	1	0	10	1	0	1	0	1	0	0	1	1	3	0	1	1	1	1	1
LATIN AMERICA	42	0	0	0	0	0	3	5	5	3	3	2	2	2	5	3	0	1	1	1	1	0
C. AMER.+CARIB.	24	0	0	0	0	0	3	4	0	2	1	1	0	2	10	0	0	1	1	1	0	0
CUBA	4	0	0	0	0	0	2	2	0	2	0	0	0	0	0	0	0	0	0	0	0	0
MEXICO	6	0	0	0	0	0	0	0	0	0	1	1	0	0	0	0	0	0	1	0	0	0
OTHER	14	0	0	0	0	0	1	2	0	0	0	0	2	2	6	1	0	0	0	1	0	0
S. AMERICA	18	0	0	0	0	0	0	0	5	1	2	0	0	0	4	1	0	0	1	1	0	0
ARGENTINA	2	0	0	0	0	0	0	0	0	0	0	0	1	0	1	0	0	0	0	0	0	0
BRAZIL	1	0	0	0	0	0	0	0	0	0	0	0	0	0	0	0	0	0	0	0	1	0
PERU	3	0	0	0	0	0	0	0	3	0	0	0	0	0	0	0	0	0	0	0	0	0
COLOMBIA	5	0	0	0	0	0	0	0	1	1	2	0	1	0	1	0	0	1	0	0	0	0
VENEZUELA	7	0	0	0	0	0	0	0	1	0	0	0	0	2	2	1	0	0	0	1	1	0
OTHER	0	0	0	0	0	0	0	0	0	0	0	0	0	0	0	0	0	0	0	0	0	0
EUROPE	42	0	1	0	3	7	6	4	1	0	2	1	3	2	2	1	0	2	1	1	5	0
EFTA	11	0	1	0	1	2	1	1	0	0	0	0	3	0	0	0	0	1	1	1	0	0
U.K.	7	0	1	0	1	2	1	1	0	0	0	0	0	0	0	0	0	0	0	0	0	0
SCANDINAVIA	4	0	0	0	0	0	0	0	0	0	0	0	3	0	0	0	0	1	0	0	0	0
SWITZERLAND	0	0	0	0	0	0	0	0	0	0	0	0	0	0	0	0	0	0	0	0	0	0
OTHER EFTA	0	0	0	0	0	0	0	0	0	0	0	0	0	0	0	0	0	0	0	0	0	0
EUROP. COMMUNITY	27	0	0	0	2	5	5	3	1	0	2	1	0	2	1	0	0	0	0	1	3	0
FRANCE	4	0	0	0	2	0	1	0	0	0	0	0	0	0	0	0	0	0	0	0	1	0
GERMANY	10	0	0	0	0	3	1	2	0	0	1	0	0	0	0	0	0	2	0	0	1	0
ITALY	1	0	0	0	0	0	0	0	1	0	0	0	0	0	0	0	0	0	0	0	0	0
BELGIUM + LUX	6	0	0	0	0	2	0	0	0	1	0	1	0	0	1	0	0	0	1	0	0	0
NETHERLANDS	6	0	0	0	0	0	1	1	0	0	1	0	0	0	0	1	0	1	0	0	1	0
SPAIN	2	0	0	0	0	0	0	0	0	0	0	0	0	0	0	0	0	0	0	0	2	0
GREECE + TURKEY	0	0	0	0	0	0	0	0	0	0	0	0	0	0	0	0	0	0	0	0	0	0
OTHER EUROPE	2	0	0	0	0	0	0	0	0	1	1	1	0	0	1	0	1	1	1	0	0	0
EUROPE Ex. U.K.	35	0	0	0	2	5	5	3	1	0	2	1	3	2	2	1	0	1	1	1	5	0
SOUTHERN DOMINIONS	10	0	1	0	0	0	1	0	3	0	0	0	0	1	2	0	0	0	0	0	0	1
S. AFRICA +RHOD.	3	0	0	0	0	0	0	0	1	0	0	0	0	1	0	0	0	0	0	0	0	1
AUSTRALIA + N.Z.	7	0	1	0	0	0	1	0	2	0	0	0	0	0	3	0	0	0	0	0	0	0
ASIA + OTHER AFRICA	13	0	0	0	0	0	0	0	0	0	0	0	0	0	3	2	0	2	0	0	0	0
JAPAN	12	0	0	0	0	0	0	0	0	0	0	0	2	2	3	0	0	2	0	0	0	0
OTHER ASIA+AFR.	1	0	0	0	0	0	0	0	0	0	0	0	0	0	0	2	1	0	0	1	0	0
BLACK AFRICA	1	0	0	0	0	0	0	0	0	0	0	0	0	0	0	1	0	1	0	0	0	0
ARAB WORLD	0	0	0	0	0	0	0	0	0	0	0	0	0	0	0	0	0	0	0	0	0	0
INDIA	0	0	0	0	0	0	0	0	0	0	0	0	0	0	0	0	1	0	0	0	0	0
PHILIPPINES	3	0	0	0	0	0	0	0	0	0	0	0	0	0	0	1	0	0	0	0	0	0
OTHER E. ASIA	1	0	0	0	0	0	0	0	0	0	0	1	1	0	0	0	0	0	0	0	0	0
OTHER ASIA	6	0	0	0	0	0	0	0	0	0	0	1	1	0	3	0	0	1	1	0	1	0

CHAPTER 3— THE PROLIFERATION OF FOREIGN SUBSIDIARIES
SECTION 4— THE FLOW OF MANUFACTURING BY INDUSTRY OF SUBSIDIARY
TABLE 3— SUBSIDIARIES MANUFACTURING
CANNED FOODS (SIC 203)
CLASSIFIED BY COUNTRY OR REGION AND BY PERIOD MANUFACTURE BEGAN

PERIOD

COUNTRY OR REGION	PRE 1968	PRE 1901	1901 -13	1914 -19	1920 -24	1925 -29	1930 -34	1935 -39	1940 -45	1946 -50	1951 -53	1954 -55	1956 -57	1958 -59	1960 -61	1962	1963	1964	1965	1966	1967	UNK
OUTSIDE U.S.	91	1	1	0	1	5	2	4	2	3	0	2	8	6	12	5	11	12	2	8	5	1
OUT. U.S. + CANADA	76	1	1	0	1	3	2	3	2	2	0	1	5	5	12	3	11	11	2	6	5	1
OUT. WEST. HEMIS.	46	.	0	0	1	3	2	3	1	2	0	1	5	4	10	2	5	2	0	2	4	0
OUT. WHITE CWEALTH	52	0	0	0	0	2	1	2	2	2	0	1	5	1	6	2	10	9	2	5	4	0
OUT. DEVLPED WORLD	34	0	0	0	0	2	1	0	1	0	0	1	3	1	2	1	6	9	2	4	1	0
CANADA	15	0	1	0	0	2	0	1	0	1	0	1	3	1	0	2	0	1	0	2	0	0
LATIN AMERICA	30	0	0	0	0	0	0	1	1	0	0	0	0	1	2	1	6	9	2	4	2	1
C. AMER.+CARIB.	19	0	0	0	0	0	0	1	1	0	0	0	0	1	2	1	6	8	1	2	4	2
CUBA	3	0	0	0	0	0	0	0	0	0	0	0	0	0	1	1	0	0	0	0	0	1
MEXICO	11	0	0	0	0	0	0	0	1	0	0	0	0	1	1	0	2	7	1	1	2	1
OTHER	5	0	0	0	0	0	0	1	0	0	0	0	0	0	0	0	0	0	1	2	1	0
S. AMERICA	11	0	0	0	0	0	0	0	0	0	0	0	0	0	1	0	0	1	0	2	0	0
ARGENTINA	0	0	0	0	0	0	0	0	0	0	0	0	0	1	0	0	0	0	0	0	0	0
BRAZIL	1	0	0	0	0	0	0	0	0	0	0	0	0	0	0	0	0	1	0	0	1	0
PERU	5	0	0	0	0	0	0	0	0	0	0	0	0	0	0	0	4	0	0	0	0	0
COLOMBIA	1	0	0	0	0	0	0	0	0	0	0	0	0	0	0	1	0	0	0	0	0	0
VENEZUELA	2	0	0	0	0	0	0	0	0	1	0	0	1	0	0	0	0	0	0	1	0	0
OTHER	2	0	0	0	0	0	0	0	0	0	0	0	0	0	0	0	0	1	1	0	0	0
EUROPE	30	1	1	0	0	1	0	2	1	2	0	0	2	2	5	1	5	1	1	0	4	1
EFTA	11	1	1	0	0	1	0	1	1	1	0	0	1	1	1	0	1	0	0	0	1	1
U.K.	10	1	0	0	0	1	0	1	1	1	0	0	1	1	1	0	1	0	0	0	1	0
SCANDINAVIA	0	0	0	0	0	0	0	0	0	0	0	0	0	0	0	0	0	0	0	0	0	0
SWITZERLAND	1	0	0	0	0	0	0	0	0	0	0	0	0	0	0	0	0	0	0	0	0	0
OTHER EFTA	0	0	0	0	0	0	0	0	0	0	0	0	0	0	0	0	0	0	0	0	0	0
EUROP. COMMUNITY	14	0	0	0	0	0	0	0	0	1	0	0	1	0	4	0	4	0	0	0	3	0
FRANCE	3	0	0	0	0	0	0	0	0	0	0	0	0	0	0	0	1	0	0	1	1	0
GERMANY	2	0	0	0	0	0	0	0	0	0	0	0	1	0	1	0	1	0	0	0	0	0
ITALY	4	0	0	0	0	0	0	0	0	0	0	0	0	0	2	0	1	0	0	1	0	0
BELGIUM + LUX	1	0	0	0	0	0	0	0	0	0	0	0	0	1	0	0	0	0	0	0	0	0
NETHERLANDS	3	0	0	0	0	0	0	0	0	1	0	0	0	0	0	1	0	0	0	0	2	0
SPAIN	3	0	0	0	0	1	1	0	0	0	0	0	0	0	0	0	0	1	0	0	0	0
GREECE + TURKEY	0	0	0	0	0	0	0	0	0	0	0	0	0	0	0	0	0	0	0	0	0	0
OTHER EUROPE	2	0	0	0	0	1	1	0	0	1	0	0	0	0	0	0	0	0	0	1	0	0
EUROPE EX. U.K.	20	0	0	0	0	1	1	1	1	1	0	0	2	2	4	1	4	1	1	1	3	0
SOUTHERN DOMINIONS	12	0	0	0	1	0	0	1	0	2	0	0	0	2	5	1	0	1	0	1	0	0
S. AFRICA +RHOD.	3	0	0	0	0	0	0	0	0	1	0	0	0	0	2	0	0	0	0	0	0	0
AUSTRALIA + N.Z.	9	0	0	0	1	0	0	1	0	1	0	0	0	2	3	1	0	1	0	1	0	0
ASIA + OTHER AFRICA	4	0	0	0	0	2	1	0	0	0	0	0	0	0	0	0	0	0	0	1	0	0
JAPAN	0	0	0	0	0	0	0	0	0	0	0	0	0	0	0	0	0	0	0	0	0	0
OTHER ASIA+AFR.	4	0	0	0	0	2	1	0	0	0	0	0	0	0	0	0	0	0	0	1	0	0
BLACK AFRICA	0	0	0	0	0	0	0	0	0	0	0	0	0	0	0	0	0	0	0	0	0	0
ARAB WORLD	1	0	0	0	0	0	0	0	0	0	0	0	0	0	0	0	0	0	0	1	0	0
INDIA	1	0	0	0	0	0	0	0	0	0	0	0	0	0	0	0	0	0	0	0	0	0
PHILIPPINES	2	0	0	0	0	2	0	0	0	0	0	0	0	0	0	0	0	0	0	0	0	0
OTHER E. ASIA	0	0	0	0	0	0	0	0	0	0	0	0	0	0	0	0	0	0	0	0	0	0
OTHER ASIA	0	0	0	0	0	0	0	0	0	0	0	0	0	0	0	0	0	0	0	0	0	0

CHAPTER 3- THE PROLIFERATION OF FOREIGN SUBSIDIARIES
SECTION 4- THE FLOW OF MANUFACTURING BY INDUSTRY OF SUBSIDIARY
TABLE 4- SUBSIDIARIES MANUFACTURING
GRAIN MILL PRODUCTS (SIC 2041)
CLASSIFIED BY COUNTRY OR REGION AND BY PERIOD MANUFACTURE BEGAN

PERIOD

COUNTRY OR REGION	PRE 1908	PRE 1901	1901 -13	1914 -19	1920 -24	1925 -29	1930 -34	1935 -39	1940 -45	1946 -50	1951 -53	1954 -55	1956 -57	1958 -59	1960 -61	1962 -63	1964	1965	1966	1967	UNK
OUTSIDE U.S.	152	0	1	1	4	10	4	9	3	3	6	9	7	7	26	10	11	6	8	18	9	0
OUT. U.S. + CANADA	129	0	0	1	3	5	4	7	3	3	1	5	7	7	25	9	11	6	8	18	8	0
OUT. WEST. HEMIS.	66	0	0	1	3	3	2	5	1	3	0	2	2	2	15	2	9	3	6	6	4	0
OUT. WHITE CWEALTH	107	0	1	2	2	4	4	3	1	5	7	6	6	18	7	9	7	7	18	7	0
OUT. DEVLPED WORLD	70	0	0	0	0	2	3	2	1	0	3	3	5	6	10	7	3	4	14	5	0
CANADA	23	0	1	0	1	5	0	2	2	0	5	4	0	0	1	0	0	0	0	1	0
LATIN AMERICA	63	0	0	0	2	2	2	2	0	0	1	3	5	5	10	3	3	2	12	4	0
C. AMER.+CARIB.	30	0	0	0	1	2	1	1	0	0	1	0	3	3	3	1	1	0	8	3	0
CUBA	1	0	0	0	0	0	0	0	0	0	0	0	0	0	0	0	0	2	0	0	0
MEXICO	14	0	0	0	0	0	1	0	0	0	1	1	1	1	3	1	2	2	6	2	0
OTHER	15	0	0	0	1	2	0	1	0	0	0	2	2	2	7	2	0	0	4	1	0
S. AMERICA	33	0	0	0	1	1	1	0	0	0	0	0	0	0	0	0	0	1	0	0	0
ARGENTINA	4	0	0	0	0	1	1	0	0	0	0	0	1	1	1	1	0	0	0	0	0
BRAZIL	5	0	0	0	1	1	0	0	0	0	0	0	0	0	0	0	0	0	0	0	0
PERU	3	0	0	0	0	0	0	0	0	0	0	1	1	1	1	0	1	0	0	0	0
COLUMBIA	7	0	0	0	0	1	0	0	0	0	0	0	0	0	3	0	0	0	0	3	0
VENEZUELA	6	0	0	0	1	0	0	0	0	0	0	1	0	1	1	0	1	1	2	0	0
OTHER	8	0	0	0	0	0	1	1	1	0	0	1	1	0	2	1	1	1	1	0	0
EUROPE	48	0	0	1	2	3	1	5	0	2	0	2	1	1	9	7	2	3	4	3	0
EFTA	18	0	1	1	0	1	1	3	0	1	0	0	1	1	2	2	1	1	1	1	0
U.K.	11	0	0	0	0	1	0	3	0	1	0	0	0	1	1	2	0	0	0	1	0
SCANDINAVIA	4	0	1	0	0	0	1	0	0	0	0	0	0	0	1	0	0	0	0	0	0
SWITZERLAND	1	0	0	0	0	0	0	0	0	0	0	0	0	0	0	0	0	0	1	0	0
OTHER EFTA	2	0	0	0	1	0	0	0	0	0	0	0	1	0	0	0	0	0	0	0	0
EUROP. COMMUNITY	25	0	0	2	2	2	0	1	0	0	0	0	0	0	7	3	1	2	2	2	0
FRANCE	4	0	0	1	1	0	0	0	0	0	0	1	0	0	1	0	0	1	1	0	0
GERMANY	8	0	0	1	1	0	0	0	0	0	0	0	0	0	3	1	0	1	0	0	0
ITALY	7	0	0	0	0	1	0	0	0	0	0	0	0	0	1	2	1	0	1	0	0
BELGIUM + LUX	2	0	0	0	0	0	0	1	0	0	0	0	0	0	1	0	0	0	0	1	0
NETHERLANDS	4	0	0	0	0	1	0	0	0	0	0	0	0	0	1	0	0	0	0	1	0
SPAIN	4	0	0	0	0	1	0	0	0	0	0	1	0	0	0	0	0	0	1	0	0
GREECE + TURKEY	0	0	0	0	0	0	0	0	0	0	0	0	0	0	0	0	0	0	0	0	0
OTHER EUROPE	37	0	1	2	2	2	1	2	0	1	0	2	2	0	8	5	2	3	4	2	0
SOUTHERN DOMINIONS	10	0	0	1	1	0	0	0	0	1	1	0	0	0	6	0	0	1	0	0	0
S. AFRICA +RHOD.	2	0	0	1	1	0	0	0	0	0	0	0	0	0	0	0	0	0	0	0	0
AUSTRALIA + N.Z.	8	0	0	0	0	0	0	0	0	1	1	0	0	0	6	0	0	1	2	1	0
ASIA + OTHER AFRICA	8	0	0	0	0	0	0	0	0	0	0	0	0	0	0	2	0	0	2	0	0
JAPAN	1	0	0	0	1	0	1	0	0	1	0	1	0	0	0	1	1	0	0	1	0
OTHER ASIA+AFR.	7	0	0	0	0	0	0	0	0	0	0	0	0	0	0	0	1	0	2	0	0
BLACK AFRICA	1	0	0	0	0	0	0	0	0	0	0	0	0	0	0	0	0	0	0	1	0
ARAB WORLD	1	0	0	0	0	0	0	0	0	0	0	0	0	1	0	0	0	0	1	0	0
INDIA	1	0	0	0	0	0	0	0	0	0	0	0	0	0	0	1	0	0	0	1	0
PHILIPPINES	3	0	0	0	0	0	1	0	0	0	0	0	0	0	0	0	0	0	1	0	0
OTHER E. ASIA	1	0	0	0	0	0	0	0	0	0	0	0	0	0	0	0	0	0	0	1	0
OTHER ASIA	0	0	0	0	0	0	0	0	0	0	0	0	0	0	0	0	0	0	0	0	0

CHAPTER 3- THE PROLIFERATION OF FOREIGN SUBSIDIARIES
SECTION 4- THE FLOW OF MANUFACTURING BY INDUSTRY OF SUBSIDIARY
TABLE 5- SUBSIDIARIES MANUFACTURING
BAKERY PRODUCTS (SIC 205)
CLASSIFIED BY COUNTRY OR REGION AND BY PERIOD MANUFACTURE BEGAN

COUNTRY OR REGION	PRE 1968	PRE 1901	1901 -13	1914 -19	1920 -24	1925 -29	1930 -34	1935 -39	1940 -45	1946 -50	1951 -53	1954 -55	1956 -57	1958 -59	1960 -61	1962	1963	1964	1965	1966	1967	UNK
OUTSIDE U.S.	54	0	1	0	1	3	0	6	1	5	3	2	0	0	7	3	3	3	8	5	3	0
OUT. U.S. + CANADA	44	0	1	0	1	1	0	4	1	5	3	1	0	0	7	2	3	3	8	5	3	0
OUT. WEST. HEMIS.	32	0	0	0	1	1	0	3	1	2	1	0	0	0	7	2	3	3	5	3	1	0
OUT. WHITE CWEALTH	36	0	0	0	1	0	0	1	1	4	1	0	0	0	7	0	0	3	3	5	3	0
OUT. DEVLPED WORLD	12	0	0	0	0	0	0	0	0	3	1	0	0	0	0	0	0	0	2	2	2	0
CANADA	10	0	1	0	0	2	0	2	0	0	2	0	0	0	0	0	0	0	0	0	0	0
LATIN AMERICA	12	0	0	0	0	2	0	2	0	3	1	1	0	0	1	0	2	0	3	2	2	0
C. AMER.+CARIB.	7	0	0	0	0	2	0	1	0	3	1	1	0	0	1	0	1	0	2	1	0	0
CUBA	1	0	0	0	0	0	0	1	0	0	1	0	0	0	0	0	0	0	0	0	0	0
MEXICO	4	0	0	0	0	2	0	1	0	0	0	1	0	0	0	0	0	0	1	1	1	0
OTHER	2	0	0	0	0	0	0	0	0	3	0	0	0	0	1	0	1	0	0	0	0	0
S. AMERICA	5	0	0	0	0	0	0	1	0	0	0	0	0	0	0	0	1	0	1	1	1	0
ARGENTINA	0	0	0	0	0	0	0	0	0	0	0	0	0	0	0	0	0	0	0	0	0	0
BRAZIL	1	0	0	0	0	0	0	0	0	0	0	0	0	0	0	0	0	0	1	0	0	0
PERU	2	0	0	0	0	0	0	1	0	1	0	0	0	0	0	0	0	0	0	0	0	0
COLOMBIA	2	0	0	0	0	0	0	1	0	1	0	0	0	0	0	0	0	0	0	0	0	0
VENEZUELA	2	0	0	0	0	0	0	1	0	1	0	0	0	0	0	0	0	0	0	1	0	0
OTHER	0	0	0	0	0	0	0	0	0	0	0	0	0	0	0	0	0	0	0	0	0	0
EUROPE	29	0	0	0	0	0	0	3	1	2	0	0	0	0	7	3	3	3	5	3	1	0
EFTA	9	0	0	0	0	0	0	3	0	1	0	0	0	0	1	1	0	0	1	0	1	0
U.K.	4	0	0	0	0	0	0	3	0	1	0	0	0	0	0	0	0	0	0	0	0	0
SCANDINAVIA	1	0	0	0	0	0	0	0	0	0	0	0	0	0	1	0	0	0	0	0	0	0
SWITZERLAND	0	0	0	0	0	0	0	0	0	0	0	0	0	0	0	0	0	0	0	0	0	0
OTHER EFTA	0	0	0	0	0	0	0	0	0	0	0	0	0	0	0	0	0	0	1	0	1	0
EUROP. COMMUNITY	16	0	0	0	0	0	0	0	1	0	0	0	0	0	6	2	2	3	3	1	0	0
FRANCE	7	0	0	0	0	0	0	0	0	0	0	0	0	0	4	2	1	1	1	1	0	0
GERMANY	2	0	0	0	0	0	0	0	0	0	0	0	0	0	0	0	0	2	1	0	0	0
ITALY	4	0	0	0	0	0	0	1	0	0	0	0	0	0	0	0	2	0	0	0	0	0
BELGIUM + LUX	3	0	0	0	0	0	0	1	0	1	0	0	0	0	2	1	0	0	3	0	0	0
NETHERLANDS	0	0	0	0	0	0	0	0	0	0	0	0	0	0	0	0	0	0	0	0	0	0
SPAIN	3	0	0	0	0	0	0	0	0	0	0	0	0	0	2	0	0	0	0	2	0	0
GREECE + TURKEY	0	0	0	0	0	0	0	0	0	1	0	0	0	0	0	0	0	1	1	0	0	0
OTHER EUROPE	1	0	0	0	0	0	0	1	0	1	0	0	0	0	0	0	0	0	0	0	1	0
EUROPE EX. U.K.	25	0	0	0	0	0	0	1	1	2	0	0	0	0	7	3	3	3	5	3	1	0
SOUTHERN DOMINIONS	3	0	0	0	1	1	0	0	0	0	0	0	0	0	0	0	0	0	0	0	0	0
S. AFRICA +RHOD.	1	0	0	0	1	1	0	0	0	0	0	0	0	0	0	0	0	0	0	0	0	0
AUSTRALIA + N.Z.	2	0	0	0	1	0	0	0	0	0	0	0	0	0	0	0	0	0	0	0	0	0
ASIA + OTHER AFRICA	0	0	0	0	0	0	0	0	0	0	0	0	0	0	0	0	0	0	0	0	0	0
JAPAN	0	0	0	0	0	0	0	0	0	0	0	0	0	0	0	0	0	0	0	0	0	0
OTHER ASIA+AFR.	0	0	0	0	0	0	0	0	0	0	0	0	0	0	0	0	0	0	0	0	0	0
BLACK AFRICA	0	0	0	0	0	0	0	0	0	0	0	0	0	0	0	0	0	0	0	0	0	0
ARAB WORLD	0	0	0	0	0	0	0	0	0	0	0	0	0	0	0	0	0	0	0	0	0	0
INDIA	0	0	0	0	0	0	0	0	0	0	0	0	0	0	0	0	0	0	0	0	0	0
PHILIPPINES	0	0	0	0	0	0	0	0	0	0	0	0	0	0	0	0	0	0	0	0	0	0
OTHER E. ASIA	0	0	0	0	0	0	0	0	0	0	0	0	0	0	0	0	0	0	0	0	0	0
OTHER ASIA	0	0	0	0	0	0	0	0	0	0	0	0	0	0	0	0	0	0	0	0	0	0

CHAPTER 3— THE PROLIFERATION OF FOREIGN SUBSIDIARIES
SECTION 4— THE FLOW OF MANUFACTURING BY INDUSTRY OF SUBSIDIARY
TABLE 6— SUBSIDIARIES MANUFACTURING
CONFECTIONERY AND RELATED PRODUCTS (SIC 207)
CLASSIFIED BY COUNTRY OR REGION AND BY PERIOD MANUFACTURE BEGAN

COUNTRY OR REGION	PRE 1968	PRE 1901	1901 -13	1914 -19	1920 -24	1925 -29	1930 -34	1935 -39	1940 -45	1946 -50	1951 -53	1954 -55	1956 -57	1958 -59	1960 -61	1962	1963	1964	1965	1966	1967	UNK
OUTSIDE U.S.	97	0	0	2	0	4	1	3	1	5	0	3	3	1	11	13	8	10	15	2	14	0
OUT. U.S. + CANADA	82	0	1	1	0	2	0	1	1	5	0	2	2	1	8	13	8	8	14	2	13	0
OUT. WEST. HEMIS.	58	0	0	1	0	2	0	0	1	4	0	2	0	1	6	8	7	7	9	2	10	0
OUT. WHITE CWEALTH	62	0	0	0	0	0	0	0	0	4	0	1	2	1	5	10	6	8	13	1	11	0
OUT. DEVLPED WORLD	30	0	0	0	0	0	0	0	0	4	0	2	2	0	2	6	2	2	7	1	3	0
CANADA	15	0	1	1	0	2	1	2	0	0	0	1	1	1	3	0	0	2	1	0	1	0
LATIN AMERICA	24	0	0	0	0	2	0	0	0	4	0	1	2	1	2	5	1	1	5	0	3	0
C. AMER.+CARIB.	13	0	0	0	0	1	0	0	0	2	0	1	0	0	1	4	0	1	4	0	3	0
CUBA	0	0	0	0	0	0	0	0	0	0	0	0	0	0	0	0	0	0	0	0	0	0
MEXICO	9	0	0	0	0	0	0	0	0	2	0	1	0	0	1	2	1	1	2	0	1	0
OTHER	4	0	0	0	0	1	0	0	0	0	0	0	0	0	0	2	0	0	2	0	2	0
S. AMERICA	11	0	0	0	0	1	0	0	0	2	0	0	2	0	2	1	0	0	1	0	0	0
ARGENTINA	0	0	0	0	0	0	0	0	0	0	0	0	0	0	0	0	0	0	0	0	0	0
BRAZIL	2	0	0	0	0	0	0	0	0	0	0	1	0	0	1	0	0	0	0	0	0	0
PERU	2	0	0	0	0	0	0	0	0	0	0	0	1	0	1	0	0	0	0	0	0	0
COLOMBIA	3	0	0	0	0	0	0	0	0	1	0	0	1	0	0	0	1	0	0	0	0	0
VENEZUELA	2	0	0	0	0	0	0	0	0	1	0	0	0	0	0	1	0	0	0	0	0	0
OTHER	2	0	0	0	0	1	0	0	0	0	0	0	0	0	0	0	0	0	1	0	0	0
EUROPE	38	0	0	0	0	1	0	0	1	1	0	0	0	1	3	5	6	6	5	1	8	0
EFTA	8	0	0	1	1	1	0	0	1	1	0	0	0	1	1	1	0	0	0	1	1	0
U.K.	6	0	0	0	1	1	0	0	1	1	0	0	0	0	0	1	0	0	0	1	0	0
SCANDINAVIA	0	0	0	0	0	0	0	0	0	0	0	0	0	0	0	0	0	0	0	0	0	0
SWITZERLAND	0	0	0	0	0	0	0	0	0	0	0	0	0	0	0	0	0	0	0	0	0	0
OTHER EFTA	2	0	0	0	0	0	0	0	0	0	0	0	0	1	0	0	0	0	0	0	1	0
EUROP. COMMUNITY	25	0	0	0	0	0	0	0	0	0	0	0	0	0	2	4	4	5	4	0	6	0
FRANCE	5	0	0	0	0	0	0	0	0	0	0	0	0	0	2	2	1	1	1	0	1	0
GERMANY	6	0	0	0	0	0	0	0	0	0	0	0	0	0	0	2	1	1	2	0	1	0
ITALY	4	0	0	0	0	0	0	0	0	0	0	0	0	0	0	0	1	1	0	0	1	0
BELGIUM + LUX	6	0	0	0	0	0	0	0	0	0	0	0	0	0	0	2	0	0	0	0	4	0
NETHERLANDS	4	0	0	0	0	0	0	0	0	0	0	0	0	0	2	0	2	1	0	0	0	0
SPAIN	1	0	0	0	0	0	0	0	0	0	0	0	0	0	0	0	0	0	0	0	0	0
GREECE + TURKEY	1	0	0	0	0	0	0	0	0	0	0	0	0	0	0	0	0	0	1	0	1	0
OTHER EUROPE	3	0	0	0	0	0	0	0	0	0	0	0	0	0	0	0	2	0	0	0	1	0
EUROPE EX. U.K.	32	0	0	0	0	0	0	0	0	0	0	0	0	1	2	4	6	6	5	0	8	0
SOUTHERN DOMINIONS	11	0	0	0	0	0	0	0	0	0	0	2	0	0	2	2	0	0	1	0	1	0
S. AFRICA +RHOD.	3	0	0	0	0	0	0	1	0	0	0	1	0	0	0	1	0	0	0	0	0	0
AUSTRALIA + N.Z.	8	0	0	0	0	0	0	1	0	0	0	1	0	0	2	1	0	1	3	0	1	0
ASIA + OTHER AFRICA	9	0	0	0	0	1	0	0	0	0	0	0	0	0	1	3	1	1	1	1	1	0
JAPAN	3	0	0	0	0	0	0	0	0	0	0	0	0	0	0	0	0	0	2	0	0	0
OTHER ASIA+AFR.	6	0	0	0	0	1	0	0	0	0	0	0	0	0	1	1	0	1	0	0	0	0
BLACK AFRICA	2	0	0	0	0	0	0	0	0	0	0	0	0	0	0	1	0	0	0	0	0	0
ARAB WORLD	0	0	0	0	0	0	0	0	0	0	0	0	0	0	0	0	0	0	0	0	0	0
INDIA	1	0	0	0	0	0	0	0	0	0	0	0	0	0	0	0	0	0	1	0	0	0
PHILIPPINES	0	0	0	0	0	0	0	0	0	0	0	0	0	0	0	0	0	0	0	0	0	0
OTHER E. ASIA	1	0	0	0	0	0	0	0	0	0	0	0	0	0	0	1	0	0	0	0	0	0
OTHER ASIA	3	0	0	0	0	0	0	0	0	0	0	0	1	0	0	1	0	0	1	0	0	0

CHAPTER 3- THE PROLIFERATION OF FOREIGN SUBSIDIARIES
SECTION 4- THE FLOW OF MANUFACTURING BY INDUSTRY OF SUBSIDIARY
TABLE 7- SUBSIDIARIES MANUFACTURING
BEVERAGES (SIC 208)
CLASSIFIED BY COUNTRY OR REGION AND BY PERIOD MANUFACTURE BEGAN

COUNTRY OR REGION	PRE 1968	PRE 1901	1901 -13	1914 -19	1920 -24	1925 -29	1930 -34	1935 -39	1940 -45	1946 -50	1951 -53	1954 -55	1956 -57	1958 -59	1960 -61	1962	1963	1964	1965	1966	1967	UNK
OUTSIDE U.S.	89	1	0	0	3	3	4	15	4	4	4	3	7	5	5	5	4	5	6	8	3	2
OUT. U.S. + CANADA	77	1	0	0	1	3	3	14	3	2	4	1	4	5	5	3	4	4	8	2	1	2
OUT. WEST. HEMIS.	50	0	0	0	1	1	3	12	3	1	2	2	6	5	3	1	3	3	7	2	1	2
OUT. WHITE CWEALTH	53	1	0	0	0	2	1	2	3	2	1	0	5	3	2	3	3	4	1	1	1	0
OUT. DEVLPED WORLD	35	1	0	0	0	1	1	2	2	3	0	1	5	1	2	3	1	1	7	1	1	0
CANADA	12	0	0	0	2	0	1	1	1	1	0	0	1	0	0	1	2	0	0	1	1	0
LATIN AMERICA	27	1	0	1	2	2	1	1	2	3	0	0	1	2	0	2	1	1	6	0	1	0
C. AMER.+CARIB.	10	0	0	0	0	0	0	1	1	1	0	1	0	2	2	1	0	3	0	0	0	0
CUBA	2	0	0	0	0	0	0	0	1	0	0	0	0	1	0	0	0	0	0	0	0	0
MEXICO	6	0	0	0	0	1	0	0	0	0	0	0	1	0	1	0	0	3	0	1	0	0
OTHER	2	0	0	0	0	0	0	0	0	0	0	0	0	1	0	0	0	0	0	0	0	0
S. AMERICA	17	1	0	0	2	2	1	2	1	2	0	0	1	0	0	2	0	1	3	0	0	0
ARGENTINA	5	0	0	0	1	1	0	0	1	1	0	0	0	1	0	0	0	0	0	0	0	0
BRAZIL	4	0	0	0	0	0	0	0	0	1	0	1	0	1	0	2	1	1	0	1	0	0
PERU	3	1	0	0	0	0	1	0	0	0	0	0	0	0	0	0	0	0	0	0	0	0
COLOMBIA	3	0	0	0	0	1	0	0	0	0	1	0	0	0	0	0	0	1	2	0	1	0
VENEZUELA	0	0	0	0	0	0	0	0	0	0	0	0	0	0	0	0	0	0	0	0	0	0
OTHER	2	0	0	0	0	0	0	0	0	0	0	0	0	0	1	0	0	0	0	0	1	0
EUROPE	29	0	0	0	0	2	2	11	1	1	3	1	0	1	0	1	2	3	0	0	1	2
EFTA	14	0	0	0	0	1	0	11	0	2	2	0	0	0	0	0	0	0	0	0	0	0
U.K.	14	0	0	0	0	1	0	11	0	2	2	0	0	0	0	0	0	0	0	0	0	0
SCANDINAVIA	0	0	0	0	0	0	0	0	0	0	0	0	0	0	0	0	0	0	0	0	0	0
SWITZERLAND	0	0	0	0	0	0	0	0	0	0	0	0	0	0	0	0	0	0	0	0	0	0
OTHER EFTA	0	0	0	0	0	0	0	0	0	0	0	0	0	0	0	0	0	0	0	0	0	0
EUROP. COMMUNITY	12	0	0	0	0	0	0	0	1	1	0	1	0	0	0	0	1	3	3	0	1	2
FRANCE	3	0	0	0	0	0	1	0	1	0	0	0	0	0	0	0	0	0	0	0	1	0
GERMANY	5	0	0	0	0	0	0	0	1	0	1	0	0	0	0	0	1	0	0	0	0	2
ITALY	2	0	0	0	0	0	0	0	0	0	0	0	0	0	0	0	0	2	0	0	0	0
BELGIUM + LUX	1	0	0	0	0	0	0	0	0	0	0	0	0	0	0	0	0	1	0	0	0	2
NETHERLANDS	2	0	0	0	0	1	0	0	0	1	0	0	0	0	1	1	0	0	0	0	0	0
SPAIN	2	0	0	0	0	0	0	0	1	0	0	0	0	0	0	0	0	0	0	0	0	0
GREECE + TURKEY	1	0	0	0	0	0	0	0	0	0	0	0	0	0	0	0	0	0	0	0	1	0
OTHER EUROPE	0	0	0	0	0	0	0	0	0	0	0	0	0	0	0	0	0	0	0	0	0	0
EUROPE EX. U.K.	15	0	0	0	0	0	2	0	1	1	1	1	0	1	1	2	2	3	0	0	1	2
SOUTHERN DOMINIONS	10	0	0	0	1	0	0	1	0	0	1	1	0	2	3	1	0	0	1	1	3	0
S. AFRICA +RHOD.	6	0	0	0	1	0	0	1	0	0	0	0	0	0	1	0	0	0	0	1	2	0
AUSTRALIA + N.Z.	4	0	0	0	0	0	0	0	0	0	1	1	0	2	2	1	0	0	1	0	1	0
ASIA + OTHER AFRICA	11	0	0	0	0	0	1	0	0	1	0	1	4	1	0	0	0	1	1	0	1	0
JAPAN	3	0	0	0	0	0	0	0	0	0	0	0	3	0	0	0	0	0	0	1	0	0
OTHER ASIA+AFR.	8	0	0	0	0	1	0	1	0	1	0	1	1	0	0	0	0	1	1	0	1	0
BLACK AFRICA	2	0	0	0	0	0	0	0	0	0	0	0	0	0	0	0	0	0	0	0	1	0
ARAB WORLD	0	0	0	0	0	0	0	0	0	0	0	0	0	0	0	0	0	0	0	0	0	0
INDIA	1	0	0	0	0	1	0	0	0	0	0	0	0	0	0	0	0	0	0	0	0	0
PHILIPPINES	4	0	0	0	0	0	1	0	0	0	0	2	0	0	0	0	0	0	0	1	0	0
OTHER E. ASIA	0	0	0	0	0	0	0	0	0	0	0	0	0	0	0	0	0	0	0	1	0	0
OTHER ASIA	1	0	0	0	0	0	0	0	0	0	0	0	0	0	0	0	0	0	0	0	0	0

CHAPTER 3- THE PROLIFERATION OF FOREIGN SUBSIDIARIES
SECTION 4- THE FLOW OF MANUFACTURING BY INDUSTRY OF SUBSIDIARY
TABLE 8- SUBSIDIARIES MANUFACTURING
OTHER FOOD PRODUCTS (SIC 206 AND 209)
CLASSIFIED BY COUNTRY OR REGION AND BY PERIOD MANUFACTURE BEGAN

PERIOD

COUNTRY OR REGION	PRE 1968	PRE 1901	1901-13	1914-19	1920-24	1925-29	1930-34	1935-39	1940-42	1946-50	1951-53	1954-55	1956-57	1958-59	1960-61	1962	1963	1964	1965	1966	1967	UNK
OUTSIDE U.S.	125	1	0	4	2	11	7	8	0	3	1	6	11	8	16	6	7	7	8	13	4	0
OUT. U.S. + CANADA	106	1	0	3	2	8	3	7	0	3	1	5	11	7	15	5	5	6	8	9	3	0
OUT. WEST. HEMIS.	78	0	0	1	2	7	1	6	0	2	0	5	9	7	14	3	5	6	6	5	1	0
OUT. WHITE CWEALTH	78	1	0	3	2	5	3	2	0	1	1	5	9	4	11	4	7	6	5	7	2	0
OUT. DEVLPED WORLD	33	1	0	2	2	2	3	2	0	1	1	2	2	0	2	3	2	1	2	4	2	0
CANADA	19	0	0	1	0	3	4	1	0	0	0	1	1	1	1	1	1	1	0	0	1	0
LATIN AMERICA	28	1	0	2	2	1	2	1	0	1	0	2	2	1	1	1	2	1	2	4	2	0
C. AMER.+CARIB.	16	0	0	0	1	1	0	1	0	1	1	0	0	0	0	0	0	0	2	2	2	0
CUBA	3	0	0	0	1	0	0	1	0	1	0	0	0	0	0	0	0	0	0	0	0	0
MEXICO	9	0	0	0	0	0	0	1	0	1	0	0	0	0	1	0	0	0	2	2	1	0
OTHER	4	1	0	0	0	1	1	0	0	0	1	0	0	0	0	0	0	0	0	0	0	0
S. AMERICA	12	1	0	2	1	1	1	0	0	1	0	0	2	0	3	0	2	1	0	2	1	0
ARGENTINA	1	0	0	0	0	0	0	0	0	1	0	0	1	0	0	0	0	0	0	0	0	0
BRAZIL	2	0	0	2	0	0	0	0	0	1	0	0	0	0	3	0	0	0	0	2	0	0
PERU	4	1	0	0	0	1	0	0	0	0	0	0	1	0	0	0	0	0	0	0	1	0
COLOMBIA	2	0	0	0	0	0	0	0	0	0	0	0	0	0	0	0	0	0	1	1	0	0
VENEZUELA	0	0	0	0	0	0	0	0	0	0	0	0	0	0	0	0	0	0	1	0	0	0
OTHER	3	0	0	0	1	0	0	0	0	0	0	0	0	0	0	1	1	1	0	0	0	0
EUROPE	58	0	0	1	0	5	0	5	0	2	0	3	8	5	9	1	5	6	4	4	4	0
EFTA	27	0	0	1	0	3	0	4	0	1	0	0	4	3	2	0	3	3	1	2	2	0
U.K.	14	0	0	0	0	2	0	4	0	1	0	0	2	1	2	0	0	0	1	1	1	0
SCANDINAVIA	11	0	0	1	0	1	0	0	0	0	0	0	1	1	2	0	3	3	0	2	1	0
SWITZERLAND	1	0	0	0	0	0	0	0	0	0	0	0	1	0	0	0	0	0	0	0	0	0
OTHER EFTA	1	0	0	0	0	0	0	0	0	0	0	0	0	0	0	0	0	0	0	0	0	0
EUROP. COMMUNITY	24	0	0	0	0	2	0	0	0	0	0	3	4	2	6	0	2	2	2	2	1	0
FRANCE	5	0	0	0	0	0	0	0	0	0	0	0	1	0	2	0	0	1	0	0	1	0
GERMANY	5	0	0	0	0	2	0	0	0	0	0	0	1	0	2	0	1	0	1	0	0	0
ITALY	6	0	0	0	0	0	0	0	0	0	0	2	1	2	1	0	1	0	1	0	0	0
BELGIUM + LUX	0	0	0	0	0	0	0	0	0	0	0	0	0	0	0	0	0	0	0	0	0	0
NETHERLANDS	8	0	0	0	0	1	0	0	0	0	0	0	1	0	1	1	1	1	1	2	0	0
SPAIN	3	0	0	0	1	0	0	0	0	0	0	0	0	0	0	0	0	0	1	1	0	0
GREECE + TURKEY	1	0	0	0	0	0	0	0	0	1	0	0	0	0	0	0	0	1	0	0	1	0
OTHER EUROPE	3	0	0	0	0	0	0	1	0	1	0	0	0	0	1	1	0	0	0	0	0	0
EUROPE EX. U.K.	44	0	0	1	0	3	0	1	0	1	0	3	6	4	7	1	5	6	3	3	3	0
SOUTHERN DOMINIONS	11	0	0	0	0	1	0	0	0	0	0	0	2	2	2	2	0	0	2	1	1	0
S. AFRICA +RHOD.	2	0	0	0	0	1	0	0	0	0	0	0	0	0	0	0	0	0	1	0	0	0
AUSTRALIA + N.Z.	9	0	0	0	0	0	0	1	0	0	0	1	2	0	3	2	0	0	1	1	1	0
ASIA + OTHER AFRICA	9	0	0	0	0	1	0	1	0	0	0	1	0	0	2	0	0	0	1	1	1	0
JAPAN	4	0	0	0	0	0	0	0	0	0	0	1	1	0	1	0	0	0	0	0	0	0
OTHER ASIA+AFR.	5	0	0	0	0	0	0	1	0	0	0	0	0	0	0	0	0	0	0	0	0	0
BLACK AFRICA	0	0	0	0	0	0	0	0	0	0	0	0	0	0	0	0	0	0	0	0	0	0
ARAB WORLD	0	0	0	0	0	0	0	0	0	0	0	0	0	0	0	0	0	0	0	0	0	0
INDIA	1	0	0	0	0	0	0	0	0	0	0	0	0	0	0	0	0	0	0	0	0	0
PHILIPPINES	2	0	0	0	1	0	1	1	0	0	0	1	1	0	0	0	0	0	0	0	0	0
OTHER E. ASIA	1	0	0	0	0	1	0	0	0	0	0	0	0	0	1	0	0	0	0	0	0	0
OTHER ASIA	1	0	0	0	0	0	0	0	0	0	0	0	0	0	1	0	0	0	0	0	0	0

CHAPTER 3- THE PROLIFERATION OF FOREIGN SUBSIDIARIES
SECTION 4- THE FLOW OF MANUFACTURING BY INDUSTRY OF SUBSIDIARY
TABLE 9- SUBSIDIARIES MANUFACTURING
TEXTILES AND APPAREL (SIC 22 AND 23)
CLASSIFIED BY COUNTRY OR REGION AND BY PERIOD MANUFACTURE BEGAN

PERIOD

COUNTRY OR REGION	PRE 1968	PRE 1901	1901 -13	1914 -19	1920 -24	1925 -29	1930 -34	1935 -39	1940 -45	1946 -50	1951 -53	1954 -55	1956 -57	1958 -59	1960 -61	1962	1963	1964	1965	1966	1967	UNK
OUTSIDE U.S.	144	0	1	1	1	2	3	3	5	12	5	5	5	12	21	8	8	9	10	14	1	18
OUT. U.S. + CANADA	117	0	1	0	1	0	2	1	3	6	4	5	5	11	20	8	6	8	10	10	1	17
OUT. WEST. HEMIS.	65	0	1	1	0	0	1	0	0	0	1	1	1	6	17	6	3	5	7	7	0	11
OUT. WHITE CWEALTH	97	0	1	0	1	0	1	1	3	6	1	5	6	9	11	5	5	7	7	9	1	16
OUT. DEVLPED WORLD	55	0	1	0	0	0	1	1	3	6	3	5	4	7	3	2	3	3	1	3	1	7
CANADA	27	0	0	1	0	0	1	2	2	6	1	0	0	1	1	0	0	1	2	4	0	1
LATIN AMERICA	52	0	1	0	2	1	1	3	3	6	3	4	4	5	3	2	3	3	1	3	1	6
C. AMER.+CARIB.	18	0	0	1	0	0	0	1	0	2	1	1	0	2	1	1	1	0	1	2	0	3
CUBA	2	0	0	0	0	0	0	0	0	0	1	0	0	1	0	0	0	0	0	0	0	1
MEXICO	14	0	0	0	0	0	0	1	1	2	0	1	1	0	1	0	0	0	2	2	0	2
OTHER	2	0	0	1	0	0	0	1	0	0	0	0	0	1	0	0	0	0	0	0	0	0
S. AMERICA	34	0	0	0	1	1	1	2	2	4	2	3	3	2	2	1	2	3	0	1	0	3
ARGENTINA	4	0	0	0	0	0	0	1	0	0	1	0	1	0	0	0	0	0	0	0	1	1
BRAZIL	4	0	0	0	0	0	0	0	0	2	0	1	0	0	0	0	0	0	0	0	0	0
PERU	3	0	0	0	0	0	0	0	0	1	0	0	0	0	0	0	0	0	0	0	0	2
COLOMBIA	6	0	0	1	0	0	0	0	0	0	0	1	0	0	0	0	0	0	0	1	1	0
VENEZUELA	14	0	0	0	1	0	0	1	2	1	2	0	2	2	2	1	1	2	0	1	0	2
OTHER	3	0	0	0	0	0	0	0	0	1	0	1	0	0	0	0	0	0	0	0	0	0
EUROPE	46	0	0	0	0	0	0	0	0	0	1	0	0	3	16	6	2	4	6	7	1	1
EFTA	21	0	0	0	0	0	0	0	0	0	1	0	0	1	9	5	1	0	2	1	1	0
U.K.	14	0	0	0	0	0	0	0	0	0	0	0	0	1	8	3	0	0	1	1	0	0
SCANDINAVIA	2	0	0	0	0	0	0	0	0	0	0	0	0	0	0	0	1	0	0	0	0	0
SWITZERLAND	4	0	0	0	0	0	0	0	0	0	1	0	0	2	0	1	0	0	1	0	0	2
OTHER EFTA	1	0	0	0	0	0	0	0	0	0	0	0	0	0	1	0	0	0	0	0	0	0
EUROP. COMMUNITY	22	0	0	0	0	0	0	0	0	0	0	0	0	1	7	1	1	2	3	3	0	1
FRANCE	9	0	0	0	0	0	0	0	0	0	0	0	0	0	3	0	0	0	4	0	0	1
GERMANY	4	0	0	0	0	0	0	0	0	0	0	0	0	2	1	1	0	1	1	1	0	1
ITALY	4	0	0	0	0	0	0	0	0	0	0	0	0	0	1	1	1	1	1	1	0	0
BELGIUM + LUX	4	0	0	0	0	0	0	0	0	0	0	0	0	1	1	1	0	1	0	0	1	0
NETHERLANDS	1	0	0	0	0	0	0	0	0	0	0	0	0	0	1	0	1	0	1	0	0	0
SPAIN	3	0	0	0	0	0	0	0	0	0	0	0	0	0	0	0	0	0	1	0	1	0
GREECE + TURKEY	0	0	0	0	0	0	0	0	0	0	0	0	0	0	0	0	0	0	0	0	0	0
OTHER EUROPE	0	0	0	0	0	0	0	0	0	0	0	0	0	0	0	0	0	0	0	0	0	0
EUROPE EX. U.K.	32	0	0	0	0	0	0	0	0	0	1	0	0	3	8	2	2	4	5	6	0	1
SOUTHERN DOMINIONS	6	0	0	0	0	0	1	0	0	0	0	0	0	0	1	0	1	1	0	0	0	1
S. AFRICA +RHOD.	3	0	0	0	0	0	0	0	0	0	0	0	0	1	1	0	1	0	0	0	0	0
AUSTRALIA + N.Z.	3	0	0	0	0	0	1	0	0	0	0	0	0	0	0	0	0	0	0	0	0	1
ASIA + OTHER AFRICA	13	0	0	0	0	0	0	0	0	0	0	1	1	2	1	0	0	0	0	0	0	9
JAPAN	10	0	0	0	0	0	0	0	0	0	0	0	1	1	1	0	0	0	0	0	0	8
OTHER ASIA+AFR.	3	0	0	0	0	0	0	0	0	0	0	1	0	2	0	0	0	0	0	0	0	1
BLACK AFRICA	0	0	0	0	0	0	0	0	0	0	0	0	0	0	0	0	0	0	0	0	0	0
ARAB WORLD	1	0	0	0	0	0	0	0	0	0	0	0	0	1	0	0	0	0	0	0	0	0
INDIA	1	0	0	0	0	0	0	0	0	0	0	0	1	0	0	0	0	0	0	0	0	0
PHILIPPINES	0	0	0	0	0	0	0	0	0	0	0	0	0	0	0	0	0	0	0	0	0	0
OTHER E. ASIA	1	0	0	0	0	0	0	0	0	0	0	0	0	0	0	0	0	0	0	0	1	1
OTHER ASIA	0	0	0	0	0	0	0	0	0	0	0	0	0	0	0	0	0	0	0	0	0	0

CHAPTER 3- THE PROLIFERATION OF FOREIGN SUBSIDIARIES
SECTION 4- THE FLOW OF MANUFACTURING BY INDUSTRY OF SUBSIDIARY
TABLE 10- SUBSIDIARIES MANUFACTURING
PAPER AND PAPERBOARD PRODUCTS, EXCEPT CONTAINERS (SIC 264)
CLASSIFIED BY COUNTRY OR REGION AND BY PERIOD MANUFACTURE BEGAN

PERIOD

COUNTRY OR REGION	PRE 1968	PRE 1901	1901 -13	1914 -19	1920 -24	1925 -29	1930 -34	1935 -39	1940 -42	1946 -50	1951 -53	1954 -55	1956 -57	1958 -59	1960 -61	1962	1963	1964	1965	1966	1967	UNK
OUTSIDE U.S.	97	1	0	2	0	2	5	1	6	4	0	11	12	4	10	3	14	7	7	3	5	0
OUT. U.S. + CANADA	83	1	0	0	0	1	4	1	1	3	0	8	10	4	9	3	14	7	7	3	5	0
OUT. WEST. HEMIS.	62	1	0	0	0	1	3	0	1	2	0	4	7	3	7	2	12	7	4	2	5	0
OUT. WHITE CWEALTH	51	0	0	0	0	1	3	1	2	1	0	5	7	3	6	2	5	2	7	2	3	0
OUT. DEVLPED WORLD	28	0	0	0	0	0	1	1	2	1	0	5	4	1	2	1	3	0	3	3	1	0
CANADA	14	0	0	2	0	1	1	0	3	1	0	3	2	0	1	1	0	0	0	0	0	0
LATIN AMERICA	21	0	0	0	0	1	1	1	2	1	0	4	3	0	2	1	2	3	1	1	0	0
C. AMER.+CARIB.	9	0	0	0	0	0	1	0	0	1	0	2	0	0	1	1	0	1	0	1	0	0
CUBA	3	0	0	0	0	0	1	0	0	1	0	0	0	0	0	0	0	0	0	0	0	0
MEXICO	5	0	0	0	0	1	1	0	0	1	0	1	0	1	1	1	0	0	0	0	0	0
OTHER	12	0	0	0	0	1	0	1	2	1	0	1	3	0	1	0	2	2	0	0	0	0
S. AMERICA	2	0	0	0	0	0	0	0	0	0	0	0	0	0	0	0	0	0	2	0	0	0
ARGENTINA	1	0	0	0	0	0	0	0	0	0	0	1	2	1	1	0	0	1	1	0	0	0
BRAZIL	2	0	0	0	0	1	0	0	0	0	0	1	0	0	0	0	0	0	0	0	0	0
PERU	1	0	0	0	0	0	0	0	0	0	0	0	0	1	0	0	0	1	0	0	0	0
COLOMBIA	4	0	0	0	0	0	0	1	2	0	0	2	2	0	0	0	0	0	0	0	0	0
VENEZUELA	4	0	0	0	0	0	0	0	0	0	0	0	0	0	1	0	0	1	0	0	1	0
OTHER	0	0	0	0	0	0	0	0	0	0	0	0	0	0	0	0	0	0	0	0	0	0
EUROPE	29	1	0	0	0	1	2	0	0	1	0	1	2	2	4	2	1	2	4	0	2	0
EFTA	8	1	0	0	0	0	0	0	0	0	0	1	2	0	1	1	0	0	1	1	0	0
U.K.	7	1	0	0	0	1	0	0	0	0	0	1	3	0	1	0	0	0	0	1	0	0
SCANDINAVIA	0	0	0	0	0	0	0	0	0	0	0	0	0	0	0	0	0	0	0	0	0	0
SWITZERLAND	0	0	0	0	0	0	0	0	0	0	0	0	0	0	1	0	0	0	0	1	0	0
OTHER EFTA	1	0	0	0	0	1	0	0	0	0	0	0	0	0	0	1	0	0	1	0	1	0
EUROP. COMMUNITY	17	0	0	0	0	2	1	0	0	0	0	3	3	2	3	1	1	2	1	0	0	0
FRANCE	9	0	0	0	0	1	1	0	0	0	0	2	1	0	1	1	1	0	0	1	0	0
GERMANY	2	0	0	0	0	0	1	0	0	0	0	1	0	2	0	0	0	2	0	0	0	0
ITALY	3	0	0	0	0	1	0	0	0	0	0	0	1	0	1	0	0	0	0	0	0	0
BELGIUM + LUX	1	0	0	0	0	0	0	0	0	0	0	0	0	0	0	0	0	0	1	0	0	0
NETHERLANDS	2	0	0	0	0	0	0	0	0	0	0	0	0	0	0	0	0	0	2	0	0	0
SPAIN	2	0	0	0	0	0	0	0	0	0	0	0	0	0	0	0	0	0	0	0	1	0
GREECE + TURKEY	1	0	0	0	0	0	0	0	0	0	0	0	0	0	0	0	0	0	0	0	0	0
OTHER EUROPE	1	0	0	0	0	0	0	0	0	1	0	0	0	0	0	0	0	0	4	0	2	0
EUROPE EX. U.K.	22	0	0	0	0	1	2	0	0	1	0	0	3	2	3	1	1	2	0	0	0	0
SOUTHERN DOMINIONS	24	0	0	0	0	1	1	1	1	1	0	2	0	1	2	0	9	5	0	0	2	0
S. AFRICA +RHOD.	14	0	0	0	0	0	0	0	0	0	0	1	0	0	1	0	9	3	0	0	0	0
AUSTRALIA + N.Z.	10	0	0	0	0	1	1	1	1	1	0	1	1	1	1	1	0	2	0	2	2	0
ASIA + OTHER AFRICA	9	0	0	0	0	0	0	0	0	0	0	1	1	0	1	0	2	0	0	0	1	0
JAPAN	2	0	0	0	0	0	0	0	0	0	0	1	0	1	1	1	1	0	0	0	0	0
OTHER ASIA+AFR.	7	0	0	0	0	0	0	0	0	0	0	0	1	0	1	0	1	0	0	0	1	0
BLACK AFRICA	0	0	0	0	0	0	0	0	0	0	0	0	0	0	0	0	0	0	0	0	0	0
ARAB WORLD	0	0	0	0	0	0	0	0	0	0	0	0	0	0	0	0	0	0	0	0	0	0
INDIA	1	0	0	0	0	0	0	0	0	0	0	0	0	0	1	1	0	0	0	0	1	0
PHILIPPINES	3	0	0	0	0	0	0	0	0	0	0	0	0	0	0	0	1	0	1	0	0	0
OTHER E. ASIA	0	0	0	0	0	0	0	0	0	0	0	0	0	0	0	0	0	0	0	0	0	0
OTHER ASIA	3	0	0	0	0	0	0	0	0	0	0	1	0	0	0	0	0	0	0	2	0	0

194

CHAPTER 3- THE PROLIFERATION OF FOREIGN SUBSIDIARIES
SECTION 4- THE FLOW OF MANUFACTURING BY INDUSTRY OF SUBSIDIARY
TABLE 11- SUBSIDIARIES MANUFACTURING
PAPERBOARD CONTAINERS AND BOXES (SIC 265)
CLASSIFIED BY COUNTRY OR REGION AND BY PERIOD MANUFACTURE BEGAN

COUNTRY OR REGION	PRE 1968	PRE 1901	1901 -13	1914 -19	1920 -24	1925 -29	1930 -34	1935 -39	1940 -45	1946 -50	1951 -53	1954 -55	1956 -57	1958 -59	1960 -61	1962	1963	1964	1965	1966	1967	UNK
OUTSIDE U.S.	106	0	0	0	0	1	2	3	3	3	7	7	10	10	10	4	16	5	12	8	4	1
OUT. U.S. + CANADA	95	0	0	0	0	1	1	1	3	2	6	7	5	10	10	4	16	5	12	7	4	1
OUT. WEST. HEMIS.	59	0	0	0	0	0	1	1	1	1	2	2	5	5	6	4	14	5	8	5	3	1
OUT. WHITE CWEALTH	68	0	0	0	0	1	1	0	0	2	5	6	5	7	7	4	13	3	10	6	1	1
OUT. DEVLPED WORLD	41	0	0	0	0	1	0	0	3	2	5	5	5	4	4	0	2	1	5	3	1	0
CANADA	11	0	0	0	0	0	1	0	0	1	1	0	5	3	2	0	0	0	0	1	0	1
LATIN AMERICA	36	0	0	0	0	1	2	0	0	1	5	5	5	3	4	0	2	4	4	2	1	0
C. AMER.+CARIB.	15	0	0	0	0	1	0	0	0	1	1	1	4	3	2	0	2	2	0	1	0	1
CUBA	1	0	0	0	0	1	0	0	0	0	0	0	0	0	0	0	0	0	0	0	0	0
MEXICO	9	0	0	0	0	0	0	0	1	0	0	0	4	0	2	0	1	0	2	0	1	0
OTHER	5	0	0	0	0	0	0	0	0	1	1	1	0	1	0	0	1	0	0	1	0	0
S. AMERICA	21	0	0	0	0	0	0	2	2	0	4	4	4	3	2	0	0	2	2	0	0	0
ARGENTINA	1	0	0	0	0	0	0	0	0	1	0	1	1	0	1	0	0	0	0	0	0	0
BRAZIL	4	0	0	0	0	0	0	0	0	0	1	0	1	3	1	0	0	0	0	1	0	0
PERU	2	0	0	0	0	0	0	0	0	0	1	0	0	0	0	0	0	0	0	1	0	0
COLOMBIA	2	0	0	0	0	0	0	1	1	0	1	0	1	0	0	0	0	0	0	1	0	1
VENEZUELA	9	0	0	0	0	0	0	0	0	0	1	3	0	3	0	1	0	0	1	0	1	0
OTHER	3	0	0	0	0	1	0	0	0	0	0	0	0	1	1	0	0	1	1	0	0	1
EUROPE	28	0	0	0	0	1	0	0	0	0	1	0	0	6	4	4	0	0	2	5	3	1
EFTA	4	0	0	0	0	1	0	0	0	0	0	0	0	0	1	0	0	0	0	0	0	1
U.K.	2	0	0	0	0	1	0	0	0	0	0	0	0	0	1	0	0	0	0	0	0	0
SCANDINAVIA	2	0	0	0	0	0	0	0	0	0	0	0	0	0	0	0	0	0	1	0	0	1
SWITZERLAND	0	0	0	0	0	0	0	0	0	0	0	0	0	0	0	0	0	0	0	0	0	0
OTHER EFTA	0	0	0	0	0	0	0	0	0	0	0	0	0	0	0	0	0	0	0	0	0	0
EUROP. COMMUNITY	18	0	0	0	0	0	0	0	0	0	0	0	0	3	3	1	0	2	2	3	0	0
FRANCE	7	0	0	0	0	0	0	0	0	0	0	0	0	0	1	0	0	0	1	0	0	0
GERMANY	7	0	0	0	0	0	0	0	0	0	1	0	0	2	1	1	0	1	0	1	0	0
ITALY	6	0	0	0	0	0	0	0	0	1	0	0	0	3	2	0	0	0	1	0	0	0
BELGIUM + LUX	3	0	0	0	0	0	0	0	0	0	0	0	0	0	0	1	0	0	0	1	0	1
NETHERLANDS	1	0	0	0	0	0	0	0	0	0	0	0	0	0	0	0	0	1	0	0	0	0
SPAIN	5	0	0	0	0	0	0	0	0	0	0	0	0	0	2	0	0	0	0	3	0	0
GREECE + TURKEY	0	0	0	0	0	0	0	0	0	0	0	0	0	0	0	0	0	0	0	0	0	0
OTHER EUROPE	1	0	0	0	0	1	0	0	0	0	0	0	0	0	0	0	0	0	0	0	0	0
EUROPE EX. U.K.	26	0	0	0	0	1	0	0	0	0	1	0	0	6	3	4	0	0	2	5	3	1
SOUTHERN DOMINIONS	24	0	0	0	0	0	1	0	0	0	0	1	0	2	2	0	13	1	2	0	3	0
S. AFRICA +RHOD.	19	0	0	0	0	0	1	0	0	1	1	0	0	2	1	0	13	1	1	0	3	0
AUSTRALIA + N.Z.	5	0	0	0	0	0	0	1	0	1	0	1	0	0	2	0	0	0	1	0	0	0
ASIA + OTHER AFRICA	7	0	0	0	0	0	0	0	0	0	0	0	0	2	0	0	1	2	1	1	0	0
JAPAN	2	0	0	0	0	0	0	0	0	1	0	0	0	0	0	0	0	1	0	1	0	0
OTHER ASIA+AFR.	5	0	0	0	0	0	0	0	0	1	0	1	0	1	2	0	1	0	1	1	0	0
BLACK AFRICA	2	0	0	0	0	0	0	0	0	0	1	0	0	0	0	0	0	0	1	1	0	0
ARAB WORLD	1	0	0	0	0	0	0	0	1	0	0	0	0	1	0	0	0	0	0	0	0	0
INDIA	0	0	0	0	0	0	0	0	0	0	0	0	0	0	0	0	0	0	0	0	0	0
PHILIPPINES	0	0	0	0	0	0	0	0	0	0	0	0	0	0	0	0	0	0	0	0	0	0
OTHER E. ASIA	1	0	0	0	0	0	0	0	0	0	0	0	0	0	1	0	0	0	0	0	0	0
OTHER ASIA	1	0	0	0	0	1	0	0	0	0	0	0	0	0	0	0	0	0	0	0	0	0

PERIOD

CHAPTER 3- THE PROLIFERATION OF FOREIGN SUBSIDIARIES
SECTION 4- THE FLOW OF MANUFACTURING BY INDUSTRY OF SUBSIDIARY
TABLE 12- SUBSIDIARIES MANUFACTURING
OTHER WOOD, FURNITURE, AND PAPER PRODUCTS (SIC 24, 25, 261-263, AND 266)
CLASSIFIED BY COUNTRY OR REGION AND BY PERIOD MANUFACTURE BEGAN

COUNTRY OR REGION	PRE 1968	PRE 1901	1901 -13	1914 -19	1920 -24	1925 -29	1930 -34	1935 -39	1940 -42	1946 -50	1951 -53	1954 -55	1956 -57	1958 -59	1960 -61	1962	1963	1964	1965	1966	1967	UNK
OUISIDE U.S.	88	3	1	4	1	6	0	0	1	2	0	8	5	12	10	2	4	6	11	7	4	1
OUT. U.S. + CANADA	56	2	1	2	1	4	0	0	1	0	0	3	3	8	6	2	3	5	5	6	4	0
OUT. WEST. HEMIS.	37	2	0	2	1	3	0	0	0	0	0	1	1	5	4	2	2	4	4	5	2	0
OUT. WHITE CMWEALTH	44	1	0	1	0	3	0	0	1	0	0	1	3	5	5	2	3	4	4	6	4	0
OUT. DEVLPED WORLD	22	0	0	0	0	1	0	0	1	0	0	2	2	3	3	2	2	1	1	2	2	0
CANADA	32	1	0	2	0	2	0	0	0	2	0	5	2	4	4	0	1	1	6	1	0	1
LATIN AMERICA	19	0	0	0	1	1	0	1	1	0	0	2	2	3	2	0	1	1	1	1	2	0
C. AMER.+CARIB.	0	0	0	0	0	0	0	0	0	0	0	0	0	0	0	0	0	0	0	0	0	0
CUBA	0	0	0	0	0	0	0	0	0	0	0	0	0	0	0	0	0	0	0	0	0	0
MEXICO	3	0	0	0	0	0	0	0	1	0	0	0	0	1	0	0	0	0	0	1	0	0
OTHER	5	0	0	0	0	1	0	1	0	0	0	1	0	1	0	0	0	1	0	0	0	0
S. AMERICA	11	0	0	0	0	0	0	0	0	0	0	1	1	1	2	0	1	0	1	1	2	0
ARGENTINA	3	0	0	0	0	0	0	0	0	0	0	0	1	0	2	0	0	0	0	0	0	0
BRAZIL	1	0	0	0	0	0	0	0	0	0	0	0	0	1	0	0	0	0	0	0	0	0
PERU	1	0	0	0	0	0	0	0	0	0	0	1	0	0	0	0	0	0	0	0	0	0
COLOMBIA	1	0	0	0	0	0	0	0	0	0	0	0	0	0	1	0	0	0	0	0	0	0
VENEZUELA	5	0	0	0	0	0	0	0	0	1	0	0	0	0	0	0	0	2	0	0	2	0
OTHER	0	0	0	0	0	0	0	0	0	0	0	0	0	0	0	0	0	0	0	0	0	0
EUROPE	27	2	1	1	0	3	0	0	0	0	0	0	1	3	2	0	2	2	4	4	2	0
EFTA	8	1	1	0	0	1	0	0	0	0	0	0	1	1	1	0	0	1	1	0	0	0
U.K.	7	1	1	0	0	1	0	0	0	0	0	0	1	1	1	0	0	1	1	0	0	0
SCANDINAVIA	1	0	0	0	0	0	0	0	0	0	0	0	0	1	0	0	0	0	0	0	0	0
SWITZERLAND	0	0	0	0	0	0	0	0	0	0	0	0	0	0	0	0	0	0	0	0	0	0
OTHER EFTA	0	0	0	0	0	0	0	0	0	0	0	0	0	0	0	0	0	0	0	0	0	0
EUROP. COMMUNITY	12	1	1	0	0	0	0	0	0	0	0	0	0	1	0	0	2	2	0	1	2	0
FRANCE	5	1	1	0	0	0	0	0	0	0	0	0	0	1	0	0	0	0	1	1	0	0
GERMANY	3	0	0	0	0	0	0	0	0	0	0	0	0	0	0	0	1	2	0	0	0	0
ITALY	3	0	0	0	0	0	0	0	0	0	0	0	0	0	1	0	1	0	1	0	0	0
BELGIUM + LUX	1	0	0	0	0	0	0	0	0	0	0	0	0	0	0	0	0	0	0	1	0	0
NETHERLANDS	0	0	0	0	0	0	0	0	0	0	0	0	0	0	0	0	0	0	0	0	0	0
SPAIN	7	0	0	1	0	2	0	0	0	0	0	0	0	1	1	0	0	0	0	1	1	0
GREECE + TURKEY	0	0	0	0	0	0	0	0	0	0	0	0	0	0	0	0	0	0	0	0	0	0
OTHER EUROPE	0	0	0	0	0	0	0	0	0	0	0	0	0	0	0	0	0	0	0	0	0	0
EUROPE EX. U.K.	20	1	0	1	0	2	0	0	0	0	0	1	2	2	1	0	2	2	3	4	2	0
SOUTHERN DOMINIONS	5	0	0	0	0	0	0	0	0	0	0	0	2	2	0	0	0	0	0	0	0	0
S. AFRICA +RHOD.	1	0	0	0	0	0	0	0	0	0	0	0	0	1	0	0	0	0	0	0	0	0
AUSTRALIA + N.Z.	4	0	0	0	0	0	0	0	0	0	0	0	2	2	0	0	0	0	0	0	0	0
ASIA + OTHER AFRICA	5	0	0	0	0	0	0	0	0	0	0	0	0	0	2	1	1	0	0	0	0	0
JAPAN	2	0	0	0	0	0	0	0	0	0	0	0	0	0	1	0	1	0	0	0	0	0
OTHER ASIA+AFR.	3	0	0	0	0	0	0	0	0	0	0	0	0	0	1	1	0	0	0	0	0	0
BLACK AFRICA	0	0	0	0	0	0	0	0	0	0	0	0	0	0	0	0	0	0	0	0	0	0
ARAB WORLD	0	0	0	0	0	0	0	0	0	0	0	0	0	0	0	0	0	0	0	0	0	0
INDIA	0	0	0	0	0	0	0	0	0	0	0	0	0	0	0	0	0	0	0	0	0	0
PHILIPPINES	3	0	0	0	0	0	0	0	0	0	0	0	0	1	1	0	0	0	0	1	0	0
OTHER E. ASIA	0	0	0	0	0	0	0	0	0	0	0	0	0	0	0	0	0	0	0	0	0	0
OTHER ASIA	0	0	0	0	0	0	0	0	0	0	0	0	0	0	0	0	0	0	0	0	0	0

PERIOD

CHAPTER 3— THE PROLIFERATION OF FOREIGN SUBSIDIARIES
SECTION 4— THE FLOW OF MANUFACTURING BY INDUSTRY OF SUBSIDIARY
TABLE 13— SUBSIDIARIES MANUFACTURING
PRINTED MATTER (SIC 27)
CLASSIFIED BY COUNTRY OR REGION AND BY PERIOD MANUFACTURE BEGAN

PERIOD

COUNTRY OR REGION	PRE 1968	PRE 1901	1901 -13	1914 -19	1920 -24	1925 -29	1930 -34	1935 -39	1940 -45	1946 -50	1951 -53	1954 -55	1956 -57	1958 -59	1960 -61	1962	1963	1964	1965	1966	1967	UNK
OUTSIDE U.S.	36	2	1	0	0	0	0	0	1	1	1	2	4	2	2	4	6	1	1	6	1	2
OUT. U.S. + CANADA	31	1	0	0	0	0	0	0	1	1	1	1	4	1	1	4	5	1	1	1	1	1
OUT. WEST. HEMIS.	25	1	0	0	0	0	0	1	1	1	0	1	3	2	1	4	4	1	1	4	1	1
OUT. WHITE CMEALTH	24	0	0	0	0	0	0	1	0	1	1	1	4	1	1	4	2	1	1	6	1	0
OUT. DEVLPED WORLD	6	0	0	0	0	0	0	1	0	0	1	0	1	0	0	0	2	0	0	2	0	0
CANADA	5	1	0	0	0	0	0	0	0	0	0	1	0	0	0	0	0	0	0	0	0	1
LATIN AMERICA	6	0	0	0	0	0	0	1	1	0	1	0	1	1	1	1	2	0	0	0	0	0
C. AMER.+CARIB.	2	0	0	0	0	0	0	1	0	1	1	0	0	1	1	0	1	0	0	1	1	0
CUBA	1	0	0	0	0	0	0	0	0	1	1	0	0	0	0	0	0	0	0	0	0	0
MEXICO	1	0	0	0	0	0	0	1	0	0	0	0	0	0	0	0	1	0	0	1	1	0
OTHER	0	0	0	0	0	0	0	0	0	0	0	0	0	1	1	0	0	0	0	0	0	0
S. AMERICA	4	0	0	0	0	0	1	1	1	0	0	0	1	1	1	1	1	1	1	1	0	0
ARGENTINA	3	0	0	0	0	0	1	1	0	0	0	0	1	1	0	0	1	0	0	1	0	0
BRAZIL	1	0	0	0	0	0	0	0	1	0	0	0	0	0	1	1	0	0	0	0	0	0
PERU	0	0	0	0	0	0	0	0	0	0	0	0	0	0	0	0	0	0	0	0	0	0
COLOMBIA	0	0	0	0	0	0	0	0	0	0	0	0	0	0	0	0	0	0	0	0	0	0
VENEZUELA	0	0	0	0	0	0	0	0	0	0	0	0	0	0	0	0	0	0	0	0	0	0
OTHER	0	0	0	0	0	0	0	0	0	0	0	0	0	0	0	0	0	0	0	0	0	0
EUROPE	20	1	0	0	0	0	0	0	1	0	0	1	3	2	1	3	4	1	1	4	1	1
EFTA	6	1	0	0	0	0	0	0	0	0	0	0	0	1	1	1	1	0	0	1	0	1
U.K.	3	1	0	0	0	0	0	0	0	0	0	0	0	1	0	1	0	0	0	0	1	1
SCANDINAVIA	2	0	0	0	0	0	0	0	0	0	0	0	0	0	1	0	1	0	0	1	0	0
SWITZERLAND	1	0	0	0	0	0	0	0	0	0	0	0	0	0	0	0	0	0	0	0	1	0
OTHER EFTA	0	0	0	0	0	0	0	0	0	0	0	0	0	0	0	0	0	0	0	0	0	0
EUROP. COMMUNITY	13	0	0	0	0	0	0	0	1	1	0	1	2	1	1	2	3	1	1	3	1	0
FRANCE	4	0	0	0	0	0	0	0	0	0	0	0	0	0	1	2	1	1	1	1	0	0
GERMANY	4	0	0	0	0	0	0	0	1	1	0	1	1	0	0	1	1	0	0	1	1	0
ITALY	4	0	0	0	0	0	0	0	0	0	0	0	0	1	0	0	1	1	1	1	1	0
BELGIUM + LUX	0	0	0	0	0	0	0	0	0	0	0	0	0	0	0	0	0	0	0	0	0	0
NETHERLANDS	1	0	0	0	0	0	0	0	0	0	0	1	0	0	0	0	1	0	0	0	0	0
SPAIN	1	0	0	0	0	0	0	0	0	0	0	0	1	0	0	0	0	0	0	0	0	0
GREECE + TURKEY	0	0	0	0	0	0	0	0	0	0	0	0	0	0	0	0	0	0	0	0	0	0
OTHER EUROPE	0	0	0	0	0	0	0	0	0	0	0	0	0	0	0	0	0	0	0	0	0	0
EUROPE EX. U.K.	17	0	0	0	0	0	0	0	1	1	0	1	3	1	1	3	3	0	0	4	1	0
SOUTHERN DOMINIONS	4	0	0	0	0	0	0	0	0	0	0	0	0	0	0	3	3	1	0	0	0	0
S. AFRICA +RHOD.	4	0	0	0	0	0	0	0	0	0	0	0	0	0	0	3	3	1	0	0	0	0
AUSTRALIA + N.Z.	0	0	0	0	0	0	0	0	0	0	0	0	0	0	0	0	0	0	0	0	0	0
ASIA + OTHER AFRICA	1	0	0	0	0	0	0	0	0	0	0	0	0	1	1	0	0	0	0	0	0	1
JAPAN	1	0	0	0	0	0	0	0	0	0	0	0	0	1	0	0	0	0	0	0	0	1
OTHER ASIA+AFR.	0	0	0	0	0	0	0	0	0	0	0	0	0	0	0	0	0	0	0	0	0	0
BLACK AFRICA	0	0	0	0	0	0	0	0	0	0	0	0	0	0	0	0	0	0	0	0	0	0
ARAB WORLD	0	0	0	0	0	0	0	0	0	0	0	0	0	0	0	0	0	0	0	0	0	0
INDIA	0	0	0	0	0	0	0	0	0	0	0	0	0	0	0	0	0	0	0	0	0	0
PHILIPPINES	0	0	0	0	0	0	0	0	0	0	0	0	0	0	0	0	0	0	0	0	0	0
OTHER E. ASIA	0	0	0	0	0	0	0	0	0	0	0	0	0	0	0	0	0	0	0	0	0	0
OTHER ASIA	0	0	0	0	0	0	0	0	0	0	0	0	0	0	0	0	0	0	0	0	0	0

CHAPTER 3- THE PROLIFERATION OF FOREIGN SUBSIDIARIES
SECTION 4- THE FLOW OF MANUFACTURING BY INDUSTRY OF SUBSIDIARY
TABLE 14- SUBSIDIARIES MANUFACTURING
INDUSTRIAL CHEMICALS (SIC 281)
CLASSIFIED BY COUNTRY OR REGION AND BY PERIOD MANUFACTURE BEGAN

PERIOD

COUNTRY OR REGION	PRE 1968	PRE 1901	1901-13	1914-19	1920-24	1925-29	1930-34	1935-39	1940-42	1946-50	1951-53	1954-55	1956-57	1958-59	1960-61	1962	1963	1964	1965	1966	1967	UNK
OUTSIDE U.S.	367	4	2	1	6	13	8	6	16	23	19	19	24	36	58	9	24	26	21	27	8	13
OUT. U.S. + CANADA	306	6	2	0	5	7	6	3	8	18	13	16	22	36	55	7	22	20	20	25	8	11
OUT. WEST. HEMIS.	198	2	2	0	4	6	3	2	6	4	6	12	10	19	36	5	17	16	20	18	7	4
OUT. WHITE CWEALTH	249	2	2	0	3	5	4	2	6	16	13	10	18	26	46	6	20	17	15	22	7	9
OUT. DEVLPED WORLD	121	0	0	0	1	1	3	1	4	14	7	5	13	17	21	3	7	5	2	8	2	7
CANADA	61	2	4	1	1	6	2	3	8	5	6	3	2	0	3	2	2	6	1	2	0	2
LATIN AMERICA	108	0	0	0	1	1	3	0	4	14	7	4	12	17	19	1	5	4	0	7	1	7
C. AMER.+CARIB.	51	0	0	0	1	0	0	1	2	5	3	2	8	10	6	1	1	3	0	4	0	4
CUBA	1	0	0	0	1	0	0	0	0	0	0	0	1	0	0	1	0	0	0	0	0	0
MEXICO	43	0	0	1	0	0	0	0	2	5	2	2	6	9	5	0	1	2	0	3	1	4
OTHER	7	0	0	0	0	0	0	0	0	0	1	0	1	1	1	0	1	1	0	1	0	0
S. AMERICA	57	0	0	0	0	1	3	1	2	9	4	2	4	7	13	0	3	0	0	3	1	3
ARGENTINA	16	0	0	0	0	0	3	0	0	2	1	1	2	2	3	0	1	1	0	0	0	2
BRAZIL	14	0	0	0	0	0	0	0	0	3	3	0	1	1	3	0	0	3	0	1	0	0
PERU	4	0	0	0	0	0	0	0	1	0	0	0	1	1	1	0	1	0	1	0	1	0
COLOMBIA	12	0	0	0	0	1	3	1	0	2	0	0	0	3	3	1	0	0	0	0	0	0
VENEZUELA	8	0	0	0	0	0	0	0	1	2	0	1	0	0	1	0	1	1	0	2	1	0
OTHER	3	0	0	0	0	0	0	0	0	0	0	0	0	0	2	0	1	0	0	0	0	0
EUROPE	135	2	2	0	4	4	3	2	3	3	4	9	8	11	28	4	10	11	13	9	4	1
EFTA	38	0	0	0	2	1	2	1	1	1	1	5	4	3	7	1	1	3	2	2	0	0
U.K.	27	0	0	0	2	0	2	1	1	1	0	4	0	3	3	1	0	1	1	1	0	0
SCANDINAVIA	8	0	0	0	0	1	2	0	1	1	1	0	0	0	3	0	0	1	2	1	0	0
SWITZERLAND	0	0	0	0	0	0	0	0	0	0	0	0	0	0	1	0	0	1	0	0	0	0
OTHER EFTA	3	0	0	0	0	0	0	0	0	0	0	1	0	0	1	0	0	0	0	0	0	0
EUROP. COMMUNITY	80	2	2	0	2	3	1	0	2	1	2	4	4	7	15	2	8	8	7	6	3	1
FRANCE	19	0	0	0	1	1	0	1	1	0	1	0	0	1	2	1	2	2	2	2	0	0
GERMANY	17	2	1	0	1	1	1	0	0	0	2	4	2	3	5	0	1	1	3	2	3	0
ITALY	21	0	0	0	1	1	0	0	1	1	1	1	1	1	3	1	4	3	1	1	0	1
BELGIUM + LUX	10	1	1	0	0	1	0	0	0	1	0	0	2	1	3	0	0	1	1	1	1	0
NETHERLANDS	13	0	1	0	0	1	0	0	0	1	0	1	0	1	2	0	1	2	1	1	0	1
SPAIN	14	0	0	0	0	0	0	0	0	1	1	1	0	1	6	0	1	0	3	0	1	0
GREECE + TURKEY	2	0	0	0	0	0	0	0	1	0	0	0	0	0	0	0	1	0	0	0	0	0
OTHER EUROPE	1	0	0	0	0	0	0	0	0	0	0	0	0	0	0	1	0	0	0	0	0	1
EUROPE EX. U.K.	108	2	2	0	2	4	1	1	2	2	4	5	4	8	25	3	9	10	11	8	4	1
SOUTHERN DOMINIONS	30	0	0	0	2	2	0	0	1	1	0	2	0	7	6	0	1	2	3	2	1	2
S. AFRICA +RHOD.	3	0	0	0	0	0	0	0	0	1	0	0	0	0	0	0	0	0	0	1	0	0
AUSTRALIA + N.Z.	27	0	0	0	2	2	0	0	1	0	2	2	1	7	6	0	1	2	3	1	1	2
ASIA + OTHER AFRICA	33	0	0	0	0	0	1	0	0	0	1	1	1	1	2	2	6	3	4	7	2	1
JAPAN	20	2	0	0	0	0	0	0	0	0	0	0	1	1	0	0	4	2	2	1	1	1
OTHER ASIA+AFR.	13	0	0	0	0	0	1	0	0	0	1	0	1	1	1	2	2	1	2	0	1	0
BLACK AFRICA	0	0	0	0	0	0	0	0	0	0	0	0	0	0	0	0	1	0	0	0	0	0
ARAB WORLD	4	0	0	0	0	0	0	0	0	0	0	0	0	0	1	0	0	0	0	0	0	0
INDIA	1	0	0	0	0	0	0	0	0	0	0	0	0	0	0	1	0	0	1	0	0	0
PHILIPPINES	3	0	0	0	0	0	0	0	0	0	0	0	0	0	1	0	1	1	1	0	0	0
OTHER E. ASIA	2	0	0	0	0	0	0	0	0	0	0	0	0	0	0	0	0	0	0	0	0	0
OTHER ASIA	3	0	0	0	0	0	0	0	0	0	0	0	0	0	1	0	0	0	0	1	0	0

CHAPTER 3- THE PROLIFERATION OF FOREIGN SUBSIDIARIES
SECTION 4- THE FLOW OF MANUFACTURING BY INDUSTRY OF SUBSIDIARY
TABLE 15- SUBSIDIARIES MANUFACTURING
PLASTICS AND SYNTHETICS (SIC 282)
CLASSIFIED BY COUNTRY OR REGION AND BY PERIOD MANUFACTURE BEGAN

PERIOD

COUNTRY OR REGION	PRE 1968	PRE 1901	1901-13	1914-19	1920-24	1925-29	1930-34	1935-39	1940-45	1946-50	1951-53	1954-55	1956-57	1958-59	1960-61	1962	1963	1964	1965	1966	1967	UNK
OUTSIDE U.S.	259	0	1	1	3	2	3	7	4	7	16	17	14	15	50	23	23	19	29	15	7	3
OUT. U.S. + CANADA	230	0	0	0	2	1	1	5	3	6	16	14	11	13	47	22	23	13	29	15	6	3
OUT. WEST. HEMIS.	164	0	0	0	1	1	1	3	0	1	7	11	6	11	38	17	20	11	17	12	3	3
OUT. WHITE CWEALTH	165	0	0	0	0	1	0	2	1	5	14	9	9	7	32	17	16	8	24	13	4	1
OUT. DEVLPED WORLD	80	0	0	0	0	0	0	2	3	5	9	4	6	3	10	7	5	3	14	5	4	0
CANADA	29	0	1	1	1	1	1	2	1	1	9	3	3	2	3	1	0	6	0	0	1	0
LATIN AMERICA	66	0	0	0	0	0	2	3	3	5	9	3	3	5	9	5	3	2	12	3	3	0
C. AMER.+CARIB.	27	0	0	0	0	0	0	2	0	3	3	3	3	3	5	2	1	2	4	2	0	0
CUBA	0	0	0	0	0	0	0	0	0	0	0	0	0	0	0	0	0	0	0	0	0	0
MEXICO	23	0	0	0	0	0	0	2	0	3	3	3	3	3	5	2	1	1	3	0	0	0
OTHER	4	0	0	0	0	0	0	0	0	0	0	0	0	0	0	0	0	1	0	2	0	0
S. AMERICA	39	0	0	0	0	0	2	1	2	0	6	3	3	2	4	3	2	0	8	0	3	3
ARGENTINA	11	0	0	0	0	0	0	1	0	1	3	1	1	1	1	0	0	0	3	0	0	0
BRAZIL	10	0	0	0	0	0	0	0	0	0	1	3	0	0	1	0	0	0	3	0	0	0
PERU	1	0	0	0	0	0	0	0	0	0	0	0	0	0	0	0	0	0	0	0	1	0
COLOMBIA	9	0	0	0	0	0	0	0	0	1	1	0	0	0	1	1	1	0	0	0	0	0
VENEZUELA	7	0	0	0	0	0	0	0	0	0	1	1	1	1	1	0	1	0	4	1	1	0
OTHER	1	0	0	0	0	0	0	0	0	0	0	0	0	0	0	0	0	0	0	0	1	0
EUROPE	99	0	0	0	2	1	1	2	0	1	5	9	4	5	24	11	13	2	11	7	0	1
EFTA	41	0	0	0	2	1	1	2	0	1	2	4	2	1	8	6	5	0	6	1	0	0
U.K.	34	0	0	0	2	1	1	2	0	1	2	4	2	1	7	5	4	0	3	1	0	0
SCANDINAVIA	5	0	0	0	0	0	0	0	0	0	0	0	0	0	1	1	1	0	1	0	0	0
SWITZERLAND	1	0	0	0	0	0	0	0	0	0	0	0	0	0	0	0	0	0	1	0	0	0
OTHER EFTA	1	0	0	0	0	0	0	0	0	0	0	0	0	0	0	0	1	0	0	0	0	0
EUROP. COMMUNITY	46	0	0	0	0	0	0	0	0	0	3	3	2	4	12	5	6	1	5	2	0	1
FRANCE	11	0	0	0	0	0	0	0	0	0	2	1	1	1	2	0	2	0	2	0	0	0
GERMANY	10	0	0	0	0	0	0	0	0	0	0	0	0	0	3	3	1	0	1	2	0	0
ITALY	9	0	0	0	0	0	0	0	0	0	1	0	0	1	3	1	1	0	1	1	0	0
BELGIUM + LUX	7	0	0	0	0	0	0	0	0	0	0	1	1	0	2	1	1	1	0	0	0	1
NETHERLANDS	9	0	0	0	0	0	0	0	0	0	0	0	0	2	2	0	1	0	1	2	0	0
SPAIN	3	0	0	0	0	0	0	0	0	0	0	0	0	0	2	0	0	1	0	0	0	0
GREECE + TURKEY	0	0	0	0	0	0	0	0	0	0	0	0	0	0	1	0	0	0	0	0	0	0
OTHER EUROPE	0	0	0	0	0	0	0	0	0	0	0	0	0	0	0	0	0	0	0	0	0	0
EUROPE EX. U.K.	65	0	0	0	1	0	0	0	0	0	3	6	2	9	17	6	9	2	8	7	0	1
SOUTHERN DOMINIONS	31	0	0	0	0	0	1	0	0	0	0	1	5	5	8	3	3	5	2	2	2	2
S. AFRICA +RHOD.	5	0	0	0	0	0	1	0	0	0	0	0	1	0	0	2	2	0	2	0	0	1
AUSTRALIA + N.Z.	26	0	0	0	0	0	0	0	0	0	0	1	5	5	8	4	2	5	2	2	2	1
ASIA + OTHER AFRICA	34	0	0	0	0	0	0	0	0	0	0	2	1	1	6	4	4	3	4	3	1	0
JAPAN	20	0	0	0	0	0	0	0	0	0	0	2	1	1	5	2	2	1	2	1	0	0
OTHER ASIA+AFR.	14	0	0	0	0	0	0	0	0	0	0	0	0	0	1	2	0	1	2	2	1	0
BLACK AFRICA	2	0	0	0	0	0	0	0	0	0	0	0	0	0	0	0	0	0	1	0	0	0
ARAB WORLD	0	0	0	0	0	0	0	0	0	0	0	0	0	0	0	0	0	0	0	0	0	0
INDIA	5	0	0	0	0	0	0	0	0	0	0	1	1	0	1	0	1	0	1	0	0	0
PHILIPPINES	2	0	0	0	0	0	0	0	0	0	0	0	0	0	0	0	0	1	0	1	0	0
OTHER E. ASIA	4	0	0	0	0	0	0	0	0	0	0	0	0	1	1	0	0	0	0	0	1	0
OTHER ASIA	1	0	0	0	0	0	0	0	0	0	0	0	0	0	1	0	0	0	0	0	0	0

CHAPTER 3- THE PROLIFERATION OF FOREIGN SUBSIDIARIES
SECTION 4- THE FLOW OF MANUFACTURING BY INDUSTRY OF SUBSIDIARY
TABLE 16- SUBSIDIARIES MANUFACTURING
DRUGS (SIC 283)
CLASSIFIED BY COUNTRY OR REGION AND BY PERIOD MANUFACTURE BEGAN

COUNTRY OR REGION	PRE 1968	PRE 1901	1901 -13	1914 -19	1920 -24	1925 -29	1930 -34	1935 -39	1940 -45	1946 -50	1951 -53	1954 -55	1956 -57	1958 -59	1960 -61	1962	1963	1964	1965	1966	1967	UNK
OUTSIDE U.S.	405	0	0	2	4	8	17	19	19	27	28	19	34	46	62	18	25	25	20	8	21	3
OUT. U.S. + CANADA	368	0	0	1	2	7	15	16	15	24	26	16	31	44	59	17	24	24	17	7	20	3
OUT. WEST. HEMIS.	241	0	0	0	2	6	14	9	3	11	17	11	20	33	36	14	18	18	9	6	14	0
OUT. WHITE CWEALTH	280	0	0	1	1	1	1	9	12	11	19	13	20	38	51	14	20	19	17	6	16	3
OUT. DEVLPED WORLD	174	0	0	1	0	1	1	7	12	17	12	5	14	20	32	7	11	9	11	4	7	3
CANADA	37	0	0	1	1	1	2	3	4	3	2	3	3	2	3	3	1	1	1	1	1	0
LATIN AMERICA	127	0	0	1	1	2	3	7	12	13	9	5	7	11	23	3	6	8	3	1	6	3
C. AMER.+CARIB.	53	0	0	1	0	1	2	2	5	5	1	1	3	6	7	0	2	5	0	0	4	1
CUBA	2	0	0	0	0	0	0	0	0	1	0	0	0	0	0	0	0	0	0	0	0	0
MEXICO	27	0	0	0	0	0	1	0	2	1	0	1	3	3	5	3	1	2	0	0	2	0
OTHER	24	0	0	0	0	1	0	2	1	1	1	0	0	3	2	0	1	3	1	0	2	1
S. AMERICA	74	0	0	0	1	1	0	5	9	8	8	3	4	5	16	3	4	3	4	0	2	2
ARGENTINA	15	0	0	0	0	1	0	1	3	1	2	1	4	1	2	1	0	1	0	0	0	0
BRAZIL	19	0	0	0	0	0	0	1	1	5	2	2	2	3	4	1	0	0	1	0	2	0
PERU	6	0	0	0	0	0	0	0	1	0	2	0	2	0	2	0	0	1	1	0	0	0
COLOMBIA	13	0	0	0	0	0	0	1	1	1	2	1	0	0	4	0	2	1	1	0	0	0
VENEZUELA	11	0	0	0	0	0	0	0	1	1	0	0	1	0	4	1	0	1	0	0	1	0
OTHER	10	0	0	0	0	0	0	2	1	1	1	0	0	1	0	1	2	0	0	0	1	0
EUROPE	138	0	0	0	2	6	7	4	0	6	9	7	11	19	20	7	10	12	4	2	12	0
EFTA	50	0	0	0	1	6	7	3	0	3	4	2	5	4	3	2	1	4	2	0	3	0
U.K.	37	0	0	0	0	6	7	2	0	3	3	1	4	1	2	0	1	2	0	0	3	0
SCANDINAVIA	5	0	0	0	1	0	0	0	0	0	0	1	1	1	1	0	0	0	0	0	0	0
SWITZERLAND	3	0	0	0	0	0	0	0	0	0	0	0	0	1	0	1	0	0	0	0	0	0
OTHER EFTA	5	0	0	0	0	0	0	1	0	0	1	0	0	1	0	1	0	2	0	0	0	0
EUROP. COMMUNITY	71	0	0	0	1	0	0	1	0	2	4	5	5	12	15	4	7	6	2	0	7	0
FRANCE	17	0	0	0	0	0	1	0	0	1	0	1	1	4	2	0	2	3	0	0	1	0
GERMANY	14	0	0	0	1	0	0	0	0	0	3	3	1	1	5	3	2	2	0	0	0	0
ITALY	25	0	0	0	0	0	0	1	0	0	3	1	3	4	4	2	2	1	1	0	3	0
BELGIUM + LUX	12	0	0	0	0	0	0	0	0	1	0	0	1	3	4	0	0	1	0	0	1	0
NETHERLANDS	3	0	0	0	0	0	0	0	0	0	0	0	0	0	0	0	1	0	0	0	0	0
SPAIN	7	0	0	0	0	0	0	0	0	0	0	0	0	2	1	0	0	2	0	0	2	0
GREECE + TURKEY	8	0	0	0	0	0	0	0	0	1	1	0	1	1	1	1	0	0	0	2	0	0
OTHER EUROPE	2	0	0	0	1	0	2	2	0	0	0	0	0	0	0	0	0	0	0	0	0	0
EUROPE EX. U.K.	101	0	0	0	1	0	0	2	0	3	6	6	7	18	18	6	9	10	4	2	9	0
SOUTHERN DOMINIONS	49	0	0	0	0	0	2	5	3	1	4	2	6	5	6	2	3	3	0	1	1	0
S. AFRICA +RHOD.	18	0	0	0	0	2	2	2	1	0	1	1	2	2	1	1	1	1	0	0	1	0
AUSTRALIA + N.Z.	31	0	0	0	0	5	5	3	1	4	4	2	3	9	5	1	2	5	2	3	1	0
ASIA + OTHER AFRICA	54	0	0	0	0	0	1	1	0	4	4	2	3	9	10	4	5	3	3	1	1	0
JAPAN	7	0	0	0	0	0	0	0	0	0	0	0	0	0	1	1	0	3	1	1	0	0
OTHER ASIA+AFR.	47	0	0	0	0	0	1	1	0	4	4	2	3	9	9	3	5	3	0	0	1	1
BLACK AFRICA	2	0	0	0	0	0	0	0	0	0	0	0	0	0	0	0	0	0	0	1	1	0
ARAB WORLD	3	0	0	0	0	0	0	0	0	0	0	1	0	0	2	0	0	0	0	0	0	0
INDIA	13	0	0	0	0	0	0	1	0	2	1	0	1	2	2	1	2	1	0	0	0	1
PHILIPPINES	3	0	0	0	0	0	0	0	0	1	0	0	0	0	0	0	1	0	0	0	1	0
OTHER E. ASIA	3	0	0	0	0	0	0	0	0	0	1	0	0	0	2	0	0	0	0	0	0	0
OTHER ASIA	18	0	0	0	0	0	0	0	0	1	1	1	1	3	5	2	1	3	0	1	1	0

CHAPTER 3- THE PROLIFERATION OF FOREIGN SUBSIDIARIES
SECTION 4— THE FLOW OF MANUFACTURING BY INDUSTRY OF SUBSIDIARY
TABLE 17— SUBSIDIARIES MANUFACTURING
SOAPS AND COSMETICS (SIC 284)
CLASSIFIED BY COUNTRY OR REGION AND BY PERIOD MANUFACTURE BEGAN

COUNTRY OR REGION	PRE 1968	PRE 1901	1901 -13	1914 -19	1920 -24	1925 -29	1930 -34	1935 -39	1940 -45	1946 -50	1951 -53	1954 -55	1956 -57	1958 -59	1960 -61	1962	1963	1964	1965	1966	1967	UNK
OUTSIDE U.S.	248	1	6	8	4	12	11	13	9	15	6	13	19	24	36	10	10	11	13	14	11	2
OUT. U.S. + CANADA	217	1	5	5	4	11	8	9	6	15	6	11	19	21	32	10	10	8	13	13	8	2
OUT. WEST. HEMIS.	158	1	4	4	4	9	8	6	2	10	5	7	9	15	24	9	9	6	9	12	7	2
OUT. WHITE CWEALTH	159	0	4	4	3	7	2	5	4	7	5	8	17	18	23	8	5	7	13	10	8	1
OUT. DEVLPED WORLD	79	0	1	4	0	2	0	4	4	5	2	4	12	8	12	5	4	4	5	2	1	0
CANADA	31	0	1	3	0	1	3	4	3	5	2	2	0	3	4	0	1	3	0	1	3	0
LATIN AMERICA	59	0	1	4	0	2	0	3	4	5	2	4	10	6	8	1	0	2	4	1	1	0
C. AMER.+CARIB.	25	0	0	1	0	1	0	0	2	3	1	0	7	3	1	0	1	2	2	1	1	0
CUBA	3	0	0	0	0	0	0	1	0	0	0	0	0	0	0	0	0	0	0	0	0	0
MEXICO	12	0	0	1	0	1	0	1	1	2	1	0	2	3	0	0	0	1	0	1	0	0
OTHER	10	0	0	0	0	0	0	0	1	1	0	0	1	0	1	0	0	1	2	0	0	0
S. AMERICA	34	0	1	3	0	1	0	3	2	2	1	4	4	3	7	1	1	0	2	0	1	0
ARGENTINA	10	0	1	1	0	0	0	1	2	0	0	1	3	3	1	1	0	0	0	0	0	0
BRAZIL	7	0	0	2	0	1	0	0	0	0	1	1	0	2	1	0	1	0	0	0	0	0
PERU	6	0	0	0	0	0	0	1	0	0	0	1	0	0	1	0	0	0	0	0	0	0
COLOMBIA	3	0	0	0	0	0	0	0	0	0	0	0	1	0	3	0	1	0	2	0	0	0
VENEZUELA	7	0	0	0	0	0	0	1	0	1	0	1	0	0	1	0	0	0	0	0	1	0
OTHER	1	0	0	0	0	0	0	0	0	0	0	0	0	1	0	0	0	0	0	0	0	0
EUROPE	110	1	4	0	4	8	6	1	0	9	4	5	6	10	16	5	4	4	6	9	7	1
EFTA	45	1	1	0	1	3	4	0	0	8	2	1	2	2	5	2	3	3	3	3	1	0
U.K.	31	1	1	0	1	3	4	0	0	7	1	0	1	0	5	2	3	1	0	1	0	0
SCANDINAVIA	9	0	0	0	0	0	0	0	0	0	0	0	1	0	0	0	0	1	2	2	1	0
SWITZERLAND	2	0	0	0	0	0	0	0	0	0	0	1	0	0	0	0	0	0	0	0	0	0
OTHER EFTA	3	0	0	0	0	0	0	0	0	1	1	0	0	2	0	0	0	0	1	0	0	0
EUROP. COMMUNITY	53	0	3	0	3	5	2	1	0	1	2	3	3	8	9	3	0	2	2	3	3	1
FRANCE	18	0	1	0	2	1	2	0	0	1	1	1	2	3	2	1	0	0	0	2	1	0
GERMANY	14	0	1	0	1	2	0	0	0	0	1	0	0	1	4	0	0	0	0	0	1	1
ITALY	12	0	1	0	0	1	2	0	0	0	0	0	1	3	1	2	0	1	1	1	1	0
BELGIUM + LUX	7	0	0	0	0	1	0	0	0	0	0	0	0	1	2	0	0	0	0	0	0	0
NETHERLANDS	2	0	0	0	0	0	0	0	0	0	0	0	0	0	0	0	0	0	1	0	0	0
SPAIN	8	0	0	0	0	0	0	0	0	0	0	2	1	0	1	0	0	1	0	1	3	0
GREECE + TURKEY	1	0	0	0	0	0	0	0	0	0	0	0	0	0	1	0	0	0	1	0	0	0
OTHER EUROPE	3	0	0	0	0	0	0	0	0	0	0	0	0	0	1	0	1	0	0	0	0	0
EUROPE EX. U.K.	79	0	3	0	3	5	2	1	0	2	3	5	5	10	11	3	1	3	6	8	7	1
SOUTHERN DOMINIONS	24	0	0	1	0	1	2	4	2	1	0	2	1	3	3	0	1	0	0	2	0	1
S. AFRICA +RHOD.	10	0	0	0	0	1	2	1	1	1	0	0	0	1	1	0	1	0	0	1	0	0
AUSTRALIA + N.Z.	14	0	0	1	0	0	0	3	1	0	0	2	1	2	2	0	0	0	0	1	0	1
ASIA + OTHER AFRICA	24	0	0	0	0	0	0	2	0	0	0	0	2	2	5	4	4	2	3	1	0	0
JAPAN	4	0	0	0	0	0	0	1	0	0	0	0	0	0	1	0	1	0	2	0	0	0
OTHER ASIA+AFR.	20	0	0	0	0	0	0	1	0	0	0	0	2	2	1	4	3	2	1	1	0	0
BLACK AFRICA	3	0	0	0	0	0	0	0	0	0	0	0	0	0	0	0	0	2	0	0	0	0
ARAB WORLD	3	0	0	0	0	0	0	0	0	0	0	0	1	2	0	0	0	0	0	1	0	0
INDIA	0	0	0	0	0	0	0	0	0	0	0	0	0	0	0	0	0	0	0	0	0	0
PHILIPPINES	2	0	0	0	0	0	0	1	0	0	0	0	1	0	0	0	0	0	0	0	0	0
OTHER E. ASIA	2	0	0	0	0	0	0	0	0	0	0	0	0	0	0	2	0	0	0	0	0	0
OTHER ASIA	10	0	0	0	0	0	0	0	0	0	0	0	0	0	3	2	3	0	1	0	0	0

CHAPTER 3- THE PROLIFERATION OF FOREIGN SUBSIDIARIES
SECTION 4- THE FLOW OF MANUFACTURING BY INDUSTRY OF SUBSIDIARY
TABLE 18- SUBSIDIARIES MANUFACTURING
PAINTS (SIC 285)
CLASSIFIED BY COUNTRY OR REGION AND BY PERIOD MANUFACTURE BEGAN

COUNTRY OR REGION	PRE 1968	PRE 1901	1901 -13	1914 -19	1920 -24	1925 -29	1930 -34	1935 -39	1940 -45	1946 -50	1951 -53	1954 -55	1956 -57	1958 -59	1960 -61	1962	1963	1964	1965	1966	1967	UNK
OUTSIDE U.S.	82	0	0	2	0	2	0	1	1	0	3	5	4	4	7	2	3	3	15	5	7	18
OUT. U.S. + CANADA	69	0	0	0	0	2	0	0	0	0	3	4	3	4	7	2	3	3	12	4	6	17
OUT. WEST. HEMIS.	45	0	0	0	0	2	0	0	0	0	3	2	3	4	5	2	3	1	7	3	4	14
OUT. WHITE CMEALTH	57	0	0	0	0	1	0	0	0	0	3	4	3	4	6	2	3	2	10	3	4	12
OUT. DEVLPED WORLD	32	0	0	0	0	0	0	0	0	0	3	3	3	2	2	0	0	1	5	1	3	9
CANADA	13	0	0	2	0	0	0	1	1	0	0	1	1	1	0	0	0	1	3	1	1	1
LATIN AMERICA	24	0	0	0	0	0	0	0	0	0	3	2	1	2	2	0	0	1	5	1	2	3
C. AMER.+CARIB.	11	0	0	0	0	0	0	0	0	0	2	1	0	0	2	0	0	1	2	0	0	1
CUBA	1	0	0	0	0	0	0	0	0	0	0	0	0	0	0	0	0	0	0	0	0	0
MEXICO	5	0	0	0	0	0	0	0	0	0	2	1	0	0	1	0	0	0	2	0	0	0
OTHER	5	0	0	0	0	0	0	0	0	0	0	0	0	1	1	0	0	1	0	0	0	1
S. AMERICA	13	0	0	0	0	0	0	0	0	0	1	1	3	2	0	0	0	0	3	1	2	2
ARGENTINA	10	0	0	0	0	0	0	0	0	0	1	0	0	2	2	0	0	0	2	0	0	0
BRAZIL	5	0	0	0	0	0	0	0	0	0	0	1	3	0	0	0	0	0	0	1	2	0
PERU	0	0	0	0	0	0	0	0	0	0	0	0	0	0	0	0	0	0	0	0	0	0
COLOMBIA	2	0	0	0	0	0	0	0	0	0	0	0	0	0	1	0	0	0	0	0	0	0
VENEZUELA	2	0	0	0	0	0	0	0	0	0	0	1	0	0	0	0	0	0	1	0	0	0
OTHER	4	0	0	0	0	0	0	0	0	0	0	0	2	0	0	0	0	0	0	0	0	2
EUROPE	27	0	0	0	0	2	0	0	0	0	0	1	0	2	3	1	3	1	7	3	2	2
EFTA	7	0	0	0	0	2	0	0	0	0	0	0	0	0	1	0	0	0	3	0	1	1
U.K.	4	0	0	0	0	1	0	0	0	0	0	0	0	0	0	0	0	0	2	0	1	0
SCANDINAVIA	2	0	0	0	0	1	0	0	0	0	0	0	0	0	0	0	0	0	0	0	0	1
SWITZERLAND	1	0	0	0	0	0	0	0	0	0	0	0	0	0	1	0	0	0	0	0	0	0
OTHER EFTA	0	0	0	0	0	0	0	0	0	0	0	0	0	0	0	0	0	0	0	0	0	0
EUROP. COMMUNITY	17	0	0	0	0	0	0	0	0	0	0	1	0	2	2	1	3	0	4	0	1	1
FRANCE	3	0	0	0	0	0	0	0	0	0	0	0	0	0	0	0	1	0	0	0	1	0
GERMANY	5	0	0	0	0	0	0	0	0	0	1	0	0	0	2	1	0	0	1	0	0	0
ITALY	2	0	0	0	0	0	0	0	0	0	0	0	0	0	0	0	1	0	0	0	0	0
BELGIUM + LUX	4	0	0	0	0	0	0	0	0	0	0	0	0	2	0	0	1	0	1	0	0	0
NETHERLANDS	4	0	0	0	0	0	0	0	0	0	0	0	0	0	0	0	0	1	2	0	0	0
SPAIN	2	0	0	0	0	0	0	0	0	0	0	0	0	0	0	0	0	0	0	2	0	1
GREECE + TURKEY	0	0	0	0	0	0	0	0	0	0	0	0	0	0	0	0	0	0	0	0	0	0
OTHER EUROPE	1	0	0	0	0	1	0	0	0	0	0	0	0	0	0	0	0	0	0	1	0	0
EUROPE EX. U.K.	23	0	0	0	0	1	0	0	0	0	1	0	0	2	3	1	3	1	5	3	1	2
SOUTHERN DOMINIONS	7	0	0	0	0	0	0	0	0	0	0	0	0	0	1	0	0	0	0	0	1	5
S. AFRICA +RHOD.	3	0	0	0	0	0	0	0	0	0	0	0	0	0	0	0	0	0	0	0	0	3
AUSTRALIA + N.Z.	4	0	0	0	0	0	0	0	0	0	0	0	0	0	1	0	0	0	0	0	1	2
ASIA + OTHER AFRICA	11	0	0	0	0	0	0	0	0	0	0	0	0	0	0	1	0	1	0	0	1	7
JAPAN	3	0	0	0	0	0	0	0	0	0	0	0	0	0	0	0	0	0	0	0	0	1
OTHER ASIA+AFR.	8	0	0	0	0	0	0	0	0	0	0	0	0	0	0	1	0	1	0	0	1	6
BLACK AFRICA	2	0	0	0	0	0	0	0	0	0	0	0	0	0	0	0	0	0	0	0	0	2
ARAB WORLD	0	0	0	0	0	0	0	0	0	0	0	0	0	0	0	0	0	0	0	0	0	0
INDIA	1	0	0	0	0	0	0	0	0	0	0	0	0	0	0	0	0	0	0	0	0	1
PHILIPPINES	1	0	0	0	0	0	0	0	0	0	0	0	0	0	1	0	0	0	0	0	0	0
OTHER E. ASIA	0	0	0	0	0	0	0	0	0	0	0	0	0	0	0	0	0	0	0	0	0	0
OTHER ASIA	4	0	0	0	0	0	0	0	0	0	0	0	0	0	0	0	0	0	0	0	1	3

CHAPTER 3- THE PROLIFERATION OF FOREIGN SUBSIDIARIES
SECTION 4- THE FLOW OF MANUFACTURING BY INDUSTRY OF SUBSIDIARY
TABLE 19- SUBSIDIARIES MANUFACTURING
AGRICULTURAL CHEMICALS (SIC 287)
CLASSIFIED BY COUNTRY OR REGION AND BY PERIOD MANUFACTURE BEGAN

COUNTRY OR REGION	PRE 1968	PRE 1901	1901 -13	1914 -19	1920 -24	1925 -29	1930 -34	1935 -39	1940 -45	1946 -50	1951 -53	1954 -55	1956 -57	1958 -59	1960 -61	1962 -63	1964	1965	1966	1967	UNK
OUTSIDE U.S.	81	0	1	1	2	1	2	1	0	4	6	1	5	6	9	1	8	8	7	7	5
OUT. U.S. + CANADA	72	0	1	1	1	0	1	1	0	3	6	1	5	6	9	1	7	6	7	7	5
OUT. WEST. HEMIS.	45	0	0	1	1	0	0	0	0	3	2	1	3	3	5	1	5	6	3	5	2
OUT. WHITE CWEALTH	61	0	1	1	1	1	1	1	0	2	6	1	4	5	7	1	6	4	6	4	4
OUT. DEVLPED WORLD	41	0	1	0	0	1	1	1	0	1	5	1	4	3	5	0	3	3	4	2	3
CANADA	9	0	0	0	1	1	0	0	0	1	0	0	0	0	0	0	1	2	0	0	2
LATIN AMERICA	27	0	1	1	0	1	1	1	0	0	4	0	2	3	4	0	2	0	4	3	3
C. AMER.+CARIB.	13	0	1	1	0	0	0	1	0	0	2	0	0	3	1	0	1	0	2	2	2
CUBA	6	0	0	1	0	1	1	1	0	0	0	0	0	0	0	0	0	0	0	0	0
MEXICO	6	0	1	0	0	0	0	0	0	0	2	0	0	1	1	0	1	0	2	2	2
OTHER	6	0	0	0	0	0	0	0	0	0	0	0	0	2	0	0	0	0	0	0	0
S. AMERICA	14	0	0	0	0	1	0	0	0	0	2	0	2	0	3	0	2	0	2	0	0
ARGENTINA	4	0	0	0	0	0	1	0	0	0	0	0	0	0	1	0	0	0	1	1	1
BRAZIL	3	0	0	0	0	0	0	0	0	0	0	0	0	0	0	0	0	1	1	0	0
PERU	1	0	0	0	0	0	0	0	0	0	0	0	0	0	1	0	1	0	0	0	1
COLOMBIA	4	0	0	0	0	0	0	0	0	1	1	0	0	2	2	0	0	0	0	0	0
VENEZUELA	2	0	0	0	0	0	0	0	0	0	0	0	0	0	0	0	0	0	0	0	0
OTHER	0	0	0	0	0	0	0	0	0	0	0	0	0	0	0	0	0	0	0	0	0
EUROPE	22	0	0	0	1	0	0	0	0	2	1	0	0	2	3	1	3	2	2	1	1
EFTA	4	0	0	0	0	0	0	0	0	1	1	0	0	1	1	0	1	1	0	0	0
U.K.	3	0	0	0	0	0	0	0	0	1	1	0	0	1	1	0	0	1	0	0	0
SCANDINAVIA	1	0	0	0	0	0	0	0	0	0	0	0	0	0	0	0	1	0	0	0	0
SWITZERLAND	0	0	0	0	0	0	0	0	0	0	0	0	0	0	0	0	0	0	0	0	0
OTHER EFTA	0	0	0	0	0	0	0	0	0	0	0	0	0	0	0	0	0	0	0	0	0
EUROP. COMMUNITY	11	0	0	0	0	0	0	0	0	1	0	0	0	0	2	0	1	0	0	1	1
FRANCE	6	0	0	0	0	0	0	0	0	1	0	0	0	0	2	0	0	0	0	1	1
GERMANY	1	0	0	0	0	0	0	0	0	0	0	0	0	0	0	0	1	0	0	0	0
ITALY	2	0	0	0	0	0	0	0	0	0	0	0	0	0	0	0	0	0	0	1	1
BELGIUM + LUX	1	0	0	0	0	0	0	0	0	0	0	0	0	1	0	0	0	0	0	0	0
NETHERLANDS	1	0	0	0	0	0	0	0	0	0	0	0	0	1	0	0	0	0	0	0	0
SPAIN	7	0	0	0	0	0	0	0	0	0	0	0	0	1	1	1	0	1	0	0	0
GREECE + TURKEY	0	0	0	0	0	0	0	0	0	0	0	0	0	0	0	0	0	0	0	0	0
OTHER EUROPE	0	0	0	0	0	0	0	0	0	0	0	0	0	0	0	0	0	0	0	2	0
EUROPE EX. U.K.	19	0	0	1	0	0	0	0	0	1	0	0	0	2	2	1	3	1	2	1	1
SOUTHERN DOMINIONS	8	0	0	0	0	0	0	0	0	0	0	1	1	0	1	1	1	1	1	1	1
S. AFRICA +RHOD.	5	0	0	0	0	0	0	0	0	0	0	1	0	1	0	0	0	0	1	0	0
AUSTRALIA + N.Z.	15	0	0	0	0	0	0	0	0	1	0	0	2	1	1	2	3	3	0	3	2
ASIA + OTHER AFRICA	15	0	0	0	0	0	0	0	0	1	0	0	2	1	1	2	3	3	0	3	2
JAPAN	1	0	0	0	0	0	0	0	0	0	0	0	0	1	0	0	0	0	0	0	1
OTHER ASIA+AFR.	14	0	0	0	0	0	0	0	0	1	1	0	2	0	1	2	2	3	0	3	0
BLACK AFRICA	4	0	0	0	0	0	0	0	0	0	0	0	0	0	1	0	0	0	1	0	0
ARAB WORLD	1	0	0	0	0	0	0	0	0	0	0	0	0	1	0	0	0	0	0	0	0
INDIA	3	0	0	0	0	0	0	0	0	1	0	0	0	0	1	0	1	0	0	0	0
PHILIPPINES	4	0	0	0	0	0	0	0	0	0	0	0	0	0	0	0	1	0	0	2	1
OTHER E. ASIA	4	0	0	0	0	0	0	0	0	0	0	0	0	1	0	1	1	0	0	0	0
OTHER ASIA	1	0	0	0	0	0	0	0	0	0	0	0	0	0	0	0	0	0	0	0	0

CHAPTER 3- THE PROLIFERATION OF FOREIGN SUBSIDIARIES
SECTION 4- THE FLOW OF MANUFACTURING BY INDUSTRY OF SUBSIDIARY
TABLE 20- SUBSIDIARIES MANUFACTURING
MISCELLANEOUS CHEMICAL PRODUCTS (SIC 289)
CLASSIFIED BY COUNTRY OR REGION AND BY PERIOD MANUFACTURE BEGAN

PERIOD

COUNTRY OR REGION	PRE 1900	PRE 1901	1901 -13	1914 -19	1920 -24	1925 -29	1930 -34	1935 -39	1940 -45	1946 -50	1951 -53	1954 -55	1956 -57	1958 -59	1960 -61	1962	1963	1964	1965	1966	1967	UNK
OUTSIDE U.S.	132	1	4	5	8	5	4	5	3	4	11	5	7	9	12	12	2	8	8	12	6	1
OUT. U.S. + CANADA	108	1	3	3	5	3	4	2	1	4	7	5	4	9	12	11	1	8	6	12	6	1
OUT. WEST. HEMIS.	73	0	3	1	2	1	1	2	0	2	4	4	2	6	6	10	1	7	4	11	5	0
OUT. WHITE CWEALTH	81	0	3	2	4	3	4	0	1	2	6	4	2	7	12	10	1	5	5	7	4	1
OUT. DEVLPED WORLD	43	0	0	2	3	2	4	0	1	2	3	1	2	4	6	2	1	3	2	2	2	1
CANADA	24	0	1	2	3	2	0	3	0	0	4	0	3	0	0	1	1	0	2	0	0	0
LATIN AMERICA	35	0	0	2	3	2	3	0	2	2	3	1	2	3	6	1	0	2	2	1	1	1
C. AMER.+CARIB.	11	0	0	0	0	1	1	0	1	1	1	0	0	1	0	1	0	2	2	1	1	1
CUBA	0	0	0	0	0	0	0	0	0	0	0	0	0	0	0	0	0	0	0	0	0	0
MEXICO	7	0	0	0	0	1	1	0	1	1	1	0	0	1	0	1	0	1	1	0	0	1
OTHER	4	0	0	0	0	0	0	0	0	0	0	0	0	0	0	0	0	1	1	1	1	0
S. AMERICA	24	0	0	2	0	1	2	0	1	1	2	1	2	2	6	1	0	0	0	0	0	1
ARGENTINA	8	0	0	0	0	0	1	0	0	0	0	0	2	0	3	0	0	0	0	1	1	0
BRAZIL	7	0	0	1	0	0	1	0	1	1	2	1	0	1	1	0	0	0	0	0	0	0
PERU	0	0	0	0	0	0	0	0	0	0	0	0	0	0	0	0	0	0	0	0	0	0
COLOMBIA	4	0	0	0	0	0	0	0	0	0	0	0	0	0	2	0	0	0	0	0	0	0
VENEZUELA	1	0	0	0	0	0	1	0	0	0	0	0	0	1	0	0	0	0	0	0	0	0
OTHER	4	0	0	1	3	0	0	0	0	0	0	0	0	0	0	0	0	1	0	0	0	0
EUROPE	48	1	3	0	1	1	0	1	1	1	3	3	0	3	5	8	0	3	2	9	4	0
EFTA	16	1	0	0	0	0	0	1	1	1	1	1	0	0	0	1	0	2	0	6	2	0
U.K.	14	1	0	0	0	0	0	1	1	1	1	1	0	0	0	1	0	2	0	4	2	0
SCANDINAVIA	0	0	0	0	0	0	0	0	0	0	0	0	0	0	0	0	0	0	0	0	0	0
SWITZERLAND	1	0	0	0	0	0	0	0	0	0	0	0	0	0	0	1	0	0	0	1	0	0
OTHER EFTA	1	0	0	0	0	0	0	0	0	0	0	0	0	0	0	0	0	0	0	1	0	0
EUROP. COMMUNITY	25	0	3	0	0	1	0	0	0	0	2	1	0	3	5	6	0	1	2	0	1	0
FRANCE	7	0	1	0	0	0	0	0	0	0	0	0	0	1	2	2	0	0	0	0	0	0
GERMANY	6	0	1	0	0	0	0	0	0	0	2	0	0	0	1	0	0	1	1	0	0	0
ITALY	9	0	1	0	0	1	0	0	0	0	0	1	0	1	1	3	0	0	1	0	0	0
BELGIUM + LUX	3	0	0	0	0	0	0	0	0	0	0	0	0	0	0	0	0	0	0	0	0	0
NETHERLANDS	6	0	0	0	0	0	0	0	0	0	0	0	0	1	1	1	0	0	0	0	0	0
SPAIN	0	0	0	0	0	0	0	0	0	0	0	0	0	0	0	1	0	0	0	3	1	0
GREECE + TURKEY	0	0	0	0	1	0	0	0	0	0	0	0	0	0	0	0	0	0	0	0	0	0
OTHER EUROPE	0	0	0	0	0	0	0	0	0	0	0	1	0	0	0	0	0	1	0	0	0	0
EUROPE EX. U.K.	34	0	3	0	0	1	0	1	0	0	2	2	0	3	5	7	0	1	2	3	2	0
SOUTHERN DOMINIONS	12	0	0	0	1	0	0	0	0	0	0	1	2	2	0	0	0	1	1	1	0	0
S. AFRICA +RHOD.	5	0	0	1	1	0	0	0	0	0	0	1	0	0	0	0	0	1	0	0	0	0
AUSTRALIA + N.Z.	7	0	0	0	0	0	0	0	0	0	0	0	2	2	0	0	0	0	1	1	0	0
ASIA + OTHER AFRICA	13	0	0	0	0	0	1	1	1	1	1	0	0	1	1	2	0	3	1	1	1	0
JAPAN	5	0	0	0	0	0	0	1	1	1	1	0	0	0	1	1	0	1	1	1	0	1
OTHER ASIA+AFR.	8	0	0	0	0	0	1	0	0	0	0	0	0	1	0	1	0	2	0	0	1	0
BLACK AFRICA	0	0	0	0	0	0	0	0	0	0	0	0	0	0	0	0	0	0	0	0	0	0
ARAB WORLD	0	0	0	0	0	0	0	0	0	0	0	0	0	0	0	0	0	0	0	0	0	0
INDIA	2	0	0	0	0	0	1	0	0	0	0	0	0	0	0	0	0	0	0	1	1	0
PHILIPPINES	3	0	0	0	0	0	0	0	0	0	0	0	0	1	0	0	0	0	2	0	0	1
OTHER E. ASIA	3	0	0	0	0	0	0	0	0	0	0	0	0	0	0	1	0	2	0	0	0	0
OTHER ASIA	0	0	0	0	0	0	0	0	0	0	0	0	0	0	0	0	0	0	0	0	0	0

CHAPTER 3- THE PROLIFERATION OF FOREIGN SUBSIDIARIES
SECTION 4- THE FLOW OF MANUFACTURING BY INDUSTRY OF SUBSIDIARY
TABLE 21- SUBSIDIARIES MANUFACTURING
REFINED PETROLEUM (SIC 291)
CLASSIFIED BY COUNTRY OR REGION AND BY PERIOD MANUFACTURE BEGAN

PERIOD

COUNTRY OR REGION	PRE 1968	PRE 1901	1901 -13	1914 -19	1920 -24	1925 -29	1930 -34	1935 -39	1940 -45	1946 -50	1951 -53	1954 -55	1956 -57	1958 -59	1960 -61	1962	1963	1964	1965	1966	1967	UNK
OUTSIDE U.S.	173	6	7	3	9	9	3	13	7	6	18	4	11	5	22	10	8	9	7	8	3	5
OUT. U.S. + CANADA	158	6	7	1	8	7	2	11	6	5	18	4	9	5	21	9	8	9	7	8	3	4
OUT. WEST. HEMIS.	126	5	4	0	6	5	2	8	2	4	16	3	7	5	18	8	6	9	6	8	2	4
OUT. WHITE CWEALTH	130	6	7	1	7	6	2	11	6	4	14	3	8	5	17	8	5	4	7	7	2	2
OUT. DEVLPED WORLD	56	4	3	1	2	3	1	5	5	2	2	2	3	3	11	2	5	1	1	0	1	2
CANADA	15	0	0	2	1	2	1	2	1	1	0	0	2	0	1	1	0	0	0	0	0	1
LATIN AMERICA	32	1	3	1	2	2	1	2	4	1	2	0	2	2	3	1	2	0	1	0	1	0
C. AMER.+CARIB.	20	1	1	1	2	2	0	3	3	1	0	0	2	2	1	1	1	0	0	0	0	0
CUBA	4	1	2	1	1	1	0	0	0	0	0	0	1	0	0	0	0	0	0	0	0	0
MEXICO	3	0	0	1	0	1	0	0	3	0	0	0	0	0	0	0	0	0	0	0	0	0
OTHER	13	0	2	0	1	0	0	3	0	1	2	0	1	2	1	1	1	0	1	0	0	0
S. AMERICA	12	0	1	0	0	0	1	0	1	0	2	0	0	0	2	1	0	0	1	0	1	0
ARGENTINA	4	0	1	0	0	0	0	0	1	0	0	0	0	0	2	0	0	0	0	0	0	0
BRAZIL	0	0	1	0	0	0	0	0	0	0	0	0	0	0	0	0	0	0	0	0	1	0
PERU	1	0	0	0	0	0	0	0	0	0	1	0	0	0	0	0	0	0	0	0	0	0
COLOMBIA	3	0	0	0	0	0	0	0	0	1	0	0	0	0	0	0	1	0	1	0	0	0
VENEZUELA	3	0	0	0	0	0	0	0	0	0	1	0	1	0	0	1	0	0	0	0	0	0
OTHER	1	0	0	0	0	0	1	0	0	0	0	0	0	0	0	0	0	0	0	0	0	0
EUROPE	80	5	4	0	3	3	2	6	3	3	10	1	6	2	5	6	7	4	6	7	0	0
EFTA	21	0	3	0	3	3	0	3	1	1	2	0	2	1	3	2	0	2	0	0	0	0
U.K.	11	0	3	0	3	3	0	3	0	0	0	0	1	1	1	0	0	0	0	0	0	0
SCANDINAVIA	0	0	0	0	0	0	0	0	0	0	0	0	0	0	0	0	0	0	0	0	0	0
SWITZERLAND	0	0	0	0	0	0	0	0	0	1	0	0	0	0	0	0	0	0	0	0	0	0
OTHER EFTA	4	0	0	0	1	0	0	0	1	0	2	0	1	0	2	0	0	0	0	0	0	0
EUROP. COMMUNITY	45	4	0	0	0	0	3	2	1	0	6	1	4	0	0	3	7	0	6	5	1	0
FRANCE	5	1	0	0	0	0	1	1	0	0	1	0	0	0	0	0	0	0	0	0	0	0
GERMANY	18	1	0	0	1	1	0	0	1	1	4	1	3	0	4	3	1	0	1	0	0	0
ITALY	16	1	0	0	0	0	0	1	1	0	1	0	0	0	0	1	4	0	4	5	0	0
BELGIUM + LUX	2	0	0	0	0	0	0	0	0	0	0	0	0	1	0	1	0	0	0	0	0	0
NETHERLANDS	4	2	0	0	0	1	0	0	1	0	0	0	1	0	1	0	1	0	0	0	1	0
SPAIN	6	0	0	0	0	0	0	0	0	0	0	0	0	0	0	0	1	0	1	0	0	0
GREECE + TURKEY	2	0	0	0	1	0	0	0	0	0	0	0	0	0	1	0	0	0	0	0	0	0
OTHER EUROPE	6	1	1	0	2	0	0	0	1	0	0	0	0	0	0	0	0	0	0	1	0	0
EUROPE EX. U.K.	69	5	1	0	3	3	2	6	3	3	8	1	5	1	6	6	7	4	6	7	0	0
SOUTHERN DOMINIONS	17	0	0	0	1	1	0	0	0	0	2	0	0	0	6	2	0	3	0	1	1	2
S. AFRICA +RHOD.	3	0	0	0	0	0	0	0	0	0	0	0	0	0	4	1	0	1	0	1	0	1
AUSTRALIA + N.Z.	14	0	0	0	1	1	0	0	0	1	2	1	1	8	4	1	0	2	0	0	1	1
ASIA + OTHER AFRICA	29	0	0	0	1	1	0	1	1	2	4	1	1	3	8	3	3	2	0	0	0	2
JAPAN	5	0	0	0	0	0	0	0	0	1	1	0	0	0	1	0	0	1	0	0	1	0
OTHER ASIA+AFR.	24	0	0	0	1	0	0	1	1	1	4	1	1	3	8	3	3	1	0	0	0	2
BLACK AFRICA	3	0	0	0	0	0	0	0	0	0	0	0	0	1	0	0	1	0	0	0	0	0
ARAB WORLD	6	0	0	0	1	0	1	0	0	0	0	1	0	1	1	0	0	0	0	0	0	1
INDIA	1	0	0	0	0	0	0	0	0	0	0	0	0	0	0	0	0	0	0	0	0	0
PHILIPPINES	3	0	0	0	0	0	0	0	0	0	2	0	0	0	1	1	0	0	0	0	0	0
OTHER E. ASIA	1	0	0	0	0	0	0	0	0	0	0	0	0	0	0	0	0	0	0	0	0	1
OTHER ASIA	10	0	0	0	1	0	0	0	0	0	3	0	0	1	3	1	0	0	0	0	1	1

CHAPTER 3- THE PROLIFERATION OF FOREIGN SUBSIDIARIES
SECTION 4- THE FLOW OF MANUFACTURING BY INDUSTRY OF SUBSIDIARY
TABLE 22- SUBSIDIARIES MANUFACTURING
OTHER PRODUCTS OF PETROLEUM AND COAL (SIC 295 AND 299)
CLASSIFIED BY COUNTRY OR REGION AND BY PERIOD MANUFACTURE BEGAN

PERIOD

COUNTRY OR REGION	PRE 1968	PRE 1901	1901-13	1914-19	1920-24	1925-29	1930-34	1935-39	1940-42	1946-50	1951-53	1954-55	1956-57	1958-59	1960-61	1962	1963	1964	1965	1966	1967	UNK
OUTSIDE U.S.	83	2	1	1	0	6	4	3	1	2	5	0	4	6	10	3	8	12	4	5	5	1
OUT. U.S. + CANADA	75	2	1	0	0	4	3	2	1	2	5	0	3	6	10	3	8	11	3	5	5	1
OUT. WEST. HEMIS.	59	2	1	0	0	4	2	2	1	1	4	0	1	5	8	2	8	10	2	2	2	1
OUT. WHITE CWEALTH	60	2	1	0	0	4	2	0	1	1	2	0	3	9	9	3	6	9	1	5	4	1
OUT. DEVLPED WORLD	22	0	0	0	0	1	1	0	0	1	1	0	2	2	4	1	2	1	1	4	1	0
CANADA	8	0	0	1	0	2	1	1	0	0	1	0	1	0	2	0	1	1	3	3	1	0
LATIN AMERICA	16	0	0	0	0	2	1	1	0	1	1	0	2	1	2	1	0	1	1	3	3	0
C. AMER.+CARIB.	5	0	0	0	0	1	1	0	0	1	0	0	1	1	2	0	0	0	0	0	0	0
CUBA	1	0	0	0	0	1	0	0	0	0	0	0	1	0	0	0	0	0	0	0	0	0
MEXICO	4	0	0	0	0	0	1	0	0	1	0	0	1	1	2	0	0	0	0	1	0	0
OTHER	0	0	0	0	0	0	0	0	0	0	0	0	0	0	0	0	0	0	0	0	0	0
S. AMERICA	11	0	0	0	0	1	0	1	0	0	1	0	1	0	0	1	1	0	1	3	3	0
ARGENTINA	1	0	0	0	0	0	1	0	0	0	0	0	1	0	0	0	0	0	0	0	0	0
BRAZIL	5	0	0	0	0	1	0	0	0	0	0	0	0	0	1	0	1	0	1	3	3	0
PERU	1	0	0	0	0	0	0	0	0	0	0	0	1	0	0	0	0	0	0	0	0	0
COLOMBIA	1	0	0	0	0	0	0	0	0	0	1	0	0	0	0	0	0	0	0	0	0	0
VENEZUELA	2	0	0	0	0	0	0	0	0	0	0	0	0	1	1	0	0	0	0	0	0	0
OTHER	1	0	0	0	0	0	0	1	0	1	0	0	0	0	0	0	0	0	0	0	0	0
EUROPE	39	2	1	0	0	3	2	2	1	1	2	0	1	3	4	1	0	1	1	1	1	0
EFTA	15	2	1	0	0	3	2	2	1	1	1	0	0	0	0	0	0	0	0	0	0	0
U.K.	8	0	1	0	0	3	1	2	0	1	0	0	0	0	0	0	0	0	0	0	0	0
SCANDINAVIA	7	0	0	0	0	0	1	0	0	0	1	0	0	0	0	0	0	0	0	0	0	0
SWITZERLAND	0	0	1	0	0	0	0	0	0	0	0	0	0	0	0	0	0	0	0	0	0	0
OTHER EFTA	0	0	0	0	0	0	0	0	0	0	0	0	0	0	0	0	0	0	0	0	0	0
EUROP. COMMUNITY	19	2	0	0	0	2	1	0	0	0	0	0	1	3	4	1	0	1	0	1	0	0
FRANCE	6	2	0	0	0	0	0	0	0	0	0	0	1	1	1	0	0	0	0	0	1	0
GERMANY	6	2	0	0	0	1	0	0	1	0	0	0	0	0	2	1	0	0	1	0	0	0
ITALY	2	0	0	0	0	1	0	0	0	0	0	0	0	1	0	0	0	0	0	0	0	0
BELGIUM + LUX	4	0	0	0	0	0	1	0	0	0	0	0	0	1	0	0	0	2	0	0	0	0
NETHERLANDS	1	0	0	0	0	0	0	0	0	0	0	0	0	0	1	0	0	0	0	0	0	0
SPAIN	3	0	0	0	0	0	0	0	0	0	0	0	0	0	0	0	0	0	0	0	1	1
GREECE + TURKEY	1	0	0	0	0	0	0	0	0	0	0	0	0	0	0	1	0	0	0	0	0	0
OTHER EUROPE	1	0	0	1	0	1	0	0	0	0	0	0	0	0	0	0	0	0	1	0	0	0
EUROPE EX. U.K.	31	2	1	0	0	3	1	0	1	0	2	0	1	3	4	1	0	1	1	1	0	0
SOUTHERN DOMINIONS	6	0	0	0	0	0	0	0	0	0	2	0	0	1	1	0	0	0	1	0	1	0
S. AFRICA +RHOD.	1	0	0	0	0	0	0	0	0	0	0	0	0	1	0	0	0	0	0	0	0	0
AUSTRALIA + N.Z.	5	0	0	0	0	0	0	0	0	0	2	0	0	0	1	0	0	0	1	0	3	0
ASIA + OTHER AFRICA	14	0	0	0	0	0	0	0	0	0	0	0	0	1	3	2	2	0	0	1	0	0
JAPAN	8	0	0	0	0	0	0	0	0	0	0	0	0	0	1	0	2	0	1	0	0	0
OTHER ASIA+AFR.	6	0	0	0	0	0	0	1	0	0	0	0	0	1	2	2	0	0	1	0	0	0
BLACK AFRICA	1	0	0	0	0	0	0	0	0	0	0	0	0	1	1	0	0	0	0	0	0	0
ARAB WORLD	0	0	0	0	0	0	0	0	0	0	0	0	0	0	0	0	0	0	1	0	0	0
INDIA	3	0	0	0	0	0	0	1	0	0	0	0	0	0	1	0	0	0	0	0	0	0
PHILIPPINES	1	0	0	0	0	0	0	0	0	0	0	0	0	0	0	1	0	0	0	0	0	0
OTHER E. ASIA	1	0	0	0	0	0	0	0	0	0	0	0	0	0	0	0	0	0	0	0	0	0
OTHER ASIA	0	0	0	0	0	0	0	0	0	0	0	0	0	0	0	0	0	0	0	0	0	0

CHAPTER 3- THE PROLIFERATION OF FOREIGN SUBSIDIARIES
SECTION 4- THE FLOW OF MANUFACTURING BY INDUSTRY OF SUBSIDIARY
TABLE 23- SUBSIDIARIES MANUFACTURING
TIRES (SIC 301)
CLASSIFIED BY COUNTRY OR REGION AND BY PERIOD MANUFACTURE BEGAN

PERIOD

COUNTRY OR REGION	PRE 1968	PRE 1901	1901 -13	1914 -19	1920 -24	1925 -29	1930 -34	1935 -39	1940 -45	1946 -50	1951 -53	1954 -55	1956 -57	1958 -59	1960 -61	1962	1963	1964	1965	1966	1967	UNK
OUTSIDE U.S.	98	0	2	2	3	3	8	12	12	12	5	4	1	11	7	3	4	2	2	4	1	0
OUT. U.S. + CANADA	91	0	2	1	2	2	7	12	12	12	5	3	1	11	7	3	4	1	1	4	1	0
OUT. WEST. HEMIS.	58	0	0	1	2	2	2	8	14	6	3	3	0	9	6	3	3	1	2	4	1	0
OUT. WHITE CWEALTH	78	0	0	1	2	2	7	10	10	7	2	2	1	9	7	3	2	1	1	3	1	0
OUT. DEVLPED WORLD	48	0	0	0	0	0	5	7	9	7	2	2	1	4	2	2	2	1	2	1	1	0
CANADA	7	0	2	1	1	1	1	0	0	0	0	1	0	0	0	0	0	1	0	0	1	0
LATIN AMERICA	33	0	0	1	0	0	0	4	8	6	2	0	1	2	1	0	1	0	2	2	0	0
C. AMER.+CARIB.	13	0	0	0	0	0	1	2	2	2	0	0	1	1	0	0	0	0	2	0	0	0
CUBA	6	0	0	0	0	0	0	1	0	0	0	0	1	0	1	0	0	0	2	0	0	0
MEXICO	4	0	0	0	0	0	1	0	1	1	0	0	0	1	0	0	0	0	0	0	0	0
OTHER	3	0	0	0	0	0	0	1	1	1	0	0	0	0	0	0	0	0	0	0	0	0
S. AMERICA	20	0	0	0	0	0	0	3	6	4	2	0	0	1	1	0	1	0	0	2	0	0
ARGENTINA	4	0	0	0	0	0	0	2	0	2	0	0	0	0	0	0	0	0	0	0	0	0
BRAZIL	5	0	0	0	0	0	0	0	2	0	0	1	0	1	0	0	1	0	0	0	0	0
PERU	2	0	0	0	0	0	0	0	0	2	0	0	0	0	0	0	0	0	0	0	0	0
COLOMBIA	3	0	0	0	0	0	0	0	0	0	2	0	0	1	0	0	0	0	0	0	0	0
VENEZUELA	4	0	0	0	0	0	0	1	2	0	0	0	0	0	1	0	0	0	0	0	0	0
OTHER	2	0	0	0	0	0	1	0	0	0	0	0	0	0	1	0	0	0	0	0	0	0
EUROPE	31	0	0	2	1	1	3	3	4	4	3	2	0	6	4	1	0	0	0	2	0	0
EFTA	10	0	0	1	1	1	2	2	1	1	0	0	0	2	1	0	1	0	0	1	0	0
U.K.	4	0	0	0	0	0	0	0	0	1	0	0	0	1	0	1	0	0	0	1	1	0
SCANDINAVIA	2	0	0	0	0	0	0	0	1	0	0	0	0	1	0	0	0	0	0	0	0	0
SWITZERLAND	1	0	0	0	0	0	0	0	0	0	0	0	0	0	0	0	1	0	0	0	0	0
OTHER EFTA	3	0	0	0	0	0	1	1	0	0	0	0	0	0	1	0	0	0	0	0	0	0
EUROP. COMMUNITY	16	0	0	1	0	0	1	0	1	3	2	1	0	2	2	0	0	0	0	0	0	0
FRANCE	4	0	0	1	0	0	0	0	0	0	1	1	0	0	1	0	0	0	0	0	0	0
GERMANY	6	0	0	0	0	0	0	0	1	1	0	0	0	2	0	0	0	0	0	1	0	0
ITALY	2	0	0	0	0	0	0	0	0	0	1	0	0	1	0	0	0	0	0	0	0	0
BELGIUM + LUX	2	0	0	0	0	0	0	0	0	0	0	1	0	1	0	0	0	0	0	0	0	0
NETHERLANDS	2	0	0	0	0	0	0	0	0	1	0	0	0	0	1	0	0	0	0	0	0	0
SPAIN	2	0	0	0	0	0	0	0	0	0	0	0	0	0	0	0	0	0	0	1	1	0
GREECE + TURKEY	1	0	0	0	0	0	0	0	0	0	1	0	0	0	1	0	0	0	0	0	0	0
OTHER EUROPE	2	0	0	0	0	0	0	0	0	0	0	0	0	0	0	1	0	0	0	0	0	0
EUROPE EX. U.K.	27	0	0	2	1	1	3	3	1	3	3	2	0	5	4	1	1	0	0	2	0	0
SOUTHERN DOMINIONS	9	0	0	0	0	0	2	2	1	1	0	0	0	1	0	0	1	0	0	0	0	0
S. AFRICA +RHOD.	3	0	0	0	0	0	1	1	1	1	0	0	0	0	0	0	0	0	0	0	0	0
AUSTRALIA + N.Z.	6	0	0	0	0	0	1	1	0	0	0	0	0	1	2	1	1	0	0	0	0	0
ASIA + OTHER AFRICA	18	0	0	0	0	0	3	3	0	1	0	0	0	2	1	2	2	1	0	0	0	0
JAPAN	3	0	0	0	0	0	0	0	0	0	0	0	0	0	0	0	1	1	0	0	0	0
OTHER ASIA+AFR.	15	0	0	0	1	0	3	3	0	1	0	0	0	2	1	1	1	0	0	0	1	0
BLACK AFRICA	2	0	0	0	0	0	0	0	0	0	0	0	0	0	0	0	1	0	0	0	1	0
ARAB WORLD	2	0	0	0	0	0	0	1	1	1	0	0	0	0	0	0	0	0	0	0	0	0
INDIA	2	0	0	0	0	0	0	0	0	0	0	0	0	1	1	0	0	0	0	0	0	0
PHILIPPINES	3	0	0	0	0	0	1	1	0	0	0	0	0	1	1	0	0	0	0	0	0	0
OTHER E. ASIA	0	0	0	0	0	0	0	0	0	0	0	0	0	0	0	0	0	0	0	0	0	0
OTHER ASIA	6	0	0	0	0	0	1	0	0	1	0	0	0	1	1	1	1	0	0	0	0	0

CHAPTER 3- THE PROLIFERATION OF FOREIGN SUBSIDIARIES
SECTION 4— THE FLOW OF MANUFACTURING BY INDUSTRY OF SUBSIDIARY
TABLE 24— SUBSIDIARIES MANUFACTURING
OTHER RUBBER PRODUCTS (OTHER SIC 30)
CLASSIFIED BY COUNTRY OR REGION AND BY PERIOD MANUFACTURE BEGAN

PERIOD

COUNTRY OR REGION	PRE 1968	PRE 1901	1901 -13	1914 -19	1920 -24	1925 -29	1930 -34	1935 -39	1940 -45	1946 -50	1951 -53	1954 -55	1956 -57	1958 -59	1960 -61	1962 -63	1964	1965	1966	1967	UNK
OUTSIDE U.S.	88	1	2	2	4	4	4	3	9	4	5	6	2	5	7	7	4	10	4	0	2
OUT. U.S. + CANADA	75	1	0	1	4	4	4	3	9	4	2	4	2	5	6	3	2	10	4	0	1
OUT. WEST. HEMIS.	47	1	0	1	4	3	3	3	6	2	4	1	2	3	5	2	2	9	3	0	1
OUT. WHITE CWEALTH	53	0	0	0	3	0	3	3	6	1	2	4	2	3	3	2	2	8	1	0	1
OUT. DEVLPED WORLD	34	0	0	0	0	0	3	3	6	1	2	3	2	3	1	2	2	4	1	0	1
CANADA	13	0	2	1	0	1	0	0	0	1	1	2	0	0	1	0	2	0	0	0	1
LATIN AMERICA	28	0	0	0	1	3	2	2	6	1	2	3	1	2	1	1	2	1	1	0	1
C. AMER.+CARIB.	13	0	0	0	0	2	1	1	2	1	0	2	0	0	0	0	0	1	0	0	0
CUBA	2	0	0	0	0	0	0	0	1	0	1	0	0	0	0	0	0	0	0	0	0
MEXICO	9	0	0	0	0	2	1	1	1	1	0	2	0	0	0	0	0	1	0	0	0
OTHER	2	0	0	0	0	0	0	0	0	0	0	0	0	0	0	1	0	0	0	0	0
S. AMERICA	15	0	0	0	1	1	1	1	4	0	1	0	0	2	1	1	0	0	1	0	1
ARGENTINA	3	0	0	0	0	0	0	0	0	0	0	0	0	0	1	0	0	0	0	0	1
BRAZIL	4	0	0	0	0	0	1	1	0	0	1	1	0	0	1	0	0	0	0	0	0
PERU	2	0	0	0	0	0	0	0	0	0	0	0	0	0	0	1	0	0	1	0	0
COLOMBIA	1	0	0	0	0	0	0	0	1	0	0	0	0	0	0	0	0	0	0	0	0
VENEZUELA	5	0	0	0	0	0	0	0	2	0	0	0	1	0	0	1	0	1	0	0	0
OTHER	0	0	0	0	0	0	0	0	0	0	0	0	0	0	0	0	0	0	0	0	0
EUROPE	28	1	0	0	4	1	1	0	2	2	1	1	0	1	3	1	5	5	1	0	0
EFTA	11	0	0	0	2	1	1	0	1	1	0	0	0	1	2	1	1	1	0	0	0
U.K.	8	0	0	0	1	1	1	0	1	0	0	0	0	0	1	1	1	1	0	0	0
SCANDINAVIA	3	0	0	0	1	0	0	0	0	1	0	0	0	0	1	0	0	0	0	0	0
SWITZERLAND	0	0	0	0	0	0	0	0	0	0	0	0	0	0	0	0	0	0	0	0	0
OTHER EFTA	0	0	0	0	0	0	0	0	0	0	0	0	0	0	0	0	0	0	0	0	0
EUROP. COMMUNITY	9	0	0	0	2	0	0	0	0	0	0	0	0	0	1	0	2	2	0	0	0
FRANCE	2	0	0	0	1	0	0	0	0	0	0	0	0	0	0	0	1	0	0	0	0
GERMANY	3	0	0	0	1	0	0	0	0	0	0	0	0	0	1	0	0	1	0	0	0
ITALY	2	0	0	0	0	0	0	0	0	0	0	0	0	0	0	0	1	1	0	0	0
BELGIUM + LUX	0	0	0	0	0	0	0	0	0	0	0	0	0	0	0	0	0	0	0	0	0
NETHERLANDS	2	0	0	0	0	0	0	0	0	0	0	0	0	0	0	0	0	0	0	0	0
SPAIN	4	0	0	0	0	0	0	0	1	0	0	0	0	1	0	0	0	0	1	1	0
GREECE + TURKEY	0	0	0	0	0	0	0	0	0	0	0	0	0	0	0	0	0	0	0	0	0
OTHER EUROPE	4	1	0	0	0	0	0	0	0	0	0	0	0	1	0	1	0	1	1	0	0
EUROPE EX. U.K.	20	1	0	0	3	0	0	1	1	1	1	1	0	1	2	0	4	4	1	0	0
SOUTHERN DOMINIONS	10	0	0	0	0	2	0	0	2	0	0	0	0	1	2	0	0	0	2	0	0
S. AFRICA +RHOD.	3	0	0	0	0	0	0	0	1	0	0	0	0	0	1	0	0	0	2	0	0
AUSTRALIA + N.Z.	7	0	0	1	0	2	0	0	1	0	0	0	0	1	1	0	4	4	0	0	0
ASIA + OTHER AFRICA	9	0	0	1	0	0	0	1	0	0	1	0	0	1	0	1	1	1	0	0	0
JAPAN	3	0	0	0	0	0	0	0	0	0	0	0	0	0	0	0	0	3	0	0	0
OTHER ASIA+AFR.	6	0	0	1	0	0	0	1	0	0	1	0	0	1	1	1	0	1	0	0	0
BLACK AFRICA	1	0	0	0	0	0	0	0	0	0	0	0	0	1	0	0	0	0	0	0	0
ARAB WORLD	2	0	0	0	0	0	0	0	0	0	0	0	0	0	1	1	0	0	0	0	0
INDIA	1	0	0	0	0	0	0	0	0	0	1	0	0	0	0	0	0	0	0	0	0
PHILIPPINES	0	0	0	0	0	0	0	0	0	0	0	0	0	0	0	0	0	0	0	0	0
OTHER E. ASIA	1	0	0	0	0	0	0	0	0	0	0	0	0	1	0	0	0	1	0	0	0
OTHER ASIA	1	0	0	0	0	0	0	1	0	0	0	0	0	0	0	0	0	0	0	0	0

CHAPTER 3- THE PROLIFERATION OF FOREIGN SUBSIDIARIES
SECTION 4- THE FLOW OF MANUFACTURING BY INDUSTRY OF SUBSIDIARY
TABLE 25- SUBSIDIARIES MANUFACTURING
GLASS PRODUCTS (SIC 321-323)
CLASSIFIED BY COUNTRY OR REGION AND BY PERIOD MANUFACTURE BEGAN

PERIOD

COUNTRY OR REGION	PRE 1968	PRE 1901	1901 -13	1914 -19	1920 -24	1925 -29	1930 -34	1935 -39	1940 -45	1946 -50	1951 -53	1954 -55	1956 -57	1958 -59	1960 -61	1962	1963	1964	1965	1966	1967	UNK
OUTSIDE U.S.	53	0	1	1	1	1	0	1	7	3	3	2	2	5	5	2	4	1	5	4	6	1
OUT. U.S. + CANADA	48	0	1	1	1	0	1	1	6	2	2	2	1	4	5	2	4	1	5	4	6	0
OUT. WEST. HEMIS.	26	0	1	1	1	0	1	1	6	1	2	0	0	3	4	2	4	1	3	4	3	0
OUT. WHITE CWEALTH	39	0	1	1	1	0	1	0	6	0	2	2	0	3	3	2	4	1	4	1	5	0
OUT. DEVLPED WORLD	24	0	0	1	0	0	1	0	6	1	2	2	0	1	1	1	3	1	2	0	3	0
CANADA	5	0	0	0	0	0	0	0	1	1	0	0	0	1	1	0	0	0	0	0	0	1
LATIN AMERICA	22	0	0	0	0	1	1	0	6	1	0	2	0	1	1	0	3	0	0	2	3	1
C. AMER.+CARIB.	5	0	0	0	0	0	0	0	0	1	2	1	1	1	1	0	0	1	0	0	3	0
CUBA	1	0	0	0	0	0	0	0	0	0	0	0	0	0	0	0	0	0	0	0	0	0
MEXICO	4	0	0	0	0	0	0	0	0	0	0	0	0	0	0	0	0	0	0	0	3	0
OTHER	0	0	0	0	0	0	0	0	0	0	0	0	0	0	0	0	0	0	0	0	0	0
S. AMERICA	17	0	0	0	0	0	0	0	6	1	0	1	0	1	1	0	3	0	0	2	0	0
ARGENTINA	1	0	0	0	0	0	0	0	1	0	0	0	0	0	0	0	0	0	0	0	0	0
BRAZIL	5	0	0	0	0	0	0	0	3	0	0	0	0	0	0	0	0	0	0	2	0	0
PERU	0	0	0	0	0	0	0	0	0	0	0	0	0	0	0	0	0	0	0	0	0	0
COLOMBIA	4	0	0	0	0	0	0	0	0	1	0	0	0	1	1	0	2	0	0	0	0	0
VENEZUELA	5	0	0	0	0	0	0	0	0	0	0	0	0	0	1	1	1	0	2	0	0	0
OTHER	2	0	0	0	0	0	0	0	2	0	0	0	0	0	0	0	0	0	0	0	0	0
EUROPE	17	1	0	0	0	0	1	0	0	1	0	1	0	3	1	1	1	0	2	1	3	0
EFTA	5	0	0	0	0	0	0	0	0	0	0	1	1	1	1	0	0	0	1	1	1	0
U.K.	5	0	0	0	0	0	0	0	0	0	0	1	1	1	1	0	0	0	1	1	1	0
SCANDINAVIA	0	0	0	0	0	0	0	0	0	0	0	0	0	0	0	0	0	0	0	0	0	0
SWITZERLAND	0	0	0	0	0	0	0	0	0	0	0	0	0	0	0	0	0	0	0	0	0	0
OTHER EFTA	0	0	0	0	0	0	0	0	0	0	0	0	0	0	0	0	0	0	0	0	0	0
EUROP. COMMUNITY	11	1	1	1	1	0	1	0	0	1	0	0	0	2	0	1	0	0	0	0	0	0
FRANCE	2	0	0	0	0	0	0	0	0	0	0	0	0	2	0	0	0	0	0	0	0	0
GERMANY	4	0	0	1	1	0	1	0	0	1	0	0	0	0	0	1	0	0	0	1	0	0
ITALY	3	1	0	0	0	0	0	0	0	0	0	0	0	0	1	0	1	0	0	0	1	0
BELGIUM + LUX	2	0	1	0	0	0	0	0	0	0	0	0	0	0	1	0	0	0	0	0	0	0
NETHERLANDS	0	0	0	0	0	0	0	0	0	0	0	0	0	0	0	0	0	0	0	0	0	0
SPAIN	1	0	0	0	0	0	0	0	0	0	0	0	0	0	1	0	0	0	0	0	1	0
GREECE + TURKEY	0	0	0	0	0	0	0	0	0	0	0	0	0	0	0	0	0	0	0	0	0	0
OTHER EUROPE	0	0	0	0	0	0	0	0	0	0	0	0	0	0	0	0	0	0	0	0	0	0
EUROPE EX. U.K.	12	1	1	1	1	1	1	0	1	0	0	0	0	2	1	1	1	0	1	0	2	0
SOUTHERN DOMINIONS	4	0	0	0	0	0	0	0	0	0	0	0	0	0	2	0	0	0	0	2	0	0
S. AFRICA +RHOD.	2	0	0	0	1	0	0	0	0	0	0	0	0	0	0	0	0	0	0	0	0	0
AUSTRALIA + N.Z.	2	0	0	0	0	0	0	0	0	0	0	0	0	0	2	0	0	0	0	0	0	0
ASIA + OTHER AFRICA	5	0	0	0	1	0	1	0	0	0	0	0	0	0	1	1	0	0	1	0	0	0
JAPAN	3	0	0	0	0	0	0	0	0	0	0	0	0	0	1	0	0	0	1	1	0	0
OTHER ASIA+AFR.	2	0	0	0	1	0	1	0	0	0	0	0	0	0	0	0	0	0	0	0	0	0
BLACK AFRICA	0	0	0	0	0	0	0	0	0	0	0	0	0	0	0	0	0	0	0	0	0	0
ARAB WORLD	0	0	0	0	0	0	0	0	0	0	0	0	0	0	0	0	0	0	0	0	0	0
INDIA	1	0	0	0	0	0	0	0	0	0	0	0	0	0	0	0	0	0	0	0	0	0
PHILIPPINES	1	0	0	0	1	0	0	0	0	0	0	0	0	0	0	0	0	0	0	0	0	0
OTHER E. ASIA	1	0	0	0	1	0	1	0	0	0	0	0	0	0	0	0	0	0	0	0	0	0
OTHER ASIA	0	0	0	0	0	0	0	0	0	0	0	0	0	0	0	0	0	0	0	0	0	0

CHAPTER 3- THE PROLIFERATION OF FOREIGN SUBSIDIARIES
SECTION 4- THE FLOW OF MANUFACTURING BY INDUSTRY OF SUBSIDIARY
TABLE 26- SUBSIDIARIES MANUFACTURING
STONE, CLAY, AND CONCRETE PRODUCTS (SIC 324-329)
CLASSIFIED BY COUNTRY OR REGION AND BY PERIOD MANUFACTURE BEGAN

COUNTRY OR REGION	PRE 1968	PRE 1901	1901 -13	1914 -19	1920 -24	1925 -29	1930 -34	1935 -39	1940 -45	1946 -50	1951 -53	1954 -55	1956 -57	1958 -59	1960 -61	1962 -63	1964	1965	1966	1967	UNK
OUTSIDE U.S.	132	0	3	1	1	6	1	5	3	6	15	11	10	9	16	8	5	2	11	12	1
OUT. U.S. + CANADA	119	0	3	1	1	5	1	5	2	5	12	10	9	8	15	8	5	2	11	10	1
OUT. WEST. HEMIS.	86	0	3	1	1	5	1	5	2	3	8	7	2	4	13	5	5	1	11	8	1
OUT. WHITE CWEALTH	88	0	1	0	1	4	1	2	1	2	7	8	9	6	11	4	4	2	9	6	1
OUT. DEVLPED WORLD	42	0	0	0	0	1	0	0	2	2	5	4	7	4	5	1	1	1	2	2	1
CANADA	13	0	0	1	0	1	0	0	1	1	3	1	1	1	1	0	0	0	0	2	0
LATIN AMERICA	33	0	0	0	0	1	2	1	2	1	3	3	1	4	2	1	2	1	0	2	0
C. AMER.+CARIB.	12	0	0	0	0	1	1	1	2	1	3	1	1	1	2	0	1	0	0	1	0
CUBA	0	0	0	0	0	0	0	0	0	0	0	0	0	0	0	0	0	0	0	0	0
MEXICO	12	0	0	0	0	1	1	1	1	0	3	1	1	1	2	0	1	0	0	1	0
OTHER	0	0	0	0	0	0	0	0	0	0	0	0	0	0	0	0	0	0	0	0	0
S. AMERICA	21	0	0	0	0	1	1	0	1	0	2	2	0	3	1	1	1	1	0	1	0
ARGENTINA	5	0	0	0	0	1	0	0	0	0	0	0	0	1	1	0	1	0	0	0	0
BRAZIL	7	0	0	0	1	0	1	0	0	0	2	0	1	1	1	0	0	0	0	0	0
PERU	1	0	0	0	0	0	0	0	0	0	0	0	0	0	0	0	0	0	0	1	0
COLOMBIA	1	0	0	0	0	0	0	0	0	0	0	1	0	0	0	0	0	0	0	0	0
VENEZUELA	2	0	0	0	0	0	0	0	0	0	0	0	1	0	0	1	0	0	0	0	0
OTHER	5	0	0	0	1	0	0	0	1	0	0	1	0	1	0	0	0	1	0	0	0
EUROPE	55	0	3	1	1	4	2	2	0	2	6	4	2	3	7	3	4	1	1	6	4
EFTA	15	0	2	0	0	2	1	1	0	0	2	0	0	1	1	1	1	0	2	1	1
U.K.	12	0	2	0	0	1	1	1	0	0	2	0	0	1	1	1	1	0	1	1	1
SCANDINAVIA	0	0	0	0	0	0	0	0	0	0	0	0	0	0	0	0	0	0	0	0	0
SWITZERLAND	0	0	0	0	0	0	0	0	0	0	0	0	0	0	0	0	0	0	0	0	0
OTHER EFTA	0	0	0	0	0	1	0	1	0	0	0	0	0	0	0	0	0	0	1	0	0
EUROP. COMMUNITY	33	0	1	1	0	0	1	1	0	2	3	4	2	2	4	3	1	1	0	1	1
FRANCE	17	0	0	1	0	0	0	0	0	1	1	3	0	1	4	1	1	1	0	1	1
GERMANY	6	0	1	0	0	1	0	0	0	0	0	1	1	1	0	1	0	0	0	0	0
ITALY	3	0	0	0	0	0	0	0	0	0	0	0	0	0	1	0	1	0	1	0	0
BELGIUM + LUX	6	0	0	0	0	0	0	0	0	0	1	1	1	0	1	0	1	0	0	1	0
NETHERLANDS	1	0	0	0	0	0	0	0	0	0	0	0	0	0	0	0	0	0	0	0	1
SPAIN	3	0	0	0	0	0	0	0	0	0	0	0	0	0	1	0	1	0	0	1	0
GREECE + TURKEY	1	0	0	0	0	0	1	0	0	0	0	0	0	0	0	0	0	0	0	0	0
OTHER EUROPE	3	0	1	0	0	0	0	0	0	0	0	0	0	1	0	1	0	0	1	1	0
EUROPE EX. U.K.	43	0	1	1	1	3	1	1	0	2	4	4	2	2	6	4	2	1	1	5	3
SOUTHERN DOMINIONS	17	0	0	0	0	3	0	0	1	1	1	2	0	1	3	1	1	0	1	3	0
S. AFRICA +RHOD.	5	0	0	0	0	0	0	0	1	1	1	1	0	1	0	1	0	0	0	0	0
AUSTRALIA + N.Z.	12	0	0	0	0	3	0	3	0	0	0	1	0	1	3	1	1	0	0	3	1
ASIA + OTHER AFRICA	14	0	0	0	0	0	0	0	0	0	0	1	0	0	3	2	2	4	0	3	1
JAPAN	5	0	0	0	0	0	0	0	0	0	0	0	0	0	3	1	1	2	0	2	0
OTHER ASIA+AFR.	9	0	0	0	0	0	0	0	0	2	0	1	0	0	0	1	1	2	0	1	0
BLACK AFRICA	1	0	0	0	0	0	0	0	0	0	0	1	0	0	0	0	0	0	0	0	0
ARAB WORLD	1	0	0	0	0	0	0	0	0	0	0	0	1	0	0	0	0	0	0	0	1
INDIA	4	0	0	0	0	0	0	0	0	1	0	0	1	0	0	0	1	0	0	1	0
PHILIPPINES	1	0	0	0	0	0	0	0	0	0	0	0	0	0	0	0	0	0	0	0	1
OTHER E. ASIA	0	0	0	0	0	0	0	0	0	0	0	0	0	0	0	0	0	0	0	0	0
OTHER ASIA	2	0	0	0	0	0	0	0	0	0	0	0	0	0	1	0	0	0	1	0	0

CHAPTER 3- THE PROLIFERATION OF FOREIGN SUBSIDIARIES
SECTION 4- THE FLOW OF MANUFACTURING BY INDUSTRY OF SUBSIDIARY
TABLE 27- SUBSIDIARIES MANUFACTURING
SMELTED AND REFINED NONFERROUS METALS (SIC 333)
CLASSIFIED BY COUNTRY OR REGION AND BY PERIOD MANUFACTURE BEGAN

PERIOD

COUNTRY OR REGION	PRE 1968	PRE 1901	1901 -13	1914 -19	1920 -24	1925 -29	1930 -34	1935 -39	1940 -45	1946 -50	1951 -53	1954 -55	1956 -57	1958 -59	1960 -61	1962	1963	1964	1965	1966	1967	UNK
OUTSIDE U.S.	66	1	2	1	2	5	3	4	0	1	2	1	3	13	9	2	4	4	6	1	2	0
OUT. U.S. + CANADA	51	1	1	1	0	0	3	3	0	0	1	1	3	11	6	2	4	3	5	1	2	0
OUT. WEST. HEMIS.	38	1	0	0	0	0	2	1	0	0	1	1	1	7	5	2	4	3	2	1	1	0
OUT. WHITE CWEALTH	32	1	1	1	2	0	1	2	0	0	0	1	2	7	3	1	3	3	2	1	1	0
OUT. DEVLPED WORLD	19	0	1	1	2	0	1	2	0	0	0	1	2	3	2	0	2	0	1	0	1	0
CANADA	15	0	1	0	0	5	0	1	0	1	0	0	2	3	3	0	1	1	1	0	0	0
LATIN AMERICA	13	0	1	1	2	0	1	2	0	0	1	0	2	2	1	0	0	0	1	1	1	0
C. AMER.-+CARIB.	4	0	1	0	0	0	1	0	0	0	0	0	0	2	0	0	0	0	0	0	0	0
CUBA	0	0	0	0	0	0	0	0	0	0	0	0	0	0	0	0	0	0	0	0	0	0
MEXICO	4	0	1	0	0	0	1	0	0	0	0	0	0	1	0	0	0	0	0	1	0	0
OTHER	0	0	0	0	0	0	0	0	0	0	0	0	0	0	0	0	0	0	0	0	0	0
S. AMERICA	9	0	0	1	2	0	0	0	0	0	1	2	2	1	1	0	0	0	1	0	0	0
ARGENTINA	3	0	0	1	0	0	1	0	0	0	0	0	0	1	0	0	0	0	0	0	0	0
BRAZIL	2	0	0	0	1	0	0	0	0	0	0	0	0	1	0	0	0	0	1	0	0	0
PERU	1	0	0	0	0	0	0	0	0	0	0	0	1	0	0	0	0	0	0	0	0	0
COLOMBIA	1	0	0	0	0	0	0	0	0	0	0	0	0	0	0	0	0	0	0	0	0	0
VENEZUELA	1	0	0	0	1	0	0	0	0	0	0	0	0	1	0	0	0	0	0	0	0	0
OTHER	1	0	0	0	0	0	0	0	0	0	0	1	0	0	1	0	0	0	0	0	0	0
EUROPE	20	1	0	0	0	0	1	0	0	0	1	1	1	7	2	1	2	2	2	1	1	0
EFTA	14	0	0	0	0	0	1	1	0	0	1	1	1	6	1	0	1	1	1	1	1	0
U.K.	9	0	0	0	0	0	1	0	0	0	0	0	0	3	1	0	1	0	1	0	1	0
SCANDINAVIA	3	0	0	0	0	0	0	0	0	0	1	0	0	2	0	0	0	1	0	0	0	0
SWITZERLAND	2	0	0	0	0	0	0	0	0	0	0	0	0	1	1	0	0	0	0	1	0	0
OTHER EFTA	0	0	0	0	0	0	0	0	0	0	0	0	0	0	0	0	0	0	0	0	0	0
EUROP. COMMUNITY	5	1	0	0	0	0	0	0	0	0	0	0	0	0	0	1	0	1	1	0	0	0
FRANCE	3	1	0	0	0	0	0	0	0	0	0	0	0	1	0	0	1	0	0	0	0	0
GERMANY	0	0	0	0	0	0	0	0	0	0	0	0	0	0	0	0	0	1	0	0	0	0
ITALY	2	0	0	0	0	0	0	0	0	0	0	0	1	0	1	1	0	0	1	0	1	0
BELGIUM + LUX	0	0	0	0	0	0	0	0	0	0	0	0	0	0	0	0	0	0	0	0	0	0
NETHERLANDS	0	1	0	0	0	0	0	0	0	0	0	0	0	0	0	0	0	0	0	0	0	0
SPAIN	1	0	0	0	0	0	0	0	0	0	0	0	0	0	1	0	0	0	0	0	0	0
GREECE + TURKEY	0	0	0	0	0	0	0	0	0	0	0	0	0	0	0	1	0	0	0	1	0	0
OTHER EUROPE	0	0	0	0	0	0	0	0	0	0	0	0	0	0	0	0	0	0	0	0	0	0
EUROPE EX. U.K.	11	1	0	0	0	0	0	0	0	0	1	1	1	4	1	1	0	2	1	1	1	0
SOUTHERN DOMINIONS	10	0	0	0	0	0	0	0	0	0	0	0	0	1	2	1	1	0	3	0	0	0
S. AFRICA +RHOD.	3	0	0	0	0	0	1	0	0	0	0	0	0	0	0	1	0	0	1	0	1	0
AUSTRALIA + N.Z.	7	0	0	0	0	0	1	0	0	0	0	0	0	1	2	0	1	1	2	0	0	0
ASIA + OTHER AFRICA	8	0	0	0	0	0	0	0	0	0	0	0	0	2	1	0	3	1	0	1	0	0
JAPAN	2	0	0	0	0	0	0	0	0	0	0	0	0	1	0	0	1	1	0	0	0	0
OTHER ASIA+AFR.	6	0	0	0	0	0	0	0	0	0	0	0	0	1	1	0	2	0	0	0	1	0
BLACK AFRICA	2	0	0	0	0	0	0	0	0	0	0	0	0	1	0	0	0	0	0	0	0	0
ARAB WORLD	2	0	0	0	0	0	0	0	0	0	0	0	0	0	1	0	0	0	0	0	1	0
INDIA	1	0	0	0	0	0	0	0	0	0	0	0	0	1	0	0	0	0	0	0	0	0
PHILIPPINES	0	0	0	0	0	0	0	0	0	0	0	0	0	0	0	0	0	0	0	0	0	0
OTHER E. ASIA	0	0	0	0	0	0	0	0	0	0	0	0	0	0	0	0	0	0	0	0	0	0
OTHER ASIA	3	0	0	0	0	0	0	0	0	0	0	0	0	0	0	0	2	0	0	0	1	0

CHAPTER 3- THE PROLIFERATION OF FOREIGN SUBSIDIARIES
SECTION 4- THE FLOW OF MANUFACTURING BY INDUSTRY OF SUBSIDIARY
TABLE 28- SUBSIDIARIES MANUFACTURING
OTHER NONFERROUS METAL PRODUCTS (SIC 334-336)
CLASSIFIED BY COUNTRY OR REGION AND BY PERIOD MANUFACTURE BEGAN

COUNTRY OR REGION	PRE 1968	PRE 1901	1901 -13	1914 -19	1920 -24	1925 -29	1930 -34	1935 -39	1940 -45	1946 -50	1951 -53	1954 -55	1956 -57	1958 -59	1960 -61	1962	1963	1964	1965	1966	1967	UNK
OUTSIDE U.S.	54	0	0	2	0	2	0	1	0	3	0	2	5	8	10	3	4	4	2	3	4	1
OUT. U.S. + CANADA	38	0	0	1	0	0	0	0	0	1	0	0	2	8	9	2	4	2	2	3	3	1
OUT. WEST. HEMIS.	27	0	0	1	0	0	0	0	0	0	0	0	2	5	6	2	3	1	1	2	3	1
OUT. WHITE CWEALTH	26	0	0	1	0	0	0	0	0	1	0	0	1	7	5	0	2	2	2	3	1	0
OUT. DEVLPED WORLD	14	0	0	0	0	0	0	0	0	1	0	0	0	4	3	0	1	2	1	2	0	0
CANADA	16	0	0	1	0	2	0	1	0	2	0	2	3	0	1	1	0	2	0	0	1	1
LATIN AMERICA	11	0	0	0	0	0	0	1	0	1	0	0	0	3	3	1	1	0	1	0	0	0
C. AMER.+CARIB.	5	0	0	0	0	0	0	0	0	1	0	0	0	1	1	0	1	1	0	0	0	0
CUBA	0	0	0	0	0	0	0	0	0	0	0	0	0	0	0	0	0	0	0	0	0	0
MEXICO	4	0	0	0	0	0	0	0	0	1	0	0	0	1	1	0	1	0	0	0	0	0
OTHER	1	0	0	0	0	0	0	0	0	0	0	0	0	0	0	0	0	1	0	1	0	0
S. AMERICA	6	0	0	0	0	0	0	0	0	1	0	0	0	2	2	0	0	1	1	0	0	0
ARGENTINA	2	0	0	0	0	0	0	0	0	0	0	0	0	0	1	1	0	0	1	1	0	0
BRAZIL	1	0	0	0	0	0	0	0	0	0	0	0	0	1	0	0	0	0	0	0	0	0
PERU	0	0	0	0	0	0	0	0	0	0	0	0	0	0	0	0	0	0	0	0	0	0
COLOMBIA	1	0	0	0	0	0	0	0	0	0	0	0	0	1	1	0	0	0	0	0	0	0
VENEZUELA	2	0	0	0	0	0	0	0	0	0	0	0	0	0	0	0	0	1	0	1	0	0
OTHER	3	0	0	0	0	0	0	0	0	0	0	0	0	0	1	0	0	0	0	0	0	0
EUROPE	17	0	0	1	0	0	0	0	0	0	0	0	2	3	2	3	3	1	1	1	1	1
EFTA	10	0	0	1	0	0	0	0	0	0	0	0	1	1	1	2	2	1	1	0	0	1
U.K.	7	0	0	0	0	0	0	0	0	0	0	0	1	1	1	0	0	1	0	0	0	1
SCANDINAVIA	1	0	0	1	0	0	0	0	0	0	0	0	0	0	1	0	0	0	0	0	0	0
SWITZERLAND	2	0	0	1	0	0	0	0	0	0	0	0	0	1	1	2	2	0	1	0	0	0
OTHER EFTA	0	0	0	0	0	0	0	0	0	0	0	0	0	0	0	0	0	0	0	0	0	0
EUROP. COMMUNITY	6	0	0	0	0	0	0	0	0	0	0	0	0	2	0	0	0	0	0	1	1	0
FRANCE	0	0	0	0	0	0	0	0	0	0	0	0	0	0	1	1	1	0	1	0	0	0
GERMANY	1	0	0	0	0	0	0	0	0	0	0	0	0	0	0	0	0	0	0	0	1	0
ITALY	1	0	0	0	0	0	0	0	0	0	0	0	0	0	1	1	0	0	0	1	0	0
BELGIUM + LUX	2	0	0	0	0	0	0	0	0	0	0	0	0	0	0	0	0	0	0	0	0	0
NETHERLANDS	2	0	0	0	0	0	0	0	0	0	0	0	0	0	1	1	0	0	1	0	0	0
SPAIN	0	0	0	0	0	0	0	0	0	0	0	0	0	0	0	0	0	0	0	0	0	0
GREECE + TURKEY	1	0	0	0	0	0	0	0	0	0	0	0	1	0	0	0	0	0	0	0	0	0
OTHER EUROPE	0	0	0	0	0	0	0	0	0	0	0	0	0	0	0	0	0	0	0	0	0	0
EUROPE EX. U.K.	10	0	0	1	1	0	0	0	0	0	0	0	2	2	1	1	0	0	1	1	1	0
SOUTHERN DOMINIONS	5	0	0	0	0	0	0	0	0	0	0	0	0	0	3	0	0	0	0	0	2	0
S. AFRICA +RHOD.	5	0	0	0	0	0	0	0	0	0	0	0	0	0	0	0	0	0	0	0	2	0
AUSTRALIA + N.Z.	5	0	0	0	0	0	0	0	0	0	0	0	2	0	3	0	0	1	1	0	0	0
ASIA + OTHER AFRICA	2	0	0	0	0	0	0	0	0	0	0	0	1	0	1	0	0	0	0	0	0	0
JAPAN	3	0	0	0	0	0	0	0	0	0	0	0	1	0	1	0	0	1	1	1	0	0
OTHER ASIA+AFR.	0	0	0	0	0	0	0	0	0	0	0	0	0	0	0	0	0	0	0	0	0	0
BLACK AFRICA	2	0	0	0	0	0	0	0	0	0	0	0	0	0	0	0	0	0	0	0	0	0
ARAB WORLD	2	0	0	0	0	0	0	0	0	0	0	0	1	1	0	1	0	0	1	0	0	0
INDIA	1	0	0	0	0	0	0	0	0	0	0	0	0	0	1	0	0	0	0	0	0	0
PHILIPPINES	0	0	0	0	0	0	0	0	0	0	0	0	0	0	0	0	0	0	0	0	0	0
OTHER F. ASIA	0	0	0	0	0	0	0	0	0	0	0	0	0	0	0	0	0	0	0	0	0	0
OTHER ASIA	0	0	0	0	0	0	0	0	0	0	0	0	0	0	0	0	0	0	0	0	0	0

PERIOD

CHAPTER 3- THE PROLIFERATION OF FOREIGN SUBSIDIARIES
SECTION 4- THE FLOW OF MANUFACTURING BY INDUSTRY OF SUBSIDIARY
TABLE 29- SUBSIDIARIES MANUFACTURING
IRON, STEEL AND MISCELLANEOUS NONFERROUS PRODUCTS (SIC 331,332, AND 339)
CLASSIFIED BY COUNTRY OR REGION AND BY PERIOD MANUFACTURE BEGAN

PERIOD

COUNTRY OR REGION	PRE 1968	PRE 1901	1901 -13	1914 -19	1920 -24	1925 -29	1930 -34	1935 -39	1940 -45	1946 -50	1951 -53	1954 -55	1956 -57	1958 -59	1960 -61	1962	1963	1964	1965	1966	1967	UNK
OUTSIDE U.S.	57	1	0	0	2	2	1	5	0	3	3	1	0	2	11	5	2	1	8	2	3	5
OUT. U.S. + CANADA	47	1	0	0	2	1	1	3	0	2	2	0	0	2	11	4	2	1	8	1	2	5
OUT. WEST. HEMIS.	35	1	0	0	0	1	1	3	0	2	2	0	0	2	8	2	2	1	8	1	2	5
OUT. WHITE CWEALTH	31	1	0	0	1	1	0	1	0	2	2	0	0	2	7	4	0	1	5	1	1	2
OUT. DEVLPED WORLD	15	0	0	0	1	0	0	0	0	2	2	0	0	2	4	3	0	0	1	0	0	0
CANADA	10	0	0	0	1	1	1	2	0	1	1	1	0	0	0	1	0	1	0	0	1	0
LATIN AMERICA	12	0	0	0	1	1	1	2	0	2	2	0	0	3	3	2	0	0	0	0	0	0
C. AMER.+CARIB.	3	0	0	0	1	0	0	0	0	0	0	0	0	1	1	1	0	0	0	0	0	0
CUBA	0	0	0	0	0	0	0	0	0	0	0	0	0	0	0	0	0	0	0	0	0	0
MEXICO	3	0	0	0	1	0	0	0	0	0	0	0	0	1	1	0	0	0	0	0	0	0
OTHER	0	0	0	0	0	0	0	0	0	0	0	0	0	0	0	1	0	0	0	0	0	0
S. AMERICA	9	0	0	0	0	1	0	2	0	2	2	1	0	2	2	2	0	1	0	1	0	2
ARGENTINA	1	0	0	0	0	0	0	0	0	0	0	0	0	0	0	0	0	0	0	0	0	1
BRAZIL	5	0	0	0	0	0	0	0	0	1	0	1	0	1	1	0	0	0	0	0	0	0
PERU	0	0	0	0	0	0	0	0	0	0	1	0	0	0	0	0	0	0	0	0	0	0
COLOMBIA	1	0	0	0	0	0	0	0	0	0	0	0	0	0	1	0	0	0	0	0	0	0
VENEZUELA	0	0	0	0	0	0	0	0	0	0	0	0	0	0	0	0	0	0	0	0	0	0
OTHER	2	0	0	0	0	0	0	0	0	1	0	0	0	1	1	0	0	0	0	0	0	0
EUROPE	27	1	0	0	0	1	1	2	0	0	0	0	0	0	6	2	2	1	6	1	1	5
EFTA	12	0	0	0	0	1	1	1	0	0	0	0	0	0	3	2	0	0	2	0	0	3
U.K.	12	0	0	0	0	1	1	1	0	0	0	0	0	0	3	2	0	0	2	0	0	3
SCANDINAVIA	0	0	0	0	0	0	0	0	0	0	0	0	0	0	0	0	0	0	0	0	0	0
SWITZERLAND	0	0	0	0	0	0	0	0	0	0	0	0	0	0	0	0	0	0	0	0	0	0
OTHER EFTA	0	0	0	0	0	0	0	0	0	0	0	0	0	0	0	0	0	0	0	0	0	0
EUROP. COMMUNITY	13	1	0	0	1	0	0	1	0	0	0	0	0	0	2	0	0	0	3	0	0	2
FRANCE	5	1	0	0	0	1	0	0	0	0	0	0	0	0	1	1	0	1	0	1	0	1
GERMANY	2	0	0	0	1	0	0	0	0	0	0	0	0	0	0	0	0	0	0	0	0	0
ITALY	2	0	0	0	0	0	1	0	0	0	0	0	0	0	0	1	0	0	0	0	0	0
BELGIUM + LUX	1	0	0	0	0	0	0	0	0	0	0	0	0	0	0	0	0	0	1	0	0	0
NETHERLANDS	3	0	0	0	0	1	0	1	0	0	0	0	0	0	2	1	1	0	0	1	1	1
SPAIN	0	0	0	0	0	0	0	0	0	0	0	0	0	0	0	0	0	0	0	0	0	0
GREECE + TURKEY	2	0	0	0	0	0	0	0	0	0	0	0	0	0	1	1	0	0	1	0	0	1
OTHER EUROPE	0	0	0	0	0	0	0	0	0	0	0	0	0	0	0	0	0	0	0	0	0	0
EUROPE EX. U.K.	15	1	0	0	1	1	1	1	0	0	0	0	0	0	3	1	1	1	4	1	1	2
SOUTHERN DOMINIONS	4	0	0	0	0	0	1	1	0	0	0	0	0	0	1	1	0	1	1	0	1	0
S. AFRICA +RHOD.	1	0	0	0	0	0	0	0	0	0	0	0	0	0	1	0	0	0	0	1	0	0
AUSTRALIA + N.Z.	3	0	0	0	0	0	1	1	0	0	0	0	0	0	0	1	0	1	1	0	1	0
ASIA + OTHER AFRICA	4	0	0	0	0	0	0	0	0	0	0	0	0	0	1	2	0	1	1	0	1	0
JAPAN	1	0	0	0	0	0	0	0	0	0	0	0	0	0	1	1	0	0	0	0	0	0
OTHER ASIA+AFR.	3	0	0	0	0	0	0	1	0	0	0	0	0	0	0	1	0	1	1	0	1	0
BLACK AFRICA	0	0	0	0	0	0	0	0	0	0	0	0	0	0	0	0	0	0	0	0	0	0
ARAB WORLD	1	0	0	0	0	0	0	0	0	0	0	0	0	0	1	0	0	0	0	0	0	0
INDIA	0	0	0	0	0	0	0	0	0	0	0	0	0	0	0	1	0	0	0	0	0	0
PHILIPPINES	1	0	0	0	0	0	0	0	0	0	0	0	0	0	0	0	0	0	0	0	0	0
OTHER E. ASIA	0	0	0	0	0	0	0	0	0	0	0	0	0	0	0	0	0	0	0	0	0	0
OTHER ASIA	1	0	0	0	0	0	0	0	0	0	0	0	0	0	0	1	0	0	1	0	0	0

CHAPTER 3- THE PROLIFERATION OF FOREIGN SUBSIDIARIES
SECTION 4- THE FLOW OF MANUFACTURING BY INDUSTRY OF SUBSIDIARY
TABLE 30- SUBSIDIARIES MANUFACTURING
METAL CANS (SIC 341)
CLASSIFIED BY COUNTRY OR REGION AND BY PERIOD MANUFACTURE BEGAN

PERIOD

COUNTRY OR REGION	PRE 1968	PRE 1901	1901 -13	1914 -19	1920 -24	1925 -29	1930 -34	1935 -39	1940 -45	1946 -50	1951 -53	1954 -55	1956 -57	1958 -59	1960 -61	1962	1963	1964	1965	1966	1967	UNK
OUTSIDE U.S.	44	0	0	0	1	0	4	1	2	2	1	2	10	0	4	6	4	1	4	2	1	0
OUT. U.S. + CANADA	35	0	0	0	1	0	4	0	1	1	1	1	9	0	3	5	3	1	3	1	1	0
OUT. WEST. HEMIS.	17	0	0	0	1	0	3	0	1	2	1	1	9	0	1	3	3	0	1	0	1	0
OUT. WHITE CWEALTH	30	0	0	0	1	0	2	0	0	1	0	0	9	0	3	5	3	1	2	2	0	0
OUT. DEVLPED WORLD	21	0	0	0	1	0	1	0	1	1	1	0	9	0	3	2	1	1	0	0	0	0
CANADA	9	0	0	0	0	0	0	1	0	0	0	1	1	0	1	1	1	0	1	2	1	0
LATIN AMERICA	18	0	0	0	1	0	1	1	1	1	1	0	6	0	2	2	1	1	1	2	1	0
C. AMER.+CARIB.	10	0	0	0	1	0	1	0	0	0	0	0	6	0	1	1	1	1	0	0	0	0
CUBA	3	0	0	0	0	0	1	0	0	0	0	0	2	0	0	0	0	0	0	0	0	0
MEXICO	6	0	0	0	1	0	1	0	0	1	1	0	4	0	1	1	1	1	0	0	0	0
OTHER	1	0	0	0	0	0	0	0	0	0	0	0	0	0	0	0	0	0	0	0	0	0
S. AMERICA	8	0	0	0	0	0	0	1	0	1	1	0	0	0	1	1	0	0	0	0	0	0
ARGENTINA	3	0	0	0	0	0	0	1	0	0	0	0	3	0	1	2	1	0	0	0	0	0
BRAZIL	3	0	0	0	0	0	0	0	0	1	0	0	2	0	1	1	0	0	0	0	0	0
PERU	0	0	0	0	0	0	0	0	0	0	0	0	0	0	0	0	0	0	0	0	0	0
COLOMBIA	2	0	0	0	0	0	0	0	0	0	1	0	1	0	1	0	0	0	0	0	0	0
VENEZUELA	2	0	0	0	1	0	0	1	0	0	0	0	0	0	0	0	0	0	0	0	0	0
OTHER	1	0	0	0	0	0	0	0	0	1	0	0	0	0	0	0	0	0	0	0	0	0
EUROPE	9	0	0	0	0	0	2	0	1	1	0	0	0	0	2	2	1	0	2	2	1	0
EFTA	4	0	0	0	0	0	1	0	1	1	0	0	0	0	0	0	1	0	0	1	1	0
U.K.	2	0	0	0	0	0	1	0	0	1	0	1	0	0	0	0	1	0	0	1	1	0
SCANDINAVIA	2	0	0	0	0	0	0	0	1	0	0	0	0	0	0	0	0	0	0	0	0	0
SWITZERLAND	0	0	0	0	0	0	0	0	0	0	0	0	0	0	0	0	0	0	0	0	0	0
OTHER EFTA	2	0	0	0	0	0	0	0	0	1	0	0	0	0	1	0	0	0	0	0	0	0
EUROP. COMMUNITY	0	0	0	0	0	0	1	0	0	0	0	0	0	0	1	0	1	0	0	0	0	0
FRANCE	1	0	0	0	0	0	0	0	0	0	0	0	0	0	0	1	0	0	0	0	0	0
GERMANY	0	0	0	0	0	0	0	0	0	0	0	0	0	0	1	0	0	0	0	0	0	0
ITALY	0	0	0	0	0	0	0	0	0	0	0	0	0	0	0	1	0	0	0	0	0	0
BELGIUM + LUX	1	0	0	0	0	0	0	0	0	0	0	0	0	0	0	0	0	0	1	0	0	0
NETHERLANDS	2	0	0	0	0	0	1	0	0	0	0	0	0	0	1	1	0	0	1	0	0	0
SPAIN	1	0	0	0	0	0	0	0	0	0	0	0	0	0	0	0	0	0	1	0	0	0
GREECE + TURKEY	0	0	0	0	0	0	0	0	0	0	0	0	0	0	0	0	0	0	0	0	0	0
OTHER EUROPE	7	0	0	0	0	0	1	0	1	0	0	0	0	0	2	1	1	0	2	0	0	0
EUROPE EX. U.K.	7	0	0	0	0	0	1	0	1	1	0	0	0	0	2	2	1	0	2	0	0	0
SOUTHERN DOMINIONS	3	0	0	0	0	0	1	0	0	0	1	0	0	0	0	0	0	0	1	0	0	0
S. AFRICA +RHOD.	2	0	0	0	0	0	1	0	0	0	1	0	0	0	0	0	0	0	0	0	0	0
AUSTRALIA + N.Z.	1	0	0	0	1	0	0	0	0	0	0	0	0	0	1	0	0	0	1	0	0	0
ASIA + OTHER AFRICA	5	0	0	0	0	0	0	0	0	0	0	0	0	0	1	1	2	0	1	0	0	0
JAPAN	2	0	0	0	0	0	0	0	0	0	0	0	0	0	0	0	1	0	0	0	0	0
OTHER ASIA+AFR.	3	0	0	0	1	0	0	0	0	0	0	0	0	0	1	0	1	0	0	0	0	0
BLACK AFRICA	0	0	0	0	0	0	0	0	0	0	0	0	0	0	0	0	0	0	0	0	0	0
ARAB WORLD	0	0	0	0	0	0	0	0	0	0	0	0	0	0	0	0	0	0	0	0	0	0
INDIA	0	0	0	0	1	0	0	0	0	0	0	0	0	0	0	0	0	0	0	0	0	0
PHILIPPINES	1	0	0	0	0	0	0	0	0	0	0	0	0	0	0	0	0	0	0	0	0	0
OTHER E. ASIA	0	0	0	0	0	0	0	0	0	0	0	0	0	0	0	0	0	0	0	0	0	0
OTHER ASIA	2	0	0	0	0	0	1	0	0	0	0	0	0	0	0	1	0	0	0	0	0	0

CHAPTER 3- THE PROLIFERATION OF FOREIGN SUBSIDIARIES
SECTION 4- THE FLOW OF MANUFACTURING BY INDUSTRY OF SUBSIDIARY
TABLE 31- SUBSIDIARIES MANUFACTURING
HEATING APPARATUS AND PLUMBING FIXTURES (SIC 343)
CLASSIFIED BY COUNTRY OR REGION AND BY PERIOD MANUFACTURE BEGAN

PERIOD

COUNTRY OR REGION	PRE 1968	PRE 1901	1901 -13	1914 -19	1920 -24	1925 -29	1930 -34	1935 -39	1940 -45	1946 -50	1951 -53	1954 -55	1956 -57	1958 -59	1960 -61	1962	1963	1964	1965	1966	1967	UNK
OUTSIDE U.S.	47	2	4	1	1	3	2	0	6	3	0	3	1	9	2	2	0	2	2	4	0
OUT. U.S. + CANADA	32	2	3	1	0	1	1	0	3	0	0	3	1	8	2	1	2	1	3	0
OUT. WEST. HEMIS.	29	2	3	1	0	1	1	0	2	0	0	2	1	6	2	1	1	1	2	0
OUT. WHITE CWEALTH	24	2	2	1	0	1	0	0	2	0	0	3	1	6	0	0	0	1	3	0
OUT. DEVLPED WORLD	6	0	0	0	0	0	0	0	2	0	0	1	0	2	0	0	0	0	0	1	0
CANADA	15	0	1	0	1	1	1	0	3	3	0	0	0	1	0	1	0	0	1	0
LATIN AMERICA	3	0	0	0	0	0	0	0	1	0	0	1	0	1	0	0	0	0	0	0
C. AMER.+CARIB.	1	0	0	0	0	0	0	0	0	0	0	0	0	0	0	0	0	0	0	1	0
CUBA	0	0	0	0	0	0	0	0	0	0	0	0	0	0	0	0	0	0	0	0
MEXICO	1	0	0	0	0	0	0	0	0	0	0	1	0	0	0	0	0	0	0	0
OTHER	0	0	0	0	0	0	0	0	0	0	0	0	0	0	0	0	0	0	0	0
S. AMERICA	2	0	0	0	0	0	0	0	1	0	0	0	0	1	0	0	0	0	0	0
ARGENTINA	1	0	0	0	0	0	0	0	1	0	0	0	0	0	0	0	0	0	0	0
BRAZIL	0	0	0	0	0	0	0	0	0	0	0	0	0	0	0	0	0	0	0	0
PERU	1	0	0	0	0	0	0	0	0	0	0	0	0	1	0	0	0	0	0	0
COLOMBIA	0	0	0	0	0	0	0	0	0	0	0	0	0	0	0	0	0	0	0	0
VENEZUELA	0	0	0	0	0	0	0	0	0	0	0	0	0	0	0	0	0	0	0	0
OTHER	0	0	0	0	0	0	0	0	0	0	0	0	0	0	0	0	0	0	0	0
EUROPE	25	2	3	1	0	1	1	0	1	1	0	2	1	6	1	1	2	2	1	2	0
EFTA	9	0	2	1	0	1	1	0	1	1	0	0	0	2	0	1	0	0	0	0
U.K.	7	0	1	1	0	1	1	0	1	0	0	0	0	2	0	0	0	0	0	0
SCANDINAVIA	0	0	0	0	0	0	0	0	0	0	0	0	0	0	0	0	0	0	0	0
SWITZERLAND	1	0	0	0	0	0	0	0	0	0	0	0	0	0	0	0	0	0	1	0
OTHER EFTA	1	0	1	0	0	0	0	0	0	0	0	0	0	0	0	0	0	0	0	0
EUROP. COMMUNITY	14	1	1	0	0	0	0	0	0	0	0	2	1	4	1	0	2	2	1	2	0
FRANCE	5	1	0	0	0	0	0	0	0	0	0	1	0	3	0	0	0	1	0	0
GERMANY	4	1	0	0	0	0	0	0	0	0	0	0	0	0	0	1	0	0	1	0
ITALY	2	0	1	0	0	0	0	0	0	0	0	1	0	0	1	0	0	0	0	0
BELGIUM + LUX	1	0	0	0	0	0	0	0	0	0	0	0	0	1	0	0	0	0	0	0
NETHERLANDS	2	0	0	0	0	0	0	0	0	0	0	0	1	0	0	1	0	0	0	0
SPAIN	1	0	0	0	0	0	0	0	0	0	0	0	0	0	0	0	0	0	1	0
GREECE + TURKEY	1	0	0	0	0	0	0	0	0	0	0	0	0	0	1	0	0	0	0	0
OTHER EUROPE	0	0	0	0	0	0	0	0	0	0	0	0	0	0	0	0	0	0	0	0
EUROPE EX. U.K.	18	2	2	0	0	1	0	0	0	0	0	2	1	4	1	1	2	2	1	2	0
SOUTHERN DOMINIONS	1	0	0	0	0	0	0	0	0	0	0	0	0	0	0	0	0	0	0	0
S. AFRICA +RHOD.	0	0	0	0	0	0	0	0	0	0	0	0	0	0	0	0	0	0	0	0
AUSTRALIA + N.Z.	1	0	0	0	0	0	0	0	0	0	0	0	2	0	0	0	0	0	0	0
ASIA + OTHER AFRICA	3	0	0	0	0	0	0	0	1	0	0	0	0	2	0	0	0	0	0	0
JAPAN	0	0	0	0	0	0	0	0	0	0	0	0	0	0	0	0	0	0	0	0
OTHER ASIA+AFR.	3	0	0	0	0	0	0	0	0	0	0	0	0	2	0	0	0	0	0	0
BLACK AFRICA	2	0	0	0	0	0	0	0	1	0	0	0	0	0	0	0	0	0	0	0
ARAB WORLD	0	0	0	0	0	0	0	0	0	0	0	0	0	0	0	0	0	0	0	0
INDIA	0	0	0	0	0	0	0	0	0	0	0	0	0	0	0	0	0	0	0	0
PHILIPPINES	0	0	0	0	0	0	0	0	0	0	0	0	0	0	0	0	0	0	0	0
OTHER E. ASIA	0	0	0	0	0	0	0	0	0	0	0	0	0	0	0	0	0	0	0	0
OTHER ASIA	1	0	0	0	0	0	0	0	1	0	0	0	0	0	0	0	0	0	0	0

CHAPTER 3- THE PROLIFERATION OF FOREIGN SUBSIDIARIES
SECTION 4- THE FLOW OF MANUFACTURING BY INDUSTRY OF SUBSIDIARY
TABLE 32- SUBSIDIARIES MANUFACTURING
OTHER FABRICATED METAL PRODUCTS (SIC 342,344-349)
CLASSIFIED BY COUNTRY OR REGION AND BY PERIOD MANUFACTURE BEGAN

COUNTRY OR REGION	PRE 1968	PRE 1901	1901 -13	1914 -19	1920 -24	1925 -29	1930 -34	1935 -39	1940 -45	1946 -50	1951 -53	1954 -55	1956 -57	1958 -59	1960 -61	1962	1963	1964	1965	1966	1967	UNK
OUTSIDE U.S.	240	1	0	5	2	5	4	14	4	19	4	10	17	20	44	21	16	14	15	13	10	2
OUT. U.S. + CANADA	195	1	0	5	2	4	2	12	1	13	3	5	13	16	39	19	14	11	13	13	9	2
OUT. WEST. HEMIS.	146	1	0	2	2	4	2	8	0	8	3	5	8	10	29	18	12	8	9	10	6	2
OUT. WHITE CWEALTH	135	0	0	2	1	3	0	7	1	9	2	5	11	10	27	13	13	9	5	8	5	1
OUT. DEVLPED WORLD	61	0	0	1	0	1	0	4	1	7	1	2	6	6	14	1	3	3	4	4	3	0
CANADA	45	0	0	3	0	1	2	2	3	6	1	4	4	4	5	2	2	3	2	0	0	0
LATIN AMERICA	49	0	0	0	0	0	0	4	1	5	0	1	5	6	10	1	2	3	4	3	3	0
C. AMER.+CARIB.	21	0	0	0	0	1	0	2	0	1	0	0	2	4	4	0	2	1	2	2	1	0
CUBA	0	0	0	0	0	0	0	1	0	1	0	0	1	0	0	0	0	0	0	1	0	0
MEXICO	17	0	0	0	0	0	0	1	0	1	0	0	1	0	4	0	2	0	2	1	1	0
OTHER	2	0	0	0	0	0	0	0	0	0	0	0	0	0	0	0	0	1	0	1	0	0
S. AMERICA	28	0	0	0	0	0	0	2	1	4	0	0	3	2	6	1	2	2	2	1	2	0
ARGENTINA	5	0	0	0	0	0	0	1	0	1	0	1	0	0	1	1	0	0	2	1	0	0
BRAZIL	6	0	0	0	0	0	0	0	1	1	0	0	3	0	1	1	0	1	0	1	1	0
PERU	2	0	0	0	0	0	0	0	0	1	0	0	0	0	0	1	0	0	0	0	0	0
COLOMBIA	5	0	0	0	0	0	0	0	0	1	0	1	0	1	1	0	0	1	0	0	1	0
VENEZUELA	6	0	0	0	0	0	0	1	0	0	0	0	2	1	1	0	0	0	2	0	0	0
OTHER	4	0	0	0	0	0	0	0	0	1	0	0	0	0	2	0	0	0	0	0	1	0
EUROPE	106	1	0	2	1	3	1	6	0	5	2	3	6	7	18	15	10	8	7	6	4	1
EFTA	39	1	0	1	0	1	1	3	0	3	1	0	1	4	5	5	2	2	5	2	2	1
U.K.	35	0	0	1	0	1	1	3	0	3	1	0	1	3	5	4	1	2	4	2	2	1
SCANDINAVIA	2	0	0	0	0	0	0	0	0	0	0	0	0	1	0	0	1	0	0	0	0	0
SWITZERLAND	0	0	0	0	0	0	0	0	0	0	0	0	0	0	0	0	0	0	0	0	0	0
OTHER EFTA	2	0	0	0	0	0	0	0	0	0	0	0	0	0	0	0	1	0	1	0	0	0
EUROP. COMMUNITY	55	0	0	0	1	2	0	3	0	2	1	5	5	3	12	8	6	5	1	3	0	0
FRANCE	11	0	0	0	1	1	0	1	0	0	0	0	3	0	4	3	2	0	1	0	1	0
GERMANY	19	0	0	0	0	2	0	0	0	2	0	2	3	3	3	2	2	5	0	0	1	0
ITALY	15	0	0	0	0	1	0	2	0	0	1	0	1	0	1	2	3	5	0	0	1	0
BELGIUM + LUX	6	0	0	0	0	0	0	1	0	0	0	0	0	0	1	1	1	0	0	1	1	0
NETHERLANDS	4	0	0	0	0	0	0	0	0	2	0	0	0	0	1	1	0	0	0	1	0	0
SPAIN	8	0	0	1	0	0	0	0	0	2	0	0	0	0	0	2	2	0	0	0	0	0
GREECE + TURKEY	2	0	1	0	0	0	0	0	0	0	0	1	0	0	1	0	0	1	0	1	1	0
OTHER EUROPE	2	0	0	0	0	0	0	0	0	0	0	0	0	0	1	0	0	0	0	0	0	0
EUROPE EX. U.K.	71	1	0	1	1	2	0	3	0	2	1	3	5	4	13	11	9	6	3	4	2	0
SOUTHERN DOMINIONS	23	0	0	0	1	0	1	2	0	1	0	1	1	3	6	2	0	0	0	3	2	0
S. AFRICA +RHOD.	7	0	0	0	1	0	0	0	0	1	0	0	1	1	1	2	0	0	0	2	0	0
AUSTRALIA + N.Z.	16	0	0	0	0	0	0	2	0	0	0	1	1	2	5	2	2	0	0	1	2	1
ASIA + OTHER AFRICA	17	0	0	0	0	0	0	0	0	2	1	1	1	0	1	1	2	0	2	1	1	1
JAPAN	12	0	0	0	0	0	0	0	0	0	0	1	0	0	4	0	1	0	1	0	0	1
OTHER ASIA+AFR.	2	0	0	0	0	0	0	0	0	2	1	0	1	0	2	0	0	0	1	0	0	0
BLACK AFRICA	1	0	0	0	0	0	0	0	0	0	0	0	0	0	0	0	0	0	0	0	0	0
ARAB WORLD	3	0	0	0	0	0	0	0	0	0	0	0	0	0	2	0	1	0	0	0	0	0
INDIA	2	0	0	0	0	0	0	0	0	0	0	1	0	0	0	0	0	0	0	0	0	0
PHILIPPINES	0	0	0	0	0	0	0	0	0	0	0	0	0	0	0	0	0	0	0	0	0	0
OTHER E. ASIA	0	0	0	0	0	0	0	0	0	0	0	0	0	0	0	0	0	0	0	0	0	0
OTHER ASIA	4	0	0	0	0	0	0	0	0	2	0	1	0	0	0	0	0	0	0	0	0	0

CHAPTER 3- THE PROLIFERATION OF FOREIGN SUBSIDIARIES
SECTION 4- THE FLOW OF MANUFACTURING BY INDUSTRY OF SUBSIDIARY
TABLE 33- SUBSIDIARIES MANUFACTURING
FARM MACHINERY (SIC 352)
CLASSIFIED BY COUNTRY OR REGION AND BY PERIOD MANUFACTURE BEGAN

PERIOD

COUNTRY OR REGION	PRE 1968	PRE 1901	1901 -13	1914 -19	1920 -24	1925 -29	1930 -34	1935 -39	1940 -45	1946 -50	1951 -53	1954 -55	1956 -57	1958 -59	1960 -61	1962	1963	1964	1965	1966	1967	UNK
OUTSIDE U.S.	55	0	5	0	0	0	1	0	1	6	2	5	2	1	11	6	3	5	1	3	1	0
OUT. U.S. + CANADA	48	0	3	0	0	0	1	1	1	5	2	5	1	1	11	5	3	5	1	2	0	0
OUT. WEST. HEMIS.	39	0	3	0	0	0	1	1	1	3	2	4	2	1	11	4	2	4	0	2	0	0
OUT. WHITE CWEALTH	33	0	3	0	0	0	0	0	0	4	0	3	1	1	8	2	2	5	1	2	0	0
OUT. DEVLPED WORLD	12	0	0	0	0	0	0	0	0	2	0	2	1	0	0	1	1	3	1	1	0	0
CANADA	7	0	2	0	0	0	1	0	0	1	0	0	1	0	0	0	0	0	0	0	0	0
LATIN AMERICA	9	0	0	0	0	0	0	0	0	2	0	1	1	0	0	1	0	1	1	0	1	0
C. AMER.+CARIB.	3	0	0	0	0	0	0	0	0	1	0	1	0	0	0	1	1	1	0	1	0	0
CUBA	0	0	0	0	0	0	0	0	0	0	0	0	0	0	0	0	0	0	0	0	0	0
MEXICO	2	0	0	0	0	0	0	0	0	1	0	1	0	0	0	1	0	0	0	0	0	0
OTHER	1	0	0	0	0	0	0	0	0	0	0	0	0	0	0	0	1	1	0	1	0	0
S. AMERICA	6	0	0	0	0	0	0	0	0	1	0	0	1	1	0	0	0	1	1	0	1	0
ARGENTINA	3	0	0	0	0	0	0	0	0	1	0	0	0	0	0	0	0	0	0	0	0	0
BRAZIL	1	0	0	0	0	0	0	0	0	0	0	0	1	1	0	0	0	0	0	0	0	0
PERU	0	0	0	0	0	0	0	0	0	0	0	0	0	0	0	0	0	0	0	0	0	0
COLOMBIA	0	0	0	0	0	0	0	0	0	0	0	0	0	0	0	0	0	1	0	0	0	0
VENEZUELA	0	0	0	0	0	0	0	0	0	0	0	0	0	0	0	0	0	0	0	0	0	0
OTHER	1	0	0	0	0	0	0	0	0	0	0	0	0	0	0	1	0	0	1	0	0	0
EUROPE	26	0	3	0	0	0	0	0	0	2	1	2	1	1	10	2	1	2	2	1	1	0
EFTA	7	0	1	0	0	0	0	0	0	1	1	1	0	0	2	1	0	0	0	1	0	0
U.K.	6	0	0	0	0	0	0	0	0	1	1	1	1	1	2	1	0	0	0	0	0	0
SCANDINAVIA	1	0	1	0	0	0	0	0	0	1	0	0	0	0	2	0	0	0	0	0	0	0
SWITZERLAND	0	0	0	0	0	0	0	0	0	0	0	0	0	0	0	0	0	0	0	0	0	0
OTHER EFTA	0	0	0	0	0	0	0	0	0	0	0	0	0	0	0	0	0	0	0	0	0	0
EUROP. COMMUNITY	15	0	2	0	0	0	0	0	0	1	0	0	0	1	8	0	0	1	1	0	0	0
FRANCE	11	0	1	0	0	0	0	0	0	1	0	1	1	1	7	1	0	0	0	0	0	0
GERMANY	2	0	1	0	0	0	0	0	0	0	0	0	0	0	1	0	0	1	0	0	0	0
ITALY	1	0	0	0	0	0	0	0	0	0	0	1	1	0	0	0	0	1	0	0	0	0
BELGIUM + LUX	1	0	0	0	0	0	0	0	0	0	0	0	0	0	0	0	0	0	0	0	0	0
NETHERLANDS	0	0	0	0	0	0	0	0	0	0	0	0	0	0	0	0	0	0	0	0	0	0
SPAIN	3	0	0	0	0	0	0	0	0	0	0	0	0	0	0	0	0	1	1	0	1	0
GREECE + TURKEY	1	0	0	0	0	0	0	0	0	0	0	1	1	0	0	0	1	0	0	0	0	0
OTHER EUROPE	0	0	0	0	0	0	0	0	0	0	0	0	0	0	0	0	0	1	0	1	0	0
EUROPE EX. U.K.	20	0	3	0	0	0	0	0	0	1	1	1	1	0	8	1	1	2	2	1	1	0
SOUTHERN DOMINIONS	9	0	0	0	0	0	1	0	1	0	0	1	0	0	1	2	1	0	1	0	0	0
S. AFRICA +RHOD.	4	0	0	0	0	0	0	0	0	0	0	0	0	0	0	2	1	0	0	1	0	0
AUSTRALIA + N.Z.	5	0	0	0	0	0	1	0	1	1	1	1	0	0	1	0	0	2	1	0	0	0
ASIA + OTHER AFRICA	4	0	0	0	0	0	0	0	1	1	0	1	0	0	0	0	0	2	0	0	0	0
JAPAN	1	0	0	0	0	0	0	0	0	1	0	0	0	0	0	0	0	0	0	0	0	0
OTHER ASIA+AFR.	3	0	0	0	0	0	1	0	1	0	0	1	0	0	0	0	0	2	0	0	0	0
BLACK AFRICA	0	0	0	0	0	0	0	0	0	0	0	0	0	0	0	0	0	0	0	0	0	0
ARAB WORLD	1	0	0	0	0	0	0	0	0	0	0	0	0	0	1	0	0	1	0	0	0	0
INDIA	1	0	0	0	0	0	1	0	1	0	0	1	0	0	0	0	0	1	0	0	0	0
PHILIPPINES	1	0	0	0	0	0	0	0	0	0	0	0	0	0	0	0	0	0	0	0	0	0
OTHER E. ASIA	0	0	0	0	0	0	0	0	0	0	0	0	0	0	0	0	0	0	0	0	0	0
OTHER ASIA	0	0	0	0	0	0	0	0	0	0	0	0	0	0	0	0	0	0	0	0	0	0

CHAPTER 3- THE PROLIFERATION OF FOREIGN SUBSIDIARIES
SECTION 4- THE FLOW OF MANUFACTURING BY INDUSTRY OF SUBSIDIARY
TABLE 34- SUBSIDIARIES MANUFACTURING
CONSTRUCTION MACHINERY (SIC 353)
CLASSIFIED BY COUNTRY OR REGION AND BY PERIOD MANUFACTURE BEGAN

PERIOD

COUNTRY OR REGION	PRE 1968	PRE 1901	1901-13	1914-19	1920-24	1925-29	1930-34	1935-39	1940-45	1946-50	1951-53	1954-55	1956-57	1958-59	1960-61	1962	1963	1964	1965	1966	1967	UNK
OUTSIDE U.S.	136	6	5	6	4	0	1	0	3	15	8	10	6	15	14	7	8	6	10	2	10	0
OUT. U.S. + CANADA	104	5	2	4	4	0	1	0	2	12	4	6	5	12	12	6	5	5	9	2	5	0
OUT. WEST. HEMIS.	78	5	2	4	4	0	1	0	2	8	3	4	5	10	10	2	4	3	8	1	1	0
OUT. WHITE CWEALTH	70	3	2	2	2	0	1	0	1	5	2	4	3	8	8	5	5	4	7	2	4	0
OUT. DEVLPED WORLD	28	0	0	0	0	0	0	0	0	4	1	3	0	4	2	4	2	2	1	1	4	0
CANADA	32	1	3	2	0	0	0	0	1	3	4	1	1	3	3	1	3	1	1	0	5	0
LATIN AMERICA	26	0	0	0	0	0	0	0	0	4	1	3	0	3	2	4	1	2	1	1	4	0
C. AMER.+CARIB.	11	0	0	0	0	0	0	0	0	1	1	1	0	1	0	0	1	2	0	1	1	0
CUBA	0	0	0	0	0	0	0	0	0	0	0	0	0	0	0	0	0	0	0	0	0	0
MEXICO	11	0	0	0	0	0	0	0	0	1	1	1	0	1	0	0	1	2	0	1	1	0
OTHER	0	0	0	0	0	0	0	0	0	0	0	0	0	0	0	0	0	0	0	0	0	0
S. AMERICA	15	0	0	0	0	0	0	0	1	3	0	2	0	2	2	0	0	0	1	0	3	0
ARGENTINA	3	0	0	0	0	0	0	0	0	0	0	0	0	0	0	1	1	0	1	0	0	0
BRAZIL	7	0	0	0	0	0	0	0	0	3	0	2	0	1	0	1	0	0	0	0	1	0
PERU	1	0	0	0	0	0	0	0	0	0	0	0	0	0	0	0	0	0	1	0	0	0
COLOMBIA	0	0	0	0	0	0	0	0	0	0	0	0	0	0	0	0	0	0	0	0	0	0
VENEZUELA	0	0	0	0	0	0	0	0	0	0	0	0	0	1	0	0	0	0	0	0	1	0
OTHER	3	0	0	0	0	0	0	0	0	0	0	0	0	0	0	1	0	0	0	0	1	0
EUROPE	48	5	2	2	2	0	0	0	0	4	2	4	4	5	7	1	2	2	5	1	0	0
EFTA	12	2	0	0	0	0	0	0	0	3	1	3	2	1	1	0	0	0	0	0	0	0
U.K.	11	2	0	0	0	0	0	0	0	3	1	3	1	1	1	0	0	0	0	0	1	0
SCANDINAVIA	0	0	0	0	0	0	0	0	0	0	0	0	0	0	0	0	0	0	0	0	0	0
SWITZERLAND	0	0	0	0	0	0	0	0	0	0	0	0	0	0	0	0	0	0	0	0	0	0
OTHER EFTA	1	0	0	0	0	0	0	0	0	0	0	0	0	0	0	0	0	0	0	0	0	0
EUROP. COMMUNITY	33	3	2	1	2	0	0	0	0	1	0	0	1	4	5	1	0	2	4	0	3	0
FRANCE	11	1	1	0	0	0	0	0	0	0	1	2	2	1	1	0	1	1	0	1	1	0
GERMANY	8	0	0	0	1	0	0	0	0	0	0	0	0	1	0	1	1	0	0	0	1	0
ITALY	5	1	1	1	0	0	0	0	0	0	0	0	0	0	1	0	1	0	0	0	0	0
BELGIUM + LUX	5	0	0	0	1	0	0	0	0	0	1	0	2	1	1	0	0	0	2	0	1	0
NETHERLANDS	4	0	1	1	0	0	0	0	0	1	0	0	0	1	0	0	1	1	1	1	1	0
SPAIN	3	0	0	0	0	0	0	0	0	0	0	0	0	0	0	0	0	0	1	1	1	0
GREECE + TURKEY	0	0	0	0	0	0	0	0	0	0	0	0	0	0	0	0	0	0	0	0	0	0
OTHER EUROPE	0	0	0	0	0	0	0	0	0	1	0	0	0	0	0	1	0	0	0	0	0	0
EUROPE Ex. U.K.	37	3	2	2	2	0	0	0	0	1	1	1	3	4	7	1	2	2	5	1	0	0
SOUTHERN DOMINIONS	23	0	0	2	2	0	0	0	1	4	1	2	1	3	2	1	0	1	2	0	1	0
S. AFRICA +RHOD.	6	0	0	1	1	0	0	0	1	2	0	0	0	0	1	0	0	0	0	0	0	0
AUSTRALIA + N.Z.	17	0	0	1	1	0	0	0	0	2	1	2	1	3	1	1	0	1	2	0	1	0
ASIA + OTHER AFRICA	7	0	0	0	0	0	1	0	1	2	1	0	0	1	1	0	2	0	1	0	1	0
JAPAN	5	0	0	0	0	0	0	0	1	0	0	0	0	0	1	0	1	1	0	0	0	0
OTHER ASIA+AFR.	0	0	0	0	0	0	0	0	0	0	0	0	0	0	0	0	0	0	0	0	0	0
BLACK AFRICA	0	0	0	0	0	0	0	0	0	0	0	0	0	0	0	0	0	0	0	0	0	0
ARAB WORLD	0	0	0	0	0	0	0	0	0	0	0	0	0	0	0	0	0	0	0	0	0	0
INDIA	2	0	0	0	0	0	1	0	0	0	0	0	0	1	0	0	0	0	0	0	0	0
PHILIPPINES	0	0	0	0	0	0	0	0	0	0	0	0	0	0	0	0	0	0	0	0	0	0
OTHER E. ASIA	0	0	0	0	0	0	0	0	0	0	0	0	0	1	0	0	0	0	0	0	0	0
OTHER ASIA	0	0	0	0	0	0	0	0	0	0	0	0	0	0	0	0	0	0	0	0	0	0

CHAPTER 3- THE PROLIFERATION OF FOREIGN SUBSIDIARIES
SECTION 4- THE FLOW OF MANUFACTURING BY INDUSTRY OF SUBSIDIARY
TABLE 35- SUBSIDIARIES MANUFACTURING
SPECIAL INDUSTRY MACHINERY (SIC 354 AND 355)
CLASSIFIED BY COUNTRY OR REGION AND BY PERIOD MANUFACTURE BEGAN

PERIOD

COUNTRY OR REGION	PRE 1968	PRE 1901	1901 -13	1914 -19	1920 -24	1925 -29	1930 -34	1935 -39	1940 -45	1946 -50	1951 -53	1954 -55	1956 -57	1958 -59	1960 -61	1962	1963	1964	1965	1966	1967	UNK
OUTSIDE U.S.	109	6	3	3	4	2	1	2	1	5	7	4	9	3	16	6	5	5	10	13	4	0
OUT. U.S. + CANADA	94	5	2	3	4	2	0	1	1	5	5	4	7	2	15	5	5	5	10	12	4	0
OUT. WEST. HEMIS.	81	5	2	3	3	2	0	1	0	4	5	4	3	2	14	4	5	2	9	11	3	0
OUT. WHITE C'WEALTH	57	2	2	1	2	1	0	0	1	2	0	3	6	0	12	1	5	2	4	7	3	0
OUT. DEVLPED WORLD	16	0	0	0	1	0	0	0	1	1	0	1	5	0	1	1	0	0	1	1	2	0
CANADA	15	1	1	0	0	1	1	0	0	0	2	0	2	1	1	1	0	3	1	1	0	0
LATIN AMERICA	13	0	0	0	1	0	0	1	1	1	0	0	4	0	1	1	1	1	0	1	1	0
C. AMER.+CARIB.	7	0	0	0	1	0	0	0	0	1	0	0	1	0	1	1	0	1	1	1	0	0
CUBA	1	0	0	0	0	0	0	0	1	0	0	0	0	0	0	0	0	0	0	0	0	0
MEXICO	5	0	0	0	1	0	0	0	0	1	0	0	1	0	1	1	0	1	0	1	0	0
OTHER	1	0	0	0	0	0	0	0	0	0	0	0	0	0	0	0	0	0	1	0	1	0
S. AMERICA	6	0	0	0	0	0	0	1	1	0	0	0	3	0	0	0	1	0	0	0	1	0
ARGENTINA	0	0	0	0	0	0	0	0	0	0	0	0	1	0	1	0	0	0	0	0	0	0
BRAZIL	2	0	0	0	0	0	0	1	0	0	0	0	0	0	0	0	1	0	0	0	0	0
PERU	0	0	0	0	0	0	0	0	0	0	0	0	1	0	0	0	0	0	0	0	0	0
COLOMBIA	1	0	0	0	0	0	0	0	0	0	0	0	0	0	0	0	0	0	0	0	1	0
VENEZUELA	1	0	0	0	0	0	0	0	0	0	0	0	0	0	0	0	0	0	0	0	0	0
OTHER	2	0	0	0	0	0	0	0	0	0	0	0	1	0	0	0	0	1	1	1	0	0
EUROPE	60	5	2	2	2	2	0	0	0	2	4	2	2	1	11	4	5	0	8	7	1	0
EFTA	26	3	1	1	1	1	0	0	0	1	4	0	1	1	3	1	0	0	5	1	1	0
U.K.	23	3	0	1	1	1	0	0	0	1	4	0	1	1	1	1	0	0	5	2	2	0
SCANDINAVIA	1	0	1	0	0	0	0	0	0	0	0	0	0	0	0	0	0	0	0	2	0	0
SWITZERLAND	1	0	0	0	0	0	0	0	0	0	0	0	0	0	1	0	0	0	0	0	0	0
OTHER EFTA	1	0	0	0	0	0	0	0	0	0	0	0	0	0	1	0	0	0	0	0	1	0
EUROP. COMMUNITY	30	2	1	0	1	0	0	0	0	1	0	0	1	0	8	3	4	0	3	4	0	0
FRANCE	8	1	0	0	1	0	0	0	0	1	0	1	0	0	2	2	1	0	1	3	0	0
GERMANY	10	0	0	0	1	0	0	0	0	0	0	1	1	1	2	0	2	0	2	0	0	0
ITALY	10	1	1	0	1	0	0	0	0	0	0	0	1	0	4	0	2	0	1	3	0	0
BELGIUM + LUX	1	0	0	0	0	0	0	0	0	0	0	0	0	0	0	1	0	0	0	0	0	0
NETHERLANDS	1	0	0	0	1	0	0	0	0	0	0	0	0	0	0	0	0	0	0	1	0	0
SPAIN	3	0	0	0	0	0	0	0	0	0	0	0	0	0	0	0	1	0	0	1	0	0
GREECE + TURKEY	1	0	0	0	0	0	0	0	0	0	0	0	0	0	0	0	0	0	0	0	1	0
OTHER EUROPE	0	0	0	0	0	0	0	0	0	0	0	0	0	0	0	0	0	0	0	0	0	0
EUROPE EX. U.K.	37	2	2	1	1	1	0	0	0	1	0	2	0	0	10	3	5	0	3	5	1	0
SOUTHERN DOMINIONS	14	0	0	1	1	0	0	1	0	2	1	1	0	1	2	0	0	0	1	3	1	0
S. AFRICA +RHOD.	4	0	0	0	1	0	0	0	0	1	1	0	1	0	0	0	0	0	0	1	1	0
AUSTRALIA + N.Z.	10	0	0	1	0	0	0	1	0	1	0	1	0	1	2	0	0	0	1	2	2	0
ASIA + OTHER AFRICA	7	0	0	0	0	0	0	0	0	1	0	0	1	1	1	0	0	1	0	1	1	0
JAPAN	4	0	0	0	0	0	0	0	0	0	0	0	1	0	1	0	0	1	0	1	0	0
OTHER ASIA+AFR.	3	0	0	0	0	0	0	0	0	1	0	1	0	1	0	0	0	0	0	0	1	0
BLACK AFRICA	0	0	0	0	0	0	0	0	0	0	0	0	0	0	0	0	0	0	0	0	0	0
ARAB WORLD	1	0	0	0	0	0	0	0	0	0	0	0	0	0	0	0	0	0	0	1	0	0
INDIA	1	0	0	0	0	0	0	0	0	0	0	1	0	0	0	0	0	0	0	0	0	0
PHILIPPINES	1	0	0	0	0	0	0	0	0	0	0	0	0	0	0	0	0	0	0	0	1	0
OTHER E. ASIA	0	0	0	0	0	0	0	0	0	0	0	0	0	0	0	0	0	0	0	0	0	0
OTHER ASIA	0	0	0	0	0	0	0	0	0	0	0	0	0	0	0	0	0	0	0	0	0	0

CHAPTER 3- THE PROLIFERATION OF FOREIGN SUBSIDIARIES
SECTION 4- THE FLOW OF MANUFACTURING BY INDUSTRY OF SUBSIDIARY
TABLE 36- SUBSIDIARIES MANUFACTURING
GENERAL INDUSTRIAL MACHINERY (SIC 356)
CLASSIFIED BY COUNTRY OR REGION AND BY PERIOD MANUFACTURE BEGAN

COUNTRY OR REGION	PRE 1968	PRE 1901	1901 -13	1914 -19	1920 -24	1925 -29	1930 -34	1935 -39	1940 -45	1946 -50	1951 -53	1954 -55	1956 -57	1958 -60	1960 -61	1962 -63	1964	1965	1966	1967	UNK
OUTSIDE U.S.	118	5	2	2	8	3	4	4	2	7	8	6	3	13	9	9	3	7	4	12	2
OUT. U.S. + CANADA	92	5	1	2	7	2	3	4	1	6	5	2	2	10	8	8	1	6	4	11	0
OUT. WEST. HEMIS.	71	5	1	2	6	2	3	3	1	3	4	1	2	7	6	7	1	3	3	7	0
OUT. WHITE CWEALTH	65	4	1	0	5	1	3	4	0	4	2	1	2	7	4	7	1	6	3	8	0
OUT. DEVLPED WORLD	25	0	0	0	1	0	0	1	0	3	1	1	1	4	2	1	0	4	2	4	0
CANADA	26	0	1	0	1	1	1	0	1	1	3	4	1	3	3	1	2	1	1	1	2
LATIN AMERICA	21	0	0	0	1	1	1	0	1	3	3	1	1	3	1	3	0	3	1	4	0
C. AMER.+CARIB.	10	0	0	0	0	0	0	0	1	1	1	0	0	1	2	1	0	2	1	1	0
CUBA	0	0	0	0	0	0	0	0	0	0	0	0	0	0	0	0	0	0	0	0	0
MEXICO	9	0	0	0	0	0	0	0	1	1	1	0	0	2	2	1	0	1	1	1	0
OTHER	1	0	0	0	0	0	0	0	0	0	0	0	0	0	0	0	0	1	0	0	0
S. AMERICA	11	0	0	0	1	0	0	1	0	2	2	1	0	1	0	1	0	1	0	3	0
ARGENTINA	3	0	0	0	0	0	0	0	0	1	1	0	0	2	0	0	0	0	0	0	0
BRAZIL	6	0	0	0	1	0	0	1	0	1	1	1	0	1	0	0	0	0	0	2	0
PERU	1	0	0	0	0	0	0	0	0	0	0	0	0	0	0	0	0	1	0	0	0
COLOMBIA	1	0	0	0	0	0	1	0	0	0	0	1	0	0	0	0	0	0	0	1	0
VENEZUELA	0	0	0	0	0	0	0	0	0	0	0	0	0	0	0	0	0	0	0	0	0
OTHER	0	0	0	0	0	0	0	0	0	0	0	0	0	0	0	0	0	0	0	0	0
EUROPE	51	5	1	2	5	2	3	3	1	0	3	0	1	3	4	6	1	2	1	6	0
EFTA	17	1	0	2	2	1	3	0	1	0	3	0	0	1	3	2	0	0	0	2	0
U.K.	14	1	0	2	1	1	0	0	1	0	3	0	0	0	0	0	0	0	0	2	0
SCANDINAVIA	1	0	0	0	0	0	0	0	0	0	0	0	0	1	0	0	0	0	0	0	0
SWITZERLAND	1	0	0	0	0	0	0	0	0	0	0	0	0	0	0	1	0	0	1	0	0
OTHER EFTA	1	0	0	0	1	0	0	0	0	0	0	0	0	0	0	0	0	1	0	0	0
EUROP. COMMUNITY	29	4	1	0	3	1	0	3	0	0	0	0	1	2	0	5	1	1	1	3	0
FRANCE	12	2	0	0	1	0	2	3	0	0	0	0	0	1	1	1	0	1	1	2	0
GERMANY	8	2	1	0	1	1	1	0	0	0	0	0	1	1	1	1	0	0	0	1	0
ITALY	5	0	0	0	0	1	1	0	0	0	0	0	0	1	0	0	2	1	0	0	0
BELGIUM + LUX	2	0	0	0	1	0	0	0	0	0	0	0	0	0	0	2	0	0	0	0	0
NETHERLANDS	2	0	0	1	0	0	0	0	0	0	0	0	0	0	0	0	0	0	0	1	0
SPAIN	5	0	0	0	0	0	0	0	0	0	0	0	0	0	1	0	1	0	1	0	0
GREECE + TURKEY	0	0	0	0	0	0	0	0	0	0	0	0	0	0	0	0	0	0	0	0	0
OTHER EUROPE	0	0	0	0	0	1	0	0	0	0	0	0	0	0	0	0	0	0	0	0	0
EUROPE EX. U.K.	37	4	1	0	4	1	3	3	0	0	3	0	1	3	1	6	1	2	1	4	0
SOUTHERN DOMINIONS	13	0	0	0	1	0	0	0	0	2	0	1	0	3	1	1	0	0	1	1	0
S. AFRICA +RHOD.	3	0	0	0	1	0	0	0	0	1	0	0	0	1	0	0	0	0	0	0	0
AUSTRALIA + N.Z.	10	0	0	0	0	0	0	0	0	1	0	1	0	2	1	1	0	0	1	1	0
ASIA + OTHER AFRICA	7	0	0	0	0	0	0	0	0	1	1	1	0	1	1	0	1	1	1	0	0
JAPAN	3	0	0	0	0	0	0	0	0	1	1	0	0	0	1	0	0	0	0	0	0
OTHER ASIA+AFR.	4	0	0	0	0	0	0	0	0	0	0	1	0	1	0	0	1	1	1	0	0
BLACK AFRICA	0	0	0	0	0	0	0	0	0	0	0	0	0	0	0	0	0	0	0	0	0
ARAB WORLD	0	0	0	0	0	0	0	0	0	0	0	0	0	0	0	0	0	0	0	0	0
INDIA	2	0	0	0	0	0	0	0	0	0	0	1	0	0	0	0	0	0	1	0	0
PHILIPPINES	1	0	0	0	0	0	0	0	0	0	0	0	0	1	0	0	0	0	0	0	0
OTHER E. ASIA	0	0	0	0	0	0	0	0	0	0	0	0	0	0	0	0	0	0	0	0	0
OTHER ASIA	1	0	0	0	0	0	0	0	0	0	0	0	0	0	0	0	0	0	0	0	0

PERIOD

CHAPTER 3- THE PROLIFERATION OF FOREIGN SUBSIDIARIES
SECTION 4- THE FLOW OF MANUFACTURING BY INDUSTRY OF SUBSIDIARY
TABLE 37- SUBSIDIARIES MANUFACTURING
OFFICE AND COMPUTING MACHINES (SIC 357)
CLASSIFIED BY COUNTRY OR REGION AND BY PERIOD MANUFACTURE BEGAN

PERIOD

COUNTRY OR REGION	PRE 1968	PRE 1901	1901 -13	1914 -19	1920 -24	1925 -29	1930 -34	1935 -39	1940 -45	1946 -50	1951 -53	1954 -55	1956 -57	1958 -59	1960 -61	1962	1963	1964	1965	1966	1967	UNK
OUTSIDE U.S.	87	1	3	6	2	6	6	9	7	9	9	1	3	8	5	1	3	1	4	3	0	0
OUT. U.S. + CANADA	76	1	3	4	1	4	6	6	6	9	8	1	3	7	4	1	3	1	3	2	0	0
OUT. WEST. HEMIS.	61	1	3	4	1	4	6	8	3	8	5	1	3	4	4	1	3	1	2	1	0	0
OUT. WHITE CWEALTH	63	0	0	4	1	4	5	8	4	7	8	0	3	6	3	0	0	1	3	1	0	0
OUT. DEVLPED WORLD	17	0	0	0	0	0	1	1	3	1	4	0	2	3	0	0	0	0	2	1	0	0
CANADA	11	0	0	2	1	2	0	0	1	0	1	0	0	1	1	0	0	0	1	1	0	0
LATIN AMERICA	15	0	0	0	0	0	0	1	3	1	3	0	2	3	1	0	0	1	1	1	0	0
C. AMER.+CARIB.	6	0	0	0	0	0	0	1	1	0	0	0	0	0	0	0	0	1	1	1	0	0
CUBA	6	0	0	0	0	0	0	0	0	0	0	0	0	0	0	0	0	0	0	0	0	0
MEXICO	6	0	0	0	0	0	0	1	1	1	1	0	0	3	0	0	0	1	1	1	0	0
OTHER	0	0	0	0	0	0	0	0	0	0	0	0	0	0	0	0	0	0	0	0	0	0
S. AMERICA	9	0	0	0	0	0	0	0	2	0	3	0	2	3	0	0	0	0	0	0	0	0
ARGENTINA	0	0	0	0	0	0	0	1	0	1	1	0	2	0	0	0	2	1	1	0	0	0
BRAZIL	6	0	0	0	0	0	0	0	2	0	2	0	0	0	0	0	0	0	0	0	0	0
PERU	0	0	0	0	0	0	0	1	0	0	1	0	0	0	0	0	0	0	0	0	0	0
COLOMBIA	1	0	0	0	0	0	0	0	0	0	0	0	0	0	0	0	0	0	0	0	0	0
VENEZUELA	1	0	0	0	0	0	0	1	0	0	1	0	0	0	0	0	0	1	1	1	0	0
OTHER	1	0	0	0	0	0	0	0	0	0	1	0	0	0	0	0	0	0	0	0	0	0
EUROPE	51	1	3	4	1	4	6	7	3	7	3	0	0	4	4	1	1	0	1	1	0	0
EFTA	18	0	3	0	0	2	1	3	1	4	0	0	0	4	2	0	0	0	1	1	0	0
U.K.	10	0	3	0	0	1	1	1	1	1	0	0	0	1	1	0	0	0	0	1	0	0
SCANDINAVIA	5	0	0	0	0	1	0	1	0	2	0	0	0	0	1	0	0	0	0	0	0	0
SWITZERLAND	2	0	0	0	0	0	0	1	1	0	0	0	0	0	1	0	0	1	1	1	0	0
OTHER EFTA	1	0	0	0	0	1	0	0	0	1	0	0	0	0	0	0	0	0	0	0	0	0
EUROP. COMMUNITY	32	1	0	4	2	5	5	4	3	3	3	0	0	3	2	0	1	1	0	1	0	0
FRANCE	8	0	0	3	1	1	1	2	1	1	1	0	0	0	1	0	0	1	0	0	0	0
GERMANY	13	1	0	3	1	3	3	1	1	1	1	0	0	1	1	0	0	0	1	1	0	0
ITALY	3	0	0	0	1	1	1	1	1	1	0	0	1	0	1	0	1	0	0	0	0	0
BELGIUM + LUX	3	0	0	0	0	0	0	0	1	1	1	0	0	0	0	0	0	0	1	0	0	0
NETHERLANDS	5	0	0	1	0	1	3	1	1	0	0	0	0	2	0	0	1	0	0	0	0	0
SPAIN	0	0	0	0	0	0	0	0	0	0	0	0	0	0	0	0	0	0	0	0	0	0
GREECE + TURKEY	0	0	0	0	0	0	0	0	0	0	0	0	0	0	0	0	0	0	1	0	0	0
OTHER EUROPE	1	0	0	0	0	0	0	0	0	0	0	0	0	0	0	0	0	1	0	1	0	0
EUROPE EX. U.K.	41	1	0	4	1	4	5	6	2	6	3	0	0	3	3	1	1	0	1	1	0	0
SOUTHERN DOMINIONS	2	0	0	0	0	0	0	0	1	1	1	1	0	0	0	0	0	0	0	0	0	0
S. AFRICA +RHOD.	1	0	0	0	0	0	0	0	0	0	0	0	0	0	0	0	0	0	1	0	0	0
AUSTRALIA + N.Z.	1	0	0	0	0	0	0	0	1	1	0	1	1	0	0	1	2	0	0	0	0	0
ASIA + OTHER AFRICA	8	0	0	0	0	0	0	1	0	0	2	0	1	0	0	1	2	0	0	0	0	0
JAPAN	6	0	0	0	0	0	0	1	0	0	2	0	0	0	0	1	0	0	0	0	0	0
OTHER ASIA+AFR.	2	0	0	0	0	0	0	0	0	0	0	0	1	0	0	0	0	0	1	0	0	0
BLACK AFRICA	0	0	0	0	0	0	0	0	0	0	0	0	0	0	0	0	0	0	0	1	0	0
ARAB WORLD	0	0	0	0	0	0	0	0	0	0	0	0	0	0	0	0	0	0	1	0	0	0
INDIA	2	0	0	0	0	0	0	0	0	1	0	0	0	0	0	0	0	0	0	0	0	0
PHILIPPINES	0	0	0	0	0	0	0	0	0	0	0	0	0	0	0	0	0	0	0	0	0	0
OTHER E. ASIA	0	0	0	0	0	0	0	0	0	0	0	0	0	0	0	0	0	0	0	0	0	0
OTHER ASIA	0	0	0	0	0	0	0	0	0	0	0	0	0	0	0	0	0	0	0	0	0	0

CHAPTER 3- THE PROLIFERATION OF FOREIGN SUBSIDIARIES
SECTION 4- THE FLOW OF MANUFACTURING BY INDUSTRY OF SUBSIDIARY
TABLE 38- SUBSIDIARIES MANUFACTURING
SERVICE INDUSTRY MACHINES (SIC 358)
CLASSIFIED BY COUNTRY OR REGION AND BY PERIOD MANUFACTURE BEGAN

PERIOD

COUNTRY OR REGION	PRE 1968	PRE 1901	1901 -13	1914 -19	1920 -24	1925 -29	1930 -34	1935 -39	1940 -45	1946 -50	1951 -53	1954 -55	1956 -57	1958 -59	1960 -61	1962	1963	1964	1965	1966	1967	UNK
OUTSIDE U.S.	51	0	0	1	0	2	1	3	0	0	0	1	3	2	3	3	10	10	3	7	1	1
OUT. U.S. + CANADA	41	0	0	1	0	1	0	3	0	0	0	1	1	2	3	3	6	9	2	5	1	1
OUT. WEST. HEMIS.	31	0	0	1	0	1	0	2	0	0	0	0	1	2	3	5	5	9	1	1	0	1
OUT. WHITE CWEALTH	29	0	0	0	0	1	0	1	0	0	0	1	1	1	1	1	6	8	2	4	1	0
OUT. DEVLPED WORLD	11	0	0	0	0	0	0	1	0	0	0	0	0	0	0	1	1	1	1	4	0	0
CANADA	10	0	0	0	0	1	1	0	0	0	0	1	1	0	0	0	4	0	1	2	0	1
LATIN AMERICA	10	0	0	0	0	0	0	1	0	0	0	1	1	0	0	1	1	1	1	4	1	1
C. AMER.+CARIB.	5	0	0	0	0	0	0	0	0	0	0	0	0	0	0	0	0	1	1	3	0	0
CUBA	0	0	0	0	0	0	0	0	0	0	0	0	0	0	0	0	0	0	0	0	0	0
MEXICO	2	0	0	0	0	0	0	0	0	0	0	1	0	0	0	0	0	0	0	0	0	0
OTHER	3	0	0	0	0	0	0	1	0	0	0	0	1	0	0	1	1	0	1	2	1	1
S. AMERICA	5	0	0	0	0	0	0	1	0	0	0	1	0	0	0	0	1	0	0	1	1	0
ARGENTINA	0	0	0	0	0	0	0	0	0	0	0	0	0	0	0	0	0	0	0	0	0	0
BRAZIL	2	0	0	0	0	0	0	1	0	0	0	0	1	0	0	0	0	0	0	0	0	0
PERU	0	0	0	0	0	0	0	0	0	0	0	0	0	0	0	0	0	0	0	0	0	0
COLOMBIA	0	0	0	0	0	0	0	0	0	0	0	0	0	0	0	0	0	0	0	0	0	0
VENEZUELA	2	0	0	0	0	0	0	0	0	0	0	0	0	0	0	1	1	0	0	0	0	0
OTHER	1	0	0	0	0	0	0	0	0	0	0	0	0	0	0	0	0	0	1	0	1	1
EUROPE	22	0	0	1	0	1	0	0	0	0	0	1	1	1	2	1	5	6	1	1	1	1
EFTA	8	0	0	1	0	0	0	0	0	0	0	1	1	0	1	1	0	3	0	1	1	1
U.K.	5	0	0	1	0	1	0	0	0	0	0	1	0	0	0	1	0	0	0	1	0	0
SCANDINAVIA	1	0	0	0	0	0	0	0	0	0	0	0	0	0	0	0	0	1	0	0	0	0
SWITZERLAND	1	0	0	0	0	0	0	0	0	0	0	1	0	0	0	0	0	1	0	0	0	0
OTHER EFTA	1	0	0	0	0	0	0	0	0	0	0	1	1	0	1	1	0	1	1	1	0	0
EUROP. COMMUNITY	14	0	0	0	0	1	0	0	0	0	0	0	0	1	1	1	5	3	1	0	0	0
FRANCE	6	0	0	0	0	1	0	0	0	0	0	0	0	0	1	1	2	1	0	0	0	0
GERMANY	4	0	0	0	0	0	0	0	0	0	0	0	0	1	0	0	1	1	0	0	0	0
ITALY	1	0	0	0	0	0	0	0	0	0	0	0	0	0	0	0	1	0	0	0	0	0
BELGIUM + LUX	1	0	0	0	0	0	0	0	0	0	0	0	0	0	0	0	1	0	0	0	0	0
NETHERLANDS	2	0	0	0	0	0	0	0	0	0	0	0	0	0	0	0	0	1	1	0	0	0
SPAIN	0	0	0	0	0	0	0	0	0	0	0	0	0	0	0	0	0	0	0	0	0	0
GREECE + TURKEY	0	0	0	0	0	0	0	0	0	0	0	0	0	0	0	0	0	0	0	0	0	0
OTHER EUROPE	0	0	0	0	0	0	0	0	0	0	0	0	0	0	0	0	0	0	0	0	0	0
EUROPE EX. U.K.	17	0	0	0	0	1	0	0	0	0	0	1	1	1	1	1	5	6	1	0	0	0
SOUTHERN DOMINIONS	7	0	0	0	0	0	0	2	0	0	0	0	0	1	1	1	0	2	0	0	0	0
S. AFRICA +RHOD.	0	0	0	0	0	0	0	0	0	0	0	0	0	0	0	0	0	0	0	0	0	0
AUSTRALIA + N.Z.	7	0	0	0	0	0	0	2	0	0	0	0	0	1	1	1	0	2	0	0	0	0
ASIA + OTHER AFRICA	2	0	0	0	0	0	0	0	0	0	0	0	0	0	0	0	0	1	1	0	0	0
JAPAN	1	0	0	0	0	0	0	0	0	0	0	0	0	0	0	0	0	1	0	0	0	0
OTHER ASIA+AFR.	1	0	0	0	0	0	0	0	0	0	0	0	0	0	0	0	0	0	1	0	0	0
BLACK AFRICA	0	0	0	0	0	0	0	0	0	0	0	0	0	0	0	0	0	0	0	0	0	0
ARAB WORLD	0	0	0	0	0	0	0	0	0	0	0	0	0	0	0	0	0	0	0	0	0	0
INDIA	1	0	0	0	0	0	0	0	0	0	0	0	0	0	0	0	0	0	1	0	0	0
PHILIPPINES	0	0	0	0	0	0	0	0	0	0	0	0	0	0	0	0	0	0	0	0	0	0
OTHER E. ASIA	0	0	0	0	0	0	0	0	0	0	0	0	0	0	0	0	0	0	0	0	0	0
OTHER ASIA	0	0	0	0	0	0	0	0	0	0	0	0	0	0	0	0	0	0	0	0	0	0

CHAPTER 3- THE PROLIFERATION OF FOREIGN SUBSIDIARIES
SECTION 4- THE FLOW OF MANUFACTURING BY INDUSTRY OF SUBSIDIARY
TABLE 39- SUBSIDIARIES MANUFACTURING
OTHER NON-ELECTRICAL MACHINERY (SIC 351 AND 359)
CLASSIFIED BY COUNTRY OR REGION AND BY PERIOD MANUFACTURE BEGAN

PERIOD

COUNTRY OR REGION	PRE 1968	PRE 1901	1901 -13	1914 -19	1920 -24	1925 -29	1930 -34	1935 -39	1940 -45	1946 -50	1951 -53	1954 -55	1956 -57	1958 -59	1960 -61	1962	1963	1964	1965	1966	1967	UNK
OUTSIDE U.S.	56	3	1	1	0	2	1	2	1	2	2	2	2	4	9	10	3	4	4	0	1	3
OUT. U.S. + CANADA	46	3	1	0	0	1	1	2	1	1	1	1	2	4	6	9	3	4	3	0	0	3
OUT. WEST. HEMIS.	39	3	1	0	0	1	1	2	1	1	1	1	2	3	6	6	3	4	3	0	0	3
OUT. WHITE CWEALTH	32	2	1	0	0	1	0	2	0	0	0	1	1	2	4	8	1	3	3	0	0	1
OUT. DEVLPED WORLD	7	0	0	0	0	1	1	0	1	0	0	1	1	0	0	3	0	0	0	0	0	0
CANADA	10	0	0	0	0	0	0	0	1	0	0	0	0	0	3	1	0	0	1	0	1	0
LATIN AMERICA	7	0	1	1	1	1	0	1	0	1	1	0	0	0	0	3	0	0	1	0	0	0
C. AMER.+CARIB.	1	0	0	0	1	1	0	0	0	0	0	0	0	0	0	0	0	0	0	0	0	0
CUBA	0	0	0	0	0	0	0	0	0	0	0	0	0	0	0	0	0	0	0	0	0	0
MEXICO	1	0	0	0	1	1	0	0	0	0	0	0	0	0	1	1	0	0	0	0	0	0
OTHER	0	0	0	0	0	0	0	0	0	0	0	0	0	0	0	0	0	0	0	0	0	0
S. AMERICA	6	0	0	0	1	0	0	1	0	0	0	1	0	1	2	2	0	0	0	0	0	0
ARGENTINA	2	0	0	0	0	1	0	0	0	0	0	0	1	1	2	2	0	0	0	0	0	0
BRAZIL	4	0	0	0	0	0	1	1	1	0	0	1	0	0	0	0	0	0	1	0	0	0
PERU	0	0	0	0	0	0	0	0	0	0	0	0	0	0	0	0	0	0	0	0	0	0
COLOMBIA	0	0	0	0	0	0	0	0	0	0	0	0	0	0	0	0	0	0	0	0	0	0
VENEZUELA	0	0	0	0	0	0	0	0	0	0	0	0	0	0	0	0	0	0	0	0	0	0
OTHER	0	0	0	0	0	0	0	0	0	0	0	0	0	0	0	0	0	0	0	0	0	0
EUROPE	34	3	1	0	0	1	2	0	0	0	1	1	3	3	5	5	3	4	3	0	0	2
EFTA	10	1	1	0	1	1	0	0	0	0	0	0	2	2	1	1	1	1	0	0	0	1
U.K.	9	1	0	0	1	1	0	0	0	1	0	0	2	2	1	1	1	1	0	0	0	1
SCANDINAVIA	1	0	0	0	0	0	0	0	0	0	0	0	0	0	0	0	0	0	0	0	0	0
SWITZERLAND	0	0	0	0	0	0	0	0	0	0	0	0	0	0	0	0	0	0	0	0	0	0
OTHER EFTA	0	0	0	0	0	0	0	0	0	0	0	0	0	0	0	0	0	0	0	0	0	0
EUROP. COMMUNITY	21	2	1	0	0	0	2	2	0	0	0	0	1	4	4	4	0	3	2	0	0	1
FRANCE	10	2	0	0	0	0	1	0	0	0	0	0	0	4	4	1	0	0	0	0	0	1
GERMANY	8	0	1	0	0	0	0	1	0	0	0	0	0	0	0	3	0	2	1	0	0	0
ITALY	1	0	0	0	0	0	0	0	0	0	0	0	1	0	0	0	0	1	0	0	0	0
BELGIUM + LUX	2	0	0	0	0	0	1	0	0	0	0	1	0	0	0	0	0	0	0	0	0	1
NETHERLANDS	0	0	0	0	0	0	0	0	0	0	0	0	0	0	0	0	0	0	0	0	0	0
SPAIN	2	0	0	0	0	0	0	0	0	0	0	0	0	0	0	0	1	0	1	0	0	0
GREECE + TURKEY	0	0	0	0	0	0	0	0	0	0	0	0	0	0	0	0	0	0	0	0	0	0
OTHER EUROPE	1	0	0	0	0	0	0	0	0	1	1	1	0	0	4	1	1	0	0	0	1	0
EUROPE EX. U.K.	25	2	1	0	0	0	2	0	0	1	1	1	1	1	4	4	2	3	3	0	0	1
SOUTHERN DOMINIONS	4	0	0	0	0	0	0	0	0	1	0	0	0	0	1	0	0	0	0	0	0	1
S. AFRICA +RHOD.	0	0	0	0	0	0	0	0	0	1	0	0	0	1	0	1	0	0	0	0	0	0
AUSTRALIA + N.Z.	4	0	0	0	0	0	0	0	0	0	0	0	0	1	1	1	0	0	0	0	0	1
ASIA + OTHER AFRICA	1	0	0	0	0	0	0	0	0	0	0	0	0	0	0	1	0	0	0	0	0	0
JAPAN	1	0	0	0	0	0	0	0	0	0	0	0	0	0	0	1	0	0	0	0	0	0
OTHER ASIA+AFR.	0	0	0	0	0	0	0	0	0	0	0	0	0	0	0	0	0	0	0	0	0	0
BLACK AFRICA	0	0	0	0	0	0	0	0	0	0	0	0	0	0	0	0	0	0	0	0	0	0
ARAB WORLD	0	0	0	0	0	0	0	0	0	0	0	0	0	0	0	0	0	0	0	0	0	0
INDIA	0	0	0	0	0	0	0	0	0	0	0	0	0	0	0	0	0	0	0	0	0	0
PHILIPPINES	0	0	0	0	0	0	0	0	0	0	0	0	0	0	0	0	0	0	0	0	0	0
OTHER E. ASIA	0	0	0	0	0	0	0	0	0	0	0	0	0	0	0	0	0	0	0	0	0	0
OTHER ASIA	0	0	0	0	0	0	0	0	0	0	0	0	0	0	0	0	0	0	0	0	0	0

CHAPTER 3— THE PROLIFERATION OF FOREIGN SUBSIDIARIES
SECTION 4— THE FLOW OF MANUFACTURING BY INDUSTRY OF SUBSIDIARY
TABLE 40— SUBSIDIARIES MANUFACTURING
HOUSEHOLD APPLIANCES (SIC 363)
CLASSIFIED BY COUNTRY OR REGION AND BY PERIOD MANUFACTURE BEGAN

COUNTRY OR REGION	PRE 1968	PRE 1901	1901-13	1914-19	1920-24	1925-29	1930-34	1935-39	1940-45	1946-50	1951-53	1954-55	1956-57	1958-59	1960-61	1962	1963	1964	1965	1966	1967	UNK
OUTSIDE U.S.	96	1	2	1	3	4	2	3	1	4	1	4	8	8	14	7	8	11	4	2	7	1
OUT. U.S. + CANADA	85	0	2	0	2	3	1	3	1	3	1	4	8	8	14	6	6	11	3	2	6	1
OUT. WEST. HEMIS.	64	0	2	0	3	3	1	1	0	2	1	3	6	4	10	5	5	8	2	2	4	1
OUT. WHITE CWEALTH	64	0	0	0	2	1	1	3	1	2	1	3	6	6	12	3	3	8	3	2	4	1
OUT. DEVLPED WORLD	35	0	1	0	0	0	0	2	1	1	1	1	2	4	9	2	1	2	3	2	4	0
CANADA	11	1	0	1	1	1	0	0	0	1	0	0	0	0	0	1	2	1	1	0	1	0
LATIN AMERICA	21	0	0	0	1	0	2	2	1	1	0	1	2	4	4	2	1	0	1	2	2	0
C. AMER.+CARIB.	8	0	0	0	0	0	1	1	1	1	0	0	1	1	1	1	1	0	1	1	0	0
CUBA	0	0	0	0	0	0	0	0	0	0	0	0	0	0	0	0	0	0	0	0	0	0
MEXICO	7	0	0	0	0	0	1	1	0	1	0	1	1	1	1	0	1	0	0	0	1	0
OTHER	1	0	0	0	0	0	0	0	1	0	0	0	0	0	0	1	0	0	0	1	0	0
S. AMERICA	13	0	0	0	0	0	1	1	0	0	0	0	1	3	3	0	0	0	0	1	1	0
ARGENTINA	4	0	0	0	0	0	1	0	0	0	0	0	1	1	1	0	1	0	0	0	0	0
BRAZIL	2	0	0	0	0	0	0	0	0	0	0	0	0	1	0	0	0	1	0	0	0	0
PERU	1	0	0	0	0	0	0	0	0	0	0	0	0	0	0	1	0	0	0	0	0	0
COLOMBIA	2	0	0	0	0	0	0	0	0	0	0	0	0	1	1	0	0	0	0	0	0	0
VENEZUELA	2	0	0	0	0	0	0	0	0	0	0	0	0	0	1	0	0	1	0	0	1	0
OTHER	2	0	0	0	0	0	0	0	0	1	0	0	0	0	0	1	1	0	1	1	0	0
EUROPE	41	0	2	0	2	2	1	1	0	2	0	2	4	4	5	3	4	7	0	0	2	0
EFTA	15	0	1	0	2	1	0	1	0	1	0	1	1	2	2	2	1	1	0	0	0	0
U.K.	14	0	1	0	2	1	0	1	0	1	0	0	1	2	2	2	1	1	0	0	0	0
SCANDINAVIA	1	0	0	0	0	0	0	0	0	0	0	0	0	0	0	0	0	0	0	0	0	0
SWITZERLAND	0	0	0	0	0	0	0	0	0	0	0	0	0	0	0	0	0	0	0	0	0	0
OTHER EFTA	0	0	0	0	0	0	0	0	0	0	0	0	0	0	0	0	0	0	0	0	0	0
EUROP. COMMUNITY	23	0	0	0	1	0	0	1	0	1	0	0	3	2	2	0	6	3	0	0	2	0
FRANCE	8	0	0	0	0	0	1	1	1	0	0	1	1	1	2	2	3	1	1	0	0	0
GERMANY	8	0	0	0	0	0	1	0	0	1	0	1	1	1	1	1	2	2	1	0	2	0
ITALY	6	0	0	0	0	0	0	0	1	0	0	0	1	1	0	1	1	1	1	0	0	0
BELGIUM + LUX	1	0	0	0	0	0	0	0	0	0	0	0	0	0	0	0	0	0	0	0	0	0
NETHERLANDS	0	0	0	0	0	0	0	0	0	0	0	0	0	0	0	0	0	0	0	0	0	0
SPAIN	0	0	0	0	0	0	0	0	0	0	0	0	0	0	0	0	0	0	0	0	0	0
GREECE + TURKEY	2	0	0	0	0	0	0	0	0	0	0	0	0	0	1	0	0	0	0	0	0	0
OTHER EUROPE	1	0	1	0	0	0	0	1	0	1	0	0	0	1	0	0	0	0	0	0	0	0
EUROPE EX. U.K.	27	0	1	0	1	1	1	0	0	1	0	2	3	2	3	6	6	6	0	0	2	0
SOUTHERN DOMINIONS	7	0	0	0	1	1	0	0	0	0	0	1	1	0	0	2	2	2	0	0	0	0
S. AFRICA +RHOD.	2	0	0	0	0	0	0	0	0	0	0	0	0	0	0	1	1	0	2	0	0	0
AUSTRALIA + N.Z.	5	0	0	0	1	1	0	0	0	0	0	1	1	0	0	1	1	2	0	0	0	0
ASIA + OTHER AFRICA	16	0	0	0	0	0	0	0	0	0	0	0	0	0	0	0	2	2	2	0	2	1
JAPAN	2	0	0	0	0	0	0	0	0	0	1	0	1	0	0	0	1	0	2	0	0	0
OTHER ASIA+AFR.	14	0	0	0	0	0	0	0	0	0	0	1	1	0	1	0	1	2	1	0	1	1
BLACK AFRICA	3	0	0	0	0	0	0	0	0	0	0	0	0	0	0	0	0	0	1	0	0	0
ARAB WORLD	2	0	0	0	0	0	0	0	0	0	0	0	0	0	0	0	0	0	1	0	0	0
INDIA	0	0	0	0	0	0	0	0	0	0	0	0	0	0	1	0	0	0	0	0	0	0
PHILIPPINES	2	0	0	0	0	0	0	0	0	0	0	0	0	0	0	1	0	1	0	0	0	0
OTHER E. ASIA	2	0	0	0	0	0	0	0	0	0	0	0	0	0	0	1	0	1	0	0	0	0
OTHER ASIA	5	0	0	0	0	0	0	0	0	0	0	0	0	0	2	1	1	1	0	0	1	0

PERIOD

CHAPTER 3- THE PROLIFERATION OF FOREIGN SUBSIDIARIES
SECTION 4- THE FLOW OF MANUFACTURING BY INDUSTRY OF SUBSIDIARY
TABLE 41- SUBSIDIARIES MANUFACTURING
COMMUNICATION EQUIPMENT (SIC 366)
CLASSIFIED BY COUNTRY OR REGION AND BY PERIOD MANUFACTURE BEGAN

COUNTRY OR REGION	PRE 1968	PRE 1901	1901 -13	1914 -19	1920 -24	1925 -29	1930 -34	1935 -39	1940 -45	1946 -50	1951 -53	1954 -55	1956 -57	1958 -59	1960 -61	1962	1963	1964	1965	1966	1967	UNK
OUTSIDE U.S.	56	0	0	0	2	9	6	1	4	3	2	5	2	3	6	1	3	3	3	3	2	0
OUT. U.S. + CANADA	47	0	0	0	1	9	6	1	4	1	2	2	1	3	5	1	2	3	3	1	2	0
OUT. WEST. HEMIS.	43	0	0	0	1	8	6	1	4	1	2	2	1	2	4	1	2	2	2	1	2	0
OUT. WHITE CWEALTH	37	0	0	0	1	6	6	1	3	0	2	2	0	2	4	1	0	0	3	1	1	0
OUT. DEVLPED WORLD	7	0	0	0	0	1	0	0	0	0	0	0	0	0	2	0	0	0	3	0	1	0
CANADA	9	0	0	0	1	1	0	0	0	2	0	0	1	0	1	1	1	1	0	0	0	0
LATIN AMERICA	4	0	0	0	1	0	0	0	0	0	0	0	0	0	1	0	0	0	1	1	1	0
C. AMER.+CARIB.	3	0	0	0	0	0	0	0	0	0	0	0	0	0	1	0	0	0	1	0	1	0
CUBA	0	0	0	0	0	0	0	0	0	0	0	0	0	0	0	0	0	0	0	0	0	0
MEXICO	3	0	0	0	0	0	0	0	0	0	0	0	0	0	1	0	0	0	1	0	1	0
OTHER	0	0	0	0	0	0	0	0	0	0	0	0	0	0	0	0	0	0	0	0	0	0
S. AMERICA	1	0	0	0	1	0	0	0	0	0	0	0	0	0	0	0	0	0	0	1	0	0
ARGENTINA	1	0	0	0	1	0	0	0	0	0	0	0	0	0	0	0	0	0	0	0	0	0
BRAZIL	0	0	0	0	0	0	0	0	0	0	0	0	0	0	0	0	0	0	0	0	0	0
PERU	0	0	0	0	0	0	0	0	0	0	0	0	0	0	0	0	0	0	0	0	0	0
COLOMBIA	0	0	0	0	0	0	0	0	0	0	0	0	0	0	0	0	0	0	0	0	0	0
VENEZUELA	0	0	0	0	0	0	0	0	0	0	0	0	0	0	0	0	0	0	0	0	0	0
OTHER	0	0	0	0	0	0	0	0	0	0	0	0	0	0	0	0	0	0	0	0	0	0
EUROPE	34	0	0	0	1	7	6	1	3	2	2	2	3	3	3	2	2	1	1	1	1	0
EFTA	14	0	0	0	0	3	3	1	1	0	0	0	1	1	1	1	1	1	1	0	0	0
U.K.	5	0	0	0	0	2	0	0	0	0	0	0	0	0	1	1	0	0	1	0	0	0
SCANDINAVIA	5	0	0	0	0	0	2	1	0	0	0	0	0	0	1	0	1	1	0	0	0	0
SWITZERLAND	0	0	0	0	0	1	0	0	1	0	0	0	0	0	0	0	0	0	0	0	0	0
OTHER EFTA	4	0	0	0	0	1	1	0	1	0	0	0	0	0	1	1	0	0	0	1	0	0
EUROP. COMMUNITY	15	0	0	0	1	3	3	0	1	0	0	1	2	2	2	0	0	0	0	0	1	0
FRANCE	4	0	0	0	1	2	1	0	0	0	0	0	0	0	0	0	0	0	0	0	0	0
GERMANY	5	0	0	0	0	1	1	0	0	0	0	1	2	0	1	1	0	0	0	1	1	0
ITALY	3	0	0	0	1	1	2	0	0	0	1	0	0	2	0	0	0	0	0	0	0	0
BELGIUM + LUX	2	0	0	0	0	0	0	0	0	0	0	0	0	0	0	0	0	0	0	0	0	0
NETHERLANDS	1	0	0	0	0	0	0	0	0	0	0	1	0	0	1	1	1	0	1	0	0	0
SPAIN	3	0	0	0	0	0	0	0	0	0	0	0	0	0	0	0	0	0	0	0	0	0
GREECE + TURKEY	1	0	0	0	0	0	0	0	0	0	0	1	0	0	0	0	0	0	0	0	0	0
OTHER EUROPE	1	0	0	0	0	0	0	0	0	0	0	0	0	0	0	0	0	0	1	0	1	0
EUROPE EX. U.K.	29	0	0	0	1	5	6	1	3	2	2	2	2	2	2	1	1	1	0	1	1	0
SOUTHERN DOMINIONS	5	0	0	0	1	0	0	0	1	1	0	0	1	0	0	0	1	1	0	0	0	0
S. AFRICA +RHOD.	2	0	0	0	0	0	0	0	0	0	0	0	1	0	0	0	0	0	0	0	0	0
AUSTRALIA + N.Z.	3	0	0	0	1	0	0	0	1	1	0	0	0	0	1	0	1	1	2	0	0	0
ASIA + OTHER AFRICA	4	0	0	0	0	0	1	0	0	0	0	0	0	0	1	0	1	1	0	0	0	0
JAPAN	1	0	0	0	0	0	0	0	0	0	0	0	0	0	0	0	0	0	0	0	0	0
OTHER ASIA+AFR.	3	0	0	0	0	0	0	0	0	0	0	0	0	0	1	0	0	0	0	0	0	0
BLACK AFRICA	0	0	0	0	0	0	0	0	0	0	0	0	0	0	0	0	0	0	0	0	0	0
ARAB WORLD	0	0	0	0	0	0	0	0	0	0	0	0	0	0	0	0	0	0	0	0	0	0
INDIA	0	0	0	0	0	0	0	0	0	0	0	0	0	0	0	0	0	0	1	0	0	0
PHILIPPINES	2	0	0	0	0	0	0	0	0	0	0	0	0	0	1	0	0	0	1	0	0	0
OTHER E. ASIA	1	0	0	0	0	0	0	0	0	0	0	0	0	0	0	0	0	0	0	0	0	0
OTHER ASIA	0	0	0	0	0	0	0	0	0	0	0	0	0	0	0	0	0	0	0	0	0	0

CHAPTER 3- THE PROLIFERATION OF FOREIGN SUBSIDIARIES
SECTION 4- THE FLOW OF MANUFACTURING BY INDUSTRY OF SUBSIDIARY
TABLE 42- SUBSIDIARIES MANUFACTURING
OTHER ELECTRONIC EQUIPMENT (SIC 365 AND 367)
CLASSIFIED BY COUNTRY OR REGION AND BY PERIOD MANUFACTURE BEGAN

COUNTRY OR REGION	PRE 1968	PRE 1901	1901 -13	1914 -19	1920 -24	1925 -29	1930 -34	1935 -39	1940 -45	1946 -50	1951 -53	1954 -55	1956 -57	1958 -59	1960 -61	1962	1963	1964	1965	1966	1967	UNK
OUTSIDE U.S.	81	0	0	0	1	4	2	2	0	0	5	4	2	8	17	6	3	5	9	4	6	1
OUT. U.S. + CANADA	72	0	0	0	0	4	2	2	0	0	5	4	1	7	15	6	3	5	7	4	6	1
OUT. WEST. HEMIS.	51	0	0	0	0	2	2	1	0	0	5	3	0	4	9	5	4	4	4	3	4	1
OUT. WHITE CWEALTH	57	0	0	0	0	3	0	1	0	0	4	2	0	6	13	4	1	5	7	2	6	1
OUT. DEVLPED WORLD	27	0	0	0	0	3	0	1	0	0	0	1	0	3	7	1	0	2	3	2	4	0
CANADA	9	0	0	0	1	0	0	0	0	2	0	1	1	1	2	0	0	0	2	0	0	0
LATIN AMERICA	21	0	0	0	1	2	0	1	2	0	0	1	1	1	2	2	0	1	2	0	2	0
C. AMER.+CARIB.	9	0	0	0	0	2	0	1	0	0	0	0	0	3	6	1	0	1	3	1	2	0
CUBA	0	0	0	0	0	0	0	0	0	0	0	0	0	0	0	0	0	0	0	0	0	0
MEXICO	7	0	0	0	0	0	0	1	0	0	0	0	0	2	3	0	0	0	1	1	0	0
OTHER	2	0	0	0	0	2	0	0	0	0	0	1	0	0	0	0	0	0	0	0	1	0
S. AMERICA	12	0	0	0	0	2	0	1	2	0	0	1	0	1	3	1	0	1	2	0	1	0
ARGENTINA	3	0	0	0	0	0	0	0	0	0	0	1	0	1	0	0	0	0	1	0	1	0
BRAZIL	5	0	0	0	1	1	0	1	0	0	0	1	0	1	2	0	0	0	0	0	0	0
PERU	0	0	0	0	0	0	0	0	0	0	0	0	0	0	0	0	0	0	0	0	0	0
COLOMBIA	0	0	0	0	0	0	0	0	0	0	0	0	0	0	0	0	0	0	0	0	0	0
VENEZUELA	2	0	0	0	0	0	0	0	0	0	0	0	0	0	1	0	0	0	1	0	1	0
OTHER	2	0	0	0	0	1	0	0	0	0	0	0	0	1	0	0	0	0	1	0	0	0
EUROPE	36	0	0	0	0	0	2	1	1	0	4	1	0	4	6	4	3	3	3	3	2	0
EFTA	13	0	0	0	0	1	2	1	1	0	1	0	0	1	2	2	1	1	0	0	0	0
U.K.	11	0	0	0	0	1	2	1	1	0	1	0	0	1	1	2	0	0	0	0	0	0
SCANDINAVIA	0	0	0	0	0	0	0	0	0	0	0	0	0	0	0	0	0	0	0	0	0	0
SWITZERLAND	2	0	0	0	0	0	2	0	0	0	0	0	0	0	1	0	0	1	0	0	0	0
OTHER EFTA	0	0	0	0	0	0	0	0	0	0	0	0	0	0	0	0	0	0	0	0	0	0
EUROP. COMMUNITY	20	0	0	0	0	0	0	0	0	0	1	0	0	3	4	2	1	2	3	3	2	0
FRANCE	4	0	0	0	0	1	0	0	0	0	0	1	0	1	1	1	1	0	1	0	1	0
GERMANY	9	0	0	0	0	1	0	0	0	0	0	0	0	1	2	1	1	0	3	1	0	0
ITALY	6	0	0	0	0	0	0	0	0	0	1	0	0	2	0	0	0	1	0	1	1	0
BELGIUM + LUX	1	0	0	0	0	0	0	0	0	0	0	0	0	0	0	0	0	0	0	0	0	0
NETHERLANDS	0	0	0	0	0	0	0	0	0	0	0	0	0	0	0	0	0	0	0	0	0	0
SPAIN	2	0	0	0	0	0	0	0	0	0	0	0	0	0	0	0	0	0	0	1	0	0
GREECE + TURKEY	1	0	0	0	0	0	0	0	0	1	1	0	1	0	1	0	0	0	0	1	0	0
OTHER EUROPE	0	0	0	0	0	0	0	0	0	0	0	0	0	0	0	0	0	0	0	0	0	0
EUROPE EX. U.K.	25	0	0	0	0	1	0	0	0	0	3	1	0	3	5	2	1	3	3	2	2	0
SOUTHERN DOMINIONS	4	0	0	0	0	0	0	0	0	0	0	2	1	0	1	0	0	0	0	0	0	0
S. AFRICA +RHOD.	0	0	0	0	0	0	0	0	0	0	0	0	0	0	0	0	0	0	0	0	0	0
AUSTRALIA + N.Z.	4	0	0	0	0	0	0	0	0	0	0	2	1	0	2	0	0	1	1	0	2	1
ASIA + OTHER AFRICA	11	0	0	0	1	1	0	0	0	0	1	0	0	0	1	1	0	1	1	1	0	1
JAPAN	5	0	0	0	0	0	0	0	0	0	0	0	0	0	2	1	0	0	1	0	0	0
OTHER ASIA+AFR.	6	0	0	0	0	1	0	0	0	0	1	1	0	0	1	1	0	1	0	0	2	0
BLACK AFRICA	1	0	0	0	0	0	0	0	0	0	0	0	0	0	0	0	0	0	0	0	0	0
ARAB WORLD	0	0	0	0	0	0	0	0	0	0	0	0	0	0	0	0	0	0	0	0	0	0
INDIA	1	0	0	0	0	0	0	0	0	0	0	0	0	1	0	0	0	0	0	0	0	1
PHILIPPINES	1	0	0	0	0	1	0	0	0	0	0	0	0	0	0	0	0	0	0	0	0	0
OTHER E. ASIA	3	0	0	0	0	0	0	0	0	0	0	0	0	0	1	0	0	0	0	0	2	0
OTHER ASIA	0	0	0	0	0	0	0	0	0	0	0	0	0	0	0	0	0	0	0	0	0	0

PERIOD

226

CHAPTER 3- THE PROLIFERATION OF FOREIGN SUBSIDIARIES
SECTION 4- THE FLOW OF MANUFACTURING BY INDUSTRY OF SUBSIDIARY
TABLE 43- SUBSIDIARIES MANUFACTURING
OTHER ELECTRICAL MACHINERY (OTHER SIC 36)
CLASSIFIED BY COUNTRY OR REGION AND BY PERIOD MANUFACTURE BEGAN

COUNTRY OR REGION	PRE 1968	PRE 1901	1901-13	1914-19	1920-24	1925-29	1930-34	1935-39	1940-45	1946-50	1951-53	1954-55	1956-57	1958-59	1960-61	1962	1963	1964	1965	1966	1967	UNK
OUTSIDE U.S.	220	4	8	6	6	5	7	10	2	15	9	9	14	25	23	14	13	9	16	7	13	5
OUT. U.S. + CANADA	176	4	6	4	3	5	6	7	1	11	5	6	11	19	19	14	13	8	14	6	10	4
OUT. WEST. HEMIS.	119	3	6	4	3	4	6	3	1	11	5	2	9	11	14	9	11	5	11	4	7	4
OUT. WHITE CWEALTH	139	3	5	1	1	5	2	5	0	10	4	6	9	14	14	13	11	8	13	7	7	4
OUT. DEVLPED WORLD	80	1	0	1	0	2	0	4	0	8	2	5	7	8	9	6	7	5	7	2	5	1
CANADA	44	0	2	2	3	0	1	3	1	4	4	3	3	6	4	0	5	1	2	1	3	1
LATIN AMERICA	57	1	0	0	0	1	0	4	0	7	0	1	6	8	5	5	5	3	3	2	3	0
C. AMER.+CARIB.	27	0	0	0	0	0	0	1	0	2	0	0	5	4	2	2	2	1	2	2	2	0
CUBA	2	0	0	0	0	0	0	0	0	0	0	0	0	2	0	0	0	0	0	0	0	0
MEXICO	18	0	0	0	0	1	0	0	0	2	0	1	3	2	2	1	3	1	2	0	1	0
OTHER	7	0	0	0	0	0	0	1	0	0	0	0	0	0	0	1	0	0	0	2	1	0
S. AMERICA	30	1	0	0	0	1	0	3	0	5	0	0	1	4	3	2	3	2	1	0	1	0
ARGENTINA	7	0	0	0	0	0	0	1	0	1	0	0	0	1	1	0	1	0	0	0	0	0
BRAZIL	13	0	0	0	1	0	2	2	0	2	0	1	0	1	2	1	1	1	0	0	0	1
PERU	1	0	0	0	0	0	0	0	0	1	0	0	0	0	0	0	0	0	0	0	0	0
COLOMBIA	3	0	0	0	0	0	0	0	0	0	0	0	0	1	0	1	0	0	0	0	0	0
VENEZUELA	5	0	0	0	0	0	0	0	0	1	0	1	1	1	0	0	0	1	0	0	0	0
OTHER	1	1	0	0	0	0	0	0	0	0	0	0	0	0	0	0	0	0	0	0	0	0
EUROPE	75	3	5	2	3	3	4	1	1	3	1	1	2	9	7	6	6	3	5	3	5	2
EFTA	30	1	2	2	2	1	2	1	1	1	0	0	1	3	4	2	2	2	2	2	3	0
U.K.	24	1	1	2	2	0	2	1	1	1	0	0	1	3	2	0	0	0	0	2	3	0
SCANDINAVIA	2	0	0	0	0	1	0	0	0	0	0	0	0	0	0	1	0	0	0	0	0	0
SWITZERLAND	2	0	1	0	1	0	0	0	0	0	0	0	0	0	2	0	0	0	0	0	0	0
OTHER EFTA	2	0	0	0	0	0	0	0	0	0	0	0	0	0	0	1	0	0	0	0	0	2
EUROP. COMMUNITY	37	1	1	0	1	2	2	0	0	2	0	0	1	3	3	4	4	2	3	1	0	2
FRANCE	14	1	3	1	1	1	1	0	0	1	0	1	0	1	1	1	1	1	0	0	0	1
GERMANY	8	0	1	0	0	0	0	0	0	0	0	0	0	1	0	2	2	0	1	0	0	0
ITALY	14	0	2	1	0	1	1	0	0	1	0	0	0	0	2	3	1	0	0	0	0	1
BELGIUM + LUX	0	0	0	0	0	0	0	0	0	0	0	0	0	1	0	0	0	0	0	0	0	0
NETHERLANDS	1	0	0	0	0	1	1	0	0	0	0	0	1	0	2	0	1	0	0	1	0	1
SPAIN	3	0	0	0	0	0	0	0	0	0	0	0	0	0	0	0	0	0	1	0	1	0
GREECE + TURKEY	3	0	0	0	0	0	0	0	0	1	1	0	0	0	0	0	0	0	0	1	1	0
OTHER EUROPE	2	1	0	0	0	0	0	0	0	0	0	1	1	0	1	0	0	0	1	0	0	0
EUROPE EX. U.K.	51	2	4	1	1	3	2	0	0	2	1	1	1	6	5	6	4	3	5	1	2	2
SOUTHERN DOMINIONS	13	0	0	1	0	0	1	1	0	0	1	0	1	2	3	1	0	0	1	0	0	0
S. AFRICA +RHOD.	2	0	0	1	0	2	0	0	0	0	1	0	1	0	0	0	0	0	0	0	0	0
AUSTRALIA + N.Z.	11	0	1	0	0	0	1	0	0	1	1	1	0	2	3	1	2	0	1	1	2	2
ASIA + OTHER AFRICA	31	0	1	1	0	1	1	0	0	0	2	1	2	2	4	2	2	2	5	1	2	1
JAPAN	8	0	0	1	1	0	1	0	0	1	0	1	1	0	0	1	1	2	1	0	2	1
OTHER ASIA+AFR.	23	0	1	1	0	0	0	0	0	0	2	0	1	0	4	2	2	0	4	0	0	0
BLACK AFRICA	2	0	0	0	0	0	0	0	0	0	0	0	0	0	0	0	0	0	2	0	0	0
ARAB WORLD	0	0	0	0	0	0	0	0	0	0	0	0	0	0	0	0	0	0	0	0	0	0
INDIA	6	0	0	0	0	0	0	0	0	0	0	1	0	3	0	0	1	0	0	0	0	0
PHILIPPINES	3	0	0	1	0	0	0	0	0	1	0	0	1	0	0	0	0	1	0	0	0	0
OTHER E. ASIA	5	0	0	1	0	0	0	0	0	0	1	0	0	0	0	1	1	0	1	0	0	0
OTHER ASIA	7	0	0	0	0	0	0	0	0	1	0	0	1	0	1	2	2	0	0	0	0	1

CHAPTER 3- THE PROLIFERATION OF FOREIGN SUBSIDIARIES
SECTION 4- THE FLOW OF MANUFACTURING BY INDUSTRY OF SUBSIDIARY
TABLE 44- SUBSIDIARIES MANUFACTURING
MOTOR VEHICLES AND MOTOR VEHICLES EQUIPMENT (SIC 371)
CLASSIFIED BY COUNTRY OR REGION AND BY PERIOD MANUFACTURE BEGAN

PERIOD

COUNTRY OR REGION	PRE 1968	PRE 1901	1901-13	1914-19	1920-24	1925-29	1930-34	1935-39	1940-45	1946-50	1951-53	1954-55	1956-57	1958-59	1960-61	1962	1963	1964	1965	1966	1967	UNK
OUTSIDE U.S.	306	1	5	7	5	23	10	9	2	13	9	6	9	39	28	18	29	26	20	29	6	12
OUT. U.S. + CANADA	258	1	3	3	4	16	8	4	2	11	7	6	9	35	27	18	26	23	13	25	6	11
OUT. WEST. HEMIS.	173	1	3	2	4	13	8	2	1	9	5	3	5	16	18	10	16	13	8	20	4	10
OUT. WHITE CWEALTH	181	1	1	3	3	8	4	2	2	8	3	5	5	32	22	14	23	16	10	12	5	10
OUT. DEVLPED WORLD	101	0	0	1	0	6	0	0	1	5	2	4	4	21	12	9	12	10	5	6	2	1
CANADA	48	0	2	4	1	7	2	5	0	2	2	0	0	4	1	0	3	3	7	4	0	1
LATIN AMERICA	85	0	0	1	0	3	0	0	1	2	2	3	4	19	9	8	10	10	5	5	2	1
C. AMER.+CARIB.	25	0	0	0	0	1	0	0	0	1	0	1	0	7	3	0	3	4	3	2	0	0
CUBA	0	0	0	0	0	0	0	0	0	0	0	0	0	0	0	0	0	0	0	0	0	0
MEXICO	23	0	0	0	0	1	0	0	0	1	0	1	0	7	3	0	3	4	3	2	0	0
OTHER	2	0	0	0	0	0	0	0	0	0	0	0	0	0	0	0	0	0	0	0	0	0
S. AMERICA	60	0	0	1	0	2	0	0	1	1	2	2	4	12	6	7	6	6	2	3	2	1
ARGENTINA	24	0	1	1	0	1	0	0	1	1	2	2	2	3	3	4	2	2	2	1	1	0
BRAZIL	20	0	1	1	0	1	0	0	1	0	0	0	2	3	1	1	2	1	1	1	0	0
PERU	2	0	0	0	0	0	0	0	0	0	0	0	0	0	0	1	1	0	0	0	0	0
COLOMBIA	5	0	0	0	0	0	0	0	0	1	0	0	2	0	1	0	1	0	0	0	0	0
VENEZUELA	7	0	0	0	0	0	0	0	0	0	2	0	0	0	1	0	1	1	1	0	1	0
OTHER	2	0	0	0	0	0	0	0	0	0	0	0	0	0	0	0	0	1	0	1	0	0
EUROPE	122	1	3	2	4	8	5	2	1	6	3	2	1	11	12	6	11	10	4	4	3	9
EFTA	52	0	2	1	0	6	1	0	0	5	3	1	0	1	2	2	1	2	2	14	3	7
U.K.	44	0	2	1	0	6	1	0	0	3	1	1	0	0	2	1	0	5	1	12	0	7
SCANDINAVIA	6	0	0	0	0	0	0	0	0	2	0	0	0	0	0	0	1	0	1	2	0	0
SWITZERLAND	1	0	0	0	0	0	0	0	0	0	0	0	0	0	0	0	0	0	0	0	0	0
OTHER EFTA	1	0	0	0	0	0	0	1	0	0	0	0	0	0	0	0	0	0	0	0	0	0
EUROP. COMMUNITY	54	1	1	1	2	2	4	1	0	1	0	1	0	9	7	3	6	3	0	0	2	0
FRANCE	29	0	0	1	2	2	3	1	0	0	0	1	0	6	2	2	2	2	0	1	2	1
GERMANY	11	1	0	1	0	0	0	1	0	0	0	0	0	0	1	1	1	1	1	1	1	0
ITALY	8	0	1	0	1	2	0	0	0	0	0	0	0	2	0	0	0	0	1	0	0	0
BELGIUM + LUX	3	0	0	0	0	0	0	0	0	0	0	0	0	2	0	0	1	0	0	0	0	0
NETHERLANDS	3	0	1	1	0	0	1	0	0	1	0	0	0	0	0	0	0	0	0	0	0	0
SPAIN	8	0	0	0	0	0	0	0	0	1	0	0	0	2	0	0	1	0	0	1	0	0
GREECE + TURKEY	3	0	0	1	0	0	1	0	0	0	0	0	1	0	0	1	0	0	1	0	0	0
OTHER EUROPE	5	0	0	0	0	0	0	1	0	0	0	0	0	0	0	0	0	0	0	0	0	1
EUROPE EX. U.K.	78	1	1	4	2	2	4	2	1	3	2	1	1	11	10	4	5	5	3	3	3	2
SOUTHERN DOMINIONS	30	0	0	0	0	2	3	2	0	0	2	0	4	3	3	2	2	2	2	1	1	1
S. AFRICA +RHOD.	12	0	0	0	0	1	1	2	0	0	0	0	4	1	1	1	1	1	1	0	1	1
AUSTRALIA + N.Z.	18	0	0	0	0	1	2	2	0	0	2	0	0	2	2	2	1	1	1	1	0	0
ASIA + OTHER AFRICA	21	0	0	0	0	3	0	0	0	3	0	0	2	2	1	2	3	1	1	1	0	0
JAPAN	5	0	0	0	0	0	0	0	0	0	0	0	0	0	0	1	1	1	2	0	0	0
OTHER ASIA+AFR.	16	0	0	0	0	3	0	0	0	3	0	0	2	2	3	1	2	0	0	0	0	0
BLACK AFRICA	2	0	0	0	0	0	0	0	0	0	0	0	0	0	1	0	0	0	0	1	0	0
ARAB WORLD	2	0	0	0	0	0	0	0	0	1	0	0	0	1	0	0	0	0	0	0	0	0
INDIA	7	0	0	0	0	2	0	0	0	0	0	0	1	1	2	0	1	1	0	0	0	0
PHILIPPINES	2	0	0	0	0	0	0	0	0	0	0	0	1	0	0	1	0	0	0	0	0	0
OTHER E. ASIA	0	0	0	0	0	0	0	0	0	0	0	0	0	0	0	0	0	0	0	0	0	0
OTHER ASIA	3	0	0	0	0	1	0	0	0	2	0	0	0	0	0	0	0	0	0	0	0	0

CHAPTER 3- THE PROLIFERATION OF FOREIGN SUBSIDIARIES
SECTION 4- THE FLOW OF MANUFACTURING BY INDUSTRY OF SUBSIDIARY
TABLE 45- SUBSIDIARIES MANUFACTURING
OTHER TRANSPORTATION EQUIPMENT (SIC 372-379)
CLASSIFIED BY COUNTRY OR REGION AND BY PERIOD MANUFACTURE BEGAN

PERIOD

COUNTRY OR REGION	PRE 1968	PRE 1901	1901 -13	1914 -19	1920 -24	1925 -29	1930 -34	1935 -39	1940 -45	1946 -50	1951 -53	1954 -55	1956 -57	1958 -59	1960 -61	1962	1963	1964	1965	1966	1967	UNK
OUTSIDE U.S.	31	3	1	1	1	1	0	0	0	2	1	1	3	4	4	2	1	1	1	1	1	2
OUT. U.S. + CANADA	22	3	1	1	0	1	0	0	0	0	1	0	2	4	5	1	1	0	1	0	0	1
OUT. WEST. HEMIS.	19	3	1	1	1	1	0	0	0	0	1	0	1	3	5	1	1	0	0	0	0	1
OUT. WHITE CWEALTH	16	3	1	0	0	1	0	0	0	0	0	0	1	1	4	1	1	0	1	0	0	0
OUT. DEVLPED WORLD	3	0	0	0	0	0	0	0	0	0	0	0	1	1	0	0	0	0	1	0	0	0
CANADA	9	0	0	0	1	0	0	0	0	2	0	0	1	0	1	1	1	1	0	1	1	1
LATIN AMERICA	3	0	0	0	0	0	0	0	0	0	0	0	1	1	0	0	1	0	0	0	0	0
C. AMER.+CARIB.	2	0	0	0	0	0	0	0	0	0	0	0	1	1	1	0	1	0	0	0	0	0
CUBA	0	0	0	0	0	0	0	0	0	0	0	0	0	0	0	0	0	0	0	0	0	0
MEXICO	2	0	0	0	0	0	0	0	0	0	0	0	1	1	0	0	1	0	0	0	0	0
OTHER	0	0	0	0	0	0	0	0	0	0	0	0	0	0	0	0	0	0	0	0	0	0
S. AMERICA	1	0	0	0	0	0	0	0	0	0	0	0	0	1	0	0	0	0	0	0	0	0
ARGENTINA	1	0	0	0	0	0	0	0	0	0	0	0	0	0	0	0	0	0	0	0	0	0
BRAZIL	1	0	0	0	0	0	0	0	0	0	0	0	1	1	0	0	0	0	0	0	0	0
PERU	0	0	0	0	0	0	0	0	0	0	0	0	0	0	0	0	0	0	0	0	0	0
COLOMBIA	0	0	0	0	0	0	0	0	0	0	0	0	0	0	0	0	0	0	0	0	0	0
VENEZUELA	0	0	0	0	0	0	0	0	0	0	0	0	0	0	0	0	0	0	0	0	0	0
OTHER	0	0	0	0	0	0	0	0	0	0	0	0	0	0	0	0	0	0	0	0	0	0
EUROPE	16	3	1	1	1	1	0	0	0	0	1	0	0	2	5	0	0	0	0	0	0	1
EFTA	4	0	0	1	0	0	0	0	0	0	1	0	0	0	1	0	0	0	1	0	0	1
U.K.	3	0	0	1	0	0	0	0	0	0	0	0	0	0	1	0	0	0	1	0	0	1
SCANDINAVIA	0	0	0	0	0	0	0	0	0	0	0	0	0	0	0	0	0	0	0	0	0	0
SWITZERLAND	0	0	0	0	0	0	0	0	0	0	0	0	0	0	0	0	0	0	0	0	0	0
OTHER EFTA	1	0	0	1	0	1	0	0	0	1	0	0	0	0	0	0	0	0	0	0	0	0
EUROP. COMMUNITY	12	3	1	0	1	1	0	0	0	0	0	1	0	2	4	0	0	0	0	0	0	0
FRANCE	3	1	0	1	0	0	0	0	0	0	0	0	0	1	1	1	0	0	0	0	0	0
GERMANY	5	2	0	0	0	0	0	0	0	0	0	0	0	0	2	0	1	0	0	0	0	0
ITALY	2	0	0	0	1	0	0	0	0	0	0	0	1	1	1	0	0	0	0	0	0	0
BELGIUM + LUX	4	0	1	0	0	1	0	0	0	0	0	0	0	0	0	0	0	1	0	0	0	0
NETHERLANDS	0	0	0	0	0	0	0	0	0	0	0	0	0	0	0	0	0	0	0	0	0	0
SPAIN	0	0	0	0	0	0	0	0	0	0	0	0	0	0	0	0	0	0	0	0	0	0
GREECE + TURKEY	0	0	0	0	0	0	0	0	0	0	0	0	0	0	0	0	0	0	0	0	0	0
OTHER EUROPE	0	0	0	0	0	0	0	0	0	0	1	0	0	0	0	1	0	0	0	0	0	0
EUROPE EX. U.K.	13	3	1	0	1	1	0	0	0	0	1	0	0	2	4	1	0	0	0	0	0	1
SOUTHERN DOMINIONS	3	0	0	0	0	0	0	0	0	0	0	0	1	1	0	0	0	0	0	1	0	0
S. AFRICA +RHOD.	1	0	0	0	0	0	0	0	0	0	0	0	0	1	0	1	0	0	0	0	0	0
AUSTRALIA + N.Z.	2	0	0	0	0	0	0	0	0	0	0	0	1	0	1	0	1	0	0	1	0	0
ASIA + OTHER AFRICA	0	0	0	0	0	0	0	0	0	0	0	0	0	0	0	0	0	0	0	0	0	0
JAPAN	0	0	0	0	0	0	0	0	0	0	0	0	0	0	0	0	0	0	0	0	0	0
OTHER ASIA+AFR.	0	0	0	0	0	0	0	0	0	0	0	0	0	0	0	0	0	0	0	0	0	0
BLACK AFRICA	0	0	0	0	0	0	0	0	0	0	0	0	0	0	0	0	0	0	0	0	0	0
ARAB WORLD	0	0	0	0	0	0	0	0	0	0	0	0	0	0	0	0	0	0	0	0	0	0
INDIA	0	0	0	0	0	0	0	0	0	0	0	0	0	0	0	0	0	0	0	0	0	0
PHILIPPINES	0	0	0	0	0	0	0	0	0	0	0	0	0	0	0	0	0	0	0	0	0	0
OTHER E. ASIA	0	0	0	0	0	0	0	0	0	0	0	0	0	0	0	0	0	0	0	0	0	0
OTHER ASIA	0	0	0	0	0	0	0	0	0	0	0	0	0	0	0	0	0	0	0	0	0	0

CHAPTER 3- THE PROLIFERATION OF FOREIGN SUBSIDIARIES
SECTION 4- THE FLOW OF MANUFACTURING BY INDUSTRY OF SUBSIDIARY
TABLE 46- SUBSIDIARIES MANUFACTURING
MEDICAL INSTRUMENTS AND SUPPLIES (SIC 384)
CLASSIFIED BY COUNTRY OR REGION AND BY PERIOD MANUFACTURE BEGAN

PERIOD

COUNTRY OR REGION	PRE 1968	PRE 1901	1901 -13	1914 -19	1920 -24	1925 -29	1930 -34	1935 -39	1940 -45	1946 -50	1951 -53	1954 -55	1956 -57	1958 -59	1960 -61	1962 -63	1964	1965	1966	1967	UNK
OUTSIDE U.S.	65	0	0	1	0	1	3	3	0	6	0	1	3	2	12	4	4	4	15	4	0
OUT. U.S. + CANADA	56	0	0	0	0	1	2	3	0	6	0	1	3	2	11	3	4	4	13	2	0
OUT. WEST. HEMIS.	43	0	0	0	0	1	1	1	0	5	0	0	2	1	9	3	4	4	10	1	0
OUT. WHITE CWEALTH	36	0	0	0	0	0	1	2	0	1	0	1	1	2	5	1	4	4	10	1	0
OUT. DEVLPED WORLD	15	0	0	0	0	0	1	2	0	1	0	1	1	2	2	0	0	0	4	1	0
CANADA	9	0	0	1	0	1	1	0	0	0	0	0	0	0	1	1	0	0	2	2	0
LATIN AMERICA	13	0	0	0	0	0	2	2	0	1	0	1	1	1	2	1	0	0	3	1	0
C. AMER.+CARIB.	3	0	0	0	0	1	1	0	0	1	0	0	0	0	1	0	0	0	0	0	0
CUBA	1	0	0	0	0	0	0	0	0	1	0	0	0	0	0	0	0	0	0	0	0
MEXICO	1	0	0	0	1	1	0	0	0	0	0	1	0	0	0	0	0	0	0	0	0
OTHER	1	0	0	0	0	0	0	0	0	0	0	0	0	0	1	0	0	0	0	0	0
S. AMERICA	10	0	0	0	0	0	2	0	0	0	0	1	1	1	1	0	0	0	3	1	0
ARGENTINA	2	0	0	0	0	0	1	0	0	0	0	1	1	0	1	0	0	0	3	0	0
BRAZIL	6	0	0	0	0	0	1	1	0	0	0	0	1	0	0	0	0	0	3	1	0
PERU	0	0	0	0	0	0	0	0	0	0	0	0	0	0	0	0	0	0	0	0	0
COLOMBIA	1	0	0	0	0	0	2	1	0	0	0	0	0	1	0	0	0	0	0	0	0
VENEZUELA	1	0	0	0	0	0	1	0	0	0	0	0	1	0	1	0	0	0	0	0	0
OTHER	0	0	0	0	0	0	0	0	0	0	0	0	0	0	0	0	0	0	0	0	0
EUROPE	36	0	0	0	1	0	0	0	0	5	0	0	2	0	7	3	1	4	8	1	0
EFTA	16	0	0	0	1	0	0	0	0	4	0	0	1	0	4	2	1	0	2	1	0
U.K.	14	0	0	0	1	0	0	0	0	4	0	0	0	0	4	2	0	0	2	1	0
SCANDINAVIA	1	0	0	0	0	0	0	0	0	0	0	0	1	0	0	0	0	0	0	0	0
SWITZERLAND	0	0	0	0	0	0	0	0	0	0	0	0	0	0	0	0	0	0	0	0	0
OTHER EFTA	1	0	0	0	0	0	0	0	0	0	0	0	0	0	0	0	0	0	0	0	0
EUROP. COMMUNITY	19	0	0	0	0	0	0	0	0	0	0	0	1	0	3	0	3	4	6	0	0
FRANCE	6	0	0	0	0	0	0	0	0	0	0	0	1	0	2	0	0	0	4	0	0
GERMANY	7	0	0	0	0	0	0	0	0	0	0	0	0	0	1	0	2	3	2	0	0
ITALY	4	0	0	0	0	0	0	0	0	0	0	0	0	0	0	0	1	1	0	0	0
BELGIUM + LUX	0	0	0	0	0	0	0	0	0	0	0	0	0	0	0	0	0	0	0	0	0
NETHERLANDS	2	0	0	0	0	0	0	0	0	0	0	0	0	0	0	0	1	0	0	0	0
SPAIN	0	0	0	0	0	0	0	0	0	0	0	0	0	0	0	0	0	0	0	0	0
GREECE + TURKEY	0	0	0	0	0	0	0	0	0	0	0	0	0	0	0	0	0	0	0	0	0
OTHER EUROPE	1	0	0	0	0	0	0	0	0	0	0	0	0	0	0	1	0	0	0	0	0
EUROPE EX. U.K.	22	0	0	0	0	0	0	0	0	1	0	0	1	2	3	1	1	4	6	0	0
SOUTHERN DOMINIONS	5	0	0	0	0	0	1	0	0	0	0	0	0	0	2	0	0	0	1	1	0
S. AFRICA +RHOD.	1	0	0	0	0	0	0	1	0	0	0	0	0	0	1	0	0	0	1	0	0
AUSTRALIA + N.Z.	4	0	0	0	0	0	1	1	0	0	0	0	0	0	1	0	0	0	1	1	0
ASIA + OTHER AFRICA	2	0	0	0	0	0	0	0	0	0	0	0	0	1	0	0	0	0	1	1	0
JAPAN	0	0	0	0	0	0	0	0	0	0	0	0	0	0	0	0	0	0	0	0	0
OTHER ASIA+AFR.	2	0	0	0	0	0	0	0	0	0	0	0	0	1	0	0	0	0	1	0	0
BLACK AFRICA	0	0	0	0	0	0	0	0	0	0	0	0	0	0	0	0	0	0	0	0	0
ARAB WORLD	0	0	0	0	0	0	0	0	0	0	0	0	0	0	0	0	0	0	0	0	0
INDIA	1	0	0	0	0	0	0	0	0	0	0	0	0	1	0	0	0	0	0	0	0
PHILIPPINES	0	0	0	0	0	0	0	0	0	0	0	0	0	0	0	0	0	0	0	0	0
OTHER E. ASIA	0	0	0	0	0	0	0	0	0	0	0	0	0	0	0	0	0	0	0	0	0
OTHER ASIA	1	0	0	0	0	0	0	0	0	0	0	0	0	0	0	0	0	0	1	0	0

CHAPTER 3- THE PROLIFERATION OF FOREIGN SUBSIDIARIES
SECTION 4- THE FLOW OF MANUFACTURING BY INDUSTRY OF SUBSIDIARY
TABLE 47- SUBSIDIARIES MANUFACTURING
OTHER INSTRUMENTS AND PRECISION GOODS (OTHER SIC 38)
CLASSIFIED BY COUNTRY OR REGION AND BY PERIOD MANUFACTURE BEGAN

COUNTRY OR REGION	PRE 1968	PRE 1901	1901 -13	1914 -19	1920 -24	1925 -29	1930 -34	1935 -39	1940 -45	1946 -50	1951 -53	1954 -55	1956 -57	1958 -59	1960 -61	1962	1963	1964	1965	1966	1967	UNK
OUTSIDE U.S.	63	3	1	0	0	3	2	1	0	1	1	2	4	3	1	17	8	7	5	2	1	1
OUT. U.S. + CANADA	59	2	1	0	0	3	2	0	0	1	1	2	4	1	1	17	8	7	5	2	1	1
OUT. WEST. HEMIS.	46	2	0	0	0	3	2	0	1	0	0	2	4	0	1	11	7	6	4	2	1	1
OUT. WHITE CWEALTH	42	1	0	0	0	3	2	0	0	0	1	2	1	1	1	15	4	6	3	1	1	0
OUT. DEVLPED WORLD	14	0	0	0	0	0	0	0	0	0	1	2	0	1	0	7	1	1	1	1	0	0
CANADA	4	1	0	0	0	0	0	1	0	0	0	0	0	0	0	0	0	0	0	0	1	0
LATIN AMERICA	13	0	0	0	0	0	0	1	0	0	1	2	0	2	1	6	0	1	0	1	0	0
C. AMER.+CARIB.	4	0	0	0	0	0	0	0	0	0	1	0	0	1	1	1	1	0	1	1	0	0
CUBA	0	0	0	0	0	0	0	0	0	0	0	0	0	0	0	0	0	0	0	0	0	0
MEXICO	3	0	0	0	0	0	0	0	0	0	0	0	0	0	0	1	1	0	1	0	0	0
OTHER	1	0	0	0	0	0	0	1	0	0	1	0	0	0	0	0	0	0	0	1	0	0
S. AMERICA	9	0	0	0	0	0	0	0	0	0	0	2	0	1	0	5	0	1	0	0	0	0
ARGENTINA	4	0	0	0	0	0	0	0	0	0	0	2	0	1	0	1	0	1	0	0	0	0
BRAZIL	2	0	0	0	0	0	0	0	0	0	0	0	0	0	0	1	1	1	1	0	0	0
PERU	1	0	0	0	0	0	0	0	0	0	0	0	0	0	0	1	1	0	0	0	0	0
COLOMBIA	1	0	0	0	0	0	0	0	0	0	0	0	0	0	0	1	1	1	0	0	0	0
VENEZUELA	0	0	0	0	0	0	0	0	0	0	0	0	0	0	0	0	1	0	0	0	0	0
OTHER	1	0	0	0	0	0	0	0	0	0	0	0	0	0	0	1	0	0	0	0	0	0
EUROPE	41	2	0	0	0	3	2	0	0	0	0	0	0	0	1	10	7	5	4	2	1	1
EFTA	14	1	0	0	0	0	0	0	0	0	0	0	0	0	0	2	5	0	2	1	0	1
U.K.	13	1	0	0	0	0	0	0	0	0	0	0	0	0	0	2	4	0	1	1	0	1
SCANDINAVIA	0	0	0	0	0	0	0	0	0	0	0	0	0	0	0	0	0	0	0	0	0	0
SWITZERLAND	0	0	0	0	0	0	0	0	0	0	0	0	0	0	0	0	0	0	0	0	0	0
OTHER EFTA	1	0	0	0	0	0	0	0	0	0	0	0	0	0	1	0	0	0	0	0	0	0
EUROP. COMMUNITY	26	1	0	0	0	3	2	0	0	0	0	0	1	0	0	7	2	5	2	0	1	0
FRANCE	7	0	0	0	0	1	2	0	0	0	0	0	1	0	0	1	0	3	0	1	0	0
GERMANY	13	1	0	0	0	2	0	0	0	0	0	0	0	0	0	4	1	1	1	0	1	0
ITALY	2	0	0	0	0	0	0	0	0	0	0	0	0	0	0	1	1	0	0	0	0	0
BELGIUM + LUX	3	0	0	0	0	0	0	0	0	0	0	0	0	0	0	1	0	1	1	0	0	0
NETHERLANDS	1	0	0	0	0	0	0	0	0	0	0	0	0	0	0	0	0	0	0	0	0	0
SPAIN	1	0	0	0	0	0	0	0	0	0	0	0	0	0	0	0	0	0	0	0	0	0
GREECE + TURKEY	0	0	0	0	0	0	0	0	0	0	0	0	0	0	0	0	0	0	0	0	0	0
OTHER EUROPE	0	0	0	0	0	0	0	0	0	0	0	0	0	0	0	0	0	0	0	0	0	1
EUROPE EX. U.K.	28	1	0	0	0	3	2	0	0	0	0	0	1	0	1	8	3	5	2	1	0	1
SOUTHERN DOMINIONS	4	0	0	0	0	0	0	0	0	1	0	0	1	0	0	0	1	0	1	0	0	0
S. AFRICA +RHOD.	1	0	0	0	0	0	0	0	0	1	0	1	0	0	0	0	0	0	0	0	0	0
AUSTRALIA + N.Z.	3	0	0	0	0	0	0	0	0	0	0	1	1	0	0	0	1	0	1	0	0	0
ASIA + OTHER AFRICA	1	0	0	0	0	0	0	0	0	0	0	0	0	0	0	0	0	0	0	0	0	0
JAPAN	0	0	0	0	0	0	0	0	0	0	0	0	0	0	0	0	0	0	0	0	0	0
OTHER ASIA+AFR.	1	0	0	0	0	0	0	0	0	0	0	0	0	0	0	1	0	0	0	0	0	0
BLACK AFRICA	0	0	0	0	0	0	0	0	0	0	0	0	0	0	0	0	0	0	0	0	0	0
ARAB WORLD	0	0	0	0	0	0	0	0	0	0	0	0	0	0	0	0	0	0	0	0	0	0
INDIA	1	0	0	0	0	0	0	0	0	0	0	0	0	0	0	1	0	0	0	0	0	0
PHILIPPINES	0	0	0	0	0	0	0	0	0	0	0	0	0	0	0	0	0	0	0	0	0	0
OTHER E. ASIA	0	0	0	0	0	0	0	0	0	0	0	0	0	0	0	0	0	0	0	0	0	0
OTHER ASIA	0	0	0	0	0	0	0	0	0	0	0	0	0	0	0	0	0	0	0	0	0	0

PERIOD

CHAPTER 3- THE PROLIFERATION OF FOREIGN SUBSIDIARIES
SECTION 4- THE FLOW OF MANUFACTURING BY INDUSTRY OF SUBSIDIARY
TABLE 48- SUBSIDIARIES MANUFACTURING
OTHER PRODUCTS (SIC 19,21,31, AND 39) OR UNKNOWN PRODUCT
CLASSIFIED BY COUNTRY OR REGION AND BY PERIOD MANUFACTURE BEGAN

PERIOD

COUNTRY OR REGION	PRE 1968	PRE 1901	1901 -13	1914 -19	1920 -24	1925 -29	1930 -34	1935 -39	1940 -45	1946 -50	1951 -53	1954 -55	1956 -57	1958 -59	1960 -61	1962	1963	1964	1965	1966	1967	UNK
OUTSIDE U.S.	431	5	6	7	10	27	15	29	11	16	16	13	20	23	61	28	26	29	21	23	19	26
OUT. U.S. + CANADA	359	4	3	6	8	23	13	22	10	13	11	8	14	21	53	26	24	22	19	21	18	20
OUT. WEST. HEMIS.	271	4	2	4	7	21	11	16	3	8	9	5	8	15	38	22	20	17	18	12	17	13
OUT. WHITE CWEALTH	265	2	2	6	8	13	11	11	8	9	7	5	12	15	42	17	21	19	12	19	14	16
OUT. DEVLPED WORLD	126	0	0	6	2	3	3	6	8	9	3	3	6	9	17	9	5	9	3	10	6	9
CANADA	72	1	3	1	2	4	2	7	1	3	5	5	6	2	8	2	2	7	2	2	1	6
LATIN AMERICA	88	0	0	2	1	2	2	6	7	5	2	3	6	6	15	4	4	5	1	9	0	7
C. AMER.+CARIB.	29	0	0	1	0	0	2	3	1	2	1	0	1	3	3	1	2	1	0	4	0	4
CUBA	3	0	0	0	0	0	0	0	0	1	1	0	0	0	0	0	0	1	0	0	0	0
MEXICO	20	0	0	0	0	0	1	2	1	2	1	0	0	1	3	2	1	1	0	0	0	2
OTHER	6	0	0	0	0	0	0	1	0	0	0	0	1	2	0	1	0	1	0	4	0	3
S. AMERICA	59	0	0	2	1	2	0	3	0	3	0	0	5	3	12	3	2	4	1	5	0	2
ARGENTINA	8	0	0	2	0	0	0	2	0	0	0	0	2	0	3	0	1	1	0	0	1	0
BRAZIL	13	0	0	0	0	1	1	1	1	1	0	0	0	0	0	1	2	0	0	3	0	0
PERU	3	0	0	0	1	0	0	1	0	0	0	0	0	0	0	0	0	1	0	0	0	0
COLOMBIA	10	0	0	1	0	0	0	0	0	1	0	0	2	0	2	0	0	0	0	3	0	1
VENEZUELA	15	0	0	0	0	0	0	0	0	1	0	1	0	3	5	1	1	0	0	1	1	0
OTHER	10	0	0	1	0	1	0	1	0	0	0	0	1	0	1	0	0	2	1	0	0	1
EUROPE	190	3	3	0	5	16	9	15	2	1	5	4	8	9	28	12	17	11	13	7	11	11
EFTA	82	2	2	0	1	10	5	14	2	1	0	2	2	1	9	4	6	2	6	2	6	5
U.K.	56	1	1	0	0	8	5	10	2	1	0	2	2	1	5	3	3	1	3	1	3	4
SCANDINAVIA	12	1	1	0	1	0	0	1	0	0	0	0	2	0	1	1	1	0	0	1	1	0
SWITZERLAND	10	0	0	0	0	1	0	1	0	0	0	0	0	0	2	0	2	1	0	0	2	1
OTHER EFTA	4	0	0	0	0	1	0	2	0	0	0	0	0	0	1	0	0	0	2	0	0	0
EUROP. COMMUNITY	84	1	1	0	4	4	3	1	0	0	3	0	5	6	15	5	10	7	4	5	3	6
FRANCE	29	1	1	0	3	4	1	1	0	0	1	1	1	1	4	3	5	5	0	2	2	2
GERMANY	23	0	0	0	0	2	0	0	0	0	0	0	2	1	5	3	5	1	1	4	2	1
ITALY	14	0	0	0	1	1	1	0	0	0	1	0	1	1	4	0	1	1	1	0	1	1
BELGIUM + LUX	7	0	0	0	0	0	0	1	0	0	0	0	0	1	0	1	0	0	0	1	0	1
NETHERLANDS	11	0	0	0	1	1	1	0	0	0	1	1	0	0	2	1	1	0	1	0	1	1
SPAIN	12	0	0	0	0	0	0	1	0	0	0	0	0	0	2	2	2	2	2	1	0	1
GREECE + TURKEY	3	0	0	0	0	0	0	0	0	0	0	0	0	0	1	1	0	0	0	0	1	0
OTHER EUROPE	9	0	0	0	0	1	1	0	0	0	0	0	0	2	0	1	0	0	2	0	0	0
EUROPE EX. U.K.	134	2	2	0	5	8	4	5	0	0	5	2	6	8	23	9	14	10	10	6	8	7
SOUTHERN DOMINIONS	32	1	0	0	0	2	1	1	0	0	3	1	0	3	5	5	0	2	3	1	1	0
S. AFRICA +RHOD.	10	0	0	0	0	1	1	0	0	2	1	0	0	1	1	2	0	0	0	0	1	0
AUSTRALIA + N.Z.	22	0	0	4	2	2	0	1	0	2	3	1	0	2	4	3	3	4	3	1	1	2
ASIA + OTHER AFRICA	49	0	0	4	1	3	1	0	0	4	1	0	0	3	5	2	2	0	2	4	5	3
JAPAN	11	0	0	4	1	1	0	0	0	0	1	1	0	0	0	0	4	4	1	0	1	0
OTHER ASIA+AFR.	38	0	0	0	2	2	1	0	0	4	0	0	0	3	3	2	3	0	2	3	5	6
BLACK AFRICA	8	0	0	0	1	1	0	0	0	0	1	1	0	0	0	0	1	0	1	1	3	2
ARAB WORLD	3	0	0	0	0	0	0	0	0	1	0	0	0	0	2	0	0	0	0	0	0	1
INDIA	2	0	0	0	0	0	0	0	0	0	0	0	0	0	0	0	1	1	0	0	0	1
PHILIPPINES	3	0	0	0	0	0	0	0	0	0	1	1	0	0	0	0	0	0	1	0	0	1
OTHER E. ASIA	4	0	0	0	1	0	1	0	0	0	0	0	0	1	2	0	0	0	0	0	0	0
OTHER ASIA	18	0	0	4	0	1	0	0	0	2	0	2	0	0	3	0	1	0	1	1	1	1

CHAPTER 3- THE PROLIFERATION OF FOREIGN SUBSIDIARIES
SECTION 5- THE FLOW OF MANUFACTURING BY CHARACTERISTIC OF SUBSIDIARY
TABLE A1- MANUFACTURING SUBSIDIARIES WHICH WERE AMONG
THE 1ST - 3RD FOREIGN MANUFACTURING SUBSIDIARIES IN THEIR PARENT SYSTEM,
CLASSIFIED BY COUNTRY OR REGION AND BY PERIOD MANUFACTURE BEGAN

COUNTRY OR REGION	PRE 1968	PRE 1901	1901 -13	1914 -19	1920 -24	1925 -29	1930 -34	1935 -39	1940 -45	1946 -50	1951 -53	1954 -55	1956 -57	1958 -59	1960 -61	1962	1963	1964	1965	1966	1967	UNK
OUTSIDE U.S.	561	37	45	45	40	89	42	43	27	43	33	33	30	30	17	3	2	0	0	0	0	2
OUT. U.S. + CANADA	374	33	22	20	30	55	26	22	17	30	23	24	24	26	15	3	2	0	0	0	0	2
OUT. WEST. HEMIS.	274	32	18	15	23	51	20	16	9	19	15	15	13	17	13	2	1	0	0	0	0	1
OUT. WHITE CWEALTH	233	20	12	13	23	23	11	9	14	18	18	15	19	19	13	3	1	0	0	0	0	2
OUT. DEVLPED WORLD	115	1	4	7	9	6	6	6	14	16	9	10	12	9	3	1	1	0	0	0	0	1
CANADA	187	4	23	25	10	34	16	21	10	13	10	9	6	4	2	0	0	0	0	0	0	0
LATIN AMERICA	100	1	4	4	7	4	4	4	14	11	8	9	11	9	9	1	1	0	0	0	0	1
C. AMER.+CARIB.	52	0	1	2	1	2	1	1	7	6	6	6	7	6	2	1	1	0	0	0	0	1
CUBA	11	0	0	1	1	1	1	1	0	0	3	0	3	0	0	0	0	0	0	0	0	0
MEXICO	40	0	1	1	0	0	3	2	7	6	1	5	4	6	2	1	1	0	0	0	0	1
OTHER	1	0	0	0	0	0	0	0	0	0	0	1	0	0	0	0	0	0	0	0	0	0
S. AMERICA	48	0	3	3	6	2	2	2	0	5	5	1	4	3	2	0	0	0	0	0	0	0
ARGENTINA	15	0	1	2	2	1	1	2	0	0	3	3	0	2	1	0	0	0	0	0	0	0
BRAZIL	10	1	1	1	1	1	0	0	1	1	0	0	0	1	0	1	0	0	0	0	0	0
PERU	4	0	0	0	1	0	0	0	0	0	2	0	0	0	0	0	0	0	0	0	0	0
COLOMBIA	5	0	0	0	0	0	0	0	1	1	0	0	2	0	1	0	0	0	0	0	0	0
VENEZUELA	9	0	0	0	0	0	0	0	2	2	2	1	2	0	0	0	0	0	0	0	0	0
OTHER	5	0	1	0	2	1	0	0	1	1	0	0	0	0	0	0	0	0	0	0	0	0
EUROPE	216	31	18	9	20	43	14	12	2	10	11	8	10	14	11	2	1	0	0	0	0	0
EFTA	112	11	11	6	8	29	9	9	2	8	5	4	4	3	2	0	1	0	0	0	0	0
U.K.	101	11	10	4	6	26	9	9	2	8	3	3	4	3	2	0	1	0	0	0	0	0
SCANDINAVIA	8	0	0	2	1	2	0	0	0	0	1	0	0	0	0	0	0	0	0	0	0	0
SWITZERLAND	8	0	0	0	0	1	0	0	0	0	1	0	0	0	2	0	0	0	0	0	0	0
OTHER EFTA	3	0	0	0	1	0	0	0	0	2	0	0	0	0	0	0	0	0	0	0	0	0
EUROP. COMMUNITY	91	17	6	3	11	10	4	3	2	2	6	3	6	9	9	2	0	0	0	0	0	0
FRANCE	29	6	3	1	7	3	1	1	0	1	2	1	1	4	0	0	0	0	0	0	0	1
GERMANY	30	8	3	2	4	4	3	1	0	0	2	0	2	2	2	2	0	0	0	0	0	0
ITALY	11	2	1	1	0	0	0	1	0	1	0	1	1	1	5	0	1	0	0	0	0	0
BELGIUM + LUX	13	1	0	0	0	2	0	0	1	0	1	1	0	1	2	0	0	0	0	0	0	0
NETHERLANDS	8	0	0	0	0	1	1	0	1	1	0	0	0	1	0	0	0	0	0	0	0	0
SPAIN	7	0	0	0	0	3	0	0	0	0	0	1	1	1	0	0	0	0	0	0	0	0
GREECE + TURKEY	0	0	0	0	0	0	0	0	0	0	0	0	0	0	0	0	0	0	0	0	0	0
OTHER EUROPE	6	3	1	0	1	1	0	0	0	2	0	0	0	1	0	0	0	0	0	0	0	0
EUROPE EX. U.K.	115	20	8	5	14	17	5	3	2	2	8	5	6	11	2	2	0	0	0	0	0	0
SOUTHERN DOMINIONS	38	1	3	3	1	6	6	4	1	4	2	6	1	3	0	0	0	0	0	0	0	0
S. AFRICA +RHOD.	10	1	0	3	0	1	2	1	1	2	2	1	1	1	0	0	0	0	0	0	0	0
AUSTRALIA + N.Z.	28	0	3	3	1	5	4	3	0	5	2	5	2	2	0	0	0	1	0	0	0	0
ASIA + OTHER AFRICA	20	0	1	1	2	2	0	0	0	5	2	1	2	0	0	0	0	0	0	0	0	0
JAPAN	15	0	2	2	2	2	0	0	0	5	1	0	1	0	1	0	0	0	0	0	0	0
OTHER ASIA+AFR.	15	0	0	0	0	0	0	0	0	0	0	0	0	0	0	0	0	0	0	0	0	0
BLACK AFRICA	0	0	0	0	0	0	0	0	0	0	0	0	0	0	0	0	0	0	0	0	0	0
ARAB WORLD	0	0	0	0	0	0	0	0	0	0	0	0	0	0	0	0	0	0	0	0	0	0
INDIA	0	0	0	0	0	0	0	0	0	0	0	0	0	0	0	0	0	0	0	0	0	0
PHILIPPINES	5	0	0	0	1	2	0	0	0	0	0	0	1	0	0	0	0	0	0	0	0	0
OTHER E. ASIA	1	0	0	0	0	0	0	0	0	0	0	1	0	0	0	0	0	0	0	0	0	0
OTHER ASIA	9	0	0	2	0	0	0	0	0	5	0	0	1	0	1	0	0	0	0	0	0	0

CHAPTER 3— THE PROLIFERATION OF FOREIGN SUBSIDIARIES
SECTION 5— THE FLOW OF MANUFACTURING BY CHARACTERISTIC OF SUBSIDIARY
TABLE A2— MANUFACTURING SUBSIDIARIES WHICH WERE AMONG
THE 4TH — 10TH FOREIGN MANUFACTURING SUBSIDIARIES IN THEIR PARENT SYSTEM,
CLASSIFIED BY COUNTRY OR REGION AND BY PERIOD MANUFACTURE BEGAN

PERIOD

COUNTRY OR REGION	PRE 1968	PRE 1901	1901-13	1914-19	1920-24	1925-29	1930-34	1935-39	1940-45	1946-50	1951-53	1954-55	1956-57	1958-59	1960-61	1962	1963	1964	1965	1966	1967	UNK
OUTSIDE U.S.	1279	11	21	20	34	85	64	104	64	102	101	82	105	153	168	59	53	25	10	15	3	0
OUT. U.S. + CANADA	1053	9	16	15	25	57	55	93	49	76	79	63	84	139	152	52	46	20	8	12	3	0
OUT. WEST. HEMIS.	694	7	16	10	23	46	43	63	14	39	50	42	39	89	112	37	33	13	6	10	3	0
OUT. WHITE CWEALTH	788	7	13	12	18	46	37	60	39	58	52	47	66	101	116	43	38	17	6	9	3	0
OUT. DEVLPED WORLD	416	2	0	8	2	15	13	36	35	41	32	28	49	57	48	18	17	7	3	3	2	0
CANADA	226	2	5	5	9	28	9	11	15	26	22	19	21	14	16	7	7	5	2	3	0	0
LATIN AMERICA	359	2	5	5	5	11	12	30	35	37	29	21	45	50	40	15	13	7	3	3	0	0
C. AMER.+CARIB.	153	1	0	0	0	2	10	17	8	13	13	7	5	7	18	8	3	4	2	1	0	0
CUBA	21	1	0	0	0	0	3	6	1	1	0	2	0	0	0	0	0	0	0	0	0	0
MEXICO	104	0	0	0	2	2	3	6	5	12	10	5	15	18	11	4	2	3	0	1	0	0
OTHER	28	0	0	0	0	0	0	5	2	0	1	0	0	3	1	5	1	1	1	0	0	0
S. AMERICA	206	1	0	5	2	9	2	13	27	24	16	14	22	28	22	6	10	3	0	1	0	0
ARGENTINA	49	0	0	2	0	3	2	4	4	4	3	2	6	5	5	3	2	2	0	1	0	0
BRAZIL	65	0	0	3	0	4	2	5	10	6	7	4	7	13	4	1	3	0	0	1	0	0
PERU	14	0	0	0	0	1	0	1	4	2	1	1	1	0	1	1	0	0	1	0	0	0
COLOMBIA	29	0	0	0	0	0	0	0	3	6	2	2	3	2	7	1	2	0	0	0	0	0
VENEZUELA	34	0	0	0	2	0	0	1	2	4	2	1	1	1	5	1	3	0	0	1	0	0
OTHER	15	1	0	0	1	1	0	2	3	2	0	2	0	1	0	0	2	0	1	0	0	0
EUROPE	484	7	13	6	19	40	34	42	6	26	31	27	23	56	83	24	22	12	5	7	1	0
EFTA	176	3	5	3	5	14	12	25	3	13	12	11	8	16	27	7	5	4	2	1	1	0
U.K.	131	2	1	2	3	9	11	19	2	9	11	9	8	13	19	4	4	2	2	0	0	0
SCANDINAVIA	23	1	2	1	1	3	1	1	0	2	0	0	0	0	4	2	0	1	0	0	0	0
SWITZERLAND	10	0	2	0	0	0	0	0	0	0	1	0	0	1	0	1	1	0	0	0	0	0
OTHER EFTA	12	0	2	0	1	2	0	3	1	2	1	0	0	0	0	0	0	1	0	1	1	0
EUROP. COMMUNITY	276	4	7	3	12	26	19	15	3	12	12	15	13	38	54	16	13	5	3	5	1	0
FRANCE	95	2	3	0	5	8	7	9	0	5	4	5	5	10	18	9	3	3	2	1	0	0
GERMANY	73	2	3	1	1	10	7	0	0	2	3	5	5	7	17	1	5	2	2	2	0	0
ITALY	52	0	2	1	3	3	1	3	0	1	3	2	3	8	13	5	4	0	1	1	1	0
BELGIUM + LUX	29	0	2	0	1	1	1	1	2	1	2	1	1	1	6	0	1	1	1	1	0	0
NETHERLANDS	27	0	0	1	1	3	3	2	1	2	1	1	1	6	4	1	0	1	1	0	1	0
SPAIN	19	0	0	0	1	0	0	1	1	1	0	0	1	0	2	0	3	2	0	0	0	0
GREECE + TURKEY	3	0	0	0	0	0	0	0	0	0	2	1	1	2	0	0	0	0	0	0	0	0
OTHER EUROPE	10	0	1	1	1	0	0	2	0	0	4	0	0	0	0	1	1	2	0	1	0	0
EUROPE FX. U.K.	353	5	12	4	16	31	23	23	4	17	20	18	15	43	64	20	18	10	3	6	1	0
SOUTHERN DOMINIONS	127	0	2	1	3	2	7	14	8	9	12	7	10	25	17	5	3	0	0	2	0	0
S. AFRICA +RHOD.	42	0	0	1	2	2	1	4	2	5	3	3	2	5	6	2	3	0	0	1	0	0
AUSTRALIA + N.Z.	85	0	2	0	1	0	4	10	6	4	9	4	8	20	11	3	0	0	0	1	0	0
ASIA + OTHER AFRICA	83	0	1	3	1	2	2	7	0	4	7	8	6	8	12	8	8	1	0	0	0	0
JAPAN	26	0	0	0	1	0	1	1	0	0	4	1	2	1	8	5	4	1	0	0	0	0
OTHER ASIA+AFR.	57	0	1	3	1	4	1	6	0	4	3	1	4	7	4	3	4	0	0	0	0	0
BLACK AFRICA	1	0	0	0	0	0	0	0	0	0	0	0	0	0	0	0	0	0	0	0	0	0
ARAB WORLD	5	0	0	0	0	0	0	0	0	0	0	0	0	1	1	0	0	1	1	0	0	0
INDIA	16	0	0	0	0	1	0	1	2	2	1	1	0	3	3	1	3	0	0	2	0	0
PHILIPPINES	12	0	0	0	0	1	0	2	1	0	2	0	1	2	0	1	1	0	1	0	1	0
OTHER F. ASIA	5	0	0	1	1	2	0	0	0	0	0	2	1	0	1	0	0	0	0	0	0	0
OTHER ASIA	18	0	0	2	0	0	1	3	4	2	0	2	2	1	3	1	0	0	0	1	1	0

CHAPTER 3- THE PROLIFERATION OF FOREIGN SUBSIDIARIES
SECTION 5- THE FLOW OF MANUFACTURING BY CHARACTERISTIC OF SUBSIDIARY
TABLE A3- MANUFACTURING SUBSIDIARIES WHICH WERE AMONG
THE 11TH - 25TH FOREIGN MANUFACTURING SUBSIDIARIES IN THE PARENT SYSTEM,
CLASSIFIED BY COUNTRY OR REGION AND BY PERIOD MANUFACTURE BEGAN

COUNTRY OR REGION	PRE 1968	PRE 1901	1901-13	1914-19	1920-24	1925-29	1930-34	1935-39	1940-45	1946-50	1951-53	1954-55	1956-57	1958-59	1960-61	1962	1963	1964	1965	1966	1967	UNK
OUTSIDE U.S.	1896	0	12	9	10	32	42	54	46	83	79	88	132	175	315	156	152	134	139	121	94	23
OUT. U.S. + CANADA	1661	0	12	6	8	28	37	46	38	72	67	68	116	160	280	140	142	114	120	110	80	17
OUT. WEST. HEMIS.	1147	0	9	3	6	22	33	32	17	40	42	41	59	108	205	106	104	78	96	74	59	13
OUT. WHITE CWEALTH	1294	0	11	4	5	21	23	26	30	55	53	57	99	129	207	111	116	94	93	93	57	10
OUT. DEVLPED WORLD	663	0	3	3	2	10	6	14	22	38	27	33	66	72	104	51	51	47	32	47	28	5
CANADA	235	0	0	3	2	4	5	8	8	11	12	20	16	15	35	16	10	20	19	11	14	6
LATIN AMERICA	514	0	3	3	2	6	4	14	21	32	25	27	57	52	75	34	38	36	24	36	21	4
C. AMER.+CARIB.	209	0	2	1	0	1	0	6	6	14	7	6	20	22	27	11	16	23	14	19	14	2
CUBA	12	0	2	0	0	0	0	0	1	0	1	0	2	1	0	0	0	0	0	0	0	2
MEXICO	130	0	2	0	0	0	0	4	4	7	4	6	9	14	13	6	9	19	8	14	11	0
OTHER	67	0	0	0	0	0	4	3	2	7	2	0	8	1	0	5	7	4	6	6	3	2
S. AMERICA	305	0	1	2	2	5	4	10	15	18	18	21	37	30	48	23	22	13	10	17	7	2
ARGENTINA	68	0	0	0	0	1	0	5	5	4	6	5	6	6	8	9	5	3	3	4	1	1
BRAZIL	77	0	1	1	0	3	3	3	5	7	6	4	13	13	9	2	5	1	1	3	3	0
PERU	21	0	0	0	0	0	0	2	2	2	1	3	1	0	9	1	1	4	2	2	1	0
COLOMBIA	47	0	0	0	1	0	1	0	3	5	5	4	1	4	2	3	4	3	2	5	1	0
VENEZUELA	58	0	0	1	1	0	0	1	2	2	3	4	8	7	12	6	4	3	2	5	2	0
OTHER	34	0	0	0	0	1	0	1	1	3	3	1	4	0	8	2	2	1	2	1	2	1
EUROPE	756	0	9	1	5	12	26	21	9	28	27	27	39	70	127	66	69	54	67	47	41	11
EFTA	252	0	5	0	2	5	12	13	2	14	8	5	16	21	41	20	18	18	22	10	14	6
U.K.	187	0	4	0	2	3	9	9	10	10	8	5	10	15	32	15	13	12	16	7	13	6
SCANDINAVIA	37	0	1	0	0	1	2	1	0	4	0	0	4	2	3	3	3	4	2	2	1	0
SWITZERLAND	13	0	0	0	0	1	0	0	0	0	0	0	1	1	4	0	1	1	1	1	0	0
OTHER EFTA	15	0	0	0	0	0	3	3	1	0	0	0	1	3	2	1	3	2	1	0	0	0
EUROP. COMMUNITY	402	0	4	1	0	6	13	6	4	12	13	17	20	44	77	39	43	28	28	24	18	5
FRANCE	120	0	1	0	1	1	5	1	0	2	3	5	3	14	32	14	11	10	8	6	8	3
GERMANY	116	0	2	1	0	5	5	6	2	3	7	8	10	9	18	10	11	9	8	8	5	2
ITALY	95	0	1	0	0	1	1	1	1	1	3	3	5	13	18	10	11	8	6	8	5	0
BELGIUM + LUX	32	0	0	0	0	0	1	2	0	1	0	0	1	3	4	2	6	1	6	4	2	0
NETHERLANDS	39	0	0	0	0	1	1	0	1	2	2	1	1	5	5	4	4	5	5	3	6	0
SPAIN	67	0	0	0	0	1	0	0	2	4	3	1	1	5	4	4	7	5	7	3	3	0
GREECE + TURKEY	17	0	0	0	0	1	0	0	2	0	1	0	1	3	3	2	1	2	1	1	0	0
OTHER EUROPE	18	0	0	0	1	1	1	0	3	2	0	0	0	0	2	1	0	1	1	1	3	5
EUROPE Ex. U.K.	569	0	8	1	3	9	17	12	8	18	19	22	29	55	95	51	56	42	51	40	28	5
SOUTHERN DOMINIONS	170	0	0	2	1	4	5	10	6	5	5	6	7	16	39	13	12	7	11	10	10	1
S. AFRICA +RHOD.	46	0	0	0	0	1	1	1	3	3	2	2	1	5	4	2	8	2	2	4	3	1
AUSTRALIA + N.Z.	124	0	0	2	1	3	3	9	3	2	3	4	6	11	35	11	4	5	9	6	7	1
ASIA + OTHER AFRICA	221	0	0	0	0	6	2	1	2	7	10	8	13	22	39	27	23	17	18	17	8	1
JAPAN	72	0	0	0	0	2	2	1	1	1	8	2	4	10	10	10	5	6	10	6	1	1
OTHER ASIA+AFR.	149	0	0	0	0	4	0	0	1	6	2	6	9	12	29	17	10	11	8	11	7	0
BLACK AFRICA	16	0	0	0	0	0	0	0	0	3	0	0	3	2	8	1	1	2	0	0	1	1
ARAB WORLD	17	0	0	0	0	0	0	0	1	3	1	0	1	2	1	0	1	2	1	3	1	0
INDIA	38	0	0	0	0	0	1	0	0	2	0	1	0	4	7	9	5	2	3	3	3	1
PHILIPPINES	25	0	0	0	2	0	0	0	1	0	0	4	1	3	2	1	2	2	1	1	2	0
OTHER E. ASIA	18	0	0	0	0	0	0	0	0	2	0	0	0	3	2	3	5	0	1	2	2	0
OTHER ASIA	35	0	0	0	2	1	1	0	0	1	0	1	1	2	9	3	4	1	0	4	2	0

CHAPTER 3- THE PROLIFERATION OF FOREIGN SUBSIDIARIES
SECTION 5- THE FLOW OF MANUFACTURING BY CHARACTERISTIC OF SUBSIDIARY
TABLE A4- MANUFACTURING SUBSIDIARIES WHICH WERE AMONG
THE MORE THAN 25TH FOREIGN MANUFACTURING SUBSIDIARIES IN THEIR PARENT SYSTEM,
CLASSIFIED BY COUNTRY OR REGION AND BY PERIOD MANUFACTURE BEGAN

COUNTRY OR REGION	PRE 1968	PRE 1901	1901-13	1914-19	1920-24	1925-29	1930-34	1935-39	1940-45	1946-50	1951-53	1954-55	1956-57	1958-59	1960-61	1962	1963	1964	1965	1966	1967	UNK
OUTSIDE U.S.	1492	0	0	0	8	14	8	13	13	22	22	25	38	64	189	102	139	177	216	193	136	116
OUT. U.S. + CANADA	1336	0	0	0	8	13	6	8	10	19	19	18	32	58	175	98	128	155	193	172	125	99
OUT. WEST. HEMIS.	965	0	0	0	6	10	4	7	6	12	12	12	21	34	123	70	100	128	132	125	83	71
OUT. WHITE CWEALTH	1033	0	0	0	5	11	3	4	8	11	17	11	22	49	137	75	87	122	164	133	106	68
OUT. DEVLPED WORLD	517	0	0	0	2	4	2	1	6	9	9	17	12	28	70	39	37	48	83	63	57	40
CANADA	156	0	0	0	2	1	0	3	3	3	3	4	6	6	14	4	11	22	23	21	11	17
LATIN AMERICA	371	0	0	0	2	3	1	4	4	7	7	6	11	24	52	28	19	27	61	47	42	28
C. AMER.+CARIB.	156	0	0	0	1	3	1	1	1	3	3	1	3	11	18	6	19	12	29	26	18	15
CUBA	4	0	0	0	0	0	0	0	0	0	0	0	1	1	0	0	0	0	0	0	0	0
MEXICO	92	0	0	1	1	2	1	1	0	0	3	0	8	7	14	6	4	7	14	15	9	10
OTHER	60	0	0	1	0	1	1	0	0	0	0	1	2	2	14	5	4	8	15	11	9	5
S. AMERICA	215	0	0	0	0	0	1	1	2	7	4	5	8	13	34	22	12	15	32	21	24	13
ARGENTINA	30	0	0	0	0	1	0	0	0	0	0	0	0	2	6	4	7	1	4	3	3	3
BRAZIL	55	0	0	0	0	0	1	0	2	6	3	3	4	3	6	11	2	5	4	4	4	2
PERU	18	0	0	0	0	0	0	1	0	0	0	0	0	1	2	0	1	1	1	10	3	3
COLOMBIA	36	0	0	0	0	0	0	0	0	0	1	1	0	3	7	2	2	3	3	2	2	3
VENEZUELA	43	0	0	1	1	0	0	0	0	1	0	0	2	3	10	5	5	3	5	4	5	2
OTHER	33	0	0	0	0	0	0	0	0	0	2	2	1	1	3	4	2	3	7	2	6	2
EUROPE	602	0	0	0	6	8	2	6	4	7	8	6	16	25	76	50	59	71	89	88	49	32
EFTA	211	0	0	0	3	1	1	6	2	5	3	1	8	9	21	20	21	21	23	38	11	17
U.K.	134	0	0	0	3	1	1	3	2	5	1	1	6	3	16	16	14	4	12	25	6	15
SCANDINAVIA	46	0	0	0	0	0	0	1	0	0	1	1	2	2	4	3	5	12	12	8	6	1
SWITZERLAND	14	0	0	0	0	0	0	1	0	0	1	0	0	2	0	0	1	1	2	2	2	1
OTHER EFTA	17	0	0	0	0	0	0	0	0	0	1	0	0	2	1	1	1	2	5	1	2	0
EUROP. COMMUNITY	307	0	0	0	0	4	2	0	2	3	4	4	7	14	43	22	31	42	54	35	28	14
FRANCE	78	0	0	0	0	0	0	0	0	1	1	1	2	2	10	4	7	15	6	11	13	4
GERMANY	84	0	0	0	0	3	1	0	0	1	2	1	3	4	11	7	8	9	16	15	4	4
ITALY	65	0	0	0	0	1	0	0	0	1	0	2	0	3	11	4	8	10	13	4	3	1
BELGIUM + LUX	45	0	0	0	0	0	1	0	0	2	2	0	3	4	7	4	7	8	11	3	7	4
NETHERLANDS	35	0	0	0	0	1	0	0	0	0	0	1	0	1	4	4	1	5	2	3	1	1
SPAIN	44	0	0	0	2	0	0	0	0	1	0	0	0	1	4	5	3	4	6	9	6	4
GREECE + TURKEY	22	0	0	0	0	1	0	0	0	0	0	0	1	2	6	3	2	2	4	3	3	0
OTHER EUROPE	18	0	0	0	1	1	0	0	0	0	0	1	0	0	4	0	2	2	2	3	1	1
EUROPE EX. U.K.	468	0	0	0	3	7	3	3	2	7	7	5	10	22	60	34	45	67	77	63	43	17
SOUTHERN DOMINIONS	154	0	0	0	1	1	2	1	0	0	3	5	3	3	20	7	25	27	15	12	12	15
S. AFRICA +RHOD.	61	0	0	0	0	0	2	0	0	2	1	5	2	1	3	6	20	12	12	9	3	8
AUSTRALIA + N.Z.	93	0	0	0	1	1	0	1	0	0	2	0	1	4	17	1	15	15	12	9	11	7
ASIA + OTHER AFRICA	209	0	0	0	0	1	2	0	2	2	2	1	2	4	27	13	25	30	28	25	22	24
JAPAN	63	0	0	0	0	0	0	0	0	2	0	0	0	4	9	2	2	9	6	7	7	12
OTHER ASIA+AFR.	146	0	0	0	0	1	2	0	2	2	2	1	1	4	18	11	18	21	22	16	15	12
BLACK AFRICA	31	0	0	0	0	0	0	0	0	0	0	0	1	0	3	2	3	9	5	2	2	2
ARAB WORLD	17	0	0	0	0	0	0	0	0	1	0	0	0	0	4	0	1	2	5	1	0	1
INDIA	14	0	0	0	0	0	0	0	0	0	0	1	0	1	2	1	3	0	3	1	0	1
PHILIPPINES	16	0	0	0	0	0	0	0	0	0	1	0	2	2	1	0	6	1	1	1	1	1
OTHER E. ASIA	15	0	0	0	1	1	0	0	0	0	0	0	1	0	1	1	1	2	1	0	4	1
OTHER ASIA	53	0	0	0	0	1	0	3	2	1	1	0	0	1	6	8	4	7	7	3	3	6

CHAPTER 3- THE PROLIFERATION OF FOREIGN SUBSIDIARIES
SECTION 5- THE FLOW OF MANUFACTURING BY CHARACTERISTIC OF SUBSIDIARY
TABLE B1- MANUFACTURING SUBSIDIARIES WHICH ENTERED A PARENT SYSTEM
WHICH HAD LESS THAN 11 YEARS "FOREIGN MANUFACTURING EXPERIENCE",
CLASSIFIED BY COUNTRY OR REGION AND BY PERIOD MANUFACTURE BEGAN

PERIOD

COUNTRY OR REGION	PRE 1968	PRE 1901	1901 -13	1914 -19	1920 -24	1925 -29	1930 -34	1935 -39	1940 -45	1946 -50	1951 -53	1954 -55	1956 -57	1958 -59	1960 -61	1962	1963	1964	1965	1966	1967	UNK
OUTSIDE U.S.	1154	34	45	51	42	128	55	45	26	54	53	55	80	97	129	53	54	45	37	50	21	0
OUT. U.S. + CANADA	864	28	22	26	27	80	36	29	14	37	34	38	66	87	112	45	50	39	30	46	18	0
OUT. WEST. HEMIS.	630	27	21	21	22	71	28	20	4	27	22	28	37	62	85	27	34	26	22	35	15	0
OUT. WHITE CWEALTH	613	15	13	18	20	42	18	14	10	22	22	27	53	66	93	38	43	30	25	31	13	0
OUT. DEVLPED WORLD	291	1	9	9	6	13	8	10	10	19	12	13	33	33	34	20	21	14	10	17	7	0
CANADA	290	6	23	25	15	48	19	16	12	17	19	17	14	10	17	8	4	6	7	4	3	0
LATIN AMERICA	234	1	1	1	5	8	6	6	12	17	14	6	15	14	12	8	4	6	7	4	3	0
C. AMER.+CARIB.	122	1	1	1	1	3	1	5	10	14	5	5	15	14	12	8	4	8	6	7	2	0
CUBA	16	0	1	0	1	1	1	1	0	6	1	4	1	2	1	0	0	0	0	0	0	0
MEXICO	80	0	1	0	0	2	1	2	6	5	4	1	10	12	8	3	3	7	4	3	1	0
OTHER	26	0	0	1	0	4	1	2	0	1	0	0	1	1	4	5	1	1	2	4	1	0
S. AMERICA	112	1	0	0	4	6	2	2	4	8	7	5	14	11	15	10	8	5	2	4	1	0
ARGENTINA	31	0	1	4	1	2	1	1	0	0	1	2	4	3	4	5	2	1	2	0	0	0
BRAZIL	26	0	0	3	0	3	0	1	1	1	5	0	1	4	2	1	3	1	0	0	1	0
PERU	9	0	0	0	1	0	0	0	0	0	0	0	1	0	1	1	0	1	1	0	0	0
COLOMBIA	16	0	0	1	1	0	0	0	1	1	0	0	2	1	4	1	2	1	1	1	0	0
VENEZUELA	21	0	0	0	0	0	0	0	1	2	0	0	3	3	3	3	0	0	0	2	1	0
OTHER	9	1	0	0	2	1	0	0	0	1	1	0	3	0	1	0	1	1	1	0	0	0
EUROPE	465	26	21	13	19	61	20	15	2	12	17	17	28	41	61	19	25	21	16	24	7	0
EFTA	181	11	10	8	6	35	10	11	2	9	6	5	9	9	11	7	7	8	3	12	1	0
U.K.	156	11	10	5	5	32	10	11	2	9	6	4	9	8	8	3	5	5	2	11	1	0
SCANDINAVIA	15	0	1	3	1	1	0	0	0	0	1	1	0	1	1	3	2	2	1	1	0	0
SWITZERLAND	5	0	0	0	0	1	0	0	0	0	0	0	0	1	1	0	0	1	0	0	0	0
OTHER EFTA	5	0	0	0	0	2	0	0	0	0	0	0	0	0	2	1	0	0	0	0	0	0
EUROP. COMMUNITY	244	13	11	5	11	22	10	4	0	3	7	11	16	27	48	11	14	11	8	8	4	0
FRANCE	86	5	3	1	1	9	4	2	0	1	3	4	6	6	17	5	3	7	4	4	2	0
GERMANY	66	7	5	3	9	7	3	1	0	0	3	3	8	2	10	1	4	2	1	1	0	0
ITALY	36	0	2	3	0	1	1	0	1	1	0	2	2	10	9	3	4	1	2	2	2	0
BELGIUM + LUX	33	1	1	0	0	4	0	1	1	1	1	1	1	6	8	1	1	1	1	1	0	0
NETHERLANDS	23	0	0	1	1	1	1	0	0	0	0	1	1	3	4	1	2	1	2	0	0	0
SPAIN	26	0	0	0	2	3	0	0	0	0	1	0	1	3	4	3	3	1	4	4	2	0
GREECE + TURKEY	6	0	0	0	0	0	0	0	0	0	1	0	0	0	1	0	0	0	0	0	1	0
OTHER EUROPE	8	0	0	0	0	1	0	0	0	0	1	1	0	0	3	0	1	1	0	0	0	0
EUROPE EX. U.K.	309	15	12	8	14	29	10	4	0	3	11	13	19	33	53	16	20	16	14	13	6	0
SOUTHERN DOMINIONS	90	1	0	3	2	6	8	4	2	6	7	4	4	13	11	4	1	3	3	4	4	0
S. AFRICA +RHOD.	32	1	0	0	1	1	5	2	1	2	3	4	2	2	1	1	1	1	1	3	3	0
AUSTRALIA + N.Z.	58	0	0	5	1	5	3	2	1	4	4	4	5	11	7	3	8	2	3	3	1	0
ASIA + OTHER AFRICA	75	0	0	1	1	4	0	1	0	5	1	4	1	8	13	4	3	1	2	3	4	0
JAPAN	18	0	0	1	0	0	0	0	0	0	0	1	1	0	6	2	3	1	1	1	0	0
OTHER ASIA+AFR.	57	0	0	0	0	4	0	1	0	5	0	3	4	8	7	2	5	0	2	6	4	0
BLACK AFRICA	2	0	0	0	0	0	0	0	0	0	0	0	0	0	0	0	0	0	0	0	0	0
ARAB WORLD	2	0	0	0	0	0	0	0	0	0	0	0	0	0	2	0	0	0	0	0	0	0
INDIA	11	0	0	0	0	0	1	0	1	0	0	2	3	3	1	2	2	2	2	0	1	0
PHILIPPINES	14	0	0	0	1	3	1	0	0	0	0	0	0	2	0	0	3	0	0	2	1	0
OTHER E. ASIA	5	0	0	0	0	1	0	0	0	0	0	0	0	0	1	0	0	1	0	0	0	0
OTHER ASIA	23	0	0	4	0	0	0	0	5	5	1	1	2	3	4	0	0	0	0	2	2	0

CHAPTER 3- THE PROLIFERATION OF FOREIGN SUBSIDIARIES
SECTION 5- THE FLOW OF MANUFACTURING BY CHARACTERISTIC OF SUBSIDIARY
TABLE 82- MANUFACTURING SUBSIDIARIES WHICH ENTERED A PARENT SYSTEM
WHICH HAD 11-20 YEARS "FOREIGN MANUFACTURING EXPERIENCE",
CLASSIFIED BY COUNTRY OR REGION AND BY PERIOD MANUFACTURE BEGAN

COUNTRY OR REGION	PRE 1968	PRE 1901	1901-13	1914-19	1920-24	1925-29	1930-34	1935-39	1940-45	1946-50	1951-53	1954-55	1956-57	1958-59	1960-61	1962	1963	1964	1965	1966	1967	UNK
OUTSIDE U.S.	872	13	20	14	15	49	63	75	45	44	35	28	33	55	83	30	45	57	60	55	53	0
OUT. U.S. + CANADA	749	13	15	9	13	40	53	63	33	34	30	22	28	51	74	28	41	51	56	51	44	0
OUT. WEST. HEMIS.	506	12	13	5	11	32	44	47	7	14	17	16	7	31	63	21	32	36	45	31	22	0
OUT. WHITE CWEALTH	584	11	12	6	9	33	31	33	28	30	24	15	27	56	56	24	35	42	45	48	36	0
OUT. DEVLPED WORLD	312	1	2	4	3	13	11	20	26	24	15	8	23	23	25	11	14	22	17	24	26	0
CANADA	123	0	5	5	2	9	10	12	12	10	5	6	5	4	9	2	4	6	4	4	9	0
LATIN AMERICA	243	1	2	4	2	8	9	16	26	20	13	6	21	20	11	7	9	15	11	20	22	0
C. AMER.+CARIB.	106	1	0	1	0	2	6	7	8	7	6	2	13	10	6	2	4	5	5	10	10	0
CUBA	9	1	0	1	0	0	2	3	0	0	1	1	1	0	0	0	0	0	2	0	0	0
MEXICO	74	0	0	0	0	0	2	3	8	7	5	1	11	9	6	2	5	6	2	6	6	0
OTHER	23	0	0	0	0	0	1	2	0	0	1	0	2	1	0	0	2	1	0	3	4	0
S. AMERICA	137	0	1	3	2	6	3	9	18	13	7	4	8	10	5	5	5	9	6	4	12	0
ARGENTINA	36	0	1	1	1	3	2	5	5	4	2	3	2	1	1	1	2	4	0	1	3	0
BRAZIL	30	0	1	1	1	2	2	2	4	3	0	1	3	3	1	1	5	1	1	5	1	0
PERU	9	0	0	2	0	0	0	1	3	1	2	0	0	2	1	0	0	0	1	0	1	0
COLOMBIA	14	0	0	0	0	0	1	0	1	1	0	0	1	0	1	0	2	3	0	0	1	0
VENEZUELA	28	0	0	0	0	0	0	1	4	3	4	0	1	0	1	3	1	1	2	3	2	0
OTHER	21	1	1	0	1	1	0	1	1	2	0	0	2	1	1	3	0	1	2	1	5	0
EUROPE	332	12	10	2	10	20	33	32	2	7	10	11	4	19	38	13	20	17	33	26	13	0
EFTA	125	3	6	0	4	7	16	23	3	3	3	4	0	6	14	4	5	7	5	4	6	0
U.K.	82	2	1	0	3	2	13	19	1	1	2	4	0	5	9	2	3	4	5	2	5	0
SCANDINAVIA	24	1	3	0	1	4	1	1	0	2	2	0	0	1	1	2	0	2	2	1	1	0
SWITZERLAND	10	0	0	0	0	0	0	1	0	0	0	0	0	0	4	0	2	1	1	1	0	0
OTHER EFTA	9	0	2	0	0	1	2	2	1	0	1	0	0	0	0	0	0	1	0	0	0	0
EUROP. COMMUNITY	172	8	4	2	5	11	15	9	1	4	4	5	3	13	20	9	12	8	17	18	5	0
FRANCE	48	3	1	1	2	2	4	3	0	2	1	3	0	5	9	5	5	1	3	1	1	0
GERMANY	51	3	0	0	1	6	8	3	0	0	0	1	1	2	3	2	3	1	5	7	2	0
ITALY	35	2	3	0	1	2	1	2	1	0	1	1	0	3	7	2	2	2	5	5	1	0
BELGIUM + LUX	22	0	0	1	1	0	1	2	0	0	0	1	1	1	1	0	1	4	5	4	1	0
NETHERLANDS	16	0	0	0	0	1	1	0	0	1	0	2	0	1	1	0	1	1	1	1	1	0
SPAIN	25	0	0	1	0	1	1	2	0	0	1	0	1	2	3	0	1	2	4	2	1	0
GREECE + TURKEY	4	1	1	0	1	0	0	0	0	0	0	0	1	0	0	0	0	0	0	1	1	0
OTHER EUROPE	6	1	0	0	0	1	0	0	0	0	1	0	0	0	1	0	0	0	1	1	0	0
EUROPE EX. U.K.	250	10	9	2	7	18	20	13	2	6	8	7	4	14	29	11	17	13	28	24	8	0
SOUTHERN DOMINIONS	79	0	2	3	0	5	9	11	5	3	3	3	1	7	9	2	3	5	5	5	3	0
S. AFRICA +RHOD.	24	0	0	1	0	1	2	3	4	2	1	1	0	3	1	2	1	1	1	4	0	0
AUSTRALIA + N.Z.	55	0	2	2	1	4	7	8	1	1	2	2	1	4	8	0	2	4	7	1	3	0
ASIA + OTHER AFRICA	95	0	1	0	1	7	2	4	0	4	4	2	2	5	16	6	9	14	6	5	6	0
JAPAN	26	0	1	0	0	2	2	4	0	0	2	2	0	2	2	2	4	7	1	1	2	0
OTHER ASIA+AFR.	69	0	0	0	1	5	0	0	0	4	3	3	0	3	14	4	5	7	6	4	4	0
BLACK AFRICA	8	0	0	0	0	0	0	1	0	0	1	1	0	1	1	1	0	1	4	0	1	0
ARAB WORLD	8	0	0	0	0	0	0	1	0	1	1	0	1	1	3	0	0	1	0	0	2	0
INDIA	17	0	0	0	1	3	1	1	0	0	0	1	0	1	0	2	2	1	1	0	1	0
PHILIPPINES	10	0	0	0	0	0	0	1	0	1	0	0	0	1	0	0	0	0	1	0	2	0
OTHER E. ASIA	10	0	0	0	1	2	1	1	0	1	0	0	2	1	3	1	1	2	1	0	0	0
OTHER ASIA	16	0	0	0	0	0	0	2	0	2	1	0	0	0	2	1	2	2	0	3	0	0

CHAPTER 3- THE PROLIFERATION OF FOREIGN SUBSIDIARIES
SECTION 5- THE FLOW OF MANUFACTURING BY CHARACTERISTIC OF SUBSIDIARY
TABLE B3- MANUFACTURING SUBSIDIARIES WHICH ENTERED A PARENT SYSTEM
WHICH HAD 21 - 40 YEARS "FOREIGN MANUFACTURING EXPERIENCE",
CLASSIFIED BY COUNTRY OR REGION AND BY PERIOD MANUFACTURE BEGAN

COUNTRY OR REGION	PRE 1968	PRE 1901	1901 -13	1914 -19	1920 -24	1925 -29	1930 -34	1935 -39	1940 -45	1946 -50	1951 -53	1954 -55	1956 -57	1958 -59	1960 -61	1962	1963	1964	1965	1966	1967	UNK
OUTSIDE U.S.	1719	0	11	9	30	30	32	82	50	114	93	88	127	173	279	116	134	96	82	100	73	0
OUT. U.S. + CANADA	1482	0	11	6	26	29	30	66	44	93	80	70	104	151	251	106	122	81	67	88	66	0
OUT. WEST. HEMIS.	1000	0	8	2	22	18	25	41	19	51	49	40	57	98	172	102	102	60	46	62	42	0
OUT. WHITE CWEALTH	1118	0	9	5	19	15	21	41	34	66	63	53	75	120	187	86	82	68	55	67	52	0
OUT. DEVLPED WORLD	579	0	3	5	4	3	6	20	27	48	36	34	53	68	93	33	34	27	25	32	28	0
CANADA	237	0	0	3	4	10	2	16	6	21	13	18	23	22	28	10	12	15	15	12	7	0
LATIN AMERICA	482	0	3	4	4	2	5	9	25	42	31	30	47	53	79	26	20	21	21	26	24	0
C. AMER.+CARIB.	190	0	2	1	1	0	1	8	6	16	12	10	20	23	26	9	5	13	8	13	15	0
CUBA	16	0	0	0	0	0	2	0	2	3	1	1	0	1	0	0	0	0	0	1	0	0
MEXICO	110	0	2	0	1	0	1	5	2	9	8	6	7	6	13	0	5	0	2	7	11	0
OTHER	64	0	0	1	0	1	3	3	2	4	3	1	7	16	13	5	4	7	6	6	4	0
S. AMERICA	292	0	0	3	3	2	3	11	19	26	19	20	27	30	53	17	15	8	13	13	9	0
ARGENTINA	58	0	1	0	1	2	0	4	6	3	2	6	3	3	10	7	5	8	3	3	1	0
BRAZIL	87	0	0	3	0	2	3	5	5	11	7	4	10	16	10	3	5	1	0	4	4	0
PERU	15	0	0	0	2	0	0	0	2	3	1	2	5	0	2	3	2	0	1	4	0	0
COLOMBIA	53	0	0	0	1	0	2	1	3	3	5	2	2	4	12	1	3	1	6	3	1	0
VENEZUELA	54	0	0	0	1	0	0	1	1	1	5	5	7	7	15	3	5	2	3	1	0	0
OTHER	25	0	0	1	0	0	0	0	2	3	2	2	0	0	0	2	0	1	4	1	3	0
EUROPE	668	0	8	1	18	16	20	31	11	36	29	25	31	63	120	59	59	44	31	37	29	0
EFTA	236	0	5	1	6	6	6	18	4	21	10	10	18	19	36	16	22	11	7	11	8	0
U.K.	164	0	2	1	4	4	7	10	3	17	8	8	13	11	29	13	15	6	5	3	6	0
SCANDINAVIA	43	0	3	0	0	1	1	1	0	3	0	0	5	2	5	3	1	1	3	5	3	0
SWITZERLAND	11	0	0	0	0	1	0	1	0	1	1	2	0	2	1	0	3	2	1	1	1	0
OTHER EFTA	18	0	0	0	2	0	0	4	1	0	1	0	0	4	1	0	2	2	1	1	0	0
EUROP. COMMUNITY	354	0	2	0	8	10	11	9	4	12	15	14	12	41	74	36	33	26	16	16	15	0
FRANCE	110	0	1	0	2	3	5	4	0	4	3	6	6	14	23	11	6	6	10	10	9	0
GERMANY	101	0	1	0	2	7	4	3	0	1	3	5	3	11	22	8	11	12	5	4	3	0
ITALY	87	0	0	0	2	4	0	3	1	2	8	1	6	11	17	12	10	5	7	1	1	0
BELGIUM + LUX	24	0	0	0	1	0	1	1	1	4	1	1	0	2	6	4	5	3	1	1	2	0
NETHERLANDS	32	0	0	0	1	0	0	1	2	2	1	1	1	2	6	2	3	3	1	1	0	0
SPAIN	40	0	0	0	3	0	1	0	2	4	3	0	1	3	6	4	3	5	3	8	1	0
GREECE + TURKEY	16	0	0	0	1	0	0	0	0	3	1	1	0	0	1	2	3	3	2	0	0	0
OTHER EUROPE	22	0	1	0	0	1	0	4	0	2	1	0	0	6	3	0	0	1	1	2	5	0
EUROPE EX. U.K.	504	0	6	0	14	12	14	21	8	19	21	17	18	52	91	46	44	42	26	30	23	0
SOUTHERN DOMINIONS	188	0	0	0	3	1	3	14	6	8	9	9	15	19	32	7	25	10	6	13	8	0
S. AFRICA +RHOD.	66	0	0	0	2	0	0	1	1	4	4	2	3	6	3	2	3	8	2	5	8	0
AUSTRALIA + N.Z.	122	0	0	0	1	1	3	13	5	4	5	7	12	13	29	5	18	8	2	4	8	0
ASIA + OTHER AFRICA	144	0	0	0	1	1	2	5	2	7	4	6	11	16	20	14	18	6	9	12	5	0
JAPAN	47	0	0	0	1	0	1	1	2	1	6	2	5	1	6	7	4	6	5	6	1	0
OTHER ASIA+AFR.	97	0	0	0	1	1	1	0	0	6	5	4	6	14	14	7	14	6	4	6	4	0
BLACK AFRICA	14	0	0	0	0	0	0	0	0	2	0	1	1	0	5	1	1	6	1	2	2	0
ARAB WORLD	15	0	0	0	0	0	0	1	1	1	1	0	1	0	2	1	2	1	1	0	0	0
INDIA	12	0	0	0	0	1	1	0	0	2	2	0	0	4	0	1	1	1	1	0	0	0
PHILIPPINES	17	0	0	0	1	0	0	0	1	1	1	1	1	3	0	1	2	1	0	1	1	0
OTHER E. ASIA	11	0	0	0	1	1	2	1	0	1	2	3	1	1	3	0	3	2	1	1	2	0
OTHER ASIA	28	0	0	0	0	0	1	1	0	1	0	0	2	3	7	3	3	3	2	2	2	0

PERIOD

CHAPTER 3- THE PROLIFERATION OF FOREIGN SUBSIDIARIES
SECTION 5- THE FLOW OF MANUFACTURING BY CHARACTERISTIC OF SUBSIDIARY
TABLE B4- MANUFACTURING SUBSIDIARIES WHICH ENTERED A PARENT SYSTEM
WHICH HAD MORE THAN 40 YEARS "FOREIGN MANUFACTURING EXPERIENCE",
CLASSIFIED BY COUNTRY OR REGION AND BY PERIOD MANUFACTURE BEGAN

PERIOD

COUNTRY OR REGION	PRE 1968	PRE 1901	1901 -13	1914 -19	1920 -24	1925 -29	1930 -34	1935 -39	1940 -45	1946 -50	1951 -53	1954 -55	1956 -57	1958 -59	1960 -61	1962	1963	1964	1965	1966	1967	UNK
OUTSIDE U.S.	1342	1	2	0	5	13	6	12	29	38	54	54	65	97	198	121	113	138	186	124	86	0
OUT. U.S. + CANADA	1211	1	2	0	5	13	5	11	23	33	44	43	58	94	185	114	105	118	168	109	80	0
OUT. WEST. HEMIS.	859	0	1	0	3	18	3	4	19	22	31	26	31	57	133	87	79	97	120	81	66	0
OUT. WHITE CWEALTH	953	1	2	0	3	11	4	11	24	24	31	35	51	73	137	84	82	93	138	89	65	0
OUT. DEVLPED WORLD	483	1	1	0	2	6	2	7	14	13	14	23	30	42	73	45	39	39	66	40	26	0
CANADA	131	0	0	0	0	0	1	1	6	5	10	11	7	3	13	7	8	20	18	15	6	0
LATIN AMERICA	352	1	1	0	2	5	2	7	13	11	13	17	27	37	52	27	26	21	48	28	14	0
C. AMER.+CARIB.	134	1	0	0	2	3	1	3	3	4	3	3	14	19	10	10	12	26	16	5	0	0
CUBA	5	0	0	0	0	1	0	0	0	0	1	0	0	1	1	0	0	0	0	0	0	0
MEXICO	91	0	0	0	2	2	1	2	2	5	2	2	9	10	6	6	7	5	15	14	5	0
OTHER	38	1	0	0	0	1	0	1	1	4	1	1	5	8	3	2	3	5	11	2	3	0
S. AMERICA	218	1	1	0	0	2	1	4	11	7	10	14	22	25	33	19	16	9	22	12	9	0
ARGENTINA	33	0	0	0	0	0	0	1	1	4	1	3	5	8	10	5	3	1	5	4	1	0
BRAZIL	62	0	0	0	0	0	0	1	7	4	5	7	3	6	9	8	3	1	4	3	1	0
PERU	22	0	0	0	0	0	0	0	1	4	5	4	1	1	2	2	2	1	6	4	3	0
COLOMBIA	33	1	0	0	0	0	0	0	1	1	2	4	1	2	7	2	3	2	3	3	1	0
VENEZUELA	39	0	0	0	1	0	0	0	0	0	1	1	6	4	9	2	3	2	4	1	3	0
OTHER	29	0	0	0	1	2	0	2	1	0	0	2	2	3	4	3	4	2	3	1	0	0
EUROPE	550	0	1	0	3	6	3	3	16	7	21	15	25	42	78	51	47	55	81	55	42	0
EFTA	186	0	0	0	2	1	1	3	7	5	8	15	6	15	30	20	11	17	28	22	10	0
U.K.	130	0	0	0	2	1	1	3	6	5	7	10	6	10	17	17	11	7	18	13	7	0
SCANDINAVIA	31	0	0	0	0	0	0	0	2	0	1	2	2	1	2	2	0	1	5	1	1	0
SWITZERLAND	10	0	0	0	0	0	1	0	0	0	0	1	1	2	1	0	0	2	1	1	2	0
OTHER EFTA	15	0	0	0	0	0	0	0	0	0	2	1	2	1	0	1	2	1	2	2	0	0
EUROP. COMMUNITY	287	0	0	0	0	3	1	2	9	1	9	15	24	41	23	23	28	30	44	22	23	0
FRANCE	71	0	0	0	0	0	0	2	2	1	2	2	5	11	6	6	7	14	5	3	9	0
GERMANY	81	0	0	0	0	3	1	2	2	4	4	6	2	11	7	7	6	6	12	13	4	0
ITALY	62	0	0	0	0	0	0	0	2	2	3	6	4	11	4	4	7	8	12	1	3	0
BELGIUM + LUX	39	0	0	0	0	2	0	0	1	1	0	0	2	3	2	2	1	7	2	2	6	0
NETHERLANDS	34	0	0	0	0	1	0	0	2	1	2	1	6	3	4	5	7	3	8	2	1	0
SPAIN	46	0	0	0	1	0	0	0	1	0	1	2	2	5	6	5	1	5	7	7	5	0
GREECE + TURKEY	16	0	0	0	0	0	0	0	0	0	2	1	0	0	0	2	3	1	1	3	1	0
OTHER EUROPE	15	1	1	0	1	1	1	0	0	1	2	1	1	1	1	1	0	2	0	1	3	0
EUROPE FX. U.K.	420	1	1	0	1	5	2	3	11	2	14	13	19	32	55	34	38	48	63	42	35	0
SOUTHERN DOMINIONS	116	0	0	0	0	1	0	2	4	4	4	5	1	10	24	12	11	16	12	7	7	0
S. AFRICA +RHOD.	29	0	0	0	0	0	0	0	3	3	1	0	1	0	5	5	6	4	4	3	1	0
AUSTRALIA + N.Z.	87	0	0	0	0	1	0	2	2	2	6	5	2	9	19	7	5	12	11	5	6	0
ASIA + OTHER AFRICA	193	0	0	0	0	1	0	1	2	2	6	6	5	10	31	24	21	26	27	19	17	0
JAPAN	62	0	0	0	0	0	0	1	0	2	1	3	3	5	10	6	8	8	19	7	12	0
OTHER ASIA+AFR.	131	0	0	0	0	1	0	1	2	2	5	5	3	5	21	18	13	18	18	12	5	0
BLACK AFRICA	22	0	0	0	0	0	0	0	0	1	1	0	0	3	3	3	1	7	3	3	4	0
ARAB WORLD	13	0	0	0	0	0	0	0	1	0	0	1	1	0	3	3	0	3	3	1	2	0
INDIA	26	0	0	0	0	1	0	0	0	1	0	1	3	1	5	5	5	2	2	2	1	0
PHILIPPINES	16	0	0	0	0	0	0	0	0	0	0	3	0	5	2	2	2	2	3	2	0	0
OTHER E. ASIA	12	0	0	0	0	0	0	0	0	0	1	0	0	1	1	1	0	2	2	2	3	0
OTHER ASIA	42	0	0	0	1	1	0	0	1	1	0	0	0	1	6	3	3	5	6	2	2	0

CHAPTER 3- THE PROLIFERATION OF FOREIGN SUBSIDIARIES
SECTION 5- THE FLOW OF MANUFACTURING BY CHARACTERISTIC OF SUBSIDIARY
TABLE C1- MANUFACTURING SUBSIDIARIES
WHICH WERE NEWLY FORMED,
CLASSIFIED BY COUNTRY OR REGION AND BY PERIOD MANUFACTURE BEGAN

PERIOD

COUNTRY OR REGION	PRE 1968	PRE 1901	1901 -13	1914 -19	1920 -24	1925 -29	1930 -34	1935 -39	1940 -45	1946 -50	1951 -53	1954 -55	1956 -57	1958 -59	1960 -61	1962	1963	1964	1965	1966	1967	UNK
OUTSIDE U.S.	2183	34	45	49	45	97	67	110	80	119	120	94	132	195	286	133	118	119	145	105	62	28
OUT. U.S. + CANADA	1937	30	34	27	36	69	56	91	61	97	97	81	124	182	280	127	110	113	134	101	59	28
OUT. WEST. HEMIS.	1288	28	30	17	29	54	43	54	21	49	59	50	58	117	198	91	86	98	118	68	38	19
OUT. WHITE CWEALTH	1553	22	25	21	26	48	30	59	48	74	75	58	106	144	237	108	95	98	118	89	51	21
OUT. DEVLPED WORLD	862	2	4	12	8	21	15	41	41	58	43	39	75	82	120	57	42	47	57	50	36	12
CANADA	246	4	11	22	9	28	11	19	19	22	23	13	8	13	6	6	8	6	4	3	3	0
LATIN AMERICA	649	2	4	10	7	15	13	37	40	48	38	31	66	65	82	36	24	27	41	33	21	9
C. AMER.+CARIB.	261	1	2	3	1	6	8	20	13	18	15	8	26	25	27	15	12	12	18	17	10	4
CUBA	22	0	1	2	0	1	0	4	0	1	1	1	0	1	0	0	0	0	2	0	0	1
MEXICO	159	0	2	1	1	5	6	11	9	17	11	7	12	20	19	8	5	5	10	6	7	1
OTHER	80	0	0	0	0	0	2	5	4	0	2	0	6	5	7	1	7	1	6	11	3	2
S. AMERICA	388	1	2	7	6	9	5	17	27	30	23	23	40	40	55	21	12	15	23	16	11	5
ARGENTINA	73	0	0	2	2	3	4	8	6	4	2	5	6	4	10	4	10	2	3	2	0	3
BRAZIL	100	0	0	4	1	4	0	7	6	11	10	5	12	17	7	7	2	0	3	6	2	2
PERU	30	1	0	1	0	0	0	1	0	0	4	3	1	1	3	4	0	4	3	6	2	0
COLOMBIA	55	0	0	0	1	0	1	1	4	3	4	5	4	5	9	0	2	5	3	5	2	2
VENEZUELA	91	0	0	0	1	0	0	1	6	6	6	6	5	11	21	2	6	3	4	4	3	0
OTHER	39	0	0	1	2	2	0	0	1	3	1	1	3	2	5	2	1	1	2	3	4	0
EUROPE	771	27	28	10	24	36	28	29	10	30	41	26	35	69	119	49	49	46	56	32	17	10
EFTA	251	7	14	3	10	16	14	19	4	15	13	8	12	14	29	14	7	15	17	12	4	4
U.K.	158	6	7	2	6	11	10	11	3	13	10	8	8	8	17	5	6	4	8	10	4	3
SCANDINAVIA	49	1	5	1	2	1	0	1	0	2	1	0	4	1	5	5	0	1	4	5	3	1
SWITZERLAND	14	0	2	0	0	2	0	2	1	0	1	0	0	1	5	0	1	0	5	4	0	0
OTHER EFTA	30	0	0	0	2	2	0	5	0	0	1	0	0	4	2	2	0	1	1	0	1	1
EUROP. COMMUNITY	415	17	12	6	11	18	11	10	5	13	18	15	19	48	82	29	34	21	25	11	4	6
FRANCE	112	7	1	1	5	4	4	2	1	4	5	3	4	14	21	7	8	7	7	5	3	3
GERMANY	107	8	6	3	9	9	5	5	2	0	3	5	3	8	24	6	6	8	5	6	3	2
ITALY	100	2	5	0	3	1	1	2	1	3	7	3	9	12	20	8	12	5	5	3	0	0
BELGIUM + LUX	48	0	0	1	1	1	1	1	0	3	1	2	1	8	7	4	1	6	6	1	1	1
NETHERLANDS	48	0	1	1	0	3	1	0	1	3	2	2	2	6	10	2	5	2	6	6	0	1
SPAIN	54	0	0	0	2	0	3	0	0	1	3	1	1	2	4	3	3	3	9	6	4	0
GREECE + TURKEY	30	2	2	0	0	0	0	0	0	1	0	1	2	2	1	0	2	3	4	2	5	0
OTHER EUROPE	21	3	0	0	1	1	1	0	0	0	3	1	2	3	1	3	2	8	4	1	0	0
EUROPE EX. U.K.	613	21	21	8	18	25	14	18	7	17	31	18	27	61	102	42	43	42	49	28	14	7
SOUTHERN DOMINIONS	213	1	2	4	4	10	12	21	9	9	9	14	9	28	25	11	9	10	9	8	5	4
S. AFRICA +RHOD.	72	1	0	1	3	0	6	5	5	8	8	4	3	7	7	4	4	2	1	3	3	3
AUSTRALIA + N.Z.	141	0	2	3	1	9	6	16	4	1	0	10	6	21	18	7	0	8	8	5	4	1
ASIA + OTHER AFRICA	304	0	0	0	1	8	3	4	2	10	0	9	14	20	54	31	28	30	28	28	16	5
JAPAN	91	0	0	1	0	2	1	0	1	0	0	4	5	3	16	10	10	12	11	1	1	2
OTHER ASIA+AFR.	213	0	0	2	1	6	2	4	1	10	0	8	9	17	38	18	18	16	17	15	3	3
BLACK AFRICA	25	0	0	1	0	0	0	0	0	0	0	0	0	0	2	8	1	4	3	1	4	1
ARAB WORLD	24	0	0	0	2	3	2	0	2	0	1	2	1	4	2	1	4	3	1	3	4	0
INDIA	40	0	0	0	0	1	1	1	0	1	2	0	5	8	8	4	7	3	4	0	3	0
PHILIPPINES	34	0	0	0	1	2	0	1	1	1	3	5	1	0	5	0	2	2	0	1	0	0
OTHER E. ASIA	21	0	1	1	0	1	0	1	0	0	0	0	1	5	2	2	3	4	2	4	3	0
OTHER ASIA	69	0	0	0	1	2	1	2	6	6	0	3	1	3	16	8	3	8	5	7	3	1

CHAPTER 3- THE PROLIFERATION OF FOREIGN SUBSIDIARIES
SECTION 5- THE FLOW OF MANUFACTURING BY CHARACTERISTIC OF SUBSIDIARY
TABLE C2- MANUFACTURING SUBSIDIARIES
WHICH WERE ACQUIRED.
CLASSIFIED BY COUNTRY OR REGION AND BY PERIOD MANUFACTURE BEGAN

PERIOD

COUNTRY OR REGION	PRE 1968	PRE 1901	1901-13	1914-19	1920-24	1925-29	1930-34	1935-39	1940-45	1946-50	1951-53	1954-55	1956-57	1958-59	1960-61	1962	1963	1964	1965	1966	1967	UNK
OUTSIDE U.S.	2199	10	22	13	27	88	56	50	38	68	85	101	118	180	312	148	180	173	178	186	147	19
OUT. U.S. + CANADA	1760	9	10	7	19	56	41	39	26	48	66	68	82	156	260	129	164	138	148	156	126	12
OUT. WEST. HEMIS.	1280	8	8	5	16	48	36	31	8	30	45	43	48	101	203	99	129	105	108	112	88	9
OUT. WHITE CWEALTH	1266	4	7	2	15	33	29	21	22	31	43	55	61	120	174	94	111	103	117	116	99	9
OUT. DEVLPED WORLD	559	1	2	2	3	11	5	9	18	21	21	27	38	62	67	37	49	38	50	50	44	4
CANADA	439	1	12	6	8	32	15	11	12	20	19	33	36	24	52	19	16	35	30	30	21	7
LATIN AMERICA	490	1	2	2	3	8	5	8	18	18	21	25	34	55	57	30	35	33	40	44	38	3
C. AMER.+CARIB.	215	0	1	0	3	2	5	1	4	6	9	10	15	29	25	9	11	21	23	25	19	1
CUBA	8	0	1	0	0	1	1	2	1	1	0	1	0	1	0	0	0	0	0	0	0	0
MEXICO	158	0	1	0	1	1	2	1	1	2	8	8	14	22	18	5	9	17	14	20	12	1
OTHER	49	0	0	0	0	0	0	0	2	1	0	1	1	2	7	4	2	4	9	5	7	1
S. AMERICA	265	1	1	2	3	6	2	6	12	14	12	15	19	26	32	21	24	12	17	19	17	2
ARGENTINA	67	0	0	1	1	2	2	2	3	3	1	4	4	8	8	6	6	3	2	9	5	1
BRAZIL	71	0	1	1	0	3	0	0	5	1	6	1	8	1	8	4	5	6	3	2	6	0
PERU	19	0	0	1	0	1	0	1	1	2	2	4	1	0	10	2	4	5	2	1	3	0
COLOMBIA	44	0	0	0	0	0	0	0	2	4	3	1	2	3	8	3	3	2	4	2	2	0
VENEZUELA	34	0	0	0	1	0	0	0	2	1	0	3	1	3	5	2	4	2	2	4	3	1
OTHER	30	1	0	0	1	0	0	3	2	3	0	1	1	0	1	4	3	2	5	0	4	0
EUROPE	955	8	7	3	15	42	30	27	6	19	26	35	35	81	146	74	82	76	81	91	64	7
EFTA	349	5	3	3	4	24	10	19	2	10	11	16	16	29	50	25	33	23	21	33	16	3
U.K.	282	0	3	3	4	20	6	16	2	9	10	7	14	23	43	23	25	13	15	26	14	3
SCANDINAVIA	41	0	0	0	0	0	3	1	0	1	1	2	1	1	4	0	3	7	4	4	1	0
SWITZERLAND	13	0	0	0	0	1	0	1	0	0	0	0	0	2	2	0	3	2	1	2	0	0
OTHER EFTA	13	0	0	0	0	0	1	1	0	0	0	2	0	2	2	2	2	1	1	1	0	0
EUROP. COMMUNITY	506	3	4	0	7	16	19	7	3	8	12	21	17	49	84	40	39	44	48	41	40	4
FRANCE	167	1	3	0	6	5	6	5	0	2	1	7	3	13	35	12	12	19	5	15	15	2
GERMANY	144	2	1	0	1	7	9	0	0	3	6	10	9	10	17	12	12	8	17	15	9	2
ITALY	100	0	0	0	0	1	1	0	1	0	4	3	3	13	19	7	7	8	11	15	5	2
BELGIUM + LUX	53	1	1	0	1	1	1	1	1	0	1	1	1	1	9	2	6	3	5	8	5	0
NETHERLANDS	42	0	0	0	2	2	2	1	1	2	0	0	1	6	4	6	2	3	3	3	5	2
SPAIN	72	0	0	0	4	2	0	0	0	0	1	5	2	3	6	8	7	5	10	13	6	0
GREECE + TURKEY	7	0	0	0	0	0	0	1	1	0	0	0	0	0	3	0	1	1	0	2	1	0
OTHER EUROPE	21	0	0	0	0	0	1	1	1	1	2	0	1	0	3	0	3	3	2	2	1	0
EUROPE FX. U.K.	673	3	4	0	11	22	24	11	4	10	16	28	21	58	103	51	59	63	66	65	50	4
SOUTHERN DOMINIONS	196	0	0	2	0	3	6	2	2	7	11	6	7	13	40	12	27	19	14	13	12	0
S. AFRICA +RHOD.	66	0	0	0	0	1	1	0	0	1	3	1	2	4	5	10	24	10	3	3	3	0
AUSTRALIA + N.Z.	130	0	1	2	1	2	5	2	1	6	8	5	5	9	35	17	3	9	11	10	9	0
ASIA + OTHER AFRICA	129	0	1	0	1	3	0	2	0	4	8	8	2	7	17	20	10	10	13	8	12	2
JAPAN	50	0	1	0	1	3	0	1	1	1	8	0	2	0	6	2	5	5	3	8	2	1
OTHER ASIA+AFR.	79	0	0	0	0	3	0	0	0	3	3	2	4	7	10	14	5	3	10	6	6	1
BLACK AFRICA	10	0	0	0	0	0	0	0	0	1	0	0	0	0	2	1	3	0	2	1	1	0
ARAB WORLD	7	0	0	0	0	0	0	0	0	0	0	1	0	0	0	1	0	0	3	0	0	0
INDIA	20	0	0	0	1	1	0	0	1	0	1	0	1	3	0	4	0	3	1	0	1	0
PHILIPPINES	15	0	0	0	0	2	0	1	0	0	0	0	1	1	5	0	0	0	1	0	3	0
OTHER E. ASIA	10	0	0	0	0	0	0	0	0	0	0	1	1	0	2	1	0	1	0	1	0	0
OTHER ASIA	17	0	0	0	0	0	0	1	0	2	2	0	2	3	0	2	2	1	1	1	3	1

CHAPTER 3- THE PROLIFERATION OF FOREIGN SUBSIDIARIES
SECTION 5- THE FLOW OF MANUFACTURING BY CHARACTERISTIC OF SUBSIDIARY
TABLE D1- MANUFACTURING SUBSIDIARIES WHICH WERE
WHOLLY OWNED AT DATE MANUFACTURE BEGAN,
CLASSIFIED BY COUNTRY OR REGION AND BY PERIOD MANUFACTURE BEGAN

PERIOD

COUNTRY OR REGION	PRE 1968	PRE 1901	1901 -13	1914 -19	1920 -24	1925 -29	1930 -34	1935 -39	1940 -45	1946 -50	1951 -53	1954 -55	1956 -57	1958 -59	1960 -61	1962	1963	1964	1965	1966	1967	UNK
OUTSIDE U.S.	2923	32	53	60	59	147	108	152	85	161	146	146	180	249	346	163	166	181	171	165	108	45
OUT. U.S. + CANADA	2293	28	31	31	41	96	81	114	57	120	107	104	142	216	296	143	144	143	139	135	90	35
OUT. WEST. HEMIS.	1626	27	25	18	36	78	65	80	22	68	68	64	81	139	212	112	116	109	103	108	67	28
OUT. WHITE CWEALTH	1600	17	23	23	28	57	44	67	42	82	75	77	108	164	210	98	91	108	108	89	69	28
OUT. DEVLPED WORLD	824	1	6	14	7	27	18	40	36	62	43	46	72	88	103	46	39	51	50	37	28	10
CANADA	630	4	22	29	18	51	27	38	28	41	39	42	38	33	50	20	22	38	32	30	18	10
LATIN AMERICA	667	1	6	13	5	18	16	34	35	52	39	40	61	77	84	31	28	34	36	27	22	7
C. AMER.+CARIB.	282	0	3	3	1	6	3	17	9	23	17	17	34	35	29	10	10	20	14	13	8	4
CUBA	28	0	0	2	0	1	1	2	1	2	2	1	6	2	0	0	0	0	0	0	0	2
MEXICO	189	0	3	1	1	5	5	10	6	17	14	15	19	26	16	7	8	16	10	10	8	1
OTHER	65	0	0	0	0	0	1	4	2	3	1	1	9	7	12	3	1	4	7	3	0	1
S. AMERICA	385	1	3	10	4	12	7	17	26	29	22	23	27	42	55	21	18	14	22	14	15	3
ARGENTINA	88	0	2	4	1	5	6	8	10	3	2	4	5	10	11	4	1	3	4	1	4	0
BRAZIL	117	0	0	5	1	5	0	8	7	11	9	9	9	17	14	4	5	4	9	4	15	0
PERU	28	1	0	0	1	1	0	1	1	3	7	1	4	1	1	1	3	1	3	0	4	0
COLOMBIA	50	0	0	0	0	1	0	1	1	5	6	2	1	11	11	3	3	4	4	0	2	0
VENEZUELA	59	0	0	0	1	0	1	1	2	4	2	6	7	7	14	5	4	2	1	3	3	2
OTHER	43	0	1	1	0	1	0	1	3	5	3	3	1	2	4	4	2	2	6	0	2	1
EUROPE	1132	26	24	11	30	57	49	50	11	44	51	39	50	97	148	76	69	67	81	79	54	19
EFTA	483	9	13	5	12	35	26	32	4	29	21	10	21	29	58	31	23	27	32	39	18	9
U.K.	357	9	7	2	8	29	23	23	2	22	17	8	16	20	44	26	18	10	23	27	13	8
SCANDINAVIA	73	0	5	3	2	4	2	2	2	5	2	2	5	6	6	4	3	4	5	7	3	0
SWITZERLAND	26	0	0	0	2	1	1	4	0	2	1	0	2	2	1	1	1	3	1	2	2	1
OTHER EFTA	27	0	1	0	2	1	1	0	0	0	1	0	0	1	1	0	1	3	3	3	0	0
EUROP. COMMUNITY	564	15	9	5	14	19	21	15	5	12	25	24	27	61	79	40	42	36	44	33	29	9
FRANCE	149	6	1	1	8	4	2	5	0	5	6	4	7	18	20	12	8	7	12	12	20	4
GERMANY	168	8	3	3	4	9	8	8	3	8	8	11	10	12	20	13	14	10	13	10	10	2
ITALY	116	1	1	0	2	2	2	2	0	1	7	5	8	13	21	13	8	10	13	12	5	2
BELGIUM + LUX	69	0	3	0	0	1	0	2	0	2	2	2	0	8	10	9	9	4	9	5	4	0
NETHERLANDS	62	0	1	1	2	1	9	2	2	2	2	2	2	8	8	9	2	5	11	3	0	1
SPAIN	38	0	0	0	2	2	2	3	0	2	2	3	2	1	4	3	0	3	5	3	3	0
GREECE + TURKEY	14	0	2	1	2	0	0	0	0	1	2	1	1	2	3	1	1	0	0	2	1	0
OTHER EUROPE	33	2	0	0	1	1	0	3	2	0	3	1	1	2	4	1	1	2	0	1	1	1
EUROPE EX. U.K.	775	17	17	9	22	28	26	27	7	22	34	31	34	77	104	50	51	57	58	52	41	11
SOUTHERN DOMINIONS	313	1	1	6	4	10	14	23	10	14	12	18	17	30	38	19	32	24	8	19	7	6
S. AFRICA +RHOD.	113	1	0	1	3	2	4	4	6	8	3	5	5	9	6	7	27	11	1	6	1	3
AUSTRALIA + N.Z.	200	0	1	5	1	8	10	19	4	6	9	13	12	21	32	12	15	13	7	13	6	3
ASIA + OTHER AFRICA	181	0	0	1	1	11	2	7	10	10	5	7	14	12	17	17	15	18	14	10	3	3
JAPAN	24	0	0	0	0	2	0	1	0	0	1	1	1	2	1	2	4	1	1	0	6	0
OTHER ASIA+AFR.	157	0	0	1	1	9	2	6	10	10	4	6	13	11	19	15	11	17	14	10	5	3
BLACK AFRICA	27	0	0	0	0	0	0	0	1	0	0	1	1	0	5	3	1	8	4	3	3	0
ARAB WORLD	17	0	0	0	0	0	0	1	0	2	0	0	0	3	1	0	0	1	3	1	0	0
INDIA	18	0	0	0	1	3	1	1	0	2	1	1	4	1	1	2	0	0	1	1	0	1
PHILIPPINES	34	0	0	0	0	0	0	0	0	2	2	0	1	4	2	2	7	1	0	0	0	1
OTHER E. ASIA	19	0	2	0	0	3	1	2	0	2	1	0	1	0	3	1	1	5	2	2	1	2
OTHER ASIA	42	0	0	1	0	3	0	3	0	4	0	0	1	3	5	8	2	3	3	3	0	2

CHAPTER 3- THE PROLIFERATION OF FOREIGN SUBSIDIARIES
SECTION 5- THE FLOW OF MANUFACTURING BY CHARACTERISTIC OF SUBSIDIARY
TABLE D2- MANUFACTURING SUBSIDIARIES WHICH WERE
JOINT VENTURES AT DATE MANUFACTURE BEGAN,
CLASSIFIED BY COUNTRY OR REGION AND BY PERIOD MANUFACTURE BEGAN

PERIOD

COUNTRY OR REGION	PRE 1968	PRE 1921	1901-13	1914-19	1920-24	1925-29	1930-34	1935-39	1940-45	1946-50	1951-53	1954-55	1956-57	1958-59	1960-61	1962	1963	1964	1965	1966	1967	UNK
OUTSIDE U.S.	1812	8	17	6	24	48	36	39	49	74	74	67	105	143	275	132	152	132	166	137	109	19
OUT. U.S. + CANADA	1696	8	14	4	21	36	33	35	45	64	69	58	97	139	265	127	146	125	157	133	104	16
OUT. WEST. HEMIS.	1161	7	13	4	15	34	28	20	13	34	44	36	47	93	201	112	112	98	112	81	67	12
OUT. WHITE CWEALTH	1411	6	8	2	14	28	23	28	38	51	57	43	81	112	219	115	126	105	132	123	88	12
OUT. DEVLPED WORLD	704	1	1	0	6	2	6	15	33	35	29	29	54	66	98	52	57	38	58	65	53	6
CANADA	116	0	3	2	3	3	3	4	4	10	5	5	8	8	8	5	5	7	9	5	5	3
LATIN AMERICA	535	1	3	1	3	12	5	7	4	10	30	22	50	46	64	37	34	27	45	52	37	4
C. AMER.+CARIB.	226	1	1	1	0	1	3	4	2	5	7	8	14	22	37	16	16	19	26	30	21	1
CUBA	13	1	0	0	0	1	3	1	1	1	0	0	0	0	0	0	0	0	0	0	0	0
MEXICO	139	0	0	0	0	0	2	1	8	5	7	5	9	17	20	27	16	9	6	13	13	2
OTHER	74	0	0	0	0	1	1	2	1	2	5	3	5	7	7	6	6	7	8	5	3	1
S. AMERICA	309	0	0	0	0	1	2	2	2	6	23	17	36	24	37	21	22	19	22	16	16	1
ARGENTINA	61	0	0	0	0	0	0	3	1	2	5	1	11	13	7	8	5	5	3	2	3	1
BRAZIL	68	0	0	0	0	1	2	3	1	5	5	7	7	11	5	5	1	3	3	2	2	1
PERU	25	0	1	0	0	0	0	1	0	2	2	1	3	0	5	2	2	2	2	3	2	1
COLOMBIA	54	0	0	0	0	0	0	0	0	4	4	3	5	2	8	3	1	4	3	4	4	1
VENEZUELA	64	1	0	0	0	0	0	0	1	3	3	3	6	4	9	3	5	6	6	2	3	0
OTHER	37	0	0	0	4	1	2	2	1	1	4	1	4	7	6	2	2	2	4	6	3	3
EUROPE	725	7	11	3	13	31	20	16	7	21	22	20	35	55	122	56	68	65	66	50	32	5
EFTA	185	3	7	2	6	9	5	7	3	6	10	9	15	14	22	12	19	14	10	9	5	2
U.K.	131	2	5	2	6	9	4	7	6	7	8	7	12	11	17	6	11	11	8	5	4	2
SCANDINAVIA	32	1	2	0	0	2	1	0	1	1	0	0	1	1	1	5	1	1	1	3	5	2
SWITZERLAND	8	0	0	0	0	0	1	0	0	0	0	0	1	1	1	0	0	0	0	1	0	0
OTHER EFTA	14	0	0	0	0	2	1	2	0	0	0	0	1	1	1	1	1	1	0	1	0	0
EUROP. COMMUNITY	408	4	4	1	6	17	13	9	3	14	9	9	16	37	88	34	35	36	33	20	17	3
FRANCE	144	1	4	1	3	5	2	3	1	5	2	2	7	11	35	13	11	11	20	8	10	1
GERMANY	101	1	2	1	5	8	5	6	1	3	5	2	5	11	20	13	13	11	6	10	8	0
ITALY	89	1	0	0	1	1	0	0	0	4	2	2	4	7	18	5	8	8	8	4	4	1
BELGIUM + LUX	35	1	1	1	1	1	2	1	0	2	2	2	4	1	8	1	1	1	3	2	1	0
NETHERLANDS	39	0	0	0	0	2	3	2	1	0	4	0	6	10	7	2	1	2	3	4	1	1
SPAIN	94	0	0	0	0	2	2	0	0	4	4	3	2	2	7	7	4	13	6	16	7	0
GREECE + TURKEY	25	0	0	0	0	1	0	0	0	0	3	0	2	0	4	2	1	0	4	3	0	0
OTHER EUROPE	13	0	0	1	1	2	0	0	0	0	0	0	0	0	1	2	3	1	3	3	2	0
EUROPE EX. U.K.	594	5	9	2	7	26	16	12	4	15	16	13	23	44	105	50	57	57	61	45	28	3
SOUTHERN DOMINIONS	146	0	1	0	1	3	6	3	4	7	3	6	4	16	29	5	8	9	9	18	12	2
S. AFRICA +RHOD.	40	0	0	1	0	1	3	1	0	3	1	1	0	3	3	3	4	4	4	4	3	2
AUSTRALIA + N.Z.	106	0	1	1	1	2	3	2	4	4	6	5	4	13	22	2	4	6	3	14	9	0
ASIA + OTHER AFRICA	290	0	1	1	1	3	2	1	2	6	6	8	8	22	50	29	36	24	27	28	23	5
JAPAN	121	0	0	1	1	3	1	0	1	1	3	1	4	4	16	5	5	13	24	15	13	9
OTHER ASIA+AFR.	169	0	1	0	1	2	2	1	1	5	5	7	4	20	34	15	23	11	13	13	16	3
BLACK AFRICA	15	0	0	0	0	0	1	0	1	0	1	1	0	0	1	3	1	2	3	2	1	0
ARAB WORLD	20	0	0	0	0	1	1	0	0	1	0	1	0	0	2	0	1	3	2	3	2	0
INDIA	47	0	0	0	0	1	1	1	1	1	0	2	0	2	12	8	8	5	4	2	1	0
PHILIPPINES	23	0	0	0	0	1	0	0	0	0	1	0	1	7	2	2	5	1	2	3	3	1
OTHER E. ASIA	12	0	0	0	0	0	0	0	0	0	2	1	0	6	1	2	1	1	0	1	1	0
OTHER ASIA	52	0	0	0	0	0	1	0	0	4	0	0	3	1	13	5	5	3	3	2	6	0

CHAPTER 3- THE PROLIFERATION OF FOREIGN SUBSIDIARIES
SECTION 6- CHANGES IN STATE OF BEING, MAIN ACTIVITY AND OWNERSHIP
TABLE 1- SUBSIDIARIES, MANUFACTURING OR NON-MANUFACTURING,
WHICH WERE LIQUIDATED OR EXPROPRIATED,
CLASSIFIED BY COUNTRY AND BY PERIOD CHANGE OCCURRED

PERIOD

COUNTRY OR REGION	PRE 1968	PRE 1901	1901 -13	1914 -19	1920 -24	1925 -29	1930 -34	1935 -39	1940 -45	1946 -50	1951 -53	1954 -55	1956 -57	1958 -59	1960 -61	1962	1963	1964	1965	1966	1967	UNK
OUTSIDE U.S.	2497	0	15	14	25	56	77	164	98	192	77	151	77	164	229	152	135	151	159	240	320	1
OUT. U.S. + CANADA	1981	0	11	8	18	32	50	114	74	160	54	116	57	135	192	124	110	128	129	216	252	0
OUT. WEST. HEMIS.	1361	0	11	3	14	29	39	85	66	121	27	86	33	94	97	84	73	70	96	159	174	1
OUT. WHITE CWEALTH	1504	0	7	7	16	27	34	88	62	122	38	80	45	103	156	86	80	106	96	160	190	0
OUT. DEVLPED WORLD	716	0	0	5	4	3	14	37	15	45	29	44	27	49	101	44	42	61	41	62	92	1
CANADA	516	0	4	6	7	24	27	50	24	32	23	35	20	29	37	28	25	23	30	24	68	0
LATIN AMERICA	620	0	0	5	4	3	11	29	8	39	27	30	24	41	95	40	37	58	33	57	78	0
C. AMER.+CARIB.	339	0	0	1	1	2	2	23	5	18	14	13	12	22	70	21	15	43	17	26	34	0
CUBA	76	0	0	1	0	0	0	2	2	0	3	4	4	7	52	2	1	0	0	0	0	0
MEXICO	183	0	0	1	0	1	0	5	5	11	4	9	8	12	10	2	6	35	12	17	22	1
OTHER	80	0	0	0	0	1	2	18	0	7	7	0	0	3	10	9	8	8	5	9	12	0
S. AMERICA	281	0	0	4	3	1	9	6	3	21	13	17	12	19	25	19	22	15	16	31	44	1
ARGENTINA	64	0	0	0	0	0	3	1	1	1	3	8	4	7	8	4	6	8	4	6	4	0
BRAZIL	60	0	0	4	1	0	1	1	1	2	1	1	3	8	7	3	6	4	6	6	11	1
PERU	19	0	0	0	0	0	1	1	2	1	3	3	1	1	2	3	1	0	4	2	3	1
COLOMBIA	39	0	0	4	1	0	0	0	0	6	2	4	0	0	2	4	2	0	2	3	7	0
VENEZUELA	64	0	0	0	0	1	1	2	1	6	2	1	2	0	4	4	6	4	3	6	15	0
OTHER	35	0	0	0	1	0	3	1	3	6	2	1	2	5	1	2	1	1	0	3	4	0
EUROPE	1047	0	10	3	14	27	34	66	57	107	19	50	24	69	79	60	60	55	68	133	112	0
EFTA	462	0	4	1	5	4	14	30	19	47	13	24	12	32	35	31	27	20	30	65	49	0
U.K.	280	0	3	1	2	2	14	12	12	31	11	16	6	20	23	18	21	16	16	34	20	0
SCANDINAVIA	81	0	0	0	1	0	0	5	1	7	0	5	2	5	5	5	2	3	8	20	13	0
SWITZERLAND	72	0	1	0	3	1	0	4	3	7	2	3	1	2	6	5	2	5	5	3	14	0
OTHER EFTA	29	0	0	0	0	1	0	2	3	3	2	0	1	2	3	1	3	1	1	3	2	0
EUROP. COMMUNITY	481	0	5	1	7	15	17	29	27	23	6	24	10	33	42	25	28	34	36	63	56	2
FRANCE	144	0	1	1	1	6	10	13	4	3	5	11	4	15	20	5	8	9	10	12	12	2
GERMANY	133	0	3	0	6	6	5	6	8	7	2	8	3	15	10	8	10	9	8	16	16	0
ITALY	94	0	0	0	0	2	1	2	7	7	2	1	2	5	6	4	6	6	8	16	16	0
BELGIUM + LUX	51	0	1	0	0	2	1	10	2	5	0	3	3	4	6	7	3	8	8	15	16	0
NETHERLANDS	59	0	0	0	0	2	1	7	2	3	1	2	3	6	4	7	3	2	2	10	6	0
SPAIN	25	0	0	0	0	2	0	0	2	1	0	3	1	4	4	1	1	1	2	6	2	0
GREECE + TURKEY	10	0	0	0	0	0	0	0	2	1	0	1	0	1	1	1	2	0	2	2	1	0
OTHER EUROPE	69	0	1	1	0	1	1	7	7	34	0	1	0	1	1	3	3	0	2	2	0	0
EUROPE EX. U.K.	767	0	7	2	12	25	20	47	45	76	8	34	18	49	56	42	39	44	52	99	92	0
SOUTHERN DOMINIONS	187	0	1	0	0	2	2	7	0	6	5	19	6	12	12	18	7	11	17	20	42	0
S. AFRICA +RHOD.	51	0	0	0	0	2	2	7	1	1	1	8	2	3	3	6	4	2	8	4	7	0
AUSTRALIA + N.Z.	136	0	1	0	0	2	2	5	5	5	4	11	4	9	9	12	3	9	9	16	35	0
ASIA + OTHER AFRICA	127	0	1	0	3	0	3	12	9	8	3	17	4	13	6	12	6	9	11	6	20	0
JAPAN	31	0	0	0	0	3	0	4	0	2	1	3	3	5	6	6	6	1	3	1	6	0
OTHER ASIA+AFR.	96	0	0	0	3	0	3	8	7	6	2	14	0	8	6	4	5	3	8	5	14	0
BLACK AFRICA	14	0	0	0	0	0	0	2	0	0	0	4	1	1	1	0	0	0	0	2	1	0
ARAB WORLD	23	0	0	0	0	0	1	1	0	0	1	2	1	1	3	0	2	3	2	0	2	0
INDIA	6	0	0	0	0	0	0	1	1	0	0	1	0	1	0	0	0	0	1	1	1	0
PHILIPPINES	13	0	0	0	1	0	1	0	1	1	1	1	1	0	0	2	2	2	1	1	1	0
OTHER E. ASIA	17	0	0	0	1	1	1	2	1	4	0	1	0	0	0	1	1	1	1	1	4	0
OTHER ASIA	23	0	0	0	1	1	2	3	1	1	0	4	1	3	2	2	2	1	3	2	2	0

CHAPTER 3- THE PROLIFERATION OF FOREIGN SUBSIDIARIES
SECTION 6- CHANGES IN STATE OF BEING, MAIN ACTIVITY AND OWNERSHIP
TABLE 2- SUBSIDIARIES, MANUFACTURING OR NON-MANUFACTURING,
WHICH WERE SOLD,
CLASSIFIED BY COUNTRY AND BY PERIOD CHANGE OCCURRED

PERIOD

COUNTRY OR REGION	PRE 1968	PRE 1901	1901-13	1914-19	1920-24	1925-29	1930-34	1935-39	1940-45	1946-50	1951-53	1954-55	1956-57	1958-59	1960-61	1962	1963	1964	1965	1966	1967	UNK
OUTSIDE U.S.	315	0	0	7	5	0	6	16	8	25	7	32	5	26	10	17	12	18	21	46	54	0
OUT. U.S. + CANADA	271	0	0	7	3	0	5	13	8	22	6	32	4	24	7	16	11	14	16	43	50	0
OUT. WEST. HEMIS.	206	0	0	4	0	0	4	12	5	17	4	20	2	18	6	16	7	10	12	32	37	0
OUT. WHITE CWEALTH	182	0	0	4	3	0	2	7	7	16	4	9	3	14	1	10	6	13	7	36	40	0
OUT. DEVLPED WORLD	79	0	0	3	3	0	1	1	3	6	2	2	2	6	1	4	6	4	5	14	15	0
CANADA	44	0	0	3	2	0	1	3	0	3	1	10	1	2	3	1	1	4	5	3	4	0
LATIN AMERICA	65	0	0	3	3	0	1	1	3	5	2	2	1	6	1	0	4	4	4	11	13	0
C. AMER.+CARIB.	27	0	0	0	2	0	0	1	1	2	0	0	1	3	1	1	1	1	1	8	4	0
CUBA	4	0	0	0	0	0	0	0	0	2	0	0	0	2	0	0	2	0	0	0	0	0
MEXICO	18	0	0	0	2	0	0	0	1	2	0	0	1	1	0	0	2	1	1	5	3	0
OTHER	5	0	0	3	0	0	1	1	0	0	0	2	0	0	1	0	0	0	0	3	1	0
S. AMERICA	38	0	0	3	1	0	1	0	2	3	2	0	0	3	0	4	2	3	3	3	9	0
ARGENTINA	8	0	0	1	1	0	1	1	0	0	0	1	1	1	1	0	1	1	0	0	2	0
BRAZIL	9	0	0	1	0	0	0	1	0	3	0	0	1	1	0	1	0	0	3	1	2	0
PERU	3	0	0	1	0	0	0	0	0	0	0	0	0	0	0	0	1	0	0	1	0	0
COLOMBIA	4	0	0	0	0	0	0	0	0	0	1	1	0	0	0	1	0	0	2	0	1	0
VENEZUELA	8	0	0	0	1	0	0	0	0	0	0	0	0	0	0	0	0	2	1	0	3	0
OTHER	6	0	0	1	0	0	0	0	2	0	1	0	1	0	0	1	0	0	0	1	1	0
EUROPE	157	0	0	2	0	0	4	9	5	14	3	20	1	13	3	8	3	10	10	26	26	0
EFTA	66	0	0	1	0	0	3	5	1	8	2	13	0	4	1	4	3	8	8	9	7	0
U.K.	54	0	0	1	0	0	3	4	1	4	2	13	0	4	1	2	3	8	8	4	4	0
SCANDINAVIA	7	0	0	0	0	0	0	1	1	1	0	0	0	0	1	1	0	0	0	2	2	0
SWITZERLAND	4	0	0	0	0	0	0	0	0	0	0	0	0	0	0	1	0	0	0	2	1	0
OTHER EFTA	1	0	0	0	0	0	1	0	0	0	1	0	0	0	0	0	0	0	0	1	0	0
EUROP. COMMUNITY	78	0	0	1	0	0	1	3	3	9	0	6	1	6	0	4	0	9	2	16	16	0
FRANCE	18	0	0	1	0	0	0	1	0	2	0	1	0	2	0	0	2	2	1	4	4	0
GERMANY	23	0	0	1	0	0	1	1	2	5	0	1	1	2	0	1	0	3	1	4	6	0
ITALY	14	0	0	0	0	0	0	1	0	2	0	1	0	3	0	0	2	2	0	4	2	0
BELGIUM + LUX	8	0	0	0	0	0	0	0	0	0	1	1	0	1	1	1	0	2	0	1	2	0
NETHERLANDS	15	0	0	0	0	0	0	0	1	2	0	1	0	1	0	2	0	0	0	5	2	0
SPAIN	6	0	0	0	0	0	0	0	1	2	1	0	0	1	2	0	0	0	0	1	3	0
GREECE + TURKEY	1	0	0	0	0	0	0	1	0	0	0	0	1	0	0	0	0	1	0	0	0	0
OTHER EUROPE	6	0	0	0	0	0	0	1	0	0	0	0	0	1	2	0	0	0	0	2	2	0
EUROPE EX. U.K.	103	0	0	1	0	0	1	5	4	10	1	7	1	9	2	6	0	10	2	22	22	0
SOUTHERN DOMINIONS	31	0	0	2	0	0	0	2	0	2	0	0	1	5	3	4	2	0	1	3	6	0
S. AFRICA +RHOD.	10	0	0	0	0	0	0	1	0	0	0	0	1	1	1	2	0	0	1	1	2	0
AUSTRALIA + N.Z.	21	0	0	2	0	0	0	1	0	2	1	0	0	4	2	2	2	0	0	2	4	0
ASIA + OTHER AFRICA	18	0	0	0	0	0	0	1	0	1	0	0	0	3	0	4	2	0	1	3	5	0
JAPAN	4	0	0	0	0	0	0	0	0	0	0	0	0	0	0	0	0	0	0	1	3	0
OTHER ASIA+AFR.	14	0	0	2	0	0	3	1	0	2	0	0	0	0	0	3	2	0	0	3	2	0
BLACK AFRICA	3	0	0	0	0	0	0	0	0	0	1	0	0	0	0	0	0	0	0	0	0	0
ARAB WORLD	1	0	0	0	0	0	0	0	0	1	0	0	0	0	0	1	0	0	0	1	1	0
INDIA	1	0	0	0	0	0	0	0	0	0	1	0	0	0	0	0	0	0	1	0	0	0
PHILIPPINES	3	0	0	0	0	0	0	0	0	0	0	0	0	0	0	1	0	0	0	1	1	0
OTHER E. ASIA	1	0	0	0	0	0	0	0	0	1	0	0	0	0	0	0	0	0	0	0	0	0
OTHER ASIA	5	0	0	0	0	0	0	0	0	0	0	0	0	0	0	1	2	0	0	2	0	0

CHAPTER 3- THE PROLIFERATION OF FOREIGN SUBSIDIARIES
SECTION 6- CHANGES IN STATE OF BEING, MAIN ACTIVITY AND OWNERSHIP
TABLE 3- MANUFACTURING SUBSIDIARIES
WHICH WERE LIQUIDATED OR EXPROPRIATED,
CLASSIFIED BY COUNTRY AND BY PERIOD CHANGE OCCURRED

PERIOD

COUNTRY OR REGION	PRE 1968	PRE 1901	1901-13	1914-19	1920-24	1925-29	1930-34	1935-39	1940-45	1946-50	1951-53	1954-55	1956-57	1958-59	1960-61	1962	1963	1964	1965	1966	1967	UNK
OUTSIDE U.S.	1127	0	8	4	7	15	41	53	34	56	36	76	37	68	113	92	63	74	94	102	153	1
OUT. U.S. + CANADA	855	0	4	2	4	9	24	31	22	42	25	53	24	52	98	70	54	61	75	89	115	1
OUT. WEST. HEMIS.	554	0	4	2	3	9	20	23	19	35	10	35	12	36	47	48	35	35	54	57	70	1
OUT. WHITE CWEALTH	637	0	3	2	3	5	17	21	17	26	19	35	17	38	86	46	34	52	50	70	95	0
OUT. DEVLPED WORLD	332	0	3	0	1	0	6	10	4	9	16	21	13	17	53	22	19	28	27	34	51	1
CANADA	272	0	4	2	3	6	17	22	12	14	11	23	13	16	15	22	9	13	19	13	38	0
LATIN AMERICA	301	0	0	0	1	0	4	8	3	7	15	18	12	16	51	22	19	26	21	32	45	1
C. AMER.+CARIB.	152	0	0	0	0	0	0	6	2	2	8	8	5	7	41	9	5	17	7	13	22	0
CUBA	39	0	0	0	0	0	0	3	1	2	1	1	1	0	30	0	0	0	0	0	0	0
MEXICO	90	0	0	0	0	0	0	3	1	1	5	6	4	7	7	7	2	15	7	11	15	0
OTHER	23	0	0	0	0	0	0	0	0	1	2	1	0	0	4	2	2	2	0	2	7	0
S. AMERICA	149	0	0	0	0	0	4	2	1	5	7	10	7	9	10	13	14	9	14	19	23	1
ARGENTINA	40	0	0	0	0	0	3	1	1	2	1	6	3	5	1	3	3	4	5	4	2	0
BRAZIL	38	0	0	0	0	0	0	0	0	0	1	2	0	3	4	5	4	3	3	4	8	0
PERU	6	0	0	0	0	0	0	0	0	1	0	0	0	0	1	1	1	0	0	1	0	0
COLOMBIA	22	0	0	0	0	0	0	0	1	1	0	0	0	0	3	2	2	2	3	6	4	1
VENEZUELA	33	0	0	0	1	0	1	0	0	1	3	2	1	1	2	4	3	1	3	0	8	0
OTHER	10	0	0	0	0	0	0	1	0	1	1	0	1	0	1	2	1	1	0	4	1	0
EUROPE	421	0	4	2	3	8	16	18	16	30	6	18	8	25	41	35	31	26	36	46	52	0
EFTA	171	0	2	0	2	2	5	12	6	17	4	7	5	7	11	13	18	5	18	16	22	0
U.K.	125	0	1	0	1	2	5	9	13	13	4	5	4	7	8	10	15	3	13	10	11	0
SCANDINAVIA	29	0	0	0	1	2	0	0	1	2	0	1	1	0	1	3	2	3	4	4	8	0
SWITZERLAND	6	0	0	0	0	0	0	0	0	1	0	0	0	0	0	0	0	0	1	0	1	0
OTHER EFTA	11	0	1	0	0	0	2	1	0	1	1	0	1	0	0	2	0	0	0	1	2	0
EUROP. COMMUNITY	218	0	2	1	0	3	10	5	8	9	2	9	2	18	30	19	11	20	16	27	26	0
FRANCE	74	0	1	1	0	1	5	2	1	1	1	2	0	10	9	4	2	9	3	4	8	0
GERMANY	56	0	0	0	0	1	2	0	4	3	1	1	0	2	17	4	3	3	5	7	9	0
ITALY	47	0	1	0	1	1	0	2	2	3	0	5	1	5	5	6	4	3	5	9	5	0
BELGIUM + LUX	22	0	0	0	0	0	1	0	0	1	1	0	1	1	2	2	1	2	1	4	3	0
NETHERLANDS	19	0	0	0	1	1	1	1	1	1	0	1	0	1	2	1	1	2	1	3	1	0
SPAIN	12	0	2	2	0	1	0	0	1	1	0	0	1	0	0	0	0	0	2	2	1	0
GREECE + TURKEY	6	0	0	0	1	1	0	0	0	0	0	1	0	0	0	1	2	0	0	0	0	0
OTHER EUROPE	14	0	0	1	2	2	1	1	2	4	0	1	1	0	1	1	2	0	0	2	1	0
EUROPE EX. U.K.	296	0	3	2	2	6	11	9	11	17	3	13	4	18	33	25	16	23	23	36	41	0
SOUTHERN DOMINIONS	88	0	0	0	0	1	2	1	0	3	3	12	3	7	4	13	3	6	12	9	9	0
S. AFRICA +RHOD.	26	0	0	0	0	0	0	1	0	1	5	5	1	3	0	3	1	1	5	2	7	0
AUSTRALIA + N.Z.	62	0	0	0	0	1	2	2	0	2	2	7	2	4	4	10	2	5	7	7	7	0
ASIA + OTHER AFRICA	45	0	0	0	0	2	2	4	3	2	2	5	2	4	2	0	1	3	6	2	9	0
JAPAN	14	0	0	0	0	2	1	1	2	2	1	2	1	3	2	0	1	1	0	2	3	0
OTHER ASIA+AFR.	31	0	0	0	0	0	1	3	1	0	1	2	0	1	0	0	0	2	6	2	6	0
BLACK AFRICA	1	0	0	0	0	0	0	0	0	0	0	0	0	0	0	0	0	0	1	0	0	0
ARAB WORLD	7	0	0	0	0	0	0	0	1	0	0	2	0	1	0	0	0	0	2	0	1	0
INDIA	4	0	0	0	0	0	0	1	0	0	1	0	0	0	0	0	1	0	0	1	1	0
PHILIPPINES	4	0	0	0	0	1	1	0	1	0	0	0	0	0	0	0	0	0	0	1	1	0
OTHER E. ASIA	7	0	0	0	0	0	1	1	0	2	0	0	0	0	1	0	0	1	0	0	2	0
OTHER ASIA	8	0	0	0	0	1	1	1	0	0	1	1	0	0	1	0	0	0	2	0	1	0

CHAPTER 3- THE PROLIFERATION OF FOREIGN SUBSIDIARIES
SECTION 6- CHANGES IN STATE OF BEING, MAIN ACTIVITY AND OWNERSHIP
TABLE 4- MANUFACTURING SUBSIDIARIES
WHICH WERE SOLD,
CLASSIFIED BY COUNTRY AND BY PERIOD CHANGE OCCURRED

PERIOD

COUNTRY OR REGION	PRE 1968	PRE 1901	1901 -13	1914 -19	1920 -24	1925 -29	1930 -34	1935 -39	1940 -45	1946 -50	1951 -53	1954 -55	1956 -57	1958 -59	1960 -61	1962	1963	1964	1965	1966	1967	UNK
OUTSIDE U.S.	190	0	0	6	2	0	3	11	2	13	3	24	3	17	7	6	7	13	13	28	32	0
OUT. U.S. + CANADA	157	0	0	6	0	0	3	9	2	10	2	17	2	15	5	5	7	11	9	26	28	0
OUT. WEST. HEMIS.	124	0	0	3	0	0	3	8	1	8	2	16	1	10	5	5	4	9	7	21	21	0
OUT. WHITE CWEALTH	106	0	0	4	0	0	1	5	2	7	1	5	2	11	5	5	4	10	4	22	23	0
OUT. DEVLPED WORLD	39	0	0	3	0	0	0	1	1	3	0	1	1	5	0	2	4	2	3	6	7	0
CANADA	33	0	0	0	2	0	0	2	0	3	1	7	1	2	2	1	0	2	2	2	4	0
LATIN AMERICA	33	0	0	3	0	0	3	1	1	2	1	1	1	5	0	0	3	2	5	5	7	0
C. AMER.+CARIB.	15	0	0	0	0	0	2	1	0	2	0	0	1	2	0	0	2	1	4	4	2	0
CUBA	4	0	0	0	0	0	0	1	0	2	0	0	0	2	0	0	0	1	0	0	0	0
MEXICO	10	0	0	0	0	0	0	0	0	0	0	0	1	0	0	0	2	0	0	3	2	0
OTHER	1	0	0	0	0	0	0	1	0	0	0	0	0	0	0	0	0	1	0	1	0	0
S. AMERICA	18	0	0	3	0	0	1	0	0	0	0	1	0	3	0	0	0	1	2	3	5	0
ARGENTINA	2	0	0	1	0	0	1	0	0	0	0	0	0	1	0	0	0	0	2	1	0	0
BRAZIL	6	0	0	1	0	0	0	0	0	0	0	1	0	2	0	0	1	0	0	0	2	0
PERU	2	0	0	0	0	0	0	0	0	0	0	0	0	0	0	0	0	0	0	0	1	0
COLOMBIA	2	0	0	0	0	0	0	0	0	0	0	1	0	0	0	1	0	3	1	1	0	0
VENEZUELA	4	0	0	0	0	0	0	0	0	0	0	0	0	0	0	0	0	1	1	0	2	0
OTHER	2	0	0	1	0	0	1	0	1	0	0	0	0	0	0	0	0	0	0	0	0	0
EUROPE	105	0	0	2	0	0	3	7	1	6	2	16	1	8	3	3	2	9	6	18	18	0
EFTA	41	0	0	1	0	0	2	4	0	2	1	12	0	2	1	0	2	0	5	4	5	0
U.K.	37	0	0	1	0	0	2	3	0	2	1	12	0	2	1	0	2	0	2	2	4	0
SCANDINAVIA	3	0	0	0	0	0	0	1	0	0	0	0	0	0	0	0	0	0	0	1	1	0
SWITZERLAND	0	0	0	0	0	0	0	0	0	0	0	0	0	0	0	0	0	0	0	0	0	0
OTHER EFTA	1	0	0	0	0	0	0	0	0	0	0	0	0	0	0	0	0	0	0	1	0	0
EUROP. COMMUNITY	55	0	0	2	0	0	1	2	1	4	1	3	1	5	0	3	0	8	1	13	11	0
FRANCE	14	0	0	1	0	0	0	1	0	1	0	0	0	2	0	0	3	2	0	4	3	0
GERMANY	18	0	0	0	0	0	1	1	1	2	0	0	1	5	1	1	1	3	1	3	1	0
ITALY	9	0	0	0	0	0	0	1	1	1	0	1	0	2	0	1	1	2	1	2	4	0
BELGIUM + LUX	4	0	0	0	0	0	0	0	0	0	0	0	0	0	1	0	0	1	0	1	2	0
NETHERLANDS	10	0	0	0	0	0	1	0	2	2	0	1	0	0	1	1	0	1	0	3	1	0
SPAIN	4	0	0	0	0	0	0	0	0	2	1	0	0	1	0	1	0	0	0	1	2	0
GREECE + TURKEY	1	0	0	0	0	0	0	0	0	0	0	0	0	0	0	0	0	1	0	0	0	0
OTHER EUROPE	4	0	0	0	0	0	0	1	0	0	0	0	0	0	2	1	1	0	0	0	0	0
EUROPE EX. U.K.	68	0	0	1	0	0	1	4	1	4	1	4	1	6	2	3	1	9	4	16	14	0
SOUTHERN DOMINIONS	11	0	0	1	0	0	0	1	0	1	0	0	0	2	2	0	1	0	0	2	1	0
S. AFRICA +RHOD.	2	0	0	0	0	0	1	0	0	0	0	0	0	0	1	0	0	0	0	1	0	0
AUSTRALIA + N.Z.	9	0	0	1	0	0	0	1	1	1	0	0	0	2	1	0	1	0	0	1	1	0
ASIA + OTHER AFRICA	8	0	0	0	0	0	0	0	0	1	0	0	0	0	1	2	1	0	1	1	2	0
JAPAN	2	0	0	0	0	0	0	0	0	0	0	0	0	0	0	2	0	0	1	0	0	0
OTHER ASIA+AFR.	6	0	0	0	0	0	0	0	0	1	0	0	0	0	1	0	1	0	0	1	0	0
BLACK AFRICA	0	0	0	0	0	0	0	0	0	0	0	0	0	0	0	0	0	0	0	0	0	0
ARAB WORLD	0	0	0	0	0	0	0	0	0	0	0	0	0	0	0	0	0	0	0	0	0	0
INDIA	1	0	0	0	0	0	0	0	0	0	0	0	0	0	0	0	1	0	1	1	0	0
PHILIPPINES	2	0	0	0	0	0	0	0	0	1	0	0	0	0	0	1	0	0	0	0	0	0
OTHER E. ASIA	1	0	0	0	0	0	0	0	0	0	0	0	0	0	1	0	0	0	0	0	0	0
OTHER ASIA	2	0	0	0	0	0	0	0	0	0	0	0	0	0	1	1	1	0	0	0	0	0

CHAPTER 3- THE PROLIFERATION OF FOREIGN SUBSIDIARIES
SECTION 6- CHANGES IN STATE OF BEING, MAIN ACTIVITY AND OWNERSHIP
TABLE 5- NON-MANUFACTURING SUBSIDIARIES
WHICH BEGAN MANUFACTURING,
CLASSIFIED BY COUNTRY AND BY PERIOD CHANGE OCCURRED

PERIOD

COUNTRY OR REGION	PRE 1968	PRE 1901	1901 -13	1914 -19	1920 -24	1925 -29	1930 -34	1935 -39	1940 -45	1946 -50	1951 -53	1954 -55	1956 -57	1958 -59	1960 -61	1962	1963	1964	1965	1966	1967	UNK
OUTSIDE U.S.	289	0	4	3	8	12	10	19	15	44	13	10	21	23	24	14	14	14	14	22	5	0
OUT. U.S. + CANADA	266	0	3	2	7	12	7	18	13	41	12	9	10	23	24	14	14	13	13	21	5	0
OUT. WEST. HEMIS.	184	0	3	1	6	10	7	15	9	29	5	7	10	14	14	9	8	9	9	14	5	0
OUT. WHITE CWEALTH	198	0	2	1	6	5	1	16	11	31	12	6	14	19	18	14	9	10	11	16	4	0
OUT. DEVLPED WORLD	109	0	0	1	1	2	0	4	6	16	7	5	9	13	12	7	7	5	6	8	0	0
CANADA	23	0	1	1	1	2	3	1	2	3	4	1	2	0	2	0	0	1	1	1	0	0
LATIN AMERICA	82	0	0	0	1	0	0	3	4	12	7	2	9	9	8	5	6	4	4	7	0	0
C. AMER.+CARIB.	38	0	0	0	0	0	0	1	1	4	2	1	6	5	4	2	2	2	2	4	0	0
CUBA	5	0	0	0	0	0	0	1	0	1	1	0	1	1	0	0	0	0	0	0	0	0
MEXICO	26	0	0	0	1	0	0	0	1	3	2	1	2	3	2	2	1	4	2	4	1	0
OTHER	7	0	0	0	0	0	0	0	0	0	1	0	1	1	0	0	1	0	0	0	1	0
S. AMERICA	44	0	0	0	1	0	0	2	3	8	5	1	3	3	4	3	4	2	2	3	1	0
ARGENTINA	9	0	0	1	1	0	0	1	1	1	0	1	0	0	1	0	0	0	1	1	1	0
BRAZIL	14	0	0	1	1	0	0	1	2	4	2	0	2	2	2	1	1	0	1	1	1	0
PERU	2	0	0	0	0	0	0	0	0	0	0	0	0	0	1	0	0	0	0	0	0	0
COLOMBIA	5	0	0	0	1	0	0	0	1	2	1	0	0	1	0	1	1	0	0	1	0	0
VENEZUELA	8	0	0	1	0	0	0	0	0	0	1	1	1	1	1	1	1	0	0	0	0	0
OTHER	6	0	0	0	0	0	0	3	0	1	2	0	0	0	1	1	1	0	0	0	0	0
EUROPE	119	0	3	1	6	8	6	10	4	21	4	2	8	6	7	7	2	4	7	9	4	0
EFTA	54	0	2	1	0	5	5	7	1	12	0	2	3	1	3	2	1	1	4	3	3	0
U.K.	36	0	1	1	0	5	5	6	0	6	0	2	0	0	1	1	1	0	2	2	1	0
SCANDINAVIA	4	0	1	0	0	0	0	0	0	3	0	0	0	1	1	0	0	1	0	1	1	0
SWITZERLAND	11	0	0	0	0	0	0	1	1	2	0	0	0	0	1	0	0	0	2	1	1	0
OTHER EFTA	3	0	0	0	0	0	0	0	0	1	0	0	0	0	0	0	0	0	0	0	0	0
EUROP. COMMUNITY	58	0	1	0	5	2	0	2	2	9	4	0	5	5	4	4	3	3	5	5	1	0
FRANCE	15	0	1	0	2	0	1	2	0	2	2	0	1	2	1	1	0	0	1	1	0	0
GERMANY	22	0	0	0	1	1	0	2	2	6	2	0	3	3	3	1	0	2	3	3	0	0
ITALY	8	0	0	0	0	1	0	0	1	0	0	0	0	0	1	1	1	2	1	0	0	0
BELGIUM + LUX	7	0	0	0	2	0	0	0	1	1	1	0	0	0	0	0	1	0	0	0	0	0
NETHERLANDS	6	0	0	0	0	1	0	0	1	0	0	0	1	0	1	0	1	0	0	1	0	0
SPAIN	3	0	0	0	0	0	0	0	0	0	0	0	0	0	0	0	0	0	0	0	0	0
GREECE + TURKEY	1	0	0	0	0	1	0	1	1	0	0	0	0	0	0	1	0	0	0	0	0	0
OTHER EUROPE	3	0	0	0	0	0	0	0	0	0	0	0	0	1	0	0	0	0	0	0	0	0
EUROPE EX. U.K.	83	0	2	0	6	3	1	4	4	15	4	0	5	6	6	7	1	4	5	7	3	0
SOUTHERN DOMINIONS	31	0	0	0	0	0	1	4	2	4	1	1	2	4	3	0	4	3	0	3	0	0
S. AFRICA +RHOD.	10	0	0	0	0	0	1	0	1	1	0	0	0	1	1	0	3	1	0	2	0	0
AUSTRALIA + N.Z.	21	0	0	0	0	2	0	4	1	3	1	1	2	3	2	0	1	2	2	2	0	0
ASIA + OTHER AFRICA	34	0	0	0	2	2	0	1	3	4	1	4	0	4	4	2	2	2	2	2	0	0
JAPAN	7	0	0	0	0	0	0	0	1	0	0	3	0	0	0	1	1	1	1	1	0	0
OTHER ASIA+AFR.	27	0	0	0	2	2	0	1	2	4	1	1	0	4	4	1	1	1	1	1	0	0
BLACK AFRICA	1	0	0	0	0	0	0	0	0	2	0	0	0	0	0	0	0	0	0	0	0	0
ARAB WORLD	6	0	0	0	0	0	0	0	0	2	0	0	0	2	2	0	0	0	0	0	0	0
INDIA	6	0	0	0	0	0	0	0	0	0	3	0	0	0	1	1	0	0	0	0	0	0
PHILIPPINES	5	0	0	0	0	0	0	0	0	0	0	3	0	2	1	0	0	2	2	0	0	0
OTHER E. ASIA	2	0	0	0	2	0	0	0	0	2	0	0	0	0	0	0	1	0	0	0	0	0
OTHER ASIA	7	0	0	0	0	2	0	1	0	0	0	0	0	2	1	0	0	0	1	1	0	0

CHAPTER 3- THE PROLIFERATION OF FOREIGN SUBSIDIARIES
SECTION 6- CHANGES IN STATE OF BEING, MAIN ACTIVITY AND OWNERSHIP
TABLE 6- MANUFACTURING JOINT VENTURES
WHICH BECAME WHOLLY OWNED BY THE PARENT SYSTEM,
CLASSIFIED BY COUNTRY AND BY PERIOD CHANGE OCCURRED

PERIOD

COUNTRY OR REGION	PRE 1968	PRE 1901	1901-13	1914-19	1920-24	1925-29	1930-34	1935-39	1940-45	1946-50	1951-53	1954-55	1956-57	1958-59	1960-61	1962	1963	1964	1965	1966	1967	UNK
OUTSIDE U.S.	464	0	0	2	2	2	11	24	9	24	14	22	20	24	38	23	24	38	22	73	92	0
OUT. U.S. + CANADA	403	0	0	1	1	1	10	17	7	17	12	15	17	21	35	4	16	34	17	70	86	0
OUT. WEST. HEMIS.	269	0	0	1	1	1	7	14	4	17	4	11	10	16	22	13	16	25	10	46	51	0
OUT. WHITE CWEALTH	314	0	0	1	1	1	7	11	7	9	10	13	13	13	25	14	15	31	16	62	66	0
OUT. DEVLPED WORLD	148	0	0	0	0	0	4	3	3	2	8	8	7	6	15	6	8	10	7	25	36	0
CANADA	61	0	0	1	1	1	1	7	2	7	2	7	3	3	3	4	1	4	5	3	6	0
LATIN AMERICA	134	0	0	0	0	0	3	3	3	0	8	4	7	5	13	6	7	9	7	24	35	0
C. AMER.+CARIB.	47	0	0	0	0	0	2	2	1	0	2	0	1	0	8	3	3	3	3	8	13	0
CUBA	7	0	0	0	0	0	1	1	1	0	2	0	0	0	0	0	0	0	0	0	1	0
MEXICO	33	0	0	0	0	0	0	0	0	0	0	3	1	0	2	3	3	2	2	7	11	0
OTHER	7	0	0	0	0	0	0	1	0	0	0	0	0	0	0	0	0	1	1	1	1	0
S. AMERICA	87	0	0	0	0	0	3	1	2	0	6	4	6	5	5	3	3	6	4	16	22	0
ARGENTINA	20	0	0	0	0	0	2	1	0	0	2	2	1	2	2	1	1	2	2	3	5	0
BRAZIL	25	0	0	0	0	0	0	0	1	0	1	1	3	1	1	2	1	3	0	5	7	0
PERU	5	0	0	0	0	0	0	0	0	1	0	0	1	0	1	0	1	0	0	2	2	0
COLOMBIA	15	0	0	0	0	0	0	0	0	0	0	1	0	1	2	1	1	1	1	2	6	0
VENEZUELA	16	0	0	0	0	1	1	0	0	0	3	0	0	1	0	1	1	2	1	6	3	0
OTHER	6	0	0	0	0	0	0	0	1	1	0	1	1	0	0	1	0	3	0	1	2	0
EUROPE	206	0	0	1	1	1	6	12	4	11	4	5	6	10	14	12	12	23	9	41	34	0
EFTA	65	0	0	1	0	0	3	7	0	4	2	1	1	4	7	4	5	8	3	8	12	0
U.K.	45	0	0	1	0	0	3	5	0	4	2	1	0	3	3	4	4	2	2	4	9	0
SCANDINAVIA	12	0	0	0	0	0	0	1	0	0	0	0	1	1	1	0	1	0	1	2	3	0
SWITZERLAND	3	0	0	0	0	0	0	0	0	0	0	0	0	0	0	0	0	0	2	1	0	0
OTHER EFTA	5	0	0	0	0	0	2	1	0	0	0	0	0	0	2	0	0	1	0	1	0	0
EUROP. COMMUNITY	129	0	0	1	1	1	2	4	4	7	2	4	5	6	6	7	6	16	6	32	20	0
FRANCE	41	0	0	0	0	0	2	0	1	2	1	0	0	3	1	3	2	7	6	12	9	0
GERMANY	33	0	0	0	0	0	2	3	3	1	1	1	3	0	1	1	1	5	3	6	3	0
ITALY	27	0	0	0	0	0	0	1	0	0	0	0	0	2	1	2	2	2	2	10	2	0
BELGIUM + LUX	14	0	0	0	0	0	0	0	0	1	0	1	1	0	2	0	1	5	1	4	4	0
NETHERLANDS	14	0	0	1	1	1	0	0	3	1	0	2	1	1	2	1	2	2	0	0	1	0
SPAIN	5	0	0	0	0	0	0	0	0	0	0	0	0	0	0	0	0	0	1	1	0	0
GREECE + TURKEY	2	0	0	0	0	0	0	0	0	0	0	0	0	0	0	1	0	0	0	0	1	0
OTHER EUROPE	5	0	0	1	0	0	1	1	0	2	2	0	0	0	0	0	1	1	0	0	0	0
EUROPE EX. U.K.	161	0	0	0	1	1	3	7	4	7	2	4	6	7	11	8	8	21	9	37	25	0
SOUTHERN DOMINIONS	40	0	0	0	0	0	0	1	0	4	0	1	4	5	6	1	3	0	1	4	10	0
S. AFRICA +RHOD.	15	0	0	0	0	0	0	0	0	1	0	0	3	0	2	0	2	0	2	2	5	0
AUSTRALIA + N.Z.	25	0	0	0	0	0	1	1	0	3	0	1	1	5	4	1	1	0	1	2	5	0
ASIA + OTHER AFRICA	23	0	0	0	0	0	0	1	3	2	0	5	0	1	2	0	1	2	1	1	7	0
JAPAN	9	0	0	0	0	0	0	1	0	0	0	4	0	0	0	1	1	1	0	0	6	0
OTHER ASIA+AFR.	14	0	0	0	0	0	0	0	1	2	0	1	0	1	2	0	0	1	1	1	1	0
BLACK AFRICA	3	0	0	0	0	0	0	0	0	0	0	0	0	0	0	0	0	1	0	0	1	0
ARAB WORLD	2	0	0	0	0	0	1	0	0	0	0	0	0	0	0	0	0	0	0	0	0	0
INDIA	1	0	0	0	0	0	0	0	0	0	0	0	0	0	0	0	0	0	0	0	0	0
PHILIPPINES	1	0	0	0	0	0	0	0	0	0	0	0	0	0	0	0	0	0	0	0	0	0
OTHER E. ASIA	3	0	0	0	0	0	1	0	0	2	0	0	0	0	0	0	1	0	0	0	0	0
OTHER ASIA	4	0	0	0	0	0	0	0	1	0	0	3	0	1	0	0	0	0	0	0	0	0

CHAPTER 3- THE PROLIFERATION OF FOREIGN SUBSIDIARIES
SECTION 6- CHANGES IN STATE OF BEING, MAIN ACTIVITY AND OWNERSHIP
TABLE 7- MANUFACTURING SUBSIDIARIES IN WHICH THE PARENT SYSTEM
"SIGNIFICANTLY" INCREASED ITS OWNERSHIP PERCENTAGE,
CLASSIFIED BY COUNTRY AND BY PERIOD CHANGE OCCURRED

PERIOD

COUNTRY OR REGION	PRE 1968	PRE 1901	1901-13	1914-19	1920-24	1925-29	1930-34	1935-39	1940-45	1946-50	1951-53	1954-55	1956-57	1958-59	1960-61	1962	1963	1964	1965	1966	1967	UNK
OUTSIDE U.S.	456	0	0	2	1	3	10	20	6	18	17	17	24	26	39	20	26	36	31	77	83	0
OUT. U.S. + CANADA	399	0	0	1	0	2	8	13	6	13	12	12	19	22	37	18	24	33	27	74	78	0
OUT. WEST. HEMIS.	263	0	0	1	0	2	6	10	3	13	4	8	10	17	22	11	19	23	17	48	49	0
OUT. WHITE CWEALTH	318	0	0	0	0	2	5	7	6	7	10	11	16	14	28	14	16	29	23	67	63	0
OUT. DEVLPED WORLD	148	0	0	0	0	0	2	3	3	0	8	5	9	6	17	7	6	11	13	28	30	0
CANADA	57	0	0	1	1	1	2	7	0	5	5	5	5	4	2	2	2	3	4	3	5	0
LATIN AMERICA	136	0	0	0	0	0	2	3	3	5	8	4	9	5	15	7	5	10	10	26	29	0
C. AMER.+CARIB.	50	0	0	0	0	0	2	2	1	0	2	0	1	0	10	3	2	4	4	10	11	0
CUBA	7	0	0	0	0	0	0	1	1	0	2	0	0	0	6	0	0	0	0	0	0	0
MEXICO	35	0	0	0	0	0	2	1	1	0	2	0	1	0	2	3	2	1	3	9	10	0
OTHER	8	0	0	0	0	0	0	0	0	0	0	0	0	0	2	0	0	1	1	1	1	0
S. AMERICA	86	0	0	0	0	2	2	1	2	0	6	4	8	5	5	3	3	6	6	16	18	0
ARGENTINA	18	0	0	0	0	0	2	1	1	0	2	2	1	2	1	0	1	0	3	3	1	0
BRAZIL	27	0	0	0	0	0	0	0	0	0	2	0	4	1	1	1	0	3	3	5	8	0
PERU	4	0	0	0	0	0	0	0	0	0	0	1	0	0	1	0	1	0	0	2	8	0
COLOMBIA	15	0	0	0	0	0	1	0	1	1	0	0	0	1	3	0	0	1	1	2	1	0
VENEZUELA	16	0	0	0	0	0	1	0	1	0	2	2	1	1	0	0	2	1	2	2	5	0
OTHER	6	0	0	0	0	0	0	0	2	2	0	0	1	1	0	1	0	2	0	2	0	0
EUROPE	202	0	0	1	2	2	6	8	3	9	4	4	7	10	14	10	15	21	12	41	35	0
EFTA	57	0	0	1	0	0	3	6	0	2	2	0	1	3	7	3	6	4	5	6	8	0
U.K.	40	0	0	1	0	0	3	5	0	2	2	0	1	3	3	3	5	5	2	2	7	0
SCANDINAVIA	10	0	0	0	0	0	1	1	0	0	0	0	0	1	1	0	1	2	2	2	1	0
SWITZERLAND	3	0	0	0	0	0	0	0	0	0	0	0	0	0	0	0	0	0	0	1	2	0
OTHER EFTA	4	0	0	0	0	0	1	0	0	0	0	0	1	1	2	0	0	1	1	1	0	0
EUROP. COMMUNITY	125	0	0	0	0	1	2	1	3	6	2	4	5	7	7	6	8	13	6	31	23	0
FRANCE	47	0	0	0	0	0	2	1	1	2	1	0	3	4	1	3	3	7	3	13	12	0
GERMANY	28	0	0	0	0	0	0	0	2	1	0	1	0	2	1	1	1	1	3	5	3	0
ITALY	25	0	0	0	0	0	2	1	0	1	0	1	1	0	2	2	3	3	2	9	3	0
BELGIUM + LUX	14	0	0	0	0	1	2	0	1	2	0	2	1	2	2	0	0	2	0	4	2	0
NETHERLANDS	11	0	0	0	0	0	0	1	0	0	1	0	0	1	1	1	1	3	1	0	3	0
SPAIN	14	0	0	0	0	1	1	0	0	2	0	0	0	0	0	1	1	3	1	3	4	0
GREECE + TURKEY	3	0	0	0	0	0	0	1	0	1	0	0	1	0	0	0	0	0	0	1	0	0
OTHER EUROPE	3	0	0	0	0	0	1	1	0	0	0	0	0	1	0	1	0	1	0	0	0	0
EUROPE EX. U.K.	162	0	0	0	0	2	3	3	3	7	2	4	7	8	11	7	10	18	10	39	28	0
SOUTHERN DOMINIONS	40	0	0	0	0	0	0	1	0	4	0	1	3	6	6	1	3	0	2	5	8	0
S. AFRICA +RHOD.	13	0	0	0	0	0	0	1	0	1	0	0	2	2	2	0	2	0	2	3	3	0
AUSTRALIA + N.Z.	27	0	0	0	0	0	0	0	0	3	0	1	1	4	4	1	1	2	3	2	5	0
ASIA + OTHER AFRICA	21	0	0	0	0	0	0	1	1	0	0	3	1	1	2	2	1	2	3	2	6	0
JAPAN	9	0	0	0	0	0	0	0	3	0	0	2	0	1	2	0	1	1	3	3	5	0
OTHER ASIA+AFR.	12	0	0	0	0	0	0	1	1	1	0	1	0	0	2	2	1	1	0	2	1	0
BLACK AFRICA	2	0	0	0	0	0	0	0	0	0	0	0	0	0	0	0	0	1	0	2	1	0
ARAB WORLD	3	0	0	0	0	0	0	0	0	0	0	0	0	0	2	0	0	1	0	1	0	0
INDIA	2	0	0	0	0	0	0	0	0	0	0	1	0	0	0	1	0	0	1	2	1	0
PHILIPPINES	4	0	0	0	0	0	0	0	0	0	0	0	0	0	0	0	0	0	2	1	0	0
OTHER E. ASIA	0	0	0	0	0	0	0	0	0	0	0	0	0	0	0	0	0	0	0	0	0	0
OTHER ASIA	1	0	0	0	0	0	0	0	0	0	0	0	0	0	1	0	0	0	0	0	0	0

CHAPTER 3- THE PROLIFERATION OF FOREIGN SUBSIDIARIES
SECTION 6- CHANGES IN STATE OF BEING, MAIN ACTIVITY AND OWNERSHIP
TABLE 8- MANUFACTURING SUBSIDIARIES IN WHICH THE PARENT SYSTEM
"SIGNIFICANTLY" DECREASED ITS OWNERSHIP PERCENTAGE,
CLASSIFIED BY COUNTRY AND BY PERIOD CHANGE OCCURRED

COUNTRY OR REGION	PRE 1968	PRE 1901	1901 -13	1914 -19	1920 -24	1925 -29	1930 -34	1935 -39	1940 -45	1946 -50	1951 -53	1954 -55	1956 -57	1958 -59	1960 -61	1962	1963	1964	1965	1966	1967	UNK
OUTSIDE U.S.	290	0	1	1	2	2	7	11	5	15	7	15	12	15	29	27	16	10	28	39	44	0
OUT. U.S. + CANADA	243	0	1	0	1	2	7	7	3	12	3	12	10	14	26	23	16	9	22	37	38	0
OUT. WEST. HEMIS.	154	0	1	0	2	1	5	6	2	8	1	8	5	9	14	14	9	7	12	27	24	0
OUT. WHITE CWEALTH	191	0	1	0	1	1	6	4	3	7	3	8	7	11	22	16	13	6	19	31	32	0
OUT. DEVLPED WORLD	103	0	0	0	1	0	3	1	1	4	2	5	5	5	12	10	7	4	12	14	17	0
CANADA	47	0	1	1	1	0	4	4	2	3	4	3	2	1	3	4	0	1	6	2	6	0
LATIN AMERICA	89	0	1	0	1	0	2	1	1	4	2	5	5	5	12	9	7	2	10	10	14	0
C. AMER.+CARIB.	42	0	1	0	0	0	0	3	1	3	2	2	0	0	1	6	2	2	4	6	6	0
CUBA	8	0	0	0	0	0	0	2	0	1	0	0	0	1	0	1	1	0	0	0	0	0
MEXICO	27	0	0	0	0	0	2	5	0	2	1	0	5	0	3	6	2	1	3	6	4	0
OTHER	7	0	0	0	0	0	0	1	1	0	0	1	1	1	1	1	0	1	1	0	2	0
S. AMERICA	47	0	0	0	1	0	2	1	0	1	1	2	1	0	1	3	5	1	6	4	8	0
ARGENTINA	12	0	0	0	0	0	2	1	0	0	1	1	3	4	2	1	1	1	1	0	1	0
BRAZIL	14	0	0	0	1	0	0	3	0	0	0	0	0	3	0	0	4	0	0	1	3	0
PERU	2	0	0	0	0	0	0	0	1	0	0	0	1	0	0	0	0	0	2	1	0	0
COLCMBIA	7	0	0	0	1	0	0	0	0	0	0	0	0	0	0	1	0	1	1	1	3	0
VENEZUELA	9	0	0	0	0	0	0	0	0	1	0	1	1	1	1	1	0	0	0	1	1	0
OTHER	3	0	0	0	0	0	0	0	1	1	0	3	0	0	1	2	0	1	0	1	0	0
EUROPE	108	0	1	0	0	2	4	5	2	5	1	4	3	8	11	8	6	2	9	20	17	0
EFTA	35	0	0	0	0	1	1	2	0	2	0	1	2	2	1	2	1	1	2	2	6	0
U.K.	24	0	0	0	0	1	0	2	0	2	0	0	1	2	1	2	2	0	0	4	3	0
SCANDINAVIA	7	0	0	0	0	0	0	0	0	0	0	1	0	0	0	0	1	1	0	2	3	0
SWITZERLAND	1	0	0	0	0	0	0	0	0	0	0	0	0	0	0	0	0	0	0	0	0	0
OTHER EFTA	3	0	1	0	0	0	0	3	0	0	0	0	0	0	0	1	1	1	0	1	0	0
EUROP. COMMUNITY	67	0	0	0	0	0	3	3	2	3	1	3	5	5	9	6	2	0	6	12	10	0
FRANCE	22	0	0	0	0	0	2	1	1	2	0	1	3	3	4	1	0	1	2	3	4	0
GERMANY	11	0	0	0	0	0	0	2	0	1	0	1	1	1	0	0	0	1	1	3	0	0
ITALY	18	0	1	0	0	0	0	2	1	0	1	0	0	0	4	1	1	0	3	3	5	0
BELGIUM + LUX	10	0	0	0	0	0	0	0	0	1	0	0	0	1	0	3	0	0	0	2	1	0
NETHERLANDS	6	0	0	0	0	0	1	0	1	0	0	0	0	0	1	0	1	0	1	2	0	0
SPAIN	4	0	0	0	0	0	0	0	0	1	0	0	0	1	1	0	0	0	0	0	1	0
GREECE + TURKEY	0	0	0	0	0	0	0	0	0	0	0	0	0	0	0	0	0	0	0	0	0	0
OTHER EUROPE	2	0	0	0	0	0	0	0	0	1	0	0	0	0	0	0	0	0	0	0	0	0
EUROPE EX. U.K.	84	0	1	0	0	1	3	3	2	3	1	3	6	6	10	6	4	2	7	16	14	0
SOUTHERN DOMINIONS	29	0	0	0	0	0	0	1	0	3	0	3	2	1	3	5	1	3	1	2	3	0
S. AFRICA +RHOD.	5	0	0	0	0	0	0	0	0	0	0	1	1	0	1	1	0	0	0	2	1	0
AUSTRALIA + N.Z.	23	0	0	0	0	0	1	1	0	3	0	1	0	1	2	4	1	3	1	2	2	0
ASIA + OTHER AFRICA	18	0	0	0	0	0	1	0	0	0	0	0	0	0	0	1	2	2	2	5	4	0
JAPAN	4	0	0	0	0	0	0	0	0	0	0	0	0	0	2	0	2	2	2	4	1	0
OTHER ASIA+AFR.	14	0	0	0	0	0	1	0	0	0	0	1	0	1	0	2	0	0	2	1	3	0
BLACK AFRICA	1	0	0	0	0	0	0	0	0	0	0	0	0	0	0	1	0	0	0	0	0	0
ARAB WORLD	2	0	0	0	0	0	0	0	0	0	0	0	0	0	1	0	0	0	1	0	0	0
INDIA	3	0	0	0	0	0	0	0	0	0	0	0	0	0	0	0	0	1	0	1	1	0
PHILIPPINES	0	0	0	0	0	0	0	0	0	0	0	0	0	0	0	0	0	0	0	1	0	0
OTHER E. ASIA	0	0	0	0	0	0	0	0	0	0	0	0	0	0	0	0	0	0	1	0	1	0
OTHER ASIA	6	0	1	0	0	0	0	3	1	0	0	2	0	0	0	0	0	1	1	2	1	0

CHAPTER 4
Varieties of Entry

CHAPTER 4- VARIETIES OF ENTRY
SECTION 1- AN OVERVIEW OF FLOW AND STOCK, MANUFACTURING AND NON-MANUFACTURING
TABLE 1- SUBSIDIARIES CLASSIFIED BY COUNTRY OR REGION,
BY PERIOD ACTIVITY BEGAN AND BY METHOD OF ENTRY

(NEW=NEWLY FORMED, ACQ=ACQUIRED, DES=DESCENDANT, UNK=UNKNOWN)

COUNTRY OR REGION	TOTAL PRE 1968 ALL	NEW	ACQ	DES	UNK	PRE 1946 ALL	NEW	ACQ	DES	UNK	1946-1957 ALL	NEW	ACQ	DES	UNK	1958-1967 ALL	NEW	ACQ	DES	UNK
OUTSIDE U.S.	11152	4841	3653	113	1959	2422	1202	576	30	614	2246	1082	635	20	509	5898	2557	2442	63	836
OUT. U.S. + CANADA	9455	4331	2938	88	1623	1885	995	418	20	452	1832	923	448	15	446	5263	2413	2072	53	725
OUT. WEST. HEMIS.	6755	3001	2194	62	1171	1377	725	308	18	326	1097	505	291	8	293	3954	1771	1595	36	552
OUT. WHITE CWEALTH	7294	3539	2145	61	1212	1366	731	294	11	330	1428	760	321	10	337	4163	2048	1530	40	545
OUT. DEVLPED WORLD	3522	1813	893	29	587	611	334	127	2	148	911	527	180	8	196	1800	952	586	19	243
CANADA	1697	510	715	25	336	537	207	158	10	162	414	159	187	5	63	635	144	370	10	111
LATIN AMERICA	2700	1330	744	26	452	508	270	110	2	126	735	418	157	7	153	1309	642	477	17	173
C. AMER.+CARIB.	1251	599	338	14	231	216	112	39	1	64	347	194	70	3	80	619	293	229	10	87
CUBA	92	36	16	2	34	47	15	10	0	22	36	19	5	2	10	5	2	1	0	2
MEXICO	625	268	225	7	89	134	69	27	1	37	156	80	49	1	26	299	119	149	5	26
OTHER	534	295	97	5	108	35	28	2	0	5	155	95	16	0	44	315	172	79	5	59
S. AMERICA	1449	731	406	12	221	292	158	71	1	62	388	224	87	4	73	690	349	248	7	86
ARGENTINA	283	122	90	4	41	74	42	15	1	16	66	35	18	1	12	117	45	57	2	13
BRAZIL	346	178	101	4	52	66	37	15	0	14	100	60	24	1	15	169	81	62	3	23
PERU	127	66	41	0	10	27	14	9	0	4	28	16	9	0	3	62	36	23	0	3
COLUMBIA	196	89	56	1	42	32	18	6	0	8	60	23	15	0	22	96	48	35	1	12
VENEZUELA	292	174	60	1	48	35	18	9	0	8	88	64	11	0	13	160	92	40	1	27
OTHER	205	102	58	2	28	58	29	17	0	12	46	26	10	2	8	86	47	31	0	8
EUROPE	4755	1981	1643	48	880	1105	549	256	16	284	693	297	194	5	197	2754	1135	1193	27	399
EFTA	2004	801	637	21	442	521	258	119	9	135	319	124	88	3	104	1061	419	430	9	203
U.K.	1189	367	443	17	282	358	155	94	8	101	204	70	67	3	64	547	142	282	6	117
SCANDINAVIA	384	173	101	0	98	96	56	14	1	26	63	23	13	0	27	213	94	74	0	45
SWITZERLAND	317	189	64	4	50	35	24	3	0	7	38	23	6	0	9	234	142	55	3	34
OTHER EFTA	114	72	29	0	12	32	23	8	0	1	14	8	2	0	4	67	41	19	0	7
EUROP. COMMUNITY	2300	963	858	25	372	464	231	112	7	114	320	139	90	2	89	1434	593	656	16	169
FRANCE	670	280	265	13	90	156	77	42	6	31	78	35	22	0	21	414	168	201	7	38
GERMANY	632	235	250	6	120	144	66	38	1	39	90	32	35	0	23	377	137	177	5	58
ITALY	434	184	160	2	69	61	31	12	0	18	69	33	13	0	23	285	120	135	2	28
BELGIUM + LUX	288	148	92	2	35	53	32	6	0	15	39	22	9	1	7	185	94	77	1	13
NETHERLANDS	276	116	91	2	58	50	25	14	0	11	44	17	11	1	15	173	74	66	1	32
SPAIN	221	92	97	1	25	41	18	13	0	10	22	8	12	0	2	152	66	72	1	13
GREECE + TURKEY	80	51	12	0	14	4	2	1	0	1	14	12	0	0	2	59	37	11	0	11
OTHER EUROPE	150	74	39	1	27	75	40	11	0	24	18	14	4	0	0	48	20	24	1	3
EUROPE EX. U.K.	3566	1614	1200	31	598	747	394	162	8	183	489	227	127	2	133	2207	993	911	21	282
SOUTHERN DOMINIONS	902	388	327	9	124	152	102	30	1	19	185	81	57	2	45	511	205	240	6	60
S. AFRICA +RHOD.	280	127	96	1	37	48	34	6	0	8	65	36	15	1	13	148	57	75	0	16
AUSTRALIA + N.Z.	622	261	231	8	87	104	68	24	1	11	120	45	42	1	32	363	148	165	6	44
ASIA + OTHER AFRICA	1098	632	224	5	167	120	74	22	1	23	219	127	40	1	51	689	431	162	3	93
JAPAN	276	149	75	2	32	17	10	5	0	1	43	18	17	0	8	198	121	53	2	23
OTHER ASIA+AFR.	822	483	149	3	135	103	64	17	1	22	176	109	23	0	43	491	310	109	2	70
BLACK AFRICA	197	110	24	1	42	7	4	1	0	2	49	33	3	1	13	121	73	20	1	27
ARAB WORLD	121	70	27	1	14	21	13	5	0	3	35	21	6	0	7	56	36	16	0	4
INDIA	95	58	25	0	8	16	13	0	0	3	17	13	2	0	2	58	32	23	0	3
PHILIPPINES	107	61	24	0	18	18	11	5	0	2	29	17	4	0	8	56	33	15	0	8
OTHER E. ASIA	96	60	18	0	14	12	6	4	0	2	11	5	1	0	5	69	49	13	0	7
OTHER ASIA	206	124	31	1	39	29	17	2	0	10	35	20	7	0	8	131	87	22	1	21

CHAPTER 4- VARIETIES OF ENTRY
SECTION 1- AN OVERVIEW OF FLOW AND STOCK, MANUFACTURING AND NON-MANUFACTURING
TABLE 2- SUBSIDIARIES CLASSIFIED BY COUNTRY OR REGION,
BY YEAR(S) SUBSIDIARY WAS ACTIVE
AND BY METHOD OF ENTRY

YEAR AND METHOD OF ENTRY
(NEW=NEWLY FORMED, ACQ=ACQUIRED, DES=DESCENDANT, UNK=UNKNOWN)

COUNTRY OR REGION	1929 ALL	1929 NEW	1929 ACQ	1929 DES	1929 UNK	1939 ALL	1939 NEW	1939 ACQ	1939 DES	1939 UNK	1957 ALL	1957 NEW	1957 ACQ	1957 DES	1957 UNK	1967 ALL	1967 NEW	1967 ACQ	1967 DES	1967 UNK
OUTSIDE U.S.	987	530	239	73	145	1763	795	339	209	420	3669	1570	797	505	797	7927	3090	2181	1347	1309
OUT. U.S. + CANADA	772	429	176	55	112	1410	655	268	172	315	2978	1311	590	416	661	6879	2798	1804	1178	1099
OUT. WEST. HEMIS.	633	361	138	47	87	1095	498	216	138	243	1921	777	402	287	455	4955	1982	1380	803	790
OUT. WHITE CWEALTH	560	314	123	39	84	999	474	177	118	230	2241	1034	411	303	493	5378	2323	1317	898	840
OUT. DEVLPED WORLD	181	91	46	11	33	396	200	65	43	88	1291	654	216	160	261	2597	1182	525	476	414
CANADA	215	101	63	18	33	353	140	71	37	105	691	259	207	89	136	1048	292	377	169	210
LATIN AMERICA	139	68	38	8	25	315	157	52	34	72	1057	534	188	129	206	1924	816	424	375	309
C. AMER.+CARIB.	55	22	14	3	16	146	68	21	19	38	478	245	76	47	110	855	365	181	162	147
CUBA	15	5	4	1	5	35	8	5	6	16	65	24	8	7	26	12	3	0	1	8
MEXICO	39	16	10	2	11	93	45	16	14	18	234	109	50	36	39	412	143	112	109	48
OTHER	1	1	0	0	0	18	15	0	1	2	179	112	18	4	45	431	219	69	52	91
S. AMERICA	84	46	24	5	9	169	89	31	15	34	579	289	112	82	96	1069	451	243	213	162
ARGENTINA	22	12	6	3	1	56	29	7	7	13	112	54	21	14	23	187	73	48	34	32
BRAZIL	19	11	7	0	1	38	23	7	1	7	151	77	34	17	23	267	110	60	56	41
PERU	8	5	3	0	0	13	9	4	0	0	46	26	11	4	5	98	54	27	11	6
COLOMBIA	5	2	0	1	2	12	6	1	1	4	78	27	16	20	15	150	53	29	41	27
VENEZUELA	5	2	2	0	1	9	4	2	0	3	108	68	12	10	18	213	91	39	44	39
OTHER	25	14	6	1	4	41	18	10	6	7	84	37	18	17	12	154	70	40	27	17
EUROPE	530	293	118	44	75	883	373	179	118	213	1355	514	290	212	339	3401	1254	1023	540	584
EFTA	242	127	57	22	36	419	179	86	57	97	653	241	135	103	174	1405	495	390	220	300
U.K.	155	70	45	16	24	284	103	68	43	70	431	137	108	75	111	800	208	268	147	177
SCANDINAVIA	56	34	8	4	10	85	42	12	9	22	137	59	18	16	44	287	121	59	35	72
SWITZERLAND	19	15	1	1	2	26	17	2	2	5	52	29	5	3	15	235	118	47	29	41
OTHER EFTA	12	8	3	1	0	24	17	4	3	0	33	16	4	9	4	83	48	16	9	10
EUROP. COMMUNITY	238	136	54	19	29	370	155	79	46	90	601	227	130	97	147	1675	614	539	273	249
FRANCE	72	41	20	5	6	117	49	31	15	22	180	71	41	33	35	493	187	157	88	61
GERMANY	84	43	21	6	14	117	44	24	18	31	175	55	44	30	46	456	141	166	67	82
ITALY	32	20	7	2	3	53	23	11	3	16	98	38	21	11	28	310	106	106	51	47
BELGIUM + LUX	26	16	2	5	3	47	27	3	4	13	76	42	10	10	14	219	106	58	35	20
NETHERLANDS	24	16	4	1	3	36	12	10	6	8	72	21	14	13	24	197	74	52	32	39
SPAIN	20	10	5	2	3	34	12	8	6	8	53	17	19	7	10	185	71	65	31	18
GREECE + TURKEY	2	2	0	0	0	3	2	1	0	0	14	10	1	1	2	66	42	7	7	10
OTHER EUROPE	29	20	2	1	6	57	25	5	9	18	34	19	5	4	6	70	32	22	9	7
EUROPE EX. U.K.	375	223	73	28	51	599	270	111	75	143	924	377	182	137	228	2601	1046	755	393	407
SOUTHERN DOMINIONS	53	41	8	0	4	120	74	23	10	13	285	125	68	37	55	648	240	202	127	79
S. AFRICA +RHOD.	17	12	2	0	3	40	26	6	2	6	99	49	19	13	18	209	77	71	37	24
AUSTRALIA + N.Z.	36	29	6	0	1	80	48	17	8	7	186	76	49	24	37	439	163	131	90	55
ASIA + OTHER AFRICA	50	27	12	3	8	92	51	14	10	17	281	138	44	38	61	906	488	155	136	127
JAPAN	8	4	4	0	0	11	8	1	1	1	47	18	16	7	6	233	122	54	35	22
OTHER ASIA+AFR.	42	23	8	3	8	81	43	13	9	16	234	120	28	31	55	673	366	101	101	105
BLACK AFRICA	6	3	1	0	2	4	0	1	2	1	49	31	2	6	10	166	86	19	25	36
ARAB WORLD	7	5	1	1	0	16	9	4	1	2	48	20	9	9	10	88	46	15	17	10
INDIA	5	5	0	0	0	14	11	0	1	2	30	19	2	4	5	86	45	21	12	8
PHILIPPINES	5	3	2	0	0	14	7	4	1	2	35	16	6	4	9	87	40	16	17	14
OTHER E. ASIA	6	2	3	0	1	9	3	2	2	2	13	6	2	0	5	76	51	6	6	10
OTHER ASIA	13	6	0	2	5	24	13	2	2	7	55	28	7	8	12	170	98	24	24	27

CHAPTER 4- VARIETIES OF ENTRY
SECTION 1- AN OVERVIEW OF FLOW AND STOCK, MANUFACTURING AND NON-MANUFACTURING
TABLE 3- MANUFACTURING SUBSIDIARIES CLASSIFIED BY COUNTRY OR REGION,
BY PERIOD MANUFACTURE BEGAN AND BY METHOD OF ENTRY

PERIOD AND METHOD OF ENTRY (NEW=NEWLY FORMED, ACQ=ACQUIRED, DES=DESCENDANT, UNK=UNKNOWN)

COUNTRY OR REGION	TOTAL PRE 1968 ALL	NEW	ACQ	DES	UNK	PRE 1946 ALL	NEW	ACQ	DES	UNK	1946-1957 ALL	NEW	ACQ	DES	UNK	1958-1967 ALL	NEW	ACQ	DES	UNK
OUTSIDE U.S.	5209	2149	2176	409	351	1031	524	303	97	107	1024	465	370	111	78	3030	1160	1503	201	166
OUT. U.S. + CANADA	4404	1904	1745	358	292	763	402	207	78	76	819	399	262	94	64	2717	1103	1276	186	152
OUT. WEST. HEMIS.	3079	1266	1270	253	214	557	275	160	67	55	479	216	165	58	40	1967	775	945	128	119
OUT. WHITE CWEALTH	3326	1527	1254	253	222	508	278	133	43	54	623	313	188	70	52	2125	936	933	140	116
OUT. DEVLPED WORLD	1685	847	553	132	112	236	143	51	16	26	395	215	106	43	31	1013	489	396	73	55
CANADA	805	245	431	51	59	268	122	96	19	31	205	66	108	17	14	313	57	227	15	14
LATIN AMERICA	1325	638	475	105	78	206	127	47	11	21	340	183	97	36	24	750	328	331	58	33
C. AMER.+CARIB.	563	256	212	49	29	78	54	14	2	8	130	67	37	16	10	338	135	161	31	11
CUBA	46	21	8	7	8	19	8	5	1	5	21	12	2	5	2	4		4		1
MEXICO	363	157	156	30	9	46	35	5	1	1	90	47	31	8	4	216	75	116	21	4
OTHER	154	78	48	12	12	13	11	0	0	1	19	8	4	3	4	118	59	44	9	6
S. AMERICA	762	382	263	56	49	128	73	33	9	13	210	116	60	20	14	412	193	170	27	22
ARGENTINA	160	69	66	15	8	45	25	11	6	3	34	17	13	3	1	79	27	42	6	4
BRAZIL	200	100	71	18	9	34	22	9	1	3	70	37	19	8	6	94	41	43	9	1
PERU	57	28	19	2	5	12	6	3	1	2	15	9	5	0	1	27	13	11	1	2
COLOMBIA	116	55	43	7	10	10	6	2	0	1	29	16	10	1	2	76	33	31	5	7
VENEZUELA	143	91	34	8	8	10	8	1	1	0	43	28	8	4	3	89	55	25	4	5
OTHER	86	39	30	6	8	17	6	7	0	4	19	9	5	4	1	47	24	18	2	3
EUROPE	2062	760	947	173	145	428	192	138	52	46	312	132	114	40	26	1285	436	695	81	73
EFTA	753	247	346	79	60	208	87	70	29	22	126	48	46	21	11	398	112	230	29	27
U.K.	555	155	279	59	42	162	60	59	26	17	101	39	40	15	7	272	56	180	18	18
SCANDINAVIA	113	49	41	11	11	25	12	1	1	5	17	7	5	3	2	70	30	29	3	4
SWITZERLAND	36	13	13	6	4	5	3	1	1	0	4	1	0	1	1	27	9	12	3	3
OTHER EFTA	49	30	13	3	3	16	12	3	1	0	4	1	1	0	1	29	17	9	1	2
EUROP. COMMUNITY	1077	408	501	85	68	186	90	59	19	18	155	65	57	19	14	721	253	385	47	36
FRANCE	324	109	143	27	17	66	26	26	9	5	38	15	13	5	5	214	68	126	13	7
GERMANY	304	104	143	32	22	64	35	19	3	7	53	12	27	10	4	184	57	97	19	11
ITALY	223	100	98	10	12	21	14	3	2	2	35	22	10	1	2	164	64	85	7	8
BELGIUM + LUX	117	48	53	8	8	19	6	5	4	4	11	7	3	1	0	87	35	45	3	4
NETHERLANDS	109	47	42	8	9	16	9	6	1	0	18	9	4	2	3	72	29	32	5	6
SPAIN	137	54	72	4	7	15	7	6	1	1	16	7	8	0	1	106	40	58	3	5
GREECE + TURKEY	42	29	7	1	5	1	0	0	0	1	6	6	0	0	0	35	23	7	1	4
OTHER EUROPE	53	22	21	4	5	18	8	3	3	4	9	6	3	0	0	25	8	15	1	1
EUROPE EX. U.K.	1507	605	668	114	103	266	132	79	26	29	211	93	74	25	19	1013	380	515	63	55
SOUTHERN DOMINIONS	488	208	196	44	26	89	62	15	8	4	86	41	31	9	5	299	105	150	27	17
S. AFRICA +RHOD.	158	69	66	11	5	26	22	2	1	1	28	18	7	2	1	97	29	57	8	3
AUSTRALIA +N.Z.	330	139	130	33	21	63	40	13	7	3	58	23	24	7	4	202	76	93	19	14
ASIA + OTHER AFRICA	529	298	127	36	43	40	21	7	7	5	81	43	20	9	9	383	234	100	20	29
JAPAN	169	89	49	9	9	10	5	3	2	0	26	11	11	2	2	120	73	35	5	7
OTHER ASIA+AFR.	360	209	78	27	34	30	16	4	5	5	55	32	9	7	7	263	161	65	15	22
BLACK AFRICA	46	24	10	1	9	0	0	0	0	0	5	3	0	0	2	39	21	10	1	7
ARAB WORLD	39	24	7	6	1	2	0	0	2	0	6	0	6	0	0	30	22	5	2	1
INDIA	68	39	20	6	1	5	5	0	0	0	20	11	2	5	2	55	28	20	6	1
PHILIPPINES	59	34	15	5	4	7	1	5	0	1	3	1	1	0	1	31	18	11	2	0
OTHER E. ASIA	39	21	10	2	5	4	1	2	0	2	5	1	0	0	0	31	19	7	2	3
OTHER ASIA	109	67	16	7	14	12	5	0	3	4	15	9	4	0	2	77	53	12	4	8

CHAPTER 4- VARIETIES OF ENTRY

SECTION 1- AN OVERVIEW OF FLOW AND STOCK, MANUFACTURING AND NON-MANUFACTURING

TABLE 4- MANUFACTURING SUBSIDIARIES CLASSIFIED BY COUNTRY OR REGION, BY YEAR(S) SUBSIDIARY ENGAGED IN MANUFACTURE AND BY METHOD OF ENTRY

YEAR AND METHOD OF ENTRY
(NEW=NEWLY FORMED, ACQ=ACQUIRED, DES=DESCENDANT, UNK=UNKNOWN)

COUNTRY OR REGION	1929 ALL	NEW	ACQ	DES	UNK	1939 ALL	NEW	ACQ	DES	UNK	1957 ALL	NEW	ACQ	DES	UNK	1967 ALL	NEW	ACQ	DES	UNK
OUTSIDE U.S.	467	239	137	49	42	715	362	174	103	76	1568	721	448	282	117	3646	1404	1277	759	206
OUT. U.S. + CANADA	330	170	94	35	31	546	277	134	80	55	1257	596	331	231	99	3203	1276	1058	678	191
OUT. WEST. HEMIS.	274	138	78	31	27	432	204	113	71	44	793	340	225	166	62	2253	862	783	468	140
OUT. WHITE CWEALTH	226	124	57	22	23	347	187	78	42	40	902	444	224	156	78	2461	1040	758	514	149
OUT. DEVLPED WORLD	74	41	19	6	8	136	85	24	12	15	534	294	116	80	44	1260	586	336	263	75
CANADA	137	69	43	14	11	169	85	40	23	21	311	125	117	51	18	443	128	219	81	15
LATIN AMERICA	56	32	16	4	4	114	73	21	9	11	464	256	106	65	37	950	414	275	210	51
C. AMER.+CARIB.	16	12	3	0	1	48	34	9	2	3	174	97	35	27	15	383	163	116	88	16
CUBA	5	3	1	0	1	13	5	5	2	1	31	15	5	5	6	2	0	1	0	1
MEXICO	11	9	2	0	0	27	22	4	0	1	114	65	26	19	4	255	100	80	69	6
OTHER	0	0	0	0	0	8	7	0	0	1	29	17	4	3	5	126	62	36	19	9
S. AMERICA	40	20	13	4	3	66	39	15	7	5	290	159	71	38	22	567	251	159	122	35
ARGENTINA	12	6	4	2	0	27	17	4	4	2	58	33	16	7	2	108	44	39	20	5
BRAZIL	12	8	4	0	0	20	15	4	1	0	96	50	23	17	6	149	63	40	41	5
PERU	3	1	2	0	0	4	4	0	0	0	25	14	6	2	3	47	22	14	4	7
COLUMBIA	1	1	0	0	0	3	3	0	0	0	36	20	10	3	3	90	38	22	21	9
VENEZUELA	2	0	1	1	0	2	2	0	0	0	46	31	7	4	4	101	52	21	23	5
OTHER	10	4	2	1	3	10	2	2	2	4	29	11	9	5	4	72	32	23	10	7
EUROPE	226	107	68	29	22	335	141	98	59	37	549	215	170	117	47	1438	482	562	303	91
EFTA	104	42	36	15	11	167	64	53	34	16	250	93	79	56	22	494	151	203	106	34
U.K.	78	26	32	13	7	128	42	45	30	11	197	68	69	46	14	356	89	168	78	21
SCANDINAVIA	19	11	3	0	5	24	12	6	1	5	34	16	8	9	1	76	34	19	16	7
SWITZERLAND	1	1	0	0	0	4	2	1	1	0	9	7	1	1	0	27	19	6	2	0
OTHER EFTA	6	4	1	0	1	11	8	1	2	0	10	2	1	2	5	35	9	10	10	6
EUROP. COMMUNITY	106	56	29	13	8	146	65	38	31	12	254	98	77	58	21	759	249	292	172	46
FRANCE	36	15	15	5	1	36	16	10	8	2	80	26	27	20	7	223	68	86	57	12
GERMANY	43	25	10	5	3	52	26	11	10	5	81	26	27	20	8	211	63	88	45	15
ITALY	13	10	1	0	2	26	11	8	5	2	47	26	12	6	3	161	57	60	34	10
BELGIUM + LUX	8	3	2	2	1	18	5	6	5	2	21	11	4	5	1	87	33	34	17	3
NETHERLANDS	6	4	1	0	1	14	7	3	3	1	25	9	7	7	2	77	28	24	19	6
SPAIN	8	4	3	0	1	12	7	3	2	0	26	12	10	2	2	119	44	49	21	5
GREECE + TURKEY	1	0	1	0	0	0	0	0	0	0	5	4	0	1	0	35	26	4	1	4
OTHER EURUPE	7	5	0	0	2	10	5	0	2	3	14	8	4	2	0	31	12	14	3	2
EUROPE EX. U.K.	148	81	36	16	15	207	99	53	29	26	352	147	101	71	33	1082	393	394	225	70
SOUTHERN DOMINIONS	25	19	5	0	1	69	47	11	8	3	147	77	35	29	6	361	137	121	83	20
S. AFRICA +RHOD.	7	6	1	0	0	20	17	2	0	1	46	31	8	7	0	123	50	25	45	3
AUSTRALIA + N.Z.	18	13	4	0	1	49	30	9	8	2	101	46	27	22	6	238	92	71	58	17
ASIA + OTHER AFRICA	23	12	5	2	4	28	16	4	4	4	97	48	20	20	9	454	243	100	82	29
JAPAN	5	3	0	2	0	6	2	1	3	0	27	10	10	2	5	144	71	39	29	5
OTHER ASIA+AFR.	18	9	5	0	4	22	12	4	2	4	70	38	10	15	7	310	172	61	53	24
BLACK AFRICA	0	0	0	0	0	0	0	0	0	0	5	3	0	0	2	43	20	10	10	3
ARAB WORLD	0	0	0	0	0	0	0	0	0	0	7	2	2	2	1	30	20	3	5	2
INDIA	3	3	0	0	0	5	4	0	1	0	9	7	0	2	0	62	32	18	8	4
PHILIPPINES	4	1	1	0	2	3	2	0	0	1	2	0	2	0	0	50	24	11	12	3
OTHER E. ASIA	4	1	2	1	0	3	1	0	1	1	23	12	1	4	6	30	19	4	3	4
OTHER ASIA	7	2	0	2	3	10	5	3	0	2	23	13	3	5	2	95	57	14	17	7

CHAPTER 4- VARIETIES OF ENTRY
SECTION 1- AN OVERVIEW OF FLOW AND STOCK, MANUFACTURING AND NON-MANUFACTURING
TABLE 5- SALES SUBSIDIARIES CLASSIFIED BY COUNTRY OR REGION,
BY PERIOD SALES BEGAN AND BY METHOD OF ENTRY

PERIOD AND METHOD OF ENTRY
(NEW=NEWLY FORMED, ACQ=ACQUIRED, DES=DESCENDANT, UNK=UNKNOWN)

COUNTRY OR REGION	TOTAL PRE 1968 ALL	NEW	ACQ	DES	UNK	PRE 1946 ALL	NEW	ACQ	DES	UNK	1946-1957 ALL	NEW	ACQ	DES	UNK	1958-1967 ALL	NEW	ACQ	DES	UNK
OUTSIDE U.S.	2217	1342	538	65	205	551	383	71	9	88	410	285	68	17	40	1189	674	399	39	77
OUT. U.S. + CANADA	1989	1251	449	52	179	484	351	57	4	72	361	254	56	13	37	1086	646	336	34	70
OUT. WEST. HEMIS.	1575	957	383	42	148	405	291	48	3	63	246	159	42	13	32	879	507	293	26	53
OUT. WHITE CWEALTH	1586	1027	341	39	140	355	261	38	2	54	289	208	36	14	31	903	558	267	23	55
OUT. DEVLPED WORLD	610	428	92	13	57	114	86	12	1	15	162	127	17	3	15	314	215	63	9	27
CANADA	228	91	89	13	26	67	32	14	5	16	49	31	12	3	3	103	28	63	5	7
LATIN AMERICA	414	294	66	10	31	79	60	9	1	9	115	95	14	1	5	207	139	43	8	17
C. AMER.+CARIB.	186	132	29	2	19	29	20	4	0	5	55	44	7	0	4	98	68	18	2	10
CUBA	14	9	2	0	2	7	4	2	0	1	5	4	0	0	1	1	1	0	0	0
MEXICO	77	44	20	0	8	16	11	1	0	4	23	15	6	0	2	35	18	13	0	4
OTHER	95	79	7	0	9	6	5	1	0	0	27	25	1	0	1	62	49	25	0	6
S. AMERICA	228	162	37	8	12	50	40	5	1	4	60	51	7	1	1	109	71	25	6	7
ARGENTINA	36	25	6	1	3	10	7	1	0	2	15	11	3	0	1	10	7	2	1	0
BRAZIL	46	33	9	3	1	11	8	2	0	1	8	8	0	0	0	27	15	7	3	2
PERU	27	20	4	0	0	5	5	0	0	0	3	3	0	0	0	16	12	4	0	0
COLOMBIA	25	18	4	2	0	8	7	1	0	0	5	5	0	0	0	11	8	1	2	0
VENEZUELA	52	36	7	0	6	3	2	1	0	0	17	17	0	0	0	29	17	6	0	6
OTHER	42	30	7	2	2	13	11	0	1	1	12	9	2	1	1	16	10	5	0	1
EUROPE	1143	681	295	31	107	324	232	36	3	53	152	98	26	10	18	638	351	233	18	36
EFTA	515	310	116	21	53	158	113	17	3	25	72	47	12	4	9	270	150	87	14	19
U.K.	205	107	54	5	24	81	54	11	2	14	29	19	8	0	2	84	34	35	7	8
SCANDINAVIA	156	99	32	6	19	50	38	4	1	8	22	12	3	3	4	83	49	25	5	7
SWITZERLAND	110	72	9	0	9	17	12	1	0	3	12	9	1	0	2	79	51	19	0	4
OTHER EFTA	44	32	9	1	1	10	9	1	0	0	9	7	0	1	1	24	16	8	0	0
EUROP. COMMUNITY	522	305	154	9	41	118	86	13	0	19	65	42	11	3	7	326	177	130	4	15
FRANCE	125	72	41	1	14	33	24	4	0	5	14	10	3	1	0	74	38	34	0	2
GERMANY	148	83	44	3	6	28	17	4	0	7	12	10	2	0	0	102	56	38	2	7
ITALY	81	48	22	2	8	25	20	0	0	1	12	5	5	1	1	54	21	18	1	2
BELGIUM + LUX	92	61	23	2	5	25	13	1	0	4	17	12	1	1	2	50	29	19	1	0
NETHERLANDS	76	41	24	0	5	16	8	3	0	2	10	5	2	0	2	46	23	8	0	4
SPAIN	43	25	13	0	3	6	2	0	0	0	3	1	1	0	0	24	16	4	0	0
GREECE + TURKEY	17	10	4	0	1	2	2	0	0	0	4	2	0	0	2	11	6	4	0	1
OTHER EUROPE	46	31	8	1	3	30	23	3	0	4	8	6	1	0	0	7	2	4	0	1
EUROPE EX. U.K.	938	574	241	22	83	243	178	25	1	39	123	79	18	10	16	554	317	198	11	28
SOUTHERN DOMINIONS	182	106	51	4	14	43	31	8	0	4	39	23	12	0	4	93	52	31	4	6
S. AFRICA +RHOD.	62	40	11	1	7	14	9	3	0	2	15	12	2	0	1	30	19	6	1	4
AUSTRALIA + N.Z.	120	66	40	3	7	29	22	5	0	2	24	11	10	0	3	63	33	25	3	2
ASIA + OTHER AFRICA	250	170	37	7	27	38	28	4	0	6	55	38	4	3	10	148	104	29	3	11
JAPAN	54	36	11	4	1	3	2	1	0	0	8	6	1	1	0	41	28	9	3	1
OTHER ASIA+AFR.	196	134	26	3	26	35	26	3	0	6	47	32	3	2	10	107	76	20	2	10
BLACK AFRICA	45	28	7	1	6	0	0	0	0	0	13	9	2	1	1	28	19	5	0	4
ARAB WORLD	36	23	4	0	6	10	9	1	0	0	11	7	0	0	2	11	7	2	0	2
INDIA	13	9	1	1	3	8	6	0	0	2	2	1	0	1	0	3	2	1	0	0
PHILIPPINES	25	14	4	0	2	5	4	0	0	0	7	3	2	0	0	11	7	2	0	2
OTHER E. ASIA	30	23	5	0	2	2	2	0	0	0	5	3	0	0	2	23	18	5	0	0
OTHER ASIA	47	37	5	1	3	6	5	0	0	1	9	8	0	0	0	31	23	5	1	2

CHAPTER 4— VARIETIES OF ENTRY

SECTION 1— AN OVERVIEW OF FLOW AND STOCK, MANUFACTURING AND NON-MANUFACTURING

TABLE 6— SALES SUBSIDIARIES CLASSIFIED BY COUNTRY OR REGION, BY YEAR(S) SUBSIDIARY ENGAGED IN SALES AND BY METHOD OF ENTRY

YEAR AND METHOD OF ENTRY

(NEW=NEWLY FORMED, ACQ=ACQUIRED, DES=DESCENDANT, UNK=UNKNOWN)

COUNTRY OR REGION	1929 ALL	NEW	ACQ	DES	UNK	1939 ALL	NEW	ACQ	DES	UNK	1957 ALL	NEW	ACQ	DES	UNK	1967 ALL	NEW	ACQ	DES	UNK
OUTSIDE U.S.	248	182	24	7	35	369	246	44	22	57	603	384	87	49	83	1358	789	336	109	124
OUT. U.S. + CANADA	222	170	19	7	26	324	226	36	19	43	527	341	75	43	68	1230	738	287	102	103
OUT. WEST. HEMIS.	207	157	18	7	25	276	188	34	18	36	388	239	55	35	59	997	578	250	84	85
OUT. WHITE CWEALTH	157	119	12	6	20	237	169	21	16	31	405	268	47	38	52	1005	620	221	82	82
OUT. DEVLPED WORLD	27	24	2	0	1	71	55	5	1	10	190	131	24	12	23	367	249	56	25	37
CANADA	26	12	5	0	9	45	20	8	3	14	76	43	12	6	15	128	51	49	7	21
LATIN AMERICA	15	13	1	0	1	48	38	2	1	7	139	102	20	8	9	233	160	37	18	18
C. AMER.+CARIB.	6	4	1	0	1	20	13	2	0	5	64	48	10	0	6	104	73	16	3	12
CUBA	3	1	1	0	1	3	1	1	0	1	5	4	1	0	0	1	1	0	0	0
MEXICO	3	3	0	0	0	15	10	1	0	4	29	17	7	0	5	31	13	11	2	5
OTHER	0	0	0	0	0	2	2	0	0	0	30	27	2	0	1	72	59	5	1	7
S. AMERICA	9	9	0	0	0	28	25	0	1	2	75	54	10	8	3	129	87	21	15	6
ARGENTINA	3	3	0	0	0	6	5	0	1	0	18	12	3	1	2	20	15	2	2	1
BRAZIL	1	1	0	0	0	5	5	0	0	0	11	8	2	0	1	25	16	5	3	1
PERU	1	1	0	0	0	5	5	0	0	0	5	5	0	0	0	18	16	2	0	0
COLOMBIA	2	2	0	0	0	2	2	0	0	0	8	3	3	2	0	14	6	3	5	0
VENEZUELA	2	2	0	0	0	1	1	0	0	0	16	16	0	0	0	28	18	6	0	4
OTHER	0	0	0	0	0	9	7	0	0	2	17	10	2	5	0	24	16	3	5	0
EUROPE	173	128	13	7	25	223	150	24	18	31	275	174	34	29	38	722	403	193	68	58
EFTA	84	60	9	4	11	115	75	13	10	17	142	88	17	16	21	336	191	83	30	32
U.K.	41	30	4	1	6	54	34	8	2	10	60	36	12	3	9	112	55	33	12	12
SCANDINAVIA	29	20	3	2	4	41	26	3	7	5	52	33	4	9	6	116	69	26	10	11
SWITZERLAND	9	6	1	1	1	12	8	1	1	2	17	10	1	1	5	78	45	18	7	8
OTHER EFTA	5	4	1	0	0	8	7	1	0	0	13	9	0	3	1	30	22	6	1	1
EUROP. COMMUNITY	68	53	4	1	10	76	54	8	5	9	103	71	12	10	10	327	179	99	31	18
FRANCE	17	14	1	0	2	20	15	3	0	2	24	17	3	3	1	81	41	28	10	2
GERMANY	16	11	1	0	4	16	10	2	3	1	21	15	0	3	3	91	49	31	3	8
ITALY	9	8	0	0	1	9	8	0	0	1	9	5	4	0	0	44	25	12	6	1
BELGIUM + LUX	11	9	0	1	1	21	17	3	0	1	33	25	1	2	5	61	39	13	6	3
NETHERLANDS	15	11	2	0	2	10	4	0	2	4	16	9	4	2	1	50	25	15	6	4
SPAIN	8	5	0	1	2	10	4	3	2	1	13	4	4	3	2	26	16	6	1	3
GREECE + TURKEY	0	0	0	0	0	2	2	0	0	0	4	2	0	0	2	14	7	2	2	3
OTHER EUROPE	13	10	0	1	2	20	15	0	1	4	13	9	1	0	3	19	10	3	4	2
EUROPE EX. U.K.	132	98	9	6	19	169	116	16	16	21	215	138	22	26	29	610	348	160	56	46
SOUTHERN DOMINIONS	21	18	3	0	0	29	20	7	0	2	55	31	16	1	7	101	56	31	6	8
S. AFRICA +RHOD.	6	5	1	0	0	11	7	3	0	1	22	13	5	1	3	34	21	5	2	6
AUSTRALIA + N.Z.	15	13	2	0	0	18	13	4	0	1	33	18	11	0	4	67	35	26	4	2
ASIA + OTHER AFRICA	13	11	2	0	0	24	18	3	0	3	58	34	5	5	14	174	119	26	10	19
JAPAN	1	1	0	0	0	1	1	0	0	0	7	5	1	1	0	40	30	7	3	0
OTHER ASIA+AFR.	12	11	1	0	0	23	17	3	0	3	51	29	4	4	14	134	89	19	7	19
BLACK AFRICA	0	0	0	0	0	7	5	0	0	2	10	8	0	0	2	37	25	5	1	6
ARAB WORLD	5	4	1	0	0	5	5	0	0	0	14	6	2	2	4	18	9	2	1	6
INDIA	2	2	0	0	0	6	4	2	0	0	8	6	1	0	1	8	4	1	1	2
PHILIPPINES	0	0	0	0	0	0	0	0	0	0	6	3	1	0	2	15	6	3	3	3
OTHER E. ASIA	1	1	0	0	0	1	1	0	0	0	4	3	0	0	1	26	20	4	0	2
OTHER ASIA	4	4	0	0	0	4	2	1	0	1	9	3	0	2	4	30	25	4	1	0

CHAPTER 4- VARIETIES OF ENTRY
SECTION 1- AN OVERVIEW OF FLOW AND STOCK, MANUFACTURING AND NON-MANUFACTURING
TABLE 7- EXTRACTION SUBSIDIARIES CLASSIFIED BY COUNTRY OR REGION,
BY PERIOD EXTRACTION BEGAN AND BY METHOD OF ENTRY

PERIOD AND METHOD OF ENTRY
(NEW=NEWLY FORMED, ACQ=ACQUIRED, DES=DESCENDANT, UNK=UNKNOWN)

COUNTRY OR REGION	TOTAL PRE 1968					PRE 1946					1946-1957					1958-1967				
	ALL	NEW	ACQ	DES	UNK	ALL	NEW	ACQ	DES	UNK	ALL	NEW	ACQ	DES	UNK	ALL	NEW	ACQ	DES	UNK
OUTSIDE U.S.	320	153	83	12	66	120	40	35	4	41	87	50	22	2	13	107	63	26	6	12
OUT. U.S. + CANADA	248	113	67	11	53	102	35	31	4	32	61	36	13	2	10	81	42	23	5	11
OUT. WEST. HEMIS.	118	63	26	8	20	38	13	12	3	10	34	23	4	2	5	45	27	10	3	5
OUT. WHITE CWEALTH	202	95	54	7	42	86	31	26	2	27	51	33	11	1	6	61	31	17	4	9
OUT. DEVLPED WORLD	187	86	49	7	41	82	30	24	2	26	46	29	10	1	6	55	27	15	4	9
CANADA	72	40	16	1	13	18	5	4	0	9	26	14	9	0	3	26	21	3	1	1
LATIN AMERICA	130	50	41	3	33	64	22	19	1	22	27	13	9	0	5	36	15	13	2	6
C. AMER.+CARIB.	81	30	23	2	25	45	15	11	0	19	16	8	5	0	3	19	7	7	2	3
CUBA	1	0	1	0	0	1	0	1	0	0	0	0	0	0	0	0	0	0	0	0
MEXICO	63	19	18	1	24	41	12	10	0	19	11	4	4	0	3	10	3	4	1	2
OTHER	17	11	4	1	1	3	3	0	0	0	5	4	1	0	0	9	4	3	1	1
S. AMERICA	49	20	18	1	8	19	7	8	1	3	11	5	4	0	2	17	8	6	0	3
ARGENTINA	7	2	2	0	2	2	1	0	0	1	3	1	0	0	2	1	0	1	0	0
BRAZIL	3	2	0	0	1	1	0	0	0	1	1	1	0	0	0	1	1	0	0	0
PERU	6	2	4	0	0	0	0	0	0	0	4	1	3	0	0	2	1	1	0	0
COLOMBIA	4	1	3	0	0	3	1	2	0	0	0	0	0	0	0	1	0	1	0	0
VENEZUELA	13	6	3	0	4	5	1	2	0	2	1	1	0	0	0	7	4	1	0	2
OTHER	16	7	7	0	1	8	4	4	0	0	2	1	1	0	0	5	2	2	0	1
EUROPE	27	14	8	3	2	11	4	4	2	1	7	4	1	0	1	9	6	3	1	0
EFTA	12	5	3	3	1	7	3	2	2	0	2	0	0	1	1	3	2	1	0	0
U.K.	12	5	3	3	1	7	3	2	2	0	2	0	0	1	1	3	2	1	0	0
SCANDINAVIA	0	0	0	0	0	0	0	0	0	0	0	0	0	0	0	0	0	0	0	0
SWITZERLAND	0	0	0	0	0	0	0	0	0	0	0	0	0	0	0	0	0	0	0	0
OTHER EFTA	0	0	0	0	0	0	0	0	0	0	0	0	0	0	0	0	0	0	0	0
EUROP. COMMUNITY	10	6	3	0	1	2	0	1	0	1	4	3	1	0	0	4	3	1	0	0
FRANCE	4	3	1	0	0	0	0	0	0	0	3	2	1	0	0	1	1	0	0	0
GERMANY	1	1	0	0	0	0	0	0	0	0	0	0	0	0	0	1	1	0	0	0
ITALY	1	0	1	0	0	0	0	0	0	0	0	0	0	0	0	1	0	1	0	0
BELGIUM + LUX	1	1	0	0	0	1	1	0	0	0	1	1	0	0	0	0	0	0	0	0
NETHERLANDS	3	2	1	0	0	0	0	0	0	0	0	0	0	0	0	2	0	1	0	1
SPAIN	1	0	1	0	0	0	0	0	0	0	1	0	1	0	0	0	0	0	0	0
GREECE + TURKEY	2	2	0	0	0	0	0	0	0	0	0	0	0	0	0	2	2	0	0	0
OTHER EUROPE	1	1	0	0	0	2	1	1	0	0	0	0	0	0	0	1	1	0	0	0
EUROPE EX. U.K.	15	9	5	0	1	4	1	2	0	1	5	4	1	0	0	6	4	2	0	0
SOUTHERN DOMINIONS	34	13	10	1	10	9	1	3	0	5	8	3	2	0	3	17	9	5	1	2
S. AFRICA +RHOD.	13	4	2	0	7	5	1	0	0	4	5	1	2	0	2	3	2	0	0	1
AUSTRALIA + N.Z.	21	9	8	1	3	4	0	3	0	1	3	2	0	0	1	14	7	5	1	1
ASIA + OTHER AFRICA	57	36	8	4	8	18	8	5	1	4	19	16	1	1	1	19	12	2	2	3
JAPAN	0	0	0	0	0	0	0	0	0	0	0	0	0	0	0	0	0	0	0	0
OTHER ASIA+AFR.	57	36	8	4	8	18	8	5	1	4	19	16	1	1	1	19	12	2	2	3
BLACK AFRICA	26	16	3	2	5	3	0	1	1	1	11	9	1	0	1	12	7	1	1	3
ARAB WORLD	15	11	2	0	2	6	3	1	0	2	5	5	0	0	0	4	3	1	0	0
INDIA	0	0	0	0	0	0	0	0	0	0	0	0	0	0	0	0	0	0	0	0
PHILIPPINES	5	3	0	1	0	3	1	1	0	1	1	1	0	0	0	1	1	0	0	0
OTHER E. ASIA	0	0	0	0	0	0	0	0	0	0	0	0	0	0	0	0	0	0	0	0
OTHER ASIA	11	6	2	0	2	6	4	1	0	1	2	1	0	1	0	3	1	1	1	1

CHAPTER 4- VARIETIES OF ENTRY
SECTION 1- AN OVERVIEW OF FLOW AND STOCK, MANUFACTURING AND NON-MANUFACTURING
TABLE 8- EXTRACTION SUBSIDIARIES CLASSIFIED BY COUNTRY OR REGION,
BY YEAR(S) SUBSIDIARY ENGAGED IN EXTRACTION
AND BY METHOD OF ENTRY

YEAR AND METHOD OF ENTRY
(NEW=NEWLY FORMED, ACQ=ACQUIRED, DES=DESCENDANT, UNK=UNKNOWN)

COUNTRY OR REGION	1929 ALL	NEW	ACQ	DES	UNK	1939 ALL	NEW	ACQ	DES	UNK	1957 ALL	NEW	ACQ	DES	UNK	1967 ALL	NEW	ACQ	DES	UNK
OUTSIDE U.S.	41	8	14	2	17	74	27	21	7	19	135	63	33	9	30	172	77	38	27	30
OUT. U.S. + CANADA	38	8	12	2	16	67	26	19	7	15	105	49	24	8	24	136	59	30	23	24
OUT. WEST. HEMIS.	15	2	5	2	6	31	10	9	5	7	53	26	10	6	11	80	39	11	17	13
OUT. WHITE CWEALTH	33	7	11	2	13	53	23	14	5	11	85	45	18	5	17	105	51	23	13	18
OUT. DEVLPED WORLD	30	6	10	1	13	50	22	13	4	11	79	41	17	4	17	95	45	20	12	18
CANADA	3	0	2	0	1	7	1	2	0	4	30	14	9	1	6	36	18	8	4	6
LATIN AMERICA	23	6	7	0	10	36	16	10	2	8	52	23	14	2	13	56	20	19	6	11
C. AMER.+CARIB.	16	1	6	0	9	24	10	6	1	7	34	15	8	1	10	28	10	4	4	10
CUBA	1	0	1	0	0	2	0	1	1	0	0	0	0	0	0	0	0	0	0	0
MEXICO	15	0	5	0	10	21	9	5	0	7	27	10	7	0	10	14	0	5	5	4
OTHER	0	0	0	0	0	1	1	0	0	0	7	5	1	1	0	14	6	0	3	5
S. AMERICA	7	5	1	0	1	12	6	4	1	1	18	8	6	1	3	28	10	15	2	1
ARGENTINA	1	1	0	0	0	2	0	1	0	1	3	1	1	0	1	4	1	2	0	1
BRAZIL	0	0	0	0	0	1	0	1	0	0	1	0	1	0	0	2	1	0	0	1
PERU	0	0	0	0	0	0	0	0	0	0	4	1	1	1	1	6	2	1	1	2
COLOMBIA	0	0	0	0	0	2	1	1	0	0	1	1	0	0	0	1	1	0	0	0
VENEZUELA	2	1	0	0	1	2	0	1	0	1	3	0	1	1	1	5	1	1	1	2
OTHER	4	3	1	0	0	5	3	1	1	0	6	3	2	0	1	10	4	2	0	4
EUROPE	5	1	3	0	1	9	4	2	0	3	13	6	4	1	2	15	9	2	1	3
EFTA	2	1	1	0	0	6	3	2	0	1	7	3	2	1	1	5	3	0	1	1
U.K.	2	1	1	0	0	6	3	2	0	1	7	3	2	1	1	5	3	0	1	1
SCANDINAVIA	0	0	0	0	0	0	0	0	0	0	0	0	0	0	0	0	0	0	0	0
SWITZERLAND	0	0	0	0	0	0	0	0	0	0	0	0	0	0	0	0	0	0	0	0
OTHER EFTA	0	0	0	0	0	0	0	0	0	0	0	0	0	0	0	0	0	0	0	0
EUROP. COMMUNITY	0	0	0	0	0	1	0	0	0	1	5	2	2	0	1	7	4	2	0	1
FRANCE	0	0	0	0	0	1	0	0	0	1	1	1	0	0	0	3	2	1	0	0
GERMANY	0	0	0	0	0	0	0	0	0	0	1	0	1	0	0	1	1	0	0	0
ITALY	0	0	0	0	0	0	0	0	0	0	1	0	0	0	1	1	0	0	0	1
BELGIUM + LUX	0	0	0	0	0	0	0	0	0	0	1	1	0	0	0	0	0	0	0	0
NETHERLANDS	0	0	0	0	0	0	0	0	0	0	1	0	1	0	0	2	1	1	0	0
SPAIN	0	0	0	0	0	0	0	0	0	0	0	0	0	0	0	1	1	0	0	0
GREECE + TURKEY	2	0	1	0	1	1	0	0	0	1	1	1	0	0	0	2	1	0	0	1
OTHER EUROPE	1	0	1	0	0	1	1	0	0	0	0	0	0	0	0	0	0	0	0	0
EUROPE EX. U.K.	3	0	2	0	1	3	1	0	0	2	6	3	2	0	1	10	6	2	0	2
SOUTHERN DOMINIONS	3	0	0	0	3	8	1	3	0	4	13	5	7	0	1	26	7	9	3	7
S. AFRICA +RHOD.	3	0	0	0	3	4	1	0	0	3	7	2	4	0	1	10	2	1	1	6
AUSTRALIA + N.Z.	0	0	0	0	0	4	0	3	0	1	6	3	3	0	0	16	5	8	2	1
ASIA + OTHER AFRICA	7	0	2	0	5	14	6	3	2	3	27	17	4	1	5	39	25	4	3	7
JAPAN	0	0	0	0	0	0	0	0	0	0	0	0	0	0	0	0	0	0	0	0
OTHER ASIA+AFR.	7	0	2	0	5	14	6	3	2	3	27	17	4	1	5	39	25	4	3	7
BLACK AFRICA	3	0	1	0	2	6	3	1	1	1	13	8	2	0	3	20	10	5	0	5
ARAB WORLD	2	0	0	0	2	1	1	0	0	0	7	5	1	0	1	10	8	0	1	1
INDIA	0	0	0	0	0	3	1	1	1	0	3	1	0	1	1	0	0	0	0	0
PHILIPPINES	1	0	0	0	1	0	0	0	0	0	0	0	0	0	0	3	3	0	0	0
OTHER E. ASIA	0	0	0	0	0	0	0	0	0	0	0	0	0	0	0	0	0	0	0	0
OTHER ASIA	1	0	1	0	0	4	1	1	0	2	4	3	1	0	0	6	4	0	0	2

CHAPTER 4- VARIETIES OF ENTRY
SECTION 1- AN OVERVIEW OF FLOW AND STOCK, MANUFACTURING AND NON-MANUFACTURING
TABLE 9- SUBSIDIARIES WITH OTHER MAIN ACTIVITY CLASSIFIED BY COUNTRY OR REGION,
BY PERIOD ACTIVITY BEGAN AND BY METHOD OF ENTRY

PERIOD AND METHOD OF ENTRY
(NEW=NEWLY FORMED, ACQ=ACQUIRED, DES=DESCENDANT, UNK=UNKNOWN)

COUNTRY OR REGION	TOTAL PRE 1968 ALL	NEW	ACQ	DES	UNK	PRE 1946 ALL	NEW	ACQ	DES	UNK	1946-1957 ALL	NEW	ACQ	DES	UNK	1958-1967 ALL	NEW	ACQ	DES	UNK
OUTSIDE U.S.	1805	784	344	408	202	317	125	43	100	49	430	190	89	78	73	991	469	212	230	80
OUT. U.S. + CANADA	1543	699	287	330	168	260	100	35	88	37	341	155	69	55	62	883	444	183	187	69
OUT. WEST. HEMIS.	1043	470	207	215	115	174	64	18	69	23	182	41	49	44	48	651	342	140	121	48
OUT. WHITE CWEALTH	1226	593	210	251	134	211	83	26	73	29	285	140	53	44	48	692	370	131	134	57
OUT. DEVLPED WORLD	629	292	92	145	70	101	41	19	26	15	200	110	27	35	28	298	141	46	84	27
CANADA	262	85	57	78	34	57	25	8	12	12	89	35	20	23	11	108	25	29	43	11
LATIN AMERICA	500	229	80	115	53	86	36	17	19	14	159	91	20	30	18	232	102	43	66	21
C. AMER.+CARIB.	260	122	33	54	38	42	12	3	16	11	82	55	11	20	14	123	55	19	36	13
CUBA	17	4	4	4	5	8	1	1	1	4	7	3	3	2	1	2	0	0	1	1
MEXICO	78	23	9	30	9	27	6	2	14	5	14	6	5	3	1	30	11	4	14	1
OTHER	165	95	20	20	24	7	5	0	0	2	61	46	9	8	10	91	44	15	20	12
S. AMERICA	240	107	47	61	15	44	24	14	3	3	77	36	2	28	4	109	47	24	30	8
ARGENTINA	43	16	10	14	3	9	4	1	1	3	13	5	3	6	0	21	6	7	7	1
BRAZIL	58	31	9	9	4	7	5	1	1	0	13	9	2	0	0	34	17	6	9	2
PERU	25	11	11	2	0	7	2	5	0	0	4	3	1	0	0	13	7	1	5	0
COLOMBIA	23	5	8	16	1	2	1	0	0	1	17	9	2	5	1	4	2	1	8	1
VENEZUELA	58	11	8	10	7	7	2	3	1	0	21	14	2	2	3	26	11	2	8	4
OTHER	33	13	7	10	0	10	5	4	0	1	9	4	1	4	0	11	4	2	5	0
EUROPE	772	353	160	152	87	148	55	15	56	22	120	39	32	19	30	484	259	113	77	35
EFTA	382	168	83	80	39	59	20	11	19	9	72	22	20	16	14	239	126	52	45	16
U.K.	197	60	47	52	26	44	14	8	14	8	41	9	10	10	12	100	37	29	28	8
SCANDINAVIA	47	15	12	11	9	7	1	1	4	1	10	4	4	2	0	30	10	7	5	8
SWITZERLAND	123	86	21	12	4	6	5	1	0	0	16	9	5	0	2	101	72	15	12	2
OTHER EFTA	15	7	3	5	0	2	0	1	1	0	5	1	1	4	0	8	7	1	0	0
EUROP. COMMUNITY	343	163	70	57	45	74	31	3	27	13	45	15	11	3	16	216	117	56	27	16
FRANCE	125	74	25	17	7	29	18	1	7	3	12	6	5	0	1	82	50	19	10	3
GERMANY	89	27	21	22	17	34	10	2	13	9	14	6	3	1	4	39	11	16	8	3
ITALY	44	20	8	6	7	4	2	0	2	0	8	2	1	1	4	29	16	7	5	1
BELGIUM + LUX	44	23	8	6	6	3	0	0	2	1	4	1	1	0	2	37	22	7	5	3
NETHERLANDS	41	19	8	5	8	4	1	0	3	0	7	0	1	1	5	29	18	7	4	1
SPAIN	15	5	3	3	3	1	0	1	0	0	1	0	0	0	1	10	4	3	3	0
GREECE + TURKEY	8	5	1	0	0	1	0	1	0	0	2	2	0	0	0	5	3	0	0	2
OTHER EUROPE	24	12	9	9	0	10	3	0	7	0	0	0	0	9	0	14	9	3	2	0
EUROPE EX. U.K.	575	293	113	152	61	104	41	7	42	14	79	30	22	19	18	384	222	84	49	29
SOUTHERN DOMINIONS	108	37	28	26	8	5	3	1	1	0	15	6	6	1	2	79	28	21	24	6
S. AFRICA +RHOD.	20	6	5	6	0	3	0	0	1	0	4	4	1	1	0	12	4	4	4	0
AUSTRALIA + N.Z.	88	31	23	20	8	4	3	1	0	0	11	2	5	0	2	67	24	17	20	6
ASIA + OTHER AFRICA	163	80	19	37	20	21	6	2	12	1	47	19	11	5	12	88	55	6	20	7
JAPAN	34	17	7	7	3	6	1	0	5	0	6	4	0	0	2	22	16	3	3	1
OTHER ASIA+AFR.	129	63	12	30	17	15	5	2	7	0	41	19	4	5	10	66	39	3	18	6
BLACK AFRICA	46	27	12	16	6	5	2	0	2	1	14	10	2	3	3	25	15	3	4	3
ARAB WORLD	20	7	2	9	2	2	0	0	2	0	11	5	1	0	2	7	2	1	4	0
INDIA	7	3	1	2	1	2	0	0	2	0	5	3	1	0	1	1	0	0	1	0
PHILIPPINES	15	6	2	5	2	2	0	0	0	0	3	1	0	3	0	9	6	0	0	1
OTHER E. ASIA	22	13	1	2	4	3	2	0	0	1	3	0	0	0	2	13	10	1	1	1
OTHER ASIA	19	7	3	7	1	5	1	0	1	0	5	0	3	0	0	11	6	0	4	1

CHAPTER 4- VARIETIES OF ENTRY
SECTION 1- AN OVERVIEW OF FLOW AND STOCK, MANUFACTURING AND NON-MANUFACTURING
TABLE 10- SUBSIDIARIES WITH OTHER MAIN ACTIVITY CLASSIFIED BY COUNTRY OR REGION, BY YEAR(S) SUBSIDIARY WAS ACTIVE AND BY METHOD OF ENTRY

YEAR AND METHOD OF ENTRY (NEW=NEWLY FORMED, ACQ=ACQUIRED, DES=DESCENDANT, UNK=UNKNOWN)

COUNTRY OR REGION	1929					1939					1957					1967				
	ALL	NEW	ACQ	DES	UNK	ALL	NEW	ACQ	DES	UNK	ALL	NEW	ACQ	DES	UNK	ALL	NEW	ACQ	DES	UNK
OUTSIDE U.S.	85	53	15	9	8	193	73	24	56	40	574	249	93	127	105	1247	542	201	363	141
OUT. U.S. + CANADA	70	45	13	7	5	154	57	19	47	31	455	196	71	103	85	1062	480	170	295	117
OUT. WEST. HEMIS.	46	33	6	4	3	100	42	10	29	19	250	91	49	55	55	724	346	130	171	77
OUT. WHITE CWEALTH	59	39	11	6	3	123	45	14	39	25	374	172	55	79	68	841	401	123	222	95
OUT. DEVLPED WORLD	27	14	8	3	2	61	17	10	21	13	249	124	28	56	41	431	182	45	150	54
CANADA	15	8	2	2	3	39	16	5	9	9	119	53	22	24	20	185	62	31	68	24
LATIN AMERICA	24	12	7	3	2	54	15	9	18	12	205	105	22	48	30	338	134	40	124	40
C. AMER.+CARIB.	8	3	1	2	2	31	5	3	14	9	111	61	10	17	23	177	76	14	62	25
CUBA	3	1	0	1	1	7	1	1	1	4	12	4	2	1	5	4	1	0	1	2
MEXICO	4	1	1	1	1	20	1	2	13	4	33	8	3	16	6	56	13	5	33	5
OTHER	1	1	0	0	0	4	3	0	0	1	66	49	5	0	12	117	62	9	28	18
S. AMERICA	16	9	6	1	0	23	10	6	4	3	94	44	12	31	7	161	58	26	62	15
ARGENTINA	3	1	1	1	0	7	2	1	2	2	14	4	2	6	2	23	6	5	9	3
BRAZIL	2	1	1	0	0	4	2	1	0	1	18	12	4	0	2	42	21	7	10	4
PERU	3	2	1	0	0	3	2	1	0	0	7	4	1	2	0	16	9	5	2	0
COLOMBIA	0	0	0	0	0	0	0	0	0	0	14	1	0	13	0	17	2	1	13	1
VENEZUELA	1	0	1	0	0	1	1	0	0	0	25	16	1	5	3	43	13	4	19	7
OTHER	7	5	2	0	0	8	3	3	2	0	16	7	4	5	0	20	7	4	9	0
EUROPE	41	29	5	4	3	87	36	8	25	18	180	65	34	41	40	529	255	102	117	55
EFTA	17	10	3	2	2	35	14	6	8	7	94	34	20	22	18	250	113	45	67	25
U.K.	10	5	2	1	2	26	9	4	7	6	63	18	11	19	15	131	42	26	47	16
SCANDINAVIA	2	0	1	1	0	3	0	1	1	1	13	5	5	2	1	28	10	5	6	7
SWITZERLAND	5	5	0	0	0	5	5	0	0	0	16	11	3	0	2	83	55	13	13	2
OTHER EFTA	0	0	0	0	0	1	0	1	0	0	2	0	1	1	0	8	6	1	1	0
EUROP. COMMUNITY	21	16	2	2	1	42	20	1	10	11	78	29	12	15	22	245	126	51	39	29
FRANCE	8	8	0	0	0	17	12	0	2	3	31	16	5	6	4	95	58	18	12	7
GERMANY	10	5	2	2	1	22	6	1	7	8	29	9	4	6	10	53	15	16	10	12
ITALY	2	2	0	0	0	2	2	0	0	0	6	3	1	1	1	29	15	6	4	4
BELGIUM + LUX	0	0	0	0	0	0	0	0	0	0	4	1	1	0	2	37	22	5	7	3
NETHERLANDS	1	1	0	0	0	1	0	0	1	0	8	0	1	2	5	31	16	6	6	3
SPAIN	1	1	0	0	0	4	0	0	4	0	4	0	1	3	0	13	4	2	6	1
GREECE + TURKEY	0	0	0	0	0	1	0	1	0	0	3	2	1	0	0	7	3	1	3	0
OTHER EUROPE	2	2	0	0	0	5	2	0	3	0	1	0	0	1	0	14	9	3	2	0
EUROPE EX. U.K.	31	24	3	3	1	61	27	4	18	12	117	47	23	22	25	398	213	76	70	39
SOUTHERN DOMINIONS	1	1	0	0	0	5	3	1	1	0	18	6	5	5	2	78	28	19	25	6
S. AFRICA +RHOD.	0	0	0	0	0	1	0	0	1	0	5	1	1	3	0	16	5	5	6	0
AUSTRALIA + N.Z.	1	1	0	0	0	4	3	1	0	0	13	5	4	2	2	62	23	14	19	6
ASIA + OTHER AFRICA	4	3	1	0	0	8	3	1	3	1	52	20	10	9	13	117	63	9	29	16
JAPAN	1	1	0	0	0	1	1	0	0	0	8	1	4	1	2	24	15	4	3	2
OTHER ASIA+AFR.	3	2	1	0	0	7	2	1	3	1	44	19	6	8	11	93	48	5	26	14
BLACK AFRICA	2	2	0	0	0	0	0	0	0	0	13	9	0	0	4	36	20	1	9	6
ARAB WORLD	0	0	0	0	0	0	0	0	0	0	12	5	1	4	2	15	7	1	7	0
INDIA	0	0	0	0	0	0	0	0	0	0	5	3	1	0	1	4	2	0	1	1
PHILIPPINES	0	0	0	0	0	1	0	0	1	0	3	0	0	2	1	9	4	0	3	2
OTHER E. ASIA	1	0	1	0	0	5	1	1	2	1	5	1	1	0	3	16	9	1	2	4
OTHER ASIA	0	0	0	0	0	1	1	0	0	0	6	1	3	2	0	13	6	2	4	1

CHAPTER 4- VARIETIES OF ENTRY
SECTION 1- AN OVERVIEW OF FLOW AND STOCK, MANUFACTURING AND NON-MANUFACTURING
TABLE 11- SUBSIDIARIES WITH UNKNOWN ACTIVITY CLASSIFIED BY COUNTRY OR REGION,
BY PERIOD ACTIVITY BEGAN AND BY METHOD OF ENTRY

PERIOD AND METHOD OF ENTRY
(NEW=NEWLY FORMED, ACQ=ACQUIRED, DES=DESCENDANT, UNK=UNKNOWN)

COUNTRY OR REGION	TOTAL PRE 1968					PRE 1946					1946-1957					1958-1967				
	ALL	NEW	ACQ	DES	UNK	ALL	NEW	ACQ	DES	UNK	ALL	NEW	ACQ	DES	UNK	ALL	NEW	ACQ	DES	UNK
OUTSIDE U.S.	2407	414	512	24	1135	593	130	124	10	329	489	92	86	6	305	1003	192	302	8	501
OUT. U.S. + CANADA	1954	365	390	19	931	438	107	88	8	235	404	79	48	4	273	863	179	254	7	423
OUT. WEST. HEMIS.	1413	245	308	17	674	335	82	70	2	175	250	43	31	4	172	659	120	207	5	327
OUT. WHITE CWEALTH	1459	298	286	15	674	321	78	71	1	166	303	66	33	4	200	649	154	182	5	308
OUT. DEVLPED WORLD	683	161	107	3	307	121	34	21	0	66	183	46	20	1	116	274	81	66	2	125
CANADA	453	49	122	5	204	155	23	36	2	94	85	13	38	2	32	140	13	48	1	78
LATIN AMERICA	541	120	82	2	257	103	25	18	0	60	154	36	17	0	101	204	59	47	1	96
C. AMER.+CARIB.	254	59	41	0	120	39	11	7	0	21	79	20	10	0	49	102	28	24	0	50
CUBA	23	2	1	0	19	15	2	1	0	12	6	0	0	0	6	1	0	0	0	1
MEXICO	100	25	22	0	39	18	5	5	0	8	27	8	5	0	14	41	12	12	0	17
OTHER	131	32	18	0	62	6	4	1	0	1	46	12	5	0	29	60	16	12	0	32
S. AMERICA	287	61	41	2	137	64	14	11	0	39	75	16	7	0	52	102	31	23	2	46
ARGENTINA	64	10	7	0	25	15	4	2	0	9	9	1	0	0	8	18	5	5	0	8
BRAZIL	66	12	11	1	37	14	2	3	0	9	15	5	2	0	8	32	5	6	1	20
PERU	16	5	3	0	5	4	1	1	0	2	3	1	0	0	2	6	3	2	0	1
COLOMBIA	52	10	5	1	31	11	3	1	0	7	25	2	3	0	20	10	5	0	1	4
VENEZUELA	45	11	8	1	22	8	1	2	0	5	12	4	1	0	7	22	6	5	1	10
OTHER	44	13	7	0	17	12	3	2	0	7	11	3	1	0	7	14	7	4	0	3
EUROPE	1077	173	233	15	539	299	66	63	8	162	170	24	21	3	122	491	83	149	4	255
EFTA	507	71	89	2	289	134	35	19	1	79	86	7	10	0	69	232	29	60	2	141
U.K.	328	40	60	2	189	101	24	14	1	62	54	3	9	0	42	136	13	37	1	85
SCANDINAVIA	96	10	16	0	59	19	5	2	0	12	22	0	1	0	21	45	5	13	1	26
SWITZERLAND	68	18	9	0	33	8	2	2	0	4	8	4	0	0	4	44	10	9	0	25
OTHER EFTA	15	3	4	0	8	6	2	3	0	1	2	0	0	0	2	7	1	1	0	5
EUROP. COMMUNITY	483	81	130	3	217	128	24	36	5	63	79	14	10	1	52	230	43	84	1	102
FRANCE	128	22	33	4	59	41	9	11	3	18	20	3	1	1	15	57	10	21	0	26
GERMANY	141	21	41	2	67	34	4	13	1	16	22	4	3	1	15	75	13	26	0	36
ITALY	103	15	32	1	44	27	4	9	1	15	16	3	2	0	12	49	9	22	0	17
BELGIUM + LUX	51	16	8	2	14	12	6	3	0	5	9	2	1	1	5	19	8	4	1	4
NETHERLANDS	60	7	16	0	33	14	2	4	0	9	12	2	1	0	5	30	3	8	0	19
SPAIN	35	8	8	0	14	10	5	2	0	3	5	2	2	0	1	17	3	3	0	9
GREECE + TURKEY	12	5	0	0	4	4	2	1	0	1	2	0	0	0	0	8	4	0	1	4
OTHER EUKOPE	40	8	6	2	17	27	10	5	2	16	1	0	0	0	0	4	0	0	0	1
EUROPE EX. U.K.	749	133	173	13	350	198	42	49	7	100	116	21	12	3	80	355	70	112	3	170
SOUTHERN DOMINIONS	157	24	42	1	66	14	5	3	0	6	45	8	6	0	31	74	11	33	1	29
S. AFRICA +RHOD.	44	8	12	0	18	4	2	1	0	1	15	3	3	0	9	19	3	8	0	8
AUSTRALIA + N.Z.	113	16	30	1	48	10	3	2	0	5	30	5	3	0	22	55	26	25	1	21
ASIA + OTHER AFRICA	179	48	33	1	69	22	11	4	0	7	35	11	4	1	19	94	26	25	0	43
JAPAN	37	7	8	0	19	4	2	1	0	1	6	1	1	0	4	24	4	6	0	14
OTHER ASIA+AFR.	142	41	25	1	50	18	9	3	0	6	29	10	3	1	15	70	22	19	0	29
BLACK AFRICA	42	15	3	0	15	8	2	0	0	2	6	2	0	0	4	25	11	3	0	11
ARAB WORLD	26	5	12	1	4	2	2	0	0	0	7	2	2	0	3	11	2	8	0	1
INDIA	16	7	3	1	4	3	3	0	0	0	5	2	1	0	1	6	2	2	0	2
PHILIPPINES	15	4	2	0	6	3	1	0	0	1	4	2	0	0	2	6	1	2	0	3
OTHER E. ASIA	8	3	0	0	6	2	1	0	0	0	0	0	0	0	0	5	2	2	0	3
OTHER ASIA	35	7	5	0	19	7	1	1	0	5	7	2	0	0	5	17	4	4	0	9

CHAPTER 4 – VARIETIES OF ENTRY
SECTION 1 – AN OVERVIEW OF FLOW AND STOCK, MANUFACTURING AND NON-MANUFACTURING
TABLE 12 – SUBSIDIARIES WITH UNKNOWN ACTIVITY CLASSIFIED BY COUNTRY OR REGION,
BY YEAR(S) SUBSIDIARY WAS ACTIVE
AND BY METHOD OF ENTRY

YEAR AND METHOD OF ENTRY
(NEW=NEWLY FORMED, ACQ=ACQUIRED, DES=DESCENDANT, UNK=UNKNOWN)

COUNTRY OR REGION	1929 ALL	NEW	ACQ	DES	UNK	1939 ALL	NEW	ACQ	DES	UNK	1957 ALL	NEW	ACQ	DES	UNK	1967 ALL	NEW	ACQ	DES	UNK
OUTSIDE U.S.	146	48	49	6	43	412	87	76	21	228	789	153	136	38	462	1504	278	329	89	808
OUT. U.S. + CANADA	112	36	38	4	34	319	69	60	19	171	634	129	89	31	385	1248	245	259	80	664
OUT. WEST. HEMIS.	91	31	31	3	26	256	54	50	15	137	437	81	63	25	268	901	157	206	63	475
OUT. WHITE CWEALTH	85	25	32	3	25	239	50	50	16	123	475	105	67	25	278	966	211	192	67	496
OUT. DEVLPED WORLD	23	6	7	1	9	78	21	13	5	39	239	64	31	8	136	444	120	68	26	230
CANADA	34	12	11	2	9	93	18	16	2	57	155	24	47	7	77	256	33	70	9	144
LATIN AMERICA	21	5	7	1	8	63	15	10	4	34	197	48	26	6	117	347	88	53	17	189
C. AMER.+CARIB.	9	2	3	1	3	23	6	6	2	9	95	24	13	2	56	163	43	26	15	89
CUBA	3	0	1	0	2	11	1	0	1	9	17	1	0	1	15	5	0	0	0	5
MEXICO	6	2	2	1	1	10	3	4	1	2	31	9	7	0	14	56	15	11	3	27
OTHER	0	0	0	0	0	2	2	2	0	0	47	14	6	0	27	102	28	15	2	57
S. AMERICA	12	3	4	0	5	40	9	6	2	23	102	24	13	0	61	184	45	27	12	100
ARGENTINA	3	1	1	0	1	15	4	2	1	8	19	4	0	0	15	32	7	7	3	21
BRAZIL	4	1	2	0	1	9	2	2	1	4	25	6	5	0	14	49	9	8	1	31
PERU	1	1	0	0	0	1	1	0	0	0	5	2	0	1	2	11	5	3	1	2
COLOMBIA	2	1	0	0	1	5	1	1	0	4	19	3	3	1	12	28	7	3	2	16
VENEZUELA	2	0	1	0	0	3	0	0	0	3	18	4	4	1	10	36	7	8	2	19
OTHER	2	0	1	0	1	7	1	1	1	4	16	5	1	2	8	28	10	4	3	11
EUROPE	85	27	30	3	25	229	43	46	13	127	338	54	49	22	213	697	105	162	50	380
EFTA	35	14	8	1	12	96	24	12	3	57	160	24	17	7	112	320	37	58	16	209
U.K.	24	8	6	1	9	70	16	9	2	43	104	13	14	5	72	196	19	40	9	128
SCANDINAVIA	6	3	1	0	2	17	4	2	0	11	38	6	1	0	31	67	8	9	3	47
SWITZERLAND	4	3	0	0	1	5	2	2	0	1	13	3	0	1	9	47	9	7	3	28
OTHER EFTA	1	0	1	0	0	2	2	0	0	0	5	2	2	0	0	10	1	2	1	6
EUROP. COMMUNITY	42	11	19	2	10	105	16	29	7	53	161	26	28	13	94	337	56	95	30	156
FRANCE	11	4	4	0	3	28	6	7	2	13	44	11	8	4	23	91	18	24	9	40
GERMANY	15	2	8	1	4	29	2	10	4	13	43	5	8	2	26	100	14	30	9	47
ITALY	8	1	6	0	1	24	2	9	0	13	35	3	8	2	22	75	8	28	7	32
BELGIUM + LUX	6	4	0	0	2	11	5	3	0	3	17	2	5	1	9	34	12	6	5	11
NETHERLANDS	2	0	1	1	0	13	1	3	0	9	22	2	5	1	14	37	4	7	0	26
SPAIN	3	0	1	0	2	7	1	3	0	3	10	1	4	1	4	26	4	7	0	15
GREECE + TURKEY	0	0	0	0	0	1	0	0	0	1	1	1	0	0	0	8	4	0	1	3
OTHER EUROPE	5	2	2	0	1	20	2	2	3	13	6	2	0	1	3	6	4	2	0	0
EUROPE EX. U.K.	61	19	24	2	16	159	27	37	11	84	234	41	35	17	141	501	86	122	41	252
SOUTHERN DOMINIONS	3	3	0	0	0	9	3	1	1	4	52	9	8	1	34	82	14	25	4	39
S. AFRICA +RHOD.	1	1	0	0	0	4	1	1	1	1	19	4	4	1	10	26	4	10	3	9
AUSTRALIA + N.Z.	2	2	0	0	0	5	2	0	0	3	33	5	4	0	24	56	10	15	1	30
ASIA + OTHER AFRICA	3	1	0	0	2	18	8	3	0	7	47	18	6	2	21	122	38	19	9	56
JAPAN	1	0	0	0	1	3	2	0	0	1	5	2	1	0	2	25	6	4	0	15
OTHER ASIA+AFR.	2	1	0	0	1	15	6	3	0	6	42	16	5	2	19	97	32	15	9	41
BLACK AFRICA	1	1	0	0	0	3	2	0	0	1	8	2	0	0	6	30	11	10	5	4
ARAB WORLD	0	0	0	0	0	3	1	2	0	0	8	2	3	0	3	15	4	3	2	6
INDIA	0	0	0	0	0	2	1	0	0	1	8	5	0	0	3	12	7	2	0	3
PHILIPPINES	0	0	0	0	0	1	1	0	0	0	4	2	1	1	0	10	2	0	0	8
OTHER E. ASIA	0	0	0	0	0	1	1	0	0	0	1	0	0	0	1	4	2	0	0	2
OTHER ASIA	1	0	0	0	1	5	0	1	0	4	13	3	1	0	9	26	6	0	2	18

CHAPTER 4— VARIETIES OF ENTRY
SECTION 2— THE FLOW OF MANUFACTURING BY INDUSTRY OF PARENT SYSTEM
TABLE 1— MANUFACTURING SUBSIDIARIES IN A SYSTEM IN THE
MEAT AND DAIRY INDUSTRIES (SIC 201 AND 202)
CLASSIFIED BY COUNTRY, PERIOD MANUFACTURE BEGAN, AND METHOD OF ENTRY

PERIOD AND METHOD OF ENTRY
(NEW=NEWLY FORMED, ACQ=ACQUIRED, DES=DESCENDANT, UNK=UNKNOWN)

COUNTRY OR REGION	TOTAL PRE 1968					PRE 1946					1946-1957					1958-1967				
	ALL	NEW	ACQ	DES	UNK	ALL	NEW	ACQ	DES	UNK	ALL	NEW	ACQ	DES	UNK	ALL	NEW	ACQ	DES	UNK
OUTSIDE U.S.	291	101	163	12	7	74	37	32	0	5	44	19	21	3	1	165	45	110	9	1
OUT. U.S. + CANADA	239	91	126	10	7	59	32	22	0	5	39	17	18	3	1	136	42	86	7	1
OUT. WEST. HEMIS.	137	53	77	3	2	36	17	17	0	2	20	7	12	1	0	79	29	48	2	0
OUT. WHITE CWEALTH	180	74	89	8	6	40	22	14	0	4	30	17	10	2	1	107	35	65	6	1
OUT. DEVLPED WORLD	120	53	55	7	5	25	15	7	0	3	23	13	7	2	1	69	22	41	5	1
CANADA	52	10	37	2	0	15	5	10	0	0	5	2	3	0	0	29	3	24	2	0
LATIN AMERICA	102	38	49	7	5	23	15	5	0	3	19	10	6	2	1	57	13	38	5	1
C. AMER.+CARIB.	48	19	21	6	0	8	6	2	0	0	10	5	3	2	0	28	8	16	4	0
CUBA	9	4	2	2	0	5	3	2	0	0	0	0	0	0	0	0	0	0	0	0
MEXICO	18	6	11	1	0	0	0	0	0	0	6	1	4	0	1	12	2	9	1	0
OTHER	21	9	8	3	0	3	3	0	0	0	1	0	2	2	0	16	6	7	3	0
S. AMERICA	54	19	28	3	5	15	9	3	0	3	9	5	3	0	1	29	5	22	1	1
ARGENTINA	9	5	4	0	0	5	4	1	0	0	1	1	0	0	0	3	2	3	0	0
BRAZIL	12	7	4	1	0	4	3	1	0	0	3	1	2	0	0	5	2	2	1	0
PERU	4	2	1	0	1	3	2	0	0	1	0	0	0	0	0	1	0	1	0	0
COLOMBIA	15	4	13	0	1	1	1	0	0	0	2	0	2	0	0	12	1	10	0	0
VENEZUELA	9	4	3	1	2	1	0	0	0	1	3	2	0	0	1	5	2	3	0	0
OTHER	5	0	3	1	1	1	0	0	0	1	0	0	0	0	0	3	0	3	0	0
EUROPE	88	33	51	2	2	26	12	12	0	2	10	4	6	0	0	52	17	33	2	0
EFTA	36	14	18	2	2	12	5	5	0	2	4	3	1	0	0	20	6	12	2	0
U.K.	26	8	16	1	1	11	5	5	0	1	4	3	1	0	0	14	3	10	1	0
SCANDINAVIA	10	6	2	1	1	1	0	0	0	1	0	0	0	0	0	6	3	2	1	0
SWITZERLAND	0	0	0	0	0	0	0	0	0	0	0	0	0	0	0	0	0	0	0	0
OTHER EFTA	0	0	0	0	0	0	0	0	0	0	0	0	0	0	0	0	0	0	0	0
EUROP. COMMUNITY	38	14	24	0	0	14	7	7	0	0	4	1	3	0	0	20	6	14	0	0
FRANCE	6	4	2	0	0	3	1	2	0	0	0	0	0	0	0	3	3	0	0	0
GERMANY	15	4	11	0	0	7	3	4	0	0	4	1	3	0	0	5	1	4	0	0
ITALY	4	2	2	0	0	0	0	0	0	0	0	0	0	0	0	4	2	2	0	0
BELGIUM + LUX	5	0	5	0	0	0	0	0	0	0	0	0	0	0	0	5	0	5	0	0
NETHERLANDS	8	2	5	0	0	4	3	1	0	0	1	1	0	0	0	3	0	3	0	0
SPAIN	7	2	5	0	0	0	0	0	0	0	0	0	0	0	0	7	2	5	0	0
GREECE + TURKEY	0	0	0	0	0	0	0	0	0	0	0	0	0	0	0	0	0	0	0	0
OTHER EUROPE	7	3	4	0	0	0	0	0	0	0	0	0	0	0	0	5	3	2	0	0
EUROPE EX. U.K.	62	25	35	1	1	15	7	7	0	1	9	4	5	0	0	38	14	23	1	0
SOUTHERN DOMINIONS	26	6	17	1	0	8	5	3	0	0	6	0	5	1	0	10	1	9	0	0
S. AFRICA +RHOD.	3	1	0	1	0	1	1	0	0	0	1	0	0	1	0	0	0	0	0	0
AUSTRALIA + N.Z.	23	14	17	0	0	7	4	3	0	0	5	0	5	0	0	10	1	9	0	0
ASIA + OTHER AFRICA	23	14	9	0	0	2	2	0	0	0	4	3	1	0	0	17	11	6	0	0
JAPAN	5	2	3	0	0	0	0	0	0	0	0	0	0	0	0	5	2	3	0	0
OTHER ASIA+AFR.	18	12	6	0	0	2	2	0	0	0	4	3	1	0	0	12	9	3	0	0
BLACK AFRICA	1	1	0	0	0	0	0	0	0	0	0	0	0	0	0	1	1	0	0	0
ARAB WORLD	2	0	1	1	0	0	0	0	0	0	0	0	0	0	0	2	0	1	1	0
INDIA	0	0	0	0	0	0	0	0	0	0	0	0	0	0	0	0	0	0	0	0
PHILIPPINES	5	4	1	0	0	0	0	0	0	0	1	1	0	0	0	3	3	0	0	0
OTHER E. ASIA	4	2	2	0	0	2	0	2	0	0	1	1	0	0	0	1	1	0	0	0
OTHER ASIA	6	5	1	0	0	0	0	0	0	0	0	0	0	0	0	5	4	1	0	0

CHAPTER 4- VARIETIES OF ENTRY
SECTION 2- THE FLOW OF MANUFACTURING BY INDUSTRY OF PARENT SYSTEM
TABLE 2- MANUFACTURING SUBSIDIARIES IN A SYSTEM IN THE
OTHER FOOD AND BEVERAGE INDUSTRIES (SIC 203-209)
CLASSIFIED BY COUNTRY, PERIOD MANUFACTURE BEGAN, AND METHOD OF ENTRY

PERIOD AND METHOD OF ENTRY
(NEW=NEWLY FORMED, ACQ=ACQUIRED, DES=DESCENDANT, UNK=UNKNOWN)

COUNTRY OR REGION	TOTAL PRE 1968					PRE 1946					1946-1957					1958-1967				
	ALL	NEW	ACQ	DES	UNK	ALL	NEW	ACQ	DES	UNK	ALL	NEW	ACQ	DES	UNK	ALL	NEW	ACQ	DES	UNK
OUTSIDE U.S.	503	150	282	20	43	105	36	46	5	18	86	33	44	4	5	304	81	192	11	20
OUT. U.S. + CANADA	402	132	209	17	38	64	25	21	4	14	63	31	25	2	5	269	76	163	11	19
OUT. WEST. HEMIS.	260	76	142	12	25	50	17	20	4	9	37	18	14	2	3	168	41	108	11	13
OUT. WHITE CWEALTH	311	104	158	13	31	32	14	8	1	9	53	26	21	1	5	221	64	129	11	17
OUT. DEVLPED WORLD	163	65	74	6	17	18	10	2	0	6	31	16	13	0	2	113	39	59	6	9
CANADA	101	18	73	3	5	41	11	25	1	4	23	2	19	2	0	35	5	29	0	1
LATIN AMERICA	142	56	67	5	13	14	8	1	0	5	26	13	11	0	2	101	35	55	5	6
C. AMER.+CARIB.	82	29	41	4	8	9	4	0	0	5	14	7	5	0	1	59	18	36	4	1
CUBA	8	3	3	1	1	4	1	0	0	3	2	1	1	0	0	2	1	1	0	0
MEXICO	50	18	26	4	2	3	2	0	0	1	10	5	4	0	1	37	11	22	4	0
OTHER	24	8	14	0	2	2	1	0	0	1	2	1	1	0	0	20	6	13	0	1
S. AMERICA	60	27	26	1	5	5	4	1	0	0	12	6	6	0	0	42	17	19	1	5
ARGENTINA	10	4	5	0	1	2	2	0	0	0	1	1	0	0	0	7	2	4	0	1
BRAZIL	10	4	6	0	0	2	1	1	0	0	2	1	0	1	0	6	2	4	0	0
PERU	8	3	4	0	1	2	1	0	1	0	2	2	0	0	0	6	1	4	0	1
COLOMBIA	8	4	3	0	1	1	0	0	0	1	2	1	1	0	0	4	4	0	0	0
VENEZUELA	14	4	7	1	2	0	0	0	0	0	4	3	0	0	1	10	4	0	1	1
OTHER	9	4	3	0	2	0	0	0	0	0	0	0	0	0	0	9	4	3	0	2
EUROPE	188	43	112	11	17	38	9	18	4	7	26	9	12	2	3	119	25	82	5	7
EFTA	70	16	41	4	8	25	5	13	3	4	8	2	4	1	1	36	9	24	0	3
U.K.	48	11	28	4	4	23	5	12	3	3	5	1	3	1	0	19	5	13	0	1
SCANDINAVIA	14	3	9	0	2	2	0	1	0	1	2	1	1	0	0	10	2	5	0	3
SWITZERLAND	2	0	1	0	1	0	0	0	0	0	1	0	0	0	1	2	0	2	0	0
OTHER EFTA	6	2	3	0	1	0	0	0	0	0	0	0	0	0	0	6	2	3	0	1
EUROP. COMMUNITY	98	21	59	7	7	10	3	5	1	1	14	7	4	2	1	70	11	50	5	4
FRANCE	26	6	17	2	1	1	0	0	0	1	4	2	2	0	0	23	4	16	2	1
GERMANY	29	7	13	2	4	3	1	1	0	1	2	2	0	0	0	17	2	11	1	3
ITALY	15	2	11	1	1	2	1	0	0	1	1	1	0	0	0	12	2	10	1	3
BELGIUM + LUX	13	4	7	1	0	2	1	1	0	0	2	1	1	0	0	9	2	7	1	0
NETHERLANDS	15	2	11	0	1	2	0	1	0	1	1	1	0	0	0	10	2	6	0	0
SPAIN	15	5	9	0	1	0	0	0	0	0	3	0	3	0	0	10	4	6	1	0
GREECE + TURKEY	2	1	0	0	0	1	1	0	0	0	0	0	0	0	0	2	1	1	0	0
OTHER EUROPE	3	0	2	0	1	0	0	0	0	0	1	1	0	0	0	1	0	0	0	0
EUROPE EX. U.K.	140	32	84	7	13	15	4	6	1	4	21	8	9	1	3	100	20	69	5	6
SOUTHERN DOMINIONS	40	17	21	0	2	8	6	1	0	1	4	4	0	0	0	28	7	20	0	1
S. AFRICA +RHOD.	15	8	7	0	0	3	2	1	0	0	2	2	0	0	0	10	4	6	0	0
AUSTRALIA + N.Z.	25	9	14	0	2	5	4	0	0	1	2	2	0	0	0	18	3	14	0	1
ASIA + OTHER AFRICA	32	16	9	0	6	4	2	0	0	1	7	5	2	0	0	21	9	6	1	5
JAPAN	11	7	2	1	2	4	2	2	0	0	2	2	0	0	0	9	5	2	0	2
OTHER ASIA+AFR.	21	9	7	1	4	0	0	0	0	0	5	3	2	0	0	12	4	4	1	3
BLACK AFRICA	2	1	1	0	0	0	0	0	0	0	1	1	0	0	0	1	0	1	0	0
ARAB WORLD	2	0	2	0	0	0	0	0	0	0	1	0	1	0	0	1	0	0	0	0
INDIA	1	1	0	0	0	1	1	0	0	0	0	0	0	0	0	0	1	1	0	0
PHILIPPINES	7	3	3	0	1	2	1	1	0	0	2	1	1	0	0	3	3	1	0	1
OTHER E. ASIA	6	3	0	1	2	1	0	0	0	1	0	0	0	0	0	5	3	0	1	1
OTHER ASIA	3	1	1	0	1	0	0	0	0	0	1	1	0	0	0	2	0	1	0	1

CHAPTER 4— VARIETIES OF ENTRY
SECTION 2— THE FLOW OF MANUFACTURING BY INDUSTRY OF PARENT SYSTEM
TABLE 3— MANUFACTURING SUBSIDIARIES IN A SYSTEM IN THE
TEXTILE AND APPAREL INDUSTRIES (SIC 22 AND 23)
CLASSIFIED BY COUNTRY, PERIOD MANUFACTURE BEGAN, AND METHOD OF ENTRY

PERIOD AND METHOD OF ENTRY
(NEW=NEWLY FORMED, ACQ=ACQUIRED, DES=DESCENDANT, UNK=UNKNOWN)

COUNTRY OR REGION	TOTAL PRE 1968					PRE 1946					1946-1957					1958-1967				
	ALL	NEW	ACQ	DES	UNK	ALL	NEW	ACQ	DES	UNK	ALL	NEW	ACQ	DES	UNK	ALL	NEW	ACQ	DES	UNK
OUTSIDE U.S.	76	47	18	4	3	6	4	1	1	0	19	13	3	3	0	47	30	14	0	3
OUT. U.S. + CANADA	58	39	11	2	3	4	4	0	0	0	12	9	1	2	0	41	28	10	0	3
OUT. WEST. HEMIS.	33	20	9	2	3	2	2	0	0	0	12	9	0	2	0	32	20	9	0	3
OUT. WHITE CWEALTH	44	31	6	2	2	2	2	0	0	0	12	9	1	1	0	27	20	5	0	2
OUT. DEVLPED WORLD	25	19	2	2	0	2	0	0	0	0	12	9	1	2	0	9	8	1	0	0
CANADA	18	8	7	2	0	4	2	1	1	0	7	4	2	1	0	6	2	4	0	0
LATIN AMERICA	25	19	2	2	0	2	2	0	0	0	12	9	1	2	0	9	8	1	0	0
C. AMER.+CARIB.	8	4	2	1	0	0	0	0	0	0	4	2	1	1	0	3	2	1	0	0
CUBA	2	0	1	1	0	0	0	0	0	0	1	0	0	1	0	0	0	0	0	0
MEXICO	6	4	0	1	0	0	0	0	0	0	3	2	1	0	0	3	2	0	1	0
OTHER	0	0	0	0	0	0	0	0	0	0	0	0	0	0	0	0	0	0	0	0
S. AMERICA	17	15	1	0	0	2	2	0	0	0	8	7	1	0	0	6	6	0	0	0
ARGENTINA	2	1	0	0	0	1	1	0	0	0	0	0	0	0	0	1	0	0	0	0
BRAZIL	3	3	0	0	0	0	0	0	0	0	2	2	0	0	0	1	1	0	0	0
PERU	0	0	0	0	0	0	0	0	0	0	0	0	0	0	0	0	0	0	0	0
COLOMBIA	4	3	0	1	0	0	0	0	0	0	1	0	1	0	0	3	3	0	0	0
VENEZUELA	6	6	0	0	0	1	1	0	0	0	3	3	0	0	0	2	2	0	0	0
OTHER	2	2	0	0	0	0	0	0	0	0	2	2	0	0	0	0	0	0	0	0
EUROPE	28	17	8	0	2	0	0	0	0	0	0	0	0	0	0	27	17	8	0	2
EFTA	14	7	6	0	1	0	0	0	0	0	0	0	0	0	0	14	7	6	0	1
U.K.	11	5	5	0	1	0	0	0	0	0	0	0	0	0	0	11	5	5	0	1
SCANDINAVIA	0	0	0	0	0	0	0	0	0	0	0	0	0	0	0	0	0	0	0	0
SWITZERLAND	2	1	0	0	0	0	0	0	0	0	0	0	0	0	0	2	1	0	0	0
OTHER EFTA	1	1	0	0	1	0	0	0	0	0	0	0	0	0	0	1	1	0	0	1
EUROP. COMMUNITY	11	7	2	0	1	0	0	0	0	0	0	0	0	0	0	10	7	2	0	1
FRANCE	4	1	1	0	1	0	0	0	0	0	0	0	0	0	0	3	1	1	0	1
GERMANY	3	2	1	0	0	0	0	0	0	0	0	0	0	0	0	3	2	1	0	0
ITALY	3	3	0	0	0	0	0	0	0	0	0	0	0	0	0	3	3	0	0	0
BELGIUM + LUX	0	0	0	0	0	0	0	0	0	0	0	0	0	0	0	0	0	0	0	0
NETHERLANDS	1	1	0	0	0	0	0	0	0	0	0	0	0	0	0	1	1	0	0	0
SPAIN	3	3	0	0	0	0	0	0	0	0	0	0	0	0	0	3	3	0	0	0
GREECE + TURKEY	0	0	0	0	0	0	0	0	0	0	0	0	0	0	0	0	0	0	0	0
OTHER EUROPE	0	0	0	0	0	0	0	0	0	0	0	0	0	0	0	0	0	0	0	0
EUROPE EX. U.K.	17	12	3	0	1	0	0	0	0	0	0	0	0	0	0	16	12	3	0	1
SOUTHERN DOMINIONS	3	3	0	0	0	0	0	0	0	0	0	0	0	0	0	3	3	0	0	0
S. AFRICA +RHOD.	2	2	0	0	0	0	0	0	0	0	0	0	0	0	0	2	2	0	0	0
AUSTRALIA + N.Z.	1	1	0	0	1	0	0	0	0	0	0	0	0	0	0	1	1	0	0	1
ASIA + OTHER AFRICA	2	2	0	1	1	0	0	0	0	0	0	0	0	0	0	2	2	0	1	1
JAPAN	2	2	0	0	0	0	0	0	0	0	0	0	0	0	0	2	2	0	0	0
OTHER ASIA+AFR.	0	0	0	0	0	0	0	0	0	0	0	0	0	0	0	0	0	0	0	0
BLACK AFRICA	0	0	0	0	0	0	0	0	0	0	0	0	0	0	0	0	0	0	0	0
ARAB WORLD	0	0	0	0	0	0	0	0	0	0	0	0	0	0	0	0	0	0	0	0
INDIA	0	0	0	0	0	0	0	0	0	0	0	0	0	0	0	0	0	0	0	0
PHILIPPINES	0	0	0	0	0	0	0	0	0	0	0	0	0	0	0	0	0	0	0	0
OTHER E. ASIA	0	0	0	0	0	0	0	0	0	0	0	0	0	0	0	0	0	0	0	0
OTHER ASIA	0	0	0	0	0	0	0	0	0	0	0	0	0	0	0	0	0	0	0	0

CHAPTER 4- VARIETIES OF ENTRY
SECTION 2- THE FLOW OF MANUFACTURING BY INDUSTRY OF PARENT SYSTEM
TABLE 4- MANUFACTURING SUBSIDIARIES IN A SYSTEM IN THE
LUMBER, FURNITURE, AND PAPER INDUSTRIES (SIC 24,25,26)
CLASSIFIED BY COUNTRY, PERIOD MANUFACTURE BEGAN, AND METHOD OF ENTRY

PERIOD AND METHOD OF ENTRY
(NEW=NEWLY FORMED, ACQ=ACQUIRED, DES=DESCENDANT, UNK=UNKNOWN)

COUNTRY OR REGION	TOTAL ALL	TOTAL NEW	PRE 1968 ACQ	TOTAL DES	TOTAL UNK	PRE 1946 ALL	NEW	ACQ	DES	UNK	1946-1957 ALL	NEW	ACQ	DES	UNK	1958-1967 ALL	NEW	ACQ	DES	UNK
OUTSIDE U.S.	182	45	123	3	8	17	7	7	0	3	35	8	25	0	2	127	30	91	3	3
OUT. U.S. + CANADA	149	37	103	1	3	8	4	4	0	2	22	8	14	0	0	118	27	85	3	3
OUT. WEST. HEMIS.	110	23	80	2	4	4	0	3	0	1	12	4	8	0	0	93	19	69	2	3
OUT. WHITE CWEALTH	94	32	56	2	3	7	3	3	0	2	15	7	8	0	0	71	23	45	2	2
OUT. DEVLPED WORLD	49	18	29	1	1	4	2	1	0	1	11	5	6	0	0	34	11	22	1	0
CANADA	33	8	20	0	3	9	5	3	0	1	13	0	11	0	2	9	3	6	0	0
LATIN AMERICA	39	14	23	1	1	4	2	1	0	1	10	4	6	0	0	25	8	16	1	0
C. AMER.+CARIB.	21	6	14	1	0	1	1	1	0	0	6	1	5	0	0	13	4	8	1	0
CUBA	1	0	1	0	0	1	0	1	0	0	0	0	0	0	0	0	0	0	0	0
MEXICO	10	3	7	0	0	0	0	0	0	0	3	1	5	0	0	6	1	2	0	0
OTHER	10	3	6	1	0	0	0	0	0	0	0	0	0	0	0	10	3	6	1	0
S. AMERICA	18	8	9	0	1	2	1	0	0	1	4	3	1	0	0	12	4	8	0	0
ARGENTINA	2	0	2	0	0	0	0	0	0	0	0	0	0	0	0	2	2	0	0	0
BRAZIL	1	0	1	0	0	0	0	0	0	0	0	0	0	0	0	1	0	1	0	0
PERU	0	0	0	0	0	0	0	0	0	0	0	0	0	0	0	0	0	0	0	0
COLUMBIA	4	3	0	0	1	2	1	0	0	1	1	0	1	0	0	1	2	0	0	0
VENEZUELA	9	4	5	0	0	0	0	0	0	0	3	0	0	0	0	4	1	4	0	0
OTHER	2	1	1	0	0	0	0	0	0	0	0	0	0	0	0	2	1	1	0	0
EUROPE	52	15	33	1	2	3	3	0	1	0	8	3	5	0	0	40	12	26	1	1
EFTA	10	4	6	0	0	0	0	0	0	0	4	1	3	0	0	6	3	3	0	0
U.K.	9	3	6	0	0	0	0	0	0	0	4	1	3	0	0	5	2	3	0	0
SCANDINAVIA	1	1	0	0	0	0	0	0	0	0	0	0	0	0	0	1	1	0	0	0
SWITZERLAND	0	0	0	0	0	0	0	0	0	0	0	0	0	0	0	0	0	0	0	0
OTHER EFTA	0	0	0	0	0	0	0	0	0	0	0	0	0	0	0	0	0	0	0	0
EUROP. COMMUNITY	33	7	23	0	3	3	3	0	0	0	4	2	2	0	0	25	5	19	0	1
FRANCE	10	1	9	0	0	1	1	0	0	0	2	0	2	0	0	7	1	6	0	0
GERMANY	6	2	4	0	0	1	1	0	0	0	2	0	2	0	0	3	2	1	0	0
ITALY	10	2	7	0	1	1	1	0	0	0	2	0	2	0	0	9	2	7	0	0
BELGIUM + LUX	5	2	2	1	0	0	0	0	0	0	0	0	0	0	0	4	2	2	1	0
NETHERLANDS	2	0	2	0	0	0	0	0	0	0	0	0	0	0	0	2	0	2	0	0
SPAIN	7	2	4	0	1	0	0	0	0	0	0	0	0	0	0	7	2	4	0	1
GREECE + TURKEY	1	1	0	0	0	0	0	0	0	0	0	0	0	0	0	1	1	0	0	0
OTHER EUROPE	1	1	0	0	0	0	0	0	0	0	0	0	0	0	0	1	0	0	0	1
EUROPE EX. U.K.	43	12	27	1	2	3	3	0	1	0	4	2	2	0	0	35	10	23	1	1
SOUTHERN DOMINIONS	46	2	41	1	2	1	0	1	0	0	3	0	3	0	0	42	2	37	1	2
S. AFRICA +RHOD.	33	1	32	0	0	1	0	1	0	0	1	0	1	0	0	31	1	31	0	0
AUSTRALIA + N.Z.	13	1	9	1	2	0	0	0	0	0	2	0	2	0	0	10	1	6	1	2
ASIA + OTHER AFRICA	12	6	6	0	0	0	0	0	0	0	1	1	0	0	0	11	5	6	0	0
JAPAN	2	2	0	0	0	0	0	0	0	0	0	0	0	0	0	2	2	0	0	0
OTHER ASIA+AFR.	10	4	6	0	0	0	0	0	0	0	1	1	0	0	0	9	3	6	0	0
BLACK AFRICA	2	0	2	0	0	0	0	0	0	0	0	0	0	0	0	2	0	2	0	0
ARAB WORLD	0	0	0	0	0	0	0	0	0	0	0	0	0	0	0	0	0	0	0	0
INDIA	1	0	1	0	0	0	0	0	0	0	0	0	0	0	0	1	0	1	0	0
PHILIPPINES	4	0	4	0	0	0	0	0	0	0	0	0	0	0	0	4	0	4	0	0
OTHER E. ASIA	0	0	0	0	0	0	0	0	0	0	0	0	0	0	0	0	0	0	0	0
OTHER ASIA	3	2	1	0	0	0	0	0	0	0	1	0	0	0	0	2	1	1	0	0

270

CHAPTER 4- VARIETIES OF ENTRY
SECTION 2- THE FLOW OF MANUFACTURING BY INDUSTRY OF PARENT SYSTEM
TABLE 5- MANUFACTURING SUBSIDIARIES IN A SYSTEM IN THE
CHEMICAL INDUSTRIES (SIC 281,282,285-289)
CLASSIFIED BY COUNTRY, PERIOD MANUFACTURE BEGAN, AND METHOD OF ENTRY

PERIOD AND METHOD OF ENTRY
(NEW=NEWLY FORMED, ACQ=ACQUIRED, DES=DESCENDANT, UNK=UNKNOWN)

COUNTRY OR REGION	TOTAL PKE 1968					PRE 1946					1946-1957					1958-1967				
	ALL	NEW	ACQ	DES	UNK	ALL	NEW	ACQ	DES	UNK	ALL	NEW	ACQ	DES	UNK	ALL	NEW	ACQ	DES	UNK
OUTSIDE U.S.	813	358	299	31	64	169	53	36	7	21	169	94	50	9	16	466	211	213	15	27
OUT. U.S. + CANADA	682	314	244	25	45	135	35	23	2	10	135	76	38	8	13	423	203	183	15	22
OUT. WEST. HEMIS.	436	196	159	16	32	67	20	12	1	6	67	37	17	3	10	297	139	130	12	16
OUT. WHITE CMWEALTH	540	254	190	16	35	106	22	17	1	9	106	61	30	6	6	340	171	143	9	17
OUT. DEVLPED WORLD	300	146	93	12	18	76	16	11	1	4	76	42	22	6	6	161	88	60	5	8
CANADA	131	44	55	6	19	34	18	13	5	11	34	18	12	1	3	43	8	30	0	5
LATIN AMERICA	246	118	85	9	13	68	15	11	1	4	68	39	21	5	3	126	64	53	3	6
C. AMER.+CARIB.	95	43	33	5	0	21	5	1	0	0	21	12	6	3	0	56	26	26	2	2
CUBA	1	1	0	0	2	1	1	0	0	0	1	0	0	0	0	0	0	0	0	1
MEXICO	72	31	28	2	5	19	5	1	0	0	19	10	6	0	0	38	16	21	0	1
OTHER	22	11	5	3	11	1	0	0	0	0	1	1	0	3	0	18	10	5	2	1
S. AMERICA	151	75	52	11	11	47	10	10	1	4	47	27	15	2	3	70	38	27	1	4
ARGENTINA	33	15	11	3	4	7	4	0	1	2	7	5	1	0	0	12	6	4	1	1
BRAZIL	41	20	16	1	3	17	2	6	0	0	17	7	8	1	1	20	11	8	0	1
PERU	14	4	8	0	1	1	0	2	0	0	1	0	1	0	0	6	2	3	0	1
COLOMBIA	25	16	8	0	0	8	2	0	0	0	8	6	2	0	0	16	10	6	0	0
VENEZUELA	16	12	2	0	2	9	0	0	0	0	9	7	1	0	1	7	5	1	1	0
OTHER	22	8	9	0	3	5	2	2	0	2	5	2	2	0	1	9	4	5	0	0
EUROPE	268	109	119	11	24	45	13	10	1	2	45	26	11	2	6	188	70	98	8	12
EFTA	83	35	32	8	6	22	7	6	1	1	22	12	5	2	2	44	16	21	5	2
U.K.	63	25	24	8	7	21	7	4	1	1	21	12	4	2	3	29	6	16	5	2
SCANDINAVIA	14	6	6	0	2	1	0	2	0	0	1	0	1	0	0	9	3	6	0	0
SWITZERLAND	3	1	2	0	0	0	0	0	0	0	0	0	0	0	0	3	1	2	0	0
OTHER EFTA	3	3	0	0	0	0	0	0	0	0	0	0	0	0	0	3	3	0	0	0
EUROP. COMMUNITY	146	60	65	3	14	18	6	3	0	4	18	11	5	0	2	111	43	57	3	8
FRANCE	35	11	15	2	6	6	1	1	0	2	6	4	3	0	1	25	6	14	2	3
GERMANY	34	15	15	1	3	6	3	0	0	1	6	3	1	0	1	24	9	12	1	2
ITALY	38	15	19	0	4	5	0	2	0	0	5	3	2	0	0	30	12	15	0	3
BELGIUM + LUX	20	10	10	0	0	0	0	0	0	0	0	0	0	0	0	19	7	10	2	0
NETHERLANDS	19	9	6	0	1	2	1	0	0	1	2	1	0	0	0	13	7	6	0	0
SPAIN	27	8	17	1	2	4	1	0	0	0	4	2	1	0	1	22	6	15	1	0
GREECE + TURKEY	6	6	0	0	1	1	0	0	0	0	1	1	0	0	0	6	5	0	0	1
OTHER EUROPE	6	0	5	0	1	0	0	0	0	0	0	0	0	0	0	6	5	5	0	1
EUROPE EX. U.K.	205	84	95	3	18	24	6	6	0	5	24	14	7	0	3	159	64	82	3	10
SOUTHERN DOMINIONS	74	35	26	1	3	8	2	2	0	0	8	3	4	0	1	49	26	20	1	2
S. AFRICA +RHOD.	13	6	1	1	1	2	1	0	0	0	2	1	1	0	0	5	3	0	1	1
AUSTRALIA + N.Z.	61	29	25	0	2	6	1	2	0	0	6	2	3	0	1	44	23	20	0	1
ASIA + OTHER AFRICA	94	52	14	4	5	14	4	0	0	0	14	8	2	1	3	60	43	12	3	2
JAPAN	40	24	8	4	5	6	1	0	0	0	6	5	1	0	0	25	19	5	1	0
OTHER ASIA+AFR.	54	28	8	3	6	8	3	0	0	0	8	3	1	1	3	35	24	7	0	2
BLACK AFRICA	7	4	0	0	1	0	0	0	0	0	0	0	0	0	0	5	4	0	0	1
ARAB WORLD	1	1	0	0	0	0	0	0	0	0	0	0	0	0	0	1	1	0	0	0
INDIA	12	5	5	0	1	2	1	0	0	0	2	2	0	0	1	8	2	3	3	0
PHILIPPINES	7	4	0	1	1	2	1	0	0	0	2	1	0	1	1	6	3	1	1	1
OTHER E. ASIA	9	4	2	1	1	1	0	0	0	0	1	0	0	0	0	3	0	1	0	0
OTHER ASIA	18	10	1	0	2	1	0	0	0	2	1	0	1	0	1	12	10	1	0	1

CHAPTER 4- VARIETIES OF ENTRY
SECTION 2- THE FLOW OF MANUFACTURING BY INDUSTRY OF PARENT SYSTEM
TABLE 6- MANUFACTURING SUBSIDIARIES IN A SYSTEM IN THE
DRUG INDUSTRY (SIC 283)
CLASSIFIED BY COUNTRY, PERIOD MANUFACTURE BEGAN, AND METHOD OF ENTRY

PERIOD AND METHOD OF ENTRY
(NEW=NEWLY FORMED, ACQ=ACQUIRED, DES=DESCENDANT, UNK=UNKNOWN)

COUNTRY OR REGION	TOTAL PRE 1968 ALL	NEW	ACQ	DES	UNK	PRE 1946 ALL	NEW	ACQ	DES	UNK	1946-1957 ALL	NEW	ACQ	DES	UNK	1958-1967 ALL	NEW	ACQ	DES	UNK
OUTSIDE U.S.	473	228	176	29	37	84	60	12	1	11	121	58	35	14	14	265	110	129	14	12
OUT. U.S. + CANADA	425	202	160	27	33	63	43	10	1	9	108	52	31	13	12	251	107	119	13	12
OUT. WEST. HEMIS.	296	139	117	16	22	43	31	6	1	5	65	33	22	4	6	186	75	89	11	11
OUT. WHITE CWEALTH	305	151	112	18	23	26	17	5	0	4	75	39	16	11	9	203	95	91	7	10
OUT. DEVLPED WORLD	175	91	53	12	18	20	12	5	0	4	52	25	11	9	7	102	54	38	3	7
CANADA	48	26	16	2	4	21	17	2	0	2	13	6	4	1	2	14	3	10	1	0
LATIN AMERICA	129	63	43	11	11	20	12	4	0	4	43	19	9	5	6	65	32	30	2	1
C. AMER.+CARIB.	57	26	18	7	5	6	4	0	1	1	19	8	1	5	3	31	14	14	2	1
CUBA	1	1	0	0	0	0	0	0	0	0	1	1	0	0	0	0	0	0	0	0
MEXICO	33	13	16	3	1	5	4	0	1	0	9	4	3	2	0	19	5	12	0	1
OTHER	23	12	2	4	3	1	0	1	0	0	9	3	0	3	3	12	9	2	1	0
S. AMERICA	72	37	25	4	6	14	8	3	0	3	24	11	6	4	3	34	18	16	0	0
ARGENTINA	15	6	7	2	0	7	4	2	1	0	5	2	2	1	0	3	0	3	0	0
BRAZIL	21	10	7	3	1	1	1	0	0	0	12	5	5	1	1	8	4	2	2	0
PERU	7	3	0	1	3	2	1	0	0	1	1	1	0	0	0	4	1	0	1	2
COLOMBIA	9	3	6	0	0	1	0	1	0	0	2	1	1	0	0	6	2	4	0	0
VENEZUELA	10	9	0	1	0	1	1	0	0	0	0	0	0	0	0	9	8	0	1	0
OTHER	10	6	1	2	1	2	1	0	1	0	4	2	0	2	2	4	3	1	0	0
EUROPE	181	68	94	9	8	24	15	6	1	2	38	17	17	2	2	117	36	71	6	4
EFTA	72	23	39	4	4	19	11	5	1	2	19	5	12	1	1	32	7	22	2	2
U.K.	60	16	35	4	3	18	10	5	1	0	17	4	12	0	1	23	2	18	2	1
SCANDINAVIA	2	1	1	0	0	0	0	0	0	0	1	0	0	0	0	2	1	0	0	1
SWITZERLAND	6	4	2	0	0	0	0	0	0	0	0	0	0	0	0	3	1	2	0	0
OTHER EFTA	4	2	2	0	0	1	1	0	0	0	1	1	0	0	0	2	0	1	0	1
EUROP. COMMUNITY	92	39	47	2	2	1	1	0	0	0	18	11	5	1	1	69	24	41	3	1
FRANCE	29	8	20	0	1	2	1	1	0	0	4	2	2	0	0	23	6	17	0	0
GERMANY	21	6	13	0	2	2	2	0	0	0	8	6	2	0	0	17	4	11	2	0
ITALY	24	13	9	0	2	0	0	0	0	0	2	0	1	0	1	16	7	8	1	0
BELGIUM + LUX	10	6	3	0	1	0	0	0	0	0	2	2	1	0	0	8	4	3	0	1
NETHERLANDS	8	2	2	2	2	1	0	0	1	0	2	2	0	1	0	5	3	2	0	0
SPAIN	10	3	7	0	0	0	0	0	0	0	2	0	0	0	0	10	2	7	1	0
GREECE + TURKEY	6	1	1	0	2	0	0	0	0	0	0	0	0	0	0	6	0	3	0	2
OTHER EUROPE	1	1	0	0	1	0	0	0	0	0	1	1	0	0	0	0	0	1	0	0
EUROPE EX. U.K.	121	52	59	5	5	6	5	1	0	1	21	13	5	2	2	94	34	53	4	3
SOUTHERN DOMINIONS	59	34	13	5	7	19	16	0	0	3	15	8	3	1	3	25	10	10	4	1
S. AFRICA +RHOD.	22	13	6	1	2	8	7	0	0	1	7	4	1	0	1	7	2	4	1	0
AUSTRALIA + N.Z.	37	21	7	4	5	11	9	0	0	2	8	4	2	1	2	18	8	6	3	1
ASIA + OTHER AFRICA	56	37	10	2	7	0	0	0	0	0	12	8	2	0	1	44	29	8	1	6
JAPAN	10	9	0	1	0	0	0	0	0	0	3	2	0	0	0	7	7	0	0	0
OTHER ASIA+AFR.	46	28	10	1	7	0	0	0	0	0	9	6	2	0	1	37	22	8	1	6
BLACK AFRICA	8	2	2	0	4	0	0	0	0	0	2	1	0	0	1	6	1	2	1	0
ARAB WORLD	3	1	2	0	0	0	0	0	0	0	0	0	0	0	0	3	1	2	0	0
INDIA	7	7	0	0	0	0	0	0	0	0	1	1	0	0	0	4	6	0	0	0
PHILIPPINES	8	6	2	0	0	0	0	0	0	0	4	4	0	0	0	4	2	2	0	0
OTHER E. ASIA	2	2	0	0	2	0	0	0	0	0	0	0	0	0	0	2	2	0	0	0
OTHER ASIA	18	10	5	1	2	0	0	0	0	0	2	0	2	0	0	16	10	3	1	2

CHAPTER 4- VARIETIES OF ENTRY
SECTION 2- THE FLOW OF MANUFACTURING BY INDUSTRY OF PARENT SYSTEM
TABLE 7- MANUFACTURING SUBSIDIARIES IN A SYSTEM IN THE
SOAP AND COSMETICS INDUSTRY (SIC 284)
CLASSIFIED BY COUNTRY, PERIOD MANUFACTURE BEGAN, AND METHOD OF ENTRY

PERIOD AND METHOD OF ENTRY
(NEW=NEWLY FORMED, ACQ=ACQUIRED, DES=DESCENDANT, UNK=UNKNOWN)

COUNTRY OR REGION	TOTAL PRE 1968					PRE 1946					1946-1957					1958-1967				
	ALL	NEW	ACQ	DES	UNK	ALL	NEW	ACQ	DES	UNK	ALL	NEW	ACQ	DES	UNK	ALL	NEW	ACQ	DES	UNK
OUTSIDE U.S.	129	60	44	12	11	22	13	5	3	1	23	11	6	3	3	82	36	33	6	7
OUT. U.S. + CANADA	112	55	32	12	11	17	9	4	3	1	19	10	3	3	3	74	36	25	6	7
OUT. WEST. HEMIS.	82	41	24	7	8	10	6	2	1	1	10	4	3	2	1	60	31	19	4	6
OUT. WHITE CWEALTH	91	50	22	9	9	12	7	3	1	1	15	10	0	3	2	63	33	19	5	6
OUT. DEVLPED WORLD	56	27	14	8	7	8	3	3	2	0	11	7	0	2	2	37	17	11	4	5
CANADA	17	5	12	0	0	5	4	1	0	0	4	1	3	0	0	8	0	8	0	0
LATIN AMERICA	30	14	8	5	3	7	4	2	1	0	9	5	3	1	0	14	5	3	3	3
C. AMER.+CARIB.	16	7	5	2	2	5	3	1	0	1	4	2	2	0	0	7	2	2	2	1
CUBA	5	2	1	1	1	2	1	1	0	0	3	1	0	1	1	0	0	0	0	0
MEXICO	7	4	3	0	0	3	2	1	0	0	1	0	1	0	0	3	2	1	0	0
OTHER	4	1	1	1	1	0	0	0	0	0	0	0	0	0	0	4	1	1	1	1
S. AMERICA	14	7	3	3	1	2	1	1	0	0	5	3	1	1	0	7	3	1	2	1
ARGENTINA	5	2	2	1	0	1	1	0	0	0	3	0	2	1	0	1	1	0	0	0
BRAZIL	2	1	1	0	0	1	0	1	0	0	0	0	0	0	0	1	1	0	0	0
PERU	3	2	1	0	0	0	0	0	0	0	2	1	1	0	0	1	1	0	0	0
COLUMBIA	0	0	0	0	0	0	0	0	0	0	0	0	0	0	0	0	0	0	0	0
VENEZUELA	3	2	0	1	0	0	0	0	0	0	2	1	0	1	0	1	1	0	0	0
OTHER	1	0	1	0	0	0	0	0	0	0	0	0	0	0	0	1	0	1	0	0
EUROPE	44	23	14	4	3	8	4	2	1	1	8	4	1	2	1	28	15	11	1	1
EFTA	16	6	6	3	1	4	0	1	2	1	3	1	2	0	0	9	5	3	1	0
U.K.	10	2	5	3	0	4	0	2	2	0	3	1	1	1	0	3	1	2	0	0
SCANDINAVIA	4	2	1	0	1	0	0	0	0	0	0	0	0	0	0	4	2	1	0	1
SWITZERLAND	0	0	0	0	0	0	0	0	0	0	0	0	0	0	0	0	0	0	0	0
OTHER EFTA	2	2	0	0	0	0	0	0	0	0	0	0	0	0	0	2	2	0	0	0
EUROP. COMMUNITY	22	14	6	0	2	4	4	0	0	0	5	3	0	0	2	13	7	6	0	0
FRANCE	9	3	5	0	1	1	1	0	0	0	2	1	0	0	1	6	1	5	0	0
GERMANY	4	3	0	1	0	1	1	0	0	0	1	1	0	0	0	2	1	0	1	0
ITALY	6	5	1	0	0	1	1	0	0	0	1	1	0	0	0	4	3	1	0	0
BELGIUM + LUX	3	3	0	0	0	1	1	0	0	0	1	1	0	0	0	1	1	0	0	0
NETHERLANDS	0	0	0	0	0	0	0	0	0	0	0	0	0	0	0	0	0	0	0	0
SPAIN	2	2	0	0	0	0	0	0	0	0	0	0	0	0	0	2	2	0	0	0
GREECE + TURKEY	2	2	0	0	0	0	0	0	0	0	0	0	0	0	0	2	2	0	0	0
OTHER EUROPE	2	0	2	0	0	0	0	0	0	0	0	0	0	0	0	2	0	2	0	0
EUROPE EX. U.K.	34	21	9	1	3	4	4	0	0	0	5	3	0	0	2	25	14	9	1	1
SOUTHERN DOMINIONS	9	3	3	2	1	3	1	1	1	0	0	0	0	0	0	6	2	2	1	1
S. AFRICA +RHOD.	4	2	1	1	0	2	0	1	1	0	0	0	0	0	0	2	2	0	0	0
AUSTRALIA + N.Z.	5	1	2	1	1	1	1	0	0	0	2	0	1	0	1	2	0	1	1	0
ASIA + OTHER AFRICA	29	15	7	3	4	2	1	1	0	0	1	0	0	1	0	26	14	6	2	4
JAPAN	3	2	1	0	0	0	0	0	0	0	0	0	0	0	0	3	2	1	0	0
OTHER ASIA+AFR.	26	13	6	3	4	2	1	1	0	0	1	0	0	1	0	23	12	5	2	4
BLACK AFRICA	4	3	0	1	0	0	0	0	0	0	0	0	0	0	0	4	3	0	1	0
ARAB WORLD	3	2	0	1	0	0	0	0	0	0	0	0	0	0	0	3	2	0	1	0
INDIA	2	1	0	1	0	0	0	0	0	0	0	0	0	0	0	2	1	0	1	0
PHILIPPINES	2	0	1	0	1	0	0	0	0	0	0	0	0	0	0	2	0	1	0	1
OTHER E. ASIA	6	2	4	0	0	0	0	0	0	0	0	0	0	0	0	6	2	4	0	0
OTHER ASIA	9	5	1	1	2	0	0	0	0	0	0	0	0	0	0	9	5	1	1	2

CHAPTER 4- VARIETIES OF ENTRY
SECTION 2- THE FLOW OF MANUFACTURING BY INDUSTRY OF PARENT SYSTEM
TABLE 8- MANUFACTURING SUBSIDIARIES IN A SYSTEM IN THE
PETROLEUM INDUSTRY (SIC 291)
CLASSIFIED BY COUNTRY, PERIOD MANUFACTURE BEGAN, AND METHOD OF ENTRY

PERIOD AND METHOD OF ENTRY
(NEW=NEWLY FORMED, ACQ=ACQUIRED, DES=DESCENDANT, UNK=UNKNOWN)

COUNTRY OR REGION	TOTAL PRE 1968					PRE 1946					1946-1957					1958-1967				
	ALL	NEW	ACQ	DES	UNK	ALL	NEW	ACQ	DES	UNK	ALL	NEW	ACQ	DES	UNK	ALL	NEW	ACQ	DES	UNK
OUTSIDE U.S.	307	183	83	32	59	87	74	56	12	6	51	20	11	7	13	219	107	60	19	33
OUT. U.S. + CANADA	336	171	70	29	59	74	47	28	8	6	48	20	8	8	5	207	104	53	17	33
OUT. WEST. HEMIS.	257	119	61	20	50	52	28	13	8	3	37	16	7	4	10	161	75	46	13	27
OUT. WHITE CWEALTH	276	150	58	23	40	63	42	13	6	5	38	15	6	4	11	170	93	46	12	19
OUT. DEVLPED WORLD	124	76	15	15	16	28	23	4	1	0	14	4	1	4	5	80	49	13	7	11
CANADA	31	12	13	3	0	13	9	3	0	0	3	0	3	1	0	12	3	7	2	0
LATIN AMERICA	79	52	9	9	9	22	19	1	2	0	11	4	0	4	3	46	29	7	4	6
C. AMER.+CARIB.	32	23	3	3	3	14	14	0	0	0	2	0	0	1	1	16	9	3	2	2
CUBA	9	7	0	1	1	3	3	0	0	0	1	0	0	1	0	5	3	0	0	1
MEXICO	9	7	0	1	1	4	4	0	0	0	1	0	0	0	1	3	3	0	0	0
OTHER	19	13	3	1	2	7	7	0	0	0	1	0	0	1	0	6	3	3	0	1
S. AMERICA	47	29	6	6	6	8	5	1	2	0	9	4	0	2	2	30	20	4	2	4
ARGENTINA	7	5	3	0	0	0	0	0	0	0	1	1	0	0	0	3	2	1	0	0
BRAZIL	8	5	3	0	0	0	0	0	0	0	1	0	1	0	0	7	4	3	0	0
PERU	2	1	0	1	0	1	1	0	0	0	0	0	0	0	0	1	1	0	0	0
COLOMBIA	8	3	0	2	3	1	0	0	1	0	2	1	0	1	1	5	2	0	0	2
VENEZUELA	18	13	1	1	3	3	3	0	0	0	4	2	1	0	1	11	9	0	1	2
OTHER	4	2	1	1	0	0	0	0	0	0	2	0	1	1	0	2	2	0	0	0
EUROPE	168	81	43	11	32	45	17	25	3	5	25	14	3	1	5	97	44	32	7	14
EFTA	52	19	10	7	16	19	6	10	3	2	6	3	0	1	1	27	6	6	2	9
U.K.	30	10	0	3	11	10	0	0	1	1	4	2	0	0	0	16	3	3	2	7
SCANDINAVIA	16	6	0	2	5	5	0	0	2	0	2	0	0	0	0	9	2	3	2	2
SWITZERLAND	2	0	0	2	0	0	0	0	0	0	0	0	0	0	0	2	0	0	2	0
OTHER EFTA	4	3	0	0	0	4	3	0	0	0	0	0	0	0	0	0	0	0	0	0
EUROP. COMMUNITY	89	45	27	4	12	17	6	9	1	1	16	8	3	2	3	55	27	23	1	4
FRANCE	19	12	6	1	1	6	3	1	0	0	6	3	1	0	3	8	5	3	1	0
GERMANY	28	13	10	0	5	6	0	5	0	1	3	1	2	0	0	17	8	9	0	1
ITALY	23	10	6	2	2	4	2	1	0	1	5	3	1	2	0	14	5	5	3	1
BELGIUM + LUX	11	6	3	0	2	1	0	1	0	0	1	1	0	0	0	9	5	3	0	1
NETHERLANDS	8	4	4	0	2	0	0	0	0	0	1	0	1	0	0	7	4	1	0	0
SPAIN	16	12	2	0	2	3	1	0	0	0	2	2	0	0	0	11	10	1	0	0
GREECE + TURKEY	3	1	0	0	2	0	0	0	0	0	0	0	0	0	0	2	1	0	0	0
OTHER EUROPE	8	4	2	0	2	5	4	1	1	0	1	0	0	0	0	2	0	2	0	0
EUROPE EX. U.K.	138	71	37	8	21	35	19	21	3	4	21	12	3	2	4	81	40	29	5	7
SOUTHERN DOMINIONS	27	10	4	3	8	1	0	0	0	0	5	2	2	0	1	19	7	2	3	7
S. AFRICA +RHOD.	4	1	0	0	2	0	0	0	0	0	0	0	0	0	0	3	1	0	0	2
AUSTRALIA + N.Z.	23	9	4	3	6	1	0	0	0	0	5	2	2	0	1	16	6	2	3	5
ASIA + OTHER AFRICA	62	28	14	6	10	6	0	2	0	2	7	2	2	0	2	45	24	12	6	6
JAPAN	17	4	4	0	7	0	0	0	0	0	3	0	0	0	0	11	4	6	0	1
OTHER ASIA+AFK.	45	24	6	6	7	6	0	2	0	2	3	2	2	0	2	34	20	6	6	5
BLACK AFRICA	4	2	1	0	1	0	0	0	0	0	0	0	0	0	0	4	2	1	0	1
ARAB WORLD	12	6	1	0	0	1	1	0	0	0	1	0	1	0	0	9	6	1	0	1
INDIA	6	5	1	2	2	0	0	0	0	0	1	0	0	1	0	6	5	1	1	1
PHILIPPINES	5	2	1	2	0	1	1	0	0	0	0	0	0	0	0	3	1	1	1	1
OTHER E. ASIA	5	2	1	0	2	0	0	0	0	0	1	0	0	0	0	5	2	1	0	2
OTHER ASIA	13	7	1	2	2	4	2	1	0	1	3	0	0	1	1	7	4	1	0	1

CHAPTER 4- VARIETIES OF ENTRY
SECTION 2- THE FLOW OF MANUFACTURING BY INDUSTRY OF PARENT SYSTEM
TABLE 9- MANUFACTURING SUBSIDIARIES IN A SYSTEM IN THE
RUBBER AND TIRE INDUSTRY (SIC 30)
CLASSIFIED BY COUNTRY, PERIOD MANUFACTURE BEGAN, AND METHOD OF ENTRY

(NEW=NEWLY FORMED, ACQ=ACQUIRED, DES=DESCENDANT, UNK=UNKNOWN)

COUNTRY OR REGION	TOTAL PRE 1968 ALL	NEW	ACQ	DES	UNK	PRE 1946 ALL	NEW	ACQ	DES	UNK	1946-1957 ALL	NEW	ACQ	DES	UNK	1958-1967 ALL	NEW	ACQ	DES	UNK
OUTSIDE U.S.	163	91	42	14	15	58	29	11	7	11	37	17	15	4	1	67	45	16	3	3
OUT. U.S. + CANADA	145	87	33	12	12	48	26	9	5	8	34	17	12	4	1	62	44	12	3	3
OUT. WEST. HEMIS.	100	58	23	9	9	29	14	4	4	7	18	8	7	2	1	52	36	12	2	1
OUT. WHITE CWEALTH	120	75	29	9	9	37	21	8	2	6	31	15	12	1	1	52	39	9	2	2
OUT. DEVLPED WORLD	71	47	11	6	7	28	16	5	2	5	18	10	5	3	0	25	21	1	1	2
CANADA	18	4	9	2	3	10	3	2	2	3	3	0	3	0	0	5	1	4	0	0
LATIN AMERICA	45	29	8	3	3	19	12	5	1	1	16	9	5	2	0	10	8	3	0	0
C. AMER.+CARIB.	18	8	6	2	2	8	3	3	1	1	6	2	3	1	0	4	3	0	0	1
CUBA	4	0	2	0	1	3	0	2	0	1	2	0	1	1	0	0	0	0	0	0
MEXICO	10	5	0	4	0	6	3	0	2	0	3	1	2	0	0	1	0	1	0	0
OTHER	4	3	4	1	1	3	2	0	2	0	1	1	0	0	0	2	1	0	0	1
S. AMERICA	27	21	2	4	0	11	9	2	0	0	10	7	2	2	0	6	5	1	0	0
ARGENTINA	6	4	0	2	0	2	2	0	0	0	3	3	0	1	0	1	1	0	0	0
BRAZIL	6	6	0	0	0	3	3	0	0	0	3	3	0	0	0	1	1	0	0	0
PERU	2	2	0	0	0	1	1	0	0	0	1	1	0	0	0	0	0	0	0	0
COLOMBIA	4	2	0	1	1	3	1	0	1	1	0	0	0	0	0	0	0	0	0	0
VENEZUELA	7	6	0	1	0	2	2	0	1	0	3	2	0	1	0	2	2	0	0	0
OTHER	2	1	0	1	0	1	0	0	0	0	0	0	0	0	0	1	1	0	0	0
EUROPE	56	31	16	4	5	14	6	3	2	3	14	6	6	1	1	28	19	7	1	1
EFTA	22	12	4	1	3	10	5	3	2	2	3	2	0	1	0	9	5	3	0	1
U.K.	12	5	1	3	3	6	2	1	2	2	2	1	0	1	0	4	2	1	0	0
SCANDINAVIA	3	2	1	0	0	1	1	0	0	0	0	0	0	0	0	2	1	2	0	0
SWITZERLAND	3	1	2	0	0	2	1	1	0	0	0	0	0	0	0	2	0	2	0	0
OTHER EFTA	4	4	0	0	0	2	2	0	0	0	0	0	0	0	0	1	1	0	0	0
EUROP. COMMUNITY	26	14	9	1	2	2	2	0	0	0	9	5	4	0	0	15	11	3	0	0
FRANCE	6	4	1	0	1	0	0	0	0	0	4	3	1	0	0	4	4	0	0	0
GERMANY	7	4	1	1	1	0	0	0	0	0	5	3	1	1	0	3	1	2	0	0
ITALY	6	4	0	1	1	0	0	0	0	0	1	1	0	0	0	5	4	2	0	1
BELGIUM + LUX	3	2	0	1	0	0	0	0	0	0	1	0	0	1	0	2	1	1	0	0
NETHERLANDS	4	3	1	0	0	0	0	0	0	0	1	1	0	0	0	1	1	0	0	0
SPAIN	4	2	2	0	0	0	0	0	0	0	2	2	0	0	0	1	1	1	0	0
GREECE + TURKEY	1	0	0	0	0	0	0	0	0	0	0	0	0	0	0	0	0	0	0	0
OTHER EUROPE	3	0	0	0	2	1	0	0	0	1	0	0	0	0	0	0	0	0	0	1
EUROPE EX. U.K.	44	26	15	1	2	8	4	3	0	1	12	5	6	1	0	24	17	6	0	1
SOUTHERN DOMINIONS	13	7	3	2	0	5	3	1	1	0	1	1	0	0	0	6	3	2	1	0
S. AFRICA +RHOD.	5	2	0	2	0	2	1	0	1	0	1	0	0	0	0	1	0	0	1	0
AUSTRALIA + N.Z.	8	5	3	0	0	3	2	1	0	0	0	0	0	0	0	5	3	2	1	0
ASIA + OTHER AFRICA	31	20	4	3	4	10	5	1	1	3	3	1	1	1	0	18	14	3	1	1
JAPAN	5	2	2	0	0	1	1	0	0	0	1	0	0	0	0	3	1	2	0	0
OTHER ASIA+AFR.	26	18	3	3	4	9	4	1	1	4	2	0	0	0	0	15	13	1	0	0
BLACK AFRICA	3	2	1	0	0	0	0	0	0	0	0	0	0	0	0	3	2	1	0	0
ARAB WORLD	2	2	0	1	0	0	0	0	0	0	0	0	0	0	0	2	2	0	0	0
INDIA	4	3	1	1	0	1	1	0	0	0	1	1	0	1	0	2	2	0	0	0
PHILIPPINES	3	0	0	0	0	0	0	0	0	0	0	0	0	0	0	3	0	0	0	0
OTHER E. ASIA	0	0	0	0	0	0	0	0	0	0	1	0	0	1	0	0	0	0	0	0
OTHER ASIA	14	9	0	1	4	6	4	0	0	4	1	1	0	0	0	7	7	0	0	0

CHAPTER 4— VARIETIES OF ENTRY
SECTION 2— THE FLOW OF MANUFACTURING BY INDUSTRY OF PARENT SYSTEM
TABLE 10— MANUFACTURING SUBSIDIARIES IN A SYSTEM IN THE
STONE, CLAY, AND GLASS INDUSTRY (SIC 32)
CLASSIFIED BY COUNTRY, PERIOD MANUFACTURE BEGAN, AND METHOD OF ENTRY

PERIOD AND METHOD OF ENTRY
(NEW=NEWLY FORMED, ACQ=ACQUIRED, DES=DESCENDANT, UNK=UNKNOWN)

COUNTRY OR REGION	TOTAL PRE 1968 ALL	NEW	ACQ	DES	UNK	PRE 1946 ALL	NEW	ACQ	DES	UNK	1946-1957 ALL	NEW	ACQ	DES	UNK	1958-1967 ALL	NEW	ACQ	DES	UNK
OUTSIDE U.S.	175	76	85	6	4	29	15	14	0	0	37	20	16	0	1	105	41	55	6	3
OUT. U.S. + CANADA	157	66	78	6	4	22	9	13	0	0	31	17	13	0	1	101	40	52	6	3
OUT. WEST. HEMIS.	108	46	53	4	3	14	8	6	0	0	12	7	4	0	1	80	31	43	4	2
OUT. WHITE CWEALTH	119	54	55	3	4	17	6	11	0	0	25	13	11	0	1	74	35	33	3	3
OUT. DEVLPED WORLD	54	23	26	2	1	8	1	7	0	0	20	11	9	0	0	24	11	10	2	1
CANADA	18	10	7	0	0	7	6	1	0	0	6	3	3	0	0	4	1	3	0	1
LATIN AMERICA	49	20	25	2	1	8	1	7	0	0	19	10	9	0	0	21	9	9	2	0
C. AMER.+CARIB.	14	8	6	0	0	1	0	1	0	0	6	4	2	0	0	7	4	3	0	0
CUBA	1	1	0	0	0	0	0	0	0	0	1	1	0	0	0	0	0	0	0	0
MEXICO	13	7	6	0	0	1	0	1	0	0	5	3	2	0	0	7	4	3	0	0
OTHER	0	0	0	0	0	0	0	0	0	0	0	0	0	0	0	0	0	0	0	0
S. AMERICA	35	12	19	2	1	7	1	6	0	0	13	6	7	0	0	14	5	6	2	1
ARGENTINA	6	1	3	1	0	2	0	1	0	0	2	1	1	0	0	2	1	0	1	0
BRAZIL	13	4	8	1	0	4	1	3	0	0	5	2	3	0	0	4	0	2	1	1
PERU	1	1	0	0	0	0	0	0	0	0	1	1	0	0	0	0	0	0	0	0
COLOMBIA	6	2	4	0	0	0	0	0	0	0	1	0	1	0	0	5	2	3	0	0
VENEZUELA	6	4	1	1	0	0	0	0	0	0	3	2	1	0	0	3	2	0	1	0
OTHER	3	0	3	0	0	2	0	2	0	0	1	0	1	0	0	0	0	0	0	0
EUROPE	78	28	43	3	3	12	6	6	0	0	8	3	4	0	0	57	19	33	3	2
EFTA	26	6	19	1	1	4	1	3	0	0	3	1	2	0	0	19	4	14	1	0
U.K.	23	4	18	1	0	3	1	2	0	0	3	1	2	0	0	17	2	14	1	0
SCANDINAVIA	3	2	0	0	0	1	1	0	0	0	0	0	0	0	0	2	2	0	0	0
SWITZERLAND	0	0	0	0	0	0	0	0	0	0	0	0	0	0	0	0	0	0	0	0
OTHER EFTA	0	0	0	0	0	0	0	0	0	0	0	0	0	0	0	0	0	0	0	0
EUROP. COMMUNITY	45	18	22	1	3	8	5	3	0	0	4	1	2	0	1	32	12	17	1	2
FRANCE	15	8	5	0	1	2	2	0	0	0	2	1	0	0	1	10	5	5	0	1
GERMANY	9	3	5	1	0	2	2	0	0	0	1	0	1	0	0	6	1	4	1	0
ITALY	10	4	4	1	1	2	2	0	0	0	1	0	1	0	0	9	3	4	1	1
BELGIUM + LUX	9	1	8	0	0	3	0	3	0	0	1	0	0	0	0	5	1	4	0	0
NETHERLANDS	2	2	0	0	0	0	0	0	0	0	1	1	0	0	0	2	2	0	0	0
SPAIN	4	2	2	0	0	0	0	0	0	0	0	0	0	0	0	4	2	2	0	0
GREECE + TURKEY	0	0	0	0	0	0	0	0	0	0	0	0	0	0	0	0	0	0	0	0
OTHER EUROPE	3	2	0	1	0	0	0	0	0	0	1	1	0	0	0	2	1	0	1	0
EUROPE EX. U.K.	55	24	25	2	3	9	5	4	0	0	5	2	2	0	1	40	17	19	2	2
SOUTHERN DOMINIONS	13	7	5	1	0	2	2	0	0	0	2	2	0	0	0	9	3	5	1	0
S. AFRICA +RHOD.	6	3	3	0	0	0	0	0	0	0	2	2	0	0	0	4	1	3	0	0
AUSTRALIA + N.Z.	7	4	2	1	0	2	2	0	0	0	2	2	0	0	0	5	2	2	1	0
ASIA + OTHER AFRICA	17	11	5	0	0	0	0	0	0	0	2	2	0	0	0	14	9	5	0	0
JAPAN	12	8	4	0	0	0	0	0	0	0	1	1	0	0	0	11	7	4	0	0
OTHER ASIA+AFR.	5	3	1	1	0	0	0	0	0	0	1	1	0	0	0	3	2	1	0	0
BLACK AFRICA	1	0	0	0	0	0	0	0	0	0	0	0	0	0	0	1	0	0	0	0
ARAB WORLD	0	0	0	0	0	0	0	0	0	0	0	0	0	0	0	0	0	0	0	0
INDIA	3	2	0	0	0	0	0	0	0	0	1	1	0	0	0	1	1	0	0	0
PHILIPPINES	0	0	0	0	0	0	0	0	0	0	0	0	0	0	0	0	0	0	0	0
OTHER E. ASIA	1	1	0	0	0	0	0	0	0	0	0	0	0	0	0	1	1	0	0	0
OTHER ASIA	0	0	0	0	0	0	0	0	0	0	0	0	0	0	0	0	0	0	0	0

CHAPTER 4- VARIETIES OF ENTRY
SECTION 2- THE FLOW OF MANUFACTURING BY INDUSTRY OF PARENT SYSTEM
TABLE 11- MANUFACTURING SUBSIDIARIES IN A SYSTEM IN THE
PRIMARY METAL INDUSTRY (SIC 33)
CLASSIFIED BY COUNTRY, PERIOD MANUFACTURE BEGAN, AND METHOD OF ENTRY

PERIOD AND METHOD OF ENTRY
(NEW=NEWLY FORMED, ACQ=ACQUIRED, DES=DESCENDANT, UNK=UNKNOWN)

COUNTRY OR REGION	TOTAL PRE 1968					PRE 1946					1946-1957					1958-1967				
	ALL	NEW	ACQ	DES	UNK	ALL	NEW	ACQ	DES	UNK	ALL	NEW	ACQ	DES	UNK	ALL	NEW	ACQ	DES	UNK
OUTSIDE U.S.	176	88	67	13	8	24	15	3	4	2	29	20	7	1	1	123	53	57	8	5
OUT. U.S. + CANADA	148	78	51	12	7	17	9	2	4	2	23	19	3	1	0	108	50	46	7	5
OUT. WEST. HEMIS.	96	46	36	8	6	8	1	1	4	2	10	9	1	0	0	78	36	34	4	4
OUT. WHITE CWEALTH	106	62	34	8	2	11	8	1	1	1	20	16	3	1	0	75	38	30	6	1
OUT. DEVLPED WORLD	65	42	18	4	1	9	8	1	0	0	17	13	3	1	0	39	21	14	3	1
CANADA	28	10	16	1	1	7	6	1	0	0	6	1	4	0	1	15	3	11	1	0
LATIN AMERICA	52	32	15	4	1	9	8	1	0	0	13	9	3	1	0	30	15	11	3	1
C. AMER.+CARIB.	23	17	6	0	0	5	4	1	0	0	5	4	1	0	0	13	9	4	0	0
CUBA	3	3	0	0	0	1	1	0	0	0	2	2	0	0	0	0	0	0	0	0
MEXICO	17	11	6	0	0	4	3	1	0	0	3	2	1	0	0	10	6	4	0	0
OTHER	3	3	0	0	0	0	0	0	0	0	0	0	0	0	0	3	3	0	0	0
S. AMERICA	29	15	9	4	1	4	4	0	0	0	8	5	2	1	0	17	6	7	3	1
ARGENTINA	3	2	1	0	0	1	1	0	0	0	1	0	1	0	0	1	1	0	0	0
BRAZIL	3	2	0	1	0	1	1	0	0	0	0	0	0	0	0	2	1	0	1	0
PERU	9	3	3	2	1	1	1	0	0	0	3	1	1	1	0	5	1	2	1	1
COLOMBIA	6	2	3	1	0	0	0	0	0	0	0	0	0	0	0	6	2	3	1	0
VENEZUELA	8	6	2	0	0	1	1	0	0	0	4	3	1	0	0	3	2	1	0	0
OTHER	0	0	0	0	0	0	0	0	0	0	0	0	0	0	0	0	0	0	0	0
EUROPE	66	24	32	6	4	6	6	0	0	0	8	4	4	0	0	52	14	28	6	4
EFTA	35	11	19	3	2	4	4	0	0	0	2	2	0	0	0	29	5	19	3	2
U.K.	29	8	16	3	2	4	4	0	0	0	2	2	0	0	0	23	2	16	3	2
SCANDINAVIA	4	2	2	0	0	0	0	0	0	0	0	0	0	0	0	4	2	2	0	0
SWITZERLAND	2	1	1	0	0	0	0	0	0	0	0	0	0	0	0	2	1	1	0	0
OTHER EFTA	0	0	0	0	0	0	0	0	0	0	0	0	0	0	0	0	0	0	0	0
EUROP. COMMUNITY	26	12	9	3	2	2	2	0	0	0	3	2	1	0	0	21	8	8	3	2
FRANCE	4	0	3	1	0	0	0	0	0	0	0	0	0	0	0	4	0	3	1	0
GERMANY	7	4	2	1	0	2	2	0	0	0	0	0	0	0	0	5	2	2	1	0
ITALY	7	6	1	0	0	0	0	0	0	0	2	2	0	0	0	5	4	1	0	0
BELGIUM + LUX	5	1	2	1	1	0	0	0	0	0	1	0	1	0	0	4	1	1	1	1
NETHERLANDS	3	1	1	0	1	0	0	0	0	0	0	0	0	0	0	3	1	1	0	1
SPAIN	3	1	2	0	0	0	0	0	0	0	1	0	1	0	0	2	1	1	0	0
GREECE + TURKEY	2	0	2	0	0	0	0	0	0	0	2	0	2	0	0	0	0	0	0	0
OTHER EUROPE	0	0	0	0	0	0	0	0	0	0	0	0	0	0	0	0	0	0	0	0
EUROPE EX. U.K.	37	16	16	3	2	2	2	0	0	0	6	2	4	0	0	29	12	12	3	2
SOUTHERN DOMINIONS	13	8	2	2	1	2	2	0	0	0	1	0	1	0	0	10	6	1	2	1
S. AFRICA +RHOD.	1	1	0	0	0	1	1	0	0	0	0	0	0	0	0	0	0	0	0	0
AUSTRALIA + N.Z.	12	7	2	2	1	1	1	0	0	0	1	0	1	0	0	10	6	1	2	1
ASIA + OTHER AFRICA	17	14	3	0	0	2	2	0	0	0	2	1	1	0	0	13	11	2	0	0
JAPAN	4	4	0	0	0	0	0	0	0	0	0	0	0	0	0	4	4	0	0	0
OTHER ASIA+AFR.	13	10	3	0	0	2	2	0	0	0	2	1	1	0	0	9	7	2	0	0
BLACK AFRICA	1	1	0	0	0	0	0	0	0	0	1	1	0	0	0	0	0	0	0	0
ARAB WORLD	4	4	0	0	0	0	0	0	0	0	0	0	0	0	0	4	4	0	0	0
INDIA	4	2	2	0	0	2	2	0	0	0	0	0	0	0	0	2	0	2	0	0
PHILIPPINES	2	2	0	0	0	0	0	0	0	0	0	0	0	0	0	2	2	0	0	0
OTHER E. ASIA	0	0	0	0	0	0	0	0	0	0	0	0	0	0	0	0	0	0	0	0
OTHER ASIA	2	1	1	0	0	0	0	0	0	0	1	0	1	0	0	1	1	0	0	0

CHAPTER 4- VARIETIES OF ENTRY
SECTION 2- THE FLOW OF MANUFACTURING BY INDUSTRY OF PARENT SYSTEM
TABLE 12- MANUFACTURING SUBSIDIARIES IN A SYSTEM IN THE
FABRICATED METAL INDUSTRY (SIC 34)
CLASSIFIED BY COUNTRY, PERIOD MANUFACTURE BEGAN, AND METHOD OF ENTRY

(NEW=NEWLY FORMED, ACQ=ACQUIRED, DES=DESCENDANT, UNK=UNKNOWN)

PERIOD AND METHOD OF ENTRY

COUNTRY OR REGION	TOTAL PRE 1968					PRE 1946					1946-1957					1958-1967				
	ALL	NEW	ACQ	DES	UNK	ALL	NEW	ACQ	DES	UNK	ALL	NEW	ACQ	DES	UNK	ALL	NEW	ACQ	DES	UNK
OUTSIDE U.S.	268	97	135	17	19	56	25	23	2	6	65	20	33	8	4	147	52	79	7	9
OUT. U.S. + CANADA	223	86	108	15	14	39	18	15	2	4	46	16	22	6	2	138	52	71	7	8
OUT. WEST. HEMIS.	164	61	80	13	10	34	17	13	2	2	25	10	8	5	2	105	34	59	6	6
OUT. WHITE CWEALTH	175	70	84	10	11	26	12	9	1	4	39	13	21	4	1	110	45	54	5	6
OUT. DEVLPED WORLD	73	34	32	2	5	5	1	2	0	2	27	10	15	1	1	41	23	15	1	2
CANADA	45	11	27	2	5	17	7	8	0	2	19	4	11	2	2	9	0	8	0	1
LATIN AMERICA	59	25	28	2	4	5	1	2	0	2	21	6	14	1	0	33	18	12	1	2
C. AMER.+CARIB.	21	0	13	2	2	2	0	1	0	1	7	1	5	1	0	12	4	7	0	1
CUBA	1	1	0	1	1	1	0	0	0	1	0	0	0	0	0	0	0	0	0	0
MEXICO	18	3	13	0	1	1	0	1	0	0	7	1	5	1	0	10	2	7	0	1
OTHER	2	2	0	1	0	1	1	0	0	0	0	0	0	0	0	2	0	2	0	0
S. AMERICA	38	20	15	1	2	3	1	1	0	1	14	5	9	0	0	21	14	5	1	1
ARGENTINA	4	1	3	0	0	0	0	0	0	0	3	2	1	0	0	1	1	2	0	0
BRAZIL	12	6	5	1	0	3	0	2	0	1	4	2	2	0	0	5	3	2	0	1
PERU	3	2	1	0	0	1	1	0	0	0	0	0	0	0	0	2	0	1	0	0
COLUMBIA	5	1	2	0	1	0	0	0	0	0	3	1	2	1	0	2	0	1	1	0
VENEZUELA	8	6	2	0	0	0	0	0	0	0	1	1	0	0	0	6	5	1	0	0
OTHER	6	4	2	0	0	0	0	0	0	0	1	0	1	0	0	5	4	1	0	0
EUROPE	128	42	68	11	7	30	15	11	2	2	16	5	6	4	1	82	22	51	5	4
EFTA	41	14	22	6	2	12	7	4	1	0	7	2	2	2	1	22	5	16	3	1
U.K.	28	7	16	3	2	9	4	4	1	0	4	2	2	1	0	15	1	12	2	1
SCANDINAVIA	6	1	4	1	0	0	0	0	0	0	2	2	0	1	0	4	1	2	1	0
SWITZERLAND	4	1	1	2	0	1	1	0	0	0	1	0	0	1	1	2	0	1	1	0
OTHER EFTA	3	2	1	0	0	2	2	0	0	0	0	0	0	0	0	1	0	1	0	0
EUROP. COMMUNITY	69	23	36	5	5	18	8	7	1	2	7	2	3	2	0	44	13	26	2	3
FRANCE	18	6	11	1	1	6	2	3	1	0	1	0	1	0	0	11	3	8	0	0
GERMANY	21	5	13	2	1	5	3	2	0	0	2	0	1	1	0	14	3	10	1	0
ITALY	13	3	5	2	3	3	1	0	0	2	1	0	0	1	0	11	4	5	1	1
BELGIUM + LUX	6	0	3	1	2	3	0	1	0	0	1	1	1	0	0	2	0	1	0	1
NETHERLANDS	11	6	4	1	0	3	2	1	0	0	2	1	1	1	0	6	3	2	0	1
SPAIN	9	3	6	0	0	0	0	0	0	0	1	0	1	0	0	8	3	5	0	0
GREECE + TURKEY	8	5	3	0	0	0	0	0	0	0	1	1	0	0	0	7	4	3	0	0
OTHER EUROPE	1	0	1	0	0	0	0	0	0	0	0	0	0	0	0	1	1	1	0	0
EUROPE EX. U.K.	100	35	52	8	5	21	11	7	1	2	12	3	6	3	0	67	21	39	4	3
SOUTHERN DOMINIONS	19	9	4	2	1	4	2	2	0	0	3	1	1	1	0	12	6	4	1	1
S. AFRICA +RHOD.	8	4	3	0	0	2	1	1	0	0	2	1	1	0	0	4	2	2	0	0
AUSTRALIA + N.Z.	11	5	1	2	1	2	1	1	0	0	1	0	0	1	0	8	4	4	1	1
ASIA + OTHER AFRICA	17	10	5	0	2	2	1	1	0	0	6	4	0	1	1	11	6	4	1	1
JAPAN	3	1	1	0	1	0	0	0	0	0	0	0	0	0	0	3	1	1	0	1
OTHER ASIA+AFR.	14	9	4	0	1	2	1	1	0	0	6	4	0	1	1	8	5	3	0	0
BLACK AFRICA	4	1	2	0	1	0	0	0	0	0	1	1	0	0	0	3	1	2	0	0
ARAB WORLD	2	0	1	0	1	0	0	0	0	0	2	1	1	0	0	0	0	0	0	0
INDIA	0	0	0	0	0	0	0	0	0	0	0	0	0	0	0	0	0	0	0	0
PHILIPPINES	3	2	1	0	0	0	0	0	0	0	1	1	0	0	0	2	1	1	1	0
OTHER E. ASIA	0	0	0	0	0	0	0	0	0	0	0	0	0	0	0	0	0	0	0	0
OTHER ASIA	5	5	0	0	0	0	0	0	0	0	2	2	0	0	0	3	0	3	0	0

CHAPTER 4- VARIETIES OF ENTRY
SECTION 2- THE FLOW OF MANUFACTURING BY INDUSTRY OF PARENT SYSTEM
TABLE 13- MANUFACTURING SUBSIDIARIES IN A SYSTEM IN THE
FARM MACHINERY INDUSTRY (SIC 352)
CLASSIFIED BY COUNTRY, PERIOD MANUFACTURE BEGAN, AND METHOD OF ENTRY

PERIOD AND METHOD OF ENTRY
(NEW=NEWLY FORMED, ACQ=ACQUIRED, DES=DESCENDANT, UNK=UNKNOWN)

COUNTRY OR REGION	TOTAL PRE 1968					PRE 1946					1946-1957					1958-1967				
	ALL	NEW	ACQ	DES	UNK	ALL	NEW	ACQ	DES	UNK	ALL	NEW	ACQ	DES	UNK	ALL	NEW	ACQ	DES	UNK
OUTSIDE U.S.	45	14	16	15	0	10	3	1	6	0	13	4	4	5	0	22	7	11	4	0
OUT. U.S. + CANADA	38	11	14	13	0	6	1	0	5	0	11	4	3	4	0	21	6	11	4	0
OUT. WEST. HEMIS.	30	8	12	10	0	6	1	0	5	0	6	2	2	2	0	18	5	10	3	0
OUT. WHITE CWEALTH	27	9	9	9	0	4	0	1	3	0	8	3	2	3	0	15	6	6	3	0
OUT. DEVLPED WORLD	11	5	2	4	0	0	0	0	0	0	6	2	1	3	0	5	3	1	1	0
CANADA	7	3	2	2	0	4	2	1	1	0	2	0	1	1	0	1	1	0	0	0
LATIN AMERICA	8	3	2	3	0	0	0	0	0	0	5	2	1	2	0	3	1	1	1	0
C. AMER.+CARIB.	5	2	1	2	0	0	0	0	0	0	3	1	1	1	0	2	1	0	1	0
CUBA	0	0	0	0	0	0	0	0	0	0	0	0	0	0	0	0	0	0	0	0
MEXICO	4	1	1	2	0	0	0	0	0	0	3	1	1	1	0	1	0	0	1	0
OTHER	1	1	0	0	0	0	0	0	0	0	0	0	0	0	0	1	1	0	0	0
S. AMERICA	3	1	1	1	0	0	0	0	0	0	2	1	0	1	0	1	0	1	0	0
ARGENTINA	2	1	0	1	0	0	0	0	0	0	2	1	0	1	0	0	0	0	0	0
BRAZIL	1	0	1	0	0	0	0	0	0	0	0	0	0	0	0	1	0	1	0	0
PERU	0	0	0	0	0	0	0	0	0	0	0	0	0	0	0	0	0	0	0	0
COLOMBIA	0	0	0	0	0	0	0	0	0	0	0	0	0	0	0	0	0	0	0	0
VENEZUELA	0	0	0	0	0	0	0	0	0	0	0	0	0	0	0	0	0	0	0	0
OTHER	0	0	0	0	0	0	0	0	0	0	0	0	0	0	0	0	0	0	0	0
EUROPE	19	4	9	6	0	5	1	0	4	0	3	0	1	2	0	11	2	8	1	0
EFTA	5	1	2	2	0	1	0	0	1	0	1	1	0	0	0	3	0	2	1	0
U.K.	4	1	2	1	0	1	0	0	1	0	1	1	0	0	0	2	0	2	0	0
SCANDINAVIA	1	0	0	1	0	0	0	0	0	0	0	0	0	0	0	1	0	0	1	0
SWITZERLAND	0	0	0	0	0	0	0	0	0	0	0	0	0	0	0	0	0	0	0	0
OTHER EFTA	0	0	0	0	0	0	0	0	0	0	0	0	0	0	0	0	0	0	0	0
EUROP. COMMUNITY	11	2	6	3	0	4	1	0	3	0	0	0	0	0	0	7	1	6	0	0
FRANCE	8	1	4	3	0	4	1	0	3	0	0	0	0	0	0	4	0	4	0	0
GERMANY	2	1	1	0	0	0	0	0	0	0	0	0	0	0	0	2	1	1	0	0
ITALY	1	0	1	0	0	0	0	0	0	0	0	0	0	0	0	1	0	1	0	0
BELGIUM + LUX	0	0	0	0	0	0	0	0	0	0	0	0	0	0	0	0	0	0	0	0
NETHERLANDS	0	0	0	0	0	0	0	0	0	0	0	0	0	0	0	0	0	0	0	0
SPAIN	2	0	1	1	0	0	0	0	0	0	0	0	0	0	0	2	0	1	1	0
GREECE + TURKEY	1	0	0	1	0	0	0	0	0	0	0	0	0	0	0	1	0	0	1	0
OTHER EUROPE	0	0	0	0	0	0	0	0	0	0	0	0	0	0	0	0	0	0	0	0
EUROPE EX. U.K.	15	3	7	5	0	4	1	0	3	0	2	0	1	1	0	9	2	6	1	0
SOUTHERN DOMINIONS	7	1	3	3	0	1	0	0	1	0	2	1	1	0	0	4	0	2	2	0
S. AFRICA +RHOD.	3	0	2	1	0	0	0	0	0	0	1	0	1	0	0	2	0	1	1	0
AUSTRALIA + N.Z.	4	1	1	2	0	1	0	0	1	0	1	1	0	0	0	2	0	1	1	0
ASIA + OTHER AFRICA	4	3	0	1	0	0	0	0	0	0	1	1	0	0	0	3	3	0	1	0
JAPAN	3	1	2	0	0	0	0	0	0	0	1	0	1	0	0	2	1	1	0	0
OTHER ASIA+AFR.	0	0	0	0	0	0	0	0	0	0	0	0	0	0	0	0	0	0	0	0
BLACK AFRICA	0	0	0	0	0	0	0	0	0	0	0	0	0	0	0	0	0	0	0	0
ARAB WORLD	1	0	1	0	0	0	0	0	0	0	1	0	1	0	0	0	0	0	0	0
INDIA	1	1	0	0	0	0	0	0	0	0	0	0	0	0	0	1	1	0	0	0
PHILIPPINES	1	1	0	0	0	0	0	0	0	0	0	0	0	0	0	1	1	0	0	0
OTHER E. ASIA	0	0	0	0	0	0	0	0	0	0	0	0	0	0	0	0	0	0	0	0
OTHER ASIA	0	0	0	0	0	0	0	0	0	0	0	0	0	0	0	0	0	0	0	0

CHAPTER 4- VARIETIES OF ENTRY
SECTION 2- THE FLOW OF MANUFACTURING BY INDUSTRY OF PARENT SYSTEM
TABLE 14- MANUFACTURING SUBSIDIARIES IN A SYSTEM IN THE
OFFICE AND COMPUTING MACHINE INDUSTRY (SIC 357)
CLASSIFIED BY COUNTRY, PERIOD MANUFACTURE BEGAN, AND METHOD OF ENTRY

PERIOD AND METHOD OF ENTRY
(NEW=NEWLY FORMED, ACQ=ACQUIRED, DES=DESCENDANT, UNK=UNKNOWN)

COUNTRY OR REGION	TOTAL PRE 1968					PRE 1946					1946-1957					1958-1967				
	ALL	NEW	ACQ	DES	UNK	ALL	NEW	ACQ	DES	UNK	ALL	NEW	ACQ	DES	UNK	ALL	NEW	ACQ	DES	UNK
OUTSIDE U.S.	73	25	29	16	3	27	12	9	5	1	18	6	7	5	0	28	7	13	6	2
OUT. U.S. + CANADA	65	22	25	15	3	22	9	8	4	1	17	6	6	5	0	26	7	11	6	2
OUT. WEST. HEMIS.	48	15	19	12	2	20	8	7	4	1	12	4	4	4	0	16	3	8	4	1
OUT. WHITE CWEALTH	54	18	20	13	3	16	7	5	3	1	16	5	6	5	0	22	6	9	5	2
OUT. DEVLPED WORLD	18	7	7	3	1	2	1	1	0	0	5	2	2	1	0	11	4	4	2	1
CANADA	8	3	4	1	0	5	3	1	1	0	1	0	1	0	0	2	0	2	0	0
LATIN AMERICA	17	7	6	3	1	2	1	1	0	0	5	2	2	1	0	10	4	3	2	1
C. AMER.+CARIB.	11	4	4	2	1	2	1	1	0	0	0	0	0	0	0	9	3	3	2	1
CUBA	1	0	1	0	0	1	0	1	0	0	0	0	0	0	0	0	0	0	0	0
MEXICO	4	2	1	1	0	1	1	0	0	0	0	0	0	0	0	3	1	1	1	0
OTHER	6	2	2	1	1	0	0	0	0	0	0	0	0	0	0	6	2	2	1	1
S. AMERICA	6	3	2	1	0	0	0	0	0	0	5	2	2	1	0	1	1	0	0	0
ARGENTINA	2	1	1	0	0	0	0	0	0	0	2	1	1	0	0	0	0	0	0	0
BRAZIL	2	1	0	1	0	0	0	0	0	0	1	0	0	1	0	1	1	0	0	0
PERU	1	1	0	0	0	0	0	0	0	0	1	1	0	0	0	0	0	0	0	0
COLOMBIA	0	0	0	0	0	0	0	0	0	0	0	0	0	0	0	0	0	0	0	0
VENEZUELA	1	0	1	0	0	0	0	0	0	0	1	0	1	0	0	0	0	0	0	0
OTHER	0	0	0	0	0	0	0	0	0	0	0	0	0	0	0	0	0	0	0	0
EUROPE	38	14	13	9	2	17	8	5	3	1	11	4	3	4	0	10	2	5	2	1
EFTA	15	6	4	3	2	5	2	1	1	1	3	2	1	0	0	7	2	2	2	1
U.K.	7	3	3	1	0	2	1	1	0	0	1	1	0	0	0	4	1	2	1	0
SCANDINAVIA	5	2	1	1	1	1	1	0	0	0	1	0	1	0	0	3	1	0	1	1
SWITZERLAND	2	1	0	1	0	1	0	0	1	0	1	1	0	0	0	0	0	0	0	0
OTHER EFTA	1	0	0	0	1	1	0	0	0	1	0	0	0	0	0	0	0	0	0	0
EUROP. COMMUNITY	23	8	9	6	0	12	6	4	2	0	8	2	2	4	0	3	0	3	0	0
FRANCE	6	2	3	1	0	3	1	2	0	0	1	1	0	0	0	2	0	1	1	0
GERMANY	10	3	3	4	0	5	2	1	2	0	3	1	1	1	0	2	0	1	1	0
ITALY	3	1	2	0	0	1	1	0	0	0	2	0	2	0	0	0	0	0	0	0
BELGIUM + LUX	3	1	1	1	0	2	1	1	0	0	0	0	0	0	0	1	0	0	1	0
NETHERLANDS	1	1	0	0	0	1	1	0	0	0	0	0	0	0	0	0	0	0	0	0
SPAIN	0	0	0	0	0	0	0	0	0	0	0	0	0	0	0	0	0	0	0	0
GREECE + TURKEY	0	0	0	0	0	0	0	0	0	0	0	0	0	0	0	0	0	0	0	0
OTHER EUROPE	0	0	0	0	0	0	0	0	0	0	0	0	0	0	0	0	0	0	0	0
EUROPE EX. U.K.	31	11	10	8	2	15	7	4	3	1	10	3	3	4	0	6	1	3	1	1
SOUTHERN DOMINIONS	4	1	2	1	0	2	0	1	1	0	0	0	0	0	0	2	1	1	0	0
S. AFRICA +RHOD.	2	1	0	1	0	1	0	0	1	0	0	0	0	0	0	1	1	0	0	0
AUSTRALIA + N.Z.	2	0	2	0	0	1	0	1	0	0	0	0	0	0	0	1	0	1	0	0
ASIA + OTHER AFRICA	6	0	4	2	0	1	0	1	0	0	1	0	1	0	0	4	0	2	2	0
JAPAN	5	0	3	2	0	1	0	1	0	0	1	0	1	0	0	3	0	1	2	0
OTHER ASIA+AFR.	1	0	1	0	0	0	0	0	0	0	0	0	0	0	0	1	0	1	0	0
BLACK AFRICA	0	0	0	0	0	0	0	0	0	0	0	0	0	0	0	0	0	0	0	0
ARAB WORLD	0	0	0	0	0	0	0	0	0	0	0	0	0	0	0	0	0	0	0	0
INDIA	1	0	1	0	0	0	0	0	0	0	0	0	0	0	0	1	0	1	0	0
PHILIPPINES	0	0	0	0	0	0	0	0	0	0	0	0	0	0	0	0	0	0	0	0
OTHER E. ASIA	0	0	0	0	0	0	0	0	0	0	0	0	0	0	0	0	0	0	0	0
OTHER ASIA	0	0	0	0	0	0	0	0	0	0	0	0	0	0	0	0	0	0	0	0

CHAPTER 4- VARIETIES OF ENTRY

SECTION 2- THE FLOW OF MANUFACTURING BY INDUSTRY OF PARENT SYSTEM

TABLE 15- MANUFACTURING SUBSIDIARIES IN A SYSTEM IN THE
OTHER NON-ELECTRICAL MACHINERY INDUSTRIES (OTHER SIC 35)
CLASSIFIED BY COUNTRY, PERIOD MANUFACTURE BEGAN, AND METHOD OF ENTRY

PERIOD AND METHOD OF ENTRY
(NEW=NEWLY FORMED, ACQ=ACQUIRED, DES=DESCENDANT, UNK=UNKNOWN)

COUNTRY OR REGION	TOTAL PRE 1968					PRE 1946					1946-1957					1958-1967				
	ALL	NEW	ACQ	DES	UNK	ALL	NEW	ACQ	DES	UNK	ALL	NEW	ACQ	DES	UNK	ALL	NEW	ACQ	DES	UNK
OUTSIDE U.S.	271	120	109	29	10	84	58	17	6	3	46	25	14	6	1	138	37	78	17	6
OUT. U.S. + CANADA	216	105	83	24	2	70	52	13	5	0	37	20	11	5	1	107	33	59	14	1
OUT. WEST. HEMIS.	174	84	70	18	2	65	47	13	5	0	27	12	11	4	0	81	25	46	9	1
OUT. WHITE CWEALTH	138	70	51	18	1	41	34	6	1	0	18	11	5	1	0	78	25	40	12	0
OUT. DEVLPED WORLD	49	25	14	8	1	5	5	0	0	0	11	9	0	1	1	32	11	14	7	0
CANADA	55	15	26	5	8	14	6	4	1	3	9	5	3	1	0	31	4	19	3	5
LATIN AMERICA	42	21	13	3	1	5	5	0	0	1	10	8	0	1	1	26	8	13	5	0
C. AMER.+CARIB.	18	11	3	0	1	1	1	0	0	1	4	3	0	0	1	13	7	3	3	0
CUBA	0	0	0	0	0	0	0	0	0	0	0	0	0	0	0	0	0	0	0	0
MEXICO	17	11	2	3	1	4	1	0	0	0	4	3	0	0	1	12	7	2	3	0
OTHER	1	0	1	0	0	0	0	0	0	0	0	0	0	0	0	1	0	1	0	0
S. AMERICA	24	10	10	3	0	3	3	0	0	0	6	5	0	1	0	13	1	10	2	0
ARGENTINA	6	1	3	1	0	0	0	0	0	0	1	1	0	0	0	4	3	3	1	0
BRAZIL	9	6	2	1	0	0	0	0	0	0	3	2	0	1	0	3	0	2	1	0
PERU	1	0	1	0	0	0	0	0	0	0	0	0	0	0	0	1	1	0	0	0
COLOMBIA	1	1	0	0	0	0	0	0	0	0	1	1	0	0	0	0	0	0	0	0
VENEZUELA	5	1	1	1	0	0	0	0	0	0	1	1	0	0	0	4	1	3	1	0
OTHER	2	1	0	0	0	1	1	0	0	0	0	0	0	0	0	1	0	1	0	0
EUROPE	127	58	56	11	1	53	36	13	4	0	17	6	9	2	0	56	16	34	5	1
EFTA	52	21	25	5	0	22	12	7	3	0	11	3	6	2	0	18	6	12	0	0
U.K.	42	13	23	5	0	18	8	7	3	0	10	3	5	2	0	13	2	11	0	0
SCANDINAVIA	6	5	1	0	0	3	3	0	0	0	0	0	0	0	0	3	2	1	0	0
SWITZERLAND	0	0	0	0	0	0	0	0	0	0	0	0	0	0	0	0	0	0	0	0
OTHER EFTA	4	3	1	0	0	1	1	0	0	0	1	0	1	0	0	2	2	0	0	0
EUROP. COMMUNITY	65	31	27	6	1	27	20	6	1	0	5	2	3	0	0	33	9	18	5	1
FRANCE	25	10	13	2	0	12	7	5	0	0	1	0	1	0	0	12	3	7	2	0
GERMANY	19	9	6	4	0	9	7	1	1	0	3	1	2	0	0	7	1	3	3	0
ITALY	11	7	4	0	0	5	5	0	0	0	0	0	0	0	0	6	2	4	0	0
BELGIUM + LUX	4	3	1	0	0	1	1	0	0	0	0	0	0	0	0	3	2	1	0	0
NETHERLANDS	6	2	3	0	1	0	0	0	0	0	1	1	0	0	0	5	3	3	0	1
SPAIN	6	3	3	0	0	3	3	0	0	0	0	0	0	0	0	3	0	3	0	0
GREECE + TURKEY	0	0	0	0	0	0	0	0	0	0	0	0	0	0	0	0	0	0	0	0
OTHER EUROPE	4	3	1	0	0	1	1	0	0	0	1	1	0	0	0	2	1	1	0	0
EUROPE EX. U.K.	85	45	33	6	1	35	28	6	1	0	7	3	4	0	0	43	14	23	5	1
SOUTHERN DOMINIONS	32	19	8	5	0	10	9	1	0	0	8	5	1	2	0	14	5	7	2	0
S. AFRICA +RHOD.	12	8	3	1	0	5	5	0	0	0	3	3	1	1	0	4	2	2	0	0
AUSTRALIA + N.Z.	20	11	5	4	0	5	4	1	0	0	5	4	0	1	0	10	3	5	2	0
ASIA + OTHER AFRICA	15	7	6	2	0	2	2	0	0	0	2	1	1	0	0	11	4	5	2	0
JAPAN	8	3	5	0	0	2	2	0	0	0	0	0	1	0	0	5	1	3	2	0
OTHER ASIA+AFR.	7	4	1	2	0	0	0	0	0	0	2	1	0	0	0	6	3	2	0	0
BLACK AFRICA	0	0	0	0	0	0	0	0	0	0	0	0	0	0	0	0	0	0	0	0
ARAB WORLD	1	1	0	0	0	0	0	0	0	0	0	0	0	0	0	1	1	1	0	0
INDIA	5	0	1	2	0	0	0	0	0	0	1	1	0	0	0	4	0	0	2	0
PHILIPPINES	0	1	0	0	0	0	0	0	0	0	0	0	0	1	0	0	0	0	0	0
OTHER E. ASIA	0	0	0	0	0	0	0	0	0	0	0	0	0	0	0	0	0	1	0	0
OTHER ASIA	1	0	0	0	0	0	0	0	0	0	0	0	0	0	0	1	0	0	0	0

CHAPTER 4- VARIETIES OF ENTRY
SECTION 2- THE FLOW OF MANUFACTURING BY INDUSTRY OF PARENT SYSTEM
TABLE 16- MANUFACTURING SUBSIDIARIES IN A SYSTEM IN THE
HOUSEHOLD APPLIANCE INDUSTRY (SIC 363)
CLASSIFIED BY COUNTRY, PERIOD MANUFACTURE BEGAN, AND METHOD OF ENTRY

(NEW=NEWLY FORMED, ACQ=ACQUIRED, DES=DESCENDANT, UNK=UNKNOWN)

PERIOD AND METHOD OF ENTRY

COUNTRY OR REGION	TOTAL PRE 1968 ALL	NEW	ACQ	DES	UNK	PRE 1946 ALL	NEW	ACQ	DES	UNK	1946-1957 ALL	NEW	ACQ	DES	UNK	1958-1967 ALL	NEW	ACQ	DES	UNK
OUTSIDE U.S.	76	40	25	10	1	8	3	0	4	1	13	7	3	3	0	55	30	22	3	0
OUT. U.S. + CANADA	67	36	21	9	1	6	2	0	3	1	11	5	3	3	0	50	29	18	3	0
OUT. WEST. HEMIS.	51	26	16	8	1	5	1	0	3	1	8	3	2	3	0	38	22	14	2	0
OUT. WHITE CWEALTH	49	32	15	2	0	3	2	1	0	0	8	5	3	0	0	38	25	11	2	0
OUT. DEVLPED WORLD	29	22	6	1	0	1	1	0	0	0	3	2	1	0	0	25	19	5	1	0
CANADA	9	4	4	1	0	2	1	0	1	0	2	2	0	0	0	5	1	4	0	0
LATIN AMERICA	16	10	5	1	0	2	1	0	1	0	3	2	1	0	0	11	7	4	0	0
C. AMER.+CARIB.	5	3	2	0	0	0	0	0	0	0	2	2	0	0	0	3	1	2	0	0
CUBA	0	0	0	0	0	0	0	0	0	0	0	0	0	0	0	0	0	0	0	0
MEXICO	4	3	1	0	0	1	1	0	0	0	1	1	0	0	0	2	1	1	0	0
OTHER	1	0	1	0	0	0	0	0	0	0	0	0	0	0	0	1	0	1	0	0
S. AMERICA	11	7	3	1	0	1	1	0	0	0	1	0	1	0	0	9	6	2	1	0
ARGENTINA	2	2	0	0	0	0	0	0	0	0	0	0	0	0	0	2	2	0	0	0
BRAZIL	3	2	1	0	0	1	1	0	0	0	0	0	0	0	0	2	1	1	0	0
PERU	1	1	0	0	0	0	0	0	0	0	0	0	0	0	0	1	1	0	0	0
COLUMBIA	1	1	0	0	0	0	0	0	0	0	0	0	0	0	0	1	1	0	0	0
VENEZUELA	2	1	1	0	0	0	0	0	0	0	0	0	0	0	0	2	1	1	0	0
OTHER	2	1	0	1	0	0	0	0	0	0	0	0	0	0	0	2	1	0	1	0
EUROPE	24	11	9	3	1	4	1	0	2	1	5	3	1	1	0	15	7	8	0	0
EFTA	7	2	2	2	1	3	0	0	2	1	1	0	1	0	0	3	2	1	0	0
U.K.	6	2	2	1	1	2	0	0	1	1	1	0	1	0	0	3	2	1	0	0
SCANDINAVIA	0	0	0	0	0	0	0	0	0	0	0	0	0	0	0	0	0	0	0	0
SWITZERLAND	1	0	0	1	0	1	0	0	1	0	0	0	0	0	0	0	0	0	0	0
OTHER EFTA	0	0	0	0	0	0	0	0	0	0	0	0	0	0	0	0	0	0	0	0
EUROP. COMMUNITY	15	7	7	1	0	1	1	0	0	0	3	3	0	0	0	11	3	7	1	0
FRANCE	5	4	0	1	0	1	0	0	1	0	1	1	0	0	0	3	3	0	0	0
GERMANY	4	2	2	0	0	0	0	0	0	0	0	0	0	0	0	4	2	2	0	0
ITALY	4	0	4	0	0	0	0	0	0	0	2	0	2	0	0	2	0	2	0	0
BELGIUM + LUX	1	0	1	0	0	0	0	0	0	0	0	0	0	0	0	1	0	1	0	0
NETHERLANDS	1	1	0	0	0	0	0	0	0	0	0	0	0	0	0	1	1	0	0	0
SPAIN	1	1	0	0	0	0	0	0	0	0	0	0	0	0	0	1	1	0	0	0
GREECE + TURKEY	1	1	0	0	0	0	0	0	0	0	0	0	0	0	0	1	1	0	0	0
OTHER EUROPE	0	0	0	0	0	0	0	0	0	0	0	0	0	0	0	0	0	0	0	0
EUROPE EX. U.K.	18	9	7	2	0	2	1	0	1	0	4	3	1	0	0	12	5	6	1	0
SOUTHERN DOMINIONS	12	2	5	5	0	1	0	0	1	0	2	0	2	0	0	9	2	3	4	0
S. AFRICA +RHOD.	2	1	0	1	0	1	0	0	1	0	0	0	0	0	0	1	1	0	0	0
AUSTRALIA + N.Z.	10	1	5	4	0	0	0	0	0	0	2	0	2	0	0	8	1	3	4	0
ASIA + OTHER AFRICA	15	13	2	0	0	0	0	0	0	0	1	1	0	0	0	14	12	2	0	0
JAPAN	13	12	1	0	0	0	0	0	0	0	1	1	0	0	0	12	11	1	0	0
OTHER ASIA+AFR.	2	1	1	0	0	0	0	0	0	0	0	0	0	0	0	2	1	1	0	0
BLACK AFRICA	0	0	0	0	0	0	0	0	0	0	0	0	0	0	0	0	0	0	0	0
ARAB WORLD	1	0	1	0	0	0	0	0	0	0	0	0	0	0	0	1	0	1	0	0
INDIA	1	1	0	0	0	0	0	0	0	0	0	0	0	0	0	1	1	0	0	0
PHILIPPINES	0	0	0	0	0	0	0	0	0	0	0	0	0	0	0	0	0	0	0	0
OTHER E. ASIA	0	0	0	0	0	0	0	0	0	0	0	0	0	0	0	0	0	0	0	0
OTHER ASIA	0	0	0	0	0	0	0	0	0	0	0	0	0	0	0	0	0	0	0	0

CHAPTER 4— VARIETIES OF ENTRY
SECTION 2— THE FLOW OF MANUFACTURING BY INDUSTRY OF PARENT SYSTEM
TABLE 17— MANUFACTURING SUBSIDIARIES IN A SYSTEM IN THE
ELECTRONICS INDUSTRY (SIC 365-367)
CLASSIFIED BY COUNTRY, PERIOD MANUFACTURE BEGAN, AND METHOD OF ENTRY

PERIOD AND METHOD OF ENTRY
(NEW=NEWLY FORMED, ACQ=ACQUIRED, DES=DESCENDANT, UNK=UNKNOWN)

COUNTRY OR REGION	TOTAL PRE 1968					PRE 1946					1946-1957					1958-1967				
	ALL	NEW	ACQ	DES	UNK	ALL	NEW	ACQ	DES	UNK	ALL	NEW	ACQ	DES	UNK	ALL	NEW	ACQ	DES	UNK
OUTSIDE U.S.	203	76	98	17	7	48	19	21	4	4	43	22	16	5	0	107	35	61	8	3
OUT. U.S. + CANADA	177	67	81	17	7	45	17	20	4	4	30	16	9	5	0	97	34	52	8	3
OUT. WEST. HEMIS.	138	46	69	12	6	39	13	19	4	3	22	11	9	2	0	72	22	41	6	3
OUT. WHITE CWEALTH	140	54	63	12	6	31	12	14	1	4	22	11	7	4	0	83	31	42	7	3
OUT. DEVLPED WORLD	49	28	15	5	1	7	5	1	0	1	9	6	0	3	0	33	17	14	2	0
CANADA	26	9	17	0	0	3	2	1	0	0	13	6	7	0	0	10	1	9	0	0
LATIN AMERICA	39	21	12	5	0	6	4	2	0	0	8	5	0	3	0	25	12	11	2	0
C. AMER.+CARIB.	15	6	7	2	0	2	2	0	0	0	1	1	0	0	0	12	3	7	2	0
CUBA	1	1	0	0	0	0	0	0	0	0	0	0	0	0	0	0	0	0	0	0
MEXICO	12	4	6	2	0	2	2	0	0	0	1	1	0	0	0	10	2	6	2	0
OTHER	2	1	1	0	0	0	0	0	0	0	0	0	0	0	0	2	1	1	0	0
S. AMERICA	24	15	5	3	1	4	2	1	0	1	7	4	0	3	0	13	9	4	0	0
ARGENTINA	8	4	3	1	0	1	1	0	0	0	2	1	0	1	0	5	3	2	0	0
BRAZIL	10	5	2	2	1	2	0	1	0	1	3	1	0	2	0	5	3	2	0	0
PERU	0	0	0	0	0	0	0	0	0	0	0	0	0	0	0	0	0	0	0	0
COLUMBIA	0	0	0	0	0	0	0	0	0	0	0	0	0	0	0	0	0	0	0	0
VENEZUELA	3	0	3	0	0	1	0	1	0	0	1	1	0	0	0	2	1	1	0	0
OTHER	3	3	0	0	0	1	1	0	0	0	1	1	0	0	0	1	1	0	0	0
EUROPE	107	29	58	10	6	36	12	17	4	3	12	6	5	1	0	55	11	36	5	3
EFTA	40	9	22	7	0	17	5	8	4	0	3	2	0	1	0	18	2	14	2	0
U.K.	25	7	13	4	0	11	4	4	3	0	2	2	0	0	0	11	1	9	1	0
SCANDINAVIA	7	1	4	2	0	3	0	2	1	0	1	0	0	1	0	3	0	2	1	0
SWITZERLAND	4	0	2	1	0	3	1	2	0	0	0	0	0	0	0	3	1	2	0	0
OTHER EFTA	4	0	3	0	0	0	0	0	0	0	0	0	0	0	0	1	0	1	0	0
EUROP. COMMUNITY	59	14	34	3	6	16	5	8	0	3	7	2	5	0	0	34	7	21	3	3
FRANCE	13	4	8	0	0	4	1	3	0	0	1	0	1	0	0	7	3	4	0	0
GERMANY	20	4	10	2	4	8	3	3	0	2	5	2	3	0	0	12	1	7	2	2
ITALY	13	5	7	1	0	2	0	1	0	1	1	0	1	0	0	8	3	4	1	0
BELGIUM + LUX	6	0	5	0	1	2	0	1	0	0	0	0	0	0	0	3	0	3	0	0
NETHERLANDS	7	1	4	0	2	1	1	0	0	0	1	1	0	0	0	4	0	3	0	1
SPAIN	5	4	1	0	0	1	1	0	0	0	1	1	0	0	0	3	2	1	0	0
GREECE + TURKEY	1	1	0	0	0	0	0	0	0	0	1	1	0	0	0	0	0	0	0	0
OTHER EUROPE	2	1	1	0	0	2	1	1	0	0	0	0	0	0	0	0	0	0	0	0
EUROPE EX. U.K.	82	22	45	6	6	25	8	13	1	3	10	4	5	1	0	44	10	27	4	3
SOUTHERN DOMINIONS	11	5	5	1	0	2	0	2	0	0	6	3	2	1	0	3	2	1	0	0
S. AFRICA +RHOD.	2	1	1	0	0	2	0	2	0	0	0	0	0	0	0	0	0	0	0	0
AUSTRALIA + N.Z.	9	4	4	1	0	0	0	0	0	0	6	3	2	1	0	3	2	1	0	0
ASIA + OTHER AFRICA	20	12	6	1	1	2	1	1	0	0	4	2	1	0	1	14	9	4	1	0
JAPAN	10	7	3	0	0	1	0	1	0	0	3	2	1	0	0	6	5	1	0	0
OTHER ASIA+AFR.	10	5	3	1	1	1	1	0	0	0	1	0	0	0	1	8	4	3	1	0
BLACK AFRICA	1	0	0	1	0	0	0	0	0	0	0	0	0	0	0	1	0	0	1	0
ARAB WORLD	0	0	0	0	0	0	0	0	0	0	0	0	0	0	0	0	0	0	0	0
INDIA	4	3	0	1	0	1	1	0	0	0	0	0	0	0	0	3	2	1	0	0
PHILIPPINES	3	1	2	0	0	0	0	0	0	0	1	0	1	0	0	2	1	1	0	0
OTHER E. ASIA	2	1	0	0	0	0	0	0	0	0	0	0	0	0	1	2	1	0	0	0
OTHER ASIA	0	0	0	0	0	0	0	0	0	0	0	0	0	0	0	0	0	0	0	0

CHAPTER 4- VARIETIES OF ENTRY
SECTION 2- THE FLOW OF MANUFACTURING BY INDUSTRY OF PARENT SYSTEM
TABLE 18- MANUFACTURING SUBSIDIARIES IN A SYSTEM IN THE
OTHER ELECTRICAL MACHINERY INDUSTRIES (OTHER SIC 36)
CLASSIFIED BY COUNTRY, PERIOD MANUFACTURE BEGAN, AND METHOD OF ENTRY

(NEW=NEWLY FORMED, ACQ=ACQUIRED, DES=DESCENDANT, UNK=UNKNOWN)

COUNTRY OR REGION	TOTAL PRE 1968 ALL	NEW	ACQ	DES	UNK	PRE 1946 ALL	NEW	ACQ	DES	UNK	1946-1957 ALL	NEW	ACQ	DES	UNK	1958-1967 ALL	NEW	ACQ	DES	UNK
OUTSIDE U.S.	223	67	108	16	26	51	19	22	4	6	40	11	18	2	9	126	37	68	10	11
OUT. U.S. + CANADA	180	62	82	13	19	37	16	15	4	2	30	11	12	0	7	109	35	55	9	10
OUT. WEST. HEMIS.	125	38	63	9	12	25	8	11	2	2	19	7	10	0	2	78	23	42	5	8
OUT. WHITE CWEALTH	138	50	61	9	15	27	14	11	2	0	20	7	7	0	6	88	29	43	7	9
OUT. DEVLPED WORLD	65	28	24	4	8	13	9	4	0	0	11	4	2	0	5	40	15	18	4	3
CANADA	43	5	26	3	7	14	3	7	0	4	10	0	6	0	2	17	2	13	1	1
LATIN AMERICA	55	24	19	4	7	12	8	4	0	0	11	4	2	0	5	31	12	13	4	2
C. AMER.+CARIB.	22	10	6	1	4	3	3	0	0	0	5	1	2	0	2	13	6	4	1	2
CUBA	2	2	0	0	0	0	0	0	0	0	0	0	0	0	0	2	0	0	0	1
MEXICO	15	7	4	0	3	3	0	3	0	0	3	0	1	0	2	8	4	3	0	1
OTHER	5	1	0	0	0	0	0	0	0	0	2	1	1	0	0	3	2	1	0	0
S. AMERICA	33	14	13	3	3	9	5	4	0	0	6	3	1	0	3	18	6	9	3	0
ARGENTINA	6	3	0	1	2	2	2	0	0	0	1	1	0	0	0	3	0	3	0	0
BRAZIL	16	7	7	0	2	5	3	2	0	0	3	1	0	0	2	8	5	0	0	3
PERU	1	1	0	0	0	0	0	0	0	0	1	1	0	0	0	1	1	0	0	0
COLOMBIA	4	1	1	1	1	0	0	0	0	0	0	0	0	0	0	3	1	0	1	1
VENEZUELA	4	3	0	1	0	0	0	0	0	0	1	0	0	0	1	3	2	0	1	0
OTHER	2	0	2	0	0	2	0	2	0	0	0	0	0	0	0	0	0	0	0	0
EUROPE	90	25	44	7	11	19	6	8	3	2	12	4	6	2	1	56	15	30	4	7
EFTA	27	6	11	3	6	9	2	3	2	1	3	0	2	1	1	14	4	6	1	3
U.K.	22	3	11	3	4	8	1	3	3	1	3	0	2	1	1	10	2	6	1	1
SCANDINAVIA	2	0	0	0	2	0	0	0	0	0	0	0	0	0	0	2	0	0	0	2
SWITZERLAND	3	3	0	0	0	0	0	0	0	0	0	0	0	0	0	3	2	0	0	0
OTHER EFTA	2	0	0	0	2	1	1	0	0	0	0	0	0	0	0	2	2	0	0	0
EUROP. COMMUNITY	52	14	30	3	3	8	3	4	1	0	6	1	4	1	0	36	10	22	2	2
FRANCE	27	5	18	3	2	6	2	3	1	0	1	0	1	0	0	19	3	14	2	0
GERMANY	16	4	11	0	2	1	1	0	0	0	3	0	3	0	0	11	3	7	0	1
ITALY	5	1	1	0	0	1	0	1	0	0	3	1	0	0	0	2	2	0	0	0
BELGIUM + LUX	1	1	0	0	0	0	0	0	0	0	0	0	0	0	0	1	1	0	0	0
NETHERLANDS	3	1	0	0	1	0	0	0	0	0	1	0	0	0	1	3	1	0	0	2
SPAIN	6	2	1	0	2	0	0	0	0	0	1	1	0	0	0	5	0	2	0	0
GREECE + TURKEY	2	2	0	0	0	0	0	0	0	0	1	1	0	0	0	1	0	0	1	0
OTHER EUROPE	3	1	2	0	0	2	0	1	0	1	1	0	0	0	1	0	0	0	0	0
EUROPE EX. U.K.	68	22	33	0	7	11	5	5	1	0	9	4	4	0	4	46	13	24	3	6
SOUTHERN DOMINIONS	19	8	10	1	0	2	1	1	0	0	6	3	3	0	0	11	4	6	1	0
S. AFRICA +RHOD.	6	3	3	0	0	1	1	0	0	0	2	1	1	0	0	3	1	2	0	0
AUSTRALIA + N.Z.	13	5	7	1	0	1	0	1	0	0	4	2	2	0	0	8	3	4	1	0
ASIA + OTHER AFRICA	16	9	9	1	0	4	1	2	1	0	1	1	0	0	0	11	4	6	1	0
JAPAN	6	4	2	0	0	3	1	2	0	0	0	0	0	0	0	2	1	1	0	0
OTHER ASIA+AFR.	10	5	5	0	0	1	0	0	1	0	1	1	0	0	0	9	3	5	0	1
BLACK AFRICA	0	0	0	0	0	0	0	0	0	0	0	0	0	0	0	0	0	0	0	0
ARAB WORLD	0	0	0	0	0	0	0	0	0	0	0	0	0	0	0	0	0	0	0	0
INDIA	4	1	4	0	0	0	0	0	0	0	0	0	0	0	0	4	1	4	0	0
PHILIPPINES	1	2	1	0	0	0	0	0	0	0	0	0	0	0	0	2	1	0	0	0
OTHER E. ASIA	2	2	0	0	0	1	0	1	0	0	0	0	0	0	0	1	1	0	0	0
OTHER ASIA	2	1	0	0	1	0	0	0	0	0	0	0	0	0	0	2	1	0	0	1

CHAPTER 4— VARIETIES OF ENTRY
SECTION 2— THE FLOW OF MANUFACTURING BY INDUSTRY OF PARENT SYSTEM
TABLE 19— MANUFACTURING SUBSIDIARIES IN A SYSTEM IN THE
MOTOR VEHICLES INDUSTRY (SIC 371)
CLASSIFIED BY COUNTRY, PERIOD MANUFACTURE BEGAN, AND METHOD OF ENTRY

(NEW=NEWLY FORMED, ACQ=ACQUIRED, DES=DESCENDANT, UNK=UNKNOWN)

COUNTRY OR REGION	TOTAL PRE 1968 ALL	NEW	ACQ	DES	UNK	PRE 1946 ALL	NEW	ACQ	DES	UNK	1946-1957 ALL	NEW	ACQ	DES	UNK	1958-1967 ALL	NEW	ACQ	DES	UNK
OUTSIDE U.S.	328	140	130	33	7	72	43	13	15	1	47	22	18	5	2	191	75	99	13	4
OUT. U.S. + CANADA	271	115	104	29	5	55	35	7	13	0	37	14	16	5	2	161	66	81	11	3
OUT. WEST. HEMIS.	197	84	71	21	4	48	30	7	11	0	27	6	15	4	2	105	48	49	6	2
OUT. WHITE CWEALTH	188	89	71	23	4	35	24	2	9	0	23	11	6	4	2	129	54	63	10	2
OUT. DEVLPED WORLD	98	44	40	12	1	12	8	0	4	0	14	10	2	0	0	71	26	38	6	1
CANADA	57	25	26	4	2	17	8	6	2	1	10	8	2	0	0	30	9	18	2	1
LATIN AMERICA	74	31	33	8	1	7	5	0	2	0	10	8	1	1	0	56	18	32	5	1
C. AMER.+CARIB.	23	6	16	0	1	2	2	0	0	0	2	0	1	1	0	19	3	15	1	0
CUBA	0	0	0	0	0	0	0	0	0	0	0	0	0	0	0	0	0	0	0	0
MEXICO	22	5	16	0	1	2	2	0	0	0	2	0	1	1	0	18	2	15	0	1
OTHER	1	1	0	0	0	0	0	0	0	0	0	0	0	0	0	1	1	0	0	0
S. AMERICA	51	25	17	7	1	5	3	0	2	0	8	7	0	1	0	37	15	17	4	1
ARGENTINA	19	10	6	2	1	2	1	0	1	0	3	3	0	0	0	14	6	6	1	1
BRAZIL	13	5	6	2	0	1	1	0	0	0	3	3	0	0	0	9	1	6	2	0
PERU	4	3	0	1	0	0	0	0	0	0	0	0	0	0	0	3	3	0	0	0
COLOMBIA	5	2	3	0	0	0	0	0	0	0	0	0	0	0	0	5	2	3	0	0
VENEZUELA	5	2	2	0	0	0	0	0	0	0	1	0	1	0	0	4	2	2	0	0
OTHER	3	3	0	0	0	1	1	0	0	0	1	1	0	0	0	1	1	0	0	0
EUROPE	130	47	48	15	4	33	19	6	8	0	17	3	9	3	2	64	25	33	4	2
EFTA	61	19	20	5	2	16	10	4	2	0	11	3	5	3	0	19	7	11	0	1
U.K.	48	11	18	3	1	11	5	4	2	0	8	2	5	1	0	14	4	9	0	1
SCANDINAVIA	8	5	2	1	0	3	1	0	2	0	2	0	0	2	0	3	1	2	0	0
SWITZERLAND	3	2	1	0	0	1	1	0	0	0	0	0	0	0	0	2	1	1	0	0
OTHER EFTA	3	1	0	1	1	1	1	0	0	0	1	1	0	0	0	1	0	0	1	0
EUROP. COMMUNITY	53	22	23	6	2	11	7	2	2	0	5	5	0	0	0	37	15	17	4	1
FRANCE	21	9	12	0	0	4	3	0	1	0	3	3	0	0	0	14	6	8	0	0
GERMANY	18	7	6	4	1	4	2	1	1	0	1	1	0	0	0	13	5	4	3	1
ITALY	7	3	5	1	0	1	1	0	0	0	0	0	0	0	0	6	2	5	1	0
BELGIUM + LUX	3	3	0	0	0	1	1	0	0	0	0	0	0	0	0	2	2	0	0	0
NETHERLANDS	4	2	0	1	1	1	1	0	0	0	1	1	0	0	0	2	0	0	1	1
SPAIN	7	2	4	1	0	2	2	0	0	0	1	0	1	0	0	5	2	4	0	0
GREECE + TURKEY	3	3	0	0	0	0	0	0	0	0	0	0	0	0	0	2	2	0	1	0
OTHER EUROPE	6	1	3	3	0	2	2	0	3	0	1	0	1	0	0	1	0	1	0	1
EUROPE EX. U.K.	82	36	30	12	3	22	14	2	6	0	9	1	4	2	2	50	21	24	4	2
SOUTHERN DOMINIONS	33	15	15	2	0	8	6	1	1	0	6	1	5	0	0	18	8	9	1	0
S. AFRICA +RHOD.	9	3	3	1	1	1	1	0	1	0	1	0	1	0	0	7	3	3	1	0
AUSTRALIA + N.Z.	24	11	12	1	0	7	5	1	0	0	5	1	5	0	0	11	5	6	0	0
ASIA + OTHER AFRICA	34	22	8	4	0	7	5	2	0	0	4	2	0	2	0	23	15	7	1	0
JAPAN	10	9	1	0	0	2	2	0	0	0	0	0	0	0	0	8	7	1	0	0
OTHER ASIA+AFR.	24	13	7	4	0	5	3	2	0	0	4	2	0	2	0	15	8	6	1	0
BLACK AFRICA	3	2	0	1	0	0	0	0	0	0	0	1	0	0	0	3	2	0	1	0
ARAB WORLD	3	1	0	2	0	1	1	0	0	0	0	0	0	0	0	3	1	0	1	1
INDIA	9	5	4	0	0	2	2	0	0	0	0	0	0	0	0	7	3	4	0	0
PHILIPPINES	2	2	0	0	0	0	0	0	0	0	0	0	0	0	0	2	2	0	0	0
OTHER E. ASIA	0	0	0	0	0	0	0	0	0	0	0	0	0	0	0	0	0	0	0	0
OTHER ASIA	7	3	3	1	0	1	1	0	1	0	3	2	0	0	0	2	0	2	0	0

CHAPTER 4- VARIETIES OF ENTRY
SECTION 2- THE FLOW OF MANUFACTURING BY INDUSTRY OF PARENT SYSTEM
TABLE 20- MANUFACTURING SUBSIDIARIES IN A SYSTEM IN THE
OTHER TRANSPORTATION EQUIPMENT INDUSTRIES (SIC 372-379)
CLASSIFIED BY COUNTRY, PERIOD MANUFACTURE BEGAN, AND METHOD OF ENTRY

PERIOD AND METHOD OF ENTRY
(NEW=NEWLY FORMED, ACQ=ACQUIRED, DES=DESCENDANT, UNK=UNKNOWN)

COUNTRY OR REGION	TOTAL PRE 1968					PRE 1946					1946-1957					1958-1967				
	ALL	NEW	ACQ	DES	UNK	ALL	NEW	ACQ	DES	UNK	ALL	NEW	ACQ	DES	UNK	ALL	NEW	ACQ	DES	UNK
OUTSIDE U.S.	125	47	59	4	11	15	6	8	0	1	20	9	8	1	2	86	32	43	3	8
OUT. U.S. + CANADA	102	44	39	4	11	8	5	2	0	1	14	9	2	1	2	76	30	35	3	8
OUT. WEST. HEMIS.	71	26	33	4	7	6	3	2	0	1	7	4	1	0	2	55	19	30	1	5
OUT. WHITE CWEALTH	74	35	21	3	11	8	5	2	0	1	9	6	1	0	2	53	24	18	3	8
OUT. DEVLPED WORLD	32	19	6	2	4	2	2	0	0	0	7	5	1	0	1	22	12	5	2	3
CANADA	23	3	20	0	0	7	1	6	0	0	6	0	6	0	0	10	2	8	0	0
LATIN AMERICA	31	18	6	2	4	2	2	0	0	0	7	5	1	0	1	21	11	5	2	3
C. AMER.+CARIB.	14	9	3	1	0	1	1	0	0	0	2	0	0	0	0	10	6	3	1	0
CUBA	0	0	0	0	0	0	0	0	0	0	0	0	0	0	0	0	0	0	0	0
MEXICO	12	7	3	1	0	1	1	0	0	0	1	1	0	0	0	9	5	3	1	0
OTHER	2	2	0	0	0	0	0	0	0	0	1	1	0	0	0	1	1	0	0	0
S. AMERICA	17	9	3	1	4	1	1	0	0	0	5	3	1	0	1	11	5	2	1	3
ARGENTINA	5	2	3	0	0	0	0	0	0	0	0	0	1	0	0	5	2	2	0	1
BRAZIL	6	4	1	1	0	1	1	0	0	0	3	2	0	0	1	3	2	1	0	0
PERU	1	0	1	0	0	0	0	0	0	0	1	0	0	0	0	0	0	1	0	0
COLOMBIA	2	1	0	0	1	0	0	0	0	0	1	1	0	0	0	1	0	0	0	1
VENEZUELA	1	1	0	0	0	0	0	0	0	0	0	0	0	0	0	0	1	0	0	0
OTHER	2	1	0	0	1	0	0	0	0	0	0	0	0	0	0	2	1	0	0	1
EUROPE	58	18	30	2	6	6	3	2	0	1	4	2	2	1	1	46	13	28	1	4
EFTA	26	5	19	1	0	1	1	0	0	0	2	1	1	0	0	23	3	19	0	1
U.K.	21	3	17	1	0	0	0	0	0	0	2	1	1	0	0	19	2	17	0	0
SCANDINAVIA	0	0	0	0	0	0	0	0	0	0	0	0	0	0	0	0	0	0	0	0
SWITZERLAND	4	2	0	1	0	1	1	0	0	0	0	0	0	0	0	3	1	1	0	1
OTHER EFTA	1	0	1	0	0	0	0	0	0	0	0	0	0	0	0	1	0	1	0	0
EUROP. COMMUNITY	29	12	11	1	3	4	2	2	0	0	1	0	0	0	0	22	10	9	1	2
FRANCE	14	6	6	1	1	2	2	0	0	0	0	0	0	0	0	10	5	5	0	0
GERMANY	6	3	2	0	1	1	1	0	0	0	0	0	0	0	0	5	3	1	1	0
ITALY	5	2	2	1	0	1	0	1	0	0	1	0	0	0	0	3	1	2	0	1
BELGIUM + LUX	3	1	1	0	1	0	0	0	0	0	1	1	0	0	1	1	0	1	0	0
NETHERLANDS	1	1	0	0	0	0	0	0	0	0	0	0	0	0	0	1	1	0	0	0
SPAIN	1	0	0	0	1	0	0	0	0	0	0	0	0	0	0	0	0	0	0	1
GREECE + TURKEY	1	1	0	0	0	0	0	0	0	0	0	0	0	0	0	0	0	0	0	0
OTHER EUROPE	1	0	0	0	1	0	0	0	0	0	1	0	0	0	0	0	0	0	1	0
EUROPE EX. U.K.	37	15	13	1	6	6	3	2	0	2	2	1	0	0	1	27	11	11	1	4
SOUTHERN DOMINIONS	7	6	1	0	0	0	0	0	0	0	3	2	1	0	0	4	4	0	0	0
S. AFRICA +RHOD.	4	4	0	0	0	0	0	0	0	0	1	1	0	0	0	3	3	0	0	0
AUSTRALIA + N.Z.	3	2	1	0	0	0	0	0	0	0	2	1	0	0	0	1	1	0	0	0
ASIA + OTHER AFRICA	6	2	2	0	1	0	0	0	0	0	0	0	0	0	0	5	2	2	0	1
JAPAN	5	2	1	0	0	0	0	0	0	0	0	0	0	0	0	4	2	2	0	0
OTHER ASIA+AFR.	1	1	0	0	0	0	0	0	0	0	0	0	0	0	0	1	1	0	0	0
BLACK AFRICA	0	0	0	0	0	0	0	0	0	0	0	0	0	0	0	0	0	0	0	0
ARAB WORLD	0	0	0	0	0	0	0	0	0	0	0	0	0	0	0	0	0	0	0	0
INDIA	0	0	0	0	0	0	0	0	0	0	0	0	0	0	0	0	0	0	0	0
PHILIPPINES	1	1	0	0	0	0	0	0	0	0	0	0	0	0	0	1	1	0	0	0
OTHER E. ASIA	1	1	0	0	0	0	0	0	0	0	1	0	0	0	0	0	0	0	0	0
OTHER ASIA	0	0	0	0	0	0	0	0	0	0	0	0	0	0	0	0	0	0	0	0

CHAPTER 4- VARIETIES OF ENTRY
SECTION 2- THE FLOW OF MANUFACTURING BY INDUSTRY OF PARENT SYSTEM
TABLE 21- MANUFACTURING SUBSIDIARIES IN A SYSTEM IN THE
INSTRUMENTS AND PRECISION GOODS INDUSTRIES (SIC 38)
CLASSIFIED BY COUNTRY, PERIOD MANUFACTURE BEGAN, AND METHOD OF ENTRY

PERIOD AND METHOD OF ENTRY
(NEW=NEWLY FORMED, ACQ=ACQUIRED, DES=DESCENDANT, UNK=UNKNOWN)

COUNTRY OR REGION	TOTAL PKE 1968					PKE 1946					1946-1957					1958-1967				
	ALL	NEW	ACQ	DES	UNK	ALL	NEW	ACQ	DES	UNK	ALL	NEW	ACQ	DES	UNK	ALL	NEW	ACQ	DES	UNK
OUTSIDE U.S.	116	58	38	12	8	19	11	5	3	0	40	19	13	5	3	57	28	20	4	5
OUT. U.S. + CANADA	99	49	33	11	6	16	8	5	2	1	31	17	9	5	0	52	24	19	4	5
OUT. WEST. HEMIS.	79	35	30	8	6	13	6	5	2	0	24	11	8	4	1	42	18	17	2	5
OUT. WHITE CMEALTH	73	35	23	10	5	8	3	2	3	0	22	11	8	3	0	43	21	13	4	5
OUT. DEVLPED WORLD	28	20	4	4	0	3	2	0	1	0	8	7	1	0	0	17	11	3	3	0
CANADA	17	9	5	1	2	9	2	4	1	2	3	3	0	0	0	5	4	1	0	0
LATIN AMERICA	20	14	3	3	0	2	2	0	0	0	8	6	1	1	0	10	6	2	2	0
C. AMER.+CARIB.	7	6	0	1	0	2	2	0	0	0	2	2	0	0	0	3	2	0	1	0
CUBA	1	1	0	0	0	1	1	0	0	0	0	0	0	0	0	0	0	0	0	0
MEXICO	5	4	0	1	0	1	1	0	0	0	2	2	0	0	0	2	1	0	1	0
OTHER	1	1	0	0	0	0	0	0	0	0	0	0	0	0	0	1	1	0	0	0
S. AMERICA	13	8	3	2	0	0	0	0	0	0	6	4	1	1	0	7	4	2	1	0
ARGENTINA	4	1	3	0	0	0	0	0	0	0	2	1	1	0	0	2	0	2	0	0
BRAZIL	3	1	1	1	0	0	0	0	0	0	2	0	1	1	0	1	1	0	0	0
PERU	1	0	1	0	0	0	0	0	0	0	0	0	0	0	0	1	0	1	0	0
COLOMBIA	2	2	0	0	0	0	0	0	0	0	0	0	0	0	0	2	2	0	0	0
VENEZUELA	2	2	0	0	0	0	0	0	0	0	1	1	0	0	0	1	1	0	0	0
OTHER	1	1	0	0	0	0	0	0	0	0	1	1	0	0	0	0	0	0	0	0
EUROPE	57	21	24	7	5	20	7	9	4	0	8	3	2	2	1	29	11	13	1	4
EFTA	18	8	6	1	2	7	1	4	1	1	3	4	0	0	1	8	3	2	0	1
U.K.	14	6	6	1	1	6	1	4	1	0	3	3	0	0	0	5	2	3	0	1
SCANDINAVIA	1	1	0	0	0	0	0	0	0	0	1	1	0	0	0	0	0	0	0	0
SWITZERLAND	1	0	1	0	0	0	0	0	0	0	0	0	0	0	0	1	0	1	0	0
OTHER EFTA	2	1	0	0	1	1	0	0	0	1	0	0	0	0	0	1	1	0	0	0
EUROP. COMMUNITY	37	12	16	6	3	11	5	5	1	0	5	2	2	2	0	21	8	9	3	1
FRANCE	13	3	6	2	2	5	1	3	1	0	2	0	0	0	1	6	2	3	1	1
GERMANY	12	4	5	3	0	5	2	2	1	0	2	0	1	1	0	7	4	2	1	0
ITALY	7	4	2	0	1	0	0	0	0	0	2	1	0	0	1	4	1	2	1	0
BELGIUM + LUX	2	0	2	0	0	0	0	0	0	0	0	0	0	0	0	2	1	1	0	0
NETHERLANDS	3	1	1	0	1	1	1	0	0	0	0	0	0	0	0	2	0	1	0	1
SPAIN	1	1	0	0	0	0	0	0	0	0	1	1	0	0	0	0	0	0	0	0
GREECE + TURKEY	0	0	0	0	0	0	0	0	0	0	0	0	0	0	0	0	0	0	0	0
OTHER EUROPE	0	0	0	0	0	0	0	0	0	0	0	0	0	0	0	0	0	0	0	0
EUROPE EX. U.K.	43	15	18	6	4	14	5	5	2	1	5	1	2	1	0	24	9	10	1	4
SOUTHERN DOMINIONS	11	7	4	0	0	2	1	1	0	0	2	2	0	0	0	4	1	3	0	0
S. AFRICA +RHOD.	3	3	0	0	0	1	1	0	0	0	0	0	0	0	0	3	0	3	0	0
AUSTRALIA + N.Z.	8	4	4	0	0	1	0	1	0	0	2	1	1	0	0	3	1	1	0	0
ASIA + OTHER AFRICA	11	7	2	1	1	2	1	1	0	0	2	1	1	0	0	6	3	1	1	1
JAPAN	3	1	1	0	1	1	1	0	0	0	1	0	0	0	0	2	0	1	0	1
OTHER ASIA+AFR.	8	6	1	1	0	1	0	1	0	0	1	1	0	0	0	4	2	1	1	0
BLACK AFRICA	1	1	0	0	0	0	0	0	0	0	0	0	0	0	0	1	1	0	0	0
ARAB WORLD	0	0	0	0	0	0	0	0	0	0	0	0	0	0	0	0	0	0	0	0
INDIA	3	1	0	1	0	1	0	0	1	0	0	0	0	0	0	2	1	0	0	0
PHILIPPINES	2	2	0	0	0	0	0	0	0	0	0	0	0	0	0	2	2	0	0	0
OTHER E. ASIA	0	0	0	0	0	0	0	0	0	0	0	0	0	0	0	0	0	0	0	0
OTHER ASIA	2	2	0	0	0	0	0	0	0	0	0	0	0	0	0	2	2	0	0	0

CHAPTER 4- VARIETIES OF ENTRY
SECTION 2- THE FLOW OF MANUFACTURING BY INDUSTRY OF PARENT SYSTEM
TABLE 22- MANUFACTURING SUBSIDIARIES IN A SYSTEM IN THE
OTHER INDUSTRIES (SIC 21,27, AND 39)
CLASSIFIED BY COUNTRY, PERIOD MANUFACTURE BEGAN, AND METHOD OF ENTRY

PERIOD AND METHOD OF ENTRY
(NEW=NEWLY FORMED, ACQ=ACQUIRED, DES=DESCENDANT, UNK=UNKNOWN)

COUNTRY OR REGION	TOTAL PRE 1968 ALL	NEW	ACQ	DES	UNK	PRE 1946 ALL	NEW	ACQ	DES	UNK	1946-1957 ALL	NEW	ACQ	DES	UNK	1958-1967 ALL	NEW	ACQ	DES	UNK
OUTSIDE U.S.	103	44	51	5	2	12	3	6	3	0	12	7	5	0	0	78	34	40	2	2
OUT. U.S. + CANADA	87	40	41	4	2	9	2	5	2	0	10	5	5	0	0	68	33	31	2	2
OUT. WEST. HEMIS.	61	29	27	3	2	6	0	4	2	0	4	3	1	0	0	51	26	22	1	2
OUT. WHITE CWEALTH	66	33	29	2	2	5	2	3	0	0	9	4	5	0	0	52	27	21	2	2
OUT. DEVLPED WORLD	31	14	15	1	1	3	2	1	0	0	7	3	4	0	0	21	9	10	1	1
CANADA	16	4	10	1	0	3	1	1	1	0	2	2	0	0	0	10	1	9	0	0
LATIN AMERICA	26	11	14	1	0	3	2	1	1	0	6	2	4	0	0	17	7	9	1	0
C. AMER.+CARIB.	11	5	5	1	0	3	2	1	1	0	2	1	1	0	0	6	2	3	1	0
CUBA	5	1	0	0	0	0	0	0	0	0	1	1	0	0	0	0	0	0	0	0
MEXICO	5	2	2	0	0	3	2	1	0	0	0	0	0	0	0	2	0	2	0	0
OTHER	4	3	3	1	0	0	0	0	1	0	1	0	1	0	0	4	2	1	1	0
S. AMERICA	11	6	1	0	0	0	0	0	0	0	4	1	3	0	0	11	5	6	0	0
ARGENTINA	5	2	0	0	0	0	0	0	0	0	0	0	0	0	0	5	2	3	0	0
BRAZIL	5	3	0	0	0	0	0	0	0	0	2	1	1	0	0	3	3	0	0	0
PERU	2	1	1	0	0	0	0	0	0	0	1	0	1	0	0	0	0	0	0	0
COLOMBIA	1	1	0	0	0	0	0	0	0	0	0	0	0	0	0	1	1	0	0	0
VENEZUELA	6	2	4	0	0	0	0	0	0	0	2	0	1	0	0	2	2	3	0	0
OTHER	0	0	0	0	0	0	0	0	0	0	0	0	0	0	0	3	0	0	0	0
EUROPE	47	20	23	3	1	6	4	2	0	0	2	2	0	0	0	39	19	18	1	1
EFTA	20	6	12	2	0	4	4	2	0	0	0	0	0	0	0	16	6	10	0	0
U.K.	13	2	9	2	0	4	4	2	0	0	0	0	0	0	0	9	2	7	0	0
SCANDINAVIA	5	4	1	0	0	0	0	0	0	0	0	0	0	0	0	5	4	1	0	0
SWITZERLAND	1	0	1	0	0	0	0	0	0	0	0	0	0	0	0	1	1	1	0	0
OTHER EFTA	1	0	1	0	1	0	0	0	0	0	0	0	0	0	0	1	0	1	0	1
EUROP. COMMUNITY	24	13	9	0	0	0	0	0	0	0	2	2	0	0	0	22	12	8	3	0
FRANCE	7	4	3	0	0	0	0	0	0	0	0	0	0	0	0	7	4	3	0	0
GERMANY	6	4	1	0	0	0	0	0	0	0	0	0	0	0	0	6	4	1	1	0
ITALY	6	2	4	0	0	0	0	0	0	0	1	1	0	0	0	5	2	3	1	0
BELGIUM + LUX	3	1	2	0	1	0	0	0	0	0	0	0	0	0	0	3	2	1	0	1
NETHERLANDS	2	2	0	0	0	0	0	0	0	0	1	1	0	0	0	1	2	0	0	0
SPAIN	2	0	2	0	0	2	0	2	0	0	0	0	0	0	0	0	0	0	0	0
GREECE + TURKEY	0	0	0	0	0	0	0	0	0	0	0	0	0	0	0	1	0	0	0	0
OTHER EUROPE	1	0	0	0	1	0	0	0	0	0	0	0	0	0	0	1	1	0	0	1
EUROPE EX. U.K.	34	18	14	1	1	2	0	2	0	0	2	2	0	0	0	30	17	11	1	1
SOUTHERN DOMINIONS	7	4	3	0	0	0	0	0	0	0	1	1	0	0	0	6	3	3	0	0
S. AFRICA +RHOD.	0	0	0	0	0	0	0	0	0	0	0	0	0	0	0	0	0	0	0	0
AUSTRALIA + N.Z.	7	4	3	0	0	0	0	0	0	0	1	1	0	0	0	6	3	3	0	0
ASIA + OTHER AFRICA	7	5	1	1	0	0	0	0	0	0	1	1	0	0	0	6	4	1	1	0
JAPAN	2	2	0	0	0	0	0	0	0	0	0	0	0	0	0	2	2	0	0	0
OTHER ASIA+AFK.	5	3	1	1	0	0	0	0	0	0	1	1	0	0	0	4	2	1	1	0
BLACK AFRICA	1	0	0	1	0	0	0	0	0	0	0	0	0	0	0	1	0	0	1	0
ARAB WORLD	1	1	0	0	0	0	0	0	0	0	0	0	0	0	0	1	1	0	0	0
INDIA	1	0	0	1	0	0	0	0	0	0	0	0	0	0	0	1	0	0	1	0
PHILIPPINES	0	0	0	0	0	0	0	0	0	0	0	0	0	0	0	0	0	0	0	0
OTHER E. ASIA	0	0	0	0	0	0	0	0	0	0	0	0	0	0	0	0	0	0	0	0
OTHER ASIA	2	2	0	0	0	0	0	0	0	0	1	1	0	0	0	1	1	0	0	0

CHAPTER 4- VARIETIES OF ENTRY
SECTION 3- THE FLOW OF MANUFACTURING BY CHARACTERISTIC OF PARENT SYSTEM
TABLE A1- MANUFACTURING SUBSIDIARIES IN A SYSTEM
WITH LOW SALES IN 1966
CLASSIFIED BY COUNTRY, PERIOD MANUFACTURE BEGAN, AND METHOD OF ENTRY

(NEW=NEWLY FORMED, ACQ=ACQUIRED, DES=DESCENDANT, UNK=UNKNOWN)

PERIOD AND METHOD OF ENTRY

COUNTRY OR REGION	TOTAL ALL	NEW	ACQ	DES	UNK	PRE 1946 ALL	NEW	ACQ	DES	UNK	1946-1957 ALL	NEW	ACQ	DES	UNK	1958-1967 ALL	NEW	ACQ	DES	UNK
OUTSIDE U.S.	2082	849	941	144	113	357	194	101	27	35	410	186	156	39	29	1280	469	684	78	49
OUT. U.S. + CANADA	1753	752	756	126	90	260	146	71	20	23	325	157	113	33	22	1139	449	572	73	45
OUT. WEST. HEMIS.	1216	514	531	87	59	204	113	56	19	16	187	83	76	21	11	800	318	399	51	32
OUT. WHITE CWEALTH	1284	577	548	79	69	143	82	41	5	15	228	118	73	21	16	922	377	434	53	38
OUT. DEVLPED WORLD	659	311	261	44	38	57	34	15	1	7	157	89	40	16	12	440	188	206	27	19
CANADA	329	97	185	18	23	97	48	30	7	12	85	29	43	6	7	141	20	112	5	4
LATIN AMERICA	537	238	225	39	31	56	33	15	1	7	138	74	37	16	11	339	131	173	22	13
C. AMER.+CARIB.	245	104	100	24	15	16	12	2	0	2	68	34	17	11	6	159	58	81	13	7
CUBA	15	7	3	4	1	12	10	2	0	1	2	1	1	0	0	1	1	0	0	1
MEXICO	159	63	76	15	4	2	1	0	0	1	43	24	13	5	1	103	29	61	10	3
OTHER	71	34	23	6	7	2	1	0	0	1	14	5	3	1	5	54	28	20	3	3
S. AMERICA	292	134	125	17	16	40	21	13	1	5	70	40	20	8	2	180	73	92	9	6
ARGENTINA	68	21	41	2	2	14	6	6	0	2	14	5	8	1	0	38	10	27	1	0
BRAZIL	81	38	31	7	5	14	8	4	1	1	25	14	5	3	0	42	16	22	4	0
PERU	19	12	5	0	2	3	1	1	0	1	5	5	0	0	0	11	6	4	0	1
COLOMBIA	39	16	18	1	4	2	2	0	0	0	8	4	3	0	1	29	10	15	1	3
VENEZUELA	55	35	16	2	2	1	1	0	0	0	14	12	2	0	0	40	22	14	2	2
OTHER	30	12	14	3	1	6	3	2	1	0	4	0	2	2	0	20	9	10	1	0
EUROPE	839	307	411	61	40	156	75	52	17	12	120	47	55	11	7	543	185	304	33	21
EFTA	319	100	157	30	17	81	35	28	13	5	56	18	27	6	4	167	47	102	10	8
U.K.	253	65	135	26	12	71	28	26	13	4	48	16	23	6	3	119	21	86	8	5
SCANDINAVIA	37	19	13	2	3	6	3	2	0	1	4	1	0	0	0	27	15	8	2	2
SWITZERLAND	11	4	5	0	2	1	0	0	0	1	2	0	1	1	0	8	5	2	1	0
OTHER EFTA	18	12	4	2	2	3	3	0	0	0	2	1	1	0	0	13	3	9	0	1
EUROP. COMMUNITY	445	175	215	29	21	69	37	22	4	6	52	21	24	4	3	319	117	169	21	12
FRANCE	143	48	80	7	6	26	11	13	1	1	11	4	4	1	2	104	33	63	5	3
GERMANY	128	49	56	14	6	25	15	6	1	3	21	4	14	2	1	79	30	36	11	2
ITALY	87	43	36	4	4	6	6	0	0	0	8	6	1	1	0	73	31	35	3	4
BELGIUM + LUX	43	17	20	2	4	6	4	1	0	2	5	3	2	0	0	32	10	17	2	2
NETHERLANDS	44	18	23	2	1	6	2	2	0	2	7	2	3	2	0	31	13	18	1	1
SPAIN	44	26	16	1	1	4	2	2	0	0	4	1	2	0	0	36	23	12	1	0
GREECE + TURKEY	14	7	5	0	2	2	1	0	0	1	1	1	0	0	0	11	5	5	0	1
OTHER EUROPE	19	10	5	1	3	1	0	0	0	1	7	5	2	0	0	10	5	4	1	0
EUROPE EX. U.K.	586	242	276	35	28	85	47	26	4	8	72	31	32	5	4	424	164	218	26	16
SOUTHERN DOMINIONS	200	101	67	20	9	45	35	4	2	4	42	18	15	6	3	110	48	48	12	2
S. AFRICA +RHOD.	61	38	15	4	2	14	13	0	0	1	15	10	3	1	1	30	15	12	3	0
AUSTRALIA + N.Z.	139	63	52	16	7	31	22	4	2	3	27	8	12	5	2	80	33	36	9	2
ASIA + OTHER AFRICA	177	106	53	10	10	2	2	0	0	0	25	18	6	0	1	147	85	47	6	9
JAPAN	55	33	17	1	3	3	3	0	0	0	6	3	3	0	0	46	28	14	4	3
OTHER ASIA+AFR.	122	73	36	5	7	2	1	1	0	0	19	15	3	0	1	101	57	33	5	6
BLACK AFRICA	13	5	5	0	2	0	0	0	0	0	2	1	1	0	0	11	5	5	0	1
ARAB WORLD	9	5	4	0	0	0	0	0	0	0	1	1	0	0	0	8	4	4	0	0
INDIA	28	15	8	3	1	1	1	0	0	0	3	3	0	0	0	24	12	8	3	1
PHILIPPINES	20	14	6	0	0	1	1	0	0	0	7	6	1	0	0	12	7	5	0	0
OTHER E. ASIA	21	10	4	0	1	0	0	0	0	0	1	1	0	0	0	20	9	9	1	1
OTHER ASIA	31	23	4	1	3	0	0	0	0	0	5	3	2	0	0	26	20	2	1	3

CHAPTER 4- VARIETIES OF ENTRY
SECTION 3- THE FLOW OF MANUFACTURING BY CHARACTERISTIC OF PARENT SYSTEM
TABLE A2- MANUFACTURING SUBSIDIARIES IN A SYSTEM
WITH HIGH SALES IN 1966
CLASSIFIED BY COUNTRY, PERIOD MANUFACTURE BEGAN, AND METHOD OF ENTRY

PERIOD AND METHOD OF ENTRY
(NEW=NEWLY FORMED, ACQ=ACQUIRED, DES=DESCENDANT, UNK=UNKNOWN)

COUNTRY OR REGION	TOTAL PRE 1968					PRE 1946					1946-1957					1958-1967				
	ALL	NEW	ACQ	DES	UNK	ALL	NEW	ACQ	DES	UNK	ALL	NEW	ACQ	DES	UNK	ALL	NEW	ACQ	DES	UNK
OUTSIDE U.S.	3150	1323	1268	208	243	668	333	203	59	73	602	280	217	55	50	1772	710	848	94	120
OUT. U.S. + CANADA	2666	1174	1010	184	207	497	258	136	49	54	486	243	151	49	43	1592	673	723	86	110
OUT. WEST. HEMIS.	1862	767	750	126	157	348	163	104	41	40	282	133	90	30	29	1170	471	556	55	88
OUT. WHITE CWEALTH	2062	971	727	137	157	360	197	92	31	40	387	196	117	37	37	1245	578	518	69	80
OUT. DEVLPED WORLD	1050	548	306	78	77	178	110	36	13	19	239	127	67	25	20	592	311	203	40	38
CANADA	484	149	258	24	36	171	75	67	10	19	116	37	66	6	7	180	37	125	8	10
LATIN AMERICA	804	407	260	58	50	149	95	32	8	14	204	110	61	19	14	422	202	167	31	22
C. AMER.+CARIB.	331	155	119	24	17	62	42	12	2	5	66	34	21	6	5	187	79	86	16	6
CUBA	33	14	7	5	7	17	7	5	1	1	12	7	1	3	1	2	0	1	0	2
MEXICO	211	96	86	13	6	34	25	7	1	1	49	24	19	3	3	118	47	60	9	2
OTHER	87	45	26	6	4	11	10	0	1	1	5	3	1	0	1	67	32	25	6	4
S. AMERICA	473	252	141	34	33	87	53	20	6	8	138	76	40	13	9	235	123	81	15	16
ARGENTINA	93	50	26	9	4	30	20	5	4	1	19	12	5	1	1	42	18	16	4	1
BRAZIL	118	62	40	10	6	20	14	5	0	1	45	23	14	6	2	51	25	21	4	1
PERU	39	17	14	2	3	8	5	2	1	1	10	4	5	1	1	17	8	7	1	1
COLOMBIA	76	39	25	5	6	8	4	2	1	1	21	12	7	1	1	46	23	16	3	4
VENEZUELA	90	57	18	6	7	9	7	1	0	1	29	16	6	4	3	50	34	11	2	3
OTHER	57	27	18	2	7	11	3	5	0	3	14	9	3	1	1	29	15	10	1	3
EUROPE	1216	460	543	83	106	268	117	86	30	35	183	85	60	19	19	741	258	397	34	52
EFTA	432	149	190	42	43	126	52	42	15	17	69	30	19	13	7	229	67	129	14	19
U.K.	298	90	144	28	30	90	32	33	12	13	53	23	17	3	4	149	35	94	7	13
SCANDINAVIA	79	32	29	4	8	19	2	5	1	4	13	6	2	3	2	46	17	22	5	2
SWITZERLAND	26	9	8	4	1	4	2	1	1	0	2	0	1	0	1	19	7	7	2	3
OTHER EFTA	29	18	9	1	1	13	9	3	1	0	1	1	0	0	0	15	8	6	0	1
EUROP. COMMUNITY	626	237	291	35	48	114	53	37	11	13	95	44	34	6	11	402	140	220	18	24
FRANCE	180	62	87	15	11	39	15	13	7	4	26	9	9	3	4	110	36	65	5	4
GERMANY	170	56	88	8	16	34	20	3	2	4	26	8	14	1	3	108	28	61	5	9
ITALY	135	58	62	4	8	14	8	3	1	2	27	16	9	0	2	91	34	50	3	2
BELGIUM + LUX	75	32	34	3	5	12	5	4	2	0	5	4	1	0	0	57	23	29	3	2
NETHERLANDS	66	29	20	5	8	10	5	4	1	3	11	4	1	2	3	41	19	15	2	5
SPAIN	95	39	46	3	7	11	5	5	1	0	12	5	6	0	1	72	29	36	2	5
GREECE + TURKEY	30	24	2	0	4	7	0	3	1	3	5	2	0	0	3	24	19	2	0	3
OTHER EUROPE	33	11	14	3	4	16	7	3	3	3	2	1	1	0	0	14	3	10	0	1
EUROPE EX. U.K.	918	370	399	55	76	178	85	53	18	22	130	62	43	10	15	592	223	303	27	39
SOUTHERN DOMINIONS	288	109	129	18	18	44	28	11	5	0	44	23	16	3	2	186	58	102	10	16
S. AFRICA +RHOD.	100	32	51	11	3	12	9	2	1	0	13	8	4	1	0	68	15	45	5	3
AUSTRALIA + N.Z.	188	77	78	11	15	32	19	9	4	0	31	15	12	2	2	118	43	57	5	13
ASIA + OTHER AFRICA	358	198	78	25	36	36	18	18	7	5	55	25	14	8	8	243	155	57	11	20
JAPAN	112	57	32	8	27	7	3	3	0	1	20	8	8	2	6	73	46	21	2	4
OTHER ASIA+AFR.	246	141	46	20	27	29	15	15	4	4	35	17	6	6	6	170	109	36	9	16
BLACK AFRICA	33	18	5	1	7	7	1	4	0	1	3	2	0	0	1	28	16	5	1	6
ARAB WORLD	30	19	3	6	1	2	0	0	0	1	5	1	2	0	1	22	18	1	1	1
INDIA	41	25	12	3	1	5	0	5	1	0	3	0	2	0	0	32	17	12	3	0
PHILIPPINES	39	21	9	4	4	5	4	1	0	0	3	1	1	1	1	20	12	4	3	2
OTHER F. ASIA	23	12	5	1	1	4	1	2	2	1	2	0	1	1	1	16	11	2	0	2
OTHER ASIA	80	46	12	5	11	12	5	2	0	3	10	6	2	1	2	52	35	10	2	5

CHAPTER 4- VARIETIES OF ENTRY
SECTION 3- THE FLOW OF MANUFACTURING BY CHARACTERISTIC OF PARENT SYSTEM
TABLE B1- MANUFACTURING SUBSIDIARIES IN A SYSTEM
WITH LOW "R&D INTENSITY" IN 1964
CLASSIFIED BY COUNTRY, PERIOD MANUFACTURE BEGAN, AND METHOD OF ENTRY

PERIOD AND METHOD OF ENTRY
(NEW=NEWLY FORMED, ACQ=ACQUIRED, DES=DESCENDANT, UNK=UNKNOWN)

COUNTRY OR REGION	TOTAL ALL	NEW	PRE 1968 ACQ	DES	UNK	PRE 1946 ALL	NEW	ACQ	DES	UNK	1946-1957 ALL	NEW	ACQ	DES	UNK	1958-1967 ALL	NEW	ACQ	DES	UNK
OUTSIDE U.S.	1462	561	591	108	138	303	146	78	25	54	281	123	111	26	21	814	292	402	57	63
OUT. U.S. + CANADA	1227	491	473	94	114	224	115	50	20	39	219	100	79	23	17	729	276	344	51	58
OUT. WEST. HEMIS.	849	315	345	64	89	152	73	34	15	30	118	52	41	12	13	543	190	270	37	46
OUT. WHITE CWEALTH	968	420	347	68	86	173	95	37	12	29	184	82	69	18	15	564	243	241	38	42
OUT. DEVLPED WORLD	475	227	142	39	39	82	45	16	7	14	113	53	41	13	6	252	129	85	19	19
CANADA	235	70	118	14	24	79	31	28	5	15	62	23	32	3	4	85	16	58	6	5
LATIN AMERICA	378	176	128	30	25	72	42	16	5	5	101	48	38	11	4	186	86	74	14	12
C. AMER.+CARIB.	161	73	58	12	9	33	21	7	1	4	32	15	12	2	3	87	37	39	8	3
CUBA	12	6	1	2	2	9	5	1	2	0	3	1	2	0	0	0	0	0	0	2
MEXICO	109	48	43	7	4	20	13	6	0	1	28	13	12	2	1	54	22	25	5	2
OTHER	40	19	14	3	3	5	4	0	0	1	1	0	1	0	1	33	15	14	3	1
S. AMERICA	217	103	70	18	16	39	21	9	4	5	69	33	26	8	2	99	49	35	6	9
ARGENTINA	35	14	13	5	1	12	6	2	3	1	7	2	5	0	0	14	6	6	2	0
BRAZIL	45	20	19	4	1	9	6	2	0	1	13	4	6	3	0	22	10	11	1	0
PERU	22	10	8	0	4	5	3	2	0	0	8	4	4	0	0	6	3	2	1	0
COLOMBIA	45	22	13	4	5	5	2	1	1	1	17	10	5	1	1	22	10	7	2	3
VENEZUELA	44	25	11	3	4	5	3	1	0	1	17	9	4	3	1	22	13	6	0	3
OTHER	26	12	6	4	2	4	3	1	0	0	7	4	2	1	0	13	7	3	1	2
EUROPE	567	204	250	44	62	127	59	31	12	25	82	38	27	8	9	351	107	192	24	28
EFTA	180	57	73	21	28	50	19	12	7	12	24	10	7	4	3	105	28	54	10	13
U.K.	118	33	52	14	19	36	10	10	7	9	16	6	3	3	1	66	14	39	4	9
SCANDINAVIA	38	11	15	5	6	6	3	1	0	2	6	1	3	1	1	24	7	11	4	2
SWITZERLAND	11	4	3	2	1	1	1	0	0	0	1	0	0	0	1	9	3	3	2	1
OTHER EFTA	11	9	3	0	2	6	5	1	0	0	1	0	1	0	0	6	4	1	0	1
EUROP. COMMUNITY	316	115	146	22	27	63	34	16	5	8	51	24	17	4	6	196	57	113	13	13
FRANCE	77	31	34	3	7	18	9	6	2	1	11	7	2	0	2	45	15	26	3	1
GERMANY	85	35	35	6	10	21	14	6	1	0	17	6	7	2	2	47	15	24	3	4
ITALY	71	26	35	4	6	11	7	2	1	1	13	8	3	0	2	47	11	30	3	3
BELGIUM + LUX	47	14	26	4	3	8	3	2	1	2	5	1	2	2	0	33	9	21	2	1
NETHERLANDS	36	9	18	2	5	5	1	1	1	2	5	2	3	1	0	24	7	12	2	4
SPAIN	40	17	23	0	2	4	4	0	0	0	5	2	3	0	0	31	14	17	0	0
GREECE + TURKEY	11	5	1	0	2	1	0	0	0	1	0	0	0	0	0	10	7	2	0	1
OTHER EUROPE	20	8	6	1	5	9	5	3	1	0	2	2	0	0	0	9	1	6	0	1
EUROPE EX. U.K.	449	171	198	30	43	91	49	21	5	16	66	29	24	5	8	285	93	153	20	19
SOUTHERN DOMINIONS	130	35	69	11	7	21	9	3	1	0	17	7	5	2	3	92	19	59	8	6
S. AFRICA +RHOD.	53	11	33	8	1	9	3	1	2	0	5	3	2	2	0	39	5	30	3	1
AUSTRALIA + N.Z.	77	24	36	8	6	12	6	2	0	0	12	4	5	2	1	53	14	29	5	5
ASIA + OTHER AFRICA	152	76	26	26	20	33	12	2	2	5	19	7	4	5	3	100	64	18	5	12
JAPAN	55	25	12	9	6	14	2	0	2	0	7	2	4	0	1	34	21	8	5	1
OTHER ASIA+AFR.	97	51	14	9	14	19	3	0	0	5	12	5	3	1	2	66	43	11	5	7
BLACK AFRICA	13	8	2	3	1	2	0	0	2	0	0	0	2	0	0	11	8	0	0	1
ARAB WORLD	15	9	2	1	0	2	0	1	0	0	4	1	1	0	0	9	8	0	0	0
INDIA	13	7	1	2	3	1	1	0	1	1	3	1	0	1	0	9	5	1	2	2
PHILIPPINES	10	5	1	1	0	2	0	0	0	1	1	1	0	0	1	7	4	0	1	2
OTHER E. ASIA	9	3	2	1	3	2	0	0	2	0	0	0	2	0	1	7	3	0	2	2
OTHER ASIA	37	19	5	3	7	10	2	0	1	4	4	2	2	0	1	23	15	4	2	2

CHAPTER 4- VARIETIES OF ENTRY
SECTION 3- THE FLOW OF MANUFACTURING BY CHARACTERISTIC OF PARENT SYSTEM
TABLE B2- MANUFACTURING SUBSIDIARIES IN A SYSTEM
WITH HIGH "R&D INTENSITY" IN 1964
CLASSIFIED BY COUNTRY, PERIOD MANUFACTURE BEGAN, AND METHOD OF ENTRY

(NEW=NEWLY FORMED, ACQ=ACQUIRED, DES=DESCENDANT, UNK=UNKNOWN)

COUNTRY OR REGION	TOTAL PRE 1968					PRE 1946					1946-1957					1958-1967				
	ALL	NEW	ACQ	DES	UNK	ALL	NEW	ACQ	DES	UNK	ALL	NEW	ACQ	DES	UNK	ALL	NEW	ACQ	DES	UNK
OUTSIDE U.S.	1216	566	464	95	67	200	103	68	17	12	274	142	87	30	15	718	321	309	48	40
OUT. U.S. + CANADA	1071	498	405	88	60	148	66	58	13	11	228	119	67	29	14	675	313	280	47	35
OUT. WEST. HEMIS.	778	347	304	62	51	122	53	47	13	9	138	66	45	15	12	504	228	212	34	30
OUT. WHITE CWEALTH	801	384	293	63	48	91	32	42	7	10	164	88	45	21	10	533	264	206	35	28
OUT. DEVLPED WORLD	379	206	117	31	18	27	14	11	0	2	109	63	25	15	6	236	129	81	16	10
CANADA	145	68	59	7	7	52	37	10	4	1	46	23	20	2	1	43	8	29	1	5
LATIN AMERICA	293	151	101	26	9	26	13	11	0	2	90	53	22	13	2	171	85	68	13	5
C. AMER.+CARIB.	127	65	41	13	4	6	0	6	0	0	33	22	6	5	0	84	37	35	8	4
CUBA	5	4	1	0	2						5	4	1	0	0	0	0	0	0	0
MEXICO	92	39	37	12	2	6	0	6	0	0	25	15	5	5	0	59	18	32	7	2
OTHER	30	22	1	2	1	0	0	0	0	0	3	3	0	0	0	25	19	3	1	2
S. AMERICA	166	86	60	13	5	29	7	11	4	1	57	31	16	8	2	87	48	33	5	1
ARGENTINA	42	18	18	3	1	7	2	4	1	0	15	8	6	1	0	19	8	9	2	1
BRAZIL	56	25	22	7	1	5	1	4	0	0	28	15	8	5	0	22	9	10	2	0
PERU	7	4	2	0	1	1	0	0	0	0	1	1	0	0	0	5	3	2	0	0
COLOMBIA	25	14	10	1	0	1	1	0	0	0	5	3	2	0	0	19	10	8	1	0
VENEZUELA	21	18	2	0	1	1	1	0	0	0	5	3	0	2	0	15	14	1	0	0
OTHER	15	7	6	0	2	5	2	3	0	0	3	1	1	0	1	7	4	3	0	0
EUROPE	502	185	232	41	35	95	34	42	11	8	86	37	33	10	6	312	114	157	20	21
EFTA	173	61	80	18	10	44	19	18	6	1	43	18	15	7	3	82	24	47	5	6
U.K.	132	44	66	13	6	32	16	12	4	1	38	16	15	5	2	59	12	39	4	4
SCANDINAVIA	19	8	6	2	3	7	1	4	1	1	3	1	0	2	0	10	6	2	1	1
SWITZERLAND	9	4	2	2	0	1	1	0	0	0	2	1	0	0	1	4	2	0	2	1
OTHER EFTA	13	5	6	1	1	2	1	2	1	0	3	1	0	0	2	9	4	4	0	1
EUROP. COMMUNITY	282	105	129	21	22	48	14	22	5	7	36	16	15	3	2	193	75	92	13	13
FRANCE	85	25	43	8	7	18	5	8	4	1	11	4	3	2	2	54	16	32	2	4
GERMANY	78	23	41	7	5	19	6	9	1	3	11	3	8	0	0	48	14	24	6	4
ITALY	63	26	27	4	3	5	3	1	1	1	9	4	4	1	0	50	21	22	3	4
BELGIUM + LUX	30	15	11	1	2	5	3	2	0	0	3	2	0	1	0	22	12	8	1	1
NETHERLANDS	26	16	7	1	2	2	2	0	0	0	2	1	0	0	1	22	12	6	2	2
SPAIN	36	11	21	2	1	5	1	4	0	0	5	1	3	0	1	29	9	17	1	2
GREECE + TURKEY	9	1	1	2	0	1	0	1	1	0	1	1	0	0	0	8	6	1	0	1
OTHER EUROPE	2	1	1	0	2	0	0	0	0	0	1	1	0	0	0	0	0	0	0	0
EUROPE EX. U.K.	370	141	166	28	29	63	18	30	7	8	48	21	18	5	4	253	102	118	16	17
SOUTHERN DOMINIONS	137	69	46	12	6	25	18	4	2	1	25	14	7	2	2	83	37	35	8	3
S. AFRICA +RHOD.	37	20	12	4	1	6	6	0	0	0	9	7	2	0	0	22	7	10	4	1
AUSTRALIA + N.Z.	100	49	34	8	5	19	12	4	2	1	16	7	5	2	2	61	30	25	4	2
ASIA + OTHER AFRICA	139	93	26	9	10	2	1	1	0	1	27	15	5	3	4	109	77	20	6	6
JAPAN	53	38	10	4	1	1	1	0	0	0	8	10	3	1	0	44	33	7	3	1
OTHER ASIA+AFR.	86	55	16	5	9	1	0	1	0	1	19	10	2	0	4	65	44	13	3	5
BLACK AFRICA	12	5	2	0	5	0	0	0	0	0	3	0	0	0	1	9	4	2	0	3
ARAB WORLD	4	2	2	0	0	0	0	0	0	0	0	2	0	0	0	4	3	2	2	0
INDIA	22	17	2	2	1	1	0	1	0	0	4	4	0	0	0	17	12	4	2	1
PHILIPPINES	14	9	2	1	1	1	0	1	0	0	7	2	1	1	1	7	6	2	0	1
OTHER E. ASIA	9	6	1	1	2	0	0	0	0	0	2	3	0	0	1	7	5	1	0	1
OTHER ASIA	25	16	5	1	2	0	0	0	0	0	3	0	2	0	1	21	16	3	1	1

CHAPTER 4— VARIETIES OF ENTRY
SECTION 3— THE FLOW OF MANUFACTURING BY CHARACTERISTIC OF PARENT SYSTEM
TABLE C1— MANUFACTURING SUBSIDIARIES IN A SYSTEM
WITH LOW "ADVERTISING INTENSITY" IN 1965
CLASSIFIED BY COUNTRY, PERIOD MANUFACTURE BEGAN, AND METHOD OF ENTRY

PERIOD AND METHOD OF ENTRY
(NEW=NEWLY FORMED, ACQ=ACQUIRED, DES=DESCENDANT, UNK=UNKNOWN)

COUNTRY OR REGION	TOTAL ALL	NEW	PRE 1968 ACQ	DES	UNK	PRE 1946 ALL	NEW	ACQ	DES	UNK	1946-1957 ALL	NEW	ACQ	DES	UNK	1958-1967 ALL	NEW	ACQ	DES	UNK
OUTSIDE U.S.	1555	711	555	122	129	362	188	96	42	36	309	146	108	30	25	846	377	351	50	68
OUT. U.S. + CANADA	1325	634	439	107	113	277	152	67	32	26	241	124	69	27	21	775	358	303	48	66
OUT. WEST. HEMIS.	942	412	340	77	92	197	101	49	26	21	139	57	48	17	17	585	254	243	34	54
OUT. WHITE CWEALTH	1023	516	315	80	88	201	112	47	20	22	191	99	53	22	17	607	305	215	38	49
OUT. DEVLPED WORLD	491	281	115	46	33	95	60	19	11	5	117	71	23	14	9	263	150	73	21	19
CANADA	230	77	116	15	16	85	36	29	10	10	68	22	39	3	4	71	19	48	2	2
LATIN AMERICA	383	222	99	30	21	80	51	18	6	5	102	67	21	10	4	190	104	60	14	12
C. AMER.+CARIB.	150	81	46	10	6	29	23	5	1	0	38	25	7	4	2	76	33	34	5	4
CUBA	15	2	2	3	0	7	5	2	0	0	5	3	0	2	0	1	0	0	1	0
MEXICO	103	55	37	2	3	17	13	3	1	0	31	21	7	2	1	52	21	27	2	2
OTHER	32	18	7	2	3	5	5	0	0	0	2	1	0	0	1	23	12	7	2	2
S. AMERICA	233	141	53	20	15	51	28	13	5	5	64	42	14	6	1	114	71	26	9	8
ARGENTINA	45	25	11	6	5	20	10	5	3	2	8	6	1	0	1	16	9	5	2	0
BRAZIL	69	44	18	6	2	13	9	3	0	1	26	17	7	1	1	29	18	8	2	1
PERU	37	5	5	0	0	2	2	0	1	0	7	2	0	2	0	3	2	0	1	0
COLOMBIA	48	22	6	3	6	4	2	0	0	1	5	5	1	1	1	26	15	5	2	4
VENEZUELA	27	33	12	3	4	4	3	1	0	0	10	1	0	0	1	29	20	4	2	3
OTHER	12	12	2	1	1	8	3	4	0	1	2	2	1	1	0	11	7	4	0	0
EUROPE	627	255	246	49	66	148	68	41	18	21	93	42	30	11	10	375	145	175	20	35
EFTA	214	82	82	23	24	68	34	18	9	7	38	18	9	6	5	105	30	55	8	12
U.K.	148	54	61	16	14	48	20	15	9	4	28	17	5	3	3	69	17	41	4	7
SCANDINAVIA	40	17	5	2	3	12	2	1	0	3	8	0	3	0	1	20	9	7	2	2
SWITZERLAND	14	4	5	2	3	2	2	0	0	0	2	0	1	0	0	12	2	5	0	3
OTHER EFTA	12	4	4	2	3	2	2	1	0	0	2	0	1	0	1	4	2	2	0	0
EUROP. COMMUNITY	333	134	137	22	33	60	27	18	5	10	45	17	19	5	4	221	90	100	12	19
FRANCE	99	36	46	6	17	19	8	8	1	1	13	4	6	1	2	63	24	33	3	3
GERMANY	87	32	36	8	11	21	10	8	2	1	13	4	4	1	2	53	18	25	5	5
ITALY	77	32	32	4	7	11	6	2	1	2	10	4	6	1	0	54	22	24	3	5
BELGIUM + LUX	37	18	15	3	3	7	2	3	1	0	6	2	1	2	0	27	14	11	1	1
NETHERLANDS	33	16	8	5	5	5	1	1	0	2	6	3	1	0	1	24	12	7	0	5
SPAIN	46	18	23	1	4	5	1	3	2	0	3	3	0	0	0	35	14	18	0	3
GREECE + TURKEY	15	12	1	1	3	1	0	0	0	1	1	1	0	0	0	11	9	2	0	1
OTHER EUROPE	19	9	3	3	3	14	6	2	3	3	3	0	0	2	0	3	2	1	0	0
EUROPE EX. U.K.	479	201	185	33	52	100	48	26	9	17	65	25	25	8	7	306	128	134	16	28
SOUTHERN DOMINIONS	149	61	63	10	11	26	19	5	2	0	21	7	11	2	1	98	35	47	6	10
S. AFRICA +RHOD.	54	12	35	3	2	6	0	5	0	0	7	3	4	1	0	42	4	34	2	2
AUSTRALIA + N.Z.	95	49	28	7	9	20	14	5	2	0	17	4	10	1	1	56	31	13	4	8
ASIA + OTHER AFRICA	166	96	31	18	15	23	14	3	6	0	25	8	7	4	6	112	74	21	8	9
JAPAN	58	37	16	2	3	8	5	1	0	1	10	4	5	0	1	39	28	8	2	1
OTHER ASIA+AFR.	108	59	16	16	12	15	9	2	5	0	15	4	4	4	5	73	46	13	7	7
BLACK AFRICA	14	8	8	1	0	0	0	0	0	0	2	0	0	0	1	12	8	1	1	2
ARAB WORLD	12	10	1	0	3	2	0	0	0	0	5	2	0	2	0	5	8	0	0	0
INDIA	22	7	8	5	3	3	3	1	2	0	5	0	2	0	2	16	4	5	3	1
PHILIPPINES	14	7	1	2	3	2	2	0	0	0	2	1	0	2	1	6	4	1	0	1
OTHER E. ASIA	15	9	4	2	3	2	1	1	0	0	2	1	1	0	0	11	6	2	1	2
OTHER ASIA	31	19	2	4	4	6	3	0	3	0	4	1	1	0	2	19	15	1	1	2

CHAPTER 4- VARIETIES OF ENTRY
SECTION 3- THE FLOW OF MANUFACTURING BY CHARACTERISTIC OF PARENT SYSTEM
TABLE C2- MANUFACTURING SUBSIDIARIES IN A SYSTEM
WITH HIGH "ADVERTISING INTENSITY" IN 1965
CLASSIFIED BY COUNTRY, PERIOD MANUFACTURE BEGAN, AND METHOD OF ENTRY

PERIOD AND METHOD OF ENTRY
(NEW=NEWLY FORMED, ACQ=ACQUIRED, DES=DESCENDANT, UNK=UNKNOWN)

COUNTRY OR REGION	TOTAL PRE 1968					PRE 1946					1946-1957					1958-1967				
	ALL	NEW	ACQ	DES	UNK	ALL	NEW	ACQ	DES	UNK	ALL	NEW	ACQ	DES	UNK	ALL	NEW	ACQ	DES	UNK
OUTSIDE U.S.	1471	563	699	79	110	293	137	99	15	42	291	123	115	28	25	867	303	485	36	43
OUT. U.S. + CANADA	1222	499	546	69	94	204	100	60	11	33	238	110	81	25	22	766	289	405	33	39
OUT. WEST. HEMIS.	823	324	381	45	62	149	68	49	10	22	138	66	48	13	11	525	190	284	22	29
OUT. WHITE CWEALTH	903	388	391	44	72	109	51	34	3	21	176	88	53	16	19	610	249	304	25	32
OUT. DEVLPED WORLD	505	230	198	26	48	65	35	13	1	16	119	58	37	12	12	318	137	148	13	20
CANADA	249	64	153	10	16	89	37	39	4	9	53	13	34	3	3	101	14	80	3	4
LATIN AMERICA	399	175	165	24	32	55	32	11	1	11	100	44	33	12	11	241	99	121	11	10
C. AMER.+CARIB.	198	83	81	16	17	28	16	5	2	4	50	22	13	9	6	119	45	63	7	4
CUBA	18	6	3	3	6	9	3	2	3	1	7	2	3	0	2	2	1	1	0	0
MEXICO	112	46	56	7	3	13	6	3	3	1	31	17	10	3	1	68	20	43	4	1
OTHER	68	31	22	6	8	6	4	0	0	2	12	3	0	3	3	49	24	19	3	3
S. AMERICA	201	92	84	8	15	27	16	6	1	4	50	22	20	3	5	122	54	58	4	6
ARGENTINA	46	17	23	2	4	11	8	2	0	1	11	3	6	1	1	23	6	15	3	2
BRAZIL	44	20	19	3	2	5	3	1	1	0	18	9	6	1	2	21	8	12	1	0
PERU	17	8	7	0	2	4	2	1	0	1	2	1	1	0	0	11	5	5	0	1
COLOMBIA	28	14	13	1	0	3	1	2	0	0	8	4	4	0	0	17	5	7	1	0
VENEZUELA	43	21	15	2	4	1	0	0	0	1	9	3	3	1	2	32	18	12	1	1
OTHER	23	12	7	1	3	3	2	1	0	2	2	2	0	0	0	18	8	7	1	2
EUROPE	537	181	280	32	35	103	37	44	9	13	91	36	38	9	8	334	108	198	14	14
EFTA	213	65	111	16	17	61	22	24	7	8	46	14	22	7	3	102	29	65	2	6
U.K.	161	42	88	15	12	58	21	23	6	7	36	8	21	6	1	63	13	44	2	4
SCANDINAVIA	28	11	14	1	1	2	0	1	0	0	7	5	1	1	0	19	6	12	0	1
SWITZERLAND	11	5	4	1	1	1	1	0	0	0	3	1	0	1	1	8	4	4	0	0
OTHER EFTA	13	7	5	0	1	0	0	0	0	0	0	0	0	0	0	12	6	5	0	1
EUROP. COMMUNITY	268	93	141	15	14	36	14	17	2	3	37	13	13	2	5	190	62	111	11	6
FRANCE	77	20	50	4	3	9	2	5	1	1	10	3	5	1	1	58	15	40	3	1
GERMANY	74	21	40	5	4	16	7	7	1	1	12	4	7	1	1	42	10	26	3	3
ITALY	55	27	24	2	2	1	0	1	0	0	10	7	1	1	2	44	20	22	2	0
BELGIUM + LUX	28	11	12	2	3	8	4	1	0	3	1	1	0	0	0	24	9	12	3	0
NETHERLANDS	34	14	15	3	1	8	4	3	1	0	4	2	1	1	0	22	8	11	1	2
SPAIN	35	11	22	1	1	5	1	1	0	3	2	1	2	0	2	27	8	17	1	0
GREECE + TURKEY	11	8	1	0	2	1	1	0	0	0	3	1	0	0	0	9	6	2	0	2
OTHER EUROPE	10	4	5	0	1	0	0	0	0	0	2	2	1	0	0	6	4	4	0	0
EUROPE EX. U.K.	376	139	192	17	23	45	16	21	2	6	55	28	17	3	7	271	95	154	12	10
SOUTHERN DOMINIONS	149	66	62	10	9	36	28	3	1	4	23	12	6	3	2	88	26	53	6	3
S. AFRICA +RHOD.	55	27	21	4	2	12	10	1	0	1	9	4	3	3	2	33	13	17	3	0
AUSTRALIA + N.Z.	94	41	41	6	7	24	18	2	1	3	14	8	3	1	1	55	13	36	3	3
ASIA + OTHER AFRICA	137	77	39	3	18	10	3	2	0	5	24	18	4	1	1	103	56	33	3	12
JAPAN	31	22	6	1	2	1	0	0	0	1	5	4	0	1	0	26	18	6	2	0
OTHER ASIA+AFR.	106	55	33	2	16	10	3	0	0	5	19	14	4	0	1	77	38	27	2	12
BLACK AFRICA	16	7	4	0	5	0	0	0	0	0	4	3	0	1	0	12	4	4	2	1
ARAB WORLD	4	2	2	0	0	1	1	0	0	0	1	0	1	0	0	3	2	1	0	0
INDIA	16	9	5	1	1	1	1	0	0	0	2	2	0	0	1	13	6	5	1	1
PHILIPPINES	23	14	8	0	1	3	3	0	0	0	2	0	2	0	0	14	7	6	0	1
OTHER E. ASIA	15	7	5	1	2	2	2	0	0	0	6	5	0	0	1	13	4	4	1	1
OTHER ASIA	32	16	9	0	7	4	2	0	0	2	6	4	2	0	0	22	12	7	0	3

CHAPTER 4- VARIETIES OF ENTRY
SECTION 3- THE FLOW OF MANUFACTURING BY CHARACTERISTIC OF PARENT SYSTEM
TABLE D1- MANUFACTURING SUBSIDIARIES IN A SYSTEM
WITH LOW "HUMAN CAPITAL INTENSITY" IN 1966
CLASSIFIED BY COUNTRY, PERIOD MANUFACTURE BEGAN, AND METHOD OF ENTRY

PERIOD AND METHOD OF ENTRY
(NEW=NEWLY FORMED, ACQ=ACQUIRED, DES=DESCENDANT, UNK=UNKNOWN)

COUNTRY OR REGION	TOTAL PRE 1968					PRE 1946					1946-1957					1958-1967				
	ALL	NEW	ACQ	DES	UNK	ALL	NEW	ACQ	DES	UNK	ALL	NEW	ACQ	DES	UNK	ALL	NEW	ACQ	DES	UNK
OUTSIDE U.S.	1316	555	545	85	116	325	160	100	20	45	265	110	106	24	25	711	285	339	41	46
OUT. U.S. + CANADA	1126	499	439	75	103	242	126	65	15	36	222	101	78	22	21	652	272	296	38	46
OUT. WEST. HEMIS.	837	348	350	51	82	178	84	52	12	30	143	56	55	14	18	510	208	243	25	34
OUT. WHITE CWEALTH	861	412	303	57	80	170	91	43	10	26	178	83	62	16	17	504	238	198	31	37
OUT. DEVLPED WORLD	396	219	104	33	35	82	50	15	6	11	90	48	24	11	7	219	121	65	16	17
CANADA	190	56	106	10	13	83	34	35	5	9	43	9	28	2	4	59	13	43	3	0
LATIN AMERICA	289	151	89	24	21	64	42	13	3	6	79	45	23	8	3	142	64	53	13	12
C. AMER.+CARIB.	132	63	43	17	7	30	19	7	1	3	27	15	3	5	1	73	29	29	11	4
CUBA	18	7	5	3	1	9	4	4	0	1	7	3	1	3	0	2	0	0	0	0
MEXICO	73	32	28	11	2	12	7	3	1	1	19	12	5	2	0	42	13	20	8	1
OTHER	41	24	10	3	4	9	8	0	0	1	1	0	1	0	0	31	16	9	3	3
S. AMERICA	157	88	46	7	14	34	23	6	2	3	52	30	16	3	3	69	35	24	2	8
ARGENTINA	28	17	10	1	0	12	10	1	1	0	6	3	3	0	0	10	4	6	0	0
BRAZIL	42	29	12	1	0	12	10	1	0	2	22	16	6	0	0	8	4	5	1	0
PERU	10	6	1	1	1	3	2	1	0	0	4	3	1	0	1	3	1	0	1	0
COLOMBIA	27	10	11	1	5	7	3	2	0	1	7	2	4	1	1	13	5	5	0	3
VENEZUELA	35	20	11	2	5	8	6	3	1	1	10	5	1	1	2	19	12	5	0	2
OTHER	15	6	5	1	2	3	1	0	1	0	3	1	1	0	1	10	5	3	0	2
EUROPE	564	215	253	35	57	134	56	45	8	25	108	41	44	10	13	318	118	164	17	19
EFTA	187	62	84	15	26	62	26	19	4	13	35	12	12	5	6	90	24	53	6	7
U.K.	129	39	63	11	16	48	18	17	4	9	26	8	9	5	3	55	13	37	2	3
SCANDINAVIA	36	14	13	2	7	9	4	1	0	4	7	4	2	0	1	20	6	10	2	2
SWITZERLAND	13	6	4	2	1	3	2	1	0	0	1	0	0	0	1	9	4	3	2	0
OTHER EFTA	9	3	4	0	2	2	2	0	0	0	1	0	1	0	0	6	1	3	0	2
EUROP. COMMUNITY	306	120	139	18	29	60	26	22	4	8	63	26	26	5	6	179	68	91	9	11
FRANCE	88	31	41	6	10	22	11	7	1	3	15	5	7	2	1	49	19	23	3	4
GERMANY	90	30	50	4	6	18	7	9	1	1	19	5	11	1	2	53	16	33	2	3
ITALY	63	31	24	4	4	10	6	2	0	2	15	9	4	1	1	37	16	18	2	1
BELGIUM + LUX	37	15	14	3	5	10	6	1	1	2	4	3	1	0	0	13	6	12	2	3
NETHERLANDS	28	13	10	4	1	6	5	1	1	0	10	4	5	3	0	13	6	5	2	0
SPAIN	45	16	26	1	2	4	1	3	0	0	7	1	5	0	1	34	14	18	1	0
GREECE + TURKEY	12	10	0	1	1	1	0	0	0	1	1	1	0	0	0	10	9	0	1	0
OTHER EUROPE	14	7	3	0	3	7	3	1	0	3	2	1	1	0	0	5	3	1	0	1
EUROPE EX. U.K.	435	176	190	24	41	86	38	28	4	16	82	33	35	5	9	263	105	127	15	16
SOUTHERN DOMINIONS	129	45	71	6	6	23	17	5	1	0	16	6	6	1	1	89	19	60	4	6
S. AFRICA +RHOD.	55	15	36	3	1	8	7	0	1	0	6	4	1	1	0	41	4	35	3	1
AUSTRALIA + N.Z.	74	30	35	3	5	15	10	5	0	0	10	5	5	0	1	48	15	25	3	5
ASIA + OTHER AFRICA	144	88	26	10	19	21	11	2	2	3	19	6	3	1	2	103	71	19	4	9
JAPAN	37	20	11	1	5	3	3	0	0	0	8	3	4	0	1	26	14	7	1	4
OTHER ASIA+AFR.	107	68	15	9	14	18	8	2	1	3	11	3	0	1	0	77	57	12	3	4
BLACK AFRICA	14	11	1	0	2	0	0	0	0	0	3	3	0	0	0	11	8	1	0	1
ARAB WORLD	11	8	0	3	0	1	1	0	0	0	1	0	0	1	0	9	8	0	3	0
INDIA	16	11	3	0	2	4	3	1	0	1	0	0	0	0	0	13	8	3	0	3
PHILIPPINES	18	9	5	2	2	4	3	1	1	1	4	1	2	0	0	10	5	4	1	1
OTHER E. ASIA	9	4	3	0	2	2	2	0	0	0	2	1	1	0	0	5	4	1	0	2
OTHER ASIA	39	25	3	2	8	8	2	0	2	4	4	2	0	0	2	26	21	3	0	2

CHAPTER 4- VARIETIES OF ENTRY
SECTION 3- THE FLOW OF MANUFACTURING BY CHARACTERISTIC OF PARENT SYSTEM
TABLE D2- MANUFACTURING SUBSIDIARIES IN A SYSTEM
WITH HIGH "HUMAN CAPITAL INTENSITY" IN 1966
CLASSIFIED BY COUNTRY, PERIOD MANUFACTURE BEGAN, AND METHOD OF ENTRY

PERIOD AND METHOD OF ENTRY
(NEW=NEWLY FORMED, ACQ=ACQUIRED, DES=DESCENDANT, UNK=UNKNOWN)

COUNTRY OR REGION	TOTAL PRE 1968					PRE 1946					1946-1957					1958-1967				
	ALL	NEW	ACQ	DES	UNK	ALL	NEW	ACQ	DES	UNK	ALL	NEW	ACQ	DES	UNK	ALL	NEW	ACQ	DES	UNK
OUTSIDE U.S.	1070	473	429	75	54	233	114	74	31	14	174	86	65	15	8	624	273	290	29	32
OUT. U.S. + CANADA	889	414	338	65	39	161	85	46	25	5	135	71	45	13	6	560	258	247	27	28
OUT. WEST. HEMIS.	608	261	246	46	29	107	51	33	21	2	69	33	24	8	4	406	177	189	17	23
OUT. WHITE CWEALTH	680	338	256	45	27	111	62	30	16	3	103	57	34	8	4	452	219	192	21	20
OUT. DEVLPED WORLD	346	188	111	27	11	62	39	14	6	3	73	42	23	6	2	202	107	74	15	6
CANADA	181	59	91	10	15	72	29	28	6	9	39	15	20	2	2	64	15	43	2	4
LATIN AMERICA	281	153	92	19	10	54	34	13	4	3	66	38	21	5	2	154	81	58	10	5
C. AMER.+CARIB.	110	61	37	5	3	16	12	3	0	1	24	14	8	1	1	66	35	26	4	1
CUBA	7	5	0	2	0	3	0	0	3	0	3	0	3	0	0	1	0	0	1	0
MEXICO	81	40	33	3	5	13	10	3	0	0	19	9	8	0	1	46	21	22	2	4
OTHER	22	16	4	0	2	0	0	0	0	0	2	2	0	0	0	19	14	4	1	0
S. AMERICA	171	92	55	14	7	38	22	10	4	2	42	24	13	4	1	88	46	32	6	4
ARGENTINA	34	15	12	4	2	13	8	2	2	1	5	3	1	1	0	15	4	9	1	1
BRAZIL	47	23	18	3	2	13	8	4	0	1	12	6	4	2	0	21	9	10	1	1
PERU	7	4	2	1	0	0	0	0	0	0	1	1	0	0	0	3	0	1	0	0
COLOMBIA	23	16	5	2	0	0	0	0	0	0	6	1	4	1	0	17	12	4	1	0
VENEZUELA	35	21	9	3	1	2	2	0	0	0	11	8	2	1	0	21	11	7	2	1
OTHER	25	13	9	1	2	9	4	4	0	1	5	2	3	0	0	11	7	2	2	1
EUROPE	418	163	181	32	22	75	31	26	16	2	49	22	18	6	3	274	110	137	10	17
EFTA	155	59	57	16	9	36	16	12	6	2	26	10	8	6	2	79	33	37	4	5
U.K.	118	37	47	14	6	30	10	12	6	2	21	9	7	4	1	53	18	28	4	3
SCANDINAVIA	21	13	6	0	2	3	1	0	0	0	4	1	1	2	0	14	9	5	0	0
SWITZERLAND	7	2	3	1	1	1	1	0	0	0	1	0	0	1	0	6	1	3	0	2
OTHER EFTA	9	7	1	0	1	2	2	0	0	0	1	0	0	0	1	6	5	1	0	0
EUROP. COMMUNITY	210	80	104	12	9	29	12	11	6	0	18	8	9	1	1	158	60	84	6	8
FRANCE	69	21	40	5	2	11	4	4	3	0	7	2	5	1	1	52	16	34	1	1
GERMANY	47	18	21	5	3	8	4	2	2	0	7	2	5	0	0	32	12	14	3	3
ITALY	43	17	20	3	3	3	1	1	1	0	5	4	1	0	0	33	11	18	3	1
BELGIUM + LUX	31	13	17	1	0	4	1	3	0	0	1	0	1	0	0	26	12	13	1	0
NETHERLANDS	20	11	6	1	2	3	1	1	1	0	1	0	1	0	0	15	12	5	0	0
SPAIN	33	11	15	3	4	4	1	2	1	0	2	2	0	0	0	27	11	12	0	4
GREECE + TURKEY	8	7	1	0	0	0	0	0	0	0	2	2	0	0	0	6	5	1	0	0
OTHER EUROPE	12	4	4	1	3	6	2	0	1	3	2	1	0	1	0	4	1	3	0	0
EUROPE EX. U.K.	300	126	134	18	16	45	21	14	10	0	28	13	11	2	2	221	92	109	6	14
SOUTHERN DOMINIONS	85	38	32	5	6	19	13	4	2	0	10	4	4	1	1	52	21	24	2	5
S. AFRICA +RHOD.	21	10	8	1	1	4	3	1	0	0	3	2	1	0	0	13	5	6	1	1
AUSTRALIA + N.Z.	64	28	24	4	5	15	10	3	2	0	7	2	3	1	1	39	16	18	1	4
ASIA + OTHER AFRICA	105	60	33	9	1	13	7	3	2	1	10	3	2	0	1	80	46	28	5	1
JAPAN	40	25	14	1	0	5	5	0	0	0	3	0	3	0	0	32	20	12	0	0
OTHER ASIA+AFR.	65	35	19	8	1	8	2	2	4	0	7	3	2	0	0	48	26	16	5	1
BLACK AFRICA	11	6	2	3	0	0	0	0	0	0	0	0	0	0	0	5	3	2	1	0
ARAB WORLD	21	9	8	2	2	1	1	0	0	0	2	0	2	0	0	18	8	8	2	0
INDIA	10	8	2	0	1	2	2	0	0	0	0	0	0	0	0	7	5	2	0	0
PHILIPPINES	5	2	2	1	0	1	1	0	0	0	0	0	0	0	0	5	2	1	0	0
OTHER E. ASIA	13	8	2	2	0	1	1	0	0	0	3	1	1	0	0	3	1	1	0	0
OTHER ASIA	13	8	2	2	0	2	1	1	0	1	3	2	0	0	1	7	5	1	0	0

CHAPTER 4- VARIETIES OF ENTRY
SECTION 3- THE FLOW OF MANUFACTURING BY CHARACTERISTIC OF PARENT SYSTEM
TABLE E1- MANUFACTURING SUBSIDIARIES IN A SYSTEM
WITH LOW "PHYSICAL CAPITAL INTENSITY" IN 1966
CLASSIFIED BY COUNTRY, PERIOD MANUFACTURE BEGAN, AND METHOD OF ENTRY

PERIOD AND METHOD OF ENTRY
(NEW=NEWLY FORMED, ACQ=ACQUIRED, DES=DESCENDANT, UNK=UNKNOWN)

COUNTRY OR REGION	TOTAL PRE 1968 ALL	NEW	ACQ	DES	UNK	PRE 1946 ALL	NEW	ACQ	DES	UNK	1946-1957 ALL	NEW	ACQ	DES	UNK	1958-1967 ALL	NEW	ACQ	DES	UNK
OUTSIDE U.S.	2548	999	1164	172	161	551	271	175	47	58	469	204	182	45	38	1476	524	807	80	65
OUT. U.S. + CANADA	2109	876	907	152	131	397	211	105	39	42	374	174	132	40	28	1295	491	670	73	61
OUT. WEST. HEMIS.	1446	570	652	101	87	284	142	80	33	29	215	91	88	22	14	911	337	484	46	44
OUT. WHITE CWEALTH	1599	703	661	113	104	257	138	70	22	27	287	144	91	30	22	1037	421	500	61	55
OUT. DEVLPED WORLD	814	392	295	62	58	132	76	29	9	18	182	99	48	21	14	493	217	218	32	26
CANADA	439	123	257	20	30	154	60	70	8	16	95	30	50	5	10	181	33	137	7	4
LATIN AMERICA	663	306	255	51	44	113	69	25	6	13	159	83	46	18	17	384	154	186	27	17
C. AMER.+CARIB.	296	122	123	28	20	44	26	9	2	7	66	32	16	11	7	183	64	98	15	6
CUBA	30	5	7	7	3	12	4	6	1	1	15	6	1	5	3	2	0	1	0	1
MEXICO	184	77	90	7	10	26	18	6	1	1	40	22	14	1	3	117	37	70	5	1
OTHER	82	35	28	8	10	6	4	0	0	2	11	4	1	3	3	64	27	27	5	5
S. AMERICA	367	184	132	23	24	69	43	16	4	6	93	51	28	7	4	201	90	88	12	11
ARGENTINA	86	40	36	5	4	25	17	5	2	1	15	5	5	1	1	45	18	22	2	2
BRAZIL	97	51	31	10	5	22	14	6	1	1	29	17	9	3	0	46	20	20	6	0
PERU	28	14	7	3	3	6	3	1	1	1	8	4	3	0	1	14	7	6	2	0
COLOMBIA	49	21	23	2	3	5	3	1	0	1	9	5	4	0	0	35	13	17	2	3
VENEZUELA	68	39	19	5	3	5	4	0	0	1	25	15	6	3	1	36	20	13	2	1
OTHER	39	19	13	2	6	6	2	2	0	2	7	5	1	0	1	25	12	10	0	3
EUROPE	1023	360	500	73	60	206	96	65	25	20	148	58	62	16	12	639	206	373	32	28
EFTA	391	128	184	33	28	101	47	29	13	12	64	23	23	16	4	208	58	132	8	10
U.K.	285	78	148	23	18	84	35	27	12	10	45	15	19	7	3	138	28	102	4	2
SCANDINAVIA	59	25	10	8	6	9	5	3	0	1	9	6	4	3	0	37	15	17	3	2
SWITZERLAND	23	10	6	3	4	5	3	0	0	2	4	1	0	0	1	16	9	6	0	1
OTHER EFTA	24	15	7	0	2	3	4	0	0	1	2	1	0	0	1	17	9	6	1	3
EUROP. COMMUNITY	523	184	270	34	24	92	44	35	8	5	66	25	31	4	6	354	115	204	22	13
FRANCE	173	55	97	12	5	33	12	15	4	2	13	4	6	2	1	123	39	76	6	6
GERMANY	150	43	81	12	10	34	17	13	1	3	24	4	17	2	1	88	34	51	3	1
ITALY	98	47	43	3	3	6	5	1	0	0	14	8	4	0	2	76	34	38	3	1
BELGIUM + LUX	47	19	22	4	1	7	4	1	2	0	5	4	1	0	0	34	11	20	2	1
NETHERLANDS	55	20	27	3	5	12	6	5	1	0	10	5	3	0	2	33	9	19	2	2
SPAIN	60	21	32	4	2	4	2	0	0	0	9	4	5	1	0	47	15	27	2	2
GREECE + TURKEY	24	19	3	0	2	0	0	0	0	0	4	4	0	0	0	20	15	3	0	2
OTHER EUROPE	25	11	11	3	2	9	3	1	3	2	5	2	3	0	0	10	7	7	0	0
EUROPE FX. U.K.	738	282	352	50	42	122	61	38	13	10	103	43	43	9	8	501	178	271	28	24
SOUTHERN DOMINIONS	208	89	90	15	8	53	37	8	4	4	37	13	19	3	2	112	39	63	8	2
S. AFRICA +RHOD.	69	36	20	7	8	16	12	2	1	1	11	7	2	1	0	38	17	16	5	2
AUSTRALIA + N.Z.	139	53	70	8	6	37	25	6	3	3	26	6	17	2	1	74	22	47	3	3
ASIA + OTHER AFRICA	215	121	62	13	19	25	9	7	1	5	30	20	7	3	0	160	92	48	14	5
JAPAN	64	35	22	2	5	16	2	3	1	3	7	4	0	0	0	51	29	16	1	9
OTHER ASIA+AFR.	151	86	40	11	14	19	7	4	0	2	23	16	7	3	0	109	63	32	5	5
BLACK AFRICA	15	7	5	1	2	0	0	0	0	0	2	1	1	0	0	14	6	5	1	1
ARAB WORLD	18	10	5	2	1	1	1	0	0	0	4	1	1	0	2	13	8	3	0	1
INDIA	23	12	8	0	3	1	0	3	0	1	2	2	0	0	0	19	8	8	0	1
PHILIPPINES	28	16	9	2	1	4	2	2	0	0	9	5	2	0	0	15	9	5	0	1
OTHER E. ASIA	21	10	10	0	1	1	1	0	0	1	1	1	0	0	0	16	8	8	0	0
OTHER ASIA	46	31	3	3	9	4	1	0	2	1	7	7	0	0	0	32	23	3	1	5

CHAPTER 4- VARIETIES OF ENTRY
SECTION 3- THE FLOW OF MANUFACTURING BY CHARACTERISTIC OF PARENT SYSTEM
TABLE E2- MANUFACTURING SUBSIDIARIES IN A SYSTEM
WITH HIGH "PHYSICAL CAPITAL INTENSITY" IN 1966
CLASSIFIED BY COUNTRY, PERIOD MANUFACTURE BEGAN, AND METHOD OF ENTRY

PERIOD AND METHOD OF ENTRY
(NEW=NEWLY FORMED, ACQ=ACQUIRED, DES=DESCENDANT, UNK=UNKNOWN)

COUNTRY OR REGION	TOTAL ALL	NEW	PRE 1968 ACQ	DES	UNK	PRE 1946 ALL	NEW	ACQ	DES	UNK	1946-1957 ALL	NEW	ACQ	DES	UNK	1958-1967 ALL	NEW	ACQ	DES	UNK
OUTSIDE U.S.	2684	1173	1045	180	195	474	256	129	39	50	543	262	191	49	41	1576	655	725	92	104
OUT. U.S. + CANADA	2310	1050	859	158	166	360	193	102	30	35	437	226	132	42	37	1436	631	625	86	94
OUT. WEST. HEMIS.	1632	711	629	112	129	268	134	80	27	27	254	125	78	25	26	1059	452	471	60	76
OUT. WHITE CWEALTH	1747	845	614	103	129	246	141	63	14	28	328	170	99	28	31	1110	534	452	61	63
OUT. DEVLPED WORLD	895	467	272	60	57	103	68	22	5	8	214	117	59	20	18	539	282	191	35	31
CANADA	374	123	186	22	29	114	63	27	9	15	106	36	59	7	4	140	24	100	6	10
LATIN AMERICA	678	339	230	46	37	92	59	22	3	8	183	101	54	17	11	377	179	154	26	18
C. AMER.+CARIB.	280	137	96	20	12	34	28	5	0	1	68	36	22	6	4	163	73	69	14	7
CUBA	18	11	3	1	2	7	4	3	0	0	8	6	1	1	0	2	1	0	0	1
MEXICO	186	82	72	15	7	20	17	3	0	0	52	26	18	5	3	104	39	51	10	4
OTHER	76	44	21	4	3	7	7	0	0	0	8	4	3	0	1	57	33	18	4	2
S. AMERICA	398	202	134	26	25	58	31	17	3	7	115	65	32	11	7	214	106	85	12	11
ARGENTINA	75	31	31	6	6	19	6	9	2	2	18	12	4	1	1	35	10	21	3	1
BRAZIL	102	49	40	7	4	12	8	3	0	1	30	18	8	2	2	58	23	29	5	1
PERU	30	15	9	4	2	6	3	2	0	1	10	6	2	2	0	14	6	5	2	1
COLOMBIA	66	34	20	9	3	5	3	2	0	0	19	13	4	1	1	42	18	14	8	2
VENEZUELA	77	53	15	6	3	5	4	0	0	1	20	12	6	2	0	52	37	9	4	2
OTHER	48	20	19	5	2	11	7	1	1	2	18	12	3	2	1	19	10	6	1	2
EUROPE	1032	407	454	71	86	218	96	73	22	27	155	74	53	14	14	645	237	328	35	45
EFTA	360	121	163	39	32	106	40	41	15	10	61	25	23	8	5	188	56	99	16	17
U.K.	266	77	131	31	24	77	25	32	14	6	56	24	21	8	3	130	28	78	10	14
SCANDINAVIA	57	26	19	4	7	16	8	5	0	3	17	8	8	0	1	24	10	6	4	4
SWITZERLAND	14	3	7	3	1	2	0	1	1	0	3	0	1	2	0	9	3	5	0	1
OTHER EFTA	23	15	6	1	1	11	7	3	0	1	2	1	1	0	0	10	7	2	1	0
EUROP. COMMUNITY	548	228	236	30	45	91	46	24	7	14	81	40	27	6	8	367	142	185	17	23
FRANCE	150	55	70	10	12	32	14	11	3	4	24	11	6	2	1	91	30	52	7	2
GERMANY	148	62	63	10	12	30	18	6	2	4	23	11	11	1	0	94	36	46	7	5
ITALY	124	54	55	5	9	14	6	4	2	2	21	11	8	1	1	88	36	42	2	8
BELGIUM + LUX	71	30	32	4	8	11	3	2	1	5	14	6	6	1	1	46	21	24	2	3
NETHERLANDS	55	27	16	4	8	4	1	1	0	2	8	3	3	2	0	43	23	12	2	6
SPAIN	79	34	41	1	3	11	5	3	0	3	10	5	5	0	0	58	24	33	1	0
GREECE + TURKEY	18	11	4	0	3	1	0	0	0	1	2	0	2	0	0	15	11	2	0	2
OTHER EUROPE	27	13	10	1	3	9	5	2	0	2	4	3	0	0	1	14	5	8	1	0
EUROPE EX. U.K.	766	330	323	40	62	141	71	41	8	21	99	50	32	6	11	515	209	250	25	31
SOUTHERN DOMINIONS	280	121	106	23	19	36	26	7	3	0	49	28	12	6	3	184	67	87	14	16
S. AFRICA +RHOD.	92	34	46	4	3	10	10	0	0	0	17	11	5	1	0	65	13	41	3	3
AUSTRALIA + N.Z.	188	87	60	19	16	26	16	7	3	0	32	17	7	5	3	124	54	46	11	13
ASIA + OTHER AFRICA	320	183	69	18	24	14	12	2	0	0	50	23	13	5	9	230	148	56	11	15
JAPAN	103	55	27	4	4	3	3	0	0	0	19	7	9	3	0	68	45	19	1	3
OTHER ASIA+AFR.	217	128	42	14	20	11	9	2	0	0	31	16	5	3	7	162	103	37	10	13
BLACK AFRICA	31	17	5	2	7	0	0	0	0	0	5	2	0	0	3	25	15	5	2	2
ARAB WORLD	21	14	2	0	0	2	2	0	0	0	4	2	0	0	0	15	13	2	0	2
INDIA	46	28	12	3	1	3	3	0	0	0	5	5	0	0	0	37	21	12	3	1
PHILIPPINES	31	19	6	3	3	1	1	0	0	0	5	5	0	0	2	25	13	6	3	1
OTHER E. ASIA	23	12	4	2	4	0	0	0	0	0	3	1	1	0	1	17	10	3	2	3
OTHER ASIA	65	38	13	3	5	5	3	2	0	0	8	5	0	0	2	46	32	9	2	3

CHAPTER 4- VARIETIES OF ENTRY

SECTION 3- THE FLOW OF MANUFACTURING BY CHARACTERISTIC OF PARENT SYSTEM

TABLE F1- MANUFACTURING SUBSIDIARIES IN A SYSTEM
WITH LOW GROWTH IN SALES 1950-1966
CLASSIFIED BY COUNTRY, PERIOD MANUFACTURE BEGAN, AND METHOD OF ENTRY

PERIOD AND METHOD OF ENTRY

(NEW=NEWLY FORMED, ACQ=ACQUIRED, DES=DESCENDANT, UNK=UNKNOWN)

COUNTRY OR REGION	TOTAL ALL	TOTAL NEW	PRE 1968 ACQ	DES	UNK	PRE 1946 ALL	NEW	ACQ	DES	UNK	1946-1957 ALL	NEW	ACQ	DES	UNK	1958-1967 ALL	NEW	ACQ	DES	UNK
OUTSIDE U.S.	2314	982	946	165	182	553	257	183	49	64	435	184	166	41	44	1287	541	597	75	74
OUT. U.S. + CANADA	1925	884	731	139	144	391	201	114	36	40	344	161	112	35	36	1163	522	505	68	68
OUT. WEST. HEMIS.	1316	578	526	87	105	273	132	83	30	28	166	75	59	12	20	857	371	384	45	57
OUT. WHITE CWEALTH	1490	720	546	99	107	252	140	68	17	27	279	132	88	28	31	941	448	390	54	49
OUT. DEVLPED WORLD	789	416	238	67	58	139	81	34	8	16	204	100	56	27	21	436	235	148	32	21
CANADA	389	98	215	26	38	162	56	69	13	24	91	23	54	6	8	124	19	92	7	6
LATIN AMERICA	609	306	205	52	39	118	69	31	6	12	178	86	53	23	16	306	151	121	23	11
C. AMER.+CARIB.	266	123	94	30	17	45	28	10	2	5	75	32	22	15	6	144	63	62	13	6
CUBA	31	12	4	8	3	11	3	3	1	4	16	8	2	5	1	3	1	0	2	0
MEXICO	158	69	69	16	8	24	16	7	1	0	47	22	17	6	2	86	31	45	9	1
OTHER	77	42	21	6	8	10	9	3	0	1	12	2	4	3	3	55	31	17	3	4
S. AMERICA	343	183	111	22	22	73	41	21	4	7	103	54	31	8	10	162	88	59	10	5
ARGENTINA	69	33	28	2	3	27	15	8	2	2	10	6	4	0	0	29	12	16	0	1
BRAZIL	93	50	29	8	6	19	12	5	1	1	36	17	11	3	5	38	21	13	4	0
PERU	25	19	3	2	1	7	4	1	2	0	10	4	2	4	0	8	11	0	1	0
COLOMBIA	38	18	14	3	3	5	3	2	0	0	10	4	4	2	0	23	11	8	1	3
VENEZUELA	79	47	19	6	6	11	4	5	0	1	29	16	6	4	3	45	28	13	2	2
OTHER	39	16	18	1	3	4	3	0	0	2	8	3	4	0	1	19	9	9	2	0
EUROPE	886	351	402	54	67	200	89	67	22	22	103	47	38	7	11	571	215	297	25	34
EFTA	323	121	142	28	28	110	44	39	15	12	43	20	13	6	4	166	57	90	7	12
U.K.	241	78	112	24	23	91	31	35	14	11	34	15	10	6	3	112	32	67	4	9
SCANDINAVIA	47	22	22	2	1	11	6	3	1	1	8	5	3	0	0	28	11	16	1	0
SWITZERLAND	15	5	6	2	2	3	2	1	0	0	0	0	0	0	0	12	3	5	2	2
OTHER EFTA	20	16	2	0	2	5	5	0	0	0	1	0	0	0	1	14	11	2	0	1
EUROP. COMMUNITY	457	181	213	24	32	77	39	23	6	9	49	21	21	1	6	324	121	169	17	17
FRANCE	134	45	67	8	11	26	10	7	4	5	8	3	3	0	2	97	32	57	4	4
GERMANY	125	49	61	6	7	23	16	6	0	1	18	8	9	1	0	82	27	46	5	5
ITALY	90	41	36	4	7	8	5	2	0	1	11	7	3	0	1	69	29	31	4	5
BELGIUM + LUX	55	20	26	4	5	12	4	4	2	2	4	2	2	0	1	39	14	20	2	3
NETHERLANDS	53	26	23	2	2	8	4	4	0	0	8	3	3	0	2	37	19	15	2	1
SPAIN	64	24	33	2	5	8	4	3	1	0	6	2	3	0	1	51	19	27	2	4
GREECE + TURKEY	20	15	4	0	1	7	0	2	0	0	2	2	0	0	0	18	13	4	0	0
OTHER EUROPE	22	10	10	0	2	6	3	2	0	1	3	2	1	0	0	12	5	7	0	1
EUROPE EX. U.K.	645	273	290	30	44	109	58	32	8	11	69	32	28	1	8	459	183	230	21	25
SOUTHERN DOMINIONS	179	79	66	16	14	47	29	11	5	2	28	12	13	1	2	100	38	42	10	10
S. AFRICA +RHOD.	55	27	15	7	4	14	10	2	4	1	9	5	2	1	1	30	12	11	5	2
AUSTRALIA + N.Z.	124	52	51	9	10	33	19	9	4	1	19	7	11	0	1	70	26	31	5	8
ASIA + OTHER AFRICA	251	148	58	17	24	26	14	5	3	4	35	16	8	4	7	186	118	45	10	13
JAPAN	71	38	25	2	5	5	2	2	1	0	9	2	5	0	2	56	34	18	1	3
OTHER ASIA+AFR.	180	110	33	15	19	21	12	3	2	4	26	14	3	4	5	130	84	27	9	10
BLACK AFRICA	23	12	6	3	0	1	0	0	0	0	4	2	1	0	0	21	11	6	2	0
ARAB WORLD	20	13	4	3	0	1	0	0	0	0	2	2	0	2	0	15	13	2	2	0
INDIA	30	18	7	3	1	3	1	1	0	0	2	2	0	0	0	24	13	5	5	1
PHILIPPINES	33	22	6	4	1	5	4	1	1	0	5	5	0	1	0	18	10	6	0	0
OTHER E. ASIA	24	11	2	6	2	3	1	0	2	0	2	0	0	4	0	19	10	2	6	2
OTHER ASIA	50	34	1	3	10	9	4	1	0	2	9	4	1	0	2	33	26	1	2	4

CHAPTER 4- VARIETIES OF ENTRY
SECTION 3- THE FLOW OF MANUFACTURING BY CHARACTERISTIC OF PARENT SYSTEM
TABLE F2- MANUFACTURING SUBSIDIARIES IN A SYSTEM
WITH HIGH GROWTH IN SALES 1950-1966
CLASSIFIED BY COUNTRY, PERIOD MANUFACTURE BEGAN, AND METHOD OF ENTRY

PERIOD AND METHOD OF ENTRY
(NEW=NEWLY FORMED, ACQ=ACQUIRED, DES=DESCENDANT, UNK=UNKNOWN)

COUNTRY OR REGION	TOTAL PRE 1968					PRE 1946					1946-1957					1958-1967				
	ALL	NEW	ACQ	DES	UNK	ALL	NEW	ACQ	DES	UNK	ALL	NEW	ACQ	DES	UNK	ALL	NEW	ACQ	DES	UNK
OUTSIDE U.S.	2351	922	1062	158	122	359	197	105	27	30	452	223	159	46	24	1453	502	798	85	68
OUT. U.S. + CANADA	2019	802	880	145	112	276	139	84	24	29	367	192	114	41	20	1296	471	682	80	63
OUT. WEST. HEMIS.	1402	520	637	105	84	206	93	69	22	22	235	112	79	30	14	905	315	480	53	48
OUT. WHITE CWEALTH	1507	657	612	98	85	193	100	57	12	12	268	153	75	26	14	991	404	480	60	47
OUT. DEVLPED WORLD	759	361	279	47	40	75	48	16	4	7	157	97	40	12	8	495	216	223	31	25
CANADA	332	120	182	13	10	83	58	21	3	1	85	31	45	5	4	157	31	116	5	5
LATIN AMERICA	617	282	243	40	28	70	46	15	2	7	132	80	35	11	6	391	156	193	27	15
C. AMER.+CARIB.	274	121	110	18	10	27	22	4	0	1	51	32	14	2	3	181	67	92	16	6
CUBA	17	9	4	1	3	8	5	2	1	0	7	4	1	2	0	1	0	1	0	0
MEXICO	185	79	80	12	14	17	15	2	0	0	38	23	13	0	2	120	41	65	10	4
OTHER	72	33	26	6	7	2	2	0	0	1	6	5	0	0	1	60	26	26	6	2
S. AMERICA	343	161	133	27	18	43	24	11	2	6	81	48	21	9	3	210	89	101	11	9
ARGENTINA	71	27	33	7	4	13	8	4	0	1	15	6	6	2	1	42	13	24	4	1
BRAZIL	83	38	34	7	2	10	6	3	0	1	25	15	6	2	2	46	17	25	3	1
PERU	30	9	15	3	3	5	2	3	0	0	4	1	1	1	2	18	6	11	2	1
COLOMBIA	65	31	25	3	5	4	2	2	0	0	16	10	6	1	0	44	19	20	2	1
VENEZUELA	57	40	13	1	3	5	4	1	0	0	13	11	2	0	0	39	25	10	1	3
OTHER	37	16	13	4	2	6	2	2	1	0	8	5	0	3	0	21	9	11	1	0
EUROPE	934	310	466	74	60	172	70	63	18	21	152	66	55	19	9	586	174	345	37	30
EFTA	349	91	180	39	24	78	29	30	12	7	65	20	30	10	5	191	42	120	17	12
U.K.	256	54	147	27	15	56	19	23	10	4	54	17	27	7	3	133	18	97	10	8
SCANDINAVIA	59	23	19	4	0	12	1	5	2	2	7	2	2	1	2	39	16	13	6	4
SWITZERLAND	14	3	6	1	0	1	0	0	1	0	2	2	0	0	0	10	3	6	0	0
OTHER EFTA	20	11	8	1	0	9	5	3	0	0	2	1	1	0	0	9	5	4	0	0
EUROP. COMMUNITY	492	180	242	33	28	80	35	29	6	10	77	39	25	9	4	326	106	188	18	14
FRANCE	157	51	88	12	4	29	10	16	2	1	25	9	9	5	1	101	32	63	5	1
GERMANY	133	43	62	13	12	33	14	11	3	6	18	6	9	1	2	79	23	42	9	5
ITALY	104	42	54	4	4	7	5	2	0	0	20	13	6	0	1	77	24	48	2	3
BELGIUM + LUX	54	25	25	0	4	6	2	1	1	0	6	6	1	0	0	42	18	23	0	1
NETHERLANDS	44	19	13	4	4	5	4	2	0	1	8	5	1	3	0	27	9	12	2	2
SPAIN	60	23	34	2	1	0	0	0	0	0	7	4	3	0	0	47	17	28	2	0
GREECE + TURKEY	14	8	2	0	4	1	1	0	0	1	2	2	0	0	0	12	7	2	0	2
OTHER EUROPE	19	8	8	0	3	7	4	1	1	2	2	0	0	0	2	10	2	7	0	0
EUROPE EX. U.K.	678	256	319	47	45	116	51	40	8	17	98	49	31	12	6	453	156	248	27	22
SOUTHERN DOMINIONS	245	87	115	20	11	26	19	4	2	1	43	20	12	8	3	164	48	99	10	7
S. AFRICA +RHOD.	89	31	48	3	3	1	0	0	0	1	15	9	5	1	0	59	13	43	2	3
AUSTRALIA + N.Z.	156	56	67	17	10	17	10	4	2	6	28	11	7	7	2	105	35	56	8	6
ASIA + OTHER AFRICA	223	123	56	11	13	8	4	2	1	1	40	26	9	3	2	155	93	45	6	11
JAPAN	81	44	20	4	12	3	2	1	0	1	15	9	4	1	1	51	33	15	2	1
OTHER ASIA+AFR.	142	79	36	7	12	5	2	1	0	3	25	17	5	2	1	104	60	30	4	10
BLACK AFRICA	16	6	4	2	4	0	0	0	0	0	1	2	0	2	1	11	4	4	0	3
ARAB WORLD	14	8	2	0	4	0	0	0	0	0	1	0	0	1	0	11	8	2	0	1
INDIA	28	17	7	3	0	2	1	0	1	0	3	4	1	0	0	23	13	7	3	0
PHILIPPINES	23	12	9	0	2	0	0	0	0	0	9	6	2	0	0	12	5	6	0	1
OTHER E. ASIA	16	8	5	0	2	2	1	0	1	0	0	0	0	0	0	14	7	5	2	0
OTHER ASIA	45	28	13	4	3	2	1	1	0	1	9	4	1	4	0	33	23	6	1	3

CHAPTER 4- VARIETIES OF ENTRY
SECTION 3- THE FLOW OF MANUFACTURING BY CHARACTERISTIC OF PARENT SYSTEM
TABLE G1- MANUFACTURING SUBSIDIARIES IN A SYSTEM
WITH LOW RETURN ON INVESTED CAPITAL IN 1966
CLASSIFIED BY COUNTRY, PERIOD MANUFACTURE BEGAN, AND METHOD OF ENTRY

PERIOD AND METHOD OF ENTRY
(NEW=NEWLY FORMED, ACQ=ACQUIRED, DES=DESCENDANT, UNK=UNKNOWN)

COUNTRY OR REGION	TOTAL PRE 1968					PRE 1946					1946-1957					1958-1967				
	ALL	NEW	ACQ	DES	UNK	ALL	NEW	ACQ	DES	UNK	ALL	NEW	ACQ	DES	UNK	ALL	NEW	ACQ	DES	UNK
OUTSIDE U.S.	2711	1128	1139	166	181	492	249	141	42	60	504	219	204	46	35	1618	660	794	78	86
OUT. U.S. + CANADA	2305	997	923	146	156	374	189	104	34	47	392	183	140	39	30	1456	625	679	73	79
OUT. WEST. HEMIS.	1613	665	675	100	119	280	130	85	29	36	212	89	81	22	20	1067	446	509	49	63
OUT. WHITE CMWEALTH	1750	814	648	104	118	259	143	63	17	36	309	143	109	31	26	1116	528	476	56	56
OUT. DEVLPED WORLD	892	444	289	62	56	111	67	21	8	15	204	103	63	22	16	536	274	205	32	25
CANADA	406	131	216	20	25	118	60	37	8	13	112	36	64	5	5	162	35	115	5	7
LATIN AMERICA	692	332	248	46	37	94	59	19	5	11	180	94	59	17	10	389	179	170	24	16
C. AMER.+CARIB.	286	122	114	23	12	39	28	6	2	3	61	28	22	7	4	171	66	86	14	5
CUBA	26	13	3	4	4	12	6	2	1	3	10	6	1	3	0	2	1	0	0	1
MEXICO	181	69	83	13	6	21	16	4	1	0	43	19	17	4	3	107	34	62	8	3
OTHER	79	40	28	6	2	6	6	0	0	0	8	3	4	0	1	62	31	24	6	1
S. AMERICA	406	210	134	23	25	55	31	13	3	8	119	66	37	10	6	218	113	84	10	11
ARGENTINA	72	39	22	6	5	13	9	2	2	0	19	13	6	0	0	36	17	14	4	1
BRAZIL	103	54	35	7	5	13	9	2	0	2	34	21	8	1	3	44	23	18	4	1
PERU	31	15	11	0	2	7	4	2	0	1	9	5	3	0	0	14	6	6	0	1
COLOMBIA	73	33	27	3	9	6	2	2	1	1	18	9	6	0	2	48	22	19	2	6
VENEZUELA	83	51	22	5	5	7	5	1	0	1	21	12	4	2	2	54	34	17	1	2
OTHER	44	18	17	4	3	9	3	2	1	3	13	5	5	1	0	22	10	10	2	0
EUROPE	1068	414	487	63	84	229	103	73	21	32	136	58	52	14	12	683	253	362	28	40
EFTA	396	133	190	31	33	112	43	41	14	14	49	23	14	7	5	226	67	135	10	14
U.K.	285	81	150	22	25	81	26	32	12	11	40	20	12	5	3	157	35	106	5	11
SCANDINAVIA	63	27	23	6	6	17	8	5	2	3	7	3	2	1	1	38	16	16	2	2
SWITZERLAND	23	8	11	2	1	2	1	1	0	0	1	0	0	1	0	19	7	10	1	1
OTHER EFTA	25	17	6	1	1	12	8	3	1	0	1	0	0	0	0	12	9	3	0	0
EUROP. COMMUNITY	539	214	244	30	41	96	48	27	7	14	75	29	33	7	6	358	137	184	16	21
FRANCE	157	61	73	11	8	31	14	10	4	3	18	7	6	2	2	104	40	57	4	3
GERMANY	142	54	68	6	13	34	21	8	0	5	23	6	13	0	4	84	27	47	3	6
ITALY	117	54	49	4	9	13	9	1	1	2	19	10	8	0	1	84	35	40	3	6
BELGIUM + LUX	62	24	28	4	6	11	4	4	1	2	5	3	2	0	0	46	20	22	2	2
NETHERLANDS	61	21	26	5	5	7	1	4	0	2	10	3	4	3	0	40	15	18	2	4
SPAIN	75	33	36	1	5	9	5	3	0	1	5	1	2	0	2	61	27	30	1	3
GREECE + TURKEY	24	20	2	0	1	1	0	0	0	0	3	2	0	0	0	21	18	2	0	1
OTHER EUROPE	34	14	15	2	3	11	7	2	1	3	5	3	2	0	0	17	4	11	1	1
EUROPE EX. U.K.	783	333	337	41	59	148	77	41	9	21	96	38	40	9	9	526	218	256	23	29
SOUTHERN DOMINIONS	246	94	112	19	12	32	18	9	5	0	38	17	17	3	1	167	59	86	11	11
S. AFRICA +RHOD.	86	25	47	3	6	7	5	1	1	0	11	7	3	1	0	63	13	43	4	8
AUSTRALIA + N.Z.	160	69	65	13	9	25	13	8	4	0	27	10	14	2	1	104	46	43	7	8
ASIA + OTHER AFRICA	299	157	76	18	23	19	13	3	1	4	38	14	12	5	7	217	134	61	10	12
JAPAN	99	45	35	2	4	2	1	1	0	0	14	5	8	0	1	70	39	26	2	3
OTHER ASIA+AFR.	200	112	41	16	19	17	8	2	1	4	24	9	4	5	6	147	95	35	8	9
BLACK AFRICA	25	16	4	0	3	0	0	0	0	0	1	0	0	1	0	22	16	4	1	2
ARAB WORLD	23	17	2	0	0	2	2	0	0	0	4	0	2	0	0	17	15	0	2	0
INDIA	35	19	12	3	0	2	1	1	0	0	2	2	0	0	0	30	15	12	3	0
PHILIPPINES	30	14	8	4	3	3	0	1	2	0	8	2	2	4	0	18	9	8	3	1
OTHER E. ASIA	24	11	6	2	4	2	1	0	0	1	2	2	0	0	0	19	8	5	2	3
OTHER ASIA	63	35	9	4	9	9	3	0	3	0	7	2	0	2	3	41	29	7	2	3

CHAPTER 4- VARIETIES OF ENTRY
SECTION 3- THE FLOW OF MANUFACTURING BY CHARACTERISTIC OF PARENT SYSTEM
TABLE G2- MANUFACTURING SUBSIDIARIES IN A SYSTEM
WITH HIGH RETURN ON INVESTED CAPITAL IN 1966
CLASSIFIED BY COUNTRY, PERIOD MANUFACTURE BEGAN, AND METHOD OF ENTRY

(NEW=NEWLY FORMED, ACQ=ACQUIRED, DES=DESCENDANT, UNK=UNKNOWN)

PERIOD AND METHOD OF ENTRY

COUNTRY OR REGION	TOTAL PRE 1968 ALL	NEW	ACQ	DES	UNK	PRE 1946 ALL	NEW	ACQ	DES	UNK	1946-1957 ALL	NEW	ACQ	DES	UNK	1958-1967 ALL	NEW	ACQ	DES	UNK
OUTSIDE U.S.	2477	1024	1050	185	172	522	273	158	44	47	502	244	167	48	43	1407	507	725	93	82
OUT. U.S. + CANADA	2076	911	826	163	139	375	211	99	35	30	413	214	122	43	34	1251	486	605	85	75
OUT. WEST. HEMIS.	1440	602	596	113	96	268	144	73	31	20	253	124	84	25	20	886	334	439	57	56
OUT. WHITE CWEALTH	1570	727	619	111	107	240	134	68	19	19	304	171	80	27	26	1020	422	471	65	62
OUT. DEVLPED WORLD	803	410	271	59	58	120	75	28	6	11	190	113	43	19	15	488	222	200	34	32
CANADA	401	113	224	22	33	147	62	59	9	17	89	30	45	5	9	156	21	120	8	7
LATIN AMERICA	636	309	230	50	43	107	67	26	4	10	160	90	38	18	14	365	152	166	28	19
C. AMER.+CARIB.	286	135	104	25	19	38	25	8	0	5	71	40	15	10	6	174	70	81	15	8
CUBA	22	8	8	4	2	7	5	2	0	0	13	3	6	4	0	2	0	0	0	2
MEXICO	186	89	78	15	3	24	18	5	0	1	47	29	14	4	0	114	42	59	11	2
OTHER	78	38	21	6	11	7	5	0	0	2	11	5	0	3	3	58	28	21	3	6
S. AMERICA	350	174	126	25	24	69	42	18	4	5	89	50	23	8	8	191	82	85	13	11
ARGENTINA	84	30	42	5	7	29	16	8	2	3	14	4	4	3	4	41	10	27	1	3
BRAZIL	92	46	33	9	3	20	13	6	1	0	26	15	4	2	1	46	18	23	5	0
PERU	27	14	8	2	3	5	2	1	1	1	8	5	2	1	1	14	7	5	1	1
COLOMBIA	42	22	16	2	1	4	4	0	0	0	11	7	4	0	0	27	11	12	3	1
VENEZUELA	62	41	12	4	4	3	3	0	0	0	22	16	4	1	1	36	22	8	3	3
OTHER	43	21	15	2	5	8	4	3	0	1	8	3	2	1	2	27	14	10	0	3
EUROPE	974	346	461	81	62	195	89	65	26	15	166	73	63	16	14	589	184	333	39	33
EFTA	346	112	152	41	27	95	44	29	14	8	75	24	32	13	6	162	44	91	14	13
U.K.	258	71	124	32	17	80	34	27	13	6	60	18	28	10	4	104	19	69	9	7
SCANDINAVIA	52	23	19	4	5	8	4	2	1	1	10	4	3	2	1	34	15	14	3	2
SWITZERLAND	14	5	5	2	2	3	2	0	0	0	3	1	1	0	1	8	2	6	0	0
OTHER EFTA	22	13	7	4	0	4	4	0	0	0	2	1	0	1	0	16	8	6	2	0
EUROP. COMMUNITY	531	197	262	34	28	87	42	32	8	5	72	36	25	3	8	362	119	205	23	15
FRANCE	166	49	94	11	9	34	12	16	4	2	19	8	5	3	3	110	29	71	6	5
GERMANY	156	51	76	16	9	30	14	11	3	2	24	6	15	3	0	98	31	50	12	5
ITALY	104	46	49	6	3	7	5	1	0	1	16	12	2	1	1	79	29	45	3	2
BELGIUM + LUX	56	25	26	1	3	7	6	1	0	0	5	4	1	0	0	43	16	24	1	2
NETHERLANDS	49	26	17	2	2	9	5	2	1	1	8	6	0	2	0	32	14	15	1	2
SPAIN	64	22	37	3	2	6	2	2	2	0	11	6	5	0	0	47	14	29	2	2
GREECE + TURKEY	17	10	4	0	3	0	0	0	0	0	6	5	1	0	0	13	6	4	0	3
OTHER EUROPE	16	5	6	3	2	7	1	1	2	3	4	3	1	0	0	5	4	4	0	0
EUROPE EX. U.K.	716	275	337	49	45	115	55	38	13	9	106	55	35	6	10	485	165	264	30	26
SOUTHERN DOMINIONS	231	110	80	19	14	53	43	4	2	4	45	22	13	6	4	125	45	63	11	6
S. AFRICA +RHOD.	74	44	19	5	2	19	17	1	1	0	16	10	4	1	1	35	17	14	4	0
AUSTRALIA + N.Z.	157	66	61	14	12	34	26	3	1	3	29	12	9	5	3	90	28	49	7	6
ASIA + OTHER AFRICA	235	146	55	13	20	20	12	4	2	1	42	29	8	3	2	172	105	43	7	17
JAPAN	68	45	14	4	5	7	4	2	2	1	12	6	3	2	1	49	35	9	1	4
OTHER ASIA+AFR.	167	101	41	9	15	13	8	2	0	1	30	23	5	1	1	123	70	34	6	13
BLACK AFRICA	21	8	6	1	6	1	0	0	0	1	4	3	0	1	0	17	5	6	1	5
ARAB WORLD	16	7	5	3	1	1	1	0	0	0	4	4	0	0	0	13	7	4	1	1
INDIA	34	21	8	3	1	3	3	0	0	0	4	4	0	0	0	26	14	4	3	1
PHILIPPINES	29	21	7	0	1	4	2	2	0	0	2	2	0	0	0	14	10	3	0	1
OTHER E. ASIA	20	11	8	0	1	2	1	0	1	0	2	2	0	0	0	17	9	8	0	0
OTHER ASIA	47	33	7	2	5	3	2	0	0	1	9	6	2	0	2	36	25	5	1	5

CHAPTER 4— VARIETIES OF ENTRY
SECTION 3— THE FLOW OF MANUFACTURING BY CHARACTERISTIC OF PARENT SYSTEM
TABLE HI- MANUFACTURING SUBSIDIARIES IN A SYSTEM
WHICH FIRST MANUFACTURED OUTSIDE U.S. AND CANADA BEFORE 1901
CLASSIFIED BY COUNTRY, PERIOD MANUFACTURE BEGAN, AND METHOD OF ENTRY

PERIOD AND METHOD OF ENTRY
(NEW=NEWLY FORMED, ACQ=ACQUIRED, DES=DESCENDANT, UNK=UNKNOWN)

COUNTRY OR REGION	TOTAL PRE 1968					PRE 1946					1946-1957					1958-1967				
	ALL	NEW	ACQ	DES	UNK	ALL	NEW	ACQ	DES	UNK	ALL	NEW	ACQ	DES	UNK	ALL	NEW	ACQ	DES	UNK
OUTSIDE U.S.	749	332	266	56	76	254	145	66	18	25	104	50	29	10	15	372	137	171	28	36
OUT. U.S. + CANADA	655	302	222	53	63	215	128	52	17	18	90	45	23	10	12	335	129	147	26	33
OUT. WEST. HEMIS.	481	210	173	37	51	164	90	44	15	15	58	28	15	7	8	249	92	114	15	28
OUT. WHITE CWEALTH	511	240	168	44	48	166	103	37	12	14	71	35	19	9	8	263	102	112	23	26
OUT. DEVLPED WORLD	224	121	59	21	17	56	40	9	4	3	36	19	8	4	5	126	62	42	13	9
CANADA	94	30	44	3	13	39	17	14	1	7	14	5	6	0	3	37	8	24	2	3
LATIN AMERICA	174	92	49	16	12	51	38	8	0	3	32	17	8	3	5	86	37	33	11	5
C. AMER.+CARIB.	62	32	17	6	5	16	16	0	0	0	5	2	0	0	2	39	14	17	6	2
CUBA	6	4	0	1	0	4	4	0	0	0	0	0	0	0	0	1	0	0	1	0
MEXICO	41	21	12	3	4	10	10	0	0	0	4	2	0	0	2	26	9	12	3	2
OTHER	15	7	5	2	1	2	2	0	0	0	1	0	0	0	1	12	5	5	2	0
S. AMERICA	112	60	32	10	7	35	22	8	2	3	27	15	8	3	1	47	23	16	5	3
ARGENTINA	17	11	3	2	0	8	7	0	2	0	4	2	2	0	0	4	2	1	1	0
BRAZIL	31	18	10	3	0	12	10	2	0	0	10	5	5	1	0	9	4	2	2	0
PERU	10	4	5	0	0	4	2	2	0	0	1	1	0	0	0	4	2	2	0	0
COLOMBIA	20	9	5	3	3	3	1	0	1	0	7	4	1	2	0	12	5	3	2	2
VENEZUELA	17	12	3	1	1	3	2	1	0	0	2	2	0	0	1	12	8	3	2	1
OTHER	17	6	6	1	3	7	1	3	0	3	3	2	0	0	0	6	3	3	2	0
EUROPE	353	143	135	28	41	143	76	40	12	15	45	22	12	5	6	159	45	83	11	20
EFTA	123	49	44	9	19	56	28	17	5	6	15	6	4	1	4	50	15	23	3	9
U.K.	79	27	32	6	12	38	14	15	5	4	10	4	3	0	3	29	9	14	3	5
SCANDINAVIA	25	10	8	2	5	9	6	1	0	2	3	2	0	0	1	13	2	7	2	2
SWITZERLAND	6	2	1	1	0	2	2	0	0	0	1	0	0	0	1	5	0	1	1	2
OTHER EFTA	13	10	3	0	0	7	6	1	0	0	1	0	1	0	0	5	4	1	0	0
EUROP. COMMUNITY	184	69	76	19	16	71	39	19	7	6	25	11	8	4	2	84	19	49	8	8
FRANCE	50	21	20	7	6	27	13	11	3	0	4	0	6	1	0	17	6	9	2	1
GERMANY	60	24	26	4	6	25	14	6	2	3	12	3	6	1	2	23	7	14	2	1
ITALY	36	18	10	2	3	12	10	0	1	1	5	4	1	0	0	17	4	9	2	2
BELGIUM + LUX	17	3	11	0	3	3	1	1	0	1	2	1	1	0	0	11	1	8	0	1
NETHERLANDS	21	3	8	2	4	6	3	0	2	1	2	1	0	1	0	16	5	9	0	2
SPAIN	19	9	6	1	2	1	1	0	0	0	2	1	1	0	1	12	4	5	2	1
GREECE + TURKEY	9	6	1	0	2	0	0	0	0	0	2	2	0	0	0	6	4	1	0	1
OTHER EUROPE	18	6	6	0	2	9	6	1	0	1	2	2	0	1	0	7	2	5	0	0
EUROPE EX. U.K.	274	116	103	22	29	105	62	25	7	11	35	18	9	5	3	130	36	69	10	15
SOUTHERN DOMINIONS	55	30	17	3	1	10	10	0	0	0	7	4	1	1	1	36	16	16	2	2
S. AFRICA +RHOD.	15	9	3	1	1	4	4	0	0	0	2	1	0	1	0	8	2	3	0	1
AUSTRALIA + N.Z.	40	21	14	2	7	6	6	0	0	0	5	3	1	0	1	28	12	13	2	1
ASIA + OTHER AFRICA	73	37	21	6	2	11	4	4	3	0	6	2	2	2	1	54	31	15	2	6
JAPAN	23	8	11	1	5	6	2	1	0	3	4	2	2	0	1	14	6	6	0	2
OTHER ASIA+AFR.	50	29	10	5	2	5	2	3	0	0	1	0	0	1	0	40	25	9	2	4
BLACK AFRICA	5	5	0	0	0	0	0	0	0	0	1	1	0	0	0	4	4	0	0	0
ARAB WORLD	7	4	0	2	0	1	0	0	1	0	1	0	0	1	0	4	4	0	0	0
INDIA	11	1	5	4	0	0	0	0	0	0	1	0	1	1	0	10	6	3	2	0
PHILIPPINES	7	3	3	2	2	0	0	0	0	0	1	1	0	0	0	6	3	2	1	1
OTHER E. ASIA	6	3	1	0	2	1	1	0	0	0	1	0	0	0	1	4	2	0	0	2
OTHER ASIA	14	9	3	1	1	2	2	0	0	1	0	0	0	0	0	12	8	3	0	1

CHAPTER 4- VARIETIES OF ENTRY

SECTION 3- THE FLOW OF MANUFACTURING BY CHARACTERISTIC OF PARENT SYSTEM

TABLE H2- MANUFACTURING SUBSIDIARIES IN A SYSTEM
WHICH FIRST MANUFACTURED OUTSIDE U.S. AND CANADA 1901-1919
CLASSIFIED BY COUNTRY, PERIOD MANUFACTURE BEGAN, AND METHOD OF ENTRY

PERIOD AND METHOD OF ENTRY
(NEW=NEWLY FORMED, ACQ=ACQUIRED, DES=DESCENDANT, UNK=UNKNOWN)

COUNTRY OR REGION	TOTAL (PRE 1968)					PRE 1946					1946-1957					1958-1967				
	ALL	NEW	ACQ	DES	UNK	ALL	NEW	ACQ	DES	UNK	ALL	NEW	ACQ	DES	UNK	ALL	NEW	ACQ	DES	UNK
OUTSIDE U.S.	905	400	287	98	105	312	163	65	40	44	188	74	64	26	24	390	163	158	32	37
OUT. U.S. + CANADA	767	350	239	87	81	237	131	48	32	26	153	60	50	23	20	367	159	141	32	35
OUT. WEST. HEMIS.	552	244	173	66	61	182	99	33	29	21	88	32	29	13	14	274	113	111	24	26
OUT. WHITE CWEALTH	569	269	172	57	65	152	83	33	17	19	122	43	43	18	18	289	143	96	22	28
OUT. DEVLPED WORLD	282	146	70	29	34	72	42	15	5	10	77	32	22	14	9	130	72	33	10	15
CANADA	138	50	48	11	24	75	32	17	8	18	35	14	14	3	4	23	4	17	0	2
LATIN AMERICA	215	106	66	21	20	55	32	15	3	5	65	28	21	10	6	93	46	30	8	9
C. AMER.+CARIB.	74	36	26	5	7	18	11	4	0	3	19	8	6	4	1	37	17	16	1	3
CUBA	6	1	2	1	2	2	0	1	0	1	3	1	1	1	0	1	0	0	0	1
MEXICO	53	26	21	4	2	12	8	3	0	1	14	6	4	1	3	27	12	14	0	0
OTHER	15	9	3	0	3	4	3	0	0	1	2	1	1	0	0	9	5	2	0	2
S. AMERICA	141	70	40	16	13	37	21	11	3	2	46	20	15	5	6	56	29	14	7	6
ARGENTINA	30	12	12	3	3	17	9	5	2	1	5	0	5	0	0	7	3	2	1	1
BRAZIL	46	22	16	4	4	9	5	3	0	1	21	9	6	3	3	16	8	7	1	0
PERU	12	6	3	2	1	2	1	0	1	0	3	2	1	0	0	7	3	2	1	1
COLOMBIA	14	6	4	2	2	4	3	1	0	0	4	1	1	1	1	6	2	2	1	1
VENEZUELA	21	14	2	3	1	1	1	0	0	0	8	5	1	1	1	11	8	1	1	1
OTHER	18	10	3	2	3	4	2	2	0	0	5	3	1	0	1	9	5	0	2	2
EUROPE	365	143	132	44	40	122	58	27	22	15	55	19	19	7	10	182	66	86	15	15
EFTA	147	55	51	23	15	60	28	14	11	7	20	8	2	7	3	64	19	35	5	5
U.K.	102	33	39	16	11	42	19	9	9	5	15	7	2	4	2	42	7	28	3	4
SCANDINAVIA	25	11	7	5	2	11	4	4	1	2	3	0	0	0	0	11	7	3	1	0
SWITZERLAND	11	6	4	1	0	3	1	1	0	0	2	0	0	1	0	4	5	3	0	1
OTHER EFTA	11	6	4	0	1	4	4	0	1	0	3	1	0	2	1	7	2	4	0	1
EUROP. COMMUNITY	180	71	70	15	21	51	26	12	7	6	29	8	15	0	6	97	37	43	8	9
FRANCE	54	21	18	8	7	17	5	12	3	1	17	6	2	1	4	37	15	11	2	9
GERMANY	49	18	22	3	6	18	12	4	1	1	18	8	7	1	3	30	15	11	1	3
ITALY	36	13	18	1	4	17	12	3	1	1	6	1	3	0	1	18	5	11	0	3
BELGIUM + LUX	22	11	6	2	3	7	5	0	1	1	5	1	2	0	2	16	8	5	2	1
NETHERLANDS	19	8	6	2	3	5	3	1	0	1	5	1	2	1	2	9	4	4	0	1
SPAIN	23	8	10	2	3	5	2	2	0	1	4	0	2	0	2	15	5	8	1	1
GREECE + TURKEY	4	4	0	0	0	0	0	0	0	0	0	2	0	1	0	4	1	0	0	0
OTHER EUROPE	11	5	1	4	1	2	1	0	2	0	2	2	0	1	0	2	1	0	1	1
EUROPE EX. U.K.	263	110	93	28	29	80	39	18	13	10	40	12	17	3	8	140	59	58	12	11
SOUTHERN DOMINIONS	89	44	28	12	4	28	12	6	6	4	14	8	5	1	0	34	17	8	6	3
S. AFRICA +RHOD.	22	11	6	2	1	6	6	0	0	0	6	5	1	1	0	8	0	5	3	1
AUSTRALIA + N.Z.	67	33	22	9	3	22	6	6	5	5	8	3	4	1	0	25	12	5	3	2
ASIA + OTHER AFRICA	98	57	13	10	17	20	13	3	3	1	19	7	1	5	5	58	39	8	3	8
JAPAN	31	17	9	2	3	3	3	0	0	0	7	1	4	1	1	21	13	5	1	2
OTHER ASIA+AFR.	67	40	4	8	14	17	10	3	3	1	12	4	1	4	4	37	26	3	2	6
BLACK AFRICA	9	5	1	1	2	1	1	0	0	0	2	0	0	1	1	6	4	1	1	0
ARAB WORLD	8	4	1	3	0	0	0	0	0	0	4	2	1	1	0	4	1	0	2	0
INDIA	11	11	0	0	0	5	5	0	0	0	2	2	0	1	0	4	4	0	0	0
PHILIPPINES	9	4	0	3	2	2	2	0	0	0	5	1	0	3	0	2	1	0	0	1
OTHER E. ASIA	3	0	1	0	2	1	0	1	0	0	0	0	0	0	0	2	0	0	1	1
OTHER ASIA	27	16	1	1	8	8	3	0	1	4	2	1	0	0	1	16	12	1	0	3

CHAPTER 4- VARIETIES OF ENTRY
SECTION 3- THE FLOW OF MANUFACTURING BY CHARACTERISTIC OF PARENT SYSTEM
TABLE H3- MANUFACTURING SUBSIDIARIES IN A SYSTEM
WHICH FIRST MANUFACTURED OUTSIDE U.S. AND CANADA 1920-1929
CLASSIFIED BY COUNTRY, PERIOD MANUFACTURE BEGAN, AND METHOD OF ENTRY

(NEW=NEWLY FORMED, ACQ=ACQUIRED, DES=DESCENDANT, UNK=UNKNOWN)

PERIOD AND METHOD OF ENTRY

COUNTRY OR REGION	TOTAL ALL	NEW	ACQ	PRE 1968 DES	UNK	PRE 1946 ALL	NEW	ACQ	DES	UNK	1946-1957 ALL	NEW	ACQ	DES	UNK	1958-1967 ALL	NEW	ACQ	DES	UNK
OUTSIDE U.S.	1524	608	682	104	93	356	154	146	23	33	296	147	95	28	26	835	307	441	53	34
OUT. U.S. + CANADA	1274	537	537	89	80	259	116	97	17	29	246	132	67	26	21	738	289	373	46	30
OUT. WEST. HEMIS.	900	364	398	55	54	182	76	76	13	18	153	81	48	12	12	536	208	274	30	24
OUT. WHITE CWEALTH	895	420	349	62	56	157	74	57	7	19	178	106	39	18	15	552	240	253	37	22
OUT. DEVLPED WORLD	482	242	158	43	36	85	45	24	5	11	110	63	22	15	10	284	134	112	23	15
CANADA	250	71	145	15	13	97	38	49	6	4	50	15	28	2	5	97	18	68	7	4
LATIN AMERICA	374	173	139	34	26	77	41	21	4	11	93	51	19	14	9	202	81	99	16	6
C. AMER.+CARIB.	169	77	64	18	9	31	18	8	2	3	40	22	7	3	4	97	37	49	9	2
CUBA	19	9	4	4	2	10	3	4	1	2	8	5	0	3	1	1	0	0	0	0
MEXICO	93	43	43	6	1	14	6	4	0	1	23	16	5	3	0	56	18	34	4	0
OTHER	57	25	17	8	6	7	7	0	1	0	9	1	2	1	3	40	18	15	5	2
S. AMERICA	205	96	75	16	17	46	23	13	1	8	53	29	12	7	5	105	44	50	7	4
ARGENTINA	54	27	21	4	2	18	9	6	1	2	11	8	1	1	0	25	10	14	4	0
BRAZIL	50	20	20	7	3	10	5	3	0	1	15	7	4	2	2	25	8	13	3	0
PERU	17	12	2	2	3	6	3	1	0	0	6	5	0	0	0	5	4	1	1	0
COLOMBIA	32	12	16	2	1	4	2	1	0	2	6	5	3	0	1	22	7	12	0	2
VENEZUELA	34	18	8	1	3	3	2	0	0	1	11	5	3	1	0	19	11	5	1	2
OTHER	18	7	8	0	5	5	2	2	0	1	4	1	1	2	0	9	5	5	1	0
EUROPE	574	203	288	33	30	142	51	66	10	15	96	50	33	7	6	316	102	189	16	9
EFTA	241	68	121	22	14	79	25	37	9	8	46	18	20	5	3	100	25	64	8	3
U.K.	191	49	100	16	11	70	22	33	8	7	37	13	18	4	2	69	14	49	4	2
SCANDINAVIA	33	13	15	3	1	5	2	2	0	1	7	5	2	0	0	21	6	11	1	1
SWITZERLAND	4	3	1	2	0	0	0	0	0	0	1	0	0	1	1	2	0	1	1	0
OTHER EFTA	13	6	5	1	0	4	1	0	0	0	1	0	0	0	0	8	5	3	0	0
EUROP. COMMUNITY	274	111	137	10	13	56	24	25	1	6	43	27	11	2	3	172	60	101	7	4
FRANCE	94	33	52	5	3	21	8	11	1	1	15	8	4	0	1	57	17	37	3	2
GERMANY	76	26	41	5	5	20	8	10	0	2	8	3	4	1	2	47	15	27	3	2
ITALY	52	26	22	2	2	1	1	0	0	0	13	10	2	0	0	38	15	20	1	2
BELGIUM + LUX	26	9	14	0	2	7	2	2	0	3	4	3	1	0	0	15	9	6	0	0
NETHERLANDS	26	17	8	1	0	5	5	2	0	0	3	3	0	0	0	20	8	5	1	0
SPAIN	35	13	21	1	1	5	2	2	0	1	4	1	1	0	0	26	8	17	0	0
GREECE + TURKEY	11	7	2	2	0	2	0	2	0	0	1	1	0	0	0	8	6	2	0	0
OTHER EUROPE	13	4	7	0	1	0	0	0	0	0	2	1	0	0	0	11	3	5	0	2
EUROPE EX. U.K.	383	154	188	17	19	72	29	33	2	8	59	37	15	3	4	247	88	140	12	7
SOUTHERN DOMINIONS	180	65	84	11	13	32	20	7	2	3	29	12	9	4	4	112	33	68	5	6
S. AFRICA +RHOD.	64	23	33	5	2	12	5	2	1	1	8	6	0	1	1	43	8	32	3	0
AUSTRALIA + N.Z.	116	42	51	6	11	20	11	6	1	2	21	6	9	3	3	69	25	36	2	6
ASIA + OTHER AFRICA	146	96	26	9	11	16	8	7	1	0	28	19	3	1	3	108	73	17	9	9
JAPAN	38	27	7	2	1	8	4	3	1	0	11	7	3	0	1	26	20	4	2	0
OTHER ASIA+AFR.	108	69	19	7	10	8	4	4	0	0	17	12	3	1	1	82	53	13	7	9
BLACK AFRICA	17	10	4	1	2	0	0	0	0	0	2	1	1	0	1	15	3	4	0	2
ARAB WORLD	10	9	5	1	1	0	0	0	0	0	3	2	0	0	0	7	3	5	1	1
INDIA	19	16	3	1	1	5	3	2	0	0	3	2	1	1	0	15	6	5	3	1
PHILIPPINES	21	9	4	1	1	1	1	0	0	0	6	4	0	0	0	10	8	1	0	1
OTHER E. ASIA	12	9	1	1	1	1	0	1	0	0	1	1	1	0	0	10	8	1	1	1
OTHER ASIA	29	20	2	3	4	1	1	0	0	0	2	1	0	0	0	25	18	1	2	4

CHAPTER 4- VARIETIES OF ENTRY

SECTION 3- THE FLOW OF MANUFACTURING BY CHARACTERISTIC OF PARENT SYSTEM

TABLE H4- MANUFACTURING SUBSIDIARIES IN A SYSTEM

WHICH FIRST MANUFACTURED OUTSIDE U.S. AND CANADA 1930-1945

CLASSIFIED BY COUNTRY, PERIOD MANUFACTURE BEGAN, AND METHOD OF ENTRY

PERIOD AND METHOD OF ENTRY

(NEW=NEWLY FORMED, ACQ=ACQUIRED, DES=DESCENDANT, UNK=UNKNOWN)

COUNTRY OR REGION	TOTAL					PRE 1946					1946-1957					1958-1967				
	ALL	NEW	ACQ	DES	UNK	ALL	NEW	ACQ	DES	UNK	ALL	NEW	ACQ	DES	UNK	ALL	NEW	ACQ	DES	UNK
OUTSIDE U.S.	890	400	350	48	35	71	43	19	5	4	208	107	81	15	5	554	250	250	28	26
OUT. U.S. + CANADA	753	358	270	41	31	46	29	10	3	4	165	91	58	12	4	489	238	202	26	23
OUT. WEST. HEMIS.	469	214	181	27	16	24	12	7	3	2	73	44	22	6	1	341	158	152	18	13
OUT. WHITE CWEALTH	605	298	210	24	26	28	19	6	0	3	130	71	49	6	4	400	208	155	18	19
OUT. DEVLPED WORLD	332	170	100	15	16	22	17	3	0	2	104	55	39	6	4	175	98	58	9	10
CANADA	137	42	80	7	4	25	14	9	2	0	43	16	23	3	1	65	12	48	2	3
LATIN AMERICA	284	144	89	14	15	22	17	3	2	0	92	47	36	4	1	148	80	50	8	10
C. AMER.+CARIB.	122	53	39	10	7	13	9	3	1	0	39	18	16	1	1	57	26	21	6	4
CUBA	10	4	1	3	0	3	1	1	1	0	6	3	3	0	0	0	0	0	0	0
MEXICO	82	31	31	8	3	10	8	2	0	0	28	11	14	2	1	35	14	15	5	1
OTHER	30	18	7	1	1	0	0	0	0	0	5	4	1	0	0	22	14	6	1	1
S. AMERICA	162	91	50	4	8	9	3	5	0	1	53	29	20	2	2	91	54	29	2	6
ARGENTINA	26	10	11	1	2	1	0	1	0	0	7	1	5	0	1	16	6	7	1	2
BRAZIL	43	23	15	1	2	3	2	1	0	0	14	7	5	1	1	24	14	9	0	1
PERU	8	1	4	0	1	0	0	0	0	0	4	1	3	0	0	4	0	1	0	1
COLOMBIA	29	19	9	0	0	1	0	1	0	0	9	6	3	0	0	18	12	6	0	0
VENEZUELA	39	29	6	2	2	3	1	2	0	0	15	10	3	0	0	16	16	3	1	1
OTHER	17	9	5	0	1	1	0	1	0	0	4	2	1	0	1	10	6	3	0	1
EUROPE	319	133	144	20	15	17	7	7	3	0	38	22	13	3	0	257	104	126	14	13
EFTA	101	35	49	11	5	12	6	5	1	0	17	8	6	3	0	71	21	41	5	4
U.K.	76	23	38	11	4	11	5	5	1	0	14	7	4	3	0	51	11	32	5	3
SCANDINAVIA	13	5	6	1	1	0	0	0	0	0	2	0	2	0	0	10	5	4	0	1
SWITZERLAND	6	2	4	0	0	0	0	0	0	0	0	0	0	0	0	6	2	4	0	0
OTHER EFTA	6	5	1	0	0	1	1	0	0	0	1	1	0	0	0	4	3	1	0	0
EUROP. COMMUNITY	181	80	79	8	8	5	1	3	1	0	14	9	5	0	0	156	70	71	8	7
FRANCE	48	18	25	2	2	2	0	1	0	1	5	2	3	0	0	44	16	24	2	2
GERMANY	51	20	22	4	3	2	1	1	0	0	5	2	2	0	1	42	17	19	4	2
ITALY	48	22	22	2	2	1	0	0	1	0	1	0	1	0	0	47	22	21	2	2
BELGIUM + LUX	15	9	5	0	1	0	0	0	0	0	3	1	2	0	0	12	8	3	0	1
NETHERLANDS	19	11	5	1	1	1	0	1	0	0	4	4	0	0	0	11	7	3	0	0
SPAIN	23	8	12	2	1	0	0	0	0	0	2	2	2	0	0	19	7	10	1	1
GREECE + TURKEY	11	3	8	0	0	0	0	0	0	0	2	2	0	0	0	9	6	3	0	0
OTHER EUROPE	3	1	1	0	1	0	0	0	0	0	1	0	0	0	1	2	0	1	0	1
EUROPE EX. U.K.	243	110	106	9	11	6	2	2	2	0	24	15	9	0	0	206	93	94	9	10
SOUTHERN DOMINIONS	69	36	21	6	0	7	5	1	1	0	20	12	5	3	0	36	19	14	3	3
S. AFRICA +RHOD.	31	15	12	2	0	4	4	0	0	0	7	4	3	0	0	15	8	5	2	2
AUSTRALIA + N.Z.	38	21	9	4	0	3	1	1	1	0	13	8	2	3	0	21	11	9	1	1
ASIA + OTHER AFRICA	81	45	16	5	1	0	0	0	0	0	15	10	4	0	1	48	35	12	1	1
JAPAN	33	19	5	1	1	0	0	0	0	0	3	2	1	0	0	21	17	4	0	0
OTHER ASIA+AFR.	48	26	11	1	0	0	0	0	0	0	12	8	3	0	1	27	18	8	1	0
BLACK AFRICA	5	5	0	0	0	0	0	0	0	0	1	1	0	0	0	4	4	0	0	0
ARAB WORLD	7	4	3	1	0	0	0	0	0	0	0	0	0	0	0	5	3	2	1	0
INDIA	9	2	6	0	0	0	0	0	0	0	5	1	4	0	1	3	1	1	1	0
PHILIPPINES	6	6	0	0	0	0	0	0	0	0	0	0	0	0	0	4	4	0	0	0
OTHER E. ASIA	6	4	2	0	0	0	0	0	0	0	1	0	1	0	0	5	4	1	0	0
OTHER ASIA	16	10	1	0	1	0	0	0	0	0	6	4	1	0	1	6	6	0	0	0

CHAPTER 4- VARIETIES OF ENTRY
SECTION 3- THE FLOW OF MANUFACTURING BY CHARACTERISTIC OF PARENT SYSTEM
TABLE H5- MANUFACTURING SUBSIDIARIES IN A SYSTEM
WHICH FIRST MANUFACTURED OUTSIDE U.S. AND CANADA AFTER 1946
CLASSIFIED BY COUNTRY, PERIOD MANUFACTURE BEGAN, AND METHOD OF ENTRY

PERIOD AND METHOD OF ENTRY
(NEW=NEWLY FORMED, ACQ=ACQUIRED, DES=DESCENDANT, UNK=UNKNOWN)

COUNTRY OR REGION	TOTAL PRE 1968					PRE 1946					1946-1957					1958-1967				
	ALL	NEW	ACQ	DES	UNK	ALL	NEW	ACQ	DES	UNK	ALL	NEW	ACQ	DES	UNK	ALL	NEW	ACQ	DES	UNK
OUTSIDE U.S.	1111	415	595	44	44	32	22	8	0	2	212	87	103	14	8	854	306	484	30	34
OUT. U.S. + CANADA	929	362	480	39	39	0	0	0	0	0	154	71	66	10	7	766	291	414	29	32
OUT. WEST. HEMIS.	651	237	346	28	33	0	0	0	0	0	97	31	52	9	5	547	206	294	19	28
OUT. WHITE CWEALTH	728	305	358	28	29	0	0	0	0	0	111	58	40	6	7	609	247	318	22	22
OUT. DEVLPED WORLD	365	171	168	13	10	0	0	0	0	0	66	46	16	1	3	296	125	152	12	7
CANADA	182	53	115	5	5	32	22	8	0	2	58	16	37	4	1	88	15	70	1	2
LATIN AMERICA	278	125	134	11	6	0	0	0	0	0	57	40	14	1	2	219	85	120	10	4
C. AMER.+CARIB.	139	59	68	8	2	0	0	0	0	0	28	17	9	1	1	109	42	59	7	1
CUBA	5	3	1	1	0	0	0	0	0	0	4	3	0	1	0	1	0	1	0	0
MEXICO	96	37	51	7	0	0	0	0	0	0	22	12	9	1	0	73	25	42	6	0
OTHER	38	19	16	1	2	0	0	0	0	0	2	2	0	0	1	35	17	16	1	1
S. AMERICA	139	66	66	3	4	0	0	0	0	0	29	23	5	0	1	110	43	61	3	3
ARGENTINA	32	10	19	2	1	0	0	0	0	0	6	4	1	1	0	26	6	18	1	1
BRAZIL	29	17	10	2	0	0	0	0	0	0	10	9	1	0	0	19	8	9	2	0
PERU	10	5	5	0	0	0	0	0	0	0	1	1	0	0	0	9	4	5	0	0
COLOMBIA	20	5	9	0	2	0	0	0	0	0	3	2	1	0	0	17	7	8	0	2
VENEZUELA	33	18	15	0	0	0	0	0	0	0	7	6	1	0	0	26	12	14	0	0
OTHER	15	7	8	0	0	0	0	0	0	0	2	1	1	0	0	13	6	7	0	0
EUROPE	431	139	249	19	20	0	0	0	0	0	69	19	38	8	4	358	120	211	11	16
EFTA	136	40	81	7	7	0	0	0	0	0	27	8	14	4	1	108	32	67	3	6
U.K.	103	23	70	5	4	0	0	0	0	0	25	8	13	4	0	77	15	57	1	4
SCANDINAVIA	17	10	5	1	1	0	0	0	0	0	0	0	0	0	0	15	10	5	0	0
SWITZERLAND	12	4	6	1	1	0	0	0	0	0	0	0	0	0	1	12	4	6	1	1
OTHER EFTA	4	3	0	1	0	0	0	0	0	0	0	0	0	0	0	4	3	0	1	0
EUROP. COMMUNITY	244	78	140	12	11	0	0	0	0	0	36	10	19	4	3	205	68	121	8	8
FRANCE	74	16	50	2	5	0	0	0	0	0	10	2	5	1	2	63	14	45	1	3
GERMANY	61	17	33	8	2	0	0	0	0	0	14	3	9	2	0	46	14	24	6	2
ITALY	49	21	26	0	1	0	0	0	0	0	5	3	2	0	0	43	18	24	0	1
BELGIUM + LUX	36	16	19	0	1	0	0	0	0	0	3	2	1	0	0	33	14	18	0	1
NETHERLANDS	24	8	12	3	1	0	0	0	0	0	4	0	2	2	0	20	8	10	1	1
SPAIN	37	15	21	0	1	0	0	0	0	0	3	0	3	0	0	34	15	18	0	1
GREECE + TURKEY	7	5	1	0	1	0	0	0	0	0	1	1	0	0	0	6	4	1	0	1
OTHER EUROPE	7	1	6	0	0	0	0	0	0	0	2	0	2	0	0	5	1	4	0	0
EUROPE EX. U.K.	328	116	179	14	16	0	0	0	0	0	44	11	25	4	4	281	105	154	10	12
SOUTHERN DOMINIONS	92	34	46	6	6	0	0	0	0	0	16	5	11	0	0	76	29	35	6	6
S. AFRICA +RHOD.	27	11	15	0	1	0	0	0	0	0	5	2	3	0	0	22	9	12	0	1
AUSTRALIA + N.Z.	65	23	31	6	5	0	0	0	0	0	11	3	8	0	0	54	20	23	6	5
ASIA + OTHER AFRICA	128	64	51	3	7	0	0	0	0	0	12	7	3	1	1	113	57	48	2	6
JAPAN	41	18	17	0	4	0	0	0	0	0	3	1	1	0	1	36	17	16	0	3
OTHER ASIA+AFR.	87	46	34	3	3	0	0	0	0	0	9	6	2	1	0	77	40	32	2	3
BLACK AFRICA	10	7	2	0	3	0	0	0	0	0	2	1	0	0	1	8	7	2	0	3
ARAB WORLD	9	7	2	0	0	0	0	0	0	0	0	0	0	0	0	9	7	2	0	0
INDIA	20	12	8	0	0	0	0	0	0	0	2	0	2	0	0	18	12	8	0	0
PHILIPPINES	12	5	7	0	0	0	0	0	0	0	2	0	2	0	0	10	5	7	0	0
OTHER E. ASIA	12	5	7	1	0	0	0	0	0	0	0	0	0	0	0	12	5	6	1	0
OTHER ASIA	24	13	9	1	0	0	0	0	0	0	5	3	2	0	0	18	10	7	1	0

CHAPTER 4- VARIETIES OF ENTRY
SECTION 3- THE FLOW OF MANUFACTURING BY CHARACTERISTIC OF PARENT SYSTEM
TABLE II- MANUFACTURING SUBSIDIARIES IN A SYSTEM
IN "ORGANIZATIONAL STAGE II" IN 1966
CLASSIFIED BY COUNTRY, PERIOD MANUFACTURE BEGAN, AND METHOD OF ENTRY

PERIOD AND METHOD OF ENTRY
(NEW=NEWLY FORMED, ACQ=ACQUIRED, DES=DESCENDANT, UNK=UNKNOWN)

COUNTRY OR REGION	TOTAL PRE 1968					PRE 1946					1946-1957					1958-1967				
	ALL	NEW	ACQ	DES	UNK	ALL	NEW	ACQ	DES	UNK	ALL	NEW	ACQ	DES	UNK	ALL	NEW	ACQ	DES	UNK
OUTSIDE U.S.	269	137	99	19	14	39	26	3	6	4	59	35	17	5	2	171	76	79	8	8
OUT. U.S. + CANADA	225	121	78	13	13	29	17	3	5	4	45	33	8	3	1	151	71	67	5	8
OUT. WEST. HEMIS.	153	76	59	8	10	24	14	2	5	3	22	14	5	2	1	107	48	52	1	6
OUT. WHITE CWEALTH	170	96	58	7	9	14	9	1	1	3	35	26	7	1	1	121	61	50	5	5
OUT. DEVLPED WORLD	94	62	23	5	4	6	4	1	0	1	28	22	4	1	1	60	36	18	4	2
CANADA	44	16	21	6	1	10	9	0	1	0	14	2	9	2	1	20	5	12	3	0
LATIN AMERICA	72	45	19	5	3	5	3	1	0	1	23	19	3	1	0	44	23	15	4	2
C. AMER.+CARIB.	33	22	8	3	0	3	2	1	0	0	13	11	1	0	0	17	9	6	2	0
CUBA	6	0	0	3	0	1	1	0	0	0	1	0	0	1	0	0	0	0	2	0
MEXICO	24	13	8	3	0	2	1	1	0	0	9	7	1	1	0	13	5	6	2	0
OTHER	3	3	0	0	0	0	0	0	0	0	0	0	0	0	0	3	3	0	0	0
S. AMERICA	39	23	11	2	3	2	1	0	0	1	10	8	2	0	0	27	14	9	2	2
ARGENTINA	4	2	2	0	0	0	0	0	0	0	1	1	0	0	0	3	1	2	0	0
BRAZIL	6	4	1	0	1	1	1	0	0	0	2	1	0	0	1	3	2	1	0	0
PERU	5	4	1	0	0	1	0	0	0	1	3	3	1	0	0	1	1	0	0	0
COLOMBIA	9	5	2	1	1	0	0	0	0	0	3	2	1	0	0	6	3	1	1	1
VENEZUELA	10	6	2	1	1	1	0	0	0	0	0	0	0	0	0	9	5	2	1	1
OTHER	5	2	3	0	0	0	0	0	0	0	0	0	0	0	0	5	2	3	0	0
EUROPE	101	38	50	7	6	17	9	2	4	2	11	5	4	2	0	73	24	44	1	4
EFTA	39	13	19	5	2	10	5	2	3	0	5	2	1	2	0	24	6	16	1	2
U.K.	31	9	16	5	1	9	4	2	3	0	5	2	1	2	0	17	3	13	0	1
SCANDINAVIA	5	2	2	0	1	0	0	0	0	0	0	0	0	0	0	5	2	2	0	1
SWITZERLAND	1	0	2	0	0	0	0	0	0	0	0	0	0	0	0	1	0	2	0	0
OTHER EFTA	2	2	0	0	0	1	1	0	0	0	0	0	0	0	0	1	1	0	0	0
EUROP. COMMUNITY	53	24	23	2	4	7	4	0	1	2	5	3	2	0	0	41	17	21	1	2
FRANCE	13	5	7	2	1	2	1	0	1	0	1	0	1	1	0	10	4	6	0	0
GERMANY	16	6	8	0	1	2	1	0	0	1	1	1	1	0	0	13	4	7	1	1
ITALY	10	6	3	0	1	2	2	0	0	0	1	1	0	0	0	7	3	3	0	1
BELGIUM + LUX	11	5	4	1	1	1	0	0	0	1	1	0	0	1	0	9	5	4	0	0
NETHERLANDS	3	1	1	0	0	0	0	0	0	0	0	0	0	0	0	2	1	1	0	0
SPAIN	7	2	1	6	0	0	0	0	0	0	1	0	0	1	0	6	2	2	0	0
GREECE + TURKEY	0	0	6	0	0	0	0	0	0	0	0	0	0	0	0	0	0	0	0	0
OTHER EUROPE	0	0	2	0	0	0	0	0	0	0	0	0	0	0	0	0	0	0	0	0
EUROPE EX. U.K.	70	29	34	2	5	8	5	0	1	2	6	3	3	0	0	56	21	31	1	3
SOUTHERN DOMINIONS	24	16	4	1	3	6	4	0	1	1	5	5	0	0	0	13	7	4	0	2
S. AFRICA +RHOD.	9	7	2	2	0	2	2	0	0	0	3	3	0	0	0	4	2	2	0	0
AUSTRALIA + N.Z.	15	9	2	1	3	4	2	0	1	1	2	2	0	0	0	9	5	2	0	2
ASIA + OTHER AFRICA	28	22	5	0	1	1	1	0	0	0	6	4	0	1	0	21	17	4	0	0
JAPAN	6	5	1	0	0	0	0	0	0	0	5	1	0	1	0	5	4	1	0	0
OTHER ASIA+AFR.	22	17	4	0	1	1	1	0	0	0	5	3	0	0	1	16	13	3	0	0
BLACK AFRICA	2	1	0	0	1	0	0	0	0	0	1	0	0	0	1	1	1	0	0	0
ARAB WORLD	5	5	0	3	0	0	0	0	0	0	0	1	0	0	0	4	4	0	0	0
INDIA	5	2	3	0	0	1	1	0	0	0	0	0	0	0	0	5	2	3	0	0
PHILIPPINES	5	5	0	0	0	0	0	0	0	0	2	2	0	0	0	5	2	2	0	0
OTHER E. ASIA	0	0	0	0	0	0	0	0	0	0	0	0	0	0	0	2	2	0	0	0
OTHER ASIA	5	4	1	0	0	0	0	0	0	0	1	0	1	0	0	4	4	0	0	0

CHAPTER 4— VARIETIES OF ENTRY
SECTION 3— THE FLOW OF MANUFACTURING BY CHARACTERISTIC OF PARENT SYSTEM
TABLE I2— MANUFACTURING SUBSIDIARIES IN A SYSTEM
IN "ORGANIZATIONAL STAGE III-ID" IN 1966
CLASSIFIED BY COUNTRY, PERIOD MANUFACTURE BEGAN, AND METHOD OF ENTRY

PERIOD AND METHOD OF ENTRY
(NEW=NEWLY FORMED, ACQ=ACQUIRED, DES=DESCENDANT, UNK=UNKNOWN)

COUNTRY OR REGION	TOTAL PRE 1968					PRE 1946					1946-1957					1958-1967				
	ALL	NEW	ACQ	DES	UNK	ALL	NEW	ACQ	DES	UNK	ALL	NEW	ACQ	DES	UNK	ALL	NEW	ACQ	DES	UNK
OUTSIDE U.S.	2409	984	1080	185	117	493	256	153	45	39	474	215	181	52	26	1399	513	746	88	52
OUT. U.S. + CANADA	2028	883	865	162	90	354	198	98	33	25	384	191	126	45	22	1262	494	641	84	43
OUT. WEST. HEMIS.	1407	582	626	114	63	253	132	75	29	17	232	111	85	24	12	900	339	466	61	34
OUT. WHITE CWEALTH	1519	717	611	108	66	229	133	64	15	17	290	156	84	32	18	983	428	463	61	31
OUT. DEVLPED WORLD	793	406	277	61	41	117	74	25	6	12	180	100	46	23	11	488	232	206	32	18
CANADA	381	101	215	46	27	139	58	55	12	14	90	24	55	7	4	137	19	105	4	9
LATIN AMERICA	621	301	239	48	27	101	66	23	4	8	152	80	41	21	10	362	155	175	23	9
C. AMER.+CARIB.	267	122	108	22	12	38	22	11	1	4	62	32	18	8	4	164	68	79	13	4
CUBA	26	8	7	3	7	11	5	6	0	0	12	6	1	3	2	2	0	1	0	1
MEXICO	162	74	70	16	2	22	15	6	1	0	43	22	14	5	2	97	37	50	10	0
OTHER	79	40	31	6	2	5	2	0	3	0	7	4	3	0	0	65	31	28	3	3
S. AMERICA	354	179	131	29	15	63	44	12	5	2	90	48	23	13	6	198	87	96	10	5
ARGENTINA	80	27	42	8	3	22	14	5	3	0	16	4	9	2	1	41	9	28	3	1
BRAZIL	89	44	31	12	2	17	13	3	1	0	27	14	5	6	2	45	17	23	5	0
PERU	25	15	6	1	3	4	2	0	1	1	7	5	1	0	1	14	8	5	0	1
COLOMBIA	51	25	21	1	4	7	5	1	0	1	11	7	2	1	1	33	13	18	0	2
VENEZUELA	72	47	20	2	3	5	5	0	0	0	22	14	5	2	1	44	28	15	0	1
OTHER	37	21	11	4	1	8	5	3	0	0	7	4	1	2	0	21	12	7	2	0
EUROPE	905	344	440	81	40	183	85	65	21	12	151	71	56	16	8	558	188	319	35	16
EFTA	319	110	154	34	16	94	41	31	14	8	62	24	25	10	3	158	45	98	10	5
U.K.	240	72	123	27	13	76	30	27	12	7	49	17	21	9	2	110	25	75	6	4
SCANDINAVIA	46	21	20	3	2	9	4	3	1	1	9	5	3	0	1	28	12	14	2	0
SWITZERLAND	16	5	7	4	0	3	1	1	1	0	2	1	0	1	0	11	5	3	2	1
OTHER EFTA	17	12	4	0	1	6	6	0	0	0	2	1	1	0	0	9	3	6	0	0
EUROP. COMMUNITY	486	190	238	34	17	80	40	30	6	4	74	38	25	6	5	325	112	183	22	8
FRANCE	155	49	83	15	6	29	8	15	5	1	21	11	5	2	3	103	30	63	8	2
GERMANY	127	47	61	13	6	29	17	9	1	2	24	8	13	2	1	70	22	39	8	1
ITALY	104	46	49	6	3	6	5	1	0	0	15	9	4	2	0	82	32	44	4	2
BELGIUM + LUX	49	21	23	2	3	7	4	2	1	0	6	4	2	0	0	36	15	19	2	0
NETHERLANDS	51	24	22	2	3	9	6	3	0	0	8	6	1	1	0	34	17	18	0	1
SPAIN	62	24	34	2	2	7	3	3	1	0	7	4	3	0	0	48	17	28	2	1
GREECE + TURKEY	19	14	3	2	0	0	0	0	0	0	2	2	0	0	0	17	12	3	2	0
OTHER EUROPE	19	6	11	1	1	1	0	1	0	0	6	2	3	0	1	10	7	2	1	0
EUROPE EX. U.K.	665	272	317	45	23	107	55	38	9	5	102	54	35	7	6	448	163	244	29	12
SOUTHERN DOMINIONS	255	90	123	26	16	49	35	7	6	1	39	15	18	4	2	162	40	98	16	8
S. AFRICA +RHOD.	86	32	45	7	2	14	12	1	1	0	12	8	3	1	0	59	12	41	5	1
AUSTRALIA + N.Z.	169	58	78	20	13	35	23	6	5	1	27	7	15	4	2	103	28	57	11	7
ASIA + OTHER AFRICA	247	148	63	16	20	21	12	3	2	4	42	25	11	4	2	180	111	49	10	10
JAPAN	75	43	25	4	3	5	4	1	0	0	14	6	6	2	1	54	34	18	1	1
OTHER ASIA+AFR.	172	105	38	13	14	16	8	2	2	4	28	20	5	2	1	126	77	31	9	9
BLACK AFRICA	22	9	10	1	2	0	0	0	0	0	1	0	0	0	1	19	9	8	1	1
ARAB WORLD	18	10	4	1	3	2	2	0	0	0	4	4	0	0	0	16	10	4	1	1
INDIA	34	23	5	4	2	2	2	0	0	0	4	4	0	0	0	27	17	5	4	1
PHILIPPINES	25	16	7	0	2	5	3	2	0	0	10	6	2	2	0	10	7	3	0	0
OTHER E. ASIA	21	13	5	2	1	0	0	0	0	0	1	1	0	0	0	20	12	5	2	1
OTHER ASIA	52	34	8	3	7	8	3	0	1	4	9	7	2	0	0	34	24	5	2	3

CHAPTER 4— VARIETIES OF ENTRY
SECTION 3— THE FLOW OF MANUFACTURING BY CHARACTERISTIC OF PARENT SYSTEM
TABLE I3— MANUFACTURING SUBSIDIARIES IN A SYSTEM
IN "ORGANIZATIONAL STAGE III-OTHER" IN 1966
CLASSIFIED BY COUNTRY, PERIOD MANUFACTURE BEGAN, AND METHOD OF ENTRY

PERIOD AND METHOD OF ENTRY
(NEW=NEWLY FORMED, ACQ=ACQUIRED, DES=DESCENDANT, UNK=UNKNOWN)

COUNTRY OR REGION	TOTAL PRE 1968 ALL	NEW	ACQ	DES	UNK	PRE 1946 ALL	NEW	ACQ	DES	UNK	1946-1957 ALL	NEW	ACQ	DES	UNK	1958-1967 ALL	NEW	ACQ	DES	UNK
OUTSIDE U.S.	2097	890	803	136	184	431	220	124	32	55	387	184	130	34	39	1195	486	549	70	90
OUT. U.S. + CANADA	1805	786	655	126	162	337	173	92	29	43	322	154	103	32	33	1070	459	460	65	86
OUT. WEST. HEMIS.	1275	530	488	84	122	245	117	72	24	31	188	80	65	20	23	791	333	351	40	67
OUT. WHITE CWEALTH	1380	629	468	96	127	235	125	59	20	31	244	117	77	24	26	841	387	332	52	70
OUT. DEVLPED WORLD	678	333	196	54	59	105	63	22	8	12	151	80	40	16	15	386	190	134	30	32
CANADA	292	104	148	10	22	94	47	32	3	12	65	30	27	2	6	125	27	89	5	4
LATIN AMERICA	530	256	167	42	40	92	56	20	5	11	134	74	38	12	10	279	126	109	25	19
C. AMER.+CARIB.	220	98	75	21	13	33	28	1	1	3	45	21	13	7	4	129	49	61	13	6
CUBA	11	7	0	4	0	6	5	0	1	0	4	2	0	2	0	1	0	0	1	0
MEXICO	148	60	65	8	5	19	17	1	1	0	30	16	12	2	0	89	27	52	6	4
OTHER	61	31	10	9	8	8	6	0	0	2	11	3	1	3	4	39	22	9	6	2
S. AMERICA	310	158	92	21	27	59	28	19	4	8	89	53	25	5	6	150	77	48	12	13
ARGENTINA	60	35	14	5	5	20	11	5	3	1	13	11	2	0	0	24	13	7	2	1
BRAZIL	86	45	29	5	5	15	9	5	0	1	34	17	12	2	3	35	19	12	3	1
PERU	26	9	11	1	2	7	3	3	0	1	4	2	2	0	0	12	4	6	3	1
COLOMBIA	48	23	16	4	5	3	1	1	1	0	13	7	5	0	1	31	15	10	1	3
VENEZUELA	52	32	8	5	6	5	3	1	1	0	17	11	2	2	2	29	18	5	3	3
OTHER	38	14	14	1	7	9	1	4	0	4	8	5	2	1	0	19	8	8	0	3
EUROPE	875	329	381	59	87	197	86	62	20	29	126	52	48	12	14	533	191	271	27	44
EFTA	326	107	148	30	34	92	37	33	9	13	50	20	16	8	6	177	50	99	13	15
U.K.	232	64	121	19	23	67	23	27	8	9	41	18	15	4	4	119	23	79	7	10
SCANDINAVIA	54	23	15	8	2	15	8	3	0	4	7	2	1	3	1	31	13	11	5	2
SWITZERLAND	15	6	3	2	3	2	2	0	0	0	2	0	0	1	0	10	4	3	0	1
OTHER EFTA	25	14	9	1	1	8	4	3	1	0	0	0	0	0	0	17	10	6	0	2
EUROP. COMMUNITY	446	173	196	25	40	81	39	24	8	10	62	23	28	4	7	291	111	144	13	23
FRANCE	131	51	60	7	8	28	14	9	2	4	13	4	6	2	1	85	33	45	2	5
GERMANY	129	44	63	8	14	29	14	9	3	4	20	12	4	1	3	80	26	42	5	7
ITALY	95	44	37	3	8	13	8	2	1	2	17	10	6	0	1	63	27	29	5	5
BELGIUM + LUX	42	16	19	2	4	6	1	2	1	2	3	2	1	0	0	32	13	16	2	2
NETHERLANDS	49	17	17	5	6	6	2	2	1	0	9	3	3	1	2	31	12	12	3	4
SPAIN	57	24	27	1	5	8	4	0	3	1	8	3	4	0	1	41	17	20	1	3
GREECE + TURKEY	18	14	1	0	3	1	0	0	0	1	4	4	0	0	0	13	10	1	0	2
OTHER EUROPE	28	11	9	3	5	6	2	3	0	1	2	2	0	0	0	11	3	7	0	1
EUROPE EX. U.K.	643	265	260	40	64	130	63	35	12	20	85	34	33	8	10	414	168	192	20	34
SOUTHERN DOMINIONS	176	86	59	10	10	31	23	6	0	2	35	17	11	4	3	99	46	42	6	5
S. AFRICA +RHOD.	52	24	24	3	4	9	8	0	0	1	9	5	3	0	1	27	11	11	3	2
AUSTRALIA + N.Z.	124	62	45	7	6	22	15	6	0	1	26	12	8	4	2	72	35	31	3	3
ASIA + OTHER AFRICA	224	115	48	15	25	17	8	4	4	1	27	11	6	4	6	159	96	38	7	18
JAPAN	76	38	19	3	6	4	1	2	1	0	10	5	4	0	1	52	32	13	2	5
OTHER ASIA+AFR.	148	77	29	12	19	13	7	2	3	1	17	6	2	4	5	107	64	25	5	13
BLACK AFRICA	19	11	0	4	4	1	0	0	1	0	3	1	0	2	0	17	11	7	1	4
ARAB WORLD	13	8	0	1	0	0	0	0	0	0	1	1	0	0	0	8	7	0	1	0
INDIA	26	12	11	2	0	3	1	0	0	2	6	2	2	2	0	21	8	11	2	0
PHILIPPINES	23	11	5	2	4	3	1	1	1	0	2	0	0	0	2	15	8	5	0	2
OTHER E. ASIA	17	8	4	0	4	4	1	1	2	0	2	2	0	1	1	10	7	1	0	5
OTHER ASIA	50	27	8	3	7	4	2	0	0	2	5	2	0	1	2	36	23	7	1	5

CHAPTER 4- VARIETIES OF ENTRY
SECTION 3- THE FLOW OF MANUFACTURING BY CHARACTERISTIC OF PARENT SYSTEM
TABLE J1 - MANUFACTURING SUBSIDIARIES IN A SYSTEM
WITH LOW "PRODUCT DIVERSITY IN THE U.S." IN 1966
CLASSIFIED BY COUNTRY, PERIOD MANUFACTURE BEGAN, AND METHOD OF ENTRY

PERIOD AND METHOD OF ENTRY
(NEW=NEWLY FORMED, ACQ=ACQUIRED, DES=DESCENDANT, UNK=UNKNOWN)

COUNTRY OR REGION	TOTAL PRE 1968 ALL	NEW	ACQ	DES	UNK	PRE 1946 ALL	NEW	ACQ	DES	UNK	1946-1957 ALL	NEW	ACQ	DES	UNK	1958-1967 ALL	NEW	ACQ	DES	UNK
OUTSIDE U.S.	2350	981	945	178	167	453	263	108	35	47	447	197	159	55	36	1371	521	678	88	84
OUT. U.S. + CANADA	2010	872	757	160	156	341	197	74	29	41	369	176	111	49	33	1235	499	572	82	82
OUT. WEST. HEMIS.	1395	572	555	109	114	248	130	61	25	32	223	98	76	28	21	879	344	418	56	61
OUT. WHITE CWEALTH	1528	695	562	109	113	224	131	51	14	28	274	139	76	33	26	981	425	435	62	59
OUT. DEVLPED WORLD	784	391	241	63	60	103	73	14	6	10	171	92	41	23	15	481	226	186	34	35
CANADA	340	109	188	18	11	112	66	34	6	6	78	21	48	6	3	136	22	106	6	2
LATIN AMERICA	615	300	202	51	42	93	67	13	4	9	146	78	35	21	12	356	155	154	26	21
C. AMER.+CARIB.	284	127	99	29	19	42	32	4	1	5	67	31	17	12	7	165	64	78	16	7
CUBA	26	13	3	5	4	10	6	3	0	1	13	6	4	1	2	2	1	1	0	0
MEXICO	165	71	68	14	5	20	16	3	0	1	43	21	16	4	1	95	34	49	9	3
OTHER	93	43	28	10	10	12	10	0	0	2	11	4	0	5	1	68	29	28	7	4
S. AMERICA	331	173	103	22	23	51	35	9	3	4	79	47	18	9	5	191	91	76	10	14
ARGENTINA	62	27	27	3	3	20	13	4	2	1	9	4	5	0	0	31	10	18	1	2
BRAZIL	76	43	24	5	3	11	8	2	0	1	24	15	4	3	2	40	20	18	2	0
PERU	29	12	10	1	4	5	3	1	0	1	7	5	1	0	1	15	4	8	1	2
COLOMBIA	58	28	19	5	5	5	4	1	0	0	12	8	2	1	1	40	16	17	3	4
VENEZUELA	73	49	14	5	5	6	5	1	0	0	20	12	5	2	1	46	32	8	2	4
OTHER	33	14	9	4	3	4	2	1	1	1	7	3	1	3	0	19	9	7	1	2
EUROPE	912	338	415	75	71	190	86	56	21	27	138	59	51	17	11	571	193	308	37	33
EFTA	321	110	132	41	33	90	40	24	14	12	53	18	21	10	4	173	52	87	17	17
U.K.	233	67	110	30	22	71	30	20	13	8	42	14	18	8	2	116	23	72	9	12
SCANDINAVIA	52	24	12	6	9	11	4	3	0	4	6	3	0	2	1	34	17	9	4	4
SWITZERLAND	14	4	4	5	1	1	0	0	1	0	4	1	3	0	0	9	3	1	4	1
OTHER EFTA	22	15	6	0	1	7	6	1	0	0	1	0	0	0	1	14	9	5	0	0
EUROP. COMMUNITY	498	190	239	33	28	87	42	29	7	9	73	35	24	7	7	330	113	186	19	12
FRANCE	151	46	87	11	5	30	9	16	3	2	17	8	5	3	1	102	29	66	5	2
GERMANY	148	54	69	11	11	30	16	8	2	4	25	8	12	2	3	90	30	49	7	4
ITALY	99	45	44	6	4	9	6	1	1	1	17	11	4	1	1	73	28	39	4	2
BELGIUM + LUX	52	27	19	2	3	8	4	1	1	2	5	5	0	0	0	38	18	18	1	1
NETHERLANDS	48	18	20	3	5	10	7	3	0	0	9	3	3	1	2	27	8	14	2	3
SPAIN	61	24	35	1	1	5	1	3	0	1	6	1	4	0	0	50	22	28	1	0
GREECE + TURKEY	12	2	7	0	4	1	0	0	0	1	2	1	1	0	0	10	1	6	0	3
OTHER EUROPE	20	8	7	0	5	7	3	0	0	4	4	4	1	0	0	9	1	6	0	1
EUROPE EX. U.K.	679	271	305	45	49	119	56	36	8	19	96	45	33	9	9	455	170	236	28	21
SOUTHERN DOMINIONS	236	105	79	21	19	45	36	3	2	4	48	20	15	8	5	131	49	61	11	10
S. AFRICA +RHOD.	76	40	21	5	4	16	14	1	1	0	15	9	3	2	1	39	17	17	2	3
AUSTRALIA + N.Z.	160	65	58	16	15	29	22	2	1	4	33	11	12	6	4	92	32	44	9	7
ASIA + OTHER AFRICA	247	129	61	13	24	13	8	2	2	1	37	19	10	3	5	177	102	49	8	18
JAPAN	78	38	22	1	6	3	2	1	0	0	12	5	4	1	2	52	31	17	0	4
OTHER ASIA+AFR.	169	91	39	12	18	10	6	0	0	0	25	14	6	2	3	125	71	32	8	14
BLACK AFRICA	19	10	6	0	3	0	0	0	0	0	2	1	0	0	1	17	9	6	0	2
ARAB WORLD	22	10	4	4	1	1	1	0	0	0	4	2	2	0	0	16	8	2	2	1
INDIA	29	18	7	3	0	1	0	1	0	0	3	3	0	0	0	24	14	7	3	0
PHILIPPINES	25	13	8	1	3	3	2	1	0	0	8	4	2	1	1	14	7	5	0	1
OTHER E. ASIA	20	11	5	0	3	1	0	0	1	0	1	1	0	0	0	17	10	5	0	3
OTHER ASIA	54	29	10	4	7	4	3	0	0	0	7	3	3	0	1	39	23	6	3	6

CHAPTER 4- VARIETIES OF ENTRY
SECTION 3- THE FLOW OF MANUFACTURING BY CHARACTERISTIC OF PARENT SYSTEM
TABLE J2- MANUFACTURING SUBSIDIARIES IN A SYSTEM
WITH HIGH "PRODUCT DIVERSITY IN THE U.S." IN 1966
CLASSIFIED BY COUNTRY, PERIOD MANUFACTURE BEGAN, AND METHOD OF ENTRY

(NEW=NEWLY FORMED, ACQ=ACQUIRED, DES=DESCENDANT, UNK=UNKNOWN)

PERIOD AND METHOD OF ENTRY

COUNTRY OR REGION	TOTAL / PRE 1968 ALL	NEW	ACQ	DES	UNK	PRE 1946 ALL	NEW	ACQ	DES	UNK	1946-1957 ALL	NEW	ACQ	DES	UNK	1958-1967 ALL	NEW	ACQ	DES	UNK
OUTSIDE U.S.	2829	1174	1235	172	186	572	264	196	51	61	561	268	213	38	42	1634	642	826	83	83
OUT. U.S. + CANADA	2368	1037	991	149	138	416	207	133	40	36	439	223	153	32	31	1460	607	705	77	71
OUT. WEST. HEMIS.	1658	697	716	104	101	304	146	99	35	24	246	118	90	19	19	1068	433	527	50	58
OUT. WHITE CWEALTH	1780	837	695	106	111	279	148	82	22	27	338	174	114	24	26	1132	515	499	60	58
OUT. DEVLPED WORLD	901	459	314	58	53	132	71	37	8	16	222	123	66	17	16	530	265	211	33	21
CANADA	461	137	244	23	48	156	57	63	11	25	122	45	60	6	11	174	35	121	6	12
LATIN AMERICA	710	340	275	45	37	112	61	34	5	12	193	105	63	13	12	392	174	178	27	13
C. AMER.+CARIB.	282	130	115	18	11	36	22	10	1	3	64	36	21	4	3	174	72	84	13	5
CUBA	20	8	5	2	4	9	6	0	1	2	8	2	5	1	0	0	0	0	0	0
MEXICO	200	87	90	14	9	26	19	6	1	0	48	26	16	3	3	122	42	68	10	2
OTHER	62	35	20	2	5	1	1	0	0	0	8	4	4	0	0	50	30	16	2	2
S. AMERICA	428	210	160	27	26	76	39	24	4	9	129	69	42	9	9	218	102	94	14	8
ARGENTINA	97	43	39	8	7	24	13	7	2	2	24	13	8	2	1	49	17	24	4	4
BRAZIL	123	57	47	12	6	23	14	7	1	1	46	22	15	5	4	53	21	25	6	1
PERU	28	16	9	1	1	7	3	2	1	1	8	4	4	0	0	12	9	3	0	0
COLOMBIA	57	27	24	2	4	5	2	2	1	0	17	8	8	0	1	35	17	14	1	3
VENEZUELA	71	42	21	4	4	5	3	2	0	0	23	16	3	2	2	43	23	17	2	1
OTHER	52	25	21	4	5	13	4	6	0	3	11	6	4	0	1	28	15	11	1	2
EUROPE	1130	423	533	69	75	234	106	82	26	20	165	73	64	13	15	701	244	387	30	40
EFTA	427	137	214	31	27	117	47	46	14	10	72	30	25	10	7	220	60	143	7	10
U.K.	318	88	169	24	20	90	30	39	12	9	59	25	22	7	5	152	33	108	5	6
SCANDINAVIA	61	25	29	5	2	14	8	4	1	1	11	4	3	3	0	36	13	22	3	0
SWITZERLAND	23	9	9	2	3	4	3	1	0	0	0	0	0	0	0	18	6	8	1	3
OTHER EFTA	25	15	7	1	2	9	6	2	1	0	2	1	0	0	1	14	8	5	0	1
EUROP. COMMUNITY	565	219	263	41	41	96	48	30	8	10	74	30	34	3	7	384	141	199	20	24
FRANCE	169	63	78	11	12	35	17	10	3	5	20	7	8	1	4	109	39	60	5	5
GERMANY	149	51	75	11	11	34	19	11	2	2	22	4	16	1	1	92	28	48	9	7
ITALY	122	55	54	3	11	11	8	2	0	1	18	11	6	0	1	90	36	46	2	6
BELGIUM + LUX	64	29	22	4	8	10	2	4	1	3	5	2	3	0	0	49	17	27	2	3
NETHERLANDS	76	30	37	3	6	6	2	2	1	1	9	6	1	1	1	44	21	18	2	3
SPAIN	30	24	5	0	1	10	6	3	1	0	10	5	4	0	1	56	19	30	2	5
GREECE + TURKEY	32	13	14	4	1	0	0	0	0	0	5	3	1	0	0	25	19	5	1	1
OTHER EUROPE	13	10	5	0	0	5	3	3	1	0	4	3	0	0	0	16	5	10	1	0
EUROPE EX. U.K.	812	335	364	45	55	144	76	43	14	11	106	48	42	6	10	549	211	279	25	34
SOUTHERN DOMINIONS	249	104	117	17	7	44	27	12	5	0	38	21	16	1	0	163	56	89	11	7
S. AFRICA +RHOD.	83	29	45	6	1	10	8	2	0	0	13	9	4	0	0	58	12	40	5	1
AUSTRALIA + N.Z.	166	75	72	11	6	34	19	11	4	0	25	12	12	0	0	105	44	49	6	6
ASIA + OTHER AFRICA	279	170	66	18	19	26	13	5	4	4	43	24	10	5	4	204	133	51	9	11
JAPAN	88	51	27	5	3	6	3	2	1	0	14	6	4	0	4	66	42	18	3	3
OTHER ASIA+AFR.	191	119	39	13	16	20	10	3	3	3	29	18	8	3	0	138	91	33	8	6
BLACK AFRICA	27	14	7	1	5	3	0	0	0	3	2	2	0	0	1	24	12	7	1	4
ARAB WORLD	17	14	1	1	1	4	4	0	1	0	3	3	0	0	0	9	12	0	0	0
INDIA	39	21	13	3	1	4	4	3	1	0	2	0	0	0	0	31	14	13	3	1
PHILIPPINES	33	21	7	3	2	3	1	1	0	0	3	3	1	0	0	17	14	6	3	1
OTHER E. ASIA	19	10	5	2	2	1	2	0	0	0	2	0	1	0	0	14	9	2	2	1
OTHER ASIA	56	39	6	2	7	2	0	2	2	4	8	6	1	0	0	38	31	5	0	2

CHAPTER 4- VARIETIES OF ENTRY
SECTION 3- THE FLOW OF MANUFACTURING BY CHARACTERISTIC OF PARENT SYSTEM
TABLE K1- MANUFACTURING SUBSIDIARIES IN A SYSTEM
WITH LOW "PRODUCT DIVERSITY ABROAD" IN 1966
CLASSIFIED BY COUNTRY, PERIOD MANUFACTURE BEGAN, AND METHOD OF ENTRY

PERIOD AND METHOD OF ENTRY
(NEW=NEWLY FORMED, ACQ=ACQUIRED, DES=DESCENDANT, UNK=UNKNOWN)

COUNTRY OR REGION	TOTAL PRE 1968 ALL	NEW	ACQ	DES	UNK	PRE 1946 ALL	NEW	ACQ	DES	UNK	1946-1957 ALL	NEW	ACQ	DES	UNK	1958-1967 ALL	NEW	ACQ	DES	UNK
OUTSIDE U.S.	1766	747	676	192	116	361	198	88	50	25	391	167	139	57	28	979	382	449	85	63
OUT. U.S. + CANADA	1510	668	536	173	102	269	146	62	41	20	328	155	96	52	25	882	367	378	80	57
OUT. WEST. HEMIS.	1041	437	388	123	68	188	92	46	37	13	201	89	70	30	12	627	256	272	56	43
OUT. WHITE CWEALTH	1147	540	395	118	78	181	104	46	19	12	244	126	61	36	21	706	310	288	63	45
OUT. DEVLPED WORLD	597	306	172	67	46	91	61	17	6	7	149	79	29	26	15	351	166	126	35	24
CANADA	256	79	140	19	14	92	52	26	9	5	63	12	43	5	3	97	15	71	5	6
LATIN AMERICA	469	231	148	50	34	81	54	16	4	7	127	66	26	22	13	255	111	106	24	14
C. AMER.+CARIB.	220	104	70	27	15	37	24	9	2	2	63	34	12	11	6	116	46	49	14	7
CUBA	26	12	5	5	4	8	2	4	1	1	15	9	0	4	2	3	1	1	0	1
MEXICO	134	61	52	14	4	21	15	5	1	0	37	21	11	4	1	73	25	36	9	3
OTHER	60	31	13	8	7	8	7	0	0	1	11	4	1	3	3	40	20	12	5	3
S. AMERICA	249	127	78	23	19	44	30	7	2	5	64	32	14	11	7	139	65	57	10	7
ARGENTINA	56	19	28	5	3	15	7	4	2	2	8	3	3	2	0	32	9	21	1	1
BRAZIL	60	28	18	7	6	10	8	1	0	1	18	7	3	4	4	31	13	14	3	1
PERU	23	14	6	2	1	5	5	0	0	0	8	5	2	1	0	10	4	4	1	1
COLOMBIA	35	23	6	2	4	5	3	1	0	1	9	2	2	2	3	21	18	3	0	0
VENEZUELA	48	30	10	5	3	4	4	0	0	0	16	10	3	0	3	28	16	7	5	0
OTHER	27	13	10	3	1	5	3	1	0	1	5	1	1	3	0	17	9	8	0	0
EUROPE	680	255	287	79	40	139	58	41	30	10	124	56	46	17	5	398	141	200	32	25
EFTA	222	70	88	37	16	63	25	15	18	5	48	15	21	11	1	100	30	52	8	10
U.K.	174	44	78	28	13	53	19	13	16	5	38	11	18	8	1	72	14	47	4	7
SCANDINAVIA	29	15	8	5	1	6	3	2	1	0	7	3	2	2	0	16	9	4	2	1
SWITZERLAND	6	0	1	4	1	1	0	0	1	0	1	0	0	1	0	4	0	1	2	1
OTHER EFTA	13	11	1	0	1	3	3	0	0	0	2	1	1	0	0	8	7	0	0	1
EUROP. COMMUNITY	388	155	167	36	22	68	31	23	9	5	64	33	21	6	5	248	91	123	21	13
FRANCE	129	37	66	14	8	25	7	11	5	2	18	8	6	2	2	82	22	49	7	4
GERMANY	110	39	47	14	7	23	11	8	2	2	20	6	10	2	2	64	22	29	10	3
ITALY	76	39	30	3	4	5	5	0	0	0	14	10	3	1	0	57	24	27	2	4
BELGIUM + LUX	33	19	10	2	1	6	3	1	1	1	3	3	0	0	0	24	13	9	1	0
NETHERLANDS	40	21	14	3	2	9	5	3	1	0	10	6	2	1	1	21	10	9	1	1
SPAIN	44	18	24	2	0	4	2	2	0	0	7	5	2	0	0	33	11	20	2	0
GREECE + TURKEY	13	9	2	2	0	0	0	0	0	0	2	1	1	0	0	12	8	1	2	0
OTHER EUROPE	13	3	6	4	0	4	0	1	3	0	4	2	1	0	0	5	1	4	1	0
EUROPE Ex. U.K.	506	211	209	51	27	86	39	28	14	5	86	45	28	9	4	326	127	153	28	18
SOUTHERN DOMINIONS	180	81	59	25	11	34	23	3	5	3	42	16	15	8	3	100	42	41	12	5
S. AFRICA +RHOD.	61	30	18	9	2	11	9	0	1	1	15	8	4	2	1	33	13	14	6	0
AUSTRALIA + N.Z.	119	51	41	16	9	23	14	3	4	2	27	8	11	6	2	67	29	27	6	5
ASIA + OTHER AFRICA	181	101	42	19	17	15	11	2	2	0	35	17	9	5	4	129	73	31	12	13
JAPAN	53	26	18	2	5	5	4	1	0	0	13	4	6	3	0	33	18	11	1	3
OTHER ASIA+AFR.	128	75	24	17	12	10	7	1	2	0	22	13	3	4	2	96	55	20	11	10
BLACK AFRICA	14	8	1	1	4	0	0	0	0	0	2	1	0	0	1	12	7	1	1	3
ARAB WORLD	14	9	1	3	1	0	0	0	0	0	3	2	0	1	0	11	7	1	2	1
INDIA	24	11	8	4	1	1	1	0	0	0	2	2	0	0	0	21	8	8	4	1
PHILIPPINES	23	14	6	3	0	1	1	0	0	0	7	4	2	1	0	15	9	4	2	0
OTHER E. ASIA	15	9	5	1	0	5	4	0	1	0	1	0	1	0	0	9	5	4	0	0
OTHER ASIA	38	24	3	5	6	4	2	0	2	0	6	3	1	1	1	28	19	2	3	5

CHAPTER 4- VARIETIES OF ENTRY
SECTION 3- THE FLOW OF MANUFACTURING BY CHARACTERISTIC OF PARENT SYSTEM
TABLE K2- MANUFACTURING SUBSIDIARIES IN A SYSTEM
WITH HIGH "PRODUCT DIVERSITY ABROAD" IN 1966
CLASSIFIED BY COUNTRY, PERIOD MANUFACTURE BEGAN, AND METHOD OF ENTRY

(NEW=NEWLY FORMED, ACQ=ACQUIRED, DES=DESCENDANT, UNK=UNKNOWN)

PERIOD AND METHOD OF ENTRY

COUNTRY OR REGION	TOTAL PRE 1968					PRE 1946					1946-1957					1958-1967				
	ALL	NEW	ACQ	DES	UNK	ALL	NEW	ACQ	DES	UNK	ALL	NEW	ACQ	DES	UNK	ALL	NEW	ACQ	DES	UNK
OUTSIDE U.S.	3413	1408	1504	158	237	664	329	216	36	83	617	298	233	36	50	2026	781	1055	86	104
OUT. U.S. + CANADA	2868	1241	1212	136	192	488	258	145	28	57	480	244	168	29	39	1813	739	899	79	96
OUT. WEST. HEMIS.	2012	832	883	90	147	364	184	114	23	43	268	127	96	17	28	1320	521	673	50	76
OUT. WHITE CWEALTH	2161	992	862	97	146	322	175	87	17	43	368	187	129	21	31	1407	630	646	59	72
OUT. DEVLPED WORLD	1098	544	383	54	67	144	83	34	8	19	244	136	78	14	16	660	325	271	32	32
CANADA	545	167	292	22	45	176	71	71	8	26	137	54	65	7	11	213	42	156	7	8
LATIN AMERICA	856	409	329	46	45	124	74	31	5	14	212	117	72	12	11	493	218	226	29	20
C. AMER.+CARIB.	346	153	144	20	15	41	30	5	0	6	68	33	26	5	4	223	90	113	15	5
CUBA	20	9	3	2	4	11	6	1	0	4	6	2	3	1	0	0	0	0	1	0
MEXICO	231	97	106	14	6	25	20	0	1	4	54	26	21	4	3	144	51	81	0	3
OTHER	95	47	35	8	4	5	4	0	0	1	8	4	3	0	1	78	39	32	4	3
S. AMERICA	510	256	185	26	30	83	44	26	5	8	144	84	46	7	7	270	128	113	14	15
ARGENTINA	103	51	38	6	5	29	19	7	2	1	25	14	10	0	1	46	18	21	4	3
BRAZIL	139	72	53	10	5	24	14	8	1	1	52	30	16	3	1	62	28	29	5	2
PERU	34	14	13	1	3	7	3	1	1	1	7	7	0	0	0	17	8	8	0	2
COLOMBIA	80	32	37	3	6	5	1	2	1	1	20	11	8	0	1	54	20	27	3	4
VENEZUELA	96	61	24	4	6	6	4	1	1	0	27	18	5	2	1	61	39	18	1	3
OTHER	58	26	20	2	7	12	3	6	0	3	13	7	4	1	1	30	11	10	1	3
EUROPE	1362	506	661	65	106	285	134	97	17	37	179	76	69	13	21	874	296	495	35	48
EFTA	526	177	258	35	44	144	62	55	10	17	77	33	25	9	10	293	82	178	16	17
U.K.	377	111	201	26	29	108	41	46	9	12	63	28	22	7	6	196	42	133	10	11
SCANDINAVIA	84	34	33	2	10	19	9	5	0	5	10	1	3	1	2	54	21	25	5	5
SWITZERLAND	31	13	12	1	2	4	3	1	0	0	3	0	0	0	1	23	9	11	1	2
OTHER EFTA	34	19	12	2	2	13	9	0	1	3	1	1	0	0	1	20	10	9	0	1
EUROP. COMMUNITY	675	254	335	28	47	115	59	36	6	14	83	32	37	4	10	466	163	262	18	23
FRANCE	191	72	99	8	9	40	19	15	3	3	19	7	7	2	1	129	46	77	3	3
GERMANY	187	66	97	8	15	41	24	11	1	5	27	6	18	1	2	118	36	68	8	8
ITALY	145	61	68	3	8	15	9	3	1	2	21	12	7	1	3	106	40	58	4	4
BELGIUM + LUX	83	29	43	3	7	12	3	4	1	4	7	4	3	0	0	60	22	36	2	5
NETHERLANDS	69	26	28	4	8	7	4	3	3	0	9	3	6	0	0	50	19	23	2	5
SPAIN	93	36	48	5	7	11	5	5	0	1	9	2	6	1	0	73	29	38	1	5
GREECE + TURKEY	29	21	5	0	3	1	0	0	0	0	5	5	0	0	0	23	16	4	1	2
OTHER EUROPE	39	15	15	1	5	14	8	2	0	4	5	4	1	0	0	19	6	12	0	1
EUROPE EX. U.K.	985	395	460	39	77	177	93	51	8	25	116	48	47	6	15	678	254	362	25	37
SOUTHERN DOMINIONS	305	128	137	13	15	55	40	12	2	1	44	25	16	1	2	194	63	109	10	12
S. AFRICA +RHOD.	98	39	48	2	3	15	13	2	0	0	13	10	3	0	0	64	16	43	2	2
AUSTRALIA + N.Z.	207	89	89	11	12	40	27	10	2	1	31	15	13	1	2	130	47	66	8	9
ASIA + OTHER AFRICA	345	198	85	12	26	24	10	2	0	5	45	26	14	3	5	252	162	69	5	16
JAPAN	113	63	31	4	4	4	1	0	0	1	13	7	7	0	1	85	55	24	3	5
OTHER ASIA+AFR.	232	135	54	8	22	20	9	2	0	5	32	19	7	3	5	167	107	45	3	12
BLACK AFRICA	32	16	6	0	5	0	0	0	0	0	3	3	2	0	0	27	14	4	0	3
ARAB WORLD	25	15	6	3	0	2	0	0	0	0	3	2	2	0	1	19	15	4	0	0
INDIA	44	28	12	0	0	2	4	0	0	0	4	4	0	0	0	34	20	12	2	0
PHILIPPINES	35	20	12	1	4	4	1	1	0	0	10	6	4	1	2	22	13	7	2	2
OTHER E. ASIA	24	12	5	1	5	4	1	1	0	0	3	1	2	0	1	16	10	2	1	2
OTHER ASIA	72	44	13	1	8	8	3	0	0	4	9	6	2	0	1	49	35	11	0	3

CHAPTER 4- VARIETIES OF ENTRY
SECTION 3- THE FLOW OF MANUFACTURING BY CHARACTERISTIC OF PARENT SYSTEM
TABLE L1- MANUFACTURING SUBSIDIARIES IN A SYSTEM
WITH LOW "GEOGRAPHICAL DIVERSITY" IN 1966
CLASSIFIED BY COUNTRY, PERIOD MANUFACTURE BEGAN, AND METHOD OF ENTRY

PERIOD AND METHOD OF ENTRY
(NEW=NEWLY FORMED, ACQ=ACQUIRED, DES=DESCENDANT, UNK=UNKNOWN)

COUNTRY OR REGION	TOTAL PRE 1968 ALL	NEW	ACQ	DES	UNK	PRE 1946 ALL	NEW	ACQ	DES	UNK	1946-1957 ALL	NEW	ACQ	DES	UNK	1958-1967 ALL	NEW	ACQ	DES	UNK
OUTSIDE U.S.	1685	653	780	146	67	266	139	90	23	14	342	137	151	40	14	1038	377	539	83	39
OUT. U.S. + CANADA	1375	565	605	125	52	182	96	58	18	10	257	115	99	32	11	908	354	448	75	31
OUT. WEST. HEMIS.	965	367	445	88	43	136	64	45	18	9	154	56	67	23	8	653	247	333	47	26
OUT. WHITE CWEALTH	1003	447	425	81	38	120	66	44	4	6	181	91	63	18	9	690	290	318	59	23
OUT. DEVLPED WORLD	471	234	179	41	11	49	35	13	0	1	111	65	33	9	4	305	134	133	32	6
CANADA	310	88	175	21	15	84	43	32	5	4	85	22	52	8	3	130	23	91	8	8
LATIN AMERICA	410	198	160	37	9	46	32	13	0	1	103	59	32	9	3	255	107	115	28	5
C. AMER.+CARIB.	195	89	80	19	4	14	12	2	0	0	46	25	15	4	2	132	52	63	15	2
CUBA	9	5	0	2	0	1	1	0	0	0	5	3	0	2	0	1	1	0	0	0
MEXICO	155	63	70	17	0	10	8	2	0	0	38	20	14	2	0	106	35	54	15	0
OTHER	31	21	10	0	0	3	3	0	0	0	3	2	1	0	0	25	16	9	0	0
S. AMERICA	215	109	80	18	5	32	20	11	0	1	57	34	17	4	2	123	55	52	13	3
ARGENTINA	55	19	28	5	0	7	4	3	0	0	11	4	4	2	1	35	11	21	3	0
BRAZIL	66	34	25	7	0	14	9	5	0	0	17	11	4	2	0	35	14	16	5	0
PERU	10	6	4	0	0	2	2	0	0	0	4	2	2	0	0	4	2	2	0	0
COLOMBIA	26	15	7	2	2	1	1	0	0	0	7	4	2	0	1	18	10	4	2	1
VENEZUELA	42	26	11	3	0	2	2	0	0	0	15	10	3	0	2	25	14	8	2	0
OTHER	16	9	5	1	0	6	3	3	0	0	3	1	1	1	0	6	4	1	1	0
EUROPE	707	243	348	64	35	113	47	42	16	8	106	37	46	17	6	471	159	260	31	21
EFTA	260	70	132	30	15	48	20	13	12	3	45	13	19	10	3	154	37	100	8	9
U.K.	214	51	114	25	11	43	16	12	12	3	38	11	17	8	2	120	24	85	5	6
SCANDINAVIA	18	7	9	4	1	1	1	0	0	0	3	0	2	2	0	14	6	6	1	1
SWITZERLAND	15	4	6	0	1	1	0	1	0	0	2	0	0	0	0	12	4	6	0	1
OTHER EFTA	13	6	3	3	2	3	3	0	0	0	2	0	0	0	1	8	3	3	0	1
EUROP. COMMUNITY	379	140	187	32	16	59	25	27	4	3	47	15	22	7	3	269	100	138	21	10
FRANCE	128	47	67	9	3	25	11	14	0	0	17	4	5	3	1	86	32	48	4	2
GERMANY	100	33	45	14	8	14	5	8	1	0	13	4	5	3	0	61	22	25	10	4
ITALY	84	11	42	4	1	8	4	3	0	0	11	3	8	0	0	69	26	38	4	1
BELGIUM + LUX	30	14	15	2	2	4	2	2	0	0	5	2	3	0	2	26	10	14	2	0
NETHERLANDS	37	22	18	2	3	4	2	2	0	0	6	2	6	0	0	27	10	13	1	3
SPAIN	52	5	25	0	1	5	1	2	0	1	9	3	3	0	0	39	15	20	3	0
GREECE + TURKEY	11	6	0	1	0	2	1	0	0	0	2	1	0	0	0	6	3	2	0	0
OTHER EUROPE	5	4	4	1	1	2	0	2	0	0	2	0	0	0	0	3	3	0	0	0
EUROPE EX. U.K.	493	192	234	39	24	70	31	30	4	5	68	26	29	9	4	351	135	175	26	15
SOUTHERN DOMINIONS	151	63	63	19	3	19	14	2	2	1	35	12	17	6	0	94	37	44	11	2
S. AFRICA +RHOD.	38	18	15	3	0	4	4	0	0	0	7	3	3	1	0	25	11	12	2	0
AUSTRALIA + N.Z.	113	45	48	16	3	15	10	2	2	1	28	9	14	5	0	69	26	32	9	2
ASIA + OTHER AFRICA	107	61	34	5	5	4	4	1	0	0	13	6	4	0	2	88	51	29	5	3
JAPAN	46	25	15	4	2	3	3	0	0	0	5	1	4	0	0	38	24	11	4	2
OTHER ASIA+AFR.	61	36	19	1	5	1	1	1	0	0	8	6	1	0	3	50	27	18	1	4
BLACK AFRICA	3	2	1	0	0	0	0	0	0	0	0	0	0	0	0	2	2	1	0	0
ARAB WORLD	7	5	1	1	0	0	0	0	0	0	2	1	0	1	0	5	5	1	0	0
INDIA	18	7	9	1	1	0	0	0	0	0	1	0	1	0	0	17	6	9	1	1
PHILIPPINES	10	6	2	1	0	0	0	0	0	0	2	2	0	0	0	7	3	2	1	0
OTHER E. ASIA	10	7	2	1	0	2	1	1	0	0	1	0	0	0	0	10	4	2	1	0
OTHER ASIA	13	9	2	1	1	1	1	0	0	0	0	0	0	0	1	7	5	1	1	0

CHAPTER 4— VARIETIES OF ENTRY
SECTION 3— THE FLOW OF MANUFACTURING BY CHARACTERISTIC OF PARENT SYSTEM
TABLE L2— MANUFACTURING SUBSIDIARIES IN A SYSTEM
WITH HIGH "GEOGRAPHICAL DIVERSITY" IN 1966
CLASSIFIED BY COUNTRY, PERIOD MANUFACTURE BEGAN, AND METHOD OF ENTRY

(NEW=NEWLY FORMED, ACQ=ACQUIRED, DES=DESCENDANT, UNK=UNKNOWN)

PERIOD AND METHOD OF ENTRY

COUNTRY OR REGION	TOTAL ALL	NEW	PRE ACQ	1968 DES	UNK	PRE 1946 ALL	NEW	ACQ	DES	UNK	1946-1957 ALL	NEW	ACQ	DES	UNK	1958-1967 ALL	NEW	ACQ	DES	UNK
OUTSIDE U.S.	3494	1502	1400	204	286	759	388	214	63	94	666	328	221	53	64	1967	786	965	88	128
OUT. U.S. + CANADA	3003	1344	1143	184	242	575	308	149	51	67	551	284	165	49	53	1787	752	829	84	122
OUT. WEST. HEMIS.	2088	902	826	125	172	416	212	115	42	47	315	160	99	24	32	1294	530	612	59	93
OUT. WHITE CWEALTH	2305	1085	832	134	186	383	213	89	32	49	431	222	127	39	43	1423	650	616	63	94
OUT. DEVLPED WORLD	1214	616	376	80	102	186	109	38	14	25	282	150	74	31	27	706	357	264	35	50
CANADA	491	158	257	20	44	184	80	65	12	27	115	44	56	4	11	180	34	136	4	6
LATIN AMERICA	915	442	317	59	70	159	96	34	9	20	236	124	66	25	21	493	222	217	25	29
C. AMER.+CARIB.	371	168	134	28	26	64	42	12	2	8	85	42	23	12	8	207	84	99	14	10
CUBA	37	16	8	5	8	18	7	5	1	5	16	3	2	8	3	3	0	1	1	1
MEXICO	210	95	88	11	6	36	27	7	1	1	53	27	18	6	2	111	41	63	4	3
OTHER	124	57	38	12	12	10	8	0	0	2	16	6	3	3	4	93	43	35	9	6
S. AMERICA	544	274	183	31	44	95	54	22	7	12	151	82	43	13	13	286	138	118	11	19
ARGENTINA	104	51	38	6	9	37	23	8	4	2	22	12	9	0	1	43	16	21	2	4
BRAZIL	133	66	46	10	9	20	13	4	1	2	53	26	15	6	6	58	27	27	3	1
PERU	47	22	15	2	5	10	4	3	2	1	11	7	3	0	1	23	11	9	1	2
COLOMBIA	89	40	36	4	8	9	5	2	1	1	22	12	7	1	2	57	23	27	2	5
VENEZUELA	102	65	23	5	7	8	6	1	0	1	28	18	5	3	2	64	41	17	2	4
OTHER	69	30	25	4	8	11	3	4	0	4	15	7	4	3	1	41	20	17	1	3
EUROPE	1335	518	600	80	111	311	145	96	31	39	197	80	69	13	20	801	278	435	36	52
EFTA	488	177	214	42	45	159	67	57	16	19	80	35	27	10	8	239	75	130	16	18
U.K.	337	104	165	29	31	118	44	47	13	14	63	28	23	7	5	148	32	95	6	12
SCANDINAVIA	95	42	32	10	10	24	12	6	1	5	14	6	0	3	2	56	24	23	6	3
SWITZERLAND	22	9	7	2	3	4	1	1	0	0	2	1	0	0	1	15	6	6	1	2
OTHER EFTA	34	22	10	1	1	13	9	3	1	0	1	0	1	0	0	20	13	6	0	1
EUROP. COMMUNITY	684	269	315	32	53	124	65	32	11	16	100	50	36	3	11	445	154	247	18	26
FRANCE	192	62	98	13	14	38	15	12	6	5	24	11	8	1	4	125	36	78	6	5
GERMANY	197	72	99	8	14	43	27	9	2	5	29	9	18	0	2	121	36	72	6	7
ITALY	137	65	56	4	11	16	10	3	1	2	26	17	6	1	2	94	38	47	2	7
BELGIUM + LUX	86	37	38	3	7	15	6	4	1	4	9	6	3	0	0	61	25	31	2	3
NETHERLANDS	72	33	24	4	7	12	6	4	1	1	12	7	1	2	2	44	19	19	2	4
SPAIN	85	32	47	2	4	11	7	4	1	0	7	1	5	0	1	67	25	38	1	3
GREECE + TURKEY	37	25	7	0	5	1	0	1	0	0	4	4	0	0	0	32	21	7	0	4
OTHER EUROPE	41	15	17	4	4	16	7	0	3	3	7	5	4	1	0	18	3	13	0	1
EUROPE EX. U.K.	998	414	435	51	80	193	101	49	18	25	134	67	46	6	15	653	246	340	27	40
SOUTHERN DOMINIONS	334	146	133	19	23	70	49	13	5	3	51	29	14	3	5	200	68	106	11	15
S. AFRICA +RHOD.	121	51	51	8	5	22	18	2	1	1	21	15	4	1	1	72	18	45	6	3
AUSTRALIA + N.Z.	213	95	82	11	18	48	31	11	4	2	30	14	10	2	4	128	50	61	5	12
ASIA + OTHER AFRICA	419	238	93	26	38	35	18	6	6	5	67	36	16	8	7	293	184	71	12	26
JAPAN	120	64	34	5	6	8	5	2	1	0	21	10	8	2	1	80	49	24	2	5
OTHER ASIA+AFR.	299	174	59	21	32	27	13	4	5	5	46	26	8	6	6	213	135	47	10	21
BLACK AFRICA	43	22	9	1	9	0	0	0	0	0	4	2	0	0	2	37	20	9	1	7
ARAB WORLD	32	19	6	5	0	2	0	0	2	0	6	2	2	0	2	23	17	4	1	1
INDIA	50	32	11	5	0	5	5	0	0	0	5	2	2	1	0	38	22	11	5	0
PHILIPPINES	48	28	11	1	4	5	3	1	1	0	18	10	1	2	1	24	15	7	0	2
OTHER E. ASIA	29	14	8	1	5	4	1	2	0	1	3	1	0	1	1	21	12	5	1	3
OTHER ASIA	97	59	14	5	13	11	4	1	2	4	10	6	3	0	1	70	49	11	2	8

CHAPTER 4— VARIETIES OF ENTRY
SECTION 4— THE FLOW OF MANUFACTURING BY INDUSTRY OF SUBSIDIARY
TABLE 1— SUBSIDIARIES MANUFACTURING
MEAT PRODUCTS (SIC 201)
CLASSIFIED BY COUNTRY, PERIOD MANUFACTURE BEGAN, AND METHOD OF ENTRY

PERIOD AND METHOD OF ENTRY
(NEW=NEWLY FORMED, ACQ=ACQUIRED, DES=DESCENDANT, UNK=UNKNOWN)

COUNTRY OR REGION	TOTAL PRE 1968 ALL	NEW	ACQ	DES	UNK	PRE 1946 ALL	NEW	ACQ	DES	UNK	1946-1957 ALL	NEW	ACQ	DES	UNK	1958-1967 ALL	NEW	ACQ	DES	UNK
OUTSIDE U.S.	72	19	47	1	2	18	9	7	0	2	14	0	14	0	0	37	10	26	1	0
OUT. U.S. + CANADA	58	17	36	1	2	17	8	7	0	2	10	0	10	0	0	29	9	19	1	0
OUT. WEST. HEMIS.	34	8	25	0	1	9	3	5	0	1	9	0	9	0	0	16	5	11	0	0
OUT. WHITE CWEALTH	32	12	16	1	1	10	5	4	0	1	3	0	3	0	0	17	7	9	1	0
OUT. DEVLPED WORLD	25	9	12	1	1	9	5	3	0	1	1	0	1	0	0	13	4	8	1	0
CANADA	14	2	11	0	1	1	1	0	0	0	4	1	4	0	0	8	1	7	0	0
LATIN AMERICA	24	9	11	1	1	8	5	2	0	1	4	1	1	0	0	13	4	8	0	0
C. AMER.+CARIB.	8	3	4	0	1	0	0	0	0	0	1	1	0	0	0	6	3	3	0	0
CUBA	1	0	1	0	0	0	0	0	0	0	1	1	0	0	0	0	0	0	0	0
MEXICO	6	3	3	0	0	0	0	0	0	0	0	0	0	0	0	5	3	2	0	0
OTHER	1	0	1	0	0	0	0	0	0	0	0	0	0	0	0	1	0	1	0	0
S. AMERICA	16	6	7	1	1	8	5	2	0	1	0	0	0	0	0	7	1	5	1	0
ARGENTINA	6	2	4	0	0	3	2	1	0	0	0	0	0	0	0	3	0	3	0	0
BRAZIL	7	3	3	1	0	4	3	0	1	0	0	0	0	0	0	3	0	3	0	0
PERU	0	0	0	0	0	0	0	0	0	0	0	0	0	0	0	0	0	0	0	0
COLOMBIA	0	0	0	0	0	0	0	0	0	0	0	0	0	0	0	0	0	0	0	0
VENEZUELA	1	1	0	0	0	0	0	0	0	0	0	0	0	0	0	1	1	0	0	0
OTHER	2	0	0	0	1	1	0	0	0	1	0	0	0	0	0	0	0	0	0	0
EUROPE	20	6	13	0	1	4	1	2	0	1	4	1	4	0	0	12	5	7	0	0
EFTA	10	2	7	0	1	3	1	1	0	1	1	1	1	0	0	6	1	5	0	0
U.K.	10	2	7	0	1	3	1	1	0	1	1	1	1	0	0	6	1	5	0	0
SCANDINAVIA	0	0	0	0	0	0	0	0	0	0	0	0	0	0	0	0	0	0	0	0
SWITZERLAND	0	0	0	0	0	0	0	0	0	0	0	0	0	0	0	0	0	0	0	0
OTHER EFTA	0	0	0	0	0	0	0	0	0	0	0	0	0	0	0	0	0	0	0	0
EUROP. COMMUNITY	5	1	4	0	0	1	0	1	0	0	2	0	2	0	0	2	1	1	0	0
FRANCE	1	0	1	0	0	0	0	0	0	0	0	0	0	0	0	1	0	1	0	0
GERMANY	2	1	2	0	0	0	0	0	0	0	2	0	2	0	0	0	1	0	0	0
ITALY	1	1	0	0	0	0	0	0	0	0	0	0	0	0	0	1	1	0	0	0
BELGIUM + LUX	1	0	1	0	0	1	0	1	0	0	0	0	0	0	0	0	0	0	0	0
NETHERLANDS	0	0	0	0	0	0	0	0	0	0	0	0	0	0	0	0	0	0	0	0
SPAIN	2	2	0	0	0	0	0	0	0	0	0	0	0	0	0	2	2	0	0	0
GREECE + TURKEY	0	0	0	0	0	0	0	0	0	0	0	0	0	0	0	0	0	0	0	0
OTHER EUROPE	3	1	2	0	0	1	0	1	0	0	0	0	0	0	0	2	1	1	0	0
EUROPE EX. U.K.	10	4	6	0	0	1	0	0	0	1	3	0	3	0	0	6	4	2	0	0
SOUTHERN DOMINIONS	13	2	11	0	0	4	0	4	0	0	5	0	5	0	0	4	0	4	0	0
S. AFRICA +RHOD.	0	0	0	0	0	0	0	0	0	0	0	0	0	0	0	0	0	0	0	0
AUSTRALIA + N.Z.	13	2	11	0	0	4	0	4	0	0	5	0	5	0	0	4	0	4	0	0
ASIA + OTHER AFRICA	1	0	1	0	0	1	0	1	0	0	0	0	0	0	0	0	0	0	0	0
JAPAN	1	0	1	0	0	1	0	1	0	0	0	0	0	0	0	0	0	0	0	0
OTHER ASIA+AFR.	0	0	0	0	0	0	0	0	0	0	0	0	0	0	0	0	0	0	0	0
BLACK AFRICA	0	0	0	0	0	0	0	0	0	0	0	0	0	0	0	0	0	0	0	0
ARAB WORLD	0	0	0	0	0	0	0	0	0	0	0	0	0	0	0	0	0	0	0	0
INDIA	0	0	0	0	0	0	0	0	0	0	0	0	0	0	0	0	0	0	0	0
PHILIPPINES	1	0	1	0	0	1	0	1	0	0	0	0	0	0	0	0	0	0	0	0
OTHER E. ASIA	0	0	0	0	0	0	0	0	0	0	0	0	0	0	0	0	0	0	0	0
OTHER ASIA	0	0	0	0	0	0	0	0	0	0	0	0	0	0	0	0	0	0	0	0

CHAPTER 4— VARIETIES OF ENTRY
SECTION 4— THE FLOW OF MANUFACTURING BY INDUSTRY OF SUBSIDIARY
TABLE 2— SUBSIDIARIES MANUFACTURING
DAIRY PRODUCTS (SIC 202)
CLASSIFIED BY COUNTRY, PERIOD MANUFACTURE BEGAN, AND METHOD OF ENTRY

PERIOD AND METHOD OF ENTRY
(NEW=NEWLY FORMED, ACQ=ACQUIRED, DES=DESCENDANT, UNK=UNKNOWN)

COUNTRY OR REGION	TOTAL PRE 1968					PRE 1946					1946-1957					1958-1967				
	ALL	NEW	ACQ	DES	UNK	ALL	NEW	ACQ	DES	UNK	ALL	NEW	ACQ	DES	UNK	ALL	NEW	ACQ	DES	UNK
OUTSIDE U.S.	134	56	69	4	3	56	27	26	1	2	19	14	14	4	0	57	15	39	3	0
OUT. U.S. + CANADA	107	51	49	3	3	41	24	14	1	2	18	13	14	4	1	47	14	31	2	0
OUT. WEST. HEMIS.	65	34	29	1	0	28	16	11	1	0	8	7	1	1	0	28	11	17	0	0
OUT. WHITE CWEALTH	88	42	40	3	3	29	16	10	1	2	18	13	13	4	0	41	13	26	2	0
OUT. DEVLPED WORLD	54	27	22	2	3	13	8	3	0	2	12	8	8	3	1	29	11	16	2	0
CANADA	27	5	20	1	0	15	3	12	0	0	1	1	1	0	0	10	1	8	1	0
LATIN AMERICA	42	17	20	2	3	13	8	3	0	2	10	6	3	1	0	19	3	14	2	0
C. AMER.+CARIB.	24	10	12	2	0	7	5	2	0	0	4	3	0	1	0	13	2	9	2	0
CUBA	4	2	2	0	0	1	0	2	0	0	0	0	0	0	0	0	0	0	0	0
MEXICO	6	3	3	0	0	0	0	0	0	0	3	3	0	0	0	3	0	3	0	0
OTHER	14	5	7	2	0	3	3	0	0	0	1	0	0	1	0	10	2	6	2	0
S. AMERICA	18	7	8	0	3	6	3	1	0	2	6	3	3	0	0	6	1	5	0	0
ARGENTINA	2	1	1	0	0	1	1	0	0	0	1	0	1	0	0	0	0	0	0	0
BRAZIL	1	1	0	0	0	0	0	0	0	1	0	0	0	0	0	0	0	1	0	0
PERU	3	3	0	0	0	2	2	0	0	0	0	0	0	0	0	0	0	0	0	0
COLOMBIA	5	0	5	0	0	1	0	1	0	0	2	0	2	0	0	2	0	2	0	0
VENEZUELA	7	3	2	2	0	1	0	0	0	1	3	2	2	0	0	3	1	2	0	0
OTHER	0	0	0	0	0	0	0	0	0	0	0	0	0	0	0	0	0	0	0	0
EUROPE	42	19	22	1	0	22	12	9	1	0	6	5	5	0	0	14	2	12	0	0
EFTA	11	7	4	0	0	6	4	2	0	0	3	3	0	0	0	2	1	1	0	0
U.K.	7	4	3	0	0	4	4	0	0	0	1	0	0	0	0	1	0	1	0	0
SCANDINAVIA	4	3	1	0	0	0	0	0	0	0	3	3	0	0	0	1	0	1	0	0
SWITZERLAND	0	0	0	0	0	0	0	0	0	0	0	0	0	0	0	0	0	0	0	0
OTHER EFTA	0	0	0	0	0	0	0	0	0	0	0	0	0	0	0	0	0	0	0	0
EUROP. COMMUNITY	27	11	15	1	0	16	8	7	1	0	3	2	3	0	0	8	1	7	0	0
FRANCE	4	4	0	0	0	3	3	0	0	0	0	0	0	0	0	1	0	1	0	0
GERMANY	10	5	5	0	0	8	4	4	0	0	2	1	1	0	0	0	0	0	0	0
ITALY	6	1	5	0	0	2	0	2	0	0	0	0	0	0	0	1	0	1	0	0
BELGIUM + LUX	6	5	1	0	0	3	1	1	1	0	0	0	0	0	0	5	1	5	0	0
NETHERLANDS	2	0	2	0	0	0	0	0	0	0	0	0	0	0	0	2	0	2	0	0
SPAIN	2	0	2	0	0	0	0	0	0	0	0	0	0	0	0	2	0	1	0	0
GREECE + TURKEY	0	0	0	0	0	0	0	0	0	0	0	0	0	0	0	0	0	0	0	0
OTHER EUROPE	2	0	1	2	0	0	0	0	1	0	0	0	0	0	0	2	1	1	0	0
EUROPE EX. U.K.	35	15	19	1	0	16	8	7	1	0	5	3	1	0	0	13	2	11	0	0
SOUTHERN DOMINIONS	10	4	5	0	0	4	2	0	0	0	0	0	0	0	0	3	0	3	0	0
S. AFRICA +RHOD.	3	1	1	0	0	1	1	0	0	0	0	0	0	0	0	1	0	1	0	0
AUSTRALIA + N.Z.	7	3	4	0	0	3	1	0	0	0	2	2	2	0	0	2	0	2	0	0
ASIA + OTHER AFRICA	13	11	2	0	0	0	0	0	0	0	2	2	0	0	0	11	9	2	0	0
JAPAN	1	1	0	0	0	0	0	0	0	0	0	0	0	0	0	1	1	0	0	0
OTHER ASIA+AFR.	12	10	2	0	0	0	0	0	0	0	2	2	0	0	0	10	8	2	0	0
BLACK AFRICA	1	1	0	0	0	0	0	0	0	0	0	0	0	0	0	1	1	0	0	0
ARAB WORLD	0	0	0	0	0	0	0	0	0	0	0	0	0	0	0	0	0	0	0	0
INDIA	1	0	1	0	0	0	0	0	0	0	0	0	0	0	0	1	0	0	0	0
PHILIPPINES	3	3	0	0	0	0	0	0	0	0	0	0	0	0	0	3	3	0	0	0
OTHER E. ASIA	1	1	0	0	0	0	0	0	0	0	0	0	0	1	0	0	0	0	0	0
OTHER ASIA	6	5	1	0	0	0	0	0	0	0	1	1	1	1	0	5	4	1	0	0

CHAPTER 4— VARIETIES OF ENTRY
SECTION 4— THE FLOW OF MANUFACTURING BY INDUSTRY OF SUBSIDIARY
TABLE 3— SUBSIDIARIES MANUFACTURING
CANNED FOODS (SIC 203)
CLASSIFIED BY COUNTRY, PERIOD MANUFACTURE BEGAN, AND METHOD OF ENTRY

PERIOD AND METHOD OF ENTRY
(NEW=NEWLY FORMED, ACQ=ACQUIRED, DES=DESCENDANT, UNK=UNKNOWN)

COUNTRY OR REGION	TOTAL PRE 1968					PRE 1946					1946-1957					1958-1967				
	ALL	NEW	ACQ	DES	UNK	ALL	NEW	ACQ	DES	UNK	ALL	NEW	ACQ	DES	UNK	ALL	NEW	ACQ	DES	UNK
OUTSIDE U.S.	91	25	55	6	4	16	7	4	2	3	13	3	8	1	1	61	15	43	3	0
OUT. U.S. + CANADA	76	23	43	5	4	12	5	2	2	3	8	3	4	0	1	55	15	37	3	0
OUT. WEST. HEMIS.	46	13	25	3	4	11	4	2	2	3	5	1	3	0	1	29	8	20	1	0
OUT. WHITE CWEALTH	52	17	29	4	2	6	3	1	1	1	6	3	2	1	0	40	11	26	3	0
OUT. DEVLPED WORLD	34	12	20	2	0	4	3	1	0	0	4	2	2	0	0	26	7	17	2	0
CANADA	15	2	12	1	0	4	2	2	0	0	5	0	4	1	0	6	0	6	0	0
LATIN AMERICA	30	10	18	2	0	1	1	0	0	0	3	2	1	0	0	26	7	17	2	0
C. AMER.+CARIB.	19	8	10	0	0	1	1	0	0	0	2	2	0	0	0	16	5	10	1	0
CUBA	3	3	0	0	0	1	1	0	0	0	2	2	0	0	0	0	0	0	0	0
MEXICO	11	2	9	0	0	0	0	0	0	0	0	0	0	0	0	11	2	9	0	0
OTHER	5	3	1	1	0	0	0	0	0	0	1	1	0	0	0	4	2	1	1	0
S. AMERICA	11	2	8	0	0	0	0	0	0	0	1	0	1	0	0	10	2	7	0	0
ARGENTINA	0	0	0	0	0	0	0	0	0	0	0	0	0	0	0	0	0	0	0	0
BRAZIL	1	1	0	0	0	0	0	0	0	0	0	0	0	0	0	1	1	0	0	0
PERU	5	0	5	0	0	0	0	0	0	0	0	0	0	0	0	5	0	5	0	0
COLOMBIA	1	1	0	0	0	0	0	0	0	0	0	0	0	0	0	1	1	0	0	0
VENEZUELA	2	1	0	1	0	0	0	0	0	0	0	0	0	0	0	2	1	0	1	0
OTHER	2	0	2	0	0	0	0	0	0	0	0	0	0	0	0	2	0	2	0	0
EUROPE	30	5	17	3	4	6	0	1	2	3	4	2	1	1	1	19	4	14	1	0
EFTA	11	0	7	1	2	3	0	1	1	1	2	0	1	0	1	5	0	5	0	0
U.K.	10	0	7	1	1	3	0	2	1	0	1	0	0	0	1	5	0	5	0	0
SCANDINAVIA	0	0	0	0	0	0	0	0	0	0	0	0	0	0	0	0	0	0	0	0
SWITZERLAND	1	0	0	0	1	0	0	0	0	0	1	0	0	0	1	0	0	0	0	0
OTHER EFTA	0	0	0	0	0	0	0	0	0	0	0	0	0	0	0	0	0	0	0	0
EUROP. COMMUNITY	14	4	8	2	0	0	0	0	0	0	2	1	0	1	0	12	3	8	1	0
FRANCE	3	1	2	0	0	0	0	0	0	0	0	0	0	0	0	3	1	2	0	0
GERMANY	2	1	0	1	0	0	0	0	0	0	0	0	0	0	0	2	1	0	1	0
ITALY	4	2	2	0	0	0	0	0	0	0	2	1	1	0	0	2	1	1	0	0
BELGIUM + LUX	1	0	3	1	0	0	0	0	0	0	0	0	0	0	0	1	0	1	0	0
NETHERLANDS	3	0	1	1	0	0	0	0	0	0	0	0	0	0	0	3	0	3	0	0
SPAIN	3	0	1	0	1	1	0	0	1	0	1	0	0	0	1	1	0	1	0	0
GREECE + TURKEY	0	0	1	1	0	0	0	0	0	0	0	0	0	0	0	0	0	0	0	0
OTHER EUROPE	2	0	0	1	1	0	0	0	0	0	1	0	0	0	1	0	0	0	0	1
EUROPE EX. U.K.	20	5	10	2	3	3	0	0	1	3	3	1	1	1	1	14	4	9	1	0
SOUTHERN DOMINIONS	12	6	6	0	0	2	2	0	0	0	0	0	0	0	0	10	4	6	0	0
S. AFRICA +RHOD.	3	3	0	0	0	1	1	0	0	0	0	0	0	0	0	2	2	0	0	0
AUSTRALIA + N.Z.	9	3	6	0	0	1	1	0	0	0	0	0	0	0	0	8	2	6	0	0
ASIA + OTHER AFRICA	4	2	2	0	0	3	2	0	1	0	1	0	1	0	0	0	0	0	0	0
JAPAN	0	0	0	0	0	0	0	0	0	0	0	0	0	0	0	0	0	0	0	0
OTHER ASIA+AFR.	4	2	2	0	0	3	2	0	1	0	1	0	1	0	0	0	0	0	0	0
BLACK AFRICA	0	0	0	0	0	0	0	0	0	0	0	0	0	0	0	0	0	0	0	0
ARAB WORLD	1	1	0	0	0	0	0	0	0	0	1	1	0	0	0	0	0	0	0	0
INDIA	1	0	1	0	0	1	0	1	0	0	0	0	0	0	0	0	0	0	0	0
PHILIPPINES	2	1	1	0	0	2	1	1	0	0	0	0	0	0	0	0	0	0	0	0
OTHER E. ASIA	0	0	0	0	0	0	0	0	0	0	0	0	0	0	0	0	0	0	0	0
OTHER ASIA	0	0	0	0	0	0	0	0	0	0	0	0	0	0	0	0	0	0	0	0

CHAPTER 4— VARIETIES OF ENTRY
SECTION 4— THE FLOW OF MANUFACTURING BY INDUSTRY OF SUBSIDIARY
TABLE 4— SUBSIDIARIES MANUFACTURING
GRAIN MILL PRODUCTS (SIC 204)
CLASSIFIED BY COUNTRY, PERIOD MANUFACTURE BEGAN, AND METHOD OF ENTRY

PERIOD AND METHOD OF ENTRY
(NEW=NEWLY FORMED, ACQ=ACQUIRED, DES=DESCENDANT, UNK=UNKNOWN)

COUNTRY OR REGION	TOTAL PRE 1968 ALL	NEW	ACQ	DES	UNK	PRE 1946 ALL	NEW	ACQ	DES	UNK	1946-1957 ALL	NEW	ACQ	DES	UNK	1958-1967 ALL	NEW	ACQ	DES	UNK
OUTSIDE U.S.	152	48	80	7	17	32	12	13	1	6	25	9	12	2	2	95	27	55	4	9
OUT. U.S. + CANADA	129	39	68	4	16	21	7	8	1	5	16	7	5	2	2	92	25	54	2	9
OUT. WEST. HEMIS.	66	12	39	4	11	14	3	6	1	4	7	2	2	1	2	45	7	31	2	5
OUT. WHITE CMEALTH	107	34	54	5	14	15	5	7	1	2	14	6	5	1	2	78	23	42	4	9
OUT. DEVLPED WORLD	70	29	32	2	7	8	5	2	0	1	9	5	4	0	0	53	19	26	2	6
CANADA	23	9	12	1	1	11	5	5	0	1	9	2	6	1	0	3	2	1	0	0
LATIN AMERICA	63	27	29	2	5	7	4	2	0	1	9	5	4	0	0	47	18	23	2	4
C. AMER.+CARIB.	30	10	16	2	2	2	0	2	0	0	3	2	0	1	0	25	7	15	2	1
CUBA	1	0	1	0	0	0	0	0	0	0	0	0	0	0	0	1	0	1	0	0
MEXICO	14	4	7	2	1	2	1	1	0	0	3	2	0	1	0	9	1	6	1	1
OTHER	15	6	8	0	1	0	0	0	0	0	0	0	0	0	0	15	6	8	0	1
S. AMERICA	33	17	13	0	3	5	3	2	0	0	6	3	3	0	0	22	11	8	0	3
ARGENTINA	4	3	1	0	0	2	2	0	0	0	1	0	1	0	0	2	1	0	0	1
BRAZIL	5	2	3	0	0	1	1	0	0	0	1	1	0	0	0	2	1	1	0	0
PERU	3	1	1	0	1	0	0	0	0	0	1	0	1	0	0	2	1	0	0	1
COLOMBIA	7	5	2	0	0	1	0	1	0	0	2	1	1	0	0	4	2	1	0	0
VENEZUELA	6	3	3	0	0	0	0	0	0	0	1	0	1	0	0	5	3	2	0	0
OTHER	8	3	3	0	2	1	0	1	0	0	0	0	0	0	0	7	3	3	0	1
EUROPE	48	7	28	4	9	12	1	6	2	3	6	2	2	0	2	30	5	20	2	3
EFTA	18	3	10	1	4	4	1	2	1	0	2	1	1	0	0	10	2	7	0	1
U.K.	11	2	7	1	1	4	1	2	1	0	1	0	1	0	0	6	1	5	0	1
SCANDINAVIA	4	0	3	0	1	0	0	0	0	0	0	0	0	0	0	2	0	2	0	0
SWITZERLAND	1	1	0	0	0	0	0	0	0	0	0	0	0	0	0	0	0	0	0	0
OTHER EFTA	2	0	0	0	2	0	0	0	0	0	1	1	0	0	0	2	1	0	0	1
EUROP. COMMUNITY	25	2	16	3	4	5	0	3	1	1	2	0	0	2	0	17	2	12	0	3
FRANCE	4	0	3	1	0	1	0	0	1	0	0	0	0	0	0	3	0	3	0	0
GERMANY	8	1	4	0	3	1	0	1	0	0	1	0	0	1	0	5	1	3	0	1
ITALY	7	1	4	1	1	1	0	1	0	0	0	0	0	0	0	5	1	3	1	0
BELGIUM + LUX	2	0	2	0	0	1	0	1	0	0	0	0	0	0	0	2	0	2	0	0
NETHERLANDS	4	0	3	1	0	1	0	1	0	0	1	0	0	1	0	2	0	2	0	0
SPAIN	4	2	2	0	0	0	0	0	0	0	1	1	0	0	0	3	2	1	0	0
GREECE + TURKEY	0	0	0	0	0	0	0	0	0	0	0	0	0	0	0	0	0	0	0	0
OTHER EUROPE	1	0	0	0	1	0	0	0	0	0	0	0	0	0	0	0	0	1	0	0
EUROPE EX. U.K.	37	5	21	3	8	8	0	4	1	3	5	1	0	0	1	24	4	15	2	3
SOUTHERN DOMINIONS	10	3	7	0	0	0	0	0	0	0	1	1	0	0	0	8	1	7	0	0
S. AFRICA +RHOD.	2	2	0	0	0	0	0	0	0	0	1	1	0	0	0	8	1	7	0	0
AUSTRALIA + N.Z.	8	1	7	0	0	0	0	0	0	0	0	0	0	0	0	7	1	4	0	2
ASIA + OTHER AFRICA	8	2	4	0	2	1	1	0	0	0	1	0	1	0	0	1	1	0	0	0
JAPAN	7	0	3	0	0	1	0	1	0	0	0	0	0	0	0	6	0	3	0	0
OTHER ASIA+AFR.	1	2	1	0	2	1	1	0	0	0	1	0	1	0	0	1	1	0	0	1
BLACK AFRICA	1	0	1	0	0	0	0	0	0	0	0	0	0	0	0	1	0	0	0	0
ARAB WORLD	1	1	0	0	0	0	0	0	0	0	0	0	0	0	0	0	0	0	0	0
INDIA	3	0	2	0	0	0	0	0	0	0	1	0	1	0	0	3	1	2	0	1
PHILIPPINES	1	1	0	0	0	0	0	0	0	0	0	0	0	0	0	1	0	0	0	0
OTHER E. ASIA	1	0	0	0	1	0	0	0	0	0	0	0	0	0	0	0	0	0	0	0
OTHER ASIA	0	0	0	0	0	0	0	0	0	0	0	0	0	0	0	0	0	0	0	0

CHAPTER 4— VARIETIES OF ENTRY
SECTION 4— THE FLOW OF MANUFACTURING BY INDUSTRY OF SUBSIDIARY
TABLE 5— SUBSIDIARIES MANUFACTURING
BAKERY PRODUCTS (SIC 205)
CLASSIFIED BY COUNTRY, PERIOD MANUFACTURE BEGAN, AND METHOD OF ENTRY

PERIOD AND METHOD OF ENTRY
(NEW=NEWLY FORMED, ACQ=ACQUIRED, DES=DESCENDANT, UNK=UNKNOWN)

COUNTRY OR REGION	TOTAL PRE 1968					PRE 1946					1946-1957					1958-1967				
	ALL	NEW	ACQ	DES	UNK	ALL	NEW	ACQ	DES	UNK	ALL	NEW	ACQ	DES	UNK	ALL	NEW	ACQ	DES	UNK
OUTSIDE U.S.	54	9	42	1	2	12	3	7	0	2	10	3	6	1	0	32	3	29	0	0
OUT. U.S. + CANADA	44	6	36	0	2	7	2	3	0	2	6	2	4	0	0	31	2	29	0	0
OUT. WEST. HEMIS.	32	3	28	0	1	6	1	3	0	2	2	0	2	0	0	24	2	24	0	0
OUT. WHITE CWEALTH	36	5	30	0	1	2	1	0	0	1	5	2	3	0	0	29	2	27	0	0
OUT. DEVLPED WORLD	12	3	8	0	1	2	0	0	0	1	4	3	3	0	0	7	2	5	0	0
CANADA	10	3	6	1	0	5	1	4	0	0	4	1	1	2	0	1	1	1	0	0
LATIN AMERICA	12	3	8	0	1	5	1	4	0	1	0	0	0	0	0	7	2	5	0	0
C. AMER.+CARIB.	7	1	5	0	1	1	0	0	0	1	1	0	1	0	0	5	1	4	0	0
CUBA	1	0	1	0	0	1	0	0	0	1	0	0	0	0	0	0	0	0	0	0
MEXICO	4	1	3	0	0	1	0	0	0	0	0	0	0	0	0	3	1	2	0	0
OTHER	2	0	2	0	0	0	0	0	0	0	0	0	0	0	0	2	0	2	0	0
S. AMERICA	5	2	3	0	0	0	0	0	0	0	0	0	0	0	0	2	0	2	0	0
ARGENTINA	0	0	0	0	0	0	0	0	0	0	0	0	0	0	0	0	0	0	0	0
BRAZIL	0	0	0	0	0	0	0	0	0	0	0	0	0	0	0	0	0	0	0	0
PERU	1	0	1	0	0	0	0	0	0	0	0	0	0	0	0	1	0	1	0	0
COLOMBIA	2	2	0	0	0	0	0	0	0	0	1	1	0	0	0	1	1	0	0	0
VENEZUELA	2	0	2	0	0	0	0	0	0	0	1	0	1	0	0	1	0	1	0	0
OTHER	0	0	0	0	0	0	0	0	0	0	0	0	0	0	0	0	0	0	0	0
EUROPE	29	3	26	0	0	4	2	2	0	0	2	1	1	0	0	23	0	23	0	0
EFTA	9	2	7	0	0	3	1	2	0	0	1	1	0	0	0	5	0	5	0	0
U.K.	4	1	3	0	0	3	1	2	0	0	0	0	0	0	0	1	0	1	0	0
SCANDINAVIA	4	1	3	0	0	0	0	0	0	0	1	1	0	0	0	3	0	3	0	0
SWITZERLAND	1	0	1	0	0	0	0	0	0	0	0	0	0	0	0	1	0	1	0	0
OTHER EFTA	0	0	0	0	0	0	0	0	0	0	0	0	0	0	0	0	0	0	0	0
EUROP. COMMUNITY	16	1	15	0	0	1	1	0	0	0	0	0	0	0	0	15	0	15	0	0
FRANCE	7	0	7	0	0	0	0	0	0	0	0	0	0	0	0	7	0	7	0	0
GERMANY	2	0	2	0	0	0	0	0	0	0	0	0	0	0	0	2	0	2	0	0
ITALY	4	0	4	0	0	0	0	0	0	0	0	0	0	0	0	4	0	4	0	0
BELGIUM + LUX	3	1	2	0	0	1	1	0	0	0	0	0	0	0	0	2	0	2	0	0
NETHERLANDS	3	0	3	0	0	0	0	0	0	0	0	0	0	0	0	3	0	3	0	0
SPAIN	3	0	3	0	0	0	0	0	0	0	0	0	0	0	0	3	0	3	0	0
GREECE + TURKEY	0	0	0	0	0	0	0	0	0	0	0	0	0	0	0	0	0	0	0	0
OTHER EUROPE	1	0	1	0	0	0	0	0	0	0	1	0	1	0	0	0	0	0	0	0
EUROPE EX. U.K.	25	2	23	0	0	1	1	0	0	0	2	1	1	0	0	22	0	22	0	0
SOUTHERN DOMINIONS	3	0	2	1	0	2	0	1	1	0	0	0	0	0	0	1	0	1	0	0
S. AFRICA +RHOD.	1	0	1	0	0	1	0	1	0	0	0	0	0	0	0	0	0	0	0	0
AUSTRALIA + N.Z.	2	0	1	1	0	1	0	0	1	0	0	0	0	0	0	1	0	1	0	0
ASIA + OTHER AFRICA	0	0	0	0	0	0	0	0	0	0	0	0	0	0	0	0	0	0	0	0
JAPAN	0	0	0	0	0	0	0	0	0	0	0	0	0	0	0	0	0	0	0	0
OTHER ASIA+AFR.	0	0	0	0	0	0	0	0	0	0	0	0	0	0	0	0	0	0	0	0
BLACK AFRICA	0	0	0	0	0	0	0	0	0	0	0	0	0	0	0	0	0	0	0	0
ARAB WORLD	0	0	0	0	0	0	0	0	0	0	0	0	0	0	0	0	0	0	0	0
INDIA	0	0	0	0	0	0	0	0	0	0	0	0	0	0	0	0	0	0	0	0
PHILIPPINES	0	0	0	0	0	0	0	0	0	0	0	0	0	0	0	0	0	0	0	0
OTHER E. ASIA	0	0	0	0	0	0	0	0	0	0	0	0	0	0	0	0	0	0	0	0
OTHER ASIA	0	0	0	0	0	0	0	0	0	0	0	0	0	0	0	0	0	0	0	0

CHAPTER 4— VARIETIES OF ENTRY
SECTION 4— THE FLOW OF MANUFACTURING BY INDUSTRY OF SUBSIDIARY

TABLE 6— SUBSIDIARIES MANUFACTURING
CONFECTIONERY AND RELATED PRODUCTS (SIC 207)
CLASSIFIED BY COUNTRY, PERIOD MANUFACTURE BEGAN, AND METHOD OF ENTRY

PERIOD AND METHOD OF ENTRY
(NEW=NEWLY FORMED, ACQ=ACQUIRED, DES=DESCENDANT, UNK=UNKNOWN)

COUNTRY OR REGION	TOTAL PRE 1968 ALL	NEW	ACQ	DES	UNK	PRE 1946 ALL	NEW	ACQ	DES	UNK	1946-1957 ALL	NEW	ACQ	DES	UNK	1958-1967 ALL	NEW	ACQ	DES	UNK
OUTSIDE U.S.	97	30	59	5	3	12	7	3	2	0	11	6	4	0	1	74	17	52	3	2
OUT. U.S. + CANADA	82	26	49	4	3	5	4	0	1	0	10	6	3	0	1	67	16	46	3	2
OUT. WEST. HEMIS.	58	19	34	3	2	5	4	0	1	0	3	3	0	0	0	50	12	34	2	2
OUT. WHITE CMEALTH	62	18	39	3	2	0	0	0	0	0	7	3	3	0	1	55	15	36	3	1
OUT. DEVLPED WORLD	30	11	17	1	1	0	0	0	0	0	7	3	3	0	1	23	8	14	1	0
CANADA	15	4	10	1	0	7	3	3	1	0	1	0	1	0	0	7	1	6	0	0
LATIN AMERICA	24	7	15	1	1	0	0	0	0	0	7	3	3	0	1	17	4	12	1	0
C. AMER.+CARIB.	13	4	7	1	1	0	0	0	0	0	3	1	1	0	1	10	3	6	1	0
CUBA	0	0	0	0	0	0	0	0	0	0	0	0	0	0	0	0	0	0	0	0
MEXICO	9	2	5	1	1	0	0	0	0	0	3	1	1	0	1	6	1	4	1	0
OTHER	4	2	2	0	0	0	0	0	0	0	0	0	0	0	0	4	2	2	0	0
S. AMERICA	11	3	8	0	0	0	0	0	0	0	4	2	2	0	0	7	1	6	0	0
ARGENTINA	0	0	0	0	0	0	0	0	0	0	0	0	0	0	0	0	0	0	0	0
BRAZIL	2	0	2	0	0	0	0	0	0	0	0	0	0	0	0	2	0	2	0	0
PERU	2	1	1	0	0	0	0	0	0	0	1	1	0	0	0	1	0	1	0	0
COLOMBIA	3	1	2	0	0	0	0	0	0	0	1	1	0	0	0	2	0	2	0	0
VENEZUELA	2	0	2	0	0	0	0	0	0	0	1	0	1	0	0	1	0	1	0	0
OTHER	2	1	1	0	0	0	0	0	0	0	1	0	1	0	0	1	1	0	0	0
EUROPE	38	8	26	3	1	2	1	0	1	0	1	1	0	0	0	35	6	26	2	1
EFTA	8	4	3	1	0	2	1	0	1	0	1	1	0	0	0	5	2	3	0	0
U.K.	6	3	2	1	0	2	1	0	1	0	1	1	0	0	0	3	1	2	0	0
SCANDINAVIA	0	0	0	0	0	0	0	0	0	0	0	0	0	0	0	0	0	0	0	0
SWITZERLAND	0	0	0	0	0	0	0	0	0	0	0	0	0	0	0	0	0	0	0	0
OTHER EFTA	2	1	1	0	0	0	0	0	0	0	0	0	0	0	0	2	1	1	0	0
EUROP. COMMUNITY	25	2	20	2	1	0	0	0	0	0	0	0	0	0	0	25	2	20	2	1
FRANCE	5	1	3	1	0	0	0	0	0	0	0	0	0	0	0	5	1	3	1	0
GERMANY	6	0	5	1	0	0	0	0	0	0	0	0	0	0	0	6	0	5	1	0
ITALY	4	1	3	0	0	0	0	0	0	0	0	0	0	0	0	4	1	3	0	0
BELGIUM + LUX	6	0	5	0	1	0	0	0	0	0	0	0	0	0	0	6	0	5	0	1
NETHERLANDS	4	0	4	0	0	0	0	0	0	0	0	0	0	0	0	4	0	4	0	0
SPAIN	1	1	0	0	0	0	0	0	0	0	0	0	0	0	0	1	1	0	0	0
GREECE + TURKEY	1	1	0	0	0	0	0	0	0	0	0	0	0	0	0	1	1	0	0	0
OTHER EUROPE	3	0	3	0	0	0	0	0	0	0	0	0	0	0	0	3	0	3	0	0
EUROPE EX. U.K.	32	5	24	2	1	0	0	0	0	0	0	0	0	0	0	32	5	24	2	1
SOUTHERN DOMINIONS	11	5	5	0	1	3	3	0	0	0	2	2	0	0	0	6	0	5	0	1
S. AFRICA +RHOD.	3	1	2	0	0	0	0	0	0	0	1	1	0	0	0	2	0	2	0	0
AUSTRALIA + N.Z.	8	4	3	0	1	3	3	0	0	0	1	1	0	0	0	4	0	3	0	1
ASIA + OTHER AFRICA	9	6	3	0	0	0	0	0	0	0	0	0	0	0	0	9	6	3	0	0
JAPAN	3	2	1	0	0	0	0	0	0	0	0	0	0	0	0	3	2	1	0	0
OTHER ASIA+AFR.	6	4	2	0	0	0	0	0	0	0	0	0	0	0	0	6	4	2	0	0
BLACK AFRICA	0	0	0	0	0	0	0	0	0	0	0	0	0	0	0	0	0	0	0	0
ARAB WORLD	2	1	1	0	0	0	0	0	0	0	0	0	0	0	0	2	1	1	0	0
INDIA	0	0	0	0	0	0	0	0	0	0	0	0	0	0	0	0	0	0	0	0
PHILIPPINES	1	1	0	0	0	0	0	0	0	0	0	0	0	0	0	1	1	0	0	0
OTHER E. ASIA	0	0	0	0	0	0	0	0	0	0	0	0	0	0	0	0	0	0	0	0
OTHER ASIA	3	2	1	0	0	0	0	0	0	0	0	0	0	0	0	3	2	1	0	1

CHAPTER 4- VARIETIES OF ENTRY
SECTION 4- THE FLOW OF MANUFACTURING BY INDUSTRY OF SUBSIDIARY
TABLE 7- SUBSIDIARIES MANUFACTURING
BEVERAGES (SIC 208)
CLASSIFIED BY COUNTRY, PERIOD MANUFACTURE BEGAN, AND METHOD OF ENTRY

PERIOD AND METHOD OF ENTRY
(NEW=NEWLY FORMED, ACQ=ACQUIRED, DES=DESCENDANT, UNK=UNKNOWN)

COUNTRY OR REGION	TOTAL PRE 1968					PRE 1946					1946-1957					1958-1967				
	ALL	NEW	ACQ	DES	UNK	ALL	NEW	ACQ	DES	UNK	ALL	NEW	ACQ	DES	UNK	ALL	NEW	ACQ	DES	UNK
OUTSIDE U.S.	89	37	43	2	5	30	14	13	0	3	18	13	5	0	0	39	10	25	2	2
OUT. U.S. + CANADA	77	34	35	1	5	25	12	10	0	3	16	12	4	0	0	34	10	21	1	2
OUT. WEST. HEMIS.	50	20	25	0	3	17	6	9	0	2	11	8	3	0	0	20	6	13	0	1
OUT. WHITE CMWEALTH	53	28	19	1	3	11	9	1	0	1	13	11	2	0	0	27	8	16	1	2
OUT. DEVLPED WORLD	35	17	14	1	3	9	7	1	0	1	8	6	2	0	0	18	4	11	1	2
CANADA	12	3	8	1	0	5	2	3	0	0	2	1	1	0	0	5	0	4	1	1
LATIN AMERICA	27	14	10	1	2	8	6	1	0	1	5	4	1	0	0	14	4	8	1	1
C. AMER.+CARIB.	10	5	3	0	2	3	2	1	0	0	3	1	2	0	0	4	2	0	0	2
CUBA	2	1	0	0	1	1	1	0	0	0	0	0	0	0	0	0	0	0	0	0
MEXICO	6	3	2	1	0	1	0	1	0	0	1	0	1	0	0	4	1	2	1	0
OTHER	2	1	1	0	0	1	1	0	0	0	2	1	1	0	0	0	0	0	0	0
S. AMERICA	17	9	7	1	0	5	4	0	0	1	2	2	0	0	0	10	3	6	1	0
ARGENTINA	5	3	1	0	1	2	1	1	0	0	1	1	0	0	0	3	1	1	0	1
BRAZIL	4	1	2	0	1	1	1	0	0	0	1	0	1	0	0	1	1	0	0	1
PERU	3	1	2	0	0	1	1	0	0	0	0	0	0	0	0	2	0	2	0	0
COLOMBIA	3	1	2	0	0	1	1	0	0	0	0	0	0	0	0	2	0	1	0	0
VENEZUELA	0	0	0	0	0	0	0	0	0	0	0	0	0	0	0	0	0	0	0	0
OTHER	2	1	1	0	0	0	0	0	0	0	0	0	0	0	0	2	1	1	0	0
EUROPE	29	9	16	0	2	14	3	9	0	2	5	3	2	0	0	8	3	5	0	0
EFTA	14	1	11	0	2	12	1	9	0	2	2	0	2	0	0	0	0	0	0	0
U.K.	14	1	11	0	2	12	1	9	0	2	2	0	2	0	0	0	0	0	0	0
SCANDINAVIA	0	0	0	0	0	0	0	0	0	0	0	0	0	0	0	0	0	0	0	0
SWITZERLAND	0	0	0	0	0	0	0	0	0	0	0	0	0	0	0	0	0	0	0	0
OTHER EFTA	0	0	0	0	0	0	0	0	0	0	0	0	0	0	0	0	0	0	0	0
EUROP. COMMUNITY	12	5	5	1	1	6	2	3	0	1	3	3	0	0	0	6	1	1	0	0
FRANCE	3	2	1	0	0	2	1	1	0	0	1	1	0	0	0	1	0	0	0	0
GERMANY	5	2	2	1	0	2	0	2	0	0	0	0	0	0	0	1	0	1	0	0
ITALY	2	0	2	0	0	1	0	1	0	0	0	0	0	0	0	2	1	1	0	0
BELGIUM + LUX	1	1	0	0	0	0	0	0	0	0	0	0	0	0	0	1	0	0	0	0
NETHERLANDS	1	0	1	0	0	0	0	0	0	0	0	0	0	0	0	1	1	0	0	0
SPAIN	2	2	0	0	0	0	0	0	0	0	0	0	0	0	0	1	1	0	0	0
GREECE + TURKEY	1	1	0	0	0	0	0	0	0	0	0	0	0	0	0	1	0	0	0	0
OTHER EUROPE	0	0	0	0	0	0	0	0	0	0	0	0	0	0	0	0	0	0	0	0
EUROPE EX. U.K.	15	8	5	0	2	3	3	0	0	0	3	3	0	0	0	8	3	5	0	0
SOUTHERN DOMINIONS	10	5	5	0	0	2	2	0	0	0	1	1	0	0	0	7	2	5	0	0
S. AFRICA +RHOD.	6	4	2	0	0	2	2	0	0	0	0	0	0	0	0	4	2	2	0	0
AUSTRALIA + N.Z.	4	3	3	1	0	0	0	0	0	0	1	1	0	0	0	3	0	3	0	0
ASIA + OTHER AFRICA	11	6	4	0	1	4	2	2	0	0	5	4	1	0	0	5	3	3	1	1
JAPAN	3	3	0	0	0	0	0	0	0	0	2	2	0	0	0	1	0	1	0	0
OTHER ASIA+AFR.	8	3	4	0	1	2	2	0	0	0	3	2	1	0	0	4	3	1	1	1
BLACK AFRICA	2	1	1	0	0	1	1	0	0	0	1	1	0	0	0	1	0	0	0	0
ARAB WORLD	0	0	0	0	0	0	0	0	0	0	1	0	1	0	0	0	0	0	1	1
INDIA	1	1	0	0	0	0	0	0	0	0	0	0	0	0	0	0	0	0	0	0
PHILIPPINES	4	1	2	0	1	0	0	0	0	0	0	0	0	0	0	2	0	2	0	0
OTHER E. ASIA	0	1	0	0	0	0	0	0	0	0	0	0	0	0	0	0	1	0	0	1
OTHER ASIA	1	0	1	0	0	0	0	0	0	0	1	0	0	0	0	1	1	0	0	0

CHAPTER 4- VARIETIES OF ENTRY
SECTION 4- THE FLOW OF MANUFACTURING BY INDUSTRY OF SUBSIDIARY
TABLE 8- SUBSIDIARIES MANUFACTURING
OTHER FOOD PRODUCTS (SIC 206 AND 209)
CLASSIFIED BY COUNTRY, PERIOD MANUFACTURE BEGAN, AND METHOD OF ENTRY

PERIOD AND METHOD OF ENTRY
(NEW=NEWLY FORMED, ACQ=ACQUIRED, DES=DESCENDANT, UNK=UNKNOWN)

COUNTRY OR REGION	TOTAL PRE 1968					PRE 1946					1946-1957					1958-1967				
	ALL	NEW	ACQ	DES	UNK	ALL	NEW	ACQ	DES	UNK	ALL	NEW	ACQ	DES	UNK	ALL	NEW	ACQ	DES	UNK
OUTSIDE U.S.	125	31	71	7	16	33	7	16	1	9	21	6	9	1	5	71	18	46	5	2
OUT. U.S. + CANADA	106	27	58	7	14	24	4	11	1	8	20	6	8	1	5	62	17	39	5	1
OUT. WEST. HEMIS.	78	20	44	5	9	15	2	8	1	4	16	5	6	1	4	47	13	30	3	1
OUT. WHITE CWEALTH	78	22	40	5	11	16	3	7	0	6	16	6	6	0	4	46	13	27	5	1
OUT. DEVLPED WORLD	33	9	17	2	5	12	3	5	0	4	5	1	3	0	1	16	5	9	2	0
CANADA	19	4	13	0	2	9	3	5	0	1	1	0	1	0	0	9	1	7	0	1
LATIN AMERICA	28	7	14	2	5	9	3	3	0	3	4	1	2	0	1	15	4	9	2	0
C. AMER.+CARIB.	16	3	9	2	2	4	0	1	0	3	2	1	1	0	0	10	2	7	2	0
CUBA	3	1	1	0	1	2	0	1	0	1	1	1	0	0	0	0	0	0	0	0
MEXICO	9	1	5	2	1	1	0	0	0	1	1	0	1	0	0	7	1	4	2	0
OTHER	4	1	3	0	1	1	0	0	0	1	0	0	0	0	0	3	0	3	0	0
S. AMERICA	12	6	5	0	1	5	2	2	0	1	2	1	1	0	0	5	3	2	0	0
ARGENTINA	1	0	1	0	0	0	0	0	0	0	1	0	1	0	0	0	0	0	0	0
BRAZIL	2	1	1	0	0	2	1	1	0	0	0	0	0	0	0	0	0	0	0	0
PERU	4	2	2	0	0	2	1	1	0	0	1	0	1	0	0	1	0	1	0	0
COLOMBIA	2	1	1	0	0	0	0	0	0	0	0	0	0	0	0	2	1	1	0	0
VENEZUELA	0	0	0	0	0	0	0	0	0	0	0	0	0	0	0	0	0	0	0	0
OTHER	3	2	0	0	1	1	0	0	0	1	0	0	0	0	0	2	2	0	0	0
EUROPE	58	12	33	5	8	11	1	5	1	4	13	3	5	2	3	34	8	23	3	0
EFTA	27	4	15	3	5	8	1	6	1	0	5	2	1	1	1	14	1	8	1	4
U.K.	14	2	8	2	2	6	1	4	1	0	3	1	1	1	0	5	0	3	0	2
SCANDINAVIA	11	2	6	1	2	2	0	2	0	0	1	0	1	0	0	8	2	5	1	0
SWITZERLAND	1	0	0	0	1	0	0	0	0	0	1	0	0	0	1	0	0	0	0	0
OTHER EFTA	1	0	1	0	0	0	0	0	0	0	0	0	0	0	0	1	0	1	0	0
EUROP. COMMUNITY	24	7	13	2	2	2	0	2	0	0	7	2	3	1	1	15	4	9	2	1
FRANCE	5	0	3	1	1	0	0	0	0	0	1	0	0	1	0	4	0	3	0	1
GERMANY	5	3	2	0	0	0	0	0	0	0	3	2	1	0	0	2	1	1	0	0
ITALY	6	2	4	0	0	1	0	1	0	0	1	1	0	0	0	4	1	3	0	0
BELGIUM + LUX	0	0	0	0	0	0	0	0	0	0	0	0	0	0	0	0	0	0	0	0
NETHERLANDS	8	2	4	1	1	1	0	0	1	0	2	0	1	0	1	5	2	3	0	0
SPAIN	3	0	3	0	0	0	0	0	0	0	0	0	0	0	0	3	0	3	0	0
GREECE + TURKEY	1	1	0	0	0	0	0	0	0	0	0	0	0	0	0	1	1	0	0	0
OTHER EUROPE	3	0	2	0	1	0	0	0	0	0	2	0	1	0	1	1	0	1	0	0
EUROPE EX. U.K.	44	10	25	3	6	5	0	1	0	4	10	2	4	1	3	29	7	19	1	3
SOUTHERN DOMINIONS	11	3	8	0	0	1	0	1	0	0	0	0	0	0	0	10	3	7	0	0
S. AFRICA +RHOD.	2	0	2	0	0	1	0	1	0	0	0	0	0	0	0	1	0	1	0	0
AUSTRALIA + N.Z.	9	3	6	0	0	0	0	0	0	0	0	0	0	0	0	9	3	6	0	0
ASIA + OTHER AFRICA	9	5	3	0	1	3	1	2	0	0	3	2	0	0	1	3	2	1	0	0
JAPAN	4	3	0	1	0	0	0	0	0	0	2	1	0	1	0	2	2	0	0	0
OTHER ASIA+AFR.	5	2	3	0	0	3	1	2	0	0	1	0	1	0	0	1	1	0	0	0
BLACK AFRICA	0	0	0	0	0	0	0	0	0	0	0	0	0	0	0	0	0	0	0	0
ARAB WORLD	0	0	0	0	0	0	0	0	0	0	0	0	0	0	0	0	0	0	0	0
INDIA	1	1	0	0	0	1	1	0	0	0	0	0	0	0	0	0	0	0	0	0
PHILIPPINES	2	0	2	0	0	1	0	1	0	0	1	0	1	0	0	0	0	0	0	0
OTHER E. ASIA	1	0	1	0	0	1	0	1	0	0	0	0	0	0	0	0	0	0	0	0
OTHER ASIA	1	1	0	0	0	0	0	0	0	0	0	0	0	0	0	1	1	0	0	0

CHAPTER 4- VARIETIES OF ENTRY
SECTION 4- THE FLOW OF MANUFACTURING BY INDUSTRY OF SUBSIDIARY
TABLE 9- SUBSIDIARIES MANUFACTURING
TEXTILES AND APPAREL (SIC 22 AND 23)
CLASSIFIED BY COUNTRY, PERIOD MANUFACTURE BEGAN, AND METHOD OF ENTRY

PERIOD AND METHOD OF ENTRY
(NEW=NEWLY FORMED, ACQ=ACQUIRED, DES=DESCENDANT, UNK=UNKNOWN)

COUNTRY OR REGION	TOTAL PRE 1968					PRE 1946					1946-1957					1958-1967				
	ALL	NEW	ACQ	DES	UNK	ALL	NEW	ACQ	DES	UNK	ALL	NEW	ACQ	DES	UNK	ALL	NEW	ACQ	DES	UNK
OUTSIDE U.S.	144	74	40	5	7	16	11	3	0	2	27	19	6	2	0	83	44	31	3	5
OUT. U.S. + CANADA	117	64	27	4	5	8	7	1	0	1	20	15	4	1	0	72	42	22	3	5
OUT. WEST. HEMIS.	65	32	16	3	4	1	1	0	1	0	2	2	0	0	0	51	29	16	2	4
OUT. WHITE CWEALTH	97	54	20	3	2	6	6	0	1	0	20	15	4	1	0	54	33	15	2	4
OUT. DEVLPED WORLD	55	33	11	2	2	7	6	1	1	0	18	13	4	1	0	23	14	6	1	2
CANADA	27	10	13	1	2	8	8	0	0	2	7	4	2	1	0	11	2	9	0	0
LATIN AMERICA	52	32	11	2	1	7	6	1	1	0	18	13	4	1	0	21	13	6	1	1
C. AMER.+CARIB.	18	8	5	2	1	1	1	0	0	0	6	4	1	1	0	8	3	4	1	0
CUBA	2	0	0	1	0	0	0	0	0	0	1	0	0	1	0	0	0	0	0	0
MEXICO	14	7	4	1	1	1	1	0	0	0	5	4	0	1	0	6	2	3	1	0
OTHER	2	1	1	0	0	0	0	0	0	0	0	0	1	0	0	2	1	0	0	1
S. AMERICA	34	24	6	1	1	6	5	1	1	0	12	9	3	0	0	13	10	2	0	1
ARGENTINA	4	3	0	1	0	2	2	0	0	0	1	1	0	0	0	0	0	0	0	0
BRAZIL	3	0	1	0	0	0	0	0	0	0	3	2	1	0	0	1	0	1	0	0
PERU	6	4	2	0	0	1	1	0	0	0	0	0	0	0	0	5	4	0	0	0
COLOMBIA	14	12	1	0	1	3	3	0	1	0	5	4	1	0	0	6	5	1	0	0
VENEZUELA	3	2	1	1	0	0	0	0	0	0	2	2	0	0	0	1	0	1	0	0
OTHER		1	0	0	0	0	0	0	0	0	1	0	1	0	0	1	1	0	0	1
EUROPE	46	27	14	2	2	0	0	0	0	0	1	1	0	0	0	44	26	14	2	2
EFTA	21	12	7	1	1	0	0	0	0	0	1	1	0	0	0	20	11	7	1	1
U.K.	14	7	5	1	1	0	0	0	0	0	0	0	0	0	0	14	7	5	1	1
SCANDINAVIA	2	1	1	0	0	0	0	0	0	0	0	0	0	0	0	2	1	1	0	0
SWITZERLAND	4	3	1	0	0	0	0	0	0	0	1	1	0	0	0	3	1	1	0	0
OTHER EFTA	1	1	0	1	0	0	0	0	0	0	0	0	0	0	0	0	0	0	1	0
EUROP. COMMUNITY	22	12	7	0	1	0	0	0	0	0	0	0	0	0	0	21	12	7	0	1
FRANCE	9	2	5	1	0	0	0	0	0	0	0	0	0	0	0	8	2	5	1	0
GERMANY	4	2	1	0	0	0	0	0	0	0	0	0	0	0	0	4	2	1	0	0
ITALY	4	3	1	1	0	0	0	0	0	0	0	0	0	0	0	4	3	1	1	0
BELGIUM + LUX	1	1	0	0	0	0	0	0	0	0	0	0	0	0	0	1	1	0	0	0
NETHERLANDS	3	3	0	0	0	0	0	0	0	0	0	0	0	0	0	3	3	0	0	0
SPAIN	0	0	0	0	0	0	0	0	0	0	0	0	0	0	0	0	0	0	0	0
GREECE + TURKEY	0	0	0	0	0	0	0	0	0	0	0	0	0	0	0	0	0	0	0	0
OTHER EUROPE	32	20	9	1	1	0	0	0	0	0	1	1	0	0	0	30	19	9	1	1
EUROPE EX. U.K.																				
SOUTHERN DOMINIONS	6	3	2	0	0	0	0	0	0	0	0	0	0	0	0	4	2	2	0	0
S. AFRICA +RHOD.	3	1	1	0	0	0	0	0	0	0	0	0	0	0	0	2	1	1	0	0
AUSTRALIA + N.Z.	3	2	1	1	1	0	0	0	0	0	0	0	0	0	0	2	1	1	0	1
ASIA + OTHER AFRICA	13	2	1	1	1	1	1	0	0	0	1	1	0	0	0	3	1	1	0	0
JAPAN	3	1	0	0	0	0	0	0	0	0	0	0	0	0	0	1	0	1	0	0
OTHER ASIA+AFR.	1	1	0	1	0	1	1	0	0	0	1	1	0	0	0	2	1	0	0	2
BLACK AFRICA	0	0	0	0	0	0	0	0	0	0	0	0	0	0	0	0	0	0	0	1
ARAB WORLD	1	1	0	0	0	0	0	0	0	0	0	0	0	0	0	1	1	0	0	1
INDIA	0	0	0	1	0	0	0	0	0	0	0	0	0	0	0	0	0	0	0	0
PHILIPPINES	1	1	0	0	0	0	0	0	0	0	0	0	0	0	0	1	1	0	0	0
OTHER E. ASIA	0	0	0	0	0	0	0	0	0	0	0	0	0	0	0	0	0	0	0	1
OTHER ASIA	0	0	0	0	0	0	0	0	0	0	0	0	0	0	0	0	0	0	0	0

CHAPTER 4— VARIETIES OF ENTRY

SECTION 4— THE FLOW OF MANUFACTURING BY INDUSTRY OF SUBSIDIARY

TABLE 10— SUBSIDIARIES MANUFACTURING

PAPER AND PAPERBOARD PRODUCTS, EXCEPT CONTAINERS (SIC 264)

CLASSIFIED BY COUNTRY, PERIOD MANUFACTURE BEGAN, AND METHOD OF ENTRY

PERIOD AND METHOD OF ENTRY

(NEW=NEWLY FORMED, ACQ=ACQUIRED, DES=DESCENDANT, UNK=UNKNOWN)

COUNTRY OR REGION	TOTAL PRE 1968 ALL	NEW	ACQ	DES	UNK	PRE 1946 ALL	NEW	ACQ	DES	UNK	1946-1957 ALL	NEW	ACQ	DES	UNK	1958-1967 ALL	NEW	ACQ	DES	UNK
OUTSIDE U.S.	97	35	55	3	4	17	10	5	0	2	27	9	17	0	1	53	16	33	3	1
OUT. U.S. + CANADA	83	30	47	3	3	10	5	3	0	2	21	9	12	0	0	52	16	32	3	1
OUT. WEST. HEMIS.	62	19	39	2	2	6	2	3	0	1	13	5	8	0	0	43	12	28	2	1
OUT. WHITE CWEALTH	51	26	21	2	1	7	3	2	0	2	13	7	6	0	0	31	16	13	2	1
OUT. DEVLPED WORLD	28	16	10	1	1	4	3	0	0	1	10	6	4	0	0	14	7	6	1	0
CANADA	14	5	8	0	1	7	5	2	0	0	6	0	5	0	1	1	0	1	0	0
LATIN AMERICA	21	11	8	1	1	4	3	1	0	0	8	4	4	0	0	9	4	4	1	1
C. AMER.+CARIB.	9	4	4	1	0	4	3	1	0	0	0	0	0	0	0	5	2	2	1	0
CUBA	1	1	0	0	0	1	1	0	0	0	0	0	0	0	0	0	0	0	0	0
MEXICO	3	1	2	0	0	1	1	0	0	0	1	0	1	0	0	1	0	1	0	0
OTHER	5	2	2	1	0	2	1	1	0	0	0	0	0	0	0	4	2	1	1	0
S. AMERICA	12	7	4	1	0	0	0	0	0	0	5	3	2	0	0	4	2	2	0	0
ARGENTINA	1	1	0	0	0	0	0	0	0	0	1	1	0	0	0	0	0	0	0	0
BRAZIL	2	1	0	1	0	0	0	0	0	0	1	0	0	1	0	1	1	0	0	0
PERU	2	0	2	0	0	0	0	0	0	0	0	0	0	0	0	2	0	2	0	0
COLOMBIA	1	1	0	0	0	0	0	0	0	0	0	0	0	0	0	1	0	1	0	0
VENEZUELA	4	3	1	0	0	0	0	0	0	0	3	3	0	0	0	0	0	0	0	0
OTHER	0	0	0	0	0	0	0	0	0	0	0	0	0	0	0	0	0	0	0	0
EUROPE	29	11	16	1	1	4	1	2	0	1	8	3	5	0	0	17	7	9	1	0
EFTA	8	3	5	0	0	1	1	0	0	0	4	1	3	0	0	3	1	2	0	0
U.K.	7	2	5	0	0	1	1	0	0	0	4	1	3	0	0	2	0	2	0	0
SCANDINAVIA	0	0	0	0	0	0	0	0	0	0	0	0	0	0	0	0	0	0	0	0
SWITZERLAND	0	0	0	0	0	0	0	0	0	0	0	0	0	0	0	0	0	0	0	0
OTHER EFTA	1	1	0	0	0	0	0	0	0	0	0	0	0	0	0	1	1	0	0	0
EUROP. COMMUNITY	17	6	9	1	1	3	0	2	0	1	3	1	2	0	0	11	5	5	1	0
FRANCE	9	1	8	0	0	1	0	1	0	0	2	0	2	0	0	6	1	5	0	0
GERMANY	3	0	3	0	0	0	0	0	0	0	0	0	0	0	0	3	0	3	0	0
ITALY	2	1	1	0	0	0	0	0	0	0	0	0	0	0	0	0	0	0	0	0
BELGIUM + LUX	1	0	0	1	0	0	0	0	0	0	0	0	0	0	0	2	1	0	1	0
NETHERLANDS	2	2	0	0	0	0	0	0	0	0	0	0	0	0	0	2	2	0	0	0
SPAIN	2	1	0	1	0	0	0	0	0	0	0	0	0	0	0	2	0	2	0	0
GREECE + TURKEY	1	1	0	0	0	0	0	0	0	0	0	0	0	0	0	1	0	0	1	0
OTHER EUROPE	1	1	0	0	0	0	0	0	0	0	0	0	0	0	0	0	0	0	0	0
EUROPE EX. U.K.	22	9	11	1	1	3	0	2	0	1	4	2	2	0	0	15	7	7	1	0
SOUTHERN DOMINIONS	24	10	14	0	0	2	1	0	0	1	3	0	3	0	0	19	9	10	1	0
S. AFRICA +RHOD.	14	7	7	0	0	2	0	1	0	1	2	0	2	0	0	13	7	6	0	0
AUSTRALIA + N.Z.	10	7	2	1	0	2	1	0	1	0	2	1	1	0	0	6	5	1	1	0
ASIA + OTHER AFRICA	9	2	7	0	0	2	0	2	0	0	0	0	0	0	0	7	2	5	0	0
JAPAN	2	0	2	0	0	0	0	0	0	0	0	0	0	0	0	2	2	0	0	0
OTHER ASIA+AFR.	7	5	0	1	1	0	0	0	0	0	2	0	2	0	0	5	3	2	0	0
BLACK AFRICA	0	0	0	0	0	0	0	0	0	0	0	0	0	0	0	0	0	0	0	0
ARAB WORLD	1	0	1	0	0	0	0	0	0	0	1	0	1	0	0	0	0	0	0	0
INDIA	1	0	1	0	0	0	0	0	0	0	0	0	0	0	0	1	0	1	0	0
PHILIPPINES	3	2	1	0	0	0	0	0	0	0	1	1	0	0	0	2	1	1	0	0
OTHER E. ASIA	0	0	0	0	0	0	0	0	0	0	0	0	0	0	0	0	0	0	0	0
OTHER ASIA	3	3	0	0	0	0	0	0	0	0	1	1	0	0	0	2	2	0	0	0

CHAPTER 4— VARIETIES OF ENTRY
SECTION 4— THE FLOW OF MANUFACTURING BY INDUSTRY OF SUBSIDIARY
TABLE 11— SUBSIDIARIES MANUFACTURING
PAPERBOARD CONTAINERS AND BOXES (SIC 265)
CLASSIFIED BY COUNTRY, PERIOD MANUFACTURE BEGAN, AND METHOD OF ENTRY

PERIOD AND METHOD OF ENTRY
(NEW=NEWLY FORMED, ACQ=ACQUIRED, DES=DESCENDANT, UNK=UNKNOWN)

COUNTRY OR REGION	TOTAL PRE 1968					PRE 1946					1946-1957					1958-1967				
	ALL	NEW	ACQ	DES	UNK	ALL	NEW	ACQ	DES	UNK	ALL	NEW	ACQ	DES	UNK	ALL	NEW	ACQ	DES	UNK
OUTSIDE U.S.	106	26	76	1	2	9	3	5	0	1	27	5	22	0	0	69	18	49	1	1
OUT. U.S. + CANADA	95	26	66	1	1	6	3	3	0	0	20	5	15	0	0	68	18	48	1	1
OUT. WEST. HEMIS.	59	13	43	1	1	2	0	2	0	0	4	2	2	0	0	52	11	39	1	1
OUT. WHITE CWEALTH	68	21	45	1	0	5	3	2	0	0	18	4	14	0	0	44	14	29	1	0
OUT. DEVLPED WORLD	41	15	26	0	0	4	3	1	0	0	17	3	14	0	0	20	9	11	0	0
CANADA	11	0	10	0	1	3	0	2	0	1	7	0	7	0	0	1	0	1	0	0
LATIN AMERICA	36	13	23	0	0	4	3	1	0	0	16	3	13	0	0	16	7	9	0	0
C. AMER.+CARIB.	15	4	11	0	0	2	1	1	0	0	6	1	5	0	0	7	2	5	0	0
CUBA	1	0	1	0	0	1	0	1	0	0	0	0	0	0	0	0	0	0	0	0
MEXICO	9	3	6	0	0	1	1	0	0	0	5	1	4	0	0	3	1	2	0	0
OTHER	5	1	4	0	0	0	0	0	0	0	1	0	1	0	0	4	1	3	0	0
S. AMERICA	21	9	12	0	0	2	2	0	0	0	10	2	8	0	0	9	5	4	0	0
ARGENTINA	4	0	4	0	0	0	0	0	0	0	2	0	2	0	0	2	0	2	0	0
BRAZIL	2	1	1	0	0	0	0	0	0	0	1	1	0	0	0	1	0	1	0	0
PERU	2	0	2	0	0	0	0	0	0	0	1	0	1	0	0	1	0	1	0	0
COLOMBIA	1	1	0	0	0	0	0	0	0	0	0	0	0	0	0	1	1	0	0	0
VENEZUELA	9	5	4	0	0	2	2	0	0	0	4	2	2	0	0	3	1	2	0	0
OTHER	3	2	1	0	0	0	0	0	0	0	2	1	1	0	0	1	1	0	0	0
EUROPE	28	7	19	1	1	1	1	0	0	0	2	0	2	0	0	25	6	18	1	1
EFTA	4	4	0	0	0	0	0	0	0	0	0	0	0	0	0	4	4	0	0	0
U.K.	2	2	0	0	0	0	0	0	0	0	0	0	0	0	0	2	2	0	0	0
SCANDINAVIA	2	2	0	0	0	0	0	0	0	0	0	0	0	0	0	2	2	0	0	0
SWITZERLAND	0	0	0	0	0	0	0	0	0	0	0	0	0	0	0	0	0	0	0	0
OTHER EFTA	0	0	0	0	0	0	0	0	0	0	0	0	0	0	0	0	0	0	0	0
EUROP. COMMUNITY	18	1	15	1	1	1	1	0	0	0	2	0	2	0	0	15	0	14	1	0
FRANCE	1	0	1	0	0	0	0	0	0	0	0	0	0	0	0	1	0	1	0	0
GERMANY	7	1	5	1	0	0	0	0	0	0	1	1	0	0	0	6	0	5	1	0
ITALY	6	0	5	1	0	1	1	0	0	0	0	0	0	0	0	5	0	5	1	0
BELGIUM + LUX	3	0	3	0	0	0	0	0	0	0	1	0	1	0	0	2	0	2	0	0
NETHERLANDS	1	0	1	0	0	0	0	0	0	0	0	0	0	0	0	1	0	1	0	0
SPAIN	5	2	3	0	0	0	0	0	0	0	2	0	2	0	0	3	2	1	0	0
GREECE + TURKEY	0	0	0	0	0	0	0	0	0	0	0	0	0	0	0	0	0	0	0	0
OTHER EUROPE	1	0	1	0	0	0	0	0	0	0	0	0	0	0	0	1	0	1	0	0
EUROPE EX. U.K.	26	5	19	1	1	1	1	0	0	0	2	0	2	0	0	23	4	18	1	1
SOUTHERN DOMINIONS	24	3	20	0	1	1	0	1	0	0	2	1	1	0	0	21	2	18	0	1
S. AFRICA +RHOD.	19	1	18	0	0	1	0	1	0	0	1	0	1	0	0	17	1	17	0	0
AUSTRALIA + N.Z.	5	2	2	0	1	0	0	0	0	0	1	1	0	0	0	3	1	1	0	1
ASIA + OTHER AFRICA	7	3	4	0	0	0	0	0	0	0	1	0	1	0	0	6	3	3	0	0
JAPAN	2	1	1	0	0	0	0	0	0	0	0	0	0	0	0	2	1	1	0	0
OTHER ASIA+AFR.	5	2	3	0	0	0	0	0	0	0	1	0	1	0	0	4	2	2	0	0
BLACK AFRICA	2	2	0	0	0	0	0	0	0	0	0	0	0	0	0	2	2	0	0	0
ARAB WORLD	0	0	0	0	0	0	0	0	0	0	0	0	0	0	0	0	0	0	0	0
INDIA	0	0	0	0	0	0	0	0	0	0	0	0	0	0	0	0	0	0	0	0
PHILIPPINES	1	0	1	0	0	0	0	0	0	0	0	0	0	0	0	1	0	1	0	0
OTHER E. ASIA	1	0	1	0	0	0	0	0	0	0	0	0	0	0	0	1	0	1	0	0
OTHER ASIA	1	0	1	0	0	0	0	0	0	0	0	0	0	0	0	1	0	1	0	0

CHAPTER 4— VARIETIES OF ENTRY

SECTION 4— THE FLOW OF MANUFACTURING BY INDUSTRY OF SUBSIDIARY

TABLE 12— SUBSIDIARIES MANUFACTURING
OTHER WOOD, FURNITURE, AND PAPER PRODUCTS (SIC 24, 25, 261-263, AND 266)
CLASSIFIED BY COUNTRY, PERIOD MANUFACTURE BEGAN, AND METHOD OF ENTRY

PERIOD AND METHOD OF ENTRY

(NEW=NEWLY FORMED, ACQ=ACQUIRED, DES=DESCENDANT, UNK=UNKNOWN)

COUNTRY OR REGION	TOTAL PRE 1968					PRE 1946					1946-1957					1958-1967				
	ALL	NEW	ACQ	DES	UNK	ALL	NEW	ACQ	DES	UNK	ALL	NEW	ACQ	DES	UNK	ALL	NEW	ACQ	DES	UNK
OUTSIDE U.S.	88	32	47	3	5	16	7	6	2	1	15	6	7	0	2	56	19	34	1	2
OUT. U.S. + CANADA	56	21	31	2	2	11	6	4	1	0	6	4	2	0	0	39	11	25	1	2
OUT. WEST. HEMIS.	37	12	21	2	2	9	5	3	1	0	2	2	0	0	0	26	5	18	1	2
OUT. WHITE CWEALTH	44	17	25	1	1	6	3	3	0	0	5	3	2	0	0	33	11	20	1	1
OUT. DEVLPED WORLD	22	9	13	0	0	2	1	1	0	0	4	2	2	0	0	16	6	10	0	0
CANADA	32	11	16	1	3	5	1	2	1	1	9	2	5	0	2	17	8	9	0	0
LATIN AMERICA	19	9	10	0	0	2	1	1	0	0	4	2	2	0	0	13	6	7	0	0
C. AMER.+CARIB.	8	3	5	0	0	2	1	1	0	0	2	1	1	0	0	4	1	3	0	0
CUBA	0	0	0	0	0	0	0	0	0	0	0	0	0	0	0	0	0	0	0	0
MEXICO	3	1	2	0	0	2	1	1	0	0	1	0	1	0	0	0	0	0	0	0
OTHER	5	2	3	0	0	0	0	0	0	0	1	1	0	0	0	4	1	3	0	0
S. AMERICA	11	6	5	0	0	0	0	0	0	0	2	1	1	0	0	9	5	4	0	0
ARGENTINA	3	1	2	0	0	0	0	0	0	0	0	0	0	0	0	3	1	2	0	0
BRAZIL	1	1	0	0	0	0	0	0	0	0	0	0	0	0	0	1	1	0	0	0
PERU	1	0	1	0	0	0	0	0	0	0	0	0	0	0	0	1	0	1	0	0
COLOMBIA	1	1	0	0	0	0	0	0	0	0	1	1	0	0	0	0	0	0	0	0
VENEZUELA	5	3	2	0	0	0	0	0	0	0	1	0	1	0	0	4	3	1	0	0
OTHER	0	0	0	0	0	0	0	0	0	0	0	0	0	0	0	0	0	0	0	0
EUROPE	27	7	16	2	2	7	3	3	1	0	1	1	0	0	0	19	3	13	1	2
EFTA	8	1	4	2	1	3	1	1	1	0	0	0	0	0	0	5	0	3	1	1
U.K.	7	1	4	1	1	3	1	1	1	0	0	0	0	0	0	4	0	3	0	1
SCANDINAVIA	1	0	0	1	0	0	0	0	0	0	0	0	0	0	0	1	0	0	1	0
SWITZERLAND	0	0	0	0	0	0	0	0	0	0	0	0	0	0	0	0	0	0	0	0
OTHER EFTA	0	0	0	0	0	0	0	0	0	0	0	0	0	0	0	0	0	0	0	0
EUROP. COMMUNITY	12	4	8	0	0	1	1	0	0	0	1	1	0	0	0	10	2	8	0	0
FRANCE	5	2	3	0	0	1	1	0	0	0	1	1	0	0	0	3	1	2	0	0
GERMANY	3	1	2	0	0	0	0	0	0	0	0	0	0	0	0	3	1	2	0	0
ITALY	3	0	3	0	0	0	0	0	0	0	0	0	0	0	0	3	0	3	0	0
BELGIUM + LUX	1	1	0	0	0	0	0	0	0	0	0	0	0	0	0	1	0	1	0	0
NETHERLANDS	0	0	0	0	0	0	0	0	0	0	0	0	0	0	0	0	0	0	0	0
SPAIN	7	2	4	0	1	3	1	2	0	0	0	0	0	0	0	4	1	2	0	1
GREECE + TURKEY	0	0	0	0	0	0	0	0	0	0	0	0	0	0	0	0	0	0	0	0
OTHER EUROPE	0	0	0	0	0	0	0	0	0	0	0	0	0	0	0	0	0	0	0	0
EUROPE EX. U.K.	20	6	12	1	1	4	2	2	0	0	1	1	0	0	0	15	3	10	1	1
SOUTHERN DOMINIONS	5	3	2	0	0	2	1	1	0	0	1	0	1	0	0	2	2	0	0	0
S. AFRICA +RHOD.	1	1	0	0	0	1	1	0	0	0	0	0	0	0	0	0	0	0	0	0
AUSTRALIA + N.Z.	4	2	2	0	0	1	0	1	0	0	1	0	1	0	0	2	2	0	0	0
ASIA + OTHER AFRICA	5	2	3	0	0	0	0	0	0	0	2	2	0	0	0	3	0	3	0	0
JAPAN	2	2	0	0	0	0	0	0	0	0	2	2	0	0	0	0	0	0	0	0
OTHER ASIA+AFR.	3	0	3	0	0	0	0	0	0	0	0	0	0	0	0	3	0	3	0	0
BLACK AFRICA	0	0	0	0	0	0	0	0	0	0	0	0	0	0	0	0	0	0	0	0
ARAB WORLD	0	0	0	0	0	0	0	0	0	0	0	0	0	0	0	0	0	0	0	0
INDIA	0	0	0	0	0	0	0	0	0	0	0	0	0	0	0	0	0	0	0	0
PHILIPPINES	3	0	3	0	0	0	0	0	0	0	0	0	0	0	0	3	0	3	0	0
OTHER E. ASIA	0	0	0	0	0	0	0	0	0	0	0	0	0	0	0	0	0	0	0	0
OTHER ASIA	0	0	0	0	0	0	0	0	0	0	0	0	0	0	0	0	0	0	0	0

CHAPTER 4- VARIETIES OF ENTRY
SECTION 4- THE FLOW OF MANUFACTURING BY INDUSTRY OF SUBSIDIARY
TABLE 13- SUBSIDIARIES MANUFACTURING
PRINTED MATTER (SIC 27)
CLASSIFIED BY COUNTRY, PERIOD MANUFACTURE BEGAN, AND METHOD OF ENTRY

PERIOD AND METHOD OF ENTRY
(NEW=NEWLY FORMED, ACQ=ACQUIRED, DES=DESCENDANT, UNK=UNKNOWN)

COUNTRY OR REGION	TOTAL PRE 1968 ALL	NEW	ACQ	DES	UNK	PRE 1946 ALL	NEW	ACQ	DES	UNK	1946-1957 ALL	NEW	ACQ	DES	UNK	1958-1967 ALL	NEW	ACQ	DES	UNK
OUTSIDE U.S.	36	14	18	1	1	4	2	2	0	0	8	5	2	0	1	22	7	14	1	0
OUT. U.S. + CANADA	31	13	16	0	1	2	1	1	0	0	7	5	1	0	1	21	7	14	0	0
OUT. WEST. HEMIS.	25	10	13	0	1	1	0	1	0	0	5	3	1	0	1	18	7	11	0	0
OUT. WHITE CWEALTH	24	12	11	0	1	1	1	0	0	0	7	5	1	0	1	16	6	10	0	0
OUT. DEVLPED WORLD	6	3	3	0	0	1	1	0	0	0	2	2	0	0	0	3	0	3	0	0
CANADA	5	1	2	1	0	2	1	1	0	0	1	0	1	0	0	1	0	0	1	0
LATIN AMERICA	6	3	3	0	0	1	1	0	0	0	2	2	0	0	0	3	0	3	0	0
C. AMER.+CARIB.	2	1	1	0	0	0	0	0	0	0	1	1	0	0	0	1	0	1	0	0
CUBA	1	1	0	0	0	0	0	0	0	0	1	1	0	0	0	0	0	0	0	0
MEXICO	1	0	1	0	0	0	0	0	0	0	0	0	0	0	0	1	0	1	0	0
OTHER	0	0	0	0	0	0	0	0	0	0	0	0	0	0	0	0	0	0	0	0
S. AMERICA	4	2	2	0	0	1	0	1	0	0	1	1	0	0	0	2	1	1	0	0
ARGENTINA	3	1	2	0	0	0	0	0	0	0	1	1	0	0	0	2	0	2	0	0
BRAZIL	1	1	0	0	0	1	1	0	0	0	0	0	0	0	0	0	0	0	0	0
PERU	0	0	0	0	0	0	0	0	0	0	0	0	0	0	0	0	0	0	0	0
COLOMBIA	0	0	0	0	0	0	0	0	0	0	0	0	0	0	0	0	0	0	0	0
VENEZUELA	0	0	0	0	0	0	0	0	0	0	0	0	0	0	0	0	0	0	0	0
OTHER	0	0	0	0	0	0	0	0	0	0	0	0	0	0	0	0	0	0	0	0
EUROPE	20	9	9	1	1	1	1	0	0	0	5	2	2	0	1	13	6	7	0	0
EFTA	6	3	2	0	1	0	0	0	0	0	2	0	1	0	1	4	3	1	0	0
U.K.	3	3	0	0	0	0	0	0	0	0	2	2	0	0	0	1	1	0	0	0
SCANDINAVIA	2	2	0	0	0	0	0	0	0	0	0	0	0	0	0	2	2	0	0	0
SWITZERLAND	1	0	1	0	0	0	0	0	0	0	0	0	0	0	0	1	0	1	0	0
OTHER EFTA	0	0	0	0	0	0	0	0	0	0	0	0	0	0	0	0	0	0	0	0
EUROP. COMMUNITY	13	5	7	0	1	0	0	0	0	0	3	2	1	0	1	9	3	6	0	0
FRANCE	4	2	2	0	0	0	0	0	0	0	0	0	0	0	0	4	2	2	0	0
GERMANY	4	2	2	0	0	0	0	0	0	0	2	2	0	0	0	2	0	2	0	0
ITALY	4	2	2	0	0	0	0	0	0	0	1	1	0	0	0	3	1	2	0	0
BELGIUM + LUX	0	0	0	0	0	0	0	0	0	0	0	0	0	0	0	0	0	0	0	0
NETHERLANDS	1	0	1	0	0	0	0	0	0	0	1	0	1	0	0	0	0	0	0	0
SPAIN	1	1	0	0	0	0	0	0	0	0	1	1	0	0	0	0	0	0	0	0
GREECE + TURKEY	0	0	0	0	0	0	0	0	0	0	0	0	0	0	0	0	0	0	0	0
OTHER EUROPE	0	0	0	0	0	0	0	0	0	0	0	0	0	0	0	0	0	0	0	0
EUROPE EX. U.K.	17	8	9	1	1	1	1	0	0	0	5	3	1	0	1	12	5	7	0	0
SOUTHERN DOMINIONS	4	0	4	0	0	0	0	0	0	0	0	0	0	0	0	4	0	4	0	0
S. AFRICA +RHOD.	4	0	4	0	0	0	0	0	0	0	0	0	0	0	0	4	0	4	0	0
AUSTRALIA + N.Z.	0	0	0	0	0	0	0	0	0	0	0	0	0	0	0	0	0	0	0	0
ASIA + OTHER AFRICA	1	1	0	0	0	0	0	0	0	0	0	0	0	0	0	1	1	0	0	0
JAPAN	1	1	0	0	0	0	0	0	0	0	0	0	0	0	0	1	1	0	0	0
OTHER ASIA+AFR.	0	0	0	0	0	0	0	0	0	0	0	0	0	0	0	0	0	0	0	0
BLACK AFRICA	0	0	0	0	0	0	0	0	0	0	0	0	0	0	0	0	0	0	0	0
ARAB WORLD	0	0	0	0	0	0	0	0	0	0	0	0	0	0	0	0	0	0	0	0
INDIA	0	0	0	0	0	0	0	0	0	0	0	0	0	0	0	0	0	0	0	0
PHILIPPINES	0	0	0	0	0	0	0	0	0	0	0	0	0	0	0	0	0	0	0	0
OTHER E. ASIA	0	0	0	0	0	0	0	0	0	0	0	0	0	0	0	0	0	0	0	0
OTHER ASIA	0	0	0	0	0	0	0	0	0	0	0	0	0	0	0	0	0	0	0	0

CHAPTER 4 - VARIETIES OF ENTRY
SECTION 4 - THE FLOW OF MANUFACTURING BY INDUSTRY OF SUBSIDIARY
TABLE 14 - SUBSIDIARIES MANUFACTURING
INDUSTRIAL CHEMICALS (SIC 281)
CLASSIFIED BY COUNTRY, PERIOD MANUFACTURE BEGAN, AND METHOD OF ENTRY

(NEW=NEWLY FORMED, ACQ=ACQUIRED, DES=DESCENDANT, UNK=UNKNOWN)

COUNTRY OR REGION	TOTAL PRE 1968					PERIOD AND METHOD OF ENTRY PRE 1946					1946-1957					1958-1967				
	ALL	NEW	ACQ	DES	UNK	ALL	NEW	ACQ	DES	UNK	ALL	NEW	ACQ	DES	UNK	ALL	NEW	ACQ	DES	UNK
OUTSIDE U.S.	367	190	114	20	30	60	28	19	3	10	85	53	20	5	7	209	109	75	12	13
OUT. U.S. + CANADA	306	168	87	17	23	33	18	9	1	5	69	46	13	5	5	193	104	65	11	13
OUT. WEST. HEMIS.	198	111	56	11	16	23	14	6	0	4	32	20	6	2	4	139	77	45	9	8
OUT. WHITE CWEALTH	249	140	74	11	15	24	14	6	1	3	57	40	11	3	3	159	86	57	7	9
OUT. DEVLPED WORLD	121	68	31	8	7	10	4	4	1	1	39	28	7	3	1	65	36	20	4	5
CANADA	61	22	27	3	7	27	10	10	2	5	16	7	7	0	2	16	5	10	1	0
LATIN AMERICA	108	57	31	6	7	10	4	4	1	1	37	26	7	3	1	54	27	20	2	5
C. AMER.+CARIB.	51	27	17	3	0	3	3	0	0	0	18	12	4	2	0	26	13	13	0	0
CUBA	1	1	0	0	0	0	0	0	0	0	1	1	0	0	0	0	0	0	0	0
MEXICO	43	21	16	2	0	3	3	0	0	0	15	9	4	2	0	21	9	12	0	0
OTHER	7	5	1	1	0	0	0	0	0	0	2	2	0	0	0	5	3	1	1	0
S. AMERICA	57	30	14	3	7	7	1	4	1	1	19	14	3	0	1	28	15	7	1	5
ARGENTINA	16	8	3	2	3	4	0	4	0	0	6	6	0	0	1	6	4	1	1	1
BRAZIL	14	7	2	2	3	2	0	2	0	0	7	3	3	1	0	5	4	0	0	2
PERU	4	1	2	0	2	0	0	0	0	0	1	1	0	0	0	2	1	0	0	1
COLOMBIA	12	5	6	0	1	1	1	0	0	0	2	0	2	0	0	8	3	5	0	0
VENEZUELA	8	8	0	0	0	1	0	1	0	0	3	3	0	0	0	4	1	0	0	1
OTHER	3	1	1	0	1	0	0	0	0	0	0	0	0	0	0	3	1	1	0	1
EUROPE	135	66	46	7	15	20	12	4	0	4	24	14	5	2	3	90	40	37	5	8
EFTA	38	15	11	5	7	7	2	3	0	2	11	5	3	2	1	20	8	5	3	4
U.K.	27	8	8	4	7	6	2	2	0	2	9	4	2	2	1	12	3	4	2	4
SCANDINAVIA	8	4	3	1	0	1	0	1	0	0	2	1	1	0	0	5	3	1	2	0
SWITZERLAND	0	0	0	0	0	0	0	0	0	0	0	0	0	0	0	0	0	0	0	0
OTHER EFTA	3	3	0	0	0	0	0	0	0	0	0	0	0	0	0	3	3	0	0	0
EUROP. COMMUNITY	80	45	26	2	6	12	9	2	0	2	11	8	2	0	1	56	28	23	2	3
FRANCE	19	11	6	0	1	5	2	2	0	1	2	2	0	0	0	15	7	6	0	1
GERMANY	17	12	4	0	1	2	2	0	0	0	2	1	1	0	0	10	5	3	0	1
ITALY	21	8	11	1	1	2	1	1	0	0	3	2	2	0	0	16	5	9	0	1
BELGIUM + LUX	10	6	2	0	2	1	1	0	0	0	2	2	0	0	0	6	3	3	0	1
NETHERLANDS	13	8	3	0	1	1	1	0	0	0	2	1	1	0	1	9	6	2	0	0
SPAIN	14	4	8	0	2	1	1	0	0	0	2	1	0	0	0	11	2	8	0	1
GREECE + TURKEY	2	2	0	0	0	0	0	0	0	0	0	0	0	0	0	2	2	0	0	0
OTHER EUROPE	1	0	1	0	0	0	0	0	0	0	0	0	0	0	0	1	0	1	0	0
EUROPE EX. U.K.	108	58	38	3	8	14	10	2	0	2	15	10	3	0	2	78	38	33	3	4
SOUTHERN DOMINIONS	30	20	5	2	1	3	2	0	0	0	5	2	1	0	1	22	16	4	2	0
S. AFRICA +RHOD.	3	3	0	1	1	0	0	0	0	0	1	1	0	0	0	2	1	0	0	0
AUSTRALIA + N.Z.	27	18	5	1	1	3	2	0	0	0	5	2	1	0	1	20	15	4	1	1
ASIA + OTHER AFRICA	33	25	5	2	0	0	0	0	0	0	5	3	1	0	0	27	21	4	2	0
JAPAN	20	14	5	2	0	0	0	0	0	0	3	2	1	0	0	16	12	4	0	0
OTHER ASIA+AFR.	13	11	0	0	2	0	0	0	0	0	2	2	0	0	0	11	9	0	2	0
BLACK AFRICA	0	0	0	0	0	0	0	0	0	0	0	0	0	0	0	0	0	0	0	0
ARAB WORLD	4	4	0	0	0	0	0	0	0	0	0	0	0	0	0	4	4	0	0	0
INDIA	3	1	0	0	1	0	0	0	0	0	1	1	0	0	0	2	1	0	0	1
PHILIPPINES	3	3	0	0	0	0	0	0	0	0	1	1	0	0	0	2	2	0	0	0
OTHER E. ASIA	2	1	0	1	0	0	0	0	0	0	0	0	0	0	0	2	1	0	1	0
OTHER ASIA	3	2	0	1	0	0	0	0	0	0	1	1	0	0	0	2	1	0	1	0

CHAPTER 4- VARIETIES OF ENTRY
SECTION 4- THE FLOW OF MANUFACTURING BY INDUSTRY OF SUBSIDIARY
TABLE 15- SUBSIDIARIES MANUFACTURING
PLASTICS AND SYNTHETICS (SIC 282)
CLASSIFIED BY COUNTRY, PERIOD MANUFACTURE BEGAN, AND METHOD OF ENTRY

PERIOD AND METHOD OF ENTRY
(NEW=NEWLY FORMED, ACQ=ACQUIRED, DES=DESCENDANT, UNK=UNKNOWN)

COUNTRY OR REGION	TOTAL PRE 1968					PRE 1946					1946-1957					1958-1967				
	ALL	NEW	ACQ	DES	UNK	ALL	NEW	ACQ	DES	UNK	ALL	NEW	ACQ	DES	UNK	ALL	NEW	ACQ	DES	UNK
OUTSIDE U.S.	259	144	85	11	16	21	11	5	3	2	54	32	17	4	1	181	101	63	4	13
OUT. U.S. + CANADA	230	135	71	7	14	12	7	3	1	1	47	31	13	2	1	168	97	55	4	12
OUT. WEST. HEMIS.	164	100	44	6	11	7	3	2	1	1	25	20	4	1	1	129	77	38	4	10
OUT. WHITE CWEALTH	165	104	48	4	8	6	4	1	0	0	37	23	12	1	1	121	77	35	3	6
OUT. DEVLPED WORLD	80	44	28	3	5	5	4	1	0	0	24	13	9	1	1	51	27	18	2	4
CANADA	29	9	14	4	2	9	4	2	2	1	7	1	4	2	0	13	4	8	0	1
LATIN AMERICA	66	35	27	1	3	5	4	1	0	0	22	11	9	1	1	39	20	17	0	2
C. AMER.+CARIB.	27	13	12	1	0	2	1	1	0	0	9	5	3	0	1	16	7	8	0	1
CUBA	0	0	0	0	0	0	0	0	0	0	0	0	0	0	0	0	0	0	0	0
MEXICO	23	10	12	0	1	2	1	1	0	0	9	5	3	0	1	12	4	8	0	0
OTHER	4	3	0	1	0	0	0	0	0	0	0	0	0	0	0	4	3	0	0	1
S. AMERICA	39	22	15	0	2	3	3	0	0	0	13	6	6	0	1	23	13	9	0	1
ARGENTINA	11	6	5	0	0	3	3	0	0	0	3	0	3	0	0	5	3	2	0	0
BRAZIL	10	4	6	0	0	3	3	0	0	0	3	0	3	0	0	4	1	3	0	0
PERU	1	0	1	0	0	0	0	0	0	0	0	0	0	0	0	1	0	1	0	0
COLOMBIA	9	6	2	1	0	0	0	0	0	0	2	2	0	0	0	7	4	2	1	0
VENEZUELA	7	5	1	1	0	0	0	0	0	0	2	1	0	1	0	5	4	1	0	0
OTHER	1	1	0	0	0	0	0	0	0	0	0	0	0	0	0	1	1	0	0	0
EUROPE	99	56	30	4	8	6	2	2	2	0	19	14	4	1	0	73	40	24	2	7
EFTA	41	21	12	3	5	5	2	2	1	0	9	7	1	1	0	27	12	9	1	5
U.K.	34	15	11	3	5	5	2	2	1	0	9	7	1	1	0	20	6	8	1	5
SCANDINAVIA	5	4	1	0	0	0	0	0	0	0	0	0	0	0	0	5	4	1	0	0
SWITZERLAND	1	1	0	0	0	0	0	0	0	0	0	0	0	0	0	1	1	0	0	0
OTHER EFTA	1	1	0	0	1	0	0	0	0	0	0	0	0	0	0	1	1	0	0	0
EUROP. COMMUNITY	46	29	12	1	3	1	0	1	0	0	9	7	2	0	0	35	22	10	1	2
FRANCE	11	6	3	1	1	0	0	0	0	0	4	3	0	0	1	7	3	2	1	1
GERMANY	10	6	2	2	0	1	0	1	0	0	3	3	0	0	0	6	3	2	2	0
ITALY	9	7	2	0	0	0	0	0	0	0	1	1	0	0	0	8	6	2	0	1
BELGIUM + LUX	7	5	2	0	0	0	0	0	0	0	0	0	0	0	0	7	5	2	0	1
NETHERLANDS	9	5	3	0	0	0	0	0	0	0	1	1	0	0	0	8	5	2	0	0
SPAIN	9	3	6	0	0	0	0	0	0	0	1	0	1	0	0	8	3	5	0	0
GREECE + TURKEY	3	3	0	0	0	0	0	0	0	0	0	0	0	0	0	3	3	0	0	0
OTHER EUROPE	0	0	0	0	0	0	0	0	0	0	0	0	0	0	0	0	0	0	0	0
EUROPE EX. U.K.	65	41	19	1	3	1	1	0	0	1	10	7	3	0	0	53	34	16	1	2
SOUTHERN DOMINIONS	31	16	12	0	1	1	1	0	0	0	1	1	0	0	0	27	14	12	0	1
S. AFRICA +RHOD.	5	4	0	0	0	0	0	0	0	0	0	0	0	0	0	2	2	0	0	0
AUSTRALIA + N.Z.	26	12	12	2	1	0	0	0	0	0	1	1	0	0	0	25	12	12	0	1
ASIA + OTHER AFRICA	34	28	2	2	2	1	1	0	0	2	5	3	2	0	0	29	23	2	2	0
JAPAN	20	19	1	0	0	1	1	0	0	0	2	2	0	0	0	17	16	1	0	1
OTHER ASIA+AFR.	14	9	1	2	2	0	0	0	0	0	3	1	1	0	1	12	7	1	0	2
BLACK AFRICA	0	0	0	0	0	0	0	0	0	0	0	0	0	0	0	0	0	0	0	0
ARAB WORLD	2	0	1	0	1	0	0	0	0	0	1	1	0	0	0	1	0	1	0	0
INDIA	5	3	1	0	1	0	0	0	0	0	1	0	1	0	0	5	3	0	1	1
PHILIPPINES	2	2	0	1	0	0	0	0	0	0	0	0	0	0	0	1	1	0	1	0
OTHER E. ASIA	4	2	0	1	0	0	0	0	0	0	0	0	0	0	0	4	2	0	1	0
OTHER ASIA	1	1	0	0	0	1	1	0	0	0	0	0	0	0	0	1	1	0	0	0

CHAPTER 4- VARIETIES OF ENTRY
SECTION 4- THE FLOW OF MANUFACTURING BY INDUSTRY OF SUBSIDIARY
TABLE 16- SUBSIDIARIES MANUFACTURING
DRUGS (SIC 283)
CLASSIFIED BY COUNTRY, PERIOD MANUFACTURE BEGAN, AND METHOD OF ENTRY

PERIOD AND METHOD OF ENTRY
(NEW=NEWLY FORMED, ACQ=ACQUIRED, DES=DESCENDANT, UNK=UNKNOWN)

COUNTRY OR REGION	TOTAL PRE 1968					PRE 1946					1946-1957					1958-1967				
	ALL	NEW	ACQ	DES	UNK	ALL	NEW	ACQ	DES	UNK	ALL	NEW	ACQ	DES	UNK	ALL	NEW	ACQ	DES	UNK
OUTSIDE U.S.	405	225	116	30	31	69	48	10	2	9	108	62	20	15	11	225	115	86	13	11
OUT. U.S. + CANADA	368	206	104	29	26	56	38	9	1	7	97	56	17	14	10	212	112	78	13	9
OUT. WEST. HEMIS.	241	138	70	17	16	34	24	5	1	4	59	37	13	5	5	148	77	52	11	8
OUT. WHITE CWEALTH	280	160	79	19	12	25	17	4	1	3	71	43	9	11	8	181	100	66	7	8
OUT. DEVLPED WORLD	174	101	45	13	12	22	14	4	1	3	48	27	6	9	6	101	60	35	3	3
CANADA	37	19	12	1	5	13	10	1	0	2	11	6	3	1	1	13	3	8	0	2
LATIN AMERICA	127	68	34	12	10	22	14	5	1	2	38	19	4	9	6	64	35	26	2	1
C. AMER.+CARIB.	53	26	12	5	10	7	5	1	0	1	15	6	2	5	2	28	15	9	2	2
CUBA	2	2	0	0	0	0	0	0	0	0	0	0	0	0	0	0	0	0	0	0
MEXICO	27	12	10	0	4	6	5	1	0	0	5	2	2	0	1	15	5	8	0	3
OTHER	24	12	2	5	5	1	0	0	0	1	10	4	0	5	1	13	8	2	0	3
S. AMERICA	74	42	22	5	5	15	9	4	0	2	23	13	3	4	3	36	20	16	0	1
ARGENTINA	15	8	6	0	1	7	5	1	0	1	4	1	1	0	0	4	2	4	0	0
BRAZIL	19	11	3	3	2	1	1	0	0	0	13	5	1	5	2	6	4	2	0	0
PERU	6	3	2	0	1	1	1	0	0	0	2	1	1	0	0	3	1	1	0	1
COLOMBIA	13	6	7	0	0	2	2	0	0	0	2	1	2	0	0	9	2	5	0	2
VENEZUELA	11	10	1	0	0	1	1	0	0	0	1	1	0	0	0	9	8	1	0	0
OTHER	10	4	3	0	1	2	1	1	0	0	3	3	1	0	0	5	3	2	0	1
EUROPE	138	69	51	10	8	19	12	5	0	1	33	20	8	3	2	86	37	38	6	5
EFTA	50	24	19	5	2	17	10	5	0	1	14	6	5	2	1	19	8	9	2	0
U.K.	37	14	17	5	1	16	9	5	0	1	11	4	4	2	0	10	1	7	2	0
SCANDINAVIA	5	2	0	0	1	0	0	0	0	0	2	1	1	0	0	3	1	1	0	1
SWITZERLAND	3	2	1	0	0	0	0	0	0	0	1	0	1	0	0	2	1	0	0	1
OTHER EFTA	5	4	1	0	0	0	0	0	0	0	1	1	0	0	0	4	3	1	0	0
EUROP. COMMUNITY	71	37	26	0	8	1	1	0	0	0	16	11	3	0	1	53	24	23	0	3
FRANCE	17	6	10	0	1	0	0	0	0	0	2	1	1	0	1	15	5	10	0	0
GERMANY	14	7	4	2	0	0	0	0	0	0	2	1	1	0	0	11	5	4	2	0
ITALY	25	14	8	0	2	1	1	0	0	0	8	5	2	0	1	17	9	5	0	1
BELGIUM + LUX	12	7	4	0	1	0	0	0	0	0	2	2	0	0	0	10	5	4	0	1
NETHERLANDS	3	3	0	0	0	0	0	0	0	0	3	3	0	0	0	0	0	0	0	0
SPAIN	7	2	4	0	1	0	0	0	0	0	0	0	0	0	0	7	2	4	0	1
GREECE + TURKEY	8	4	2	0	2	0	0	0	0	0	1	1	0	0	0	7	2	2	0	2
OTHER EUROPE	2	2	0	0	0	0	0	0	0	0	2	2	0	0	0	0	0	0	0	0
EUROPE EX. U.K.	101	55	34	5	7	3	3	0	0	0	22	16	4	1	2	76	36	31	4	5
SOUTHERN DOMINIONS	49	30	8	5	6	15	12	0	0	3	13	7	3	1	2	21	11	5	4	0
S. AFRICA +RHOD.	18	13	3	1	1	6	5	0	0	1	5	4	1	0	0	7	4	2	1	0
AUSTRALIA + N.Z.	31	17	5	4	5	9	7	0	0	2	8	3	2	1	2	14	7	3	3	1
ASIA + OTHER AFRICA	54	39	11	2	2	0	0	0	0	0	13	10	1	0	2	41	29	10	2	0
JAPAN	7	6	0	1	0	0	0	0	0	0	3	2	0	1	0	4	4	0	0	0
OTHER ASIA+AFR.	47	33	11	0	3	0	0	0	0	0	10	8	1	0	1	37	25	10	0	2
BLACK AFRICA	3	2	1	0	0	0	0	0	0	0	1	0	1	0	0	2	2	0	0	0
ARAB WORLD	2	0	2	0	0	0	0	0	0	0	0	0	0	0	0	2	0	2	0	0
INDIA	13	10	3	0	0	0	0	0	0	0	3	2	1	0	0	10	7	2	0	1
PHILIPPINES	8	7	1	0	0	0	0	0	0	0	4	3	1	0	0	4	4	0	0	0
OTHER E. ASIA	3	3	0	0	0	0	0	0	0	0	0	0	0	0	0	3	3	0	0	0
OTHER ASIA	18	11	4	1	2	0	0	0	0	0	2	1	0	1	0	16	11	3	0	2

CHAPTER 4- VARIETIES OF ENTRY
SECTION 4- THE FLOW OF MANUFACTURING BY INDUSTRY OF SUBSIDIARY
TABLE 17- SUBSIDIARIES MANUFACTURING
SOAPS AND COSMETICS (SIC 284)
CLASSIFIED BY COUNTRY, PERIOD MANUFACTURE BEGAN, AND METHOD OF ENTRY

PERIOD AND METHOD OF ENTRY
(NEW=NEWLY FORMED, ACQ=ACQUIRED, DES=DESCENDANT, UNK=UNKNOWN)

COUNTRY OR REGION	TOTAL PRE 1968					PRE 1946					1946-1957					1958-1967				
	ALL	NEW	ACQ	DES	UNK	ALL	NEW	ACQ	DES	UNK	ALL	NEW	ACQ	DES	UNK	ALL	NEW	ACQ	DES	UNK
OUTSIDE U.S.	248	134	82	13	17	64	43	18	0	3	53	29	10	9	5	129	62	54	4	9
OUT. U.S. + CANADA	217	121	66	13	15	49	33	15	0	1	51	27	10	9	5	115	61	41	4	9
OUT. WEST. HEMIS.	158	90	51	6	9	35	25	10	0	0	30	14	9	5	2	91	51	32	1	7
OUT. WHITE CWEALTH	159	93	41	10	14	29	18	10	0	1	37	22	4	6	5	92	53	27	4	8
OUT. DEVLPED WORLD	79	45	17	7	10	15	8	6	0	1	23	15	1	4	3	41	22	10	3	6
CANADA	31	13	16	0	2	15	10	3	0	2	2	2	0	0	0	14	1	13	0	0
LATIN AMERICA	59	31	15	7	6	14	8	5	0	1	21	13	2	4	2	24	10	9	3	2
C. AMER.+CARIB.	25	10	6	5	4	5	2	2	0	1	11	5	1	4	1	9	3	4	1	1
CUBA	3	1	0	2	0	1	1	0	0	0	2	1	0	1	0	0	0	0	0	0
MEXICO	12	7	3	2	0	3	2	1	0	0	4	3	1	0	0	5	2	2	0	1
OTHER	10	2	2	3	3	1	0	1	0	0	5	1	0	3	1	4	1	2	1	0
S. AMERICA	34	21	9	2	2	9	6	3	0	0	10	8	1	0	1	15	7	5	2	1
ARGENTINA	10	6	4	0	0	5	4	1	0	0	1	1	0	0	0	4	1	3	0	0
BRAZIL	7	3	3	1	0	3	2	1	0	0	2	1	1	0	0	4	2	0	1	1
PERU	6	4	1	0	1	1	0	1	0	0	2	1	0	1	0	3	3	0	0	0
COLOMBIA	3	0	1	1	1	0	0	0	0	0	0	0	0	0	0	3	3	0	0	0
VENEZUELA	7	7	0	0	0	0	0	0	0	0	4	4	0	0	0	3	3	0	0	0
OTHER	1	1	0	0	0	0	0	0	0	0	1	1	0	0	0	0	0	0	0	0
EUROPE	110	57	43	5	5	24	16	8	0	0	24	10	8	4	2	61	31	27	1	2
EFTA	45	21	20	3	1	10	6	4	0	0	13	4	5	3	1	22	11	11	0	0
U.K.	31	12	17	2	0	10	6	4	0	0	9	2	5	2	0	12	4	8	0	0
SCANDINAVIA	9	5	3	1	0	0	0	0	0	0	2	1	0	0	1	7	4	3	0	0
SWITZERLAND	2	1	0	0	1	0	0	0	0	0	2	1	0	0	0	0	0	0	0	0
OTHER EFTA	3	3	0	0	0	0	0	0	0	0	0	0	0	0	0	3	3	0	0	0
EUROP. COMMUNITY	53	31	17	1	4	14	10	4	0	0	9	5	2	1	1	29	16	11	1	1
FRANCE	18	8	8	1	1	4	2	2	0	0	5	1	2	2	0	9	5	4	0	0
GERMANY	14	7	5	0	2	6	4	2	0	0	1	1	0	0	0	6	2	3	1	0
ITALY	12	9	3	0	0	2	2	0	0	0	1	1	0	0	0	9	6	3	0	0
BELGIUM + LUX	7	5	1	0	1	1	1	0	0	0	2	2	0	0	0	4	2	1	1	0
NETHERLANDS	2	2	0	0	0	1	1	0	0	0	0	0	0	0	0	1	1	0	0	0
SPAIN	8	4	4	0	0	0	0	0	0	0	0	0	0	0	0	7	4	3	0	0
GREECE + TURKEY	1	0	0	1	0	0	0	0	0	0	0	0	0	0	0	1	0	0	1	0
OTHER EUROPE	3	1	2	0	0	0	0	0	0	0	1	1	0	0	0	2	0	2	0	0
EUROPE EX. U.K.	79	45	26	3	5	14	10	4	0	0	15	8	3	2	2	49	27	19	1	2
SOUTHERN DOMINIONS	24	15	6	1	1	10	9	1	0	0	5	2	1	1	0	9	4	4	0	1
S. AFRICA +RHOD.	10	7	3	0	0	5	4	1	0	0	1	1	0	0	0	4	2	2	0	0
AUSTRALIA + N.Z.	14	8	2	1	0	5	5	0	0	0	4	1	1	1	0	5	2	2	1	0
ASIA + OTHER AFRICA	24	18	2	0	4	1	1	0	0	0	2	1	1	0	0	21	16	1	0	4
JAPAN	4	4	0	0	0	0	0	0	0	0	0	0	0	0	0	4	4	0	0	0
OTHER ASIA+AFR.	20	14	2	0	4	1	1	0	0	0	2	1	1	0	0	17	12	1	0	4
BLACK AFRICA	3	3	0	0	0	0	0	0	0	0	0	0	0	0	0	3	3	0	0	0
ARAB WORLD	3	2	0	0	1	0	0	0	0	0	1	0	1	0	0	2	2	0	0	0
INDIA	1	1	0	0	0	1	1	0	0	0	0	0	0	0	0	0	0	0	0	0
PHILIPPINES	0	0	0	0	0	0	0	0	0	0	0	0	0	0	0	0	0	0	0	0
OTHER E. ASIA	2	2	0	0	0	0	0	0	0	0	0	0	0	0	0	2	2	0	0	0
OTHER ASIA	10	6	1	0	3	0	0	0	0	0	0	0	0	0	0	10	6	1	0	3

CHAPTER 4- VARIETIES OF ENTRY
SECTION 4- THE FLOW OF MANUFACTURING BY INDUSTRY OF SUBSIDIARY
TABLE 18- SUBSIDIARIES MANUFACTURING
PAINTS (SIC 285)
CLASSIFIED BY COUNTRY, PERIOD MANUFACTURE BEGAN, AND METHOD OF ENTRY

PERIOD AND METHOD OF ENTRY
(NEW=NEWLY FORMED, ACQ=ACQUIRED, DES=DESCENDANT, UNK=UNKNOWN)

COUNTRY OR REGION	TOTAL / PRE 1968					PRE 1946					1946-1957					1958-1967				
	ALL	NEW	ACQ	DES	UNK	ALL	NEW	ACQ	DES	UNK	ALL	NEW	ACQ	DES	UNK	ALL	NEW	ACQ	DES	UNK
OUTSIDE U.S.	82	16	41	1	6	12	6	2	3	1	7	2	2	0	0	46	7	34	0	5
OUT. U.S. + CANADA	69	15	31	1	5	10	5	2	2	1	6	1	3	1	0	40	7	28	0	5
OUT. WEST. HEMIS.	45	7	21	0	3	2	2	2	0	0	1	1	0	0	0	27	4	20	0	3
OUT. WHITE CWEALTH	57	14	27	1	3	10	1	1	1	0	6	3	1	1	0	34	7	24	0	3
OUT. DEVLPED WORLD	32	10	10	1	2	9	0	0	0	0	6	2	2	0	0	14	4	8	0	2
CANADA	13	1	10	0	1	2	0	0	0	1	2	1	1	0	0	6	0	6	0	0
LATIN AMERICA	24	8	10	1	2	3	0	0	0	0	8	5	1	1	0	13	3	8	0	2
C. AMER.+CARIB.	11	0	5	1	2	1	0	0	0	0	1	0	0	1	0	7	1	4	0	2
CUBA	1	1	0	0	0	0	0	0	0	0	0	0	0	0	0	0	0	0	0	0
MEXICO	5	1	2	1	1	2	0	0	0	0	0	0	0	0	0	3	0	2	0	1
OTHER	5	1	1	0	1	0	0	0	0	0	1	0	1	0	0	4	1	2	0	1
S. AMERICA	13	6	5	0	0	0	0	0	0	0	5	4	1	0	0	6	2	4	0	0
ARGENTINA	0	0	0	0	0	0	0	0	0	0	0	0	0	0	0	0	0	0	0	0
BRAZIL	5	0	4	0	0	0	0	0	0	0	0	0	0	0	0	6	2	4	0	0
PERU	0	0	0	0	0	0	0	0	0	0	0	0	0	0	0	0	0	0	0	0
COLOMBIA	2	1	0	0	0	0	0	0	0	0	1	0	1	0	0	5	1	4	0	0
VENEZUELA	2	2	0	0	0	0	0	0	0	0	2	2	0	0	0	1	1	0	0	0
OTHER	4	2	0	0	0	0	0	0	0	0	2	2	0	0	0	0	0	0	0	0
EUROPE	27	5	17	0	3	1	0	0	0	0	1	0	0	0	0	22	3	16	0	3
EFTA	7	1	4	1	1	0	0	0	0	0	0	0	0	0	0	5	0	4	0	1
U.K.	4	1	2	1	1	0	0	0	0	0	0	0	0	0	0	3	0	2	0	1
SCANDINAVIA	2	0	2	0	0	0	0	0	0	0	0	0	0	0	0	1	0	1	0	0
SWITZERLAND	0	0	0	0	0	0	0	0	0	0	0	0	0	0	0	1	0	1	0	0
OTHER EFTA	1	0	0	0	0	0	0	0	0	0	1	0	1	0	0	0	0	0	0	0
EUROP. COMMUNITY	17	4	11	0	1	1	0	0	0	0	1	0	1	0	0	14	3	10	0	1
FRANCE	3	0	3	0	0	0	0	0	0	0	0	0	0	0	0	3	0	3	0	0
GERMANY	4	2	2	0	0	1	0	0	0	0	0	1	1	0	0	1	0	1	0	0
ITALY	2	0	2	0	0	0	0	0	0	0	0	0	0	0	0	2	1	1	0	0
BELGIUM + LUX	4	2	2	0	0	1	0	0	0	0	0	0	0	0	0	2	0	2	0	0
NETHERLANDS	4	0	2	0	0	1	0	0	0	0	0	0	0	0	0	4	2	2	0	0
SPAIN	2	0	2	0	0	0	0	0	0	0	0	0	0	0	0	3	0	2	0	0
GREECE + TURKEY	0	0	0	0	0	0	0	0	0	0	0	0	0	0	0	0	0	0	0	0
OTHER EUROPE	1	0	0	0	1	0	0	0	0	0	1	0	0	0	0	1	0	0	0	1
EUROPE EX. U.K.	23	4	15	0	2	1	0	0	0	0	1	0	1	0	0	19	3	14	0	2
SOUTHERN DOMINIONS	7	0	2	0	0	0	0	0	0	0	0	0	0	0	0	2	0	2	0	0
S. AFRICA +RHOD.	3	0	0	0	0	0	0	0	0	0	0	0	0	0	0	2	0	2	0	0
AUSTRALIA + N.Z.	4	2	2	0	0	0	0	0	0	0	0	1	1	0	0	2	0	2	0	0
ASIA + OTHER AFRICA	11	2	2	0	0	0	0	0	0	0	1	0	1	0	0	2	2	2	0	0
JAPAN	3	2	0	0	0	0	0	0	0	0	0	0	0	0	0	2	2	0	0	0
OTHER ASIA+AFR.	8	2	2	0	0	0	0	0	0	0	1	1	1	0	0	2	0	2	0	0
BLACK AFRICA	2	0	0	0	0	0	0	0	0	0	0	0	0	0	0	0	0	0	0	0
ARAB WORLD	0	0	0	0	0	0	0	0	0	0	0	0	0	0	0	0	0	0	0	0
INDIA	1	1	0	0	0	0	0	0	0	0	1	0	0	0	0	0	0	0	0	0
PHILIPPINES	1	0	0	0	0	0	0	0	0	0	0	0	0	0	0	0	0	0	0	0
OTHER E. ASIA	0	0	0	0	0	0	0	0	0	0	0	0	0	0	0	0	0	0	0	0
OTHER ASIA	4	1	0	0	0	0	0	0	0	0	0	0	0	0	0	1	1	0	0	0

CHAPTER 4-- VARIETIES OF ENTRY
SECTION 4-- THE FLOW OF MANUFACTURING BY INDUSTRY OF SUBSIDIARY
TABLE 19-- SUBSIDIARIES MANUFACTURING
AGRICULTURAL CHEMICALS (SIC 287)
CLASSIFIED BY COUNTRY, PERIOD MANUFACTURE BEGAN, AND METHOD OF ENTRY

PERIOD AND METHOD OF ENTRY
(NEW=NEWLY FORMED, ACQ=ACQUIRED, DES=DESCENDANT, UNK=UNKNOWN)

COUNTRY OR REGION	TOTAL PRE 1968					PRE 1946					1946-1957					1958-1967				
	ALL	NEW	ACQ	DES	UNK	ALL	NEW	ACQ	DES	UNK	ALL	NEW	ACQ	DES	UNK	ALL	NEW	ACQ	DES	UNK
OUTSIDE U.S.	81	40	22	4	8	7	2	3	1	1	16	11	2	2	1	51	27	17	1	6
OUT. U.S. + CANADA	72	39	18	3	7	4	2	1	0	1	15	11	1	2	1	48	26	16	1	5
OUT. WEST. HEMIS.	45	21	15	2	5	4	1	1	1	0	9	6	1	1	1	33	15	13	0	5
OUT. WHITE CMEALTH	61	35	14	1	7	4	2	2	0	0	13	11	0	1	1	40	22	13	0	5
OUT. DEVLPED WORLD	41	27	4	1	6	3	2	0	0	1	11	9	0	0	1	24	16	4	0	4
CANADA	9	1	4	1	1	3	3	0	0	0	0	0	0	0	0	3	1	3	0	1
LATIN AMERICA	27	18	3	3	2	2	2	0	0	1	6	6	0	1	0	15	11	3	0	0
C. AMER.+CARIB.	13	11	0	0	3	2	2	0	0	0	2	2	0	0	0	7	7	0	0	0
CUBA	0	0	0	0	0	0	0	0	0	0	0	0	0	0	0	0	0	0	0	0
MEXICO	6	4	0	0	2	1	1	0	0	0	2	2	0	0	0	1	1	0	0	0
OTHER	6	6	3	0	0	0	0	0	0	0	0	0	0	0	0	6	6	0	0	0
S. AMERICA	14	7	1	3	2	1	0	0	1	0	3	3	0	0	0	8	4	3	0	1
ARGENTINA	4	1	1	1	1	0	0	0	0	0	1	1	0	0	0	1	0	1	0	0
BRAZIL	3	0	0	2	1	0	0	0	0	0	0	0	0	0	0	3	2	0	1	0
PERU	4	0	2	1	1	0	0	0	0	0	1	1	0	0	0	0	0	0	0	0
COLUMBIA	2	3	0	0	0	0	0	0	0	0	1	1	0	0	0	3	2	2	0	0
VENEZUELA	2	2	0	0	0	0	0	0	0	0	0	0	0	0	0	1	1	0	0	0
OTHER	0	0	0	0	0	0	0	0	0	0	0	0	0	0	0	0	0	0	0	0
EUROPE	22	10	9	1	1	1	0	0	0	0	3	3	0	0	0	17	8	8	0	1
EFTA	4	3	0	1	1	0	0	0	0	0	1	1	0	1	0	3	3	0	0	0
U.K.	3	2	0	1	1	0	0	0	0	0	1	1	0	1	0	2	2	0	0	0
SCANDINAVIA	0	0	0	0	0	0	0	0	0	0	0	0	0	0	0	1	1	0	0	0
SWITZERLAND	0	0	0	0	0	0	0	0	0	0	0	0	0	0	0	0	0	0	0	0
OTHER EFTA	0	0	0	0	0	0	0	0	0	0	0	0	0	0	0	0	0	0	0	0
EUROP. COMMUNITY	11	4	5	0	2	0	0	0	0	0	2	2	0	0	0	8	2	5	0	1
FRANCE	6	2	2	0	2	0	0	0	0	0	1	1	0	0	0	4	2	2	0	0
GERMANY	1	1	0	0	0	0	0	0	0	0	0	0	0	0	0	0	0	0	0	0
ITALY	2	1	1	0	0	0	0	0	0	0	0	0	0	0	0	2	1	1	0	0
BELGIUM + LUX	1	1	1	0	0	0	0	0	0	0	1	1	0	0	0	1	0	1	0	0
NETHERLANDS	1	0	1	0	0	0	0	0	0	0	0	0	0	0	0	1	1	0	0	0
SPAIN	7	3	4	0	0	1	1	0	0	0	0	0	0	0	0	6	3	3	0	0
GREECE + TURKEY	0	0	0	0	0	0	0	0	0	0	0	0	0	0	0	0	0	0	0	0
OTHER EUROPE	0	0	0	0	1	1	1	0	0	0	0	0	0	0	0	0	0	0	0	0
EUROPE EX. U.K.	19	8	9	0	1	1	1	0	0	0	2	2	0	0	0	15	8	8	0	1
SOUTHERN DOMINIONS	8	2	4	1	0	0	0	0	0	0	1	1	0	0	0	6	2	3	0	0
S. AFRICA +RHOD.	3	1	1	1	0	0	0	0	0	0	1	1	0	0	0	2	1	1	0	0
AUSTRALIA + N.Z.	5	1	3	0	0	0	0	0	0	0	0	0	0	0	0	4	1	2	0	0
ASIA + OTHER AFRICA	15	9	2	4	0	0	0	0	0	0	5	5	0	1	0	10	4	1	0	5
JAPAN	1	0	1	0	4	0	0	0	0	0	0	0	0	0	0	1	5	0	0	0
OTHER ASIA+AFR.	14	9	1	1	3	0	0	0	0	0	5	5	0	1	0	9	5	1	0	3
BLACK AFRICA	4	1	0	0	0	0	0	0	0	0	2	2	0	1	0	2	1	0	0	2
ARAB WORLD	1	1	0	0	0	0	0	0	0	0	0	0	0	0	0	1	0	1	0	0
INDIA	3	2	1	1	0	0	0	0	0	0	2	2	0	0	0	1	0	0	0	0
PHILIPPINES	1	1	0	0	0	0	0	0	0	0	1	1	0	0	0	1	1	0	0	0
OTHER E. ASIA	4	3	0	1	0	0	0	0	0	0	0	0	0	0	0	4	3	0	0	1
OTHER ASIA	1	1	0	0	0	0	0	0	0	0	0	0	0	0	0	1	1	0	0	0

CHAPTER 4- VARIETIES OF ENTRY
SECTION 4- THE FLOW OF MANUFACTURING BY INDUSTRY OF SUBSIDIARY
TABLE 20- SUBSIDIARIES MANUFACTURING
MISCELLANEOUS CHEMICAL PRODUCTS (SIC 289)
CLASSIFIED BY COUNTRY, PERIOD MANUFACTURE BEGAN, AND METHOD OF ENTRY

PERIOD AND METHOD OF ENTRY
(NEW=NEWLY FORMED, ACQ=ACQUIRED, DES=DESCENDANT, UNK=UNKNOWN)

COUNTRY OR REGION	TOTAL ALL	NEW	ACQ	DES	UNK	PRE 1946 ALL	NEW	ACQ	DES	UNK	1946-1957 ALL	NEW	ACQ	DES	UNK	1958-1967 ALL	NEW	ACQ	DES	UNK
OUTSIDE U.S.	132	63	52	8	8	35	14	11	4	6	27	18	7	2	0	69	31	34	2	2
OUT. U.S. + CANADA	108	58	40	5	5	22	13	6	0	3	20	14	4	2	0	65	31	30	2	2
OUT. WEST. HEMIS.	73	38	30	2	3	11	8	2	0	1	12	9	3	0	0	50	21	25	2	2
OUT. WHITE CWEALTH	81	44	29	4	4	17	9	6	0	2	12	7	3	2	0	51	28	20	1	2
OUT. DEVLPED WORLD	43	24	12	3	4	12	6	4	0	2	8	5	1	2	0	22	13	7	0	2
CANADA	24	5	12	4	3	13	5	5	0	3	7	4	3	0	0	4	0	4	0	0
LATIN AMERICA	35	20	10	2	3	11	5	4	0	2	8	2	5	1	0	15	10	3	0	0
C. AMER.+CARIB.	11	5	4	1	1	2	0	1	0	1	2	0	2	0	0	6	3	0	0	0
CUBA	7	3	2	0	1	2	2	0	1	1	2	2	0	0	0	2	1	1	0	0
MEXICO	4	2	2	0	0	2	0	0	0	0	0	0	2	0	0	4	2	2	0	0
OTHER	24	15	6	2	1	9	5	3	1	0	6	3	2	1	1	9	7	2	0	0
S. AMERICA	8	2	4	0	2	3	0	2	0	1	2	0	3	0	1	3	2	1	0	0
ARGENTINA	7	6	0	0	1	1	1	0	1	0	4	3	0	1	0	2	2	0	0	0
BRAZIL	0	0	0	0	0	0	0	0	0	0	0	0	0	0	0	0	0	0	0	0
PERU	4	3	1	0	0	1	1	0	0	0	0	0	1	0	0	3	2	1	0	0
COLOMBIA	1	1	0	1	1	0	0	0	0	0	0	0	0	0	0	1	1	0	0	0
VENEZUELA	4	3	0	0	0	4	3	1	0	0	0	0	0	0	0	0	0	0	0	0
OTHER	4	3	0	0	0	4	3	1	1	1	0	0	0	0	0	0	0	0	0	0
EUROPE	48	24	21	2	1	7	4	2	1	2	7	3	6	1	0	34	14	18	2	0
EFTA	16	7	7	1	1	2	1	1	1	0	3	3	3	0	0	11	3	7	1	0
U.K.	14	6	6	1	1	2	1	1	1	1	3	3	3	0	0	9	2	6	1	0
SCANDINAVIA	0	0	0	0	0	0	0	0	0	0	0	0	0	0	0	0	0	0	0	0
SWITZERLAND	1	0	1	0	0	0	0	0	0	0	0	0	0	0	0	1	0	1	0	0
OTHER EFTA	1	1	0	1	1	0	0	0	0	0	0	0	0	0	0	1	1	0	0	0
EUROP. COMMUNITY	25	12	12	0	1	4	2	2	0	0	3	2	2	0	0	18	8	9	0	0
FRANCE	7	2	4	2	1	1	0	1	1	0	0	0	1	0	0	6	2	3	1	0
GERMANY	6	4	2	0	0	2	1	0	0	0	2	1	0	0	0	3	2	1	0	0
ITALY	9	4	5	0	0	0	0	1	0	1	2	1	1	0	0	6	2	4	0	0
BELGIUM + LUX	3	0	0	0	0	0	0	0	0	0	0	0	0	0	0	3	2	0	1	0
NETHERLANDS	6	4	2	0	1	1	1	0	0	0	2	1	1	0	0	5	3	2	0	0
SPAIN	0	0	0	0	0	0	0	0	0	0	0	0	0	0	0	0	0	0	0	0
GREECE + TURKEY	1	1	2	0	0	0	0	0	0	0	0	0	1	0	0	0	0	0	0	0
OTHER EUROPE	0	0	0	0	0	0	0	0	0	0	0	0	0	0	0	0	0	0	0	0
EUROPE EX. U.K.	34	18	15	1	0	5	3	1	0	1	4	3	3	1	0	25	12	12	1	0
SOUTHERN DOMINIONS	12	7	5	0	0	3	3	0	0	0	4	3	1	0	0	5	1	4	0	0
S. AFRICA +RHOD.	5	4	4	2	0	2	2	0	0	0	2	2	1	0	0	1	1	1	0	0
AUSTRALIA + N.Z.	7	3	4	2	0	1	1	0	0	0	2	1	1	0	0	4	1	3	0	0
ASIA + OTHER AFRICA	13	7	4	0	2	1	1	0	0	0	1	1	1	0	0	11	6	3	0	2
JAPAN	5	3	2	0	0	0	0	0	0	0	0	0	0	0	0	5	3	2	0	0
OTHER ASIA+AFR.	8	4	2	0	2	1	1	0	0	0	1	0	1	0	0	7	3	2	0	2
BLACK AFRICA	0	0	0	0	0	0	0	0	0	0	0	0	0	0	0	0	0	0	0	0
ARAB WORLD	0	0	0	0	0	0	0	0	0	0	0	0	0	0	0	0	0	0	0	0
INDIA	3	2	1	0	1	1	1	0	0	0	0	0	0	0	0	2	1	1	0	1
PHILIPPINES	2	2	1	1	1	0	0	0	0	0	0	0	0	0	0	2	2	0	1	1
OTHER E. ASIA	3	2	0	1	0	0	0	0	0	0	0	0	0	0	0	3	2	0	1	0
OTHER ASIA	0	0	0	0	0	0	0	0	0	0	0	0	0	0	0	0	0	0	0	0

CHAPTER 4- VARIETIES OF ENTRY
SECTION 4- THE FLOW OF MANUFACTURING BY INDUSTRY OF SUBSIDIARY
TABLE 21- SUBSIDIARIES MANUFACTURING
REFINED PETROLEUM (SIC 291)
CLASSIFIED BY COUNTRY, PERIOD MANUFACTURE BEGAN, AND METHOD OF ENTRY

PERIOD AND METHOD OF ENTRY
(NEW=NEWLY FORMED, ACQ=ACQUIRED, DES=DESCENDANT, UNK=UNKNOWN)

COUNTRY OR REGION	TOTAL PRE 1968					PRE 1946					1946-1957					1958-1967				
	ALL	NEW	ACQ	DES	UNK	ALL	NEW	ACQ	DES	UNK	ALL	NEW	ACQ	DES	UNK	ALL	NEW	ACQ	DES	UNK
OUTSIDE U.S.	173	78	34	22	34	57	39	6	6	6	39	13	9	6	11	72	26	19	10	17
OUT. U.S. + CANADA	158	72	27	21	34	48	33	4	5	6	36	13	5	6	11	70	26	17	10	17
OUT. WEST. HEMIS.	126	51	25	15	31	32	19	4	3	6	30	11	5	4	10	60	21	16	8	15
OUT. WHITE CWEALTH	130	62	26	16	24	46	31	4	5	6	29	9	6	5	9	53	22	16	6	9
OUT. DEVLPED WORLD	56	31	4	11	8	21	17	0	4	0	9	2	1	3	3	24	12	3	4	5
CANADA	15	6	7	7	0	9	6	2	1	0	3	2	3	0	0	2	0	2	0	0
LATIN AMERICA	32	21	2	6	3	16	14	0	2	0	6	2	0	2	1	10	5	1	2	2
C. AMER.+CARIB.	20	15	1	2	2	12	12	0	0	0	2	0	0	1	1	6	3	1	1	1
CUBA	4	3	0	0	0	3	3	0	0	0	1	0	0	1	0	0	0	0	0	0
MEXICO	3	3	0	1	0	3	3	0	0	0	0	0	0	0	0	0	0	0	0	0
OTHER	13	9	1	4	2	6	6	0	2	0	1	2	0	0	1	6	3	1	1	1
S. AMERICA	12	6	3	1	1	4	2	2	0	0	4	0	0	1	0	4	2	0	0	1
ARGENTINA	4	3	0	0	0	3	2	0	0	0	0	0	0	0	0	1	1	0	0	0
BRAZIL	0	0	0	0	0	0	0	0	0	0	0	0	0	0	0	0	0	0	0	0
PERU	1	1	0	0	0	0	0	0	0	0	0	0	0	0	0	1	1	0	0	0
COLOMBIA	3	1	0	0	1	1	0	0	1	0	1	1	0	0	0	1	0	0	0	1
VENEZUELA	3	1	0	2	0	0	0	0	0	0	2	1	0	1	0	1	0	0	1	0
OTHER	1	0	1	0	0	0	0	0	0	0	1	0	1	0	0	0	0	0	0	0
EUROPE	80	36	21	7	16	26	15	4	1	6	20	9	3	3	5	34	12	14	3	5
EFTA	21	10	2	3	6	8	6	1	0	1	5	2	0	1	2	8	2	1	2	3
U.K.	11	5	0	1	3	1	1	0	0	0	4	2	0	1	1	6	2	1	1	2
SCANDINAVIA	6	2	0	2	3	3	2	0	0	1	1	0	0	0	1	2	0	0	1	1
SWITZERLAND	0	0	1	0	0	0	0	1	0	0	0	0	0	0	0	0	0	0	0	0
OTHER EFTA	4	3	1	0	0	4	3	0	1	0	0	0	0	0	0	0	0	0	0	0
EUROP. COMMUNITY	45	19	16	6	6	9	6	1	0	2	13	5	3	2	3	23	8	13	0	1
FRANCE	5	5	0	1	1	3	2	0	0	1	1	0	0	1	0	1	0	1	0	0
GERMANY	18	7	7	0	3	4	2	0	1	0	5	4	1	0	0	11	4	7	0	0
ITALY	16	6	8	2	1	2	2	0	0	1	5	3	2	0	0	7	1	5	1	0
BELGIUM + LUX	2	2	0	0	0	0	0	0	1	0	1	1	0	0	0	1	1	0	0	0
NETHERLANDS	4	2	0	2	1	0	0	0	0	0	1	0	0	1	0	3	2	0	1	0
SPAIN	6	3	3	0	0	3	0	0	1	0	2	2	0	0	0	1	1	0	0	0
GREECE + TURKEY	2	1	0	0	1	0	0	0	0	0	0	0	0	0	0	2	1	0	0	1
OTHER EUROPE	6	0	0	2	3	6	0	0	0	0	0	0	0	0	1	0	1	0	0	0
EUROPE EX. U.K.	69	31	20	5	13	25	14	4	1	6	16	7	3	2	4	28	10	13	2	3
SOUTHERN DOMINIONS	17	5	0	3	7	1	1	0	0	0	3	2	0	0	1	11	2	0	3	6
S. AFRICA +RHOD.	3	0	0	0	2	0	0	0	0	0	0	0	0	0	0	2	0	0	0	2
AUSTRALIA + N.Z.	14	5	0	3	5	1	1	0	0	0	3	2	0	0	1	9	2	0	3	4
ASIA + OTHER AFRICA	29	10	4	5	8	5	3	0	2	0	7	0	2	1	4	15	7	2	3	4
JAPAN	5	0	0	0	5	0	0	0	0	0	4	0	2	0	2	1	0	2	0	1
OTHER ASIA+AFR.	24	10	2	5	5	5	3	0	2	0	3	0	0	1	2	14	7	2	2	3
BLACK AFRICA	3	2	0	0	1	0	0	0	0	0	0	0	0	0	0	3	2	0	0	1
ARAB WORLD	6	1	0	4	0	1	0	0	1	0	1	0	0	1	0	3	1	0	2	0
INDIA	1	1	0	0	0	0	0	0	0	0	0	0	0	0	0	1	1	0	0	0
PHILIPPINES	3	1	0	0	2	0	0	0	0	0	1	0	0	1	1	1	1	0	0	1
OTHER E. ASIA	1	0	0	0	0	0	0	0	0	0	0	0	0	0	0	1	0	0	0	0
OTHER ASIA	10	5	1	1	2	4	3	0	1	1	1	0	0	0	1	4	2	1	0	1

CHAPTER 4- VARIETIES OF ENTRY

SECTION 4- THE FLOW OF MANUFACTURING BY INDUSTRY OF SUBSIDIARY

TABLE 22- SUBSIDIARIES MANUFACTURING

OTHER PRODUCTS OF PETROLEUM AND COAL (SIC 295 AND 299)

CLASSIFIED BY COUNTRY, PERIOD MANUFACTURE BEGAN, AND METHOD OF ENTRY

PERIOD AND METHOD OF ENTRY

(NEW=NEWLY FORMED, ACQ=ACQUIRED, DES=DESCENDANT, UNK=UNKNOWN)

COUNTRY OR REGION	TOTAL PRE 1968					PRE 1946					1946-1957					1958-1967				
	ALL	NEW	ACQ	DES	UNK	ALL	NEW	ACQ	DES	UNK	ALL	NEW	ACQ	DES	UNK	ALL	NEW	ACQ	DES	UNK
OUTSIDE U.S.	83	51	19	7	6	18	10	3	1	4	11	6	2	2	1	53	35	14	3	1
OUT. U.S. + CANADA	75	48	17	5	5	13	9	1	0	3	10	5	2	2	1	51	34	14	2	1
OUT. WEST. HEMIS.	59	38	15	2	4	11	7	1	0	3	6	3	2	1	0	41	28	12	0	1
OUT. WHITE CWEALTH	60	37	14	4	5	10	6	1	0	3	6	4	2	0	0	43	27	12	2	2
OUT. DEVLPED WORLD	22	16	2	3	1	2	2	0	0	0	4	2	0	2	0	16	14	2	0	0
CANADA	8	3	3	0	2	5	3	2	0	0	1	1	0	0	0	2	1	0	1	0
LATIN AMERICA	16	10	2	1	3	2	2	0	0	0	4	2	1	1	0	10	6	2	2	0
C. AMER.+CARIB.	5	3	0	2	0	1	1	0	0	0	1	0	0	1	0	3	2	0	1	0
CUBA	1	0	0	1	0	0	0	0	0	0	1	0	0	1	0	0	0	0	0	0
MEXICO	4	3	0	1	0	1	1	0	0	0	0	0	0	0	0	3	2	0	1	0
OTHER	0	0	0	0	0	0	0	0	0	0	0	0	0	0	0	0	0	0	0	0
S. AMERICA	11	7	2	2	0	1	1	0	0	0	3	2	1	0	0	7	4	2	1	0
ARGENTINA	1	1	0	0	0	0	0	0	0	0	0	0	0	0	0	1	1	0	0	0
BRAZIL	5	3	0	2	0	0	0	0	0	0	1	1	0	0	0	4	3	0	1	0
PERU	1	1	0	0	0	0	0	0	0	0	0	0	0	0	0	1	1	0	0	0
COLOMBIA	1	0	1	0	0	0	0	0	0	0	0	0	0	0	0	1	0	1	0	0
VENEZUELA	2	1	1	0	0	0	0	0	0	0	2	1	1	0	0	0	0	0	0	0
OTHER	1	1	0	0	0	0	0	0	0	0	0	0	0	0	0	1	1	0	0	0
EUROPE	39	26	8	1	4	11	7	1	0	3	4	3	0	1	0	24	16	7	0	1
EFTA	15	10	4	0	1	4	3	0	0	1	2	1	0	1	0	9	5	4	0	0
U.K.	8	4	3	0	1	3	3	0	0	0	1	1	0	0	0	4	3	1	0	0
SCANDINAVIA	7	4	1	1	1	1	0	0	0	1	1	0	0	1	0	5	2	3	0	0
SWITZERLAND	0	0	0	0	0	0	0	0	0	0	0	0	0	0	0	0	0	0	0	0
OTHER EFTA	0	0	0	0	0	0	0	0	0	0	0	0	0	0	0	0	0	0	0	0
EUROP. COMMUNITY	19	12	4	0	3	6	3	1	0	2	1	1	0	0	0	12	8	3	0	1
FRANCE	6	4	2	0	0	2	1	1	0	0	1	1	0	0	0	3	2	1	0	0
GERMANY	6	4	1	1	0	3	2	0	1	0	0	0	0	0	0	3	2	1	0	0
ITALY	2	2	0	0	0	0	0	0	0	0	0	0	0	0	0	2	2	0	0	0
BELGIUM + LUX	4	1	1	2	0	1	0	0	1	0	0	0	0	0	0	3	1	1	1	0
NETHERLANDS	1	1	0	0	0	0	0	0	0	0	0	0	0	0	0	1	1	0	0	0
SPAIN	3	3	0	0	0	0	0	0	0	0	0	0	0	0	0	3	3	0	0	0
GREECE + TURKEY	1	1	0	0	0	0	0	0	0	0	1	1	0	0	0	0	0	0	0	0
OTHER EUROPE	1	1	0	0	0	0	0	0	0	0	0	0	0	0	0	1	1	0	0	0
EUROPE EX. U.K.	31	20	2	5	4	8	4	1	0	3	3	3	0	0	0	20	13	6	0	1
SOUTHERN DOMINIONS	6	4	2	0	0	0	0	0	0	0	0	0	0	0	0	6	4	2	0	0
S. AFRICA +RHOD.	1	1	0	0	0	0	0	0	0	0	0	0	0	0	0	1	1	0	0	0
AUSTRALIA + N.Z.	5	3	2	0	0	0	0	0	0	0	0	0	0	0	0	5	3	2	0	0
ASIA + OTHER AFRICA	14	8	5	1	0	0	0	0	0	0	0	0	0	0	0	14	8	5	1	0
JAPAN	8	2	5	1	0	0	0	0	0	0	0	0	0	0	0	8	2	5	1	0
OTHER ASIA+AFR.	6	6	0	0	0	0	0	0	0	0	0	0	0	0	0	6	6	0	0	0
BLACK AFRICA	1	1	0	0	0	0	0	0	0	0	0	0	0	0	0	1	1	0	0	0
ARAB WORLD	0	0	0	0	0	0	0	0	0	0	0	0	0	0	0	0	0	0	0	0
INDIA	3	3	0	0	0	0	0	0	0	0	0	0	0	0	0	3	3	0	0	0
PHILIPPINES	1	1	0	0	0	0	0	0	0	0	0	0	0	0	0	1	1	0	0	0
OTHER E. ASIA	1	1	0	0	0	0	0	0	0	0	0	0	0	0	0	1	1	0	0	0
OTHER ASIA	0	0	0	0	0	0	0	0	0	0	0	0	0	0	0	0	0	0	0	0

CHAPTER 4- VARIETIES OF ENTRY
SECTION 4- THE FLOW OF MANUFACTURING BY INDUSTRY OF SUBSIDIARY
TABLE 23- SUBSIDIARIES MANUFACTURING
TIRES (SIC 301)
CLASSIFIED BY COUNTRY, PERIOD MANUFACTURE BEGAN, AND METHOD OF ENTRY

PERIOD AND METHOD OF ENTRY
(NEW=NEWLY FORMED, ACQ=ACQUIRED, DES=DESCENDANT, UNK=UNKNOWN)

COUNTRY OR REGION	TOTAL PRE 1968					PRE 1946					1946-1957					1958-1967				
	ALL	NEW	ACQ	DES	UNK	ALL	NEW	ACQ	DES	UNK	ALL	NEW	ACQ	DES	UNK	ALL	NEW	ACQ	DES	UNK
OUTSIDE U.S.	98	58	26	11	3	42	25	10	5	2	22	12	6	4	0	34	21	10	2	1
OUT. U.S. + CANADA	91	56	24	9	2	36	23	9	3	1	22	12	6	4	0	33	21	9	2	1
OUT. WEST. HEMIS.	58	33	17	7	1	19	11	4	3	1	12	6	4	2	0	27	16	9	2	2
OUT. WHITE CWEALTH	78	49	21	6	2	29	19	8	1	1	20	11	6	3	0	29	19	7	1	1
OUT. DEVLPED WORLD	48	35	7	5	1	21	15	5	1	0	12	7	2	3	0	15	13	0	2	1
CANADA	7	2	2	2	1	6	2	1	2	1	0	0	0	0	0	1	0	1	0	0
LATIN AMERICA	33	23	7	2	1	17	12	2	2	1	10	6	2	1	0	6	5	1	0	0
C. AMER.+CARIB.	13	7	4	1	1	6	3	1	1	1	3	1	1	1	0	4	3	2	0	0
CUBA	3	3	0	0	0	1	1	0	0	0	2	2	0	0	0	0	0	0	0	0
MEXICO	6	4	2	0	0	5	3	2	0	0	0	0	0	0	0	1	1	0	0	0
OTHER	4	3	0	1	0	0	0	0	0	0	1	1	0	0	0	3	2	0	1	0
S. AMERICA	20	16	3	1	0	11	9	2	0	0	7	5	1	1	0	2	2	0	0	0
ARGENTINA	4	3	0	0	0	2	2	0	0	0	2	1	1	0	0	0	0	0	0	0
BRAZIL	5	5	0	0	0	2	2	0	0	0	2	2	0	0	0	1	1	0	0	0
PERU	2	2	0	0	0	2	2	0	0	0	0	0	0	0	0	0	0	0	0	0
COLOMBIA	3	2	1	0	0	1	1	0	0	0	1	0	1	0	0	1	1	0	0	0
VENEZUELA	4	2	1	1	0	2	2	0	0	0	2	0	0	1	0	0	0	0	0	0
OTHER	2	1	1	0	0	1	0	1	0	0	0	0	0	0	0	1	1	0	0	0
EUROPE	31	15	12	3	1	9	4	3	1	1	9	4	4	1	0	13	7	5	1	0
EFTA	10	5	3	2	0	3	3	0	1	0	1	0	1	1	0	4	2	1	1	0
U.K.	4	2	0	2	0	1	1	0	1	0	1	0	0	1	0	2	1	0	0	0
SCANDINAVIA	2	0	2	0	0	0	0	0	0	0	0	0	2	0	0	2	0	0	0	0
SWITZERLAND	1	0	1	0	0	0	0	0	0	0	0	0	1	0	0	1	0	0	0	0
OTHER EFTA	3	3	0	0	0	2	2	0	0	0	1	1	0	0	0	0	0	0	0	0
EUROP. COMMUNITY	16	6	8	1	1	2	2	0	0	0	7	1	4	1	1	7	3	3	1	0
FRANCE	4	2	1	0	1	1	0	1	0	0	1	1	0	0	1	2	2	0	0	0
GERMANY	6	0	6	0	0	1	0	1	0	0	3	0	3	0	0	2	0	2	0	0
ITALY	2	1	1	0	0	0	0	0	0	0	0	0	0	0	0	1	1	0	0	0
BELGIUM + LUX	2	2	0	0	0	0	0	0	0	0	1	1	0	0	0	0	0	0	0	0
NETHERLANDS	2	2	0	0	0	0	0	0	0	0	2	2	0	0	0	0	0	0	0	0
SPAIN	2	2	0	0	0	0	0	0	0	0	1	1	0	0	0	2	2	0	0	0
GREECE + TURKEY	1	0	0	1	0	0	0	0	0	0	0	0	0	0	0	0	0	0	1	0
OTHER EUROPE	2	2	0	0	0	1	1	0	0	0	0	0	0	0	0	2	2	0	0	0
EUROPE EX. U.K.	27	13	12	1	1	7	3	3	0	1	8	4	4	0	0	12	6	5	1	0
SOUTHERN DOMINIONS	9	5	3	1	0	5	3	1	1	0	1	1	0	0	0	3	1	2	0	0
S. AFRICA +RHOD.	3	2	0	1	0	3	1	0	1	0	1	1	0	0	0	0	0	0	0	0
AUSTRALIA + N.Z.	6	3	3	0	0	2	2	0	0	0	0	0	0	0	0	3	1	2	0	0
ASIA + OTHER AFRICA	18	13	2	3	0	5	4	1	1	0	2	1	0	1	0	11	8	1	2	0
JAPAN	3	1	0	2	0	1	1	0	0	0	0	0	0	0	0	2	0	0	2	0
OTHER ASIA+AFR.	15	12	0	3	0	4	3	0	1	0	2	1	0	1	0	9	8	0	2	0
BLACK AFRICA	2	2	0	0	0	0	0	0	0	0	0	0	0	0	0	2	2	0	0	0
ARAB WORLD	2	2	0	0	0	0	0	0	0	0	0	0	0	0	0	2	2	0	0	0
INDIA	2	2	0	1	0	2	0	0	1	0	0	0	0	0	0	1	2	0	0	0
PHILIPPINES	3	2	0	1	0	0	0	0	0	0	1	0	0	1	0	0	0	0	1	0
OTHER E. ASIA	0	0	0	0	0	1	1	0	0	0	0	0	0	0	0	0	0	0	0	0
OTHER ASIA	6	5	0	1	0	0	0	0	1	0	1	1	0	0	0	4	4	0	0	0

CHAPTER 4- VARIETIES OF ENTRY
SECTION 4- THE FLOW OF MANUFACTURING BY INDUSTRY OF SUBSIDIARY
TABLE 24- SUBSIDIARIES MANUFACTURING
OTHER RUBBER PRODUCTS (OTHER SIC 30)
CLASSIFIED BY COUNTRY, PERIOD MANUFACTURE BEGAN, AND METHOD OF ENTRY

PERIOD AND METHOD OF ENTRY
(NEW=NEWLY FORMED, ACQ=ACQUIRED, DES=DESCENDANT, UNK=UNKNOWN)

COUNTRY OR REGION	TOTAL PRE 1968					PRE 1946					1946-1957					1958-1967				
	ALL	NEW	ACQ	DES	UNK	ALL	NEW	ACQ	DES	UNK	ALL	NEW	ACQ	DES	UNK	ALL	NEW	ACQ	DES	UNK
OUTSIDE U.S.	88	38	31	9	8	29	16	3	5	5	17	6	8	2	1	40	16	20	2	2
OUT. U.S. + CANADA	75	37	25	8	4	25	16	3	4	2	13	6	4	2	1	36	15	18	2	1
OUT. WEST. HEMIS.	47	18	20	6	3	14	8	2	3	1	5	1	2	1	1	28	9	16	2	1
OUT. WHITE CMWEALTH	53	29	16	4	3	16	11	2	2	1	12	6	4	1	1	24	12	10	1	1
OUT. DEVLPED WORLD	34	20	8	4	1	12	8	1	2	1	8	5	2	1	0	13	7	5	1	0
CANADA	13	1	6	2	4	4	0	0	3	1	4	0	4	0	0	4	1	2	1	0
LATIN AMERICA	28	19	5	2	1	11	8	1	1	1	8	5	2	1	0	8	6	2	0	0
C. AMER.+CARIB.	13	6	4	2	1	5	2	1	1	1	5	2	2	1	0	3	2	1	0	0
CUBA	2	0	0	1	1	1	0	0	0	1	1	0	0	1	0	0	0	0	0	0
MEXICO	9	4	4	1	0	4	2	1	1	0	3	1	2	0	0	2	1	1	0	0
OTHER	2	2	0	0	0	0	0	0	0	0	1	1	0	0	0	1	1	0	0	0
S. AMERICA	15	13	1	0	0	6	6	0	0	0	3	3	0	0	0	5	4	1	0	0
ARGENTINA	3	1	1	0	0	1	1	0	0	0	1	1	0	0	0	1	1	0	0	0
BRAZIL	4	4	0	0	0	1	1	0	0	0	1	0	1	0	0	2	2	0	0	0
PERU	2	2	0	0	0	1	1	0	0	0	0	0	0	0	0	1	1	0	0	0
COLOMBIA	1	1	0	0	0	1	1	0	0	0	0	0	0	0	0	0	0	0	0	0
VENEZUELA	5	5	0	0	0	2	2	0	0	0	1	1	0	0	0	2	2	0	0	0
OTHER	0	0	0	0	0	0	0	0	0	0	0	0	0	0	0	0	0	0	0	0
EUROPE	28	11	12	2	3	8	5	1	1	1	4	1	1	1	1	16	5	10	0	1
EFTA	11	3	4	2	2	5	3	1	1	0	1	1	0	0	0	5	0	4	0	1
U.K.	8	2	3	2	1	4	2	0	1	1	1	1	0	0	0	3	0	3	1	0
SCANDINAVIA	3	1	1	0	1	1	1	0	0	0	0	0	0	0	0	2	0	1	0	1
SWITZERLAND	0	0	0	0	0	0	0	0	0	0	0	0	0	0	0	0	0	0	0	0
OTHER EFTA	0	0	0	0	0	0	0	0	0	0	0	0	0	0	0	0	0	0	0	0
EUROP. COMMUNITY	9	3	5	0	1	2	1	1	0	0	2	0	2	0	0	5	2	3	0	0
FRANCE	2	2	0	0	0	1	1	0	0	0	0	0	0	0	0	1	1	0	0	0
GERMANY	3	2	0	0	1	1	0	0	0	1	0	0	0	0	0	2	2	0	0	0
ITALY	2	0	2	0	0	1	0	1	0	0	0	0	0	0	0	1	0	1	0	0
BELGIUM + LUX	0	0	0	0	0	0	0	0	0	0	0	0	0	0	0	0	0	0	0	0
NETHERLANDS	2	1	0	0	1	0	0	0	0	0	0	0	0	0	0	2	1	0	1	1
SPAIN	4	0	2	0	0	0	0	0	0	0	1	0	1	0	0	3	0	2	0	1
GREECE + TURKEY	0	3	0	0	0	0	0	0	0	0	0	0	0	0	0	0	0	0	0	0
OTHER EUROPE	4	2	2	0	0	1	1	0	0	0	1	0	1	0	0	3	1	2	0	0
EUROPE EX. U.K.	20	9	9	0	2	4	3	1	0	0	3	1	1	0	1	13	5	7	0	1
SOUTHERN DOMINIONS	10	4	4	2	0	4	1	0	2	1	0	0	0	0	0	6	2	3	1	1
S. AFRICA +RHOD.	3	1	0	2	0	1	0	0	1	0	0	0	0	0	0	2	1	1	0	1
AUSTRALIA + N.Z.	7	3	4	0	0	3	1	0	1	1	0	0	0	0	0	4	1	3	0	0
ASIA + OTHER AFRICA	9	4	4	2	0	2	0	2	1	0	2	1	0	1	0	6	2	3	0	1
JAPAN	3	2	1	0	0	1	1	0	0	0	1	1	0	0	0	3	1	3	0	0
OTHER ASIA+AFR.	6	1	0	1	0	1	0	1	0	0	1	0	0	0	0	3	1	3	0	0
BLACK AFRICA	1	1	1	0	0	1	1	0	0	0	0	0	0	0	0	1	0	1	0	0
ARAB WORLD	2	1	1	0	0	0	0	0	0	0	1	1	0	0	0	1	0	1	0	0
INDIA	1	0	0	1	0	0	0	0	0	0	0	0	0	0	0	1	0	0	1	0
PHILIPPINES	0	0	0	0	0	0	0	0	0	0	0	0	0	0	0	0	0	0	0	0
OTHER E. ASIA	1	0	0	1	0	0	0	0	0	0	0	0	0	0	0	1	0	1	0	0
OTHER ASIA	1	1	0	0	1	1	1	0	0	1	0	0	0	0	0	0	0	0	0	0

CHAPTER 4-- VARIETIES OF ENTRY
SECTION 4-- THE FLOW OF MANUFACTURING BY INDUSTRY OF SUBSIDIARY
TABLE 25-- SUBSIDIARIES MANUFACTURING
GLASS PRODUCTS (SIC 321-323)
CLASSIFIED BY COUNTRY, PERIOD MANUFACTURE BEGAN, AND METHOD OF ENTRY

PERIOD AND METHOD OF ENTRY
(NEW=NEWLY FORMED, ACQ=ACQUIRED, DES=DESCENDANT, UNK=UNKNOWN)

COUNTRY OR REGION	TOTAL PRE 1968					PRE 1946					1946-1957					1958-1967				
	ALL	NEW	ACQ	DES	UNK	ALL	NEW	ACQ	DES	UNK	ALL	NEW	ACQ	DES	UNK	ALL	NEW	ACQ	DES	UNK
OUTSIDE U.S.	53	18	33	0	2	13	2	9	0	2	8	4	4	0	0	32	12	20	0	0
OUT. U.S. + CANADA	48	15	32	0	1	10	1	8	0	1	7	3	4	0	0	31	11	20	0	0
OUT. WEST. HEMIS.	26	9	16	0	1	4	1	2	0	1	2	1	1	0	0	20	7	13	0	0
OUT. WHITE CWEALTH	39	14	24	0	1	10	1	8	0	1	6	3	3	0	0	23	10	13	0	0
OUT. DEVLPED WORLD	24	8	16	0	0	7	1	6	0	0	5	2	3	0	0	12	5	7	0	0
CANADA	5	3	1	0	1	3	1	1	0	1	1	1	0	0	0	1	1	0	0	0
LATIN AMERICA	22	6	16	0	0	6	0	6	0	0	5	2	3	0	0	11	4	7	0	0
C. AMER.+CARIB.	5	1	4	0	0	0	0	0	0	0	2	1	1	0	0	3	0	3	0	0
CUBA	1	1	0	0	0	0	0	0	0	0	1	1	0	0	0	0	0	0	0	0
MEXICO	4	0	4	0	0	0	0	0	0	0	1	0	1	0	0	3	0	3	0	0
OTHER	0	0	0	0	0	0	0	0	0	0	0	0	0	0	0	0	0	0	0	0
S. AMERICA	17	5	12	0	0	6	0	6	0	0	3	1	2	0	0	8	4	4	0	0
ARGENTINA	1	0	1	0	0	0	0	0	0	0	1	0	1	0	0	0	0	0	0	0
BRAZIL	5	0	5	0	0	4	0	4	0	0	0	0	0	0	0	1	0	1	0	0
PERU	0	0	0	0	0	0	0	0	0	0	0	0	0	0	0	0	0	0	0	0
COLOMBIA	4	1	3	0	0	0	0	0	0	0	1	1	0	0	0	3	0	3	0	0
VENEZUELA	5	4	1	0	0	0	0	0	0	0	1	0	1	0	0	4	4	0	0	0
OTHER	2	0	2	0	0	2	0	2	0	0	0	0	0	0	0	0	0	0	0	0
EUROPE	17	4	12	0	1	3	0	2	0	1	2	1	1	0	0	12	3	9	0	0
EFTA	5	0	5	0	0	0	0	0	0	0	1	0	1	0	0	4	0	4	0	0
U.K.	5	0	5	0	0	0	0	0	0	0	1	0	1	0	0	4	0	4	0	0
SCANDINAVIA	0	0	0	0	0	0	0	0	0	0	0	0	0	0	0	0	0	0	0	0
SWITZERLAND	0	0	0	0	0	0	0	0	0	0	0	0	0	0	0	0	0	0	0	0
OTHER EFTA	0	0	0	0	0	0	0	0	0	0	0	0	0	0	0	0	0	0	0	0
EUROP. COMMUNITY	11	4	6	0	1	3	0	2	0	1	1	1	0	0	0	7	3	4	0	0
FRANCE	2	1	0	0	1	1	0	0	0	1	1	1	0	0	0	0	0	0	0	0
GERMANY	4	3	1	0	0	0	0	0	0	0	0	0	0	0	0	4	3	1	0	0
ITALY	3	0	3	0	0	0	0	0	0	0	0	0	0	0	0	3	0	3	0	0
BELGIUM + LUX	2	0	2	0	0	2	0	2	0	0	0	0	0	0	0	0	0	0	0	0
NETHERLANDS	0	0	0	0	0	0	0	0	0	0	0	0	0	0	0	0	0	0	0	0
SPAIN	1	0	1	0	0	0	0	0	0	0	0	0	0	0	0	1	0	1	0	0
GREECE + TURKEY	0	0	0	0	0	0	0	0	0	0	0	0	0	0	0	0	0	0	0	0
OTHER EUROPE	0	0	0	0	0	0	0	0	0	0	0	0	0	0	0	0	0	0	0	0
EUROPE EX. U.K.	12	4	7	0	1	3	0	2	0	1	1	1	0	0	0	8	3	5	0	0
SOUTHERN DOMINIONS	4	1	3	0	0	0	0	0	0	0	0	0	0	0	0	4	1	3	0	0
S. AFRICA +RHOD.	2	1	1	0	0	0	0	0	0	0	0	0	0	0	0	2	1	1	0	0
AUSTRALIA + N.Z.	2	0	2	0	0	0	0	0	0	0	0	0	0	0	0	2	0	2	0	0
ASIA + OTHER AFRICA	5	4	1	0	0	1	1	0	0	0	0	0	0	0	0	4	3	1	0	0
JAPAN	3	2	1	0	0	0	0	0	0	0	0	0	0	0	0	3	2	1	0	0
OTHER ASIA+AFR.	2	2	0	0	0	1	1	0	0	0	0	0	0	0	0	1	1	0	0	0
BLACK AFRICA	0	0	0	0	0	0	0	0	0	0	0	0	0	0	0	0	0	0	0	0
ARAB WORLD	0	0	0	0	0	0	0	0	0	0	0	0	0	0	0	0	0	0	0	0
INDIA	1	1	0	0	0	0	0	0	0	0	0	0	0	0	0	1	1	0	0	0
PHILIPPINES	0	0	0	0	0	0	0	0	0	0	0	0	0	0	0	0	0	0	0	0
OTHER E. ASIA	1	1	0	0	0	1	1	0	0	0	0	0	0	0	0	0	0	0	0	0
OTHER ASIA	0	0	0	0	0	0	0	0	0	0	0	0	0	0	0	0	0	0	0	0

CHAPTER 4- VARIETIES OF ENTRY

SECTION 4- THE FLOW OF MANUFACTURING BY INDUSTRY OF SUBSIDIARY

TABLE 26- SUBSIDIARIES MANUFACTURING
STONE, CLAY, AND CONCRETE PRODUCTS (SIC 324-329)
CLASSIFIED BY COUNTRY, PERIOD MANUFACTURE BEGAN, AND METHOD OF ENTRY

PERIOD AND METHOD OF ENTRY
(NEW=NEWLY FORMED, ACQ=ACQUIRED, DES=DESCENDANT, UNK=UNKNOWN)

COUNTRY OR REGION	TOTAL PRE 1968					PRE 1946					1946-1957					1958-1967				
	ALL	NEW	ACQ	DES	UNK	ALL	NEW	ACQ	DES	UNK	ALL	NEW	ACQ	DES	UNK	ALL	NEW	ACQ	DES	UNK
OUTSIDE U.S.	132	67	55	4	5	20	12	7	0	1	42	24	16	0	2	69	31	32	4	2
OUT. U.S. + CANADA	119	59	50	4	5	17	9	7	0	1	36	21	13	0	2	65	29	30	4	2
OUT. WEST. HEMIS.	86	45	35	3	2	14	9	5	0	0	19	12	6	0	1	52	24	24	3	1
OUT. WHITE CWEALTH	88	41	39	2	5	9	3	5	0	1	29	14	13	0	2	49	24	21	2	2
OUT. DEVLPED WORLD	42	18	19	1	3	3	0	2	0	1	18	10	7	0	1	20	8	10	1	1
CANADA	13	8	5	0	0	3	3	0	0	0	6	3	3	0	0	4	2	2	0	0
LATIN AMERICA	33	14	15	1	3	3	3	0	0	0	17	9	6	1	1	13	2	9	0	2
C. AMER.+CARIB.	12	6	6	0	0	1	0	1	0	0	5	3	2	0	0	6	3	3	0	0
CUBA	0	0	0	0	0	0	0	0	0	0	0	0	0	0	0	0	0	0	0	0
MEXICO	12	6	6	0	0	1	0	1	0	0	5	3	2	0	0	6	3	3	0	0
OTHER	0	0	0	0	0	0	0	0	0	0	0	0	0	0	0	0	0	0	0	0
S. AMERICA	21	8	9	1	3	2	2	0	0	0	12	6	5	0	1	7	2	3	1	1
ARGENTINA	5	1	3	0	1	2	2	0	0	0	2	1	1	0	0	1	0	1	0	1
BRAZIL	7	4	3	0	0	0	0	0	0	0	6	3	3	0	0	1	1	0	0	0
PERU	1	1	0	0	0	0	0	0	0	0	1	1	0	0	0	0	0	0	0	0
COLOMBIA	1	0	1	0	0	0	0	0	0	0	0	0	0	0	0	1	0	1	0	0
VENEZUELA	2	1	1	0	0	0	0	0	0	0	1	0	1	0	0	1	1	0	0	0
OTHER	5	1	2	1	2	0	0	0	0	0	2	1	0	0	1	3	0	2	1	1
EUROPE	55	27	25	1	2	11	6	5	0	0	14	7	6	0	1	30	14	14	1	1
EFTA	15	8	7	0	0	6	3	3	0	0	2	2	0	0	0	7	3	4	0	0
U.K.	12	6	6	0	0	5	3	2	0	0	2	2	0	0	0	5	1	4	0	0
SCANDINAVIA	3	2	1	0	0	1	0	1	0	0	0	0	0	0	0	2	2	0	0	0
SWITZERLAND	0	0	0	0	0	0	0	0	0	0	0	0	0	0	0	0	0	0	0	0
OTHER EFTA	0	0	0	0	0	0	0	0	0	0	0	0	0	0	0	0	0	0	0	0
EUROP. COMMUNITY	33	15	16	0	2	5	3	2	0	0	11	4	6	0	1	17	8	8	0	1
FRANCE	17	9	7	0	1	2	1	1	0	0	5	2	2	0	1	10	6	4	0	0
GERMANY	6	3	3	0	0	2	2	0	0	0	3	1	2	0	0	1	0	1	0	0
ITALY	3	1	1	0	1	0	0	0	0	0	1	1	0	0	0	2	0	1	0	1
BELGIUM + LUX	6	1	5	0	0	1	1	0	0	0	2	0	2	0	0	3	0	3	0	0
NETHERLANDS	1	1	0	0	0	0	0	0	0	0	0	0	0	0	0	1	1	0	0	0
SPAIN	3	1	2	0	0	0	0	0	0	0	2	0	2	0	0	1	1	0	0	0
GREECE + TURKEY	1	1	0	0	0	0	0	0	0	0	0	0	0	0	0	1	1	0	0	0
OTHER EUROPE	3	2	0	0	1	0	0	0	0	0	1	1	0	0	0	2	1	0	0	1
EUROPE EX. U.K.	43	21	19	1	2	6	3	3	0	0	12	5	6	0	1	25	13	10	1	1
SOUTHERN DOMINIONS	17	11	5	1	0	3	3	0	0	0	4	4	0	0	0	10	4	5	1	0
S. AFRICA +RHOD.	5	4	1	0	0	0	0	0	0	0	3	3	0	0	0	2	1	1	0	0
AUSTRALIA + N.Z.	12	7	4	0	1	3	3	0	0	0	1	1	0	0	0	8	3	4	1	1
ASIA + OTHER AFRICA	14	7	5	1	1	0	0	0	0	0	1	1	0	0	0	13	6	5	1	1
JAPAN	5	3	1	0	1	0	0	0	0	0	1	1	0	0	0	4	2	1	0	1
OTHER ASIA+AFR.	9	4	4	1	0	0	0	0	0	0	0	0	0	0	0	9	4	4	1	0
BLACK AFRICA	1	1	0	0	0	0	0	0	0	0	0	0	0	0	0	1	1	0	0	0
ARAB WORLD	1	0	1	0	0	0	0	0	0	0	0	0	0	0	0	1	0	1	0	0
INDIA	4	2	1	0	1	0	0	0	0	0	0	0	0	0	0	4	2	1	0	1
PHILIPPINES	1	1	0	0	0	0	0	0	0	0	0	0	0	0	0	1	1	0	0	0
OTHER E. ASIA	0	0	0	0	0	0	0	0	0	0	0	0	0	0	0	0	0	0	0	0
OTHER ASIA	2	1	0	0	1	0	0	0	0	0	0	0	0	0	0	2	1	0	0	1

CHAPTER 4— VARIETIES OF ENTRY
SECTION 4— THE FLOW OF MANUFACTURING BY INDUSTRY OF SUBSIDIARY
TABLE 27— SUBSIDIARIES MANUFACTURING
SMELTED AND REFINED NONFERROUS METALS (SIC 333)
CLASSIFIED BY COUNTRY, PERIOD MANUFACTURE BEGAN, AND METHOD OF ENTRY

(NEW=NEWLY FORMED, ACQ=ACQUIRED, DES=DESCENDANT, UNK=UNKNOWN)

PERIOD AND METHOD OF ENTRY

COUNTRY OR REGION	TOTAL PRE 1968					PRE 1946					1946-1957					1958-1967				
	ALL	NEW	ACQ	DES	UNK	ALL	NEW	ACQ	DES	UNK	ALL	NEW	ACQ	DES	UNK	ALL	NEW	ACQ	DES	UNK
OUTSIDE U.S.	66	32	26	1	7	18	10	3	1	4	7	5	1	0	1	41	17	22	0	2
OUT. U.S. + CANADA	51	26	21	1	3	11	6	3	1	1	5	4	1	0	0	35	16	17	0	2
OUT. WEST. HEMIS.	38	17	17	1	3	4	1	1	1	1	3	3	0	0	0	31	13	16	0	2
OUT. WHITE CWEALTH	32	20	11	0	1	8	5	2	0	1	3	2	1	0	0	21	13	8	0	0
OUT. DEVLPED WORLD	19	14	5	0	0	7	5	2	0	0	3	2	1	0	0	9	7	2	0	0
CANADA																				
LATIN AMERICA	15	6	5	0	4	7	4	0	3	0	2	1	0	0	1	6	1	5	0	0
C. AMER.+CARIB.	13	9	4	0	0	7	5	2	0	0	2	1	1	0	0	4	3	1	0	0
CUBA	4	3	1	0	0	3	3	0	0	0	0	0	0	0	0	1	0	1	0	0
MEXICO	0	0	0	0	0	0	0	0	0	0	0	0	0	0	0	0	0	0	0	0
OTHER	4	3	1	0	0	3	2	1	0	0	0	0	0	0	0	1	1	0	0	0
S. AMERICA	3	1	2	0	0	0	0	0	0	0	0	0	0	0	0	3	2	1	0	0
ARGENTINA	2	2	0	0	0	0	0	0	0	0	1	1	0	0	0	1	1	0	0	0
BRAZIL	2	2	0	0	0	1	1	0	0	0	0	0	0	0	0	1	1	0	0	0
PERU	1	1	0	0	0	0	0	0	0	0	1	1	0	0	0	0	0	0	0	0
COLOMBIA	1	1	0	0	0	0	0	0	0	0	0	0	0	0	0	1	1	0	0	0
VENEZUELA	1	1	0	0	0	0	0	0	0	0	1	1	0	0	0	0	0	0	0	0
OTHER	1	0	1	0	0	0	0	0	0	0	1	0	1	0	0	0	0	0	0	0
EUROPE	20	7	10	1	2	2	1	0	1	0	2	2	0	0	0	16	5	10	0	1
EFTA	14	4	8	1	1	1	1	0	1	0	2	2	0	0	0	11	2	8	0	1
U.K.	9	2	5	1	1	1	1	0	1	0	2	2	0	0	0	6	1	5	0	0
SCANDINAVIA	3	1	2	0	0	0	0	0	0	0	0	0	0	0	0	3	1	2	0	0
SWITZERLAND	2	1	1	0	0	0	0	0	0	0	0	0	0	0	0	2	1	1	0	0
OTHER EFTA	0	0	0	0	0	0	0	0	0	0	0	0	0	0	0	0	0	0	0	0
EUROP. COMMUNITY	5	3	1	0	1	1	0	0	0	1	0	0	0	0	0	4	3	1	0	0
FRANCE	0	0	0	0	0	0	0	0	0	0	0	0	0	0	0	0	0	0	0	0
GERMANY	3	2	1	0	0	0	0	0	0	0	0	0	0	0	0	3	2	1	0	0
ITALY	0	0	0	0	0	0	0	0	0	0	0	0	0	0	0	0	0	0	0	0
BELGIUM + LUX	2	0	1	0	1	1	0	0	0	1	0	0	0	0	0	1	1	0	0	0
NETHERLANDS	0	0	0	0	0	0	0	0	0	0	0	0	0	0	0	0	0	0	0	0
SPAIN	1	0	1	0	0	0	0	0	0	0	0	0	0	0	0	1	1	0	0	0
GREECE + TURKEY	0	0	0	0	0	0	0	0	0	0	0	0	0	0	0	0	0	0	0	0
OTHER EUROPE	0	0	0	0	0	0	0	0	0	0	0	0	0	0	0	0	0	0	0	0
EUROPE EX. U.K.	11	5	5	0	1	1	1	0	0	0	0	0	0	0	0	10	5	5	0	1
SOUTHERN DOMINIONS	10	4	5	0	1	2	1	1	0	0	0	0	0	0	0	8	3	4	0	1
S. AFRICA +RHOD.	3	1	1	0	1	1	1	0	0	0	0	0	0	0	0	2	2	0	0	1
AUSTRALIA + N.Z.	7	3	4	0	0	1	0	1	0	0	0	0	0	0	0	6	3	3	0	0
ASIA + OTHER AFRICA	8	6	2	0	0	0	0	0	0	0	1	1	0	0	0	7	5	2	0	0
JAPAN	2	1	1	0	0	0	0	0	0	0	0	0	0	0	0	2	1	1	0	0
OTHER ASIA+AFR.	6	5	1	0	0	0	0	0	0	0	1	1	0	0	0	5	4	1	0	0
BLACK AFRICA	2	2	0	0	0	0	0	0	0	0	1	1	0	0	0	1	1	0	0	0
ARAB WORLD	2	2	0	0	0	0	0	0	0	0	1	1	0	0	0	1	1	0	0	0
INDIA	1	0	1	0	0	0	0	0	0	0	0	0	0	0	0	1	0	1	0	0
PHILIPPINES	0	0	0	0	0	0	0	0	0	0	0	0	0	0	0	0	0	0	0	0
OTHER E. ASIA	0	0	0	0	0	0	0	0	0	0	0	0	0	0	0	0	0	0	0	0
OTHER ASIA	3	2	1	0	0	0	0	0	0	0	0	0	0	0	0	3	2	1	0	0

CHAPTER 4- VARIETIES OF ENTRY
SECTION 4- THE FLOW OF MANUFACTURING BY INDUSTRY OF SUBSIDIARY
TABLE 28- SUBSIDIARIES MANUFACTURING
OTHER NONFERROUS METAL PRODUCTS (SIC 334-336)
CLASSIFIED BY COUNTRY, PERIOD MANUFACTURE BEGAN, AND METHOD OF ENTRY

PERIOD AND METHOD OF ENTRY
(NEW=NEWLY FORMED, ACQ=ACQUIRED, DES=DESCENDANT, UNK=UNKNOWN)

COUNTRY OR REGION	TOTAL					PRE 1946					1946-1957					1958-1967				
	ALL	NEW	ACQ	PRE 1968 DES	UNK	ALL	NEW	ACQ	DES	UNK	ALL	NEW	ACQ	DES	UNK	ALL	NEW	ACQ	DES	UNK
OUTSIDE U.S.	54	24	22	2	5	5	1	1	0	3	10	5	4	0	1	38	18	17	2	1
OUT. U.S. + CANADA	38	21	13	1	2	1	1	0	0	1	3	3	0	0	0	33	18	13	1	1
OUT. WEST. HEMIS.	27	13	10	1	1	1	0	0	0	1	2	2	0	0	0	23	11	10	1	1
OUT. WHITE CWEALTH	26	17	8	1	0	1	0	0	0	1	2	2	0	0	0	23	15	8	0	0
OUT. DEVLPED WORLD	14	10	4	0	0	0	0	0	0	0	1	1	0	0	0	13	9	4	0	0
CANADA	16	3	9	1	3	4	1	1	0	2	7	2	4	0	1	5	0	4	1	0
LATIN AMERICA	11	8	3	0	0	0	0	0	0	0	1	1	0	0	0	10	7	3	0	0
C. AMER.+CARIB.	5	4	1	0	0	0	0	0	0	0	1	1	0	0	0	4	3	1	0	0
CUBA	0	0	0	0	0	0	0	0	0	0	0	0	0	0	0	0	0	0	0	0
MEXICO	4	3	1	0	0	0	0	0	0	0	1	1	0	0	0	3	2	1	0	0
OTHER	1	1	0	0	0	0	0	0	0	0	0	0	0	0	0	1	1	0	0	0
S. AMERICA	6	4	2	0	0	0	0	0	0	0	0	0	0	0	0	6	4	2	0	0
ARGENTINA	2	1	1	0	0	0	0	0	0	0	0	0	0	0	0	2	1	1	0	0
BRAZIL	1	1	0	0	0	0	0	0	0	0	0	0	0	0	0	1	1	0	0	0
PERU	0	0	0	0	0	0	0	0	0	0	0	0	0	0	0	0	0	0	0	0
COLOMBIA	1	0	0	1	0	0	0	0	0	0	0	0	0	0	0	1	0	0	1	0
VENEZUELA	2	2	0	0	0	0	0	0	0	0	0	0	0	0	0	2	2	0	0	0
OTHER	0	0	0	0	0	0	0	0	0	0	0	0	0	0	0	0	0	0	0	0
EUROPE	17	8	7	0	1	1	0	0	0	1	2	2	0	0	0	13	6	7	0	0
EFTA	10	4	4	0	1	1	0	0	0	1	1	1	0	0	0	7	3	4	0	0
U.K.	7	3	3	0	1	1	0	0	0	1	1	1	0	0	0	5	2	3	0	0
SCANDINAVIA	1	0	1	0	0	0	0	0	0	0	0	0	0	0	0	1	0	1	0	0
SWITZERLAND	2	1	1	0	0	0	0	0	0	0	0	0	0	0	0	2	1	1	0	0
OTHER EFTA	0	0	0	0	0	0	0	0	0	0	0	0	0	0	0	0	0	0	0	0
EUROP. COMMUNITY	6	3	3	0	0	0	0	0	0	0	0	0	0	0	0	6	3	3	0	0
FRANCE	0	0	0	0	0	0	0	0	0	0	0	0	0	0	0	0	0	0	0	0
GERMANY	1	0	1	0	0	0	0	0	0	0	0	0	0	0	0	1	0	1	0	0
ITALY	1	1	0	0	0	0	0	0	0	0	0	0	0	0	0	1	1	0	0	0
BELGIUM + LUX	2	1	1	0	0	0	0	0	0	0	0	0	0	0	0	2	1	1	0	0
NETHERLANDS	2	1	1	0	0	0	0	0	0	0	0	0	0	0	0	2	1	1	0	0
SPAIN	0	0	0	0	0	0	0	0	0	0	0	0	0	0	0	0	0	0	0	0
GREECE + TURKEY	1	1	0	0	0	0	0	0	0	0	1	1	0	0	0	0	0	0	0	0
OTHER EUROPE	0	0	0	0	0	0	0	0	0	0	0	0	0	0	0	0	0	0	0	0
EUROPE EX. U.K.	10	5	4	0	1	0	0	0	0	0	1	1	0	0	0	8	4	4	0	0
SOUTHERN DOMINIONS	5	1	2	1	1	0	0	0	0	0	0	0	0	0	0	5	1	2	1	1
S. AFRICA +RHOD.	0	0	0	0	0	0	0	0	0	0	0	0	0	0	0	0	0	0	0	0
AUSTRALIA + N.Z.	5	1	2	1	1	0	0	0	0	0	0	0	0	0	0	5	1	2	1	1
ASIA + OTHER AFRICA	5	4	1	0	0	0	0	0	0	0	0	0	0	0	0	5	4	1	0	0
JAPAN	2	2	0	0	0	0	0	0	0	0	0	0	0	0	0	2	2	0	0	0
OTHER ASIA+AFR.	3	2	1	0	0	0	0	0	0	0	0	0	0	0	0	3	2	1	0	0
BLACK AFRICA	0	0	0	0	0	0	0	0	0	0	0	0	0	0	0	0	0	0	0	0
ARAB WORLD	2	2	0	0	0	0	0	0	0	0	0	0	0	0	0	2	2	0	0	0
INDIA	1	0	1	0	0	0	0	0	0	0	0	0	0	0	0	1	0	1	0	0
PHILIPPINES	0	0	0	0	0	0	0	0	0	0	0	0	0	0	0	0	0	0	0	0
OTHER E. ASIA	0	0	0	0	0	0	0	0	0	0	0	0	0	0	0	0	0	0	0	0
OTHER ASIA	0	0	0	0	0	0	0	0	0	0	0	0	0	0	0	0	0	0	0	0

CHAPTER 4- VARIETIES OF ENTRY
SECTION 4- THE FLOW OF MANUFACTURING BY INDUSTRY OF SUBSIDIARY
TABLE 29- SUBSIDIARIES MANUFACTURING
IRON, STEEL AND MISCELLANEOUS NONFERROUS PRODUCTS (SIC 331,332, AND 339)
CLASSIFIED BY COUNTRY, PERIOD MANUFACTURE BEGAN, AND METHOD OF ENTRY

PERIOD AND METHOD OF ENTRY
(NEW=NEWLY FORMED, ACQ=ACQUIRED, DES=DESCENDANT, UNK=UNKNOWN)

COUNTRY OR REGION	TOTAL PRE 1968					PRE 1946					1946-1957					1958-1967				
	ALL	NEW	ACQ	DES	UNK	ALL	NEW	ACQ	DES	UNK	ALL	NEW	ACQ	DES	UNK	ALL	NEW	ACQ	DES	UNK
OUTSIDE U.S.	57	22	21	3	6	11	7	1	0	3	7	3	3	1	0	34	12	17	2	3
OUT. U.S. + CANADA	47	17	16	3	6	7	4	0	0	3	4	1	2	1	0	31	12	14	2	3
OUT. WEST. HEMIS.	35	10	13	1	6	6	3	0	0	3	4	0	2	2	0	24	7	13	1	3
OUT. WHITE CWEALTH	31	13	9	3	4	4	3	0	0	1	4	1	2	1	0	21	9	7	2	3
OUT. DEVLPED WORLD	15	9	3	2	1	1	1	0	0	0	4	4	0	2	0	10	7	1	1	1
CANADA	10	5	5	0	0	4	3	1	0	0	3	2	2	1	0	3	0	3	1	0
LATIN AMERICA	12	7	2	2	0	1	1	0	0	0	4	1	1	1	0	7	5	1	1	0
C. AMER.+CARIB.	3	2	0	1	0	0	0	0	0	0	1	1	0	0	0	2	1	0	1	0
CUBA	0	0	0	0	0	0	0	0	0	0	0	0	0	0	0	0	0	0	0	0
MEXICO	3	2	0	1	0	0	0	0	0	0	1	1	0	0	0	2	1	0	1	0
OTHER	0	0	0	0	0	0	0	0	0	0	0	0	0	0	0	0	0	0	0	0
S. AMERICA	9	5	3	1	0	0	0	0	0	0	4	0	2	1	0	5	4	1	0	0
ARGENTINA	1	0	1	0	0	0	0	0	0	0	0	0	0	0	0	1	0	1	0	0
BRAZIL	5	4	1	0	0	0	0	0	0	0	2	0	1	0	0	3	3	0	0	0
PERU	0	0	0	0	0	0	0	0	0	0	0	0	0	0	0	0	0	0	0	0
COLOMBIA	1	0	0	1	0	0	0	0	0	0	1	0	1	0	0	0	0	0	0	0
VENEZUELA	0	0	0	0	0	0	0	0	0	0	0	0	0	0	0	0	0	0	0	0
OTHER	2	1	1	0	0	0	0	0	0	0	1	0	0	1	0	1	1	0	0	0
EUROPE	27	5	11	1	5	5	2	0	0	3	0	0	0	0	0	17	3	11	1	2
EFTA	12	2	5	1	2	2	2	0	0	2	0	0	0	0	0	7	2	5	0	0
U.K.	12	2	5	1	2	2	2	0	0	2	0	0	0	0	0	7	2	5	0	0
SCANDINAVIA	0	0	0	0	0	0	0	0	0	0	0	0	0	0	0	0	0	0	0	0
SWITZERLAND	0	0	0	0	0	0	0	0	0	0	0	0	0	0	0	0	0	0	0	0
OTHER EFTA	0	0	0	0	0	0	0	0	0	0	0	0	0	0	0	0	0	0	0	0
EUROP. COMMUNITY	13	2	5	1	3	3	2	0	0	1	0	0	0	0	0	8	2	5	1	0
FRANCE	5	1	2	0	1	2	1	0	0	1	0	0	0	0	0	2	1	1	0	0
GERMANY	2	1	0	0	1	1	1	0	0	0	0	0	0	0	0	2	2	0	0	0
ITALY	2	0	1	0	1	1	0	0	0	1	0	0	0	0	0	1	0	1	0	1
BELGIUM + LUX	1	0	1	0	0	0	0	0	0	0	0	0	0	0	0	1	0	1	0	0
NETHERLANDS	3	0	1	1	0	1	0	0	0	0	0	0	0	0	0	2	0	1	1	0
SPAIN	0	0	0	0	0	0	0	0	0	0	0	0	0	0	0	0	0	0	0	0
GREECE + TURKEY	2	1	1	0	1	0	0	0	0	0	0	0	0	0	0	2	1	1	0	1
OTHER EUROPE	0	0	0	0	0	0	0	0	0	0	0	0	0	0	0	0	0	0	0	0
EUROPE EX. U.K.	15	3	6	1	3	3	0	0	0	1	0	0	0	0	0	10	1	6	1	2
SOUTHERN DOMINIONS	4	2	2	0	0	1	1	0	0	0	0	0	0	0	0	3	1	2	0	0
S. AFRICA +RHOD.	1	1	1	0	0	0	0	0	0	0	0	0	0	0	0	1	0	1	0	0
AUSTRALIA + N.Z.	3	2	1	0	0	1	1	0	0	0	0	0	0	0	0	2	1	1	0	0
ASIA + OTHER AFRICA	4	3	0	1	0	0	0	0	0	0	0	0	0	0	0	4	3	1	0	0
JAPAN	1	1	0	0	0	0	0	0	0	0	0	0	0	0	0	1	1	0	0	0
OTHER ASIA+AFR.	3	2	0	1	0	0	0	0	0	0	0	0	0	0	0	3	2	1	0	0
BLACK AFRICA	1	1	0	0	0	0	0	0	0	0	0	0	0	0	0	1	1	0	0	0
ARAB WORLD	0	0	0	0	0	0	0	0	0	0	0	0	0	0	0	0	0	0	0	0
INDIA	1	1	0	0	0	0	0	0	0	0	0	0	0	0	0	1	0	1	0	0
PHILIPPINES	1	0	0	1	0	0	0	0	0	0	1	0	0	1	0	0	0	0	0	0
OTHER E. ASIA	0	0	0	0	0	0	0	0	0	0	0	0	0	0	0	0	0	0	0	0
OTHER ASIA	1	0	0	0	1	0	0	0	0	0	0	0	0	0	0	1	0	0	0	1

CHAPTER 4- VARIETIES OF ENTRY
SECTION 4- THE FLOW OF MANUFACTURING BY INDUSTRY OF SUBSIDIARY
TABLE 30- SUBSIDIARIES MANUFACTURING
METAL CANS (SIC 341)
CLASSIFIED BY COUNTRY, PERIOD MANUFACTURE BEGAN, AND METHOD OF ENTRY

(NEW=NEWLY FORMED, ACQ=ACQUIRED, DES=DESCENDANT, UNK=UNKNOWN)

PERIOD AND METHOD OF ENTRY

COUNTRY OR REGION	TOTAL PRE 1968					PRE 1946					1946-1957					1958-1967				
	ALL	NEW	ACQ	DES	UNK	ALL	NEW	ACQ	DES	UNK	ALL	NEW	ACQ	DES	UNK	ALL	NEW	ACQ	DES	UNK
OUTSIDE U.S.	44	14	23	5	2	7	1	5	0	1	15	4	8	3	0	22	9	10	2	1
OUT. U.S. + CANADA	35	11	18	4	2	6	1	4	0	1	13	3	7	3	0	16	7	7	1	1
OUT. WEST. HEMIS.	17	6	9	1	1	4	1	3	0	0	2	0	1	1	1	11	5	5	0	0
OUT. WHITE CWEALTH	30	11	15	3	1	4	1	2	0	1	12	3	7	2	0	14	7	6	1	0
OUT. DEVLPED WORLD	21	8	9	3	1	3	1	1	0	1	11	3	6	2	0	7	4	2	1	0
CANADA	9	3	5	1	0	1	0	1	0	0	5	1	3	1	0	3	2	1	0	0
LATIN AMERICA	18	5	9	3	1	2	1	1	0	0	11	1	6	3	1	5	3	2	0	0
C. AMER.+CARIB.	10	0	6	3	1	1	0	0	1	0	6	0	4	2	0	3	0	2	0	1
CUBA	3	0	0	3	0	1	0	0	1	0	2	0	0	2	0	0	0	0	0	0
MEXICO	6	0	6	0	0	0	0	0	0	0	4	0	4	0	0	2	0	2	0	0
OTHER	1	0	0	1	0	0	0	0	0	0	0	0	0	0	0	1	0	0	1	0
S. AMERICA	8	5	3	0	0	1	0	1	0	0	5	1	2	0	0	2	4	0	0	0
ARGENTINA	3	0	3	0	0	0	0	0	0	0	3	0	3	0	0	0	0	0	0	0
BRAZIL	1	0	1	0	0	0	0	0	0	0	0	0	0	0	0	1	0	1	0	0
PERU	0	0	0	0	0	0	0	0	0	0	0	0	0	0	0	0	0	0	0	0
COLOMBIA	2	2	0	0	0	0	0	0	0	0	0	0	0	0	0	2	2	0	0	0
VENEZUELA	2	2	0	0	0	0	0	0	0	0	1	1	0	0	0	1	1	0	0	0
OTHER	1	0	0	1	0	0	0	0	0	0	0	0	0	0	0	1	0	0	1	0
EUROPE	9	2	7	0	0	2	2	0	0	0	1	0	1	0	0	6	0	6	0	0
EFTA	4	0	4	0	0	1	0	1	0	0	1	0	1	0	0	2	0	2	0	0
U.K.	2	0	2	0	0	1	0	1	0	0	0	0	0	0	0	1	0	1	0	0
SCANDINAVIA	2	0	2	0	0	0	0	0	0	0	1	0	1	0	0	1	0	1	0	0
SWITZERLAND	0	0	0	0	0	0	0	0	0	0	0	0	0	0	0	0	0	0	0	0
OTHER EFTA	0	0	0	0	0	0	0	0	0	0	0	0	0	0	0	0	0	0	0	0
EUROP. COMMUNITY	2	0	2	0	0	1	0	1	0	0	0	0	0	0	0	1	0	1	0	0
FRANCE	0	0	0	0	0	0	0	0	0	0	0	0	0	0	0	0	0	0	0	0
GERMANY	1	0	1	0	0	1	0	1	0	0	0	0	0	0	0	0	0	0	0	0
ITALY	0	0	0	0	0	0	0	0	0	0	0	0	0	0	0	0	0	0	0	0
BELGIUM + LUX	0	0	0	0	0	0	0	0	0	0	0	0	0	0	0	0	0	0	0	0
NETHERLANDS	1	0	1	0	0	0	0	0	0	0	0	0	0	0	0	1	0	1	0	0
SPAIN	2	1	1	0	0	0	0	0	0	0	0	0	0	0	0	2	1	1	0	0
GREECE + TURKEY	1	1	0	0	0	0	0	0	0	0	0	0	0	0	0	1	1	0	0	0
OTHER EUROPE	0	0	0	0	0	0	0	0	0	0	0	0	0	0	0	0	0	0	0	0
EUROPE EX. U.K.	7	2	5	0	0	1	0	1	0	0	1	0	1	0	0	5	2	3	0	0
SOUTHERN DOMINIONS	3	0	3	0	0	1	0	1	0	0	1	0	1	0	0	1	0	1	0	0
S. AFRICA +RHOD.	2	0	2	0	0	1	0	1	0	0	1	0	1	0	0	0	0	0	0	0
AUSTRALIA + N.Z.	1	0	1	0	0	0	0	0	0	0	0	0	0	0	0	1	0	1	0	0
ASIA + OTHER AFRICA	5	4	1	0	0	1	1	0	0	0	1	1	0	0	0	3	2	1	0	0
JAPAN	2	1	1	0	0	0	0	0	0	0	1	0	1	0	0	1	1	0	0	0
OTHER ASIA+AFR.	3	3	0	0	0	1	1	0	0	0	0	0	0	0	0	2	2	0	0	0
BLACK AFRICA	0	0	0	0	0	0	0	0	0	0	0	0	0	0	0	0	0	0	0	0
ARAB WORLD	0	0	0	0	0	0	0	0	0	0	0	0	0	0	0	0	0	0	0	0
INDIA	1	0	1	0	0	0	0	0	0	0	1	0	1	0	0	0	0	0	0	0
PHILIPPINES	0	0	0	0	0	0	0	0	0	0	0	0	0	0	0	0	0	0	0	0
OTHER E. ASIA	1	0	1	0	0	0	0	0	0	0	0	0	0	0	0	1	0	1	0	0
OTHER ASIA	2	2	0	0	0	0	0	0	0	0	0	0	0	0	0	2	2	0	0	0

CHAPTER 4- VARIETIES OF ENTRY

SECTION 4- THE FLOW OF MANUFACTURING BY INDUSTRY OF SUBSIDIARY

TABLE 31- SUBSIDIARIES MANUFACTURING
HEATING APPARATUS AND PLUMBING FIXTURES (SIC 343)
CLASSIFIED BY COUNTRY, PERIOD MANUFACTURE BEGAN, AND METHOD OF ENTRY

PERIOD AND METHOD OF ENTRY

(NEW=NEWLY FORMED, ACQ=ACQUIRED, DES=DESCENDANT, UNK=UNKNOWN)

COUNTRY OR REGION	TOTAL PRE 1968					PRE 1946					1946-1957					1958-1967				
	ALL	NEW	ACQ	DES	UNK	ALL	NEW	ACQ	DES	UNK	ALL	NEW	ACQ	DES	UNK	ALL	NEW	ACQ	DES	UNK
OUTSIDE U.S.	47	15	25	3	4	13	8	3	0	2	12	2	5	3	2	22	5	17	0	0
OUT. U.S. + CANADA	32	14	15	3	0	8	7	1	0	0	6	2	1	3	0	18	5	13	0	0
OUT. WEST. HEMIS.	29	13	13	3	0	8	7	1	0	0	4	1	0	3	0	17	5	12	0	0
OUT. WHITE CWEALTH	24	11	11	2	0	5	5	0	0	0	5	2	1	2	0	14	4	10	0	0
OUT. DEVLPED WORLD	6	2	4	0	0	0	0	0	0	0	3	2	1	0	0	3	0	3	0	0
CANADA	15	1	10	0	4	5	1	2	0	2	6	0	4	0	2	4	0	4	0	0
LATIN AMERICA	3	1	2	0	0	0	0	0	0	0	2	1	1	0	0	1	0	1	0	0
C. AMER.+CARIB.	1	0	1	0	0	0	0	0	0	0	0	0	0	0	0	1	0	1	0	0
CUBA	0	0	0	0	0	0	0	0	0	0	0	0	0	0	0	0	0	0	0	0
MEXICO	1	0	1	0	0	0	0	0	0	0	0	0	0	0	0	1	0	1	0	0
OTHER	0	0	0	0	0	0	0	0	0	0	0	0	0	0	0	0	0	0	0	0
S. AMERICA	2	1	1	0	0	0	0	0	0	0	1	1	0	0	0	1	0	1	0	0
ARGENTINA	1	0	1	0	0	0	0	0	0	0	0	0	0	0	0	1	0	1	0	0
BRAZIL	0	0	0	0	0	0	0	0	0	0	0	0	0	0	0	0	0	0	0	0
PERU	1	1	0	0	0	0	0	0	0	0	1	1	0	0	0	0	0	0	0	0
COLOMBIA	0	0	0	0	0	0	0	0	0	0	0	0	0	0	0	0	0	0	0	0
VENEZUELA	0	0	0	0	0	0	0	0	0	0	0	0	0	0	0	0	0	0	0	0
OTHER	0	0	0	0	0	0	0	0	0	0	0	0	0	0	0	0	0	0	0	0
EUROPE	25	11	11	3	0	8	7	1	0	0	3	0	0	3	0	14	4	10	0	0
EFTA	9	4	4	1	0	5	4	1	0	0	1	0	0	1	0	3	0	3	0	0
U.K.	7	2	4	1	0	3	2	1	0	0	1	0	0	1	0	3	0	3	0	0
SCANDINAVIA	0	0	0	0	0	0	0	0	0	0	0	0	0	0	0	0	0	0	0	0
SWITZERLAND	1	1	0	0	0	1	1	0	0	0	0	0	0	0	0	0	0	0	0	0
OTHER EFTA	1	1	0	0	0	1	1	0	0	0	0	0	0	0	0	0	0	0	0	0
EUROP. COMMUNITY	14	7	5	2	0	3	3	1	0	0	2	0	0	2	0	9	4	5	0	0
FRANCE	5	3	1	1	0	1	1	1	0	0	1	0	0	1	0	3	2	1	0	0
GERMANY	4	2	1	1	0	1	1	0	0	0	1	0	0	1	0	2	1	1	0	0
ITALY	2	1	1	0	0	1	1	0	0	0	0	0	0	0	0	1	0	1	0	0
BELGIUM + LUX	1	0	1	0	0	0	0	0	0	0	0	0	0	0	0	1	0	1	0	0
NETHERLANDS	2	1	1	0	0	0	0	0	0	0	0	0	0	0	0	2	1	1	0	0
SPAIN	1	0	1	0	0	0	0	0	0	0	0	0	0	0	0	1	0	1	0	0
GREECE + TURKEY	0	0	0	0	0	0	0	0	0	0	0	0	0	0	0	0	0	0	0	0
OTHER EUROPE	0	0	0	0	0	0	0	0	0	0	0	0	0	0	0	0	0	0	0	0
EUROPE EX. U.K.	18	9	7	2	0	5	5	0	0	0	2	0	0	2	0	11	4	7	0	0
SOUTHERN DOMINIONS	1	1	0	0	0	0	0	0	0	0	0	0	0	0	0	1	1	0	0	0
S. AFRICA +RHOD.	0	0	0	0	0	0	0	0	0	0	0	0	0	0	0	0	0	0	0	0
AUSTRALIA + N.Z.	1	1	0	0	0	0	0	0	0	0	0	0	0	0	0	1	1	0	0	0
ASIA + OTHER AFRICA	3	1	2	0	0	0	0	0	0	0	0	0	0	0	0	2	1	2	0	0
JAPAN	3	1	2	0	0	0	0	0	0	0	0	0	0	0	0	2	1	2	0	0
OTHER ASIA+AFR.	2	0	2	0	0	0	0	0	0	0	0	0	0	0	0	2	0	2	0	0
BLACK AFRICA	2	0	2	0	0	0	0	0	0	0	0	0	0	0	0	2	0	2	0	0
ARAB WORLD	0	0	0	0	0	0	0	0	0	0	0	0	0	0	0	0	0	0	0	0
INDIA	0	0	0	0	0	0	0	0	0	0	0	0	0	0	0	0	0	0	0	0
PHILIPPINES	0	0	0	0	0	0	0	0	0	0	0	0	0	0	0	0	0	0	0	0
OTHER E. ASIA	0	0	0	0	0	0	0	0	0	0	0	0	0	0	0	0	0	0	0	0
OTHER ASIA	1	1	0	0	0	0	0	0	0	0	1	1	0	0	0	0	0	0	0	0

347

PERIOD AND METHOD OF ENTRY
(NEW=NEWLY FORMED, ACQ=ACQUIRED, DES=DESCENDANT, UNK=UNKNOWN)

COUNTRY OR REGION	TOTAL PRE 1968					PRE 1946					1946-1957					1958-1967				
	ALL	NEW	ACQ	DES	UNK	ALL	NEW	ACQ	DES	UNK	ALL	NEW	ACQ	DES	UNK	ALL	NEW	ACQ	DES	UNK
OUTSIDE U.S.	240	93	106	22	17	35	20	9	4	2	50	28	16	4	2	153	45	81	14	13
OUT. U.S. + CANADA	195	80	84	16	13	24	14	6	3	1	35	23	9	2	1	134	43	69	11	11
OUT. WEST. HEMIS.	146	53	66	13	12	18	9	5	3	1	24	15	6	2	1	102	29	55	8	10
OUT. WHITE CWEALTH	135	63	52	11	8	13	8	2	1	1	27	17	8	2	0	94	37	42	8	7
OUT. DEVLPED WORLD	61	35	22	3	1	6	5	1	0	0	16	12	4	0	0	39	18	17	3	1
CANADA	45	13	22	6	4	11	6	3	1	1	15	5	7	2	1	19	2	12	3	2
LATIN AMERICA	49	27	18	3	1	6	5	1	0	0	11	8	3	0	0	32	14	14	3	1
C. AMER.+CARIB.	21	10	9	1	1	2	2	0	0	0	3	3	0	0	0	16	5	9	1	1
CUBA	2	2	0	0	0	1	1	0	0	0	1	1	0	0	0	0	0	0	0	0
MEXICO	17	6	9	1	1	1	1	0	0	0	2	2	0	0	0	14	3	9	1	1
OTHER	2	2	0	0	0	0	0	0	0	0	0	0	0	0	0	2	2	0	0	0
S. AMERICA	28	17	9	2	0	4	3	1	0	0	8	5	3	0	0	16	9	5	2	0
ARGENTINA	5	2	3	0	0	1	1	0	0	0	1	0	1	0	0	3	1	2	0	0
BRAZIL	6	4	2	0	0	1	1	0	0	0	2	1	1	0	0	3	2	1	0	0
PERU	2	1	1	0	0	0	0	0	0	0	2	1	1	0	0	0	0	0	0	0
COLOMBIA	5	3	1	1	0	2	1	1	0	0	0	0	0	0	0	3	2	0	1	0
VENEZUELA	6	4	2	0	0	0	0	0	0	0	2	1	1	0	0	4	3	1	0	0
OTHER	4	3	0	1	0	1	0	0	1	0	0	1	0	0	0	3	2	0	1	0
EUROPE	106	36	49	10	10	14	6	5	2	1	16	9	4	2	1	75	21	40	6	8
EFTA	39	9	21	3	5	6	1	4	1	0	5	4	0	0	2	27	3	17	2	4
U.K.	35	8	20	2	4	6	1	4	1	0	5	4	0	0	2	23	3	16	1	3
SCANDINAVIA	2	0	1	0	1	0	0	0	0	0	0	0	0	0	0	2	0	1	1	0
SWITZERLAND	0	0	0	0	0	0	0	0	0	0	0	0	0	0	0	0	0	0	0	0
OTHER EFTA	2	1	0	0	1	0	0	0	0	0	0	0	0	0	0	2	1	0	0	1
EUROP. COMMUNITY	55	22	21	7	5	6	3	1	1	1	10	5	3	2	0	39	14	17	4	4
FRANCE	11	3	5	1	2	3	2	0	1	0	5	0	3	2	0	8	1	5	0	2
GERMANY	19	7	8	4	0	1	0	1	0	0	5	4	1	0	0	13	5	6	2	0
ITALY	15	10	3	1	1	0	0	0	0	0	3	1	0	2	0	12	7	3	2	1
BELGIUM + LUX	6	0	4	1	1	2	1	0	0	1	0	0	0	0	0	4	0	3	1	0
NETHERLANDS	4	2	1	0	1	0	0	0	0	0	2	1	1	0	0	2	1	0	0	1
SPAIN	8	3	5	0	0	1	1	0	0	0	1	0	1	0	0	6	2	4	0	0
GREECE + TURKEY	2	1	1	0	0	0	0	0	0	0	0	0	0	0	0	1	1	0	0	0
OTHER EUROPE	2	1	1	0	0	1	0	0	0	1	0	0	0	0	0	1	0	1	0	0
EUROPE EX. U.K.	71	28	29	8	6	8	5	1	1	1	11	5	4	2	0	52	18	24	5	5
SOUTHERN DOMINIONS	23	8	11	3	1	4	3	1	0	0	3	2	0	1	0	16	3	10	2	1
S. AFRICA +RHOD.	7	5	2	0	0	2	2	0	0	0	1	1	0	0	0	4	2	2	0	0
AUSTRALIA + N.Z.	16	3	9	3	1	2	1	1	0	0	2	1	0	1	0	12	1	8	2	1
ASIA + OTHER AFRICA	17	9	6	0	1	0	0	0	0	0	6	4	1	0	0	11	5	5	0	1
JAPAN	5	1	2	1	1	0	0	0	0	0	1	0	0	1	0	4	1	2	0	1
OTHER ASIA+AFR.	12	8	4	0	0	0	0	0	0	0	5	4	1	0	0	7	4	3	0	0
BLACK AFRICA	2	1	1	0	0	0	0	0	0	0	0	0	0	0	0	2	1	1	0	0
ARAB WORLD	1	0	1	0	0	0	0	0	0	0	0	0	0	0	0	1	0	1	0	0
INDIA	3	2	1	0	0	0	0	0	0	0	0	0	0	0	0	3	2	1	0	0
PHILIPPINES	2	2	0	0	0	0	0	0	0	0	2	2	0	0	0	0	0	0	0	0
OTHER E. ASIA	0	0	0	0	0	0	0	0	0	0	0	0	0	0	0	0	0	0	0	0
OTHER ASIA	4	3	0	1	0	0	0	0	0	0	3	2	0	1	0	1	1	0	0	0

CHAPTER 4- VARIETIES OF ENTRY
SECTION 4- THE FLOW OF MANUFACTURING BY INDUSTRY OF SUBSIDIARY
TABLE 33- SUBSIDIARIES MANUFACTURING
FARM MACHINERY (SIC 352)
CLASSIFIED BY COUNTRY, PERIOD MANUFACTURE BEGAN, AND METHOD OF ENTRY

PERIOD AND METHOD OF ENTRY
(NEW=NEWLY FORMED, ACQ=ACQUIRED, DES=DESCENDANT, UNK=UNKNOWN)

COUNTRY OR REGION	TOTAL PRE 1968					PRE 1946					1946-1957					1958-1967				
	ALL	NEW	ACQ	DES	UNK	ALL	NEW	ACQ	DES	UNK	ALL	NEW	ACQ	DES	UNK	ALL	NEW	ACQ	DES	UNK
OUTSIDE U.S.	55	20	21	14	0	9	4	0	5	0	15	7	4	4	0	31	9	17	5	0
OUT. U.S. + CANADA	48	15	20	13	0	5	1	0	4	0	14	6	4	4	0	29	8	16	5	0
OUT. WEST. HEMIS.	39	10	19	10	0	3	1	0	2	0	12	4	4	4	0	24	5	15	4	0
OUT. WHITE CWEALTH	33	12	12	9	0	3	1	0	2	0	9	3	3	3	0	21	8	9	4	0
OUT. DEVLPED WORLD	12	7	1	4	0	0	0	0	0	0	5	2	0	3	0	7	5	1	1	0
CANADA	7	5	1	1	0	4	3	0	1	0	1	1	0	0	0	2	1	1	0	0
LATIN AMERICA	9	5	1	3	0	0	0	0	0	0	4	2	0	2	0	5	3	1	1	0
C. AMER.+CARIB.	3	2	0	1	0	0	0	0	0	0	2	1	0	1	0	1	1	0	0	0
CUBA	0	0	0	0	0	0	0	0	0	0	0	0	0	0	0	0	0	0	0	0
MEXICO	2	1	0	1	0	0	0	0	0	0	2	1	0	1	0	0	0	0	0	0
OTHER	1	1	0	0	0	0	0	0	0	0	0	0	0	0	0	1	1	0	0	0
S. AMERICA	6	3	1	2	0	0	0	0	0	0	2	1	0	1	0	4	2	1	1	0
ARGENTINA	3	2	0	1	0	0	0	0	0	0	1	1	0	0	0	2	1	0	1	0
BRAZIL	1	0	1	0	0	0	0	0	0	0	0	0	0	0	0	1	0	1	0	0
PERU	0	0	0	0	0	0	0	0	0	0	0	0	0	0	0	0	0	0	0	0
COLOMBIA	1	1	0	0	0	0	0	0	0	0	0	0	0	0	0	1	1	0	0	0
VENEZUELA	0	0	0	0	0	0	0	0	0	0	0	0	0	0	0	0	0	0	0	0
OTHER	1	0	0	1	0	0	0	0	0	0	1	0	0	1	0	0	0	0	0	0
EUROPE	26	7	13	6	0	3	1	0	2	0	6	3	1	2	0	17	3	12	2	0
EFTA	7	2	3	2	0	1	0	0	1	0	3	2	0	1	0	3	0	3	0	0
U.K.	6	2	3	1	0	0	0	0	0	0	3	2	0	1	0	3	0	3	0	0
SCANDINAVIA	1	0	0	1	0	1	0	0	1	0	0	0	0	0	0	0	0	0	0	0
SWITZERLAND	0	0	0	0	0	0	0	0	0	0	0	0	0	0	0	0	0	0	0	0
OTHER EFTA	0	0	0	0	0	0	0	0	0	0	0	0	0	0	0	0	0	0	0	0
EUROP. COMMUNITY	15	4	8	3	0	2	1	0	1	0	2	1	1	0	0	11	2	7	2	0
FRANCE	11	2	6	3	0	1	0	0	1	0	1	1	0	0	0	9	1	6	2	0
GERMANY	2	1	1	0	0	1	1	0	0	0	0	0	0	0	0	1	0	1	0	0
ITALY	1	1	0	0	0	0	0	0	0	0	0	0	0	0	0	1	1	0	0	0
BELGIUM + LUX	1	0	1	0	0	0	0	0	0	0	1	0	1	0	0	0	0	0	0	0
NETHERLANDS	0	0	0	0	0	0	0	0	0	0	0	0	0	0	0	0	0	0	0	0
SPAIN	3	1	2	0	0	0	0	0	0	0	0	0	0	0	0	3	1	2	0	0
GREECE + TURKEY	1	0	0	1	0	0	0	0	0	0	1	0	0	1	0	0	0	0	0	0
OTHER EUROPE	0	0	0	0	0	0	0	0	0	0	0	0	0	0	0	0	0	0	0	0
EUROPE EX. U.K.	20	5	10	5	0	3	1	0	2	0	3	1	1	1	0	14	3	9	2	0
SOUTHERN DOMINIONS	9	1	5	3	0	2	0	0	2	0	2	0	2	0	0	5	1	3	1	0
S. AFRICA +RHOD.	4	0	3	1	0	0	0	0	0	0	1	0	1	0	0	3	0	2	1	0
AUSTRALIA + N.Z.	5	1	2	2	0	2	0	0	2	0	1	0	1	0	0	2	1	1	0	0
ASIA + OTHER AFRICA	4	2	1	1	0	0	0	0	0	0	2	1	1	0	0	2	1	0	1	0
JAPAN	1	0	1	0	0	0	0	0	0	0	1	0	1	0	0	0	0	0	0	0
OTHER ASIA+AFR.	3	2	0	1	0	0	0	0	0	0	1	1	0	0	0	2	1	0	1	0
BLACK AFRICA	0	0	0	0	0	0	0	0	0	0	0	0	0	0	0	0	0	0	0	0
ARAB WORLD	1	1	0	0	0	0	0	0	0	0	0	0	0	0	0	1	1	0	0	0
INDIA	1	1	0	0	0	0	0	0	0	0	1	1	0	0	0	0	0	0	0	0
PHILIPPINES	1	0	0	1	0	0	0	0	0	0	0	0	0	0	0	1	0	0	1	0
OTHER E. ASIA	0	0	0	0	0	0	0	0	0	0	0	0	0	0	0	0	0	0	0	0
OTHER ASIA	0	0	0	0	0	0	0	0	0	0	0	0	0	0	0	0	0	0	0	0

CHAPTER 4- VARIETIES OF ENTRY
SECTION 4- THE FLOW OF MANUFACTURING BY INDUSTRY OF SUBSIDIARY
TABLE 34- SUBSIDIARIES MANUFACTURING
CONSTRUCTION MACHINERY (SIC 353)
CLASSIFIED BY COUNTRY, PERIOD MANUFACTURE BEGAN, AND METHOD OF ENTRY

PERIOD AND METHOD OF ENTRY
(NEW=NEWLY FORMED, ACQ=ACQUIRED, DES=DESCENDANT, UNK=UNKNOWN)

COUNTRY OR REGION	TOTAL PRE 1968					PRE 1946					1946-1957					1958-1967				
	ALL	NEW	ACQ	DES	UNK	ALL	NEW	ACQ	DES	UNK	ALL	NEW	ACQ	DES	UNK	ALL	NEW	ACQ	DES	UNK
OUTSIDE U.S.	136	63	50	20	3	25	16	6	2	1	39	21	12	5	1	72	26	32	13	1
OUT. U.S. + CANADA	104	50	36	17	2	18	13	3	2	0	30	16	9	4	1	56	21	24	11	1
OUT. WEST. HEMIS.	78	35	30	13	1	18	13	3	2	0	22	10	9	3	0	38	12	18	8	0
OUT. WHITE CWEALTH	70	35	22	12	1	11	8	2	1	0	14	6	6	1	1	45	18	17	10	0
OUT. DEVLPED WORLD	28	15	7	5	1	0	0	0	0	0	8	6	0	1	1	20	9	7	4	0
CANADA	32	13	14	3	2	7	3	3	0	1	9	5	3	1	0	16	5	8	2	1
LATIN AMERICA	26	15	6	4	1	0	0	0	0	0	8	6	0	1	1	18	9	6	3	0
C. AMER.+CARIB.	11	8	1	2	0	0	0	0	0	0	3	3	0	0	0	8	5	1	2	0
CUBA	1	0	1	0	0	0	0	0	0	0	0	0	0	0	0	1	0	1	0	0
MEXICO	11	8	1	2	0	0	0	0	0	0	3	3	0	0	0	8	5	1	2	0
OTHER	0	0	0	0	0	0	0	0	0	0	0	0	0	0	0	0	0	0	0	0
S. AMERICA	15	7	5	1	0	0	0	0	0	0	5	3	0	0	0	10	4	5	1	0
ARGENTINA	7	2	4	1	0	0	0	0	0	0	3	3	0	0	0	3	1	2	1	0
BRAZIL	3	4	1	0	0	0	0	0	0	0	1	1	0	0	0	2	1	1	0	0
PERU	1	0	1	0	0	0	0	0	0	0	0	0	0	0	0	1	0	1	0	0
COLOMBIA	0	0	0	0	0	0	0	0	0	0	0	0	0	0	0	0	0	0	0	0
VENEZUELA	3	1	0	1	0	0	0	0	0	0	0	0	0	0	0	3	1	1	1	0
OTHER	1	0	1	0	0	0	0	0	0	0	0	0	0	0	0	1	0	1	0	0
EUROPE	48	19	19	10	0	11	6	3	2	0	14	6	6	2	0	23	7	10	6	0
EFTA	12	3	6	3	0	2	0	0	2	0	3	3	4	2	0	1	1	1	0	0
U.K.	11	3	5	3	0	2	0	0	1	0	3	3	3	2	0	1	1	1	0	0
SCANDINAVIA	0	0	0	0	0	0	0	0	0	0	0	0	0	0	0	0	0	0	0	0
SWITZERLAND	0	0	0	0	0	0	0	0	0	0	0	0	0	0	0	0	0	0	0	0
OTHER EFTA	1	1	1	0	0	1	0	1	0	0	1	1	1	0	0	0	0	0	0	0
EUROP. COMMUNITY	33	14	12	7	0	8	5	2	1	0	4	2	2	0	0	21	7	8	6	0
FRANCE	11	4	5	2	0	3	1	1	1	0	0	0	0	0	0	8	3	3	2	0
GERMANY	8	2	2	4	0	1	0	1	0	0	3	1	0	2	0	8	8	2	3	0
ITALY	5	2	3	0	0	2	0	1	0	0	0	0	2	0	0	3	0	0	3	0
BELGIUM + LUX	5	2	3	1	0	1	1	0	0	0	0	0	0	0	0	4	2	1	1	0
NETHERLANDS	4	3	1	1	0	1	1	0	1	0	1	1	0	0	0	3	1	1	1	0
SPAIN	3	2	1	0	0	0	0	0	0	0	1	1	0	0	0	1	1	0	0	0
GREECE + TURKEY	0	0	0	0	0	0	0	0	0	0	0	0	0	0	0	0	0	0	0	0
OTHER EUROPE	0	0	0	0	0	0	0	0	0	0	0	0	0	0	0	0	0	0	0	0
EUROPE EX. U.K.	37	16	14	7	0	9	6	2	1	0	6	3	2	3	0	22	7	9	6	0
SOUTHERN DOMINIONS	23	12	9	2	0	5	5	0	0	0	8	4	3	1	0	10	3	6	1	0
S. AFRICA +RHOD.	6	5	1	0	0	3	3	0	0	0	2	1	1	0	0	1	1	1	0	0
AUSTRALIA + N.Z.	17	7	8	2	0	2	2	0	0	0	6	3	2	1	0	9	2	6	1	0
ASIA + OTHER AFRICA	7	4	2	1	0	2	2	0	0	0	0	0	0	0	0	5	2	1	2	0
JAPAN	5	4	0	1	0	2	2	0	0	0	0	0	0	0	0	3	2	0	1	0
OTHER ASIA+AFR.	2	0	0	1	0	0	0	0	0	0	0	0	0	0	0	2	0	1	1	0
BLACK AFRICA	0	0	0	0	0	0	0	0	0	0	0	0	0	0	0	0	0	0	0	0
ARAB WORLD	0	0	0	0	0	0	0	0	0	0	0	0	0	0	0	0	0	0	0	0
INDIA	2	0	0	1	0	0	0	0	0	0	0	0	0	0	0	2	0	1	1	0
PHILIPPINES	0	0	0	0	0	0	0	0	0	0	0	0	0	0	0	0	0	0	0	0
OTHER E. ASIA	0	0	0	0	0	0	0	0	0	0	0	0	0	0	0	0	0	0	0	0
OTHER ASIA	0	0	0	0	0	0	0	0	0	0	0	0	0	0	0	0	0	0	0	0

CHAPTER 4- VARIETIES OF ENTRY
SECTION 4- THE FLOW OF MANUFACTURING BY INDUSTRY OF SUBSIDIARY
TABLE 35- SUBSIDIARIES MANUFACTURING
SPECIAL INDUSTRY MACHINERY (SIC 354 AND 355)
CLASSIFIED BY COUNTRY, PERIOD MANUFACTURE BEGAN, AND METHOD OF ENTRY

(NEW=NEWLY FORMED, ACQ=ACQUIRED, DES=DESCENDANT, UNK=UNKNOWN)

PERIOD AND METHOD OF ENTRY

COUNTRY OR REGION	TOTAL PRE 1968					PRE 1946					1946-1957					1958-1967				
	ALL	NEW	ACQ	DES	UNK	ALL	NEW	ACQ	DES	UNK	ALL	NEW	ACQ	DES	UNK	ALL	NEW	ACQ	DES	UNK
OUTSIDE U.S.	109	37	61	7	4	22	11	8	2	1	25	11	11	2	1	62	15	42	3	2
OUT. U.S. + CANADA	94	36	50	6	2	18	11	5	2	0	21	11	8	1	1	55	14	37	3	1
OUT. WEST. HEMIS.	81	28	46	5	2	16	9	5	2	0	16	7	7	1	1	49	12	34	2	1
OUT. WHITE CWEALTH	57	28	26	2	1	9	7	2	0	0	11	8	3	0	0	37	13	21	2	1
OUT. DEVLPED WORLD	16	11	4	1	0	2	2	0	0	0	7	6	1	0	0	7	3	3	1	0
CANADA	15	1	11	1	2	4	0	3	0	1	4	0	3	1	0	7	1	5	0	1
LATIN AMERICA	13	8	4	1	0	2	1	0	1	0	5	4	1	0	0	6	3	3	0	0
C. AMER.+CARIB.	7	5	1	0	1	1	1	0	0	0	2	2	0	0	0	4	2	1	0	1
CUBA	1	1	0	0	0	1	1	0	0	0	0	0	0	0	0	0	0	0	0	0
MEXICO	5	3	1	1	0	0	0	0	0	0	1	1	0	0	0	3	1	1	0	1
OTHER	1	1	0	0	0	0	0	0	0	0	1	1	0	0	0	0	0	0	0	0
S. AMERICA	6	3	3	0	0	1	1	0	0	0	3	2	1	0	0	2	0	2	0	0
ARGENTINA	0	0	0	0	0	0	0	0	0	0	0	0	0	0	0	0	0	0	0	0
BRAZIL	2	2	0	0	0	1	1	0	0	0	0	0	0	0	0	1	1	0	0	0
PERU	0	0	0	0	0	0	0	0	0	0	0	0	0	0	0	0	0	0	0	0
COLOMBIA	1	0	0	0	1	0	0	0	0	0	1	0	0	0	1	0	0	0	0	0
VENEZUELA	1	1	0	0	0	0	0	0	0	0	0	0	0	0	0	0	0	0	0	0
OTHER	2	0	2	0	0	0	0	0	0	0	0	0	0	0	0	2	0	2	0	0
EUROPE	60	19	38	2	1	13	7	5	0	1	10	4	5	0	1	37	8	28	1	0
EFTA	26	6	18	1	1	7	3	3	0	1	6	2	3	0	1	13	1	12	1	0
U.K.	23	4	17	1	1	6	2	3	0	1	6	2	3	0	1	11	0	11	1	0
SCANDINAVIA	1	1	0	0	0	1	1	0	0	0	0	0	0	0	0	0	0	0	0	0
SWITZERLAND	1	1	0	0	0	0	0	0	0	0	0	0	0	0	0	1	1	0	0	0
OTHER EFTA	1	0	1	0	0	0	0	0	0	0	0	0	0	0	0	1	0	1	0	0
EUROP. COMMUNITY	30	11	18	0	1	5	3	2	0	0	3	1	2	0	0	22	7	14	0	1
FRANCE	8	4	5	0	0	2	2	0	0	0	2	1	1	0	0	4	1	3	0	0
GERMANY	10	3	5	1	0	2	1	1	0	0	1	0	1	0	0	8	3	4	1	0
ITALY	10	3	7	0	0	1	1	0	0	0	0	0	0	0	0	8	2	6	0	0
BELGIUM + LUX	1	1	0	0	0	0	0	0	0	0	0	0	0	0	0	1	1	0	0	0
NETHERLANDS	3	2	1	0	0	0	0	0	0	0	1	1	0	0	0	1	0	1	0	0
SPAIN	3	2	1	0	0	0	0	0	0	0	1	1	0	0	0	1	0	1	0	0
GREECE + TURKEY	0	0	0	0	0	0	0	0	0	0	0	0	0	0	0	0	0	0	0	0
OTHER EUROPE	0	0	0	0	0	0	0	0	0	0	0	0	0	0	0	0	0	0	0	0
EUROPE EX. U.K.	37	15	21	1	0	7	5	2	0	0	4	2	2	0	0	26	8	17	0	1
SOUTHERN DOMINIONS	14	4	7	3	0	3	2	1	0	0	4	1	2	1	0	7	1	5	1	1
S. AFRICA +RHOD.	4	1	3	2	0	1	1	1	0	0	2	0	1	1	0	1	0	1	0	0
AUSTRALIA + N.Z.	10	3	6	1	0	2	1	0	0	0	2	1	1	0	0	6	1	5	1	1
ASIA + OTHER AFRICA	7	5	0	1	1	2	2	0	0	0	2	2	0	0	0	5	3	0	1	1
JAPAN	4	3	0	0	1	0	0	0	0	0	2	2	0	0	0	4	2	0	0	1
OTHER ASIA+AFR.	3	2	0	0	1	0	0	0	0	0	2	0	0	0	0	1	1	0	0	1
BLACK AFRICA	0	0	0	0	0	0	0	0	0	0	0	0	0	0	0	0	0	0	0	0
ARAB WORLD	1	0	0	0	0	0	0	0	0	0	0	0	0	0	0	1	1	0	0	0
INDIA	1	1	0	0	0	0	0	0	0	0	1	1	0	0	0	1	1	0	0	0
PHILIPPINES	1	1	0	0	0	0	0	0	0	0	0	0	0	0	0	0	0	0	0	0
OTHER E. ASIA	0	0	0	0	0	0	0	0	0	0	0	0	0	0	0	0	0	0	0	0
OTHER ASIA	0	0	0	0	0	0	0	0	0	0	0	0	0	0	0	0	0	0	0	0

CHAPTER 4- VARIETIES OF ENTRY
SECTION 4- THE FLOW OF MANUFACTURING BY INDUSTRY OF SUBSIDIARY
TABLE 36- SUBSIDIARIES MANUFACTURING
GENERAL INDUSTRIAL MACHINERY (SIC 356)
CLASSIFIED BY COUNTRY, PERIOD MANUFACTURE BEGAN, AND METHOD OF ENTRY

PERIOD AND METHOD OF ENTRY
(NEW=NEWLY FORMED, ACQ=ACQUIRED, DES=DESCENDANT, UNK=UNKNOWN)

COUNTRY OR REGION	TOTAL PRE 1968					PRE 1946					1946-1957					1958-1967				
	ALL	NEW	ACQ	DES	UNK	ALL	NEW	ACQ	DES	UNK	ALL	NEW	ACQ	DES	UNK	ALL	NEW	ACQ	DES	UNK
OUTSIDE U.S.	118	52	44	13	7	30	21	7	1	1	24	11	8	4	1	62	20	29	8	5
OUT. U.S. + CANADA	92	46	29	12	5	25	19	5	1	0	15	7	4	3	1	52	20	20	8	4
OUT. WEST. HEMIS.	71	34	24	9	4	23	17	5	1	0	10	3	4	2	1	38	14	15	6	3
OUT. WHITE CWEALTH	65	35	18	8	4	18	16	2	0	0	9	5	2	2	0	38	14	14	6	4
OUT. DEVLPED WORLD	25	15	5	4	1	2	2	0	0	0	6	5	0	1	0	17	8	5	3	1
CANADA	26	6	15	2	1	5	2	2	0	1	9	4	4	1	0	10	0	9	1	0
LATIN AMERICA	21	12	5	3	1	2	2	0	0	0	5	4	1	0	0	14	6	3	3	1
C. AMER.+CARIB.	10	5	3	1	1	0	0	0	0	0	2	2	0	0	0	8	3	3	1	1
CUBA	0	0	0	0	0	0	0	0	0	0	0	0	0	0	0	0	0	0	0	0
MEXICO	9	4	3	1	0	0	0	0	0	0	2	2	0	0	0	7	2	3	1	0
OTHER	1	1	0	0	0	0	0	0	0	0	0	0	0	0	0	1	1	0	0	0
S. AMERICA	11	7	2	2	1	2	2	0	0	0	3	2	1	0	0	6	3	1	2	1
ARGENTINA	3	2	0	1	0	0	0	0	0	0	1	1	0	0	0	2	1	0	1	0
BRAZIL	6	3	2	1	0	2	2	0	0	0	1	1	0	0	0	3	0	2	1	0
PERU	1	1	0	0	0	0	0	0	0	0	0	0	0	0	0	1	1	0	0	0
COLOMBIA	1	1	0	0	0	0	0	0	0	0	1	1	0	0	0	0	0	0	0	0
VENEZUELA	0	0	0	0	0	0	0	0	0	0	0	0	0	0	0	0	0	0	0	0
OTHER	0	0	0	0	0	0	0	0	0	0	0	0	0	0	0	0	0	0	0	0
EUROPE	51	24	18	5	4	22	16	5	1	0	4	1	1	1	1	25	7	12	3	3
EFTA	17	6	8	2	1	7	3	3	1	1	3	1	1	1	1	7	2	4	1	0
U.K.	14	4	8	1	1	6	2	3	0	1	3	1	1	1	0	5	1	4	0	0
SCANDINAVIA	1	0	0	1	0	0	0	0	0	0	0	0	0	0	0	1	0	0	1	0
SWITZERLAND	1	1	0	0	0	0	0	0	0	0	0	0	0	0	0	1	1	0	0	0
OTHER EFTA	1	1	0	0	0	1	1	0	0	0	0	0	0	0	0	0	0	0	0	0
EUROP. COMMUNITY	29	16	7	3	3	14	12	2	0	0	1	0	1	0	0	14	4	5	3	3
FRANCE	12	6	5	1	0	5	4	1	0	0	0	0	0	0	0	7	2	4	1	0
GERMANY	8	5	1	0	2	5	5	0	0	0	1	0	1	0	0	2	0	0	0	2
ITALY	5	4	0	0	1	2	2	0	0	0	0	0	0	0	0	3	2	0	0	1
BELGIUM + LUX	2	1	1	0	0	2	1	1	0	0	0	0	0	0	0	0	0	0	0	0
NETHERLANDS	2	0	0	2	0	0	0	0	0	0	0	0	0	0	0	2	0	0	2	0
SPAIN	5	2	3	0	0	1	1	0	0	0	0	0	0	0	0	4	1	3	0	0
GREECE + TURKEY	0	0	0	0	0	0	0	0	0	0	0	0	0	0	0	0	0	0	0	0
OTHER EUROPE	0	0	0	0	0	0	0	0	0	0	0	0	0	0	0	0	0	0	0	0
EUROPE EX. U.K.	37	20	10	4	3	16	14	2	0	0	1	0	1	0	1	20	6	8	3	3
SOUTHERN DOMINIONS	13	7	3	3	0	1	1	0	0	0	3	1	0	2	0	9	5	2	2	0
S. AFRICA +RHOD.	3	2	0	1	0	1	1	0	0	0	0	0	0	0	0	2	1	0	1	0
AUSTRALIA + N.Z.	10	5	3	2	0	0	0	0	0	0	3	1	0	2	0	7	4	3	0	0
ASIA + OTHER AFRICA	7	6	0	1	0	0	0	0	0	0	0	0	0	0	0	7	6	0	1	0
JAPAN	3	3	0	0	0	0	0	0	0	0	0	0	0	0	0	3	3	0	0	0
OTHER ASIA+AFR.	4	3	0	1	0	0	0	0	0	0	0	0	0	0	0	4	3	0	1	0
BLACK AFRICA	0	0	0	0	0	0	0	0	0	0	0	0	0	0	0	0	0	0	0	0
ARAB WORLD	0	0	0	0	0	0	0	0	0	0	0	0	0	0	0	0	0	0	0	0
INDIA	2	1	0	1	0	0	0	0	0	0	0	0	0	0	0	2	1	0	1	0
PHILIPPINES	1	1	0	0	0	0	0	0	0	0	0	0	0	0	0	1	1	0	0	0
OTHER E. ASIA	0	0	0	0	0	0	0	0	0	0	0	0	0	0	0	0	0	0	0	0
OTHER ASIA	1	1	0	0	0	0	0	0	0	0	0	0	0	0	0	1	1	0	0	0

CHAPTER 4- VARIETIES OF ENTRY

SECTION 4- THE FLOW OF MANUFACTURING BY INDUSTRY OF SUBSIDIARY

TABLE 37- SUBSIDIARIES MANUFACTURING

OFFICE AND COMPUTING MACHINES (SIC 357)

CLASSIFIED BY COUNTRY, PERIOD MANUFACTURE BEGAN, AND METHOD OF ENTRY

PERIOD AND METHOD OF ENTRY

(NEW=NEWLY FORMED, ACQ=ACQUIRED, DES=DESCENDANT, UNK=UNKNOWN)

COUNTRY OR REGION	TOTAL PRE 1968					PRE 1946					1946-1957					1958-1967				
	ALL	NEW	ACQ	DES	UNK	ALL	NEW	ACQ	DES	UNK	ALL	NEW	ACQ	DES	UNK	ALL	NEW	ACQ	DES	UNK
OUTSIDE U.S.	87	34	34	16	3	40	19	12	6	3	22	11	4	7	0	25	4	18	3	0
OUT. U.S. + CANADA	76	30	28	15	3	34	15	11	5	3	21	11	3	7	0	21	4	14	3	0
OUT. WEST. HEMIS.	61	23	25	11	2	30	13	10	5	2	15	7	3	5	0	16	3	12	1	0
OUT. WHITE CWEALTH	63	24	24	12	3	27	11	10	3	3	18	9	3	6	0	18	4	11	3	0
OUT. DEVLPED WORLD	17	8	4	4	1	4	2	1	0	1	7	5	0	2	0	6	1	3	2	0
CANADA	11	4	6	1	0	6	4	1	1	0	1	0	1	0	0	4	0	4	0	0
LATIN AMERICA	15	7	3	4	1	4	2	1	1	0	6	4	0	1	1	5	1	2	2	0
C. AMER.+CARIB.	6	2	2	2	0	1	1	0	0	0	0	0	0	0	0	5	1	2	2	0
CUBA	0	0	0	0	0	0	0	0	0	0	0	0	0	0	0	0	0	0	0	0
MEXICO	6	2	2	2	0	1	1	0	0	0	0	0	0	0	0	5	1	2	2	0
OTHER	0	0	0	0	0	0	0	0	0	0	0	0	0	0	0	0	0	0	0	0
S. AMERICA	9	5	1	2	1	3	1	1	0	1	6	4	0	2	0	0	0	0	0	0
ARGENTINA	0	0	0	0	0	0	0	0	0	0	0	0	0	0	0	0	0	0	0	0
BRAZIL	6	3	1	1	1	3	1	1	0	1	3	2	0	1	0	0	0	0	0	0
PERU	0	0	0	0	0	0	0	0	0	0	0	0	0	0	0	0	0	0	0	0
COLOMBIA	1	0	0	1	0	0	0	0	0	0	1	0	0	1	0	0	0	0	0	0
VENEZUELA	1	1	0	0	0	0	0	0	0	0	1	1	0	0	0	0	0	0	0	0
OTHER	1	1	0	0	0	0	0	0	0	0	1	1	0	0	0	0	0	0	0	0
EUROPE	51	19	22	8	2	29	13	9	5	2	10	4	3	3	0	12	2	10	0	0
EFTA	18	7	6	5	0	10	5	2	3	0	4	2	1	1	0	4	0	3	1	0
U.K.	10	4	4	2	0	6	3	2	1	0	1	1	0	0	0	3	0	2	1	0
SCANDINAVIA	5	2	2	1	0	2	1	0	1	0	2	1	1	0	0	1	0	1	0	0
SWITZERLAND	2	0	0	2	0	1	0	0	1	0	1	0	0	1	0	0	0	0	0	0
OTHER EFTA	1	1	0	0	0	1	1	0	0	0	0	0	0	0	0	0	0	0	0	0
EUROP. COMMUNITY	32	11	16	3	2	18	7	7	2	2	6	2	3	1	0	8	2	6	0	0
FRANCE	13	4	7	1	1	8	3	4	0	1	2	0	1	1	0	3	1	2	0	0
GERMANY	8	4	4	0	0	4	2	2	0	0	1	1	0	0	0	3	1	2	0	0
ITALY	5	1	2	2	0	3	1	1	1	0	1	0	0	1	0	1	0	1	0	0
BELGIUM + LUX	3	1	2	0	0	1	0	1	0	0	1	1	0	0	0	1	0	1	0	0
NETHERLANDS	3	1	1	0	1	2	1	0	0	1	1	0	1	0	0	0	0	0	0	0
SPAIN	0	0	0	0	0	0	0	0	0	0	0	0	0	0	0	0	0	0	0	0
GREECE + TURKEY	1	1	0	0	0	1	1	0	0	0	0	0	0	0	0	0	0	0	0	0
OTHER EUROPE	0	0	0	0	0	0	0	0	0	0	0	0	0	0	0	0	0	0	0	0
EUROPE EX. U.K.	41	15	18	6	2	23	10	7	4	2	9	3	3	3	0	9	2	8	0	0
SOUTHERN DOMINIONS	2	1	0	1	0	1	0	0	1	0	1	1	0	0	0	0	0	0	0	0
S. AFRICA +RHOD.	1	1	0	0	0	0	0	0	0	0	1	1	0	0	0	0	0	0	0	0
AUSTRALIA + N.Z.	1	0	0	1	0	1	0	0	1	0	0	0	0	0	0	0	0	0	0	0
ASIA + OTHER AFRICA	8	3	3	2	0	1	0	0	1	0	3	2	1	0	0	4	1	2	1	0
JAPAN	6	2	2	2	0	1	0	0	1	0	3	2	1	0	0	2	0	1	1	0
OTHER ASIA+AFR.	2	1	1	0	0	0	0	0	0	0	0	0	0	0	0	2	1	1	0	0
BLACK AFRICA	0	0	0	0	0	0	0	0	0	0	0	0	0	0	0	0	0	0	0	0
ARAB WORLD	0	0	0	0	0	0	0	0	0	0	0	0	0	0	0	0	0	0	0	0
INDIA	2	1	1	0	0	0	0	0	0	0	0	0	0	0	0	2	1	1	0	0
PHILIPPINES	0	0	0	0	0	0	0	0	0	0	0	0	0	0	0	0	0	0	0	0
OTHER E. ASIA	0	0	0	0	0	0	0	0	0	0	0	0	0	0	0	0	0	0	0	0
OTHER ASIA	0	0	0	0	0	0	0	0	0	0	0	0	0	0	0	0	0	0	0	0

CHAPTER 4- VARIETIES OF ENTRY
SECTION 4- THE FLOW OF MANUFACTURING BY INDUSTRY OF SUBSIDIARY
TABLE 38- SUBSIDIARIES MANUFACTURING
SERVICE INDUSTRY MACHINES (SIC 358)
CLASSIFIED BY COUNTRY, PERIOD MANUFACTURE BEGAN, AND METHOD OF ENTRY

PERIOD AND METHOD OF ENTRY
(NEW=NEWLY FORMED, ACQ=ACQUIRED, DES=DESCENDANT, UNK=UNKNOWN)

COUNTRY OR REGION	TOTAL PRE 1968 ALL	NEW	ACQ	DES	UNK	PRE 1946 ALL	NEW	ACQ	DES	UNK	1946-1957 ALL	NEW	ACQ	DES	UNK	1958-1967 ALL	NEW	ACQ	DES	UNK
OUTSIDE U.S.	51	15	33	1	2	7	4	3	0	0	5	2	3	0	0	39	9	27	1	2
OUT. U.S. + CANADA	41	12	26	1	2	5	3	2	0	0	4	1	3	0	0	32	8	21	1	2
OUT. WEST. HEMIS.	31	9	19	1	2	4	2	2	0	0	3	1	2	0	0	24	6	15	1	2
OUT. WHITE CWEALTH	29	7	19	1	2	2	1	1	0	0	2	0	2	0	0	25	6	16	1	2
OUT. DEVLPED WORLD	11	4	7	0	0	1	1	0	0	0	1	0	1	0	0	9	3	6	0	0
CANADA	10	3	7	0	0	2	1	1	0	0	1	1	0	0	0	7	1	6	0	0
LATIN AMERICA	10	3	7	0	0	1	1	0	0	0	1	0	1	0	0	8	2	6	0	0
C. AMFR.+CARIB.	5	2	3	0	0	0	0	0	0	0	0	0	0	0	0	5	2	3	0	0
CUBA	0	0	0	0	0	0	0	0	0	0	0	0	0	0	0	0	0	0	0	0
MEXICO	2	0	2	0	0	0	0	0	0	0	0	0	0	0	0	2	0	2	0	0
OTHER	3	2	1	0	0	0	0	0	0	0	0	0	0	0	0	3	2	1	0	0
S. AMERICA	5	1	4	0	0	1	1	0	0	0	1	0	1	0	0	3	0	3	0	0
ARGENTINA	0	0	0	0	0	0	0	0	0	0	0	0	0	0	0	0	0	0	0	0
BRAZIL	2	1	1	0	0	1	1	0	0	0	1	0	1	0	0	0	0	0	0	0
PERU	0	0	0	0	0	0	0	0	0	0	0	0	0	0	0	0	0	0	0	0
COLOMBIA	0	0	0	0	0	0	0	0	0	0	0	0	0	0	0	0	0	0	0	0
VENEZUELA	2	0	2	0	0	0	0	0	0	0	0	0	0	0	0	2	0	2	0	0
OTHER	1	0	1	0	0	0	0	0	0	0	0	0	0	0	0	1	0	1	0	0
EUROPE	22	3	16	1	2	2	1	1	0	0	3	0	3	0	0	17	2	12	1	2
EFTA	8	1	7	0	0	1	1	0	0	0	2	0	2	0	0	5	0	5	0	0
U.K.	5	1	4	0	0	1	1	0	0	0	2	0	2	0	0	2	0	2	0	0
SCANDINAVIA	1	0	1	0	0	0	0	0	0	0	0	0	0	0	0	1	0	1	0	0
SWITZERLAND	1	0	1	0	0	0	0	0	0	0	0	0	0	0	0	1	0	1	0	0
OTHER EFTA	1	0	1	0	0	0	0	0	0	0	0	0	0	0	0	1	0	1	0	0
EUROP. COMMUNITY	14	2	9	1	2	1	0	1	0	0	1	0	1	0	0	12	2	7	1	2
FRANCE	6	2	4	0	0	1	0	1	0	0	0	0	0	0	0	5	2	3	0	0
GERMANY	4	0	3	1	0	0	0	0	0	0	1	0	1	0	0	3	0	2	1	0
ITALY	1	0	0	0	1	0	0	0	0	0	0	0	0	0	0	1	0	0	0	1
BELGIUM + LUX	1	0	0	0	1	0	0	0	0	0	0	0	0	0	0	1	0	0	0	1
NETHERLANDS	2	0	2	0	0	0	0	0	0	0	0	0	0	0	0	2	0	2	0	0
SPAIN	0	0	0	0	0	0	0	0	0	0	0	0	0	0	0	0	0	0	0	0
GREECE + TURKEY	0	0	0	0	0	0	0	0	0	0	0	0	0	0	0	0	0	0	0	0
OTHER EUROPE	0	0	0	0	0	0	0	0	0	0	0	0	0	0	0	0	0	0	0	0
EUROPE EX. U.K.	17	2	12	1	2	1	0	1	0	0	1	0	1	0	0	15	2	10	1	2
SOUTHERN DOMINIONS	7	4	3	0	0	2	2	0	0	0	0	0	0	0	0	5	2	3	0	0
S. AFRICA +RHOD.	5	2	3	0	0	2	2	0	0	0	0	0	0	0	0	3	0	3	0	0
AUSTRALIA + N.Z.	2	2	0	0	0	0	0	0	0	0	0	0	0	0	0	2	2	0	0	0
ASIA + OTHER AFRICA	2	2	0	0	0	0	0	0	0	0	0	0	0	0	0	2	2	0	0	0
JAPAN	1	1	0	0	0	0	0	0	0	0	0	0	0	0	0	1	1	0	0	0
OTHER ASIA+AFR.	1	1	0	0	0	0	0	0	0	0	0	0	0	0	0	1	1	0	0	0
BLACK AFRICA	0	0	0	0	0	0	0	0	0	0	0	0	0	0	0	0	0	0	0	0
ARAB WORLD	0	0	0	0	0	0	0	0	0	0	0	0	0	0	0	0	0	0	0	0
INDIA	1	1	0	0	0	0	0	0	0	0	0	0	0	0	0	1	1	0	0	0
PHILIPPINES	0	0	0	0	0	0	0	0	0	0	0	0	0	0	0	0	0	0	0	0
OTHER E. ASIA	0	0	0	0	0	0	0	0	0	0	0	0	0	0	0	0	0	0	0	0
OTHER ASIA	0	0	0	0	0	0	0	0	0	0	0	0	0	0	0	0	0	0	0	0

CHAPTER 4- VARIETIES OF ENTRY
SECTION 4- THE FLOW OF MANUFACTURING BY INDUSTRY OF SUBSIDIARY
TABLE 39- SUBSIDIARIES MANUFACTURING
OTHER NON-ELECTRICAL MACHINERY (SIC 351 AND 359)
CLASSIFIED BY COUNTRY, PERIOD MANUFACTURE BEGAN, AND METHOD OF ENTRY

PERIOD AND METHOD OF ENTRY
(NEW=NEWLY FORMED, ACQ=ACQUIRED, DES=DESCENDANT, UNK=UNKNOWN)

COUNTRY OR REGION	TOTAL PRE 1968					PRE 1946					1946-1957					1958-1967				
	ALL	NEW	ACQ	DES	UNK	ALL	NEW	ACQ	DES	UNK	ALL	NEW	ACQ	DES	UNK	ALL	NEW	ACQ	DES	UNK
OUTSIDE U.S.	56	22	26	4	1	11	9	2	0	0	7	0	6	1	0	35	13	18	3	1
OUT. U.S. + CANADA	46	19	21	3	0	9	7	2	0	0	5	0	5	0	0	29	12	14	3	0
OUT. WEST. HEMIS.	39	14	19	3	0	7	5	2	0	0	4	0	4	0	0	25	9	13	3	0
OUT. WHITE CWEALTH	32	16	13	2	0	7	5	2	0	0	3	0	3	0	0	21	11	8	2	0
OUT. DEVLPED WORLD	7	5	2	0	0	2	2	0	0	0	1	0	1	0	0	4	3	1	0	0
CANADA	10	3	5	1	1	2	2	0	0	0	2	0	1	0	1	6	1	4	1	0
LATIN AMERICA	7	5	2	0	0	2	2	0	0	0	1	0	1	0	0	4	3	1	0	0
C. AMER.+CARIB.	1	1	0	0	0	0	0	0	0	0	0	0	0	0	0	1	1	0	0	0
CUBA	0	0	0	0	0	0	0	0	0	0	0	0	0	0	0	0	0	0	0	0
MEXICO	1	1	0	0	0	0	0	0	0	0	0	0	0	0	0	1	1	0	0	0
OTHER	0	0	0	0	0	0	0	0	0	0	0	0	0	0	0	0	0	0	0	0
S. AMERICA	6	4	2	0	0	2	2	0	0	0	1	0	1	0	0	3	2	1	0	0
ARGENTINA	2	1	1	0	0	0	0	0	0	0	1	0	1	0	0	1	1	0	0	0
BRAZIL	4	3	1	0	0	2	2	0	0	0	0	0	0	0	0	2	1	1	0	0
PERU	0	0	0	0	0	0	0	0	0	0	0	0	0	0	0	0	0	0	0	0
COLOMBIA	0	0	0	0	0	0	0	0	0	0	0	0	0	0	0	0	0	0	0	0
VENEZUELA	0	0	0	0	0	0	0	0	0	0	0	0	0	0	0	0	0	0	0	0
OTHER	0	0	0	0	0	0	0	0	0	0	0	0	0	0	0	0	0	0	0	0
EUROPE	34	13	16	3	0	7	5	2	0	0	2	0	2	0	0	23	8	12	3	0
EFTA	10	3	6	0	0	2	2	0	0	0	1	0	1	0	0	6	1	5	0	0
U.K.	9	3	5	0	0	2	2	0	0	0	1	0	1	0	0	6	1	5	0	0
SCANDINAVIA	1	0	1	0	0	0	0	0	0	0	0	0	0	0	0	0	0	0	0	0
SWITZERLAND	0	0	0	0	0	0	0	0	0	0	0	0	0	0	0	0	0	0	0	0
OTHER EFTA	0	0	0	0	0	0	0	0	0	0	0	0	0	0	0	0	0	0	0	0
EUROP. COMMUNITY	21	9	9	3	0	5	3	2	0	0	1	0	1	0	0	14	6	6	2	0
FRANCE	10	2	6	2	0	3	2	1	0	0	1	0	1	0	0	6	2	4	2	0
GERMANY	8	5	2	1	0	1	1	0	0	0	0	0	0	0	0	4	3	2	1	0
ITALY	1	1	0	0	0	0	0	0	0	0	0	0	0	0	0	1	1	0	0	0
BELGIUM + LUX	1	1	0	0	0	0	0	0	0	0	0	0	0	0	0	1	1	0	0	0
NETHERLANDS	1	0	1	0	0	1	0	1	0	0	0	0	0	0	0	0	0	0	0	0
SPAIN	2	1	0	0	0	0	0	0	0	0	0	0	0	0	0	2	1	0	0	0
GREECE + TURKEY	1	0	1	0	0	0	0	0	0	0	0	0	0	0	0	1	0	1	0	0
OTHER EUROPE	0	0	0	0	0	0	0	0	0	0	0	0	0	0	0	0	0	0	0	0
EUROPE EX. U.K.	25	10	11	3	0	5	3	2	0	0	2	0	2	0	0	17	7	7	3	0
SOUTHERN DOMINIONS	4	0	3	0	0	0	0	0	0	0	2	0	2	0	0	1	0	1	0	0
S. AFRICA +RHOD.	0	0	0	0	0	0	0	0	0	0	0	0	0	0	0	0	0	0	0	0
AUSTRALIA + N.Z.	4	0	3	0	0	0	0	0	0	0	3	0	3	0	0	1	0	1	0	0
ASIA + OTHER AFRICA	1	1	0	0	0	0	0	0	0	0	0	0	0	0	0	1	1	0	0	0
JAPAN	1	1	0	0	0	0	0	0	0	0	0	0	0	0	0	1	1	0	0	0
OTHER ASIA+AFR.	0	0	0	0	0	0	0	0	0	0	0	0	0	0	0	0	0	0	0	0
BLACK AFRICA	0	0	0	0	0	0	0	0	0	0	0	0	0	0	0	0	0	0	0	0
ARAB WORLD	0	0	0	0	0	0	0	0	0	0	0	0	0	0	0	0	0	0	0	0
INDIA	0	0	0	0	0	0	0	0	0	0	0	0	0	0	0	0	0	0	0	0
PHILIPPINES	0	0	0	0	0	0	0	0	0	0	0	0	0	0	0	0	0	0	0	0
OTHER E. ASIA	0	0	0	0	0	0	0	0	0	0	0	0	0	0	0	0	0	0	0	0
OTHER ASIA	0	0	0	0	0	0	0	0	0	0	0	0	0	0	0	0	0	0	0	0

CHAPTER 4— VARIETIES OF ENTRY
SECTION 4— THE FLOW OF MANUFACTURING BY INDUSTRY OF SUBSIDIARY
TABLE 40— SUBSIDIARIES MANUFACTURING
HOUSEHOLD APPLIANCES (SIC 363)
CLASSIFIED BY COUNTRY, PERIOD MANUFACTURE BEGAN, AND METHOD OF ENTRY

PERIOD AND METHOD OF ENTRY
(NEW=NEWLY FORMED, ACQ=ACQUIRED, DES=DESCENDANT, UNK=UNKNOWN)

COUNTRY OR REGION	TOTAL PRE 1968					PRE 1946					1946-1957					1958-1967				
	ALL	NEW	ACQ	DES	UNK	ALL	NEW	ACQ	DES	UNK	ALL	NEW	ACQ	DES	UNK	ALL	NEW	ACQ	DES	UNK
OUTSIDE U.S.	96	49	31	9	6	17	10	1	3	3	17	7	5	3	2	61	32	25	3	1
OUT. U.S. + CANADA	85	43	27	8	6	12	6	1	2	3	16	6	5	3	2	56	31	21	3	1
OUT. WEST. HEMIS.	64	30	22	6	5	9	3	2	2	3	12	4	4	3	1	42	23	17	1	1
OUT. WHITE CWEALTH	64	36	21	3	3	6	4	1	1	0	12	5	5	0	2	45	27	15	2	1
OUT. DEVLPED WORLD	35	25	6	2	2	3	3	0	0	0	5	2	1	0	2	27	20	5	2	0
CANADA	11	6	4	1	0	5	4	0	1	0	1	1	2	0	1	5	1	4	0	0
LATIN AMERICA	21	13	5	2	1	3	3	0	0	0	4	2	2	0	0	14	8	4	2	0
C. AMER.+CARIB.	8	4	3	0	1	1	1	0	0	0	3	2	0	0	1	4	0	3	0	0
CUBA	0	0	0	0	0	0	0	0	0	0	0	0	0	0	0	0	0	0	0	0
MEXICO	7	4	2	0	1	1	1	0	0	0	3	2	0	0	1	3	1	2	0	0
OTHER	1	0	1	0	0	0	0	0	0	0	0	0	0	0	0	1	0	1	0	0
S. AMERICA	13	9	2	1	0	2	2	0	0	0	1	0	1	0	0	10	7	1	2	0
ARGENTINA	4	3	1	0	0	1	1	0	0	0	1	0	1	0	0	2	2	0	0	0
BRAZIL	2	2	0	0	0	1	1	0	0	0	0	0	0	0	0	1	1	0	0	0
PERU	1	1	0	0	0	0	0	0	0	0	0	0	0	0	0	1	1	0	0	0
COLOMBIA	2	1	1	0	0	0	0	0	0	0	0	0	0	0	0	2	1	1	0	0
VENEZUELA	2	1	0	1	0	0	0	0	0	0	0	0	0	0	0	2	1	0	1	0
OTHER	2	1	0	1	0	0	0	0	0	0	0	0	0	0	0	2	1	0	1	0
EUROPE	41	15	19	3	4	8	2	2	3	3	8	4	3	1	0	25	9	15	0	0
EFTA	15	4	6	2	3	5	1	1	1	3	3	1	1	1	0	7	2	5	0	0
U.K.	14	4	5	2	3	5	1	0	1	3	2	1	1	0	0	7	2	5	0	0
SCANDINAVIA	1	0	0	0	0	0	0	0	0	0	1	1	0	0	0	0	0	0	0	0
SWITZERLAND	0	0	0	0	0	0	0	0	0	0	0	0	0	0	0	0	0	0	0	0
OTHER EFTA	0	0	0	0	0	0	0	0	0	0	0	0	0	0	0	0	0	0	0	0
EUROP. COMMUNITY	23	9	12	1	1	2	0	0	1	0	5	3	2	0	0	16	6	9	0	0
FRANCE	8	6	1	1	0	1	0	0	1	0	1	1	0	0	0	6	5	1	0	0
GERMANY	8	1	6	1	0	0	0	0	0	0	1	0	1	0	0	7	1	5	1	0
ITALY	6	2	4	0	0	0	0	0	0	0	3	2	1	0	0	3	0	3	0	0
BELGIUM + LUX	1	0	1	0	0	1	0	1	0	0	0	0	0	0	0	0	0	0	0	0
NETHERLANDS	0	0	0	0	0	0	0	0	0	0	0	0	0	0	0	0	0	0	0	0
SPAIN	0	0	0	0	0	0	0	0	0	0	0	0	0	0	0	0	0	0	0	0
GREECE + TURKEY	2	1	0	1	0	0	0	0	0	0	0	0	0	0	0	2	1	0	1	0
OTHER EUROPE	1	1	0	0	0	1	1	0	0	0	0	0	0	0	0	0	0	0	0	0
EUROPE EX. U.K.	27	11	14	1	1	3	1	1	1	0	6	3	3	0	0	18	7	10	0	1
SOUTHERN DOMINIONS	7	3	1	3	0	1	1	0	0	0	2	0	2	0	0	4	2	1	1	0
S. AFRICA +RHOD.	2	1	0	1	0	0	0	0	0	0	0	0	0	0	0	2	1	0	1	0
AUSTRALIA + N.Z.	5	2	1	2	0	1	1	0	0	0	2	0	2	0	0	2	1	1	0	0
ASIA + OTHER AFRICA	16	12	2	2	0	0	0	0	0	0	2	0	2	0	0	13	12	1	0	0
JAPAN	2	0	1	1	0	0	0	0	0	0	1	0	1	0	0	0	0	0	1	0
OTHER ASIA+AFR.	14	12	1	0	1	0	0	0	0	0	1	0	1	0	0	13	12	1	0	0
BLACK AFRICA	3	3	0	0	0	0	0	0	0	0	0	0	0	0	0	3	3	0	0	0
ARAB WORLD	2	2	0	0	0	0	0	0	0	0	0	0	0	0	0	2	2	0	0	0
INDIA	2	2	0	0	0	0	0	0	0	0	0	0	0	0	0	2	2	0	0	0
PHILIPPINES	2	2	0	0	0	0	0	0	0	0	1	1	0	0	0	1	1	0	0	0
OTHER E. ASIA	1	1	0	0	0	0	0	0	0	0	0	0	0	0	0	1	1	0	0	0
OTHER ASIA	5	4	1	0	0	0	0	0	0	0	0	0	0	0	0	5	4	1	0	0

CHAPTER 4- VARIETIES OF ENTRY
SECTION 4- THE FLOW OF MANUFACTURING BY INDUSTRY OF SUBSIDIARY
TABLE 41- SUBSIDIARIES MANUFACTURING
COMMUNICATION EQUIPMENT (SIC 366)
CLASSIFIED BY COUNTRY, PERIOD MANUFACTURE BEGAN, AND METHOD OF ENTRY

(NEW=NEWLY FORMED, ACQ=ACQUIRED, DES=DESCENDANT, UNK=UNKNOWN)

PERIOD AND METHOD OF ENTRY

COUNTRY OR REGION	TOTAL PRE 1968					PRE 1946					1946-1957					1958-1967				
	ALL	NEW	ACQ	DES	UNK	ALL	NEW	ACQ	DES	UNK	ALL	NEW	ACQ	DES	UNK	ALL	NEW	ACQ	DES	UNK
OUTSIDE U.S.	56	18	33	4	1	22	4	15	2	1	12	7	5	0	0	22	7	13	2	0
OUT. U.S. + CANADA	47	15	27	4	1	21	4	14	2	1	6	4	2	0	0	20	7	11	2	0
OUT. WEST. HEMIS.	43	14	25	3	1	20	4	13	2	1	6	4	2	0	0	17	6	10	1	0
OUT. WHITE CWEALTH	37	12	20	4	1	17	4	10	2	1	4	2	2	0	0	16	6	8	2	0
OUT. DEVLPED WORLD	7	4	2	1	0	1	0	1	0	0	0	0	0	0	0	6	4	1	1	0
CANADA	9	3	6	0	0	1	0	1	0	0	6	3	3	0	0	2	0	2	0	0
LATIN AMERICA	4	1	2	1	0	1	0	1	0	0	0	0	0	0	0	3	1	1	1	0
C. AMER.+CARIB.	3	1	1	1	0	0	0	0	0	0	0	0	0	0	0	3	1	1	1	0
CUBA	0	0	0	0	0	0	0	0	0	0	0	0	0	0	0	0	0	0	0	0
MEXICO	3	1	1	1	0	0	0	0	0	0	0	0	0	0	0	3	1	1	1	0
OTHER	0	0	0	0	0	0	0	0	0	0	0	0	0	0	0	0	0	0	0	0
S. AMERICA	1	0	1	0	0	1	0	1	0	0	0	0	0	0	0	0	0	0	0	0
ARGENTINA	1	0	1	0	0	1	0	1	0	0	0	0	0	0	0	0	0	0	0	0
BRAZIL	0	0	0	0	0	0	0	0	0	0	0	0	0	0	0	0	0	0	0	0
PERU	0	0	0	0	0	0	0	0	0	0	0	0	0	0	0	0	0	0	0	0
COLOMBIA	0	0	0	0	0	0	0	0	0	0	0	0	0	0	0	0	0	0	0	0
VENEZUELA	0	0	0	0	0	0	0	0	0	0	0	0	0	0	0	0	0	0	0	0
OTHER	0	0	0	0	0	0	0	0	0	0	0	0	0	0	0	0	0	0	0	0
EUROPE	34	9	21	3	1	18	4	11	2	1	4	2	2	0	0	12	3	8	1	0
EFTA	14	2	10	2	0	8	1	6	1	0	0	0	0	0	0	6	1	4	1	0
U.K.	5	1	4	0	0	2	0	2	0	0	0	0	0	0	0	3	1	2	0	0
SCANDINAVIA	5	1	3	1	0	3	1	2	0	0	0	0	0	0	0	2	0	1	1	0
SWITZERLAND	0	0	0	0	0	0	0	0	0	0	0	0	0	0	0	0	0	0	0	0
OTHER EFTA	4	0	3	0	1	3	0	2	0	1	0	0	0	0	0	1	0	1	0	0
EUROP. COMMUNITY	15	3	10	1	1	8	2	4	1	1	2	0	2	0	0	5	1	4	0	0
FRANCE	4	1	2	1	0	4	1	2	1	0	0	0	0	0	0	0	0	0	0	0
GERMANY	5	2	2	0	1	3	1	1	0	1	0	0	0	0	0	2	1	1	0	0
ITALY	3	0	3	0	0	0	0	0	0	0	1	0	1	0	0	2	0	2	0	0
BELGIUM + LUX	2	0	2	0	0	1	0	1	0	0	0	0	0	0	0	1	0	1	0	0
NETHERLANDS	1	0	1	0	0	0	0	0	0	0	1	0	1	0	0	0	0	0	0	0
SPAIN	3	3	0	0	0	1	1	0	0	0	1	1	0	0	0	1	1	0	0	0
GREECE + TURKEY	1	1	0	0	0	0	0	0	0	0	1	1	0	0	0	0	0	0	0	0
OTHER EUROPE	1	0	1	0	0	1	0	1	0	0	0	0	0	0	0	0	0	0	0	0
EUROPE EX. U.K.	29	8	17	3	1	16	4	9	2	1	4	2	2	0	0	9	2	6	1	0
SOUTHERN DOMINIONS	5	2	3	0	0	2	0	2	0	0	2	2	0	0	0	1	0	1	0	0
S. AFRICA +RHOD.	2	1	1	0	0	0	0	0	0	0	1	1	0	0	0	1	0	1	0	0
AUSTRALIA +N.Z.	3	1	2	0	0	2	0	2	0	0	1	1	0	0	0	0	0	0	0	0
ASIA + OTHER AFRICA	4	3	1	0	0	0	0	0	0	0	0	0	0	0	0	4	3	1	0	0
JAPAN	1	0	1	0	0	0	0	0	0	0	0	0	0	0	0	1	0	1	0	0
OTHER ASIA+AFR.	3	3	0	0	0	0	0	0	0	0	0	0	0	0	0	3	3	0	0	0
BLACK AFRICA	0	0	0	0	0	0	0	0	0	0	0	0	0	0	0	0	0	0	0	0
ARAB WORLD	0	0	0	0	0	0	0	0	0	0	0	0	0	0	0	0	0	0	0	0
INDIA	0	0	0	0	0	0	0	0	0	0	0	0	0	0	0	0	0	0	0	0
PHILIPPINES	2	2	0	0	0	0	0	0	0	0	0	0	0	0	0	2	2	0	0	0
OTHER E. ASIA	1	1	0	0	0	0	0	0	0	0	0	0	0	0	0	1	1	0	0	0
OTHER ASIA	0	0	0	0	0	0	0	0	0	0	0	0	0	0	0	0	0	0	0	0

CHAPTER 4- VARIETIES OF ENTRY
SECTION 4- THE FLOW OF MANUFACTURING BY INDUSTRY OF SUBSIDIARY
TABLE 42- SUBSIDIARIES MANUFACTURING
OTHER ELECTRONIC EQUIPMENT (SIC 365 AND 367)
CLASSIFIED BY COUNTRY, PERIOD MANUFACTURE BEGAN, AND METHOD OF ENTRY

PERIOD AND METHOD OF ENTRY
(NEW=NEWLY FORMED, ACQ=ACQUIRED, DES=DESCENDANT, UNK=UNKNOWN)

COUNTRY OR REGION	TOTAL PRE 1968					PRE 1946					1946-1957					1958-1967				
	ALL	NEW	ACQ	DES	UNK	ALL	NEW	ACQ	DES	UNK	ALL	NEW	ACQ	DES	UNK	ALL	NEW	ACQ	DES	UNK
OUTSIDE U.S.	81	29	45	4	2	9	7	1	1	0	13	6	6	1	0	58	16	38	2	2
OUT. U.S. + CANADA	72	26	39	4	2	8	6	1	1	0	10	5	4	1	0	53	15	34	2	2
OUT. WEST. HEMIS.	51	15	30	3	2	5	3	1	1	0	9	4	4	2	0	36	8	25	1	2
OUT. WHITE CWEALTH	57	23	30	3	2	4	4	0	0	0	6	4	2	0	0	46	15	28	1	2
OUT. DEVLPED WORLD	27	15	11	1	0	4	4	0	0	0	1	1	0	0	0	22	10	11	1	0
CANADA	9	3	6	0	0	1	1	0	0	0	3	1	2	0	0	5	1	4	0	0
LATIN AMERICA	21	11	9	1	0	3	3	0	0	0	1	1	0	0	0	17	7	9	1	0
C. AMER.+CARIB.	9	3	6	0	0	1	1	0	0	0	0	0	0	0	0	8	2	6	0	0
CUBA	0	0	0	0	0	0	0	0	0	0	0	0	0	0	0	0	0	0	0	0
MEXICO	7	2	5	0	0	1	0	1	0	0	0	0	0	0	0	6	1	5	0	0
OTHER	2	1	1	0	0	0	0	0	0	0	0	0	0	0	0	2	1	1	0	0
S. AMERICA	12	8	3	1	0	2	2	0	0	0	1	1	0	0	0	9	5	3	1	0
ARGENTINA	3	2	1	0	0	0	0	0	0	0	1	1	0	0	0	2	1	1	0	0
BRAZIL	5	2	2	1	0	1	1	0	0	0	0	0	0	0	0	4	1	2	1	0
PERU	0	0	0	0	0	0	0	0	0	0	0	0	0	0	0	0	0	0	0	0
COLOMBIA	0	0	0	0	0	0	0	0	0	0	0	0	0	0	0	0	0	0	0	0
VENEZUELA	2	2	0	0	0	0	0	0	0	0	0	0	0	0	0	2	2	0	0	0
OTHER	2	2	0	0	0	1	1	0	0	0	0	0	0	0	0	1	1	0	0	0
EUROPE	36	9	23	2	2	4	2	1	1	0	5	3	2	0	0	27	4	20	1	2
EFTA	13	2	8	2	1	4	2	1	1	0	1	0	1	0	0	8	1	6	1	1
U.K.	11	2	7	2	0	4	2	1	1	0	1	0	1	0	0	6	0	5	1	0
SCANDINAVIA	0	0	0	0	0	0	0	0	0	0	0	0	0	0	0	0	0	0	0	0
SWITZERLAND	2	0	1	0	1	0	0	0	0	0	0	0	0	0	0	2	0	1	0	1
OTHER EFTA	0	0	0	0	0	0	0	0	0	0	0	0	0	0	0	0	0	0	0	0
EUROP. COMMUNITY	20	5	14	1	0	0	0	0	0	0	2	1	1	0	0	18	4	13	1	0
FRANCE	4	3	1	0	0	0	0	0	0	0	0	0	0	0	0	4	3	1	0	0
GERMANY	9	2	8	0	0	0	0	0	0	0	1	1	0	0	0	8	0	7	0	0
ITALY	6	2	4	0	0	0	0	0	0	0	1	1	1	0	0	5	1	4	0	0
BELGIUM + LUX	1	0	1	0	0	0	0	0	0	0	0	0	0	0	0	1	0	1	0	0
NETHERLANDS	0	0	0	0	0	0	0	0	0	0	0	0	0	0	0	0	0	0	0	0
SPAIN	2	1	1	0	0	0	0	0	0	0	1	1	1	0	0	1	0	1	0	0
GREECE + TURKEY	1	1	0	0	0	0	0	0	0	0	1	0	1	0	0	0	0	0	0	0
OTHER EUROPE	0	0	0	0	0	0	0	0	0	0	0	0	0	0	0	0	0	0	0	0
EUROPE EX. U.K.	25	7	16	0	2	0	0	0	0	0	4	3	1	0	0	21	4	15	0	2
SOUTHERN DOMINIONS	4	1	2	1	0	0	0	0	0	0	3	1	1	1	0	1	0	1	0	0
S. AFRICA +RHOD.	0	0	0	0	0	0	0	0	0	0	0	0	0	0	0	0	0	0	0	0
AUSTRALIA + N.Z.	4	1	2	1	0	0	0	0	0	0	3	1	1	1	0	1	0	1	0	0
ASIA + OTHER AFRICA	11	5	5	1	0	1	1	0	0	0	1	1	1	1	0	8	4	4	0	0
JAPAN	5	1	3	1	0	1	0	0	0	0	1	0	0	1	0	3	1	2	0	0
OTHER ASIA+AFR.	6	4	2	0	0	1	1	0	0	0	0	0	0	0	0	5	3	2	0	0
BLACK AFRICA	1	0	1	0	0	0	0	0	0	0	0	0	0	0	0	1	0	1	0	0
ARAB WORLD	0	0	0	0	0	0	0	0	0	0	0	0	0	0	0	0	0	0	0	0
INDIA	1	1	0	0	0	1	1	0	0	0	0	0	0	0	0	1	1	0	0	0
PHILIPPINES	1	1	0	0	0	0	0	0	0	0	1	1	0	0	0	0	0	0	0	0
OTHER E. ASIA	3	2	1	0	0	0	0	0	0	0	0	0	0	0	0	3	2	1	0	0
OTHER ASIA	0	0	0	0	0	0	0	0	0	0	0	0	0	0	0	0	0	0	0	0

358

(NEW=NEWLY FORMED, ACQ=ACQUIRED, DES=DESCENDANT, UNK=UNKNOWN)

PERIOD AND METHOD OF ENTRY

COUNTRY OR REGION	TOTAL PRE 1968					PRE 1946					1946-1957					1958-1967				
	ALL	NEW	ACQ	DES	UNK	ALL	NEW	ACQ	DES	UNK	ALL	NEW	ACQ	DES	UNK	ALL	NEW	ACQ	DES	UNK
OUTSIDE U.S.	220	86	89	18	22	48	22	15	6	5	47	15	18	5	9	120	49	56	7	8
OUT. U.S. + CANADA	176	76	64	15	17	36	19	11	4	2	33	10	11	4	8	103	47	42	7	7
OUT. WEST. HEMIS.	119	53	44	8	10	30	16	8	4	2	16	8	3	2	3	69	34	28	2	5
OUT. WHITE CWEALTH	139	59	49	11	16	22	11	8	1	2	29	8	10	3	8	84	40	31	7	6
OUT. DEVLPED WORLD	80	35	25	8	11	8	5	3	0	0	22	7	4	3	8	49	23	18	5	3
CANADA	44	10	25	3	5	12	4	4	2	3	14	5	5	1	2	17	2	14	0	1
LATIN AMERICA	57	23	20	7	7	6	3	3	0	0	17	7	7	2	5	34	13	14	5	2
C. AMER.+CARIB.	27	11	9	3	4	1	1	0	0	0	8	2	2	1	2	18	8	6	2	2
CUBA	2	0	0	1	1	0	0	0	0	0	0	0	0	0	0	2	0	0	1	1
MEXICO	18	6	7	2	3	1	1	0	0	0	6	1	1	1	2	11	4	5	1	1
OTHER	7	5	2	0	0	0	0	0	0	0	2	1	1	0	0	5	4	1	0	0
S. AMERICA	30	12	11	4	3	5	2	3	0	0	9	5	5	1	3	16	5	8	3	2
ARGENTINA	7	2	4	1	0	1	0	1	0	0	1	0	2	0	0	6	1	3	1	1
BRAZIL	13	4	6	2	1	3	2	2	0	0	4	2	2	1	0	6	0	3	1	0
PERU	1	1	0	0	0	0	0	0	0	0	0	0	0	0	0	1	1	0	0	0
COLOMBIA	3	1	0	1	1	0	0	0	0	0	2	1	0	1	0	1	0	0	1	1
VENEZUELA	5	4	0	1	0	0	0	0	0	0	2	2	0	1	0	3	2	0	0	0
OTHER	1	0	1	0	0	1	0	0	0	1	0	0	0	0	0	0	0	0	0	0
EUROPE	75	34	29	5	5	22	13	5	2	2	7	2	2	1	0	44	19	20	2	3
EFTA	30	16	11	3	0	12	8	2	2	0	2	2	1	0	0	16	7	9	0	0
U.K.	24	12	9	3	0	10	7	1	2	0	2	1	1	1	0	12	4	8	0	0
SCANDINAVIA	2	1	1	0	0	0	0	0	0	0	1	0	0	0	0	1	1	0	0	0
SWITZERLAND	2	1	1	0	0	0	0	0	0	0	0	0	0	0	0	2	1	1	0	0
OTHER EFTA	2	2	0	0	0	1	1	0	0	0	0	0	0	0	0	1	1	0	0	0
EUROP. COMMUNITY	37	14	15	4	4	9	4	3	0	2	4	2	0	0	2	22	10	8	2	2
FRANCE	14	5	7	1	1	5	2	2	0	1	2	1	0	0	1	6	3	3	0	0
GERMANY	8	3	3	1	1	2	0	2	0	0	1	1	1	0	0	7	3	3	2	0
ITALY	14	6	4	2	2	4	2	0	0	2	1	0	0	0	0	8	4	2	1	1
BELGIUM + LUX	0	0	0	0	0	0	0	0	0	0	0	0	0	0	0	0	0	0	0	0
NETHERLANDS	1	0	1	0	0	0	0	0	0	0	0	0	0	0	0	1	0	0	1	0
SPAIN	3	0	2	0	1	0	0	0	0	0	0	0	0	0	0	3	0	2	0	1
GREECE + TURKEY	3	3	0	1	0	0	0	0	0	0	2	2	1	0	0	2	2	0	1	0
OTHER EUROPE	2	1	0	0	0	1	1	0	0	0	0	0	0	0	0	1	1	0	0	0
EUROPE EX. U.K.	51	22	20	2	5	12	6	4	0	2	5	1	2	0	0	32	15	12	2	3
SOUTHERN DOMINIONS	13	5	6	1	1	4	1	2	0	1	2	1	1	0	0	7	3	3	0	1
S. AFRICA +RHOD.	2	1	1	0	0	0	0	0	0	0	2	1	1	0	0	0	0	0	0	0
AUSTRALIA + N.Z.	11	4	5	1	1	4	1	2	0	1	0	0	0	0	0	7	3	3	0	1
ASIA + OTHER AFRICA	31	14	9	2	4	4	2	1	0	0	7	2	3	1	3	18	12	5	1	0
JAPAN	8	2	4	1	0	2	1	0	0	0	3	0	3	2	0	3	1	2	1	0
OTHER ASIA+AFR.	23	12	5	1	4	2	1	1	0	0	5	2	0	1	3	15	10	4	0	0
BLACK AFRICA	2	2	0	0	0	0	0	0	0	0	0	0	0	0	0	2	2	0	0	0
ARAB WORLD	0	0	0	0	0	0	0	0	0	0	0	0	0	0	0	0	0	0	0	0
INDIA	6	3	3	0	1	1	0	1	0	0	0	0	0	0	0	5	2	3	0	1
PHILIPPINES	3	0	1	1	1	1	0	0	1	0	1	0	0	0	1	1	0	0	1	1
OTHER E. ASIA	5	3	1	0	1	1	1	0	0	0	2	1	1	0	1	2	2	0	0	0
OTHER ASIA	7	4	0	0	2	0	0	0	0	0	1	0	0	0	1	5	4	0	0	1

CHAPTER 4- VARIETIES OF ENTRY

SECTION 4- THE FLOW OF MANUFACTURING BY INDUSTRY OF SUBSIDIARY

TABLE 44- SUBSIDIARIES MANUFACTURING

MOTOR VEHICLES AND MOTOR VEHICLES EQUIPMENT (SIC 371)

CLASSIFIED BY COUNTRY, PERIOD MANUFACTURE BEGAN, AND METHOD OF ENTRY

PERIOD AND METHOD OF ENTRY

(NEW=NEWLY FORMED, ACQ=ACQUIRED, DES=DESCENDANT, UNK=UNKNOWN)

COUNTRY OR REGION	TOTAL PRE 1968					PRE 1946					1946-1957					1958-1967				
	ALL	NEW	ACQ	DES	UNK	ALL	NEW	ACQ	DES	UNK	ALL	NEW	ACQ	DES	UNK	ALL	NEW	ACQ	DES	UNK
OUTSIDE U.S.	306	108	148	31	7	62	29	18	12	3	37	19	10	6	2	195	60	120	13	2
OUT. U.S. + CANADA	258	90	124	28	5	41	21	10	9	1	33	15	10	6	2	173	54	105	12	2
OUT. WEST. HEMIS.	173	51	92	18	2	36	17	9	9	1	22	7	10	4	1	105	27	73	5	0
OUT. WHITE CWEALTH	181	71	82	22	4	24	14	6	6	0	21	10	3	6	2	134	47	75	10	2
OUT. DEVLPED WORLD	101	46	37	14	3	8	6	0	2	0	15	9	1	4	1	77	31	36	8	2
CANADA	48	18	24	3	2	21	8	9	2	2	4	4	0	0	0	22	6	15	1	0
LATIN AMERICA	85	39	32	10	3	5	4	0	1	0	11	8	0	2	1	68	27	32	7	2
C. AMER.+CARIB.	25	12	10	2	1	1	1	0	0	0	2	0	0	1	1	22	11	10	1	0
CUBA	2	0	2	0	1	0	0	0	0	0	0	0	0	0	0	0	0	0	0	0
MEXICO	23	10	10	2	0	1	1	0	0	0	2	0	0	1	1	20	9	10	0	1
OTHER	2	2	0	0	0	0	0	0	0	0	0	0	0	0	0	2	2	0	0	0
S. AMERICA	60	27	22	8	2	4	3	0	1	0	9	8	0	1	0	46	16	22	6	2
ARGENTINA	24	9	11	3	1	2	2	0	0	0	3	3	0	0	0	19	5	11	2	1
BRAZIL	20	10	6	4	0	2	1	0	1	0	5	4	0	1	0	13	4	6	3	0
PERU	2	2	0	0	0	0	0	0	0	0	0	0	0	0	0	2	2	0	0	0
COLOMBIA	5	2	3	0	0	0	0	0	0	0	0	0	0	0	0	5	2	3	0	0
VENEZUELA	7	2	2	1	1	0	0	0	0	0	1	1	0	0	0	6	2	2	1	1
OTHER	2	2	0	1	0	0	0	0	0	0	0	1	0	0	0	1	1	0	0	0
EUROPE	122	29	72	10	2	26	11	8	6	1	12	4	5	2	1	75	14	59	2	0
EFTA	52	5	34	3	1	10	4	4	1	1	7	2	3	2	1	28	1	27	0	0
U.K.	44	2	30	1	1	9	3	4	1	1	5	2	3	2	0	23	1	23	0	0
SCANDINAVIA	6	2	2	2	0	1	1	0	0	0	2	0	0	2	0	3	1	2	0	0
SWITZERLAND	1	0	1	0	0	0	0	0	0	0	0	0	0	0	0	1	0	1	0	0
OTHER EFTA	1	1	0	0	0	0	0	0	0	0	0	0	0	0	0	1	1	0	0	0
EUROP. COMMUNITY	54	16	33	3	1	12	6	4	2	0	3	3	2	0	0	38	10	27	1	1
FRANCE	29	10	18	0	0	5	3	2	0	0	3	2	2	0	0	21	7	14	0	0
GERMANY	11	1	8	2	0	3	2	0	1	0	0	0	0	0	0	8	1	6	1	0
ITALY	8	2	6	0	0	2	1	1	0	0	0	0	0	0	0	6	1	6	0	0
BELGIUM + LUX	3	3	0	0	0	1	1	0	0	0	0	0	0	0	0	2	2	0	0	0
NETHERLANDS	3	0	1	1	1	1	0	0	1	0	0	0	0	0	0	2	0	1	0	1
SPAIN	8	2	5	1	0	1	1	0	0	0	1	0	1	0	0	7	1	5	1	0
GREECE + TURKEY	3	3	0	0	0	0	0	0	0	0	1	1	0	0	0	2	2	0	0	0
OTHER EUROPE	5	1	0	3	1	3	0	0	3	0	1	1	0	0	1	0	0	0	0	0
EUROPE EX. U.K.	78	24	42	9	1	17	8	4	5	0	7	2	2	0	2	52	14	36	2	1
SOUTHERN DOMINIONS	30	13	12	4	0	7	4	1	2	0	6	2	4	0	0	16	7	7	2	0
S. AFRICA +RHOD.	12	7	3	1	0	2	2	0	0	0	0	2	0	0	0	9	5	3	1	1
AUSTRALIA + N.Z.	18	6	9	3	0	5	2	1	2	0	6	2	4	0	0	7	2	4	1	1
ASIA + OTHER AFRICA	21	9	8	4	0	3	2	0	1	0	4	2	1	1	0	14	6	7	1	0
JAPAN	16	7	5	4	0	3	2	0	1	0	4	1	0	3	0	9	3	4	0	0
OTHER ASIA+AFR.	2	1	0	1	0	0	0	0	0	0	0	0	0	0	0	7	3	4	1	0
BLACK AFRICA	2	1	1	0	0	0	0	0	0	0	1	1	0	0	0	1	0	1	0	0
ARAB WORLD	2	1	0	0	0	0	0	0	0	0	0	0	0	0	0	2	2	0	1	1
INDIA	7	3	4	0	0	2	2	0	0	0	1	1	0	0	0	5	1	4	0	0
PHILIPPINES	2	1	0	1	0	0	0	0	0	0	1	1	0	0	0	1	0	0	0	0
OTHER E. ASIA	0	0	0	0	0	0	0	0	0	0	0	0	0	0	0	0	0	0	0	0
OTHER ASIA	3	1	1	1	0	1	0	0	1	0	2	1	1	0	0	0	0	0	0	0

CHAPTER 4- VARIETIES OF ENTRY
SECTION 4- THE FLOW OF MANUFACTURING BY INDUSTRY OF SUBSIDIARY
TABLE 45- SUBSIDIARIES MANUFACTURING
OTHER TRANSPORTATION EQUIPMENT (SIC 372-379)
CLASSIFIED BY COUNTRY, PERIOD MANUFACTURE BEGAN, AND METHOD OF ENTRY

PERIOD AND METHOD OF ENTRY
(NEW=NEWLY FORMED, ACQ=ACQUIRED, DES=DESCENDANT, UNK=UNKNOWN)

COUNTRY OR REGION	TOTAL PRE 1968					PRE 1946					1946-1957					1958-1967				
	ALL	NEW	ACQ	DES	UNK	ALL	NEW	ACQ	DES	UNK	ALL	NEW	ACQ	DES	UNK	ALL	NEW	ACQ	DES	UNK
OUTSIDE U.S.	31	13	13	2	1	7	4	2	1	0	9	2	4	2	1	15	7	7	1	0
OUT. U.S. + CANADA	22	10	8	2	1	6	3	2	1	0	4	1	1	0	1	12	6	5	1	0
OUT. WEST. HEMIS.	19	8	7	2	1	6	3	2	1	0	3	1	1	0	1	10	5	4	1	0
OUT. WHITE CWEALTH	16	8	6	1	1	5	3	2	0	0	2	1	0	0	1	9	4	4	1	0
OUT. DEVLPED WORLD	3	2	1	0	0	0	0	0	0	0	1	1	0	0	0	2	1	1	0	0
CANADA	9	3	5	1	0	1	0	0	1	0	5	2	3	0	0	3	1	2	0	0
LATIN AMERICA	3	2	1	0	0	1	1	0	0	0	0	0	0	0	0	2	1	1	0	0
C. AMER.+CARIB.	2	1	1	0	0	0	0	0	0	0	0	0	0	0	0	2	1	1	0	0
CUBA	0	0	0	0	0	0	0	0	0	0	0	0	0	0	0	0	0	0	0	0
MEXICO	2	1	1	0	0	0	0	0	0	0	0	0	0	0	0	2	1	1	0	0
OTHER	0	0	0	0	0	0	0	0	0	0	0	0	0	0	0	0	0	0	0	0
S. AMERICA	1	0	1	0	0	1	1	0	0	0	0	0	0	0	0	0	0	0	0	0
ARGENTINA	0	0	0	0	0	0	0	0	0	0	0	0	0	0	0	0	0	0	0	0
BRAZIL	1	0	1	0	0	1	1	0	0	0	0	0	0	0	0	0	0	0	0	0
PERU	0	0	0	0	0	0	0	0	0	0	0	0	0	0	0	0	0	0	0	0
COLOMBIA	0	0	0	0	0	0	0	0	0	0	0	0	0	0	0	0	0	0	0	0
VENEZUELA	0	0	0	0	0	0	0	0	0	0	0	0	0	0	0	0	0	0	0	0
OTHER	0	0	0	0	0	0	0	0	0	0	0	0	0	0	0	0	0	0	0	0
EUROPE	16	6	6	1	1	6	3	2	1	0	2	0	0	1	1	8	3	4	1	0
EFTA	4	0	1	1	1	1	1	0	0	0	2	0	1	1	0	1	0	1	0	0
U.K.	3	0	1	1	1	1	1	0	0	0	1	0	0	1	0	1	0	1	0	0
SCANDINAVIA	0	0	0	0	0	0	0	0	0	0	0	0	0	0	0	0	0	0	0	0
SWITZERLAND	0	0	0	0	0	0	0	0	0	0	0	0	0	0	0	0	0	0	0	0
OTHER EFTA	1	0	1	0	0	0	0	0	0	0	1	0	1	0	0	0	0	0	0	0
EUROP. COMMUNITY	12	6	5	1	0	5	3	1	1	0	0	0	0	0	0	7	3	3	1	0
FRANCE	3	1	2	0	0	1	0	1	0	0	0	0	0	0	0	2	1	1	0	0
GERMANY	5	2	3	0	0	3	1	1	1	0	0	0	0	0	0	2	1	2	0	0
ITALY	4	3	1	0	0	1	1	0	0	0	0	0	0	0	0	3	1	1	0	0
BELGIUM + LUX	0	0	0	0	0	0	0	0	0	0	0	0	0	0	0	0	0	0	0	0
NETHERLANDS	0	0	0	0	0	0	0	0	0	0	0	0	0	0	0	0	0	0	0	0
SPAIN	0	0	0	0	0	0	0	0	0	0	0	0	0	0	0	0	0	0	0	0
GREECE + TURKEY	0	0	0	0	0	0	0	0	0	0	0	0	0	0	0	0	0	0	0	0
OTHER EUROPE	0	0	0	0	0	0	0	0	0	0	0	0	0	0	0	0	0	0	0	0
EUROPE EX. U.K.	13	6	5	1	1	5	3	2	0	1	1	0	0	0	1	7	3	3	1	0
SOUTHERN DOMINIONS	3	2	1	0	0	0	0	0	0	0	1	0	1	0	0	2	2	0	0	0
S. AFRICA +RHOD.	1	1	0	0	0	0	0	0	0	0	0	0	0	0	0	1	1	0	0	0
AUSTRALIA + N.Z.	2	1	1	0	0	0	0	0	0	0	1	0	1	0	0	1	1	0	0	0
ASIA + OTHER AFRICA	0	0	0	0	0	0	0	0	0	0	0	0	0	0	0	0	0	0	0	0
JAPAN	0	0	0	0	0	0	0	0	0	0	0	0	0	0	0	0	0	0	0	0
OTHER ASIA+AFR.	0	0	0	0	0	0	0	0	0	0	0	0	0	0	0	0	0	0	0	0
BLACK AFRICA	0	0	0	0	0	0	0	0	0	0	0	0	0	0	0	0	0	0	0	0
ARAB WORLD	0	0	0	0	0	0	0	0	0	0	0	0	0	0	0	0	0	0	0	0
INDIA	0	0	0	0	0	0	0	0	0	0	0	0	0	0	0	0	0	0	0	0
PHILIPPINES	0	0	0	0	0	0	0	0	0	0	0	0	0	0	0	0	0	0	0	0
OTHER E. ASIA	0	0	0	0	0	0	0	0	0	0	0	0	0	0	0	0	0	0	0	0
OTHER ASIA	0	0	0	0	0	0	0	0	0	0	0	0	0	0	0	0	0	0	0	0

CHAPTER 4- VARIETIES OF ENTRY
SECTION 4- THE FLOW OF MANUFACTURING BY INDUSTRY OF SUBSIDIARY
TABLE 46- SUBSIDIARIES MANUFACTURING
MEDICAL INSTRUMENTS AND SUPPLIES (SIC 384)
CLASSIFIED BY COUNTRY, PERIOD MANUFACTURE BEGAN, AND METHOD OF ENTRY

PERIOD AND METHOD OF ENTRY
(NEW=NEWLY FORMED, ACQ=ACQUIRED, DES=DESCENDANT, UNK=UNKNOWN)

COUNTRY OR REGION	TOTAL PRE 1968					PRE 1946					1946-1957					1958-1967				
	ALL	NEW	ACQ	DES	UNK	ALL	NEW	ACQ	DES	UNK	ALL	NEW	ACQ	DES	UNK	ALL	NEW	ACQ	DES	UNK
OUTSIDE U.S.	65	24	38	3	0	7	4	2	1	0	11	5	5	1	0	47	15	31	1	0
OUT. U.S. + CANADA	56	22	32	2	0	5	3	2	0	0	11	5	5	1	0	40	14	25	1	0
OUT. WEST. HEMIS.	43	14	28	1	0	3	1	2	0	0	7	3	4	0	0	33	10	22	1	0
OUT. WHITE CWEALTH	36	16	18	2	0	3	2	0	1	0	5	3	2	0	0	28	11	16	1	0
OUT. DEVLPED WORLD	15	9	4	2	0	3	2	0	1	0	3	2	1	0	0	9	5	3	1	0
CANADA	9	2	6	1	0	2	1	0	1	0	0	0	0	0	0	7	1	6	0	0
LATIN AMERICA	13	8	4	1	0	2	2	0	0	0	4	2	1	1	0	7	4	3	0	0
C. AMER.+CARIB.	3	3	0	0	0	2	2	0	0	0	0	0	0	0	0	1	1	0	0	0
CUBA	1	1	0	0	0	1	1	0	0	0	0	0	0	0	0	0	0	0	0	0
MEXICO	1	1	0	0	0	1	1	0	0	0	0	0	0	0	0	0	0	0	0	0
OTHER	1	1	0	0	0	0	0	0	0	0	0	0	0	0	0	1	1	0	0	0
S. AMERICA	10	5	4	1	0	0	0	0	0	0	4	2	1	1	0	6	3	3	0	0
ARGENTINA	2	1	1	0	0	0	0	0	0	0	1	0	1	0	0	1	1	0	0	0
BRAZIL	6	2	3	1	0	0	0	0	0	0	1	0	0	1	0	5	2	3	0	0
PERU	0	0	0	0	0	0	0	0	0	0	0	0	0	0	0	0	0	0	0	0
COLOMBIA	1	1	0	0	0	0	0	0	0	0	1	1	0	0	0	0	0	0	0	0
VENEZUELA	1	1	0	0	0	0	0	0	0	0	1	1	0	0	0	0	0	0	0	0
OTHER	0	0	0	0	0	0	0	0	0	0	0	0	0	0	0	0	0	0	0	0
EUROPE	36	10	25	1	0	1	0	1	0	0	7	3	4	0	0	28	7	20	1	0
EFTA	16	4	12	0	0	1	0	1	0	0	5	2	3	0	0	10	2	8	0	0
U.K.	14	2	12	0	0	1	0	1	0	0	4	1	3	0	0	9	1	8	0	0
SCANDINAVIA	1	1	0	0	0	0	0	0	0	0	1	1	0	0	0	0	0	0	0	0
SWITZERLAND	0	0	0	0	0	0	0	0	0	0	0	0	0	0	0	0	0	0	0	0
OTHER EFTA	1	1	0	0	0	0	0	0	0	0	0	0	0	0	0	1	1	0	0	0
EUROP. COMMUNITY	19	5	13	1	0	0	0	0	0	0	1	0	1	0	0	18	5	12	1	0
FRANCE	6	1	5	0	0	0	0	0	0	0	0	0	0	0	0	6	1	5	0	0
GERMANY	7	0	6	1	0	0	0	0	0	0	1	0	1	0	0	6	0	5	1	0
ITALY	4	3	1	0	0	0	0	0	0	0	0	0	0	0	0	4	3	1	0	0
BELGIUM + LUX	0	0	0	0	0	0	0	0	0	0	0	0	0	0	0	0	0	0	0	0
NETHERLANDS	2	1	1	0	0	0	0	0	0	0	0	0	0	0	0	2	1	1	0	0
SPAIN	0	0	0	0	0	0	0	0	0	0	0	0	0	0	0	0	0	0	0	0
GREECE + TURKEY	0	0	0	0	0	0	0	0	0	0	0	0	0	0	0	0	0	0	0	0
OTHER EUROPE	1	1	0	0	0	0	0	0	0	0	1	1	0	0	0	0	0	0	0	0
EUROPE EX. U.K.	22	8	13	1	0	0	0	0	0	0	3	2	1	0	0	19	6	12	1	0
SOUTHERN DOMINIONS	5	3	2	0	0	2	1	1	0	0	0	0	0	0	0	3	2	1	0	0
S. AFRICA +RHOD.	1	1	0	0	0	0	0	0	0	0	0	0	0	0	0	1	1	0	0	0
AUSTRALIA + N.Z.	4	2	2	0	0	2	1	1	0	0	0	0	0	0	0	2	1	1	0	0
ASIA + OTHER AFRICA	2	1	1	0	0	0	0	0	0	0	0	0	0	0	0	2	1	1	0	0
JAPAN	0	0	0	0	0	0	0	0	0	0	0	0	0	0	0	0	0	0	0	0
OTHER ASIA+AFR.	2	1	1	0	0	0	0	0	0	0	0	0	0	0	0	2	1	1	0	0
BLACK AFRICA	0	0	0	0	0	0	0	0	0	0	0	0	0	0	0	0	0	0	0	0
ARAB WORLD	0	0	0	0	0	0	0	0	0	0	0	0	0	0	0	0	0	0	0	0
INDIA	1	1	0	0	0	0	0	0	0	0	0	0	0	0	0	1	1	0	0	0
PHILIPPINES	0	0	0	0	0	0	0	0	0	0	0	0	0	0	0	0	0	0	0	0
OTHER E. ASIA	0	0	0	0	0	0	0	0	0	0	0	0	0	0	0	0	0	0	0	0
OTHER ASIA	1	0	1	0	0	0	0	0	0	0	0	0	0	0	0	1	0	1	0	0

CHAPTER 4- VARIETIES OF ENTRY
SECTION 4- THE FLOW OF MANUFACTURING BY INDUSTRY OF SUBSIDIARY
TABLE 47- SUBSIDIARIES MANUFACTURING
OTHER INSTRUMENTS AND PRECISION GOODS (OTHER SIC 38)
CLASSIFIED BY COUNTRY, PERIOD MANUFACTURE BEGAN, AND METHOD OF ENTRY

PERIOD AND METHOD OF ENTRY
(NEW=NEWLY FORMED, ACQ=ACQUIRED, DES=DESCENDANT, UNK=UNKNOWN)

COUNTRY OR REGION	TOTAL ALL	TOTAL NEW	TOTAL ACQ (PRE 1968)	TOTAL DES	TOTAL UNK	PRE 1946 ALL	PRE 1946 NEW	PRE 1946 ACQ	PRE 1946 DES	PRE 1946 UNK	1946-1957 ALL	1946-1957 NEW	1946-1957 ACQ	1946-1957 DES	1946-1957 UNK	1958-1967 ALL	1958-1967 NEW	1958-1967 ACQ	1958-1967 DES	1958-1967 UNK
OUTSIDE U.S.	63	13	42	7	0	10	6	2	2	0	8	1	7	0	0	44	6	33	5	0
OUT. U.S. + CANADA	59	11	41	6	0	8	4	2	2	0	8	1	7	0	0	42	6	32	4	0
OUT. WEST. HEMIS.	46	10	30	5	0	8	4	2	2	0	5	1	4	0	0	32	5	24	3	0
OUT. WHITE CMEALTH	42	8	30	4	0	6	2	2	2	0	4	0	4	0	0	32	6	24	2	0
OUT. DEVLPED WORLD	14	1	12	1	0	0	0	0	0	0	3	0	3	0	0	11	1	9	1	0
CANADA	4	2	1	1	0	2	2	0	0	0	0	0	0	0	0	2	0	1	1	0
LATIN AMERICA	13	1	11	1	0	0	0	0	0	0	3	0	3	0	0	10	1	8	1	0
C. AMER.+CARIB.	4	1	2	1	0	0	0	0	0	0	1	0	1	0	0	3	1	1	1	0
CUBA	0	0	0	0	0	0	0	0	0	0	0	0	0	0	0	0	0	0	0	0
MEXICO	3	1	1	1	0	0	0	0	0	0	1	0	1	0	0	2	1	0	1	0
OTHER	1	0	1	0	0	0	0	0	0	0	0	0	0	0	0	1	0	1	0	0
S. AMERICA	9	0	9	0	0	0	0	0	0	0	2	0	2	0	0	7	0	7	0	0
ARGENTINA	4	0	4	0	0	0	0	0	0	0	2	0	2	0	0	2	0	2	0	0
BRAZIL	2	0	2	0	0	0	0	0	0	0	0	0	0	0	0	2	0	2	0	0
PERU	1	0	1	0	0	0	0	0	0	0	0	0	0	0	0	1	0	1	0	0
COLOMBIA	1	0	1	0	0	0	0	0	0	0	0	0	0	0	0	1	0	1	0	0
VENEZUELA	0	0	0	0	0	0	0	0	0	0	0	0	0	0	0	0	0	0	0	0
OTHER	1	0	1	0	0	0	0	0	0	0	0	0	0	0	0	1	0	1	0	0
EUROPE	41	8	27	5	0	7	3	2	2	0	3	0	3	0	0	30	5	22	3	0
EFTA	14	1	10	2	0	1	1	0	0	0	2	0	2	0	0	10	0	8	2	0
U.K.	13	1	9	2	0	1	1	0	0	0	2	0	2	0	0	9	0	7	2	0
SCANDINAVIA	0	0	0	0	0	0	0	0	0	0	0	0	0	0	0	0	0	0	0	0
SWITZERLAND	0	0	0	0	0	0	0	0	0	0	0	0	0	0	0	0	0	0	0	0
OTHER EFTA	1	1	0	0	0	0	0	0	0	0	0	0	0	0	0	1	1	0	0	0
EUROP. COMMUNITY	26	7	16	3	0	6	2	2	2	0	1	0	1	0	0	19	5	13	1	0
FRANCE	7	3	3	1	0	3	1	1	1	0	0	0	0	0	0	4	2	2	0	0
GERMANY	13	2	9	2	0	3	1	1	1	0	1	0	1	0	0	9	1	7	1	0
ITALY	2	1	1	0	0	0	0	0	0	0	0	0	0	0	0	2	1	1	0	0
BELGIUM + LUX	3	2	1	0	0	0	0	0	0	0	0	0	0	0	0	3	2	1	0	0
NETHERLANDS	1	1	0	0	0	0	0	0	0	0	0	0	0	0	0	1	1	0	0	0
SPAIN	1	0	1	0	0	0	0	0	0	0	0	0	0	0	0	1	0	1	0	0
GREECE + TURKEY	0	0	0	0	0	0	0	0	0	0	0	0	0	0	0	0	0	0	0	0
OTHER EUROPE	0	0	0	0	0	0	0	0	0	0	0	0	0	0	0	0	0	0	0	0
EUROPE Ex. U.K.	28	7	18	3	0	6	2	2	2	0	1	0	1	0	0	21	5	15	1	0
SOUTHERN DOMINIONS	4	2	2	0	0	2	1	1	0	0	1	1	0	0	0	1	0	1	0	0
S. AFRICA +RHOD.	1	1	0	0	0	0	0	0	0	0	1	1	0	0	0	0	0	0	0	0
AUSTRALIA + N.Z.	3	1	2	0	0	2	1	1	0	0	0	0	0	0	0	1	0	1	0	0
ASIA + OTHER AFRICA	1	0	1	0	0	0	0	0	0	0	0	0	0	0	0	1	0	1	0	0
JAPAN	0	0	0	0	0	0	0	0	0	0	0	0	0	0	0	0	0	0	0	0
OTHER ASIA+AFR.	1	0	1	0	0	0	0	0	0	0	0	0	0	0	0	1	0	1	0	0
BLACK AFRICA	0	0	0	0	0	0	0	0	0	0	0	0	0	0	0	0	0	0	0	0
ARAB WORLD	0	0	0	0	0	0	0	0	0	0	0	0	0	0	0	0	0	0	0	0
INDIA	1	0	1	0	0	0	0	0	0	0	0	0	0	0	0	1	0	1	0	0
PHILIPPINES	0	0	0	0	0	0	0	0	0	0	0	0	0	0	0	0	0	0	0	0
OTHER E. ASIA	0	0	0	0	0	0	0	0	0	0	0	0	0	0	0	0	0	0	0	0
OTHER ASIA	0	0	0	0	0	0	0	0	0	0	0	0	0	0	0	0	0	0	0	0

CHAPTER 4- VARIETIES OF ENTRY

SECTION 4- THE FLOW OF MANUFACTURING BY INDUSTRY OF SUBSIDIARY

TABLE 48- SUBSIDIARIES MANUFACTURING
OTHER PRODUCTS (SIC 19,21,31, AND 39) OR UNKNOWN PRODUCT
CLASSIFIED BY COUNTRY, PERIOD MANUFACTURE BEGAN, AND METHOD OF ENTRY

PERIOD AND METHOD OF ENTRY
(NEW=NEWLY FORMED, ACQ=ACQUIRED, DES=DESCENDANT, UNK=UNKNOWN)

COUNTRY OR REGION	TOTAL (PRE 1968) ALL	NEW	ACQ	DES	UNK	PRE 1946 ALL	NEW	ACQ	DES	UNK	1946-1957 ALL	NEW	ACQ	DES	UNK	1958-1967 ALL	NEW	ACQ	DES	UNK
OUTSIDE U.S.	431	155	151	46	53	110	48	28	16	18	65	24	26	8	7	230	83	97	22	28
OUT. U.S. + CANADA	359	136	116	42	45	89	39	21	15	14	46	17	17	7	5	204	80	78	20	26
OUT. WEST. HEMIS.	271	100	91	31	36	69	28	17	12	12	30	11	13	2	4	159	61	61	17	20
OUT. WHITE CWEALTH	265	102	78	30	39	57	27	11	8	11	33	13	13	7	3	159	62	57	15	25
OUT. DEVLPED WORLD	126	52	32	15	18	28	13	4	4	7	21	9	4	6	2	68	30	24	5	9
CANADA	72	19	35	4	8	21	9	7	1	4	19	7	9	1	2	26	3	19	2	2
LATIN AMERICA	88	36	25	11	9	20	11	4	3	2	16	6	4	5	1	45	19	17	3	6
C. AMER.+CARIB.	29	12	8	4	1	6	4	1	1	0	5	3	1	1	0	14	5	6	2	1
CUBA	3	2	0	1	0	1	0	0	1	0	2	2	0	0	0	0	0	0	0	0
MEXICO	20	8	7	2	1	4	3	1	0	0	3	1	1	1	0	11	4	5	1	1
OTHER	6	2	1	1	0	1	1	0	0	0	0	0	0	0	0	3	1	1	1	0
S. AMERICA	59	24	17	7	8	14	7	3	2	2	11	3	3	4	1	31	14	11	1	5
ARGENTINA	8	3	1	1	1	3	1	0	1	1	2	0	0	0	0	3	2	1	0	0
BRAZIL	13	7	3	2	1	5	4	0	0	1	2	0	1	1	0	6	3	2	1	0
PERU	3	1	1	1	0	1	0	0	1	0	2	1	1	0	0	0	0	0	0	0
COLOMBIA	10	1	4	0	5	1	0	1	0	0	2	1	1	0	0	7	1	2	0	4
VENEZUELA	15	5	6	2	1	1	1	0	0	0	3	0	1	2	0	10	4	5	0	1
OTHER	10	7	2	1	0	3	2	1	0	0	2	1	0	1	0	5	4	1	0	0
EUROPE	190	61	71	23	24	53	19	16	11	7	18	4	11	1	2	108	38	44	11	15
EFTA	82	25	28	14	10	36	15	10	7	4	5	0	4	0	1	36	10	14	7	5
U.K.	56	12	26	9	5	27	9	7	7	2	5	0	4	0	1	20	3	15	2	2
SCANDINAVIA	12	7	0	2	3	5	1	0	2	2	0	0	0	0	0	7	5	0	0	1
SWITZERLAND	10	3	1	3	2	2	2	0	0	0	0	0	0	0	0	7	1	1	3	2
OTHER EFTA	4	3	1	0	0	2	2	0	0	0	0	0	0	0	0	2	1	1	0	0
EUROP. COMMUNITY	84	28	30	8	12	14	5	5	3	1	9	4	3	1	1	55	21	22	4	8
FRANCE	29	7	13	3	4	7	2	3	1	1	3	1	1	0	1	17	4	10	1	2
GERMANY	23	7	10	2	3	2	2	0	0	0	2	0	2	0	0	18	5	8	2	3
ITALY	14	8	4	0	1	1	0	0	0	1	3	3	0	0	0	9	5	4	0	0
BELGIUM + LUX	7	4	1	2	2	3	1	1	0	1	0	0	0	0	0	3	2	0	1	1
NETHERLANDS	11	2	8	1	2	1	0	1	0	0	1	0	0	1	0	8	1	5	0	2
SPAIN	12	1	1	2	2	1	0	0	1	0	3	0	3	0	0	8	2	4	1	1
GREECE + TURKEY	3	2	0	1	0	0	0	0	0	0	0	0	0	0	0	3	2	0	1	0
OTHER EUROPE	9	5	1	0	0	2	1	0	0	1	1	0	1	0	0	6	4	1	0	1
EUROPE EX. U.K.	134	49	45	14	19	26	12	6	4	4	13	4	7	1	1	88	33	32	9	14
SOUTHERN DOMINIONS	32	19	9	3	1	5	5	0	0	0	7	4	2	0	1	20	10	7	3	0
S. AFRICA +RHOD.	10	4	4	1	1	2	2	0	0	0	2	1	1	0	0	6	1	3	1	1
AUSTRALIA + N.Z.	22	15	5	2	0	3	3	0	0	0	5	3	2	0	0	14	9	3	2	0
ASIA + OTHER AFRICA	49	20	11	5	11	11	4	1	2	4	5	3	0	0	2	31	13	10	3	5
JAPAN	11	4	4	1	2	3	2	0	1	0	0	0	0	0	0	8	2	4	0	2
OTHER ASIA+AFR.	38	16	7	4	9	8	2	1	0	5	5	3	0	0	2	23	11	7	3	2
BLACK AFRICA	8	3	2	0	3	0	0	0	0	0	1	0	0	0	1	7	3	2	0	2
ARAB WORLD	3	2	0	1	0	0	0	0	0	0	1	1	0	0	0	2	1	0	1	0
INDIA	2	1	1	1	0	0	0	0	0	0	0	0	0	0	0	2	1	1	0	0
PHILIPPINES	3	0	0	0	0	0	0	0	0	0	1	0	0	0	1	3	1	1	0	1
OTHER E. ASIA	4	0	3	1	0	1	0	0	1	0	0	0	0	0	0	3	0	3	0	0
OTHER ASIA	18	10	1	1	5	6	2	0	0	4	2	2	0	0	0	9	6	1	1	1

CHAPTER 4- VARIETIES OF ENTRY
SECTION 5- THE FLOW OF MANUFACTURING BY CHARACTERISTIC OF SUBSIDIARY
TABLE A1- MANUFACTURING SUBSIDIARIES WHICH WERE AMONG
THE 1ST - 3RD FOREIGN MANUFACTURING SUBSIDIARIES IN THEIR PARENT SYSTEM,
CLASSIFIED BY COUNTRY, PERIOD MANUFACTURE BEGAN, AND METHOD OF ENTRY

(NEW=NEWLY FORMED, ACQ=ACQUIRED, DES=DESCENDANT, UNK=UNKNOWN)

PERIOD AND METHOD OF ENTRY

COUNTRY OR REGION	TOTAL PRE 1968					PRE 1946					1946-1957					1958-1967				
	ALL	NEW	ACQ	DES	UNK	ALL	NEW	ACQ	DES	UNK	ALL	NEW	ACQ	DES	UNK	ALL	NEW	ACQ	DES	UNK
OUTSIDE U.S.	561	289	193	37	40	368	199	112	22	35	139	64	56	14	5	52	26	25	1	0
OUT. U.S. + CANADA	374	190	125	26	31	225	118	66	15	26	101	48	38	10	5	46	24	21	1	0
OUT. WEST. HEMIS.	274	129	98	22	24	178	87	56	15	20	62	24	28	6	4	33	18	14	1	0
OUT. WHITE CWEALTH	233	129	72	7	23	125	75	30	2	18	70	35	25	5	5	36	19	17	0	0
OUT. DEVLPED WORLD	115	73	28	4	9	53	35	10	0	8	47	31	11	4	1	14	7	7	0	0
CANADA	187	99	68	11	9	143	81	46	7	9	38	16	18	4	0	6	2	4	0	0
LATIN AMERICA	100	61	27	4	7	47	31	10	0	6	39	24	10	4	1	13	6	7	0	0
C. AMER.+CARIB.	52	31	13	3	4	21	15	3	0	3	22	12	6	3	1	8	4	4	0	0
CUBA	11	5	1	1	4	6	2	1	0	3	5	3	0	1	1	0	0	0	0	0
MEXICO	40	26	11	2	0	15	13	2	0	0	16	9	5	2	0	8	4	4	0	0
OTHER	1	0	1	0	0	0	0	0	0	0	1	0	1	0	0	0	0	0	0	0
S. AMERICA	48	30	14	1	3	26	16	7	0	3	17	13	4	1	0	5	2	3	0	0
ARGENTINA	15	7	7	0	1	12	6	5	0	1	0	0	0	0	0	3	1	2	0	0
BRAZIL	10	8	1	1	0	4	3	1	0	0	5	4	0	1	0	1	1	0	0	0
PERU	4	2	2	0	0	3	2	1	0	0	1	0	1	0	0	0	0	0	0	0
COLOMBIA	5	3	2	0	0	1	1	0	0	0	3	2	1	0	0	1	0	1	0	0
VENEZUELA	9	8	1	0	0	2	2	0	0	0	7	6	1	0	0	0	0	0	0	0
OTHER	5	2	1	0	2	4	2	1	0	1	1	1	0	0	0	0	0	0	0	0
EUROPE	216	95	83	18	20	149	71	49	13	16	39	10	20	5	4	28	14	14	0	0
EFTA	112	43	42	16	11	85	34	30	12	9	21	7	8	4	2	6	2	4	0	0
U.K.	101	40	40	15	6	77	31	29	11	6	18	7	7	4	0	6	2	4	0	0
SCANDINAVIA	8	1	2	1	4	6	1	1	1	3	2	0	1	0	1	0	0	0	0	0
SWITZERLAND	0	0	0	0	0	0	0	0	0	0	0	0	0	0	0	0	0	0	0	0
OTHER EFTA	3	2	0	0	1	2	2	0	0	0	1	0	0	0	1	0	0	0	0	0
EUROP. COMMUNITY	91	46	36	2	7	54	32	16	1	5	17	3	11	1	2	20	11	9	0	0
FRANCE	29	16	11	1	1	20	12	7	1	0	5	1	3	0	1	4	3	1	0	0
GERMANY	30	17	10	0	3	25	16	6	0	3	4	1	3	0	0	1	0	1	0	0
ITALY	11	6	5	0	0	5	0	3	0	2	3	0	2	1	0	3	3	0	0	0
BELGIUM + LUX	13	3	8	0	2	1	1	0	0	0	4	1	1	0	2	8	1	7	0	0
NETHERLANDS	8	4	2	1	1	5	1	3	0	1	1	1	0	0	0	2	2	0	0	0
SPAIN	7	1	5	0	1	5	0	3	0	2	0	0	0	0	0	2	0	2	0	0
GREECE + TURKEY	0	0	0	0	0	0	0	0	0	0	0	0	0	0	0	0	0	0	0	0
OTHER EUROPE	6	5	0	0	1	5	4	0	0	1	0	0	0	0	0	1	1	0	0	0
EUROPE EX. U.K.	115	55	43	3	14	72	40	20	2	10	21	3	13	1	4	22	12	10	0	0
SOUTHERN DOMINIONS	38	19	13	4	2	22	11	7	2	2	13	6	6	1	0	3	2	0	1	0
S. AFRICA +RHOD.	10	6	3	0	1	6	3	2	0	1	3	2	1	0	0	1	1	0	0	0
AUSTRALIA + N.Z.	28	13	10	4	1	16	8	5	2	1	10	4	5	1	0	2	1	0	1	0
ASIA + OTHER AFRICA	20	15	2	0	2	7	5	1	0	1	10	8	1	0	1	2	2	0	0	0
JAPAN	5	3	1	0	1	1	1	0	0	0	2	1	1	0	0	1	1	0	0	0
OTHER ASIA+AFR.	15	12	0	0	2	6	4	1	0	1	8	7	0	0	1	1	1	0	0	0
BLACK AFRICA	0	0	0	0	0	0	0	0	0	0	0	0	0	0	0	0	0	0	0	0
ARAB WORLD	0	0	0	0	0	0	0	0	0	0	0	0	0	0	0	0	0	0	0	0
INDIA	0	0	0	0	0	0	0	0	0	0	0	0	0	0	0	0	0	0	0	0
PHILIPPINES	5	5	0	0	0	3	3	0	0	0	2	2	0	0	0	0	0	0	0	0
OTHER E. ASIA	1	0	0	0	1	1	0	0	0	1	0	0	0	0	0	0	0	0	0	0
OTHER ASIA	9	7	1	0	1	2	1	1	0	0	6	5	1	0	0	1	1	0	0	0

CHAPTER 4- VARIETIES OF ENTRY
SECTION 5- THE FLOW OF MANUFACTURING BY CHARACTERISTIC OF SUBSIDIARY
TABLE A2- MANUFACTURING SUBSIDIARIES WHICH WERE AMONG
THE 4TH - 10TH FOREIGN MANUFACTURING SUBSIDIARIES IN THEIR PARENT SYSTEM,
CLASSIFIED BY COUNTRY, PERIOD MANUFACTURE BEGAN, AND METHOD OF ENTRY

PERIOD AND METHOD OF ENTRY
(NEW=NEWLY FORMED, ACQ=ACQUIRED, DES=DESCENDANT, UNK=UNKNOWN)

COUNTRY OR REGION	TOTAL					PRE 1946					1946-1957					1958-1967				
	ALL	NEW	ACQ	DES	UNK	ALL	NEW	ACQ	DES	UNK	ALL	NEW	ACQ	DES	UNK	ALL	NEW	ACQ	DES	UNK
OUTSIDE U.S.	1279	589	511	106	73	403	190	142	37	34	390	199	138	34	19	486	200	231	35	20
OUT. U.S. + CANADA	1053	526	385	87	55	319	167	101	29	22	302	169	91	27	15	432	190	193	31	18
OUT. WEST. HEMIS.	694	336	264	61	33	222	112	71	25	14	170	87	59	18	6	302	137	134	18	13
OUT. WHITE CWEALTH	788	404	283	56	45	232	121	78	16	17	223	133	60	17	13	333	150	145	23	15
OUT. DEVLPED WORLD	416	226	136	28	26	111	62	34	5	10	150	95	36	9	10	155	69	66	14	6
CANADA	226	63	126	19	18	84	23	41	8	12	88	30	47	7	4	54	10	38	4	2
LATIN AMERICA	359	190	121	26	22	97	55	30	4	8	132	82	32	5	9	130	53	59	13	5
C. AMER.+CARIB.	153	77	53	16	7	38	21	11	2	4	56	32	16	5	3	59	24	26	9	0
CUBA	21	11	6	2	2	17	5	4	1	1	8	5	1	1	1	2	1	1	0	0
MEXICO	104	49	38	14	3	17	7	6	1	1	44	23	15	4	2	43	17	17	9	0
OTHER	28	17	9	0	2	10	1	1	0	2	4	4	0	0	0	14	6	8	0	0
S. AMERICA	206	113	68	10	15	59	34	19	2	4	76	50	16	4	6	71	29	33	4	5
ARGENTINA	49	26	18	3	2	16	11	4	1	0	15	9	3	2	1	18	6	11	0	1
BRAZIL	65	38	18	5	4	22	11	7	1	3	24	16	4	1	3	19	11	7	3	0
PERU	14	6	6	0	2	6	3	1	1	1	5	3	2	0	0	3	0	3	0	0
COLOMBIA	29	18	7	0	4	3	2	0	0	1	12	8	3	0	1	14	8	4	0	2
VENEZUELA	34	19	11	2	2	3	3	0	0	0	16	11	3	1	1	15	5	8	1	1
OTHER	15	6	8	0	1	9	2	6	0	1	4	3	1	0	0	2	1	1	0	0
EUROPE	484	213	199	46	26	167	74	59	22	12	107	52	37	14	4	210	87	103	10	10
EFTA	176	70	73	24	9	70	29	25	11	5	44	18	16	9	1	62	23	32	4	3
U.K.	131	44	61	19	7	49	16	18	10	5	37	15	14	7	1	45	13	29	2	1
SCANDINAVIA	23	14	8	1	0	10	6	4	0	0	4	2	2	0	0	9	6	2	1	0
SWITZERLAND	10	3	2	4	1	3	1	1	1	0	2	0	2	0	0	5	2	0	2	1
OTHER EFTA	12	9	2	0	1	8	6	2	0	0	1	1	0	0	0	3	2	0	1	1
EUROP. COMMUNITY	276	127	113	21	15	89	40	33	10	6	52	27	17	5	3	135	60	63	6	3
FRANCE	95	33	45	9	8	34	9	17	6	2	17	8	8	0	1	44	16	25	3	0
GERMANY	73	34	29	8	3	23	12	8	2	1	16	6	8	0	0	34	16	13	6	1
ITALY	52	32	16	1	3	12	9	1	2	0	9	6	3	0	0	31	17	12	1	1
BELGIUM + LUX	29	17	9	2	1	10	5	2	0	3	6	5	1	0	0	13	7	6	2	0
NETHERLANDS	27	11	14	0	1	10	4	5	0	1	4	2	2	0	0	13	4	6	1	1
SPAIN	19	10	8	0	0	4	1	0	0	0	4	2	2	0	0	11	4	6	0	0
GREECE + TURKEY	3	3	0	0	1	1	0	0	0	1	3	3	0	0	0	0	0	0	0	0
OTHER EUROPE	10	3	5	1	1	4	1	0	1	0	2	2	0	0	0	2	0	2	0	0
EUROPE EX. U.K.	353	169	138	27	19	118	58	41	12	7	70	37	23	7	3	165	74	74	8	9
SOUTHERN DOMINIONS	127	76	37	11	3	37	30	5	2	0	38	19	15	3	1	52	27	17	6	2
S. AFRICA +RHOD.	42	31	9	2	0	12	12	0	0	0	13	9	3	1	0	17	10	6	1	0
AUSTRALIA + N.Z.	85	45	28	9	3	25	18	5	2	0	25	10	12	2	1	35	17	11	5	2
ASIA + OTHER AFRICA	83	47	28	4	4	18	8	7	2	1	25	16	7	1	1	40	23	14	2	1
JAPAN	26	11	13	2	0	4	1	3	0	0	7	3	4	0	0	15	7	7	1	1
OTHER ASIA+AFR.	57	36	15	0	4	14	7	4	0	0	18	13	4	1	0	25	16	7	0	0
BLACK AFRICA	1	1	0	0	0	0	0	0	0	0	1	1	0	0	0	0	0	0	0	0
ARAB WORLD	5	4	1	0	0	2	2	0	0	0	1	0	1	0	0	4	4	0	0	0
INDIA	16	11	4	0	1	2	1	0	0	0	4	4	0	1	0	10	5	4	0	1
PHILIPPINES	12	8	4	0	0	3	1	2	0	0	5	4	1	0	0	4	3	1	0	0
OTHER E. ASIA	5	2	3	0	0	1	0	0	1	0	1	1	0	0	0	1	1	0	0	0
OTHER ASIA	18	10	3	2	3	6	3	0	1	2	6	3	2	0	0	6	4	1	1	0

CHAPTER 4- VARIETIES OF ENTRY
SECTION 5- THE FLOW OF MANUFACTURING BY CHARACTERISTIC OF SUBSIDIARY
TABLE A3- MANUFACTURING SUBSIDIARIES WHICH WERE AMONG
THE 11TH - 25TH FOREIGN MANUFACTURING SUBSIDIARIES IN THR PARENT SYSTEM,
CLASSIFIED BY COUNTRY, PERIOD MANUFACTURE BEGAN, AND METHOD OF ENTRY

PERIOD AND METHOD OF ENTRY
(NEW=NEWLY FORMED, ACQ=ACQUIRED, DES=DESCENDANT, UNK=UNKNOWN)

COUNTRY OR REGION	TOTAL PRE 1968					PRE 1946					1946-1957					1958-1967				
	ALL	NEW	ACQ	DES	UNK	ALL	NEW	ACQ	DES	UNK	ALL	NEW	ACQ	DES	UNK	ALL	NEW	ACQ	DES	UNK
OUTSIDE U.S.	1896	776	844	126	127	205	120	40	19	26	382	155	150	33	44	1286	501	654	74	57
OUT. U.S. + CANADA	1661	721	697	121	105	175	104	33	17	21	323	144	112	33	34	1146	473	552	71	50
OUT. WEST. HEMIS.	1147	480	501	80	73	122	70	24	14	14	182	78	64	18	22	830	332	413	48	37
OUT. WHITE CWEALTH	1294	595	517	93	79	120	70	25	11	14	264	125	88	25	26	900	400	404	57	39
OUT. DEVLPED WORLD	663	326	237	54	41	60	39	9	4	8	164	78	51	19	16	434	209	177	31	17
CANADA	235	55	147	5	22	30	16	7	2	5	59	11	38	0	10	140	28	102	3	7
LATIN AMERICA	514	241	196	41	32	53	34	9	3	7	141	66	48	15	12	316	141	139	23	13
C. AMER.+CARIB.	209	89	86	18	14	14	12	1	0	1	47	20	14	7	6	146	57	71	11	7
CUBA	12	4	1	3	2	2	1	1	0	0	7	3	1	2	1	1	0	0	1	1
MEXICO	130	54	64	7	5	10	9	1	0	0	26	13	10	1	2	94	32	53	6	3
OTHER	67	31	21	8	7	2	2	0	0	0	14	4	3	3	4	51	25	18	5	3
S. AMERICA	305	152	110	23	18	39	22	8	3	6	94	46	34	8	6	170	84	68	12	6
ARGENTINA	68	28	30	5	4	15	8	3	2	2	15	7	8	0	0	37	13	19	3	2
BRAZIL	77	34	32	7	4	9	6	2	0	1	30	13	11	3	3	38	15	19	4	0
PERU	21	12	7	0	2	2	1	0	1	0	9	6	2	1	0	10	5	5	0	0
COLOMBIA	47	21	20	4	2	6	3	2	0	1	12	5	6	0	1	29	13	12	2	2
VENEZUELA	58	41	10	3	4	3	2	0	1	0	17	9	4	2	2	38	30	6	1	1
OTHER	34	16	11	4	2	4	2	1	0	1	11	6	3	2	0	18	8	7	2	1
EUROPE	756	284	365	49	47	83	40	22	10	11	121	54	47	8	12	541	190	296	31	24
EFTA	252	84	128	16	18	39	20	11	5	4	43	14	18	6	5	164	50	101	5	8
U.K.	187	52	104	11	14	25	11	6	4	1	33	11	15	3	4	123	30	83	4	6
SCANDINAVIA	37	18	12	4	3	8	5	2	0	1	8	3	2	3	0	21	10	8	1	2
SWITZERLAND	13	5	7	0	1	1	1	0	0	0	1	0	0	1	0	11	4	7	0	0
OTHER EFTA	15	9	5	1	0	5	3	1	1	0	1	0	1	0	0	9	6	3	0	0
EUROP. COMMUNITY	402	152	193	28	24	34	17	9	3	5	62	30	23	2	7	301	105	161	23	12
FRANCE	120	40	63	9	7	9	7	2	0	0	11	6	3	0	2	97	31	56	8	3
GERMANY	116	41	58	10	5	14	8	4	2	0	24	6	14	1	3	78	27	40	8	3
ITALY	95	40	44	4	4	4	2	4	0	1	16	11	2	1	2	73	27	40	2	3
BELGIUM + LUX	32	12	14	2	4	2	1	1	0	0	3	2	1	0	0	27	9	13	2	3
NETHERLANDS	39	19	14	2	3	5	3	1	1	0	8	5	1	0	2	26	11	12	2	1
SPAIN	67	28	35	2	2	3	1	2	0	0	10	4	5	0	1	54	22	28	2	2
GREECE + TURKEY	17	12	3	0	2	1	1	0	0	0	3	2	1	0	0	14	9	3	0	0
OTHER EUROPE	18	8	6	3	1	7	2	2	2	1	3	0	2	0	1	8	4	3	1	0
EUROPE EX. U.K.	569	232	261	38	33	58	29	16	6	7	88	43	32	5	8	418	160	213	27	18
SOUTHERN DOMINIONS	170	69	73	16	11	28	22	2	2	2	23	6	8	5	4	118	41	63	9	5
S. AFRICA +RHOD.	46	20	19	6	1	8	7	0	0	1	8	3	3	1	1	30	10	16	4	0
AUSTRALIA + N.Z.	124	49	54	10	10	20	15	2	2	1	15	3	5	4	3	88	31	47	5	5
ASIA + OTHER AFRICA	221	127	63	15	15	11	8	0	0	2	38	18	9	5	6	171	101	54	8	8
JAPAN	72	42	22	2	6	4	4	0	0	0	15	6	6	0	2	53	33	16	2	4
OTHER ASIA+AFR.	149	85	41	13	9	7	5	0	0	1	23	12	3	4	4	118	68	38	8	4
BLACK AFRICA	16	10	4	0	2	0	0	0	0	0	4	2	0	0	2	12	8	4	0	0
ARAB WORLD	17	12	2	2	1	0	0	0	0	0	2	2	0	0	0	13	10	1	1	1
INDIA	38	20	13	4	1	3	1	0	1	1	2	0	2	0	0	32	15	13	4	0
PHILIPPINES	25	13	8	3	1	1	1	0	0	0	10	5	5	0	0	14	7	7	2	0
OTHER E. ASIA	18	11	5	0	2	1	1	0	0	0	2	0	0	2	0	18	11	5	2	0
OTHER ASIA	35	19	9	2	5	3	1	0	0	1	3	1	0	3	1	29	17	8	1	3

CHAPTER 4- VARIETIES OF ENTRY

SECTION 5- THE FLOW OF MANUFACTURING BY CHARACTERISTIC OF SUBSIDIARY

TABLE A4- MANUFACTURING SUBSIDIARIES WHICH WERE AMONG THE MORE THAN 25TH FOREIGN MANUFACTURING SUBSIDIARIES IN THEIR PARENT SYSTEM, CLASSIFIED BY COUNTRY, PERIOD MANUFACTURE BEGAN, AND METHOD OF ENTRY

(NEW=NEWLY FORMED, ACQ=ACQUIRED, DES=DESCENDANT, UNK=UNKNOWN)

COUNTRY OR REGION	TOTAL PRE 1968 ALL	NEW	ACQ	DES	UNK	PERIOD AND METHOD OF ENTRY — PRE 1946 ALL	NEW	ACQ	DES	UNK	1946-1957 ALL	NEW	ACQ	DES	UNK	1958-1967 ALL	NEW	ACQ	DES	UNK
OUTSIDE U.S.	1492	531	649	81	115	104	54	28	12	10	56	22	13	8	13	1216	455	608	61	92
OUT. U.S. + CANADA	1336	499	558	75	105	88	44	23	11	10	45	19	10	8	8	1104	436	525	56	87
OUT. WEST. HEMIS.	965	341	417	50	86	57	29	15	5	8	33	15	6	3	8	804	302	393	39	70
OUT. WHITE CWEALTH	1033	426	401	59	79	61	26	17	10	8	31	15	5	10	1	873	385	381	42	65
OUT. DEVLPED WORLD	517	237	167	35	38	37	16	9	8	4	15	9	1	4	1	425	212	157	22	34
CANADA	156	32	91	6	10	16	10	5	1	0	11	3	3	3	2	112	19	83	5	5
LATIN AMERICA	371	158	141	25	19	31	15	8	6	2	12	7	1	2	2	300	134	132	17	17
C. AMER.+CARIB.	156	63	63	10	5	7	4	2	1	0	7	1	2	2	2	127	52	61	9	5
CUBA	4	3	0	1	0	2	2	0	0	0	1	0	0	1	0	1	0	0	1	0
MEXICO	92	30	45	5	2	5	2	2	1	0	4	2	2	0	0	73	24	43	4	2
OTHER	60	30	18	4	3	0	0	0	0	0	2	0	0	1	1	53	28	18	4	3
S. AMERICA	215	95	78	15	14	24	11	6	5	2	5	2	2	0	1	173	82	71	8	12
ARGENTINA	30	10	12	3	2	3	1	2	0	0	2	0	0	2	0	22	8	10	2	1
BRAZIL	55	22	26	4	1	13	6	4	3	0	0	0	0	0	0	40	16	22	1	1
PERU	18	8	4	2	0	0	0	0	0	0	0	0	0	0	0	14	8	4	1	1
COLOMBIA	36	15	14	2	4	2	1	0	0	1	0	0	0	0	0	33	14	14	2	3
VENEZUELA	43	23	12	3	1	3	0	0	0	1	0	0	0	0	0	36	20	11	2	3
OTHER	33	17	10	1	3	3	1	0	1	1	0	0	0	0	0	28	10	10	0	2
EUROPE	602	180	305	31	54	37	17	11	3	6	26	8	6	6	6	507	155	286	26	40
EFTA	211	51	105	16	22	17	9	4	1	3	13	4	4	1	3	164	38	95	15	16
U.K.	134	20	75	9	15	13	6	4	1	2	10	2	6	0	2	96	12	65	8	11
SCANDINAVIA	46	16	20	5	4	3	2	0	1	0	1	0	0	0	2	41	14	20	5	2
SWITZERLAND	14	6	4	2	2	1	1	0	0	0	2	1	0	0	0	11	3	4	2	2
OTHER EFTA	17	10	6	0	1	0	0	0	0	0	1	1	0	0	0	16	9	6	0	1
EUROP. COMMUNITY	307	94	162	13	24	17	6	7	2	2	7	2	1	1	3	269	86	154	10	19
FRANCE	78	22	46	3	3	4	0	2	1	1	2	2	0	0	0	68	20	44	9	2
GERMANY	84	17	49	4	10	3	0	3	0	0	1	0	0	2	3	74	17	46	2	7
ITALY	65	23	33	3	5	7	4	1	0	2	2	0	2	1	0	56	19	30	2	5
BELGIUM + LUX	45	19	22	2	2	1	1	0	0	0	2	0	0	1	1	42	18	22	1	1
NETHERLANDS	35	13	12	2	4	2	1	1	0	0	4	0	0	0	0	29	12	12	2	2
SPAIN	44	15	24	0	3	0	0	0	0	0	3	1	1	0	1	40	14	23	1	2
GREECE + TURKEY	22	15	4	0	2	0	0	0	0	0	2	0	0	0	1	21	15	4	0	1
OTHER EUROPE	18	5	10	0	2	3	2	0	1	0	3	1	0	0	0	13	2	10	0	4
EUROPE EX. U.K.	468	160	230	22	39	24	11	7	2	4	16	6	2	1	7	411	143	221	18	29
SOUTHERN DOMINIONS	154	49	73	7	10	12	10	2	0	0	4	2	1	1	0	123	37	70	6	10
S. AFRICA +RHOD.	61	12	35	3	3	4	4	0	0	0	2	0	0	2	0	49	8	35	3	3
AUSTRALIA + N.Z.	93	37	38	4	7	8	8	2	1	1	4	2	1	1	1	74	29	35	3	7
ASIA + OTHER AFRICA	209	112	39	12	22	8	2	1	3	3	3	0	0	0	0	174	110	37	7	20
JAPAN	63	33	13	2	3	2	1	0	0	0	3	0	0	0	0	49	32	12	2	3
OTHER ASIA+AFR.	146	79	26	10	19	6	1	1	3	3	3	0	0	0	0	125	78	25	5	17
BLACK AFRICA	31	14	7	1	7	0	0	0	0	0	2	2	0	0	0	29	14	4	1	7
ARAB WORLD	17	8	4	4	0	1	0	0	1	0	2	1	0	1	0	13	8	4	1	0
INDIA	14	8	3	1	0	0	0	0	0	0	1	0	1	0	0	13	8	3	0	2
PHILIPPINES	16	8	3	0	3	0	0	0	0	0	0	0	0	0	0	13	8	3	0	2
OTHER E. ASIA	15	8	2	2	0	2	2	0	0	0	0	0	0	0	0	12	8	1	0	3
OTHER ASIA	53	33	7	2	5	1	1	0	1	0	1	0	0	0	0	45	32	7	1	5

CHAPTER 4- VARIETIES OF ENTRY
SECTION 5- THE FLOW OF MANUFACTURING BY CHARACTERISTIC OF SUBSIDIARY
TABLE B1- MANUFACTURING SUBSIDIARIES WHICH ENTERED A PARENT SYSTEM
WHICH HAD LESS THAN 11 YEARS "FOREIGN MANUFACTURING EXPERIENCE",
CLASSIFIED BY COUNTRY, PERIOD MANUFACTURE BEGAN, AND METHOD OF ENTRY

PERIOD AND METHOD OF ENTRY
(NEW=NEWLY FORMED, ACQ=ACQUIRED, DES=DESCENDANT, UNK=UNKNOWN)

COUNTRY OR REGION	TOTAL PRE 1968 ALL	NEW	ACQ	DES	UNK	PRE 1946 ALL	NEW	ACQ	DES	UNK	1946-1957 ALL	NEW	ACQ	DES	UNK	1958-1967 ALL	NEW	ACQ	DES	UNK
OUTSIDE U.S.	1154	466	560	69	59	426	215	151	28	32	242	103	112	18	9	486	148	297	23	18
OUT. U.S. + CANADA	864	356	406	54	48	262	135	85	18	24	175	84	69	14	8	427	137	252	22	16
OUT. WEST. HEMIS.	630	237	310	44	39	214	103	74	17	20	110	40	53	12	5	306	94	183	15	14
OUT. WHITE CWEALTH	613	265	279	28	41	150	84	43	5	18	124	68	41	7	8	339	113	195	16	15
OUT. DEVLPED WORLD	291	145	120	12	14	58	35	14	1	8	77	53	18	2	4	156	57	88	9	2
CANADA	290	110	154	15	11	164	80	66	10	8	67	19	43	4	1	59	11	45	1	2
LATIN AMERICA	234	119	96	10	9	48	32	11	1	4	65	44	16	2	3	121	43	69	7	2
C. AMER.+CARIB.	122	59	50	7	6	26	18	4	0	4	31	18	9	2	2	65	23	37	5	0
CUBA	16	6	3	1	6	8	2	2	0	4	7	4	0	1	2	1	0	1	0	0
MEXICO	80	40	35	5	0	16	14	2	0	0	23	13	9	1	0	41	13	24	4	0
OTHER	26	13	12	1	0	2	2	0	0	0	1	1	0	0	0	23	10	12	1	0
S. AMERICA	112	60	46	3	3	22	14	7	1	0	34	26	7	0	1	56	20	32	2	2
ARGENTINA	31	13	15	2	1	9	7	2	0	0	7	2	3	1	1	15	4	10	1	0
BRAZIL	26	18	7	1	0	5	4	1	0	0	12	9	3	1	0	9	5	3	0	0
PERU	9	5	4	0	0	2	2	0	0	0	2	1	1	0	0	5	2	3	0	0
COLOMBIA	16	8	6	0	2	1	0	1	0	0	4	3	1	0	0	11	5	4	0	2
VENEZUELA	21	12	9	0	0	1	0	1	0	0	7	4	3	0	0	13	8	5	0	0
OTHER	9	4	5	0	0	4	1	2	1	0	2	1	1	0	0	3	2	2	0	0
EUROPE	465	162	238	34	31	177	82	63	17	15	74	23	37	10	4	214	57	138	7	12
EFTA	181	58	89	22	12	93	36	35	14	8	30	14	13	6	1	58	13	40	2	3
U.K.	156	49	82	19	6	85	33	34	13	5	28	9	15	3	1	43	7	33	3	0
SCANDINAVIA	15	5	5	1	4	6	1	1	1	3	2	2	0	0	0	7	2	4	0	1
SWITZERLAND	5	1	2	1	1	0	0	0	0	0	0	0	0	0	0	5	1	2	1	1
OTHER EFTA	5	3	1	0	1	2	1	0	0	1	0	0	0	0	0	3	2	1	0	0
EUROP. COMMUNITY	244	89	127	12	16	76	42	25	3	6	37	12	18	4	3	131	35	84	5	7
FRANCE	86	25	51	5	5	31	15	11	1	4	11	3	5	3	0	44	7	35	1	1
GERMANY	66	27	29	6	4	28	18	7	3	0	14	5	9	0	0	24	4	13	3	4
ITALY	36	17	17	0	2	3	3	0	0	0	4	1	3	0	0	29	13	14	0	2
BELGIUM + LUX	33	12	18	0	3	8	3	5	0	0	4	3	1	0	0	21	6	12	0	3
NETHERLANDS	23	8	12	0	3	6	3	3	0	0	4	2	2	0	0	13	3	7	0	3
SPAIN	26	7	18	0	1	5	2	3	0	0	3	2	1	0	0	18	3	14	0	1
GREECE + TURKEY	6	5	0	0	1	0	0	0	0	0	2	2	0	0	0	4	3	0	0	1
OTHER EUROPE	8	3	4	0	1	3	2	1	0	0	2	1	1	0	0	3	0	2	0	1
EUROPE EX. U.K.	309	113	156	15	25	92	49	29	4	10	46	14	24	4	4	171	50	103	7	11
SOUTHERN DOMINIONS	90	41	41	7	1	26	17	8	0	1	21	13	7	1	0	43	11	26	6	0
S. AFRICA +RHOD.	32	17	15	0	0	11	9	2	0	0	7	3	4	0	0	14	5	9	0	0
AUSTRALIA + N.Z.	58	24	26	7	1	15	8	6	0	1	14	10	3	1	0	29	6	17	6	0
ASIA + OTHER AFRICA	75	34	31	3	7	11	8	3	0	0	15	10	3	1	1	49	16	25	2	6
JAPAN	18	8	7	1	2	1	1	0	0	0	3	1	2	0	0	14	6	5	1	2
OTHER ASIA+AFR.	57	26	24	2	5	10	7	3	0	0	12	9	1	1	1	35	10	20	1	4
BLACK AFRICA	2	1	1	0	0	0	0	0	0	0	0	0	0	0	0	2	1	1	0	0
ARAB WORLD	2	1	0	0	1	0	0	0	0	0	2	1	0	0	1	0	0	0	0	0
INDIA	11	5	6	0	0	4	3	1	0	0	2	1	1	0	0	5	1	4	0	0
PHILIPPINES	14	6	8	0	0	2	2	0	0	0	3	2	1	0	0	9	2	7	0	0
OTHER E. ASIA	5	2	1	1	1	1	0	0	0	1	1	1	0	0	0	3	1	1	1	0
OTHER ASIA	23	11	8	1	3	3	2	1	0	0	4	2	1	0	1	16	7	6	1	2

CHAPTER 4- VARIETIES OF ENTRY
SECTION 5- THE FLOW OF MANUFACTURING BY CHARACTERISTIC OF SUBSIDIARY
TABLE B2- MANUFACTURING SUBSIDIARIES WHICH ENTERED A PARENT SYSTEM
WHICH HAD 11 -20 YEARS "FOREIGN MANUFACTURING EXPERIENCE",
CLASSIFIED BY COUNTRY, PERIOD MANUFACTURE BEGAN, AND METHOD OF ENTRY

PERIOD AND METHOD OF ENTRY
(NEW=NEWLY FORMED, ACQ=ACQUIRED, DES=DESCENDANT, UNK=UNKNOWN)

COUNTRY OR REGION	TOTAL PRE 1968					PRE 1946					1946-1957					1958-1967				
	ALL	NEW	ACQ	DES	UNK	ALL	NEW	ACQ	DES	UNK	ALL	NEW	ACQ	DES	UNK	ALL	NEW	ACQ	DES	UNK
OUTSIDE U.S.	872	436	338	42	56	294	167	72	20	35	140	76	51	8	5	438	193	215	14	16
OUT. U.S. + CANADA	749	396	276	33	44	239	143	56	15	25	114	65	40	5	4	396	188	180	13	15
OUT. WEST. HEMIS.	506	273	185	18	30	171	103	41	11	16	54	33	19	5	2	281	137	125	7	12
OUT. WHITE CWEALTH	584	316	213	26	29	163	99	39	11	16	96	52	35	5	4	325	165	139	12	9
OUT. DEVLPED WORLD	312	167	108	18	19	80	49	15	6	10	70	38	24	5	3	162	90	69	7	6
CANADA	123	40	62	9	12	55	24	16	5	10	26	11	11	3	1	42	5	35	1	1
LATIN AMERICA	243	123	91	15	14	68	40	15	4	9	60	32	21	5	2	115	51	55	6	3
C. AMER.+CARIB.	106	47	47	9	3	25	13	8	2	2	28	13	12	2	1	53	21	27	5	0
CUBA	9	4	3	2	0	7	4	3	0	0	0	0	0	0	0	2	0	0	2	0
MEXICO	74	30	37	6	1	14	6	6	1	1	23	11	11	1	0	37	13	20	4	0
OTHER	23	13	7	1	2	4	3	1	0	0	5	2	1	0	2	14	8	5	1	0
S. AMERICA	137	76	44	6	11	43	27	7	2	7	32	19	9	3	1	62	30	28	1	3
ARGENTINA	36	19	13	1	3	16	13	3	0	0	3	2	1	0	0	17	4	9	1	3
BRAZIL	30	16	8	3	3	10	5	3	1	1	6	3	2	1	0	14	8	3	1	2
PERU	8	4	2	0	2	4	3	1	0	0	1	0	1	0	0	3	1	0	0	2
COLOMBIA	14	9	4	0	1	4	2	1	0	1	5	4	1	0	0	5	3	2	0	0
VENEZUELA	28	17	7	2	2	4	3	1	0	0	8	5	1	1	1	16	9	6	1	0
OTHER	21	11	9	0	1	5	3	1	0	1	4	2	1	1	0	12	6	6	0	0
EUROPE	332	165	135	13	19	121	64	37	7	13	32	19	12	0	1	179	82	86	6	5
EFTA	125	59	53	4	9	60	30	20	3	7	10	7	3	0	0	55	22	30	1	2
U.K.	82	30	39	4	9	40	16	14	3	7	7	5	1	1	0	35	9	24	0	2
SCANDINAVIA	24	17	5	2	0	14	11	2	1	0	1	1	0	0	0	9	5	3	1	0
SWITZERLAND	10	8	1	0	1	4	2	1	0	1	1	1	0	0	0	5	5	0	0	0
OTHER EFTA	9	4	4	0	1	2	1	1	0	0	1	0	1	0	0	6	3	2	0	1
EUROP. COMMUNITY	172	85	70	7	10	54	29	17	2	6	16	8	7	0	1	102	48	46	5	3
FRANCE	48	19	20	3	6	15	5	6	1	3	3	1	1	0	1	30	13	13	2	2
GERMANY	51	25	22	3	1	20	12	7	1	0	5	2	3	0	0	26	11	12	2	1
ITALY	35	18	16	0	1	9	6	2	0	1	2	0	2	0	0	24	12	12	0	0
BELGIUM + LUX	22	13	7	1	1	9	6	2	0	1	1	1	0	0	0	12	6	5	1	0
NETHERLANDS	16	10	5	0	1	6	4	2	0	0	2	1	1	0	0	8	5	2	0	1
SPAIN	25	15	9	1	0	4	3	1	0	0	4	4	0	0	0	17	8	8	1	0
GREECE + TURKEY	4	3	1	0	0	1	1	0	0	0	1	1	0	0	0	2	1	1	0	0
OTHER EUROPE	6	3	2	1	0	3	2	1	0	0	1	0	0	0	0	2	0	2	1	0
EUROPE EX. U.K.	250	135	96	9	10	81	48	23	4	6	25	14	10	0	1	144	73	63	5	3
SOUTHERN DOMINIONS	79	49	22	2	6	35	28	3	2	2	10	7	3	0	0	34	14	16	0	4
S. AFRICA +RHOD.	24	17	5	0	2	11	10	1	0	0	4	3	1	0	0	9	4	3	0	2
AUSTRALIA + N.Z.	55	32	17	2	4	24	18	2	2	2	6	4	2	0	0	25	10	13	0	2
ASIA + OTHER AFRICA	95	59	28	3	5	15	11	1	1	2	12	7	4	1	0	68	41	23	1	3
JAPAN	26	11	11	0	4	3	1	2	0	0	2	1	0	0	1	21	9	9	0	3
OTHER ASIA+AFR.	69	44	17	3	5	12	9	2	0	1	10	6	1	1	2	47	29	14	2	2
BLACK AFRICA	8	3	2	0	3	0	0	0	0	0	2	2	0	0	0	6	1	2	0	3
ARAB WORLD	8	6	2	0	0	5	5	0	0	0	0	0	0	0	0	3	1	2	0	0
INDIA	17	13	3	1	0	2	2	0	0	0	4	4	0	0	0	11	7	3	1	0
PHILIPPINES	10	3	6	1	0	2	1	1	0	0	0	0	0	0	0	8	2	5	1	0
OTHER E. ASIA	10	4	6	0	0	2	2	0	0	0	2	1	1	0	0	6	1	5	0	0
OTHER ASIA	16	9	3	2	2	5	2	2	1	0	3	1	1	1	0	8	6	0	0	2

CHAPTER 4- VARIETIES OF ENTRY
SECTION 5- THE FLOW OF MANUFACTURING BY CHARACTERISTIC OF SUBSIDIARY
TABLE B3- MANUFACTURING SUBSIDIARIES WHICH ENTERED A PARENT SYSTEM
WHICH HAD 21 - 80 YEARS "FOREIGN MANUFACTURING EXPERIENCE",
CLASSIFIED BY COUNTRY, PERIOD MANUFACTURE BEGAN, AND METHOD OF ENTRY

(NEW=NEWLY FORMED, ACQ=ACQUIRED, DES=DESCENDANT, UNK=UNKNOWN)
PERIOD AND METHOD OF ENTRY

COUNTRY OR REGION	TOTAL PRE 1968 ALL	NEW	ACQ	DES	UNK	PRE 1946 ALL	NEW	ACQ	DES	UNK	1946-1957 ALL	NEW	ACQ	DES	UNK	1958-1967 ALL	NEW	ACQ	DES	UNK
OUTSIDE U.S.	1719	721	754	127	117	244	115	66	31	32	422	195	144	42	41	1053	411	544	54	44
OUT. U.S. + CANADA	1482	658	618	115	91	203	101	54	29	19	347	170	106	39	32	932	387	458	47	40
OUT. WEST. HEMIS.	1000	420	443	80	57	141	63	39	26	13	197	95	62	22	18	662	262	342	32	26
OUT. WHITE CWEALTH	1118	539	434	77	68	144	72	43	16	13	257	133	74	25	25	717	334	317	36	30
OUT. DEVLPED WORLD	579	301	195	41	42	68	42	16	4	6	171	87	47	19	18	340	172	132	18	18
CANADA	237	63	136	12	26	41	14	12	2	13	75	25	38	3	9	121	24	86	7	4
LATIN AMERICA	482	238	175	35	34	62	38	15	3	6	150	75	44	17	14	270	125	116	15	14
C. AMER.+CARIB.	190	92	68	18	12	20	9	4	3	4	58	28	22	5	3	112	55	42	10	5
CUBA	16	10	2	2	2	4	2	0	0	2	2	2	0	0	0	10	6	2	2	0
MEXICO	110	51	44	10	5	11	3	3	3	2	34	16	13	3	2	65	32	28	4	1
OTHER	64	31	22	6	5	5	4	1	0	0	22	10	9	2	1	37	17	12	4	4
S. AMERICA	292	146	107	17	22	42	23	12	3	4	92	47	32	5	8	158	76	63	9	10
ARGENTINA	58	23	27	4	4	14	5	7	1	1	14	5	7	1	1	30	13	13	2	2
BRAZIL	87	45	30	5	7	15	10	3	1	1	32	17	11	2	2	40	18	16	2	4
PERU	15	7	5	1	2	2	1	1	0	0	5	3	1	0	1	8	3	3	1	1
COLOMBIA	53	25	24	2	2	5	3	1	1	0	20	9	10	0	1	28	13	13	1	1
VENEZUELA	54	33	13	3	5	3	1	0	0	2	11	6	5	0	0	40	26	8	3	3
OTHER	25	13	8	2	2	3	3	0	0	0	10	7	3	0	0	12	3	5	2	2
EUROPE	668	255	320	56	37	105	40	32	21	12	121	56	43	13	9	442	159	245	22	16
EFTA	236	76	117	29	14	46	19	12	11	4	57	22	22	11	2	133	35	83	7	8
U.K.	164	43	90	21	10	30	9	8	11	2	46	17	19	7	3	88	17	63	3	5
SCANDINAVIA	43	16	19	5	3	6	3	2	1	0	10	4	3	2	1	27	9	14	2	2
SWITZERLAND	11	5	4	2	0	4	2	1	1	0	2	1	1	0	0	5	2	2	1	0
OTHER EFTA	18	12	4	1	1	7	5	1	0	1	6	4	1	1	0	5	3	2	0	0
EUROP. COMMUNITY	354	148	167	23	16	44	16	14	6	8	53	29	18	2	4	257	103	135	15	4
FRANCE	110	38	63	7	2	15	5	8	1	1	16	8	6	1	1	79	25	49	5	0
GERMANY	101	38	48	9	6	14	5	6	2	1	11	3	6	2	0	76	30	36	5	5
ITALY	87	41	36	4	6	7	3	3	1	0	16	11	3	1	1	64	27	30	2	5
BELGIUM + LUX	24	12	9	2	1	3	1	1	1	0	3	1	1	0	1	18	10	7	1	0
NETHERLANDS	32	19	11	1	1	5	3	2	0	0	11	6	3	1	1	16	10	6	0	0
SPAIN	40	12	23	2	3	4	2	2	0	0	5	1	3	1	0	31	9	18	2	2
GREECE + TURKEY	16	11	4	0	1	1	1	0	0	0	3	2	1	0	0	12	8	3	0	1
OTHER EUROPE	22	8	9	2	3	10	3	6	1	0	3	1	1	0	1	9	4	2	1	2
EUROPE EX. U.K.	504	212	230	35	27	75	31	24	10	10	75	39	24	6	6	354	142	182	19	11
SOUTHERN DOMINIONS	188	71	89	17	11	27	18	4	4	1	41	19	11	7	4	120	34	74	6	6
S. AFRICA +RHOD.	66	22	37	6	1	3	3	0	0	0	14	9	2	2	1	49	10	35	4	0
AUSTRALIA + N.Z.	122	49	52	11	10	24	15	4	4	1	27	10	9	5	3	71	24	39	2	6
ASIA + OTHER AFRICA	144	94	34	7	9	9	5	3	0	1	35	20	13	1	1	100	69	18	6	7
JAPAN	47	31	14	1	1	3	1	2	0	0	14	8	5	0	1	30	22	7	1	0
OTHER ASIA+AFR.	97	63	20	6	8	6	4	1	0	1	21	12	8	1	0	70	47	11	5	7
BLACK AFRICA	14	7	6	0	1	0	0	0	0	0	2	1	1	0	0	12	6	5	0	1
ARAB WORLD	15	9	3	2	1	1	1	0	0	0	4	2	1	1	0	10	6	2	1	1
INDIA	12	7	3	1	1	0	0	0	0	0	2	1	1	0	0	10	6	2	1	1
PHILIPPINES	17	11	4	1	1	3	2	1	0	0	6	4	1	1	0	8	5	2	0	1
OTHER E. ASIA	11	7	2	1	1	1	1	0	0	0	3	2	1	0	0	7	4	1	1	1
OTHER ASIA	28	22	2	1	3	1	1	0	0	0	4	3	0	0	1	23	18	2	1	2

CHAPTER 4- VARIETIES OF ENTRY
SECTION 5- THE FLOW OF MANUFACTURING BY CHARACTERISTIC OF SUBSIDIARY
TABLE B4- MANUFACTURING SUBSIDIARIES WHICH ENTERED A PARENT SYSTEM
WHICH HAD MORE THAN 40 YEARS "FOREIGN MANUFACTURING EXPERIENCE",
CLASSIFIED BY COUNTRY, PERIOD MANUFACTURE BEGAN, AND METHOD OF ENTRY

PERIOD AND METHOD OF ENTRY
(NEW=NEWLY FORMED, ACQ=ACQUIRED, DES=DESCENDANT, UNK=UNKNOWN)

COUNTRY OR REGION	TOTAL ALL	TOTAL NEW	PRE 1968 ACQ	DES	UNK	PRE 1946 ALL	NEW	ACQ	DES	UNK	1946-1957 ALL	NEW	ACQ	DES	UNK	1958-1967 ALL	NEW	ACQ	DES	UNK
OUTSIDE U.S.	1342	562	545	112	123	68	34	18	7	9	211	98	65	25	23	1063	430	462	80	91
OUT. U.S. + CANADA	1211	526	465	107	113	60	29	15	7	9	178	86	49	23	20	973	411	401	77	84
OUT. WEST. HEMIS.	859	356	342	71	90	29	10	10	6	7	110	50	32	13	15	720	296	304	52	68
OUT. WHITE CWEALTH	953	434	347	84	88	51	26	11	6	8	141	66	40	20	15	761	342	296	58	65
OUT. DEVLPED WORLD	483	249	145	50	39	33	19	9	3	2	80	42	18	14	6	370	188	118	33	31
CANADA	131	36	80	5	10	8	5	3	0	0	33	12	16	2	3	90	19	61	3	7
LATIN AMERICA	352	170	123	36	23	31	19	9	1	2	68	36	17	10	5	253	115	97	25	16
C. AMER.+CARIB.	134	62	50	13	9	9	1	3	0	5	15	9	2	1	3	110	44	50	10	6
CUBA	5	3	2	0	0	3	1	0	0	0	1	2	0	0	0	1	1	0	0	0
MEXICO	91	38	42	7	4	5	1	0	0	0	11	7	0	2	2	75	26	42	5	2
OTHER	38	21	8	4	5	1	1	0	0	0	3	0	0	0	3	34	18	8	4	2
S. AMERICA	218	108	73	23	14	22	10	9	1	2	53	27	17	7	2	143	71	47	15	10
ARGENTINA	33	16	12	4	1	6	4	1	1	0	6	2	4	0	0	21	10	7	3	1
BRAZIL	62	23	31	8	0	5	3	2	0	0	20	8	7	5	0	37	12	22	3	0
PERU	22	12	8	1	1	4	2	2	0	0	4	2	2	0	0	14	8	4	1	1
COLOMBIA	33	15	9	5	4	0	0	0	0	0	8	4	2	1	1	25	11	7	4	3
VENEZUELA	39	29	5	3	2	2	1	0	0	1	8	7	1	0	0	29	21	4	3	1
OTHER	29	13	8	3	5	5	0	3	0	2	7	4	1	1	1	17	9	4	2	2
EUROPE	550	190	259	41	60	22	7	6	2	7	77	35	23	7	12	451	148	230	32	41
EFTA	186	55	89	17	25	7	1	4	0	2	26	11	6	3	6	153	43	79	14	17
U.K.	130	34	69	10	17	6	1	4	0	1	20	9	5	2	4	104	24	60	8	12
SCANDINAVIA	31	11	12	4	4	1	0	0	0	1	3	2	0	0	1	27	9	12	4	2
SWITZERLAND	10	7	7	0	3	0	0	0	0	0	2	0	1	0	1	8	7	1	0	0
OTHER EFTA	15	7	7	0	1	0	0	0	0	0	1	1	0	0	0	14	6	6	2	1
EUROP. COMMUNITY	287	97	140	22	28	10	4	1	1	4	42	17	15	5	6	235	76	124	16	19
FRANCE	71	29	31	4	7	4	3	0	0	1	7	2	1	2	2	60	23	30	3	4
GERMANY	81	19	47	4	11	3	1	1	0	1	17	4	9	1	3	61	14	38	3	6
ITALY	62	25	29	4	4	1	0	0	0	1	13	8	4	1	0	48	17	25	3	3
BELGIUM + LUX	39	14	19	3	6	1	0	0	1	0	2	1	1	0	0	36	13	18	3	3
NETHERLANDS	34	10	14	3	3	0	0	0	0	0	4	2	1	0	1	30	17	13	3	5
SPAIN	46	20	22	1	2	2	1	0	0	0	4	2	2	0	0	40	17	19	1	2
GREECE + TURKEY	16	11	2	0	3	1	0	1	0	0	2	2	0	0	0	13	9	2	0	2
OTHER EUROPE	15	7	6	2	3	2	0	0	0	1	3	3	0	0	0	10	3	6	1	0
EUROPE EX. U.K.	420	156	190	31	43	16	6	2	1	6	57	26	18	5	8	347	124	170	24	29
SOUTHERN DOMINIONS	116	52	44	12	8	3	2	0	0	1	14	8	4	1	1	99	42	40	10	7
S. AFRICA +RHOD.	29	13	9	5	2	0	0	0	0	0	4	3	0	1	0	25	10	9	4	2
AUSTRALIA + N.Z.	87	39	35	7	6	3	2	0	0	1	10	5	4	0	1	74	32	31	6	5
ASIA + OTHER AFRICA	193	114	39	18	22	4	1	3	1	3	19	7	5	2	5	170	106	34	10	20
JAPAN	62	35	17	14	6	2	1	1	1	1	7	6	4	4	1	53	33	13	2	5
OTHER ASIA+AFR.	131	79	22	14	16	2	0	2	0	0	12	1	1	1	4	117	73	21	16	15
BLACK AFRICA	22	14	3	1	4	0	0	0	0	0	1	1	0	0	0	21	13	3	3	4
ARAB WORLD	13	8	1	4	0	1	0	1	0	0	1	0	1	1	0	11	8	3	3	0
INDIA	26	14	8	4	0	0	0	0	0	0	3	3	0	0	0	23	11	11	8	0
PHILIPPINES	16	8	8	4	0	0	0	0	0	0	4	0	3	0	1	12	8	8	0	0
OTHER E. ASIA	12	8	1	0	3	0	0	0	0	0	1	0	0	0	1	11	8	2	0	2
OTHER ASIA	42	27	7	2	6	1	0	0	0	1	2	2	0	0	0	39	25	7	1	6

CHAPTER 4- VARIETIES OF ENTRY

SECTION 5- THE FLOW OF MANUFACTURING BY CHARACTERISTIC OF SUBSIDIARY

TABLE C1- MANUFACTURING SUBSIDIARIES WHICH WERE
WHOLLY OWNED AT DATE MANUFACTURE BEGAN,
CLASSIFIED BY COUNTRY, PERIOD MANUFACTURE BEGAN, AND METHOD OF ENTRY

(NEW=NEWLY FORMED, ACQ=ACQUIRED, DES=DESCENDANT, UNK=UNKNOWN)

PERIOD AND METHOD OF ENTRY

COUNTRY OR REGION	TOTAL PRE 1968					PRE 1946					1946-1957					1958-1967				
	ALL	NEW	ACQ	DES	UNK	ALL	NEW	ACQ	DES	UNK	ALL	NEW	ACQ	DES	UNK	ALL	NEW	ACQ	DES	UNK
OUTSIDE U.S.	2923	1222	1234	238	184	696	392	186	54	64	633	292	227	68	46	1549	538	821	116	74
OUT. U.S. + CANADA	2293	1019	889	208	142	479	285	109	43	42	473	242	136	59	36	1306	492	644	106	64
OUT. WEST. HEMIS.	1626	670	678	143	107	351	198	86	37	30	281	129	91	36	25	966	343	501	70	52
OUT. WHITE CWEALTH	1600	776	561	141	102	301	186	62	23	30	342	187	88	41	26	937	403	411	77	46
OUT. DEVLPED WORLD	824	440	239	82	53	149	100	25	10	14	223	128	52	28	15	442	212	162	44	24
CANADA	630	203	345	30	42	217	107	77	11	22	160	50	91	9	10	243	46	177	10	10
LATIN AMERICA	667	349	211	65	35	128	87	23	6	12	192	113	45	23	11	340	149	143	36	12
C. AMER.+CARIB.	282	132	99	32	15	48	33	8	1	6	91	50	24	11	6	139	49	67	20	3
CUBA	28	12	5	5	6	11	8	3	0	0	12	1	5	3	3	3	3	0	0	0
MEXICO	189	86	78	20	5	31	24	5	1	1	65	38	21	5	1	92	24	52	14	2
OTHER	65	34	16	8	7	6	3	0	0	3	14	5	2	3	4	44	24	14	6	0
S. AMERICA	385	217	112	33	20	80	54	15	5	6	101	63	21	12	5	201	100	76	16	9
ARGENTINA	88	44	32	6	6	36	23	8	3	2	14	7	5	1	1	38	14	19	2	3
BRAZIL	117	66	33	13	5	23	19	3	0	1	36	23	5	5	3	58	24	25	8	1
PERU	28	17	8	1	2	7	3	2	0	2	6	4	1	0	1	15	10	5	0	0
COLOMBIA	50	28	16	4	2	4	3	0	0	1	14	9	4	1	0	32	16	12	2	2
VENEZUELA	59	42	9	5	3	3	3	0	0	0	19	14	3	2	0	35	25	6	3	1
OTHER	43	20	14	4	5	7	3	2	2	0	12	6	3	3	0	23	11	9	1	2
EUROPE	1132	434	515	89	75	258	131	75	26	26	184	85	62	21	16	671	218	378	42	33
EFTA	483	163	235	41	35	136	65	44	14	13	81	32	28	13	8	257	66	163	14	14
U.K.	357	100	193	31	33	105	45	38	13	9	63	24	25	9	5	181	31	130	9	11
SCANDINAVIA	73	34	28	5	6	18	10	3	1	4	14	7	3	2	2	41	17	21	3	0
SWITZERLAND	26	10	8	5	3	4	3	1	0	0	3	1	0	2	0	18	6	8	2	2
OTHER EFTA	27	19	6	0	2	9	7	2	0	0	1	0	0	0	1	17	12	4	0	1
EUROP. COMMUNITY	564	227	255	41	41	103	56	29	8	10	88	43	29	8	8	364	128	197	25	14
FRANCE	149	55	69	12	13	34	14	14	3	3	22	11	4	4	3	89	30	51	5	3
GERMANY	168	57	82	17	12	39	22	9	3	5	30	5	19	3	3	97	28	54	11	4
ITALY	116	57	48	5	6	12	9	2	1	0	22	16	4	1	1	80	32	43	4	1
BELGIUM + LUX	69	30	33	4	2	6	4	1	1	0	6	5	1	0	0	57	21	31	2	3
NETHERLANDS	62	30	23	4	5	12	4	7	1	0	8	6	1	1	0	41	17	18	3	3
SPAIN	38	18	13	3	4	7	3	2	1	1	7	4	3	0	0	24	11	8	2	3
GREECE + TURKEY	14	11	1	0	2	0	0	0	0	0	1	1	0	0	0	13	10	1	0	2
OTHER EUROPE	33	15	11	4	3	12	7	2	2	1	7	5	2	0	0	13	3	7	2	1
EUROPE EX. U.K.	775	334	322	58	61	153	86	37	13	17	121	61	37	12	11	490	187	248	33	22
SOUTHERN DOMINIONS	313	133	126	34	14	69	52	9	6	2	61	26	21	9	5	177	55	96	19	7
S. AFRICA +RHOD.	113	50	46	11	3	21	19	1	1	0	21	13	5	2	1	68	18	40	8	2
AUSTRALIA + N.Z.	200	83	80	23	11	48	33	8	5	2	40	13	16	7	4	109	37	56	11	5
ASIA + OTHER AFRICA	181	103	37	20	18	24	12	4	5	2	36	18	8	6	4	118	70	27	9	12
JAPAN	24	12	9	3	0	3	3	0	0	0	5	3	1	1	0	16	7	8	1	0
OTHER ASIA+AFR.	157	91	28	17	18	21	13	2	5	1	31	15	7	5	4	102	63	19	8	12
BLACK AFRICA	27	15	5	1	6	0	0	0	0	0	3	1	2	0	0	24	13	5	1	5
ARAB WORLD	17	7	7	6	1	1	0	0	1	0	3	1	0	1	1	12	6	3	3	0
INDIA	18	11	4	3	0	5	5	0	0	0	4	4	0	0	0	9	2	3	4	0
PHILIPPINES	34	21	7	4	2	6	4	0	1	1	13	6	2	4	1	14	11	2	0	1
OTHER E. ASIA	19	11	5	0	3	1	1	0	0	0	2	0	1	0	1	16	11	4	0	1
OTHER ASIA	42	26	3	4	7	8	6	2	0	0	5	2	2	0	1	27	20	2	1	4

CHAPTER 4- VARIETIES OF ENTRY
SECTION 5- THE FLOW OF MANUFACTURING BY CHARACTERISTIC OF SUBSIDIARY
TABLE C2- MANUFACTURING SUBSIDIARIES WHICH WERE
JOINT VENTURES AT DATE MANUFACTURE BEGAN,
CLASSIFIED BY COUNTRY, PERIOD MANUFACTURE BEGAN, AND METHOD OF ENTRY

PERIOD AND METHOD OF ENTRY
(NEW=NEWLY FORMED, ACQ=ACQUIRED, DES=DESCENDANT, UNK=UNKNOWN)

COUNTRY OR REGION	TOTAL PRE 1968					PRE 1946					1946-1957					1958-1967				
	ALL	NEW	ACQ	DES	UNK	ALL	NEW	ACQ	DES	UNK	ALL	NEW	ACQ	DES	UNK	ALL	NEW	ACQ	DES	UNK
OUTSIDE U.S.	1812	818	818	62	95	227	104	79	18	26	320	161	123	13	23	1246	553	616	31	46
OUT. U.S. + CANADA	1696	780	753	58	89	196	90	68	15	23	288	146	110	12	20	1196	544	575	31	46
OUT. WEST. HEMIS.	1161	531	512	40	66	134	56	50	12	16	161	81	61	6	13	854	394	401	22	37
OUT. WHITE CWEALTH	1411	665	620	42	72	147	71	50	8	18	232	117	89	8	18	1020	477	481	26	36
OUT. DEVLPED WORLD	704	358	287	24	29	64	35	18	4	7	147	81	51	6	9	487	242	218	14	13
CANADA	116	38	65	4	6	31	14	11	3	3	32	15	13	1	3	50	9	41	0	0
LATIN AMERICA	535	249	241	18	23	62	34	18	3	7	127	65	49	6	7	342	150	174	9	9
C. AMER.+CARIB.	226	108	105	7	5	24	17	5	1	1	32	16	13	2	1	169	75	87	4	3
CUBA	13	9	2	1	1	7	4	1	1	1	6	5	1	0	0	0	0	0	0	0
MEXICO	139	61	72	4	2	12	8	4	0	0	21	8	10	2	0	106	45	58	2	1
OTHER	74	38	31	2	2	5	5	0	0	0	5	3	2	0	0	63	30	29	2	2
S. AMERICA	309	141	136	11	18	38	17	13	2	6	95	49	36	4	6	173	75	87	5	6
ARGENTINA	61	24	31	3	2	7	3	2	1	1	19	10	8	1	0	34	11	21	1	1
BRAZIL	68	32	30	3	2	8	3	4	1	0	29	14	11	2	2	30	15	15	1	0
PERU	25	10	11	1	2	5	3	1	1	0	9	5	4	0	0	10	2	6	1	1
COLOMBIA	54	23	27	1	2	6	3	2	0	1	13	6	6	0	1	35	14	19	1	1
VENEZUELA	64	35	22	2	5	4	3	0	0	1	19	11	5	1	2	41	21	17	1	2
OTHER	37	17	15	1	4	8	2	4	0	2	6	3	2	0	1	23	12	9	1	1
EUROPE	725	278	366	31	45	108	42	41	11	14	98	43	40	6	9	514	193	285	14	22
EFTA	185	65	85	18	15	42	14	16	8	4	36	14	14	5	3	105	37	55	3	8
U.K.	131	43	63	14	9	31	9	12	7	3	31	14	11	4	2	67	20	40	3	4
SCANDINAVIA	32	13	12	4	3	7	0	3	1	3	3	0	2	0	1	22	11	7	0	2
SWITZERLAND	8	2	4	0	2	0	0	0	0	0	1	0	0	1	0	7	2	4	0	1
OTHER EFTA	14	7	6	0	1	3	1	1	0	1	1	0	1	0	0	9	4	4	1	1
EUROP. COMMUNITY	408	159	211	12	23	57	25	22	3	7	48	21	21	2	5	300	113	168	8	11
FRANCE	144	47	84	6	6	21	8	10	2	1	12	4	6	1	2	110	35	68	4	3
GERMANY	101	41	54	1	4	18	10	7	0	1	15	7	5	1	1	67	24	40	1	2
ITALY	89	40	41	3	5	5	4	0	1	0	12	6	5	1	0	72	30	36	2	4
BELGIUM + LUX	39	15	18	1	5	9	1	3	0	5	3	2	1	0	1	27	12	14	1	0
NETHERLANDS	35	16	14	2	3	4	3	2	0	0	6	2	2	1	0	24	12	10	0	2
SPAIN	94	33	57	1	3	5	3	2	0	0	9	3	5	0	1	80	27	50	1	2
GREECE + TURKEY	25	17	6	0	2	0	0	0	0	0	5	0	5	0	0	19	12	6	0	1
OTHER EUROPE	13	4	7	0	2	3	0	1	0	2	0	0	0	0	0	10	4	6	0	0
EUROPE EX. U.K.	594	235	303	17	36	77	33	29	4	11	67	29	29	2	7	447	173	245	11	18
SOUTHERN DOMINIONS	146	70	64	2	8	18	10	6	0	2	25	10	10	2	2	101	45	48	2	6
S. AFRICA +RHOD.	40	18	20	0	2	4	2	2	0	0	7	5	2	0	0	29	11	17	0	1
AUSTRALIA + N.Z.	106	52	44	2	6	14	8	4	0	2	18	10	8	1	1	72	34	31	2	5
ASIA + OTHER AFRICA	290	183	82	7	13	8	4	3	0	1	38	23	11	0	4	239	156	68	6	9
JAPAN	121	74	36	2	7	6	4	1	0	1	18	7	9	0	2	94	64	24	1	5
OTHER ASIA+AFR.	169	109	46	6	6	2	0	2	0	0	20	16	2	0	2	145	92	44	5	4
BLACK AFRICA	15	9	4	0	1	0	0	0	0	0	2	1	1	0	0	13	8	4	0	1
ARAB WORLD	20	16	2	1	0	2	2	0	0	0	1	1	0	0	0	17	15	2	0	0
INDIA	47	27	16	2	1	1	0	0	1	0	6	2	2	2	0	44	25	16	2	1
PHILIPPINES	23	12	8	0	3	0	0	0	0	1	6	5	1	0	2	17	7	8	2	0
OTHER E. ASIA	12	8	3	1	0	1	1	0	0	0	1	1	0	0	0	11	7	3	1	0
OTHER ASIA	52	37	13	2	0	1	1	0	0	0	8	6	2	0	0	43	30	11	2	0

CHAPTER 4- VARIETIES OF ENTRY
SECTION 6- CHANGES IN STATE OF BEING, MAIN ACTIVITY AND OWNERSHIP
TABLE 1- SUBSIDIARIES, MANUFACTURING OR NON-MANUFACTURING,
WHICH WERE LIQUIDATED OR EXPROPRIATED,
CLASSIFIED BY COUNTRY, PERIOD CHANGE OCCURRED, AND METHOD OF ENTRY

(NEW=NEWLY FORMED, ACQ=ACQUIRED, DES=DESCENDANT, UNK=UNKNOWN)

PERIOD AND METHOD OF ENTRY

COUNTRY OR REGION	TOTAL ALL	NEW	PRE 1968 ACQ	DES	UNK	PRE 1946 ALL	NEW	ACQ	DES	UNK	1946-1957 ALL	NEW	ACQ	DES	UNK	1958-1967 ALL	NEW	ACQ	DES	UNK
OUTSIDE U.S.	2497	855	892	282	464	449	149	135	40	125	497	211	121	67	98	1551	499	636	175	241
OUT. U.S. + CANADA	1981	732	648	243	358	307	127	75	30	75	387	175	80	55	77	1287	430	493	158	206
OUT. WEST. HEMIS.	1361	474	462	162	263	247	110	52	25	60	267	121	54	39	53	847	243	356	98	150
OUT. WHITE CWEALTH	1504	593	465	192	254	241	105	55	23	58	285	126	58	43	58	978	362	352	126	138
OUT. DEVLPED WORLD	716	300	210	99	107	78	27	25	9	17	145	71	29	19	26	493	202	156	71	64
CANADA	516	127	244	39	106	142	22	60	10	50	110	36	41	12	21	264	69	143	17	35
LATIN AMERICA	620	258	186	81	95	60	17	23	5	15	120	54	26	16	24	440	187	137	60	56
C. AMER.+CARIB.	339	143	100	37	59	34	11	11	2	12	57	29	13	4	8	248	103	75	31	39
CUBA	76	28	14	12	22	8	3	3	1	1	10	3	3	2	2	58	22	8	9	19
MEXICO	183	68	68	18	29	25	8	6	1	10	35	15	13	2	5	123	45	49	15	14
OTHER	80	47	18	7	8	1	0	0	0	1	12	11	0	0	1	67	36	18	7	6
S. AMERICA	281	115	86	44	36	26	6	14	3	3	63	25	10	5	16	192	84	62	29	17
ARGENTINA	64	21	21	15	7	5	0	2	0	0	16	4	5	1	4	43	17	14	8	4
BRAZIL	60	25	19	7	9	4	2	0	0	0	9	5	1	0	3	47	18	18	7	4
PERU	19	4	11	1	3	5	1	2	0	2	4	1	0	0	3	10	2	6	1	1
COLOMBIA	39	14	11	11	3	1	0	0	0	1	12	6	1	3	2	26	8	10	8	0
VENEZUELA	64	40	11	7	6	5	1	4	0	0	10	5	3	1	1	49	34	6	4	5
OTHER	35	11	13	3	8	6	2	3	0	0	12	4	2	3	4	17	5	8	1	3
EUROPE	1047	363	348	129	207	211	89	44	21	57	200	81	43	33	43	636	193	261	75	107
EFTA	462	151	157	53	101	77	26	20	8	23	96	38	25	15	18	289	87	112	30	60
U.K.	280	74	103	37	66	53	14	17	6	16	64	25	15	10	14	163	35	71	21	36
SCANDINAVIA	81	19	28	9	25	8	1	1	1	5	14	3	5	3	3	59	15	22	6	16
SWITZERLAND	72	46	16	2	8	7	7	0	0	0	12	8	2	1	1	51	31	12	1	7
OTHER EFTA	29	12	10	5	2	7	4	2	1	0	6	2	3	2	0	16	6	7	2	1
EUROP. COMMUNITY	481	175	162	59	85	101	52	17	9	23	63	24	13	9	17	317	99	132	41	45
FRANCE	144	49	49	24	22	36	16	10	2	8	17	7	3	2	5	91	26	36	20	9
GERMANY	133	44	43	17	29	31	15	6	2	8	22	5	7	5	5	80	24	30	10	16
ITALY	94	38	32	8	16	15	10	0	0	5	11	5	5	1	0	68	23	31	7	7
BELGIUM + LUX	51	24	15	6	6	14	5	1	1	7	9	4	1	2	2	37	18	14	3	2
NETHERLANDS	59	20	23	4	12	7	2	4	3	0	4	3	1	0	0	41	8	21	1	11
SPAIN	25	4	16	3	1	1	0	0	0	1	3	1	2	0	0	21	3	14	3	0
GREECE + TURKEY	10	6	2	1	1	1	0	0	0	1	3	3	0	0	0	6	3	2	1	0
OTHER EUROPE	69	28	11	13	17	25	10	3	3	9	35	15	5	8	7	9	3	3	2	1
EUROPE EX. U.K.	767	289	245	92	141	158	75	27	15	41	136	56	28	23	29	473	158	190	54	71
SOUTHERN DOMINIONS	187	60	77	13	37	12	8	3	0	1	36	22	7	2	5	139	30	67	11	31
S. AFRICA +RHOD.	51	22	19	1	9	2	0	0	0	1	12	10	1	1	0	37	11	18	0	8
AUSTRALIA + N.Z.	136	38	58	12	28	10	7	3	0	0	24	12	6	1	5	102	19	49	11	23
ASIA + OTHER AFRICA	127	51	37	20	19	24	13	5	4	2	31	18	4	4	5	72	20	28	12	12
JAPAN	31	9	13	2	7	6	3	3	0	0	6	1	1	0	4	19	5	9	2	3
OTHER ASIA+AFR.	96	42	24	18	12	18	10	2	4	2	25	17	3	3	2	53	15	19	11	8
BLACK AFRICA	14	8	3	1	2	2	2	0	0	0	4	3	0	0	1	8	3	3	1	1
ARAB WORLD	23	11	5	5	2	1	1	0	1	0	5	3	1	1	0	15	5	5	3	2
INDIA	6	3	3	0	0	4	3	1	0	0	2	0	2	0	0	3	0	3	0	0
PHILIPPINES	13	6	3	2	2	4	1	2	0	1	4	2	1	0	1	5	3	1	2	0
OTHER E. ASIA	17	4	5	4	4	4	1	1	1	1	5	1	1	2	1	8	2	3	1	2
OTHER ASIA	23	10	5	5	3	3	1	1	0	1	6	3	1	2	0	14	4	4	4	2

CHAPTER 4— VARIETIES OF ENTRY
SECTION 6— CHANGES IN STATE OF BEING, MAIN ACTIVITY AND OWNERSHIP
TABLE 2— SUBSIDIARIES, MANUFACTURING OR NON-MANUFACTURING,
WHICH WERE SOLD,
CLASSIFIED BY COUNTRY, PERIOD CHANGE OCCURRED, AND METHOD OF ENTRY

PERIOD AND METHOD OF ENTRY
(NEW=NEWLY FORMED, ACQ=ACQUIRED, DES=DESCENDANT, UNK=UNKNOWN)

COUNTRY OR REGION	TOTAL PRE 1968 ALL	NEW	ACQ	DES	UNK	PRE 1946 ALL	NEW	ACQ	DES	UNK	1946-1957 ALL	NEW	ACQ	DES	UNK	1958-1967 ALL	NEW	ACQ	DES	UNK
OUTSIDE U.S.	315	106	110	39	60	42	15	15	5	7	69	16	19	7	27	204	75	76	27	26
OUT. U.S. + CANADA	271	92	89	34	56	36	14	11	4	7	54	12	15	4	23	181	66	63	26	26
OUT. WEST. HEMIS.	206	70	65	23	48	25	9	8	3	5	43	10	11	4	18	138	51	46	16	25
OUT. WHITE CWEALTH	182	68	64	26	24	23	9	8	3	3	32	9	10	2	11	127	50	46	21	10
OUT. DEVLPED WORLD	79	26	28	13	12	11	5	3	1	2	13	2	6	0	5	55	19	19	12	5
CANADA	44	14	21	5	4	6	1	4	1	0	15	4	4	3	4	23	9	13	1	0
LATIN AMERICA	65	22	24	11	8	11	5	3	1	2	11	2	4	0	5	43	15	17	10	1
C. AMER.+CARIB.	27	8	12	5	2	4	2	1	0	1	3	0	1	1	1	20	6	10	4	0
CUBA	4	1	1	0	2	2	1	1	0	0	0	0	0	0	0	2	0	0	0	2
MEXICO	18	4	10	4	0	4	1	2	1	0	1	1	0	0	0	13	2	8	3	0
OTHER	5	3	1	1	0	0	0	0	0	0	1	0	0	1	0	4	3	1	0	0
S. AMERICA	38	14	12	6	6	7	3	3	0	1	8	2	2	0	4	23	9	7	6	1
ARGENTINA	8	3	3	2	0	2	1	1	0	0	5	1	2	2	0	1	1	0	0	0
BRAZIL	9	4	3	2	0	2	1	0	1	0	0	0	0	0	0	7	3	3	1	0
PERU	3	3	0	0	0	0	0	0	0	0	0	0	0	0	0	3	3	0	0	0
COLOMBIA	4	1	3	0	0	0	0	0	0	0	1	0	1	0	0	3	1	2	0	0
VENEZUELA	8	3	2	2	1	1	1	0	0	0	0	0	0	0	0	7	2	2	2	1
OTHER	6	0	2	2	2	2	0	0	0	2	2	0	0	2	0	2	0	2	0	0
EUROPE	157	52	51	17	37	20	7	7	3	3	38	8	8	4	18	99	37	36	10	16
EFTA	66	19	18	4	25	10	3	4	2	1	20	2	4	1	13	36	14	10	1	11
U.K.	54	10	15	4	25	9	3	3	2	1	19	2	4	1	12	26	5	8	1	11
SCANDINAVIA	7	4	0	0	0	1	1	0	0	0	1	1	0	0	0	5	3	2	0	0
SWITZERLAND	4	1	0	0	0	0	0	0	0	0	0	0	0	0	0	4	1	0	0	0
OTHER EFTA	1	0	1	0	0	0	0	0	0	0	0	0	1	0	0	1	0	0	0	0
EUROP. COMMUNITY	78	28	29	12	9	8	4	4	0	0	17	5	3	2	6	53	19	22	9	3
FRANCE	18	8	5	5	0	2	2	0	0	0	3	1	0	2	0	13	5	5	3	0
GERMANY	23	5	12	6	0	4	1	2	1	0	2	0	1	1	0	17	4	9	4	0
ITALY	14	6	4	1	2	4	1	1	0	2	3	1	0	1	0	7	4	3	0	0
BELGIUM + LUX	8	2	3	1	2	1	0	0	0	1	1	1	0	0	0	6	1	3	0	1
NETHERLANDS	15	6	5	2	2	1	0	1	0	0	4	1	2	1	0	10	5	2	1	2
SPAIN	6	3	1	1	0	0	0	0	0	0	1	1	0	1	0	5	2	1	0	0
GREECE + TURKEY	1	0	1	0	0	0	0	0	0	0	0	0	0	0	0	1	0	1	0	0
OTHER EUROPE	6	2	2	1	1	0	0	0	0	0	2	0	0	1	1	4	2	2	0	0
EUROPE EX. U.K.	103	42	36	13	12	11	4	4	1	2	19	7	4	3	5	73	31	28	9	5
SOUTHERN DOMINIONS	31	12	8	4	7	4	2	0	0	2	3	2	1	0	0	24	8	7	4	5
S. AFRICA +RHOD.	10	4	2	1	3	1	0	1	0	0	1	0	0	0	1	8	4	1	1	2
AUSTRALIA + N.Z.	21	8	6	3	4	3	2	0	0	1	2	2	0	0	0	16	4	6	3	3
ASIA + OTHER AFRICA	18	6	6	2	4	1	0	0	0	1	2	0	2	0	0	15	6	4	2	4
JAPAN	4	2	2	0	0	0	0	0	0	0	1	0	1	0	0	3	2	1	0	0
OTHER ASIA+AFR.	14	4	4	2	4	1	0	1	0	0	1	0	1	2	0	12	4	2	0	4
BLACK AFRICA	3	0	1	0	2	1	0	1	0	0	1	0	0	0	0	1	0	0	0	2
ARAB WORLD	1	1	0	0	0	0	0	0	0	0	0	0	0	0	0	1	1	0	0	0
INDIA	1	1	0	0	0	0	0	0	0	0	0	0	0	0	0	1	1	0	0	0
PHILIPPINES	3	0	1	0	0	0	0	0	0	0	0	0	0	0	0	3	0	1	2	0
OTHER E. ASIA	1	0	0	2	1	0	0	0	0	0	0	0	0	0	0	1	0	0	0	1
OTHER ASIA	5	2	2	0	1	0	0	0	0	0	0	0	0	0	0	5	2	2	0	1

CHAPTER 4- VARIETIES OF ENTRY
SECTION 6- CHANGES IN STATE OF BEING, MAIN ACTIVITY AND OWNERSHIP
TABLE 3- MANUFACTURING SUBSIDIARIES
WHICH WERE LIQUIDATED OR EXPROPRIATED,
CLASSIFIED BY COUNTRY, PERIOD CHANGE OCCURRED, AND METHOD OF ENTRY

(NEW=NEWLY FORMED, ACQ=ACQUIRED, DES=DESCENDANT, UNK=UNKNOWN)

COUNTRY OR REGION	TOTAL PRE 1968					PERIOD AND METHOD OF ENTRY — PRE 1946					1946-1957					1958-1967				
	ALL	NEW	ACQ	DES	UNK	ALL	NEW	ACQ	DES	UNK	ALL	NEW	ACQ	DES	UNK	ALL	NEW	ACQ	DES	UNK
OUTSIDE U.S.	1127	373	512	146	96	162	54	68	19	21	205	87	71	25	22	760	232	373	102	53
OUT. U.S. + CANADA	855	301	365	131	58	96	42	31	13	10	144	63	46	22	13	615	196	288	96	35
OUT. WEST. HEMIS.	554	179	251	85	39	80	33	26	11	10	92	43	28	13	8	382	103	197	61	21
OUT. WHITE CWEALTH	637	234	258	103	42	68	31	21	11	5	97	40	31	16	10	472	163	206	76	27
OUT. DEVLPED WORLD	332	135	125	51	21	21	10	6	4	1	59	25	19	9	6	252	100	100	38	14
CANADA	272	72	147	15	38	66	12	37	6	11	61	24	25	3	9	145	36	85	6	18
LATIN AMERICA	301	122	114	46	19	16	9	5	2	0	52	20	18	9	5	233	93	91	35	14
C. AMER.+CARIB.	152	61	62	21	8	8	6	2	0	0	23	10	10	2	1	121	45	50	19	7
CUBA	39	18	7	8	6	4	2	2	0	0	3	1	0	0	2	32	15	5	8	4
MEXICO	90	31	49	9	1	4	4	0	0	0	16	6	10	0	0	70	21	39	9	1
OTHER	23	12	6	4	1	0	0	0	0	0	4	3	0	0	1	19	9	6	4	0
S. AMERICA	149	61	52	25	11	8	3	3	2	0	29	10	8	7	4	112	48	41	16	7
ARGENTINA	40	13	13	11	3	4	0	2	2	0	11	2	4	3	2	25	11	7	6	1
BRAZIL	38	16	15	4	3	1	1	0	0	0	6	4	1	0	1	31	11	14	4	2
PERU	6	2	4	0	0	1	1	0	0	0	1	0	1	0	0	4	1	3	0	0
COLOMBIA	22	9	9	4	0	0	0	0	0	0	2	2	0	0	0	20	7	9	4	0
VENEZUELA	33	19	8	4	2	1	0	1	0	0	6	2	1	3	0	26	17	6	1	2
OTHER	10	2	3	2	3	1	1	0	0	0	3	0	1	1	1	6	1	2	1	2
EUROPE	421	127	192	72	30	67	27	22	9	9	62	24	21	11	6	292	76	149	52	15
EFTA	171	46	83	28	14	28	11	10	1	6	33	11	13	7	2	110	24	60	20	6
U.K.	125	33	62	19	11	23	8	9	1	5	25	9	10	4	2	77	16	43	14	4
SCANDINAVIA	29	7	13	6	3	3	1	2	0	0	4	1	2	1	0	22	5	9	5	3
SWITZERLAND	6	2	3	1	0	1	1	0	0	0	2	1	1	0	0	3	0	2	1	0
OTHER EFTA	11	4	5	2	0	1	0	1	0	0	2	1	1	0	0	8	3	3	2	0
EUROP. COMMUNITY	218	72	93	39	14	29	14	8	6	1	22	9	7	2	4	167	49	78	31	9
FRANCE	74	18	34	19	3	11	5	5	1	0	4	2	1	0	1	59	11	28	18	2
GERMANY	56	20	22	8	6	12	6	3	2	1	9	2	4	1	2	35	12	15	5	3
ITALY	47	19	19	7	2	3	2	0	0	1	3	2	0	1	0	41	15	19	6	1
BELGIUM + LUX	22	8	8	4	2	3	1	0	2	0	1	0	1	0	0	18	7	7	2	2
NETHERLANDS	19	7	10	1	1	2	1	1	0	0	3	2	1	0	0	14	4	8	1	1
SPAIN	12	1	10	1	0	3	0	3	0	0	1	0	0	1	0	8	1	7	0	0
GREECE + TURKEY	6	2	2	1	1	1	0	0	0	1	1	1	0	0	0	4	1	2	1	0
OTHER EUROPE	14	6	4	3	1	6	2	2	1	1	5	3	0	2	0	3	1	2	0	0
EUROPE EX. U.K.	296	94	130	53	19	44	19	13	8	4	37	15	11	7	4	215	60	106	38	11
SOUTHERN DOMINIONS	88	32	43	8	5	4	3	1	0	0	21	13	5	2	1	63	16	37	6	4
S. AFRICA +RHOD.	26	12	13	1	0	0	0	0	0	0	8	6	1	1	0	18	6	12	0	0
AUSTRALIA + N.Z.	62	20	30	7	5	4	3	1	0	0	13	7	4	1	1	45	10	25	6	4
ASIA + OTHER AFRICA	45	20	16	5	4	9	3	3	1	2	9	6	2	1	0	27	11	11	3	2
JAPAN	14	7	5	2	0	5	2	2	1	0	1	0	1	0	0	8	5	2	1	0
OTHER ASIA+AFR.	31	13	11	5	2	5	1	0	2	2	7	5	2	0	0	19	7	9	3	0
BLACK AFRICA	1	1	0	0	0	0	0	0	0	0	0	0	0	0	0	1	1	0	0	0
ARAB WORLD	7	3	3	1	0	1	0	0	1	0	0	0	0	0	0	6	3	3	0	0
INDIA	4	2	2	0	0	0	0	0	0	0	2	0	2	0	0	2	2	0	0	0
PHILIPPINES	4	3	1	0	0	1	1	0	0	0	1	1	0	0	0	2	1	1	0	0
OTHER E. ASIA	7	2	4	0	1	1	0	1	0	0	2	1	0	0	1	4	1	3	0	0
OTHER ASIA	8	3	1	0	3	2	0	1	1	0	2	1	0	0	1	4	2	0	2	0

CHAPTER 4- VARIETIES OF ENTRY
SECTION 6- CHANGES IN STATE OF BEING, MAIN ACTIVITY AND OWNERSHIP
TABLE 4- MANUFACTURING SUBSIDIARIES
WHICH WERE SOLD, PERIOD CHANGE OCCURRED, AND METHOD OF ENTRY
CLASSIFIED BY COUNTRY, PERIOD CHANGE OCCURRED, AND METHOD OF ENTRY

(NEW=NEWLY FORMED, ACQ=ACQUIRED, DES=DESCENDANT, UNK=UNKNOWN)

PERIOD AND METHOD OF ENTRY

COUNTRY OR REGION	TOTAL PRE 1968					PRE 1946					1946-1957					1958-1967				
	ALL	NEW	ACQ	DES	UNK	ALL	NEW	ACQ	DES	UNK	ALL	NEW	ACQ	DES	UNK	ALL	NEW	ACQ	DES	UNK
OUTSIDE U.S.	190	65	74	23	28	24	11	9	2	2	43	10	12	6	15	123	44	53	15	11
OUT. U.S. + CANADA	157	55	58	18	26	20	11	6	1	2	31	6	9	3	13	106	38	43	14	11
OUT. WEST. HEMIS.	124	42	46	14	22	15	8	5	1	1	27	6	7	3	11	82	28	34	10	10
OUT. WHITE CWEALTH	106	40	43	13	10	12	6	4	0	2	15	4	7	1	3	79	30	32	12	5
OUT. DEVLPED WORLD	39	15	13	5	6	5	3	1	0	1	5	0	3	0	2	29	12	9	5	3
CANADA	33	10	16	5	2	4	0	3	1	0	12	4	3	3	2	17	6	10	1	0
LATIN AMERICA	33	13	12	4	4	5	3	1	0	1	4	2	2	0	0	24	10	9	4	1
C. AMER.+CARIB.	15	5	6	2	2	1	1	0	0	0	3	1	1	0	1	11	4	5	2	0
CUBA	4	1	1	0	2	0	0	0	0	0	2	0	0	0	2	2	1	1	0	0
MEXICO	10	3	5	2	0	1	1	0	0	0	1	1	0	0	0	8	2	4	2	0
OTHER	1	1	0	0	0	0	0	0	0	0	0	0	0	0	0	1	1	0	0	0
S. AMERICA	18	8	6	2	2	4	2	1	0	1	1	1	0	0	0	13	6	4	2	1
ARGENTINA	2	2	0	0	0	1	1	0	0	0	0	0	0	0	0	1	1	0	0	0
BRAZIL	6	3	2	1	0	1	0	1	0	0	1	1	0	0	0	5	2	2	1	0
PERU	2	2	0	0	0	0	0	0	0	0	0	0	0	0	0	2	2	0	0	0
COLOMBIA	2	0	2	0	0	0	0	0	0	0	0	0	0	0	0	1	0	2	0	0
VENEZUELA	4	1	1	1	1	0	0	0	0	0	1	0	0	1	0	4	1	1	1	1
OTHER	2	0	1	0	1	2	1	0	0	1	0	0	0	0	0	0	0	0	0	0
EUROPE	105	32	42	11	20	13	6	5	1	1	25	5	6	3	11	67	21	31	7	8
EFTA	41	10	12	3	16	7	3	3	1	0	15	1	2	2	10	19	6	7	0	6
U.K.	37	8	10	3	16	6	3	2	1	0	15	1	2	2	10	16	4	6	0	6
SCANDINAVIA	3	1	2	0	0	1	0	1	0	0	0	0	0	0	0	2	1	1	0	0
SWITZERLAND	0	0	0	0	0	0	0	0	0	0	0	0	0	0	0	0	0	0	0	0
OTHER EFTA	1	1	0	0	0	0	0	0	0	0	0	0	0	0	0	1	1	0	0	0
EUROP. COMMUNITY	55	19	26	8	2	5	3	2	0	0	9	3	4	1	1	41	13	20	7	1
FRANCE	14	6	4	4	0	2	2	0	0	0	1	0	0	1	0	11	4	4	3	0
GERMANY	18	3	12	3	0	2	1	1	0	0	1	0	1	0	0	14	2	9	3	0
ITALY	9	5	2	2	0	0	0	0	0	0	2	1	0	1	0	7	4	3	0	0
BELGIUM + LUX	4	1	2	0	1	0	0	0	0	0	1	0	1	0	0	3	1	2	0	0
NETHERLANDS	10	4	4	1	1	0	0	0	0	0	4	2	2	0	0	6	2	2	1	1
SPAIN	4	2	1	0	1	0	0	0	0	0	1	1	0	0	0	3	1	1	0	1
GREECE + TURKEY	1	0	1	0	0	0	0	0	0	0	0	0	0	0	0	1	0	0	0	1
OTHER EUROPE	4	1	2	1	0	1	0	0	0	1	0	0	0	0	0	3	1	2	0	0
EUROPE EX. U.K.	68	24	32	8	4	7	3	3	0	1	10	4	4	1	1	51	17	25	7	2
SOUTHERN DOMINIONS	11	6	3	2	0	2	2	0	0	0	1	0	1	0	0	8	3	3	2	0
S. AFRICA +RHOD.	2	0	3	0	0	0	0	0	0	0	0	0	0	0	0	2	0	3	0	0
AUSTRALIA + N.Z.	9	4	3	2	0	2	2	0	0	0	1	1	0	0	0	6	2	3	2	0
ASIA + OTHER AFRICA	8	4	1	1	2	2	0	2	0	0	1	0	1	0	0	7	4	1	1	2
JAPAN	2	2	0	0	0	2	2	0	0	0	0	0	0	0	0	2	2	0	0	0
OTHER ASIA+AFR.	6	2	3	1	0	0	0	0	0	0	1	0	1	0	0	5	2	0	1	2
BLACK AFRICA	0	0	0	0	0	0	0	0	0	0	0	0	0	0	0	0	0	0	0	0
ARAB WORLD	0	0	0	0	0	0	0	0	0	0	0	0	0	0	0	0	0	0	0	0
INDIA	1	1	0	0	0	0	0	0	0	0	1	1	0	0	0	1	1	0	0	0
PHILIPPINES	2	0	1	1	0	0	0	0	0	0	0	0	0	0	0	2	0	0	1	1
OTHER E. ASIA	1	0	1	0	1	0	0	0	0	0	1	1	0	0	0	0	0	0	0	0
OTHER ASIA	2	1	1	0	1	0	0	0	0	0	0	0	0	0	0	2	1	1	0	1

CHAPTER 4- VARIETIES OF ENTRY
SECTION 6- CHANGES IN STATE OF BEING, MAIN ACTIVITY AND OWNERSHIP
TABLE 5- NON-MANUFACTURING SUBSIDIARIES
WHICH BEGAN MANUFACTURING, PERIOD CHANGE OCCURRED, AND METHOD OF ENTRY
CLASSIFIED BY COUNTRY, PERIOD CHANGE OCCURRED, AND METHOD OF ENTRY

(NEW=NEWLY FORMED, ACQ=ACQUIRED, DES=DESCENDANT, UNK=UNKNOWN)

PERIOD AND METHOD OF ENTRY

COUNTRY OR REGION	TOTAL PRE 1968					PRE 1946					1946-1957					1958-1967				
	ALL	NEW	ACQ	DES	UNK	ALL	NEW	ACQ	DES	UNK	ALL	NEW	ACQ	DES	UNK	ALL	NEW	ACQ	DES	UNK
OUTSIDE U.S.	289	190	27	55	17	71	53	6	10	2	88	53	6	23	6	130	84	15	22	9
OUT. U.S. + CANADA	266	176	22	52	16	60	46	4	8	2	81	48	5	23	5	125	82	13	21	9
OUT. WEST. HEMIS.	184	115	13	47	9	51	39	2	8	2	51	26	3	22	0	82	50	8	17	7
OUT. WHITE CWEALTH	198	128	18	40	12	34	22	4	6	2	63	38	3	17	5	101	68	11	17	5
OUT. DEVLPED WORLD	109	79	10	10	10	14	11	2	0	1	37	27	2	3	5	58	41	6	7	4
CANADA	23	14	5	3	1	11	7	2	2	0	7	5	1	0	1	5	2	2	1	0
LATIN AMERICA	82	61	9	5	7	9	7	2	0	0	30	22	2	1	5	43	32	5	4	2
C. AMER.+CARIB.	38	27	4	1	6	2	1	1	0	0	13	8	1	0	4	23	18	2	1	2
CUBA	5	3	1	1	0	1	1	0	0	0	3	2	1	0	0	1	0	0	1	0
MEXICO	26	20	3	0	3	1	0	1	0	0	7	6	0	0	1	18	14	2	0	2
OTHER	7	4	0	0	3	0	0	0	0	0	3	0	0	0	3	4	4	0	0	0
S. AMERICA	44	34	5	4	1	7	6	1	0	0	17	14	1	1	1	20	14	3	3	0
ARGENTINA	9	7	1	1	0	4	4	0	0	0	1	1	0	0	0	4	2	1	1	0
BRAZIL	14	13	1	0	0	1	1	0	0	0	7	7	0	0	0	6	5	1	0	0
PERU	2	2	0	0	0	1	1	0	0	0	0	0	0	0	0	1	1	0	0	0
COLOMBIA	5	3	1	1	0	1	0	0	1	0	1	1	0	0	0	3	2	1	0	0
VENEZUELA	8	5	1	1	1	0	0	0	0	0	3	1	0	1	1	5	4	1	0	0
OTHER	6	4	1	1	0	0	0	0	0	0	5	3	1	1	0	1	1	0	0	0
EUROPE	119	74	8	34	3	38	28	2	7	1	35	17	1	17	0	46	29	5	10	2
EFTA	54	36	3	14	1	21	19	1	1	0	17	10	0	7	0	16	7	2	6	1
U.K.	36	28	1	6	1	18	17	0	1	0	11	7	0	4	0	7	4	1	1	1
SCANDINAVIA	11	4	1	6	0	1	1	0	0	0	3	1	0	2	0	7	2	1	4	0
SWITZERLAND	4	4	0	0	0	1	1	0	0	0	2	2	0	0	0	1	1	0	0	0
OTHER EFTA	3	0	1	2	0	1	0	1	0	0	1	0	0	1	0	1	0	0	1	0
EUROP. COMMUNITY	58	32	5	19	2	13	6	1	5	1	18	7	1	10	0	27	19	3	4	1
FRANCE	15	6	2	7	0	5	2	1	2	0	5	1	0	4	0	5	3	1	1	0
GERMANY	22	15	2	5	0	2	2	0	0	0	9	3	1	5	0	11	10	1	0	0
ITALY	8	4	1	2	1	2	1	0	1	0	1	1	0	0	0	5	2	1	1	1
BELGIUM + LUX	7	3	1	2	1	2	1	0	0	1	1	0	0	1	0	4	2	1	1	0
NETHERLANDS	6	4	0	2	0	2	0	0	2	0	2	2	0	0	0	2	2	0	0	0
SPAIN	3	3	0	0	0	1	1	0	0	0	0	0	0	0	0	2	2	0	0	0
GREECE + TURKEY	1	1	0	0	0	0	0	0	0	0	0	0	0	0	0	1	1	0	0	0
OTHER EUROPE	3	2	0	1	0	3	2	0	1	0	0	0	0	0	0	0	0	0	0	0
EUROPE EX. U.K.	83	46	7	28	2	20	11	2	6	1	24	10	1	13	0	39	25	4	9	1
SOUTHERN DOMINIONS	31	20	3	5	3	7	7	0	0	0	9	3	1	4	1	15	10	2	1	2
S. AFRICA +RHOD.	10	6	1	2	1	1	1	0	0	0	3	1	0	2	0	6	4	1	0	1
AUSTRALIA + N.Z.	21	14	2	3	2	6	6	0	0	0	6	2	1	2	1	9	6	1	1	1
ASIA + OTHER AFRICA	34	21	2	8	3	6	4	1	0	1	9	6	0	3	0	19	11	1	5	2
JAPAN	7	3	1	3	0	1	0	1	0	0	2	1	0	1	0	4	2	0	2	0
OTHER ASIA+AFR.	27	18	1	5	3	5	4	0	0	1	7	5	0	2	0	15	9	1	3	2
BLACK AFRICA	1	1	0	0	0	0	0	0	0	0	0	0	0	0	0	1	1	0	0	0
ARAB WORLD	6	3	0	1	2	2	2	0	0	0	2	1	0	1	0	2	0	0	0	2
INDIA	6	2	1	3	0	0	0	0	0	0	0	0	0	0	0	6	2	1	3	0
PHILIPPINES	5	4	0	1	0	0	0	0	0	0	3	3	0	0	0	2	1	0	1	0
OTHER E. ASIA	2	2	0	0	0	0	0	0	0	0	1	1	0	0	0	1	1	0	0	0
OTHER ASIA	7	6	0	0	1	3	2	0	0	1	1	1	0	0	0	3	3	0	0	0

CHAPTER 4- VARIETIES OF ENTRY
SECTION 6- CHANGES IN STATE OF BEING, MAIN ACTIVITY AND OWNERSHIP
TABLE 6- MANUFACTURING JOINT VENTURES
WHICH BECAME WHOLLY OWNED BY THE PARENT SYSTEM,
CLASSIFIED BY COUNTRY, PERIOD CHANGE OCCURRED, AND METHOD OF ENTRY

PERIOD AND METHOD OF ENTRY
(NEW=NEWLY FORMED, ACQ=ACQUIRED, DES=DESCENDANT, UNK=UNKNOWN)

COUNTRY OR REGION	TOTAL PRE 1968					PRE 1946					1946-1957					1958-1967				
	ALL	NEW	ACQ	DES	UNK	ALL	NEW	ACQ	DES	UNK	ALL	NEW	ACQ	DES	UNK	ALL	NEW	ACQ	DES	UNK
OUTSIDE U.S.	464	165	159	91	49	50	13	22	9	6	80	30	15	20	15	334	122	122	62	28
OUT. U.S. + CANADA	403	150	136	77	40	37	11	14	8	4	61	24	10	15	12	305	115	112	54	24
OUT. WEST. HEMIS.	269	101	89	50	29	28	9	9	7	3	42	16	7	8	11	199	76	73	35	15
OUT. WHITE CWEALTH	314	118	108	57	31	27	8	12	4	3	45	19	8	10	8	242	91	88	43	20
OUT. DEVLPED WORLD	148	55	50	27	16	10	2	6	1	1	25	10	4	7	4	113	43	40	19	11
CANADA	61	15	23	14	9	13	2	8	1	2	19	6	5	5	3	29	7	10	8	4
LATIN AMERICA	134	49	47	27	11	9	2	5	1	1	19	8	3	7	1	106	39	39	19	9
C. AMER.+CARIB.	47	17	17	7	6	3	1	1	1	0	3	3	0	0	0	41	12	16	7	6
CUBA	7	4	1	0	2	1	1	0	0	0	0	0	0	0	0	6	0	0	0	2
MEXICO	33	10	14	6	3	2	0	1	1	0	3	3	0	0	0	28	6	13	6	3
OTHER	7	3	2	1	1	0	0	0	0	0	0	0	0	0	0	7	3	3	1	1
S. AMERICA	87	32	30	20	5	6	0	4	1	1	16	5	3	7	1	65	27	23	12	3
ARGENTINA	20	5	10	4	1	3	0	2	1	0	5	2	1	1	1	12	5	5	2	1
BRAZIL	25	7	8	9	1	1	0	0	0	1	5	2	1	2	0	19	5	7	7	3
PERU	5	2	1	1	1	0	0	0	0	0	1	0	0	1	0	4	1	1	0	0
COLCMBIA	15	8	7	0	0	0	0	0	0	0	0	0	0	0	0	15	8	7	0	1
VENEZUELA	16	10	3	3	0	1	0	1	0	0	4	1	1	2	0	11	9	1	1	0
OTHER	6	0	1	3	2	0	0	0	0	0	1	0	1	1	0	4	0	0	1	2
EUROPE	206	73	71	44	18	25	9	6	7	3	26	9	5	6	6	155	55	60	31	9
EFTA	65	17	21	19	8	11	4	2	4	1	8	1	2	3	2	46	12	17	12	5
U.K.	45	14	13	14	4	9	3	1	4	1	7	1	1	3	2	29	10	11	7	1
SCANDINAVIA	12	2	4	3	3	1	0	1	0	0	1	0	1	0	0	10	2	2	3	3
SWITZERLAND	3	0	2	0	1	0	0	0	0	0	0	0	0	0	0	3	0	2	0	1
OTHER EFTA	5	1	2	2	0	1	1	0	0	0	0	0	0	0	0	4	0	2	2	0
EUROP. COMMUNITY	129	54	44	24	7	12	5	5	3	0	18	8	3	3	4	99	41	37	18	3
FRANCE	41	13	17	10	1	5	0	3	1	1	3	1	1	1	0	37	12	16	8	1
GERMANY	33	11	12	9	1	3	3	0	0	0	6	3	1	1	1	19	5	7	6	1
ITALY	27	15	10	2	0	3	1	1	1	0	4	3	1	0	0	24	13	7	1	0
BELGIUM + LUX	14	7	3	2	2	0	0	0	0	0	4	2	1	0	1	10	6	3	1	1
NETHERLANDS	14	8	2	1	3	1	1	0	0	0	2	2	0	0	0	9	5	5	1	2
SPAIN	5	0	5	0	0	0	0	0	0	0	0	0	0	0	0	5	0	5	0	0
GREECE + TURKEY	2	0	1	1	1	0	0	0	0	1	0	0	0	0	0	1	0	1	1	0
OTHER EUROPE	5	2	2	0	2	1	0	0	1	0	0	0	0	0	0	4	2	1	0	1
EUROPE EX. U.K.	161	59	58	30	14	16	6	5	3	2	19	8	4	3	4	126	45	49	24	8
SOUTHERN DOMINIONS	40	16	14	6	4	1	0	1	0	0	9	4	1	2	2	30	12	12	4	2
S. AFRICA +RHOD.	15	8	3	1	3	0	0	0	0	0	4	2	0	0	2	11	6	3	1	1
AUSTRALIA + N.Z.	25	8	11	5	1	1	0	1	0	0	5	2	1	2	0	19	6	9	3	1
ASIA + OTHER AFRICA	23	12	4	0	7	2	1	2	0	0	7	3	1	0	3	14	9	1	0	4
JAPAN	9	6	1	0	2	1	1	1	0	0	6	2	1	0	3	7	5	1	0	2
OTHER ASIA+AFR.	14	6	3	0	5	1	0	1	0	0	1	1	0	0	0	7	4	0	1	2
BLACK AFRICA	3	1	0	0	2	0	0	0	0	0	0	0	0	0	0	3	1	0	0	2
ARAB WORLD	2	2	0	0	0	0	0	0	0	0	0	0	0	0	0	2	2	0	0	0
INDIA	1	1	0	0	0	0	0	0	0	0	1	1	0	0	0	0	0	0	0	0
PHILIPPINES	1	0	1	0	0	0	0	0	0	0	0	0	0	0	0	1	0	1	0	0
OTHER E. ASIA	3	1	2	0	0	1	0	1	0	0	1	1	0	0	0	0	0	0	0	0
OTHER ASIA	4	1	0	0	3	0	0	0	0	0	3	0	1	0	3	1	1	0	0	0

CHAPTER 4- VARIETIES OF ENTRY
SECTION 6- CHANGES IN STATE OF BEING, MAIN ACTIVITY AND OWNERSHIP
TABLE 7- MANUFACTURING SUBSIDIARIES IN WHICH THE PARENT SYSTEM
"SIGNIFICANTLY" INCREASED ITS OWNERSHIP PERCENTAGE,
CLASSIFIED BY COUNTRY, PERIOD CHANGE OCCURRED, AND METHOD OF ENTRY

(NEW=NEWLY FORMED, ACQ=ACQUIRED, DES=DESCENDANT, UNK=UNKNOWN)

COUNTRY OR REGION	TOTAL PRE 1968					PERIOD AND METHOD OF ENTRY — PRE 1946					1946-1957					1958-1967				
	ALL	NEW	ACQ	DES	UNK	ALL	NEW	ACQ	DES	UNK	ALL	NEW	ACQ	DES	UNK	ALL	NEW	ACQ	DES	UNK
OUTSIDE U.S.	456	160	178	99	19	42	9	20	10	3	76	31	17	21	7	338	120	141	68	9
OUT. U.S. + CANADA	399	146	155	81	17	30	7	12	8	3	56	25	12	13	6	313	114	131	60	8
OUT. WEST. HEMIS.	263	94	104	50	15	22	5	8	6	3	35	14	9	7	5	206	75	87	37	7
OUT. WHITE CWEALTH	318	118	123	64	13	20	4	10	4	2	44	21	10	9	4	254	93	103	51	7
OUT. DEVLPED WORLD	148	61	52	32	3	8	2	4	2	0	22	12	3	6	1	118	47	45	24	2
CANADA	57	14	23	18	2	12	2	8	2	0	20	6	5	8	1	25	6	10	8	1
LATIN AMERICA	136	52	51	31	2	8	2	4	2	0	21	11	3	6	1	107	39	44	23	1
C. AMER.+CARIB.	50	18	21	10	1	3	2	1	0	0	3	3	0	0	0	44	13	20	10	1
CUBA	7	5	1	1	0	1	1	0	0	0	0	0	0	0	0	6	4	1	1	0
MEXICO	35	9	17	9	0	2	1	1	0	0	3	3	0	0	0	30	5	16	9	0
OTHER	8	4	3	1	0	0	0	0	0	0	0	0	0	0	0	8	4	3	1	0
S. AMERICA	86	34	30	21	1	5	0	3	2	0	18	8	3	6	1	63	26	24	13	0
ARGENTINA	18	3	10	4	1	3	0	2	1	0	5	1	1	3	0	10	2	7	0	1
BRAZIL	27	11	7	9	0	0	0	0	0	0	7	3	1	3	0	20	8	6	6	0
PERU	4	2	1	1	0	0	0	0	0	0	1	1	0	0	0	3	1	1	1	0
COLOMBIA	15	7	7	1	0	0	0	0	0	0	0	0	0	0	0	15	7	7	1	0
VENEZUELA	16	10	4	2	0	0	0	0	0	0	4	2	1	1	0	12	8	3	1	0
OTHER	6	1	1	4	0	2	0	1	1	0	1	0	0	1	0	3	1	0	2	0
EUROPE	202	64	83	43	12	20	5	6	6	3	24	8	7	5	4	158	51	70	32	5
EFTA	57	13	23	16	5	10	3	2	4	1	5	0	2	2	1	42	10	19	10	3
U.K.	40	12	15	11	2	9	3	1	4	1	4	0	1	2	1	27	9	13	5	0
SCANDINAVIA	10	1	4	3	2	1	0	0	0	1	1	0	0	0	1	8	1	4	3	0
SWITZERLAND	3	0	2	0	1	0	0	0	0	0	0	0	0	0	0	3	0	2	0	1
OTHER EFTA	4	0	2	2	0	0	0	0	0	0	0	0	0	0	0	4	0	2	2	0
EUROP. COMMUNITY	125	49	46	26	4	7	2	4	1	0	17	8	2	4	3	101	39	40	21	1
FRANCE	47	13	21	12	1	1	0	1	0	0	3	1	0	1	1	43	12	20	11	0
GERMANY	28	8	11	9	0	5	1	3	1	0	6	3	1	2	0	17	4	7	6	0
ITALY	25	14	9	2	0	0	0	0	0	0	1	1	0	0	0	24	13	9	2	0
BELGIUM + LUX	14	7	3	2	2	0	0	0	0	0	4	1	0	1	2	10	6	3	1	0
NETHERLANDS	11	7	2	1	1	1	1	0	0	0	3	2	1	0	0	7	4	1	1	1
SPAIN	14	1	12	0	1	1	0	1	0	0	1	0	1	0	0	12	1	10	0	1
GREECE + TURKEY	3	1	1	1	0	1	0	0	1	0	0	0	0	0	0	2	1	1	0	0
OTHER EUROPE	3	0	1	1	1	1	0	0	0	1	1	0	0	1	0	1	0	1	0	0
EUROPE EX. U.K.	162	52	68	32	10	11	2	5	3	1	20	8	6	2	4	131	42	57	27	5
SOUTHERN DOMINIONS	40	15	17	6	2	1	0	1	0	0	8	5	3	0	0	31	10	13	6	2
S. AFRICA +RHOD.	13	7	4	1	1	0	0	0	0	0	3	2	1	0	0	10	5	3	1	1
AUSTRALIA + N.Z.	27	8	13	5	1	1	0	1	0	0	5	3	2	0	0	21	5	10	5	1
ASIA + OTHER AFRICA	21	15	4	2	0	0	0	0	0	0	4	2	2	0	0	17	13	2	2	0
JAPAN	9	6	3	0	0	0	0	0	0	0	3	2	1	0	0	6	4	2	0	0
OTHER ASIA+AFR.	12	9	1	2	0	0	0	0	0	0	1	0	1	0	0	11	9	0	2	0
BLACK AFRICA	2	1	0	1	0	0	0	0	0	0	0	0	0	0	0	2	1	0	1	0
ARAB WORLD	3	3	0	0	0	0	0	0	0	0	0	0	0	0	0	3	3	0	0	0
INDIA	2	2	0	0	0	0	0	0	0	0	0	0	0	0	0	2	2	0	0	0
PHILIPPINES	4	2	1	1	0	0	0	0	0	0	1	0	1	0	0	3	2	0	1	0
OTHER E. ASIA	0	0	0	0	0	0	0	0	0	0	0	0	0	0	0	0	0	0	0	0
OTHER ASIA	1	1	0	0	0	0	0	0	0	0	0	0	0	0	0	1	1	0	0	0

CHAPTER 4- VARIETIES OF ENTRY
SECTION 6- CHANGES IN STATE OF BEING, MAIN ACTIVITY AND OWNERSHIP
TABLE 8- MANUFACTURING SUBSIDIARIES IN WHICH THE PARENT SYSTEM
"SIGNIFICANTLY" DECREASED ITS OWNERSHIP PERCENTAGE,
CLASSIFIED BY COUNTRY, PERIOD CHANGE OCCURRED, AND METHOD OF ENTRY

PERIOD AND METHOD OF ENTRY
(NEW=NEWLY FORMED, ACQ=ACQUIRED, DES=DESCENDANT, UNK=UNKNOWN)

COUNTRY OR REGION	TOTAL PRE 1968					PRE 1946					1946-1957					1958-1967				
	ALL	NEW	ACQ	DES	UNK	ALL	NEW	ACQ	DES	UNK	ALL	NEW	ACQ	DES	UNK	ALL	NEW	ACQ	DES	UNK
OUTSIDE U.S.	290	101	128	48	13	33	13	11	7	2	49	23	18	5	3	208	65	99	36	8
OUT. U.S. + CANADA	243	91	100	43	9	21	12	5	4	0	37	18	12	5	2	185	61	83	34	7
OUT. WEST. HEMIS.	154	55	71	23	5	16	10	4	2	0	22	9	9	4	0	116	36	58	17	5
OUT. WHITE CWEALTH	191	75	75	33	8	16	8	5	3	0	25	14	7	2	2	150	53	63	28	6
OUT. DEVLPED WORLD	103	44	34	21	4	6	3	1	2	0	16	9	4	1	2	81	32	29	18	2
CANADA	47	10	28	5	4	12	1	6	3	2	12	5	5	0	1	23	4	16	2	1
LATIN AMERICA	89	36	29	20	4	5	2	1	2	0	15	9	3	1	2	69	25	25	17	2
C. AMER.+CARIB.	42	17	13	9	3	0	0	0	0	0	6	5	0	0	1	36	12	13	9	2
CUBA	8	5	0	0	3	0	0	0	0	0	1	0	0	0	1	7	5	0	0	2
MEXICO	27	9	10	8	0	0	0	0	0	0	3	3	0	0	0	24	6	10	8	0
OTHER	7	3	3	1	0	0	0	0	0	0	2	2	0	0	0	5	1	3	1	0
S. AMERICA	47	19	16	11	1	5	2	3	0	0	9	4	3	1	1	33	13	12	8	0
ARGENTINA	12	1	5	5	1	3	0	2	1	0	2	2	1	1	0	7	1	3	3	0
BRAZIL	14	8	4	2	0	0	0	0	2	0	4	2	1	1	0	10	6	3	1	0
PERU	2	2	0	0	0	1	1	0	0	0	0	0	0	0	0	1	1	0	0	0
COLOMBIA	7	1	4	2	0	0	0	0	0	0	1	0	1	0	0	6	1	3	2	0
VENEZUELA	9	5	2	2	0	1	0	1	0	0	2	2	0	2	0	7	3	2	2	0
OTHER	3	2	1	0	0	1	1	0	0	0	0	0	0	0	0	2	1	1	0	0
EUROPE	108	35	53	15	5	14	8	4	2	0	13	6	5	2	0	81	21	44	11	5
EFTA	35	11	19	4	1	4	3	0	1	0	5	2	2	1	0	26	6	17	2	1
U.K.	24	6	13	4	1	4	3	0	1	0	4	2	2	1	0	16	2	11	2	1
SCANDINAVIA	7	2	5	0	0	0	0	0	0	0	0	0	0	0	0	7	2	5	0	0
SWITZERLAND	1	1	0	0	0	0	0	0	0	0	0	0	0	0	0	1	0	1	0	0
OTHER EFTA	3	3	0	0	0	0	0	0	0	0	1	1	0	0	0	2	2	0	0	0
EUROP. COMMUNITY	67	22	31	11	3	9	4	4	1	0	7	3	3	0	1	51	15	24	9	3
FRANCE	22	8	11	2	1	5	3	1	0	1	1	1	1	1	0	16	5	9	2	1
GERMANY	11	2	7	2	0	2	0	2	0	0	4	1	3	0	0	5	1	2	2	0
ITALY	18	7	7	3	1	1	1	0	1	0	0	0	0	0	0	17	6	7	3	1
BELGIUM + LUX	10	4	4	1	1	1	0	0	1	0	2	1	0	0	1	3	4	4	1	0
NETHERLANDS	6	1	2	3	0	0	0	0	0	0	0	0	0	0	0	5	2	2	1	0
SPAIN	4	0	3	0	0	1	0	1	0	0	2	1	1	0	0	4	0	3	0	1
GREECE + TURKEY	0	0	0	0	0	0	0	0	0	0	0	0	0	0	0	0	0	0	0	0
OTHER EUROPE	2	2	0	0	0	0	0	0	0	0	1	1	0	0	0	0	0	0	0	0
EUROPE EX. U.K.	84	29	40	11	4	10	5	4	1	1	9	5	3	1	0	65	19	33	9	4
SOUTHERN DOMINIONS	28	10	12	6	0	1	1	0	0	0	8	3	3	2	0	19	6	9	4	0
S. AFRICA +RHOD.	5	3	1	1	0	0	0	0	0	0	2	1	0	1	0	3	2	1	0	0
AUSTRALIA + N.Z.	23	7	11	5	0	1	1	0	0	0	6	2	3	1	0	16	4	8	4	0
ASIA + OTHER AFRICA	18	10	6	2	0	1	1	0	0	0	1	0	1	0	0	16	9	5	2	0
JAPAN	4	2	1	1	0	1	1	0	0	0	1	1	0	0	0	4	2	1	1	0
OTHER ASIA+AFR.	14	8	5	1	0	1	1	0	0	0	0	0	0	0	0	12	7	4	1	0
BLACK AFRICA	1	1	0	0	0	0	0	0	0	0	0	0	0	0	0	1	1	0	0	0
ARAB WORLD	2	1	1	0	0	0	0	0	0	0	0	0	0	0	0	2	1	1	0	0
INDIA	2	1	1	0	0	0	0	0	0	0	0	0	0	0	0	1	1	0	0	0
PHILIPPINES	3	2	1	0	0	0	0	0	0	0	0	0	0	0	0	3	2	1	0	0
OTHER E. ASIA	0	0	0	0	0	0	0	0	0	0	0	0	0	0	0	0	0	0	0	0
OTHER ASIA	6	3	2	1	0	0	0	0	0	0	1	0	1	0	0	5	3	1	1	0

CHAPTER 5
Patterns of Ownership

CHAPTER 5- PATTERNS OF OWNERSHIP
SECTION 1- AN OVERVIEW OF FLOW AND STOCK, MANUFACTURING AND NON-MANUFACTURING
TABLE 1- SUBSIDIARIES CLASSIFIED BY COUNTRY OR REGION,
BY PERIOD ACTIVITY BEGAN AND BY SYSTEM OWNERSHIP %

PERIOD AND OWNERSHIP PERCENTAGE
(WHL=95-100%, MAJ=50-94%, MIN=5-49%, UNK=UNKNOWN)

COUNTRY OR REGION	TOTAL PRE 1968					PRE 1946					1946-1957					1958-1967				
	ALL	WHL	MAJ	MIN	UNK	ALL	WHL	MAJ	MIN	UNK	ALL	WHL	MAJ	MIN	UNK	ALL	WHL	MAJ	MIN	UNK
OUTSIDE U.S.	11152	6894	1895	828	949	2422	1648	324	117	333	2246	1576	363	143	164	5898	3670	1208	568	452
OUT. U.S. + CANADA	9455	5637	1765	767	811	1885	1234	290	106	255	1832	1238	324	126	144	5263	3165	1151	535	412
OUT. WEST. HEMIS.	6755	4076	1278	522	552	1377	903	212	72	190	1097	743	197	77	80	3954	2430	869	373	282
OUT. WHITE CWEALTH	7294	4209	1439	661	648	1366	868	214	86	198	1428	938	266	97	127	4163	2403	959	478	323
OUT. DEVLPED WORLD	3522	2006	652	338	326	611	401	87	36	87	911	606	165	58	82	1800	999	400	244	157
CANADA	1697	1257	130	61	138	537	414	34	11	78	414	338	39	17	20	635	505	57	33	40
LATIN AMERICA	2700	1561	487	245	259	508	331	78	34	65	735	495	127	49	64	1309	735	282	162	130
C. AMER.+CARIB.	1251	753	199	113	117	216	148	25	16	27	347	256	45	14	32	619	349	129	83	58
CUBA	92	62	12	5	9	47	32	7	3	5	36	26	5	2	3	5	4	0	0	1
MEXICO	625	337	110	72	70	134	92	15	8	19	156	101	25	7	23	299	144	70	57	28
OTHER	534	354	77	36	38	35	24	3	5	3	155	129	15	5	6	315	201	59	26	29
S. AMERICA	1449	808	288	132	142	292	183	53	18	38	388	239	82	35	32	690	386	153	79	72
ARGENTINA	283	155	52	27	23	74	54	13	0	7	66	37	18	7	4	117	64	21	20	12
BRAZIL	346	205	66	27	37	66	41	9	6	10	100	57	25	8	10	169	107	32	13	17
PERU	127	82	24	7	4	27	21	5	1	0	28	17	5	5	1	62	44	14	1	3
COLOMBIA	196	101	51	17	19	32	19	6	3	4	60	41	11	4	4	96	41	34	10	11
VENEZUELA	292	147	58	33	45	35	14	10	7	10	88	52	17	7	12	160	81	31	25	23
OTHER	205	118	37	21	14	58	34	10	7	7	46	35	6	4	1	86	49	21	10	6
EUROPE	4755	2948	892	306	406	1105	700	182	60	163	693	483	112	49	49	2754	1765	598	197	194
EFTA	2004	1407	265	69	160	521	353	86	17	65	319	250	34	18	17	1061	804	145	34	78
U.K.	1189	783	170	50	106	358	233	60	12	53	204	153	25	17	9	547	397	85	21	44
SCANDINAVIA	384	285	49	10	28	96	72	15	3	6	63	54	4	1	4	213	159	30	6	18
SWITZERLAND	317	262	29	4	12	35	27	4	2	2	38	34	4	0	0	234	201	21	2	10
OTHER EFTA	114	77	17	5	14	32	21	7	0	4	14	9	1	0	4	67	47	9	5	6
EUROP. COMMUNITY	2300	1322	509	178	209	464	271	86	32	75	320	200	67	23	30	1434	851	356	123	104
FRANCE	670	324	184	82	58	156	76	25	22	33	78	46	22	7	3	414	202	137	53	22
GERMANY	632	385	126	30	70	144	86	32	3	23	90	55	20	6	9	377	244	74	21	38
ITALY	434	248	102	29	36	61	38	11	2	10	69	46	12	5	6	285	164	79	22	20
BELGIUM + LUX	288	187	49	20	21	53	35	10	4	4	39	26	6	1	6	185	126	33	15	11
NETHERLANDS	276	178	48	17	24	50	36	8	1	5	44	27	7	4	6	173	115	33	12	13
SPAIN	221	89	76	34	16	41	26	4	2	9	22	13	3	6	0	152	50	69	26	7
GREECE + TURKEY	80	36	26	13	3	4	3	1	0	0	14	6	6	2	0	59	27	19	10	3
OTHER EUROPE	150	94	16	13	18	75	47	5	9	14	18	14	4	0	2	48	33	4	4	2
EUROPE EX. U.K.	3566	2165	722	256	300	747	467	122	48	110	489	330	87	32	40	2207	1368	513	176	150
SOUTHERN DOMINIONS	902	594	148	53	53	152	125	15	8	4	185	134	33	12	6	511	335	100	33	43
S. AFRICA +RHOD.	280	195	34	22	10	48	39	3	3	3	65	47	10	5	3	148	109	21	14	4
AUSTRALIA + N.Z.	622	399	114	31	43	104	86	12	5	1	120	87	23	7	3	363	226	79	19	39
ASIA + OTHER AFRICA	1098	534	238	163	93	120	78	15	5	23	219	126	52	16	25	689	330	171	143	45
JAPAN	276	89	73	70	26	17	8	6	2	1	43	15	14	7	7	198	66	53	61	18
OTHER ASIA+AFR.	822	445	165	93	67	103	70	9	3	22	176	111	38	9	18	491	264	118	82	27
BLACK AFRICA	197	113	35	20	9	7	3	1	0	3	49	29	15	3	2	121	81	19	17	4
ARAB WORLD	121	65	25	14	8	21	13	3	1	4	35	24	6	2	3	56	28	16	11	1
INDIA	95	35	22	29	5	16	15	2	1	0	17	11	2	1	3	58	9	19	28	1
PHILIPPINES	107	63	22	9	9	18	13	2	2	0	29	17	6	1	0	58	33	14	8	3
OTHER E. ASIA	96	63	11	4	14	12	6	1	2	0	11	9	1	1	0	69	48	9	4	9
OTHER ASIA	206	106	50	17	22	29	20	1	1	7	35	21	8	1	5	131	65	41	15	10

CHAPTER 5- PATTERNS OF OWNERSHIP
SECTION 1- AN OVERVIEW OF FLOW AND STOCK, MANUFACTURING AND NON-MANUFACTURING
TABLE 2- SUBSIDIARIES CLASSIFIED BY COUNTRY OR REGION,
BY YEAR(S) SUBSIDIARY WAS ACTIVE
AND BY SYSTEM OWNERSHIP %

YEAR AND OWNERSHIP PERCENTAGE
(WHL=95-100%, MAJ=50-94%, MIN=5-49%, UNK=UNKNOWN)

COUNTRY OR REGION	1929 ALL	WHL	MAJ	MIN	UNK	1939 ALL	WHL	MAJ	MIN	UNK	1957 ALL	WHL	MAJ	MIN	UNK	1967 ALL	WHL	MAJ	MIN	UNK
OUTSIDE U.S.	987	657	141	48	141	1763	1222	250	75	216	3669	2533	557	218	361	7927	5143	1457	660	667
OUT. U.S. + CANADA	772	490	125	41	116	1410	945	224	69	172	2978	1982	496	198	302	6879	4326	1356	616	581
OUT. WEST. HEMIS.	633	401	109	35	88	1095	730	177	55	133	1921	1280	324	122	195	4955	3131	991	419	414
OUT. WHITE CWEALTH	560	342	89	31	98	999	650	161	55	133	2241	1453	388	157	243	5378	3269	1108	538	463
OUT. DEVLPED WORLD	181	115	19	8	39	396	269	56	17	54	1291	851	217	89	134	2597	1573	521	287	216
CANADA	215	167	16	7	25	353	277	26	6	44	691	551	61	20	59	1048	817	101	44	86
LATIN AMERICA	139	89	16	6	28	315	215	47	14	39	1057	702	172	76	107	1924	1195	365	197	167
C. AMER.+CARIB.	55	33	9	2	11	146	105	16	8	17	478	348	52	30	48	855	542	152	90	71
CUBA	15	7	5	0	3	35	27	5	2	1	65	47	7	5	6	12	11	1	0	0
MEXICO	39	26	3	2	8	93	67	8	3	15	234	157	28	15	34	412	230	79	61	42
OTHER	1	0	1	0	0	18	11	3	3	1	179	144	17	10	8	431	301	72	29	29
S. AMERICA	84	56	7	4	17	169	110	31	6	22	579	354	120	46	59	1069	653	213	107	96
ARGENTINA	22	18	1	0	3	56	43	7	0	6	112	78	19	6	9	187	115	36	20	16
BRAZIL	19	14	1	0	4	38	24	9	2	3	151	89	33	11	18	267	173	48	16	30
PERU	8	6	0	0	2	13	11	1	0	1	46	29	10	6	1	98	66	20	7	5
COLUMBIA	5	3	0	0	2	12	7	1	2	2	78	44	18	8	8	150	84	34	14	18
VENEZUELA	5	1	0	0	4	9	3	2	0	4	108	60	23	7	18	213	123	40	32	18
OTHER	25	14	3	4	4	41	22	10	6	3	84	54	17	8	5	154	92	35	18	9
EUROPE	530	326	100	29	75	883	570	154	45	114	1355	896	222	86	151	3401	2221	651	227	302
EFTA	242	162	51	11	18	419	288	75	13	43	653	466	97	28	62	1405	1037	196	53	119
U.K.	155	100	32	7	16	284	188	51	9	36	431	293	66	25	47	800	554	129	38	79
SCANDINAVIA	56	40	14	2	0	85	62	17	2	4	137	108	18	3	8	287	224	32	8	23
SWITZERLAND	19	15	1	2	1	26	21	1	2	2	52	45	5	0	2	235	204	21	2	8
OTHER EFTA	12	7	4	0	1	24	17	6	0	1	33	20	8	0	5	83	55	14	5	9
EUROP. COMMUNITY	238	138	42	12	46	370	220	69	25	56	601	366	108	49	78	1675	1025	351	137	162
FRANCE	72	39	9	8	16	117	57	19	17	24	180	94	35	27	24	493	256	133	62	42
GERMANY	84	48	19	2	15	117	72	26	1	18	175	106	38	7	24	456	293	84	26	53
ITALY	32	17	5	1	9	53	34	9	2	8	98	62	15	7	14	310	188	70	19	33
BELGIUM + LUX	26	18	5	1	2	47	31	10	4	2	76	54	11	4	7	219	159	29	16	15
NETHERLANDS	24	16	4	0	4	36	26	5	1	4	72	50	9	4	9	197	129	35	14	19
SPAIN	20	12	3	0	5	34	22	6	0	6	53	34	9	5	5	185	76	76	21	12
GREECE + TURKEY	1	0	0	0	1	3	3	0	0	0	14	7	5	2	0	66	34	18	11	3
OTHER EUROPE	29	14	4	6	5	57	37	4	7	9	34	23	3	2	6	70	49	10	5	6
EUROPE EX. U.K.	375	226	68	22	59	599	382	103	36	78	924	603	156	61	104	2601	1667	522	189	223
SOUTHERN DOMINIONS	53	45	3	3	2	120	100	12	5	3	285	217	42	16	10	648	460	113	37	38
S. AFRICA +RHOD.	17	15	0	1	1	40	33	3	2	2	99	78	10	6	5	209	164	24	12	9
AUSTRALIA + N.Z.	36	30	3	2	1	80	67	9	3	1	186	139	32	10	5	439	296	89	25	29
ASIA + OTHER AFRICA	50	30	6	3	11	92	60	11	5	16	281	167	60	20	34	906	450	227	155	74
JAPAN	8	4	2	1	1	11	6	2	2	1	47	18	15	7	7	233	72	71	65	25
OTHER ASIA+AFK.	42	26	4	2	10	81	54	9	3	15	234	149	45	13	27	673	378	156	90	49
BLACK AFRICA	6	2	1	0	3	16	8	3	1	4	49	28	15	2	4	166	112	28	20	6
ARAB WORLD	7	2	2	0	3	13	10	2	0	1	48	30	8	4	6	88	50	20	12	6
INDIA	5	5	0	0	0	14	10	1	0	3	30	22	4	1	3	86	29	23	28	6
PHILIPPINES	5	5	0	0	0	6	6	0	0	0	39	23	8	3	5	87	52	22	7	8
OTHER E. ASIA	6	2	0	0	4	8	4	1	1	2	13	11	1	1	0	76	52	11	5	8
OTHER ASIA	13	10	0	0	3	24	16	2	1	5	55	35	9	2	9	170	83	52	18	17

CHAPTER 5- PATTERNS OF OWNERSHIP
SECTION 1- AN OVERVIEW OF FLOW AND STOCK, MANUFACTURING AND NON-MANUFACTURING
TABLE 3- MANUFACTURING SUBSIDIARIES CLASSIFIED BY COUNTRY OR REGION,
BY PERIOD MANUFACTURE BEGAN AND BY SYSTEM OWNERSHIP %

PERIOD AND OWNERSHIP PERCENTAGE
(WHL=95-100%, MAJ=50-94%, MIN=5-49%, UNK=UNKNOWN)

COUNTRY OR REGION	TOTAL PRE 1968 ALL	WHL	MAJ	MIN	UNK	PRE 1946 ALL	WHL	MAJ	MIN	UNK	1946-1957 ALL	WHL	MAJ	MIN	UNK	1958-1967 ALL	WHL	MAJ	MIN	UNK
OUTSIDE U.S.	5209	2914	1224	586	361	1031	704	157	70	100	1024	641	224	105	54	3030	1569	843	411	207
OUT. U.S. + CANADA	4404	2287	1137	557	318	763	487	133	62	81	819	477	197	99	46	2717	1323	807	396	191
OUT. WEST. HEMIS.	3079	1621	804	360	218	557	358	100	33	66	479	285	107	61	26	1967	978	597	266	126
OUT. WHITE CWEALTH	3326	1599	930	482	245	508	307	96	51	54	623	346	163	77	37	2125	946	671	354	154
OUT. DEVLPED WORLD	1685	818	439	262	125	236	150	35	29	22	395	223	106	44	22	1013	445	298	189	81
CANADA	805	627	87	29	43	268	217	24	8	19	205	164	27	6	8	313	246	36	15	16
LATIN AMERICA	1325	666	333	197	100	206	129	33	29	15	340	192	90	38	20	750	345	210	130	65
C. AMER.+CARIB.	563	276	134	91	45	78	48	10	14	6	130	90	24	8	8	338	138	100	69	31
CUBA	46	26	8	5	5	19	11	4	1	3	21	12	4	4	1	4	3	0	0	1
MEXICO	363	186	80	59	27	46	31	6	6	3	90	64	17	4	5	216	91	57	49	19
OTHER	154	64	46	27	13	13	6	0	5	2	19	14	3	2	0	118	44	43	20	11
S. AMERICA	762	390	199	106	55	128	81	23	15	9	210	102	66	30	12	412	207	110	61	34
ARGENTINA	160	91	38	23	6	45	37	3	5	0	34	14	13	7	0	79	40	22	11	6
BRAZIL	200	118	45	22	13	34	23	7	3	1	70	36	13	11	10	96	59	25	8	2
PERU	57	28	17	7	2	12	7	4	1	0	15	6	2	5	2	30	15	11	1	0
COLOMBIA	116	52	36	17	10	10	4	3	3	0	29	14	9	4	2	77	34	24	10	8
VENEZUELA	143	58	41	22	21	10	3	3	1	3	43	19	14	4	6	90	36	24	17	12
OTHER	86	43	22	15	3	17	7	3	5	2	19	13	5	3	1	50	23	14	7	0
EUROPE	2062	1135	531	195	164	428	265	80	26	57	312	190	59	42	21	1285	680	392	127	86
EFTA	753	481	139	45	67	208	138	34	7	29	126	82	20	16	8	398	261	85	22	30
U.K.	555	354	93	36	52	162	107	24	6	25	101	64	17	13	7	272	183	52	17	20
SCANDINAVIA	113	73	28	5	6	25	18	4	0	3	17	13	3	1	0	70	42	21	4	3
SWITZERLAND	36	25	7	1	3	5	4	0	0	1	4	3	1	0	0	27	18	6	1	2
OTHER EFTA	49	29	11	3	6	16	9	4	0	3	4	2	1	0	1	29	18	6	3	2
EUROP. COMMUNITY	1077	569	307	103	83	186	108	41	15	22	155	93	33	18	11	721	368	233	70	50
FRANCE	324	146	104	44	24	66	36	11	10	9	38	21	10	4	3	214	89	83	30	12
GERMANY	304	172	80	22	27	64	39	17	1	7	53	34	13	3	3	184	99	50	18	17
ITALY	223	116	72	17	15	21	13	5	1	2	35	22	7	4	2	164	81	60	12	11
BELGIUM + LUX	117	72	27	11	7	19	8	5	3	3	11	7	2	2	0	87	57	20	6	4
NETHERLANDS	109	63	24	9	10	16	12	3	1	0	18	9	5	3	1	72	42	16	5	9
SPAIN	137	38	64	30	5	15	7	1	3	4	16	7	5	3	1	106	24	58	24	0
GREECE + TURKEY	42	14	15	10	3	1	0	1	0	0	6	1	3	2	0	35	13	11	8	3
OTHER EUROPE	53	33	7	6	6	18	12	0	3	3	9	7	0	1	1	25	14	7	2	2
EUROPE EX. U.K.	1507	781	438	159	112	266	158	56	20	32	211	126	44	27	14	1013	497	338	112	66
SOUTHERN DOMINIONS	488	311	109	36	18	89	69	13	5	2	86	60	19	7	0	299	182	77	24	16
S. AFRICA +RHOD.	158	110	26	14	1	26	21	3	1	1	28	21	5	2	0	97	68	18	11	0
AUSTRALIA + N.Z.	330	201	83	22	17	63	48	10	4	1	58	39	14	5	0	202	114	59	13	16
ASIA + OTHER AFRICA	529	175	164	129	36	40	24	7	5	4	81	35	29	12	5	383	116	128	112	27
JAPAN	169	23	58	64	11	10	3	2	5	0	26	4	13	5	4	120	16	43	54	7
OTHER ASIA+AFR.	360	152	106	65	25	30	21	5	0	4	55	31	16	7	1	263	100	85	58	20
BLACK AFRICA	46	27	8	7	2	0	0	0	0	0	6	4	2	0	0	40	23	6	7	2
ARAB WORLD	39	16	11	9	2	2	1	1	0	0	6	4	1	1	0	31	11	9	8	2
INDIA	68	16	23	25	2	5	2	1	0	2	20	4	8	7	1	43	10	14	18	1
PHILIPPINES	59	33	15	9	1	6	6	0	0	0	13	6	5	2	0	40	21	10	7	1
OTHER E. ASIA	39	19	8	4	7	1	1	0	0	0	5	3	1	1	0	33	15	7	3	7
OTHER ASIA	109	40	41	11	12	8	8	2	0	2	20	13	5	2	1	77	27	33	10	7

CHAPTER 5- PATTERNS OF OWNERSHIP
SECTION I- AN OVERVIEW OF FLOW AND STOCK, MANUFACTURING AND NON-MANUFACTURING
TABLE 4- MANUFACTURING SUBSIDIARIES CLASSIFIED BY COUNTRY OR REGION,
BY YEAR(S) SUBSIDIARY ENGAGED IN MANUFACTURE
AND BY SYSTEM OWNERSHIP %

YEAR AND OWNERSHIP PERCENTAGE
(WHL=95-100%, MAJ=50-94%, MIN=5-49%, UNK=UNKNOWN)

COUNTRY OR REGION	1929 ALL	WHL	MAJ	MIN	UNK	1939 ALL	WHL	MAJ	MIN	UNK	1957 ALL	WHL	MAJ	MIN	UNK	1967 ALL	WHL	MAJ	MIN	UNK
OUTSIDE U.S.	467	322	73	24	48	715	506	113	36	60	1568	1008	312	148	100	3646	2048	924	443	231
OUT. U.S. + CANADA	330	212	61	17	40	546	368	95	32	51	1257	757	271	141	88	3203	1700	865	428	210
OUT. WEST. HEMIS.	274	172	55	14	33	432	286	82	21	43	793	487	166	81	59	2253	1199	624	277	153
OUT. WHITE CWEALTH	226	140	42	11	33	347	225	65	25	32	902	519	212	111	60	2461	1212	715	373	161
OUT. DEVLPED WORLD	74	52	6	3	13	136	97	15	11	13	534	313	123	66	32	1260	627	347	211	75
CANADA	137	110	12	7	8	169	138	18	4	9	311	251	41	7	12	443	348	59	15	21
LATIN AMERICA	56	40	6	3	7	114	82	13	11	8	464	270	105	60	29	950	501	241	151	57
C. AMER.+CARIB.	16	13	2	0	1	48	34	2	4	7	174	116	24	22	12	383	183	102	72	26
CUBA	5	3	1	0	1	13	8	2	2	1	31	18	4	5	4	2	2	0	0	0
MEXICO	11	10	0	0	0	27	22	2	2	2	114	80	17	10	7	255	128	62	50	15
OTHER	0	0	0	0	0	8	4	0	3	1	29	18	3	7	1	126	53	40	22	11
S. AMERICA	40	27	4	3	6	66	48	10	4	4	290	154	81	38	17	567	318	139	79	31
ARGENTINA	12	11	1	0	0	27	24	0	0	3	58	39	12	6	1	108	63	25	17	3
BRAZIL	12	10	1	0	2	20	15	3	0	2	96	54	26	9	7	149	97	31	12	9
PERU	3	2	0	0	0	4	3	1	0	0	25	12	7	6	0	47	24	13	7	3
COLOMBIA	1	1	0	0	0	3	3	0	0	0	36	14	13	7	2	90	48	21	12	9
VENEZUELA	2	0	0	0	2	2	1	0	0	1	46	20	15	5	6	101	50	28	18	5
OTHER	10	3	2	0	3	10	2	2	4	2	29	15	8	5	1	72	36	21	13	2
EUROPE	226	138	50	11	27	335	214	68	17	36	549	332	108	58	51	1438	814	380	134	110
EFTA	104	69	23	4	8	167	115	30	4	18	250	155	47	20	28	494	321	93	34	46
U.K.	78	51	16	4	7	128	87	20	4	17	197	122	32	19	24	356	232	62	27	35
SCANDINAVIA	19	14	5	0	0	24	18	6	0	0	34	25	8	1	0	76	52	17	3	4
SWITZERLAND	1	0	0	0	1	4	3	0	0	1	6	4	1	0	1	27	19	5	1	2
OTHER EFTA	6	3	2	0	0	11	7	4	0	0	13	4	6	0	3	35	18	9	3	5
EUROP. COMMUNITY	106	60	24	5	17	146	85	34	12	15	254	154	51	30	19	759	427	207	68	57
FRANCE	36	18	6	4	8	52	27	10	8	7	80	43	15	14	8	223	111	68	27	17
GERMANY	43	26	11	1	5	50	32	13	0	5	81	54	15	4	8	211	124	52	18	17
ITALY	13	8	3	0	2	18	13	3	0	2	47	30	9	5	3	161	87	51	10	13
BELGIUM + LUX	8	3	3	0	2	14	9	4	0	1	21	12	4	4	1	87	59	16	7	5
NETHERLANDS	6	5	1	0	0	12	7	2	1	2	25	15	3	4	3	77	46	20	6	5
SPAIN	8	5	2	0	1	12	7	4	0	1	26	13	8	5	0	119	34	64	19	2
GREECE + TURKEY	1	0	0	0	1	0	0	0	0	0	5	1	2	2	0	35	12	12	8	3
CTHER EUROPE	7	4	0	2	1	10	7	0	1	2	14	9	2	1	2	31	20	4	5	2
EUROPE EX. U.K.	148	87	34	7	20	207	127	48	13	19	352	210	76	39	27	1082	582	318	107	75
SOUTHERN DOMINIONS	25	20	3	2	0	69	54	10	3	2	147	107	27	11	2	361	238	84	25	14
S. AFRICA +RHOD.	7	7	0	0	0	20	15	3	1	1	46	37	5	3	1	123	97	18	7	1
AUSTRALIA + N.Z.	18	13	3	2	0	49	39	7	2	1	101	70	22	8	1	238	141	66	18	13
ASIA + OTHER AFRICA	23	14	2	1	6	28	18	4	1	5	97	48	31	12	6	454	147	160	118	29
JAPAN	5	2	2	1	0	6	3	2	1	0	27	5	13	6	3	144	21	54	58	11
OTHER ASIA+AFR.	18	12	0	0	6	22	15	2	0	5	70	43	18	6	3	310	126	106	60	18
BLACK AFRICA	0	0	0	0	0	0	0	0	0	0	5	3	0	2	0	43	28	5	8	2
ARAB WORLD	0	0	0	0	0	0	0	0	0	0	7	4	2	1	0	30	13	8	8	1
INDIA	3	3	0	0	0	5	4	1	0	0	9	2	1	1	0	62	14	22	24	2
PHILIPPINES	4	4	0	0	0	4	4	0	0	0	23	15	5	2	1	50	26	17	6	1
OTHER E. ASIA	4	1	0	0	3	3	1	0	0	2	3	2	0	0	1	30	14	7	5	4
OTHER ASIA	7	4	0	0	3	10	6	1	0	3	23	12	8	1	2	95	31	44	12	8

CHAPTER 5- PATTERNS OF OWNERSHIP
SECTION 1- AN OVERVIEW OF FLOW AND STOCK, MANUFACTURING AND NON-MANUFACTURING
TABLE 5- SALES SUBSIDIARIES CLASSIFIED BY COUNTRY OR REGION,
BY PERIOD SALES BEGAN AND BY SYSTEM OWNERSHIP %

PERIOD AND OWNERSHIP PERCENTAGE
(WHL=95-100%, MAJ=50-94%, MIN=5-49%, UNK=UNKNOWN)

COUNTRY OR REGION	TOTAL PRE 1968					PRE 1946					1946-1957					1958-1967				
	ALL	WHL	MAJ	MIN	UNK	ALL	WHL	MAJ	MIN	UNK	ALL	WHL	MAJ	MIN	UNK	ALL	WHL	MAJ	MIN	UNK
OUTSIDE U.S.	2217	1743	243	51	113	551	444	64	10	33	410	352	37	6	15	1189	947	142	35	65
OUT. U.S. + CANADA	1989	1542	237	49	103	484	383	62	10	29	361	305	36	5	15	1086	854	139	34	59
OUT. WEST. HEMIS.	1575	1206	199	41	84	405	318	54	9	24	246	205	29	2	10	879	683	116	30	50
OUT. WHITE CMWEALTH	1586	1228	191	45	83	355	281	43	9	22	289	242	29	4	14	903	705	119	32	47
OUT. DEVLPED WORLD	610	495	56	14	25	114	92	14	1	7	162	143	9	3	7	314	260	33	10	11
CANADA	228	201	6	2	10	67	61	1	0	4	49	47	1	1	0	103	93	3	1	6
LATIN AMERICA	414	336	38	8	19	79	65	8	1	5	115	100	7	3	5	207	171	23	4	9
C. AMER.+CARIB.	186	156	11	3	12	29	26	0	0	3	55	47	2	2	4	98	83	9	1	5
CUBA	14	13	0	0	0	7	7	0	0	0	5	5	0	0	0	1	0	0	0	1
MEXICO	77	59	6	2	7	16	13	0	0	3	23	18	1	1	3	35	28	5	1	0
OTHER	95	84	5	1	5	6	6	0	0	0	27	24	1	1	1	62	54	4	0	4
S. AMERICA	228	180	27	5	7	50	39	8	1	2	60	53	5	1	1	109	88	14	3	4
ARGENTINA	36	27	5	5	3	10	8	4	1	0	15	11	0	3	1	10	8	1	1	0
BRAZIL	46	36	8	2	0	11	6	4	0	1	8	7	1	0	0	27	23	3	0	1
PERU	27	23	1	0	0	5	5	0	0	0	3	3	0	0	0	16	15	1	0	0
COLOMBIA	25	18	6	0	0	8	7	1	0	0	5	5	0	0	0	11	6	5	0	0
VENEZUELA	52	42	4	2	1	3	2	1	1	0	17	16	1	0	0	29	24	2	2	1
OTHER	42	34	3	1	3	13	11	1	0	1	12	11	0	1	0	16	12	2	0	2
EUROPE	1143	862	163	26	63	324	246	48	9	21	152	122	23	2	5	638	494	92	15	37
EFTA	515	406	62	5	27	158	117	31	2	8	72	59	8	1	4	270	230	23	2	15
U.K.	205	145	36	2	11	81	56	18	1	2	29	24	4	1	0	84	65	14	0	5
SCANDINAVIA	156	131	13	2	9	50	39	8	1	0	22	18	2	0	2	83	74	3	1	5
SWITZERLAND	110	95	9	0	4	17	13	4	0	0	12	10	2	0	0	79	72	3	0	4
OTHER EFTA	44	35	4	1	3	10	9	1	0	0	9	7	1	0	2	24	19	3	1	1
EURUP. COMMUNITY	522	381	79	16	33	118	90	14	3	11	65	52	11	1	1	326	239	54	12	21
FRANCE	125	78	28	8	7	33	25	4	0	4	14	11	3	0	0	74	42	24	2	3
GERMANY	148	112	19	3	8	28	24	4	0	0	12	8	3	1	0	102	80	12	2	8
ITALY	81	61	12	3	3	13	9	3	0	1	12	11	1	0	0	54	41	8	2	2
BELGIUM + LUX	92	76	9	1	6	25	21	2	0	2	17	16	1	0	0	50	39	6	1	4
NETHERLANDS	76	54	11	3	9	19	11	4	0	4	10	6	3	0	0	46	37	9	1	4
SPAIN	43	30	9	2	2	16	14	0	1	1	3	3	0	0	0	24	13	7	0	1
GREECE + TURKEY	17	11	6	0	0	2	2	0	0	0	4	2	2	0	0	11	7	4	0	0
OTHER EUROPE	46	34	7	3	1	30	23	3	3	1	8	6	2	0	0	7	5	2	0	0
EUROPE EX. U.K.	938	717	127	24	52	243	190	30	8	15	123	98	19	1	5	554	429	78	15	32
SOUTHERN DOMINIONS	182	156	8	2	9	43	42	0	0	1	39	35	3	0	1	93	79	5	2	7
S. AFRICA +RHOD.	62	55	1	0	3	14	14	0	0	0	15	14	1	0	0	30	27	0	0	3
AUSTRALIA + N.Z.	120	101	7	2	12	29	28	0	0	1	24	21	2	0	1	63	52	5	2	4
ASIA + OTHER AFRICA	250	188	28	13	12	38	30	6	0	2	55	48	3	0	4	148	110	19	13	6
JAPAN	54	29	10	7	6	3	3	0	0	0	8	5	2	0	2	41	21	9	7	4
OTHER ASIA+AFR.	196	159	18	6	9	35	27	6	0	2	47	43	2	0	2	107	89	10	6	2
BLACK AFRICA	45	35	3	3	3	0	0	0	0	0	13	13	0	0	0	28	22	3	3	0
ARAB WORLD	36	26	4	1	0	12	8	2	0	2	11	8	2	0	0	11	10	0	1	0
INDIA	13	11	1	1	0	8	7	1	0	0	2	2	0	0	0	3	2	0	0	1
PHILLIPPINES	25	20	5	0	0	7	5	2	0	0	7	7	0	0	0	11	8	3	0	0
OTHER E. ASIA	30	26	2	0	2	2	1	1	0	0	5	5	0	0	1	23	20	1	2	0
OTHER ASIA	47	41	3	1	1	6	6	0	0	0	9	8	0	0	0	31	27	3	1	0

CHAPTER 5- PATTERNS OF OWNERSHIP
SECTION 1- AN OVERVIEW OF FLOW AND STOCK, MANUFACTURING AND NON-MANUFACTURING
TABLE 6- SALES SUBSIDIARIES CLASSIFIED BY COUNTRY OR REGION,
BY YEAR(S) SUBSIDIARY ENGAGED IN SALES
AND BY SYSTEM OWNERSHIP %

YEAR AND OWNERSHIP PERCENTAGE
(WHL=95-100%, MAJ=50-94%, MIN=5-49%, UNK=UNKNOWN)

COUNTRY OR REGION	1929					1939					1957					1967				
	ALL	WHL	MAJ	MIN	UNK	ALL	WHL	MAJ	MIN	UNK	ALL	WHL	MAJ	MIN	UNK	ALL	WHL	MAJ	MIN	UNK
OUTSIDE U.S.	248	191	37	5	15	369	300	46	5	18	603	504	67	9	23	1358	1103	152	37	66
OUT. U.S. + CANADA	222	168	36	5	13	324	259	45	5	15	527	431	65	8	23	1230	985	148	35	62
OUT. WEST. HEMIS.	207	154	36	5	12	276	218	43	5	10	388	315	55	4	14	997	794	126	29	48
OUT. WHITE CWEALTH	157	120	23	5	9	237	190	30	4	13	405	330	47	7	21	1005	799	121	32	53
OUT. DEVLPED WORLD	27	23	2	0	2	71	58	6	0	7	190	157	16	4	13	367	302	35	11	19
CANADA	26	23	1	0	2	45	41	1	0	3	76	73	2	1	0	128	118	4	2	4
LATIN AMERICA	15	14	0	0	1	48	41	2	0	5	139	116	10	4	9	233	191	22	6	14
C. AMER.+CARIB.	6	6	0	0	0	20	17	0	0	3	64	55	2	2	5	104	88	7	2	7
CUBA	3	3	0	0	0	3	3	0	0	0	5	5	0	0	0	1	1	0	0	0
MEXICO	3	3	0	0	0	15	12	0	0	3	29	23	2	0	4	31	25	4	0	2
OTHER	0	0	0	0	0	2	2	0	0	0	30	27	0	2	1	72	62	3	2	5
S. AMERICA	9	8	0	0	1	28	24	2	0	2	75	61	8	2	4	129	103	15	4	7
ARGENTINA	3	2	0	0	1	6	5	1	0	0	18	14	2	0	2	20	14	3	0	3
BRAZIL	1	1	0	0	0	5	4	1	0	0	11	8	2	1	0	25	21	3	1	0
PERU	1	1	0	0	0	5	5	0	0	0	8	5	3	0	0	18	17	1	0	0
COLOMBIA	2	2	0	0	0	2	2	0	0	0	5	5	0	0	0	14	8	6	0	0
VENEZUELA	0	0	0	0	0	1	1	0	0	0	16	15	1	0	0	28	24	1	2	1
OTHER	2	2	0	0	0	9	7	0	0	2	17	14	0	1	2	24	19	1	1	3
EUROPE	173	124	34	5	10	223	171	39	5	8	275	218	45	4	8	722	572	98	17	35
EFTA	84	58	22	1	3	115	85	26	2	2	142	110	26	2	4	336	283	36	4	13
U.K.	41	26	12	0	3	54	36	15	0	2	60	43	15	1	1	112	84	22	1	5
SCANDINAVIA	29	20	8	1	0	41	31	9	1	0	52	41	8	1	2	116	102	6	2	6
SWITZERLAND	9	8	1	0	0	12	11	1	0	0	17	14	3	0	0	78	72	5	0	1
OTHER EFTA	5	4	1	0	0	8	7	1	0	0	13	12	0	0	1	30	25	3	1	1
EUROP. COMMUNITY	68	51	9	2	6	76	60	11	1	4	103	86	13	2	2	327	250	46	13	18
FRANCE	17	13	3	0	1	20	18	2	0	0	24	20	2	1	1	81	52	21	3	5
GERMANY	16	13	3	0	0	16	13	3	0	0	21	15	5	0	1	91	71	12	3	5
ITALY	9	6	2	0	1	9	6	3	0	0	9	7	2	0	0	44	35	4	3	2
BELGIUM + LUX	11	10	1	0	0	21	18	3	0	0	33	31	2	0	0	61	53	4	1	3
NETHERLANDS	15	9	0	2	4	10	8	2	0	0	16	13	2	1	0	50	39	5	3	3
SPAIN	8	7	1	0	0	10	8	1	1	0	13	11	1	1	0	26	16	8	0	2
GREECE + TURKEY	0	0	0	0	0	0	0	0	0	0	4	2	2	0	0	14	10	4	0	0
OTHER EUROPE	13	8	2	2	1	20	16	2	1	1	13	9	3	1	0	19	13	4	1	2
EUROPE EX. U.K.	132	98	22	5	7	169	135	24	4	6	215	175	30	3	7	610	488	76	16	30
SOUTHERN DOMINIONS	21	20	0	0	1	29	29	0	0	0	55	51	3	0	1	101	91	4	2	4
S. AFRICA +RHOD.	6	6	0	0	0	11	11	0	0	0	22	21	1	0	0	34	31	0	0	3
AUSTRALIA + N.Z.	15	14	0	0	1	18	18	0	0	0	33	30	2	0	1	67	60	4	2	1
ASIA + OTHER AFRICA	13	10	2	0	1	24	18	4	0	2	58	46	7	1	5	174	131	24	10	9
JAPAN	1	1	0	0	0	1	1	0	0	0	7	5	1	0	1	40	20	11	5	4
OTHER ASIA+AFR.	12	9	2	0	1	23	17	4	0	2	51	41	6	0	4	134	111	13	5	5
BLACK AFRICA	0	0	0	0	0	0	0	0	0	0	10	10	0	0	0	37	32	2	3	0
ARAB WORLD	5	2	2	0	1	3	3	0	0	0	14	9	2	0	3	18	14	2	0	2
INDIA	0	0	0	0	0	6	6	0	0	0	8	6	2	0	0	8	6	1	1	0
PHILIPPINES	1	1	0	0	0	4	4	0	0	0	6	4	2	0	0	15	12	2	1	0
OTHER E. ASIA	0	0	0	0	0	0	0	0	0	0	4	4	0	0	0	26	22	2	2	0
OTHER ASIA	4	4	0	0	0	4	4	0	0	0	9	8	0	0	1	30	25	3	1	1

CHAPTER 5- PATTERNS OF OWNERSHIP
SECTION 1- AN OVERVIEW OF FLOW AND STOCK, MANUFACTURING AND NON-MANUFACTURING
TABLE 7- EXTRACTION SUBSIDIARIES CLASSIFIED BY COUNTRY OR REGION,
BY PERIOD EXTRACTION BEGAN AND BY SYSTEM OWNERSHIP %

PERIOD AND OWNERSHIP PERCENTAGE
(WHL=95-100%, MAJ=50-94%, MIN=5-49%, UNK=UNKNOWN)

COUNTRY OR REGION	TOTAL PRE 1968					PRE 1946					1946-1957					1958-1967				
	ALL	WHL	MAJ	MIN	UNK	ALL	WHL	MAJ	MIN	UNK	ALL	WHL	MAJ	MIN	UNK	ALL	WHL	MAJ	MIN	UNK
OUTSIDE U.S.	320	193	56	31	34	120	75	15	10	20	87	53	23	3	8	107	65	18	18	6
OUT. U.S. + CANADA	248	143	47	25	29	102	63	13	9	17	61	32	19	3	7	81	48	15	13	5
OUT. WEST. HEMIS.	118	63	26	18	10	38	20	4	8	6	34	12	15	3	4	45	31	7	7	5
OUT. WHITE CWEALTH	202	116	39	18	25	86	56	11	4	15	51	29	16	1	5	61	31	12	13	5
OUT. DEVLPED WORLD	187	109	34	16	24	82	55	10	3	14	46	27	13	1	5	55	27	11	12	5
CANADA	72	50	9	6	5	18	12	2	1	3	26	21	4	0	1	26	17	3	5	1
LATIN AMERICA	130	80	21	7	19	64	43	9	1	11	27	20	4	0	3	36	17	8	6	5
C. AMER.+CARIB.	81	53	13	4	10	45	31	6	0	8	16	12	3	0	1	19	10	4	4	1
CUBA	1	1	-	0	0	1	1	-	0	0	0	0	0	0	0	0	0	0	0	0
MEXICO	63	42	7	3	10	41	29	4	0	8	11	8	2	0	1	10	5	1	3	1
OTHER	17	11	5	1	0	3	2	3	0	0	5	4	1	0	0	9	5	3	1	0
S. AMERICA	49	27	8	3	9	19	12	3	1	3	11	8	1	0	2	17	7	4	2	4
ARGENTINA	7	6	0	0	0	2	2	0	0	0	3	3	0	0	0	1	1	0	0	0
BRAZIL	3	0	0	1	2	1	0	0	0	1	1	0	0	0	1	1	0	0	1	0
PERU	6	4	2	0	0	0	0	0	0	0	4	3	1	0	0	2	1	1	0	0
COLOMBIA	4	3	1	0	0	3	2	1	0	0	0	0	0	0	0	1	1	0	0	0
VENEZUELA	13	4	3	0	6	5	2	1	0	2	1	0	0	0	1	7	2	0	1	3
OTHER	16	10	2	2	1	8	6	1	1	0	2	2	0	0	0	5	2	1	1	1
EUROPE	27	13	6	4	4	11	3	2	3	3	7	3	3	0	1	9	7	1	1	0
EFTA	12	6	1	2	3	7	2	1	2	2	2	1	0	0	1	3	3	0	0	0
U.K.	12	6	1	2	3	7	2	1	2	2	2	1	0	0	1	3	3	0	0	0
SCANDINAVIA	0	0	0	0	0	0	0	0	0	0	0	0	0	0	0	0	0	0	0	0
SWITZERLAND	0	0	0	0	0	0	0	0	0	0	0	0	0	0	0	0	0	0	0	0
OTHER EFTA	0	0	0	0	0	0	0	0	0	0	0	0	0	0	0	0	0	0	0	0
EUROP. COMMUNITY	10	5	5	3	0	0	0	0	0	0	4	1	3	0	0	4	3	1	0	0
FRANCE	4	2	2	0	0	2	1	1	0	0	1	0	1	0	0	3	2	1	0	0
GERMANY	1	1	0	0	0	0	0	0	0	0	1	1	0	0	0	0	0	0	0	0
ITALY	1	1	0	0	0	0	0	0	0	0	1	0	0	0	0	0	0	0	0	0
BELGIUM + LUX	3	2	1	0	0	1	0	1	0	0	0	0	0	0	0	1	1	0	0	0
NETHERLANDS	1	0	0	0	0	0	0	0	0	0	1	0	1	0	0	1	0	0	1	0
SPAIN	2	2	0	0	0	0	0	0	0	0	0	0	0	0	0	1	1	0	0	0
GREECE + TURKEY	2	0	0	0	0	0	1	0	0	0	1	0	0	0	0	1	1	0	0	0
OTHER EUROPE	2	2	0	0	0	0	0	0	0	0	0	0	0	0	0	0	0	0	0	0
EUROPE EX. U.K.	15	7	5	2	1	4	1	1	1	1	5	2	3	0	0	6	4	1	1	0
SOUTHERN DOMINIONS	34	21	7	5	1	9	5	1	3	0	8	2	3	2	1	17	14	3	0	0
S. AFRICA +RHOD.	13	7	1	4	1	5	3	0	2	0	5	1	1	2	1	3	3	0	0	0
AUSTRALIA + N.Z.	21	14	6	1	0	4	2	1	1	0	3	1	2	0	0	14	11	3	0	0
ASIA + OTHER AFRICA	57	29	13	9	5	18	12	1	2	3	19	7	9	1	2	19	10	3	6	0
JAPAN	0	0	0	0	0	0	0	0	0	0	0	0	0	0	0	0	0	0	0	0
OTHER ASIA+AFR.	57	29	13	9	5	18	12	1	2	3	19	7	9	1	2	19	10	3	6	0
BLACK AFRICA	26	7	11	5	3	6	3	0	0	2	11	5	9	1	1	12	6	2	4	0
ARAB WORLD	15	9	2	2	1	6	6	0	2	0	5	0	0	0	0	3	3	0	0	0
INDIA	0	0	0	0	0	0	0	0	0	0	0	0	0	0	0	0	0	0	0	0
PHILIPPINES	5	4	0	0	1	3	3	0	0	0	1	0	0	0	1	1	1	0	0	0
OTHER E. ASIA	0	0	0	0	0	0	0	0	0	0	0	0	0	0	0	0	0	0	0	0
OTHER ASIA	11	9	0	2	0	6	5	0	1	0	2	2	0	0	0	3	2	0	1	0

CHAPTER 5— PATTERNS OF OWNERSHIP
SECTION 1— AN OVERVIEW OF FLOW AND STOCK, MANUFACTURING AND NON-MANUFACTURING
TABLE 8— EXTRACTION SUBSIDIARIES CLASSIFIED BY COUNTRY OR REGION,
BY YEAR(S) SUBSIDIARY ENGAGED IN EXTRACTION
AND BY SYSTEM OWNERSHIP %

YEAR AND OWNERSHIP PERCENTAGE
(WHL=95-100%, MAJ=50-94%, MIN=5-49%, UNK=UNKNOWN)

COUNTRY OR REGION	1929					1939					1957					1967				
	ALL	WHL	MAJ	MIN	UNK	ALL	WHL	MAJ	MIN	UNK	ALL	WHL	MAJ	MIN	UNK	ALL	WHL	MAJ	MIN	UNK
OUTSIDE U.S.	41	21	4	5	11	74	45	12	10	7	135	90	25	7	13	172	110	28	24	10
OUT. U.S. + CANADA	38	19	3	5	11	67	41	10	9	7	105	66	20	7	12	136	86	23	18	9
OUT. WEST. HEMIS.	15	6	1	5	3	31	15	3	8	5	53	24	15	7	7	80	47	15	13	5
OUT. WHITE CWEALTH	33	16	3	3	11	53	34	9	5	5	85	56	18	2	9	105	64	19	14	8
OUT. DEVLPED WORLD	30	16	2	2	10	50	34	8	4	4	79	54	14	2	9	95	59	16	13	7
CANADA	3	2	1	0	0	7	4	2	1	0	30	24	5	0	1	36	24	5	6	1
LATIN AMERICA	23	13	2	1	7	36	26	7	1	2	52	42	5	0	5	56	39	8	5	4
C. AMER.+CARIB.	16	8	1	0	7	24	19	4	0	1	34	29	3	0	2	28	20	4	3	1
CUBA	1	0	1	0	0	2	0	2	0	0	7	6	1	0	0	14	9	1	3	1
MEXICO	15	8	0	0	7	21	19	1	0	1	27	23	2	0	2	14	11	3	0	0
OTHER	0	0	0	0	0	1	0	1	0	0	0	0	0	0	0	0	0	0	0	0
S. AMERICA	7	5	1	1	0	12	7	3	1	1	18	13	2	0	3	28	19	4	2	3
ARGENTINA	1	1	0	0	0	0	0	0	0	0	3	3	0	0	0	4	3	0	0	1
BRAZIL	0	0	0	0	0	0	0	0	0	0	1	0	0	0	1	2	0	1	1	0
PERU	0	0	0	0	0	2	1	0	0	1	4	3	0	0	1	6	5	0	0	1
COLOMBIA	0	0	0	0	0	2	0	1	1	0	1	1	0	0	0	1	1	0	0	0
VENEZUELA	2	1	0	1	0	7	5	1	0	1	3	1	1	0	1	5	4	1	0	0
OTHER	4	3	1	0	0	1	1	0	0	0	6	5	1	0	0	10	6	2	1	1
EUROPE	5	3	0	1	1	9	2	1	2	4	13	5	4	2	2	15	9	3	2	1
EFTA	2	1	0	1	0	6	2	0	2	2	7	3	2	2	0	5	4	0	1	0
U.K.	2	1	0	1	0	6	2	0	2	2	7	3	2	2	0	5	4	0	1	0
SCANDINAVIA	0	0	0	0	0	0	0	0	0	0	0	0	0	0	0	0	0	0	0	0
SWITZERLAND	0	0	0	0	0	0	0	0	0	0	0	0	0	0	0	0	0	0	0	0
OTHER EFTA	0	0	0	0	0	0	0	0	0	0	0	0	0	0	0	0	0	0	0	0
EUROP. COMMUNITY	1	1	0	0	0	1	0	1	0	0	5	1	2	0	2	7	3	3	0	1
FRANCE	0	0	0	0	0	0	0	0	0	0	1	0	1	0	0	3	1	2	0	0
GERMANY	0	0	0	0	0	0	0	0	0	0	1	1	0	0	0	1	0	1	0	0
ITALY	0	0	0	0	0	0	0	0	0	0	1	0	1	0	0	1	1	0	0	0
BELGIUM + LUX	1	1	0	0	0	1	0	1	0	0	1	0	0	0	1	0	0	0	0	0
NETHERLANDS	0	0	0	0	0	0	0	0	0	0	1	0	0	0	1	2	1	0	0	1
SPAIN	0	0	0	0	0	0	0	0	0	0	1	1	0	0	0	1	0	0	1	0
GREECE + TURKEY	0	0	0	0	0	0	0	0	0	0	0	0	0	0	0	2	2	0	0	0
OTHER EUROPE	2	1	0	0	1	2	0	0	0	2	0	0	0	0	0	0	0	0	0	0
EUROPE EX. U.K.	3	2	0	0	1	3	0	1	0	2	6	2	2	0	2	10	5	3	1	1
SOUTHERN DOMINIONS	3	2	0	1	0	8	5	2	1	0	13	7	2	2	2	26	18	4	4	0
S. AFRICA +RHOD.	3	2	0	1	0	5	3	1	1	0	7	4	2	1	0	10	8	0	2	0
AUSTRALIA + N.Z.	0	0	0	0	0	3	2	1	0	0	6	3	0	1	2	16	10	4	2	0
ASIA + OTHER AFRICA	7	3	0	2	2	14	8	3	3	0	27	12	7	1	7	39	20	8	8	3
JAPAN	0	0	0	0	0	0	0	0	0	0	0	0	0	0	0	0	0	0	0	0
OTHER ASIA+AFR.	7	3	0	2	2	14	8	3	3	0	27	12	7	1	7	39	20	8	8	3
BLACK AFRICA	3	1	0	0	2	8	4	1	3	0	13	6	7	0	0	20	7	7	4	2
ARAB WORLD	2	0	0	2	0	1	1	0	0	0	7	6	0	1	0	10	7	0	2	1
INDIA	0	0	0	0	0	1	0	1	0	0	3	0	0	0	3	0	0	0	0	0
PHILIPPINES	1	1	0	0	0	0	0	0	0	0	0	0	0	0	0	3	2	0	1	0
OTHER E. ASIA	0	0	0	0	0	1	0	1	0	0	4	0	0	0	4	0	0	0	0	0
OTHER ASIA	1	1	0	0	0	3	3	0	0	0	0	0	0	0	0	6	4	1	1	0

CHAPTER 5- PATTERNS OF OWNERSHIP
SECTION 1- AN OVERVIEW OF FLOW AND STOCK, MANUFACTURING AND NON-MANUFACTURING
TABLE 9- SUBSIDIARIES WITH OTHER MAIN ACTIVITY CLASSIFIED BY COUNTRY OR REGION,
BY PERIOD ACTIVITY BEGAN AND BY SYSTEM OWNERSHIP %

PERIOD AND OWNERSHIP PERCENTAGE
(WHL=95-100%, MAJ=50-94%, MIN=5-49%, UNK=UNKNOWN)

COUNTRY OR REGION	TOTAL PRE 1968					PRE 1946					1946-1957					1958-1967				
	ALL	WHL	MAJ	MIN	UNK	ALL	WHL	MAJ	MIN	UNK	ALL	WHL	MAJ	MIN	UNK	ALL	WHL	MAJ	MIN	UNK
OUTSIDE U.S.	1805	1296	204	110	128	317	224	40	17	36	430	340	41	16	33	991	732	123	77	59
OUT. U.S. + CANADA	1543	1090	186	96	112	260	179	36	16	29	341	266	38	10	27	883	645	112	70	56
OUT. WEST. HEMIS.	1043	728	127	78	74	174	123	18	15	18	182	137	21	8	16	651	468	88	55	40
OUT. WHITE CWEALTH	1226	863	154	79	92	211	139	34	14	24	285	223	33	7	22	692	501	87	58	46
OUT. DEVLPED WORLD	629	441	75	28	55	101	68	18	4	14	200	153	25	4	18	298	220	32	23	23
CANADA	262	206	18	14	16	57	45	4	1	7	89	74	3	6	6	108	87	11	7	3
LATIN AMERICA	500	362	59	18	38	86	56	18	1	11	159	129	17	2	11	232	177	24	15	16
C. AMER.+CARIB.	260	197	29	5	16	42	27	10	0	5	82	65	10	1	6	123	105	9	4	5
CUBA	17	13	4	0	0	8	5	3	0	0	7	6	1	0	0	2	2	0	0	0
MEXICO	78	50	9	2	10	27	16	6	0	5	14	8	2	1	3	30	26	1	0	2
OTHER	165	134	16	3	6	7	6	1	0	0	61	51	7	0	3	91	77	8	0	3
S. AMERICA	240	165	30	13	22	44	29	8	1	6	77	64	7	1	5	109	72	15	11	11
ARGENTINA	43	33	3	4	3	9	6	1	0	2	13	12	1	0	0	21	15	1	4	1
BRAZIL	58	42	7	1	4	7	5	2	0	0	13	10	2	0	1	34	27	1	0	3
PERU	25	19	4	0	1	7	6	0	0	0	4	4	0	0	0	13	9	3	0	1
COLOMBIA	23	18	5	0	0	2	2	0	0	0	17	16	1	0	0	4	0	4	0	0
VENEZUELA	58	29	8	7	12	9	3	3	0	3	21	14	2	1	4	26	12	4	6	5
OTHER	33	24	3	1	2	10	7	1	1	1	9	8	1	0	0	11	9	1	0	1
EUROPE	772	556	90	56	50	148	103	16	14	15	120	101	7	4	8	484	352	67	38	27
EFTA	382	309	23	12	26	59	47	1	4	7	72	66	0	1	5	239	196	22	7	14
U.K.	197	149	15	7	14	44	36	1	2	5	41	36	0	1	4	100	77	14	4	5
SCANDINAVIA	47	35	4	1	7	7	6	0	0	1	10	9	0	0	0	30	20	4	1	5
SWITZERLAND	123	113	4	3	3	6	6	0	2	0	16	16	0	0	0	101	93	4	1	3
OTHER EFTA	15	12	0	1	2	2	1	0	0	1	5	5	0	0	0	8	6	0	1	1
EUROP. COMMUNITY	343	215	57	40	23	74	46	13	8	7	45	33	6	3	3	216	136	38	29	13
FRANCE	125	68	23	27	7	29	15	4	8	2	12	7	2	3	0	82	46	17	16	3
GERMANY	89	63	17	4	6	34	23	9	0	2	14	10	2	0	2	39	30	6	1	2
ITALY	44	29	4	4	5	4	3	0	0	1	8	8	0	0	0	30	18	6	4	3
BELGIUM + LUX	44	27	8	4	5	3	3	0	0	0	4	4	0	0	0	37	23	6	4	4
NETHERLANDS	41	28	5	2	1	4	3	0	0	1	7	7	0	0	0	29	19	5	4	1
SPAIN	15	11	2	1	0	4	4	0	0	0	7	7	0	1	0	4	0	2	0	0
GREECE + TURKEY	8	3	4	1	0	1	1	0	0	0	2	1	1	0	0	5	1	3	1	0
OTHER EUROPE	24	18	4	2	0	10	6	2	2	0	2	2	0	0	0	12	10	2	0	0
EUROPE EX. U.K.	575	407	75	49	36	104	67	15	12	10	79	65	7	3	4	384	275	53	34	22
SOUTHERN DOMINIONS	108	67	16	10	6	5	4	1	0	0	15	7	5	2	1	79	56	10	8	5
S. AFRICA +RHOD.	20	11	3	2	1	1	1	0	0	0	4	2	1	1	0	12	8	2	2	0
AUSTRALIA + N.Z.	88	56	13	8	5	4	3	1	0	0	11	5	4	2	0	67	48	8	6	5
ASIA + OTHER AFRICA	163	105	21	12	18	21	16	1	1	3	47	29	9	2	7	88	60	11	9	8
JAPAN	34	26	5	2	1	6	4	0	1	0	6	5	1	2	0	22	17	3	3	1
OTHER ASIA+AFR.	129	79	16	10	17	15	12	1	0	3	41	24	8	2	7	66	43	8	6	7
BLACK AFRICA	46	25	6	4	3	2	1	0	0	0	14	10	3	1	0	25	14	3	3	2
ARAB WORLD	20	13	4	0	2	2	2	0	0	0	11	5	3	1	2	7	6	0	0	1
INDIA	7	4	1	1	0	1	1	0	0	0	5	3	1	1	0	1	0	0	0	0
PHILIPPINES	15	11	1	0	3	1	1	0	0	0	3	3	0	0	0	9	8	1	0	3
OTHER E. ASIA	22	13	2	2	2	5	3	0	0	2	3	2	1	0	0	13	8	1	2	1
OTHER ASIA	19	13	2	1	2	2	2	0	0	0	5	4	0	0	1	11	7	2	1	1

CHAPTER 5- PATTERNS OF OWNERSHIP
SECTION 1- AN OVERVIEW OF FLOW AND STOCK, MANUFACTURING AND NON-MANUFACTURING
TABLE 10- SUBSIDIARIES WITH OTHER MAIN ACTIVITY CLASSIFIED BY COUNTRY OR REGION,
BY YEAR(S) SUBSIDIARY WAS ACTIVE
AND BY SYSTEM OWNERSHIP %

YEAR AND OWNERSHIP PERCENTAGE
(WHL=95-100%, MAJ=50-94%, MIN=5-49%, UNK=UNKNOWN)

COUNTRY OR REGION	1929 ALL	WHL	MAJ	MIN	UNK	1939 ALL	WHL	MAJ	MIN	UNK	1957 ALL	WHL	MAJ	MIN	UNK	1967 ALL	WHL	MAJ	MIN	UNK
OUTSIDE U.S.	85	56	11	7	11	193	133	29	13	18	574	436	60	28	50	1247	924	150	93	80
OUT. U.S. + CANADA	70	43	11	7	9	154	99	27	13	15	455	338	55	20	42	1062	775	133	80	74
OUT. WEST. HEMIS.	46	30	4	6	6	100	67	13	12	8	250	183	27	16	24	724	517	91	61	55
OUT. WHITE CWEALTH	59	33	11	6	9	123	74	25	12	12	374	275	48	18	33	841	609	106	70	56
OUT. DEVLPED WORLD	27	14	7	1	5	61	37	16	1	7	249	183	36	7	23	431	324	53	26	28
CANADA	15	13	0	0	2	39	34	2	0	3	119	98	5	8	8	185	149	17	13	6
LATIN AMERICA	24	13	7	1	3	54	32	14	1	7	205	155	28	4	18	338	258	42	19	19
C. AMER.+CARIB.	8	3	5	0	0	31	18	8	0	5	111	83	16	2	10	177	142	21	6	8
CUBA	3	1	2	0	0	7	5	2	0	0	12	9	2	0	0	4	3	1	0	0
MEXICO	4	2	2	0	0	20	10	5	0	5	33	19	5	2	7	56	39	5	4	8
OTHER	1	0	1	0	0	4	3	1	0	0	66	55	8	0	3	117	100	15	2	0
S. AMERICA	16	10	2	1	3	23	14	6	1	2	94	72	12	2	8	161	116	21	11	13
ARGENTINA	3	1	2	0	0	7	5	1	0	1	14	12	1	0	1	23	17	2	1	3
BRAZIL	2	1	0	1	0	4	2	2	0	0	18	15	2	0	1	42	35	4	0	3
PERU	3	2	1	0	0	4	2	2	0	0	7	5	2	0	0	16	12	3	0	1
COLOMBIA	0	0	0	0	0	0	0	1	0	0	14	14	0	0	0	17	13	4	0	0
VENEZUELA	1	0	0	0	1	0	0	0	0	0	25	14	4	1	6	43	23	6	9	5
OTHER	7	5	0	1	1	8	5	2	1	0	16	12	3	1	0	20	16	2	1	1
EUROPE	41	27	6	4	4	87	57	10	12	8	180	139	12	12	17	529	377	64	48	40
EFTA	17	14	1	2	0	35	26	1	3	5	94	83	1	1	9	250	201	20	8	21
U.K.	10	9	0	1	0	26	21	1	1	3	63	54	1	1	7	131	99	14	5	13
SCANDINAVIA	2	2	0	0	0	3	3	0	0	0	13	11	0	0	2	28	18	3	1	6
SWITZERLAND	5	3	1	1	0	5	2	0	2	1	16	16	0	0	0	83	78	3	1	1
OTHER EFTA	0	0	0	0	0	1	0	0	0	1	2	2	0	0	0	8	6	0	1	1
EUROP. COMMUNITY	21	13	3	2	3	42	26	6	7	3	78	49	10	11	8	245	150	39	37	19
FRANCE	8	5	1	0	2	17	8	1	7	1	31	15	4	11	1	95	47	18	26	4
GERMANY	10	6	2	2	0	22	16	5	0	1	29	21	5	0	3	53	42	4	2	5
ITALY	2	1	0	0	1	2	1	0	0	1	4	1	0	0	3	29	19	6	1	3
BELGIUM + LUX	0	0	0	0	0	0	0	0	0	0	8	7	0	0	1	37	23	5	4	5
NETHERLANDS	1	1	0	0	0	1	1	0	0	0	6	5	1	0	0	31	19	6	4	2
SPAIN	1	0	0	1	0	4	3	1	0	0	3	2	1	0	0	13	10	2	1	0
GREECE + TURKEY	0	0	0	0	0	1	0	1	0	0	1	1	0	0	0	7	4	1	2	0
OTHER EUROPE	2	0	1	0	1	5	2	1	2	0	4	4	0	0	0	14	12	2	0	0
EUROPE EX. U.K.	31	18	6	3	4	61	36	9	11	5	117	85	11	11	10	398	278	50	43	27
SOUTHERN DOMINIONS	1	1	0	0	0	5	4	1	0	0	18	9	6	1	2	78	56	12	5	5
S. AFRICA +RHOD.	0	0	0	0	0	4	3	1	0	0	5	2	2	0	1	16	10	3	2	1
AUSTRALIA + N.Z.	1	1	0	0	0	1	1	0	0	0	13	7	4	1	1	62	46	9	3	4
ASIA + OTHER AFRICA	4	2	0	0	2	8	6	2	0	0	52	35	9	3	5	117	84	15	8	10
JAPAN	1	1	0	0	0	1	1	0	0	0	8	7	1	0	0	24	18	4	1	1
OTHER ASIA+AFR.	3	1	0	0	2	7	5	2	0	0	44	28	8	3	5	93	66	11	7	9
BLACK AFRICA	2	1	0	0	1	5	3	2	0	0	13	9	3	1	0	36	25	4	5	2
ARAB WORLD	0	0	0	0	0	0	0	0	0	0	12	6	3	2	1	15	9	3	1	2
INDIA	0	0	0	0	0	0	0	0	0	0	5	3	1	0	1	4	2	0	0	2
PHILIPPINES	0	0	0	0	0	0	0	0	0	0	3	1	0	0	2	9	7	1	0	1
OTHER E. ASIA	1	0	0	0	1	1	1	0	0	0	5	4	1	0	0	16	13	2	0	1
OTHER ASIA	0	0	0	0	0	1	1	0	0	0	6	5	0	0	1	13	10	1	1	1

CHAPTER 5- PATTERNS OF OWNERSHIP
SECTION 1- AN OVERVIEW OF FLOW AND STOCK, MANUFACTURING AND NON-MANUFACTURING
TABLE 11- SUBSIDIARIES WITH UNKNOWN ACTIVITY CLASSIFIED BY COUNTRY OR REGION,
BY PERIOD ACTIVITY BEGAN AND BY SYSTEM OWNERSHIP %

PERIOD AND OWNERSHIP PERCENTAGE
(WHL=95-100%, MAJ=50-94%, MIN=5-49%, UNK=UNKNOWN)

COUNTRY OR REGION	TOTAL (PRE 1968)					PRE 1946					1946-1957					1958-1967				
	ALL	WHL	MAJ	MIN	UNK	ALL	WHL	MAJ	MIN	UNK	ALL	WHL	MAJ	MIN	UNK	ALL	WHL	MAJ	MIN	UNK
OUTSIDE U.S.	2407	1367	264	75	379	593	343	70	14	166	489	345	57	16	71	1003	679	137	45	142
OUT. U.S. + CANADA	1954	1091	244	65	305	438	242	65	13	118	404	279	52	12	61	863	570	127	40	126
OUT. WEST. HEMIS.	1413	806	187	47	204	335	184	51	11	89	250	174	37	6	33	659	448	99	30	82
OUT. WHITE CWEALTH	1459	782	192	58	241	321	169	46	12	94	303	195	41	11	56	649	418	105	35	91
OUT. DEVLPED WORLD	683	349	80	30	119	121	68	15	2	36	183	120	20	9	34	274	161	45	19	49
CANADA	453	276	20	10	74	155	101	5	1	48	85	66	5	4	10	140	109	10	5	16
LATIN AMERICA	541	285	57	18	101	103	58	14	2	29	154	105	15	6	28	204	122	28	10	44
C. AMER.+CARIB.	254	142	22	10	46	39	25	2	2	10	79	55	7	3	14	102	62	13	0	22
CUBA	23	17	1	0	4	15	10	1	0	4	6	6	0	0	0	1	1	0	0	0
MEXICO	100	42	12	6	26	18	11	1	0	5	27	10	4	1	12	41	21	8	3	9
OTHER	131	83	9	4	16	6	4	0	0	1	46	39	3	2	2	60	40	5	2	13
S. AMERICA	287	143	35	8	55	64	33	12	0	19	75	50	8	3	14	102	60	15	5	22
ARGENTINA	64	23	7	0	12	15	8	4	0	3	9	4	2	0	3	18	11	1	1	6
BRAZIL	66	30	10	2	19	14	7	1	0	6	15	8	2	1	4	32	15	7	0	9
PERU	16	11	1	0	1	4	4	0	0	0	3	2	0	1	0	6	5	1	0	0
COLOMBIA	52	32	5	0	9	11	6	1	0	4	25	21	2	0	2	10	5	2	0	3
VENEZUELA	45	26	4	4	8	8	4	2	0	2	12	7	1	1	3	22	15	3	3	3
OTHER	44	21	8	2	6	12	4	4	0	4	11	8	1	1	1	14	9	3	1	1
EUROPE	1077	630	148	29	153	299	161	49	10	79	170	120	28	1	21	491	349	71	18	53
EFTA	507	331	60	6	55	134	82	23	2	27	86	72	10	0	4	232	177	27	4	24
U.K.	328	208	39	4	40	101	59	19	1	22	54	45	7	0	2	136	104	13	3	16
SCANDINAVIA	96	67	10	0	7	19	13	2	0	3	22	19	2	0	1	45	35	6	1	3
SWITZERLAND	68	47	9	2	4	8	7	0	0	1	8	7	1	0	0	44	33	8	0	3
OTHER EFTA	15	9	2	0	4	6	3	2	1	1	2	1	0	0	1	7	5	0	0	2
EUROP. COMMUNITY	483	252	85	20	80	128	57	26	6	39	79	43	18	1	17	230	152	41	13	24
FRANCE	128	54	37	6	23	41	9	12	1	19	20	12	8	0	0	57	33	17	3	4
GERMANY	141	76	19	4	32	34	11	7	2	14	22	13	8	0	1	75	52	9	1	13
ITALY	103	56	17	5	14	27	16	4	2	5	16	7	4	1	5	49	33	9	3	4
BELGIUM + LUX	51	27	5	4	4	12	9	2	1	0	9	4	1	0	4	19	14	2	3	0
NETHERLANDS	60	39	7	3	7	14	12	1	0	1	12	7	2	0	0	30	20	4	0	3
SPAIN	35	19	2	0	8	10	6	0	0	4	2	2	0	0	0	17	11	2	1	4
GREECE + TURKEY	12	7	1	1	0	0	0	0	0	0	2	2	0	0	0	8	6	1	0	1
OTHER EUROPE	40	21	0	2	10	27	16	2	0	9	2	2	0	1	0	4	3	0	0	2
EUROPE EX. U.K.	749	422	109	25	113	198	102	30	9	57	116	75	21	1	19	355	245	58	15	37
SOUTHERN DOMINIONS	157	94	13	3	23	14	12	0	0	2	45	37	4	1	3	74	45	9	2	18
S. AFRICA +RHOD.	44	28	4	1	4	4	2	0	0	2	15	11	2	1	1	19	15	2	1	1
AUSTRALIA + N.Z.	113	66	9	1	19	10	10	0	0	0	30	26	2	0	1	55	30	7	1	17
ASIA + OTHER AFRICA	179	82	26	15	28	22	11	2	1	8	35	17	5	4	9	94	54	19	10	11
JAPAN	37	18	3	3	10	4	1	1	1	1	6	2	1	1	1	24	15	2	1	6
OTHER ASIA+AFR.	142	64	23	12	18	18	10	1	0	7	29	15	5	1	6	70	39	17	9	5
BLACK AFRICA	42	21	8	2	8	2	1	0	0	1	6	3	1	1	1	25	17	6	1	1
ARAB WORLD	26	9	8	0	3	3	2	1	0	0	7	3	2	0	1	11	4	2	3	2
INDIA	16	8	0	4	1	3	3	0	0	0	5	3	1	0	1	6	2	4	0	0
PHILIPPINES	15	6	1	0	4	2	1	0	0	2	4	2	0	2	0	6	4	0	1	1
OTHER E. ASIA	8	5	0	1	1	1	1	0	0	0	0	0	0	0	1	5	4	0	0	1
OTHER ASIA	35	15	6	2	8	7	3	0	0	4	7	4	1	0	2	17	8	5	2	2

CHAPTER 5- PATTERNS OF OWNERSHIP
SECTION 1- AN OVERVIEW OF FLOW AND STOCK, MANUFACTURING AND NON-MANUFACTURING
TABLE 12- SUBSIDIARIES WITH UNKNOWN ACTIVITY CLASSIFIED BY COUNTRY OR REGION,
BY YEAR(S) SUBSIDIARY WAS ACTIVE
AND BY SYSTEM OWNERSHIP %

YEAR AND OWNERSHIP PERCENTAGE
(WHL=95-100%, MAJ=50-94%, MIN=5-49%, UNK=UNKNOWN)

COUNTRY OR REGION	1929					1939					1957					1967				
	ALL	WHL	MAJ	MIN	UNK	ALL	WHL	MAJ	MIN	UNK	ALL	WHL	MAJ	MIN	UNK	ALL	WHL	MAJ	MIN	UNK
OUTSIDE U.S.	146	67	16	7	56	412	238	50	11	113	789	495	93	26	175	1504	958	203	63	280
OUT. U.S. + CANADA	112	48	14	7	43	319	178	47	10	84	634	390	85	22	137	1248	780	187	55	226
OUT. WEST. HEMIS.	91	39	13	5	34	256	144	36	9	67	437	271	61	14	91	901	574	135	39	153
OUT. WHITE CWEALTH	85	33	10	6	36	239	127	32	9	71	475	273	63	19	120	966	585	147	49	185
OUT. DEVLPED WORLD	23	10	2	2	9	78	43	11	1	23	239	144	28	10	57	444	261	70	26	87
CANADA	34	19	2	0	13	93	60	3	1	29	155	105	8	4	38	256	178	16	8	54
LATIN AMERICA	21	9	1	2	9	63	34	11	1	17	197	119	24	8	46	347	206	52	16	73
C. AMER.+CARIB.	9	3	1	2	3	23	17	1	1	4	95	65	7	4	19	163	109	18	7	29
CUBA	3	0	1	0	2	11	11	0	0	0	17	15	0	0	2	5	5	0	0	0
MEXICO	6	3	0	2	1	10	4	1	1	4	31	12	3	2	14	56	29	8	4	15
OTHER	0	0	0	0	0	2	2	0	0	0	47	38	4	2	3	102	75	10	3	14
S. AMERICA	12	6	0	0	6	40	17	10	0	13	102	54	17	4	27	184	97	34	9	44
ARGENTINA	3	2	0	0	1	15	8	5	0	2	19	10	4	0	5	32	17	6	0	9
BRAZIL	4	2	0	0	2	9	3	1	0	5	25	12	3	1	9	49	20	10	2	17
PERU	1	0	0	0	1	3	1	1	0	1	5	2	3	0	0	11	8	2	0	1
COLOMBIA	2	0	0	0	2	5	1	1	0	3	19	10	0	1	8	28	14	3	3	8
VENEZUELA	0	0	0	0	0	1	1	0	0	0	18	12	2	1	3	36	23	4	3	6
OTHER	2	1	0	0	1	7	3	2	0	2	16	8	5	1	2	28	15	9	1	3
EUROPE	85	36	11	5	33	229	126	36	8	59	338	202	53	10	73	697	449	106	26	116
EFTA	35	20	6	2	7	96	60	18	2	16	160	115	23	3	19	320	228	47	6	39
U.K.	24	13	4	1	6	70	42	15	1	12	104	71	18	2	13	196	135	31	4	26
SCANDINAVIA	6	4	1	1	0	17	11	2	1	3	38	31	2	1	4	67	52	6	2	7
SWITZERLAND	4	3	0	0	1	5	4	0	0	1	13	11	1	0	1	47	35	8	0	4
OTHER EFTA	1	0	1	0	0	4	3	1	0	0	5	2	2	0	1	10	6	2	0	2
EUROP. COMMUNITY	42	14	5	3	20	105	49	17	5	34	161	76	30	6	49	337	195	56	19	67
FRANCE	11	3	3	0	5	28	11	7	1	9	44	16	12	1	15	91	45	24	4	18
GERMANY	15	3	0	1	11	29	11	5	1	12	43	16	8	2	17	100	56	13	4	27
ITALY	8	2	2	1	3	24	14	3	1	6	35	17	6	2	10	75	46	11	4	14
BELGIUM + LUX	6	5	0	1	0	11	9	1	1	0	17	10	2	1	4	34	24	4	3	3
NETHERLANDS	2	1	0	0	1	13	4	1	1	7	22	17	2	0	3	37	24	4	4	5
SPAIN	3	0	0	0	3	8	4	0	0	4	10	6	0	1	3	26	16	2	0	8
GREECE + TURKEY	0	0	0	0	0	0	0	0	0	0	1	1	0	0	0	8	6	1	0	1
OTHER EUROPE	5	2	0	0	3	20	13	1	1	5	6	4	0	0	2	6	4	0	1	1
EUROPE EX. U.K.	61	23	7	4	27	159	84	21	7	47	234	131	35	8	60	501	314	75	22	90
SOUTHERN DOMINIONS	3	2	0	0	1	9	8	0	0	1	52	43	4	1	4	82	57	9	2	14
S. AFRICA +RHOD.	1	0	0	0	1	4	3	0	0	1	19	14	2	1	2	26	18	3	2	3
AUSTRALIA + N.Z.	2	2	0	0	0	5	5	0	0	0	33	29	2	0	2	56	39	6	0	11
ASIA + OTHER AFRICA	3	1	2	0	0	18	10	1	0	7	47	26	4	3	14	122	68	20	11	23
JAPAN	1	0	1	0	0	3	1	0	0	2	5	1	0	1	3	25	13	2	1	9
OTHER ASIA+AFR.	2	1	1	0	0	15	9	1	0	5	42	25	4	2	11	97	55	18	10	14
BLACK AFRICA	1	1	0	0	0	3	3	0	0	0	8	5	1	0	2	30	20	3	3	4
ARAB WORLD	0	0	0	0	0	3	3	0	0	0	8	5	1	0	2	15	7	6	0	2
INDIA	0	0	0	0	0	2	2	0	0	0	8	6	0	0	2	12	7	1	3	1
PHILIPPINES	0	0	0	0	0	1	1	0	0	0	4	1	0	0	3	10	5	2	1	2
OTHER E. ASIA	0	0	0	0	0	1	0	0	0	1	1	1	0	0	0	4	3	1	0	0
OTHER ASIA	1	0	1	0	0	5	0	1	0	4	13	7	2	2	2	26	13	5	3	5

CHAPTER 5- PATTERNS OF OWNERSHIP
SECTION 2- THE FLOW OF MANUFACTURING BY INDUSTRY OF PARENT SYSTEM
TABLE 1- MANUFACTURING SUBSIDIARIES IN A SYSTEM IN THE
MEAT AND DAIRY INDUSTRIES (SIC 201 AND 202)
CLASSIFIED BY COUNTRY, PERIOD MANUFACTURE BEGAN, AND SYSTEM OWNERSHIP %

PERIOD AND OWNERSHIP PERCENTAGE
(WHL=95-100%, MAJ=50-94%, MIN=5-49%, UNK=UNKNOWN)

COUNTRY OR REGION	TOTAL PRE 1968					PRE 1946					1946-1957					1958-1967				
	ALL	WHL	MAJ	MIN	UNK	ALL	WHL	MAJ	MIN	UNK	ALL	WHL	MAJ	MIN	UNK	ALL	WHL	MAJ	MIN	UNK
OUTSIDE U.S.	291	167	79	29	8	74	57	8	6	3	44	30	6	5	3	165	80	65	18	2
OUT. U.S. + CANADA	239	126	71	29	8	59	43	7	6	3	39	25	6	5	3	136	58	58	18	2
OUT. WEST. HEMIS.	137	75	44	11	5	36	31	2	0	3	20	16	2	1	1	79	28	40	10	1
OUT. WHITE CWEALTH	180	84	59	27	7	40	26	5	6	3	30	17	6	5	2	107	41	48	16	2
OUT. DEVLPED WORLD	120	53	37	22	5	25	12	5	6	2	23	10	6	5	2	69	31	26	11	1
CANADA	52	41	8	0	0	15	14	1	0	0	5	5	0	0	0	29	22	7	0	0
LATIN AMERICA	102	51	27	18	3	23	12	5	6	0	19	9	4	4	2	57	30	18	8	1
C. AMER.+CARIB.	48	25	9	9	2	8	3	0	5	0	10	7	0	1	2	28	15	9	3	1
CUBA	9	4	0	2	0	5	3	0	2	0	3	1	0	0	0	0	0	0	0	0
MEXICO	18	14	1	1	1	0	0	0	0	0	6	6	0	0	0	12	8	3	1	0
OTHER	21	7	6	6	0	3	0	0	3	0	1	0	0	1	0	16	7	6	2	1
S. AMERICA	54	26	18	9	0	15	9	5	1	0	9	2	4	3	0	29	15	9	5	0
ARGENTINA	9	6	2	0	0	5	4	1	0	0	1	1	0	0	0	3	2	0	1	0
BRAZIL	12	10	2	0	0	4	4	0	0	0	3	3	0	0	0	5	3	0	1	0
PERU	4	0	0	3	0	3	0	0	1	0	0	0	0	0	0	1	0	0	0	0
COLOMBIA	15	6	5	4	0	1	1	0	0	0	2	1	1	0	0	12	6	4	2	0
VENEZUELA	9	2	5	2	0	1	0	1	0	0	3	0	0	2	0	5	1	3	1	0
OTHER	5	2	1	1	0	1	1	0	0	0	1	0	0	1	0	3	1	1	1	0
EUROPE	88	54	28	3	3	26	25	0	0	1	10	9	0	0	1	52	20	28	3	1
EFTA	36	27	9	0	0	12	12	0	0	0	4	4	0	0	0	20	11	9	0	0
U.K.	26	21	5	0	0	11	11	0	0	0	3	3	0	0	0	14	9	5	0	0
SCANDINAVIA	10	6	4	0	0	1	1	0	0	0	3	1	0	0	0	6	2	4	0	0
SWITZERLAND	0	0	0	0	0	0	0	0	0	0	0	0	0	0	0	0	0	0	0	0
OTHER EFTA	0	0	0	0	0	0	0	0	0	0	0	0	0	0	0	0	0	0	0	0
EUROP. COMMUNITY	38	25	10	1	2	14	13	0	0	1	4	4	0	0	0	20	8	10	1	1
FRANCE	6	4	2	0	0	3	3	0	0	0	0	0	0	0	0	3	1	2	0	0
GERMANY	15	10	4	1	0	7	6	0	0	1	3	3	0	0	0	5	1	4	0	0
ITALY	4	0	3	1	0	0	0	0	0	0	0	0	0	0	0	4	0	3	1	0
BELGIUM + LUX	5	4	1	0	0	0	0	0	0	0	0	0	0	0	0	5	4	1	0	0
NETHERLANDS	8	7	0	0	1	4	4	0	0	0	0	0	0	0	0	4	2	0	1	1
SPAIN	7	0	7	0	0	0	0	0	0	0	0	0	0	0	0	7	0	7	0	0
GREECE + TURKEY	0	0	0	0	0	0	0	0	0	0	0	0	0	0	0	0	0	0	0	0
OTHER EUROPE	7	2	2	2	1	0	0	0	0	0	2	1	0	1	1	5	1	2	2	0
EUROPE EX. U.K.	62	33	23	3	3	15	14	0	0	1	9	8	0	0	1	38	11	23	3	1
SOUTHERN DOMINIONS	26	19	5	0	0	8	6	2	0	0	6	6	0	0	0	10	7	3	0	0
S. AFRICA +RHOD.	3	2	0	0	0	1	1	0	0	0	1	1	0	0	0	0	0	0	0	0
AUSTRALIA + N.Z.	23	17	5	0	2	7	5	2	0	0	5	5	0	0	0	10	7	3	0	0
ASIA + OTHER AFRICA	23	2	11	8	2	2	0	0	0	2	4	1	2	1	0	17	1	9	7	0
JAPAN	5	0	1	4	0	0	0	0	0	0	0	0	0	0	0	5	0	1	4	0
OTHER ASIA+AFR.	18	2	10	4	0	2	0	0	0	2	4	1	2	1	0	12	1	8	3	0
BLACK AFRICA	1	0	1	0	0	0	0	0	0	0	0	0	0	0	0	1	0	1	0	0
ARAB WORLD	2	0	2	0	0	0	0	0	0	0	0	0	0	0	0	2	0	2	0	0
INDIA	2	0	0	2	0	0	0	0	0	0	0	0	0	0	0	2	0	0	2	0
PHILIPPINES	5	2	3	0	0	0	0	0	0	0	2	1	1	0	0	3	1	2	0	0
OTHER E. ASIA	4	0	0	2	2	2	0	0	0	2	1	0	0	1	0	1	0	0	1	0
OTHER ASIA	6	0	4	2	0	0	0	0	0	0	1	0	1	0	0	5	0	3	2	0

CHAPTER 5- PATTERNS OF OWNERSHIP
SECTION 2- THE FLOW OF MANUFACTURING BY INDUSTRY OF PARENT SYSTEM
TABLE 2- MANUFACTURING SUBSIDIARIES IN A SYSTEM IN THE
OTHER FOOD AND BEVERAGE INDUSTRIES (SIC 203-209)
CLASSIFIED BY COUNTRY, PERIOD MANUFACTURE BEGAN, AND SYSTEM OWNERSHIP %

PERIOD AND OWNERSHIP PERCENTAGE
(WHL=95-100%, MAJ=50-94%, MIN=5-49%, UNK=UNKNOWN)

COUNTRY OR REGION	TOTAL PRE 1968					PRE 1946					1946-1957					1958-1967				
	ALL	WHL	MAJ	MIN	UNK	ALL	WHL	MAJ	MIN	UNK	ALL	WHL	MAJ	MIN	UNK	ALL	WHL	MAJ	MIN	UNK
OUTSIDE U.S.	503	300	129	34	32	105	81	8	1	15	86	58	19	3	6	304	161	102	30	11
OUT. U.S. + CANADA	402	218	121	29	28	64	47	5	0	12	63	38	17	3	5	269	133	99	26	11
OUT. WEST. HEMIS.	260	143	73	19	20	50	36	4	0	10	37	21	17	3	4	168	86	60	16	6
OUT. WHITE CWEALTH	311	159	107	24	16	32	25	4	0	3	53	33	14	2	3	221	101	89	21	10
OUT. DEVLPED WORLD	163	88	53	11	10	18	15	1	0	2	31	21	9	0	1	113	52	43	11	7
CANADA	101	82	8	5	4	41	34	3	1	3	23	20	2	0	1	35	28	3	4	0
LATIN AMERICA	142	75	48	10	8	14	11	1	0	2	26	17	8	0	1	101	47	39	10	5
C. AMER.+CARIB.	82	38	30	7	0	9	6	1	0	2	14	9	4	1	0	59	23	25	7	4
CUBA	8	6	2	0	0	4	3	1	0	0	2	1	1	0	0	2	2	0	0	0
MEXICO	50	29	13	4	4	3	3	0	0	0	10	7	1	2	0	37	19	11	4	3
OTHER	24	3	15	3	3	2	0	0	0	2	2	1	1	0	0	20	2	14	3	1
S. AMERICA	60	37	18	3	1	5	5	0	0	0	12	8	4	0	0	42	24	14	3	1
ARGENTINA	10	8	1	0	1	2	2	0	0	0	1	1	0	0	0	7	5	1	0	1
BRAZIL	10	9	0	1	0	2	2	0	0	0	2	2	0	0	0	6	5	0	1	0
PERU	8	5	3	0	0	0	0	0	0	0	2	1	1	0	0	6	4	2	0	0
COLUMBIA	9	6	3	0	0	1	1	0	0	0	4	3	1	0	0	4	2	2	0	0
VENEZUELA	14	4	6	3	0	0	0	0	0	0	4	3	1	2	0	10	3	4	3	0
OTHER	9	5	4	0	0	0	0	0	0	0	3	0	1	0	0	9	5	4	0	0
EUROPE	188	97	55	14	17	38	24	4	0	10	26	13	6	3	4	119	60	45	11	3
EFTA	70	40	13	5	11	25	15	1	0	9	8	3	3	0	2	36	22	9	5	0
U.K.	48	27	11	4	11	23	13	1	0	9	5	2	1	0	2	19	8	3	4	0
SCANDINAVIA	14	11	3	0	0	2	2	0	0	0	1	1	0	0	0	10	8	2	0	0
SWITZERLAND	2	0	2	1	0	0	0	0	0	0	0	0	1	0	0	1	0	1	0	0
OTHER EFTA	6	2	3	0	0	0	0	0	0	1	0	0	0	0	0	6	2	3	1	0
EUROP. COMMUNITY	98	47	35	6	10	10	6	3	0	1	14	8	3	1	2	70	33	29	5	3
FRANCE	26	8	15	2	1	1	1	1	0	0	2	2	0	0	0	23	6	14	2	1
GERMANY	29	16	6	2	2	3	2	1	1	0	6	4	0	1	1	17	10	4	2	0
ITALY	15	8	6	2	2	1	0	0	0	0	2	2	1	1	0	12	7	5	2	1
BELGIUM + LUX	13	7	5	2	0	2	2	0	0	0	2	2	1	0	0	9	5	4	0	0
NETHERLANDS	15	8	6	0	2	3	2	2	0	0	1	0	1	0	0	9	5	5	2	1
SPAIN	15	6	0	3	0	2	0	1	0	0	3	1	1	0	0	10	3	2	1	0
GREECE + TURKEY	2	1	1	0	0	0	0	0	0	0	0	0	0	0	0	2	1	1	0	0
OTHER EUROPE	3	3	0	0	0	1	0	0	0	0	1	0	0	0	0	1	0	0	0	0
EUROPE EX. U.K.	140	70	50	10	6	15	11	3	0	1	21	11	5	3	2	100	48	42	7	3
SOUTHERN DOMINIONS	40	29	9	1	1	8	8	0	0	0	4	2	2	0	0	28	19	7	1	1
S. AFRICA +RHOD.	15	11	3	1	0	3	3	0	0	0	2	1	1	0	0	10	7	2	1	0
AUSTRALIA + N.Z.	25	18	6	0	1	5	5	0	0	0	2	1	1	0	0	18	12	5	0	1
ASIA + OTHER AFRICA	32	17	9	4	2	4	4	0	0	0	7	6	1	0	0	21	7	8	4	2
JAPAN	11	4	4	3	1	0	0	0	0	0	2	2	0	0	0	9	2	4	3	0
OTHER ASIA+AFR.	21	13	5	1	0	4	4	0	0	0	5	4	1	1	0	12	5	4	0	2
BLACK AFRICA	2	2	0	0	0	0	0	0	0	0	1	1	0	0	0	1	1	0	0	0
ARAB WORLD	2	2	0	0	0	0	0	0	0	0	1	1	0	0	0	1	1	0	0	0
INDIA	1	1	0	1	0	1	1	0	0	0	0	0	0	0	0	0	0	0	0	0
PHILIPPINES	7	5	1	0	2	2	2	0	0	0	2	2	0	0	0	3	1	1	1	0
OTHER E. ASIA	6	2	2	2	0	1	1	0	0	0	0	0	0	0	0	5	1	2	0	2
OTHER ASIA	3	1	2	0	0	0	0	0	0	0	1	1	0	0	0	2	1	1	0	0

CHAPTER 5- PATTERNS OF OWNERSHIP
SECTION 2- THE FLOW OF MANUFACTURING BY INDUSTRY OF PARENT SYSTEM
TABLE 3- MANUFACTURING SUBSIDIARIES IN A SYSTEM IN THE
TEXTILE AND APPAREL INDUSTRIES (SIC 22 AND 23)
CLASSIFIED BY COUNTRY, PERIOD MANUFACTURE BEGAN, AND SYSTEM OWNERSHIP %

PERIOD AND OWNERSHIP PERCENTAGE
(WHL=95-100%, MAJ=50-94%, MIN=5-49%, UNK=UNKNOWN)

COUNTRY OR REGION	TOTAL PRE 1968					PRE 1946					1946-1957					1958-1967				
	ALL	WHL	MAJ	MIN	UNK	ALL	WHL	MAJ	MIN	UNK	ALL	WHL	MAJ	MIN	UNK	ALL	WHL	MAJ	MIN	UNK
OUTSIDE U.S.	76	48	18	2	4	6	4	2	0	0	19	16	2	0	1	47	28	14	2	3
OUT. U.S. + CANADA	58	33	17	2	3	4	1	1	0	0	12	9	2	0	0	41	23	14	2	2
OUT. WEST. HEMIS.	33	18	10	2	2	2	0	1	0	0	0	0	0	0	0	32	18	10	2	2
OUT. WHITE CMWEALTH	44	23	14	2	2	1	1	0	1	0	12	9	2	0	0	27	13	11	2	1
OUT. DEVLPED WORLD	25	15	7	0	1	1	1	0	1	0	12	9	2	0	0	9	5	4	0	0
CANADA	18	15	1	0	1	4	3	1	1	0	7	7	0	0	0	6	5	0	0	0
LATIN AMERICA	25	15	7	1	1	2	1	1	0	0	12	7	2	0	1	9	5	4	0	0
C. AMER.+CARIB.	8	4	2	0	1	0	0	0	0	0	4	3	1	0	0	3	1	2	0	0
CUBA	2	1	1	0	0	0	0	0	0	0	1	1	0	0	0	0	0	0	0	0
MEXICO	6	3	2	0	0	0	0	0	0	0	3	1	2	0	0	3	1	2	0	0
OTHER	0	0	0	0	0	0	0	0	0	0	0	0	0	0	0	0	0	0	0	0
S. AMERICA	17	11	5	0	0	2	1	1	0	0	8	6	2	0	0	6	4	2	0	0
ARGENTINA	2	1	1	0	0	1	1	0	0	0	0	0	0	0	0	1	0	1	0	0
BRAZIL	3	2	1	0	0	0	0	0	0	0	2	1	0	0	0	1	0	1	0	0
PERU	0	0	0	0	0	0	0	0	0	0	0	0	0	0	0	0	0	0	0	0
COLOMBIA	4	1	3	0	0	0	0	0	0	0	1	0	1	0	0	3	1	2	0	0
VENEZUELA	6	5	1	0	0	1	0	1	0	0	3	3	0	0	0	2	2	0	0	0
OTHER	2	2	0	0	0	0	0	0	0	0	2	2	0	0	0	0	0	0	0	0
EUROPE	28	16	8	0	2	0	0	0	0	0	0	0	0	0	0	27	16	8	1	2
EFTA	14	10	2	0	2	0	0	0	0	0	0	0	0	0	0	14	10	2	0	2
U.K.	11	8	2	0	1	0	0	0	0	0	0	0	0	0	0	11	10	2	0	1
SCANDINAVIA	0	0	0	0	0	0	0	0	0	0	0	0	0	0	0	0	0	0	0	0
SWITZERLAND	2	1	0	0	0	0	0	0	0	0	0	0	0	0	0	2	0	2	0	0
OTHER EFTA	1	1	0	0	0	0	0	0	0	0	0	0	0	0	0	1	1	0	0	0
EUROP. COMMUNITY	11	5	4	1	1	0	0	0	0	0	0	0	0	0	0	10	5	4	1	1
FRANCE	4	1	1	1	1	0	0	0	0	0	0	0	0	0	0	3	1	1	1	1
GERMANY	3	2	1	0	0	0	0	0	0	0	0	0	0	0	0	3	1	2	0	0
ITALY	3	2	1	0	0	0	0	0	0	0	0	0	0	0	0	3	2	1	0	0
BELGIUM + LUX	0	0	0	0	0	0	0	0	0	0	0	0	0	0	0	0	0	0	0	0
NETHERLANDS	1	1	0	0	0	0	0	0	0	0	0	0	0	0	0	1	0	1	0	0
SPAIN	3	1	2	0	0	0	0	0	0	0	0	0	0	0	0	3	1	2	0	0
GREECE + TURKEY	0	0	0	0	0	0	0	0	0	0	0	0	0	0	0	0	0	0	0	0
OTHER EUROPE	0	0	0	0	0	0	0	0	0	0	0	0	0	0	0	0	0	0	0	0
EUROPE EX. U.K.	17	8	6	0	1	0	0	0	0	0	0	0	0	0	0	16	8	6	0	1
SOUTHERN DOMINIONS	3	2	1	0	0	0	0	0	0	0	0	0	0	0	0	3	2	1	0	0
S. AFRICA +RHOD.	2	1	1	0	0	0	0	0	0	0	0	0	0	0	0	2	1	1	0	0
AUSTRALIA + N.Z.	1	1	0	0	0	0	0	0	0	0	0	0	0	0	0	1	1	0	0	0
ASIA + OTHER AFRICA	2	0	1	0	1	0	0	0	0	0	0	0	0	0	0	2	0	1	0	1
JAPAN	2	0	1	0	1	0	0	0	0	0	0	0	0	0	0	2	0	1	0	1
OTHER ASIA+AFR.	0	0	0	0	0	0	0	0	0	0	0	0	0	0	0	0	0	0	0	0
BLACK AFRICA	0	0	0	0	0	0	0	0	0	0	0	0	0	0	0	0	0	0	0	0
ARAB WORLD	0	0	0	0	0	0	0	0	0	0	0	0	0	0	0	0	0	0	0	0
INDIA	0	0	0	0	0	0	0	0	0	0	0	0	0	0	0	0	0	0	0	0
PHILIPPINES	0	0	0	0	0	0	0	0	0	0	0	0	0	0	0	0	0	0	0	0
OTHER E. ASIA	0	0	0	0	0	0	0	0	0	0	0	0	0	0	0	0	0	0	0	0
OTHER ASIA	0	0	0	0	0	0	0	0	0	0	0	0	0	0	0	0	0	0	0	0

CHAPTER 5- PATTERNS OF OWNERSHIP
SECTION 2- THE FLOW OF MANUFACTURING BY INDUSTRY OF PARENT SYSTEM
TABLE 4- MANUFACTURING SUBSIDIARIES IN A SYSTEM IN THE
LUMBER, FURNITURE, AND PAPER INDUSTRIES (SIC 24,25,26)
CLASSIFIED BY COUNTRY, PERIOD MANUFACTURE BEGAN, AND SYSTEM OWNERSHIP %

PERIOD AND OWNERSHIP PERCENTAGE
(WHL=95-100%, MAJ=50-94%, MIN=5-49%, UNK=UNKNOWN)

COUNTRY OR REGION	TOTAL PRE 1968					PRE 1946					1946-1957					1958-1967				
	ALL	WHL	MAJ	MIN	UNK	ALL	WHL	MAJ	MIN	UNK	ALL	WHL	MAJ	MIN	UNK	ALL	WHL	MAJ	MIN	UNK
OUTSIDE U.S.	182	84	63	25	7	17	9	5	1	2	35	17	11	5	2	127	58	47	19	3
OUT. U.S. + CANADA	149	64	59	21	4	8	3	3	1	1	22	10	10	2	0	118	51	46	18	3
OUT. WEST. HEMIS.	110	53	43	11	2	4	3	1	0	0	12	5	5	2	0	93	45	37	9	2
OUT. WHITE CWEALTH	94	28	48	15	2	7	2	3	1	1	15	6	8	1	0	71	20	37	13	1
OUT. DEVLPED WORLD	49	12	22	13	2	4	0	2	1	1	11	5	6	0	0	34	7	14	12	1
CANADA	33	20	4	4	3	9	6	2	0	1	13	7	1	3	2	9	7	1	1	0
LATIN AMERICA	39	11	16	10	2	4	0	2	1	1	10	5	5	0	0	25	6	9	9	1
C. AMER.+CARIB.	21	9	6	5	1	2	0	1	0	1	6	5	1	0	0	13	4	4	5	0
CUBA	1	0	0	0	1	1	0	0	0	1	0	0	0	0	0	0	0	0	0	0
MEXICO	10	7	2	1	0	0	0	1	0	0	6	5	1	0	0	3	2	0	1	0
OTHER	10	2	4	4	0	1	0	0	1	0	0	0	0	0	0	10	2	4	4	0
S. AMERICA	18	2	10	5	1	2	0	1	0	0	4	0	4	0	0	12	2	5	4	1
ARGENTINA	2	1	1	0	0	0	0	0	0	0	0	0	0	0	0	2	1	1	0	0
BRAZIL	1	0	1	0	0	0	0	0	0	0	0	0	0	0	0	1	0	1	0	0
PERU	0	0	0	0	0	0	0	0	0	0	0	0	0	0	0	0	0	0	0	0
COLOMBIA	4	0	3	0	0	2	0	1	0	0	1	0	1	0	0	1	0	1	0	0
VENEZUELA	9	1	6	1	1	0	0	0	0	0	3	0	3	0	0	6	1	3	1	1
OTHER	2	0	0	2	0	0	0	0	0	0	0	0	0	0	0	2	0	0	2	0
EUROPE	52	20	28	2	1	3	2	1	0	0	8	3	4	1	0	40	15	23	1	1
EFTA	10	5	4	0	1	0	0	0	0	0	4	2	2	0	0	6	3	2	0	1
U.K.	9	4	4	0	1	0	0	0	0	0	4	2	2	0	0	5	2	2	0	1
SCANDINAVIA	1	1	0	0	0	0	0	0	0	0	0	0	0	0	0	1	1	0	0	0
SWITZERLAND	0	0	0	0	0	0	0	0	0	0	0	0	0	0	0	0	0	0	0	0
OTHER EFTA	0	0	0	0	0	0	0	0	0	0	0	0	0	0	0	0	0	0	0	0
EUROP. COMMUNITY	33	14	16	2	1	3	2	1	0	0	4	1	2	1	0	25	11	13	1	1
FRANCE	10	3	6	1	0	1	1	0	0	0	2	1	1	0	0	7	1	5	1	0
GERMANY	6	2	3	1	0	1	1	0	0	0	2	0	1	1	0	3	1	2	0	0
ITALY	10	5	4	1	0	1	0	1	0	0	0	0	0	0	0	9	5	4	0	0
BELGIUM + LUX	5	2	3	0	0	0	0	0	0	0	0	0	0	0	0	4	2	2	0	0
NETHERLANDS	2	2	0	0	0	1	1	0	0	0	0	0	0	0	0	2	1	0	0	0
SPAIN	7	1	6	0	0	0	0	0	0	0	0	0	0	0	0	7	1	6	0	0
GREECE + TURKEY	1	0	1	0	0	0	0	0	0	0	0	0	0	0	0	1	0	1	0	0
OTHER EUROPE	1	0	1	1	0	0	0	0	0	0	0	0	0	0	0	1	0	1	1	0
EUROPE EX. U.K.	43	16	24	2	0	3	2	1	1	0	4	1	2	1	0	35	13	21	1	0
SOUTHERN DOMINIONS	46	32	7	6	1	1	1	0	0	0	3	2	1	1	0	42	29	7	5	1
S. AFRICA +RHOD.	33	27	2	4	0	1	0	0	0	0	1	1	0	1	0	32	26	2	4	0
AUSTRALIA + N.Z.	13	5	5	2	1	0	1	0	0	0	2	1	1	0	0	10	3	5	3	1
ASIA + OTHER AFRICA	12	1	8	3	0	0	0	0	0	0	1	0	1	0	0	11	1	7	3	0
JAPAN	2	0	2	0	1	0	0	0	0	0	0	0	0	0	0	2	0	2	0	1
OTHER ASIA+AFR.	10	0	6	3	0	0	0	0	0	0	1	1	1	0	0	9	0	5	3	0
BLACK AFRICA	2	0	1	1	0	0	0	0	0	0	0	0	0	0	0	2	0	1	1	0
ARAB WORLD	0	0	0	0	0	0	0	0	0	0	0	0	0	0	0	0	0	0	0	0
INDIA	1	1	0	1	1	0	0	0	0	0	1	1	1	0	0	1	0	1	1	0
PHILIPPINES	4	0	2	1	0	0	0	0	0	0	0	0	0	0	0	4	0	2	1	0
OTHER E. ASIA	0	0	0	0	0	0	0	0	0	0	0	0	0	0	0	0	0	0	0	0
OTHER ASIA	3	0	3	0	0	0	0	0	0	0	1	0	0	0	0	2	0	2	0	0

CHAPTER 5- PATTERNS OF OWNERSHIP
SECTION 2- THE FLOW OF MANUFACTURING BY INDUSTRY OF PARENT SYSTEM
TABLE 5- MANUFACTURING SUBSIDIARIES IN A SYSTEM IN THE
CHEMICAL INDUSTRIES (SIC 281,282;285-289)
CLASSIFIED BY COUNTRY, PERIOD MANUFACTURE BEGAN, AND SYSTEM OWNERSHIP %

PERIOD AND OWNERSHIP PERCENTAGE
(WHL=95-100%, MAJ=50-94%, MIN=5-49%, UNK=UNKNOWN)

COUNTRY OR REGION	TOTAL (PRE 1968)					PRE 1946					1946-1957					1958-1967				
	ALL	WHL	MAJ	MIN	UNK	ALL	WHL	MAJ	MIN	UNK	ALL	WHL	MAJ	MIN	UNK	ALL	WHL	MAJ	MIN	UNK
OUTSIDE U.S.	813	380	219	90	63	117	67	29	11	10	169	83	53	21	12	466	230	137	58	41
OUT. U.S. + CANADA	682	288	202	85	53	70	34	24	8	4	135	61	44	20	10	423	193	134	57	39
OUT. WEST. HEMIS.	436	190	129	51	33	39	20	12	4	3	67	33	17	14	3	297	137	100	33	27
OUT. WHITE CWEALTH	540	217	168	73	37	49	24	17	5	3	106	47	37	13	9	340	146	114	55	25
OUT. DEVLPED WORLD	300	117	87	42	23	32	15	12	4	1	76	34	29	6	7	161	68	46	32	15
CANADA	131	92	17	5	10	47	33	5	3	6	34	22	9	1	2	43	37	3	1	2
LATIN AMERICA	246	98	73	34	20	31	14	12	4	1	68	28	27	6	7	126	56	34	24	12
C. AMER.+CARIB.	95	34	21	22	6	6	3	1	2	0	21	12	6	2	1	56	19	14	19	4
CUBA	1	0	1	0	0	0	0	0	0	0	1	0	1	0	0	0	0	0	0	0
MEXICO	72	28	13	18	4	6	3	0	1	0	19	12	4	2	0	38	13	8	15	2
OTHER	22	6	7	4	2	0	0	0	1	0	1	0	1	0	0	18	6	6	4	2
S. AMERICA	151	64	52	12	14	25	11	11	0	3	47	16	21	4	6	70	37	20	5	8
ARGENTINA	33	18	11	2	3	13	8	5	0	0	7	2	5	0	0	12	8	1	2	3
BRAZIL	41	18	14	4	3	4	2	1	1	0	17	6	5	3	3	20	11	8	1	0
PERU	14	6	4	1	1	2	1	0	0	0	6	4	1	0	0	6	1	1	0	1
COLOMBIA	25	12	7	3	3	4	0	2	0	0	8	3	3	0	0	16	8	4	2	2
VENEZUELA	16	6	6	2	4	0	0	0	0	0	9	4	1	0	0	7	3	2	2	0
OTHER	22	4	10	6	0	6	0	3	0	3	5	1	3	1	0	9	3	3	4	0
EUROPE	268	135	85	25	18	30	16	10	2	2	45	22	10	11	2	188	97	65	12	14
EFTA	83	45	22	9	6	16	9	6	1	0	22	9	5	1	1	44	27	11	1	5
U.K.	63	35	16	7	5	13	7	5	1	0	21	9	5	6	1	29	19	6	0	4
SCANDINAVIA	14	1	4	9	1	3	2	1	0	0	0	0	0	0	0	9	3	2	3	1
SWITZERLAND	3	1	2	0	0	0	0	0	0	0	0	0	0	0	0	3	1	2	0	0
OTHER EFTA	3	2	0	1	0	0	0	0	0	0	0	0	0	0	0	3	2	0	1	0
EUROP. COMMUNITY	146	73	47	11	11	13	6	4	1	2	18	11	3	1	0	111	56	40	7	8
FRANCE	35	18	14	0	3	4	1	2	0	1	5	4	1	0	0	25	13	11	0	1
GERMANY	34	20	6	3	5	4	1	2	0	1	6	4	1	1	0	24	15	3	2	4
ITALY	38	15	13	6	4	3	2	1	0	0	5	2	0	0	3	30	11	12	6	1
BELGIUM + LUX	20	13	7	0	0	1	1	0	0	0	0	0	0	0	0	19	12	7	0	0
NETHERLANDS	19	7	7	1	4	1	1	0	0	1	2	0	2	0	0	13	5	5	0	3
SPAIN	27	10	12	5	0	1	1	0	0	0	4	2	0	1	0	22	7	11	4	0
GREECE + TURKEY	6	3	3	0	0	0	0	0	0	0	2	0	1	0	0	5	3	2	0	0
OTHER EUROPE	6	4	1	0	1	0	0	0	0	0	0	0	0	0	0	6	4	1	0	1
EUROPE EX. U.K.	205	100	69	18	13	17	9	5	1	2	24	13	5	5	1	159	78	59	12	10
SOUTHERN DOMINIONS	74	33	17	5	10	8	3	2	1	1	8	5	1	1	0	49	25	13	2	9
S. AFRICA +RHOD.	13	6	2	0	0	2	1	1	0	0	2	1	0	1	0	5	4	1	0	0
AUSTRALIA + N.Z.	61	27	15	5	9	6	2	1	1	1	6	4	1	0	0	44	21	12	2	9
ASIA + OTHER AFRICA	94	22	27	21	5	6	2	2	2	0	14	6	0	4	1	60	15	22	19	4
JAPAN	40	3	13	13	2	1	0	1	0	0	0	0	0	0	0	25	3	10	11	1
OTHER ASIA+AFR.	54	19	14	8	3	1	0	1	0	0	8	6	2	0	0	35	12	8	8	3
BLACK AFRICA	7	4	0	0	0	0	0	0	0	0	0	0	0	0	0	5	4	0	0	0
ARAB WORLD	1	0	0	0	1	0	0	0	0	0	0	0	0	0	0	1	0	0	0	0
INDIA	12	4	3	5	0	1	0	1	1	0	2	2	0	1	0	8	1	2	5	1
PHILIPPINES	7	3	1	0	0	1	1	0	0	0	3	2	1	0	0	3	0	0	0	3
OTHER E. ASIA	9	4	3	1	0	0	0	0	0	0	2	2	0	0	0	6	2	3	1	0
OTHER ASIA	18	4	6	0	3	0	0	0	0	0	1	1	0	0	0	12	3	6	0	3

CHAPTER 5- PATTERNS OF OWNERSHIP
SECTION 2- THE FLOW OF MANUFACTURING BY INDUSTRY OF PARENT SYSTEM
TABLE 6- MANUFACTURING SUBSIDIARIES IN A SYSTEM IN THE
DRUG INDUSTRY (SIC 283)
CLASSIFIED BY COUNTRY, PERIOD MANUFACTURE BEGAN, AND SYSTEM OWNERSHIP %

PERIOD AND OWNERSHIP PERCENTAGE
(WHL=95-100%, MAJ=50-94%, MIN=5-49%, UNK=UNKNOWN)

COUNTRY OR REGION	TOTAL PRE 1968					PRE 1946					1946-1957					1958-1967				
	ALL	WHL	MAJ	MIN	UNK	ALL	WHL	MAJ	MIN	UNK	ALL	WHL	MAJ	MIN	UNK	ALL	WHL	MAJ	MIN	UNK
OUTSIDE U.S.	473	352	88	9	21	84	74	7	1	2	121	104	14	0	3	265	174	67	8	16
OUT. U.S. + CANADA	425	308	85	9	20	63	54	6	1	2	108	92	13	0	3	251	162	66	8	15
OUT. WEST. HEMIS.	296	213	61	7	15	43	37	5	0	1	65	59	4	0	2	186	117	52	7	10
OUT. WHITE CWEALTH	305	205	76	8	15	26	21	2	1	2	75	61	12	0	2	203	123	62	7	11
OUT. DEVLPED WORLD	175	120	41	3	10	20	17	1	1	1	52	42	9	0	1	102	61	31	2	8
CANADA	48	44	3	0	1	21	20	1	0	0	13	12	1	0	0	14	12	1	0	1
LATIN AMERICA	129	95	24	2	7	20	17	1	1	1	43	33	9	0	1	65	45	14	1	5
C. AMER.+CARIB.	57	47	7	0	2	6	6	0	0	0	19	18	1	0	0	31	23	6	0	2
CUBA	3	1	1	0	1	0	0	0	0	0	1	1	0	0	0	0	0	0	0	0
MEXICO	33	25	7	0	1	5	5	0	0	0	9	8	1	0	0	19	12	6	0	1
OTHER	23	21	0	1	1	1	1	0	0	0	9	9	0	0	0	12	11	0	0	1
S. AMERICA	72	48	17	2	5	14	11	1	0	1	24	15	8	0	1	34	22	8	1	3
ARGENTINA	15	11	3	0	1	7	6	0	0	1	5	3	2	0	0	3	2	1	0	0
BRAZIL	21	13	5	1	2	1	0	1	0	0	12	6	5	0	1	8	7	1	0	1
PERU	7	4	1	1	0	2	2	0	0	0	2	2	0	0	0	4	1	1	1	1
COLOMBIA	9	5	4	0	0	1	1	0	0	0	2	2	0	0	0	6	3	3	0	0
VENEZUELA	10	7	3	0	0	1	1	0	0	0	0	0	0	0	0	9	6	3	0	0
OTHER	10	8	1	0	1	2	2	0	0	0	4	3	1	0	0	4	3	0	0	1
EUROPE	181	135	33	5	6	24	21	2	0	1	38	34	3	0	1	117	80	28	5	4
EFTA	72	59	6	1	4	19	18	1	0	0	19	17	1	0	1	32	24	4	1	3
U.K.	60	51	3	1	3	18	17	1	0	0	17	15	1	0	1	23	19	2	1	1
SCANDINAVIA	4	3	1	0	0	0	0	0	0	0	1	1	0	0	0	3	1	1	0	0
SWITZERLAND	2	2	0	0	0	0	0	0	0	0	1	1	0	0	0	1	1	0	0	0
OTHER EFTA	6	3	2	0	1	1	1	0	0	0	0	0	0	0	0	5	2	2	0	1
EUROP. COMMUNITY	92	69	19	3	1	5	3	1	0	0	18	16	2	0	1	69	50	16	3	0
FRANCE	29	13	14	1	1	2	0	1	0	1	4	2	2	0	0	23	11	11	1	0
GERMANY	21	19	2	0	0	2	2	0	0	0	2	2	0	0	0	17	15	1	1	0
ITALY	24	22	2	0	0	1	1	0	0	0	8	8	0	0	0	16	14	1	0	1
BELGIUM + LUX	10	9	0	1	0	0	0	0	0	0	2	2	0	0	0	8	6	0	1	0
NETHERLANDS	8	6	2	0	0	0	0	0	0	0	2	2	0	0	0	5	3	2	0	0
SPAIN	10	3	7	0	0	0	0	0	0	0	0	0	0	0	0	10	3	7	0	0
GREECE + TURKEY	6	3	1	1	0	0	0	0	0	0	0	0	0	0	0	6	3	1	1	0
OTHER EUROPE	1	1	0	0	0	0	0	0	0	0	0	0	0	0	0	0	0	0	0	0
EUROPE EX. U.K.	121	84	30	4	3	6	4	1	0	1	21	19	2	0	1	94	61	27	4	2
SOUTHERN DOMINIONS	59	51	6	0	2	19	16	3	0	0	15	15	0	0	0	25	20	3	0	2
S. AFRICA +RHOD.	22	19	3	0	0	8	6	2	0	0	7	7	0	0	0	7	6	1	0	0
AUSTRALIA + N.Z.	37	32	3	0	2	11	10	1	0	0	8	8	0	0	0	18	14	2	0	2
ASIA + OTHER AFRICA	56	27	22	2	5	0	0	0	0	0	12	10	1	0	1	44	17	21	2	4
JAPAN	10	2	5	1	2	0	0	0	0	0	3	1	1	0	1	7	1	4	1	1
OTHER ASIA+AFR.	46	25	17	1	3	0	0	0	0	0	9	9	0	0	0	37	16	17	1	3
BLACK AFRICA	8	6	0	1	1	0	0	0	0	0	2	2	0	0	0	6	4	0	1	1
ARAB WORLD	3	3	0	0	0	0	0	0	0	0	0	0	0	0	0	3	3	0	0	0
INDIA	7	2	5	0	0	0	0	0	0	0	1	1	0	0	0	6	1	5	0	0
PHILIPPINES	8	6	2	0	0	0	0	0	0	0	4	4	0	0	0	4	2	2	0	0
OTHER E. ASIA	2	2	0	0	0	0	0	0	0	0	0	0	0	0	0	2	2	0	0	0
OTHER ASIA	18	6	10	0	2	0	0	0	0	0	2	2	0	0	0	16	4	10	0	2

CHAPTER 5- PATTERNS OF OWNERSHIP
SECTION 2- THE FLOW OF MANUFACTURING BY INDUSTRY OF PARENT SYSTEM
TABLE 7- MANUFACTURING SUBSIDIARIES IN A SYSTEM IN THE
SOAP AND COSMETICS INDUSTRY (SIC 284)
CLASSIFIED BY COUNTRY, PERIOD MANUFACTURE BEGAN, AND SYSTEM OWNERSHIP %

PERIOD AND OWNERSHIP PERCENTAGE
(WHL=95-100%, MAJ=50-94%, MIN=5-49%, UNK=UNKNOWN)

COUNTRY OR REGION	TOTAL PRE 1968					PRE 1946					1946-1957					1958-1967				
	ALL	WHL	MAJ	MIN	UNK	ALL	WHL	MAJ	MIN	UNK	ALL	WHL	MAJ	MIN	UNK	ALL	WHL	MAJ	MIN	UNK
OUTSIDE U.S.	129	109	7	2	9	22	20	2	0	0	23	20	1	0	2	82	69	4	2	7
OUT. U.S. + CANADA	112	95	7	2	6	17	15	2	0	0	19	17	1	0	0	74	63	4	2	5
OUT. WEST. HEMIS.	82	71	4	2	3	10	9	1	0	0	10	10	0	0	0	60	52	3	2	3
OUT. WHITE CWEALTH	91	75	7	2	6	12	10	2	0	0	15	13	1	0	0	63	52	4	2	5
OUT. DEVLPED WORLD	56	48	4	1	3	8	7	1	0	0	11	9	1	0	1	37	32	2	1	2
CANADA	17	14	0	0	3	5	5	0	0	0	4	3	0	0	1	8	6	0	0	2
LATIN AMERICA	30	24	3	0	3	7	6	1	0	0	9	7	1	0	1	14	11	1	0	2
C. AMER.+CARIB.	16	10	3	2	1	4	3	1	0	0	5	3	1	1	0	7	4	1	1	1
CUBA	5	2	2	0	1	2	1	1	0	0	3	1	1	0	1	0	0	0	0	0
MEXICO	7	5	1	0	1	2	2	0	0	0	2	2	0	0	0	3	3	0	0	0
OTHER	4	3	0	0	1	0	0	0	0	0	0	0	0	0	0	4	3	0	1	0
S. AMERICA	14	14	0	0	0	3	3	0	0	0	4	4	0	0	0	7	7	0	0	0
ARGENTINA	5	5	0	0	0	2	2	0	0	0	0	0	0	0	0	3	3	0	0	0
BRAZIL	2	2	0	0	0	1	1	0	0	0	0	0	0	0	0	1	1	0	0	0
PERU	3	3	0	0	0	0	0	0	0	0	2	2	0	0	0	1	1	0	0	0
COLUMBIA	0	0	0	0	0	0	0	0	0	0	0	0	0	0	0	0	0	0	0	0
VENEZUELA	3	3	0	0	0	0	0	0	0	0	2	2	0	0	0	1	1	0	0	0
OTHER	1	1	0	0	0	0	0	0	0	0	0	0	0	0	0	1	1	0	0	0
EUROPE	44	36	3	1	3	8	7	0	0	1	7	7	0	0	0	28	22	2	0	3
EFTA	16	16	0	0	0	4	4	0	0	0	3	3	0	0	0	9	9	0	0	0
U.K.	10	10	0	0	0	4	4	0	0	0	3	3	0	0	0	3	3	0	0	0
SCANDINAVIA	4	4	0	0	0	0	0	0	0	0	0	0	0	0	0	4	4	0	0	0
SWITZERLAND	0	0	0	0	0	0	0	0	0	0	0	0	0	0	0	0	0	0	0	0
OTHER EFTA	2	2	0	0	0	0	0	0	0	0	0	0	0	0	0	2	2	0	0	0
EUROP. COMMUNITY	22	15	3	1	2	4	3	0	0	1	4	4	0	0	0	13	8	2	1	2
FRANCE	9	6	1	1	1	1	1	0	0	0	2	2	0	0	0	6	3	1	1	1
GERMANY	4	2	1	1	0	1	0	1	0	0	0	0	0	0	0	2	2	0	0	0
ITALY	6	4	1	0	1	1	1	0	0	0	1	1	0	0	0	4	2	1	0	1
BELGIUM + LUX	3	3	0	0	0	1	1	0	0	0	1	1	0	0	0	1	1	0	0	0
NETHERLANDS	0	0	0	0	0	0	0	0	0	0	0	0	0	0	0	0	0	0	0	0
SPAIN	2	1	0	0	1	0	0	0	0	0	0	0	0	0	0	2	1	0	0	1
GREECE + TURKEY	2	2	0	0	0	0	0	0	0	0	0	0	0	0	0	2	2	0	0	0
OTHER EUROPE	2	2	0	0	0	0	0	0	0	0	0	0	0	0	0	2	2	0	0	0
EUROPE EX. U.K.	34	26	3	1	3	4	3	0	0	1	4	4	0	0	0	25	19	2	0	3
SOUTHERN DOMINIONS	9	8	0	0	0	1	1	0	0	0	1	1	0	0	0	6	6	0	0	0
S. AFRICA +RHOD.	4	4	0	0	0	0	0	0	0	0	0	0	0	0	0	4	4	0	0	0
AUSTRALIA + N.Z.	5	4	0	0	1	1	1	0	0	0	1	1	0	0	0	2	2	0	0	0
ASIA + OTHER AFRICA	29	27	0	1	0	1	1	0	0	0	2	2	0	0	0	26	24	1	1	0
JAPAN	3	3	0	0	0	0	0	0	0	0	0	0	0	0	0	3	3	0	0	0
OTHER ASIA+AFR.	26	24	0	1	0	1	1	0	0	0	2	2	0	0	0	23	21	1	1	0
BLACK AFRICA	4	4	0	0	0	0	0	0	0	0	0	0	0	0	0	4	4	0	0	0
ARAB WORLD	3	3	0	0	0	0	0	0	0	0	1	1	0	0	0	2	2	0	0	0
INDIA	2	1	1	0	0	0	0	0	0	0	0	0	0	0	0	2	1	1	0	0
PHILIPPINES	2	2	0	0	0	1	1	0	0	0	1	1	0	0	0	0	0	0	0	0
OTHER E. ASIA	6	6	0	0	0	0	0	0	0	0	0	0	0	0	0	6	6	0	0	0
OTHER ASIA	9	8	0	0	1	0	0	0	0	0	0	0	0	0	0	9	8	0	0	1

CHAPTER 5- PATTERNS OF OWNERSHIP

SECTION 2- THE FLOW OF MANUFACTURING BY INDUSTRY OF PARENT SYSTEM

TABLE 8- MANUFACTURING SUBSIDIARIES IN A SYSTEM IN THE

PETROLEUM INDUSTRY (SIC 291)

CLASSIFIED BY COUNTRY, PERIOD MANUFACTURE BEGAN, AND SYSTEM OWNERSHIP %

PERIOD AND OWNERSHIP PERCENTAGE

(WHL=95-100%, MAJ=50-94%, MIN=5-49%, UNK=UNKNOWN)

COUNTRY OR REGION	TOTAL PRE 1968					PRE 1946					1946-1957					1958-1967				
	ALL	WHL	MAJ	MIN	UNK	ALL	WHL	MAJ	MIN	UNK	ALL	WHL	MAJ	MIN	UNK	ALL	WHL	MAJ	MIN	UNK
OUTSIDE U.S.	367	151	105	59	42	87	51	16	9	11	51	28	16	2	5	219	72	73	48	26
OUT. U.S. + CANADA	336	134	101	56	38	74	41	15	9	9	48	26	15	2	5	207	67	71	45	24
OUT. WEST. HEMIS.	257	101	85	43	21	52	26	13	7	6	37	19	13	2	3	161	56	59	34	12
OUT. WHITE CWEALTH	276	105	81	52	33	63	36	13	7	7	38	20	13	1	4	170	49	55	44	22
OUT. DEVLPED WORLD	124	47	29	26	20	28	19	4	2	3	14	8	2	0	4	80	20	23	24	13
CANADA	31	17	4	3	4	13	10	1	0	2	3	2	1	0	0	12	5	2	3	2
LATIN AMERICA	79	33	16	13	17	22	15	2	2	3	11	7	2	2	0	46	11	12	11	12
C. AMER.+CARIB.	32	18	8	6	0	14	10	1	2	0	2	2	0	0	0	16	6	6	6	0
CUBA	4	3	1	0	0	3	2	1	0	0	0	0	0	0	0	0	0	0	0	0
MEXICO	9	5	3	1	0	3	2	1	0	0	1	1	0	0	0	5	4	2	1	0
OTHER	19	10	4	5	0	7	5	0	2	0	1	1	0	0	0	11	5	4	3	0
S. AMERICA	47	15	8	7	17	8	5	1	0	3	9	5	2	2	0	30	5	6	7	12
ARGENTINA	7	5	2	0	0	4	4	0	0	0	0	0	0	0	0	3	2	0	2	0
BRAZIL	8	3	2	2	1	0	0	0	0	0	1	1	0	0	0	7	2	2	2	1
PERU	2	0	2	0	0	0	0	0	0	0	0	0	0	0	0	2	0	2	0	0
COLOMBIA	8	3	2	0	3	1	0	0	1	0	2	1	0	1	0	5	1	2	0	3
VENEZUELA	18	1	1	3	13	3	1	1	0	1	4	2	2	0	0	11	1	0	3	8
OTHER	4	3	1	0	0	0	0	0	0	0	2	2	0	0	0	2	1	1	0	0
EUROPE	168	73	53	25	16	45	21	11	7	6	25	15	7	2	1	97	37	35	16	9
EFTA	52	27	16	3	6	19	8	7	2	2	6	4	0	1	1	27	15	9	0	3
U.K.	30	15	8	3	4	10	4	2	2	2	4	2	0	1	1	16	9	6	0	1
SCANDINAVIA	16	8	6	0	2	5	2	3	0	0	2	2	0	0	0	9	4	3	0	2
SWITZERLAND	2	2	0	0	0	2	2	0	0	0	0	0	0	0	0	2	2	0	0	0
OTHER EFTA	4	2	2	0	0	2	0	2	0	0	0	0	0	0	0	0	0	0	0	0
EUROP. COMMUNITY	89	39	29	14	6	17	9	3	3	2	16	8	7	1	0	55	22	19	10	4
FRANCE	19	9	3	6	1	6	3	0	3	0	5	4	1	0	0	8	5	3	0	0
GERMANY	28	13	10	2	3	6	2	3	0	1	5	1	1	0	0	17	8	6	3	2
ITALY	23	10	11	1	1	4	1	4	0	0	5	1	3	0	0	14	6	8	0	1
BELGIUM + LUX	11	4	2	4	1	1	0	1	0	0	1	0	1	0	0	9	4	1	3	1
NETHERLANDS	8	4	3	0	0	0	0	0	0	0	1	2	1	0	0	7	4	2	1	0
SPAIN	16	2	5	6	3	3	0	0	1	2	2	0	0	0	0	11	5	5	3	1
GREECE + TURKEY	3	0	1	1	1	1	0	0	0	0	0	0	0	1	0	2	0	0	0	1
OTHER EUROPE	8	5	2	0	0	5	4	1	0	0	1	1	0	0	0	2	2	0	0	0
EUROPE EX. U.K.	138	58	45	22	12	35	17	9	5	4	21	13	7	1	1	81	28	29	16	8
SOUTHERN DOMINIONS	27	13	10	1	1	1	1	0	0	0	5	3	2	0	0	19	9	8	1	1
S. AFRICA +RHOD.	4	1	1	1	0	0	1	0	0	0	0	0	0	0	0	3	1	1	0	1
AUSTRALIA + N.Z.	23	12	9	0	1	1	0	0	0	0	5	3	2	0	0	16	8	7	1	1
ASIA + OTHER AFRICA	62	15	22	17	4	6	4	2	0	2	7	1	4	2	2	45	10	16	17	2
JAPAN	17	9	1	4	1	6	4	0	2	0	4	1	0	0	0	11	5	1	4	1
OTHER ASIA+AFR.	45	14	13	13	3	0	0	0	0	0	3	0	0	2	2	34	9	15	13	1
BLACK AFRICA	12	3	4	2	0	0	0	0	0	0	0	0	0	0	0	4	1	3	1	0
ARAB WORLD	9	0	4	3	1	0	0	0	0	0	0	0	0	1	0	9	3	3	2	0
INDIA	6	0	2	4	0	0	0	0	0	0	1	0	0	0	1	6	1	2	4	0
PHILIPPINES	5	3	2	0	1	1	1	0	0	0	0	0	0	0	0	3	2	0	0	1
OTHER E. ASIA	5	1	1	2	1	0	0	0	0	0	1	0	0	0	1	5	1	2	2	0
OTHER ASIA	13	6	4	1	1	4	3	1	0	0	1	0	0	0	1	7	3	3	1	0

CHAPTER 5- PATTERNS OF OWNERSHIP
SECTION 2- THE FLOW OF MANUFACTURING BY INDUSTRY OF PARENT SYSTEM
TABLE 9- MANUFACTURING SUBSIDIARIES IN A SYSTEM IN THE
RUBBER AND TIRE INDUSTRY (SIC 30)
CLASSIFIED BY COUNTRY, PERIOD MANUFACTURE BEGAN, AND SYSTEM OWNERSHIP %

PERIOD AND OWNERSHIP PERCENTAGE
(WHL=95-100%, MAJ=50-94%, MIN=5-49%, UNK=UNKNOWN)

COUNTRY OR REGION	TOTAL PRE 1968					PRE 1946					1946-1957					1958-1967				
	ALL	WHL	MAJ	MIN	UNK	ALL	WHL	MAJ	MIN	UNK	ALL	WHL	MAJ	MIN	UNK	ALL	WHL	MAJ	MIN	UNK
OUTSIDE U.S.	163	71	29	28	34	58	33	2	11	12	37	17	5	10	5	67	21	22	7	17
OUT. U.S. + CANADA	145	60	26	28	30	48	26	1	11	10	34	14	5	10	5	62	20	20	7	15
OUT. WEST. HEMIS.	100	39	22	16	22	29	15	1	4	9	18	6	2	7	3	52	18	19	5	10
OUT. WHITE CWEALTH	120	51	20	23	26	37	19	1	9	8	31	14	4	8	5	52	18	15	6	13
OUT. DEVLPED WORLD	71	32	10	14	15	28	16	0	7	5	18	9	4	3	2	25	7	6	4	8
CANADA	18	11	3	0	4	10	7	1	0	2	3	3	0	0	0	5	1	2	0	2
LATIN AMERICA	45	21	4	12	8	19	11	0	7	1	16	8	3	3	2	10	2	1	2	5
C. AMER.+CARIB.	18	6	2	5	5	8	3	0	4	1	6	3	1	1	1	4	0	1	0	3
CUBA	4	3	0	1	0	2	1	0	1	0	2	1	0	1	0	0	0	0	0	0
MEXICO	10	3	1	3	3	6	2	0	3	1	3	1	1	0	1	1	0	0	0	1
OTHER	4	0	1	1	2	0	0	0	0	0	1	0	0	1	0	3	0	1	0	2
S. AMERICA	27	15	2	7	3	11	8	0	3	0	10	5	2	2	1	6	2	0	2	2
ARGENTINA	6	3	1	2	0	2	2	0	0	0	3	3	0	0	0	1	1	0	0	0
BRAZIL	6	1	0	2	3	2	2	0	0	0	3	1	0	1	0	1	0	0	0	0
PERU	2	1	0	0	1	2	2	0	0	0	1	1	0	0	0	1	1	0	0	0
COLOMBIA	4	1	0	2	1	3	1	0	2	0	0	0	0	0	0	1	0	0	0	1
VENEZUELA	7	3	0	1	1	1	1	0	0	0	3	0	2	1	0	2	1	0	0	1
OTHER	2	1	0	1	0	1	1	0	0	0	0	0	0	0	0	1	0	0	1	0
EUROPE	56	22	13	8	13	14	6	1	2	5	14	5	1	6	2	28	11	11	1	6
EFTA	22	8	4	2	8	10	5	0	1	4	3	0	1	1	1	9	3	3	0	3
U.K.	12	3	3	2	4	6	3	0	1	2	1	0	0	1	0	4	0	2	0	2
SCANDINAVIA	3	1	0	0	1	1	1	0	0	0	0	0	0	0	0	2	0	1	0	1
SWITZERLAND	3	2	1	0	1	1	0	0	0	1	1	0	1	0	0	2	1	0	0	0
OTHER EFTA	4	2	0	0	2	2	1	0	0	1	1	0	0	0	1	1	1	0	0	0
EUROP. COMMUNITY	26	13	5	4	4	2	1	0	1	0	9	5	0	3	1	15	7	5	0	3
FRANCE	6	4	0	0	2	1	1	0	0	0	1	0	0	0	1	3	3	0	0	0
GERMANY	7	2	0	3	2	0	0	0	0	0	3	1	0	2	0	5	1	3	0	1
ITALY	6	2	4	0	0	0	0	0	0	0	1	1	0	0	0	5	0	5	0	0
BELGIUM + LUX	3	2	0	0	0	0	0	0	0	0	1	1	0	0	0	2	2	0	0	0
NETHERLANDS	4	3	1	0	0	1	1	0	0	0	1	1	0	0	0	2	1	0	1	0
SPAIN	4	0	1	2	1	0	0	0	0	0	3	2	0	1	0	1	0	1	0	0
GREECE + TURKEY	3	1	2	0	0	0	0	0	0	0	0	0	0	0	0	2	1	0	0	1
OTHER EUROPE	1	0	2	0	1	1	1	0	0	0	0	0	0	0	0	0	0	0	0	0
EUROPE EX. U.K.	44	19	10	6	9	8	3	1	1	3	12	5	1	5	2	24	11	9	1	4
SOUTHERN DOMINIONS	13	6	3	3	0	5	4	0	0	1	3	1	0	2	0	6	2	3	1	0
S. AFRICA +RHOD.	5	3	3	1	0	2	2	0	0	0	1	0	0	1	0	1	1	0	0	0
AUSTRALIA + N.Z.	8	3	3	2	0	3	2	0	0	1	2	1	0	1	0	5	1	3	1	0
ASIA + OTHER AFRICA	31	11	6	5	9	10	5	0	2	3	3	1	0	1	0	18	5	5	4	4
JAPAN	5	0	0	3	2	2	0	0	2	0	0	0	0	0	0	3	0	0	2	1
OTHER ASIA+AFR.	26	11	6	2	7	9	5	0	0	4	2	1	0	0	1	15	5	5	2	3
BLACK AFRICA	3	2	1	0	0	0	0	0	0	0	1	0	1	0	0	3	2	1	0	0
ARAB WORLD	2	0	1	0	1	0	0	0	0	0	0	0	0	0	0	2	0	1	0	1
INDIA	4	2	0	1	1	1	1	0	0	0	2	0	0	1	1	3	1	0	0	0
PHILIPPINES	3	2	0	0	1	2	0	0	1	0	0	0	0	0	0	0	0	0	0	0
OTHER E. ASIA	0	0	0	0	0	0	0	0	0	0	0	0	0	0	0	0	0	0	0	0
OTHER ASIA	14	5	4	1	4	6	3	0	0	3	1	0	0	0	1	7	2	3	1	1

CHAPTER 5- PATTERNS OF OWNERSHIP
SECTION 2- THE FLOW OF MANUFACTURING BY INDUSTRY OF PARENT SYSTEM
TABLE 10- MANUFACTURING SUBSIDIARIES IN A SYSTEM IN THE
STONE, CLAY, AND GLASS INDUSTRY (SIC 32)
CLASSIFIED BY COUNTRY, PERIOD MANUFACTURE BEGAN, AND SYSTEM OWNERSHIP %

PERIOD AND OWNERSHIP PERCENTAGE
(WHL=95-100%, MAJ=50-94%, MIN=5-49%, UNK=UNKNOWN)

COUNTRY OR REGION	TOTAL PRE 1968					PRE 1946					1946-1957					1958-1967				
	ALL	WHL	MAJ	MIN	UNK	ALL	WHL	MAJ	MIN	UNK	ALL	WHL	MAJ	MIN	UNK	ALL	WHL	MAJ	MIN	UNK
OUTSIDE U.S.	175	72	43	50	6	29	15	6	8	0	37	13	6	16	2	105	44	31	26	4
OUT. U.S. + CANADA	157	59	40	50	5	22	10	4	8	0	31	9	5	16	1	101	40	31	26	4
OUT. WEST. HEMIS.	108	44	28	31	3	14	6	4	4	0	12	3	1	7	1	80	35	23	20	2
OUT. WHITE CWEALTH	119	39	33	40	4	17	6	4	7	0	25	8	4	13	0	74	25	25	20	4
OUT. DEVLPED WORLD	54	16	12	22	2	8	4	0	4	0	20	6	4	10	0	24	6	8	8	2
CANADA	18	13	3	0	1	7	5	2	0	0	6	4	1	0	1	4	4	0	0	0
LATIN AMERICA	49	15	12	19	2	8	4	0	4	0	19	6	4	9	0	21	5	8	6	2
C. AMER.+CARIB.	14	5	4	5	0	1	0	0	1	0	6	4	0	2	0	7	1	4	2	0
CUBA	1	1	0	0	0	0	0	0	0	0	1	1	0	0	0	0	0	0	0	0
MEXICO	13	4	4	5	0	1	0	0	1	0	5	3	0	2	0	7	1	4	0	2
OTHER	0	0	0	0	0	0	0	0	0	0	0	0	0	0	0	0	0	0	0	0
S. AMERICA	35	10	8	14	2	7	4	0	3	0	13	2	4	7	0	14	4	4	4	2
ARGENTINA	6	1	3	2	1	1	1	0	0	0	2	0	1	1	0	2	0	2	0	1
BRAZIL	13	4	3	5	1	4	2	0	2	0	5	1	3	1	0	4	0	0	2	1
PERU	1	0	0	1	0	0	0	0	0	0	1	0	0	1	0	0	0	0	0	0
COLOMBIA	6	3	2	1	0	0	0	0	0	0	1	1	0	0	0	5	2	2	1	0
VENEZUELA	6	1	2	3	0	0	0	0	0	0	3	0	0	2	0	3	0	2	1	0
OTHER	3	1	0	2	0	2	1	0	1	0	1	0	0	1	0	0	0	0	0	0
EUROPE	78	37	21	16	3	12	5	4	3	0	8	2	0	5	1	57	30	17	8	2
EFTA	26	16	4	6	0	4	3	1	0	0	3	0	0	3	0	19	13	3	3	0
U.K.	23	15	3	5	0	3	3	0	0	0	3	0	0	3	0	17	12	3	2	0
SCANDINAVIA	3	0	1	0	2	1	0	1	0	0	0	0	0	0	0	2	0	0	1	1
SWITZERLAND	0	0	0	0	0	0	0	0	0	0	0	0	0	0	0	0	0	0	0	0
OTHER EFTA	0	0	0	0	0	0	0	0	0	0	0	0	0	0	0	0	0	0	0	0
EUROP. COMMUNITY	45	20	14	8	2	8	2	3	3	0	4	2	0	2	0	32	16	11	3	1
FRANCE	15	7	3	4	1	2	0	2	0	0	2	1	0	1	0	10	6	3	1	0
GERMANY	10	3	6	0	1	2	1	1	0	0	1	0	0	1	0	6	3	2	1	0
ITALY	9	4	1	4	0	3	1	0	2	0	0	0	0	0	0	5	3	1	0	0
BELGIUM + LUX	2	1	1	0	0	0	0	0	0	0	0	0	0	0	0	2	1	1	0	0
NETHERLANDS	4	0	3	1	0	0	0	0	0	0	1	0	0	1	0	3	1	0	2	0
SPAIN	4	0	0	4	0	0	0	0	0	0	0	0	0	0	0	4	2	0	2	0
GREECE + TURKEY	0	0	0	0	0	0	0	0	0	0	0	0	0	0	0	0	0	0	0	0
OTHER EUROPE	3	1	0	1	1	0	0	0	0	0	0	0	0	0	0	2	1	0	1	0
EUROPE EX. U.K.	55	22	18	11	3	9	2	4	3	0	5	2	0	2	1	40	18	14	6	2
SOUTHERN DOMINIONS	13	4	4	5	0	2	1	0	1	0	2	1	1	0	0	9	2	3	4	0
S. AFRICA +RHOD.	6	2	2	2	0	0	0	0	0	0	2	1	1	0	0	4	1	1	2	0
AUSTRALIA + N.Z.	7	2	2	3	0	2	1	0	1	0	0	0	0	0	0	5	1	2	2	0
ASIA + OTHER AFRICA	17	3	3	10	2	0	0	0	0	0	2	0	0	2	0	14	3	3	8	0
JAPAN	12	2	3	7	1	0	0	0	0	0	1	1	0	0	0	11	2	3	6	0
OTHER ASIA+AFR.	5	1	0	3	1	0	0	0	0	0	1	0	0	1	0	3	1	0	2	0
BLACK AFRICA	1	0	0	1	0	0	0	0	0	0	0	0	0	0	0	1	0	0	1	0
ARAB WORLD	0	0	0	0	0	0	0	0	0	0	0	0	0	0	0	0	0	0	0	0
INDIA	0	0	0	2	0	0	0	0	0	0	0	0	0	0	0	0	0	0	1	0
PHILIPPINES	1	0	0	1	0	0	0	0	0	0	1	0	0	1	0	0	0	0	0	0
OTHER E. ASIA	0	0	0	0	0	0	0	0	0	0	0	0	0	0	0	1	0	0	0	0
OTHER ASIA	0	0	0	0	0	0	0	0	0	0	0	0	0	0	0	0	0	0	0	0

CHAPTER 5- PATTERNS OF OWNERSHIP
SECTION 2- THE FLOW OF MANUFACTURING BY INDUSTRY OF PARENT SYSTEM
TABLE 11- MANUFACTURING SUBSIDIARIES IN A SYSTEM IN THE
PRIMARY METAL INDUSTRY (SIC 33)
CLASSIFIED BY COUNTRY, PERIOD MANUFACTURE BEGAN, AND SYSTEM OWNERSHIP %

PERIOD AND OWNERSHIP PERCENTAGE
(WHL=95-100%, MAJ=50-94%, MIN=5-49%, UNK=UNKNOWN)

COUNTRY OR REGION	TOTAL PRE 1968					PRE 1946					1946-1957					1958-1967				
	ALL	WHL	MAJ	MIN	UNK	ALL	WHL	MAJ	MIN	UNK	ALL	WHL	MAJ	MIN	UNK	ALL	WHL	MAJ	MIN	UNK
OUTSIDE U.S.	176	82	58	33	3	24	16	7	1	0	29	13	11	5	0	123	53	40	27	3
OUT. U.S. + CANADA	148	65	50	30	3	17	11	6	0	0	23	9	9	5	0	108	45	35	25	3
OUT. WEST. HEMIS.	96	45	35	15	1	8	4	4	0	0	10	3	7	0	0	78	38	24	15	1
OUT. WHITE CWEALTH	106	41	36	27	2	11	8	3	0	0	20	7	8	5	0	75	26	25	22	2
OUT. DEVLPED WORLD	65	22	21	20	2	9	7	2	0	0	17	6	6	5	0	39	9	13	15	2
CANADA	28	17	8	3	0	7	5	1	1	0	6	4	2	0	0	15	8	5	2	0
LATIN AMERICA	52	20	15	15	2	9	8	1	0	0	13	3	4	4	2	30	9	10	11	0
C. AMER.+CARIB.	23	10	7	6	0	5	4	1	0	0	5	2	2	1	0	13	4	4	5	0
CUBA	3	1	1	1	0	1	1	0	0	0	2	0	1	1	0	0	0	0	0	0
MEXICO	17	8	4	5	0	4	3	1	0	0	3	2	1	0	0	10	3	2	5	0
OTHER	3	1	2	0	0	0	0	0	0	0	0	0	0	0	0	3	1	2	0	0
S. AMERICA	29	10	8	9	2	4	4	0	0	0	8	1	2	3	2	17	5	6	6	0
ARGENTINA	2	2	0	0	0	1	1	0	0	0	0	0	0	0	0	1	1	0	0	0
BRAZIL	3	1	1	1	0	1	1	0	0	0	0	0	0	0	0	2	0	1	1	0
PERU	3	1	0	2	0	1	1	0	0	0	2	0	0	2	0	0	0	0	0	0
COLOMBIA	9	3	2	2	2	0	0	0	0	0	4	1	0	1	2	5	2	2	1	0
VENEZUELA	8	2	3	3	0	1	1	0	0	0	1	0	1	0	0	6	1	2	3	0
OTHER	4	1	2	1	0	0	0	0	0	0	1	0	1	0	0	3	1	1	1	0
EUROPE	66	37	22	6	1	4	2	2	0	0	7	2	3	2	0	55	33	17	4	1
EFTA	35	22	10	2	1	4	2	2	0	0	2	1	1	0	0	29	19	7	2	1
U.K.	29	18	8	2	1	4	2	2	0	0	2	1	1	0	0	23	15	5	2	1
SCANDINAVIA	4	2	2	0	0	0	0	0	0	0	0	0	0	0	0	4	2	2	0	0
SWITZERLAND	2	2	0	0	0	0	0	0	0	0	0	0	0	0	0	2	2	0	0	0
OTHER EFTA	0	0	0	0	0	0	0	0	0	0	0	0	0	0	0	0	0	0	0	0
EUROP. COMMUNITY	26	14	8	4	0	0	0	0	0	0	5	1	2	2	0	21	13	6	2	0
FRANCE	4	2	2	0	0	0	0	0	0	0	1	0	1	0	0	3	2	1	0	0
GERMANY	7	3	2	2	0	0	0	0	0	0	1	0	0	1	0	6	3	2	1	0
ITALY	7	4	2	1	0	0	0	0	0	0	2	1	1	0	0	5	3	1	1	0
BELGIUM + LUX	5	3	1	1	0	0	0	0	0	0	1	0	0	1	0	4	3	1	0	0
NETHERLANDS	3	2	1	0	0	0	0	0	0	0	0	0	0	0	0	3	2	1	0	0
SPAIN	3	1	2	0	0	0	0	0	0	0	0	0	0	0	0	3	1	2	0	0
GREECE + TURKEY	2	0	2	0	0	0	0	0	0	0	0	0	0	0	0	2	0	2	0	0
OTHER EUROPE	0	0	0	0	0	0	0	0	0	0	0	0	0	0	0	0	0	0	0	0
EUROPE EX. U.K.	37	19	14	4	0	0	0	0	0	0	5	1	2	2	0	32	18	12	2	0
SOUTHERN DOMINIONS	13	6	6	1	0	2	2	0	0	0	1	0	1	0	0	10	4	5	1	0
S. AFRICA +RHOD.	1	1	0	0	0	1	1	0	0	0	0	0	0	0	0	0	0	0	0	0
AUSTRALIA + N.Z.	12	5	6	1	0	1	1	0	0	0	1	0	1	0	0	10	4	5	1	0
ASIA + OTHER AFRICA	17	2	7	8	0	2	0	1	1	0	2	0	0	2	0	13	2	6	5	0
JAPAN	4	0	2	2	0	2	0	1	1	0	0	0	0	0	0	2	0	1	1	0
OTHER ASIA+AFR.	13	2	5	6	0	0	0	0	0	0	2	0	0	2	0	11	2	5	4	0
BLACK AFRICA	1	0	0	1	0	0	0	0	0	0	0	0	0	0	0	1	0	0	1	0
ARAB WORLD	4	0	1	3	0	0	0	0	0	0	1	0	0	1	0	3	0	1	2	0
INDIA	4	2	1	1	0	0	0	0	0	0	1	0	0	1	0	3	2	1	0	0
PHILIPPINES	2	0	2	0	0	0	0	0	0	0	0	0	0	0	0	2	0	2	0	0
OTHER E. ASIA	0	0	0	0	0	0	0	0	0	0	0	0	0	0	0	0	0	0	0	0
OTHER ASIA	2	0	1	1	0	0	0	0	0	0	0	0	0	0	0	2	0	1	1	0

CHAPTER 5- PATTERNS OF OWNERSHIP
SECTION 2- THE FLOW OF MANUFACTURING BY INDUSTRY OF PARENT SYSTEM
TABLE 12- MANUFACTURING SUBSIDIARIES IN A SYSTEM IN THE
FABRICATED METAL INDUSTRY (SIC 34)
CLASSIFIED BY COUNTRY, PERIOD MANUFACTURE BEGAN, AND SYSTEM OWNERSHIP %

PERIOD AND OWNERSHIP PERCENTAGE
(WHL=95-100%, MAJ=50-94%, MIN=5-49%, UNK=UNKNOWN)

COUNTRY OR REGION	TOTAL PRE 1968					PRE 1946					1946-1957					1958-1967				
	ALL	WHL	MAJ	MIN	UNK	ALL	WHL	MAJ	MIN	UNK	ALL	WHL	MAJ	MIN	UNK	ALL	WHL	MAJ	MIN	UNK
OUTSIDE U.S.	268	137	57	43	31	56	29	12	6	9	65	35	17	11	2	147	73	28	26	20
OUT. U.S. + CANADA	223	101	52	43	27	39	16	10	6	7	46	19	14	11	2	138	66	28	26	18
OUT. WEST. HEMIS.	164	76	35	30	23	34	14	10	4	6	25	11	5	7	2	105	51	20	19	15
OUT. WHITE CWEALTH	175	70	46	37	22	26	7	8	5	6	39	15	13	9	2	110	48	25	23	14
OUT. DEVLPED WORLD	73	30	22	17	4	5	2	0	2	1	27	9	13	5	0	41	19	9	10	3
CANADA	45	36	5	0	4	17	13	2	0	2	19	16	3	0	0	9	7	0	0	2
LATIN AMERICA	59	25	17	13	4	5	2	0	2	1	21	7	9	4	0	33	15	8	7	3
C. AMER.+CARIB.	21	5	9	5	2	2	1	0	1	0	7	2	5	0	0	12	2	4	4	2
CUBA	1	1	0	0	0	1	1	0	0	0	0	0	0	0	0	0	0	0	0	0
MEXICO	18	4	7	5	2	0	0	0	1	0	7	2	5	0	0	10	2	2	0	2
OTHER	2	0	2	0	0	0	0	0	0	0	0	0	0	0	0	2	0	2	0	0
S. AMERICA	38	20	8	8	2	3	0	0	1	1	14	6	4	4	0	21	13	4	3	1
ARGENTINA	4	2	0	2	0	0	0	0	0	0	3	1	0	2	0	4	3	0	0	0
BRAZIL	12	6	3	1	2	3	1	0	1	1	4	2	1	1	0	5	3	2	0	1
PERU	3	1	1	1	0	0	0	0	0	0	1	1	0	0	0	3	0	1	1	0
COLOMBIA	5	4	0	1	0	0	0	0	0	0	2	1	1	0	1	4	3	0	0	0
VENEZUELA	8	3	3	2	0	0	0	0	0	0	2	0	1	1	0	6	3	2	1	0
OTHER	6	4	1	1	0	0	0	0	0	0	1	1	0	0	0	5	3	0	1	0
EUROPE	126	60	26	21	21	30	12	9	3	6	16	9	0	5	2	82	39	17	13	13
EFTA	41	29	4	4	4	12	8	2	0	2	7	6	0	1	0	22	15	2	0	5
U.K.	28	21	2	1	4	9	7	1	0	1	4	3	0	0	1	15	11	1	0	3
SCANDINAVIA	6	4	0	1	1	1	0	1	0	0	2	2	0	0	0	4	2	0	1	1
SWITZERLAND	4	3	1	0	0	2	1	0	0	1	1	0	0	2	0	2	1	0	0	0
OTHER EFTA	3	1	1	0	1	0	0	0	0	0	1	1	0	0	0	1	0	0	0	1
EUROP. COMMUNITY	69	27	18	10	14	18	4	7	3	4	7	3	0	2	2	44	20	11	5	8
FRANCE	18	7	5	4	2	6	2	2	1	1	1	1	0	0	0	11	4	3	3	1
GERMANY	21	10	5	1	5	5	1	2	0	2	2	1	0	0	1	14	8	3	0	2
ITALY	13	7	3	1	2	5	1	2	0	2	2	1	0	0	0	11	6	3	0	2
BELGIUM + LUX	6	0	1	2	2	1	1	0	0	1	1	0	0	1	0	2	0	0	1	1
NETHERLANDS	11	3	4	2	2	3	0	0	1	1	1	0	0	0	1	6	2	2	2	0
SPAIN	9	1	1	5	0	0	0	0	0	0	1	0	0	1	0	8	3	0	4	0
GREECE + TURKEY	8	0	3	0	0	0	0	0	0	0	1	0	0	1	0	7	1	3	3	0
OTHER EUROPE	1	0	0	1	0	0	0	0	0	0	0	0	0	0	0	1	0	0	1	0
EUROPE EX. U.K.	100	39	24	20	17	21	5	8	3	5	12	6	0	4	2	67	28	16	13	10
SOUTHERN DOMINIONS	19	10	4	4	1	4	2	1	1	0	3	1	1	1	0	12	7	2	2	1
S. AFRICA +RHOD.	8	2	3	3	0	2	2	1	0	0	2	0	0	1	0	4	2	1	1	0
AUSTRALIA + N.Z.	11	8	1	1	1	2	2	0	0	0	1	1	0	0	0	8	5	1	1	1
ASIA + OTHER AFRICA	17	6	5	5	1	0	0	0	0	0	6	1	4	1	1	11	5	1	4	1
JAPAN	3	1	0	1	1	0	0	0	0	0	0	0	0	0	0	3	1	0	1	1
OTHER ASIA+AFR.	14	5	5	4	0	0	0	0	0	0	6	1	4	1	0	8	4	1	3	1
BLACK AFRICA	4	2	1	1	0	0	0	0	0	0	1	1	1	0	0	3	2	0	1	0
ARAB WORLD	2	1	1	0	0	0	0	0	0	0	2	0	1	1	0	0	0	0	0	0
INDIA	0	0	0	0	0	0	0	0	0	0	0	0	0	0	0	0	0	0	0	0
PHILIPPINES	3	0	1	2	0	0	0	0	0	0	1	0	0	1	0	2	0	0	2	0
OTHER E. ASIA	0	0	0	0	0	0	0	0	0	0	0	0	0	0	0	0	0	0	0	0
OTHER ASIA	5	2	2	0	0	0	0	0	0	0	2	0	2	0	0	3	2	1	1	0

CHAPTER 5- PATTERNS OF OWNERSHIP
SECTION 2- THE FLOW OF MANUFACTURING BY INDUSTRY OF PARENT SYSTEM
TABLE 13- MANUFACTURING SUBSIDIARIES IN A SYSTEM IN THE
FARM MACHINERY INDUSTRY (SIC 352)
CLASSIFIED BY COUNTRY, PERIOD MANUFACTURE BEGAN, AND SYSTEM OWNERSHIP %

PERIOD AND OWNERSHIP PERCENTAGE
(WHL=95-100%, MAJ=50-94%, MIN=5-49%, UNK=UNKNOWN)

COUNTRY OR REGION	TOTAL PRE 1968					PRE 1946					1946-1957					1958-1967				
	ALL	WHL	MAJ	MIN	UNK	ALL	WHL	MAJ	MIN	UNK	ALL	WHL	MAJ	MIN	UNK	ALL	WHL	MAJ	MIN	UNK
OUTSIDE U.S.	45	25	11	5	4	10	7	1	0	2	13	11	2	0	0	22	7	8	5	2
OUT. U.S. + CANADA	38	18	11	5	4	6	3	1	0	2	11	9	2	0	0	21	6	8	5	2
OUT. WEST. HEMIS.	30	11	11	4	4	6	3	1	0	2	6	4	2	0	0	18	4	8	4	2
OUT. WHITE CWEALTH	27	7	7	5	4	4	1	1	0	2	8	7	1	0	0	15	3	5	5	2
OUT. DEVLPED WORLD	11	8	1	2	0	0	0	0	0	0	6	6	0	0	0	5	2	1	2	0
CANADA	7	7	0	0	0	4	4	0	0	0	2	2	0	0	0	1	1	0	0	0
LATIN AMERICA	8	7	0	1	0	4	4	0	0	0	5	5	0	0	0	3	1	2	1	0
C. AMER.+CARIB.	5	5	0	0	0	0	0	0	0	0	3	3	0	0	0	2	2	0	0	0
CUBA	0	0	0	0	0	0	0	0	0	0	0	0	0	0	0	0	0	1	1	0
MEXICO	4	4	0	0	0	0	0	0	0	0	3	3	0	0	0	1	1	0	0	0
OTHER	1	1	0	0	0	0	0	0	0	0	0	0	0	0	0	1	1	1	1	0
S. AMERICA	3	2	0	1	0	0	0	0	0	0	2	2	0	0	0	1	0	0	0	0
ARGENTINA	2	1	0	1	0	0	0	0	0	0	1	1	0	0	0	1	0	0	1	0
BRAZIL	1	1	0	0	0	0	0	0	0	0	1	1	0	0	0	0	0	0	0	0
PERU	0	0	0	0	0	0	0	0	0	0	0	0	0	0	0	0	0	0	0	0
COLOMBIA	0	0	0	0	0	0	0	0	0	0	0	0	0	0	0	0	0	0	0	0
VENEZUELA	0	0	0	0	0	0	0	0	0	0	0	0	0	0	0	0	0	0	0	0
OTHER	0	0	0	0	0	0	0	0	0	0	0	0	0	0	0	0	0	0	0	0
EUROPE	19	5	7	3	4	4	1	1	0	2	4	4	2	0	0	11	2	4	3	2
EFTA	5	2	3	0	0	1	0	1	0	0	2	2	1	0	0	2	1	1	0	0
U.K.	4	2	2	0	0	0	0	0	0	0	1	1	1	0	0	2	1	1	0	0
SCANDINAVIA	1	0	1	0	0	1	0	1	0	0	1	1	0	0	0	0	0	0	0	0
SWITZERLAND	0	0	0	0	0	0	0	0	0	0	0	0	0	0	0	0	0	0	0	0
OTHER EFTA	0	0	0	0	0	0	0	0	0	0	0	0	0	0	0	0	0	0	0	0
EUROP. COMMUNITY	11	1	4	2	4	3	0	1	0	2	1	1	0	0	0	7	0	3	2	2
FRANCE	8	1	3	1	3	2	0	1	0	1	0	0	0	0	0	6	0	3	2	1
GERMANY	2	0	1	0	1	1	0	0	0	1	1	1	0	0	0	0	0	0	0	0
ITALY	1	0	0	1	0	0	0	0	0	0	0	0	0	0	0	1	0	0	1	0
BELGIUM + LUX	0	0	0	0	0	0	0	0	0	0	0	0	0	0	0	0	0	0	0	0
NETHERLANDS	0	0	0	0	0	0	0	0	0	0	0	0	0	0	0	0	0	0	0	0
SPAIN	2	2	0	1	0	0	0	0	0	0	0	0	1	0	0	1	1	0	1	0
GREECE + TURKEY	0	0	0	0	0	0	0	0	0	0	0	0	0	0	0	0	0	0	0	0
OTHER EUROPE	1	0	0	1	0	0	0	0	0	0	1	1	0	0	0	0	1	0	1	0
EUROPE EX. U.K.	15	3	5	3	4	4	1	1	0	2	2	2	1	0	0	9	1	3	3	2
SOUTHERN DOMINIONS	7	5	2	0	0	2	2	0	0	0	1	1	0	0	0	4	2	2	0	0
S. AFRICA +RHOD.	3	1	1	0	0	2	2	0	0	0	0	0	0	0	0	3	1	2	0	0
AUSTRALIA + N.Z.	4	4	1	1	0	2	2	0	0	0	1	1	0	0	0	1	1	1	1	0
ASIA + OTHER AFRICA	4	1	2	1	0	0	0	0	0	0	1	1	0	0	0	3	0	2	1	0
JAPAN	1	1	0	0	0	0	0	0	0	0	1	1	0	0	0	1	0	1	1	0
OTHER ASIA+AFR.	3	0	1	1	0	0	0	0	0	0	0	0	0	0	0	2	0	1	0	0
BLACK AFRICA	0	1	0	0	0	0	0	0	0	0	1	1	1	0	0	1	0	0	1	0
ARAB WORLD	1	1	0	0	0	0	0	0	0	0	0	0	0	0	0	0	0	0	0	0
INDIA	1	0	1	0	0	0	0	0	0	0	1	1	0	0	0	1	0	1	1	0
PHILIPPINES	1	0	0	1	0	0	0	0	0	0	0	0	0	0	0	1	0	0	0	0
OTHER E. ASIA	0	0	0	0	0	0	0	0	0	0	0	0	0	0	0	0	0	0	0	0
OTHER ASIA	0	0	0	0	0	0	0	0	0	0	0	0	0	0	0	0	0	0	0	0

CHAPTER 5- PATTERNS OF OWNERSHIP
SECTION 2- THE FLOW OF MANUFACTURING BY INDUSTRY OF PARENT SYSTEM
TABLE 14- MANUFACTURING SUBSIDIARIES IN A SYSTEM IN THE
OFFICE AND COMPUTING MACHINE INDUSTRY (SIC 357)
CLASSIFIED BY COUNTRY, PERIOD MANUFACTURE BEGAN, AND SYSTEM OWNERSHIP %

PERIOD AND OWNERSHIP PERCENTAGE
(WHL=95-100%, MAJ=50-99%, MIN=5-49%, UNK=UNKNOWN)

COUNTRY OR REGION	TOTAL PRE 1968					PRE 1946					1946-1957					1958-1967				
	ALL	WHL	MAJ	MIN	UNK	ALL	WHL	MAJ	MIN	UNK	ALL	WHL	MAJ	MIN	UNK	ALL	WHL	MAJ	MIN	UNK
OUTSIDE U.S.	73	54	11	6	2	27	21	4	1	1	18	15	2	1	0	28	18	5	4	1
OUT. U.S. + CANADA	65	46	11	6	2	22	16	4	1	1	17	14	2	1	0	26	16	5	4	1
OUT. WEST. HEMIS.	48	36	7	3	2	20	15	4	0	1	12	11	1	0	0	16	10	2	3	1
OUT. WHITE CWEALTH	54	36	10	6	2	19	14	3	1	1	14	11	2	1	0	21	11	5	4	1
OUT. DEVLPED WORLD	18	11	4	3	0	2	1	0	1	0	5	3	1	1	0	11	7	3	1	0
CANADA	8	8	0	0	0	5	5	0	0	0	1	1	0	0	0	2	2	0	0	0
LATIN AMERICA	17	11	3	2	1	2	2	0	0	0	4	4	0	0	0	11	5	3	2	1
C. AMER.+CARIB.	11	7	2	2	0	1	1	0	0	0	1	1	0	0	0	9	5	2	2	0
CUBA	1	1	0	0	0	1	1	0	0	0	0	0	0	0	0	0	0	0	0	0
MEXICO	6	5	0	1	0	0	0	0	0	0	1	1	0	0	0	5	4	0	1	0
OTHER	4	1	2	1	0	0	0	0	0	0	0	0	0	0	0	4	1	2	1	0
S. AMERICA	6	4	1	0	1	1	1	0	0	0	3	3	0	0	0	2	0	1	0	1
ARGENTINA	1	1	0	0	0	1	1	0	0	0	0	0	0	0	0	0	0	0	0	0
BRAZIL	2	1	0	0	1	0	0	0	0	0	1	1	0	0	0	1	0	0	0	1
PERU	1	1	0	0	0	0	0	0	0	0	1	1	0	0	0	0	0	0	0	0
COLOMBIA	1	1	0	0	0	0	0	0	0	0	1	1	0	0	0	0	0	0	0	0
VENEZUELA	1	0	1	0	0	0	0	0	0	0	0	0	0	0	0	1	0	1	0	0
OTHER	0	0	0	0	0	0	0	0	0	0	0	0	0	0	0	0	0	0	0	0
EUROPE	38	29	6	2	1	19	15	3	0	1	8	7	1	0	0	11	7	2	2	0
EFTA	15	13	1	1	0	7	6	1	0	0	3	3	0	0	0	5	4	0	1	0
U.K.	7	6	1	0	0	3	2	1	0	0	1	1	0	0	0	3	3	0	0	0
SCANDINAVIA	5	4	0	1	0	2	2	0	0	0	1	1	0	0	0	2	1	0	1	0
SWITZERLAND	2	2	0	0	0	1	1	0	0	0	1	1	0	0	0	0	0	0	0	0
OTHER EFTA	1	1	0	0	0	1	1	0	0	0	0	0	0	0	0	0	0	0	0	0
EUROP. COMMUNITY	23	16	5	1	1	12	9	2	0	1	5	4	1	0	0	6	3	2	1	0
FRANCE	6	4	1	1	0	2	1	1	0	0	1	1	0	0	0	3	2	0	1	0
GERMANY	10	6	2	1	1	5	3	1	0	1	4	3	0	1	0	1	0	1	0	0
ITALY	3	2	1	0	0	1	1	0	0	0	1	0	1	0	0	1	1	0	0	0
BELGIUM + LUX	3	2	1	0	0	1	1	0	0	0	1	1	0	0	0	1	0	1	0	0
NETHERLANDS	1	1	0	0	0	1	1	0	0	0	0	0	0	0	0	0	0	0	0	0
SPAIN	0	0	0	0	0	0	0	0	0	0	0	0	0	0	0	0	0	0	0	0
GREECE + TURKEY	0	0	0	0	0	0	0	0	0	0	0	0	0	0	0	0	0	0	0	0
OTHER EUROPE	0	0	0	0	0	0	0	0	0	0	0	0	0	0	0	0	0	0	0	0
EUROPE EX. U.K.	31	23	5	2	1	16	13	2	0	1	7	6	1	0	0	8	4	2	2	0
SOUTHERN DOMINIONS	4	4	0	0	0	0	0	0	0	0	2	2	0	0	0	2	2	0	0	0
S. AFRICA +RHOD.	2	2	0	0	0	0	0	0	0	0	1	1	0	0	0	1	1	0	0	0
AUSTRALIA + N.Z.	2	2	0	0	0	0	0	0	0	0	1	1	0	0	0	1	1	0	0	0
ASIA + OTHER AFRICA	6	3	1	1	1	1	1	0	0	0	2	1	0	0	1	3	1	1	1	0
JAPAN	2	1	0	1	0	0	0	0	0	0	0	0	0	0	0	2	1	0	1	0
OTHER ASIA+AFR.	4	2	1	0	1	1	1	0	0	0	2	1	0	0	1	1	0	1	0	0
BLACK AFRICA	0	0	0	0	0	0	0	0	0	0	0	0	0	0	0	0	0	0	0	0
ARAB WORLD	0	0	0	0	0	0	0	0	0	0	0	0	0	0	0	0	0	0	0	0
INDIA	1	0	1	0	0	0	0	0	0	0	0	0	0	0	0	1	0	1	0	0
PHILIPPINES	1	1	0	0	0	1	1	0	0	0	0	0	0	0	0	0	0	0	0	0
OTHER E. ASIA	1	0	0	0	1	0	0	0	0	0	1	0	0	0	1	0	0	0	0	0
OTHER ASIA	1	1	0	0	0	0	0	0	0	0	1	1	0	0	0	0	0	0	0	0

CHAPTER 5- PATTERNS OF OWNERSHIP
SECTION 2- THE FLOW OF MANUFACTURING BY INDUSTRY OF PARENT SYSTEM
TABLE 15- MANUFACTURING SUBSIDIARIES IN A SYSTEM IN THE
OTHER NON-ELECTRICAL MACHINERY INDUSTRIES (OTHER SIC 35)
CLASSIFIED BY COUNTRY, PERIOD MANUFACTURE BEGAN, AND SYSTEM OWNERSHIP %

PERIOD AND OWNERSHIP PERCENTAGE
(WHL=95-100%, MAJ=50-94%, MIN=5-49%, UNK=UNKNOWN)

COUNTRY OR REGION	TOTAL PRE 1968					PRE 1946					1946-1957					1958-1967				
	ALL	WHL	MAJ	MIN	UNK	ALL	WHL	MAJ	MIN	UNK	ALL	WHL	MAJ	MIN	UNK	ALL	WHL	MAJ	MIN	UNK
OUTSIDE U.S.	271	181	52	19	16	84	62	14	0	8	46	36	6	2	2	138	83	32	17	6
OUT. U.S. + CANADA	216	139	46	17	12	70	50	14	0	6	37	29	5	2	1	107	60	27	15	5
OUT. WEST. HEMIS.	174	116	40	8	9	65	45	14	0	6	27	21	4	1	1	81	50	22	7	2
OUT. WHITE CWEALTH	138	76	37	16	8	41	29	10	0	2	18	11	4	2	1	78	36	23	14	5
OUT. DEVLPED WORLD	49	25	10	10	3	5	5	0	0	0	11	9	1	1	0	32	11	9	9	3
CANADA	55	42	6	2	4	14	12	0	0	2	10	7	1	0	1	31	23	5	2	1
LATIN AMERICA	42	23	6	9	3	5	5	0	0	0	11	8	1	1	0	26	10	5	8	3
C. AMER.+CARIB.	18	9	0	6	2	1	1	0	0	0	4	3	0	1	0	13	5	0	6	2
CUBA	0	0	0	0	0	0	0	0	0	0	0	0	0	0	0	0	0	0	0	0
MEXICO	17	9	0	5	2	1	1	0	0	0	4	3	0	1	0	12	5	0	5	2
OTHER	1	0	0	1	0	0	0	0	0	0	0	0	0	0	0	1	0	0	1	0
S. AMERICA	24	14	5	3	1	4	4	0	0	0	6	5	1	1	0	13	5	5	2	1
ARGENTINA	6	3	2	0	1	0	0	0	0	0	1	1	0	0	0	4	2	2	0	0
BRAZIL	9	7	1	0	1	3	3	0	0	0	3	3	0	0	0	3	1	1	1	0
PERU	1	1	0	0	0	0	0	0	0	0	0	0	0	0	0	1	1	0	0	0
COLOMBIA	1	0	1	0	0	0	0	0	0	0	1	0	1	0	0	0	0	0	0	0
VENEZUELA	5	3	0	2	0	0	0	0	0	0	1	1	0	0	0	4	2	0	2	0
OTHER	2	1	1	0	0	1	1	0	0	0	0	0	0	0	0	1	0	1	0	0
EUROPE	127	88	26	4	8	53	37	11	0	5	17	13	3	0	1	56	38	12	4	2
EFTA	52	43	5	0	3	22	16	3	0	3	11	10	1	0	0	18	17	1	0	0
U.K.	42	34	4	0	3	18	12	3	0	3	10	10	0	0	0	13	12	1	0	0
SCANDINAVIA	6	6	0	0	0	0	0	0	0	0	0	0	0	0	0	3	3	0	0	0
SWITZERLAND	0	0	0	0	0	0	0	0	0	0	0	0	0	0	0	0	0	0	0	0
OTHER EFTA	4	3	1	0	0	1	1	0	0	0	1	0	1	0	0	2	2	0	0	0
EUROP. COMMUNITY	65	38	18	4	5	27	18	7	0	2	5	2	2	0	1	33	18	9	4	2
FRANCE	25	13	6	3	3	12	8	2	0	2	1	0	0	0	1	12	5	4	3	0
GERMANY	19	11	7	0	1	9	6	3	0	0	3	0	2	0	1	7	5	2	0	0
ITALY	11	8	3	0	0	5	4	1	0	0	0	0	0	0	0	6	4	2	0	0
BELGIUM + LUX	4	3	1	0	0	1	0	1	0	0	0	0	0	0	0	3	3	0	0	0
NETHERLANDS	6	3	1	0	0	0	0	0	0	0	1	0	1	0	0	5	3	1	1	0
SPAIN	6	3	3	0	0	3	2	1	0	0	0	0	0	0	0	3	1	2	0	0
GREECE + TURKEY	0	0	0	0	0	0	0	0	0	0	0	0	0	0	0	0	0	0	0	0
OTHER EUROPE	4	4	0	0	0	1	1	0	0	0	1	1	0	0	0	2	2	0	0	0
EUROPE EX. U.K.	85	54	22	4	5	35	25	8	0	2	7	3	3	0	1	43	26	11	4	2
SOUTHERN DOMINIONS	32	25	5	1	1	10	8	1	0	1	8	7	1	0	0	14	10	3	1	0
S. AFRICA +RHOD.	12	10	1	1	0	5	5	0	0	0	3	2	1	0	0	4	3	0	1	0
AUSTRALIA + N.Z.	20	15	4	1	0	5	3	1	0	1	5	5	0	0	0	10	7	3	0	0
ASIA + OTHER AFRICA	15	3	9	3	0	2	0	2	0	0	2	1	0	1	0	11	2	7	2	0
JAPAN	8	1	5	2	0	2	0	2	0	0	1	0	0	1	0	5	1	3	1	0
OTHER ASIA+AFR.	7	2	4	1	0	0	0	0	0	0	1	1	0	0	0	6	1	4	1	0
BLACK AFRICA	0	0	0	0	0	0	0	0	0	0	0	0	0	0	0	0	0	0	0	0
ARAB WORLD	1	0	0	1	0	0	0	0	0	0	0	0	0	0	0	1	0	0	1	0
INDIA	5	2	3	0	0	0	0	0	0	0	1	1	0	0	0	4	1	3	0	0
PHILIPPINES	0	0	0	0	0	0	0	0	0	0	0	0	0	0	0	0	0	0	0	0
OTHER E. ASIA	0	0	0	0	0	0	0	0	0	0	0	0	0	0	0	0	0	0	0	0
OTHER ASIA	1	1	0	0	0	0	0	0	0	0	0	0	0	0	0	1	1	0	0	0

CHAPTER 5- PATTERNS OF OWNERSHIP
SECTION 2- THE FLOW OF MANUFACTURING BY INDUSTRY OF PARENT SYSTEM
TABLE 16- MANUFACTURING SUBSIDIARIES IN A SYSTEM IN THE
HOUSEHOLD APPLIANCE INDUSTRY (SIC 363)
CLASSIFIED BY COUNTRY, PERIOD MANUFACTURE BEGAN, AND SYSTEM OWNERSHIP %

PERIOD AND OWNERSHIP PERCENTAGE
(WHL=95-100%, MAJ=50-94%, MIN=5-49%, UNK=UNKNOWN)

COUNTRY OR REGION	TOTAL PRE 1968					PRE 1946					1946-1957					1958-1967				
	ALL	WHL	MAJ	MIN	UNK	ALL	WHL	MAJ	MIN	UNK	ALL	WHL	MAJ	MIN	UNK	ALL	WHL	MAJ	MIN	UNK
OUTSIDE U.S.	76	60	12	4	0	8	6	2	0	0	13	11	2	0	0	55	43	8	4	0
OUT. U.S. + CANADA	67	52	11	4	0	6	4	2	0	0	11	10	1	0	0	50	38	8	4	0
OUT. WEST. HEMIS.	51	38	11	2	0	5	3	2	0	0	8	7	1	0	0	38	28	8	2	0
OUT. WHITE CMEALTH	49	37	8	4	0	3	3	0	0	0	8	7	1	0	0	38	27	7	4	0
OUT. DEVLPED WORLD	29	24	1	4	0	1	1	0	0	0	3	3	0	0	0	25	20	1	4	0
CANADA	9	8	1	0	0	2	2	0	0	0	2	1	1	0	0	5	5	0	0	0
LATIN AMERICA	16	14	0	2	0	1	1	0	0	0	3	3	0	0	0	12	10	0	2	0
C. AMER.+CARIB.	5	4	0	1	0	0	0	0	0	0	2	2	0	0	0	3	2	0	1	0
CUBA	0	0	0	0	0	0	0	0	0	0	0	0	0	0	0	0	0	0	0	0
MEXICO	4	4	0	0	0	0	0	0	0	0	2	2	0	0	0	2	2	0	0	0
OTHER	1	0	0	1	0	0	0	0	0	0	0	0	0	0	0	1	0	0	1	0
S. AMERICA	11	10	0	1	0	1	1	0	0	0	1	1	0	0	0	9	8	0	1	0
ARGENTINA	2	2	0	0	0	0	0	0	0	0	1	1	0	0	0	1	1	0	0	0
BRAZIL	3	3	0	0	0	1	1	0	0	0	0	0	0	0	0	2	2	0	0	0
PERU	1	1	0	0	0	0	0	0	0	0	0	0	0	0	0	1	1	0	0	0
COLOMBIA	1	1	0	0	0	0	0	0	0	0	0	0	0	0	0	1	1	0	0	0
VENEZUELA	2	1	0	1	0	0	0	0	0	0	0	0	0	0	0	2	1	0	1	0
OTHER	2	2	0	0	0	0	0	0	0	0	0	0	0	0	0	2	2	0	0	0
EUROPE	24	15	9	0	0	4	2	2	0	0	5	2	2	1	0	15	8	7	0	0
EFTA	7	4	3	0	0	2	0	2	0	0	2	1	1	0	0	3	3	2	0	0
U.K.	6	3	3	0	0	2	0	2	0	0	1	1	0	0	0	3	2	1	0	0
SCANDINAVIA	1	0	0	0	0	0	0	0	0	0	1	1	0	0	0	0	0	0	0	0
SWITZERLAND	0	0	0	0	0	0	0	0	0	0	0	0	0	0	0	0	0	0	0	0
OTHER EFTA	0	0	0	0	0	0	0	0	0	0	0	0	0	0	0	0	0	0	0	0
EUROP. COMMUNITY	15	9	6	0	0	1	1	0	0	0	3	0	3	0	0	11	5	6	0	0
FRANCE	5	4	1	0	0	1	1	0	0	0	1	0	1	0	0	3	2	1	0	0
GERMANY	4	1	3	0	0	0	0	0	0	0	0	0	0	0	0	4	1	3	0	0
ITALY	4	2	2	0	0	0	0	0	0	0	2	0	2	0	0	2	1	1	0	0
BELGIUM + LUX	1	1	0	0	0	0	0	0	0	0	0	0	0	0	0	1	1	0	0	0
NETHERLANDS	1	1	0	0	0	0	0	0	0	0	0	0	0	0	0	1	1	0	0	0
SPAIN	0	0	0	0	0	0	0	0	0	0	0	0	0	0	0	0	0	0	0	0
GREECE + TURKEY	1	1	0	0	0	0	0	0	0	0	0	0	0	0	0	1	1	0	0	0
OTHER EUROPE	1	1	0	0	0	1	1	0	0	0	0	0	0	0	0	0	0	0	0	0
EUROPE EX. U.K.	18	12	6	0	0	2	2	0	0	0	4	0	4	0	0	12	6	6	0	0
SOUTHERN DOMINIONS	12	12	0	0	0	1	1	0	0	0	2	2	0	0	0	9	9	0	0	0
S. AFRICA +RHOD.	2	2	0	0	0	0	0	0	0	0	0	0	0	0	0	2	2	0	0	0
AUSTRALIA + N.Z.	10	10	0	0	0	1	1	0	0	0	2	2	0	0	0	7	7	0	0	0
ASIA + OTHER AFRICA	15	11	2	2	0	0	0	0	0	0	1	1	0	0	0	14	11	1	2	0
JAPAN	2	1	1	0	0	0	0	0	0	0	1	1	0	0	0	1	1	0	0	0
OTHER ASIA+AFR.	13	10	1	2	0	0	0	0	0	0	0	0	0	0	0	13	10	1	2	0
BLACK AFRICA	3	3	0	0	0	0	0	0	0	0	0	0	0	0	0	3	3	0	0	0
ARAB WORLD	2	2	0	0	0	0	0	0	0	0	0	0	0	0	0	2	2	0	0	0
INDIA	1	0	0	1	0	0	0	0	0	0	0	0	0	0	0	1	1	0	1	0
PHILIPPINES	1	1	0	0	0	0	0	0	0	0	0	0	0	0	0	1	1	0	0	0
OTHER E. ASIA	1	1	0	1	0	0	0	0	0	0	0	0	0	0	0	1	1	0	1	0
OTHER ASIA	5	3	1	1	0	0	0	0	0	0	0	0	0	0	0	5	3	1	1	0

CHAPTER 5- PATTERNS OF OWNERSHIP
SECTION 2- THE FLOW OF MANUFACTURING BY INDUSTRY OF PARENT SYSTEM
TABLE 17- MANUFACTURING SUBSIDIARIES IN A SYSTEM IN THE
ELECTRONICS INDUSTRY (SIC 365-367)
CLASSIFIED BY COUNTRY, PERIOD MANUFACTURE BEGAN, AND SYSTEM OWNERSHIP %

PERIOD AND OWNERSHIP PERCENTAGE
(WHL=95-100%, MAJ=50-94%, MIN=5-49%, UNK=UNKNOWN)

COUNTRY OR REGION	TOTAL PRE 1968					PRE 1946					1946-1957					1958-1967				
	ALL	WHL	MAJ	MIN	UNK	ALL	WHL	MAJ	MIN	UNK	ALL	WHL	MAJ	MIN	UNK	ALL	WHL	MAJ	MIN	UNK
OUTSIDE U.S.	203	125	34	24	15	48	32	8	4	4	43	28	9	5	1	107	65	17	15	10
OUT. U.S. + CANADA	177	102	31	24	15	45	29	8	4	4	30	17	7	5	1	97	56	16	15	10
OUT. WEST. HEMIS.	138	73	28	21	11	39	23	8	4	4	22	11	6	5	0	72	39	14	12	7
OUT. WHITE CWEALTH	140	75	25	22	14	31	20	4	3	4	22	11	6	4	1	83	44	15	15	9
OUT. DEVLPED WORLD	49	33	5	6	5	7	7	0	0	0	9	6	2	0	1	33	20	3	6	4
CANADA	26	23	3	0	0	3	3	0	0	0	13	11	2	0	0	10	9	1	0	0
LATIN AMERICA	39	29	3	3	4	6	6	0	0	0	8	6	1	0	1	25	17	2	3	3
C. AMER.+CARIB.	15	10	2	0	3	2	2	0	0	0	1	1	0	0	0	12	7	2	0	3
CUBA	1	1	0	0	0	0	0	0	0	0	1	1	0	0	0	0	0	0	0	0
MEXICO	12	7	2	0	3	2	2	0	0	0	0	0	0	0	0	10	5	2	0	3
OTHER	2	2	0	0	0	0	0	0	0	0	0	0	0	0	0	2	2	0	0	0
S. AMERICA	24	19	1	3	1	4	4	0	0	0	7	5	1	1	0	13	10	0	3	0
ARGENTINA	8	5	1	2	0	1	1	0	0	0	2	2	1	0	0	5	3	0	2	0
BRAZIL	10	8	0	1	1	2	2	0	0	0	3	3	0	0	0	5	4	0	1	0
PERU	0	0	0	0	0	0	0	0	0	0	0	0	0	0	0	0	0	0	0	0
COLOMBIA	0	0	0	0	0	0	0	0	0	0	0	0	0	0	0	0	0	0	0	0
VENEZUELA	3	3	0	0	0	0	0	0	0	0	1	1	0	0	0	2	2	0	0	0
OTHER	3	3	0	0	0	1	1	0	0	0	1	1	0	0	0	1	1	0	0	0
EUROPE	107	62	22	9	10	36	21	7	4	4	12	7	3	2	0	55	34	12	3	6
EFTA	40	27	5	3	3	17	10	4	2	1	3	3	0	0	0	18	14	1	1	2
U.K.	25	19	3	1	1	11	7	3	1	0	2	2	0	0	0	11	10	1	0	1
SCANDINAVIA	7	4	1	1	0	3	2	0	1	0	1	1	0	0	0	3	1	1	0	1
SWITZERLAND	4	2	0	1	1	1	1	0	0	0	0	0	0	0	0	3	2	0	1	0
OTHER EFTA	4	2	1	0	1	3	0	1	1	1	0	0	0	0	0	1	1	0	0	0
EUROP. COMMUNITY	59	34	11	5	7	16	10	2	1	3	7	4	1	2	0	34	20	8	1	4
FRANCE	13	7	1	2	2	4	2	0	1	1	1	0	0	1	0	7	6	1	0	0
GERMANY	20	12	4	1	3	8	6	1	0	1	0	0	0	0	0	12	6	3	1	2
ITALY	13	7	4	2	0	0	0	0	0	0	5	3	1	0	0	8	4	3	1	0
BELGIUM + LUX	6	3	2	0	1	2	2	0	0	0	1	1	0	0	0	3	2	1	0	0
NETHERLANDS	7	5	0	0	1	2	2	0	0	0	0	0	0	0	0	4	3	0	0	1
SPAIN	5	0	5	0	0	1	0	1	0	0	1	0	1	0	0	3	0	3	0	0
GREECE + TURKEY	1	0	1	0	0	1	0	1	0	0	0	0	0	0	0	0	0	0	0	0
OTHER EUROPE	2	1	0	1	0	2	1	0	1	0	0	0	0	0	0	0	0	0	0	0
EUROPE EX. U.K.	82	43	19	8	9	25	14	4	3	4	10	5	3	2	0	44	24	12	3	5
SOUTHERN DOMINIONS	11	7	3	1	0	2	1	0	1	0	6	4	1	1	0	3	2	1	0	0
S. AFRICA +RHOD.	2	2	0	0	0	0	0	0	0	0	1	1	0	0	0	1	1	0	0	0
AUSTRALIA + N.Z.	9	5	3	1	0	2	1	0	1	0	5	3	1	1	0	2	1	1	0	0
ASIA + OTHER AFRICA	20	4	3	11	1	1	1	0	0	0	4	3	0	1	0	14	3	1	9	1
JAPAN	10	4	1	8	0	1	1	0	0	0	3	1	0	2	0	6	3	0	3	0
OTHER ASIA+AFR.	10	1	2	3	1	0	0	0	0	0	1	0	0	0	0	8	1	1	6	0
BLACK AFRICA	1	0	0	0	1	1	0	0	0	0	0	0	0	0	0	1	0	0	1	0
ARAB WORLD	0	0	0	0	0	0	0	0	0	0	0	0	0	0	0	0	0	0	0	0
INDIA	4	0	1	3	0	0	0	0	0	0	1	0	1	0	0	3	0	0	3	0
PHILIPPINES	3	3	0	0	0	0	0	0	0	0	1	1	0	0	0	2	2	0	0	0
OTHER E. ASIA	2	0	1	0	1	0	0	0	0	0	0	0	0	0	0	2	0	1	1	0
OTHER ASIA	0	0	0	0	0	0	0	0	0	0	0	0	0	0	0	0	0	0	0	0

CHAPTER 5- PATTERNS OF OWNERSHIP
SECTION 2- THE FLOW OF MANUFACTURING BY INDUSTRY OF PARENT SYSTEM
TABLE 18- MANUFACTURING SUBSIDIARIES IN A SYSTEM IN THE
OTHER ELECTRICAL MACHINERY INDUSTRIES (OTHER SIC 36)
CLASSIFIED BY COUNTRY, PERIOD MANUFACTURE BEGAN, AND SYSTEM OWNERSHIP %

PERIOD AND OWNERSHIP PERCENTAGE
(WHL=95-100%, MAJ=50-94%, MIN=5-49%, UNK=UNKNOWN)

COUNTRY OR REGION	TOTAL PRE 1968 ALL	WHL	MAJ	MIN	UNK	PRE 1946 ALL	WHL	MAJ	MIN	UNK	1946-1957 ALL	WHL	MAJ	MIN	UNK	1958-1967 ALL	WHL	MAJ	MIN	UNK
OUTSIDE U.S.	223	99	58	26	34	51	26	6	3	16	40	21	11	5	3	126	52	41	18	15
OUT. U.S. + CANADA	180	66	54	25	31	37	14	5	3	15	30	13	10	4	3	109	39	39	18	13
OUT. WEST. HEMIS.	125	39	42	21	20	25	8	4	2	11	19	7	8	3	1	78	24	30	16	8
OUT. WHITE CWEALTH	138	49	41	22	23	27	10	5	3	9	20	8	7	2	3	88	31	29	17	8
OUT. DEVLPED WORLD	65	28	15	7	14	13	6	1	1	5	11	6	2	1	2	40	16	12	5	7
CANADA	43	33	4	1	3	14	12	1	0	1	10	8	1	1	0	17	13	2	0	2
LATIN AMERICA	55	27	12	4	11	12	6	1	0	4	11	6	2	1	2	31	15	9	2	5
C. AMER.+CARIB.	22	8	6	0	7	3	2	0	1	1	5	3	2	0	1	13	3	5	0	5
CUBA	2	1	0	0	1	0	0	0	0	0	0	0	0	0	0	2	1	0	0	1
MEXICO	15	5	5	0	4	0	0	0	0	1	3	1	2	0	0	8	2	4	0	2
OTHER	5	2	1	0	2	0	0	0	0	0	2	2	0	0	0	3	0	1	0	2
S. AMERICA	33	19	6	1	7	9	4	1	0	3	6	3	0	1	0	18	12	4	2	0
ARGENTINA	6	5	1	0	0	2	2	1	0	0	1	1	0	0	0	3	2	0	0	0
BRAZIL	16	9	4	1	2	5	2	0	0	2	3	2	0	1	0	8	5	3	0	0
PERU	1	1	0	1	0	0	0	0	0	0	0	0	0	0	0	1	1	0	0	0
COLOMBIA	4	1	1	0	2	0	0	0	0	0	0	0	0	0	0	3	1	1	2	0
VENEZUELA	4	3	0	1	0	0	0	0	0	0	1	1	0	0	0	3	3	0	0	0
OTHER	2	0	1	0	1	2	0	1	0	1	0	0	0	0	0	0	0	0	0	0
EUROPE	90	26	29	15	17	19	5	2	2	10	12	4	1	2	1	56	17	22	11	6
EFTA	27	10	7	1	8	9	3	0	0	6	3	1	1	1	0	14	6	6	0	2
U.K.	22	5	0	1	8	8	2	0	0	6	3	1	1	1	0	10	2	6	0	2
SCANDINAVIA	0	0	0	0	0	0	0	0	0	0	0	0	0	0	0	2	2	0	0	0
SWITZERLAND	2	2	0	0	0	0	0	0	0	0	0	0	0	0	0	2	2	0	0	0
OTHER EFTA	3	3	0	0	0	1	1	0	0	0	0	0	0	0	0	2	2	0	0	0
EUROP. COMMUNITY	52	13	21	10	6	8	2	2	2	2	6	1	0	1	1	36	10	16	7	3
FRANCE	27	7	8	5	6	6	2	1	0	2	1	0	0	1	0	19	5	8	3	3
GERMANY	16	3	9	4	0	1	0	1	1	0	4	1	0	0	0	11	2	5	4	0
ITALY	5	0	3	0	0	1	0	0	1	0	1	0	0	0	0	2	0	2	0	0
BELGIUM + LUX	1	1	0	0	0	0	0	0	0	0	0	0	0	0	0	1	1	0	0	0
NETHERLANDS	3	2	1	0	0	0	0	0	0	0	0	0	0	0	0	5	1	0	0	0
SPAIN	6	2	0	4	0	0	0	0	0	0	1	1	0	0	0	3	1	0	4	0
GREECE + TURKEY	2	0	1	0	2	2	0	1	0	0	1	0	1	0	0	1	0	0	0	1
OTHER EUROPE	3	1	0	0	2	0	0	0	0	2	1	1	0	0	0	0	0	0	0	0
EUROPE EX. U.K.	68	21	22	14	9	11	3	2	2	4	9	3	0	1	1	46	15	16	11	4
SOUTHERN DOMINIONS	19	11	6	2	0	2	2	0	0	0	6	3	2	1	0	11	6	4	1	0
S. AFRICA +RHOD.	6	6	0	0	0	2	1	1	0	0	2	2	0	0	0	3	3	0	0	0
AUSTRALIA + N.Z.	13	5	6	2	3	1	1	1	1	0	4	1	2	1	0	8	3	4	1	1
ASIA + OTHER AFRICA	16	2	7	4	3	4	1	1	2	1	1	1	1	1	1	11	1	4	4	2
JAPAN	6	1	4	1	0	3	1	2	0	0	1	1	0	0	0	2	0	2	1	0
OTHER ASIA+AFR.	10	1	3	3	3	1	0	0	2	1	0	0	1	1	1	9	1	3	3	3
BLACK AFRICA	0	0	0	0	0	0	0	0	0	0	0	0	0	0	0	0	0	0	0	0
ARAB WORLD	0	0	0	0	0	0	0	0	0	0	0	0	0	0	0	0	0	0	0	0
INDIA	4	0	1	2	1	0	0	0	1	1	1	1	0	0	0	4	1	1	2	0
PHILIPPINES	2	0	1	0	0	1	0	1	0	0	0	0	0	0	0	2	0	1	0	0
OTHER E. ASIA	2	1	0	1	0	0	0	0	0	1	0	0	0	0	0	1	0	0	0	0
OTHER ASIA	2	0	1	0	1	0	0	0	0	0	0	0	0	0	0	2	0	1	0	1

414

CHAPTER 5- PATTERNS OF OWNERSHIP
SECTION 2- THE FLOW OF MANUFACTURING BY INDUSTRY OF PARENT SYSTEM
TABLE 19- MANUFACTURING SUBSIDIARIES IN A SYSTEM IN THE
MOTOR VEHICLES INDUSTRY (SIC 371)
CLASSIFIED BY COUNTRY, PERIOD MANUFACTURE BEGAN, AND SYSTEM OWNERSHIP %

PERIOD AND OWNERSHIP PERCENTAGE
(WHL=95-100%, MAJ=50-94%, MIN=5-49%, UNK=UNKNOWN)

COUNTRY OR REGION	TOTAL PRE 1968					PRE 1946					1946-1957					1958-1967				
	ALL	WHL	MAJ	MIN	UNK	ALL	WHL	MAJ	MIN	UNK	ALL	WHL	MAJ	MIN	UNK	ALL	WHL	MAJ	MIN	UNK
OUTSIDE U.S.	328	174	61	64	11	72	58	6	4	4	47	25	9	11	2	191	91	46	49	5
OUT. U.S. + CANADA	271	127	59	58	9	55	45	5	1	4	37	16	9	10	2	161	66	45	47	3
OUT. WEST. HEMIS.	197	98	39	39	8	48	39	5	1	3	27	11	8	6	2	105	48	26	28	3
OUT. WHITE CWEALTH	188	91	40	49	7	35	30	2	0	3	23	10	4	8	1	129	51	34	41	3
OUT. DEVLPED WORLD	98	39	25	31	2	12	11	0	0	1	14	7	1	5	1	71	21	24	26	0
CANADA	57	47	2	6	2	17	13	1	3	0	10	9	0	1	0	30	25	1	2	2
LATIN AMERICA	74	29	20	23	2	7	6	1	0	0	10	5	1	4	0	56	18	19	19	0
C. AMER.+CARIB.	23	8	5	10	0	2	2	0	0	0	2	2	0	0	0	19	4	5	10	0
CUBA	0	0	0	0	0	0	0	0	0	0	0	0	0	0	0	0	0	0	0	0
MEXICO	22	8	5	9	0	2	2	0	0	0	2	2	0	0	0	18	4	5	9	0
OTHER	1	0	0	1	0	0	0	0	0	0	0	0	0	0	0	1	0	0	1	0
S. AMERICA	51	21	15	13	2	5	4	1	0	0	8	3	1	4	0	37	14	14	9	0
ARGENTINA	19	6	6	7	0	2	2	0	0	0	3	1	1	1	0	14	4	6	4	0
BRAZIL	13	7	2	4	0	2	2	0	0	0	3	1	0	2	0	9	5	2	2	0
PERU	4	3	1	0	0	1	1	0	0	0	0	0	0	0	0	3	2	1	0	0
COLOMBIA	5	1	3	1	0	0	0	0	0	0	0	0	0	0	0	5	1	3	1	0
VENEZUELA	7	3	2	1	1	0	0	0	0	0	1	0	0	1	0	5	2	2	1	0
OTHER	3	1	1	0	1	1	0	0	0	1	1	1	0	0	0	1	0	1	0	0
EUROPE	130	69	21	18	6	33	24	5	1	3	17	8	4	4	1	64	37	12	13	2
EFTA	61	27	10	7	2	16	11	3	1	1	11	7	2	1	1	19	9	5	4	1
U.K.	48	18	7	6	2	11	6	3	1	1	8	5	1	1	1	14	7	3	4	0
SCANDINAVIA	8	5	2	1	0	3	3	0	0	0	2	1	1	0	0	3	1	1	1	0
SWITZERLAND	3	2	0	0	0	1	1	0	0	0	0	0	0	0	0	2	1	0	1	0
OTHER EFTA	2	2	0	0	0	1	1	0	0	0	1	1	0	0	0	0	0	0	0	0
EUROP. COMMUNITY	53	35	9	9	3	11	8	2	0	1	5	1	2	2	0	37	26	5	4	2
FRANCE	21	13	4	4	0	4	4	0	0	0	3	1	1	1	0	14	9	3	1	1
GERMANY	18	13	3	1	1	4	4	0	0	0	1	0	1	0	0	13	10	1	2	0
ITALY	7	5	1	1	1	1	1	0	0	0	1	0	0	1	0	6	4	1	1	0
BELGIUM + LUX	3	1	1	0	1	1	0	0	0	1	0	0	0	0	0	2	1	1	0	0
NETHERLANDS	4	1	1	1	1	1	1	0	0	0	0	0	0	0	0	5	2	1	1	1
SPAIN	7	1	1	4	0	2	1	0	0	1	1	0	0	1	0	4	0	1	3	0
GREECE + TURKEY	3	3	1	1	0	0	0	0	0	0	0	0	0	0	0	3	1	1	1	0
OTHER EUROPE	6	2	0	0	0	4	4	0	0	0	1	0	0	1	0	1	0	0	0	0
EUROPE EX. U.K.	82	51	14	12	4	22	18	2	0	2	9	3	3	3	0	50	30	9	9	2
SOUTHERN DOMINIONS	33	17	12	3	0	8	8	0	0	0	6	1	4	1	0	18	8	8	2	0
S. AFRICA +RHOD.	9	3	4	1	0	1	1	0	0	0	0	0	0	0	0	7	2	4	1	1
AUSTRALIA + N.Z.	24	14	8	2	2	7	7	0	0	0	6	1	4	1	0	11	6	4	1	0
ASIA + OTHER AFRICA	34	12	6	14	2	7	7	0	0	0	4	2	0	2	0	23	6	3	13	1
JAPAN	10	2	1	6	1	2	2	0	0	0	0	0	0	0	0	8	0	1	6	1
OTHER ASIA+AFR.	24	10	5	8	0	5	5	0	0	0	4	2	0	2	0	15	5	7	3	0
BLACK AFRICA	3	1	2	0	0	0	0	0	0	0	1	1	0	0	0	3	1	2	0	0
ARAB WORLD	3	3	0	0	0	2	2	0	0	0	0	0	0	0	0	1	1	0	0	0
INDIA	9	2	3	4	0	0	0	0	0	0	2	1	0	1	0	7	3	4	0	0
PHILIPPINES	2	1	0	1	0	2	2	0	0	0	0	0	0	0	0	0	0	0	0	0
OTHER E. ASIA	0	0	0	0	0	0	0	0	0	0	0	0	0	0	0	0	0	0	0	0
OTHER ASIA	7	3	0	3	1	2	2	0	0	0	1	0	0	1	0	2	0	1	2	0

CHAPTER 5- PATTERNS OF OWNERSHIP
SECTION 2- THE FLOW OF MANUFACTURING BY INDUSTRY OF PARENT SYSTEM
TABLE 20- MANUFACTURING SUBSIDIARIES IN A SYSTEM IN THE
OTHER TRANSPORTATION EQUIPMENT INDUSTRIES (SIC 372-379)
CLASSIFIED BY COUNTRY, PERIOD MANUFACTURE BEGAN, AND SYSTEM OWNERSHIP %

PERIOD AND OWNERSHIP PERCENTAGE
(WHL=95-100%, MAJ=50-94%, MIN=5-49%, UNK=UNKNOWN)

COUNTRY OR REGION	TOTAL PRE 1968					PRE 1946					1946-1957					1958-1967				
	ALL	WHL	MAJ	MIN	UNK	ALL	WHL	MAJ	MIN	UNK	ALL	WHL	MAJ	MIN	UNK	ALL	WHL	MAJ	MIN	UNK
OUTSIDE U.S.	125	67	35	15	4	15	8	4	2	1	20	13	6	1	0	86	46	25	12	3
OUT. U.S. + CANADA	102	46	33	15	4	8	1	4	2	1	14	8	5	1	0	76	37	24	12	3
OUT. WEST. HEMIS.	71	36	20	11	1	6	1	2	2	1	7	4	2	1	0	55	31	16	8	0
OUT. WHITE CWEALTH	74	28	26	12	4	8	1	4	2	1	9	6	3	0	0	53	21	19	10	3
OUT. DEVLPED WORLD	32	11	13	4	3	2	0	2	1	0	7	4	3	0	0	22	7	8	4	3
CANADA	23	21	2	0	0	7	7	0	0	0	6	5	1	1	0	10	9	1	0	0
LATIN AMERICA	31	10	13	4	3	2	0	2	0	0	7	7	3	1	0	21	6	8	4	3
C. AMER.+CARIB.	14	4	5	2	2	1	0	1	0	0	2	0	1	0	0	10	3	3	2	2
CUBA	0	0	0	0	0	0	0	0	0	0	0	0	0	0	0	0	0	0	0	0
MEXICO	12	3	4	2	2	1	0	1	0	0	1	1	0	0	0	9	2	3	2	2
OTHER	2	1	1	0	0	0	0	0	0	0	1	1	1	0	0	1	1	0	0	0
S. AMERICA	17	6	8	2	1	1	0	1	0	0	5	5	3	2	0	11	3	5	2	1
ARGENTINA	5	2	2	1	0	0	0	0	0	0	0	0	0	0	0	5	1	3	1	0
BRAZIL	6	2	3	1	0	0	0	0	0	0	3	3	2	1	0	3	0	2	1	0
PERU	1	1	0	0	0	1	0	1	0	0	0	0	0	0	0	0	0	0	0	0
COLOMBIA	2	0	2	0	0	0	0	0	0	0	1	1	0	0	0	1	0	1	0	0
VENEZUELA	1	1	0	0	0	0	0	0	0	0	0	0	0	0	0	0	0	0	0	0
OTHER	2	2	0	0	0	1	0	1	0	0	0	0	0	0	0	2	2	0	0	0
EUROPE	58	32	14	9	1	6	1	2	2	1	4	4	2	1	1	46	29	11	6	0
EFTA	26	19	2	3	0	1	1	0	0	0	2	2	1	1	1	23	18	3	2	0
U.K.	21	15	0	3	0	0	0	0	0	0	2	2	1	1	1	19	15	2	2	0
SCANDINAVIA	0	0	0	0	0	0	0	0	0	0	0	0	0	0	0	0	0	0	0	0
SWITZERLAND	4	3	1	0	0	1	1	0	0	0	0	0	0	0	0	3	2	1	0	0
OTHER EFTA	1	1	1	0	1	0	0	0	0	0	0	0	0	0	0	1	1	0	0	0
EUROP. COMMUNITY	29	11	10	5	1	4	0	2	1	1	1	1	0	0	0	22	10	8	4	0
FRANCE	14	5	4	4	0	2	0	1	1	0	1	1	1	1	0	10	4	3	3	0
GERMANY	6	3	3	0	1	1	0	1	0	1	0	0	0	0	0	5	3	2	0	0
ITALY	5	1	1	3	0	1	0	0	1	0	0	0	0	0	0	3	1	1	1	0
BELGIUM + LUX	3	2	1	1	0	0	0	0	0	0	0	0	0	0	0	3	2	1	0	0
NETHERLANDS	1	1	1	0	0	0	0	0	0	0	0	0	0	0	0	1	0	1	0	0
SPAIN	1	0	0	0	0	0	0	0	0	0	0	0	0	0	0	1	1	0	0	0
GREECE + TURKEY	1	1	0	0	0	0	0	0	0	0	0	0	0	0	0	0	0	0	0	0
OTHER EUROPE	1	0	0	1	0	1	0	1	0	0	1	0	1	0	0	0	0	0	0	0
EUROPE EX. U.K.	37	17	11	6	1	6	1	2	2	1	2	2	1	0	0	27	14	9	4	0
SOUTHERN DOMINIONS	7	3	4	0	0	0	0	0	0	0	3	2	1	0	0	4	1	3	0	0
S. AFRICA +RHOD.	4	2	2	0	0	0	0	0	0	0	1	1	1	0	0	3	1	1	1	0
AUSTRALIA + N.Z.	3	1	2	0	0	0	0	0	0	0	1	1	0	0	0	1	0	2	0	0
ASIA + OTHER AFRICA	6	1	2	2	0	0	0	0	0	0	1	0	1	0	0	5	1	2	2	0
JAPAN	5	0	2	2	0	0	0	0	0	0	1	0	1	0	0	4	1	1	2	0
OTHER ASIA+AFR.	1	1	0	0	0	0	0	0	0	0	0	0	0	0	0	1	0	1	0	0
BLACK AFRICA	0	0	0	0	0	0	0	0	0	0	0	0	0	0	0	0	0	0	0	0
ARAB WORLD	0	0	0	0	0	0	0	0	0	0	0	0	0	0	0	0	0	0	0	0
INDIA	0	0	0	0	0	0	0	0	0	0	0	0	0	0	0	0	0	0	0	0
PHILIPPINES	1	1	0	0	0	0	0	0	0	0	1	1	0	0	0	0	0	0	0	0
OTHER E. ASIA	1	1	0	0	0	0	0	0	0	0	0	0	0	0	0	1	1	0	0	0
OTHER ASIA	0	0	0	0	0	0	0	0	0	0	0	0	0	0	0	0	0	0	0	0

CHAPTER 5- PATTERNS OF OWNERSHIP
SECTION 2- THE FLOW OF MANUFACTURING BY INDUSTRY OF PARENT SYSTEM
TABLE 21- MANUFACTURING SUBSIDIARIES IN A SYSTEM IN THE
INSTRUMENTS AND PRECISION GOODS INDUSTRIES (SIC 38)
CLASSIFIED BY COUNTRY, PERIOD MANUFACTURE BEGAN, AND SYSTEM OWNERSHIP %

PERIOD AND OWNERSHIP PERCENTAGE
(WHL=95-100%, MAJ=50-94%, MIN=5-49%, UNK=UNKNOWN)

COUNTRY OR REGION	TOTAL PRE 1968					PRE 1946					1946-1957					1958-1967				
	ALL	WHL	MAJ	MIN	UNK	ALL	WHL	MAJ	MIN	UNK	ALL	WHL	MAJ	MIN	UNK	ALL	WHL	MAJ	MIN	UNK
OUTSIDE U.S.	116	84	22	7	3	19	12	7	0	0	40	32	6	0	2	57	40	9	7	1
OUT. U.S. + CANADA	99	68	21	7	3	16	10	6	0	0	31	23	6	0	2	52	35	9	7	1
OUT. WEST. HEMIS.	79	54	16	6	3	13	9	4	0	0	24	18	4	0	2	42	27	8	6	1
OUT. WHITE CWEALTH	73	50	15	6	2	8	5	3	0	0	22	16	5	0	1	43	29	7	6	1
OUT. DEVLPED WORLD	28	19	8	1	0	3	1	2	0	0	8	6	2	0	0	17	12	4	1	0
CANADA	17	16	1	0	0	3	2	1	0	0	9	9	0	0	0	5	5	0	0	0
LATIN AMERICA	20	14	5	1	0	3	2	1	0	0	7	5	2	0	0	10	7	2	1	0
C. AMER.+CARIB.	7	6	1	0	0	2	1	1	0	0	2	2	0	0	0	3	3	0	0	0
CUBA	1	0	1	0	0	1	0	1	0	0	0	0	0	0	0	0	0	0	0	0
MEXICO	5	5	0	0	0	1	1	0	0	0	2	2	0	0	0	2	2	0	0	0
OTHER	1	1	0	0	0	0	0	0	0	0	0	0	0	0	0	1	1	0	0	0
S. AMERICA	13	8	4	1	0	1	1	0	0	0	5	3	2	0	0	7	4	2	1	0
ARGENTINA	4	0	3	1	0	0	0	0	0	0	2	0	2	0	0	2	0	1	1	0
BRAZIL	3	2	1	0	0	1	1	0	0	0	1	1	0	0	0	1	0	1	0	0
PERU	1	1	0	0	0	0	0	0	0	0	0	0	0	0	0	1	1	0	0	0
COLOMBIA	2	2	0	0	0	0	0	0	0	0	1	1	0	0	0	1	1	0	0	0
VENEZUELA	2	2	0	0	0	0	0	0	0	0	1	1	0	0	0	1	1	0	0	0
OTHER	1	1	0	0	0	0	0	0	0	0	0	0	0	0	0	1	1	0	0	0
EUROPE	57	41	9	5	2	8	6	2	0	0	20	15	3	0	2	29	20	4	5	0
EFTA	18	12	4	1	1	3	2	1	0	0	7	5	1	0	1	8	5	2	1	0
U.K.	14	10	3	1	0	3	2	1	0	0	5	4	1	0	0	6	4	1	1	0
SCANDINAVIA	1	0	1	0	0	0	0	0	0	0	0	0	0	0	0	1	0	1	0	0
SWITZERLAND	2	1	0	0	1	0	0	0	0	0	1	0	0	0	1	1	1	0	0	0
OTHER EFTA	1	1	0	0	0	0	0	0	0	0	1	1	0	0	0	0	0	0	0	0
EUROP. COMMUNITY	37	28	4	4	1	5	4	1	0	0	11	9	1	0	1	21	15	2	4	0
FRANCE	13	8	2	2	1	2	1	1	0	0	5	4	0	0	1	6	3	1	2	0
GERMANY	12	11	1	0	0	3	3	0	0	0	5	5	0	0	0	4	3	1	0	0
ITALY	7	5	0	2	0	0	0	0	0	0	0	0	0	0	0	7	5	0	2	0
BELGIUM + LUX	2	2	0	0	0	0	0	0	0	0	0	0	0	0	0	2	2	0	0	0
NETHERLANDS	3	2	1	0	0	0	0	0	0	0	1	0	1	0	0	2	2	0	0	0
SPAIN	1	0	1	0	0	0	0	0	0	0	1	0	1	0	0	0	0	0	0	0
GREECE + TURKEY	0	0	0	0	0	0	0	0	0	0	0	0	0	0	0	0	0	0	0	0
OTHER EUROPE	1	1	0	0	0	0	0	0	0	0	1	1	0	0	0	0	0	0	0	0
EUROPE EX. U.K.	43	31	6	4	2	5	4	1	0	0	15	11	2	0	2	23	16	3	4	0
SOUTHERN DOMINIONS	11	7	3	0	1	5	2	3	0	0	2	2	0	0	0	4	3	0	0	1
S. AFRICA +RHOD.	3	3	0	0	0	1	1	0	0	0	1	1	0	0	0	1	1	0	0	0
AUSTRALIA + N.Z.	8	4	3	0	1	4	1	3	0	0	1	1	0	0	0	3	2	0	0	1
ASIA + OTHER AFRICA	11	6	4	0	1	0	0	0	0	0	2	1	1	0	0	9	5	3	0	1
JAPAN	3	1	1	0	1	0	0	0	0	0	1	0	1	0	0	2	1	0	0	1
OTHER ASIA+AFR.	8	5	3	0	0	0	0	0	0	0	1	1	0	0	0	7	4	3	0	0
BLACK AFRICA	1	1	0	0	0	0	0	0	0	0	0	0	0	0	0	1	1	0	0	0
ARAB WORLD	0	0	0	0	0	0	0	0	0	0	0	0	0	0	0	0	0	0	0	0
INDIA	3	2	1	0	0	0	0	0	0	0	1	1	0	0	0	2	1	1	0	0
PHILIPPINES	2	2	0	0	0	0	0	0	0	0	0	0	0	0	0	2	2	0	0	0
OTHER E. ASIA	0	0	0	0	0	0	0	0	0	0	0	0	0	0	0	0	0	0	0	0
OTHER ASIA	2	0	2	0	0	0	0	0	0	0	0	0	0	0	0	2	0	2	0	0

CHAPTER 5- PATTERNS OF OWNERSHIP
SECTION 2- THE FLOW OF MANUFACTURING BY INDUSTRY OF PARENT SYSTEM
TABLE 22- MANUFACTURING SUBSIDIARIES IN A SYSTEM IN THE
OTHER INDUSTRIES (SIC 21,27, AND 39)
CLASSIFIED BY COUNTRY, PERIOD MANUFACTURE BEGAN, AND SYSTEM OWNERSHIP %

PERIOD AND OWNERSHIP PERCENTAGE
(WHL=95-100%, MAJ=50-94%, MIN=5-49%, UNK=UNKNOWN)

COUNTRY OR REGION	TOTAL PRE 1968					PRE 1946					1946-1957					1958-1967				
	ALL	WHL	MAJ	MIN	UNK	ALL	WHL	MAJ	MIN	UNK	ALL	WHL	MAJ	MIN	UNK	ALL	WHL	MAJ	MIN	UNK
OUTSIDE U.S.	103	56	20	8	18	12	8	2	0	2	12	7	3	0	2	78	41	15	8	14
OUT. U.S. + CANADA	87	43	19	8	17	9	6	1	0	1	10	5	3	0	2	68	32	14	8	14
OUT. WEST. HEMIS.	61	29	11	6	15	6	4	1	0	1	4	1	1	0	2	51	24	9	6	12
OUT. WHITE CWEALTH	66	30	17	1	13	5	3	2	0	0	9	5	2	0	2	52	22	13	6	11
OUT. DEVLPED WORLD	31	16	10	2	3	3	2	1	0	0	7	5	2	0	0	21	9	7	2	3
CANADA	16	13	1	0	1	3	2	0	0	1	2	2	0	0	0	10	9	1	0	0
LATIN AMERICA	26	14	8	2	2	3	2	1	0	0	6	4	2	0	0	17	8	5	2	2
C. AMER.+CARIB.	11	7	2	1	1	3	0	1	0	0	2	2	0	0	0	6	3	1	1	1
CUBA	5	3	1	0	0	3	2	1	0	0	0	0	0	0	0	2	1	0	0	0
MEXICO	5	3	1	0	1	0	0	0	0	0	1	1	0	0	0	4	2	1	0	1
OTHER	1	1	0	0	0	0	0	0	0	0	0	0	0	0	0	0	0	0	0	0
S. AMERICA	15	7	6	1	1	0	0	0	0	0	4	2	2	0	0	11	5	4	1	1
ARGENTINA	5	2	2	0	1	0	0	0	0	0	0	0	0	0	0	5	2	2	0	1
BRAZIL	2	1	1	0	0	0	0	0	0	0	2	1	1	0	0	0	0	0	0	0
PERU	1	1	0	0	0	0	0	0	0	0	0	0	0	0	0	1	1	0	0	0
COLUMBIA	1	0	1	0	0	0	0	0	0	0	0	0	0	0	0	1	0	1	0	0
VENEZUELA	6	4	1	0	1	0	0	0	0	0	0	0	0	0	0	5	3	1	0	1
OTHER	0	0	0	0	0	0	0	0	0	0	0	0	0	0	0	0	0	0	0	0
EUROPE	47	24	7	3	13	6	4	1	0	1	2	0	0	0	2	39	20	6	3	10
EFTA	20	13	2	0	5	4	3	0	0	1	0	0	0	0	0	16	10	2	0	4
U.K.	13	9	1	0	3	4	3	0	0	1	0	0	0	0	0	9	6	1	0	2
SCANDINAVIA	5	4	1	0	0	0	0	0	0	0	0	0	0	0	0	5	4	1	0	0
SWITZERLAND	1	0	0	0	1	0	0	0	0	0	0	0	0	0	0	1	0	0	0	1
OTHER EFTA	1	0	1	0	0	0	0	0	0	0	0	0	0	0	0	1	0	1	0	0
EUROP. COMMUNITY	24	9	4	3	8	0	0	0	0	0	2	0	0	0	2	22	9	4	3	6
FRANCE	7	2	2	1	2	0	0	0	0	0	0	0	0	0	0	7	2	2	1	2
GERMANY	6	2	2	0	2	0	0	0	0	0	2	0	0	0	2	4	2	2	0	0
ITALY	6	2	2	0	2	0	0	0	0	0	0	0	0	0	0	6	2	2	0	2
BELGIUM + LUX	3	2	0	0	1	0	0	0	0	0	0	0	0	0	0	3	2	0	0	1
NETHERLANDS	2	1	1	0	1	0	0	0	0	0	0	0	0	0	0	2	1	1	0	1
SPAIN	2	1	1	0	0	0	0	0	0	0	0	0	0	0	0	2	1	1	0	0
GREECE + TURKEY	0	0	0	0	0	0	0	0	0	0	0	0	0	0	0	0	0	0	0	0
OTHER EUROPE	1	1	0	0	0	0	0	0	0	0	1	0	0	0	0	0	0	0	0	0
EUROPE EX. U.K.	34	15	6	3	10	2	1	0	0	1	2	0	0	0	2	30	14	5	3	8
SOUTHERN DOMINIONS	7	3	1	2	1	0	0	0	0	0	1	0	1	0	0	6	3	0	2	1
S. AFRICA +RHOD.	0	0	0	0	0	0	0	0	0	0	0	0	0	0	0	0	0	0	0	0
AUSTRALIA + N.Z.	7	3	1	2	1	0	0	0	0	0	1	0	1	0	0	6	3	0	2	1
ASIA + OTHER AFRICA	7	2	3	1	1	0	0	0	0	0	1	1	0	0	0	6	1	3	1	1
JAPAN	2	2	0	0	0	0	0	0	0	0	1	1	0	0	0	1	1	0	0	0
OTHER ASIA+AFR.	5	2	2	0	1	0	0	0	0	0	0	0	0	0	0	4	1	2	1	1
BLACK AFRICA	1	0	1	0	0	0	0	0	0	0	0	0	0	0	0	1	0	0	0	0
ARAB WORLD	1	0	1	0	0	0	0	0	0	0	0	0	0	0	0	1	0	0	0	0
INDIA	1	1	0	0	0	0	0	0	0	0	0	0	0	0	0	1	1	0	0	0
PHILIPPINES	0	0	0	0	0	0	0	0	0	0	0	0	0	0	0	0	0	0	0	0
OTHER E. ASIA	0	0	0	0	0	0	0	0	0	0	0	0	0	0	0	0	0	0	0	0
OTHER ASIA	2	2	0	0	0	0	0	0	0	0	1	1	0	0	0	1	0	0	0	0

418

CHAPTER 5- PATTERNS OF OWNERSHIP
SECTION 3- THE FLOW OF MANUFACTURING BY CHARACTERISTIC OF PARENT SYSTEM
TABLE A1- MANUFACTURING SUBSIDIARIES IN A SYSTEM
WITH LOW SALES IN 1966
CLASSIFIED BY COUNTRY, PERIOD MANUFACTURE BEGAN, AND SYSTEM OWNERSHIP %

PERIOD AND OWNERSHIP PERCENTAGE
(WHL=95-100%, MAJ=50-94%, MIN=5-49%, UNK=UNKNOWN)

COUNTRY OR REGION	TOTAL PRE 1968 ALL	WHL	MAJ	MIN	UNK	PRE 1946 ALL	WHL	MAJ	MIN	UNK	1946-1957 ALL	WHL	MAJ	MIN	UNK	1958-1967 ALL	WHL	MAJ	MIN	UNK
OUTSIDE U.S.	2082	1241	437	218	151	357	235	67	22	33	410	271	75	41	23	1280	735	295	155	95
OUT. U.S. + CANADA	1753	982	405	205	132	260	157	57	18	28	325	205	64	38	18	1139	620	284	149	86
OUT. WEST. HEMIS.	1216	693	279	122	97	204	122	47	14	26	187	123	30	24	10	800	448	202	89	61
OUT. WHITE CWEALTH	1284	654	342	177	100	143	78	40	14	11	228	128	56	30	14	902	448	246	133	75
OUT. DEVLPED WORLD	659	340	171	100	43	57	36	10	9	2	157	91	41	17	8	440	213	120	74	33
CANADA	329	259	32	13	19	97	78	10	3	5	85	66	11	3	5	141	115	11	6	9
LATIN AMERICA	537	289	126	83	35	56	35	10	9	2	138	82	34	14	8	339	172	82	60	25
C. AMER.+CARIB.	245	131	52	37	23	16	10	3	3	0	68	49	10	4	5	159	72	39	30	18
CUBA	15	4	3	3	5	2	0	1	1	0	11	3	2	2	4	2	1	0	0	1
MEXICO	159	88	32	26	12	12	9	2	1	0	43	34	6	2	1	103	45	24	23	11
OTHER	71	39	17	8	6	2	1	0	1	0	14	12	2	0	0	54	26	15	7	6
S. AMERICA	292	158	74	46	12	40	25	7	6	2	70	33	24	10	3	180	100	43	30	7
ARGENTINA	68	35	16	13	2	14	11	2	1	0	14	7	5	2	0	40	17	9	10	2
BRAZIL	81	49	17	10	5	14	8	2	2	2	25	12	9	3	1	42	29	6	5	2
PERU	19	11	5	2	1	3	2	0	1	0	5	2	2	1	0	11	7	3	0	1
COLOMBIA	39	19	14	4	2	2	0	1	0	1	8	4	2	1	1	29	15	10	3	1
VENEZUELA	55	26	18	9	2	1	1	0	0	0	14	5	6	2	1	40	20	12	7	1
OTHER	30	18	4	8	0	6	3	0	3	0	4	3	0	1	0	20	12	4	4	0
EUROPE	839	490	180	69	80	156	87	37	7	25	120	78	16	16	10	543	325	127	46	45
EFTA	319	214	40	18	32	81	51	11	2	17	56	43	4	7	2	167	120	25	9	13
U.K.	253	173	26	13	26	71	44	9	2	16	48	37	3	6	2	119	92	14	5	8
SCANDINAVIA	37	26	3	4	1	6	5	1	0	0	4	2	0	1	0	27	18	4	3	2
SWITZERLAND	11	7	6	0	3	1	1	0	0	0	2	1	0	0	0	8	4	6	0	1
OTHER EFTA	18	8	6	1	3	3	1	1	0	1	2	1	1	0	0	13	6	4	1	2
EUROP. COMMUNITY	445	244	117	37	42	69	32	25	4	8	52	28	12	6	6	319	184	80	27	28
FRANCE	143	69	35	18	14	26	11	7	4	4	11	6	3	0	1	104	52	30	13	9
GERMANY	128	73	22	6	11	25	12	10	0	3	21	13	7	0	1	79	48	18	6	7
ITALY	87	55	11	5	5	6	4	2	0	0	8	5	0	2	1	73	46	20	3	4
BELGIUM + LUX	43	24	9	4	4	6	4	1	0	1	5	2	1	1	1	32	21	6	3	3
NETHERLANDS	44	23	17	4	8	6	4	4	0	0	7	2	1	2	2	31	17	12	2	6
SPAIN	44	17	18	7	2	4	0	2	2	0	4	2	0	2	0	36	12	17	6	2
GREECE + TURKEY	12	1	4	5	2	0	0	0	0	0	1	0	0	1	0	11	1	4	4	2
OTHER EUROPE	19	14	1	2	2	2	1	0	1	0	7	5	0	0	2	10	8	1	1	0
EUROPE EX. U.K.	586	317	154	56	54	85	43	28	5	9	72	41	13	10	8	424	233	113	41	37
SOUTHERN DOMINIONS	200	142	36	15	4	45	34	8	2	1	42	35	5	2	0	110	73	23	11	3
S. AFRICA +RHOD.	61	44	11	4	0	14	11	3	0	0	15	12	3	0	0	30	21	5	4	0
AUSTRALIA + N.Z.	139	98	25	11	4	31	23	5	2	1	27	23	2	2	0	80	52	18	7	3
ASIA + OTHER AFRICA	177	61	63	38	13	3	1	2	0	0	25	10	9	6	0	147	50	52	32	13
JAPAN	55	18	18	21	5	2	1	1	2	0	6	1	2	3	0	46	9	14	18	5
OTHER ASIA+AFR.	122	51	45	17	8	1	0	1	0	0	19	9	7	3	0	101	41	38	14	8
BLACK AFRICA	13	4	3	4	2	0	0	0	0	0	2	0	2	0	0	11	4	2	4	2
ARAB WORLD	9	4	3	2	0	0	0	0	0	0	1	0	0	1	0	8	4	2	2	0
INDIA	28	6	15	5	1	1	1	0	0	0	3	1	2	0	0	24	4	15	4	1
PHILIPPINES	20	12	5	3	0	7	5	1	0	0	7	5	0	1	0	6	2	4	2	0
OTHER E. ASIA	21	15	3	1	2	1	0	1	0	0	1	0	1	0	0	19	15	1	1	2
OTHER ASIA	31	10	16	2	3	0	0	0	0	0	5	2	3	0	0	26	8	13	2	3

CHAPTER 5- PATTERNS OF OWNERSHIP
SECTION 3- THE FLOW OF MANUFACTURING BY CHARACTERISTIC OF PARENT SYSTEM
TABLE A2- MANUFACTURING SUBSIDIARIES IN A SYSTEM
WITH HIGH SALES IN 1966
CLASSIFIED BY COUNTRY, PERIOD MANUFACTURE BEGAN, AND SYSTEM OWNERSHIP %

(WHL=95-100%, MAJ=50-94%, MIN=5-49%, UNK=UNKNOWN)

| COUNTRY OR REGION | TOTAL | | | | | PERIOD AND OWNERSHIP PERCENTAGE | | | | | | | | | | | | | | |
| | | | PRE 1968 | | | PRE 1946 | | | | | 1946-1957 | | | | | 1958-1967 | | | | |
	ALL	WHL	MAJ	MIN	UNK	ALL	WHL	MAJ	MIN	UNK	ALL	WHL	MAJ	MIN	UNK	ALL	WHL	MAJ	MIN	UNK
OUTSIDE U.S.	3150	1671	780	366	225	668	461	91	47	69	602	363	142	62	35	1772	847	547	257	121
OUT. U.S. + CANADA	2666	1301	728	359	196	497	322	78	43	54	486	269	127	59	31	1592	710	523	248	111
OUT. WEST. HEMIS.	1862	921	519	233	127	348	229	55	23	41	282	158	72	35	17	1170	534	392	175	69
OUT. WHITE CWEALTH	2062	949	585	203	155	360	223	57	36	44	387	215	101	45	26	1245	511	427	222	85
OUT. DEVLPED WORLD	1050	489	270	163	87	178	113	25	20	20	239	133	64	25	17	592	243	181	118	50
CANADA	484	370	52	16	29	171	139	13	4	15	116	94	15	3	4	180	137	24	9	10
LATIN AMERICA	904	380	209	117	69	149	93	23	20	13	204	111	55	24	14	422	176	131	73	42
C. AMER.+CARIB.	331	152	82	56	25	62	38	11	11	6	66	43	14	4	5	187	71	61	41	14
CUBA	33	22		2	2	17	11	3			12	9	2	0	1					
MEXICO	211	103	47	35	16	34	22	4	5	3	49	32	11	2	2	118	49	32	28	9
OTHER	87	27	30	19	7	11	5	4		2	5	2	1	2	0	67	20	29	13	5
S. AMERICA	473	228	127	61	44	87	55	16	9	7	138	68	41	20	9	235	105	70	32	28
ARGENTINA	93	55	21	10	5	30	25	5	0	0	19	7	7	5	0	42	23	9	4	5
BRAZIL	118	68	28	12	8	20	15	1	2	2	45	24	13	4	4	51	29	14	6	2
PERU	39	18	12	5		9	5	3	1		10	4	2	3	1	17	9	7	0	1
COLOMBIA	76	31	13	13	8	8	4	1	3	0	21	10	7	3	0	46	17	15	7	7
VENEZUELA	90	31	25	13	19	9	2	3	1	3	29	14	8	3	4	50	15	14	9	12
OTHER	57	25	18	8	3	11	4	3	2	2	14	9	4	1	0	29	12	11	5	1
EUROPE	1216	630	347	126	89	268	171	45	19	33	183	106	40	26	11	741	353	262	81	45
EFTA	432	262	99	27	36	126	85	24	5	12	69	38	16	9	6	229	139	59	13	18
U.K.	298	176	67	23	26	90	61	16	4	9	53	26	13	9	5	149	89	38	10	12
SCANDINAVIA	79	49	18	4	5	19	13	5	1	0	13	11	2	0	0	46	25	16	0	5
SWITZERLAND	25	18	4	1	2	4	3	0	0	1	2	1	0	0	1	19	14	3	1	1
OTHER EFTA	29	19	5	2	3	13	8	3	0	2	1	0	1	0	0	15	11	2	1	0
EUROP. COMMUNITY	626	316	185	66	44	114	71	17	11	15	95	60	18	12	5	402	185	150	43	24
FRANCE	180	78	59	26	12	39	23	4	6	5	26	16	5	3	2	110	39	50	17	4
GERMANY	170	93	43	16	16	39	27	7	1	4	26	17	4	4	1	103	49	32	11	11
ITALY	135	60	50	10	10	14	8	2	1	3	27	17	7	1	1	91	35	40	9	7
BELGIUM + LUX	75	47	17	7	3	12	5	2	3	2	5	4	1	0	0	57	38	14	4	1
NETHERLANDS	66	38	16	5	3	10	8	1	1	0	11	6	3	2	0	41	24	14	2	1
SPAIN	95	21	47	23	4	11	4	3	1	3	12	5	5	2	0	72	12	41	18	1
GREECE + TURKEY	30	13	11	5	1	11		0	0	3	5	1	3	1	0	24	12	7	4	1
OTHER EUROPE	33	18	5	5	4	16	11	0	2	3	2	2	0	0	0	14	5	3	3	1
EUROPE EX. U.K.	918	454	280	103	63	178	110	29	15	24	130	80	27	17	6	592	264	224	71	33
SOUTHERN DOMINIONS	288	167	72	21	14	44	35	5	3	1	44	26	13	5	0	186	106	54	13	13
S. AFRICA +RHOD.	100	67	15	11	3	12	10	0	1	1	13	9	2	2	0	68	48	13	7	0
AUSTRALIA + N.Z.	188	100	57	11	13	32	25	5	2	0	31	17	11	3	0	118	58	41	6	13
ASIA + OTHER AFRICA	358	124	100	86	24	36	23	3	1	7	55	26	19	4	6	243	75	76	81	11
JAPAN	112	15	39	40	6	7	3	3	1	0	20	4	9	4	3	173	8	26	36	3
OTHER ASIA+AFR.	246	109	61	46	18	29	20	0	0	7	35	22	10	0	3	170	67	50	45	8
BLACK AFRICA	33	23	5	6	2	2	1	1	0	0	5	3	2	0	0	28	20	5	3	0
ARAB WORLD	30	13	8	6	1	2	1	1	0	0	3	4	0	1	0	22	8	5	6	1
INDIA	41	12	7	20	1	6	5	1	0	0	12	8	1	2	1	32	5	6	20	1
PHILIPPINES	39	21	11	5	1	6	5	1	0	0						20	6	7	5	2
OTHER E. ASIA	23	9	5	3	5	4	1	0	0	3	2	2	0	0	0	16	6	5	3	2
OTHER ASIA	80	31	25	9	9	12	8	1	0	3	10	3	4	0	2	52	20	20	8	4

CHAPTER 5- PATTERNS OF OWNERSHIP
SECTION 3- THE FLOW OF MANUFACTURING BY CHARACTERISTIC OF PARENT SYSTEM
TABLE B1- MANUFACTURING SUBSIDIARIES IN A SYSTEM
WITH LOW "R&D INTENSITY" IN 1964
CLASSIFIED BY COUNTRY, PERIOD MANUFACTURE BEGAN, AND SYSTEM OWNERSHIP %

PERIOD AND OWNERSHIP PERCENTAGE
(WHL=95-100%, MAJ=50-94%, MIN=5-49%, UNK=UNKNOWN)

COUNTRY OR REGION	TOTAL (PRE 1968)					PRE 1946					1946-1957					1958-1967				
	ALL	WHL	MAJ	MIN	UNK	ALL	WHL	MAJ	MIN	UNK	ALL	WHL	MAJ	MIN	UNK	ALL	WHL	MAJ	MIN	UNK
OUTSIDE U.S.	1462	767	343	174	114	303	183	62	23	35	281	161	76	25	19	814	423	205	126	60
OUT. U.S. + CANADA	1227	592	316	167	97	224	123	55	22	24	219	114	66	25	14	729	355	195	120	59
OUT. WEST. HEMIS.	849	432	214	102	65	152	84	37	13	18	118	61	31	16	10	543	287	146	73	37
OUT. WHITE C'WEALTH	968	430	267	141	83	173	92	44	17	20	184	94	59	19	12	564	244	164	105	51
OUT. DEVLPED WORLD	475	202	126	81	38	82	44	20	9	9	113	59	39	9	6	252	99	67	63	23
CANADA	235	175	27	7	17	79	60	7	1	11	62	47	10	0	5	85	68	10	6	1
LATIN AMERICA	378	160	102	65	32	72	39	18	9	6	101	53	35	9	4	186	68	49	47	22
C. AMER.+CARIB.	161	71	36	34	11	33	18	7	5	3	32	23	8	0	1	87	30	21	29	7
CUBA	12	6	4	0	1	8	4	3	0	1	3	2	1	0	0	0	0	0	0	0
MEXICO	109	51	22	23	6	20	11	4	4	1	28	20	7	0	1	54	20	11	19	4
OTHER	40	14	10	11	4	5	3	0	1	1	1	1	0	0	0	33	10	10	10	3
S. AMERICA	217	89	66	31	21	39	21	11	4	3	69	30	27	9	3	99	38	28	18	15
ARGENTINA	35	19	7	5	2	12	8	4	0	0	7	3	2	2	0	14	8	1	5	0
BRAZIL	45	26	11	5	2	9	7	1	1	0	13	8	4	1	0	22	11	6	3	2
PERU	22	7	8	4	3	5	3	2	0	0	8	1	3	4	0	6	3	3	0	0
COLOMBIA	45	20	15	6	3	5	2	1	2	0	17	9	7	1	0	22	4	7	8	3
VENEZUELA	44	10	13	4	16	4	1	0	0	3	17	5	9	0	3	22	4	4	4	10
OTHER	26	7	12	5	0	4	0	3	1	0	7	4	2	1	0	13	3	7	3	0
EUROPE	567	297	151	59	53	127	70	31	11	15	82	43	20	12	7	351	184	100	36	31
EFTA	180	111	38	14	16	50	28	14	3	5	24	13	6	4	1	105	70	18	7	10
U.K.	118	68	28	13	8	36	20	9	3	4	16	4	4	4	1	66	41	15	6	4
SCANDINAVIA	38	28	5	0	4	7	4	3	0	0	6	6	0	0	0	24	18	2	0	4
SWITZERLAND	11	7	2	0	2	1	1	0	0	0	1	0	1	0	0	9	6	0	1	2
OTHER EFTA	13	8	3	1	1	6	3	2	0	1	1	1	0	0	0	6	5	0	1	0
EUROP. COMMUNITY	316	162	90	27	31	63	35	15	5	8	51	27	14	5	5	196	100	61	17	18
FRANCE	77	35	23	11	5	18	11	4	2	1	11	6	1	3	1	45	18	18	6	3
GERMANY	85	44	24	6	11	21	14	3	0	4	17	10	5	0	2	47	20	16	6	5
ITALY	71	37	24	3	7	11	4	3	2	2	13	9	4	0	0	47	23	16	3	5
BELGIUM + LUX	47	30	4	4	3	8	5	2	0	1	5	1	2	1	1	33	27	4	1	1
NETHERLANDS	36	16	10	4	5	3	0	3	0	0	5	1	0	3	1	24	12	7	1	4
SPAIN	40	7	19	11	3	4	0	1	1	2	5	2	2	0	1	31	5	18	7	1
GREECE + TURKEY	11	4	3	1	2	1	0	1	0	0	2	1	0	1	0	10	4	2	3	1
OTHER EUROPE	20	13	1	4	1	7	7	0	0	0	2	1	0	0	1	9	5	1	2	1
EUROPE EX. U.K.	449	229	123	46	44	91	50	22	8	11	66	36	16	8	6	285	143	85	30	27
SOUTHERN DOMINIONS	130	87	20	12	3	13	9	2	2	0	17	12	3	2	0	92	66	15	8	3
S. AFRICA +RHOD.	53	41	7	6	0	4	3	0	1	0	5	3	1	1	0	39	35	0	4	0
AUSTRALIA + N.Z.	77	46	19	6	3	9	6	2	1	0	12	9	2	1	0	53	31	15	4	3
ASIA + OTHER AFRICA	152	48	43	31	9	12	5	4	1	3	19	6	8	2	3	100	37	31	29	3
JAPAN	55	6	19	15	3	2	0	2	0	0	7	0	4	2	1	34	6	13	13	2
OTHER ASIA+AFR.	97	42	24	16	6	10	5	2	0	3	12	6	4	0	2	66	31	18	16	1
BLACK AFRICA	13	7	1	3	0	0	0	0	0	0	4	3	0	0	1	11	7	1	3	0
ARAB WORLD	15	6	4	3	0	0	0	0	0	0	1	0	1	0	0	9	3	3	3	0
INDIA	13	4	4	3	1	1	1	0	0	0	3	2	1	0	0	9	3	3	3	0
PHILIPPINES	10	4	2	1	1	1	1	0	0	0	0	0	0	0	0	7	3	1	3	0
OTHER E. ASIA	9	3	5	1	1	1	1	0	0	0	2	1	0	0	1	7	2	3	1	1
OTHER ASIA	37	17	10	3	4	7	3	1	0	3	4	1	2	0	1	23	13	7	3	0

CHAPTER 5- PATTERNS OF OWNERSHIP
SECTION 3- THE FLOW OF MANUFACTURING BY CHARACTERISTIC OF PARENT SYSTEM
TABLE 82- MANUFACTURING SUBSIDIARIES IN A SYSTEM
WITH HIGH "R&D INTENSITY" IN 1964
CLASSIFIED BY COUNTRY, PERIOD MANUFACTURE BEGAN, AND SYSTEM OWNERSHIP %

PERIOD AND OWNERSHIP PERCENTAGE
(WHL=95-100%, MAJ=50-94%, MIN=5-49%, UNK=UNKNOWN)

COUNTRY OR REGION	TOTAL PRE 1968					PRE 1946					1946-1957					1958-1967				
	ALL	WHL	MAJ	MIN	UNK	ALL	WHL	MAJ	MIN	UNK	ALL	WHL	MAJ	MIN	UNK	ALL	WHL	MAJ	MIN	UNK
OUTSIDE U.S.	1216	690	275	145	82	200	134	35	20	11	274	193	47	24	10	718	363	193	101	61
OUT. U.S. + CANADA	1071	568	263	140	80	148	89	30	18	11	228	154	41	23	10	675	325	192	99	59
OUT. WEST. HEMIS.	778	415	194	99	56	122	73	28	11	10	138	99	23	13	3	504	243	143	75	43
OUT. WHITE CWEALTH	801	399	212	117	60	91	49	17	15	10	164	106	34	15	9	533	244	161	87	41
OUT. DEVLPED WORLD	379	195	96	53	28	27	17	2	7	1	109	71	20	11	7	236	107	74	35	20
CANADA	145	122	12	5	2	52	45	5	2	0	46	39	6	1	0	43	38	1	2	2
LATIN AMERICA	293	153	69	41	24	26	16	2	7	1	90	55	18	10	7	171	82	49	24	16
C. AMER.+CARIB.	127	68	31	17	7	6	4	0	2	0	33	25	3	4	1	84	39	27	13	5
CUBA	5	3	1	0	0	0	0	0	0	0	5	3	1	1	0	0	0	0	0	0
MEXICO	92	47	23	14	6	6	4	0	2	0	25	19	3	2	1	59	24	20	11	4
OTHER	30	18	7	2	1	0	0	0	0	0	3	3	0	0	0	25	15	7	2	1
S. AMERICA	166	85	38	24	17	20	12	1	7	0	57	30	15	6	6	87	43	22	11	11
ARGENTINA	42	20	11	6	4	7	5	1	1	0	15	7	5	1	2	19	6	5	4	4
BRAZIL	56	31	10	8	6	5	1	0	4	0	28	14	8	2	4	22	16	2	2	2
PERU	7	3	2	1	1	1	1	0	0	0	1	1	0	0	0	5	1	2	1	1
COLOMBIA	25	13	7	2	3	1	0	1	0	0	5	4	0	0	1	19	9	6	2	2
VENEZUELA	21	10	6	3	2	1	1	0	0	0	5	2	2	0	1	15	7	6	1	1
OTHER	15	8	2	3	2	2	2	0	0	0	3	2	0	1	0	7	4	1	1	1
EUROPE	502	291	117	49	36	95	55	22	9	9	86	61	14	9	2	312	175	81	31	25
EFTA	173	114	26	18	11	44	30	11	2	1	43	31	4	7	1	82	53	11	9	9
U.K.	132	91	19	12	7	32	23	8	1	0	38	26	4	7	1	59	42	7	4	6
SCANDINAVIA	19	10	4	3	2	7	4	2	1	0	2	2	0	0	0	10	4	3	2	1
SWITZERLAND	9	7	0	1	0	1	1	0	0	0	3	3	0	0	0	4	3	0	1	0
OTHER EFTA	13	6	3	2	2	4	2	1	1	0	0	0	0	0	0	9	4	2	1	2
EUROP. COMMUNITY	282	158	70	24	25	48	24	10	6	8	36	25	8	2	1	193	109	52	16	16
FRANCE	85	38	25	11	11	18	6	3	5	4	11	7	4	0	0	54	25	18	6	5
GERMANY	78	54	14	2	8	19	12	2	3	2	11	8	3	0	0	48	34	6	4	4
ITALY	63	33	16	7	6	9	3	5	0	1	9	5	1	3	0	50	25	10	4	6
BELGIUM + LUX	30	17	8	1	2	5	3	1	0	1	3	3	0	0	0	22	13	6	1	1
NETHERLANDS	26	16	7	3	0	4	1	1	1	0	3	2	1	0	0	19	11	7	1	0
SPAIN	36	13	10	4	2	2	1	0	1	0	5	2	2	0	1	29	9	16	4	0
GREECE + TURKEY	9	5	2	2	0	0	0	0	0	0	1	1	0	0	0	8	4	2	2	0
OTHER EUROPE	2	1	0	1	0	0	0	0	0	0	1	1	0	0	0	0	0	0	0	0
EUROPE FX. U.K.	370	200	98	37	29	63	32	14	8	9	48	35	10	2	1	253	133	74	27	19
SOUTHERN DOMINIONS	137	77	32	11	13	17	13	4	0	0	25	21	3	1	0	83	39	24	8	12
S. AFRICA +RHOD.	37	25	9	2	1	6	6	0	0	0	9	8	1	0	0	22	13	7	2	0
AUSTRALIA + N.Z.	100	52	23	9	12	19	13	4	2	0	16	13	2	1	0	61	26	17	6	12
ASIA + OTHER AFRICA	139	47	45	39	7	2	1	0	1	0	27	17	6	3	1	109	29	38	36	6
JAPAN	53	5	18	27	3	1	0	1	0	0	8	1	4	2	1	44	4	13	25	2
OTHER ASIA+AFR.	86	42	27	12	4	1	1	0	0	0	19	16	2	1	0	65	25	25	11	4
BLACK AFRICA	12	10	1	1	0	1	1	0	0	0	3	2	0	1	0	9	8	1	0	0
ARAB WORLD	4	3	1	0	0	0	0	0	0	0	0	0	0	0	0	4	3	1	0	0
INDIA	22	5	8	9	0	1	1	0	0	0	4	0	3	1	0	17	1	8	8	1
PHILIPPINES	14	10	3	1	1	1	1	0	0	0	7	6	1	0	0	7	4	1	1	1
OTHER E. ASIA	9	5	2	1	1	0	0	0	0	0	2	2	0	0	0	7	3	2	1	3
OTHER ASIA	25	9	12	0	3	0	0	0	0	0	3	3	0	0	0	21	6	12	0	3

CHAPTER 5- PATTERNS OF OWNERSHIP
SECTION 3- THE FLOW OF MANUFACTURING BY CHARACTERISTIC OF PARENT SYSTEM
TABLE C1- MANUFACTURING SUBSIDIARIES IN A SYSTEM
WITH LOW "ADVERTISING INTENSITY" IN 1965
CLASSIFIED BY COUNTRY, PERIOD MANUFACTURE BEGAN, AND SYSTEM OWNERSHIP %

PERIOD AND OWNERSHIP PERCENTAGE
(WHL=95-100%, MAJ=50-94%, MIN=5-49%, UNK=UNKNOWN)

COUNTRY OR REGION	TOTAL PRE 1968 ALL	WHL	MAJ	MIN	UNK	PRE 1946 ALL	WHL	MAJ	MIN	UNK	1946-1957 ALL	WHL	MAJ	MIN	UNK	1958-1967 ALL	WHL	MAJ	MIN	UNK
OUTSIDE U.S.	1555	772	381	228	136	362	223	63	35	41	309	166	75	44	24	846	383	243	149	71
OUT. U.S. + CANADA	1325	605	351	221	116	277	161	53	31	32	241	114	65	43	19	775	330	233	147	65
OUT. WEST. HEMIS.	942	434	268	147	72	197	110	45	20	22	139	64	39	27	9	585	260	184	100	41
OUT. WHITE CMFALTH	1023	439	278	184	98	201	117	35	22	27	191	90	54	32	15	607	232	189	130	56
OUT. DEVLPED WORLD	491	209	111	101	54	95	61	10	11	13	117	58	30	17	12	263	90	71	73	29
CANADA	230	167	30	7	20	85	62	10	4	9	68	52	10	1	5	71	53	10	2	6
LATIN AMERICA	383	171	83	74	44	80	51	8	11	10	102	50	26	16	10	190	70	49	47	24
C. AMER.+CARIB.	150	65	32	36	10	29	19	3	4	3	38	22	9	4	3	76	24	20	28	4
CUBA	15	8	3	3	1	7	3	2	1	1	5	4	1	0	0	3	1	0	2	0
MEXICO	103	47	21	25	7	17	12	1	2	2	31	17	7	4	3	52	18	13	19	2
OTHER	32	10	8	10	2	5	4	0	1	0	2	1	1	0	0	23	5	7	9	2
S. AMERICA	233	106	51	38	34	51	32	5	7	7	64	28	17	12	7	114	46	29	19	20
ARGENTINA	45	22	13	5	5	20	16	4	0	0	8	1	6	1	0	17	5	3	4	5
BRAZIL	69	39	13	10	7	13	9	1	1	2	26	14	5	4	3	30	16	7	5	2
PERU	7	4	1	2	0	4	2	1	0	0	2	0	0	2	0	1	2	0	0	0
COLOMBIA	37	15	10	6	6	4	2	0	2	0	7	2	0	2	1	26	11	6	4	5
VENEZUELA	48	15	12	6	16	4	1	0	0	3	14	6	3	3	3	29	8	8	3	10
OTHER	27	11	4	9	2	8	2	0	4	2	5	5	2	0	0	11	4	4	3	0
EUROPE	627	305	179	77	55	148	79	36	15	18	93	44	23	20	6	375	182	120	42	31
EFTA	214	119	53	21	18	68	38	21	5	4	38	18	7	9	4	105	63	25	7	10
U.K.	148	79	36	18	12	48	24	15	5	4	28	11	5	8	4	69	44	16	5	4
SCANDINAVIA	40	23	12	2	3	12	8	4	0	0	8	6	1	1	0	20	9	7	1	3
SWITZERLAND	14	9	2	1	1	6	4	0	1	0	0	0	0	0	0	8	5	2	0	1
OTHER EFTA	12	8	3	0	1	2	2	0	0	0	2	1	1	0	0	8	5	0	1	2
EUROP. COMMUNITY	333	162	96	38	30	60	31	14	7	8	45	21	12	10	2	221	110	70	21	20
FRANCE	99	49	25	15	6	19	10	2	4	3	13	7	3	2	0	63	32	20	8	3
GERMANY	87	44	25	8	10	21	13	5	1	2	13	8	3	3	1	53	23	17	5	8
ITALY	77	34	23	9	2	11	5	4	1	1	10	3	1	3	0	54	26	16	6	6
BELGIUM + LUX	37	18	12	5	3	5	2	2	1	0	6	1	2	1	1	27	16	8	2	1
NETHERLANDS	33	17	11	1	3	2	2	0	0	0	3	2	2	1	0	24	13	8	0	2
SPAIN	46	8	23	12	3	1	0	0	1	0	6	3	2	1	0	35	4	21	10	0
GREECE + TURKEY	15	5	7	2	1	1	0	0	0	1	3	1	2	0	0	11	4	4	2	1
OTHER EUROPE	19	11	0	4	3	1	1	0	0	0	1	1	0	0	2	3	1	0	2	0
EUROPE EX. U.K.	479	226	143	59	43	100	55	21	10	14	65	33	18	12	2	306	138	104	37	27
SOUTHERN DOMINIONS	149	84	37	18	6	26	18	3	4	1	21	12	6	3	0	98	54	28	11	5
S. AFRICA +RHOD.	54	43	4	6	1	6	5	0	1	0	4	2	2	0	0	42	34	2	6	0
AUSTRALIA + N.Z.	95	43	33	12	5	20	13	3	4	0	17	10	4	3	0	56	20	26	5	5
ASIA + OTHER AFRICA	166	45	52	52	11	23	13	6	4	0	25	8	10	4	3	112	24	36	47	5
JAPAN	58	7	24	25	2	8	3	4	1	0	10	0	6	3	1	39	4	14	21	0
OTHER ASIA+AFR.	108	38	28	27	10	15	10	2	3	0	15	8	4	1	2	73	20	22	26	5
BLACK AFRICA	12	6	1	5	0	2	1	0	1	0	2	0	1	0	1	12	6	3	3	0
ARAB WORLD	14	4	6	4	1	2	1	0	1	0	1	0	0	1	0	9	2	3	4	0
INDIA	22	6	8	4	1	3	1	1	1	0	5	3	2	0	0	16	3	5	7	1
PHILIPPINES	14	5	4	3	1	2	1	1	0	0	2	2	0	0	0	6	1	2	3	0
OTHER E. ASIA	15	5	4	3	3	0	0	0	0	0	2	2	0	0	0	11	3	4	3	1
OTHER ASIA	31	12	9	4	4	6	5	1	0	1	4	1	1	0	2	19	5	7	4	3

CHAPTER 5- PATTERNS OF OWNERSHIP
SECTION 3- THE FLOW OF MANUFACTURING BY CHARACTERISTIC OF PARENT SYSTEM
TABLE C2- MANUFACTURING SUBSIDIARIES IN A SYSTEM
WITH HIGH "ADVERTISING INTENSITY" IN 1965
CLASSIFIED BY COUNTRY, PERIOD MANUFACTURE BEGAN, AND SYSTEM OWNERSHIP %

PERIOD AND OWNERSHIP PERCENTAGE
(WHL=95-100%, MAJ=50-94%, MIN=5-49%, UNK=UNKNOWN)

COUNTRY OR REGION	TOTAL PRE 1968					PRE 1946					1946-1957					1958-1967				
	ALL	WHL	MAJ	MIN	UNK	ALL	WHL	MAJ	MIN	UNK	ALL	WHL	MAJ	MIN	UNK	ALL	WHL	MAJ	MIN	UNK
OUTSIDE U.S.	1471	943	332	93	83	293	220	34	11	28	291	211	50	14	16	867	512	248	68	39
OUT. U.S. + CANADA	1222	742	313	81	72	204	147	26	9	22	238	165	48	11	14	766	430	239	61	36
OUT. WEST. HEMIS.	823	512	206	47	47	149	114	17	0	18	138	102	23	6	7	525	296	166	41	22
OUT. WHITE CWEALTH	903	510	262	70	53	109	73	16	9	11	176	116	39	10	11	610	321	207	51	31
OUT. DEVLPED WORLD	505	282	141	43	36	65	39	9	9	8	119	76	29	6	8	318	167	103	28	20
CANADA	249	201	19	12	11	89	73	8	2	6	53	46	2	3	2	101	82	7	7	3
LATIN AMERICA	399	230	107	34	25	55	33	9	9	4	100	63	25	5	7	241	134	73	20	14
C. AMER.+CARIB.	198	115	47	18	17	28	16	3	6	3	50	39	5	1	3	119	60	39	11	9
CUBA	18	11	2	2	1	13	9	3	1	0	3	1	1	0	1	2	2	0	0	0
MEXICO	112	73	25	6	8	13	9	2	1	1	31	26	3	1	0	68	38	20	5	4
OTHER	68	31	20	10	8	2	1	0	0	1	16	9	1	4	2	49	20	19	6	2
S. AMERICA	201	115	60	16	10	27	17	6	3	1	50	24	20	4	2	122	74	34	9	4
ARGENTINA	46	30	10	2	2	11	9	2	0	0	11	6	4	1	0	23	15	5	2	1
BRAZIL	44	28	12	2	2	5	3	1	1	0	13	10	2	1	0	26	15	9	0	2
PERU	17	9	6	0	1	4	1	2	1	0	5	4	1	0	0	8	4	3	0	1
COLOMBIA	28	14	9	5	0	3	1	2	0	0	7	5	1	1	0	17	8	6	3	0
VENEZUELA	43	19	17	4	2	1	0	1	0	0	8	4	4	0	0	32	15	12	4	1
OTHER	23	15	6	1	1	3	3	0	0	0	9	5	3	1	0	11	7	3	0	1
EUROPE	537	346	130	21	31	103	78	11	0	14	91	67	14	5	5	334	201	105	16	12
EFTA	213	151	35	6	17	61	46	4	0	11	46	35	7	1	3	102	70	24	5	3
U.K.	161	117	19	5	16	58	43	4	0	11	36	27	5	1	3	63	47	10	4	2
SCANDINAVIA	28	21	7	0	0	2	2	0	0	0	7	6	1	0	0	19	13	6	0	0
SWITZERLAND	11	7	4	0	0	0	0	0	0	0	3	2	1	0	0	8	5	3	0	0
OTHER EFTA	13	6	5	1	1	1	1	0	0	0	0	0	0	0	0	12	5	5	1	1
EUROP. COMMUNITY	268	170	71	10	12	36	27	6	0	3	37	28	5	2	2	190	115	60	8	7
FRANCE	77	35	35	3	4	9	3	6	0	0	10	6	3	0	1	58	24	29	3	2
GERMANY	74	55	8	3	8	16	14	0	1	1	12	10	0	1	1	42	31	7	2	1
ITALY	55	36	16	1	2	6	4	0	0	2	8	6	2	0	0	41	26	14	1	0
BELGIUM + LUX	28	21	5	1	1	2	2	0	0	0	2	2	0	0	0	24	17	6	1	1
NETHERLANDS	34	23	7	1	3	3	2	0	0	1	5	4	1	1	0	26	13	4	1	2
SPAIN	35	13	18	3	1	5	4	0	1	0	4	1	3	0	0	27	8	16	2	1
GREECE + TURKEY	11	4	5	1	1	0	0	0	0	0	2	0	1	1	0	9	4	4	0	1
OTHER EUROPE	10	8	1	1	0	1	1	0	0	0	3	3	0	0	0	6	4	1	1	0
EUROPE EX. U.K.	376	229	111	16	15	45	35	7	0	3	55	40	9	4	2	271	154	95	12	10
SOUTHERN DOMINIONS	149	107	32	5	3	36	30	6	0	0	23	19	4	0	0	88	58	22	5	3
S. AFRICA +RHOD.	55	39	12	3	3	12	10	2	0	0	9	8	1	0	0	33	21	9	3	0
AUSTRALIA + N.Z.	94	68	20	2	3	24	20	4	0	0	14	11	3	0	0	55	37	13	2	3
ASIA + OTHER AFRICA	137	59	44	21	13	10	6	2	0	2	24	16	3	1	4	103	37	39	20	7
JAPAN	31	7	10	12	2	1	0	0	1	0	4	2	1	0	1	26	5	9	12	0
OTHER ASIA+AFR.	106	52	34	9	11	10	6	1	0	3	19	13	3	1	2	77	33	30	8	6
BLACK AFRICA	16	11	3	0	2	0	0	0	0	0	4	3	1	0	0	12	8	2	0	2
ARAB WORLD	4	3	1	0	0	0	0	0	0	0	1	1	0	0	0	3	2	1	0	0
INDIA	16	6	6	4	0	1	1	0	0	0	2	2	0	0	0	13	3	6	4	0
PHILIPPINES	23	13	9	1	0	3	3	0	0	0	6	5	1	0	0	14	5	8	1	0
OTHER E. ASIA	15	9	3	0	3	1	1	0	0	0	1	0	0	0	1	13	8	3	0	2
OTHER ASIA	32	10	12	4	6	4	1	0	0	3	5	2	2	1	0	22	7	10	3	2

CHAPTER 5- PATTERNS OF OWNERSHIP
SECTION 3- THE FLOW OF MANUFACTURING BY CHARACTERISTIC OF PARENT SYSTEM
TABLE D1- MANUFACTURING SUBSIDIARIES IN A SYSTEM
WITH LOW "HUMAN CAPITAL INTENSITY" IN 1966
CLASSIFIED BY COUNTRY, PERIOD MANUFACTURE BEGAN, AND SYSTEM OWNERSHIP %

PERIOD AND OWNERSHIP PERCENTAGE
(WHL=95-100%, MAJ=50-94%, MIN=5-49%, UNK=UNKNOWN)

COUNTRY OR REGION	TOTAL PRE 1968					PRE 1946					1946-1957					1958-1967				
	ALL	WHL	MAJ	MIN	UNK	ALL	WHL	MAJ	MIN	UNK	ALL	WHL	MAJ	MIN	UNK	ALL	WHL	MAJ	MIN	UNK
OUTSIDE U.S.	1316	703	325	151	122	325	205	50	30	40	265	159	60	22	24	711	339	215	99	58
OUT. U.S. + CANADA	1126	560	302	145	109	242	140	41	29	33	222	126	54	20	22	652	294	207	97	54
OUT. WEST. HEMIS.	837	423	233	102	73	178	100	35	17	26	143	79	34	16	14	510	244	164	69	33
OUT. WHITE CWEALTH	861	394	246	119	93	170	91	29	24	26	178	101	46	13	18	504	202	171	82	49
OUT. DEVLPED WORLD	396	182	99	62	48	82	52	7	11	12	90	53	23	4	10	219	77	69	47	26
CANADA	190	143	23	6	13	83	65	6	2	7	43	33	6	2	2	59	45	8	2	4
LATIN AMERICA	289	137	69	43	36	64	40	9	11	7	79	47	20	4	8	142	50	43	28	21
C. AMER.+CARIB.	132	67	30	20	13	30	16	3	7	4	27	22	2	1	2	73	29	25	12	7
CUBA	18	11	1	0	6	9	7	1	0	1	7	6	0	0	1	2	0	0	0	4
MEXICO	73	43	18	6	6	12	7	2	2	1	19	16	2	0	1	42	20	14	6	3
OTHER	41	13	11	12	5	9	4	3	3	2	0	0	0	1	0	31	9	11	8	3
S. AMERICA	157	70	39	23	23	34	24	3	4	3	52	25	18	3	6	69	21	18	16	14
ARGENTINA	28	15	9	4	4	12	12	0	0	0	6	1	5	0	0	10	2	4	4	0
BRAZIL	42	29	6	3	4	6	6	0	0	0	22	14	5	0	3	14	9	1	3	1
PERU	10	3	0	3	0	3	1	1	1	0	4	1	0	1	0	3	1	2	0	0
COLOMBIA	27	8	7	8	4	7	3	1	3	0	7	2	2	1	2	13	3	3	3	3
VENEZUELA	35	8	8	3	15	5	1	1	0	3	10	4	4	2	0	19	3	4	3	3
OTHER	15	7	4	3	0	1	1	0	0	0	3	3	0	0	0	10	3	4	0	3
EUROPE	564	287	164	55	54	134	70	29	15	20	108	59	24	14	11	318	158	111	26	23
EFTA	187	113	43	12	19	62	39	12	3	8	35	18	9	5	3	90	56	22	4	8
U.K.	129	78	30	9	12	48	30	6	3	6	26	12	6	5	3	55	36	15	1	3
SCANDINAVIA	36	22	11	0	3	9	6	3	0	0	7	6	1	0	0	20	10	7	0	3
SWITZERLAND	13	8	1	1	3	3	2	0	0	1	1	0	1	0	0	9	6	0	1	2
OTHER EFTA	9	5	1	2	1	2	1	0	0	1	1	0	1	0	0	6	4	0	2	0
EUROP. COMMUNITY	306	153	90	30	29	60	27	15	9	9	63	36	13	7	7	179	90	62	14	13
FRANCE	88	39	30	11	6	22	9	5	6	2	15	10	3	0	2	49	20	22	5	2
GERMANY	90	51	21	8	10	18	11	2	1	4	19	12	2	3	2	53	28	17	4	4
ITALY	63	27	23	7	5	10	4	4	0	2	15	9	2	2	2	37	14	15	5	3
BELGIUM + LUX	37	22	9	2	5	5	3	2	0	1	4	1	4	0	1	27	21	7	5	1
NETHERLANDS	28	14	7	2	5	5	3	2	0	0	10	4	2	2	2	13	7	3	0	3
SPAIN	45	8	25	9	0	4	0	2	2	0	7	3	2	2	0	34	5	22	6	1
GREECE + TURKEY	12	6	1	0	1	1	0	0	0	1	1	1	0	0	0	10	5	5	0	0
OTHER EUROPE	14	7	1	4	2	0	0	0	0	0	2	1	1	0	0	10	3	4	1	2
EUROPE EX. U.K.	435	209	134	46	42	86	40	20	12	14	82	47	18	9	8	263	122	96	25	20
SOUTHERN DOMINIONS	129	84	26	15	3	23	18	3	1	1	16	12	2	2	0	89	54	21	12	2
S. AFRICA +RHOD.	55	45	3	6	1	8	7	0	0	1	6	6	0	0	0	41	32	3	6	0
AUSTRALIA + N.Z.	74	39	23	9	2	15	11	3	1	0	10	6	8	2	0	48	22	18	6	2
ASIA + OTHER AFRICA	144	52	43	32	16	21	12	2	2	5	19	8	5	0	3	103	32	32	31	8
JAPAN	37	7	13	13	4	3	0	2	1	0	8	2	3	0	1	26	5	6	12	3
OTHER ASIA+AFR.	107	45	30	19	12	18	12	0	1	5	11	6	0	0	0	77	27	26	19	5
BLACK AFRICA	14	9	3	0	2	0	0	0	0	0	1	0	0	0	1	14	9	2	3	0
ARAB WORLD	11	3	3	3	1	0	0	0	0	0	0	0	0	0	0	9	3	1	5	1
INDIA	16	4	5	6	1	3	3	0	0	0	1	0	2	0	0	13	1	3	6	3
PHILIPPINES	18	9	6	2	1	4	3	1	0	0	4	2	0	0	0	10	4	4	2	0
OTHER E. ASIA	9	4	2	2	1	2	2	0	0	0	2	2	0	0	0	5	1	2	2	0
OTHER ASIA	39	16	12	3	7	8	5	0	0	3	4	2	1	0	1	26	9	11	3	3

CHAPTER 5- PATTERNS OF OWNERSHIP
SECTION 3- THE FLOW OF MANUFACTURING BY CHARACTERISTIC OF PARENT SYSTEM
TABLE D2- MANUFACTURING SUBSIDIARIES IN A SYSTEM
WITH HIGH "HUMAN CAPITAL INTENSITY" IN 1966
CLASSIFIED BY COUNTRY, PERIOD MANUFACTURE BEGAN, AND SYSTEM OWNERSHIP %

PERIOD AND OWNERSHIP PERCENTAGE
(WHL=95-100%, MAJ=50-94%, MIN=5-49%, UNK=UNKNOWN)

COUNTRY OR REGION	TOTAL PRE 1968 ALL	WHL	MAJ	MIN	UNK	PRE 1946 ALL	WHL	MAJ	MIN	UNK	1946-1957 ALL	WHL	MAJ	MIN	UNK	1958-1967 ALL	WHL	MAJ	MIN	UNK
OUTSIDE U.S.	1070	498	269	176	88	233	150	35	19	29	174	97	44	25	8	624	251	190	132	51
OUT. U.S. + CANADA	889	371	246	168	71	161	100	26	15	20	135	66	39	24	6	560	205	181	129	45
OUT. WEST. HEMIS.	608	249	176	106	51	107	70	16	7	14	69	35	21	10	3	406	144	139	89	34
OUT. WHITE CWEALTH	680	275	198	144	49	111	66	18	11	16	103	48	32	19	4	452	161	148	114	29
OUT. DEVLPED WORLD	346	144	92	79	22	62	36	10	8	8	73	35	21	14	3	202	73	61	57	11
CANADA	181	127	23	8	17	72	50	9	4	9	39	31	5	1	2	64	46	9	3	6
LATIN AMERICA	281	122	70	62	20	54	30	10	8	6	66	31	18	14	3	154	61	42	40	11
C. AMER.+CARIB.	110	45	28	27	6	16	10	2	2	2	24	11	9	2	2	66	24	17	23	2
CUBA	7	4	3	0	0	3	2	1	0	0	3	1	2	0	0	1	1	0	0	0
MEXICO	81	37	12	24	5	13	8	1	2	2	19	10	5	2	2	46	19	6	20	1
OTHER	22	4	13	3	1	1	0	0	0	0	2	0	2	0	0	19	4	11	3	1
S. AMERICA	171	77	42	35	14	38	20	8	6	4	42	20	9	12	1	88	37	25	17	3
ARGENTINA	34	14	10	6	3	13	8	1	2	2	5	2	1	2	0	15	4	6	4	1
BRAZIL	47	19	11	11	5	13	7	1	2	2	7	4	3	0	0	21	7	4	6	3
PERU	7	5	0	2	0	1	1	0	0	0	2	1	0	1	0	4	3	0	1	0
COLOMBIA	23	12	6	2	3	0	0	0	0	0	6	3	3	0	0	17	9	3	2	3
VENEZUELA	35	14	10	9	1	2	1	0	1	0	12	5	3	2	1	21	8	7	6	0
OTHER	25	13	5	5	2	9	3	2	1	3	3	3	0	0	0	11	6	5	0	0
EUROPE	418	179	118	63	38	75	47	11	5	12	49	25	14	7	3	274	107	93	51	23
EFTA	155	77	34	16	14	36	25	5	2	4	26	15	5	1	4	79	37	24	10	8
U.K.	118	53	26	13	12	30	19	5	3	4	21	11	4	4	2	53	23	17	7	6
SCANDINAVIA	21	13	5	2	1	3	3	0	0	0	4	3	1	0	0	14	7	4	2	1
SWITZERLAND	7	6	1	0	1	1	1	0	0	1	0	0	0	0	0	6	5	1	0	0
OTHER EFTA	9	5	1	1	0	2	2	0	0	0	1	1	0	0	0	6	2	1	2	1
EUROP. COMMUNITY	210	89	62	33	21	29	16	7	1	5	18	8	6	1	3	158	65	51	27	15
FRANCE	69	26	16	19	6	11	7	1	1	2	4	1	1	2	0	52	18	14	16	4
GERMANY	47	21	16	2	6	8	5	2	0	1	7	4	3	0	0	32	12	11	4	5
ITALY	43	16	17	2	6	4	1	1	0	2	5	2	2	1	0	33	13	14	2	4
BELGIUM + LUX	31	15	7	6	3	3	1	1	1	0	5	2	2	0	1	26	14	6	4	2
NETHERLANDS	20	11	6	2	0	4	2	1	1	0	1	1	0	0	0	15	8	6	1	0
SPAIN	33	6	16	10	1	4	2	2	0	0	2	1	1	0	0	27	3	14	10	0
GREECE + TURKEY	8	2	4	0	2	0	0	0	0	0	2	2	0	0	0	6	2	2	2	0
OTHER EUROPE	12	5	2	2	2	0	0	0	0	0	2	2	0	0	0	4	0	2	2	0
EUROPE EX. U.K.	300	126	92	50	26	45	28	6	2	8	28	14	10	3	1	221	84	76	44	17
SOUTHERN DOMINIONS	85	41	20	10	10	19	14	3	2	0	10	6	3	1	0	52	21	14	7	10
S. AFRICA +RHOD.	21	12	2	4	0	4	3	1	0	0	3	2	1	0	0	13	7	2	4	0
AUSTRALIA + N.Z.	64	29	18	6	10	15	11	2	1	1	7	4	2	1	0	39	14	12	4	10
ASIA + OTHER AFRICA	105	29	38	33	3	13	9	2	0	2	10	3	4	1	2	80	16	32	31	1
JAPAN	40	7	16	16	1	5	3	1	1	0	3	1	1	1	0	32	4	13	14	1
OTHER ASIA+AFR.	65	22	22	17	2	8	6	1	0	1	7	4	3	0	0	48	12	19	17	0
BLACK AFRICA	5	2	1	2	0	0	0	0	0	0	0	0	0	0	0	5	2	1	2	0
ARAB WORLD	11	6	3	2	0	2	1	0	1	0	2	2	0	0	0	8	3	3	2	0
INDIA	21	5	6	8	2	2	1	0	1	0	1	0	1	0	0	18	4	6	8	2
PHILIPPINES	10	5	0	2	1	2	1	0	0	1	1	1	0	0	0	7	3	0	2	1
OTHER E. ASIA	15	0	2	1	2	2	0	1	0	2	0	0	0	0	0	3	0	2	1	0
OTHER ASIA	13	3	7	2	0	2	2	0	0	0	3	1	2	0	0	7	0	5	2	0

CHAPTER 5- PATTERNS OF OWNERSHIP
SECTION 3- THE FLOW OF MANUFACTURING BY CHARACTERISTIC OF PARENT SYSTEM
TABLE E1- MANUFACTURING SUBSIDIARIES IN A SYSTEM
WITH LOW "PHYSICAL CAPITAL INTENSITY" IN 1966
CLASSIFIED BY COUNTRY, PERIOD MANUFACTURE BEGAN, AND SYSTEM OWNERSHIP %

PERIOD AND OWNERSHIP PERCENTAGE
(WHL=95-100%, MAJ=50-94%, MIN=5-49%, UNK=UNKNOWN)

COUNTRY OR REGION	TOTAL PRE 1968 ALL	WHL	MAJ	MIN	UNK	PRE 1946 ALL	WHL	MAJ	MIN	UNK	1946-1957 ALL	WHL	MAJ	MIN	UNK	1958-1967 ALL	WHL	MAJ	MIN	UNK
OUTSIDE U.S.	2548	1539	552	253	152	551	406	63	29	53	469	309	94	41	25	1476	824	395	183	74
OUT. U.S. + CANADA	2109	1184	510	243	129	397	274	54	24	45	374	230	83	40	21	1295	680	373	179	63
OUT. WEST. HEMIS.	1446	826	339	153	92	284	200	38	10	36	215	135	40	28	12	911	491	261	115	44
OUT. WHITE CWEALTH	1599	832	428	210	111	257	158	42	21	36	287	171	68	30	18	1037	503	318	159	57
OUT. DEVLPED WORLD	814	437	213	108	49	132	86	16	14	16	182	108	51	14	9	493	243	146	80	24
CANADA	439	355	42	10	23	154	132	9	5	8	95	79	11	1	4	181	144	22	4	11
LATIN AMERICA	663	358	171	90	37	113	74	16	14	9	159	95	43	12	9	384	189	112	64	19
C. AMER.+CARIB.	296	156	70	43	24	44	28	4	8	4	66	45	11	3	7	183	83	55	32	13
CUBA	30	17	4	3	0	12	8	1	2	1	15	6	3	1	5	2	2	0	0	0
MEXICO	184	104	39	28	12	26	18	3	1	4	40	31	7	2	0	117	55	29	25	8
OTHER	82	35	27	7	7	6	1	0	0	5	11	8	1	0	2	64	26	26	7	5
S. AMERICA	367	202	101	47	13	69	46	12	6	5	93	50	32	9	2	201	106	57	32	6
ARGENTINA	86	50	17	15	5	25	21	3	1	0	15	6	4	5	0	45	23	10	10	2
BRAZIL	97	61	24	7	5	22	16	2	1	3	29	16	12	0	1	46	29	10	5	2
PERU	28	17	9	2	0	6	3	2	1	0	8	5	2	1	0	14	9	5	0	0
COLOMBIA	49	22	18	8	1	5	2	2	1	0	9	4	3	2	0	35	16	13	5	1
VENEZUELA	68	30	24	10	2	5	2	2	1	0	25	13	10	2	0	36	16	11	8	1
OTHER	39	22	9	5	2	6	3	0	1	2	7	6	1	0	0	25	13	8	4	0
EUROPE	1023	584	238	95	76	206	138	30	9	29	148	92	24	20	12	639	354	184	66	35
EFTA	391	266	63	22	22	101	79	9	2	11	64	43	11	7	3	208	144	43	13	8
U.K.	285	194	40	17	16	84	66	7	2	9	45	29	8	6	2	138	99	25	9	5
SCANDINAVIA	59	42	13	3	1	9	3	3	0	3	13	10	1	1	1	37	25	9	2	1
SWITZERLAND	23	13	6	1	1	5	3	0	0	2	4	1	1	0	2	16	11	3	1	1
OTHER EFTA	24	13	6	6	4	5	3	0	0	2	2	1	0	0	1	17	9	6	1	1
EUROP. COMMUNITY	523	277	142	47	46	92	50	21	6	15	66	42	10	6	8	354	185	111	35	23
FRANCE	173	74	58	22	15	33	14	8	4	7	13	2	1	2	8	123	52	49	16	6
GERMANY	150	84	37	16	13	34	20	10	0	4	24	16	6	2	0	88	48	21	12	7
ITALY	98	54	30	12	6	6	4	0	0	2	14	5	2	1	2	76	41	27	4	4
BELGIUM + LUX	47	31	9	2	4	7	4	2	0	1	5	3	1	0	1	34	24	8	1	1
NETHERLANDS	55	34	21	5	8	12	9	0	1	2	10	5	3	0	2	33	20	6	2	5
SPAIN	60	19	20	17	3	4	3	0	0	1	9	2	0	6	1	47	14	20	11	2
GREECE + TURKEY	24	7	2	4	2	3	0	0	0	3	4	1	0	1	2	20	6	8	4	2
OTHER EUROPE	25	15	4	2	3	9	6	0	1	2	5	4	1	0	0	10	6	2	3	0
EUROPE EX. U.K.	738	390	198	78	60	122	72	23	7	20	103	63	16	14	10	501	255	159	57	30
SOUTHERN DOMINIONS	208	148	40	13	1	53	47	5	1	0	37	26	7	4	0	112	75	28	8	1
S. AFRICA +RHOD.	69	47	11	7	0	16	14	1	1	0	11	8	1	2	0	38	25	9	4	0
AUSTRALIA + N.Z.	139	101	29	6	15	37	33	4	0	0	26	18	6	4	0	74	50	19	4	1
ASIA + OTHER AFRICA	215	94	61	45	15	25	15	3	4	3	30	17	9	2	2	160	62	49	41	8
JAPAN	64	15	19	27	3	6	3	0	3	0	7	4	3	0	0	51	8	15	25	3
OTHER ASIA+AFR.	151	79	42	18	12	19	12	0	3	4	23	13	8	2	0	109	54	34	16	5
BLACK AFRICA	15	12	5	1	1	0	0	0	0	0	1	1	0	0	0	14	11	1	1	1
ARAB WORLD	18	11	1	5	1	3	1	0	3	0	4	4	0	0	0	13	6	5	2	0
INDIA	23	7	10	2	3	4	3	0	0	1	9	6	1	1	1	19	5	9	4	1
PHILIPPINES	28	14	8	5	1	4	3	0	0	1	1	0	0	1	0	15	5	6	1	3
OTHER E. ASIA	21	15	2	2	3	7	4	0	1	2	7	2	5	0	0	16	14	1	1	0
OTHER ASIA	46	20	17	3	6	7	4	0	0	3	7	2	5	0	0	32	14	12	3	3

CHAPTER 5— PATTERNS OF OWNERSHIP
SECTION 3— THE FLOW OF MANUFACTURING BY CHARACTERISTIC OF PARENT SYSTEM
TABLE E2— MANUFACTURING SUBSIDIARIES IN A SYSTEM
WITH HIGH "PHYSICAL CAPITAL INTENSITY" IN 1966
CLASSIFIED BY COUNTRY, PERIOD MANUFACTURE BEGAN, AND SYSTEM OWNERSHIP %

PERIOD AND OWNERSHIP PERCENTAGE
(WHL=95-100%, MAJ=50-94%, MIN=5-49%, UNK=UNKNOWN)

COUNTRY OR REGION	TOTAL PRE 1968 ALL	WHL	MAJ	MIN	UNK	PRE 1946 ALL	WHL	MAJ	MIN	UNK	1946-1957 ALL	WHL	MAJ	MIN	UNK	1958-1967 ALL	WHL	MAJ	MIN	UNK
OUTSIDE U.S.	2684	1373	665	331	224	474	290	95	40	49	543	325	123	62	33	1576	758	447	229	142
OUT. U.S. + CANADA	2310	1099	623	312	199	360	205	81	37	37	437	244	108	57	28	1436	650	434	218	134
OUT. WEST. HEMIS.	1632	788	459	202	132	268	151	64	22	31	254	146	62	31	15	1059	491	333	149	86
OUT. WHITE CWEALTH	1747	771	499	270	144	246	143	55	29	19	328	172	89	45	22	1110	456	355	196	103
OUT. DEVLPED WORLD	895	392	228	155	81	103	63	19	15	6	214	116	54	28	16	539	213	155	112	59
CANADA	374	274	42	19	25	114	85	14	3	12	106	81	15	5	5	140	108	13	11	8
LATIN AMERICA	678	311	164	110	67	92	54	17	15	6	183	98	46	26	13	377	159	101	69	48
C. AMER.+CARIB.	280	127	64	50	24	34	20	6	6	2	68	47	13	5	3	163	60	45	39	19
CUBA	18	9	4	4	1	7	5	0	2	0	8	6	2	0	0	2	1	1	0	0
MEXICO	186	87	40	33	16	20	13	3	3	1	52	35	10	4	3	104	39	27	26	12
OTHER	76	31	20	15	6	7	2	3	1	1	8	6	2	0	0	57	20	18	13	6
S. AMERICA	398	184	100	60	43	58	34	11	9	4	115	51	33	21	10	214	99	56	30	29
ARGENTINA	75	40	20	8	4	19	15	1	3	0	18	8	8	2	0	35	17	8	6	4
BRAZIL	102	56	21	15	8	12	7	3	1	1	41	20	10	8	3	47	29	8	6	4
PERU	30	12	8	5	2	6	4	1	1	0	7	4	2	1	0	14	7	4	2	1
COLOMBIA	66	28	19	9	9	5	2	1	2	0	20	10	6	2	2	40	16	12	5	7
VENEZUELA	77	27	19	12	19	5	2	2	0	1	18	6	4	4	4	54	19	15	8	12
OTHER	48	21	13	11	1	11	7	2	1	1	11	3	5	3	0	24	11	7	5	1
EUROPE	1032	536	289	100	93	218	120	52	17	29	155	92	32	22	9	645	324	205	61	55
EFTA	360	210	76	23	46	106	57	26	5	18	61	38	9	9	5	188	115	41	6	23
U.K.	266	155	53	19	36	77	39	20	3	15	56	34	13	4	5	130	82	20	11	18
SCANDINAVIA	57	33	15	2	6	16	11	3	0	2	4	0	0	0	0	36	18	11	2	5
SWITZERLAND	14	8	3	0	2	2	1	0	0	1	0	0	0	0	0	11	7	3	0	1
OTHER EFTA	23	14	5	2	2	11	6	1	2	1	1	0	1	0	0	11	8	0	2	1
EUROP. COMMUNITY	548	283	160	56	40	91	53	21	9	8	81	46	20	12	3	367	184	119	35	29
FRANCE	150	73	41	22	11	32	21	6	3	1	24	14	7	2	1	91	39	31	14	7
GERMANY	148	82	41	10	14	30	19	7	1	3	23	14	5	1	3	94	49	29	8	7
ITALY	124	61	42	11	9	14	7	3	1	3	21	12	5	3	1	88	40	33	8	7
BELGIUM + LUX	71	40	19	9	3	11	9	1	0	1	5	3	2	0	0	55	35	12	6	2
NETHERLANDS	55	27	17	4	3	4	2	1	0	1	8	5	1	2	0	39	21	14	2	2
SPAIN	79	19	44	13	3	11	4	4	2	1	7	0	5	2	0	61	10	38	12	1
GREECE + TURKEY	18	7	5	5	1	1	0	1	0	0	2	0	2	0	0	15	7	3	4	1
OTHER EUROPE	27	17	4	3	3	9	6	0	2	1	4	3	0	1	0	15	8	4	0	4
EUROPE EX. U.K.	766	381	236	81	57	141	81	34	13	13	99	58	24	13	4	515	242	178	55	40
SOUTHERN DOMINIONS	280	161	68	23	17	36	22	8	4	2	49	35	11	3	0	184	104	49	16	15
S. AFRICA +RHOD.	92	64	15	7	1	10	8	2	0	0	17	13	4	0	0	60	44	9	7	0
AUSTRALIA + N.Z.	188	97	53	16	16	26	15	6	4	1	32	22	7	3	0	124	60	40	9	15
ASIA + OTHER AFRICA	320	91	102	79	22	14	4	2	4	4	50	19	19	8	3	230	63	79	72	16
JAPAN	103	10	38	34	8	3	1	0	2	0	19	1	9	8	1	68	8	25	29	6
OTHER ASIA+AFR.	217	81	64	45	14	11	3	2	2	4	31	18	10	0	3	162	54	54	43	11
BLACK AFRICA	31	15	7	6	2	1	1	0	0	0	4	2	0	1	1	25	13	5	6	1
ARAB WORLD	21	6	6	6	2	1	0	1	0	0	2	0	1	0	1	17	5	5	6	1
INDIA	46	11	12	20	1	2	1	0	1	0	5	0	2	3	0	37	5	12	19	1
PHILIPPINES	31	19	8	3	0	3	2	1	0	0	10	8	1	1	0	17	9	5	3	0
OTHER E. ASIA	23	9	7	2	4	0	0	0	0	0	2	0	1	1	0	20	7	7	3	3
OTHER ASIA	65	21	24	8	6	4	2	1	0	1	8	2	3	2	1	46	14	21	7	4

CHAPTER 5- PATTERNS OF OWNERSHIP
SECTION 3- THE FLOW OF MANUFACTURING BY CHARACTERISTIC OF PARENT SYSTEM
TABLE F1- MANUFACTURING SUBSIDIARIES IN A SYSTEM
WITH LOW GROWTH IN SALES 1950-1966
CLASSIFIED BY COUNTRY, PERIOD MANUFACTURE BEGAN, AND SYSTEM OWNERSHIP %

PERIOD AND OWNERSHIP PERCENTAGE
(WHL=95-100%, MAJ=50-94%, MIN=5-49%, UNK=UNKNOWN)

COUNTRY OR REGION	TOTAL PRE 1968					PRE 1946					1946-1957					1958-1967				
	ALL	WHL	MAJ	MIN	UNK	ALL	WHL	MAJ	MIN	UNK	ALL	WHL	MAJ	MIN	UNK	ALL	WHL	MAJ	MIN	UNK
OUTSIDE U.S.	2314	1227	564	294	190	553	371	73	40	69	435	256	99	51	29	1287	600	392	203	92
OUT. U.S. + CANADA	1925	927	532	279	160	391	242	62	34	53	344	181	87	50	26	1163	504	383	195	81
OUT. WEST. HEMIS.	1316	636	381	167	112	273	173	43	13	44	166	86	45	24	11	857	377	293	130	57
OUT. WHITE CWEALTH	1490	663	437	244	128	252	148	42	28	34	279	142	74	41	22	941	373	321	175	72
OUT. DEVLPED WORLD	789	367	201	143	68	139	83	19	21	16	204	109	52	27	16	436	175	130	95	36
CANADA	389	300	32	15	30	162	129	11	6	16	91	75	12	1	3	124	96	9	8	11
LATIN AMERICA	609	291	151	112	48	118	69	19	21	3	178	95	42	26	15	306	127	90	65	24
C. AMER.+CARIB.	266	128	63	47	26	45	26	4	12	3	75	50	15	3	7	144	52	44	32	16
CUBA	31	15	6	4	5	11	6	2	3	0	16	7	4	1	4	3	2	0	0	1
MEXICO	158	82	32	31	12	24	16	2	4	2	47	34	9	1	3	86	32	21	26	7
OTHER	77	31	25	12	9	10	4	0	5	1	12	9	2	1	0	55	18	23	6	8
S. AMERICA	343	163	88	65	22	73	43	15	9	6	103	45	27	23	8	162	75	46	33	8
ARGENTINA	69	36	15	14	1	27	19	7	0	1	10	2	3	5	0	29	15	5	9	3
BRAZIL	93	50	20	13	10	19	12	2	2	3	36	17	10	5	4	38	21	8	5	3
PERU	25	12	7	6	0	7	4	2	1	0	10	3	2	5	0	8	5	3	0	0
COLOMBIA	38	14	10	9	5	5	1	2	2	0	10	4	1	3	2	23	8	7	5	3
VENEZUELA	79	31	29	14	4	4	2	2	0	0	29	13	10	4	2	45	16	17	10	2
OTHER	39	20	7	9	2	11	5	2	4	2	8	6	1	1	0	19	9	6	4	0
EUROPE	886	439	256	95	84	200	121	34	9	36	103	54	21	19	9	571	264	201	67	39
EFTA	323	198	67	19	35	110	71	16	3	20	43	26	6	7	4	166	101	45	9	11
U.K.	241	144	45	17	31	91	57	13	3	18	34	19	5	6	4	112	68	27	8	9
SCANDINAVIA	47	31	14	0	1	11	9	2	0	0	8	6	1	1	0	28	16	11	1	0
SWITZERLAND	15	10	4	1	2	3	3	0	0	1	1	0	0	0	0	12	8	4	0	1
OTHER EFTA	20	13	4	1	2	5	3	1	0	1	1	1	0	0	0	14	9	3	1	1
EUROP. COMMUNITY	457	211	147	48	44	77	43	16	5	13	49	22	13	9	5	324	146	118	34	26
FRANCE	134	54	48	17	12	26	15	4	1	6	18	8	3	2	1	97	37	41	14	5
GERMANY	125	64	36	11	12	23	11	7	1	4	18	10	5	2	1	82	43	24	8	7
ITALY	90	36	39	12	8	12	6	5	1	0	11	6	4	1	1	69	24	34	4	7
BELGIUM + LUX	55	29	12	6	5	8	6	3	1	2	4	1	1	1	1	39	23	8	6	2
NETHERLANDS	53	28	12	9	7	8	5	1	2	0	8	3	0	3	2	37	19	11	2	5
SPAIN	64	15	31	17	1	0	0	0	0	0	6	3	1	1	0	51	5	28	15	1
GREECE + TURKEY	20	10	8	6	1	6	2	2	1	1	2	0	1	1	0	18	5	7	4	0
OTHER EUROPE	22	10	3	5	3	0	0	0	0	3	3	3	1	0	0	12	3	3	4	0
EUROPE EX. U.K.	645	295	211	78	53	109	64	21	6	18	69	35	16	13	5	459	196	174	59	30
SOUTHERN DOMINIONS	179	112	47	15	1	47	36	7	3	1	28	17	8	3	0	100	59	32	9	0
S. AFRICA +RHOD.	55	34	13	5	1	14	10	2	1	1	9	6	2	1	0	30	18	9	3	0
AUSTRALIA + N.Z.	124	78	34	10	0	33	26	5	2	0	19	11	6	2	0	70	41	23	6	0
ASIA + OTHER AFRICA	251	85	78	57	27	26	16	2	5	2	35	15	16	2	2	186	54	60	54	18
JAPAN	71	9	28	26	7	5	2	2	0	1	9	1	6	1	1	56	6	20	24	6
OTHER ASIA+AFR.	180	76	50	31	20	21	14	0	5	1	26	14	10	1	1	130	48	40	30	12
BLACK AFRICA	23	13	4	4	2	1	0	1	0	0	2	0	2	0	0	21	13	2	4	2
ARAB WORLD	20	9	5	5	1	1	1	0	0	0	4	3	1	0	0	15	5	4	5	1
INDIA	30	9	9	10	1	3	3	0	0	0	4	2	0	1	0	24	4	8	10	1
PHILIPPINES	33	15	10	6	1	5	4	0	0	1	10	5	4	0	0	18	6	6	6	0
OTHER E. ASIA	24	10	6	3	5	5	0	0	0	3	4	2	2	0	0	19	8	6	3	2
OTHER ASIA	50	20	16	2	10	9	6	0	0	3	3	2	3	0	1	33	12	13	2	6

CHAPTER 5- PATTERNS OF OWNERSHIP
SECTION 3- THE FLOW OF MANUFACTURING BY CHARACTERISTIC OF PARENT SYSTEM
TABLE F2- MANUFACTURING SUBSIDIARIES IN A SYSTEM
WITH HIGH GROWTH IN SALES 1950-1966
CLASSIFIED BY COUNTRY, PERIOD MANUFACTURE BEGAN, AND SYSTEM OWNERSHIP %

PERIOD AND OWNERSHIP PERCENTAGE
(WHL=95-100%, MAJ=50-94%, MIN=5-49%, UNK=UNKNOWN)

COUNTRY OR REGION	TOTAL PRE 1968					PRE 1946					1946-1957					1958-1967				
	ALL	WHL	MAJ	MIN	UNK	ALL	WHL	MAJ	MIN	UNK	ALL	WHL	MAJ	MIN	UNK	ALL	WHL	MAJ	MIN	UNK
OUTSIDE U.S.	2351	1331	536	239	158	359	238	71	28	22	452	303	89	36	24	1453	790	376	175	112
OUT. U.S. + CANADA	2019	1076	490	229	144	276	169	61	26	20	367	241	76	32	18	1296	666	353	171	106
OUT. WEST. HEMIS.	1402	763	337	153	93	206	123	50	18	15	235	155	43	25	12	905	485	244	110	66
OUT. WHITE CWEALTH	1507	750	402	191	109	193	112	45	21	15	268	172	61	20	15	991	466	296	150	79
OUT. DEVLPED WORLD	759	373	203	96	55	75	49	13	8	5	157	102	39	9	7	495	222	151	79	43
CANADA	332	255	46	10	14	83	69	10	2	2	85	62	13	4	6	157	124	23	4	6
LATIN AMERICA	617	313	153	76	51	70	46	11	8	5	132	86	33	7	6	391	181	109	61	40
C. AMER.+CARIB.	274	137	63	41	18	27	18	5	2	2	51	39	6	4	2	181	80	52	35	14
CUBA	17	11	2	-	2	8	5	-	2	1	-	5	-	-	-	1	1	-	-	-
MEXICO	185	93	41	27	14	17	11	2	2	1	38	29	6	2	1	120	53	32	23	12
OTHER	72	33	20	13	2	2	2	-	-	-	6	5	-	1	-	60	26	20	12	2
S. AMERICA	343	176	90	35	33	43	28	6	6	3	81	47	27	3	4	210	101	57	26	26
ARGENTINA	71	41	15	8	6	13	13	-	-	-	15	10	4	1	-	42	18	11	7	6
BRAZIL	83	50	20	8	3	10	7	3	-	-	25	15	8	3	1	46	28	12	4	2
PERU	30	15	9	1	2	5	3	2	-	-	4	2	1	-	-	18	10	5	1	2
COLOMBIA	65	31	24	5	4	4	1	2	1	-	16	9	2	5	-	44	20	16	4	4
VENEZUELA	57	23	10	7	17	5	1	-	1	3	13	6	7	1	3	39	16	6	5	11
OTHER	37	16	12	6	1	6	2	3	1	-	8	5	3	-	-	21	9	6	1	1
EUROPE	934	541	215	85	69	172	103	39	16	14	152	101	26	16	9	586	337	150	53	46
EFTA	349	225	54	25	30	78	51	17	4	6	65	42	10	9	4	191	132	27	12	20
U.K.	256	169	37	19	18	56	39	10	3	4	54	33	9	9	3	133	97	18	7	11
SCANDINAVIA	59	37	11	4	6	12	7	4	1	-	7	7	-	-	-	39	23	7	3	6
SWITZERLAND	14	10	0	1	2	-	1	1	-	-	2	2	-	-	1	10	7	-	1	2
OTHER EFTA	20	9	6	1	4	9	4	3	-	2	2	-	1	-	-	9	5	2	1	1
EUROP. COMMUNITY	492	281	125	44	33	80	45	20	9	6	77	55	13	4	5	326	181	92	31	22
FRANCE	157	78	43	24	10	29	14	5	8	2	25	17	5	1	1	101	47	33	15	6
GERMANY	133	76	32	9	13	33	22	9	-	2	18	14	3	1	-	79	40	21	8	10
ITALY	104	65	27	8	2	7	4	3	-	-	20	15	2	2	1	77	46	22	6	3
BELGIUM + LUX	54	37	13	2	1	6	5	1	-	-	6	5	1	-	1	42	31	9	1	1
NETHERLANDS	44	25	10	2	4	5	4	1	-	-	8	4	2	2	-	27	17	7	1	2
SPAIN	60	16	29	11	4	1	-	1	-	-	7	2	2	2	3	47	12	26	7	2
GREECE + TURKEY	14	6	3	4	1	-	-	-	-	-	1	-	2	1	-	12	6	2	3	1
OTHER EUROPE	19	13	3	2	1	5	5	-	-	-	2	2	-	-	-	10	6	3	-	1
EUROPE EX. U.K.	678	372	178	66	51	116	64	29	13	10	98	68	17	7	6	453	240	132	46	35
SOUTHERN DOMINIONS	245	149	49	19	16	26	17	6	2	1	43	34	6	3	-	164	98	37	14	15
S. AFRICA +RHOD.	89	65	9	9	0	9	8	-	-	-	15	12	2	1	-	59	45	6	8	-
AUSTRALIA + N.Z.	156	84	40	10	16	17	9	5	2	1	28	22	4	2	-	105	53	31	6	15
ASIA + OTHER AFRICA	223	73	73	49	8	8	3	5	-	-	40	20	11	6	3	155	50	57	43	5
JAPAN	81	13	23	29	4	3	3	-	-	-	15	4	5	4	2	51	9	15	25	2
OTHER ASIA+AFR.	142	60	50	20	4	3	-	3	-	-	25	16	6	2	1	104	41	42	18	3
BLACK AFRICA	16	9	2	3	0	-	-	-	-	-	3	3	-	-	-	11	3	5	3	-
ARAB WORLD	14	3	6	8	1	1	1	-	-	-	1	-	2	-	1	11	3	5	3	-
INDIA	28	7	12	8	0	-	-	-	-	-	4	2	1	1	-	23	11	11	7	-
PHILIPPINES	23	17	5	1	0	2	2	-	-	-	9	8	-	1	-	12	7	4	1	-
OTHER E. ASIA	16	10	2	1	2	-	-	-	-	-	1	1	-	1	-	14	10	2	-	2
OTHER ASIA	45	14	23	4	1	2	1	1	-	-	7	3	4	-	-	33	10	18	4	1

CHAPTER 5- PATTERNS OF OWNERSHIP
SECTION 3- THE FLOW OF MANUFACTURING BY CHARACTERISTIC OF PARENT SYSTEM
TABLE G1- MANUFACTURING SUBSIDIARIES IN A SYSTEM
WITH LOW RETURN ON INVESTED CAPITAL IN 1966
CLASSIFIED BY COUNTRY, PERIOD MANUFACTURE BEGAN, AND SYSTEM OWNERSHIP %

PERIOD AND OWNERSHIP PERCENTAGE
(WHL=95-100%, MAJ=50-94%, MIN=5-49%, UNK=UNKNOWN)

COUNTRY OR REGION	TOTAL ALL	WHL	MAJ	MIN	UNK	PRE 1946 ALL	WHL	MAJ	MIN	UNK	1946-1957 ALL	WHL	MAJ	MIN	UNK	1958-1967 ALL	WHL	MAJ	MIN	UNK
OUTSIDE U.S.	2711	1384	674	333	223	492	317	83	38	54	504	293	120	58	33	1618	774	471	237	136
OUT. U.S. + CANADA	2305	1076	626	315	205	374	222	68	37	47	392	201	106	54	31	1456	653	452	224	127
OUT. WEST. HEMIS.	1613	773	440	208	138	280	168	52	20	40	212	112	52	30	18	1067	493	336	158	80
OUT. WHITE CWEALTH	1750	743	508	270	163	259	148	49	31	31	309	150	90	45	24	1116	445	369	194	108
OUT. DEVLPED WORLD	892	376	237	151	87	111	63	18	17	13	204	100	62	26	16	536	213	157	108	58
CANADA	406	308	48	18	18	118	95	15	1	7	112	92	14	4	2	162	121	19	13	9
LATIN AMERICA	692	303	186	107	67	94	54	16	17	7	180	89	54	24	13	389	160	116	66	47
C. AMER.+CARIB.	286	123	72	49	27	39	20	7	9	3	61	35	17	4	5	171	68	48	36	19
CUBA	26	12	7	4	3	12	5	4	2	1	10	6	3	0	1	2	1	0	0	1
MEXICO	181	80	46	27	18	21	12	3	4	2	43	24	12	3	4	107	44	31	20	12
OTHER	79	31	19	20	6	6	3	0	3	0	8	5	2	1	0	62	23	17	16	6
S. AMERICA	406	180	114	58	40	55	34	9	8	4	119	54	37	20	8	218	92	68	30	28
ARGENTINA	72	35	19	9	8	13	13	0	0	0	19	7	8	4	0	36	15	11	5	5
BRAZIL	103	57	21	15	8	13	10	0	2	1	44	21	12	7	4	44	26	11	6	3
PERU	31	12	12	3	1	7	3	3	1	0	7	1	4	2	0	14	8	5	0	1
COLOMBIA	73	25	24	14	9	6	2	1	3	0	18	8	5	5	0	48	15	18	8	7
VENEZUELA	83	29	26	10	17	7	2	2	0	3	21	10	6	3	2	54	17	18	7	12
OTHER	44	22	12	7	0	9	4	3	2	0	10	7	2	1	0	22	11	7	4	0
EUROPE	1068	545	300	98	105	229	135	45	16	33	136	76	27	20	13	683	334	228	62	59
EFTA	396	241	82	20	44	112	66	24	4	18	49	32	7	5	5	226	143	51	11	21
U.K.	285	173	55	17	33	81	48	15	3	15	40	23	7	5	5	157	102	33	9	13
SCANDINAVIA	63	37	17	2	6	17	11	5	1	0	7	1	0	0	0	38	19	12	1	6
SWITZERLAND	23	14	5	1	2	2	1	0	0	1	1	1	0	0	0	19	12	5	1	1
OTHER EFTA	25	17	5	0	3	12	6	4	0	2	1	0	0	0	0	12	10	1	0	1
EUROP. COMMUNITY	539	259	165	54	51	96	59	17	9	11	75	38	18	13	6	358	162	130	32	34
FRANCE	157	73	43	21	16	31	22	4	0	5	18	10	5	2	1	104	41	38	15	10
GERMANY	142	72	44	10	15	34	20	9	1	4	23	12	6	4	1	84	40	29	5	10
ITALY	117	51	47	10	8	13	9	3	0	1	19	10	4	4	1	84	32	39	6	7
BELGIUM + LUX	62	32	17	7	6	11	3	4	1	3	5	2	2	0	1	46	27	12	4	3
NETHERLANDS	61	31	14	10	6	7	5	1	1	0	10	4	2	1	1	40	22	12	2	4
SPAIN	75	18	40	14	3	9	3	5	1	0	5	3	1	1	0	61	12	36	12	1
GREECE + TURKEY	24	8	9	5	2	1	0	1	0	0	2	0	1	1	0	21	8	7	4	2
OTHER EUROPE	34	19	4	5	5	11	7	0	2	2	5	3	0	0	2	17	9	4	3	1
EUROPE Ex. U.K.	783	372	245	81	72	148	87	30	13	18	96	53	20	15	8	526	232	195	53	46
SOUTHERN DOMINIONS	246	146	60	25	6	32	24	4	3	1	38	25	9	4	0	167	97	47	18	5
S. AFRICA +RHOD.	86	55	15	10	5	7	4	1	1	1	11	7	3	3	0	63	44	11	8	0
AUSTRALIA + N.Z.	160	91	45	15	5	25	20	3	1	0	27	18	6	3	0	104	53	36	10	5
ASIA + OTHER AFRICA	299	82	80	85	27	19	9	3	1	6	38	11	16	6	5	217	62	61	78	16
JAPAN	99	29	29	41	7	2	0	1	0	1	14	0	8	4	2	70	9	20	36	5
OTHER ASIA+AFR.	200	73	51	44	20	17	9	2	0	6	24	11	8	2	3	147	53	41	42	11
BLACK AFRICA	25	13	6	3	3	1	0	1	0	0	4	0	1	0	3	22	13	5	3	1
ARAB WORLD	23	7	8	5	2	1	0	0	1	0	4	2	0	2	0	17	5	6	3	1
INDIA	35	7	7	19	1	2	0	2	0	0	2	0	0	1	1	30	5	5	18	0
PHILIPPINES	30	14	8	6	1	3	2	0	1	0	8	5	1	1	1	18	6	6	5	0
OTHER E. ASIA	24	8	6	3	6	2	0	1	0	0	2	2	0	0	2	19	6	5	6	4
OTHER ASIA	63	24	16	8	9	9	5	1	2	3	7	2	2	1	2	41	17	13	7	4

CHAPTER 5- PATTERNS OF OWNERSHIP
SECTION 3- THE FLOW OF MANUFACTURING BY CHARACTERISTIC OF PARENT SYSTEM
TABLE G2- MANUFACTURING SUBSIDIARIES IN A SYSTEM
WITH HIGH RETURN ON INVESTED CAPITAL IN 1966
CLASSIFIED BY COUNTRY, PERIOD MANUFACTURE BEGAN, AND SYSTEM OWNERSHIP %

PERIOD AND OWNERSHIP PERCENTAGE
(WHL=95-100%, MAJ=50-94%, MIN=5-49%, UNK=UNKNOWN)

COUNTRY OR REGION	TOTAL PRE 1968 ALL	WHL	MAJ	MIN	UNK	PRE 1946 ALL	WHL	MAJ	MIN	UNK	1946-1957 ALL	WHL	MAJ	MIN	UNK	1958-1967 ALL	WHL	MAJ	MIN	UNK
OUTSIDE U.S.	2477	1498	532	250	151	522	370	73	31	48	502	339	94	45	24	1407	789	365	174	79
OUT. U.S. + CANADA	2076	1182	497	239	121	375	251	65	24	35	413	271	82	43	17	1251	660	350	172	69
OUT. WEST. HEMIS.	1440	826	350	146	85	268	180	49	12	27	253	168	47	29	9	886	478	254	105	49
OUT. WHITE CWEALTH	1579	846	417	210	91	240	150	47	19	24	304	192	67	30	15	1020	504	303	161	52
OUT. DEVLPED WORLD	803	442	202	112	42	120	83	16	12	9	190	123	43	16	8	488	236	143	84	25
CANADA	401	316	35	11	30	147	119	8	7	13	89	68	12	2	7	156	129	15	2	10
LATIN AMERICA	636	356	147	93	36	107	71	16	12	8	160	103	35	14	8	365	182	96	67	20
C. AMER.+CARIB.	286	158	61	44	20	38	27	3	5	3	71	56	7	4	4	174	75	51	35	13
CUBA	22	14	1	1	4	7	6	0	1	0	13	6	1	2	4	2	2	0	0	0
MEXICO	186	109	33	34	9	24	18	3	2	1	47	41	5	1	0	114	50	25	31	8
OTHER	78	35	27	7	7	7	3	0	2	2	11	9	1	1	0	58	23	26	4	5
S. AMERICA	350	198	86	49	16	69	44	13	7	5	89	47	28	10	4	191	107	45	32	7
ARGENTINA	84	51	17	14	2	29	22	6	0	1	14	7	4	3	0	41	22	7	11	1
BRAZIL	92	56	24	7	5	20	12	3	3	2	26	15	10	0	1	46	29	11	4	2
PERU	27	17	5	4	1	5	4	1	0	0	8	5	0	3	0	14	8	4	1	1
COLOMBIA	42	25	13	3	1	4	2	1	0	0	11	6	4	0	0	27	17	7	2	1
VENEZUELA	62	28	17	12	4	3	1	1	1	0	22	9	8	2	3	36	18	8	9	1
OTHER	43	21	10	9	3	8	3	1	0	3	8	5	2	1	0	27	13	8	5	1
EUROPE	974	567	222	97	64	195	123	37	10	25	166	108	28	22	8	589	336	157	65	31
EFTA	346	230	53	25	24	95	70	11	3	11	75	49	12	11	3	162	111	30	11	10
U.K.	258	172	34	19	19	80	57	10	3	10	60	40	8	10	2	104	75	16	6	7
SCANDINAVIA	52	37	11	3	1	8	7	1	0	0	10	7	2	1	0	34	23	8	2	1
SWITZERLAND	14	11	2	0	1	3	3	0	0	0	3	2	1	0	0	8	6	0	1	1
OTHER EFTA	22	10	6	3	3	4	3	0	0	1	2	0	1	0	1	16	7	5	3	1
EUROP. COMMUNITY	531	300	137	49	35	87	44	25	6	12	72	50	12	5	5	362	206	100	38	18
FRANCE	166	74	56	23	10	34	12	11	6	5	19	12	3	2	2	110	50	42	15	3
GERMANY	156	94	34	12	12	30	19	8	0	3	24	18	5	0	1	98	57	21	12	8
ITALY	104	63	25	7	7	7	3	1	0	3	16	12	3	0	1	79	48	21	6	4
BELGIUM + LUX	56	39	11	4	1	7	3	3	0	1	5	4	0	1	0	43	32	8	3	0
NETHERLANDS	49	30	11	3	5	9	7	2	0	0	8	4	1	2	1	32	19	8	2	3
SPAIN	64	20	25	16	1	6	4	0	2	0	11	4	2	5	0	47	12	22	11	2
GREECE + TURKEY	17	5	6	5	1	0	0	0	0	0	4	1	2	1	0	13	4	4	4	1
OTHER EUROPE	16	12	1	2	3	5	5	0	0	0	4	4	0	0	0	5	4	1	0	0
EUROPE EX. U.K.	716	395	188	78	45	115	66	27	7	15	106	68	20	12	6	485	261	141	59	24
SOUTHERN DOMINIONS	231	157	45	10	11	53	42	8	2	1	45	35	7	3	0	125	80	30	5	10
S. AFRICA +RHOD.	74	56	10	4	0	19	17	2	0	0	16	14	1	1	0	35	25	7	3	0
AUSTRALIA + N.Z.	157	101	35	6	11	34	25	6	2	1	29	21	6	2	0	90	55	23	2	10
ASIA + OTHER AFRICA	235	102	83	39	10	20	15	4	0	1	42	25	12	4	1	172	62	67	35	8
JAPAN	68	16	28	20	4	7	3	4	0	0	12	5	4	2	1	49	8	20	18	3
OTHER ASIA+AFR.	167	86	55	19	6	13	12	0	0	1	30	20	8	2	0	123	54	47	17	5
BLACK AFRICA	21	14	5	2	1	0	0	0	0	0	4	3	1	0	0	17	11	1	4	1
ARAB WORLD	16	10	3	3	0	1	1	0	0	0	2	2	0	0	0	13	7	3	3	0
INDIA	34	11	15	6	1	3	3	0	0	0	4	4	0	0	0	26	4	15	6	1
PHILIPPINES	29	19	8	2	0	3	4	0	0	0	4	4	0	0	0	14	7	4	7	0
OTHER E. ASIA	20	16	2	1	1	2	1	1	0	0	11	8	2	1	0	17	15	1	0	0
OTHER ASIA	47	16	25	5	3	3	3	0	0	0	8	3	5	0	0	36	10	20	3	3

CHAPTER 5- PATTERNS OF OWNERSHIP
SECTION 3- THE FLOW OF MANUFACTURING BY CHARACTERISTIC OF PARENT SYSTEM
TABLE H1- MANUFACTURING SUBSIDIARIES IN A SYSTEM
WHICH FIRST MANUFACTURED OUTSIDE U.S. AND CANADA BEFORE 1901
CLASSIFIED BY COUNTRY, PERIOD MANUFACTURE BEGAN, AND SYSTEM OWNERSHIP %

PERIOD AND OWNERSHIP PERCENTAGE
(WHL=95-100%, MAJ=50-94%, MIN=5-49%, UNK=UNKNOWN)

COUNTRY OR REGION	TOTAL PRE 1968					PRE 1946					1946-1957					1958-1967				
	ALL	WHL	MAJ	MIN	UNK	ALL	WHL	MAJ	MIN	UNK	ALL	WHL	MAJ	MIN	UNK	ALL	WHL	MAJ	MIN	UNK
OUTSIDE U.S.	749	423	186	52	69	254	157	53	11	33	104	70	25	4	5	372	196	108	37	31
OUT. U.S. + CANADA	655	352	176	48	64	215	126	50	10	29	90	57	24	4	5	335	169	102	34	30
OUT. WEST. HEMIS.	481	257	137	37	40	164	92	41	9	22	58	37	15	3	3	249	128	81	25	15
OUT. WHITE CWEALTH	511	255	145	43	57	166	94	41	8	23	71	40	23	3	5	263	121	81	32	29
OUT. DEVLPED WORLD	224	115	52	22	29	56	35	11	1	9	36	22	10	1	3	126	58	31	20	17
CANADA	94	71	10	4	5	39	31	3	1	4	14	13	1	0	0	37	27	6	3	1
LATIN AMERICA	174	95	39	11	24	51	34	9	1	7	32	20	9	1	2	86	41	21	9	15
C. AMER.+CARIB.	62	36	12	6	6	16	12	3	0	1	5	3	1	0	1	39	21	8	6	4
CUBA	6	4	1	0	0	4	3	1	0	0	0	0	0	0	0	1	1	0	0	0
MEXICO	41	24	8	2	6	10	7	2	0	1	4	1	1	0	1	26	15	5	2	4
OTHER	15	8	3	2	0	2	2	0	0	0	1	1	0	0	0	12	5	3	4	0
S. AMERICA	112	59	27	5	18	35	22	6	1	6	27	17	8	1	1	47	20	13	3	11
ARGENTINA	17	16	0	0	0	8	8	0	0	0	4	4	0	0	0	4	4	0	0	0
BRAZIL	31	22	6	0	3	12	9	1	0	2	10	9	0	1	0	9	4	4	0	1
PERU	10	5	4	2	0	4	2	2	0	0	1	0	1	0	0	4	3	1	0	0
COLOMBIA	20	9	7	0	2	1	1	0	0	0	7	3	3	1	0	12	5	4	1	2
VENEZUELA	17	2	2	2	12	3	0	0	0	3	2	0	1	0	1	12	2	1	1	8
OTHER	17	5	8	2	1	7	2	3	1	1	3	1	2	0	0	6	2	3	1	0
EUROPE	353	197	98	20	32	143	82	32	9	20	45	29	12	2	2	159	86	54	9	10
EFTA	123	85	24	3	9	56	35	12	2	7	15	13	1	1	0	50	37	11	0	2
U.K.	79	52	16	3	6	38	23	7	2	6	10	9	0	1	0	29	20	9	0	0
SCANDINAVIA	25	18	5	0	2	9	6	3	0	0	3	3	0	0	0	13	9	2	0	2
SWITZERLAND	6	6	0	0	0	2	2	0	0	0	1	1	0	0	0	3	3	0	0	0
OTHER EFTA	13	9	3	0	1	7	4	2	0	1	1	0	1	0	0	5	5	0	0	0
EUROP. COMMUNITY	184	89	62	11	18	71	39	18	5	9	25	12	10	1	2	84	38	34	5	7
FRANCE	50	23	14	6	5	27	15	4	4	4	4	4	0	0	0	17	10	4	2	1
GERMANY	60	28	25	2	5	25	15	7	0	3	12	5	6	1	0	23	8	12	2	1
ITALY	36	17	13	3	3	12	7	4	0	1	5	3	1	0	1	17	7	8	1	1
BELGIUM + LUX	17	8	5	1	3	7	4	2	1	0	2	0	2	0	0	11	8	1	1	1
NETHERLANDS	21	13	5	0	3	3	2	1	0	0	2	0	1	0	1	16	11	2	0	3
SPAIN	19	6	8	1	1	6	2	4	0	0	1	1	0	0	0	12	3	7	1	1
GREECE + TURKEY	9	4	3	1	1	1	1	0	0	0	2	0	2	0	0	6	3	1	2	0
OTHER EUROPE	18	13	1	1	2	9	6	0	1	2	2	2	0	0	0	7	1	3	2	1
EUROPE EX. U.K.	274	145	82	17	26	105	59	25	7	14	35	20	12	1	2	130	66	45	9	10
SOUTHERN DOMINIONS	55	37	14	1	1	10	8	2	0	0	7	6	1	0	0	36	23	11	1	1
S. AFRICA +RHOD.	15	12	2	0	0	4	4	0	0	0	2	1	1	0	0	8	7	1	0	0
AUSTRALIA + N.Z.	40	25	12	16	1	6	4	2	2	0	5	5	0	2	0	28	16	10	15	4
ASIA + OTHER AFRICA	73	23	25	5	7	11	1	5	0	0	6	2	2	1	1	54	19	16	4	2
JAPAN	23	3	12	2	2	6	1	5	0	0	2	0	1	1	0	14	2	6	11	2
OTHER ASIA+AFR.	50	20	13	11	5	5	0	2	0	0	4	2	1	0	1	40	17	10	4	0
BLACK AFRICA	5	3	1	1	1	0	0	0	0	0	1	1	0	0	0	4	2	1	1	0
ARAB WORLD	7	2	2	2	0	1	0	1	0	0	1	0	1	0	0	4	2	1	1	0
INDIA	11	3	5	2	1	0	0	0	0	0	1	1	0	0	0	10	4	1	3	1
PHILIPPINES	7	3	1	1	0	0	0	0	0	0	1	1	0	0	0	6	2	1	3	1
OTHER E. ASIA	6	2	0	1	3	2	1	0	0	2	0	0	0	0	0	4	2	3	0	0
OTHER ASIA	14	8	4	2	0	2	1	1	1	0	0	0	0	0	0	12	7	3	2	0

CHAPTER 5- PATTERNS OF OWNERSHIP
SECTION 3- THE FLOW OF MANUFACTURING BY CHARACTERISTIC OF PARENT SYSTEM
TABLE H2- MANUFACTURING SUBSIDIARIES IN A SYSTEM
WHICH FIRST MANUFACTURED OUTSIDE U.S. AND CANADA 1901-1919
CLASSIFIED BY COUNTRY, PERIOD MANUFACTURE BEGAN, AND SYSTEM OWNERSHIP %

PERIOD AND OWNERSHIP PERCENTAGE
(WHL=95-100%, MAJ=50-94%, MIN=5-49%, UNK=UNKNOWN)

COUNTRY OR REGION	TOTAL PRE 1968					PRE 1946					1946-1957					1958-1967				
	ALL	WHL	MAJ	MIN	UNK	ALL	WHL	MAJ	MIN	UNK	ALL	WHL	MAJ	MIN	UNK	ALL	WHL	MAJ	MIN	UNK
OUTSIDE U.S.	905	535	186	69	100	312	219	39	18	36	188	114	43	17	14	390	202	104	34	50
OUT. U.S. + CANADA	767	441	172	65	79	237	166	33	15	23	153	86	37	17	13	367	189	102	33	43
OUT. WEST. HEMIS.	552	315	134	37	58	182	129	26	7	20	88	51	22	8	7	274	135	86	22	31
OUT. WHITE CWEALTH	569	308	134	57	64	152	103	21	10	18	122	64	30	17	11	289	141	83	30	35
OUT. DEVLPED WORLD	282	164	51	34	30	72	51	7	8	6	77	43	18	10	6	130	70	26	16	18
CANADA	138	94	14	4	21	75	53	6	3	13	35	28	6	0	1	23	13	2	1	7
LATIN AMERICA	215	126	38	28	21	55	37	7	8	3	65	35	15	9	6	93	54	16	11	12
C. AMER.+CARIB.	74	43	8	13	10	18	12	0	4	2	19	13	4	1	1	37	18	4	8	7
CUBA	6	3	1	1	1	2	1	0	1	0	3	1	1	0	1	1	0	0	0	1
MEXICO	53	33	5	11	4	12	9	0	2	1	14	9	3	1	0	27	15	2	8	2
OTHER	15	6	2	1	5	4	2	0	1	1	2	2	0	0	1	9	3	2	0	4
S. AMERICA	141	83	30	15	11	37	25	7	4	1	46	22	11	8	5	56	36	12	3	5
ARGENTINA	30	17	10	1	1	17	11	6	0	0	5	1	4	0	0	7	5	1	0	1
BRAZIL	46	32	6	4	4	9	7	1	1	0	21	11	4	3	3	16	14	0	0	2
PERU	12	6	0	3	0	2	2	0	0	0	3	2	0	0	1	7	4	3	0	0
COLOMBIA	14	7	0	3	4	2	2	0	0	0	4	0	0	3	0	6	3	0	1	2
VENEZUELA	21	10	6	3	1	1	1	0	0	0	8	4	2	2	0	11	5	4	1	1
OTHER	18	11	5	1	1	4	2	0	1	1	5	4	1	0	0	9	5	4	0	0
EUROPE	365	204	94	16	45	122	79	24	3	16	55	31	12	6	6	182	94	58	7	23
EFTA	147	90	34	4	16	60	40	13	2	5	20	13	6	0	1	64	37	15	2	10
U.K.	102	61	23	3	12	42	26	10	2	4	15	10	4	0	1	42	25	9	1	7
SCANDINAVIA	25	16	7	0	2	11	8	3	0	0	3	2	1	0	0	11	6	3	0	2
SWITZERLAND	9	6	2	0	1	3	2	0	0	1	2	1	0	0	0	4	3	2	0	0
OTHER EFTA	11	7	2	1	1	4	4	0	0	0	0	0	0	0	0	7	3	1	1	1
EUROP. COMMUNITY	180	94	47	10	26	51	31	10	1	9	29	15	5	5	4	97	48	32	4	13
FRANCE	54	24	16	3	9	17	8	4	0	5	7	5	0	1	1	30	14	12	2	3
GERMANY	49	28	8	5	8	17	11	4	1	1	8	4	4	2	1	24	13	3	2	6
ITALY	36	16	8	0	5	7	4	1	0	2	11	6	4	0	1	18	10	3	0	2
BELGIUM + LUX	22	14	4	1	2	5	4	0	0	1	1	0	0	0	1	16	10	4	1	1
NETHERLANDS	19	12	4	1	2	5	4	1	0	0	5	3	0	1	1	16	5	8	0	1
SPAIN	23	11	10	1	1	4	2	2	0	0	4	2	1	0	0	15	7	3	0	0
GREECE + TURKEY	4	1	2	1	0	0	0	0	0	0	0	0	0	0	0	4	1	2	1	0
OTHER EUROPE	11	8	1	0	2	7	6	0	0	1	2	1	1	0	1	2	1	0	0	0
EUROPE EX. U.K.	263	143	71	13	33	80	53	14	1	12	40	21	8	6	5	140	69	49	6	16
SOUTHERN DOMINIONS	89	67	14	5	2	40	34	2	3	1	14	11	3	0	0	34	22	9	2	1
S. AFRICA +RHOD.	22	17	3	1	1	6	5	0	0	1	6	5	1	0	0	9	7	2	0	0
AUSTRALIA + N.Z.	67	50	11	5	1	34	29	2	3	0	8	6	2	0	0	25	15	7	2	1
ASIA + OTHER AFRICA	98	44	26	16	12	20	16	0	1	3	19	9	7	2	1	58	19	19	13	7
JAPAN	31	6	13	10	2	3	2	0	1	0	7	1	4	1	1	21	3	9	8	1
OTHER ASIA+AFR.	67	38	13	6	9	17	14	0	0	3	12	8	3	1	0	37	16	10	5	6
BLACK AFRICA	9	7	1	1	0	0	1	0	0	0	1	0	1	0	0	9	7	1	1	0
ARAB WORLD	8	5	1	1	1	1	0	0	0	0	1	1	0	0	0	6	3	0	2	1
INDIA	11	5	2	3	1	5	5	0	0	0	2	0	1	1	0	4	0	1	1	1
PHILIPPINES	9	6	3	0	0	2	1	0	0	0	5	3	2	0	0	2	1	1	0	0
OTHER E. ASIA	3	3	0	0	0	1	2	0	0	0	2	2	0	0	0	0	0	2	0	0
OTHER ASIA	27	12	6	1	7	8	5	0	0	3	2	2	0	0	0	16	5	6	1	4

CHAPTER 5- PATTERNS OF OWNERSHIP
SECTION 3- THE FLOW OF MANUFACTURING BY CHARACTERISTIC OF PARENT SYSTEM
TABLE H3- MANUFACTURING SUBSIDIARIES IN A SYSTEM
WHICH FIRST MANUFACTURED OUTSIDE U.S. AND CANADA 1920-1929
CLASSIFIED BY COUNTRY, PERIOD MANUFACTURE BEGAN, AND SYSTEM OWNERSHIP %

PERIOD AND OWNERSHIP PERCENTAGE
(WHL=95-100%, MAJ=50-94%, MIN=5-49%, UNK=UNKNOWN)

COUNTRY OR REGION	TOTAL PRE 1968					PRE 1946					1946-1957					1958-1967				
	ALL	WHL	MAJ	MIN	UNK	ALL	WHL	MAJ	MIN	UNK	ALL	WHL	MAJ	MIN	UNK	ALL	WHL	MAJ	MIN	UNK
OUTSIDE U.S.	1524	907	318	175	87	356	250	48	29	29	296	187	59	34	16	835	470	211	112	42
OUT. U.S. + CANADA	1274	701	297	167	78	259	167	40	25	27	246	151	51	33	11	738	383	206	109	40
OUT. WEST. HEMIS.	900	508	206	99	58	182	117	31	11	23	153	93	32	23	5	536	298	143	65	30
OUT. WHITE CWEALTH	895	463	234	140	50	157	96	26	23	12	178	113	37	20	8	552	254	171	97	30
OUT. DEVLPED WORLD	482	249	123	79	28	85	56	9	14	6	110	70	23	11	6	284	123	91	54	16
CANADA	250	206	21	8	9	97	83	8	4	2	50	36	8	1	5	97	87	5	3	2
LATIN AMERICA	374	193	91	68	20	77	50	9	14	4	93	58	19	10	6	202	85	63	44	10
C. AMER.+CARIB.	169	81	43	30	14	31	20	2	7	2	40	30	5	2	3	97	31	36	21	9
CUBA	19	10	4	2	3	10	5	2	2	1	8	4	2	1	1	1	1	0	0	0
MEXICO	93	51	21	16	5	14	13	0	1	0	23	19	2	1	1	56	19	19	14	4
OTHER	57	20	18	12	6	7	2	0	4	1	9	7	1	1	0	40	11	17	7	5
S. AMERICA	205	112	48	38	6	46	30	7	7	2	53	28	14	8	3	105	54	27	23	1
ARGENTINA	54	32	12	9	1	18	16	1	1	0	11	4	4	3	0	25	12	7	6	0
BRAZIL	50	29	11	7	3	10	6	1	0	3	15	7	6	0	2	25	16	6	5	0
PERU	17	9	5	3	0	6	3	2	1	0	6	4	1	1	0	5	2	4	1	0
COLOMBIA	32	14	11	7	0	4	1	2	1	0	6	4	4	2	0	22	9	2	4	0
VENEZUELA	34	19	8	4	2	3	2	1	0	0	11	6	3	1	1	19	11	9	3	1
OTHER	18	9	1	8	0	5	2	0	3	0	4	3	0	1	0	9	4	1	4	0
EUROPE	574	334	123	59	38	142	89	23	10	20	96	59	15	17	5	316	186	85	32	13
EFTA	241	149	35	20	21	79	54	8	2	15	46	24	7	12	3	100	71	20	6	3
U.K.	191	119	23	16	18	70	49	6	1	14	37	17	6	11	3	69	53	11	4	1
SCANDINAVIA	33	21	8	3	1	5	4	0	1	0	7	5	1	1	0	21	12	7	1	1
SWITZERLAND	4	3	0	0	1	4	1	0	0	0	1	1	0	0	0	2	2	0	1	0
OTHER EFTA	13	6	4	1	2	4	0	2	0	1	1	1	0	0	0	8	4	2	1	1
EUROP. COMMUNITY	274	161	70	24	16	56	32	13	6	5	43	30	6	5	2	172	99	51	13	9
FRANCE	94	45	31	13	4	21	11	3	6	1	15	8	3	2	2	57	26	25	13	1
GERMANY	76	51	14	5	5	20	12	5	0	3	8	7	1	0	0	47	32	8	5	2
ITALY	52	32	13	3	4	1	1	0	0	0	13	9	2	2	0	38	22	11	5	4
BELGIUM + LUX	26	16	7	2	1	7	2	4	0	0	4	3	0	1	0	15	11	3	1	0
NETHERLANDS	26	17	5	1	2	5	3	2	0	0	3	3	0	0	0	15	8	4	1	2
SPAIN	35	10	15	10	0	3	0	2	0	0	4	1	1	2	0	26	4	12	10	0
GREECE + TURKEY	11	6	3	1	1	0	0	0	0	0	1	0	0	1	0	10	6	2	1	1
OTHER EUROPE	13	8	0	4	0	0	0	0	2	0	2	2	0	0	0	8	6	0	2	0
EUROPE EX. U.K.	383	215	100	43	20	72	40	17	9	6	59	42	9	6	2	247	133	74	28	12
SOUTHERN DOMINIONS	180	113	40	10	10	32	22	8	1	1	29	19	8	2	0	112	72	24	7	9
S. AFRICA +RHOD.	64	51	8	4	0	12	10	2	0	0	8	6	2	0	0	43	35	4	4	0
AUSTRALIA + N.Z.	116	62	32	6	10	20	12	6	1	1	21	13	6	2	0	69	37	20	3	9
ASIA + OTHER AFRICA	146	61	43	30	10	8	6	0	0	2	28	15	9	4	0	108	40	34	26	8
JAPAN	38	5	11	19	2	0	0	0	0	0	11	3	5	3	0	26	2	6	16	2
OTHER ASIA+AFR.	108	56	32	11	8	8	6	0	0	2	17	12	4	1	0	82	38	28	10	6
BLACK AFRICA	17	10	3	3	1	0	0	0	0	0	2	1	1	0	0	15	9	2	3	1
ARAB WORLD	10	7	0	3	0	0	0	0	0	0	3	2	0	1	0	7	5	2	0	0
INDIA	19	7	7	4	0	5	4	0	0	1	3	3	0	0	0	15	5	7	4	0
PHILIPPINES	21	14	5	1	1	5	4	0	0	1	6	5	1	0	0	10	5	4	1	3
OTHER E. ASIA	12	4	3	1	4	1	0	0	1	0	1	0	1	0	0	10	0	3	0	2
OTHER ASIA	29	14	11	2	2	2	2	0	0	0	2	1	1	0	0	25	11	10	2	2

CHAPTER 5- PATTERNS OF OWNERSHIP
SECTION 3- THE FLOW OF MANUFACTURING BY CHARACTERISTIC OF PARENT SYSTEM
TABLE H4- MANUFACTURING SUBSIDIARIES IN A SYSTEM
WHICH FIRST MANUFACTURED OUTSIDE U.S. AND CANADA 1930-1945
CLASSIFIED BY COUNTRY, PERIOD MANUFACTURE BEGAN, AND SYSTEM OWNERSHIP %

PERIOD AND OWNERSHIP PERCENTAGE
(WHL=95-100%, MAJ=50-94%, MIN=5-49%, UNK=UNKNOWN)

COUNTRY OR REGION	TOTAL PRE 1968					PRE 1946					1946-1957					1958-1967				
	ALL	WHL	MAJ	MIN	UNK	ALL	WHL	MAJ	MIN	UNK	ALL	WHL	MAJ	MIN	UNK	ALL	WHL	MAJ	MIN	UNK
OUTSIDE U.S.	890	452	206	113	62	71	43	14	11	3	208	112	59	26	11	554	297	133	76	48
OUT. U.S. + CANADA	753	349	184	109	58	46	20	12	11	3	165	81	49	25	10	489	248	123	73	45
OUT. WEST. HEMIS.	469	215	112	74	37	24	13	4	5	2	73	34	17	16	6	341	168	91	53	29
OUT. WHITE CWEALTH	605	260	162	92	44	28	8	9	9	2	130	63	41	18	8	400	189	112	65	34
OUT. DEVLPED WORLD	332	148	85	44	24	22	7	8	6	1	104	52	37	10	5	175	89	40	28	18
CANADA	137	103	22	4	4	25	23	2	0	0	43	31	10	1	1	65	49	10	3	3
LATIN AMERICA	284	134	72	35	21	22	8	7	6	1	92	47	32	9	4	148	80	32	20	16
C. AMER.+CARIB.	122	61	25	15	8	13	4	5	3	1	39	27	7	3	2	57	30	13	9	5
CUBA	10	7	1	1	0	3	2	1	0	0	5	5	0	1	0	0	0	0	0	0
MEXICO	82	36	19	11	7	10	2	4	3	1	28	19	6	1	2	35	15	9	7	4
OTHER	30	18	5	3	1	0	0	0	0	0	5	3	1	1	0	22	15	4	2	1
S. AMERICA	162	73	47	20	13	9	3	3	3	0	53	20	25	6	2	91	50	19	11	11
ARGENTINA	26	9	4	7	4	1	1	0	0	0	7	2	2	3	0	16	6	2	4	4
BRAZIL	43	19	15	6	1	3	1	0	2	0	14	4	11	2	0	24	16	4	3	1
PERU	8	3	1	1	1	0	0	0	0	0	2	2	0	1	0	2	1	0	0	1
COLOMBIA	29	15	10	1	2	1	0	0	1	0	9	5	4	0	0	18	10	5	1	2
VENEZUELA	39	17	15	5	5	3	1	2	0	0	15	6	7	1	2	21	11	6	1	3
OTHER	17	10	2	3	0	1	1	0	1	0	4	3	0	0	0	10	6	2	2	0
EUROPE	319	157	79	46	30	17	8	3	4	2	38	17	6	11	4	257	132	70	31	24
EFTA	101	63	14	9	14	12	7	2	1	2	17	8	3	3	3	71	48	9	5	9
U.K.	76	47	11	8	10	11	7	2	1	1	14	6	3	3	2	51	34	6	4	7
SCANDINAVIA	13	9	1	1	1	0	0	0	0	0	2	2	0	0	0	10	7	1	1	1
SWITZERLAND	6	4	1	0	0	0	0	0	0	0	0	0	0	0	0	6	4	1	0	1
OTHER EFTA	6	3	1	0	2	0	0	0	0	0	1	0	0	0	1	4	3	1	0	0
EUROP. COMMUNITY	181	87	51	23	14	5	1	1	3	0	14	8	2	3	1	156	78	48	17	13
FRANCE	48	23	17	5	2	2	1	0	0	1	3	2	1	1	0	44	21	16	5	2
GERMANY	51	24	10	8	7	2	0	1	1	0	5	3	1	0	0	42	20	8	7	7
ITALY	48	24	15	5	4	0	0	0	0	0	1	0	1	1	0	47	24	15	4	4
BELGIUM + LUX	15	9	3	0	3	0	0	0	0	0	1	1	0	0	0	12	8	3	1	0
NETHERLANDS	19	7	6	2	1	1	0	0	0	1	4	2	0	1	1	11	5	6	0	0
SPAIN	23	5	9	8	1	0	0	0	0	0	4	0	0	4	0	19	5	9	4	1
GREECE + TURKEY	11	1	5	5	0	0	0	0	0	0	1	0	1	0	0	9	4	4	0	1
OTHER EUROPE	3	1	0	1	1	0	0	0	0	0	1	1	0	0	0	2	0	0	1	1
EUROPE EX. U.K.	243	110	68	38	20	6	1	1	3	1	24	11	3	8	2	206	98	64	27	17
SOUTHERN DOMINIONS	69	41	11	8	3	7	5	1	1	0	20	11	5	4	0	36	25	5	3	3
S. AFRICA +RHOD.	31	9	3	4	4	4	2	1	1	0	7	4	1	2	0	15	13	1	0	1
AUSTRALIA + N.Z.	38	22	8	4	3	3	3	0	0	0	13	7	4	2	1	21	12	4	2	3
ASIA + OTHER AFRICA	81	17	22	20	4	0	0	0	0	0	15	6	6	1	2	48	11	16	19	2
JAPAN	33	9	9	11	1	0	0	0	0	0	3	1	1	0	1	21	2	8	11	0
OTHER ASIA+AFR.	48	14	13	9	3	0	0	0	0	0	12	5	5	1	1	27	9	8	8	2
BLACK AFRICA	5	1	1	0	1	0	0	0	0	0	1	0	0	0	0	4	0	1	2	1
ARAB WORLD	7	3	1	2	0	0	0	0	0	0	1	0	0	1	0	6	3	2	0	1
INDIA	9	5	2	2	0	0	0	0	0	0	1	1	0	0	0	3	1	0	2	0
PHILIPPINES	6	2	1	1	2	0	0	0	0	0	5	3	1	0	1	3	2	2	1	0
OTHER E. ASIA	6	2	2	2	0	0	0	0	0	0	3	0	1	0	0	5	2	2	1	1
OTHER ASIA	16	2	7	1	2	0	0	0	0	0	6	1	4	0	1	6	1	3	1	1

CHAPTER 5- PATTERNS OF OWNERSHIP
SECTION 3- THE FLOW OF MANUFACTURING BY CHARACTERISTIC OF PARENT SYSTEM
TABLE H5- MANUFACTURING SUBSIDIARIES IN A SYSTEM
WHICH FIRST MANUFACTURED OUTSIDE U.S. AND CANADA AFTER 1946
CLASSIFIED BY COUNTRY, PERIOD MANUFACTURE BEGAN, AND SYSTEM OWNERSHIP %

PERIOD AND OWNERSHIP PERCENTAGE
(WHL=95-100%, MAJ=50-94%, MIN=5-49%, UNK=UNKNOWN)

COUNTRY OR REGION	TOTAL PRE 1968					PRE 1946					1946-1957					1958-1967				
	ALL	WHL	MAJ	MIN	UNK	ALL	WHL	MAJ	MIN	UNK	ALL	WHL	MAJ	MIN	UNK	ALL	WHL	MAJ	MIN	UNK
OUTSIDE U.S.	1111	561	315	173	49	32	27	4	0	1	212	150	31	22	9	854	384	280	151	39
OUT. U.S. + CANADA	929	415	298	164	43	0	0	0	0	0	154	98	30	18	8	766	317	268	146	35
OUT. WEST. HEMIS.	651	303	205	108	28	0	0	0	0	0	97	66	16	9	6	547	237	189	99	22
OUT. WHITE CWEALTH	728	294	246	146	34	0	0	0	0	0	111	62	26	17	6	609	232	220	129	28
OUT. DEVLPED WORLD	365	138	126	82	16	0	0	0	0	0	66	36	17	10	3	296	102	109	72	13
CANADA	182	146	17	9	6	32	27	4	0	1	58	52	1	4	1	88	67	12	5	4
LATIN AMERICA	278	112	93	56	15	0	0	0	0	0	57	32	14	9	2	219	80	79	47	13
C. AMER.+CARIB.	139	57	45	28	7	0	0	0	0	0	28	18	7	2	1	109	39	38	26	6
CUBA	5	2	1	1	1	0	0	0	0	0	4	1	1	1	1	1	1	0	0	0
MEXICO	96	44	26	20	5	0	0	0	0	0	22	16	1	1	0	73	28	21	19	5
OTHER	38	11	18	7	1	0	0	0	0	0	2	0	1	0	1	35	10	17	7	1
S. AMERICA	139	55	48	28	8	0	0	0	0	0	29	14	7	7	1	110	41	41	21	7
ARGENTINA	32	14	11	6	1	0	0	0	0	0	6	3	2	1	0	26	11	9	5	1
BRAZIL	29	15	7	5	2	0	0	0	0	0	10	7	0	3	0	19	8	7	5	2
PERU	10	5	4	0	1	0	0	0	0	0	1	0	1	0	0	9	5	3	0	1
COLOMBIA	20	5	9	4	2	0	0	0	0	0	3	0	2	1	0	17	5	7	3	2
VENEZUELA	33	9	11	12	1	0	0	0	0	0	7	3	1	2	1	26	6	10	10	0
OTHER	15	7	6	1	1	0	0	0	0	0	2	1	1	0	0	13	6	5	1	1
EUROPE	431	221	131	54	21	0	0	0	0	0	69	48	11	6	4	358	173	120	48	17
EFTA	136	87	31	9	8	0	0	0	0	0	27	23	3	0	1	108	64	28	9	7
U.K.	103	70	20	6	6	0	0	0	0	0	25	21	3	0	1	77	49	17	6	5
SCANDINAVIA	17	9	6	1	1	0	0	0	0	0	2	2	0	0	0	15	7	6	1	1
SWITZERLAND	12	6	4	1	1	0	0	0	0	0	0	0	0	0	0	12	6	4	1	1
OTHER EFTA	4	2	1	1	0	0	0	0	0	0	0	0	0	0	0	4	2	1	1	0
EUROP. COMMUNITY	244	124	72	35	10	0	0	0	0	0	36	23	7	4	2	205	101	65	31	8
FRANCE	74	30	21	17	5	0	0	0	0	0	11	6	4	0	0	63	24	17	17	5
GERMANY	61	35	21	2	2	0	0	0	0	0	15	11	2	1	0	46	24	19	1	2
ITALY	49	25	16	7	0	0	0	0	0	0	6	4	0	1	0	43	21	16	6	0
BELGIUM + LUX	36	22	9	4	1	0	0	0	0	0	3	2	1	0	1	33	20	8	4	0
NETHERLANDS	24	12	5	5	2	0	0	0	0	0	4	0	0	2	2	20	12	5	3	0
SPAIN	37	12	22	8	1	0	0	0	0	0	3	1	1	2	0	34	15	21	7	1
GREECE + TURKEY	7	2	2	2	1	0	0	0	0	0	1	0	1	0	0	6	2	2	2	1
OTHER EUROPE	7	2	4	0	1	0	0	0	0	0	2	0	0	1	0	5	1	4	0	2
EUROPE EX. U.K.	328	151	111	48	15	0	0	0	0	0	44	27	8	6	3	281	124	103	42	12
SOUTHERN DOMINIONS	92	49	29	12	2	0	0	0	0	0	16	14	1	1	0	76	35	28	11	2
S. AFRICA +RHOD.	27	11	10	6	0	0	0	0	0	0	5	5	0	0	0	22	6	10	6	0
AUSTRALIA + N.Z.	65	38	19	6	2	0	0	0	0	0	11	9	1	1	0	54	29	18	5	2
ASIA + OTHER AFRICA	128	33	45	42	5	0	0	0	0	0	12	4	4	2	2	113	29	41	40	3
JAPAN	41	7	12	16	4	0	0	0	0	0	3	0	1	1	1	36	7	11	15	3
OTHER ASIA+AFR.	87	26	33	26	1	0	0	0	0	0	9	4	0	2	1	77	22	30	25	0
BLACK AFRICA	10	2	6	4	0	0	0	0	0	0	2	2	0	0	0	8	2	3	4	0
ARAB WORLD	9	1	3	4	0	0	0	0	0	0	0	0	0	0	0	9	1	3	3	0
INDIA	20	1	6	13	0	0	0	0	0	0	0	0	0	0	0	20	1	6	13	0
PHILIPPINES	12	5	5	2	0	0	0	0	0	0	2	1	1	0	0	10	4	4	2	0
OTHER E. ASIA	12	8	3	1	0	0	0	0	0	0	0	0	0	0	0	12	8	3	1	0
OTHER ASIA	24	4	13	5	1	0	0	0	0	0	5	1	2	1	1	18	3	11	4	0

CHAPTER 5— PATTERNS OF OWNERSHIP
SECTION 3— THE FLOW OF MANUFACTURING BY CHARACTERISTIC OF PARENT SYSTEM
TABLE II— MANUFACTURING SUBSIDIARIES IN A SYSTEM
IN "ORGANIZATIONAL STAGE II" IN 1966
CLASSIFIED BY COUNTRY, PERIOD MANUFACTURE BEGAN, AND SYSTEM OWNERSHIP %

PERIOD AND OWNERSHIP PERCENTAGE
(WHL=95-100%, MAJ=50-94%, MIN=5-49%, UNK=UNKNOWN)

COUNTRY OR REGION	TOTAL PRE 1968					PRE 1946					1946-1957					1958-1967				
	ALL	WHL	MAJ	MIN	UNK	ALL	WHL	MAJ	MIN	UNK	ALL	WHL	MAJ	MIN	UNK	ALL	WHL	MAJ	MIN	UNK
OUTSIDE U.S.	269	140	78	39	12	39	25	12	0	2	59	31	17	8	3	171	84	49	31	7
OUT. U.S. + CANADA	225	110	68	38	9	29	17	10	0	2	45	23	13	8	1	151	70	45	30	6
OUT. WEST. HEMIS.	153	76	50	21	6	24	14	9	0	1	22	11	8	2	1	107	51	33	19	4
OUT. WHITE CWEALTH	170	76	54	32	8	14	6	7	0	1	35	15	11	8	1	121	55	36	24	6
OUT. DEVLPED WORLD	94	41	28	22	3	6	4	1	0	1	28	12	10	6	0	60	25	17	16	2
CANADA	44	30	10	1	3	10	8	2	0	0	14	8	4	0	2	20	14	4	1	1
LATIN AMERICA	72	34	18	17	3	5	3	2	0	0	23	12	5	6	0	44	19	12	11	2
C. AMER.+CARIB.	33	16	9	7	1	3	2	1	0	0	13	8	3	2	0	17	6	5	5	1
CUBA	6	3	2	1	0	1	1	0	0	0	4	2	1	1	0	1	0	1	0	0
MEXICO	24	12	5	6	1	2	2	0	0	0	9	6	2	1	0	13	4	3	5	1
OTHER	3	1	2	0	0	0	0	0	0	0	0	0	0	0	0	3	1	2	0	0
S. AMERICA	39	18	9	10	2	2	1	1	0	0	10	4	2	4	0	27	13	7	6	1
ARGENTINA	4	2	0	2	0	0	0	0	0	0	1	1	0	0	0	3	1	0	2	0
BRAZIL	6	4	1	0	1	0	0	0	0	0	2	2	0	0	0	3	2	1	0	0
PERU	5	2	2	1	0	1	1	0	0	0	3	0	1	1	1	1	1	0	0	0
COLOMBIA	9	4	2	2	1	1	1	0	0	0	3	1	1	0	1	6	3	1	2	0
VENEZUELA	10	3	4	3	0	0	0	0	0	0	1	0	0	1	0	9	3	4	2	0
OTHER	5	3	1	1	0	0	0	0	0	0	0	0	0	0	0	5	3	1	1	0
EUROPE	101	54	33	9	5	17	9	8	0	0	11	7	2	1	1	73	38	23	8	4
EFTA	39	24	12	3	0	10	7	3	0	0	5	4	1	0	0	24	13	8	3	0
U.K.	31	21	8	2	0	9	7	2	0	0	5	4	1	0	0	17	10	5	2	0
SCANDINAVIA	5	1	3	1	0	0	0	0	0	0	0	0	0	0	0	5	1	3	1	0
SWITZERLAND	1	1	0	0	0	0	0	0	0	0	0	0	0	0	0	1	1	0	0	0
OTHER EFTA	2	1	1	0	0	1	0	1	0	0	0	0	0	0	0	1	1	0	0	0
EUROP. COMMUNITY	53	27	17	4	5	7	2	5	0	0	5	2	1	1	1	41	23	11	3	4
FRANCE	13	5	4	2	2	2	1	1	0	0	1	0	1	0	0	10	4	2	2	2
GERMANY	16	6	8	0	2	2	1	1	0	0	1	1	0	0	0	13	4	7	0	2
ITALY	10	6	1	1	2	0	0	0	0	0	3	1	0	1	1	7	5	1	0	1
BELGIUM + LUX	11	9	2	0	0	2	1	1	0	0	0	0	0	0	0	9	8	1	0	0
NETHERLANDS	3	1	2	0	0	1	0	1	0	0	0	0	0	0	0	2	1	1	0	0
SPAIN	7	3	4	0	0	0	0	0	0	0	1	0	1	0	0	6	3	3	0	0
GREECE + TURKEY	2	0	0	2	0	0	0	0	0	0	0	0	0	0	0	2	0	0	2	0
OTHER EUROPE	0	0	0	0	0	0	0	0	0	0	0	0	0	0	0	0	0	0	0	0
EUROPE EX. U.K.	70	33	25	7	5	8	2	6	0	0	6	3	1	1	1	56	28	18	6	4
SOUTHERN DOMINIONS	24	13	6	4	1	6	4	1	1	0	5	3	1	0	1	13	6	4	3	0
S. AFRICA +RHOD.	9	5	3	1	0	2	1	1	0	0	3	2	1	0	0	4	2	1	1	0
AUSTRALIA + N.Z.	15	8	3	3	1	4	3	0	1	0	2	1	0	0	1	9	4	3	2	0
ASIA + OTHER AFRICA	28	9	11	8	0	1	1	0	0	0	6	2	2	2	0	21	8	6	7	0
JAPAN	6	2	1	3	0	1	1	0	0	0	0	0	0	0	0	5	2	1	2	0
OTHER ASIA+AFR.	22	7	10	5	0	0	0	0	0	0	6	2	2	2	0	16	6	5	5	0
BLACK AFRICA	2	1	0	1	0	0	0	0	0	0	1	1	0	0	0	1	0	0	1	0
ARAB WORLD	5	2	2	1	0	0	0	0	0	0	1	0	0	1	0	4	2	2	0	0
INDIA	5	2	2	1	0	0	0	0	0	0	0	0	0	0	0	5	2	2	1	0
PHILIPPINES	5	3	0	2	0	0	0	0	0	0	3	1	0	2	0	2	2	0	0	0
OTHER E. ASIA	0	0	0	0	0	0	0	0	0	0	0	0	0	0	0	0	0	0	0	0
OTHER ASIA	5	1	3	0	1	0	0	0	0	0	1	1	0	0	0	4	0	3	0	1

CHAPTER 5- PATTERNS OF OWNERSHIP
SECTION 3- THE FLOW OF MANUFACTURING BY CHARACTERISTIC OF PARENT SYSTEM
TABLE I2- MANUFACTURING SUBSIDIARIES IN A SYSTEM
IN "ORGANIZATIONAL STAGE III-ID" IN 1966
CLASSIFIED BY COUNTRY, PERIOD MANUFACTURE BEGAN, AND SYSTEM OWNERSHIP %

PERIOD AND OWNERSHIP PERCENTAGE
(WHL=95-100%, MAJ=50-94%, MIN=5-49%, UNK=UNKNOWN)

COUNTRY OR REGION	TOTAL PRE 1968					PRE 1946					1946-1957					1958-1967				
	ALL	WHL	MAJ	MIN	UNK	ALL	WHL	MAJ	MIN	UNK	ALL	WHL	MAJ	MIN	UNK	ALL	WHL	MAJ	MIN	UNK
OUTSIDE U.S.	2409	1384	539	285	158	493	341	61	40	51	474	312	89	48	25	1399	731	389	197	82
OUT. U.S. + CANADA	2028	1087	508	270	135	354	228	51	36	39	384	239	80	45	20	1262	620	377	189	76
OUT. WEST. HEMIS.	1407	758	360	171	96	253	165	37	16	35	232	142	43	34	13	900	451	280	121	48
OUT. WHITE CWEALTH	1519	799	423	228	93	229	141	38	29	21	290	180	66	30	14	983	437	319	169	58
OUT. DEVLPED WORLD	793	411	199	125	50	117	75	14	20	8	180	117	42	14	7	488	219	143	91	35
CANADA	381	297	31	15	23	139	113	10	4	12	90	73	9	3	5	137	111	12	8	6
LATIN AMERICA	621	329	148	99	39	101	63	14	20	4	152	97	37	11	7	362	169	97	68	28
C. AMER.+CARIB.	267	128	65	48	23	38	23	3	9	3	62	46	10	2	4	164	59	52	37	16
CUBA	26	16	3	2	3	11	7	1	2	1	12	8	2	0	2	2	0	0	0	1
MEXICO	162	84	36	31	11	22	15	2	4	1	43	33	7	1	2	97	36	27	26	8
OTHER	79	28	26	15	8	5	1	0	3	1	7	5	1	1	0	65	22	25	11	7
S. AMERICA	354	201	83	51	16	63	40	11	11	1	90	51	27	9	3	198	110	45	31	12
ARGENTINA	80	47	19	11	2	22	17	5	0	0	16	7	6	3	0	41	23	8	8	2
BRAZIL	89	57	20	10	2	17	12	2	3	0	27	16	10	1	0	45	29	8	6	2
PERU	25	16	4	3	2	4	3	1	0	0	7	4	0	2	1	14	9	2	1	2
COLOMBIA	51	25	16	7	3	7	2	2	3	0	11	7	2	1	1	33	16	12	3	2
VENEZUELA	72	36	19	11	5	5	3	1	1	0	22	12	2	7	1	44	21	11	9	3
OTHER	37	20	5	9	2	8	3	0	4	1	7	5	1	1	0	21	12	4	4	1
EUROPE	905	493	232	98	69	183	113	28	11	31	151	91	26	23	11	558	289	178	64	27
EFTA	319	205	48	25	36	94	62	7	3	20	62	36	10	11	5	158	107	29	11	11
U.K.	240	149	34	21	31	76	48	7	0	18	49	27	8	10	4	110	74	19	8	9
SCANDINAVIA	46	36	8	1	1	9	7	2	0	0	9	7	1	1	0	28	22	5	0	1
SWITZERLAND	16	11	2	1	2	3	2	0	0	1	2	2	0	0	0	11	7	2	1	1
OTHER EFTA	17	9	4	2	2	6	5	0	0	1	2	0	1	0	1	9	4	3	2	0
EUROP. COMMUNITY	486	262	137	51	29	80	46	16	8	10	74	49	13	8	4	325	167	108	35	15
FRANCE	155	70	48	23	12	29	13	6	6	5	21	13	4	2	2	103	44	39	15	5
GERMANY	127	77	27	12	7	29	20	5	1	3	24	17	5	2	0	70	40	17	9	5
ITALY	104	54	40	6	4	6	2	3	0	1	15	11	3	1	0	82	40	35	4	3
BELGIUM + LUX	49	32	8	4	2	7	8	2	0	1	6	5	0	1	0	36	25	5	5	1
NETHERLANDS	51	29	14	7	4	9	7	3	2	0	8	3	2	3	1	34	18	12	2	2
SPAIN	62	11	35	15	1	7	4	3	0	0	7	2	2	2	0	48	5	30	12	1
GREECE + TURKEY	19	5	3	2	3	2	1	0	0	0	2	2	1	2	0	17	5	8	4	0
OTHER EUROPE	19	10	3	2	5	0	0	0	0	1	6	4	0	2	2	10	5	2	0	0
EUROPE EX. U.K.	665	344	198	77	38	107	65	21	8	13	102	64	18	13	7	448	215	159	56	18
SOUTHERN DOMINIONS	255	173	48	20	9	49	39	6	4	0	39	28	6	5	0	162	106	36	11	9
S. AFRICA +RHOD.	86	67	10	8	0	14	13	1	0	0	12	10	1	1	0	59	44	8	7	0
AUSTRALIA + N.Z.	169	106	38	12	9	35	26	5	4	0	27	18	5	4	0	103	62	28	4	9
ASIA + OTHER AFRICA	247	92	80	53	18	21	13	3	1	4	42	23	11	6	2	180	56	66	46	12
JAPAN	75	10	29	27	7	5	1	3	0	1	14	3	6	3	2	54	6	20	23	5
OTHER ASIA+AFR.	172	82	51	26	11	16	12	0	0	4	28	20	5	3	0	126	50	46	23	7
BLACK AFRICA	22	13	4	4	1	0	0	0	0	0	3	3	0	0	0	19	10	4	4	1
ARAB WORLD	18	10	7	0	1	1	1	0	0	0	1	1	0	0	0	16	8	7	0	1
INDIA	34	11	9	12	1	2	2	2	0	0	4	3	0	1	1	27	6	8	11	1
PHILIPPINES	25	18	3	3	1	5	4	0	0	0	10	9	0	1	0	10	5	3	2	1
OTHER E. ASIA	21	11	5	3	2	6	0	0	0	1	1	0	2	1	1	20	11	2	2	2
OTHER ASIA	52	19	23	4	5	8	5	0	0	3	9	4	5	0	0	34	10	18	4	2

CHAPTER 5- PATTERNS OF OWNERSHIP
SECTION 3- THE FLOW OF MANUFACTURING BY CHARACTERISTIC OF PARENT SYSTEM
TABLE I3- MANUFACTURING SUBSIDIARIES IN A SYSTEM
IN "ORGANIZATIONAL STAGE III-OTHER" IN 1966
CLASSIFIED BY COUNTRY, PERIOD MANUFACTURE BEGAN, AND SYSTEM OWNERSHIP %

PERIOD AND OWNERSHIP PERCENTAGE
(WHL=95-100%, MAJ=50-94%, MIN=5-49%, UNK=UNKNOWN)

COUNTRY OR REGION	TOTAL PRE 1968 ALL	WHL	MAJ	MIN	UNK	PRE 1946 ALL	WHL	MAJ	MIN	UNK	1946-1957 ALL	WHL	MAJ	MIN	UNK	1958-1967 ALL	WHL	MAJ	MIN	UNK
OUTSIDE U.S.	2097	1163	475	192	183	431	294	72	20	45	387	236	88	39	24	1195	633	315	133	114
OUT. U.S. + CANADA	1805	942	439	184	164	337	218	63	19	37	322	184	78	37	23	1070	540	298	128	104
OUT. WEST. HEMIS.	1275	679	312	125	108	245	159	47	12	27	188	111	43	22	12	791	409	222	91	69
OUT. WHITE CWEALTH	1380	660	354	167	139	235	145	42	17	31	244	128	65	31	20	841	387	247	119	88
OUT. DEVLPED WORLD	678	320	164	87	71	105	67	18	7	13	151	82	39	16	14	386	171	107	64	44
CANADA	292	221	36	8	19	94	76	9	1	8	65	52	10	2	1	125	93	17	5	10
LATIN AMERICA	530	263	127	59	56	92	59	16	7	10	134	73	35	15	11	279	131	76	37	35
C. AMER.+CARIB.	220	122	40	27	18	33	21	5	4	3	45	34	6	3	2	129	67	29	20	13
CUBA	11	6	3	1	1	6	3	3	1	0	4	2	1	0	1	1	1	0	0	0
MEXICO	148	83	27	16	12	19	13	3	1	2	30	23	4	2	1	89	47	20	13	9
OTHER	61	33	10	10	5	8	5	0	2	1	11	9	1	1	0	39	19	9	7	4
S. AMERICA	310	141	87	32	38	59	38	11	3	7	89	39	29	12	9	150	64	47	17	22
ARGENTINA	60	33	13	6	5	20	18	1	1	0	13	5	5	3	0	24	10	7	3	4
BRAZIL	86	49	18	7	10	15	11	1	1	2	34	15	10	4	5	35	23	7	2	3
PERU	26	10	12	1	0	7	3	3	1	0	4	2	2	0	0	12	12	7	0	0
COLOMBIA	48	19	15	7	6	3	2	1	0	0	13	5	5	2	1	31	12	8	5	5
VENEZUELA	52	14	15	6	16	5	0	2	0	3	17	7	5	2	3	29	7	8	4	10
OTHER	38	16	14	5	1	9	4	3	1	1	8	5	2	1	0	19	7	9	3	0
EUROPE	875	504	206	64	82	197	125	37	12	23	126	75	25	18	8	533	304	144	34	51
EFTA	326	220	60	12	27	92	61	21	3	7	50	35	7	5	3	177	124	32	4	17
U.K.	232	160	40	10	17	67	45	15	2	5	41	28	5	5	0	119	87	20	3	9
SCANDINAVIA	54	33	13	1	6	15	11	3	1	0	7	6	1	0	0	31	16	9	0	6
SWITZERLAND	15	12	2	0	0	2	2	0	0	0	2	0	1	0	0	10	9	1	0	0
OTHER EFTA	25	15	5	1	4	8	3	3	0	2	0	0	0	0	0	17	12	2	1	2
EUROP. COMMUNITY	446	235	118	35	46	81	50	14	5	12	62	33	15	9	5	291	152	89	21	29
FRANCE	131	63	41	13	9	28	17	8	3	4	13	8	3	2	0	85	38	35	7	5
GERMANY	129	71	33	8	17	29	18	7	0	4	20	11	5	2	2	80	42	21	6	11
ITALY	95	49	25	9	10	13	9	2	0	2	17	9	4	3	1	63	31	19	6	7
BELGIUM + LUX	42	23	11	2	5	6	4	1	0	1	3	0	2	0	1	32	21	8	1	2
NETHERLANDS	49	29	8	3	5	5	2	1	2	0	9	5	3	1	0	31	20	6	1	4
SPAIN	57	21	21	11	3	8	4	1	0	3	4	1	2	3	0	41	14	19	7	1
GREECE + TURKEY	18	8	5	2	2	1	0	0	0	1	2	2	0	1	0	13	7	2	1	3
OTHER EUROPE	28	20	2	4	2	11	11	0	0	0	2	0	0	0	0	11	7	2	1	1
EUROPE EX. U.K.	643	344	166	54	65	130	80	22	10	18	85	47	20	13	5	414	217	124	31	42
SOUTHERN DOMINIONS	176	109	43	6	7	31	24	6	0	1	35	26	8	1	0	99	59	29	5	6
S. AFRICA +RHOD.	52	33	10	1	1	9	7	1	0	1	9	7	2	0	0	27	19	7	1	0
AUSTRALIA + N.Z.	124	76	33	5	6	22	17	5	0	0	26	19	6	1	0	72	40	22	4	6
ASIA + OTHER AFRICA	224	66	63	55	19	17	10	4	0	3	27	10	10	3	4	159	46	49	52	12
JAPAN	76	9	26	27	4	4	2	2	0	0	10	1	6	2	1	52	6	18	25	3
OTHER ASIA+AFR.	148	57	37	28	15	13	8	2	0	3	17	9	4	1	3	107	40	31	27	9
BLACK AFRICA	19	12	2	2	1	1	0	1	0	0	0	0	0	0	0	17	12	2	2	1
ARAB WORLD	13	5	2	4	1	3	1	1	0	1	3	2	0	1	0	8	3	1	4	0
INDIA	26	4	9	11	1	3	1	1	1	0	1	0	1	0	0	21	8	1	11	1
PHILIPPINES	23	9	8	1	5	1	1	0	0	0	6	4	0	2	0	15	4	6	5	2
OTHER E. ASIA	17	8	2	1	5	4	1	1	0	3	2	2	0	0	0	10	5	1	1	0
OTHER ASIA	50	19	14	5	7	4	3	1	0	0	5	1	1	0	2	36	15	12	4	5

CHAPTER 5- PATTERNS OF OWNERSHIP
SECTION 3- THE FLOW OF MANUFACTURING BY CHARACTERISTIC OF PARENT SYSTEM
TABLE J1- MANUFACTURING SUBSIDIARIES IN A SYSTEM
WITH LOW "PRODUCT DIVERSITY IN THE U.S." IN 1966
CLASSIFIED BY COUNTRY, PERIOD MANUFACTURE BEGAN, AND SYSTEM OWNERSHIP %

PERIOD AND OWNERSHIP PERCENTAGE
(WHL=95-100%, MAJ=50-94%, MIN=5-49%, UNK=UNKNOWN)

COUNTRY OR REGION	TOTAL PRE 1968 ALL	WHL	MAJ	MIN	UNK	PRE 1946 ALL	WHL	MAJ	MIN	UNK	1946-1957 ALL	WHL	MAJ	MIN	UNK	1958-1967 ALL	WHL	MAJ	MIN	UNK
OUTSIDE U.S.	2350	1358	545	226	142	453	320	81	25	27	447	304	89	33	21	1371	734	375	168	94
OUT. U.S. + CANADA	2010	1099	507	215	124	341	228	69	24	20	369	246	75	30	18	1235	625	363	161	86
OUT. WEST. HEMIS.	1395	763	363	143	81	248	163	58	13	14	223	146	45	22	10	879	454	260	108	57
OUT. WHITE CWEALTH	1528	778	419	189	93	224	140	50	20	14	274	172	62	24	16	981	466	307	145	63
OUT. DEVLPED WORLD	784	409	195	101	50	103	73	13	11	6	171	115	34	11	11	481	221	148	79	33
CANADA	340	259	38	11	18	112	92	12	1	7	78	58	14	3	3	136	109	12	7	8
LATIN AMERICA	615	336	144	72	43	93	65	11	11	6	146	100	30	8	8	356	171	103	53	29
C. AMER.+CARIB.	284	150	68	40	16	42	28	5	8	1	67	52	8	2	5	165	70	55	30	10
CUBA	26	15	4	4	3	10	6	2	2	0	13	7	2	1	3	2	2	0	0	0
MEXICO	165	90	38	22	8	20	16	1	3	0	43	34	6	1	2	95	40	29	20	6
OTHER	93	45	26	15	5	12	6	2	3	1	11	11	0	0	0	68	28	26	10	4
S. AMERICA	331	186	76	32	27	51	37	6	3	5	79	48	22	6	3	191	101	48	23	19
ARGENTINA	62	41	9	7	3	20	18	0	1	1	11	6	3	1	1	31	17	6	6	2
BRAZIL	76	48	13	9	5	11	9	0	0	2	25	13	8	2	2	40	26	5	6	3
PERU	29	13	10	3	1	5	3	2	0	0	9	3	3	2	1	15	7	3	2	3
COLOMBIA	58	32	19	2	4	5	3	2	0	0	13	11	1	0	1	40	18	14	7	1
VENEZUELA	73	30	20	8	14	6	2	1	2	1	21	10	7	1	3	46	18	12	14	2
OTHER	33	22	5	3	0	4	2	1	0	1	10	5	0	0	5	19	13	5	1	0
EUROPE	912	529	238	74	58	190	120	45	12	13	138	90	28	14	6	571	319	165	48	39
EFTA	321	216	60	18	22	90	64	18	3	5	53	40	7	5	1	173	112	35	10	16
U.K.	233	164	36	12	17	71	52	11	3	5	42	32	5	4	1	116	80	20	5	11
SCANDINAVIA	52	32	12	3	4	11	7	4	0	0	6	5	0	1	0	34	20	8	2	4
SWITZERLAND	14	10	3	1	0	1	1	0	0	0	4	3	1	0	0	9	6	2	1	0
OTHER EFTA	22	10	9	2	1	7	4	3	0	0	1	0	1	0	0	14	5	5	2	1
EUROP. COMMUNITY	498	279	143	40	28	87	49	26	6	6	73	42	21	6	4	330	188	96	28	18
FRANCE	151	74	47	19	9	30	14	8	4	4	17	11	4	1	1	102	49	35	14	4
GERMANY	148	88	39	8	10	30	19	10	0	1	25	15	8	1	1	90	54	21	7	8
ITALY	99	59	33	3	4	8	5	3	0	0	17	10	5	2	0	73	44	25	3	3
BELGIUM + LUX	52	32	13	3	4	10	4	4	2	0	5	3	2	0	0	38	25	9	2	1
NETHERLANDS	48	26	11	5	1	9	7	0	0	2	9	3	2	2	2	27	16	4	2	2
SPAIN	61	20	28	10	3	7	2	0	2	3	6	4	0	2	0	50	14	28	7	1
GREECE + TURKEY	12	3	3	3	0	1	0	0	0	0	1	0	0	1	0	10	3	4	2	2
OTHER EUROPE	20	11	4	3	2	7	5	0	2	0	5	4	0	1	0	8	2	2	1	1
EUROPE EX. U.K.	679	365	202	62	41	119	68	34	9	8	96	58	23	10	5	455	239	145	43	28
SOUTHERN DOMINIONS	236	151	48	13	12	45	35	8	1	1	48	38	8	2	0	131	78	32	10	11
S. AFRICA +RHOD.	76	49	15	6	0	16	13	3	0	0	15	12	3	0	0	39	24	9	6	0
AUSTRALIA + N.Z.	160	102	33	7	12	29	22	5	1	1	33	26	5	2	0	92	54	23	4	11
ASIA + OTHER AFRICA	247	83	77	56	11	13	8	5	0	0	37	18	9	6	4	177	57	63	50	7
JAPAN	78	10	26	27	8	3	0	0	3	0	12	3	5	3	1	52	7	18	24	3
OTHER ASIA+AFR.	169	73	51	29	7	10	8	2	0	0	25	15	4	3	3	125	50	45	26	4
BLACK AFRICA	19	8	5	3	1	1	0	0	0	0	2	2	0	0	0	15	6	3	5	1
ARAB WORLD	22	11	7	2	1	1	0	0	0	1	3	1	1	1	0	16	10	4	3	3
INDIA	29	6	11	11	0	3	1	1	0	1	8	2	3	2	1	24	3	5	11	0
PHILIPPINES	25	16	6	3	3	1	1	0	0	0	1	1	0	0	0	14	3	6	4	0
OTHER E. ASIA	20	11	4	3	1	1	1	0	0	0	4	3	0	1	0	17	10	4	2	1
OTHER ASIA	54	21	18	7	4	4	3	1	0	0	7	6	1	1	1	39	16	15	6	2

CHAPTER 5- PATTERNS OF OWNERSHIP
SECTION 3- THE FLOW OF MANUFACTURING BY CHARACTERISTIC OF PARENT SYSTEM
TABLE J2- MANUFACTURING SUBSIDIARIES IN A SYSTEM
WITH HIGH "PRODUCT DIVERSITY IN THE U.S." IN 1966
CLASSIFIED BY COUNTRY, PERIOD MANUFACTURE BEGAN, AND SYSTEM OWNERSHIP %

PERIOD AND OWNERSHIP PERCENTAGE
(WHL=95-100%, MAJ=50-94%, MIN=5-49%, UNK=UNKNOWN)

COUNTRY OR REGION	TOTAL PRE 1968					PRE 1946					1946-1957					1958-1967				
	ALL	WHL	MAJ	MIN	UNK	ALL	WHL	MAJ	MIN	UNK	ALL	WHL	MAJ	MIN	UNK	ALL	WHL	MAJ	MIN	UNK
OUTSIDE U.S.	2829	1520	666	356	225	572	376	77	44	75	561	329	128	70	34	1634	815	461	242	116
OUT. U.S. + CANADA	2368	1159	620	338	198	416	251	66	37	62	439	227	116	67	29	1460	681	438	234	107
OUT. WEST. HEMIS.	1658	835	431	212	140	304	188	44	19	53	246	135	57	37	17	1068	512	330	156	70
OUT. WHITE CWEALTH	1780	802	502	289	156	279	161	47	30	41	338	170	95	51	22	1132	471	360	208	93
OUT. DEVLPED WORLD	901	405	242	160	77	132	76	22	18	16	222	108	71	31	12	530	221	149	111	49
CANADA	461	361	46	18	27	156	125	11	7	13	122	102	12	3	5	174	134	23	8	9
LATIN AMERICA	710	324	189	126	58	112	63	22	18	9	193	92	59	30	12	392	169	108	78	37
C. AMER.+CARIB.	282	128	65	52	29	36	20	5	6	5	64	39	16	6	3	174	69	44	40	21
CUBA	20	11	4	2	2	9	5	2	1	1	8	5	2	1	0	2	1	0	0	1
MEXICO	200	98	41	38	19	26	15	5	5	1	48	31	11	3	3	122	52	25	30	13
OTHER	62	19	20	12	8	1	1	0	0	0	8	3	3	2	0	50	15	17	10	7
S. AMERICA	428	196	124	74	29	76	43	17	12	4	129	53	43	24	9	218	100	64	38	16
ARGENTINA	97	47	28	16	4	24	18	6	0	0	24	8	10	6	0	47	21	12	10	4
BRAZIL	123	69	32	13	8	23	14	3	4	2	46	23	14	5	4	53	32	15	4	2
PERU	28	15	7	4	1	7	2	2	2	1	8	3	3	3	0	12	10	2	1	1
COLOMBIA	57	18	18	15	6	5	1	1	1	1	17	5	2	1	2	35	12	15	12	4
VENEZUELA	71	27	22	14	7	4	1	1	3	0	23	9	6	4	3	43	17	15	7	4
OTHER	52	20	17	12	3	13	5	3	3	2	11	5	4	2	0	28	10	10	7	1
EUROPE	1130	584	287	121	108	234	138	37	14	45	165	94	28	28	15	701	352	222	79	48
EFTA	427	258	78	27	46	117	72	17	4	24	72	41	13	11	7	220	145	48	12	15
U.K.	318	185	57	24	35	90	53	14	3	20	59	31	11	11	6	152	101	32	10	9
SCANDINAVIA	61	41	15	4	3	14	11	3	0	0	11	0	0	0	0	36	30	12	4	3
SWITZERLAND	23	15	5	0	3	4	3	1	0	1	0	0	0	0	0	18	12	4	0	0
OTHER EFTA	25	17	2	1	1	9	5	0	3	1	2	1	0	0	1	14	11	2	0	1
EUROP. COMMUNITY	565	276	159	63	56	96	54	16	9	17	74	46	9	12	7	384	176	134	42	32
FRANCE	169	71	52	25	16	35	20	9	6	6	20	11	4	3	2	109	40	39	16	8
GERMANY	149	78	39	14	17	34	20	7	6	6	22	15	3	3	1	92	43	29	5	10
ITALY	122	55	39	14	11	11	7	2	2	0	18	12	2	2	1	90	36	35	10	8
BELGIUM + LUX	64	37	15	6	6	10	5	2	4	1	5	3	0	1	1	49	29	13	1	2
NETHERLANDS	61	35	14	4	6	6	5	0	1	0	9	5	3	0	2	44	25	11	3	4
SPAIN	76	18	36	20	2	10	4	5	0	0	10	3	3	2	2	56	11	28	18	1
GREECE + TURKEY	30	11	12	7	0	0	0	0	0	0	5	3	1	1	0	25	8	11	6	0
OTHER EUROPE	32	21	2	4	4	11	7	0	1	3	4	3	0	0	1	16	11	2	0	0
EUROPE EX. U.K.	812	399	230	97	73	144	85	23	11	25	106	63	17	17	9	549	251	190	69	39
SOUTHERN DOMINIONS	249	156	60	23	6	44	34	5	4	1	38	23	10	5	0	163	99	45	14	5
S. AFRICA +RHOD.	83	61	11	8	1	10	8	0	1	0	13	9	2	2	0	58	44	9	5	5
AUSTRALIA + N.Z.	166	95	49	15	5	34	26	5	3	1	25	14	8	4	2	105	55	36	6	5
ASIA + OTHER AFRICA	279	95	84	68	26	26	16	6	2	7	43	18	19	4	2	204	61	59	62	17
JAPAN	88	14	31	34	7	6	3	3	1	0	14	2	1	3	0	66	9	27	30	5
OTHER ASIA+AFR.	191	81	53	34	19	20	13	0	0	7	29	16	12	1	0	138	52	41	33	12
BLACK AFRICA	27	19	3	4	1	1	1	0	0	0	2	2	2	0	0	24	16	1	4	1
ARAB WORLD	17	6	4	6	1	1	1	0	0	0	3	2	1	0	0	14	3	3	6	1
INDIA	39	12	10	14	2	4	6	0	0	1	11	5	5	1	0	31	6	5	10	2
PHILIPPINES	33	17	9	5	1	4	3	0	0	1	8	2	2	4	0	17	9	7	1	0
OTHER E. ASIA	19	8	4	1	8	3	0	0	0	3	2	2	2	0	0	14	6	2	1	3
OTHER ASIA	56	19	23	4	8	8	5	0	0	5	8	3	5	0	0	38	11	18	4	5

CHAPTER 5- PATTERNS OF OWNERSHIP
SECTION 3- THE FLOW OF MANUFACTURING BY CHARACTERISTIC OF PARENT SYSTEM
TABLE K1- MANUFACTURING SUBSIDIARIES IN A SYSTEM
WITH LOW "PRODUCT DIVERSITY ABROAD" IN 1966
CLASSIFIED BY COUNTRY, PERIOD MANUFACTURE BEGAN, AND SYSTEM OWNERSHIP %

PERIOD AND OWNERSHIP PERCENTAGE
(WHL=95-100%, MAJ=50-94%, MIN=5-49%, UNK=UNKNOWN)

COUNTRY OR REGION	TOTAL PRE 1968 ALL	WHL	MAJ	MIN	UNK	PRE 1946 ALL	WHL	MAJ	MIN	UNK	1946-1957 ALL	WHL	MAJ	MIN	UNK	1958-1967 ALL	WHL	MAJ	MIN	UNK
OUTSIDE U.S.	1766	1056	373	172	130	361	256	56	26	23	391	268	69	31	23	979	532	248	115	84
OUT. U.S. + CANADA	1510	865	341	162	111	269	182	45	23	19	328	220	60	28	20	882	463	236	111	72
OUT. WEST. HEMIS.	1041	594	248	98	76	188	124	39	9	16	201	133	40	17	11	627	337	169	72	49
OUT. WHITE CWEALTH	1147	627	280	138	86	181	120	29	19	13	244	155	52	22	15	706	352	199	97	58
OUT. DEVLPED WORLD	597	336	132	80	43	91	67	6	14	4	149	103	25	11	10	351	166	101	55	29
CANADA	256	191	32	10	19	92	74	11	3	4	63	48	9	3	3	97	69	12	4	12
LATIN AMERICA	469	271	93	64	35	81	58	6	14	3	127	87	20	11	9	255	126	67	39	23
C. AMER.+CARIB.	220	121	45	32	18	37	25	3	8	1	63	47	7	4	5	116	49	35	20	12
CUBA	26	16	4	3	3	8	5	1	2	0	15	9	3	1	2	3	2	0	0	1
MEXICO	134	74	29	18	10	21	16	2	2	1	37	28	4	1	4	73	30	23	14	6
OTHER	60	31	12	11	5	8	4	0	4	0	11	10	0	1	0	40	17	12	6	5
S. AMERICA	249	150	48	32	17	44	33	3	6	2	64	40	13	7	4	139	77	32	19	11
ARGENTINA	56	33	8	9	5	15	14	0	0	1	8	5	2	1	0	32	14	6	8	4
BRAZIL	60	42	7	6	5	10	7	1	2	0	18	13	3	1	1	31	22	3	3	2
PERU	23	14	5	4	0	5	4	0	0	1	8	5	2	1	0	10	7	2	1	0
COLOMBIA	35	17	11	2	5	5	2	1	2	0	8	3	3	1	1	21	10	7	0	4
VENEZUELA	48	26	12	7	3	4	3	2	0	0	16	9	4	2	1	28	14	8	5	1
OTHER	27	18	5	4	0	4	3	0	1	0	5	5	0	0	0	17	10	5	2	0
EUROPE	680	397	150	55	59	139	91	28	6	14	124	79	23	13	9	398	227	99	36	36
EFTA	222	144	33	12	22	63	45	10	2	6	48	33	6	5	4	100	66	17	5	12
U.K.	174	110	26	8	19	53	38	8	2	5	38	27	4	4	3	72	45	14	2	11
SCANDINAVIA	29	23	3	0	3	6	5	1	0	0	7	5	1	1	0	16	13	1	2	0
SWITZERLAND	6	4	2	0	0	1	1	0	0	0	1	1	0	0	0	4	2	2	0	0
OTHER EFTA	13	7	2	3	1	3	1	1	0	1	2	0	1	0	1	8	6	0	1	1
EUROP. COMMUNITY	388	223	93	34	30	68	41	17	4	6	64	40	15	6	3	248	142	61	24	21
FRANCE	129	65	33	17	10	25	14	5	2	4	18	11	2	2	1	82	40	24	13	5
GERMANY	110	61	28	6	12	23	14	6	1	2	20	12	6	2	0	64	35	16	3	10
ITALY	76	48	19	4	5	5	3	2	0	0	14	9	4	1	0	57	36	13	3	5
BELGIUM + LUX	33	26	4	3	0	6	3	2	1	0	4	3	0	1	0	24	20	2	2	0
NETHERLANDS	40	23	9	6	2	9	7	2	0	0	9	5	1	2	1	21	11	6	3	1
SPAIN	44	16	20	6	2	4	2	2	0	0	7	4	1	2	0	33	10	18	4	1
GREECE + TURKEY	13	4	4	3	2	0	0	0	0	0	1	0	1	0	0	12	4	3	3	2
OTHER EUROPE	13	10	0	0	3	0	0	0	0	0	0	0	0	0	0	12	4	3	3	0
EUROPE EX. U.K.	506	287	124	47	40	86	53	20	4	9	86	52	19	9	6	326	182	85	34	25
SOUTHERN DOMINIONS	180	121	35	16	4	34	23	8	2	1	42	36	4	2	0	100	62	23	12	3
S. AFRICA +RHOD.	61	44	9	6	0	11	8	3	0	0	15	13	1	1	0	33	23	5	5	0
AUSTRALIA + N.Z.	119	77	26	10	4	23	15	5	2	1	27	23	3	1	0	67	39	18	7	3
ASIA + OTHER AFRICA	181	76	63	27	13	15	10	3	1	1	35	18	13	2	2	129	48	47	24	10
JAPAN	53	11	24	11	5	5	1	3	0	1	13	2	8	2	1	33	8	13	8	4
OTHER ASIA+AFR.	128	65	39	16	8	10	9	0	1	0	22	16	5	0	1	96	40	34	16	6
BLACK AFRICA	14	10	1	2	1	0	0	0	0	0	2	2	0	0	0	12	9	1	1	1
ARAB WORLD	14	7	5	2	0	0	0	0	0	0	3	2	0	1	0	11	5	4	2	0
INDIA	24	5	12	6	1	1	1	0	1	0	2	2	0	0	0	21	2	12	6	1
PHILIPPINES	23	16	4	2	1	5	4	0	1	0	9	8	2	0	0	9	3	2	2	2
OTHER E. ASIA	15	9	4	2	0	0	0	0	0	0	0	0	0	0	0	15	9	4	2	0
OTHER ASIA	38	18	13	2	5	4	4	0	0	0	6	3	2	0	1	28	11	11	2	4

CHAPTER 5- PATTERNS OF OWNERSHIP
SECTION 3- THE FLOW OF MANUFACTURING BY CHARACTERISTIC OF PARENT SYSTEM
TABLE K2- MANUFACTURING SUBSIDIARIES IN A SYSTEM
WITH HIGH "PRODUCT DIVERSITY ABROAD" IN 1966
CLASSIFIED BY COUNTRY, PERIOD MANUFACTURE BEGAN, AND SYSTEM OWNERSHIP %

PERIOD AND OWNERSHIP PERCENTAGE
(WHL=95-100%, MAJ=50-94%, MIN=5-49%, UNK=UNKNOWN)

COUNTRY OR REGION	TOTAL PRE 1968					PRE 1946					1946-1957					1958-1967				
	ALL	WHL	MAJ	MIN	UNK	ALL	WHL	MAJ	MIN	UNK	ALL	WHL	MAJ	MIN	UNK	ALL	WHL	MAJ	MIN	UNK
OUTSIDE U.S.	3413	1822	838	410	237	664	440	102	43	79	617	365	148	72	32	2026	1017	588	295	126
OUT. U.S. + CANADA	2868	1393	786	391	211	488	297	90	38	63	480	253	131	69	27	1813	843	565	284	121
OUT. WEST. HEMIS.	2012	1004	546	257	145	364	227	63	23	51	268	148	62	42	16	1320	629	421	192	78
OUT. WHITE CWEALTH	2161	953	641	340	163	322	181	68	31	42	368	187	105	53	23	1407	585	468	256	98
OUT. DEVLPED WORLD	1088	478	305	181	84	144	82	29	15	18	244	120	80	31	13	660	276	196	135	53
CANADA	545	429	52	19	26	176	143	12	5	16	137	112	17	3	5	213	174	23	11	5
LATIN AMERICA	856	389	240	134	66	124	70	27	15	12	212	105	69	27	11	493	214	144	92	43
C. AMER.+CARIB.	346	157	88	60	27	41	23	7	6	5	68	44	17	4	3	223	90	64	50	19
CUBA	20	10	4	2	2	11	6	3	1	1	6	3	1	1	1	1	1	0	0	0
MEXICO	231	114	50	42	17	25	15	4	4	2	54	37	13	2	2	144	62	33	36	13
OTHER	95	33	34	16	8	5	2	0	1	2	8	4	3	1	0	78	27	31	14	6
S. AMERICA	510	232	152	74	39	83	47	20	9	7	144	61	52	23	8	270	124	80	42	24
ARGENTINA	103	55	29	14	2	29	22	7	0	0	25	9	10	6	0	46	24	12	8	2
BRAZIL	139	75	38	16	9	24	16	3	3	2	52	23	19	6	4	62	36	16	7	3
PERU	34	14	12	3	2	7	3	3	1	0	7	3	2	2	0	17	8	7	0	2
COLOMBIA	80	33	26	15	5	5	2	1	1	1	20	9	7	2	1	54	22	18	10	4
VENEZUELA	96	31	30	15	18	6	0	3	1	2	27	10	10	4	3	61	21	11	11	12
OTHER	58	24	17	11	3	12	4	4	3	2	13	7	4	2	0	30	13	10	6	1
EUROPE	1362	716	375	140	107	285	167	54	20	44	179	105	33	29	12	874	444	288	91	51
EFTA	526	330	105	33	46	144	91	25	5	23	77	48	14	11	4	293	191	66	17	19
U.K.	377	239	67	28	33	108	67	17	4	20	63	36	12	11	4	196	136	38	13	9
SCANDINAVIA	84	50	24	2	3	19	13	5	1	0	10	9	1	0	0	54	28	18	1	7
SWITZERLAND	31	21	5	1	3	4	3	0	0	1	1	2	1	0	0	23	16	4	2	1
OTHER EFTA	34	20	9	2	3	13	8	3	0	2	1	1	0	0	0	20	11	6	2	1
EUROP. COMMUNITY	675	332	209	69	54	115	62	25	11	17	83	48	15	12	8	466	222	169	46	29
FRANCE	191	80	66	27	15	40	20	6	6	8	19	11	4	2	2	129	49	56	17	7
GERMANY	187	105	50	16	15	41	25	11	0	5	27	18	5	2	2	118	62	34	14	8
ITALY	145	66	53	13	10	15	9	3	0	3	21	13	3	4	1	106	44	47	9	6
BELGIUM + LUX	83	43	24	8	7	12	3	4	2	3	7	3	2	1	1	63	37	18	5	3
NETHERLANDS	69	38	16	8	7	7	5	1	1	0	9	3	1	4	1	50	30	14	1	5
SPAIN	93	22	44	24	3	11	5	3	2	1	9	3	2	4	0	73	14	39	19	1
GREECE + TURKEY	29	10	11	7	1	1	0	1	0	0	5	1	2	2	0	23	9	8	5	1
OTHER EUROPE	39	22	6	7	3	14	9	1	0	4	5	5	0	0	0	19	6	6	6	1
EUROPE EX. U.K.	985	477	308	112	74	177	100	37	16	24	116	69	21	18	8	678	308	250	78	42
SOUTHERN DOMINIONS	305	186	73	20	14	55	46	5	3	1	44	25	14	5	0	194	115	54	12	13
S. AFRICA +RHOD.	98	66	17	8	1	15	13	0	1	1	13	8	4	1	0	64	45	13	6	0
AUSTRALIA + N.Z.	207	120	56	12	13	40	33	5	2	0	31	17	10	4	0	130	70	41	6	13
ASIA + OTHER AFRICA	345	102	98	97	24	24	14	4	2	6	45	18	15	8	4	252	70	79	89	14
JAPAN	113	13	33	50	6	4	2	0	2	0	13	3	4	4	2	85	8	27	46	4
OTHER ASIA+AFR.	232	89	65	47	18	20	12	2	0	6	32	15	11	4	2	167	62	52	43	10
BLACK AFRICA	32	17	7	5	2	2	0	0	2	0	3	2	2	0	0	27	15	8	4	0
ARAB WORLD	25	10	6	6	1	4	2	1	0	1	4	2	1	1	0	19	7	5	6	1
INDIA	44	13	9	19	2	4	2	0	2	0	3	2	2	1	1	34	7	8	18	1
PHILIPPINES	35	17	11	6	0	2	2	0	0	0	10	5	4	1	0	22	10	7	5	0
OTHER E. ASIA	24	10	4	2	7	4	1	1	1	1	3	0	0	1	1	16	7	4	5	0
OTHER ASIA	72	22	28	9	7	8	4	4	1	3	9	2	5	1	1	49	16	22	8	3

CHAPTER 5- PATTERNS OF OWNERSHIP
SECTION 3- THE FLOW OF MANUFACTURING BY CHARACTERISTIC OF PARENT SYSTEM
TABLE L1- MANUFACTURING SUBSIDIARIES IN A SYSTEM
WITH LOW "GEOGRAPHICAL DIVERSITY" IN 1966
CLASSIFIED BY COUNTRY, PERIOD MANUFACTURE BEGAN, AND SYSTEM OWNERSHIP %

PERIOD AND OWNERSHIP PERCENTAGE
(WHL=95-100%, MAJ=50-94%, MIN=5-49%, UNK=UNKNOWN)

COUNTRY OR REGION	TOTAL PRE 1968					PRE 1946					1946-1957					1958-1967				
	ALL	WHL	MAJ	MIN	UNK	ALL	WHL	MAJ	MIN	UNK	ALL	WHL	MAJ	MIN	UNK	ALL	WHL	MAJ	MIN	UNK
OUTSIDE U.S.	1685	922	399	218	107	266	171	46	26	23	342	215	70	37	20	1038	536	283	155	64
OUT. U.S. + CANADA	1375	679	368	205	95	182	103	38	23	18	257	149	58	33	17	908	427	272	149	60
OUT. WEST. HEMIS.	965	481	259	130	73	136	77	30	11	18	154	90	34	19	11	653	314	195	100	44
OUT. WHITE CWEALTH	1003	445	303	174	69	120	64	29	20	7	181	96	47	24	14	690	285	227	130	48
OUT. DEVLPED WORLD	471	215	134	90	26	49	29	8	12	0	111	63	27	14	7	305	123	99	64	19
CANADA	310	243	31	13	12	84	68	8	3	5	85	66	12	4	3	130	109	11	6	4
LATIN AMERICA	410	198	109	75	22	46	26	8	12	0	103	59	24	14	6	255	113	77	49	16
C. AMER.+CARIB.	195	98	48	34	12	14	7	3	4	0	46	30	9	4	3	132	61	36	26	9
CUBA	9	3	2	1	1	1	0	0	1	0	5	2	2	0	1	1	1	0	0	0
MEXICO	155	86	32	27	9	10	6	3	1	0	38	27	6	3	2	106	53	23	23	7
OTHER	31	9	14	6	2	3	1	0	2	0	3	1	1	1	0	25	7	13	3	2
S. AMERICA	215	100	61	41	10	32	19	5	8	0	57	29	15	10	3	123	52	41	23	7
ARGENTINA	55	26	13	13	1	7	6	1	0	0	11	8	2	1	0	35	12	10	12	1
BRAZIL	66	40	12	12	2	14	9	1	4	0	17	11	2	4	0	35	20	9	4	2
PERU	10	3	5	2	0	2	1	1	0	0	4	0	2	2	0	4	2	0	0	2
COLOMBIA	26	8	12	4	2	1	0	0	1	0	7	3	2	1	1	18	5	8	3	2
VENEZUELA	42	15	17	5	5	2	0	1	1	0	15	4	3	2	3	25	11	10	2	2
OTHER	16	8	7	2	0	6	3	0	3	0	4	3	1	0	0	6	3	2	2	0
EUROPE	707	365	185	78	62	113	61	25	10	17	106	61	22	13	10	471	243	138	55	35
EFTA	260	163	38	18	28	48	30	5	2	11	45	32	5	5	3	154	101	28	11	14
U.K.	214	135	31	14	21	43	26	5	2	10	38	26	5	5	2	120	83	21	7	9
SCANDINAVIA	18	12	2	1	2	1	1	0	0	0	3	3	0	0	0	14	8	2	1	2
SWITZERLAND	15	9	3	2	1	1	1	0	0	0	2	2	0	0	1	12	6	3	1	1
OTHER EFTA	13	7	2	1	3	3	2	0	0	1	2	1	0	0	1	8	4	2	1	1
EUROP. COMMUNITY	379	180	121	44	30	59	29	18	7	5	47	22	15	4	6	269	129	88	33	19
FRANCE	128	53	40	22	11	27	11	6	7	3	13	6	4	1	2	86	36	30	14	6
GERMANY	100	49	35	8	8	21	11	9	0	1	18	10	8	0	0	61	28	18	8	7
ITALY	84	40	28	8	6	4	2	1	0	1	9	4	2	2	1	69	34	25	6	4
BELGIUM + LUX	30	17	9	3	1	3	3	0	0	0	6	2	1	2	1	26	15	8	1	0
NETHERLANDS	37	21	9	3	4	4	2	2	0	0	9	4	0	1	4	24	15	7	1	3
SPAIN	52	16	21	14	1	4	0	2	2	0	6	1	1	4	0	39	10	18	10	1
GREECE + TURKEY	5	1	3	0	1	0	0	0	0	0	3	2	0	0	0	3	0	2	0	1
OTHER EUROPE	11	5	2	2	2	2	0	0	1	1	2	2	0	0	1	6	3	1	2	0
EUROPE EX. U.K.	493	230	154	64	41	70	35	20	8	7	68	35	17	8	8	351	160	117	48	26
SOUTHERN DOMINIONS	151	95	33	16	4	19	13	4	1	1	35	25	6	4	0	94	57	23	11	3
S. AFRICA +RHOD.	38	22	9	5	0	4	3	1	1	0	7	5	1	1	0	25	14	7	4	0
AUSTRALIA + N.Z.	113	73	24	11	4	15	10	3	1	1	28	20	5	3	0	69	43	16	7	3
ASIA + OTHER AFRICA	107	21	41	36	7	4	3	1	0	0	13	4	6	2	1	88	14	34	34	6
JAPAN	46	4	16	21	4	1	0	1	0	0	5	0	3	2	0	38	4	12	19	3
OTHER ASIA+AFR.	61	17	25	15	3	3	3	0	0	0	8	4	3	0	1	50	10	22	15	3
BLACK AFRICA	3	0	1	1	1	0	0	0	0	0	1	0	0	0	0	2	0	1	1	1
ARAB WORLD	7	2	3	2	0	0	0	0	0	0	0	0	1	0	0	7	2	3	2	0
INDIA	18	8	7	2	1	2	0	0	2	0	1	1	0	0	0	17	7	3	7	0
PHILIPPINES	10	6	2	2	0	0	0	0	0	0	1	1	0	0	0	7	4	1	2	0
OTHER E. ASIA	10	3	4	3	0	0	0	0	0	0	0	0	0	0	0	10	3	3	4	0
OTHER ASIA	13	4	7	0	2	1	1	0	0	0	5	2	2	0	1	7	1	5	0	1

CHAPTER 5— PATTERNS OF OWNERSHIP
SECTION 3— THE FLOW OF MANUFACTURING BY CHARACTERISTIC OF PARENT SYSTEM
TABLE L2— MANUFACTURING SUBSIDIARIES IN A SYSTEM
WITH HIGH "GEOGRAPHICAL DIVERSITY" IN 1966
CLASSIFIED BY COUNTRY, PERIOD MANUFACTURE BEGAN, AND SYSTEM OWNERSHIP %

PERIOD AND OWNERSHIP PERCENTAGE
(WHL=95-100%, MAJ=50-94%, MIN=5-49%, UNK=UNKNOWN;

COUNTRY OR REGION	TOTAL PRE 1968					PRE 1946					1946-1957					1958-1967				
	ALL	WHL	MAJ	MIN	UNK	ALL	WHL	MAJ	MIN	UNK	ALL	WHL	MAJ	MIN	UNK	ALL	WHL	MAJ	MIN	UNK
OUTSIDE U.S.	3494	1956	812	364	260	759	525	112	43	79	666	418	147	66	35	1967	1013	553	255	146
OUT. U.S. + CANADA	3003	1579	759	348	227	575	376	97	38	64	551	324	133	64	30	1787	879	529	246	133
OUT. WEST. HEMIS.	2088	1117	535	225	148	416	274	72	21	49	315	191	68	40	16	1294	652	395	164	83
OUT. WHITE CWEALTH	2305	1135	618	304	180	383	237	68	30	48	431	246	110	51	24	1423	652	440	223	108
OUT. DEVLPED WORLD	1214	599	303	171	101	186	120	27	17	22	282	160	78	28	16	706	319	198	126	63
CANADA	491	377	53	16	33	184	149	15	5	15	115	94	14	2	5	180	134	24	9	13
LATIN AMERICA	915	462	224	123	79	159	102	25	17	15	236	133	65	24	14	493	227	134	82	50
C. AMER.+CARIB.	371	180	85	58	33	64	41	7	10	6	85	61	15	4	5	207	78	63	44	22
CUBA	37	23	6	4	4	18	11	4	2	1	16	10	2	2	2	3	2	0	0	1
MEXICO	210	102	47	33	18	36	25	3	5	3	53	38	11	1	3	111	39	33	27	12
OTHER	124	55	32	21	11	10	5	0	3	2	16	13	2	1	0	93	37	30	17	9
S. AMERICA	544	282	139	65	46	95	61	18	7	9	151	72	50	20	9	286	149	71	38	28
ARGENTINA	104	62	24	10	6	37	30	6	0	1	22	6	10	3	3	43	26	8	4	5
BRAZIL	133	77	33	10	11	20	14	6	0	0	53	25	20	6	2	58	38	11	6	3
PERU	47	25	12	5	2	10	6	3	1	0	11	6	2	0	3	23	13	7	1	2
COLOMBIA	89	42	25	13	8	9	4	2	3	0	22	11	6	3	2	57	27	17	15	6
VENEZUELA	102	42	25	17	16	8	3	2	0	3	28	15	8	3	2	64	24	15	14	11
OTHER	69	34	20	10	3	11	4	3	2	2	15	9	4	0	2	41	21	13	6	1
EUROPE	1335	748	340	117	104	311	197	57	16	41	197	123	34	29	11	801	428	249	72	52
EFTA	488	311	100	27	40	159	106	30	5	18	80	49	15	11	5	239	156	55	11	17
U.K.	337	214	62	25	31	118	79	20	4	15	63	37	11	10	1	148	98	31	8	11
SCANDINAVIA	95	61	25	3	5	24	17	6	1	0	14	11	2	1	0	56	33	17	2	5
SWITZERLAND	22	16	4	0	1	4	3	0	0	2	2	1	1	0	0	15	12	3	0	0
OTHER EFTA	34	20	9	2	3	13	7	4	0	2	1	0	1	0	0	20	13	4	2	1
EUROP. COMMUNITY	684	375	181	59	54	124	74	24	8	18	100	66	15	14	5	445	235	142	37	31
FRANCE	192	92	59	22	14	38	23	5	2	8	24	16	4	3	1	125	53	50	16	6
GERMANY	197	117	43	14	19	43	28	8	1	6	29	20	3	3	3	121	69	32	9	11
ITALY	137	74	44	9	9	16	10	4	0	2	26	18	5	1	2	94	46	35	6	7
BELGIUM + LUX	86	52	19	8	6	15	4	5	3	3	9	6	3	0	0	61	42	13	4	2
NETHERLANDS	72	40	16	6	6	12	9	2	1	0	12	6	2	2	1	44	25	12	3	5
SPAIN	85	22	43	16	4	11	9	1	0	1	7	4	2	0	1	67	14	39	13	2
GREECE + TURKEY	37	13	12	10	2	1	0	1	0	0	4	0	2	2	0	32	13	9	8	2
OTHER EUROPE	41	27	4	1	4	16	12	2	1	1	6	5	0	0	1	18	4	13	4	6
EUROPE EX. U.K.	998	534	278	95	73	193	118	37	12	26	134	86	23	19	6	653	330	218	64	41
SOUTHERN DOMINIONS	334	212	75	20	14	70	56	9	2	0	51	36	12	3	0	200	120	54	13	13
S. AFRICA +RHOD.	121	88	17	9	9	22	18	2	1	0	21	16	4	1	0	72	54	11	7	0
AUSTRALIA + N.Z.	213	124	58	11	13	48	38	7	1	3	30	20	8	2	0	128	66	43	6	13
ASIA + OTHER AFRICA	419	157	120	88	30	35	21	6	6	1	67	32	22	8	5	293	104	92	79	18
JAPAN	120	20	41	40	8	8	1	4	2	0	21	5	9	4	2	80	12	28	35	5
OTHER ASIA+AFR.	299	137	79	48	22	27	18	2	4	0	46	27	13	4	0	213	92	64	44	13
BLACK AFRICA	43	27	7	6	2	0	0	0	0	0	6	4	1	1	0	37	24	6	6	1
ARAB WORLD	32	15	8	6	1	2	1	0	1	0	4	1	1	1	0	23	10	6	4	1
INDIA	50	16	13	18	1	5	5	0	0	0	5	3	1	0	1	38	8	12	17	1
PHILIPPINES	48	27	13	6	1	5	4	0	1	0	18	12	5	1	0	24	11	8	5	0
OTHER E. ASIA	29	16	4	1	7	4	1	1	1	1	3	2	0	1	0	21	13	4	0	4
OTHER ASIA	97	36	34	11	10	11	7	1	1	0	10	3	5	1	1	70	26	28	10	6

CHAPTER 5- PATTERNS OF OWNERSHIP
SECTION 4- THE FLOW OF MANUFACTURING BY INDUSTRY OF SUBSIDIARY
TABLE 1- SUBSIDIARIES MANUFACTURING
MEAT PRODUCTS (SIC 201)
CLASSIFIED BY COUNTRY, PERIOD MANUFACTURE BEGAN, AND SYSTEM OWNERSHIP %

PERIOD AND OWNERSHIP PERCENTAGE
(WHL=95-100%, MAJ=50-94%, MIN=5-49%, UNK=UNKNOWN)

COUNTRY OR REGION	TOTAL PRE 1968					PRE 1946					1946-1957					1958-1967				
	ALL	WHL	MAJ	MIN	UNK	ALL	WHL	MAJ	MIN	UNK	ALL	WHL	MAJ	MIN	UNK	ALL	WHL	MAJ	MIN	UNK
OUTSIDE U.S.	72	51	14	3	1	18	16	1	0	1	14	14	0	0	0	37	21	13	3	0
OUT. U.S. + CANADA	58	41	11	3	1	17	15	1	0	1	10	10	0	0	0	29	16	10	3	0
OUT. WEST. HEMIS.	34	24	7	2	1	9	7	1	0	1	9	9	0	0	0	16	8	6	2	0
OUT. WHITE CWEALTH	32	20	8	1	1	10	9	1	0	0	3	3	0	0	0	17	8	8	1	0
OUT. DEVLPED WORLD	25	17	4	1	1	9	8	0	0	0	1	1	0	0	0	13	8	4	1	0
CANADA	14	10	3	0	0	1	1	0	0	0	4	4	0	0	0	8	5	3	0	0
LATIN AMERICA	24	17	4	1	0	8	8	0	0	0	1	1	0	0	0	13	8	4	1	0
C. AMER.+CARIB.	8	3	4	0	0	0	0	0	0	0	1	1	0	0	0	6	2	4	0	0
CUBA	1	0	0	0	0	0	0	0	0	0	0	0	0	0	0	0	0	0	0	0
MEXICO	6	3	3	0	0	0	0	0	0	0	1	1	0	0	0	5	2	3	0	0
OTHER	1	0	1	0	0	0	0	0	0	0	0	0	0	0	0	1	0	1	0	0
S. AMERICA	16	14	0	1	0	8	8	0	0	0	0	0	0	0	0	7	6	0	1	0
ARGENTINA	6	6	0	0	0	3	3	0	0	0	0	0	0	0	0	3	3	0	0	0
BRAZIL	7	6	0	0	0	4	4	0	0	0	0	0	0	0	0	3	3	0	0	0
PERU	0	0	0	0	0	0	0	0	0	0	0	0	0	0	0	0	0	0	0	0
COLOMBIA	0	0	0	0	0	0	0	0	0	0	0	0	0	0	0	0	0	0	0	0
VENEZUELA	1	0	0	1	0	0	0	0	0	0	0	0	0	0	0	1	0	0	1	0
OTHER	2	1	0	0	0	1	1	0	0	0	0	0	0	0	0	0	0	0	0	0
EUROPE	20	12	6	2	0	4	4	0	0	0	4	4	0	0	0	12	4	6	2	0
EFTA	10	8	2	0	0	3	3	0	0	0	1	1	0	0	0	6	4	2	0	0
U.K.	10	8	2	0	0	3	3	0	0	0	1	1	0	0	0	6	4	2	0	0
SCANDINAVIA	0	0	0	0	0	0	0	0	0	0	0	0	0	0	0	0	0	0	0	0
SWITZERLAND	0	0	0	0	0	0	0	0	0	0	0	0	0	0	0	0	0	0	0	0
OTHER EFTA	5	3	2	0	0	0	0	0	0	0	0	0	0	0	0	2	0	2	0	0
EUROP. COMMUNITY	1	0	1	0	0	1	1	0	0	0	2	2	0	0	0	1	0	1	0	0
FRANCE	2	2	0	0	0	0	0	0	0	0	0	0	0	0	0	2	2	0	0	0
GERMANY	1	0	0	1	0	0	0	0	0	0	2	2	0	0	0	1	0	0	1	0
ITALY	0	0	0	0	0	0	0	0	0	0	0	0	0	0	0	0	0	0	0	0
BELGIUM + LUX	1	0	0	1	0	1	1	0	0	0	0	0	0	0	0	1	0	0	1	0
NETHERLANDS	0	0	0	0	0	0	0	0	0	0	0	0	0	0	0	0	0	0	0	0
SPAIN	2	0	2	0	0	0	0	0	0	0	0	0	0	0	0	2	0	2	0	0
GREECE + TURKEY	0	0	0	0	0	0	0	0	0	0	0	0	0	0	0	0	0	0	0	0
OTHER EUROPE	3	1	0	2	0	0	0	0	0	0	1	1	0	0	0	2	0	0	2	0
EUROPE EX. U.K.	10	4	4	2	0	1	1	0	0	0	3	3	0	0	0	6	0	4	2	0
SOUTHERN DOMINIONS	13	12	1	0	0	4	3	1	0	0	5	5	0	0	0	4	4	0	0	0
S. AFRICA +RHOD.	0	0	0	0	0	0	0	0	0	0	0	0	0	0	0	0	0	0	0	0
AUSTRALIA + N.Z.	13	12	1	0	0	4	3	1	0	0	5	5	0	0	0	4	4	0	0	0
ASIA + OTHER AFRICA	1	0	0	1	0	1	0	0	1	0	0	0	0	0	0	0	0	0	0	0
JAPAN	0	0	0	0	0	0	0	0	0	0	0	0	0	0	0	0	0	0	0	0
OTHER ASIA+AFR.	1	0	0	1	0	1	0	0	1	0	0	0	0	0	0	0	0	0	0	0
BLACK AFRICA	0	0	0	0	0	0	0	0	0	0	0	0	0	0	0	0	0	0	0	0
ARAB WORLD	0	0	0	0	0	0	0	0	0	0	0	0	0	0	0	0	0	0	0	0
INDIA	0	0	0	0	0	0	0	0	0	0	0	0	0	0	0	0	0	0	0	0
PHILIPPINES	0	0	0	0	0	0	0	0	0	0	0	0	0	0	0	0	0	0	0	0
OTHER E. ASIA	1	0	0	1	0	1	0	0	1	0	0	0	0	0	0	0	0	0	0	0
OTHER ASIA	0	0	0	0	0	0	0	0	0	0	0	0	0	0	0	0	0	0	0	0

CHAPTER 5- PATTERNS OF OWNERSHIP
SECTION 4-- THE FLOW OF MANUFACTURING BY INDUSTRY OF SUBSIDIARY
TABLE 2-- SUBSIDIARIES MANUFACTURING
DAIRY PRODUCTS (SIC 202)
CLASSIFIED BY COUNTRY, PERIOD MANUFACTURE BEGAN, AND SYSTEM OWNERSHIP %

PERIOD AND OWNERSHIP PERCENTAGE
(WHL=95-100%, MAJ=50-94%, MIN=5-49%, UNK=UNKNOWN)

COUNTRY OR REGION	TOTAL PRE 1968					PRE 1946					1946-1957					1958-1967				
	ALL	WHL	MAJ	MIN	UNK	ALL	WHL	MAJ	MIN	UNK	ALL	WHL	MAJ	MIN	UNK	ALL	WHL	MAJ	MIN	UNK
OUTSIDE U.S.	134	82	29	20	1	56	43	6	6	1	19	11	3	5	0	57	28	20	9	0
OUT. U.S. + CANADA	107	57	28	20	1	41	28	6	6	1	18	10	3	5	0	47	19	19	9	0
OUT. WEST. HEMIS.	65	43	16	4	1	28	25	2	0	1	8	6	1	1	0	28	12	13	3	0
OUT. WHITE CWEALTH	88	41	26	20	1	29	17	5	6	1	18	10	3	5	0	41	14	18	9	0
OUT. DEVLPED WORLD	54	15	20	19	0	13	3	4	6	0	12	4	3	5	0	29	8	13	8	0
CANADA	27	25	1	0	0	15	15	0	0	0	1	1	0	0	0	10	9	1	0	0
LATIN AMERICA	42	14	12	16	0	13	3	4	6	0	10	4	2	4	0	19	7	6	6	0
C. AMER.+CARIB.	24	11	5	8	0	7	2	0	5	0	4	3	0	1	0	13	6	5	2	0
CUBA	6	4	0	2	0	4	2	0	2	0	0	0	0	0	0	0	0	0	0	0
MEXICO	4	5	1	0	0	3	0	0	3	0	3	3	0	0	0	3	2	1	0	0
OTHER	14	4	4	6	0	3	0	0	3	0	1	0	0	1	0	10	4	4	2	0
S. AMERICA	18	3	7	8	0	6	1	4	1	0	6	1	2	3	0	6	1	1	4	0
ARGENTINA	2	1	0	1	0	1	1	0	0	0	0	0	0	0	0	1	0	1	0	0
BRAZIL	1	0	0	1	0	0	0	0	0	0	1	0	1	0	0	0	0	0	0	0
PERU	3	0	1	2	0	3	1	2	0	0	0	0	0	0	0	0	0	0	0	0
COLOMBIA	5	0	2	4	0	1	0	0	1	0	2	0	0	2	0	2	0	0	1	0
VENEZUELA	7	2	3	2	0	1	0	1	0	0	3	1	1	1	0	3	1	0	2	0
OTHER	0	0	0	0	0	0	0	0	0	0	0	0	0	0	0	0	0	0	0	0
EUROPE	42	35	5	1	1	22	20	1	0	1	6	6	0	0	0	14	9	4	1	0
EFTA	11	11	0	0	0	6	6	0	0	0	3	3	0	0	0	2	2	0	0	0
U.K.	7	7	0	0	0	6	6	0	0	0	3	3	0	0	0	1	1	0	0	0
SCANDINAVIA	4	4	0	0	0	0	0	0	0	0	0	0	0	0	0	1	1	0	0	0
SWITZERLAND	0	0	0	0	0	0	0	0	0	0	0	0	0	0	0	0	0	0	0	0
OTHER EFTA	0	0	0	0	0	0	0	0	0	0	0	0	0	0	0	0	0	0	0	0
EUROP. COMMUNITY	27	22	3	1	1	16	14	1	0	1	3	3	0	0	0	8	5	2	1	0
FRANCE	4	3	0	1	0	3	3	0	0	0	0	0	0	0	0	1	0	0	1	0
GERMANY	10	8	1	0	1	8	6	1	0	1	2	2	0	0	0	0	0	0	0	0
ITALY	1	0	1	0	0	0	0	0	0	0	0	0	0	0	0	1	0	1	0	0
BELGIUM + LUX	6	5	1	0	0	1	1	0	0	0	0	0	0	0	0	5	4	1	0	0
NETHERLANDS	6	6	0	0	0	4	4	0	0	0	1	1	0	0	0	1	1	0	0	0
SPAIN	2	0	2	0	0	0	0	0	0	0	0	0	0	0	0	2	0	2	0	0
GREECE + TURKEY	0	0	0	0	0	0	0	0	0	0	0	0	0	0	0	0	0	0	0	0
OTHER EUROPE	2	2	0	0	0	0	0	0	0	0	0	0	0	0	0	2	2	0	0	0
EUROPE Ex. U.K.	35	28	5	1	1	16	14	1	0	1	6	6	0	0	0	13	8	4	1	0
SOUTHERN DOMINIONS	10	7	2	0	0	6	5	1	0	0	0	0	0	0	0	3	2	1	0	0
S. AFRICA +RHOD.	3	2	2	0	0	1	1	0	0	0	0	0	0	0	0	1	1	0	0	0
AUSTRALIA + N.Z.	7	5	2	0	0	5	4	1	0	0	0	0	0	0	0	2	1	1	0	0
ASIA + OTHER AFRICA	13	9	1	3	0	0	0	0	0	0	2	2	0	0	0	11	7	1	2	0
JAPAN	12	8	1	3	0	0	0	0	0	0	2	2	0	0	0	10	6	1	2	0
OTHER ASIA+AFR.	1	1	0	0	0	0	0	0	0	0	0	0	0	0	0	1	1	0	0	0
BLACK AFRICA	1	0	1	0	0	0	0	0	0	0	0	0	0	0	0	1	0	1	0	0
ARAB WORLD	0	0	0	0	0	0	0	0	0	0	0	0	0	0	0	0	0	0	0	0
INDIA	3	1	2	1	0	0	0	0	0	0	2	1	1	0	0	3	1	2	0	0
PHILIPPINES	1	0	0	2	1	0	0	0	0	0	0	0	0	1	0	0	0	0	0	0
OTHER E. ASIA	6	0	4	2	0	0	0	0	0	0	1	1	1	1	0	5	0	3	2	0
OTHER ASIA																				

CHAPTER 5- PATTERNS OF OWNERSHIP
SECTION 4- THE FLOW OF MANUFACTURING BY INDUSTRY OF SUBSIDIARY
TABLE 3- SUBSIDIARIES MANUFACTURING
CANNED FOODS (SIC 203)
CLASSIFIED BY COUNTRY, PERIOD MANUFACTURE BEGAN, AND SYSTEM OWNERSHIP %

PERIOD AND OWNERSHIP PERCENTAGE
(WHL=95-100%, MAJ=50-94%, MIN=5-49%, UNK=UNKNOWN)

COUNTRY OR REGION	TOTAL PRE 1968					PRE 1946					1946-1957					1958-1967				
	ALL	WHL	MAJ	MIN	UNK	ALL	WHL	MAJ	MIN	UNK	ALL	WHL	MAJ	MIN	UNK	ALL	WHL	MAJ	MIN	UNK
OUTSIDE U.S.	91	59	23	5	3	16	13	0	1	2	13	9	4	0	0	61	37	19	4	1
OUT. U.S. + CANADA	76	49	21	3	2	12	11	0	0	1	8	5	3	0	0	55	33	18	3	1
OUT. WEST. HEMIS.	46	30	13	1	1	11	11	0	0	0	5	4	1	0	0	29	15	12	1	1
OUT. WHITE CWEALTH	52	30	18	2	2	6	5	0	0	1	6	3	3	0	0	40	22	15	2	1
OUT. DEVLPED WORLD	34	23	8	2	1	4	3	0	0	1	4	2	2	0	0	26	18	6	2	0
CANADA	15	10	2	2	1	4	2	0	1	1	5	4	1	0	0	6	4	1	1	0
LATIN AMERICA	30	19	8	2	1	1	1	0	0	0	3	1	2	0	0	26	18	6	1	1
C. AMER.+CARIB.	19	14	2	1	1	1	1	0	0	0	2	1	1	0	0	16	13	1	0	2
CUBA	3	2	1	0	0	0	0	0	0	0	2	1	1	0	0	1	1	0	0	0
MEXICO	11	9	1	1	0	1	1	0	0	0	0	0	0	0	0	11	9	1	0	1
OTHER	5	3	0	1	1	0	0	0	0	0	0	0	0	0	0	4	3	0	1	0
S. AMERICA	11	5	6	0	0	0	0	0	0	0	1	0	1	0	0	10	5	5	0	0
ARGENTINA	1	0	1	0	0	0	0	0	0	0	0	0	0	0	0	0	0	0	0	0
BRAZIL	1	1	0	0	0	0	0	0	0	0	0	0	0	0	0	1	1	0	0	0
PERU	5	3	2	0	0	0	0	0	0	0	1	0	1	0	0	5	3	2	0	0
COLOMBIA	1	0	1	0	0	0	0	0	0	0	0	0	0	0	0	1	0	1	0	0
VENEZUELA	2	0	2	0	0	0	0	0	0	0	0	0	0	0	0	2	0	2	0	0
OTHER	2	1	1	0	0	0	0	0	0	0	0	0	0	0	0	2	1	1	0	0
EUROPE	30	17	11	0	1	6	6	0	0	0	4	3	1	0	0	19	8	10	0	1
EFTA	11	8	2	0	1	3	3	0	0	0	2	1	1	0	0	5	4	1	0	0
U.K.	10	8	1	0	0	3	3	0	0	0	1	1	0	0	0	5	4	1	0	0
SCANDINAVIA	0	0	0	0	0	0	0	0	0	0	0	0	0	0	0	0	0	0	0	0
SWITZERLAND	1	0	1	0	0	0	0	0	0	0	1	0	1	0	0	0	0	0	0	0
OTHER EFTA	0	0	0	0	0	0	0	0	0	0	0	0	0	0	0	0	0	0	0	0
EUROP. COMMUNITY	14	5	8	0	0	1	1	0	0	0	1	1	0	0	0	12	3	8	0	1
FRANCE	3	0	3	0	0	0	0	0	0	0	0	0	0	0	0	3	0	3	0	0
GERMANY	2	1	1	0	0	1	1	0	0	0	0	0	0	0	0	1	0	1	0	0
ITALY	4	2	2	0	0	0	0	0	0	0	1	1	0	0	0	3	1	2	0	0
BELGIUM + LUX	1	0	0	0	1	0	0	0	0	0	0	0	0	0	0	1	0	0	0	1
NETHERLANDS	3	2	0	0	0	0	0	0	0	0	0	0	0	0	0	1	1	0	0	0
SPAIN	1	0	1	0	0	0	0	0	0	0	0	0	0	0	0	1	0	1	0	0
GREECE + TURKEY	2	2	0	0	0	1	1	0	0	0	1	1	0	0	0	0	0	0	0	0
OTHER EUROPE	2	2	0	0	0	1	1	0	0	0	0	0	0	0	0	0	0	0	0	0
EUROPE EX. U.K.	20	9	10	0	1	3	3	0	0	0	3	2	1	0	0	14	4	9	0	1
SOUTHERN DOMINIONS	12	9	2	1	0	2	2	0	0	0	0	0	0	0	0	10	7	2	1	1
S. AFRICA +RHOD.	3	2	0	1	0	1	1	0	0	0	0	0	0	0	0	2	1	1	1	1
AUSTRALIA + N.Z.	9	7	2	0	0	1	1	0	0	0	0	0	0	0	0	8	6	2	0	0
ASIA + OTHER AFRICA	4	4	0	0	0	3	3	0	0	0	0	0	0	0	0	0	0	0	0	0
JAPAN	0	0	0	0	0	0	0	0	0	0	0	0	0	0	0	0	0	0	0	0
OTHER ASIA+AFR.	4	4	0	0	0	3	3	0	0	0	0	0	0	0	0	0	0	0	0	0
BLACK AFRICA	1	1	0	0	0	0	0	0	0	0	0	0	0	0	0	0	0	0	0	0
ARAB WORLD	1	1	0	0	0	0	0	0	0	0	0	0	0	0	0	0	0	0	0	0
INDIA	1	1	0	0	0	1	1	0	0	0	0	0	0	0	0	0	0	0	0	0
PHILIPPINES	2	2	0	0	0	2	2	0	0	0	0	0	0	0	0	0	0	0	0	0
OTHER E. ASIA	0	0	0	0	0	0	0	0	0	0	0	0	0	0	0	0	0	0	0	0
OTHER ASIA	0	0	0	0	0	0	0	0	0	0	0	0	0	0	0	0	0	0	0	0

CHAPTER 5- PATTERNS OF OWNERSHIP
SECTION 4- THE FLOW OF MANUFACTURING BY INDUSTRY OF SUBSIDIARY
TABLE 4- SUBSIDIARIES MANUFACTURING
GRAIN MILL PRODUCTS (SIC 204)
CLASSIFIED BY COUNTRY, PERIOD MANUFACTURE BEGAN, AND SYSTEM OWNERSHIP %

PERIOD AND OWNERSHIP PERCENTAGE
(WHL=95-100%, MAJ=50-94%, MIN=5-49%, UNK=UNKNOWN)

COUNTRY OR REGION	TOTAL PRE 1968					PRE 1946					1946-1957					1958-1967				
	ALL	WHL	MAJ	MIN	UNK	ALL	WHL	MAJ	MIN	UNK	ALL	WHL	MAJ	MIN	UNK	ALL	WHL	MAJ	MIN	UNK
OUTSIDE U.S.	152	85	48	9	10	32	25	5	0	2	25	18	5	1	1	95	42	38	8	7
OUT. U.S. + CANADA	129	67	45	9	8	21	16	4	0	1	16	11	4	1	0	92	40	37	8	7
OUT. WEST. HEMIS.	66	39	19	5	3	14	11	2	0	1	7	4	2	1	0	45	24	15	4	2
OUT. WHITE CWEALTH	107	50	42	7	8	15	10	4	0	1	14	9	4	1	0	78	31	34	6	7
OUT. DEVLPED WORLD	70	31	29	5	5	8	6	2	0	0	9	7	2	0	0	53	18	25	5	5
CANADA	23	18	3	0	2	11	9	1	0	1	9	7	1	0	1	3	2	1	0	0
LATIN AMERICA	63	28	26	4	5	7	5	2	0	0	9	7	2	0	0	47	16	22	4	5
C. AMER.+CARIB.	30	10	14	3	3	2	2	0	0	0	3	2	1	0	0	25	6	13	3	3
CUBA	1	1	0	0	0	0	0	0	0	0	0	0	0	0	0	1	1	0	0	0
MEXICO	14	7	6	0	1	2	2	0	0	0	3	2	1	0	0	9	3	5	0	1
OTHER	15	2	8	3	2	0	0	0	0	0	0	0	0	0	0	15	2	8	3	2
S. AMERICA	33	18	12	1	2	5	3	2	0	0	6	5	1	0	0	22	10	9	1	2
ARGENTINA	4	3	1	0	0	2	1	1	0	0	1	1	0	0	0	1	1	0	0	0
BRAZIL	5	5	0	0	0	1	1	0	0	0	2	2	0	0	0	2	2	0	0	0
PERU	3	1	2	0	0	0	0	0	0	0	2	1	1	0	0	1	0	1	0	0
COLOMBIA	7	4	3	0	0	1	0	1	0	0	2	2	0	0	0	4	2	2	0	0
VENEZUELA	6	3	1	1	1	0	0	0	0	0	1	0	1	0	0	5	2	2	1	0
OTHER	8	2	5	0	1	1	1	0	0	0	0	0	0	0	0	7	2	4	0	1
EUROPE	48	28	13	4	3	12	9	2	0	1	6	3	2	1	0	30	16	9	3	2
EFTA	18	14	2	2	0	6	6	0	0	0	2	1	1	0	0	10	7	1	2	0
U.K.	11	9	0	2	0	4	4	0	0	0	1	1	0	0	0	6	4	0	2	0
SCANDINAVIA	4	4	0	0	0	2	2	0	0	0	0	0	0	0	0	2	2	0	0	0
SWITZERLAND	1	0	1	0	0	0	0	0	0	0	1	0	1	0	0	0	0	0	0	0
OTHER EFTA	2	1	1	0	0	0	0	0	0	0	0	0	0	0	0	2	1	1	0	0
EUROP. COMMUNITY	25	13	9	0	3	5	2	2	0	1	3	2	0	1	0	17	9	6	0	2
FRANCE	4	3	1	0	0	1	1	0	0	0	0	0	0	0	0	3	2	1	0	0
GERMANY	8	5	3	0	0	1	0	1	0	0	2	2	0	0	0	5	3	2	0	0
ITALY	7	3	2	2	0	1	0	0	1	0	1	0	0	1	0	5	3	2	0	0
BELGIUM + LUX	2	1	1	0	0	0	0	0	0	0	0	0	0	0	0	2	1	1	0	0
NETHERLANDS	4	3	1	0	0	2	1	1	0	0	0	0	0	0	0	2	1	0	0	1
SPAIN	4	0	2	2	0	0	0	0	0	0	1	0	1	0	0	3	0	2	1	0
GREECE + TURKEY	0	0	0	0	0	0	0	0	0	0	0	0	0	0	0	0	0	0	0	0
OTHER EUROPE	1	1	0	0	0	1	1	0	0	0	0	0	0	0	0	0	0	0	0	0
EUROPE EX. U.K.	37	19	13	2	3	8	5	2	0	1	5	2	2	1	0	24	12	9	1	2
SOUTHERN DOMINIONS	10	7	3	0	0	1	1	0	0	0	1	1	0	0	0	8	5	3	0	0
S. AFRICA +RHOD.	2	2	0	0	0	1	1	0	0	0	1	1	0	0	0	0	0	0	0	0
AUSTRALIA + N.Z.	8	5	3	0	0	0	0	0	0	0	0	0	0	0	0	8	5	3	0	0
ASIA + OTHER AFRICA	8	4	3	1	0	1	1	0	0	0	1	0	1	0	0	7	3	3	1	0
JAPAN	1	1	0	0	0	0	0	0	0	0	0	0	0	0	0	1	1	0	0	0
OTHER ASIA+AFR.	7	3	3	1	0	1	1	0	0	0	1	0	1	0	0	6	2	3	1	0
BLACK AFRICA	1	1	0	0	0	1	1	0	0	0	0	0	0	0	0	1	1	0	0	0
ARAB WORLD	1	1	0	0	0	0	0	0	0	0	0	0	0	0	0	1	1	0	0	0
INDIA	1	0	0	1	0	1	0	0	1	0	0	0	0	0	0	0	0	0	0	0
PHILIPPINES	3	3	0	0	0	0	0	0	0	0	0	0	0	0	0	3	1	2	0	0
OTHER E. ASIA	1	1	0	0	0	0	0	0	0	0	0	0	0	0	0	1	0	1	0	0
OTHER ASIA	0	0	0	0	0	0	0	0	0	0	0	0	0	0	0	0	0	0	0	0

CHAPTER 5- PATTERNS OF OWNERSHIP
SECTION 4- THE FLOW OF MANUFACTURING BY INDUSTRY OF SUBSIDIARY
TABLE 5- SUBSIDIARIES MANUFACTURING
BAKERY PRODUCTS (SIC 205)
CLASSIFIED BY COUNTRY, PERIOD MANUFACTURE BEGAN, AND SYSTEM OWNERSHIP %

PERIOD AND OWNERSHIP PERCENTAGE
(WHL=95-100%, MAJ=50-94%, MIN=5-49%, UNK=UNKNOWN)

COUNTRY OR REGION	TOTAL PRE 1968					PRE 1946					1946-1957					1958-1967				
	ALL	WHL	MAJ	MIN	UNK	ALL	WHL	MAJ	MIN	UNK	ALL	WHL	MAJ	MIN	UNK	ALL	WHL	MAJ	MIN	UNK
OUTSIDE U.S.	54	30	20	2	2	12	12	0	0	0	10	6	3	0	1	32	12	17	2	1
OUT. U.S. + CANADA	44	21	20	1	1	7	7	0	0	0	6	3	3	0	0	31	11	17	2	1
OUT. WEST. HEMIS.	32	19	11	1	1	6	6	0	0	0	2	2	0	0	0	24	11	11	1	1
OUT. WHITE CWEALTH	36	13	20	2	1	2	2	0	0	0	5	2	3	0	0	29	9	17	2	0
OUT. DEVLPED WORLD	12	2	9	1	0	1	1	0	0	0	4	1	3	0	0	7	0	6	1	0
CANADA	10	9	0	0	1	5	5	0	0	0	4	3	0	0	1	1	1	0	0	0
LATIN AMERICA	12	2	9	1	0	1	1	0	0	0	4	1	3	0	0	7	1	6	0	0
C. AMER.+CARIB.	7	1	5	1	0	1	1	0	0	0	1	0	1	0	0	5	0	4	1	0
CUBA	1	1	0	1	0	1	1	0	0	0	0	0	0	0	0	0	0	0	0	0
MEXICO	4	0	3	0	1	0	0	0	0	0	1	0	1	0	0	3	0	2	1	0
OTHER	2	1	2	0	0	0	0	0	0	0	0	0	0	0	0	2	0	2	0	0
S. AMERICA	5	1	4	0	0	0	0	0	0	0	3	1	2	0	0	2	1	2	0	0
ARGENTINA	0	0	0	0	0	0	0	0	0	0	0	0	0	0	0	0	0	0	0	0
BRAZIL	0	0	0	0	0	0	0	0	0	0	0	0	0	0	0	0	0	0	0	0
PERU	1	0	1	0	0	0	0	0	0	0	1	0	1	0	0	0	0	0	0	0
COLOMBIA	2	0	1	1	0	0	0	0	0	0	1	0	0	1	0	1	0	1	0	0
VENEZUELA	2	1	2	0	0	0	0	0	0	0	1	1	0	0	0	1	0	1	0	0
OTHER	0	0	0	0	0	0	0	0	0	0	0	0	0	0	0	0	0	0	0	0
EUROPE	29	16	11	1	1	4	4	0	0	0	2	2	0	0	0	23	10	11	1	1
EFTA	9	4	2	1	0	3	3	0	0	0	1	1	0	0	0	5	3	2	0	0
U.K.	4	4	0	0	0	3	3	0	0	0	1	1	0	0	0	1	1	0	0	0
SCANDINAVIA	4	3	1	0	0	0	0	0	0	0	0	0	0	0	0	3	2	1	0	0
SWITZERLAND	1	0	1	0	0	0	0	0	0	0	0	0	0	0	0	1	0	1	0	0
OTHER EFTA	0	0	0	0	0	0	0	0	0	0	0	0	0	0	0	0	0	0	0	0
EUROP. COMMUNITY	16	8	6	1	1	1	1	0	0	0	1	0	1	0	0	15	7	6	1	1
FRANCE	7	1	4	1	1	0	0	0	0	0	0	0	0	0	0	7	1	4	1	1
GERMANY	2	1	1	0	0	0	0	0	0	0	0	0	0	0	0	2	1	1	0	0
ITALY	4	3	1	0	0	1	1	0	0	0	0	0	0	0	0	4	3	1	0	0
BELGIUM + LUX	3	3	0	0	0	0	0	0	0	0	0	0	0	0	0	2	2	0	0	0
NETHERLANDS	0	0	0	0	0	0	0	0	0	0	0	0	0	0	0	0	0	0	0	0
SPAIN	3	0	3	0	0	0	0	0	0	0	0	0	0	0	0	3	0	3	0	0
GREECE + TURKEY	0	0	0	0	0	0	0	0	0	0	0	0	0	0	0	0	0	0	0	0
OTHER EUROPE	1	1	0	0	0	0	0	0	0	0	0	1	0	1	0	0	0	0	0	1
EUROPE EX. U.K.	25	12	11	1	1	1	1	0	0	0	1	2	0	2	0	22	9	11	1	1
SOUTHERN DOMINIONS	3	3	0	0	0	2	2	0	0	0	0	0	0	0	0	1	1	0	0	0
S. AFRICA +RHOD.	1	1	0	0	0	1	1	0	0	0	0	0	0	0	0	0	0	0	0	0
AUSTRALIA + N.Z.	2	2	0	0	0	1	1	0	0	0	0	0	0	0	0	1	1	0	0	0
ASIA + OTHER AFRICA	0	0	0	0	0	0	0	0	0	0	0	0	0	0	0	0	0	0	0	0
JAPAN	0	0	0	0	0	0	0	0	0	0	0	0	0	0	0	0	0	0	0	0
OTHER ASIA+AFR.	0	0	0	0	0	0	0	0	0	0	0	0	0	0	0	0	0	0	0	0
BLACK AFRICA	0	0	0	0	0	0	0	0	0	0	0	0	0	0	0	0	0	0	0	0
ARAB WORLD	0	0	0	0	0	0	0	0	0	0	0	0	0	0	0	0	0	0	0	0
INDIA	0	0	0	0	0	0	0	0	0	0	0	0	0	0	0	0	0	0	0	0
PHILIPPINES	0	0	0	0	0	0	0	0	0	0	0	0	0	0	0	0	0	0	0	0
OTHER E. ASIA	0	0	0	0	0	0	0	0	0	0	0	0	0	0	0	0	0	0	0	0
OTHER ASIA	0	0	0	0	0	0	0	0	0	0	0	0	0	0	0	0	0	0	0	0

CHAPTER 5- PATTERNS OF OWNERSHIP
SECTION 4-- THE FLOW OF MANUFACTURING BY INDUSTRY OF SUBSIDIARY
TABLE 6-- SUBSIDIARIES MANUFACTURING
CONFECTIONERY AND RELATED PRODUCTS (SIC 207)
CLASSIFIED BY COUNTRY, PERIOD MANUFACTURE BEGAN, AND SYSTEM OWNERSHIP %

PERIOD AND OWNERSHIP PERCENTAGE
(WHL=95-100%, MAJ=50-94%, MIN=5-49%, UNK=UNKNOWN)

COUNTRY OR REGION	TOTAL PRE 1968					PRE 1946					1946-1957					1958-1967				
	ALL	WHL	MAJ	MIN	UNK	ALL	WHL	MAJ	MIN	UNK	ALL	WHL	MAJ	MIN	UNK	ALL	WHL	MAJ	MIN	UNK
OUTSIDE U.S.	97	58	34	2	3	12	12	0	0	0	11	5	5	0	1	74	41	29	2	2
OUT: U.S. + CANADA	82	43	34	2	3	5	5	0	0	0	10	4	5	0	1	67	34	29	2	2
OUT: WEST. HEMIS.	58	32	23	2	1	5	5	0	0	0	3	0	3	0	0	50	27	20	2	1
OUT: WHITE CWEALTH	62	34	25	1	2	0	0	0	0	0	7	4	2	0	1	55	30	23	1	1
OUT: DEVLPED WORLD	30	16	12	0	2	0	0	0	0	0	7	4	2	0	1	23	12	10	0	1
CANADA	15	15	0	0	0	7	7	0	0	0	1	1	0	0	0	7	7	0	0	0
LATIN AMERICA	24	11	11	0	2	0	0	0	0	0	7	4	2	0	1	17	7	9	0	1
C. AMER.+CARIB.	13	4	7	0	2	0	0	0	0	0	3	2	0	0	1	10	2	7	0	1
CUBA	0	0	0	0	0	0	0	0	0	0	0	0	0	0	0	0	0	0	0	0
MEXICO	9	3	4	0	2	0	0	0	0	0	3	2	0	0	1	6	1	4	0	1
OTHER	4	1	3	0	0	0	0	0	0	0	0	0	0	0	0	4	1	3	0	0
S. AMERICA	11	7	4	0	0	0	0	0	0	0	4	2	2	0	0	7	5	2	0	0
ARGENTINA	0	0	0	0	0	0	0	0	0	0	0	0	0	0	0	2	2	0	0	0
BRAZIL	2	2	0	0	0	0	0	0	0	0	0	0	0	0	0	2	2	0	0	0
PERU	2	1	1	0	0	0	0	0	0	0	2	1	1	0	0	0	0	0	0	0
COLOMBIA	3	2	1	0	0	0	0	0	0	0	1	1	0	0	0	2	1	0	1	0
VENEZUELA	2	1	1	0	0	0	0	0	0	0	1	0	1	0	0	1	1	0	0	0
OTHER	2	1	1	0	0	0	0	0	0	0	0	0	0	0	0	2	1	1	0	0
EUROPE	38	22	14	2	0	2	2	0	0	0	1	0	1	0	0	35	20	13	2	0
EFTA	8	3	4	1	0	2	2	0	0	0	1	0	1	0	0	5	1	3	1	0
U.K.	6	2	3	1	0	2	2	0	0	0	1	0	1	0	0	3	0	2	1	0
SCANDINAVIA	0	0	0	0	0	0	0	0	0	0	0	0	0	0	0	0	0	0	0	0
SWITZERLAND	0	0	0	0	0	0	0	0	0	0	0	0	0	0	0	0	0	0	0	0
OTHER EFTA	2	1	1	0	0	0	0	0	0	0	0	0	0	0	0	2	1	1	0	0
EUROP. COMMUNITY	25	16	8	1	0	0	0	0	0	0	0	0	0	0	0	25	16	8	1	0
FRANCE	5	1	4	0	0	0	0	0	0	0	0	0	0	0	0	5	1	4	0	0
GERMANY	6	4	1	1	0	0	0	0	0	0	0	0	0	0	0	6	4	1	1	0
ITALY	4	4	0	0	0	0	0	0	0	0	0	0	0	0	0	4	4	0	0	0
BELGIUM + LUX	6	5	1	0	0	0	0	0	0	0	0	0	0	0	0	6	5	1	0	0
NETHERLANDS	4	2	2	0	0	0	0	0	0	0	0	0	0	0	0	4	2	2	0	0
SPAIN	1	1	0	0	0	0	0	0	0	0	0	0	0	0	0	1	1	0	0	0
GREECE + TURKEY	1	0	1	0	0	0	0	0	0	0	0	0	0	0	0	1	0	1	0	0
OTHER EUROPE	3	2	1	0	0	0	0	0	0	0	0	0	0	0	0	3	2	1	0	0
EUROPE EX. U.K.	32	20	11	1	1	2	2	0	0	0	0	0	0	0	0	32	20	11	1	0
SOUTHERN DOMINIONS	11	5	5	0	1	3	3	0	0	0	2	0	2	0	0	6	2	3	0	1
S. AFRICA +RHOD.	3	1	2	0	0	0	0	0	0	0	1	0	1	0	0	2	1	1	0	0
AUSTRALIA + N.Z.	8	4	3	0	1	3	3	0	0	0	1	0	1	0	0	4	1	2	0	1
ASIA + OTHER AFRICA	9	5	4	0	0	0	0	0	0	0	0	0	0	0	0	9	5	4	0	0
JAPAN	3	0	3	0	0	0	0	0	0	0	0	0	0	0	0	3	0	3	0	0
OTHER ASIA+AFR.	6	5	1	0	0	0	0	0	0	0	0	0	0	0	0	6	5	1	0	0
BLACK AFRICA	0	0	0	0	0	0	0	0	0	0	0	0	0	0	0	0	0	0	0	0
ARAB WORLD	2	2	0	0	0	0	0	0	0	0	0	0	0	0	0	2	2	0	0	0
INDIA	0	0	0	0	0	0	0	0	0	0	0	0	0	0	0	0	0	0	0	0
PHILIPPINES	1	1	0	0	0	0	0	0	0	0	0	0	0	0	0	1	1	0	0	0
OTHER E. ASIA	0	0	0	0	0	0	0	0	0	0	0	0	0	0	0	0	0	0	0	0
OTHER ASIA	3	2	1	0	0	0	0	0	0	0	0	0	0	0	0	3	2	1	0	0

CHAPTER 5- PATTERNS OF OWNERSHIP
SECTION 4- THE FLOW OF MANUFACTURING BY INDUSTRY OF SUBSIDIARY
TABLE 7- SUBSIDIARIES MANUFACTURING
BEVERAGES (SIC 208)
CLASSIFIED BY COUNTRY, PERIOD MANUFACTURE BEGAN, AND SYSTEM OWNERSHIP %

PERIOD AND OWNERSHIP PERCENTAGE
(WHL=95-100%, MAJ=50-94%, MIN=5-49%, UNK=UNKNOWN)

COUNTRY OR REGION	TOTAL PRE 1968					PRE 1946					1946-1957					1958-1967				
	ALL	WHL	MAJ	MIN	UNK	ALL	WHL	MAJ	MIN	UNK	ALL	WHL	MAJ	MIN	UNK	ALL	WHL	MAJ	MIN	UNK
OUTSIDE U.S.	89	55	17	0	15	30	19	2	0	9	18	15	1	0	2	39	21	14	0	4
OUT. U.S. + CANADA	77	46	15	0	14	25	15	1	0	9	16	13	1	0	2	34	18	13	0	3
OUT. WEST. HEMIS.	50	29	8	0	11	17	7	1	0	9	11	9	0	0	2	20	13	7	0	0
OUT. WHITE CWEALTH	53	35	13	0	3	11	11	0	0	0	13	12	1	0	0	27	12	12	0	3
OUT. DEVLPED WORLD	35	22	10	0	3	9	9	0	0	0	8	7	1	0	0	18	6	9	0	3
CANADA	12	9	2	0	1	5	4	1	0	0	2	2	0	0	0	5	3	1	0	1
LATIN AMERICA	27	17	7	0	3	8	8	0	0	0	5	4	1	0	0	14	5	6	0	3
C. AMER.+CARIB.	10	5	3	0	2	3	3	0	0	0	3	2	1	0	0	4	0	2	0	2
CUBA	2	2	0	0	0	2	2	0	0	0	0	0	0	0	0	0	0	0	0	0
MEXICO	6	2	2	0	2	0	0	0	0	0	2	1	1	0	0	4	0	2	0	2
OTHER	2	1	1	0	0	2	2	0	0	0	1	1	0	0	0	0	0	0	0	0
S. AMERICA	17	12	4	0	1	5	5	0	0	0	2	2	0	0	0	10	5	4	0	1
ARGENTINA	5	4	0	0	1	2	2	0	0	0	0	0	0	0	0	3	2	0	0	1
BRAZIL	4	3	1	0	0	1	1	0	0	0	1	1	0	0	0	2	1	1	0	0
PERU	3	2	1	0	0	2	2	0	0	0	0	0	0	0	0	1	0	1	0	0
COLOMBIA	3	1	2	0	0	0	0	0	0	0	1	0	1	0	0	2	0	2	0	0
VENEZUELA	0	0	0	0	0	0	0	0	0	0	0	0	0	0	0	0	0	0	0	0
OTHER	2	2	0	0	0	0	0	0	0	0	0	0	0	0	0	2	2	0	0	0
EUROPE	29	12	4	0	11	14	4	1	0	9	7	3	2	0	2	8	5	3	0	0
EFTA	14	2	1	0	11	12	2	1	0	9	2	0	0	0	2	0	0	0	0	0
U.K.	14	2	1	0	11	12	2	1	0	9	2	0	0	0	2	0	0	0	0	0
SCANDINAVIA	0	0	0	0	0	0	0	0	0	0	0	0	0	0	0	0	0	0	0	0
SWITZERLAND	0	0	0	0	0	0	0	0	0	0	0	0	0	0	0	0	0	0	0	0
OTHER EFTA	0	0	0	0	0	0	0	0	0	0	0	0	0	0	0	0	0	0	0	0
EUROP. COMMUNITY	12	8	2	0	0	1	1	0	0	0	5	3	2	0	0	6	4	2	0	0
FRANCE	3	2	1	0	0	0	0	0	0	0	2	2	0	0	0	1	0	1	0	0
GERMANY	5	3	1	0	0	1	1	0	0	0	2	1	1	0	0	2	1	1	0	0
ITALY	2	1	1	0	0	0	0	0	0	0	1	0	1	0	0	1	1	0	0	0
BELGIUM + LUX	1	1	0	0	0	0	0	0	0	0	0	0	0	0	0	1	1	0	0	0
NETHERLANDS	1	1	0	0	0	0	0	0	0	0	0	0	0	0	0	1	1	0	0	0
SPAIN	2	2	0	0	0	1	1	0	0	0	0	0	0	0	0	1	0	1	0	0
GREECE + TURKEY	1	0	1	0	0	0	0	0	0	0	1	0	1	0	0	0	0	0	0	0
OTHER EUROPE	0	0	0	0	0	0	0	0	0	0	0	0	0	0	0	0	0	0	0	0
EUROPE EX. U.K.	15	10	3	0	0	2	2	0	0	0	5	3	2	0	0	8	5	3	0	0
SOUTHERN DOMINIONS	10	9	1	0	0	2	2	0	0	0	1	1	0	0	0	7	6	1	0	0
S. AFRICA +RHOD.	6	6	1	0	0	2	2	0	0	0	0	0	0	0	0	4	4	0	0	0
AUSTRALIA + N.Z.	4	3	1	0	0	0	0	0	0	0	1	1	0	0	0	3	2	1	0	0
ASIA + OTHER AFRICA	11	8	3	0	0	1	1	0	0	0	5	2	3	0	0	5	2	3	0	0
JAPAN	3	3	0	0	0	0	0	0	0	0	1	1	0	0	0	2	1	0	0	0
OTHER ASIA+AFR.	8	5	3	0	0	1	1	0	0	0	3	1	2	0	0	4	1	3	0	0
BLACK AFRICA	2	2	0	0	0	0	0	0	0	0	1	1	0	0	0	1	1	0	0	0
ARAB WORLD	0	0	0	0	0	0	0	0	0	0	0	0	0	0	0	0	0	0	0	0
INDIA	1	1	0	0	0	1	1	0	0	0	0	0	0	0	0	0	0	0	0	0
PHILIPPINES	4	2	2	0	0	0	0	0	0	0	2	0	2	0	0	2	0	2	0	0
OTHER E. ASIA	0	0	0	0	0	0	0	0	0	0	0	0	0	0	0	0	0	0	0	0
OTHER ASIA	1	0	1	0	0	0	0	0	0	0	0	0	0	0	0	1	1	0	0	0

CHAPTER 5- PATTERNS OF OWNERSHIP
SECTION 4- THE FLOW OF MANUFACTURING BY INDUSTRY OF SUBSIDIARY
TABLE 8- SUBSIDIARIES MANUFACTURING
OTHER FOOD PRODUCTS (SIC 206 AND 209)
CLASSIFIED BY COUNTRY, PERIOD MANUFACTURE BEGAN, AND SYSTEM OWNERSHIP %

PERIOD AND OWNERSHIP PERCENTAGE
(WHL=95-100%, MAJ=50-94%, MIN=5-49%, UNK=UNKNOWN)

COUNTRY OR REGION	TOTAL PRE 1968					PRE 1946					1946-1957					1958-1967				
	ALL	WHL	MAJ	MIN	UNK	ALL	WHL	MAJ	MIN	UNK	ALL	WHL	MAJ	MIN	UNK	ALL	WHL	MAJ	MIN	UNK
OUTSIDE U.S.	125	75	39	3	8	33	26	4	0	3	21	13	6	0	2	71	36	29	3	3
OUT. U.S. + CANADA	106	58	37	3	8	24	18	3	0	3	20	12	6	0	2	62	28	28	3	3
OUT. WEST. HEMIS.	78	45	24	3	6	15	12	1	0	2	16	10	4	0	2	47	23	19	3	2
OUT. WHITE CWEALTH	78	38	30	3	7	16	10	3	0	3	16	9	5	0	2	46	19	22	3	2
OUT. DEVLPED WORLD	33	17	13	0	3	12	8	2	0	2	5	3	2	0	0	16	6	9	0	1
CANADA	19	17	2	0	0	9	8	1	0	0	1	1	0	0	0	9	8	1	0	0
LATIN AMERICA	28	13	13	0	2	9	6	2	0	1	4	2	2	0	0	15	5	9	0	1
C. AMER.+CARIB.	16	7	8	0	1	4	2	1	0	1	2	1	1	0	0	10	4	6	0	0
CUBA	3	2	1	0	0	2	1	1	0	0	1	1	0	0	0	0	0	0	0	0
MEXICO	9	5	4	0	0	1	1	0	0	0	1	1	0	0	0	7	3	4	0	0
OTHER	4	0	3	0	1	1	0	0	0	1	0	0	0	0	0	3	0	3	0	0
S. AMERICA	12	6	5	0	1	5	4	1	0	0	2	1	1	0	0	5	1	3	0	1
ARGENTINA	2	2	0	0	0	2	2	0	0	0	0	0	0	0	0	0	0	0	0	0
BRAZIL	2	2	0	0	0	2	2	0	0	0	0	0	0	0	0	0	0	0	0	0
PERU	4	2	2	0	0	0	0	0	0	0	1	0	1	0	0	3	2	1	0	0
COLOMBIA	2	1	0	0	1	1	0	1	0	0	1	1	0	0	0	0	0	0	0	0
VENEZUELA	0	0	0	0	0	0	0	0	0	0	0	0	0	0	0	0	0	0	0	0
OTHER	3	0	2	0	1	0	0	0	0	0	0	0	0	0	0	2	0	2	0	1
EUROPE	58	33	20	1	4	11	9	1	0	1	13	7	4	0	2	34	17	15	1	1
EFTA	27	20	6	0	1	8	8	0	0	0	5	2	3	0	0	14	10	3	0	1
U.K.	14	12	2	0	0	6	6	0	0	0	3	2	1	0	0	5	4	1	0	0
SCANDINAVIA	11	8	3	0	0	2	2	0	0	0	1	0	1	0	0	8	6	2	0	0
SWITZERLAND	1	0	0	0	1	0	0	0	0	0	1	0	0	0	1	0	0	0	0	0
OTHER EFTA	1	0	1	0	0	0	0	0	0	0	0	0	0	0	0	1	0	1	0	0
EUROP. COMMUNITY	24	9	11	0	4	2	0	0	0	2	7	4	1	0	2	15	5	9	0	1
FRANCE	5	2	3	0	0	0	0	0	0	0	2	1	1	0	0	3	1	2	0	0
GERMANY	5	1	2	0	2	0	0	0	0	0	1	1	0	0	0	4	0	2	0	2
ITALY	6	0	4	0	2	0	0	0	0	0	1	0	1	0	0	4	0	4	0	2
BELGIUM + LUX	0	0	0	0	0	0	0	0	0	0	0	0	0	0	0	0	0	0	0	0
NETHERLANDS	8	4	2	0	2	0	0	0	0	0	3	1	0	0	2	5	3	2	0	0
SPAIN	3	1	2	0	0	0	0	0	0	0	0	0	0	0	0	3	1	2	0	0
GREECE + TURKEY	1	1	0	0	0	0	0	0	0	0	0	0	0	0	0	1	1	0	0	0
OTHER EUROPE	3	2	0	0	1	0	0	0	0	0	1	1	0	0	0	1	0	1	0	1
EUROPE EX. U.K.	44	21	18	1	4	5	3	1	0	1	10	5	3	0	2	29	13	14	1	1
SOUTHERN DOMINIONS	11	6	4	1	0	1	1	0	0	0	0	0	0	0	0	10	5	4	0	1
S. AFRICA +RHOD.	2	1	1	0	0	1	0	1	0	0	0	0	0	0	0	1	1	0	0	0
AUSTRALIA + N.Z.	9	5	3	0	1	0	0	0	0	0	0	0	0	0	0	9	5	3	0	1
ASIA + OTHER AFRICA	9	6	2	0	2	3	2	0	0	0	3	3	0	0	0	3	2	0	2	2
JAPAN	4	2	2	0	0	0	0	0	0	0	2	2	0	0	0	2	0	2	0	0
OTHER ASIA+AFR.	5	4	0	0	1	3	2	0	0	1	1	1	0	0	0	1	1	0	0	0
BLACK AFRICA	0	0	0	0	0	0	0	0	0	0	0	0	0	0	0	0	0	0	0	0
ARAB WORLD	0	0	0	0	0	0	0	0	0	0	0	0	0	0	0	0	0	0	0	0
INDIA	1	1	0	0	0	1	1	0	0	0	0	0	0	0	0	0	0	0	0	0
PHILIPPINES	2	2	0	0	0	1	1	0	0	0	0	0	0	0	0	1	1	0	0	0
OTHER E. ASIA	1	0	0	0	1	1	0	0	0	1	0	0	0	0	0	0	0	0	0	0
OTHER ASIA	1	1	0	0	0	1	1	0	0	0	0	0	0	0	0	0	0	0	0	0

CHAPTER 5- PATTERNS OF OWNERSHIP
SECTION 4- THE FLOW OF MANUFACTURING BY INDUSTRY OF SUBSIDIARY
TABLE 9- SUBSIDIARIES MANUFACTURING
TEXTILES AND APPAREL (SIC 22 AND 23)
CLASSIFIED BY COUNTRY, PERIOD MANUFACTURE BEGAN, AND SYSTEM OWNERSHIP %

PERIOD AND OWNERSHIP PERCENTAGE
(WHL=95-100%, MAJ=50-94%, MIN=5-49%, UNK=UNKNOWN)

COUNTRY OR REGION	TOTAL PRE 1968					PRE 1946					1946-1957					1958-1967				
	ALL	WHL	MAJ	MIN	UNK	ALL	WHL	MAJ	MIN	UNK	ALL	WHL	MAJ	MIN	UNK	ALL	WHL	MAJ	MIN	UNK
OUTSIDE U.S.	144	68	35	12	11	16	6	7	1	2	27	19	3	4	1	83	43	25	7	8
OUT. U.S. + CANADA	117	46	32	11	11	8	1	4	1	2	20	12	3	4	1	72	33	25	6	8
OUT. WEST. HEMIS.	65	25	19	5	5	8	0	4	0	0	2	0	0	0	0	51	25	18	4	4
OUT. WHITE CWEALTH	97	37	26	9	9	7	1	3	1	2	20	12	3	4	1	54	24	20	4	6
OUT. DEVLPED WORLD	55	21	15	6	6	7	1	3	1	2	18	12	3	3	0	23	8	9	2	4
CANADA	27	22	3	1	0	8	5	3	0	0	7	7	0	0	0	11	10	0	1	0
LATIN AMERICA	52	21	13	6	6	7	1	3	0	2	18	12	3	3	0	21	8	7	2	4
C. AMER.+CARIB.	18	9	4	2	0	1	0	0	1	0	6	5	1	0	0	8	4	4	0	0
CUBA	2	1	0	0	0	0	0	0	0	0	1	1	0	0	0	0	0	0	0	0
MEXICO	14	7	3	2	0	1	0	0	1	0	5	4	1	0	0	6	3	3	0	0
OTHER	2	1	1	0	0	0	0	0	0	0	0	0	0	0	0	2	1	1	0	0
S. AMERICA	34	12	9	4	6	6	1	3	0	2	12	7	3	2	0	13	4	3	2	4
ARGENTINA	4	1	1	1	0	2	1	1	0	0	1	0	0	1	0	1	1	0	0	0
BRAZIL	4	2	1	1	0	0	0	0	0	0	3	2	0	1	0	0	0	0	0	0
PERU	3	2	1	0	0	1	1	0	0	0	1	0	1	0	0	1	1	0	0	0
COLOMBIA	6	1	4	1	0	0	0	0	0	0	1	0	0	1	0	5	1	3	1	0
VENEZUELA	14	6	2	2	6	3	0	1	0	2	5	4	1	0	0	6	2	3	1	0
OTHER	3	2	0	1	0	0	0	0	0	0	2	2	0	0	0	1	0	0	0	0
EUROPE	46	24	14	2	5	0	0	0	0	0	1	1	0	0	0	44	24	14	2	4
EFTA	21	12	4	1	4	0	0	0	0	0	1	1	0	0	0	20	12	4	1	3
U.K.	14	8	4	0	2	0	0	0	0	0	0	0	0	0	0	14	8	4	1	2
SCANDINAVIA	2	1	0	1	0	0	0	0	0	0	0	0	0	0	0	2	1	0	0	0
SWITZERLAND	4	3	0	0	1	0	0	0	0	0	0	0	0	0	0	4	3	0	0	1
OTHER EFTA	1	0	0	1	1	0	0	0	0	0	1	1	0	0	0	0	0	0	0	0
EUROP. COMMUNITY	22	11	8	0	1	0	0	0	0	0	0	0	0	0	0	21	11	8	1	1
FRANCE	9	3	4	1	1	0	0	0	0	0	0	0	0	0	0	8	3	4	1	0
GERMANY	4	2	1	1	0	0	0	0	0	0	0	0	0	0	0	4	2	1	0	1
ITALY	4	2	2	0	0	0	0	0	0	0	0	0	0	0	0	4	2	2	0	0
BELGIUM + LUX	4	4	0	0	0	0	0	0	0	0	0	0	0	0	0	4	4	2	0	0
NETHERLANDS	1	0	1	0	0	0	0	0	0	0	0	0	0	0	0	1	0	1	0	0
SPAIN	3	1	2	0	0	0	0	0	0	0	0	0	0	0	0	3	1	2	0	0
GREECE + TURKEY	0	0	0	0	0	0	0	0	0	0	0	0	0	0	0	0	0	0	0	0
OTHER EUROPE	0	0	0	0	0	0	0	0	0	0	0	0	0	0	0	0	0	0	0	0
EUROPE EX. U.K.	32	16	10	2	3	0	0	0	0	0	1	1	0	0	1	30	16	10	2	2
SOUTHERN DOMINIONS	6	1	2	2	0	1	0	0	0	0	1	0	0	0	0	4	1	1	1	1
S. AFRICA +RHOD.	3	0	1	1	0	0	0	0	0	0	1	0	0	0	0	2	0	1	1	0
AUSTRALIA + N.Z.	3	1	1	1	0	1	0	0	0	0	0	0	0	0	0	2	1	0	0	1
ASIA + OTHER AFRICA	13	0	3	1	0	0	0	0	0	0	0	0	0	0	0	3	1	1	0	1
JAPAN	10	0	2	1	0	0	0	0	0	0	0	0	0	0	0	1	1	0	0	0
OTHER ASIA+AFR.	3	0	1	2	0	0	0	0	0	0	0	0	0	0	0	2	0	2	0	0
BLACK AFRICA	0	0	0	0	0	0	0	0	0	0	0	0	0	0	0	1	1	0	0	0
ARAB WORLD	1	0	1	1	0	0	0	0	0	0	0	0	0	0	0	1	0	1	1	0
INDIA	1	1	0	1	1	0	0	0	0	0	0	0	0	0	0	0	0	0	0	0
PHILIPPINES	1	0	1	1	0	0	0	0	0	0	1	1	0	0	0	0	0	0	0	0
OTHER E. ASIA	1	0	0	0	0	0	0	0	0	0	0	0	0	0	0	1	1	0	0	0
OTHER ASIA	0	0	0	0	0	0	0	0	0	0	0	0	0	0	0	0	0	0	0	0

CHAPTER 5- PATTERNS OF OWNERSHIP
SECTION 4- THE FLOW OF MANUFACTURING BY INDUSTRY OF SUBSIDIARY
TABLE 10- SUBSIDIARIES MANUFACTURING
PAPER AND PAPERBOARD PRODUCTS, EXCEPT CONTAINERS (SIC 264)
CLASSIFIED BY COUNTRY, PERIOD MANUFACTURE BEGAN, AND SYSTEM OWNERSHIP %

PERIOD AND OWNERSHIP PERCENTAGE
(WHL=95-100%, MAJ=50-94%, MIN=5-49%, UNK=UNKNOWN)

COUNTRY OR REGION	TOTAL PRE 1968					PRE 1946					1946-1957					1958-1967				
	ALL	WHL	MAJ	MIN	UNK	ALL	WHL	MAJ	MIN	UNK	ALL	WHL	MAJ	MIN	UNK	ALL	WHL	MAJ	MIN	UNK
OUTSIDE U.S.	97	45	37	12	3	17	9	6	1	1	27	13	9	4	1	53	23	22	7	1
OUT. U.S. + CANADA	83	38	34	10	1	10	6	3	0	1	21	10	9	2	0	52	22	22	7	1
OUT. WEST. HEMIS.	62	31	23	7	1	6	5	1	0	0	13	7	4	2	0	43	19	18	5	1
OUT. WHITE CWEALTH	51	16	29	6	0	7	3	3	1	1	13	5	7	1	0	31	8	19	4	0
OUT. DEVLPED WORLD	28	8	16	4	0	4	1	2	1	1	10	4	6	0	0	14	3	8	3	0
CANADA	14	7	3	2	2	7	3	3	0	1	6	3	0	2	1	1	1	0	0	0
LATIN AMERICA	21	7	11	3	0	4	1	2	1	0	8	3	5	0	0	9	3	4	2	0
C. AMER.+CARIB.	9	4	4	1	0	1	1	0	0	0	3	1	1	1	0	5	1	3	1	0
CUBA	1	1	0	0	0	1	1	0	0	0	0	0	0	0	0	0	0	0	0	0
MEXICO	3	2	0	1	0	0	0	0	0	0	1	1	0	0	0	1	0	0	1	0
OTHER	5	2	3	0	0	0	0	0	0	0	1	0	1	0	0	4	1	3	0	0
S. AMERICA	12	3	7	2	0	3	0	2	1	0	5	1	4	0	0	4	2	1	1	0
ARGENTINA	2	0	2	0	0	1	0	1	0	0	1	0	1	0	0	0	0	0	0	0
BRAZIL	2	1	1	0	0	0	0	0	0	0	1	0	1	0	0	0	0	0	0	0
PERU	1	0	0	1	0	0	0	0	0	0	0	0	0	0	0	1	1	0	0	0
COLOMBIA	4	1	2	1	0	2	0	1	1	0	0	0	0	0	0	2	1	0	1	0
VENEZUELA	4	1	2	1	0	0	0	0	0	0	2	0	2	0	0	1	0	1	0	0
OTHER	0	0	0	0	0	0	0	0	0	0	0	0	0	0	0	0	0	0	0	0
EUROPE	29	13	14	2	0	4	3	1	0	0	8	4	3	1	0	17	6	10	1	0
EFTA	8	4	4	0	0	1	1	0	0	0	4	2	2	0	0	3	1	2	0	0
U.K.	7	4	3	0	0	1	1	0	0	0	4	2	2	0	0	2	1	1	0	0
SCANDINAVIA	0	0	0	0	0	0	0	0	0	0	0	0	0	0	0	0	0	0	0	0
SWITZERLAND	0	0	0	0	0	0	0	0	0	0	0	0	0	0	0	0	0	0	0	0
OTHER EFTA	1	0	1	0	0	0	0	0	0	0	0	0	0	0	0	1	0	1	0	0
EUROP. COMMUNITY	17	8	7	2	0	3	2	1	0	0	3	1	1	1	0	11	5	5	1	0
FRANCE	9	3	5	1	0	1	1	0	0	0	2	1	1	0	0	6	1	5	0	0
GERMANY	2	1	0	1	0	1	0	1	0	0	0	0	0	0	0	1	0	0	1	0
ITALY	3	2	1	0	0	1	1	0	0	0	1	0	0	1	0	1	1	0	0	0
BELGIUM + LUX	1	1	0	0	0	0	0	0	0	0	0	0	0	0	0	1	1	0	0	0
NETHERLANDS	2	0	2	0	0	0	0	0	0	0	0	0	0	0	0	2	0	2	0	0
SPAIN	2	2	0	0	0	0	0	0	0	0	0	0	0	0	0	2	2	0	0	0
GREECE + TURKEY	1	1	0	0	0	0	0	0	0	0	0	0	0	0	0	1	1	0	0	0
OTHER EUROPE	1	0	1	0	0	0	0	0	0	0	1	0	1	0	0	0	0	0	0	0
EUROPE EX. U.K.	22	9	11	2	0	3	2	1	0	0	4	2	2	0	0	15	5	9	1	0
SOUTHERN DOMINIONS	24	17	2	4	1	2	2	0	0	0	3	2	0	0	1	19	13	2	3	1
S. AFRICA +RHOD.	14	11	0	3	0	2	2	0	0	0	1	1	0	0	0	13	10	0	3	0
AUSTRALIA + N.Z.	10	6	2	1	1	0	0	0	0	0	2	1	0	0	1	6	3	2	0	1
ASIA + OTHER AFRICA	9	2	7	0	0	2	0	2	0	0	2	1	1	0	0	7	0	6	1	0
JAPAN	2	1	1	0	0	0	0	0	0	0	0	0	0	0	0	2	0	2	0	0
OTHER ASIA+AFR.	7	1	5	1	0	2	0	2	0	0	2	1	1	0	0	5	0	4	1	0
BLACK AFRICA	0	0	0	0	0	0	0	0	0	0	0	0	0	0	0	0	0	0	0	0
ARAB WORLD	0	0	0	0	0	0	0	0	0	0	0	0	0	0	0	0	0	0	0	0
INDIA	1	1	0	0	0	0	0	0	0	0	1	1	0	0	0	0	0	0	0	0
PHILIPPINES	3	0	2	1	0	2	0	2	0	0	0	0	0	0	0	2	0	2	0	0
OTHER E. ASIA	0	0	0	0	0	0	0	0	0	0	0	0	0	0	0	0	0	0	0	0
OTHER ASIA	3	0	3	0	0	0	0	0	0	0	1	0	1	0	0	2	0	2	0	0

CHAPTER 5- PATTERNS OF OWNERSHIP
SECTION 4- THE FLOW OF MANUFACTURING BY INDUSTRY OF SUBSIDIARY
TABLE 11- SUBSIDIARIES MANUFACTURING
PAPERBOARD CONTAINERS AND BOXES (SIC 265)
CLASSIFIED BY COUNTRY, PERIOD MANUFACTURE BEGAN, AND SYSTEM OWNERSHIP %

PERIOD AND OWNERSHIP PERCENTAGE
(WHL=95-100%, MAJ=50-94%, MIN=5-49%, UNK=UNKNOWN)

COUNTRY OR REGION	TOTAL					PRE 1946					1946-1957					1958-1967				
	ALL	WHL	MAJ	MIN	UNK	ALL	WHL	MAJ	MIN	UNK	ALL	WHL	MAJ	MIN	UNK	ALL	WHL	MAJ	MIN	UNK
OUTSIDE U.S.	106	54	29	19	3	9	4	3	1	1	27	16	8	3	0	69	34	18	15	2
OUT. U.S. + CANADA	95	43	29	19	3	6	1	3	1	1	20	9	8	3	0	68	33	18	15	2
OUT. WEST. HEMIS.	59	31	16	10	1	2	1	0	1	0	4	2	1	1	0	52	28	15	8	1
OUT. WHITE CWEALTH	68	25	26	14	2	5	0	3	1	1	18	8	8	2	0	44	17	15	11	1
OUT. DEVLPED WORLD	41	14	15	10	2	4	0	3	0	1	17	8	7	2	0	20	6	5	8	1
CANADA	11	11	0	0	0	3	3	0	0	0	7	7	0	0	0	1	1	0	0	0
LATIN AMERICA	36	12	13	9	2	4	2	1	0	1	16	6	7	3	0	16	4	5	6	1
C. AMER.+CARIB.	15	8	2	4	1	2	0	1	0	1	6	5	1	0	0	7	3	0	4	0
CUBA	1	0	0	0	1	1	0	0	0	1	0	0	0	0	0	0	0	0	0	0
MEXICO	9	6	2	1	0	1	0	1	0	0	5	4	1	0	0	3	2	0	1	0
OTHER	5	2	0	3	0	0	0	0	0	0	1	1	0	0	0	4	1	0	3	0
S. AMERICA	21	4	11	5	1	2	2	0	0	0	10	1	6	3	0	9	1	5	2	1
ARGENTINA	1	0	0	1	0	0	0	0	0	0	0	0	0	0	0	1	0	0	1	0
BRAZIL	4	2	1	1	0	2	2	0	0	0	2	0	1	1	0	0	0	0	0	0
PERU	2	0	1	1	0	0	0	0	0	0	2	0	1	1	0	0	0	0	0	0
COLOMBIA	2	1	0	1	0	0	0	0	0	0	2	1	0	1	0	0	0	0	0	0
VENEZUELA	9	1	7	0	1	0	0	0	0	0	4	0	4	0	0	5	1	3	0	1
OTHER	3	0	2	1	0	0	0	0	0	0	0	0	0	0	0	3	0	2	1	0
EUROPE	28	11	11	4	2	1	0	1	0	0	2	1	0	1	0	25	10	10	3	2
EFTA	4	2	1	0	1	0	0	0	0	0	0	0	0	0	0	4	2	1	0	1
U.K.	2	1	0	0	1	0	0	0	0	0	0	0	0	0	0	2	1	0	0	1
SCANDINAVIA	2	1	1	0	0	0	0	0	0	0	0	0	0	0	0	2	1	1	0	0
SWITZERLAND	0	0	0	0	0	0	0	0	0	0	0	0	0	0	0	0	0	0	0	0
OTHER EFTA	0	0	0	0	0	0	0	0	0	0	0	0	0	0	0	0	0	0	0	0
EUROP. COMMUNITY	18	8	7	3	0	1	0	1	0	0	2	1	0	1	0	15	7	6	2	0
FRANCE	1	0	1	0	0	0	0	0	0	0	0	0	0	0	0	1	0	1	0	0
GERMANY	7	3	3	1	0	0	0	0	0	0	1	0	0	1	0	6	3	3	0	0
ITALY	6	3	2	1	0	1	0	1	0	0	0	0	0	0	0	5	3	1	1	0
BELGIUM + LUX	3	1	1	1	0	0	0	0	0	0	1	1	0	0	0	2	0	1	1	0
NETHERLANDS	1	1	0	0	0	0	0	0	0	0	0	0	0	0	0	1	1	0	0	0
SPAIN	5	1	3	1	0	0	0	0	0	0	0	0	0	0	0	5	1	3	1	0
GREECE + TURKEY	0	0	0	0	0	0	0	0	0	0	0	0	0	0	0	0	0	0	0	0
OTHER EUROPE	1	0	0	0	1	0	0	0	0	0	0	0	0	0	0	1	0	0	0	1
EUROPE EX. U.K.	26	10	11	4	1	1	0	1	0	0	2	1	0	1	0	23	9	10	3	1
SOUTHERN DOMINIONS	24	17	3	4	0	1	1	0	0	0	2	1	1	0	0	21	15	2	4	0
S. AFRICA +RHOD.	19	14	2	3	0	1	1	0	0	0	0	0	0	0	0	18	13	2	3	0
AUSTRALIA + N.Z.	5	3	1	1	0	0	0	0	0	0	2	1	1	0	0	3	2	0	1	0
ASIA + OTHER AFRICA	7	3	2	2	0	1	1	0	0	0	0	0	0	0	0	6	2	2	2	0
JAPAN	2	1	0	1	0	0	0	0	0	0	0	0	0	0	0	2	1	0	1	0
OTHER ASIA+AFR.	5	2	2	1	0	1	1	0	0	0	0	0	0	0	0	4	1	2	1	0
BLACK AFRICA	2	0	1	1	0	0	0	0	0	0	0	0	0	0	0	2	0	1	1	0
ARAB WORLD	1	1	0	0	0	1	1	0	0	0	0	0	0	0	0	0	0	0	0	0
INDIA	0	0	0	0	0	0	0	0	0	0	0	0	0	0	0	0	0	0	0	0
PHILIPPINES	0	0	0	0	0	0	0	0	0	0	0	0	0	0	0	0	0	0	0	0
OTHER E. ASIA	1	1	0	0	0	0	0	0	0	0	0	0	0	0	0	1	1	0	0	0
OTHER ASIA	1	0	1	0	0	0	0	0	0	0	0	0	0	0	0	1	0	1	0	0

CHAPTER 5- PATTERNS OF OWNERSHIP
SECTION 4- THE FLOW OF MANUFACTURING BY INDUSTRY OF SUBSIDIARY
TABLE 12- SUBSIDIARIES MANUFACTURING
OTHER WOOD, FURNITURE, AND PAPER PRODUCTS (SIC 24, 25, 261-263, AND 266)
CLASSIFIED BY COUNTRY, PERIOD MANUFACTURE BEGAN, AND SYSTEM OWNERSHIP %

PERIOD AND OWNERSHIP PERCENTAGE
(WHL=95-100%, MAJ=50-94%, MIN=5-49%, UNK=UNKNOWN)

COUNTRY OR REGION	TOTAL PRE 1968					PRE 1946					1946-1957					1958-1967				
	ALL	WHL	MAJ	MIN	UNK	ALL	WHL	MAJ	MIN	UNK	ALL	WHL	MAJ	MIN	UNK	ALL	WHL	MAJ	MIN	UNK
OUTSIDE U.S.	88	44	26	10	7	16	12	2	1	1	15	7	6	1	1	56	25	18	8	5
OUT. U.S. + CANADA	56	24	21	7	4	11	8	2	1	0	6	3	3	0	0	39	13	16	6	4
OUT. WEST. HEMIS.	37	18	15	3	1	9	7	2	0	0	2	2	0	0	0	26	9	13	3	1
OUT. WHITE CWEALTH	44	14	19	7	4	6	4	1	1	0	5	2	3	0	0	33	8	15	6	4
OUT. DEVLPED WORLD	22	7	7	5	3	2	1	0	1	0	4	1	3	0	0	16	5	4	4	3
CANADA	32	20	5	3	3	5	4	0	0	1	9	4	3	1	1	17	12	2	2	1
LATIN AMERICA	19	6	6	4	3	2	1	1	0	0	4	1	3	0	0	13	4	2	4	3
C. AMER.+CARIB.	8	1	4	3	0	2	1	0	1	0	2	0	2	0	0	4	0	2	2	0
CUBA	0	0	0	0	0	0	0	0	0	0	0	0	0	0	0	0	0	0	0	0
MEXICO	3	1	1	1	0	1	0	0	1	0	2	1	1	0	0	0	0	0	0	0
OTHER	5	0	3	2	0	1	1	0	1	0	0	0	0	0	0	4	0	2	2	0
S. AMERICA	11	5	2	1	3	0	0	0	0	0	2	1	1	0	0	9	4	1	1	3
ARGENTINA	3	2	0	1	0	0	0	0	0	0	0	0	0	0	0	3	2	0	1	0
BRAZIL	1	0	1	0	0	0	0	0	0	0	0	0	0	0	0	1	0	1	0	0
PERU	1	1	0	0	0	0	0	0	0	0	1	1	0	0	0	0	0	0	0	0
COLOMBIA	1	0	1	0	0	0	0	0	0	0	1	0	1	0	0	0	0	0	0	0
VENEZUELA	5	2	0	0	3	0	0	0	0	0	0	0	0	0	0	5	2	0	0	3
OTHER	0	0	0	0	0	0	0	0	0	0	0	0	0	0	0	0	0	0	0	0
EUROPE	27	11	14	1	1	7	5	2	0	0	1	1	0	0	0	19	5	12	1	1
EFTA	8	5	2	1	0	3	2	1	0	0	0	0	0	0	0	5	3	1	1	0
U.K.	7	5	2	0	0	3	2	1	0	0	0	0	0	0	0	4	3	1	0	0
SCANDINAVIA	1	0	0	1	0	0	0	0	0	0	0	0	0	0	0	1	0	0	1	0
SWITZERLAND	0	0	0	0	0	0	0	0	0	0	0	0	0	0	0	0	0	0	0	0
OTHER EFTA	0	0	0	0	0	0	0	0	0	0	0	0	0	0	0	0	0	0	0	0
EUROP. COMMUNITY	12	4	8	0	0	1	0	1	0	0	1	0	1	0	0	10	4	6	0	0
FRANCE	5	2	3	0	0	1	0	1	0	0	1	1	0	0	0	3	1	2	0	0
GERMANY	3	1	2	0	0	0	0	0	0	0	0	0	0	0	0	3	1	2	0	0
ITALY	3	2	1	0	0	0	0	0	0	0	0	0	0	0	0	3	2	1	0	0
BELGIUM + LUX	1	0	1	0	0	0	0	0	0	0	0	0	0	0	0	1	0	1	0	0
NETHERLANDS	0	0	0	0	0	0	0	0	0	0	0	0	0	0	0	0	0	0	0	0
SPAIN	7	2	4	1	0	0	0	0	0	0	3	2	1	0	0	4	0	3	1	0
GREECE + TURKEY	0	0	0	0	0	0	0	0	0	0	0	0	0	0	0	0	0	0	0	0
OTHER EUROPE	0	0	0	0	0	0	0	0	0	0	0	0	0	0	0	0	0	0	0	0
EUROPE EX. U.K.	20	6	12	1	1	4	3	1	0	0	1	1	0	0	0	15	2	11	1	1
SOUTHERN DOMINIONS	5	5	0	0	0	2	2	0	0	0	1	1	0	0	0	2	2	0	0	0
S. AFRICA +RHOD.	1	1	0	0	0	1	1	0	0	0	0	0	0	0	0	0	0	0	0	0
AUSTRALIA + N.Z.	4	4	0	0	0	1	1	0	0	0	1	1	0	0	0	2	2	0	0	0
ASIA + OTHER AFRICA	5	2	1	2	0	0	0	0	0	0	0	0	0	0	0	5	2	1	2	0
JAPAN	2	1	0	1	0	0	0	0	0	0	0	0	0	0	0	2	1	0	1	0
OTHER ASIA+AFR.	3	1	1	1	0	0	0	0	0	0	0	0	0	0	0	3	1	1	1	0
BLACK AFRICA	0	0	0	0	0	0	0	0	0	0	0	0	0	0	0	0	0	0	0	0
ARAB WORLD	0	0	0	0	0	0	0	0	0	0	0	0	0	0	0	0	0	0	0	0
INDIA	0	0	0	0	0	0	0	0	0	0	0	0	0	0	0	0	0	0	0	0
PHILIPPINES	3	1	1	1	0	0	0	0	0	0	0	0	0	0	0	3	1	1	1	0
OTHER E. ASIA	0	0	0	0	0	0	0	0	0	0	0	0	0	0	0	0	0	0	0	0
OTHER ASIA	0	0	0	0	0	0	0	0	0	0	0	0	0	0	0	0	0	0	0	0

CHAPTER 5- PATTERNS OF OWNERSHIP
SECTION 4- THE FLOW OF MANUFACTURING BY INDUSTRY OF SUBSIDIARY
TABLE 13- SUBSIDIARIES MANUFACTURING
PRINTED MATTER (SIC 27)
CLASSIFIED BY COUNTRY, PERIOD MANUFACTURE BEGAN, AND SYSTEM OWNERSHIP %

PERIOD AND OWNERSHIP PERCENTAGE
(WHL=95-100%, MAJ=50-94%, MIN=5-49%, UNK=UNKNOWN)

COUNTRY OR REGION	TOTAL PRE 1968					PRE 1946					1946-1957					1958-1967				
	ALL	WHL	MAJ	MIN	UNK	ALL	WHL	MAJ	MIN	UNK	ALL	WHL	MAJ	MIN	UNK	ALL	WHL	MAJ	MIN	UNK
OUTSIDE U.S.	36	20	6	5	3	4	3	0	0	1	8	4	2	1	1	22	13	4	4	1
OUT. U.S. + CANADA	31	16	6	5	3	2	1	0	0	1	7	3	2	1	1	21	12	4	4	1
OUT. WEST. HEMIS.	25	13	5	3	3	1	0	0	0	1	5	3	2	2	1	18	12	3	2	1
OUT. WHITE CWEALTH	24	12	6	5	1	1	1	0	0	0	7	3	2	1	1	16	8	4	4	0
OUT. DEVLPED WORLD	6	3	1	2	0	1	1	0	0	0	2	2	0	0	0	3	0	1	2	0
CANADA	5	4	1	0	0	2	2	0	0	0	1	1	0	0	0	1	1	0	0	0
LATIN AMERICA	6	3	1	2	0	1	1	0	0	0	2	1	1	0	0	3	1	1	1	0
C. AMER.+CARIB.	2	1	0	1	0	0	0	0	0	0	1	1	0	0	0	1	0	0	1	0
CUBA	1	1	0	0	0	0	0	0	0	0	1	1	0	0	0	0	0	0	0	0
MEXICO	1	0	0	1	0	0	0	0	0	0	0	0	0	0	0	1	0	0	1	0
OTHER	0	0	0	0	0	0	0	0	0	0	0	0	0	0	0	0	0	0	0	0
S. AMERICA	4	2	1	1	0	1	1	0	0	0	1	0	1	0	0	2	0	1	1	0
ARGENTINA	3	1	1	1	0	0	0	0	0	0	1	0	1	0	0	2	0	1	1	0
BRAZIL	1	1	0	0	0	1	1	0	0	0	0	0	0	0	0	0	0	0	0	0
PERU	0	0	0	0	0	0	0	0	0	0	0	0	0	0	0	0	0	0	0	0
COLOMBIA	0	0	0	0	0	0	0	0	0	0	0	0	0	0	0	0	0	0	0	0
VENEZUELA	0	0	0	0	0	0	0	0	0	0	0	0	0	0	0	0	0	0	0	0
OTHER	0	0	0	0	0	0	0	0	0	0	0	0	0	0	0	0	0	0	0	0
EUROPE	20	9	4	3	3	1	1	0	0	0	5	2	2	0	1	13	8	2	2	1
EFTA	6	3	0	0	3	1	1	0	0	0	1	0	0	0	1	4	3	0	0	1
U.K.	3	2	0	0	2	1	1	0	0	0	1	0	0	0	1	1	0	0	0	1
SCANDINAVIA	2	1	0	0	0	0	0	0	0	0	0	0	0	0	0	2	2	0	0	0
SWITZERLAND	1	0	0	0	1	0	0	0	0	0	0	0	0	0	0	1	1	0	0	0
OTHER EFTA	0	0	0	0	0	0	0	0	0	0	0	0	0	0	0	0	0	0	0	0
EUROP. COMMUNITY	13	5	4	3	1	0	0	0	0	0	4	2	2	0	0	9	5	2	2	0
FRANCE	4	2	1	1	0	0	0	0	0	0	0	0	0	0	0	4	2	1	1	0
GERMANY	4	2	1	0	0	0	0	0	0	0	2	1	1	0	0	2	1	0	1	0
ITALY	4	2	1	0	1	0	0	0	0	0	1	0	0	0	1	3	2	1	0	0
BELGIUM + LUX	0	0	0	0	0	0	0	0	0	0	0	0	0	0	0	0	0	0	0	0
NETHERLANDS	1	1	0	0	0	0	0	0	0	0	1	1	0	0	0	0	0	0	0	0
SPAIN	1	0	0	0	1	0	0	0	0	0	0	0	0	0	0	0	0	0	0	0
GREECE + TURKEY	0	0	0	0	0	0	0	0	0	0	0	0	0	0	0	0	0	0	0	0
OTHER EUROPE	0	0	0	0	0	0	0	0	0	0	0	0	0	0	0	0	0	0	0	0
EUROPE EX. U.K.	17	9	4	3	1	0	0	0	0	0	5	2	2	0	1	12	8	2	2	0
SOUTHERN DOMINIONS	4	4	0	0	0	0	0	0	0	0	0	0	0	0	0	4	4	0	0	0
S. AFRICA +RHOD.	4	4	0	0	0	0	0	0	0	0	0	0	0	0	0	4	4	0	0	0
AUSTRALIA + N.Z.	0	0	0	0	0	0	0	0	0	0	0	0	0	0	0	0	0	0	0	0
ASIA + OTHER AFRICA	1	0	1	0	0	0	0	0	0	0	0	0	0	0	0	1	0	1	0	0
JAPAN	1	0	1	0	0	0	0	0	0	0	0	0	0	0	0	1	0	1	0	0
OTHER ASIA+AFR.	0	0	0	0	0	0	0	0	0	0	0	0	0	0	0	0	0	0	0	0
BLACK AFRICA	0	0	0	0	0	0	0	0	0	0	0	0	0	0	0	0	0	0	0	0
ARAB WORLD	0	0	0	0	0	0	0	0	0	0	0	0	0	0	0	0	0	0	0	0
INDIA	0	0	0	0	0	0	0	0	0	0	0	0	0	0	0	0	0	0	0	0
PHILLIPPINES	0	0	0	0	0	0	0	0	0	0	0	0	0	0	0	0	0	0	0	0
OTHER E. ASIA	0	0	0	0	0	0	0	0	0	0	0	0	0	0	0	0	0	0	0	0
OTHER ASIA	0	0	0	0	0	0	0	0	0	0	0	0	0	0	0	0	0	0	0	0

CHAPTER 5- PATTERNS OF OWNERSHIP
SECTION 4- THE FLOW OF MANUFACTURING BY INDUSTRY OF SUBSIDIARY
TABLE 14- SUBSIDIARIES MANUFACTURING
INDUSTRIAL CHEMICALS (SIC 281)
CLASSIFIED BY COUNTRY, PERIOD MANUFACTURE BEGAN, AND SYSTEM OWNERSHIP %

PERIOD AND OWNERSHIP PERCENTAGE
(WHL=95-100%, MAJ=50-94%, MIN=5-49%, UNK=UNKNOWN)

COUNTRY OR REGION	TOTAL / PRE 1968 ALL	WHL	MAJ	MIN	UNK	PRE 1946 ALL	WHL	MAJ	MIN	UNK	1946-1957 ALL	WHL	MAJ	MIN	UNK	1958-1967 ALL	WHL	MAJ	MIN	UNK
OUTSIDE U.S.	367	154	127	44	42	60	33	17	4	6	85	35	32	11	7	209	86	78	29	16
OUT. U.S. + CANADA	306	113	118	42	33	33	14	14	3	2	69	25	28	11	5	193	74	76	28	15
OUT. WEST. HEMIS.	198	74	85	24	15	23	11	9	2	1	32	12	12	7	1	139	51	64	15	9
OUT. WHITE CWEALTH	249	85	100	38	26	24	9	11	2	2	57	20	23	9	5	159	56	66	27	10
OUT. DEVLPED WORLD	121	41	40	22	18	10	3	5	1	1	39	13	18	4	4	65	25	17	17	6
CANADA	61	41	9	2	9	27	19	3	1	4	16	10	4	0	2	16	12	2	1	1
LATIN AMERICA	108	39	33	18	18	10	3	5	1	1	37	13	16	4	4	54	23	12	13	6
C. AMER.+CARIB.	51	20	10	13	8	3	1	1	0	1	18	6	6	4	2	26	10	3	11	2
CUBA	1	0	1	0	0	0	0	0	0	0	1	0	1	0	0	0	0	0	0	0
MEXICO	43	18	6	12	7	3	1	0	1	1	15	9	3	2	1	21	8	2	10	1
OTHER	7	2	3	1	1	0	0	0	0	0	2	0	2	1	0	5	2	1	1	1
S. AMERICA	57	19	23	5	10	7	2	4	1	0	19	4	10	2	3	28	13	9	2	4
ARGENTINA	16	5	8	0	3	4	2	1	0	1	6	1	6	0	0	6	2	1	0	3
BRAZIL	14	4	4	2	4	1	0	0	0	1	4	1	2	2	0	9	3	2	0	2
PERU	4	3	0	0	1	1	1	0	0	0	1	0	0	0	1	2	2	0	0	0
COLOMBIA	12	2	7	2	1	1	0	1	0	0	2	0	2	0	0	8	2	5	1	0
VENEZUELA	8	2	3	1	2	1	0	0	1	0	3	0	1	2	0	4	2	1	1	0
OTHER	3	2	1	0	0	0	0	0	0	0	0	0	0	0	0	3	1	1	0	1
EUROPE	135	56	60	11	8	20	11	7	1	1	24	9	8	6	1	90	36	43	5	6
EFTA	38	21	11	4	2	7	5	2	0	0	11	4	4	3	0	20	12	3	1	4
U.K.	27	15	8	2	2	6	5	1	0	0	9	3	4	2	0	12	7	3	0	2
SCANDINAVIA	8	4	3	1	0	1	0	1	0	0	1	1	0	0	0	5	3	0	0	2
SWITZERLAND	0	0	0	0	0	0	0	0	0	0	0	0	0	0	0	3	2	0	1	0
OTHER EFTA	3	2	0	1	0	0	0	0	0	0	0	0	0	0	0	0	0	0	0	0
EUROP. COMMUNITY	80	29	40	6	5	12	5	5	1	1	11	4	3	3	1	56	20	32	2	2
FRANCE	19	6	11	2	0	2	1	0	1	0	2	1	0	1	0	15	5	10	0	0
GERMANY	17	5	9	2	1	5	3	1	0	1	2	1	1	0	0	10	3	5	1	1
ITALY	21	9	9	1	2	2	1	1	0	0	3	1	1	1	0	16	7	8	0	1
BELGIUM + LUX	10	5	4	1	0	2	0	2	0	0	2	1	1	0	0	6	3	2	1	0
NETHERLANDS	13	4	7	1	1	1	0	1	0	0	2	0	0	1	1	9	2	7	0	0
SPAIN	14	5	8	0	1	1	1	0	0	0	2	1	1	0	0	11	3	7	1	0
GREECE + TURKEY	2	0	1	1	0	0	0	0	0	0	0	0	0	0	0	2	1	0	1	0
OTHER EUROPE	1	1	0	0	0	0	0	0	0	0	0	0	0	0	0	1	0	1	0	0
EUROPE EX. U.K.	108	41	52	9	6	14	6	6	1	1	15	6	4	4	1	78	29	42	4	3
SOUTHERN DOMINIONS	30	13	10	2	5	3	3	0	0	0	3	2	1	0	0	22	11	7	1	3
S. AFRICA +RHOD.	3	3	0	0	0	3	3	0	0	0	0	0	0	0	0	2	2	0	0	0
AUSTRALIA + N.Z.	27	10	10	2	5	0	0	0	0	0	3	2	1	0	0	20	9	7	1	3
ASIA + OTHER AFRICA	33	5	15	11	2	0	0	0	0	0	3	1	1	1	0	27	4	12	10	1
JAPAN	20	3	8	7	2	0	0	0	0	0	2	0	0	2	0	16	2	7	6	1
OTHER ASIA+AFR.	13	2	7	4	0	0	0	0	0	0	1	1	0	0	0	11	2	5	4	0
BLACK AFRICA	0	0	0	0	0	0	0	0	0	0	0	0	0	0	0	0	0	0	0	0
ARAB WORLD	4	1	2	0	1	0	0	0	0	0	0	0	0	0	0	4	1	2	0	1
INDIA	3	1	1	0	1	0	0	0	0	0	1	1	0	0	0	1	0	1	0	0
PHILIPPINES	2	1	1	0	0	0	0	0	0	0	0	0	0	0	0	2	1	1	0	0
OTHER E. ASIA	2	0	1	1	0	0	0	0	0	0	0	0	0	0	0	2	0	1	1	0
OTHER ASIA	2	0	2	0	0	0	0	0	0	0	0	0	0	0	0	2	0	1	0	1

CHAPTER 5- PATTERNS OF OWNERSHIP
SECTION 4- THE FLOW OF MANUFACTURING BY INDUSTRY OF SUBSIDIARY
TABLE 15- SUBSIDIARIES MANUFACTURING
PLASTICS AND SYNTHETICS (SIC 282)
CLASSIFIED BY COUNTRY, PERIOD MANUFACTURE BEGAN, AND SYSTEM OWNERSHIP %

PERIOD AND OWNERSHIP PERCENTAGE
(WHL=95-100%, MAJ=50-94%, MIN=5-49%, UNK=UNKNOWN)

COUNTRY OR REGION	TOTAL PRE 1968					PRE 1946					1946-1957					1958-1967				
	ALL	WHL	MAJ	MIN	UNK	ALL	WHL	MAJ	MIN	UNK	ALL	WHL	MAJ	MIN	UNK	ALL	WHL	MAJ	MIN	UNK
OUTSIDE U.S.	259	113	75	44	24	21	12	5	2	2	54	29	12	9	4	181	72	58	33	18
OUT. U.S. + CANADA	230	92	70	42	23	12	6	4	1	1	47	24	10	9	4	168	62	56	32	18
OUT. WEST. HEMIS.	164	65	48	32	16	7	4	2	0	1	25	10	7	6	2	129	51	39	26	13
OUT. WHITE CWEALTH	165	57	53	35	19	6	2	2	1	1	37	20	9	5	3	121	35	42	29	15
OUT. DEVLPED WORLD	80	31	26	13	10	5	2	2	1	0	24	15	4	3	2	51	14	20	9	8
CANADA	29	21	5	2	1	9	6	1	1	1	7	5	2	0	0	13	10	2	1	0
LATIN AMERICA	66	27	22	10	7	5	2	2	1	0	22	14	3	3	2	39	11	17	6	5
C. AMER.+CARIB.	27	9	9	7	2	2	0	0	1	1	9	6	1	1	1	16	3	7	5	1
CUBA	0	0	0	0	0	0	0	0	0	0	0	0	0	0	0	0	0	0	0	0
MEXICO	23	8	8	6	1	2	0	0	1	1	9	6	1	1	1	12	2	6	4	0
OTHER	4	1	1	1	1	0	0	0	0	0	0	0	0	0	0	4	1	1	1	1
S. AMERICA	39	18	13	3	5	3	2	1	0	0	13	8	2	2	1	23	8	10	1	4
ARGENTINA	11	7	2	2	0	3	2	1	0	0	3	2	0	1	0	5	3	1	1	0
BRAZIL	10	5	3	1	1	0	0	0	0	0	6	4	1	1	0	4	1	2	1	0
PERU	1	1	0	0	0	0	0	0	0	0	0	0	0	0	0	1	1	0	0	0
COLOMBIA	9	4	2	0	3	0	0	0	0	0	2	0	2	0	0	7	2	2	0	3
VENEZUELA	7	1	5	0	1	0	0	0	0	0	2	0	1	0	1	5	1	4	0	0
OTHER	1	0	1	0	0	0	0	0	0	0	0	0	0	0	0	1	0	1	0	0
EUROPE	99	45	25	18	10	6	3	2	0	1	19	8	4	6	1	73	34	19	12	8
EFTA	41	24	9	5	3	5	3	2	0	0	9	3	1	4	1	27	18	6	1	2
U.K.	34	20	7	5	2	5	3	2	0	0	9	3	1	4	1	20	14	4	1	1
SCANDINAVIA	5	2	2	0	1	0	0	0	0	0	0	0	0	0	0	5	2	2	0	1
SWITZERLAND	1	1	0	0	0	0	0	0	0	0	0	0	0	0	0	1	1	0	0	0
OTHER EFTA	1	1	0	0	0	0	0	0	0	0	0	0	0	0	0	1	1	0	0	0
EUROP. COMMUNITY	46	13	15	10	7	1	0	0	0	1	9	4	3	2	0	35	9	12	8	6
FRANCE	11	4	4	1	2	0	0	0	0	0	4	2	1	0	0	7	2	3	1	2
GERMANY	10	3	3	3	1	1	0	0	0	1	2	2	0	0	0	7	1	3	3	0
ITALY	9	3	3	3	0	0	0	0	0	0	1	0	1	0	0	8	3	2	3	0
BELGIUM + LUX	7	2	3	1	1	0	0	0	0	0	1	0	0	1	0	6	2	3	0	1
NETHERLANDS	9	2	4	3	0	0	0	0	0	0	1	0	1	0	0	8	2	3	3	0
SPAIN	9	5	3	1	0	0	0	0	0	0	1	1	0	0	0	8	4	3	1	0
GREECE + TURKEY	3	3	0	0	0	0	0	0	0	0	0	0	0	0	0	3	3	0	0	0
OTHER EUROPE	0	0	0	0	0	0	0	0	0	0	0	0	0	0	0	0	0	0	0	0
EUROPE EX. U.K.	65	25	18	13	8	1	0	0	0	1	10	5	3	2	0	53	20	15	11	7
SOUTHERN DOMINIONS	31	15	10	2	2	1	1	0	0	0	3	1	2	0	0	27	13	10	2	2
S. AFRICA +RHOD.	5	4	0	0	0	1	1	0	0	0	2	1	1	0	0	2	2	0	0	0
AUSTRALIA + N.Z.	26	11	10	2	2	0	0	0	0	0	1	0	1	0	0	25	11	10	2	2
ASIA + OTHER AFRICA	34	5	13	12	4	0	0	0	0	0	5	1	3	0	1	29	4	10	12	3
JAPAN	20	1	9	9	1	0	0	0	0	0	3	0	2	0	1	17	1	7	9	0
OTHER ASIA+AFR.	14	4	4	3	3	0	0	0	0	0	2	1	1	0	0	12	3	3	3	3
BLACK AFRICA	2	2	0	0	0	0	0	0	0	0	1	1	0	0	0	1	1	0	0	0
ARAB WORLD	0	0	0	0	0	0	0	0	0	0	0	0	0	0	0	0	0	0	0	0
INDIA	5	0	3	1	1	0	0	0	0	0	0	0	0	0	0	5	0	3	1	1
PHILIPPINES	2	1	1	0	0	0	0	0	0	0	1	0	1	0	0	1	1	0	0	0
OTHER E. ASIA	4	1	1	0	2	0	0	0	0	0	0	0	0	0	0	4	1	1	0	2
OTHER ASIA	1	1	0	0	0	0	0	0	0	0	0	0	0	0	0	1	1	0	0	0

CHAPTER 5- PATTERNS OF OWNERSHIP
SECTION 4— THE FLOW OF MANUFACTURING BY INDUSTRY OF SUBSIDIARY
TABLE 16— SUBSIDIARIES MANUFACTURING
DRUGS (SIC 283)
CLASSIFIED BY COUNTRY, PERIOD MANUFACTURE BEGAN, AND SYSTEM OWNERSHIP %

PERIOD AND OWNERSHIP PERCENTAGE
(WHL=95-100%, MAJ=50-94%, MIN=5-49%, UNK=UNKNOWN)

COUNTRY OR REGION	TOTAL PRE 1968					PRE 1946					1946-1957					1958-1967				
	ALL	WHL	MAJ	MIN	UNK	ALL	WHL	MAJ	MIN	UNK	ALL	WHL	MAJ	MIN	UNK	ALL	WHL	MAJ	MIN	UNK
OUTSIDE U.S.	405	292	84	9	17	69	56	11	1	1	108	91	13	2	2	225	145	60	6	14
OUT. U.S. + CANADA	368	263	79	7	14	56	46	8	1	1	97	81	12	2	2	212	136	59	6	11
OUT. WEST. HEMIS.	241	170	57	7	7	34	29	3	0	1	59	52	4	2	1	148	89	48	5	6
OUT. WHITE CWEALTH	280	186	70	8	13	25	20	3	1	1	71	55	12	2	2	181	111	55	5	10
OUT. DEVLPED WORLD	174	116	42	4	9	22	17	3	1	1	48	39	8	0	1	101	60	31	3	7
CANADA	37	29	5	0	3	13	10	3	0	0	11	10	1	0	0	13	9	1	0	3
LATIN AMERICA	127	93	22	2	7	22	17	3	0	0	38	29	8	0	1	64	47	11	1	5
C. AMER.+CARIB.	53	43	4	0	3	7	7	0	0	0	15	14	1	0	0	28	22	3	0	3
CUBA	2	1	1	0	0	0	0	0	0	0	2	1	1	0	0	0	0	0	0	0
MEXICO	27	22	2	0	2	6	6	0	0	0	5	5	0	0	0	15	11	2	0	2
OTHER	24	20	2	0	2	6	6	0	0	0	8	8	0	0	0	13	11	1	1	0
S. AMERICA	74	50	18	2	4	15	10	3	1	1	23	15	7	0	1	36	25	8	1	2
ARGENTINA	15	10	4	0	1	7	5	1	0	1	4	2	2	0	0	4	3	1	0	0
BRAZIL	19	10	6	1	2	2	2	0	1	0	11	5	5	0	0	6	3	1	0	2
PERU	6	4	0	1	1	2	2	0	0	0	1	1	0	0	1	3	1	0	1	0
COLOMBIA	13	9	4	0	0	1	1	0	0	0	3	3	0	0	0	9	6	3	0	0
VENEZUELA	11	7	4	0	0	1	0	1	0	0	1	1	1	0	0	9	5	4	0	0
OTHER	10	10	0	0	0	2	2	0	0	0	3	3	0	0	0	5	5	0	0	0
EUROPE	138	105	24	5	4	19	18	1	0	0	33	29	2	2	0	86	58	21	3	4
EFTA	50	44	3	1	2	17	16	1	0	0	14	14	0	0	0	19	14	2	1	2
U.K.	37	34	4	1	1	16	15	1	0	0	11	11	0	0	0	10	8	2	1	1
SCANDINAVIA	5	3	1	0	1	0	0	0	0	0	2	2	0	0	0	3	2	0	0	1
SWITZERLAND	3	3	0	0	0	1	1	0	0	0	1	1	0	0	0	2	2	1	0	0
OTHER EFTA	5	3	1	0	1	0	0	0	0	0	0	0	0	0	0	4	2	1	0	1
EUROP. COMMUNITY	71	53	14	3	1	2	2	0	0	0	16	13	2	1	0	53	38	13	0	1
FRANCE	17	8	9	0	0	0	1	1	0	0	2	1	1	0	0	15	7	8	0	1
GERMANY	14	12	1	1	0	1	1	0	0	0	2	1	1	0	0	11	10	0	1	0
ITALY	25	21	3	1	0	0	1	0	0	0	8	7	0	1	0	17	14	3	0	0
BELGIUM + LUX	12	9	1	1	1	0	0	0	0	0	2	2	0	0	0	10	7	1	1	1
NETHERLANDS	3	3	0	0	0	1	1	0	0	0	2	2	0	0	0	0	0	0	0	0
SPAIN	7	2	5	0	0	0	0	0	0	0	0	0	0	0	0	7	2	5	0	0
GREECE + TURKEY	8	4	2	0	2	0	0	0	0	0	1	0	0	1	0	7	4	1	1	1
OTHER EUROPE	2	2	0	0	0	0	0	0	0	0	2	2	0	0	0	0	0	0	0	0
EUROPE EX. U.K.	101	71	23	4	3	3	3	0	0	0	22	18	2	2	0	76	50	21	2	3
SOUTHERN DOMINIONS	49	41	8	0	0	15	11	4	0	0	13	13	0	0	0	21	17	4	0	0
S. AFRICA +RHOD.	18	14	4	0	0	6	4	2	0	0	5	5	0	0	0	7	5	2	0	0
AUSTRALIA + N.Z.	31	27	4	0	0	9	7	2	0	0	8	8	0	0	0	14	12	2	0	0
ASIA + OTHER AFRICA	54	24	25	2	3	0	0	0	0	0	13	10	2	0	1	41	14	23	2	2
JAPAN	7	1	5	0	1	0	0	0	0	0	3	0	2	0	1	4	1	3	0	0
OTHER ASIA+AFR.	47	23	20	2	2	0	0	0	0	0	10	10	0	0	0	37	13	20	2	2
BLACK AFRICA	3	3	0	0	0	0	0	0	0	0	1	1	0	0	0	2	2	0	0	0
ARAB WORLD	2	1	1	0	0	0	0	0	0	0	0	0	0	0	0	2	1	1	0	0
INDIA	13	5	6	2	0	0	0	0	0	0	3	0	3	0	0	10	2	6	2	0
PHILIPPINES	8	7	1	0	0	0	0	0	0	0	4	4	0	0	0	4	3	1	0	0
OTHER E. ASIA	3	2	1	0	0	0	0	0	0	0	0	0	0	0	0	3	3	1	0	0
OTHER ASIA	18	5	11	0	2	0	0	0	0	0	2	2	0	0	0	16	3	11	0	2

CHAPTER 5- PATTERNS OF OWNERSHIP
SECTION 4- THE FLOW OF MANUFACTURING BY INDUSTRY OF SUBSIDIARY
TABLE 17- SUBSIDIARIES MANUFACTURING
SOAPS AND COSMETICS (SIC 284)
CLASSIFIED BY COUNTRY, PERIOD MANUFACTURE BEGAN, AND SYSTEM OWNERSHIP %

PERIOD AND OWNERSHIP PERCENTAGE
(WHL=95-100%, MAJ=50-94%, MIN=5-49%, UNK=UNKNOWN)

COUNTRY OR REGION	TOTAL PRE 1968					PRE 1946					1946-1957					1958-1967				
	ALL	WHL	MAJ	MIN	UNK	ALL	WHL	MAJ	MIN	UNK	ALL	WHL	MAJ	MIN	UNK	ALL	WHL	MAJ	MIN	UNK
OUTSIDE U.S.	248	205	23	6	12	64	56	4	2	2	53	45	4	1	3	129	104	15	3	7
OUT. U.S. + CANADA	217	176	23	6	10	49	42	4	2	1	51	43	4	1	3	115	91	15	3	6
OUT. WEST. HEMIS.	158	124	19	6	7	35	28	4	2	1	30	25	3	1	1	91	71	12	3	5
OUT. WHITE CWEALTH	159	128	19	4	7	29	25	3	0	1	37	32	2	1	2	92	71	14	1	4
OUT. DEVLPED WORLD	79	68	6	1	4	15	15	0	0	0	23	20	1	0	2	41	33	5	1	2
CANADA	31	29	0	0	2	15	14	0	0	1	2	2	0	0	0	14	13	0	0	1
LATIN AMERICA	59	52	4	0	3	14	14	0	0	0	21	18	1	0	2	24	20	3	0	1
C. AMER.+CARIB.	25	23	1	0	1	5	5	0	0	0	11	10	0	0	1	9	8	1	0	0
CUBA	3	3	0	0	0	1	1	0	0	0	1	1	0	0	0	0	0	0	0	0
MEXICO	12	11	0	1	0	3	3	0	0	0	4	4	0	0	0	5	4	0	1	0
OTHER	10	10	0	0	0	1	1	0	0	0	5	5	0	0	0	4	4	0	0	0
S. AMERICA	34	29	3	0	2	9	9	0	0	0	10	8	1	0	1	15	12	2	1	0
ARGENTINA	10	9	1	0	0	5	5	0	0	0	1	1	0	0	0	4	3	1	0	0
BRAZIL	7	6	1	0	0	3	3	0	0	0	1	1	0	0	0	2	2	0	0	0
PERU	6	5	1	0	0	1	1	0	0	0	2	2	0	0	0	3	3	0	0	0
COLUMBIA	3	3	0	0	0	0	0	0	0	0	0	0	0	0	0	3	3	0	0	0
VENEZUELA	7	5	1	0	1	0	0	0	0	0	4	3	0	0	1	3	2	0	0	1
OTHER	1	1	0	0	0	0	0	0	0	0	1	1	0	0	0	0	0	0	0	0
EUROPE	110	85	14	5	5	24	17	4	2	1	24	20	2	1	1	61	48	8	2	3
EFTA	45	37	4	2	2	10	7	1	2	0	13	11	1	0	1	22	19	2	0	1
U.K.	31	24	3	2	2	10	7	1	2	0	9	7	1	0	1	12	10	1	0	1
SCANDINAVIA	9	9	0	0	0	0	0	0	0	0	2	2	0	0	0	7	7	0	0	0
SWITZERLAND	2	2	0	0	0	0	0	0	0	0	2	2	0	0	0	0	0	0	0	0
OTHER EFTA	3	2	1	0	0	0	0	0	0	0	0	0	0	0	0	3	2	1	0	0
EUROP. COMMUNITY	53	41	8	1	2	14	10	3	1	1	9	8	0	0	1	29	23	4	1	0
FRANCE	18	12	4	0	2	4	2	1	1	0	5	4	1	0	0	9	6	2	0	1
GERMANY	14	11	2	1	0	6	4	2	0	0	1	1	0	0	0	6	6	0	0	0
ITALY	12	11	0	1	0	2	2	0	0	0	1	1	0	0	0	9	7	2	0	0
BELGIUM + LUX	7	6	1	0	0	1	1	0	0	0	2	2	0	0	0	4	3	1	0	0
NETHERLANDS	2	2	0	0	0	1	1	0	0	0	0	0	0	0	0	1	1	0	0	0
SPAIN	8	3	2	2	1	0	0	0	0	0	1	0	0	0	1	7	3	2	1	1
GREECE + TURKEY	1	1	0	0	0	0	0	0	0	0	0	0	0	0	0	1	1	0	0	0
OTHER EUROPE	3	3	0	0	0	0	0	0	0	0	1	1	0	0	0	2	2	0	0	0
EUROPE EX. U.K.	79	61	11	3	3	14	10	3	0	1	15	13	1	1	1	49	38	7	2	2
SOUTHERN DOMINIONS	24	21	1	0	1	10	10	0	0	0	4	3	1	0	0	9	8	0	0	1
S. AFRICA +RHOD.	10	9	1	0	0	5	5	0	0	0	1	1	0	0	0	4	4	0	0	0
AUSTRALIA + N.Z.	14	12	0	1	1	5	5	0	0	0	3	3	0	0	0	5	4	0	0	1
ASIA + OTHER AFRICA	24	18	4	1	1	1	1	0	0	0	2	2	0	0	0	21	15	4	1	1
JAPAN	4	2	2	0	0	1	1	0	0	0	2	2	0	0	0	4	2	2	0	0
OTHER ASIA+AFR.	20	16	2	1	0	0	0	0	0	0	2	2	0	0	0	17	13	2	1	1
BLACK AFRICA	3	3	0	0	0	0	0	0	0	0	0	0	0	0	0	3	3	0	0	0
ARAB WORLD	3	3	0	0	0	0	0	0	0	0	1	1	0	0	0	3	3	0	0	0
INDIA	0	0	0	0	0	0	0	0	0	0	0	0	0	0	0	0	0	0	0	0
PHILIPPINES	2	2	0	0	0	0	0	0	0	0	1	1	0	0	0	0	0	0	0	0
OTHER E. ASIA	2	2	0	0	1	0	0	0	0	0	0	0	0	0	0	2	2	0	0	0
OTHER ASIA	10	6	2	1	1	0	0	0	0	0	0	0	0	0	0	10	6	2	2	1

CHAPTER 5- PATTERNS OF OWNERSHIP
SECTION 4- THE FLOW OF MANUFACTURING BY INDUSTRY OF SUBSIDIARY
TABLE 18- SUBSIDIARIES MANUFACTURING
PAINTS (SIC 285)
CLASSIFIED BY COUNTRY, PERIOD MANUFACTURE BEGAN, AND SYSTEM OWNERSHIP %

PERIOD AND OWNERSHIP PERCENTAGE
(WHL=95-100%, MAJ=50-94%, MIN=5-49%, UNK=UNKNOWN)

COUNTRY OR REGION	TOTAL PRE 1968					PRE 1946					1946-1957					1958-1967				
	ALL	WHL	MAJ	MIN	UNK	ALL	WHL	MAJ	MIN	UNK	ALL	WHL	MAJ	MIN	UNK	ALL	WHL	MAJ	MIN	UNK
OUTSIDE U.S.	82	33	18	10	3	6	4	0	1	1	12	5	4	3	0	46	24	14	6	2
OUT. U.S. + CANADA	69	22	18	9	3	2	0	0	1	1	10	3	1	3	0	40	19	14	5	2
OUT. WEST. HEMIS.	45	13	10	5	3	2	0	0	1	1	2	1	1	0	0	27	12	9	4	2
OUT. WHITE CWEALTH	57	19	17	8	1	1	0	0	0	1	10	3	4	3	0	34	16	13	5	0
OUT. DEVLPED WORLD	32	9	10	4	0	0	0	0	0	0	9	2	4	3	0	14	7	6	1	0
CANADA	13	11	0	1	0	4	4	0	0	0	2	2	0	0	0	6	5	0	1	0
LATIN AMERICA	24	9	8	4	0	0	0	0	0	0	8	2	3	3	0	13	7	5	1	1
C. AMER.+CARIB.	11	5	2	3	0	0	0	0	0	0	3	1	0	2	0	7	4	2	1	0
CUBA	1	0	0	1	0	0	0	0	0	0	1	0	0	1	0	0	0	0	0	0
MEXICO	5	3	1	1	0	0	0	0	0	0	2	1	0	1	0	3	2	1	0	0
OTHER	5	1	1	1	1	0	0	0	0	0	0	0	0	0	0	4	2	1	1	0
S. AMERICA	13	4	6	0	0	0	0	0	0	0	5	1	3	1	0	6	3	3	0	0
ARGENTINA	0	0	0	0	0	0	0	0	0	0	0	0	0	0	0	0	0	0	0	0
BRAZIL	5	2	3	0	0	0	0	0	0	0	0	0	0	0	0	5	2	3	0	0
PERU	0	0	0	0	0	0	0	0	0	0	0	0	0	0	0	0	0	0	0	0
COLOMBIA	2	0	1	0	0	0	0	0	0	0	1	0	0	1	0	1	0	0	0	0
VENEZUELA	2	1	1	0	0	0	0	0	0	0	2	1	1	0	0	0	0	0	0	0
OTHER	4	0	2	2	0	0	0	0	0	0	2	0	2	0	0	0	0	0	0	0
EUROPE	27	11	8	3	3	2	1	0	1	1	1	0	0	1	0	22	10	8	2	2
EFTA	7	2	2	1	1	1	1	0	1	0	0	0	0	0	0	5	2	2	0	1
U.K.	4	1	1	1	1	1	1	0	1	0	0	0	0	0	0	3	1	1	0	1
SCANDINAVIA	2	1	0	1	0	0	0	0	0	0	0	0	0	0	0	1	1	0	0	0
SWITZERLAND	1	0	1	0	0	0	0	0	0	0	0	0	0	0	0	1	0	1	0	0
OTHER EFTA	0	0	0	0	0	0	0	0	0	0	0	0	0	0	0	0	0	0	0	0
EUROP. COMMUNITY	17	9	4	2	1	1	0	0	1	0	1	0	0	1	0	14	8	4	2	0
FRANCE	3	2	1	0	0	0	0	0	0	0	0	0	0	0	0	3	2	1	0	0
GERMANY	2	1	0	1	0	1	0	0	1	0	0	0	0	0	0	2	1	0	1	0
ITALY	2	0	2	0	1	0	0	0	0	0	0	0	0	0	0	2	1	0	0	1
BELGIUM + LUX	4	2	1	1	0	0	0	0	0	0	0	0	0	0	0	4	2	1	1	0
NETHERLANDS	4	3	0	0	1	0	0	0	0	0	0	0	0	0	0	3	3	0	0	0
SPAIN	2	0	2	0	0	0	0	0	0	0	0	0	0	0	0	2	0	0	2	0
GREECE + TURKEY	0	0	0	0	0	0	0	0	0	0	0	0	0	0	0	0	0	0	0	0
OTHER EUROPE	1	0	1	0	1	0	0	0	0	1	0	0	0	0	0	1	0	0	0	1
EUROPE EX. U.K.	23	10	7	2	2	1	0	0	0	1	1	1	0	0	0	19	9	7	2	1
SOUTHERN DOMINIONS	7	2	0	0	0	0	0	0	0	0	0	0	0	0	0	2	2	0	0	0
S. AFRICA +RHOD.	3	0	0	0	0	0	0	0	0	0	0	0	0	0	0	0	0	0	0	0
AUSTRALIA + N.Z.	4	2	2	2	0	0	0	0	0	0	0	0	0	0	0	2	2	0	2	0
ASIA + OTHER AFRICA	11	0	2	2	0	0	0	0	0	0	1	0	1	0	0	3	1	1	0	2
JAPAN	3	0	0	2	0	0	0	0	0	0	0	0	0	0	0	2	0	1	0	0
OTHER ASIA+AFR.	8	0	2	0	0	0	0	0	0	0	1	0	1	0	0	1	0	0	0	0
BLACK AFRICA	2	0	0	0	0	0	0	0	0	0	0	0	0	0	0	0	0	0	0	0
ARAB WORLD	0	0	0	0	0	0	0	0	0	0	0	0	0	0	0	0	0	0	0	0
INDIA	1	0	0	1	0	0	0	0	0	0	0	0	0	0	0	0	0	0	0	0
PHILIPPINES	1	0	0	0	0	0	0	0	0	0	1	0	1	0	0	0	0	0	0	0
OTHER E. ASIA	0	0	0	0	0	0	0	0	0	0	0	0	0	0	0	0	0	0	0	0
OTHER ASIA	4	0	1	1	0	0	0	0	0	0	1	0	0	1	0	1	0	1	0	0

CHAPTER 5- PATTERNS OF OWNERSHIP
SECTION 4- THE FLOW OF MANUFACTURING BY INDUSTRY OF SUBSIDIARY
TABLE 19- SUBSIDIARIES MANUFACTURING
AGRICULTURAL CHEMICALS (SIC 287)
CLASSIFIED BY COUNTRY, PERIOD MANUFACTURE BEGAN, AND SYSTEM OWNERSHIP %

PERIOD AND OWNERSHIP PERCENTAGE
(WHL=95-100%, MAJ=50-94%, MIN=5-49%, UNK=UNKNOWN)

COUNTRY OR REGION	TOTAL PRE 1968					PRE 1946					1946-1957					1958-1967				
	ALL	WHL	MAJ	MIN	UNK	ALL	WHL	MAJ	MIN	UNK	ALL	WHL	MAJ	MIN	UNK	ALL	WHL	MAJ	MIN	UNK
OUTSIDE U.S.	81	35	25	10	4	7	6	1	0	0	16	13	3	0	0	51	16	21	10	4
OUT. U.S. + CANADA	72	30	23	10	4	4	4	0	0	0	15	12	3	0	0	48	14	20	10	4
OUT. WEST. HEMIS.	45	21	14	6	2	1	1	0	0	0	9	9	0	0	0	33	11	11	6	2
OUT. WHITE CMEALTH	61	23	21	10	3	4	4	0	0	0	13	10	3	0	0	40	9	18	10	3
OUT. DEVLPED WORLD	41	17	12	6	3	3	3	0	0	0	11	8	3	0	0	24	6	9	6	3
CANADA	9	5	2	0	2	3	2	1	0	0	1	1	0	0	0	3	2	1	0	0
LATIN AMERICA	27	9	9	4	2	3	3	1	0	0	6	4	2	0	0	15	3	6	4	2
C. AMER.+CARIB.	13	4	3	4	0	2	2	0	0	0	2	2	0	0	0	7	0	3	3	0
CUBA	1	0	0	0	0	1	1	0	0	0	0	0	0	0	0	0	0	0	0	0
MEXICO	6	3	0	3	0	0	0	0	0	0	2	2	0	0	0	6	0	3	3	0
OTHER	6	0	3	0	2	1	1	0	0	0	0	0	0	0	0	1	0	3	0	0
S. AMERICA	14	5	6	0	2	1	1	0	0	0	4	2	2	0	0	8	3	3	0	2
ARGENTINA	4	1	2	0	1	1	1	0	0	0	1	0	1	0	0	3	2	1	0	1
BRAZIL	3	0	3	0	0	0	0	0	0	0	0	0	0	0	0	3	0	3	0	0
PERU	1	0	0	0	0	0	0	0	0	0	0	0	0	0	0	1	0	0	0	1
COLOMBIA	4	3	0	0	1	0	0	0	0	0	1	1	0	0	0	3	2	0	1	0
VENEZUELA	2	1	1	0	0	0	0	0	0	0	0	0	0	0	0	1	1	0	0	0
OTHER	0	0	0	0	0	0	0	0	0	0	0	0	0	0	0	0	0	0	0	0
EUROPE	22	6	10	3	0	1	1	0	0	0	3	3	0	0	0	17	4	10	3	0
EFTA	4	2	2	0	0	0	0	0	0	0	1	1	0	0	0	3	1	2	0	0
U.K.	3	2	1	0	0	0	0	0	0	0	0	0	0	0	0	2	1	1	0	0
SCANDINAVIA	1	0	1	0	0	0	0	0	0	0	0	0	0	0	0	1	0	1	0	0
SWITZERLAND	0	0	0	0	0	0	0	0	0	0	0	0	0	0	0	0	0	0	0	0
OTHER EFTA	0	0	0	0	0	0	0	0	0	0	0	0	0	0	0	0	0	0	0	0
EUROP. COMMUNITY	11	5	4	1	0	0	0	0	0	0	2	2	0	0	0	8	3	4	1	0
FRANCE	6	3	2	1	0	0	0	0	0	0	1	1	0	0	0	4	2	2	1	0
GERMANY	1	1	0	0	0	0	0	0	0	0	1	1	0	0	0	2	2	0	0	0
ITALY	2	1	1	0	0	0	0	0	0	0	0	0	0	0	0	1	0	1	0	0
BELGIUM + LUX	1	0	0	1	0	0	0	0	0	0	0	0	0	0	0	1	1	0	1	0
NETHERLANDS	1	1	0	0	0	0	0	0	0	0	0	0	0	0	0	1	0	1	0	0
SPAIN	7	0	4	2	0	0	0	0	0	0	0	0	0	0	0	6	0	4	2	0
GREECE + TURKEY	1	0	0	0	0	0	0	0	0	0	0	0	0	0	0	0	0	0	0	0
OTHER EUROPE	0	0	0	0	0	0	0	0	0	0	0	0	0	0	0	0	0	0	0	0
EUROPE EX. U.K.	19	6	9	3	0	1	1	0	0	0	2	2	0	0	0	15	3	9	3	0
SOUTHERN DOMINIONS	8	5	1	1	1	0	0	0	0	0	1	1	0	0	0	6	4	1	0	1
S. AFRICA +RHOD.	3	3	0	0	0	0	0	0	0	0	1	1	0	0	0	2	2	0	0	0
AUSTRALIA + N.Z.	5	2	1	1	1	0	0	0	0	0	0	0	0	0	0	4	2	1	0	1
ASIA + OTHER AFRICA	15	8	3	3	1	1	1	0	0	0	5	5	0	0	0	10	3	3	3	1
JAPAN	1	0	0	1	0	0	0	0	0	0	0	0	0	0	0	1	0	0	1	0
OTHER ASIA+AFR.	14	8	3	2	1	1	1	0	0	0	5	5	0	0	0	9	3	3	2	1
BLACK AFRICA	4	4	0	0	0	0	0	0	0	0	2	2	0	0	0	2	2	0	0	0
ARAB WORLD	1	0	1	0	0	0	0	0	0	0	0	0	0	0	0	1	0	1	0	0
INDIA	3	2	0	1	0	0	0	0	0	0	2	2	0	0	0	1	0	0	1	0
PHILIPPINES	1	1	0	0	0	0	0	0	0	0	1	1	0	0	0	0	0	0	0	0
OTHER E. ASIA	4	1	2	1	0	1	1	0	0	0	0	0	0	0	0	4	1	2	1	0
OTHER ASIA	1	1	0	0	0	0	0	0	0	0	0	0	0	0	0	1	1	0	0	1

CHAPTER 5- PATTERNS OF OWNERSHIP
SECTION 4- THE FLOW OF MANUFACTURING BY INDUSTRY OF SUBSIDIARY
TABLE 20- SUBSIDIARIES MANUFACTURING
MISCELLANEOUS CHEMICAL PRODUCTS (SIC 289)
CLASSIFIED BY COUNTRY, PERIOD MANUFACTURE BEGAN, AND SYSTEM OWNERSHIP %

PERIOD AND OWNERSHIP PERCENTAGE
(WHL=95-100%, MAJ=50-94%, MIN=5-49%, UNK=UNKNOWN)

COUNTRY OR REGION	TOTAL PRE 1968					PRE 1946					1946-1957					1958-1967				
	ALL	WHL	MAJ	MIN	UNK	ALL	WHL	MAJ	MIN	UNK	ALL	WHL	MAJ	MIN	UNK	ALL	WHL	MAJ	MIN	UNK
OUTSIDE U.S.	132	74	33	17	7	35	25	1	5	4	27	18	6	1	2	69	31	26	11	1
OUT. U.S. + CANADA	108	59	32	14	5	22	18	0	3	1	20	13	6	1	0	65	28	26	10	1
OUT. WEST. HEMIS.	73	40	23	8	2	11	10	0	0	1	12	9	2	1	0	50	21	21	7	1
OUT. WHITE CWEALTH	81	42	23	13	2	17	13	0	3	1	12	7	4	1	0	51	22	19	9	1
OUT. DEVLPED WORLD	43	23	12	7	0	12	9	0	3	0	8	4	4	0	0	22	10	8	4	0
CANADA	24	15	1	3	5	13	7	1	2	3	7	5	0	0	2	4	3	0	1	0
LATIN AMERICA	35	19	9	6	0	11	8	0	3	0	8	4	4	0	0	15	7	5	3	0
C. AMER.+CARIB.	11	6	4	0	0	2	2	0	0	0	2	2	0	0	0	6	2	4	0	0
CUBA	0	0	0	0	0	0	0	0	0	0	0	0	0	0	0	0	0	0	0	0
MEXICO	7	5	1	0	0	2	2	0	0	0	2	2	0	0	0	2	1	1	0	0
OTHER	4	1	3	0	0	0	0	0	0	0	0	0	0	0	0	4	1	3	0	0
S. AMERICA	24	13	5	6	0	9	6	0	3	0	6	2	4	0	0	9	5	1	3	0
ARGENTINA	8	4	2	2	0	3	3	0	0	0	2	0	1	1	0	3	1	1	1	0
BRAZIL	7	4	2	1	0	3	1	0	1	1	2	2	0	0	0	2	1	0	1	0
PERU	0	0	0	0	0	0	0	0	0	0	0	0	0	0	0	0	0	0	0	0
COLOMBIA	4	3	1	0	0	1	1	0	0	0	2	2	0	0	0	3	2	1	0	0
VENEZUELA	1	1	0	0	0	0	0	0	0	0	0	0	0	0	0	1	1	0	0	0
OTHER	4	1	0	3	0	4	1	0	3	0	0	0	0	0	0	0	0	0	0	0
EUROPE	48	28	15	3	2	7	6	0	0	1	7	6	1	0	0	34	16	14	3	1
EFTA	16	10	6	0	0	2	2	0	0	0	3	2	1	0	0	11	6	5	0	0
U.K.	14	8	6	0	0	2	2	0	0	0	3	2	1	0	0	9	4	5	0	0
SCANDINAVIA	0	0	0	0	0	0	0	0	0	0	0	0	0	0	0	0	0	0	0	0
SWITZERLAND	1	1	0	0	0	0	0	0	0	0	0	0	0	0	0	1	1	0	0	0
OTHER EFTA	1	1	0	0	0	0	0	0	0	0	0	0	0	0	0	1	1	0	0	1
EUROP. COMMUNITY	25	15	6	3	1	4	3	0	0	1	3	3	0	0	0	18	9	6	3	0
FRANCE	7	5	2	0	0	1	1	0	0	0	0	0	0	0	0	6	3	2	1	0
GERMANY	6	4	2	0	0	1	1	0	0	0	2	2	0	0	0	3	1	2	0	0
ITALY	9	6	0	1	0	2	1	1	0	0	1	0	1	0	0	6	4	1	1	0
BELGIUM + LUX	0	0	0	0	0	0	0	0	0	0	0	0	0	0	0	0	0	0	0	0
NETHERLANDS	3	1	1	2	0	1	0	0	1	0	0	0	0	0	0	3	1	1	1	0
SPAIN	6	2	3	0	1	0	0	0	0	0	0	0	0	0	0	5	0	3	2	1
GREECE + TURKEY	0	0	0	0	0	0	0	0	0	0	0	0	0	0	0	0	0	0	0	0
OTHER EUROPE	0	0	0	0	0	0	0	0	0	0	0	0	0	0	0	0	0	0	0	0
EUROPE EX. U.K.	34	20	9	3	2	5	4	0	0	1	4	4	0	0	0	25	12	9	3	1
SOUTHERN DOMINIONS	12	8	3	1	0	3	3	0	0	0	4	3	1	0	0	5	2	2	1	0
S. AFRICA +RHOD.	5	4	1	0	0	2	2	0	0	0	2	1	1	0	0	1	1	0	0	0
AUSTRALIA + N.Z.	7	4	2	1	0	1	1	0	0	0	2	2	0	0	0	4	1	2	1	0
ASIA + OTHER AFRICA	13	4	5	4	0	1	1	0	0	0	1	1	0	1	0	11	3	5	3	0
JAPAN	5	0	2	3	0	0	0	0	0	0	1	0	0	1	0	4	0	2	2	0
OTHER ASIA+AFR.	8	4	3	1	0	1	1	0	0	0	0	0	0	0	0	7	3	3	1	0
BLACK AFRICA	0	0	0	0	0	0	0	0	0	0	0	0	0	0	0	0	0	0	0	0
ARAB WORLD	0	0	0	0	0	0	0	0	0	0	0	0	0	0	0	0	0	0	0	0
INDIA	3	1	1	1	0	1	1	0	0	0	0	0	0	0	0	2	0	1	1	0
PHILIPPINES	2	1	1	0	0	0	0	0	0	0	0	0	0	0	0	2	1	1	0	0
OTHER E. ASIA	3	2	1	0	0	0	0	0	0	0	0	0	0	0	0	3	2	1	0	0
OTHER ASIA	0	0	0	0	0	0	0	0	0	0	0	0	0	0	0	0	0	0	0	0

466

CHAPTER 5- PATTERNS OF OWNERSHIP
SECTION 4-- THE FLOW OF MANUFACTURING BY INDUSTRY OF SUBSIDIARY
TABLE 21- SUBSIDIARIES MANUFACTURING
REFINED PETROLEUM (SIC 291)
CLASSIFIED BY COUNTRY, PERIOD MANUFACTURE BEGAN, AND SYSTEM OWNERSHIP %

PERIOD AND OWNERSHIP PERCENTAGE
(WHL=95-100%, MAJ=50-94%, MIN=5-49%, UNK=UNKNOWN)

COUNTRY OR REGION	TOTAL PRE 1968					PRE 1946					1946-1957					1958-1967				
	ALL	WHL	MAJ	MIN	UNK	ALL	WHL	MAJ	MIN	UNK	ALL	WHL	MAJ	MIN	UNK	ALL	WHL	MAJ	MIN	UNK
OUTSIDE U.S.	173	86	44	24	14	57	36	11	5	5	39	21	13	1	4	72	29	20	18	5
OUT. U.S. + CANADA	158	78	41	23	12	48	30	10	3	5	36	19	12	1	4	70	29	19	17	5
OUT. WEST. HEMIS.	126	58	35	18	11	32	18	8	3	3	30	14	12	1	3	60	26	15	14	5
OUT. WHITE CWEALTH	130	64	33	21	10	46	28	10	2	3	29	16	10	0	3	53	20	13	16	4
OUT. DEVLPED WORLD	56	29	9	13	3	21	15	4	2	0	9	6	0	0	3	24	8	5	11	0
CANADA	15	8	3	1	2	9	6	1	0	2	3	2	1	0	0	2	0	1	1	0
LATIN AMERICA	32	20	6	5	1	16	12	2	2	0	6	5	1	0	0	10	3	4	3	0
C. AMER.+CARIB.	20	12	4	4	0	12	8	2	2	0	2	2	0	0	0	6	2	2	2	0
CUBA	4	3	1	0	0	3	2	1	0	0	1	1	0	0	0	0	0	0	0	0
MEXICO	3	2	1	0	0	3	2	1	0	0	0	0	0	0	0	0	0	0	0	0
OTHER	13	7	2	4	0	6	4	1	1	0	1	1	0	0	0	6	2	2	2	0
S. AMERICA	12	8	2	1	1	4	4	0	0	0	4	3	0	0	1	4	1	2	1	0
ARGENTINA	4	4	0	0	0	3	3	0	0	0	0	0	0	0	0	1	1	0	0	0
BRAZIL	0	0	0	0	0	0	0	0	0	0	0	0	0	0	0	0	0	0	0	0
PERU	1	0	0	1	0	0	0	0	0	0	0	0	0	0	0	1	0	0	1	0
COLOMBIA	3	2	1	0	0	1	1	0	0	0	1	1	0	0	0	1	1	0	0	0
VENEZUELA	3	1	0	1	1	0	0	0	0	0	2	1	0	1	0	1	0	1	0	0
OTHER	1	1	0	0	0	0	0	0	0	0	1	1	0	0	0	0	0	0	0	0
EUROPE	80	41	21	9	9	26	14	6	3	3	20	12	6	1	1	34	15	9	5	5
EFTA	21	16	2	1	2	8	5	3	0	0	5	3	0	1	1	8	3	3	0	2
U.K.	11	6	2	1	2	3	1	1	0	1	4	1	0	1	1	6	3	2	1	1
SCANDINAVIA	6	3	2	1	0	3	2	0	0	0	0	0	0	0	0	2	0	1	0	0
SWITZERLAND	0	0	0	0	0	0	0	0	0	0	0	0	0	0	0	0	0	0	0	0
OTHER EFTA	4	2	0	2	0	2	2	0	0	0	0	0	0	0	0	2	0	0	2	0
EUROP. COMMUNITY	45	24	15	3	3	9	5	3	0	1	13	7	6	0	0	23	12	6	3	2
FRANCE	5	3	0	1	1	3	2	0	0	1	1	1	0	0	0	1	1	0	1	0
GERMANY	18	9	5	2	2	2	1	1	0	0	5	4	1	0	0	11	4	3	1	0
ITALY	16	8	8	0	0	4	2	2	0	0	5	2	3	0	0	7	4	3	0	0
BELGIUM + LUX	2	1	1	0	0	0	0	0	0	0	1	1	0	0	0	1	1	0	0	0
NETHERLANDS	4	3	1	0	0	0	0	0	0	0	1	0	1	0	0	3	0	0	3	0
SPAIN	6	2	0	2	2	3	0	0	2	1	2	2	0	0	0	1	1	0	0	1
GREECE + TURKEY	2	0	0	2	0	0	0	0	0	0	0	0	0	0	0	2	0	0	1	0
OTHER EUROPE	6	4	0	2	0	6	4	0	2	0	0	0	0	0	0	0	0	0	0	4
EUROPE EX. U.K.	69	35	19	8	7	25	13	6	3	3	16	10	6	0	0	28	12	7	5	4
SOUTHERN DOMINIONS	17	8	6	1	2	1	1	0	0	0	3	1	2	0	0	11	6	4	1	0
S. AFRICA +RHOD.	3	1	0	1	1	0	0	0	0	0	0	1	0	0	0	2	1	0	1	0
AUSTRALIA + N.Z.	14	7	6	0	0	1	1	0	0	0	3	1	2	0	0	9	5	4	0	0
ASIA + OTHER AFRICA	29	9	8	8	2	5	3	2	0	0	7	1	4	0	2	15	5	2	8	0
JAPAN	5	0	5	0	0	5	3	3	0	0	1	0	1	0	0	1	1	0	0	0
OTHER ASIA+AFR.	24	9	3	8	2	5	3	0	0	0	3	1	4	0	2	14	5	1	8	0
BLACK AFRICA	3	2	0	1	0	0	0	0	0	0	0	0	0	0	0	3	1	0	2	0
ARAB WORLD	6	2	0	2	2	1	0	0	0	0	1	0	0	0	1	3	0	0	3	0
INDIA	1	0	0	1	0	0	0	0	0	0	0	0	0	0	0	1	0	0	1	0
PHILIPPINES	3	1	0	2	0	0	0	0	0	0	1	0	0	0	1	1	0	0	1	0
OTHER E. ASIA	1	1	0	0	0	0	0	0	0	0	0	0	0	0	0	1	2	0	0	0
OTHER ASIA	10	5	2	1	1	4	3	0	0	1	1	1	0	0	0	4	2	1	1	0

CHAPTER 5- PATTERNS OF OWNERSHIP
SECTION 4- THE FLOW OF MANUFACTURING BY INDUSTRY OF SUBSIDIARY

TABLE 22- SUBSIDIARIES MANUFACTURING
OTHER PRODUCTS OF PETROLEUM AND COAL (SIC 295 AND 299)
CLASSIFIED BY COUNTRY, PERIOD MANUFACTURE BEGAN, AND SYSTEM OWNERSHIP %

PERIOD AND OWNERSHIP PERCENTAGE
(WHL=95-100%, MAJ=50-94%, MIN=5-49%, UNK=UNKNOWN)

COUNTRY OR REGION	TOTAL PRE 1968 ALL	WHL	MAJ	MIN	UNK	PRE 1946 ALL	WHL	MAJ	MIN	UNK	1946-1957 ALL	WHL	MAJ	MIN	UNK	1958-1967 ALL	WHL	MAJ	MIN	UNK
OUTSIDE U.S.	83	35	26	15	6	18	11	2	2	3	11	9	2	0	0	53	15	22	13	3
OUT. U.S. + CANADA	75	29	25	15	5	13	8	1	2	2	10	8	2	0	0	51	13	22	13	3
OUT. WEST. HEMIS.	59	20	23	12	3	11	6	1	2	2	6	5	1	0	0	41	9	21	10	1
OUT. WHITE CWEALTH	60	23	19	15	2	10	7	1	2	0	6	4	2	0	0	43	12	16	13	2
OUT. DEVLPED WORLD	22	10	5	5	2	2	2	0	0	0	4	3	1	0	0	16	5	4	5	2
CANADA	8	6	1	0	1	5	3	1	0	1	1	1	0	0	0	2	2	0	0	0
LATIN AMERICA	16	9	2	3	2	2	2	0	0	0	4	3	1	0	0	10	4	1	3	2
C. AMER.+CARIB.	5	4	0	1	0	1	1	0	0	0	1	1	0	0	0	3	2	0	1	0
CUBA	1	1	0	0	0	0	0	0	0	0	1	1	0	0	0	0	0	0	0	0
MEXICO	4	3	0	1	0	1	1	0	0	0	0	0	0	0	0	3	2	0	1	0
OTHER	0	0	0	0	0	0	0	0	0	0	0	0	0	0	0	0	0	0	0	0
S. AMERICA	11	5	2	2	2	1	1	0	0	0	3	2	1	0	0	7	2	1	2	2
ARGENTINA	5	1	0	2	2	0	0	0	0	0	0	0	0	0	0	4	1	0	2	1
BRAZIL	1	1	0	0	0	0	0	0	0	0	1	1	0	0	0	1	1	0	0	0
PERU	1	1	0	0	0	0	0	0	0	0	0	0	0	0	0	1	1	0	0	0
COLOMBIA	1	1	0	0	0	0	0	0	0	0	0	0	0	0	0	1	1	0	0	0
VENEZUELA	2	0	2	0	0	0	0	0	0	0	0	0	0	0	0	1	0	1	0	1
OTHER	1	1	0	0	0	0	0	0	0	0	1	0	0	0	0	0	1	0	0	0
EUROPE	39	16	14	6	3	11	6	1	2	2	4	3	1	0	0	24	7	12	4	1
EFTA	15	8	4	0	3	4	2	0	0	2	2	2	0	0	0	9	4	4	0	1
U.K.	8	2	3	0	3	3	1	0	0	2	1	1	0	0	0	4	4	3	0	0
SCANDINAVIA	7	6	1	0	0	0	0	0	0	0	1	1	0	0	0	5	4	2	0	0
SWITZERLAND	0	0	0	0	0	0	0	0	0	0	0	0	0	0	0	0	0	0	0	0
OTHER EFTA	0	0	0	0	0	0	0	0	0	0	0	0	0	0	0	0	0	0	0	0
EUROP. COMMUNITY	19	7	8	4	0	6	4	2	0	0	1	0	1	0	0	12	3	7	2	0
FRANCE	6	2	3	1	0	2	1	1	0	0	0	0	1	0	0	3	1	2	0	0
GERMANY	6	3	2	1	0	3	3	0	0	0	0	0	0	0	0	3	2	1	0	0
ITALY	2	1	1	0	0	0	0	0	0	0	0	0	0	0	0	2	1	1	0	0
BELGIUM + LUX	4	1	1	2	0	1	0	1	0	0	0	0	0	0	0	3	1	1	1	0
NETHERLANDS	1	0	1	0	0	0	0	0	0	0	0	0	0	0	0	1	0	0	1	0
SPAIN	3	1	1	0	1	1	0	0	1	0	0	0	0	0	0	3	1	1	0	0
GREECE + TURKEY	1	0	1	0	0	0	0	0	0	0	0	0	0	0	0	0	0	0	2	0
OTHER EUROPE	1	0	0	1	0	0	0	1	1	0	1	0	0	0	0	0	0	1	0	0
EUROPE EX. U.K.	31	14	11	6	0	8	5	0	2	0	3	0	1	0	0	20	7	9	4	0
SOUTHERN DOMINIONS	6	3	3	0	0	0	0	0	0	0	2	2	0	0	0	4	1	3	0	0
S. AFRICA +RHOD.	1	0	1	0	0	0	0	0	0	0	0	0	0	0	0	1	0	1	0	0
AUSTRALIA + N.Z.	5	3	2	0	0	0	0	0	0	0	2	2	0	0	0	3	1	2	0	0
ASIA + OTHER AFRICA	14	1	6	6	0	0	0	0	0	0	0	0	0	0	0	13	1	3	6	0
JAPAN	8	1	3	4	0	0	0	0	0	0	0	0	0	0	0	7	1	3	4	0
OTHER ASIA+AFR.	6	1	3	2	0	0	0	0	0	0	0	0	0	0	0	6	1	3	2	0
BLACK AFRICA	1	0	1	0	0	0	0	0	0	0	0	0	0	0	0	1	0	2	0	0
ARAB WORLD	0	0	0	0	0	0	0	0	0	0	0	0	0	0	0	0	0	0	0	0
INDIA	3	0	2	0	1	0	0	0	0	0	0	0	0	0	0	3	1	0	1	0
PHILIPPINES	1	0	0	1	0	0	0	0	0	0	0	0	0	0	0	1	0	0	1	0
OTHER E. ASIA	1	0	0	1	0	0	0	0	0	0	0	0	0	0	0	1	1	1	0	0
OTHER ASIA	0	0	0	0	0	0	0	0	0	0	0	0	0	0	0	0	0	0	0	0

CHAPTER 5- PATTERNS OF OWNERSHIP
SECTION 4- THE FLOW OF MANUFACTURING BY INDUSTRY OF SUBSIDIARY
TABLE 23- SUBSIDIARIES MANUFACTURING
TIRES (SIC 301)
CLASSIFIED BY COUNTRY, PERIOD MANUFACTURE BEGAN, AND SYSTEM OWNERSHIP %

PERIOD AND OWNERSHIP PERCENTAGE
(WHL=95-100%, MAJ=50-94%, MIN=5-49%, UNK=UNKNOWN)

COUNTRY OR REGION	TOTAL PRE 1968					PRE 1946					1946-1957					1958-1967				
	ALL	WHL	MAJ	MIN	UNK	ALL	WHL	MAJ	MIN	UNK	ALL	WHL	MAJ	MIN	UNK	ALL	WHL	MAJ	MIN	UNK
OUTSIDE U.S.	98	47	16	19	16	42	24	1	10	7	22	11	4	6	1	34	12	11	3	8
OUT. U.S. + CANADA	91	42	16	19	14	36	20	1	10	5	22	11	4	6	1	33	11	11	3	8
OUT. WEST. HEMIS.	58	26	13	9	10	19	11	1	3	4	12	5	2	4	1	27	10	10	2	5
OUT. WHITE CWEALTH	78	34	14	16	14	29	14	1	9	5	20	11	3	5	1	29	9	10	2	8
OUT. DEVLPED WORLD	48	22	9	10	7	21	12	0	7	2	12	7	3	2	0	15	3	6	1	5
CANADA	7	5	0	0	2	6	4	0	0	2	0	0	0	0	0	1	1	0	0	0
LATIN AMERICA	33	16	3	10	4	17	9	0	7	1	10	6	2	2	0	6	1	1	1	3
C. AMER.+CARIB.	13	3	1	5	4	6	1	0	1	4	3	2	0	1	0	4	0	1	3	0
CUBA	6	2	0	0	4	5	1	0	0	4	1	1	0	0	0	0	0	0	0	0
MEXICO	4	1	0	3	0	0	0	0	0	0	2	1	0	1	0	2	0	0	2	0
OTHER	3	0	1	2	0	1	0	0	1	0	0	0	0	0	0	2	0	1	1	0
S. AMERICA	20	13	2	5	0	11	8	0	3	0	7	4	2	1	0	2	1	0	1	0
ARGENTINA	4	3	1	0	0	2	2	0	0	0	2	1	1	0	0	0	0	0	0	0
BRAZIL	5	5	0	0	0	2	2	0	0	0	3	3	0	0	0	0	0	0	0	0
PERU	2	1	0	1	0	2	1	0	1	0	0	0	0	0	0	0	0	0	0	0
COLOMBIA	3	1	1	1	0	2	1	0	1	0	1	0	1	0	0	0	0	0	0	0
VENEZUELA	4	2	0	2	0	2	1	0	1	0	1	0	0	1	0	1	1	0	0	0
OTHER	2	1	0	1	0	1	1	0	0	0	0	0	0	0	0	1	0	0	1	0
EUROPE	31	15	6	4	6	9	5	1	1	2	9	6	2	1	0	13	4	3	2	4
EFTA	10	3	2	1	4	5	2	1	0	2	1	1	0	0	0	4	0	1	1	2
U.K.	4	2	1	1	0	2	1	1	0	0	1	1	0	0	0	1	0	0	1	0
SCANDINAVIA	2	0	0	0	2	0	0	0	0	0	0	0	0	0	0	2	0	0	0	2
SWITZERLAND	1	0	0	0	1	1	0	0	0	1	0	0	0	0	0	0	0	0	0	0
OTHER EFTA	3	1	1	0	1	2	1	0	0	1	0	0	0	0	0	1	0	1	0	0
EUROP. COMMUNITY	16	10	3	2	1	1	1	0	0	0	8	5	2	1	0	7	4	1	1	1
FRANCE	4	3	0	0	1	1	1	0	0	0	1	1	0	0	0	2	1	0	0	1
GERMANY	6	3	2	1	0	0	0	0	0	0	4	2	2	0	0	2	1	0	1	0
ITALY	2	1	1	0	0	0	0	0	0	0	0	0	0	0	0	2	1	1	0	0
BELGIUM + LUX	2	2	0	0	0	0	0	0	0	0	1	1	0	0	0	1	1	0	0	0
NETHERLANDS	2	1	0	1	0	0	0	0	0	0	2	1	0	1	0	0	0	0	0	0
SPAIN	2	1	0	0	1	1	1	0	0	0	0	0	0	0	0	1	0	0	0	1
GREECE + TURKEY	2	0	1	1	0	1	0	0	1	0	0	0	0	0	0	1	0	1	0	0
OTHER EUROPE	1	1	0	0	0	1	1	0	0	0	0	0	0	0	0	0	0	0	0	0
EUROPE EX. U.K.	27	13	5	3	6	7	4	0	1	2	8	5	2	1	0	12	4	3	1	4
SOUTHERN DOMINIONS	9	5	1	3	0	5	3	1	1	0	1	1	0	0	0	3	1	0	2	0
S. AFRICA +RHOD.	3	2	1	0	0	2	1	1	0	0	1	1	0	0	0	0	0	0	0	0
AUSTRALIA + N.Z.	6	3	0	3	0	3	2	0	1	0	0	0	0	0	0	3	1	0	2	0
ASIA + OTHER AFRICA	18	6	6	2	4	5	3	1	0	1	2	1	1	0	0	11	2	4	2	3
JAPAN	3	0	3	0	0	0	0	0	0	0	1	0	1	0	0	2	0	2	0	0
OTHER ASIA+AFR.	15	6	3	2	4	5	3	1	0	1	1	1	0	0	0	9	2	2	2	3
BLACK AFRICA	2	1	0	1	0	0	0	0	0	0	0	0	0	0	0	2	1	0	1	0
ARAB WORLD	2	0	1	0	1	0	0	0	0	0	0	0	0	0	0	2	0	1	0	1
INDIA	2	2	0	0	0	1	1	0	0	0	0	0	0	0	0	1	1	0	0	0
PHILIPPINES	3	2	1	0	0	2	1	1	0	0	1	1	0	0	0	0	0	0	0	0
OTHER E. ASIA	0	0	0	0	0	0	0	0	0	0	0	0	0	0	0	0	0	0	0	0
OTHER ASIA	6	1	1	1	3	2	1	0	0	1	0	0	0	0	0	4	0	1	1	2

CHAPTER 5— PATTERNS OF OWNERSHIP
SECTION 4— THE FLOW OF MANUFACTURING BY INDUSTRY OF SUBSIDIARY
TABLE 24— SUBSIDIARIES MANUFACTURING
OTHER RUBBER PRODUCTS (OTHER SIC 30)
CLASSIFIED BY COUNTRY, PERIOD MANUFACTURE BEGAN, AND SYSTEM OWNERSHIP %

PERIOD AND OWNERSHIP PERCENTAGE
(WHL=95-100%, MAJ=50-94%, MIN=5-49%, UNK=UNKNOWN)

COUNTRY OR REGION	TOTAL PRE 1968 ALL	WHL	MAJ	MIN	UNK	PRE 1946 ALL	WHL	MAJ	MIN	UNK	1946-1957 ALL	WHL	MAJ	MIN	UNK	1958-1967 ALL	WHL	MAJ	MIN	UNK
OUTSIDE U.S.	88	44	16	19	7	29	19	0	8	2	17	9	2	4	2	40	16	14	7	3
OUT. U.S. + CANADA	75	35	16	19	4	25	17	0	8	0	13	5	2	4	2	36	13	14	7	2
OUT. WEST. HEMIS.	47	21	13	11	2	14	9	0	5	0	5	1	1	2	1	28	11	12	4	1
OUT. WHITE CWEALTH	53	21	11	16	4	16	11	0	5	0	12	5	1	4	2	24	5	10	7	2
OUT. DEVLPED WORLD	34	16	7	8	2	12	9	0	3	0	8	4	1	2	1	13	3	6	3	1
CANADA	13	9	0	0	3	4	2	0	0	2	4	4	0	0	0	4	3	0	0	1
LATIN AMERICA	28	14	3	8	2	11	8	0	3	0	8	4	1	2	1	8	2	2	3	0
C. AMER.+CARIB.	13	6	3	4	0	5	3	0	2	0	5	3	1	0	1	3	0	2	1	0
CUBA	2	2	0	0	0	1	1	0	0	0	1	1	0	0	0	0	0	0	0	0
MEXICO	9	4	2	3	0	4	2	0	2	0	3	1	1	0	1	2	0	1	1	0
OTHER	2	0	0	1	0	0	0	0	0	0	1	1	0	0	0	1	0	1	0	0
S. AMERICA	15	8	0	4	2	6	5	0	1	0	3	1	0	1	0	5	2	0	2	1
ARGENTINA	3	1	0	1	0	1	1	0	0	0	1	0	0	1	0	2	2	0	0	0
BRAZIL	4	1	0	2	0	1	1	0	0	0	1	0	0	1	0	2	0	0	1	1
PERU	2	1	0	1	0	1	1	0	0	0	0	0	0	0	0	1	0	0	1	0
COLOMBIA	1	1	0	0	0	1	1	0	0	0	0	0	0	0	0	0	0	0	0	0
VENEZUELA	5	1	0	2	2	2	1	0	1	0	1	0	0	1	0	2	0	0	1	1
OTHER	0	0	0	0	0	0	0	0	0	0	0	0	0	0	0	0	0	0	0	0
EUROPE	28	12	8	8	0	8	6	0	2	0	4	1	1	2	0	16	5	5	4	0
EFTA	11	6	2	2	1	5	4	0	1	0	1	1	0	0	0	5	3	2	1	0
U.K.	8	5	1	1	1	4	3	0	1	0	1	1	0	0	0	3	2	1	0	1
SCANDINAVIA	3	1	0	1	0	1	1	0	0	0	0	0	0	0	0	2	0	1	1	0
SWITZERLAND	0	0	0	0	0	0	0	0	0	0	0	0	0	0	0	0	0	0	0	0
OTHER EFTA	0	0	0	0	0	0	0	0	0	0	0	0	0	0	0	0	0	0	0	0
EUROP. COMMUNITY	9	4	0	4	0	2	1	0	1	0	2	0	1	1	0	5	2	0	2	0
FRANCE	2	1	0	1	0	1	0	0	1	0	1	0	1	0	0	1	0	1	1	0
GERMANY	3	1	0	2	0	1	1	0	0	0	0	0	0	0	0	2	1	0	1	0
ITALY	2	1	0	0	0	0	0	0	0	0	1	0	0	1	0	1	0	1	0	0
BELGIUM + LUX	0	0	0	0	0	0	0	0	0	0	0	0	0	0	0	0	0	0	0	0
NETHERLANDS	2	1	0	1	0	0	0	0	0	0	0	0	0	0	0	1	0	0	0	1
SPAIN	4	0	2	2	0	0	0	0	0	0	1	1	0	0	0	3	0	2	1	0
GREECE + TURKEY	0	0	0	0	0	0	0	0	0	0	0	0	0	0	0	0	0	0	0	0
OTHER EUROPE	4	2	2	0	0	1	1	0	0	0	1	0	1	0	0	3	1	2	0	0
EUROPE EX. U.K.	20	7	6	7	0	4	3	0	1	0	3	0	1	2	0	13	3	6	4	0
SOUTHERN DOMINIONS	10	7	1	2	0	4	2	0	2	0	0	0	0	0	0	6	5	1	0	0
S. AFRICA +RHOD.	3	3	0	0	0	3	1	0	1	0	0	0	0	0	0	2	2	0	0	0
AUSTRALIA + N.Z.	7	4	1	2	0	2	1	0	1	0	0	0	0	0	0	4	3	1	0	0
ASIA + OTHER AFRICA	9	2	4	1	2	1	1	0	0	0	1	1	0	0	0	6	1	4	0	1
JAPAN	3	2	0	1	0	1	1	0	0	0	1	1	0	0	0	1	0	0	1	0
OTHER ASIA+AFR.	6	0	4	0	2	0	0	0	0	0	0	0	0	0	0	5	0	4	0	1
BLACK AFRICA	1	1	1	0	0	1	1	0	0	0	0	0	0	0	0	1	1	1	0	0
ARAB WORLD	2	0	2	0	0	0	0	0	0	0	0	0	0	0	0	2	0	2	0	0
INDIA	1	0	1	0	0	0	0	0	0	0	1	0	1	0	0	1	0	1	0	0
PHILIPPINES	1	0	0	2	0	0	0	0	0	0	0	0	0	0	0	1	0	0	0	0
OTHER E. ASIA	1	1	0	0	0	0	0	0	0	0	0	0	0	0	0	1	0	1	0	0
OTHER ASIA	1	1	0	0	0	1	1	0	0	0	0	0	0	0	0	0	0	0	0	0

CHAPTER 5— PATTERNS OF OWNERSHIP
SECTION 4— THE FLOW OF MANUFACTURING BY INDUSTRY OF SUBSIDIARY
TABLE 25— SUBSIDIARIES MANUFACTURING
GLASS PRODUCTS (SIC 321-323)
CLASSIFIED BY COUNTRY, PERIOD MANUFACTURE BEGAN, AND SYSTEM OWNERSHIP %

PERIOD AND OWNERSHIP PERCENTAGE
(WHL=95-100%, MAJ=50-94%, MIN=5-49%, UNK=UNKNOWN)

COUNTRY OR REGION	TOTAL PRE 1968					PRE 1946					1946-1957					1958-1967				
	ALL	WHL	MAJ	MIN	UNK	ALL	WHL	MAJ	MIN	UNK	ALL	WHL	MAJ	MIN	UNK	ALL	WHL	MAJ	MIN	UNK
OUTSIDE U.S.	53	20	17	14	1	12	5	1	5	1	8	5	0	3	0	32	10	16	6	0
OUT. U.S. + CANADA	48	17	16	14	1	10	4	0	5	1	7	4	0	3	0	31	9	16	6	0
OUT. WEST. HEMIS.	26	8	8	9	1	4	1	0	2	1	2	0	0	2	0	20	7	8	5	0
OUT. WHITE C'WEALTH	39	13	14	11	1	10	4	0	5	1	6	4	0	2	0	23	5	14	4	0
OUT. DEVLPED WORLD	24	9	8	6	1	7	3	0	3	1	5	4	0	1	0	12	2	8	2	0
CANADA	5	3	1	0	0	2	1	1	0	0	1	1	0	0	0	1	1	0	0	0
LATIN AMERICA	22	9	8	5	0	6	3	0	3	0	5	4	0	1	0	11	2	8	1	0
C. AMER.+CARIB.	5	2	3	0	0	0	0	0	0	0	2	2	0	0	0	3	0	3	0	0
CUBA	1	1	0	0	0	0	0	0	0	0	1	1	0	0	0	0	0	0	0	0
MEXICO	4	1	3	0	0	0	0	0	0	0	1	1	0	0	0	3	0	3	0	0
OTHER	0	0	0	0	0	0	0	0	0	0	0	0	0	0	0	0	0	0	0	0
S. AMERICA	17	7	5	5	0	6	3	0	3	0	3	2	0	1	0	8	2	5	1	0
ARGENTINA	1	1	0	0	0	1	1	0	0	0	0	0	0	0	0	0	0	0	0	0
BRAZIL	5	1	0	4	0	3	1	0	2	0	1	0	0	1	0	1	0	0	1	0
PERU	0	0	0	0	0	0	0	0	0	0	0	0	0	0	0	0	0	0	0	0
COLOMBIA	4	3	1	0	0	0	0	0	0	0	1	1	0	0	0	3	2	1	0	0
VENEZUELA	5	1	4	0	0	0	0	0	0	0	1	1	0	0	0	4	0	4	0	0
OTHER	2	1	0	1	0	2	1	0	1	0	0	0	0	0	0	0	0	0	0	0
EUROPE	17	7	5	5	0	3	1	0	2	0	2	0	0	2	0	12	6	5	1	0
EFTA	5	3	0	2	0	0	0	0	0	0	1	0	0	1	0	4	3	0	1	0
U.K.	5	3	0	2	0	0	0	0	0	0	1	0	0	1	0	4	3	0	1	0
SCANDINAVIA	0	0	0	0	0	0	0	0	0	0	0	0	0	0	0	0	0	0	0	0
SWITZERLAND	0	0	0	0	0	0	0	0	0	0	0	0	0	0	0	0	0	0	0	0
OTHER EFTA	0	0	0	0	0	0	0	0	0	0	0	0	0	0	0	0	0	0	0	0
EUROP. COMMUNITY	11	4	4	3	0	3	1	0	2	0	1	0	0	1	0	7	3	4	0	0
FRANCE	2	2	0	0	0	1	1	0	0	0	0	0	0	0	0	1	1	0	0	0
GERMANY	4	2	2	0	0	0	0	0	0	0	0	0	0	0	0	2	0	2	0	0
ITALY	3	1	2	0	0	0	0	0	0	0	0	0	0	0	0	3	1	2	0	0
BELGIUM + LUX	2	0	0	1	0	2	0	0	1	0	0	0	0	0	0	0	0	0	0	0
NETHERLANDS	0	0	0	0	0	0	0	0	0	0	0	0	0	0	0	0	0	0	0	0
SPAIN	1	0	1	0	0	0	0	0	0	0	0	0	0	0	0	1	0	1	0	0
GREECE + TURKEY	0	0	0	0	0	0	0	0	0	0	0	0	0	0	0	0	0	0	0	0
OTHER EUROPE	0	0	0	0	0	0	0	0	0	0	0	0	0	0	0	0	0	0	0	0
EUROPE EX. U.K.	12	4	5	3	0	3	1	0	2	0	1	0	0	1	0	8	3	5	0	0
SOUTHERN DOMINIONS	4	1	2	1	0	0	0	0	0	0	0	0	0	0	0	4	1	2	1	0
S. AFRICA +RHOD.	2	1	1	0	0	0	0	0	0	0	0	0	0	0	0	2	1	0	1	0
AUSTRALIA + N.Z.	2	0	2	0	0	0	0	0	0	0	0	0	0	0	0	2	0	2	0	0
ASIA + OTHER AFRICA	5	0	1	3	1	1	0	0	1	0	0	0	0	0	0	4	0	1	3	0
JAPAN	3	0	1	2	0	0	0	0	0	0	0	0	0	0	0	3	1	2	0	0
OTHER ASIA+AFR.	2	0	0	2	0	1	0	0	1	0	0	0	0	0	0	1	0	0	0	0
BLACK AFRICA	0	0	0	0	0	0	0	0	0	0	0	0	0	0	0	0	0	0	0	0
ARAB WORLD	0	0	0	0	0	0	0	0	0	0	0	0	0	0	0	0	0	0	0	0
INDIA	1	0	0	1	0	0	0	0	0	0	0	0	0	0	0	1	0	0	1	0
PHILIPPINES	0	0	0	0	0	0	0	0	0	0	0	0	0	0	0	0	0	0	0	0
OTHER E. ASIA	1	0	0	1	0	1	0	0	0	1	0	0	0	0	0	0	0	0	0	0
OTHER ASIA	0	0	0	0	0	0	0	0	0	0	0	0	0	0	0	0	0	0	0	0

CHAPTER 5- PATTERNS OF OWNERSHIP
SECTION 4- THE FLOW OF MANUFACTURING BY INDUSTRY OF SUBSIDIARY
TABLE 26- SUBSIDIARIES MANUFACTURING
STONE, CLAY, AND CONCRETE PRODUCTS (SIC 324-329)
CLASSIFIED BY COUNTRY, PERIOD MANUFACTURE BEGAN, AND SYSTEM OWNERSHIP %

PERIOD AND OWNERSHIP PERCENTAGE
(WHL=95-100%, MAJ=50-94%, MIN=5-49%, UNK=UNKNOWN)

COUNTRY OR REGION	TOTAL ALL	WHL	MAJ	MIN	UNK	PRE 1968 ALL	WHL	MAJ	MIN	UNK	PRE 1946 ALL	WHL	MAJ	MIN	UNK	1946-1957 ALL	WHL	MAJ	MIN	UNK	1958-1967 ALL	WHL	MAJ	MIN	UNK
OUTSIDE U.S.	132	60	30	32	9	131	60	30	32	9	20	10	5	4	1	42	22	10	7	3	69	28	15	21	5
OUT. U.S. + CANADA	119	49	30	32	7	118	49	30	32	7	17	7	5	4	1	36	17	10	7	2	65	25	15	21	4
OUT. WEST. HEMIS.	86	40	20	21	4	85	40	20	21	4	14	7	4	2	1	19	10	8	4	1	52	23	13	15	1
OUT. WHITE CWEALTH	88	30	21	30	6	87	30	21	30	6	9	0	5	3	1	29	14	8	6	1	49	16	8	21	4
OUT. DEVLPED WORLD	42	9	11	18	3	41	9	11	18	3	3	0	1	2	0	18	7	7	4	0	20	2	3	12	3
CANADA	13	11	0	0	2	11	11	0	0	0	3	3	0	0	0	6	5	0	0	1	4	3	0	0	1
LATIN AMERICA	33	9	10	11	3	33	9	10	11	3	3	0	1	2	0	17	7	7	3	0	13	2	2	6	3
C. AMER.+CARIB.	12	6	2	4	0	12	6	2	4	0	1	0	0	1	0	5	5	0	0	0	6	1	2	3	0
CUBA	0	0	0	0	0	0	0	0	0	0	0	0	0	0	0	0	0	0	0	0	0	0	0	0	0
MEXICO	12	6	2	4	0	12	6	2	4	0	1	0	0	1	0	5	5	0	0	0	6	1	2	3	0
OTHER	0	0	0	0	0	0	0	0	0	0	0	0	0	0	0	0	0	0	0	0	0	0	0	0	0
S. AMERICA	21	3	8	7	3	21	3	8	7	3	2	0	1	1	0	12	2	7	3	0	7	1	0	3	3
ARGENTINA	5	1	1	3	1	5	1	1	3	1	0	0	0	0	0	2	0	2	0	0	3	0	0	2	1
BRAZIL	7	1	5	1	0	7	1	5	1	0	0	0	0	0	0	6	1	5	0	0	1	0	0	1	0
PERU	1	0	0	1	0	1	0	0	1	0	0	0	0	0	0	0	0	0	0	0	1	1	0	0	0
COLOMBIA	1	0	0	1	0	1	0	0	1	0	0	0	0	0	0	1	1	0	0	0	0	0	0	0	0
VENEZUELA	2	1	0	0	1	2	1	0	0	1	0	0	0	0	0	1	0	0	1	0	1	0	0	1	0
OTHER	5	1	2	2	0	5	1	2	2	0	2	0	1	1	0	2	0	1	1	0	1	1	0	0	0
EUROPE	55	30	12	9	4	55	30	12	9	4	11	5	4	1	1	14	7	2	3	2	30	18	6	5	1
EFTA	15	11	3	1	0	15	11	3	1	0	6	5	1	0	0	2	0	1	1	0	7	6	1	0	0
U.K.	12	9	2	1	0	12	9	2	1	0	5	5	0	0	0	2	0	1	1	0	5	4	1	0	0
SCANDINAVIA	3	2	1	0	0	3	2	1	0	0	1	0	1	0	0	0	0	0	0	0	2	2	0	0	0
SWITZERLAND	0	0	0	0	0	0	0	0	0	0	0	0	0	0	0	0	0	0	0	0	0	0	0	0	0
OTHER EFTA	0	0	0	0	0	0	0	0	0	0	0	0	0	0	0	0	0	0	0	0	0	0	0	0	0
EUROP. COMMUNITY	33	17	8	5	3	33	17	8	5	3	5	0	3	1	1	11	7	1	2	1	17	10	4	2	1
FRANCE	17	9	5	3	0	17	9	5	3	0	2	0	1	1	0	5	3	1	1	0	10	6	3	1	0
GERMANY	6	4	1	0	1	6	4	1	0	1	2	0	1	0	1	3	3	0	0	1	1	1	0	0	0
ITALY	3	1	1	1	0	3	1	1	1	0	0	0	0	0	0	1	1	0	0	0	2	1	0	1	0
BELGIUM + LUX	6	2	2	2	0	6	2	2	2	0	1	0	1	0	0	2	2	0	0	0	3	2	1	0	0
NETHERLANDS	1	1	0	0	0	1	1	0	0	0	0	0	0	0	0	0	0	0	0	0	1	1	0	0	0
SPAIN	3	0	2	1	0	3	0	2	1	0	0	0	0	0	0	0	0	0	0	0	3	1	2	0	0
GREECE + TURKEY	1	1	0	0	0	1	1	0	0	0	0	0	0	0	0	0	0	0	0	0	1	1	0	0	0
OTHER EUROPE	3	1	0	1	1	3	1	0	1	1	0	0	0	0	0	0	0	0	0	0	2	1	0	1	0
EUROPE EX. U.K.	43	21	10	8	4	43	21	10	8	4	6	0	4	1	1	12	7	1	2	2	25	14	5	5	1
SOUTHERN DOMINIONS	17	9	7	1	0	17	9	7	1	0	3	2	0	1	0	4	3	1	0	0	10	4	6	0	0
S. AFRICA +RHOD.	5	3	2	0	0	5	3	2	0	0	0	0	0	0	0	3	2	1	0	0	2	1	1	0	0
AUSTRALIA + N.Z.	12	6	5	1	0	12	6	5	1	0	3	2	0	1	0	1	1	0	0	0	8	3	5	0	0
ASIA + OTHER AFRICA	14	1	1	11	1	13	1	1	11	0	0	0	0	0	0	1	0	0	1	0	12	1	1	10	0
JAPAN	5	1	0	4	0	5	1	0	4	0	0	0	0	0	0	0	0	0	0	0	5	1	0	4	0
OTHER ASIA+AFR.	9	0	1	7	1	8	0	1	7	0	0	0	0	0	0	1	0	0	1	0	7	0	1	6	0
BLACK AFRICA	1	0	0	1	0	1	0	0	1	0	0	0	0	0	0	0	0	0	0	0	1	0	0	1	0
ARAB WORLD	1	0	0	1	0	1	0	0	1	0	0	0	0	0	0	0	0	0	0	0	1	0	0	1	0
INDIA	4	0	0	3	1	3	0	0	3	0	0	0	0	0	0	1	0	0	1	0	2	0	0	2	0
PHILIPPINES	1	0	0	1	0	1	0	0	1	0	0	0	0	0	0	0	0	0	0	0	1	0	0	1	0
OTHER E. ASIA	1	0	0	1	0	1	0	0	1	0	0	0	0	0	0	0	0	0	0	0	1	0	0	1	0
OTHER ASIA	2	0	1	1	0	2	0	1	1	0	0	0	0	0	0	0	0	0	0	0	2	0	1	1	0

CHAPTER 5- PATTERNS OF OWNERSHIP
SECTION 4- THE FLOW OF MANUFACTURING BY INDUSTRY OF SUBSIDIARY
TABLE 27- SUBSIDIARIES MANUFACTURING
SMELTED AND REFINED NONFERROUS METALS (SIC 333)
CLASSIFIED BY COUNTRY, PERIOD MANUFACTURE BEGAN, AND SYSTEM OWNERSHIP %

PERIOD AND OWNERSHIP PERCENTAGE
(WHL=95-100%, MAJ=50-94%, MIN=5-49%, UNK=UNKNOWN)

COUNTRY OR REGION	TOTAL PRE 1968					PRE 1946					1946-1957					1958-1967				
	ALL	WHL	MAJ	MIN	UNK	ALL	WHL	MAJ	MIN	UNK	ALL	WHL	MAJ	MIN	UNK	ALL	WHL	MAJ	MIN	UNK
OUTSIDE U.S.	66	29	25	11	1	18	11	5	1	1	7	3	3	1	0	41	15	17	9	0
OUT. U.S. + CANADA	51	18	24	8	1	11	5	5	0	1	5	1	3	1	0	35	12	16	7	0
OUT. WEST. HEMIS.	38	13	18	6	1	4	1	2	1	0	3	1	2	0	0	31	11	14	6	0
OUT. WHITE CWEALTH	32	10	15	7	0	8	4	4	0	0	3	2	2	0	0	21	6	9	6	0
OUT. DEVLPED WORLD	19	5	9	5	0	7	4	3	0	0	3	3	2	0	0	9	1	4	4	0
CANADA	15	11	1	3	0	7	6	0	1	0	2	2	0	0	0	6	3	1	2	0
LATIN AMERICA	13	5	6	2	0	7	4	3	0	0	2	0	1	1	0	4	1	2	1	0
C. AMER.+CARIB.	4	2	1	1	0	3	2	1	0	0	1	0	0	1	0	1	0	0	0	0
CUBA	4	0	4	0	0	3	0	2	0	0	1	0	2	0	0	0	0	0	0	0
MEXICO	0	2	0	1	0	0	1	0	1	0	0	0	0	0	0	0	0	0	0	0
OTHER	0	3	0	0	0	0	2	0	0	0	0	0	0	0	0	1	0	2	1	0
S. AMERICA	9	2	5	0	0	4	2	2	0	0	2	0	0	0	0	3	1	2	0	0
ARGENTINA	3	1	2	0	1	2	1	1	0	0	0	0	0	0	0	1	0	0	0	0
BRAZIL	2	0	2	0	1	1	0	1	0	0	0	0	0	0	0	1	0	0	1	0
PERU	1	0	0	0	0	1	0	0	0	0	0	1	0	0	0	0	0	0	0	0
COLOMBIA	1	0	2	0	0	0	0	0	0	0	1	0	1	0	0	0	0	0	1	0
VENEZUELA	1	0	1	0	0	0	0	0	0	0	0	1	0	0	0	1	0	0	0	0
OTHER	1	0	0	1	0	0	0	0	0	0	1	1	1	1	1	0	0	0	0	0
EUROPE	20	8	10	2	0	2	1	1	0	0	2	1	1	1	0	16	7	7	2	0
EFTA	14	6	7	1	0	1	1	1	0	0	2	1	1	1	0	11	5	5	1	0
U.K.	9	4	4	1	0	1	1	0	0	0	2	1	0	0	0	6	3	2	1	0
SCANDINAVIA	3	1	2	0	0	1	0	1	0	0	0	0	0	0	0	3	1	2	0	0
SWITZERLAND	2	1	1	0	0	1	1	0	0	0	0	0	0	0	0	2	1	1	0	0
OTHER EFTA	5	2	3	0	0	1	0	1	0	0	1	0	0	0	0	0	0	0	0	0
EUROP. COMMUNITY	5	2	3	0	0	1	0	1	0	0	0	0	0	0	0	4	2	2	2	0
FRANCE	3	2	0	0	0	0	0	0	0	0	0	0	0	0	0	0	0	0	0	0
GERMANY	2	0	1	1	0	0	0	0	0	0	0	0	0	0	0	3	2	2	1	0
ITALY	2	0	2	0	0	1	0	1	0	0	0	0	0	0	0	3	0	0	0	0
BELGIUM + LUX	0	0	0	1	0	0	0	0	0	0	0	0	0	0	0	1	0	1	1	0
NETHERLANDS	1	0	2	0	0	0	0	1	0	0	0	1	0	0	0	0	0	0	0	0
SPAIN	0	0	0	1	0	0	0	0	0	0	0	0	0	0	0	1	0	0	1	0
GREECE + TURKEY	0	0	0	0	0	0	0	0	0	0	0	0	0	0	0	0	0	0	0	0
OTHER EUROPE	0	0	0	0	0	0	0	0	0	0	0	0	0	0	0	0	0	0	0	0
EUROPE EX. U.K.	11	4	6	1	0	1	0	1	0	0	1	1	1	1	0	10	4	5	1	0
SOUTHERN DOMINIONS	10	4	5	0	1	2	1	0	0	1	2	1	0	0	0	8	3	5	0	0
S. AFRICA +RHOD.	3	1	1	1	1	1	0	1	0	0	0	0	0	1	0	2	1	1	0	0
AUSTRALIA + N.Z.	7	3	4	0	0	1	1	0	0	0	1	1	0	1	0	6	2	4	0	0
ASIA + OTHER AFRICA	8	1	2	4	0	0	0	0	0	0	0	0	0	0	0	7	1	2	4	0
JAPAN	2	1	1	1	0	0	0	0	0	0	0	0	0	0	0	2	1	2	1	0
OTHER ASIA+AFR.	6	0	3	3	0	0	0	0	0	0	0	1	0	0	0	5	0	2	3	0
BLACK AFRICA	2	0	2	0	0	0	0	0	0	0	0	1	0	0	0	1	1	1	1	0
ARAB WORLD	0	0	0	0	0	0	0	0	0	0	0	0	0	0	0	0	0	0	0	0
INDIA	1	0	1	1	0	0	0	0	0	0	0	1	0	0	0	1	0	0	0	0
PHILIPPINES	0	0	0	0	0	0	0	0	0	0	0	0	0	0	0	0	0	0	1	0
OTHER E. ASIA	0	0	0	2	0	0	0	0	0	0	0	0	0	0	0	0	0	0	0	0
OTHER ASIA	3	0	1	2	0	0	0	0	0	0	0	0	0	0	0	3	0	2	2	0

CHAPTER 5- PATTERNS OF OWNERSHIP
SECTION 4- THE FLOW OF MANUFACTURING BY INDUSTRY OF SUBSIDIARY
TABLE 28- SUBSIDIARIES MANUFACTURING
OTHER NONFERROUS METAL PRODUCTS (SIC 334-336)
CLASSIFIED BY COUNTRY, PERIOD MANUFACTURE BEGAN, AND SYSTEM OWNERSHIP %

PERIOD AND OWNERSHIP PERCENTAGE
(WHL=95-100%, MAJ=50-94%, MIN=5-49%, UNK=UNKNOWN)

COUNTRY OR REGION	TOTAL PRE 1968					PRE 1946					1946-1957					1958-1967				
	ALL	WHL	MAJ	MIN	UNK	ALL	WHL	MAJ	MIN	UNK	ALL	WHL	MAJ	MIN	UNK	ALL	WHL	MAJ	MIN	UNK
OUTSIDE U.S.	54	26	15	10	2	5	5	0	0	0	10	4	4	2	0	38	17	11	8	2
OUT. U.S. + CANADA	38	14	11	10	2	5	5	0	0	0	3	1	0	2	0	33	12	11	8	2
OUT. WEST. HEMIS.	27	11	8	5	2	1	1	0	0	0	2	0	0	2	0	23	10	8	3	2
OUT. WHITE CWEALTH	26	10	7	9	0	1	1	0	0	0	2	1	0	1	0	23	8	7	8	0
OUT. DEVLPED WORLD	14	4	4	6	0	0	0	0	0	0	1	1	0	0	0	13	3	4	6	0
CANADA	16	12	4	0	0	4	4	0	0	0	7	3	4	0	0	5	5	0	0	0
LATIN AMERICA	11	3	3	5	0	4	4	0	0	0	1	1	1	0	0	10	5	3	5	0
C. AMER.+CARIB.	5	1	2	2	0	0	0	0	0	0	1	1	1	0	0	4	2	2	2	0
CUBA	0	0	0	0	0	0	0	0	0	0	0	0	0	0	0	0	0	0	0	0
MEXICO	4	1	1	2	0	0	0	0	0	0	1	1	1	0	0	3	0	1	2	0
OTHER	1	0	1	0	0	0	0	0	0	0	0	0	0	0	0	1	0	1	0	0
S. AMERICA	6	2	1	3	0	0	0	0	0	0	0	0	0	0	0	6	2	1	3	0
ARGENTINA	2	1	0	1	0	0	0	0	0	0	0	0	0	0	0	2	1	0	1	0
BRAZIL	1	0	1	0	0	0	0	0	0	0	0	0	0	0	0	1	0	1	0	0
PERU	0	0	0	0	0	0	0	0	0	0	0	0	0	0	0	0	0	0	0	0
COLOMBIA	1	0	0	1	0	0	0	0	0	0	0	0	0	0	0	1	0	0	1	0
VENEZUELA	2	1	1	1	0	0	0	0	0	0	0	0	0	0	0	2	1	0	1	0
OTHER	0	0	0	0	0	0	0	0	0	0	0	0	0	0	0	0	0	0	0	0
EUROPE	17	9	5	2	0	1	1	0	0	0	2	1	0	2	0	13	8	5	0	0
EFTA	10	5	3	1	0	1	1	0	0	0	1	1	0	1	0	7	4	3	0	0
U.K.	7	3	2	1	0	0	0	0	0	0	1	0	0	1	0	5	3	2	0	0
SCANDINAVIA	1	1	0	0	0	1	1	0	0	0	0	0	0	0	0	0	0	0	0	0
SWITZERLAND	2	1	1	0	0	0	0	0	0	0	0	0	0	0	0	2	1	1	0	0
OTHER EFTA	0	0	0	0	0	0	0	0	0	0	0	0	0	0	0	0	0	0	0	0
EUROP. COMMUNITY	6	4	2	0	0	0	0	0	0	0	0	0	0	0	0	6	4	2	0	0
FRANCE	0	0	0	0	0	0	0	0	0	0	0	0	0	0	0	0	0	0	0	0
GERMANY	1	1	0	0	0	0	0	0	0	0	0	0	0	0	0	1	1	0	0	0
ITALY	1	1	1	0	0	0	0	0	0	0	0	0	0	0	0	1	1	1	0	0
BELGIUM + LUX	2	1	1	1	0	0	0	0	0	0	0	0	0	0	0	2	1	1	1	0
NETHERLANDS	2	1	1	1	0	0	0	0	0	0	0	0	0	0	0	2	1	1	1	0
SPAIN	0	0	0	0	0	0	0	0	0	0	0	0	0	0	0	0	0	0	0	0
GREECE + TURKEY	1	1	0	1	0	0	0	0	0	0	1	0	0	1	0	0	0	0	0	0
OTHER EUROPE	0	0	0	0	0	0	0	0	0	0	0	0	0	0	0	0	0	0	0	0
EUROPE EX. U.K.	10	6	3	1	0	1	1	0	0	0	1	1	0	1	0	8	5	3	0	0
SOUTHERN DOMINIONS	5	1	2	2	0	0	0	0	0	0	0	0	0	0	0	5	1	2	0	2
S. AFRICA +RHOD.	0	0	0	0	0	0	0	0	0	0	0	0	0	0	0	0	0	0	0	0
AUSTRALIA + N.Z.	5	2	2	2	0	0	0	0	0	0	0	0	0	0	0	5	1	2	0	2
ASIA + OTHER AFRICA	5	1	1	3	0	1	1	0	0	0	1	0	0	1	0	5	1	1	3	0
JAPAN	2	0	0	2	0	0	0	0	0	0	0	0	0	0	0	2	0	0	1	0
OTHER ASIA+AFR.	3	1	1	1	0	0	0	0	0	0	0	0	0	0	0	3	1	1	1	0
BLACK AFRICA	0	0	0	0	0	0	0	0	0	0	0	0	0	0	0	0	0	0	1	0
ARAB WORLD	2	1	1	1	0	0	0	0	0	0	0	0	0	0	0	2	0	1	1	0
INDIA	1	0	0	0	0	0	0	0	0	0	0	0	0	0	0	1	1	0	0	0
PHILIPPINES	0	1	0	1	0	0	0	0	0	0	0	0	0	0	0	0	0	0	0	0
OTHER E. ASIA	0	0	0	0	0	0	0	0	0	0	0	0	0	0	0	0	0	0	0	0
OTHER ASIA	0	0	0	0	0	0	0	0	0	0	0	0	0	0	0	0	0	0	0	0

CHAPTER 5- PATTERNS OF OWNERSHIP
SECTION 4- THE FLOW OF MANUFACTURING BY INDUSTRY OF SUBSIDIARY
TABLE 29- SUBSIDIARIES MANUFACTURING
IRON, STEEL AND MISCELLANEOUS NONFERROUS PRODUCTS (SIC 331,332, AND 339)
CLASSIFIED BY COUNTRY, PERIOD MANUFACTURE BEGAN, AND SYSTEM OWNERSHIP %

PERIOD AND OWNERSHIP PERCENTAGE
(WHL=95-100%, MAJ=50-94%, MIN=5-49%, UNK=UNKNOWN)

COUNTRY OR REGION	TOTAL PRE 1968 ALL	WHL	MAJ	MIN	UNK	PRE 1946 ALL	WHL	MAJ	MIN	UNK	1946-1957 ALL	WHL	MAJ	MIN	UNK	1958-1967 ALL	WHL	MAJ	MIN	UNK
OUTSIDE U.S.	57	28	12	8	4	11	6	3	1	1	7	4	2	1	0	34	18	7	6	3
OUT. U.S. + CANADA	47	20	11	7	4	7	3	2	1	1	4	2	2	0	0	31	15	7	6	3
OUT. WEST. HEMIS.	35	15	6	5	4	6	2	2	1	1	4	0	2	2	0	24	13	4	4	3
OUT. WHITE CWEALTH	31	12	7	7	3	4	1	1	1	1	4	2	2	0	0	21	9	4	6	2
OUT. DEVLPED WORLD	15	6	5	4	0	1	1	1	0	0	4	2	2	0	0	10	3	3	4	0
CANADA	10	8	1	1	0	4	3	1	0	0	3	3	0	0	0	3	3	0	0	0
LATIN AMERICA	12	5	5	2	0	1	1	1	0	0	4	0	2	1	1	7	2	3	2	0
C. AMER.+CARIB.	3	2	0	1	0	1	1	0	0	0	0	0	0	0	0	2	1	0	1	0
CUBA	0	0	0	0	0	0	0	0	0	0	0	0	0	0	0	0	0	0	0	0
MEXICO	3	2	0	0	0	1	1	0	0	0	0	0	0	0	0	2	1	1	0	0
OTHER	0	0	0	0	0	0	0	0	0	0	0	0	0	0	0	0	0	0	0	0
S. AMERICA	9	3	4	2	0	0	0	0	0	0	4	2	2	0	0	5	1	2	2	0
ARGENTINA	1	1	0	1	0	0	0	0	0	0	0	0	0	0	0	1	0	0	1	0
BRAZIL	5	0	3	1	0	0	0	0	0	0	2	2	0	0	0	3	1	1	0	0
PERU	0	0	0	0	0	0	0	0	0	0	0	0	0	0	0	0	0	0	0	0
COLOMBIA	1	1	0	0	0	0	0	0	0	0	1	0	0	1	0	0	1	0	0	0
VENEZUELA	0	0	0	0	0	0	0	0	0	0	0	0	0	0	0	0	0	0	0	0
OTHER	2	1	1	0	0	0	0	0	0	0	1	1	1	0	0	1	0	1	0	0
EUROPE	27	12	4	2	4	5	2	2	1	1	0	0	0	0	0	17	10	3	1	3
EFTA	12	6	2	0	2	2	2	1	0	0	0	0	0	0	0	7	4	2	0	1
U.K.	12	6	2	0	1	2	2	1	0	0	0	0	0	0	0	7	4	2	0	1
SCANDINAVIA	0	0	0	0	0	0	0	0	0	0	0	0	0	0	0	0	0	0	0	0
SWITZERLAND	0	0	0	0	0	0	0	0	0	0	0	0	0	0	0	0	0	0	0	0
OTHER EFTA	0	0	0	0	0	0	0	0	0	0	0	0	0	0	0	0	0	0	0	0
EUROP. COMMUNITY	13	6	1	1	3	3	0	1	1	1	0	0	0	0	0	8	6	0	0	2
FRANCE	5	2	1	1	0	2	0	1	1	0	0	0	0	0	0	2	2	0	0	0
GERMANY	2	1	0	0	2	1	0	0	0	1	0	0	0	0	0	1	2	0	0	2
ITALY	2	1	0	1	0	1	0	0	0	0	0	0	0	0	0	2	0	0	1	0
BELGIUM + LUX	1	1	0	0	0	0	0	0	0	0	0	0	0	0	0	1	1	0	0	1
NETHERLANDS	3	2	0	0	0	0	0	0	0	0	0	0	0	0	0	2	2	0	0	1
SPAIN	0	0	0	0	0	0	0	0	0	0	0	0	0	0	0	0	0	0	0	0
GREECE + TURKEY	2	0	1	0	0	0	0	0	0	0	0	0	0	0	0	2	0	1	0	0
OTHER EUROPE	0	0	0	0	0	0	0	0	0	0	0	0	0	0	0	0	0	0	0	0
EUROPE EX. U.K.	15	6	1	0	3	3	0	1	0	1	0	0	0	0	0	10	6	1	0	2
SOUTHERN DOMINIONS	4	2	2	0	0	1	0	1	0	0	0	0	0	0	0	3	2	1	0	0
S. AFRICA +RHOD.	1	1	0	0	0	0	0	0	0	0	0	0	0	0	0	1	1	0	0	0
AUSTRALIA + N.Z.	3	1	2	3	0	1	0	1	0	0	0	0	0	0	0	2	1	1	3	0
ASIA + OTHER AFRICA	4	1	0	1	0	0	0	0	0	0	0	0	0	0	0	4	1	0	1	0
JAPAN	1	0	0	2	0	0	0	0	0	0	0	0	0	0	0	1	0	0	1	0
OTHER ASIA+AFR.	3	1	0	2	0	0	0	0	0	0	0	0	0	0	0	3	1	0	2	0
BLACK AFRICA	1	0	0	0	0	0	0	0	0	0	0	0	0	0	0	1	0	0	1	0
ARAB WORLD	0	0	0	0	0	0	0	0	0	0	0	0	0	0	0	0	0	0	0	0
INDIA	1	0	0	1	0	0	0	0	0	0	0	0	0	0	0	1	0	0	1	0
PHILIPPINES	0	0	0	0	0	0	0	0	0	0	0	0	0	0	0	0	0	0	0	0
OTHER E. ASIA	0	0	0	0	0	0	0	0	0	0	0	0	0	0	0	0	1	0	0	0
OTHER ASIA	1	1	0	0	0	1	0	0	1	1	0	0	0	0	0	1	1	0	1	2

CHAPTER 5- PATTERNS OF OWNERSHIP
SECTION 4- THE FLOW OF MANUFACTURING BY INDUSTRY OF SUBSIDIARY
TABLE 30- SUBSIDIARIES MANUFACTURING
METAL CANS (SIC 341)
CLASSIFIED BY COUNTRY, PERIOD MANUFACTURE BEGAN, AND SYSTEM OWNERSHIP %

PERIOD AND OWNERSHIP PERCENTAGE
(WHL=95-100%, MAJ=50-94%, MIN=5-49%, UNK=UNKNOWN)

COUNTRY OR REGION	TOTAL PRE 1968					PRE 1946					1946-1957					1958-1967				
	ALL	WHL	MAJ	MIN	UNK	ALL	WHL	MAJ	MIN	UNK	ALL	WHL	MAJ	MIN	UNK	ALL	WHL	MAJ	MIN	UNK
OUTSIDE U.S.	44	21	8	11	4	7	4	0	3	0	15	7	5	1	2	22	10	3	7	2
OUT. U.S. + CANADA	35	16	6	11	2	6	3	0	3	0	13	6	4	1	2	16	7	2	7	0
OUT. WEST. HEMIS.	17	7	2	8	0	4	2	0	2	0	2	2	0	0	0	11	3	2	6	0
OUT. WHITE CWEALTH	30	13	5	10	2	4	2	0	2	0	12	5	4	1	2	14	6	1	7	0
OUT. DEVLPED WORLD	21	10	5	4	2	3	2	0	1	0	11	4	4	1	2	7	4	1	2	0
CANADA	9	5	2	0	2	1	1	0	0	0	2	1	1	0	0	6	3	1	0	2
LATIN AMERICA	18	9	4	3	2	2	1	0	1	0	11	4	4	1	2	5	4	0	1	0
C. AMER.+CARIB.	10	5	3	0	2	1	1	0	0	0	6	1	3	0	2	3	3	0	0	0
CUBA	3	1	0	0	2	0	0	0	0	0	2	0	0	0	2	1	1	0	0	0
MEXICO	6	3	3	0	0	1	1	0	0	0	4	1	3	0	0	1	1	0	0	0
OTHER	1	1	0	0	0	0	0	0	0	0	0	0	0	0	0	1	1	0	0	0
S. AMERICA	8	4	1	3	0	1	0	0	1	0	5	3	1	1	0	2	1	0	1	0
ARGENTINA	3	2	0	1	0	0	0	0	0	0	2	2	0	0	0	1	0	0	1	0
BRAZIL	3	2	1	0	0	1	0	0	1	0	2	2	1	0	0	0	0	0	0	0
PERU	0	0	0	0	0	0	0	0	0	0	0	0	0	0	0	0	0	0	0	0
COLOMBIA	2	0	0	1	1	0	0	0	0	0	0	0	0	0	0	0	0	0	1	0
VENEZUELA	2	1	0	1	0	0	0	0	0	0	1	0	0	1	0	1	1	0	0	0
OTHER	1	1	0	0	0	0	0	0	0	0	0	0	0	0	0	0	0	0	0	0
EUROPE	9	3	1	5	0	2	1	0	1	0	1	1	0	0	0	6	1	1	4	0
EFTA	4	3	1	0	0	1	1	0	0	0	1	1	0	0	0	2	1	1	0	0
U.K.	2	1	1	0	0	1	1	0	0	0	0	0	0	0	0	1	0	1	0	0
SCANDINAVIA	0	0	0	0	0	0	0	0	0	0	0	0	0	0	0	0	0	0	0	0
SWITZERLAND	0	0	0	0	0	0	0	0	0	0	0	0	0	0	0	0	0	0	0	0
OTHER EFTA	2	2	0	0	0	0	0	0	0	0	1	1	0	0	0	1	1	0	0	0
EUROP. COMMUNITY	2	0	0	2	0	1	0	0	1	0	0	0	0	0	0	1	0	0	1	0
FRANCE	1	0	0	1	0	0	0	0	0	0	0	0	0	0	0	1	0	0	1	0
GERMANY	0	0	0	0	0	0	0	0	0	0	0	0	0	0	0	0	0	0	0	0
ITALY	1	0	0	1	0	1	0	0	1	0	0	0	0	0	0	0	0	0	0	0
BELGIUM + LUX	0	0	0	0	0	0	0	0	0	0	0	0	0	0	0	0	0	0	0	0
NETHERLANDS	0	0	0	0	0	0	0	0	0	0	0	0	0	0	0	0	0	0	0	0
SPAIN	1	0	0	1	0	0	0	0	0	0	0	0	0	0	0	2	0	0	2	0
GREECE + TURKEY	2	0	0	1	0	0	0	0	0	0	0	0	0	0	0	1	0	0	1	0
OTHER EUROPE	1	0	0	1	0	0	0	0	0	0	0	0	0	0	0	0	0	0	0	0
EUROPE EX. U.K.	7	2	0	5	0	1	0	0	1	0	1	1	0	0	0	5	1	0	4	0
SOUTHERN DOMINIONS	3	2	0	1	0	1	1	0	0	0	1	1	0	0	0	1	0	0	1	0
S. AFRICA +RHOD.	2	1	0	1	0	1	1	0	0	0	0	0	0	0	0	1	0	0	1	0
AUSTRALIA + N.Z.	5	2	1	2	0	1	1	0	0	0	2	1	1	0	0	2	0	0	2	0
ASIA + OTHER AFRICA	2	1	0	1	0	0	0	0	0	0	1	1	0	0	0	1	0	0	1	0
JAPAN	3	1	1	1	0	0	0	0	0	0	1	1	0	0	0	2	0	1	1	0
OTHER ASIA+AFR.	0	0	0	0	0	0	0	0	0	0	0	0	0	0	0	0	0	0	0	0
BLACK AFRICA	0	0	0	0	0	0	0	0	0	0	0	0	0	0	0	0	0	0	0	0
ARAB WORLD	0	0	0	0	0	0	0	0	0	0	0	0	0	0	0	0	0	0	0	0
INDIA	0	0	0	0	0	0	0	0	0	0	0	0	0	0	0	0	0	0	0	0
PHILIPPINES	1	1	0	0	0	0	0	0	0	0	0	0	0	0	0	1	1	0	0	0
OTHER E. ASIA	0	0	0	0	0	0	0	0	0	0	0	0	0	0	0	0	0	0	0	0
OTHER ASIA	2	0	0	1	0	0	0	0	0	0	0	0	0	0	0	2	0	0	1	0

CHAPTER 5- PATTERNS OF OWNERSHIP
SECTION 4- THE FLOW OF MANUFACTURING BY INDUSTRY OF SUBSIDIARY
TABLE 31- SUBSIDIARIES MANUFACTURING
HEATING APPARATUS AND PLUMBING FIXTURES (SIC 343)
CLASSIFIED BY COUNTRY, PERIOD MANUFACTURE BEGAN, AND SYSTEM OWNERSHIP %

PERIOD AND OWNERSHIP PERCENTAGE
(WHL=95-100%, MAJ=50-94%, MIN=5-49%, UNK=UNKNOWN)

COUNTRY OR REGION	TOTAL PRE 1968 ALL	WHL	MAJ	MIN	UNK	PRE 1946 ALL	WHL	MAJ	MIN	UNK	1946-1957 ALL	WHL	MAJ	MIN	UNK	1958-1967 ALL	WHL	MAJ	MIN	UNK
OUTSIDE U.S.	47	23	7	5	12	13	7	0	0	6	12	6	3	2	1	22	10	4	3	5
OUT. U.S. + CANADA	32	12	5	5	10	8	4	0	0	4	6	2	1	2	1	18	6	4	3	5
OUT. WEST. HEMIS.	29	12	5	5	6	8	4	0	0	4	4	2	1	2	1	17	6	4	3	5
OUT. WHITE CWEALTH	24	8	5	5	6	5	2	0	0	3	5	2	1	2	0	14	4	4	3	3
OUT. DEVLPED WORLD	6	1	1	3	1	0	0	0	0	0	3	0	0	2	1	3	1	1	1	0
CANADA	15	11	2	2	2	5	3	0	0	2	6	4	2	0	0	4	4	0	0	0
LATIN AMERICA	3	2	0	0	1	0	0	0	0	0	2	0	0	2	0	1	1	0	0	0
C. AMER.+CARIB.	1	0	0	0	1	0	0	0	0	0	0	0	0	0	0	1	1	0	0	0
CUBA	0	0	0	0	0	0	0	0	0	0	0	0	0	0	0	0	0	0	0	0
MEXICO	1	0	0	0	1	0	0	0	0	0	0	0	0	0	0	1	1	0	0	0
OTHER	0	0	0	0	0	0	0	0	0	0	0	0	0	0	0	0	0	0	0	0
S. AMERICA	2	2	0	0	0	0	0	0	0	0	2	0	0	2	0	0	0	0	0	0
ARGENTINA	1	0	0	0	0	0	0	0	0	0	0	0	0	0	0	0	0	0	0	0
BRAZIL	0	0	0	1	0	0	0	0	0	0	1	0	0	1	0	0	0	0	0	0
PERU	1	1	0	0	0	0	0	0	0	0	0	0	0	0	0	0	0	0	0	0
COLOMBIA	0	0	0	1	0	0	0	0	0	0	1	0	0	1	0	0	0	0	0	0
VENEZUELA	0	0	0	0	0	0	0	0	0	0	0	0	0	0	0	0	0	0	0	0
OTHER	0	0	0	0	0	0	0	0	0	0	0	0	0	0	0	0	0	0	0	0
EUROPE	25	10	4	2	9	8	4	0	0	4	3	2	0	0	1	14	4	4	2	4
EFTA	9	4	0	0	5	5	3	0	0	2	1	1	0	0	0	3	1	0	0	2
U.K.	7	3	0	0	4	3	2	0	0	1	1	1	0	0	0	3	1	0	0	2
SCANDINAVIA	0	0	0	0	0	0	0	0	0	0	0	0	0	0	0	0	0	0	0	0
SWITZERLAND	1	1	0	0	0	1	1	0	0	0	0	0	0	0	0	0	0	0	0	0
OTHER EFTA	1	0	0	1	0	0	0	0	0	0	1	0	0	1	0	0	0	0	0	0
EUROP. COMMUNITY	14	6	3	3	2	3	1	0	0	2	2	2	0	0	0	9	3	3	3	0
FRANCE	5	2	2	0	1	1	0	0	0	1	1	1	0	0	0	3	1	2	0	0
GERMANY	4	2	0	0	2	1	1	0	0	0	1	1	0	0	0	2	0	0	0	2
ITALY	2	2	0	2	0	1	0	0	0	0	0	0	0	0	0	1	1	0	0	0
BELGIUM + LUX	1	0	0	0	0	0	0	0	0	0	0	0	0	0	0	1	1	0	0	0
NETHERLANDS	2	0	1	0	1	0	0	0	0	0	0	0	0	0	0	2	0	1	1	0
SPAIN	1	0	1	0	0	0	0	0	0	0	0	0	0	0	0	1	0	1	0	0
GREECE + TURKEY	1	0	1	0	0	0	0	0	0	0	0	0	0	0	0	0	0	1	0	0
OTHER EUROPE	0	0	0	1	0	0	0	0	0	0	0	0	0	0	0	0	0	0	0	0
EUROPE EX. U.K.	18	7	4	2	5	5	2	0	0	3	2	2	0	0	0	11	3	3	2	2
SOUTHERN DOMINIONS	1	1	1	0	0	0	0	0	0	0	0	0	0	0	0	1	1	0	0	0
S. AFRICA +RHOD.	0	0	0	0	0	0	0	0	0	0	0	0	0	0	0	0	0	0	0	0
AUSTRALIA + N.Z.	1	1	1	0	0	0	0	0	0	0	0	0	0	0	0	1	1	0	0	0
ASIA + OTHER AFRICA	3	1	0	0	0	0	0	0	0	0	1	0	1	0	0	2	1	1	0	0
JAPAN	0	0	0	1	0	0	0	0	0	0	0	0	0	0	0	0	0	0	1	0
OTHER ASIA+AFR.	3	1	0	1	0	0	0	0	0	0	1	0	1	0	0	2	1	0	1	0
BLACK AFRICA	2	1	0	0	0	0	0	0	0	0	1	0	1	0	0	2	1	0	1	0
ARAB WORLD	0	0	0	1	0	0	0	0	0	0	0	0	0	0	0	0	0	0	0	0
INDIA	0	0	0	0	0	0	0	0	0	0	0	0	0	0	0	0	0	0	0	0
PHILIPPINES	0	0	0	0	0	0	0	0	0	0	0	0	0	0	0	0	0	0	0	0
OTHER E. ASIA	0	0	0	0	0	0	0	0	0	0	0	0	0	0	0	0	0	0	0	0
OTHER ASIA	1	0	1	0	0	0	0	0	0	0	1	0	1	0	0	0	0	0	0	0

CHAPTER 5- PATTERNS OF OWNERSHIP
SECTION 4- THE FLOW OF MANUFACTURING BY INDUSTRY OF SUBSIDIARY
TABLE 32- SUBSIDIARIES MANUFACTURING
OTHER FABRICATED METAL PRODUCTS (SIC 342,344-349)
CLASSIFIED BY COUNTRY, PERIOD MANUFACTURE BEGAN, AND SYSTEM OWNERSHIP %

PERIOD AND OWNERSHIP PERCENTAGE
(WHL=95-100%, MAJ=50-94%, MIN=5-49%, UNK=UNKNOWN)

COUNTRY OR REGION	TOTAL PRE 1968 ALL	WHL	MAJ	MIN	UNK	PRE 1946 ALL	WHL	MAJ	MIN	UNK	1946-1957 ALL	WHL	MAJ	MIN	UNK	1958-1967 ALL	WHL	MAJ	MIN	UNK
OUTSIDE U.S.	240	138	48	36	16	35	27	6	1	1	50	31	12	7	0	153	80	30	28	15
OUT. U.S. + CANADA	195	101	43	35	14	24	16	6	1	1	35	18	10	7	0	134	67	27	27	13
OUT. WEST. HEMIS.	146	80	32	21	11	18	12	5	1	0	24	13	7	4	0	102	55	20	16	11
OUT. WHITE CWEALTH	135	60	37	30	7	13	7	4	1	1	27	12	9	6	0	94	41	24	23	6
OUT. DEVLPED WORLD	61	24	16	18	3	6	4	1	0	1	16	5	7	4	0	39	15	8	14	2
CANADA	45	37	5	1	2	11	11	0	0	0	15	13	2	0	0	19	13	3	1	2
LATIN AMERICA	49	21	11	14	3	6	4	1	0	1	11	5	3	3	0	32	12	7	11	2
C. AMER.+CARIB.	21	9	5	6	1	2	1	1	0	0	3	2	1	0	0	16	6	3	6	1
CUBA	2	1	1	0	0	1	0	1	0	0	1	1	0	0	0	0	0	0	0	0
MEXICO	17	8	2	6	1	1	1	0	0	0	2	1	0	1	0	14	6	1	6	1
OTHER	2	0	2	0	0	0	0	0	0	0	0	0	0	0	0	2	1	2	0	0
S. AMERICA	28	12	6	8	2	4	3	0	1	0	8	3	0	3	0	16	6	6	4	0
ARGENTINA	5	3	2	0	0	1	1	0	0	0	1	0	1	0	0	3	2	1	0	0
BRAZIL	6	3	1	2	0	2	1	0	1	0	1	1	0	0	0	3	2	1	0	0
PERU	2	1	0	1	0	0	0	0	0	0	2	1	0	1	0	0	0	0	0	0
COLOMBIA	5	2	1	1	1	0	0	0	0	0	2	1	0	1	0	3	2	0	1	1
VENEZUELA	6	3	1	1	0	1	0	1	0	0	1	0	1	0	0	4	2	0	2	0
OTHER	4	1	2	1	0	0	0	0	0	0	1	1	0	1	0	3	0	2	1	0
EUROPE	106	63	25	11	6	14	8	5	1	0	16	10	3	3	0	75	45	17	7	6
EFTA	39	26	5	3	4	6	4	2	0	0	5	3	1	1	0	27	19	2	2	4
U.K.	35	25	4	2	3	6	4	2	0	0	5	3	1	1	0	23	18	1	1	3
SCANDINAVIA	2	0	0	2	0	0	0	0	0	0	0	0	0	0	0	2	0	0	2	0
SWITZERLAND	0	0	0	0	0	0	0	0	0	0	0	0	0	0	0	0	0	0	0	0
OTHER EFTA	2	1	1	0	0	0	0	0	0	0	0	0	0	0	0	2	1	1	0	0
EUROP. COMMUNITY	55	31	15	7	2	6	2	3	1	0	10	7	2	1	0	39	22	10	5	2
FRANCE	11	5	3	2	1	3	2	1	0	0	0	0	0	0	0	8	3	2	2	1
GERMANY	19	14	5	0	0	2	0	1	1	0	4	4	2	0	0	13	10	2	0	0
ITALY	15	8	5	2	0	0	0	0	0	0	3	2	1	0	0	12	6	4	2	0
BELGIUM + LUX	6	3	1	2	0	0	0	0	0	0	2	1	0	0	0	4	3	1	0	0
NETHERLANDS	4	1	1	1	1	1	0	0	0	1	1	0	0	1	0	2	2	0	0	0
SPAIN	8	4	3	1	0	1	1	0	0	0	1	0	1	0	0	6	3	3	0	0
GREECE + TURKEY	2	2	0	0	0	0	0	0	0	0	0	0	0	0	0	2	2	0	0	0
OTHER EUROPE	2	2	0	0	0	1	1	0	0	0	0	0	0	0	0	1	1	0	0	0
EUROPE EX. U.K.	71	38	21	9	3	8	4	3	1	0	11	7	2	2	0	52	27	16	6	3
SOUTHERN DOMINIONS	23	14	2	3	4	4	4	0	0	0	3	3	0	0	0	16	7	2	3	4
S. AFRICA +RHOD.	7	5	1	1	0	2	2	0	0	0	1	1	0	0	0	4	2	1	1	0
AUSTRALIA + N.Z.	16	9	1	2	4	2	2	0	0	0	2	2	0	0	0	12	5	2	2	4
ASIA + OTHER AFRICA	17	5	5	7	1	0	0	0	0	0	6	2	4	1	0	11	3	1	6	1
JAPAN	5	3	0	1	0	0	0	0	0	0	1	0	0	1	0	4	3	0	1	0
OTHER ASIA+AFR.	12	3	5	3	1	0	0	0	0	0	5	2	4	1	0	7	1	1	5	0
BLACK AFRICA	2	1	0	1	0	0	0	0	0	0	0	0	0	0	0	1	1	0	0	0
ARAB WORLD	1	0	1	0	0	0	0	0	0	0	0	0	0	0	0	1	0	1	0	0
INDIA	3	0	1	1	0	0	0	0	0	0	0	0	0	0	0	3	1	1	1	0
PHILIPPINES	2	0	1	1	0	0	0	0	0	0	1	0	1	0	0	1	0	0	1	0
OTHER E. ASIA	0	0	0	0	0	0	0	0	0	0	0	0	0	0	0	0	0	0	0	0
OTHER ASIA	4	1	3	0	0	0	0	0	0	0	3	0	3	0	0	1	0	0	0	0

478

PERIOD AND OWNERSHIP PERCENTAGE
(WHL=95-100%, MAJ=50-94%, MIN=5-49%, UNK=UNKNOWN)

COUNTRY OR REGION	TOTAL PRE 1968					PRE 1946					1946-1957					1958-1967				
	ALL	WHL	MAJ	MIN	UNK	ALL	WHL	MAJ	MIN	UNK	ALL	WHL	MAJ	MIN	UNK	ALL	WHL	MAJ	MIN	UNK
OUTSIDE U.S.	55	29	13	9	4	9	7	1	0	1	15	11	3	1	0	31	11	9	8	3
OUT. U.S. + CANADA	48	22	13	9	4	5	3	1	0	1	14	10	3	1	0	29	9	9	8	3
OUT. WEST. HEMIS.	39	16	11	8	4	5	3	1	0	1	10	6	3	1	0	24	7	7	7	3
OUT. WHITE CWEALTH	33	13	8	8	4	3	1	1	0	1	9	7	1	1	0	21	5	6	7	3
OUT. DEVLPED WORLD	12	7	3	2	0	0	0	0	0	0	5	5	0	0	0	7	2	3	2	0
CANADA	7	7	0	0	0	4	4	0	0	0	1	1	0	0	0	2	2	0	0	0
LATIN AMERICA	9	6	2	1	0	0	0	0	0	0	4	4	0	0	0	5	2	2	1	0
C. AMER.+CARIB.	3	3	0	0	0	0	0	0	0	0	2	2	0	0	0	1	1	0	0	0
CUBA	0	0	0	0	0	0	0	0	0	0	0	0	0	0	0	0	0	0	0	0
MEXICO	2	2	0	0	0	0	0	0	0	0	2	2	0	0	0	0	0	0	0	0
OTHER	1	1	0	0	0	0	0	0	0	0	0	0	0	0	0	1	1	0	0	0
S. AMERICA	6	3	2	1	0	0	0	0	0	0	2	2	0	0	0	4	1	2	1	0
ARGENTINA	3	1	2	0	0	0	0	0	0	0	1	1	0	0	0	2	0	2	0	0
BRAZIL	1	1	0	0	0	0	0	0	0	0	0	0	0	0	0	1	1	0	0	0
PERU	1	0	0	1	0	0	0	0	0	0	0	0	0	0	0	1	0	0	1	0
COLOMBIA	0	0	0	0	0	0	0	0	0	0	0	0	0	0	0	0	0	0	0	0
VENEZUELA	1	1	0	0	0	0	0	0	0	0	1	1	0	0	0	0	0	0	0	0
OTHER	0	0	0	0	0	0	0	0	0	0	0	0	0	0	0	0	0	0	0	0
EUROPE	26	10	7	5	4	3	1	1	0	1	6	3	2	1	0	17	6	4	4	3
EFTA	7	4	3	0	0	0	0	0	0	0	3	1	2	0	0	4	3	1	0	0
U.K.	6	4	2	0	0	0	0	0	0	0	2	1	1	0	0	4	3	1	0	0
SCANDINAVIA	1	0	1	0	0	0	0	0	0	0	1	0	1	0	0	0	0	0	0	0
SWITZERLAND	0	0	0	0	0	0	0	0	0	0	0	0	0	0	0	0	0	0	0	0
OTHER EFTA	0	0	0	0	0	0	0	0	0	0	0	0	0	0	0	0	0	0	0	0
EUROP. COMMUNITY	15	4	4	3	4	3	1	1	0	1	0	0	0	0	0	12	3	3	3	3
FRANCE	11	2	2	3	4	2	0	1	0	1	0	0	0	0	0	9	2	1	3	3
GERMANY	2	1	1	0	0	1	1	0	0	0	0	0	0	0	0	1	0	1	0	0
ITALY	1	1	0	0	0	0	0	0	0	0	0	0	0	0	0	1	1	0	0	0
BELGIUM + LUX	1	0	1	0	0	0	0	0	0	0	0	0	0	0	0	1	0	1	0	0
NETHERLANDS	0	0	0	0	0	0	0	0	0	0	0	0	0	0	0	0	0	0	0	0
SPAIN	3	2	0	1	0	0	0	0	0	0	2	2	0	0	0	1	0	0	1	0
GREECE + TURKEY	1	0	0	1	0	0	0	0	0	0	1	0	0	1	0	0	0	0	0	0
OTHER EUROPE	0	0	0	0	0	0	0	0	0	0	0	0	0	0	0	0	0	0	0	0
EUROPE EX. U.K.	20	6	5	5	4	3	1	1	0	1	4	2	1	1	0	13	3	3	4	3
SOUTHERN DOMINIONS	9	5	3	1	0	2	2	0	0	0	3	2	1	0	0	4	1	2	1	0
S. AFRICA +RHOD.	4	1	3	0	0	0	0	0	0	0	1	0	1	0	0	3	1	2	0	0
AUSTRALIA + N.Z.	5	4	0	1	0	2	2	0	0	0	2	2	0	0	0	1	0	0	1	0
ASIA + OTHER AFRICA	4	1	1	2	0	0	0	0	0	0	1	1	0	0	0	3	0	1	2	0
JAPAN	1	0	0	1	0	0	0	0	0	0	0	0	0	0	0	1	0	0	1	0
OTHER ASIA+AFR.	3	1	1	1	0	0	0	0	0	0	1	1	0	0	0	2	0	1	1	0
BLACK AFRICA	0	0	0	0	0	0	0	0	0	0	0	0	0	0	0	0	0	0	0	0
ARAB WORLD	1	0	1	0	0	0	0	0	0	0	0	0	0	0	0	1	0	1	0	0
INDIA	1	0	0	1	0	0	0	0	0	0	0	0	0	0	0	1	0	0	1	0
PHILIPPINES	1	1	0	0	0	0	0	0	0	0	1	1	0	0	0	0	0	0	0	0
OTHER E. ASIA	0	0	0	0	0	0	0	0	0	0	0	0	0	0	0	0	0	0	0	0
OTHER ASIA	0	0	0	0	0	0	0	0	0	0	0	0	0	0	0	0	0	0	0	0

CHAPTER 5- PATTERNS OF OWNERSHIP
SECTION 4- THE FLOW OF MANUFACTURING BY INDUSTRY OF SUBSIDIARY
TABLE 34- SUBSIDIARIES MANUFACTURING
CONSTRUCTION MACHINERY (SIC 353)
CLASSIFIED BY COUNTRY, PERIOD MANUFACTURE BEGAN, AND SYSTEM OWNERSHIP %

PERIOD AND OWNERSHIP PERCENTAGE
(WHL=95-100%, MAJ=50-94%, MIN=5-49%, UNK=UNKNOWN)

COUNTRY OR REGION	TOTAL PRE 1968 ALL	WHL	MAJ	MIN	UNK	PRE 1946 ALL	WHL	MAJ	MIN	UNK	1946-1957 ALL	WHL	MAJ	MIN	UNK	1958-1967 ALL	WHL	MAJ	MIN	UNK
OUTSIDE U.S.	136	77	43	9	7	25	15	8	0	2	39	31	6	1	1	72	31	29	8	4
OUT. U.S. + CANADA	104	52	37	9	6	18	9	8	0	1	30	23	5	1	1	56	20	24	8	4
OUT. WEST. HEMIS.	78	39	30	4	5	18	9	8	0	1	22	16	4	1	1	38	14	18	3	3
OUT. WHITE CWEALTH	70	29	27	9	5	11	5	5	0	1	14	9	4	1	0	45	15	18	8	4
OUT. DEVLPED WORLD	28	13	9	5	1	0	0	0	0	0	8	7	1	0	0	20	6	8	5	1
CANADA	32	25	6	0	1	7	6	0	0	1	9	8	1	0	0	16	11	5	0	0
LATIN AMERICA	26	13	7	5	1	0	0	0	0	0	8	7	1	0	0	18	6	6	5	1
C. AMER.+CARIB.	11	6	2	3	0	0	0	0	0	0	3	2	1	0	0	8	4	1	3	0
CUBA	0	0	0	0	0	0	0	0	0	0	0	0	0	0	0	0	0	0	0	0
MEXICO	11	6	2	3	0	0	0	0	0	0	3	2	1	0	0	8	4	1	3	0
OTHER	0	0	0	0	0	0	0	0	0	0	0	0	0	0	0	0	0	0	0	0
S. AMERICA	15	7	5	2	1	0	0	0	0	0	5	5	0	0	0	10	2	5	2	1
ARGENTINA	3	1	2	0	0	0	0	0	0	0	0	0	0	0	0	3	1	2	0	0
BRAZIL	7	5	1	1	0	0	0	0	0	0	5	5	0	0	0	2	0	1	1	0
PERU	1	0	1	0	0	0	0	0	0	0	0	0	0	0	0	1	0	1	0	0
COLOMBIA	0	0	0	0	0	0	0	0	0	0	0	0	0	0	0	0	0	0	0	0
VENEZUELA	3	1	0	2	0	0	0	0	0	0	0	0	0	0	0	3	1	0	2	0
OTHER	1	0	1	0	0	0	0	0	0	0	0	0	0	0	0	1	0	1	0	0
EUROPE	48	24	16	3	5	11	5	5	0	1	14	9	3	1	1	23	10	8	2	3
EFTA	12	8	3	0	1	2	0	2	0	0	9	7	1	0	1	1	1	0	0	0
U.K.	11	8	2	0	1	2	0	2	0	0	8	7	0	0	1	1	1	0	0	0
SCANDINAVIA	0	0	0	0	0	0	0	0	0	0	0	0	0	0	0	0	0	0	0	0
SWITZERLAND	0	0	0	0	0	0	0	0	0	0	0	0	0	0	0	0	0	0	0	0
OTHER EFTA	1	0	1	0	0	0	0	0	0	0	1	0	1	0	0	0	0	0	0	0
EUROP. COMMUNITY	33	15	12	2	4	8	4	3	0	1	4	2	2	0	0	21	9	7	2	3
FRANCE	11	4	6	1	0	3	2	1	0	0	0	0	0	0	0	8	2	5	1	0
GERMANY	8	6	2	0	0	2	2	0	0	0	3	2	1	0	0	3	2	1	0	0
ITALY	5	0	1	1	3	2	0	1	0	1	0	0	0	0	0	3	0	0	1	2
BELGIUM + LUX	5	3	2	0	0	1	0	1	0	0	0	0	0	0	0	4	3	1	0	0
NETHERLANDS	4	2	1	0	1	0	0	0	0	0	1	0	1	0	0	3	2	0	0	1
SPAIN	3	1	1	1	0	1	0	1	0	0	0	0	0	0	0	2	1	0	1	0
GREECE + TURKEY	0	0	0	0	0	0	0	0	0	0	0	0	0	0	0	0	0	0	0	0
OTHER EUROPE	0	0	0	0	0	0	0	0	0	0	0	0	0	0	0	0	0	0	0	0
EUROPE EX. U.K.	37	16	14	3	4	9	5	3	0	1	6	2	3	1	0	22	9	8	2	3
SOUTHERN DOMINIONS	23	15	8	0	0	5	4	1	0	0	8	7	1	0	0	10	4	6	0	0
S. AFRICA +RHOD.	6	5	1	0	0	3	3	0	0	0	2	2	0	0	0	1	0	1	0	0
AUSTRALIA + N.Z.	17	10	7	0	0	2	1	1	0	0	6	5	1	0	0	9	4	5	0	0
ASIA + OTHER AFRICA	7	0	6	1	0	2	0	2	0	0	0	0	0	0	0	5	0	4	1	0
JAPAN	5	0	4	1	0	2	0	2	0	0	0	0	0	0	0	3	0	2	1	0
OTHER ASIA+AFR.	2	0	2	0	0	0	0	0	0	0	0	0	0	0	0	2	0	2	0	0
BLACK AFRICA	0	0	0	0	0	0	0	0	0	0	0	0	0	0	0	0	0	0	0	0
ARAB WORLD	2	0	2	0	0	0	0	0	0	0	0	0	0	0	0	2	0	2	0	0
INDIA	0	0	0	0	0	0	0	0	0	0	0	0	0	0	0	0	0	0	0	0
PHILIPPINES	0	0	0	0	0	0	0	0	0	0	0	0	0	0	0	0	0	0	0	0
OTHER E. ASIA	0	0	0	0	0	0	0	0	0	0	0	0	0	0	0	0	0	0	0	0
OTHER ASIA	0	0	0	0	0	0	0	0	0	0	0	0	0	0	0	0	0	0	0	0

CHAPTER 5- PATTERNS OF OWNERSHIP
SECTION 4- THE FLOW OF MANUFACTURING BY INDUSTRY OF SUBSIDIARY
TABLE 35- SUBSIDIARIES MANUFACTURING
SPECIAL INDUSTRY MACHINERY (SIC 354 AND 355)
CLASSIFIED BY COUNTRY, PERIOD MANUFACTURE BEGAN, AND SYSTEM OWNERSHIP %

PERIOD AND OWNERSHIP PERCENTAGE
(WHL=95-100%, MAJ=50-94%, MIN=5-49%, UNK=UNKNOWN)

COUNTRY OR REGION	TOTAL PRE 1968					PRE 1946					1946-1957					1958-1967				
	ALL	WHL	MAJ	MIN	UNK	ALL	WHL	MAJ	MIN	UNK	ALL	WHL	MAJ	MIN	UNK	ALL	WHL	MAJ	MIN	UNK
OUTSIDE U.S.	109	64	17	12	16	22	19	2	0	1	25	12	6	4	3	62	33	9	8	12
OUT. U.S. + CANADA	94	53	16	12	13	18	15	2	0	1	21	10	5	4	2	55	28	9	8	10
OUT. WEST. HEMIS.	81	50	12	7	12	16	13	2	1	0	16	9	4	1	2	49	28	6	6	9
OUT. WHITE CWEALTH	57	25	12	11	9	9	8	1	0	0	11	3	2	4	2	37	14	9	7	7
OUT. DEVLPED WORLD	16	4	5	6	1	2	2	0	0	0	7	2	2	3	0	7	3	3	1	1
CANADA	15	11	1	0	3	4	4	0	0	0	4	2	1	0	1	7	5	0	2	2
LATIN AMERICA	13	3	4	5	1	2	2	0	0	0	5	1	1	3	0	6	0	3	2	1
C. AMER.+CARIB.	7	1	3	2	1	1	1	0	0	0	2	0	1	1	0	4	0	2	1	1
CUBA	1	0	0	1	0	0	0	0	0	0	1	0	0	1	0	0	0	0	0	0
MEXICO	5	1	2	0	1	1	1	0	0	0	1	1	1	0	0	3	0	1	1	1
OTHER	1	0	1	0	0	0	0	0	0	0	0	0	0	0	0	1	0	1	0	0
S. AMERICA	6	2	0	3	0	1	1	0	0	0	3	1	0	2	0	2	0	0	1	1
ARGENTINA	0	0	0	0	0	0	0	0	0	0	0	0	0	0	0	0	0	0	0	0
BRAZIL	2	2	0	0	0	1	1	0	0	0	1	1	0	0	0	0	0	0	0	0
PERU	0	0	0	0	0	0	0	0	0	0	0	0	0	0	0	0	0	0	0	0
COLOMBIA	1	0	0	0	0	0	0	0	0	0	1	0	0	1	0	0	0	0	0	0
VENEZUELA	1	0	0	1	0	0	0	0	0	0	0	0	0	0	0	0	0	0	0	0
OTHER	2	0	1	1	0	0	0	0	0	0	1	0	0	1	0	2	0	1	1	0
EUROPE	60	40	8	5	7	13	11	2	0	0	10	6	1	1	2	37	23	5	4	5
EFTA	26	21	2	1	2	7	6	1	0	0	6	5	1	0	0	13	10	0	1	2
U.K.	23	19	2	1	1	6	5	1	0	0	6	5	1	0	0	11	9	0	1	1
SCANDINAVIA	1	1	0	0	0	0	0	0	0	0	0	0	0	0	0	1	0	0	0	0
SWITZERLAND	1	1	0	0	0	0	0	0	0	0	0	0	0	0	0	1	1	0	0	0
OTHER EFTA	1	0	1	0	1	0	0	0	0	0	0	0	0	0	0	1	0	1	0	1
EUROP. COMMUNITY	30	18	5	2	5	5	4	1	0	0	3	1	0	1	2	22	13	4	2	3
FRANCE	8	4	1	2	1	2	2	0	0	0	2	1	0	0	1	4	1	3	0	0
GERMANY	10	4	3	3	0	2	1	1	0	0	2	0	0	1	0	8	3	2	0	3
ITALY	10	8	1	0	1	1	1	0	0	0	1	0	0	0	1	8	7	0	1	0
BELGIUM + LUX	1	1	0	0	0	0	0	0	0	0	0	0	0	1	0	1	1	0	0	0
NETHERLANDS	1	1	0	0	0	0	0	0	0	0	1	0	0	0	0	1	0	1	0	0
SPAIN	3	1	0	1	1	1	1	0	0	0	0	0	0	0	0	1	0	0	1	0
GREECE + TURKEY	1	1	0	0	0	0	0	0	0	0	0	0	0	0	0	1	0	0	0	1
OTHER EUROPE	0	0	0	0	0	0	0	0	0	0	0	0	0	0	0	0	0	0	0	0
EUROPE EX. U.K.	37	21	6	4	6	7	6	1	0	0	4	1	0	1	2	26	14	5	3	4
SOUTHERN DOMINIONS	14	9	2	0	3	3	2	0	0	1	4	2	2	0	0	7	5	0	0	2
S. AFRICA +RHOD.	4	3	1	0	0	1	1	0	0	0	2	1	1	0	0	1	1	0	0	0
AUSTRALIA + N.Z.	10	6	2	0	3	2	1	0	0	1	2	1	1	0	0	6	4	0	0	2
ASIA + OTHER AFRICA	7	1	1	2	2	0	0	0	0	0	2	1	1	0	0	5	0	1	2	2
JAPAN	4	1	1	2	2	0	0	0	0	0	2	1	1	0	0	4	0	1	2	2
OTHER ASIA+AFR.	3	1	1	1	0	0	0	0	0	0	2	1	0	0	0	1	0	0	1	0
BLACK AFRICA	0	0	0	0	0	0	0	0	0	0	0	0	0	0	0	0	0	0	0	0
ARAB WORLD	1	0	0	0	0	0	0	0	0	0	0	0	0	0	0	1	0	1	0	0
INDIA	1	1	0	0	0	0	0	0	0	0	1	1	0	0	0	0	0	0	0	0
PHILIPPINES	1	0	1	0	0	0	0	0	0	0	1	0	1	0	0	0	0	0	0	0
OTHER E. ASIA	0	0	0	0	0	0	0	0	0	0	0	0	0	0	0	0	0	0	0	0
OTHER ASIA	0	0	0	0	0	0	0	0	0	0	0	0	0	0	0	0	0	0	0	0

CHAPTER 5- PATTERNS OF OWNERSHIP
SECTION 4- THE FLOW OF MANUFACTURING BY INDUSTRY OF SUBSIDIARY
TABLE 36- SUBSIDIARIES MANUFACTURING
GENERAL INDUSTRIAL MACHINERY (SIC 356)
CLASSIFIED BY COUNTRY, PERIOD MANUFACTURE BEGAN, AND SYSTEM OWNERSHIP %

PERIOD AND OWNERSHIP PERCENTAGE
(WHL=95-100%, MAJ=50-94%, MIN=5-49%, UNK=UNKNOWN)

COUNTRY OR REGION	TOTAL PRE 1968					PRE 1946					1946-1957					1958-1967				
	ALL	WHL	MAJ	MIN	UNK	ALL	WHL	MAJ	MIN	UNK	ALL	WHL	MAJ	MIN	UNK	ALL	WHL	MAJ	MIN	UNK
OUTSIDE U.S.	118	71	24	10	11	30	21	8	0	1	24	17	4	3	0	62	33	12	7	10
OUT. U.S. + CANADA	92	50	23	9	10	25	17	7	0	1	15	8	4	3	0	52	25	12	6	9
OUT. WEST. HEMIS.	71	41	16	6	8	23	15	7	0	1	10	6	2	2	0	38	20	7	4	7
OUT. WHITE CWEALTH	65	31	18	8	8	18	13	5	0	0	9	4	2	3	0	38	14	11	5	8
OUT. DEVLPED WORLD	25	11	8	4	2	2	2	0	0	0	6	3	2	1	0	17	6	6	3	2
CANADA	26	21	1	1	1	5	4	1	0	0	9	9	0	0	0	10	8	0	1	1
LATIN AMERICA	21	9	7	3	2	2	2	0	0	0	5	2	2	1	0	14	5	5	2	2
C. AMER.+CARIB.	10	2	4	2	2	0	0	0	0	0	2	0	2	0	0	8	2	2	2	2
CUBA	0	0	0	0	0	0	0	0	0	0	0	0	0	0	0	0	0	0	0	0
MEXICO	9	2	3	2	2	0	0	0	0	0	2	0	2	0	0	7	2	1	2	2
OTHER	1	0	1	0	0	0	0	0	0	0	0	0	0	0	0	1	0	1	0	0
S. AMERICA	11	7	3	1	0	2	2	0	0	0	3	2	0	1	0	6	3	3	0	0
ARGENTINA	3	2	1	0	0	0	0	0	0	0	1	1	0	0	0	2	1	1	0	0
BRAZIL	6	5	1	0	0	2	2	0	0	0	1	1	0	0	0	3	2	1	0	0
PERU	1	1	0	0	0	0	0	0	0	0	1	1	0	0	0	0	0	0	0	0
COLOMBIA	1	0	1	0	0	0	0	0	0	0	0	0	0	0	0	1	0	0	1	0
VENEZUELA	0	0	0	0	0	0	0	0	0	0	0	0	0	0	0	0	0	0	0	0
OTHER	0	0	0	0	0	0	0	0	0	0	0	0	0	0	0	0	0	0	0	0
EUROPE	51	28	14	2	7	22	14	7	0	1	4	3	1	0	0	25	11	6	2	6
EFTA	17	10	5	0	2	7	4	2	0	1	3	2	1	0	0	7	4	2	0	1
U.K.	14	9	4	0	1	6	3	2	0	1	3	2	1	0	0	5	4	1	0	0
SCANDINAVIA	1	0	1	0	0	0	0	0	0	0	0	0	0	0	0	1	0	1	0	0
SWITZERLAND	1	1	0	0	0	0	0	0	0	0	0	0	0	0	0	1	0	0	0	1
OTHER EFTA	1	1	0	0	0	1	1	0	0	0	0	0	0	0	0	0	0	0	0	0
EUROP. COMMUNITY	29	16	7	1	5	14	10	4	0	0	1	0	1	0	0	14	5	3	1	5
FRANCE	12	5	3	1	3	6	4	2	0	0	1	0	1	0	0	6	1	1	1	3
GERMANY	8	6	2	0	0	5	4	1	0	0	0	0	0	0	0	2	1	1	0	0
ITALY	5	3	1	0	1	2	2	0	0	0	0	0	0	0	0	3	1	1	0	1
BELGIUM + LUX	2	1	1	0	0	0	0	0	0	0	1	1	0	0	0	1	0	0	0	1
NETHERLANDS	2	1	0	1	0	1	1	0	0	0	0	0	0	0	0	1	0	0	1	0
SPAIN	5	2	2	0	0	0	0	0	0	0	0	0	0	0	0	4	2	1	0	0
GREECE + TURKEY	2	2	0	0	0	0	0	0	0	0	0	0	0	0	0	0	0	0	0	0
OTHER EUROPE	0	0	0	0	0	0	0	0	0	0	0	0	0	0	0	0	0	0	0	0
EUROPE EX. U.K.	37	19	10	2	6	16	11	5	0	1	1	1	0	0	0	20	7	5	2	6
SOUTHERN DOMINIONS	13	10	1	1	1	1	1	0	0	0	3	2	1	0	0	9	7	0	1	1
S. AFRICA +RHOD.	3	3	0	0	0	1	1	0	0	0	1	1	0	0	0	1	1	0	0	0
AUSTRALIA + N.Z.	10	7	1	1	1	0	0	0	0	0	2	1	1	0	0	8	6	0	1	1
ASIA + OTHER AFRICA	7	3	1	3	0	0	0	0	0	0	3	2	0	1	0	4	2	1	0	1
JAPAN	3	1	2	0	0	0	0	0	0	0	2	2	0	0	0	1	1	0	0	0
OTHER ASIA+AFR.	4	2	0	2	0	0	0	0	0	0	1	0	0	2	0	3	1	0	1	1
BLACK AFRICA	0	0	0	0	0	0	0	0	0	0	0	0	0	0	0	0	0	0	0	0
ARAB WORLD	0	0	0	0	0	0	0	0	0	0	0	0	0	0	0	0	0	0	0	0
INDIA	2	2	0	0	0	0	0	0	0	0	1	1	0	0	0	1	1	0	0	0
PHILIPPINES	1	0	0	1	0	0	0	0	0	0	0	0	0	0	0	1	0	0	0	0
OTHER E. ASIA	0	0	0	0	0	0	0	0	0	0	0	0	0	0	0	0	0	0	0	0
OTHER ASIA	1	0	0	1	0	0	0	0	0	0	0	0	0	0	0	1	0	1	0	0

CHAPTER 5- PATTERNS OF OWNERSHIP
SECTION 4- THE FLOW OF MANUFACTURING BY INDUSTRY OF SUBSIDIARY
TABLE 37- SUBSIDIARIES MANUFACTURING
OFFICE AND COMPUTING MACHINES (SIC 357)
CLASSIFIED BY COUNTRY, PERIOD MANUFACTURE BEGAN, AND SYSTEM OWNERSHIP %

PERIOD AND OWNERSHIP PERCENTAGE
(WHL=95-100%, MAJ=50-94%, MIN=5-49%, UNK=UNKNOWN)

COUNTRY OR REGION	TOTAL PRE 1968					PRE 1946					1946-1957					1958-1967				
	ALL	WHL	MAJ	MIN	UNK	ALL	WHL	MAJ	MIN	UNK	ALL	WHL	MAJ	MIN	UNK	ALL	WHL	MAJ	MIN	UNK
OUTSIDE U.S.	87	68	11	6	2	40	33	5	1	1	22	18	4	0	0	25	17	2	5	1
OUT. U.S. + CANADA	76	57	11	6	2	34	27	5	1	1	21	17	4	0	0	21	13	2	5	1
OUT. WEST. HEMIS.	61	45	9	5	2	30	24	5	0	1	15	12	3	0	0	16	9	1	5	1
OUT. WHITE CWEALTH	63	46	9	6	2	27	22	3	1	1	18	14	4	0	0	18	10	2	5	1
OUT. DEVLPED WORLD	17	12	3	2	0	4	3	0	1	0	7	5	2	0	0	6	4	1	1	0
CANADA	11	11	0	0	0	6	6	0	0	0	1	1	0	0	0	4	4	0	0	0
LATIN AMERICA	15	12	2	1	0	4	3	0	1	0	6	5	1	0	0	5	4	1	0	0
C. AMER.+CARIB.	6	5	1	0	0	1	1	0	0	0	0	0	0	0	0	5	4	1	0	0
CUBA	0	0	0	0	0	0	0	0	0	0	0	0	0	0	0	0	0	0	0	0
MEXICO	6	5	1	0	0	1	1	0	0	0	0	0	0	0	0	5	4	1	0	0
OTHER	0	0	0	0	0	0	0	0	0	0	0	0	0	0	0	0	0	0	0	0
S. AMERICA	9	7	1	1	0	3	2	0	1	0	6	5	1	0	0	0	0	0	0	0
ARGENTINA	0	0	0	0	0	0	0	0	0	0	0	0	0	0	0	0	0	0	0	0
BRAZIL	6	4	1	1	0	2	1	0	1	0	4	3	1	0	0	0	0	0	0	0
PERU	0	0	0	0	0	0	0	0	0	0	0	0	0	0	0	0	0	0	0	0
COLOMBIA	1	1	0	0	0	1	1	0	0	0	0	0	0	0	0	0	0	0	0	0
VENEZUELA	1	1	0	0	0	0	0	0	0	0	1	1	0	0	0	0	0	0	0	0
OTHER	1	1	0	0	0	0	0	0	0	0	1	1	0	0	0	0	0	0	0	0
EUROPE	51	42	6	2	1	29	24	4	1	0	10	9	1	0	0	12	9	1	1	1
EFTA	18	16	2	0	0	10	8	2	0	0	4	4	0	0	0	4	4	0	0	0
U.K.	10	8	2	0	0	6	4	2	0	0	1	1	0	0	0	3	3	0	0	0
SCANDINAVIA	5	5	0	0	0	2	2	0	0	0	2	2	0	0	0	1	1	0	0	0
SWITZERLAND	2	2	0	0	0	1	1	0	0	0	1	1	0	0	0	0	0	0	0	0
OTHER EFTA	1	1	0	0	0	1	1	0	0	0	0	0	0	0	0	0	0	0	0	0
EUROP. COMMUNITY	32	25	4	2	1	18	15	2	1	0	6	5	1	0	0	8	5	1	1	1
FRANCE	8	5	1	2	0	5	4	0	1	0	1	1	0	0	0	2	0	1	1	0
GERMANY	13	9	3	0	1	9	7	2	0	0	2	1	1	0	0	2	1	0	0	1
ITALY	3	3	0	0	0	1	1	0	0	0	1	1	0	0	0	1	1	0	0	0
BELGIUM + LUX	3	3	0	0	0	1	1	0	0	0	1	1	0	0	0	1	1	0	0	0
NETHERLANDS	5	5	0	0	0	2	2	0	0	0	1	1	0	0	0	2	2	0	0	0
SPAIN	0	0	0	0	0	0	0	0	0	0	0	0	0	0	0	0	0	0	0	0
GREECE + TURKEY	0	0	0	0	0	0	0	0	0	0	0	0	0	0	0	0	0	0	0	0
OTHER EUROPE	1	1	0	0	0	1	1	0	0	0	0	0	0	0	0	0	0	0	0	0
EUROPE EX. U.K.	41	34	4	2	1	23	20	2	1	0	9	8	1	0	0	9	6	1	1	1
SOUTHERN DOMINIONS	2	2	0	0	0	0	0	0	0	0	2	2	0	0	0	0	0	0	0	0
S. AFRICA +RHOD.	1	1	0	0	0	0	0	0	0	0	1	1	0	0	0	0	0	0	0	0
AUSTRALIA + N.Z.	1	1	0	0	0	0	0	0	0	0	1	1	0	0	0	0	0	0	0	0
ASIA + OTHER AFRICA	8	1	3	3	1	1	0	0	1	0	3	1	2	0	0	4	0	1	2	1
JAPAN	6	1	2	2	1	1	0	0	1	0	2	1	1	0	0	3	0	1	1	1
OTHER ASIA+AFR.	2	0	1	1	0	0	0	0	0	0	1	0	1	0	0	1	0	0	1	0
BLACK AFRICA	0	0	0	0	0	0	0	0	0	0	0	0	0	0	0	0	0	0	0	0
ARAB WORLD	0	0	0	0	0	0	0	0	0	0	0	0	0	0	0	0	0	0	0	0
INDIA	2	0	1	1	0	0	0	0	0	0	1	0	1	0	0	1	0	0	1	0
PHILIPPINES	0	0	0	0	0	0	0	0	0	0	0	0	0	0	0	0	0	0	0	0
OTHER E. ASIA	0	0	0	0	0	0	0	0	0	0	0	0	0	0	0	0	0	0	0	0
OTHER ASIA	0	0	0	0	0	0	0	0	0	0	0	0	0	0	0	0	0	0	0	0

CHAPTER 5- PATTERNS OF OWNERSHIP
SECTION 4- THE FLOW OF MANUFACTURING BY INDUSTRY OF SUBSIDIARY
TABLE 38- SUBSIDIARIES MANUFACTURING
SERVICE INDUSTRY MACHINES (SIC 358)
CLASSIFIED BY COUNTRY, PERIOD MANUFACTURE BEGAN, AND SYSTEM OWNERSHIP %

PERIOD AND OWNERSHIP PERCENTAGE
(WHL=95-100%, MAJ=50-94%, MIN=5-49%, UNK=UNKNOWN)

COUNTRY OR REGION	TOTAL					PRE 1968					PRE 1946					1946-1957					1958-1967				
	ALL	WHL	MAJ	MIN	UNK	ALL	WHL	MAJ	MIN	UNK	ALL	WHL	MAJ	MIN	UNK	ALL	WHL	MAJ	MIN	UNK	ALL	WHL	MAJ	MIN	UNK
OUTSIDE U.S.	51	28	7	8	7	7	5	0	2	0	2	0	0	0	2	4	2	1	1	0	39	21	6	8	4
OUT. U.S. + CANADA	41	19	7	7	7	5	3	2	0	0	2	0	0	0	2	3	1	1	0	1	32	15	6	7	4
OUT. WEST. HEMIS.	31	15	5	3	7	4	2	2	0	0	2	0	0	0	2	2	1	1	0	0	24	12	5	3	4
OUT. WHITE CWEALTH	29	12	6	5	6	2	1	1	0	0	1	0	0	0	1	2	1	0	1	0	25	11	4	6	4
OUT. DEVLPED WORLD	11	4	3	4	0	1	1	0	0	0	0	0	0	0	0	1	1	0	0	0	9	3	2	4	0
CANADA	10	9	0	1	0	1	0	0	0	1	0	0	0	0	0	1	1	0	0	0	7	6	0	1	0
LATIN AMERICA	10	4	2	4	0	2	1	0	1	0	0	0	0	0	0	1	1	0	0	0	8	3	1	4	0
C. AMER.+CARIB.	5	2	1	2	0	0	0	0	0	0	0	0	0	0	0	0	0	0	0	0	5	2	1	2	0
CUBA	0	0	0	0	0	0	0	0	0	0	0	0	0	0	0	0	0	0	0	0	0	0	0	0	0
MEXICO	2	1	0	1	0	0	0	0	0	0	0	0	0	0	0	0	0	0	0	0	2	1	0	1	0
OTHER	3	1	1	1	0	0	0	0	0	0	0	0	0	0	0	0	0	0	0	0	3	1	1	1	0
S. AMERICA	5	2	1	2	0	1	1	0	0	0	0	0	0	0	0	1	1	0	0	0	3	1	0	2	0
ARGENTINA	0	0	0	0	0	0	0	0	0	0	0	0	0	0	0	0	0	0	0	0	0	0	0	0	0
BRAZIL	2	1	0	1	0	1	1	0	0	0	0	0	0	0	0	1	1	0	0	0	0	0	0	0	0
PERU	0	0	0	0	0	0	0	0	0	0	0	0	0	0	0	0	0	0	0	0	0	0	0	0	0
COLOMBIA	0	0	0	0	0	0	0	0	0	0	0	0	0	0	0	0	0	0	0	0	0	0	0	0	0
VENEZUELA	2	1	0	1	0	0	0	0	0	0	0	0	0	0	0	0	0	0	0	0	2	1	0	1	0
OTHER	1	0	0	0	1	0	0	0	0	0	0	0	0	0	0	0	0	0	0	0	1	0	0	1	0
EUROPE	22	10	3	2	7	2	1	1	0	1	0	0	0	0	0	2	1	1	0	0	17	9	3	1	4
EFTA	8	5	1	1	1	1	1	0	0	0	0	0	0	0	0	1	1	0	0	0	5	4	1	0	0
U.K.	5	2	2	0	1	1	0	1	0	1	0	0	0	0	0	1	1	0	0	0	2	1	1	0	0
SCANDINAVIA	1	1	0	0	0	0	0	0	0	0	0	0	0	0	0	0	0	0	0	0	1	1	0	0	0
SWITZERLAND	1	1	0	0	0	0	0	0	0	0	0	0	0	0	0	0	0	0	0	0	1	1	0	0	0
OTHER EFTA	1	1	0	0	0	0	0	0	0	0	0	0	0	0	0	0	0	0	0	0	1	1	0	0	0
EUROP. COMMUNITY	14	5	2	1	6	1	0	1	0	1	0	0	0	0	0	1	0	1	0	0	12	5	2	1	4
FRANCE	6	2	1	0	3	1	1	0	0	0	0	0	0	0	0	0	0	0	0	0	5	2	1	0	2
GERMANY	4	2	0	1	1	0	0	0	0	0	0	0	0	0	0	1	0	0	1	0	3	2	0	1	0
ITALY	1	1	0	0	0	0	0	0	0	0	0	0	0	0	0	0	0	0	0	0	1	1	0	0	0
BELGIUM + LUX	1	0	0	0	1	0	0	0	0	0	0	0	0	0	0	0	0	0	0	0	1	0	0	0	1
NETHERLANDS	2	0	1	0	1	0	0	0	0	0	0	0	0	0	0	0	0	0	0	0	2	0	1	0	1
SPAIN	0	0	0	0	0	0	0	0	0	0	0	0	0	0	0	0	0	0	0	0	0	0	0	0	0
GREECE + TURKEY	0	0	0	0	0	0	0	0	0	0	0	0	0	0	0	0	0	0	0	0	0	0	0	0	0
OTHER EUROPE	0	0	0	0	0	0	0	0	0	0	0	0	0	0	0	0	0	0	0	0	0	0	0	0	0
EUROPE EX. U.K.	17	8	2	1	6	1	1	0	0	1	0	0	0	0	0	1	0	1	0	0	15	8	2	1	4
SOUTHERN DOMINIONS	7	5	1	1	0	1	0	1	0	0	0	0	0	0	0	1	1	0	0	0	5	3	1	1	0
S. AFRICA +RHOD.	0	0	0	0	0	0	0	0	0	0	0	0	0	0	0	0	0	0	0	0	0	0	0	0	0
AUSTRALIA + N.Z.	7	5	1	1	0	1	0	1	0	0	0	0	0	0	0	1	1	0	0	0	5	3	1	1	0
ASIA + OTHER AFRICA	2	2	0	0	0	0	0	0	0	0	0	0	0	0	0	0	0	0	0	0	2	2	0	0	0
JAPAN	1	1	0	0	0	0	0	0	0	0	0	0	0	0	0	0	0	0	0	0	1	1	0	0	0
OTHER ASIA+AFR.	1	1	0	0	0	0	0	0	0	0	0	0	0	0	0	0	0	0	0	0	1	1	0	0	0
BLACK AFRICA	0	0	0	0	0	0	0	0	0	0	0	0	0	0	0	0	0	0	0	0	0	0	0	0	0
ARAB WORLD	0	0	0	0	0	0	0	0	0	0	0	0	0	0	0	0	0	0	0	0	0	0	0	0	0
INDIA	1	1	0	0	0	0	0	0	0	0	0	0	0	0	0	0	0	0	0	0	1	1	0	0	0
PHILIPPINES	0	0	0	0	0	0	0	0	0	0	0	0	0	0	0	0	0	0	0	0	0	0	0	0	0
OTHER E. ASIA	0	0	0	0	0	0	0	0	0	0	0	0	0	0	0	0	0	0	0	0	0	0	0	0	0
OTHER ASIA	0	0	0	0	0	0	0	0	0	0	0	0	0	0	0	0	0	0	0	0	0	0	0	0	0

CHAPTER 5- PATTERNS OF OWNERSHIP
SECTION 4- THE FLOW OF MANUFACTURING BY INDUSTRY OF SUBSIDIARY
TABLE 39- SUBSIDIARIES MANUFACTURING
OTHER NON-ELECTRICAL MACHINERY (SIC 351 AND 359)
CLASSIFIED BY COUNTRY, PERIOD MANUFACTURE BEGAN, AND SYSTEM OWNERSHIP %

PERIOD AND OWNERSHIP PERCENTAGE
(WHL=95-100%, MAJ=50-94%, MIN=5-49%, UNK=UNKNOWN)

COUNTRY OR REGION	TOTAL PRE 1968					PRE 1946					1946-1957					1958-1967				
	ALL	WHL	MAJ	MIN	UNK	ALL	WHL	MAJ	MIN	UNK	ALL	WHL	MAJ	MIN	UNK	ALL	WHL	MAJ	MIN	UNK
OUTSIDE U.S.	56	32	13	4	4	11	8	2	1	0	7	5	2	0	0	35	19	9	3	4
OUT. U.S. + CANADA	46	23	13	4	3	9	6	2	1	0	5	3	2	0	0	29	14	9	3	3
OUT. WEST. HEMIS.	39	20	10	3	3	7	4	2	1	0	4	3	1	0	0	25	13	7	2	3
OUT. WHITE CWEALTH	32	16	10	3	2	7	4	2	1	0	3	2	1	0	0	21	10	7	2	2
OUT. DEVLPED WORLD	7	3	3	1	0	2	2	0	0	0	1	0	1	0	0	4	3	2	1	0
CANADA	10	9	0	0	1	2	2	0	0	0	2	2	0	0	0	6	5	0	1	0
LATIN AMERICA	7	3	3	0	0	2	2	0	0	0	1	0	1	0	0	4	1	2	0	1
C. AMER.+CARIB.	1	1	0	1	0	0	0	0	0	0	0	0	0	0	0	1	0	1	0	0
CUBA	0	0	0	0	0	0	0	0	0	0	0	0	0	0	0	0	0	0	0	0
MEXICO	1	0	0	0	0	0	0	0	0	0	0	0	0	0	0	1	0	1	0	0
OTHER	0	0	0	0	0	0	0	0	0	0	0	0	0	0	0	0	0	0	0	0
S. AMERICA	6	2	3	1	0	2	2	0	0	0	1	0	1	0	0	3	1	1	0	1
ARGENTINA	2	2	1	1	0	2	2	0	0	0	0	0	0	0	0	2	0	1	1	0
BRAZIL	4	2	2	0	0	0	0	0	0	0	1	0	1	0	0	1	1	0	0	0
PERU	0	0	0	0	0	0	0	0	0	0	0	0	0	0	0	0	0	0	0	0
COLOMBIA	0	0	0	0	0	0	0	0	0	0	0	0	0	0	0	0	0	0	0	0
VENEZUELA	0	0	0	0	0	0	0	0	0	0	0	0	0	0	0	0	0	0	0	0
OTHER	0	0	0	0	0	0	0	0	0	0	0	0	0	0	0	0	0	0	0	0
EUROPE	34	19	8	3	2	7	4	2	1	0	2	1	1	0	0	23	13	6	2	2
EFTA	10	6	2	1	1	2	2	0	0	0	1	1	0	0	0	6	3	2	1	0
U.K.	9	5	2	1	0	2	2	0	0	0	0	0	0	0	0	6	3	3	0	0
SCANDINAVIA	1	1	0	0	0	0	0	0	0	0	1	1	0	0	0	0	0	0	0	0
SWITZERLAND	0	0	0	0	0	0	0	0	0	0	0	0	0	0	0	0	0	0	0	0
OTHER EFTA	0	0	0	0	0	0	0	0	0	0	0	0	0	0	0	0	0	0	0	0
EUROP. COMMUNITY	21	12	5	1	2	5	2	2	1	0	1	0	1	0	0	14	9	3	0	2
FRANCE	10	3	3	1	2	1	0	1	0	0	0	0	0	0	0	8	3	3	0	2
GERMANY	8	7	1	0	0	3	2	1	0	0	1	0	1	0	0	4	4	0	0	0
ITALY	1	1	0	0	0	1	0	0	0	1	0	0	0	0	0	0	0	0	0	0
BELGIUM + LUX	2	2	0	0	0	0	0	0	0	0	0	0	0	0	0	2	2	0	0	0
NETHERLANDS	0	0	0	0	0	0	0	0	0	0	0	0	0	0	0	0	0	0	0	0
SPAIN	2	0	1	1	0	0	0	0	0	0	0	0	0	0	0	2	0	1	1	0
GREECE + TURKEY	0	0	0	0	0	0	0	0	0	0	0	0	0	0	0	0	0	0	0	0
OTHER EUROPE	1	1	0	0	0	0	0	0	0	0	0	0	0	0	0	1	0	0	0	1
EUROPE EX. U.K.	25	14	6	2	2	5	2	2	1	0	2	1	1	0	0	17	10	4	1	2
SOUTHERN DOMINIONS	4	1	1	0	1	1	0	0	1	0	2	1	1	0	0	1	0	0	0	1
S. AFRICA +RHOD.	0	0	0	0	0	0	0	0	0	0	0	0	0	0	0	0	0	0	0	0
AUSTRALIA + N.Z.	4	1	1	1	1	1	0	0	1	0	2	1	1	0	0	1	0	0	0	1
ASIA + OTHER AFRICA	1	0	1	0	0	0	0	0	0	0	0	0	0	0	0	1	0	1	0	0
JAPAN	1	0	1	0	0	0	0	0	0	0	0	0	0	0	0	1	0	1	0	0
OTHER ASIA+AFR.	0	0	0	0	0	0	0	0	0	0	0	0	0	0	0	0	0	0	0	0
BLACK AFRICA	0	0	0	0	0	0	0	0	0	0	0	0	0	0	0	0	0	0	0	0
ARAB WORLD	0	0	0	0	0	0	0	0	0	0	0	0	0	0	0	0	0	0	0	0
INDIA	0	0	0	0	0	0	0	0	0	0	0	0	0	0	0	0	0	0	0	0
PHILIPPINES	0	0	0	0	0	0	0	0	0	0	0	0	0	0	0	0	0	0	0	0
OTHER E. ASIA	0	0	0	0	0	0	0	0	0	0	0	0	0	0	0	0	0	0	0	0
OTHER ASIA	0	0	0	0	0	0	0	0	0	0	0	0	0	0	0	0	0	0	0	0

CHAPTER 5- PATTERNS OF OWNERSHIP
SECTION 4- THE FLOW OF MANUFACTURING BY INDUSTRY OF SUBSIDIARY
TABLE 40- SUBSIDIARIES MANUFACTURING
HOUSEHOLD APPLIANCES (SIC 363)
CLASSIFIED BY COUNTRY, PERIOD MANUFACTURE BEGAN, AND SYSTEM OWNERSHIP %

PERIOD AND OWNERSHIP PERCENTAGE
(WHL=95-100%, MAJ=50-94%, MIN=5-49%, UNK=UNKNOWN)

COUNTRY OR REGION	TOTAL PRE 1968					PRE 1946					1946-1957					1958-1967				
	ALL	WHL	MAJ	MIN	UNK	ALL	WHL	MAJ	MIN	UNK	ALL	WHL	MAJ	MIN	UNK	ALL	WHL	MAJ	MIN	UNK
OUTSIDE U.S.	96	69	15	6	5	17	11	3	0	3	18	15	1	0	1	61	43	11	6	1
OUT. U.S. + CANADA	85	59	15	6	4	12	7	3	0	2	17	14	1	0	1	56	38	11	6	1
OUT. WEST. HEMIS.	64	42	14	4	3	9	4	3	0	2	12	11	1	0	0	42	27	10	4	1
OUT. WHITE CWEALTH	64	46	10	5	2	6	5	0	0	1	12	10	1	0	1	45	31	9	5	0
OUT. DEVLPED WORLD	35	28	2	4	1	3	3	0	0	0	5	4	0	0	1	27	21	2	4	0
CANADA	11	10	0	0	1	5	4	0	0	1	1	1	0	0	0	5	5	0	0	0
LATIN AMERICA	21	17	1	2	1	3	3	0	0	0	4	3	0	0	1	14	11	1	2	0
C. AMER.+CARIB.	8	5	1	2	0	1	1	0	0	0	3	2	0	1	0	4	2	1	1	0
CUBA	0	0	0	0	0	0	0	0	0	0	0	0	0	0	0	0	0	0	0	0
MEXICO	7	5	0	1	1	1	1	0	0	0	3	2	0	0	1	3	2	0	0	1
OTHER	1	0	1	0	0	0	0	0	0	0	0	0	0	0	0	1	0	1	0	0
S. AMERICA	13	12	0	1	0	2	2	0	0	0	1	1	0	0	0	10	9	0	1	0
ARGENTINA	4	4	0	0	0	1	1	0	0	0	1	1	0	0	0	2	2	0	0	0
BRAZIL	2	2	0	0	0	1	1	0	0	0	0	0	0	0	0	1	1	0	0	0
PERU	1	1	0	0	0	0	0	0	0	0	0	0	0	0	0	1	1	0	0	0
COLOMBIA	2	2	0	0	0	0	0	0	0	0	0	0	0	0	0	2	2	0	0	0
VENEZUELA	2	1	0	1	0	0	0	0	0	0	0	0	0	0	0	2	1	0	1	0
OTHER	2	2	0	0	0	0	0	0	0	0	0	0	0	0	0	2	2	0	0	0
EUROPE	41	24	12	2	3	8	3	3	0	2	8	8	0	0	0	25	13	9	2	1
EFTA	15	7	5	1	2	5	1	3	0	1	3	3	0	0	0	7	3	2	1	1
U.K.	14	6	5	1	2	5	1	3	0	1	2	2	0	0	0	7	3	2	1	1
SCANDINAVIA	1	1	0	0	0	0	0	0	0	0	1	1	0	0	0	0	0	0	0	0
SWITZERLAND	0	0	0	0	0	0	0	0	0	0	0	0	0	0	0	0	0	0	0	0
OTHER EFTA	0	0	0	0	0	0	0	0	0	0	0	0	0	0	0	0	0	0	0	0
EUROP. COMMUNITY	23	15	7	1	1	2	1	0	0	1	5	5	0	0	0	16	9	7	0	0
FRANCE	8	7	1	0	0	1	1	0	0	0	1	1	0	0	0	6	5	1	0	0
GERMANY	8	4	4	0	0	1	1	0	0	0	0	0	0	0	0	7	3	4	0	0
ITALY	6	4	2	0	0	0	0	0	0	0	3	3	0	0	0	3	1	2	0	0
BELGIUM + LUX	1	0	0	1	0	0	0	0	0	0	1	0	0	1	0	0	0	0	0	0
NETHERLANDS	0	0	0	0	0	0	0	0	0	0	0	0	0	0	0	0	0	0	0	0
SPAIN	0	0	0	0	0	0	0	0	0	0	0	0	0	0	0	0	0	0	0	0
GREECE + TURKEY	2	1	0	1	0	0	0	0	0	0	0	0	0	0	0	2	1	0	1	0
OTHER EUROPE	1	1	0	0	0	0	0	0	0	0	0	0	0	0	0	1	1	0	0	0
EUROPE EX. U.K.	27	18	7	1	0	3	2	0	0	1	6	6	0	0	0	18	10	7	1	0
SOUTHERN DOMINIONS	7	7	0	0	0	1	1	0	0	0	2	2	0	0	0	4	4	0	0	0
S. AFRICA +RHOD.	2	2	0	0	0	0	0	0	0	0	0	0	0	0	0	2	2	0	0	0
AUSTRALIA + N.Z.	5	5	0	0	0	1	1	0	0	0	2	2	0	0	0	2	2	0	0	0
ASIA + OTHER AFRICA	16	11	2	2	0	0	0	0	0	0	3	1	1	1	0	13	10	1	2	0
JAPAN	2	0	1	1	0	0	0	0	0	0	2	0	1	1	0	0	0	0	0	0
OTHER ASIA+AFR.	14	11	1	2	0	0	0	0	0	0	1	1	0	0	0	13	10	1	2	0
BLACK AFRICA	3	3	0	0	0	0	0	0	0	0	0	0	0	0	0	3	3	0	0	0
ARAB WORLD	2	2	0	0	0	0	0	0	0	0	0	0	0	0	0	2	2	0	0	0
INDIA	0	0	0	0	0	0	0	0	0	0	0	0	0	0	0	0	0	0	0	0
PHILIPPINES	2	1	0	1	0	0	0	0	0	0	0	0	0	0	0	2	1	0	1	0
OTHER E. ASIA	2	2	0	0	0	0	0	0	0	0	1	1	0	0	0	1	1	0	0	0
OTHER ASIA	5	3	1	0	1	0	0	0	0	0	0	0	0	0	0	5	3	1	1	0

CHAPTER 5- PATTERNS OF OWNERSHIP
SECTION 4- THE FLOW OF MANUFACTURING BY INDUSTRY OF SUBSIDIARY
TABLE 41- SUBSIDIARIES MANUFACTURING
COMMUNICATION EQUIPMENT (SIC 366)
CLASSIFIED BY COUNTRY, PERIOD MANUFACTURE BEGAN, AND SYSTEM OWNERSHIP %

PERIOD AND OWNERSHIP PERCENTAGE
(WHL=95-100%, MAJ=50-94%, MIN=5-49%, UNK=UNKNOWN)

COUNTRY OR REGION	TOTAL PRE 1968					PRE 1946					1946-1957					1958-1967				
	ALL	WHL	MAJ	MIN	UNK	ALL	WHL	MAJ	MIN	UNK	ALL	WHL	MAJ	MIN	UNK	ALL	WHL	MAJ	MIN	UNK
OUTSIDE U.S.	56	35	10	5	6	22	13	4	3	2	12	9	3	0	0	22	13	3	2	4
OUT. U.S. + CANADA	47	28	9	5	5	21	12	4	3	2	6	4	2	0	0	20	12	3	2	3
OUT. WEST. HEMIS.	43	26	8	5	4	20	11	4	3	2	6	4	2	0	0	17	11	2	2	2
OUT. WHITE CWEALTH	37	21	7	4	5	17	9	3	3	2	4	3	1	0	0	16	9	3	1	3
OUT. DEVLPED WORLD	7	4	1	0	2	1	1	0	0	0	0	0	0	0	0	6	3	1	0	2
CANADA	9	7	1	0	1	1	1	0	0	0	6	5	1	0	0	2	1	0	0	1
LATIN AMERICA	4	2	1	0	1	1	1	0	0	0	0	0	0	0	0	3	1	1	0	1
C. AMER.+CARIB.	3	1	1	1	0	1	1	0	0	0	0	0	0	0	0	3	0	1	1	0
CUBA	0	0	0	0	0	0	0	0	0	0	0	0	0	0	0	0	0	0	0	0
MEXICO	3	1	1	0	1	0	0	0	0	0	0	0	0	0	0	3	1	1	0	1
OTHER	0	0	0	0	0	0	0	0	0	0	0	0	0	0	0	0	0	0	0	0
S. AMERICA	1	1	0	0	0	1	1	0	0	0	0	0	0	0	0	0	0	0	0	0
ARGENTINA	1	1	0	0	0	1	1	0	0	0	0	0	0	0	0	0	0	0	0	0
BRAZIL	0	0	0	0	0	0	0	0	0	0	0	0	0	0	0	0	0	0	0	0
PERU	0	0	0	0	0	0	0	0	0	0	0	0	0	0	0	0	0	0	0	0
COLOMBIA	0	0	0	0	0	0	0	0	0	0	0	0	0	0	0	0	0	0	0	0
VENEZUELA	0	0	0	0	0	0	0	0	0	0	0	0	0	0	0	0	0	0	0	0
OTHER	0	0	0	0	0	0	0	0	0	0	0	0	0	0	0	0	0	0	0	0
EUROPE	34	21	6	4	3	18	10	3	3	2	4	3	1	0	0	12	8	2	1	1
EFTA	14	8	2	2	2	8	5	1	1	1	0	0	0	0	0	6	3	1	1	1
U.K.	5	4	0	1	0	2	2	0	1	0	0	0	0	0	0	3	2	1	0	0
SCANDINAVIA	5	4	0	1	1	2	2	0	0	0	0	0	0	0	0	3	2	0	1	0
SWITZERLAND	0	2	0	0	0	3	2	0	1	0	0	0	0	0	0	2	0	0	0	1
OTHER EFTA	4	2	1	0	1	3	1	1	0	1	2	2	0	0	0	0	0	0	0	0
EUROP. COMMUNITY	15	12	1	1	1	8	5	1	1	1	0	0	0	0	0	5	5	0	0	0
FRANCE	5	4	1	0	1	4	2	1	1	0	0	0	0	0	0	2	0	0	0	0
GERMANY	5	3	0	1	1	3	2	0	0	1	1	1	0	0	0	2	2	0	0	0
ITALY	3	2	1	0	0	0	0	0	0	0	1	1	0	0	0	1	2	0	0	0
BELGIUM + LUX	2	2	0	0	0	0	0	0	0	0	0	0	0	0	0	0	0	0	0	0
NETHERLANDS	1	1	0	0	0	1	1	0	0	0	1	1	0	0	0	0	0	0	0	0
SPAIN	3	0	3	0	0	0	0	0	0	0	1	0	1	0	0	1	0	1	0	0
GREECE + TURKEY	1	1	0	0	0	0	0	0	0	0	0	0	0	0	0	0	0	0	0	0
OTHER EUROPE	1	0	0	1	1	1	0	0	1	2	1	0	0	1	1	0	0	0	0	1
EUROPE EX. U.K.	29	17	6	3	3	16	8	3	3	2	4	3	1	0	0	9	6	2	1	1
SOUTHERN DOMINIONS	5	3	2	0	0	2	1	0	1	0	2	1	1	0	0	1	1	0	0	0
S. AFRICA +RHOD.	2	2	0	0	0	2	1	1	0	0	1	1	0	0	0	1	1	0	0	0
AUSTRALIA + N.Z.	3	1	2	0	0	2	0	1	1	1	1	0	1	0	0	0	0	0	0	1
ASIA + OTHER AFRICA	4	2	0	1	1	0	0	0	0	0	0	0	0	0	0	4	2	2	1	0
JAPAN	1	0	0	1	0	0	0	0	0	0	0	0	0	0	0	1	0	0	1	1
OTHER ASIA+AFR.	3	2	0	0	1	0	0	0	0	0	0	0	0	0	0	3	2	2	0	0
BLACK AFRICA	0	0	0	0	0	0	0	0	0	0	0	0	0	0	0	0	0	0	0	0
ARAB WORLD	0	0	0	0	0	0	0	0	0	0	0	0	0	0	0	0	0	0	0	0
INDIA	0	0	0	0	0	0	0	0	0	0	0	0	0	0	0	0	0	0	0	0
PHILIPPINES	2	2	0	0	0	0	0	0	0	0	0	0	0	0	0	2	2	0	0	0
OTHER E. ASIA	1	0	0	0	1	0	0	0	0	0	0	0	0	0	0	1	0	0	0	1
OTHER ASIA	0	0	0	0	0	0	0	0	0	0	0	0	0	0	0	0	0	0	0	0

CHAPTER 5- PATTERNS OF OWNERSHIP
SECTION 4- THE FLOW OF MANUFACTURING BY INDUSTRY OF SUBSIDIARY
TABLE 42- SUBSIDIARIES MANUFACTURING
OTHER ELECTRONIC EQUIPMENT (SIC 365 AND 367)
CLASSIFIED BY COUNTRY, PERIOD MANUFACTURE BEGAN, AND SYSTEM OWNERSHIP %

PERIOD AND OWNERSHIP PERCENTAGE
(WHL=95-100%, MAJ=50-94%, MIN=5-49%, UNK=UNKNOWN)

COUNTRY OR REGION	TOTAL PRE 1968					PRE 1946					1946-1957					1958-1967				
	ALL	WHL	MAJ	MIN	UNK	ALL	WHL	MAJ	MIN	UNK	ALL	WHL	MAJ	MIN	UNK	ALL	WHL	MAJ	MIN	UNK
OUTSIDE U.S.	81	47	15	13	5	9	8	0	1	0	13	5	4	4	0	58	34	11	8	5
OUT. U.S. + CANADA	72	40	14	12	5	8	7	0	1	0	10	3	4	3	0	53	30	10	8	5
OUT. WEST. HEMIS.	51	26	11	10	3	5	4	0	1	0	9	3	3	3	0	36	19	8	6	3
OUT. WHITE CWEALTH	57	31	13	9	3	4	4	0	0	0	6	1	4	1	0	46	26	9	8	3
OUT. DEVLPED WORLD	27	18	4	3	2	4	4	0	0	0	1	0	1	0	0	22	14	3	3	2
CANADA	9	7	1	1	0	1	1	0	0	0	3	2	0	1	0	5	4	1	0	0
LATIN AMERICA	21	14	3	2	2	3	3	0	0	0	1	0	1	0	0	17	11	2	2	2
C. AMER.+CARIB.	9	6	2	0	1	1	1	0	0	0	0	0	0	0	0	8	5	2	0	1
CUBA	0	0	0	0	0	0	0	0	0	0	0	0	0	0	0	0	0	0	0	0
MEXICO	7	4	2	0	1	1	1	0	0	0	0	0	0	0	0	6	3	2	0	1
OTHER	2	2	0	0	0	0	0	0	0	0	0	0	0	0	0	2	2	0	0	0
S. AMERICA	12	8	1	2	1	2	2	0	0	0	1	0	1	0	0	9	6	0	2	1
ARGENTINA	3	1	1	1	0	0	0	0	0	0	1	0	1	0	0	2	1	0	1	0
BRAZIL	5	4	0	1	0	1	1	0	0	0	0	0	0	0	0	4	3	0	1	0
PERU	0	0	0	0	0	0	0	0	0	0	0	0	0	0	0	0	0	0	0	0
COLOMBIA	0	0	0	0	0	0	0	0	0	0	0	0	0	0	0	0	0	0	0	0
VENEZUELA	2	1	0	0	1	0	0	0	0	0	0	0	0	0	0	2	1	0	0	1
OTHER	2	2	0	0	0	1	1	0	0	0	0	0	0	0	0	1	1	0	0	0
EUROPE	36	21	10	3	2	4	3	0	1	0	5	2	3	0	0	27	16	7	2	2
EFTA	13	10	1	1	1	4	3	0	1	0	1	1	0	0	0	8	6	1	0	1
U.K.	11	8	1	1	1	4	3	0	1	0	1	1	0	0	0	6	4	1	0	1
SCANDINAVIA	0	0	0	0	0	0	0	0	0	0	0	0	0	0	0	0	0	0	0	0
SWITZERLAND	2	2	0	0	0	0	0	0	0	0	0	0	0	0	0	2	2	0	0	0
OTHER EFTA	0	0	0	0	0	0	0	0	0	0	0	0	0	0	0	0	0	0	0	0
EUROP. COMMUNITY	20	11	6	2	1	0	0	0	0	0	2	1	1	0	0	18	10	5	2	1
FRANCE	4	3	1	0	0	0	0	0	0	0	0	0	0	0	0	4	3	1	0	0
GERMANY	9	5	2	2	0	0	0	0	0	0	1	0	1	0	0	8	5	1	2	0
ITALY	6	2	3	0	1	0	0	0	0	0	1	0	1	0	0	5	2	2	0	1
BELGIUM + LUX	1	1	0	0	0	0	0	0	0	0	0	0	0	0	0	1	1	0	0	0
NETHERLANDS	0	0	0	0	0	0	0	0	0	0	0	0	0	0	0	0	0	0	0	0
SPAIN	2	0	2	0	0	0	0	0	0	0	1	0	1	0	0	1	0	1	0	0
GREECE + TURKEY	1	0	1	0	0	0	0	0	0	0	1	0	1	0	0	0	0	0	0	0
OTHER EUROPE	0	0	0	0	0	0	0	0	0	0	0	0	0	0	0	0	0	0	0	0
EUROPE Ex. U.K.	25	13	9	2	1	0	0	0	0	0	4	1	3	0	0	21	12	6	2	1
SOUTHERN DOMINIONS	4	1	0	2	1	0	0	0	0	0	3	0	0	2	1	1	1	0	0	0
S. AFRICA +RHOD.	0	0	0	0	0	0	0	0	0	0	0	0	0	0	0	0	0	0	0	0
AUSTRALIA + N.Z.	4	1	0	2	1	0	0	0	0	0	3	0	0	2	1	1	1	0	0	0
ASIA + OTHER AFRICA	11	4	1	5	1	1	1	0	0	0	2	1	0	1	0	8	2	1	4	1
JAPAN	5	0	0	4	1	0	0	0	0	0	0	0	0	0	0	5	0	0	4	1
OTHER ASIA+AFR.	6	4	1	1	0	1	1	0	0	0	2	1	0	1	0	3	2	1	0	0
BLACK AFRICA	1	1	0	0	0	0	0	0	0	0	1	1	0	0	0	0	0	0	0	0
ARAB WORLD	0	0	0	0	0	0	0	0	0	0	0	0	0	0	0	0	0	0	0	0
INDIA	1	0	0	1	0	0	0	0	0	0	1	0	0	1	0	0	0	0	0	0
PHILIPPINES	1	1	0	0	0	1	1	0	0	0	0	0	0	0	0	0	0	0	0	0
OTHER E. ASIA	3	2	1	0	0	0	0	0	0	0	0	0	0	0	0	3	2	1	0	0
OTHER ASIA	0	0	0	0	0	0	0	0	0	0	0	0	0	0	0	0	0	0	0	0

CHAPTER 5- PATTERNS OF OWNERSHIP
SECTION 4- THE FLOW OF MANUFACTURING BY INDUSTRY OF SUBSIDIARY
TABLE 43- SUBSIDIARIES MANUFACTURING
OTHER ELECTRICAL MACHINERY (OTHER SIC 36)
CLASSIFIED BY COUNTRY, PERIOD MANUFACTURE BEGAN, AND SYSTEM OWNERSHIP %

PERIOD AND OWNERSHIP PERCENTAGE
(WHL=95-100%, MAJ=50-94%, MIN=5-49%, UNK=UNKNOWN)

COUNTRY OR REGION	TOTAL PRE 1968					PRE 1946					1946-1957					1958-1967				
	ALL	WHL	MAJ	MIN	UNK	ALL	WHL	MAJ	MIN	UNK	ALL	WHL	MAJ	MIN	UNK	ALL	WHL	MAJ	MIN	UNK
OUTSIDE U.S.	220	128	39	18	30	48	32	8	2	6	47	30	9	3	5	120	66	22	13	19
OUT. U.S. + CANADA	176	89	36	18	29	36	20	7	2	6	33	17	8	3	5	103	52	20	13	18
OUT. WEST. HEMIS.	119	56	29	14	16	30	17	7	2	4	16	8	5	2	1	69	31	17	10	11
OUT. WHITE CWEALTH	139	68	27	15	25	22	12	3	1	6	29	13	8	3	5	84	43	16	11	14
OUT. DEVLPED WORLD	80	42	12	6	19	8	4	1	0	3	22	13	4	1	4	49	25	7	5	12
CANADA	44	39	3	0	1	12	12	0	0	0	14	13	1	0	0	17	14	2	0	1
LATIN AMERICA	57	33	7	4	13	6	3	1	0	2	17	9	3	1	4	34	21	3	3	7
C. AMER.+CARIB.	27	15	4	1	7	1	1	0	0	0	8	5	2	0	1	18	9	2	1	6
CUBA	2	1	0	0	1	0	0	0	0	0	0	0	0	0	0	2	1	0	0	1
MEXICO	18	10	3	1	4	1	1	0	0	0	6	3	2	0	1	11	6	1	1	3
OTHER	7	4	1	0	2	0	0	0	0	0	2	2	0	0	0	5	2	1	0	2
S. AMERICA	30	18	3	3	6	5	2	1	0	2	9	4	1	1	3	16	12	1	2	1
ARGENTINA	7	4	1	1	1	2	1	0	0	1	1	1	0	0	0	5	2	1	1	0
BRAZIL	13	10	1	2	0	3	1	1	1	0	4	3	0	1	0	6	6	0	0	0
PERU	1	1	0	0	0	0	0	0	0	0	0	0	0	0	0	1	1	0	0	0
COLOMBIA	3	1	1	0	1	0	0	0	0	0	2	1	0	0	1	1	0	1	0	0
VENEZUELA	5	2	1	0	2	0	0	0	0	0	2	1	1	0	0	3	1	0	0	2
OTHER	1	0	0	0	1	1	0	0	0	1	0	0	0	0	0	0	0	0	0	0
EUROPE	75	37	20	9	7	22	11	6	2	3	7	2	2	2	1	44	24	12	5	3
EFTA	30	17	9	3	1	12	6	5	1	0	2	2	0	0	0	16	9	4	2	1
U.K.	24	13	8	2	1	10	4	5	1	0	2	2	0	0	0	12	7	3	1	1
SCANDINAVIA	2	1	1	0	0	1	1	0	0	0	0	0	0	0	0	2	0	1	0	0
SWITZERLAND	2	1	0	1	0	0	0	0	0	0	0	0	0	0	0	1	1	0	1	0
OTHER EFTA	2	2	0	0	0	1	1	0	0	0	0	0	0	0	0	1	1	0	0	0
EUROP. COMMUNITY	37	17	9	5	4	9	5	1	1	2	4	0	1	2	1	22	12	7	2	1
FRANCE	14	7	2	2	2	5	3	1	1	0	2	0	0	1	1	6	4	2	0	2
GERMANY	8	5	3	2	2	2	2	0	0	0	1	0	0	1	0	7	5	2	0	0
ITALY	14	4	4	3	2	0	0	0	0	0	1	0	0	1	0	8	2	3	3	0
BELGIUM + LUX	0	0	0	0	0	0	0	0	0	0	0	0	0	0	0	0	0	0	0	0
NETHERLANDS	1	1	0	0	0	0	0	0	0	0	1	1	0	0	0	1	1	0	0	0
SPAIN	3	1	1	0	1	0	0	0	0	0	0	0	0	0	0	3	1	1	1	1
GREECE + TURKEY	2	1	1	0	0	0	0	0	0	0	0	0	0	0	0	2	1	1	0	0
OTHER EUROPE	2	0	0	0	1	1	1	0	0	0	1	0	0	0	1	1	0	0	0	0
EUROPE EX. U.K.	51	24	12	7	6	12	7	1	1	3	5	2	2	1	1	32	17	9	2	2
SOUTHERN DOMINIONS	13	8	1	1	3	4	4	0	0	0	2	2	0	0	0	7	2	1	1	3
S. AFRICA +RHOD.	2	2	0	0	0	0	0	0	0	0	2	2	0	0	0	0	0	0	0	0
AUSTRALIA + N.Z.	11	6	1	1	3	4	4	0	0	0	0	0	0	0	0	7	2	1	1	3
ASIA + OTHER AFRICA	31	11	8	4	6	4	2	0	1	1	7	4	3	0	0	18	5	4	2	5
JAPAN	8	2	3	2	6	2	1	0	0	1	2	1	1	0	0	3	1	0	2	0
OTHER ASIA+AFR.	23	9	5	2	6	2	1	0	0	1	5	3	2	0	0	15	4	2	0	5
BLACK AFRICA	2	2	0	0	0	0	0	0	0	0	0	0	0	0	0	2	2	0	0	0
ARAB WORLD	0	0	0	0	0	0	0	0	0	0	0	0	0	0	0	0	0	0	0	0
INDIA	6	1	2	1	2	1	1	0	0	0	0	0	0	0	0	5	2	2	0	1
PHILIPPINES	1	1	0	0	0	0	0	0	0	0	2	2	0	0	0	1	0	0	0	0
OTHER E. ASIA	5	4	0	0	0	1	1	0	0	0	0	0	0	0	0	2	2	1	0	0
OTHER ASIA	7	1	1	0	4	0	0	0	0	0	1	0	0	1	0	5	0	0	0	4

CHAPTER 5- PATTERNS OF OWNERSHIP
SECTION 4- THE FLOW OF MANUFACTURING BY INDUSTRY OF SUBSIDIARY
TABLE 44-- SUBSIDIARIES MANUFACTURING
MOTOR VEHICLES AND MOTOR VEHICLES EQUIPMENT (SIC 371)
CLASSIFIED BY COUNTRY, PERIOD MANUFACTURE BEGAN, AND SYSTEM OWNERSHIP %

PERIOD AND OWNERSHIP PERCENTAGE
(WHL=95-100%, MAJ=50-94%, MIN=5-49%, UNK=UNKNOWN)

COUNTRY OR REGION	TOTAL PRE 1968 ALL	WHL	MAJ	MIN	UNK	PRE 1946 ALL	WHL	MAJ	MIN	UNK	1946-1957 ALL	WHL	MAJ	MIN	UNK	1958-1967 ALL	WHL	MAJ	MIN	UNK
OUTSIDE U.S.	306	149	68	62	15	62	47	5	5	5	37	16	9	10	2	195	86	54	47	8
OUT. U.S. + CANADA	258	114	64	57	12	41	31	3	2	5	33	12	9	10	2	173	71	52	45	5
OUT. WEST. HEMIS.	173	81	39	34	9	36	26	3	2	5	22	6	8	6	2	105	49	28	26	2
OUT. WHITE CWEALTH	181	74	47	49	9	24	18	2	1	3	21	9	3	8	1	134	47	42	40	5
OUT. DEVLPED WORLD	101	41	29	26	4	8	8	0	0	0	15	8	1	5	1	77	25	28	21	3
CANADA	48	35	4	5	3	21	16	2	3	0	4	4	0	0	0	22	15	2	2	3
LATIN AMERICA	85	33	25	23	2	5	5	0	0	0	11	6	1	4	0	68	22	24	19	3
C. AMER.+CARIB.	25	7	7	9	2	1	1	0	0	0	2	2	0	0	0	22	3	7	9	2
CUBA	0	0	0	0	0	0	0	0	0	0	0	0	0	0	0	0	0	0	0	0
MEXICO	23	6	7	8	2	1	1	0	0	0	2	2	0	0	0	20	3	7	8	2
OTHER	2	1	0	1	0	0	0	0	0	0	0	0	0	0	0	2	1	0	1	0
S. AMERICA	60	26	18	14	1	4	4	0	0	0	9	4	1	4	0	46	18	17	10	1
ARGENTINA	24	8	8	7	1	2	2	0	0	0	3	0	0	3	0	19	6	8	4	1
BRAZIL	20	11	5	4	0	2	2	0	0	0	5	3	1	1	0	13	6	4	3	0
PERU	2	2	0	0	0	0	0	0	0	0	0	0	0	0	0	2	2	0	0	0
COLOMBIA	5	1	2	2	0	0	0	0	0	0	0	0	0	0	0	5	1	2	2	0
VENEZUELA	7	3	2	2	0	0	0	0	0	0	1	0	0	1	0	6	3	2	1	0
OTHER	2	1	1	0	0	0	0	0	0	0	1	0	1	0	0	1	1	0	0	0
EUROPE	122	57	22	27	7	26	16	3	2	5	12	4	3	4	1	75	37	16	21	1
EFTA	52	28	7	7	3	10	6	1	1	2	7	3	2	1	1	28	19	4	5	0
U.K.	44	23	5	6	3	9	5	1	1	2	5	2	1	1	1	23	16	3	4	0
SCANDINAVIA	6	3	2	1	0	1	1	0	0	0	2	1	1	0	0	3	1	1	1	0
SWITZERLAND	1	1	0	0	0	0	0	0	0	0	0	0	0	0	0	1	1	0	0	0
OTHER EFTA	1	1	0	0	0	0	0	0	0	0	0	0	0	0	0	1	1	0	0	0
EUROP. COMMUNITY	54	23	14	13	3	12	7	2	1	2	3	1	1	1	0	38	16	11	10	1
FRANCE	29	14	6	8	1	5	4	1	0	0	3	0	0	2	1	21	10	5	6	0
GERMANY	11	2	5	3	1	2	1	1	0	0	1	0	1	0	0	8	2	3	3	0
ITALY	8	3	3	1	1	2	1	0	1	0	0	0	0	0	0	6	2	3	0	1
BELGIUM + LUX	3	2	0	0	1	1	1	0	0	0	0	0	0	0	0	2	1	0	0	1
NETHERLANDS	3	2	0	1	0	1	1	0	0	0	0	0	0	0	0	2	1	0	1	0
SPAIN	8	1	1	6	0	0	0	0	0	0	1	0	0	1	0	7	1	1	5	0
GREECE + TURKEY	3	1	1	0	1	1	0	0	0	1	0	0	0	0	0	2	1	1	0	0
OTHER EUROPE	5	4	0	0	0	3	3	0	0	0	0	0	0	0	0	2	1	0	0	0
EUROPE EX. U.K.	78	34	17	21	4	17	11	2	1	3	7	2	2	2	1	52	21	13	17	1
SOUTHERN DOMINIONS	30	15	12	2	0	7	7	0	0	0	6	0	5	1	0	16	8	7	1	0
S. AFRICA +RHOD.	12	6	4	1	0	2	2	0	0	0	1	0	0	1	0	9	4	4	1	0
AUSTRALIA + N.Z.	18	9	8	1	0	5	5	0	0	0	5	0	5	0	0	7	4	3	0	0
ASIA + OTHER AFRICA	21	9	5	5	2	3	3	0	0	0	2	1	0	0	1	14	5	4	4	1
JAPAN	5	1	1	2	1	0	0	0	0	0	0	0	0	0	0	5	1	1	2	1
OTHER ASIA+AFR.	16	8	4	3	1	3	3	0	0	0	4	2	0	2	0	9	3	4	2	0
BLACK AFRICA	2	2	0	0	0	0	0	0	0	0	0	0	0	0	0	2	1	1	0	0
ARAB WORLD	2	2	0	0	0	0	0	0	0	0	0	0	0	0	0	2	2	0	0	0
INDIA	7	2	3	2	0	2	2	0	0	0	0	0	0	0	0	5	0	3	2	0
PHILIPPINES	2	2	0	0	0	0	0	0	0	0	1	1	0	0	0	1	1	0	0	0
OTHER E. ASIA	0	0	0	0	0	0	0	0	0	0	0	0	0	0	0	0	0	0	0	0
OTHER ASIA	3	1	0	0	1	1	1	0	0	0	2	0	0	0	0	0	0	0	0	1

CHAPTER 5- PATTERNS OF OWNERSHIP
SECTION 4- THE FLOW OF MANUFACTURING BY INDUSTRY OF SUBSIDIARY
TABLE 45- SUBSIDIARIES MANUFACTURING
OTHER TRANSPORTATION EQUIPMENT (SIC 372-379)
CLASSIFIED BY COUNTRY, PERIOD MANUFACTURE BEGAN, AND SYSTEM OWNERSHIP %

PERIOD AND OWNERSHIP PERCENTAGE
(WHL=95-100%, MAJ=50-94%, MIN=5-49%, UNK=UNKNOWN)

COUNTRY OR REGION	TOTAL PRE 1968					PRE 1946					1946-1957					1958-1967				
	ALL	WHL	MAJ	MIN	UNK	ALL	WHL	MAJ	MIN	UNK	ALL	WHL	MAJ	MIN	UNK	ALL	WHL	MAJ	MIN	UNK
OUTSIDE U.S.	31	11	9	7	2	7	0	4	1	1	7	5	1	1	0	15	5	4	5	1
OUT. U.S. + CANADA	22	6	8	6	1	6	0	4	1	1	3	3	0	0	0	12	3	4	5	0
OUT. WEST. HEMIS.	19	5	8	4	1	6	0	4	1	1	2	2	0	0	0	10	3	4	3	0
OUT. WHITE CWEALTH	16	4	6	5	1	5	0	3	1	1	2	2	0	0	0	9	2	3	4	0
OUT. DEVLPED WORLD	3	1	0	2	0	0	0	0	0	0	1	1	0	0	0	2	0	0	2	0
CANADA	9	5	1	1	1	1	0	1	0	0	4	2	1	1	0	3	2	0	0	1
LATIN AMERICA	3	1	0	2	0	0	0	0	0	0	1	0	0	1	0	2	0	0	2	0
C. AMER.+CARIB.	2	0	0	2	0	0	0	0	0	0	0	0	0	0	0	2	0	0	2	0
CUBA	0	0	0	0	0	0	0	0	0	0	0	0	0	0	0	0	0	0	0	0
MEXICO	2	0	0	2	0	0	0	0	0	0	0	0	0	0	0	2	0	0	2	0
OTHER	0	0	0	0	0	0	0	0	0	0	0	0	0	0	0	0	0	0	0	0
S. AMERICA	1	1	0	0	0	0	0	0	0	0	1	1	0	0	0	0	0	0	0	0
ARGENTINA	0	0	0	0	0	0	0	0	0	0	0	0	0	0	0	0	0	0	0	0
BRAZIL	1	1	0	0	0	0	0	0	0	0	1	1	0	0	0	0	0	0	0	0
PERU	0	0	0	0	0	0	0	0	0	0	0	0	0	0	0	0	0	0	0	0
COLOMBIA	0	0	0	0	0	0	0	0	0	0	0	0	0	0	0	0	0	0	0	0
VENEZUELA	0	0	0	0	0	0	0	0	0	0	0	0	0	0	0	0	0	0	0	0
OTHER	0	0	0	0	0	0	0	0	0	0	0	0	0	0	0	0	0	0	0	0
EUROPE	16	3	8	3	1	6	0	4	1	1	1	1	0	0	0	8	2	4	2	0
EFTA	4	1	2	0	1	1	0	1	0	0	1	1	0	0	0	1	1	1	0	0
U.K.	3	0	2	0	0	1	0	0	0	0	0	0	0	0	0	1	0	1	0	0
SCANDINAVIA	0	0	0	0	0	0	0	0	0	0	0	0	0	0	0	0	0	0	0	0
SWITZERLAND	1	1	0	0	0	0	0	0	0	0	0	0	0	0	0	1	1	0	0	0
OTHER EFTA	1	1	0	0	0	0	0	0	0	0	0	0	0	0	0	0	0	0	0	0
EUROP. COMMUNITY	12	2	6	3	1	5	0	3	1	1	0	0	0	0	0	7	2	3	2	0
FRANCE	3	1	2	0	0	1	0	1	0	0	0	0	0	0	0	2	1	1	0	0
GERMANY	5	0	5	0	0	3	0	3	0	0	0	0	0	0	0	2	0	2	0	0
ITALY	4	1	1	1	1	3	0	0	1	1	0	1	0	0	0	1	0	0	1	0
BELGIUM + LUX	0	0	0	0	0	0	0	0	0	0	0	0	0	0	0	0	0	0	0	0
NETHERLANDS	0	0	0	0	0	0	0	0	0	0	0	0	0	0	0	0	0	0	0	0
SPAIN	0	0	0	0	0	0	0	0	0	0	0	0	0	0	0	0	0	0	0	0
GREECE + TURKEY	0	0	0	0	0	0	0	0	0	0	0	0	0	0	0	0	0	0	0	0
OTHER EUROPE	0	0	0	0	0	0	0	0	0	0	0	0	0	0	0	0	0	0	0	0
EUROPE EX. U.K.	13	3	6	3	1	5	0	4	1	1	1	1	0	0	0	7	2	2	2	0
SOUTHERN DOMINIONS	3	2	0	1	0	0	0	0	0	0	1	1	0	0	0	2	1	0	1	0
S. AFRICA +RHOD.	1	1	0	1	0	0	0	0	0	0	0	0	0	0	0	1	0	0	1	0
AUSTRALIA + N.Z.	2	2	0	0	0	0	0	0	0	0	1	1	0	0	0	1	1	0	0	0
ASIA + OTHER AFRICA	0	0	0	0	0	0	0	0	0	0	0	0	0	0	0	0	0	0	0	0
JAPAN	0	0	0	0	0	0	0	0	0	0	0	0	0	0	0	0	0	0	0	0
OTHER ASIA+AFR.	0	0	0	0	0	0	0	0	0	0	0	0	0	0	0	0	0	0	0	0
BLACK AFRICA	0	0	0	0	0	0	0	0	0	0	0	0	0	0	0	0	0	0	0	0
ARAB WORLD	0	0	0	0	0	0	0	0	0	0	0	0	0	0	0	0	0	0	0	0
INDIA	0	0	0	0	0	0	0	0	0	0	0	0	0	0	0	0	0	0	0	0
PHILIPPINES	0	0	0	0	0	0	0	0	0	0	0	0	0	0	0	0	0	0	0	0
OTHER E. ASIA	0	0	0	0	0	0	0	0	0	0	0	0	0	0	0	0	0	0	0	0
OTHER ASIA	0	0	0	0	0	0	0	0	0	0	0	0	0	0	0	0	0	0	0	0

CHAPTER 5- PATTERNS OF OWNERSHIP
SECTION 4- THE FLOW OF MANUFACTURING BY INDUSTRY OF SUBSIDIARY
TABLE 46- SUBSIDIARIES MANUFACTURING
MEDICAL INSTRUMENTS AND SUPPLIES (SIC 384)
CLASSIFIED BY COUNTRY, PERIOD MANUFACTURE BEGAN, AND SYSTEM OWNERSHIP %

PERIOD AND OWNERSHIP PERCENTAGE
(WHL=95-100%, MAJ=50-94%, MIN=5-49%, UNK=UNKNOWN)

COUNTRY OR REGION	TOTAL PRE 1968					PRE 1946					1946-1957					1958-1967				
	ALL	WHL	MAJ	MIN	UNK	ALL	WHL	MAJ	MIN	UNK	ALL	WHL	MAJ	MIN	UNK	ALL	WHL	MAJ	MIN	UNK
OUTSIDE U.S.	65	55	10	0	0	8	4	4	0	0	10	8	2	0	0	47	43	4	0	0
OUT. U.S. + CANADA	56	47	9	0	0	6	3	3	0	0	10	8	2	0	0	40	36	4	0	0
OUT. WEST. HEMIS.	43	38	5	0	0	3	2	1	0	0	7	7	0	0	0	33	29	4	0	0
OUT. WHITE CWEALTH	36	29	7	0	0	3	1	2	0	0	5	3	2	0	0	28	25	3	0	0
OUT. DEVLPED WORLD	15	10	5	0	0	3	1	2	0	0	3	1	2	0	0	9	8	1	0	0
CANADA	9	8	1	0	0	2	1	1	0	0	0	0	0	0	0	7	7	0	0	0
LATIN AMERICA	13	9	4	0	0	3	1	2	0	0	3	1	2	0	0	7	7	0	0	0
C. AMER.+CARIB.	3	2	1	0	0	1	1	0	0	0	1	0	1	0	0	1	0	1	0	0
CUBA	1	0	1	0	0	0	0	0	0	0	0	0	0	0	0	1	0	1	0	0
MEXICO	1	1	0	0	0	1	1	0	0	0	0	0	0	0	0	0	0	0	0	0
OTHER	1	1	0	0	0	0	0	0	0	0	1	1	0	0	0	0	0	0	0	0
S. AMERICA	10	7	3	0	0	2	0	2	0	0	2	1	1	0	0	6	5	1	0	0
ARGENTINA	2	0	2	0	0	1	0	1	0	0	1	0	1	0	0	0	0	0	0	0
BRAZIL	6	5	1	0	0	1	0	1	0	0	0	0	0	0	0	5	5	0	0	0
PERU	0	0	0	0	0	0	0	0	0	0	0	0	0	0	0	0	0	0	0	0
COLOMBIA	1	1	0	0	0	0	0	0	0	0	0	0	0	0	0	1	1	0	0	0
VENEZUELA	1	1	0	0	0	0	0	0	0	0	1	1	0	0	0	0	0	0	0	0
OTHER	0	0	0	0	0	0	0	0	0	0	0	0	0	0	0	0	0	0	0	0
EUROPE	36	33	3	0	0	1	1	0	0	0	7	7	0	0	0	28	25	3	0	0
EFTA	16	15	1	0	0	1	1	0	0	0	5	5	0	0	0	10	9	1	0	0
U.K.	14	13	1	0	0	1	1	0	0	0	4	4	0	0	0	9	8	1	0	0
SCANDINAVIA	1	1	0	0	0	0	0	0	0	0	1	1	0	0	0	0	0	0	0	0
SWITZERLAND	0	0	0	0	0	0	0	0	0	0	0	0	0	0	0	0	0	0	0	0
OTHER EFTA	1	1	0	0	0	0	0	0	0	0	0	0	0	0	0	1	1	0	0	0
EUROP. COMMUNITY	19	17	2	0	0	0	0	0	0	0	1	1	0	0	0	18	16	2	0	0
FRANCE	7	5	2	0	0	0	0	0	0	0	1	1	0	0	0	6	4	2	0	0
GERMANY	7	7	0	0	0	0	0	0	0	0	1	1	0	0	0	6	6	0	0	0
ITALY	4	3	1	0	0	0	0	0	0	0	0	0	0	0	0	4	3	1	0	0
BELGIUM + LUX	0	0	0	0	0	0	0	0	0	0	0	0	0	0	0	0	0	0	0	0
NETHERLANDS	2	2	0	0	0	0	0	0	0	0	0	0	0	0	0	2	2	0	0	0
SPAIN	0	0	0	0	0	0	0	0	0	0	0	0	0	0	0	0	0	0	0	0
GREECE + TURKEY	0	0	0	0	0	0	0	0	0	0	0	0	0	0	0	0	0	0	0	0
OTHER EUROPE	1	1	0	0	0	0	0	0	0	0	1	1	0	0	0	0	0	0	0	0
EUROPE EX. U.K.	22	20	2	0	0	0	0	0	0	0	3	3	0	0	0	19	17	2	0	0
SOUTHERN DOMINIONS	5	4	1	0	0	2	1	1	0	0	0	0	0	0	0	3	3	0	0	0
S. AFRICA +RHOD.	1	1	0	0	0	0	0	0	0	0	0	0	0	0	0	1	1	0	0	0
AUSTRALIA + N.Z.	4	3	1	0	0	2	1	1	0	0	0	0	0	0	0	2	2	0	0	0
ASIA + OTHER AFRICA	2	2	0	0	0	0	0	0	0	0	0	0	0	0	0	2	2	0	0	0
JAPAN	0	0	0	0	0	0	0	0	0	0	0	0	0	0	0	0	0	0	0	0
OTHER ASIA+AFR.	2	1	1	0	0	0	0	0	0	0	0	0	0	0	0	2	1	1	0	0
BLACK AFRICA	0	0	0	0	0	0	0	0	0	0	0	0	0	0	0	0	0	0	0	0
ARAB WORLD	0	0	0	0	0	0	0	0	0	0	0	0	0	0	0	0	0	0	0	0
INDIA	1	1	0	0	0	0	0	0	0	0	0	0	0	0	0	1	1	0	0	0
PHILIPPINES	0	0	0	0	0	0	0	0	0	0	0	0	0	0	0	0	0	0	0	0
OTHER E. ASIA	0	0	0	0	0	0	0	0	0	0	0	0	0	0	0	0	0	0	0	0
OTHER ASIA	1	0	1	0	0	0	0	0	0	0	0	0	0	0	0	1	1	0	0	0

CHAPTER 5- PATTERNS OF OWNERSHIP
SECTION 4- THE FLOW OF MANUFACTURING BY INDUSTRY OF SUBSIDIARY
TABLE 47- SUBSIDIARIES MANUFACTURING
OTHER INSTRUMENTS AND PRECISION GOODS (OTHER SIC 38)
CLASSIFIED BY COUNTRY, PERIOD MANUFACTURE BEGAN, AND SYSTEM OWNERSHIP %

PERIOD AND OWNERSHIP PERCENTAGE
(WHL=95-100%, MAJ=50-94%, MIN=5-49%, UNK=UNKNOWN)

COUNTRY OR REGION	TOTAL PRE 1968					PRE 1946					1946-1957					1958-1967				
	ALL	WHL	MAJ	MIN	UNK	ALL	WHL	MAJ	MIN	UNK	ALL	WHL	MAJ	MIN	UNK	ALL	WHL	MAJ	MIN	UNK
OUTSIDE U.S.	63	45	11	5	1	10	7	2	1	0	8	2	5	1	0	44	36	4	3	1
OUT. U.S. + CANADA	59	41	11	5	1	8	5	2	1	0	8	2	5	1	0	42	34	4	3	1
OUT. WEST. HEMIS.	46	33	6	5	1	8	5	2	1	0	5	2	2	1	0	32	26	2	3	1
OUT. WHITE CWEALTH	42	29	8	4	1	6	4	1	1	0	4	1	3	0	0	32	24	4	3	1
OUT. DEVLPED WORLD	14	9	5	0	0	0	0	0	0	0	3	0	3	0	0	11	9	2	0	0
CANADA	4	4	0	0	0	2	2	0	0	0	0	0	0	0	0	2	2	0	0	0
LATIN AMERICA	13	8	5	0	0	0	0	0	0	0	3	0	3	0	0	10	8	2	0	0
C. AMER.+CARIB.	4	3	1	0	0	0	0	0	0	0	1	0	1	0	0	3	3	0	0	0
CUBA	0	0	0	0	0	0	0	0	0	0	0	0	0	0	0	0	0	0	0	0
MEXICO	3	2	1	0	0	0	0	0	0	0	1	0	1	0	0	2	1	1	0	0
OTHER	1	1	0	0	0	0	0	0	0	0	0	0	0	0	0	1	1	0	0	0
S. AMERICA	9	5	4	0	0	0	0	0	0	0	2	0	2	0	0	7	5	2	0	0
ARGENTINA	4	1	3	0	0	0	0	0	0	0	2	0	2	0	0	2	1	1	0	0
BRAZIL	2	1	1	0	0	0	0	0	0	0	0	0	0	0	0	2	1	1	0	0
PERU	1	1	0	0	0	0	0	0	0	0	0	0	0	0	0	1	1	0	0	0
COLOMBIA	1	1	0	0	0	0	0	0	0	0	0	0	0	0	0	1	1	0	0	0
VENEZUELA	0	0	0	0	0	0	0	0	0	0	0	0	0	0	0	0	0	0	0	0
OTHER	1	1	0	0	0	0	0	0	0	0	0	0	0	0	0	1	1	0	0	0
EUROPE	41	30	4	5	1	7	5	1	1	0	3	1	1	1	0	30	24	2	3	1
EFTA	14	10	2	1	0	1	1	0	0	0	2	0	1	1	0	10	9	1	0	0
U.K.	13	10	1	1	0	1	1	0	0	0	2	0	1	1	0	9	9	0	0	0
SCANDINAVIA	0	0	0	0	0	0	0	0	0	0	0	0	0	0	0	0	0	0	0	0
SWITZERLAND	0	0	0	0	0	0	0	0	0	0	0	0	0	0	0	0	0	0	0	0
OTHER EFTA	1	0	1	0	0	0	0	0	0	0	0	0	0	0	0	1	0	1	0	0
EUROP. COMMUNITY	26	19	2	4	1	6	4	1	1	0	1	1	0	0	0	19	14	1	3	1
FRANCE	7	2	2	3	0	3	1	1	1	0	0	0	0	0	0	4	1	1	2	0
GERMANY	13	11	2	0	0	3	3	0	0	0	1	1	0	0	0	9	7	2	0	0
ITALY	2	2	0	0	0	0	0	0	0	0	0	0	0	0	0	2	2	0	0	0
BELGIUM + LUX	3	3	0	0	0	0	0	0	0	0	0	0	0	0	0	3	3	0	0	0
NETHERLANDS	1	1	0	0	0	0	0	0	0	0	0	0	0	0	0	1	1	0	0	0
SPAIN	1	1	0	0	0	0	0	0	0	0	0	0	0	0	0	1	1	0	0	0
GREECE + TURKEY	0	0	0	0	0	0	0	0	0	0	0	0	0	0	0	0	0	0	0	0
OTHER EUROPE	0	0	0	0	0	0	0	0	0	0	0	0	0	0	0	0	0	0	0	0
EUROPE EX. U.K.	28	20	3	4	1	6	4	1	1	0	1	1	0	0	0	21	15	2	3	1
SOUTHERN DOMINIONS	4	2	2	0	0	1	1	0	0	0	1	0	1	0	0	2	1	1	0	0
S. AFRICA +RHOD.	1	1	0	0	0	0	0	0	0	0	0	0	0	0	0	1	1	0	0	0
AUSTRALIA + N.Z.	3	1	2	0	0	1	1	0	0	0	1	0	1	0	0	1	0	1	0	0
ASIA + OTHER AFRICA	1	1	0	0	0	0	0	0	0	0	1	1	0	0	0	0	0	0	0	0
JAPAN	0	0	0	0	0	0	0	0	0	0	0	0	0	0	0	0	0	0	0	0
OTHER ASIA+AFR.	1	1	0	0	0	0	0	0	0	0	1	1	0	0	0	0	0	0	0	0
BLACK AFRICA	0	0	0	0	0	0	0	0	0	0	0	0	0	0	0	0	0	0	0	0
ARAB WORLD	0	0	0	0	0	0	0	0	0	0	0	0	0	0	0	0	0	0	0	0
INDIA	1	1	0	0	0	0	0	0	0	0	1	1	0	0	0	0	0	0	0	0
PHILIPPINES	0	0	0	0	0	0	0	0	0	0	0	0	0	0	0	0	0	0	0	0
OTHER E. ASIA	0	0	0	0	0	0	0	0	0	0	0	0	0	0	0	0	0	0	0	0
OTHER ASIA	0	0	0	0	0	0	0	0	0	0	0	0	0	0	0	0	0	0	0	0

CHAPTER 5- PATTERNS OF OWNERSHIP
SECTION 4- THE FLOW OF MANUFACTURING BY INDUSTRY OF SUBSIDIARY
TABLE 48- SUBSIDIARIES MANUFACTURING
OTHER PRODUCTS (SIC 19,21,31, AND 39) OR UNKNOWN PRODUCT
CLASSIFIED BY COUNTRY, PERIOD MANUFACTURE BEGAN, AND SYSTEM OWNERSHIP %

PERIOD AND OWNERSHIP PERCENTAGE
(WHL=95-100%, MAJ=50-94%, MIN=5-49%, UNK=UNKNOWN)

COUNTRY OR REGION	TOTAL PRE 1968 ALL	WHL	MAJ	MIN	UNK	PRE 1946 ALL	WHL	MAJ	MIN	UNK	1946-1957 ALL	WHL	MAJ	MIN	UNK	1958-1967 ALL	WHL	MAJ	MIN	UNK
OUTSIDE U.S.	431	239	80	32	54	110	64	17	4	25	65	39	15	6	5	230	136	48	22	24
OUT. U.S. + CANADA	359	186	73	30	50	89	48	16	3	22	46	23	13	5	5	204	115	44	22	23
OUT. WEST. HEMIS.	271	144	53	24	37	69	37	13	1	18	30	17	6	5	2	159	90	34	18	17
OUT. WHITE CWEALTH	265	128	60	23	38	57	29	11	1	14	33	17	10	2	4	159	82	39	18	20
OUT. DEVLPED WORLD	126	66	24	9	18	28	16	3	2	7	21	9	9	0	3	68	41	12	7	8
CANADA	72	53	7	2	4	21	16	1	1	3	19	16	2	1	0	26	21	4	0	1
LATIN AMERICA	88	42	20	6	13	20	11	3	2	4	16	6	7	0	3	45	25	10	4	6
C. AMER.+CARIB.	29	12	5	3	5	6	3	2	0	1	2	2	2	0	1	14	7	1	0	3
CUBA	3	1	2	0	0	1	0	1	0	0	0	0	1	0	0	1	0	0	0	0
MEXICO	20	9	3	3	3	4	2	0	0	1	3	1	1	0	1	11	6	1	0	1
OTHER	6	2	0	0	2	1	1	0	0	0	0	0	0	0	0	3	1	0	1	2
S. AMERICA	59	30	15	5	8	14	8	1	2	3	11	4	5	0	2	31	18	9	3	3
ARGENTINA	8	5	1	1	0	3	1	0	0	0	2	0	0	0	0	3	2	1	0	0
BRAZIL	13	9	0	1	3	5	3	1	0	1	2	0	0	0	2	6	6	0	0	0
PERU	3	1	1	0	0	1	1	0	0	0	2	0	0	0	0	0	0	0	0	0
COLOMBIA	10	2	2	1	2	1	0	0	1	0	2	1	2	0	0	7	1	4	0	2
VENEZUELA	15	7	5	1	2	1	0	0	0	1	3	2	1	0	0	10	5	3	1	1
OTHER	10	6	2	1	1	3	1	0	1	1	2	1	1	0	0	5	4	1	0	0
EUROPE	190	94	37	17	31	53	26	11	1	15	18	11	1	4	2	108	57	25	12	14
EFTA	82	48	12	4	13	36	21	7	0	8	5	3	0	2	0	36	24	5	2	5
U.K.	56	33	5	4	10	27	15	4	0	8	0	0	0	2	0	20	15	1	2	2
SCANDINAVIA	12	7	3	0	2	5	3	2	0	0	0	0	0	0	0	7	4	2	0	1
SWITZERLAND	10	6	2	0	1	2	2	0	0	0	0	0	0	0	0	7	4	2	1	0
OTHER EFTA	4	2	2	0	0	2	1	1	0	0	0	0	0	0	0	2	2	0	0	0
EUROP. COMMUNITY	84	37	18	7	16	14	3	4	1	6	9	7	0	1	1	55	27	14	5	9
FRANCE	29	14	5	3	5	7	3	0	1	3	3	3	0	0	0	17	8	5	2	2
GERMANY	23	11	5	2	3	5	0	1	0	1	2	2	0	1	0	18	9	4	1	4
ITALY	14	6	2	2	1	2	0	0	0	1	3	2	1	0	0	9	4	2	1	2
BELGIUM + LUX	7	2	3	0	1	3	1	0	0	1	0	0	0	0	0	3	2	1	0	0
NETHERLANDS	11	4	5	1	1	1	0	1	0	0	1	0	1	0	0	8	4	1	2	1
SPAIN	12	3	5	4	0	0	0	0	0	0	3	1	1	1	0	8	2	4	2	0
GREECE + TURKEY	3	2	0	0	0	2	1	0	0	0	0	0	0	0	0	1	1	0	0	0
OTHER EUROPE	9	4	2	1	2	0	0	0	0	0	1	0	1	0	0	8	4	1	1	2
EUROPE EX. U.K.	134	61	32	13	21	26	11	7	1	7	13	8	1	2	2	88	42	24	10	12
SOUTHERN DOMINIONS	32	22	7	2	1	5	4	1	1	0	7	3	3	1	0	20	15	3	1	1
S. AFRICA +RHOD.	10	8	2	0	0	1	1	0	1	0	2	1	1	0	0	6	6	0	0	0
AUSTRALIA + N.Z.	22	14	5	2	1	3	3	1	0	0	5	2	2	1	0	14	9	3	1	1
ASIA + OTHER AFRICA	49	28	9	5	5	11	7	1	1	3	5	3	2	0	0	31	18	6	5	2
JAPAN	11	4	3	1	5	3	1	1	0	0	0	0	0	0	0	8	2	4	2	2
OTHER ASIA+AFR.	38	24	4	3	5	8	5	0	0	3	5	3	2	0	0	23	16	2	3	2
BLACK AFRICA	8	4	1	1	2	0	0	0	0	0	1	0	1	0	0	7	4	0	1	2
ARAB WORLD	3	1	1	1	0	1	0	0	0	0	1	1	0	0	0	1	0	0	0	0
INDIA	2	1	0	1	0	0	1	0	0	0	0	0	0	0	0	2	1	1	0	0
PHILIPPINES	3	2	0	0	0	0	0	0	0	0	1	1	0	0	0	1	1	0	0	0
OTHER E. ASIA	4	4	0	0	0	1	1	0	0	0	0	0	0	0	0	3	3	0	0	0
OTHER ASIA	18	12	2	0	3	6	3	0	0	3	2	2	0	0	0	9	7	2	0	0

CHAPTER 5- PATTERNS OF OWNERSHIP
SECTION 5- THE FLOW OF MANUFACTURING BY CHARACTERISTIC OF SUBSIDIARY
TABLE A1- MANUFACTURING SUBSIDIARIES WHICH WERE AMONG
THE 1ST - 3RD FOREIGN MANUFACTURING SUBSIDIARIES IN THEIR PARENT SYSTEM,
CLASSIFIED BY COUNTRY, PERIOD MANUFACTURE BEGAN, AND SYSTEM OWNERSHIP %

PERIOD AND OWNERSHIP PERCENTAGE
(WHL=95-100%, MAJ=50-94%, MIN=5-49%, UNK=UNKNOWN)

COUNTRY OR REGION	TOTAL PRE 1968					PRE 1946					1946-1957					1958-1967				
	ALL	WHL	MAJ	MIN	UNK	ALL	WHL	MAJ	MIN	UNK	ALL	WHL	MAJ	MIN	UNK	ALL	WHL	MAJ	MIN	UNK
OUTSIDE U.S.	561	376	107	41	35	368	257	64	22	25	139	96	22	11	10	52	23	21	8	0
OUT. U.S. + CANADA	374	222	89	33	28	225	141	48	17	19	101	63	20	9	7	46	18	21	7	0
OUT. WEST. HEMIS.	274	168	61	20	24	178	113	37	11	17	62	39	11	5	7	33	16	13	4	0
OUT. WHITE CWEALTH	233	122	65	27	17	125	73	29	13	10	70	39	16	8	7	36	10	20	6	0
OUT. DEVLPED WORLD	115	61	33	14	6	53	33	11	6	3	47	26	13	5	3	14	2	9	3	0
CANADA	187	154	18	8	7	143	116	16	5	6	38	33	2	2	1	6	5	0	1	0
LATIN AMERICA	100	54	28	13	4	47	28	11	6	2	39	24	9	4	2	13	2	8	3	0
C. AMER.+CARIB.	52	29	12	6	2	21	11	6	2	2	22	16	2	2	1	8	2	4	2	0
CUBA	11	6	2	1	2	6	3	2	0	1	5	3	0	1	1	0	0	0	0	0
MEXICO	40	22	10	5	0	15	8	4	2	1	16	12	2	1	1	8	2	4	2	0
OTHER	1	1	0	0	0	0	0	0	0	0	1	1	0	0	0	0	0	0	0	0
S. AMERICA	48	25	16	7	0	26	17	5	4	0	17	8	7	2	0	5	0	4	1	0
ARGENTINA	15	10	3	2	0	12	10	1	1	0	1	0	1	0	0	3	0	2	1	0
BRAZIL	10	7	2	1	0	4	3	0	1	0	5	4	0	0	0	1	0	1	0	0
PERU	4	2	2	0	0	3	1	1	1	0	1	0	1	0	0	0	0	0	0	0
COLOMBIA	5	0	4	1	0	1	0	1	0	0	3	0	2	1	0	1	0	1	0	0
VENEZUELA	9	3	2	2	0	2	0	1	1	0	7	3	1	1	0	0	0	0	0	0
OTHER	5	3	1	1	0	4	2	2	0	0	1	1	0	1	0	0	0	0	0	0
EUROPE	216	134	47	14	21	149	93	33	8	15	39	27	3	3	6	28	14	11	3	0
EFTA	112	79	19	4	10	85	57	18	2	8	21	17	3	1	2	6	5	0	1	0
U.K.	101	71	16	4	10	77	52	15	2	8	18	14	1	1	2	6	5	0	1	0
SCANDINAVIA	8	6	2	0	0	6	4	2	0	0	2	2	0	0	0	0	0	0	0	0
SWITZERLAND	0	0	0	0	0	0	0	0	0	0	0	1	0	0	0	0	0	0	0	0
OTHER EFTA	3	2	1	0	0	2	1	1	0	0	1	0	1	0	0	0	0	0	0	0
EUROP. COMMUNITY	91	46	26	9	10	54	30	13	5	6	17	9	2	2	4	20	7	11	2	1
FRANCE	29	16	6	3	4	20	12	2	3	3	5	4	2	0	1	4	2	2	0	0
GERMANY	30	20	7	1	2	25	15	7	1	2	4	2	2	0	0	1	1	0	0	0
ITALY	11	4	4	2	1	3	1	1	0	1	3	1	0	1	0	5	1	3	1	0
BELGIUM + LUX	13	4	7	1	3	3	1	1	1	0	3	2	0	1	0	7	2	4	0	3
NETHERLANDS	8	2	1	2	3	1	1	0	1	0	4	1	0	1	0	3	1	2	0	0
SPAIN	7	5	2	0	0	5	3	2	0	0	1	0	0	0	0	1	1	0	0	0
GREECE + TURKEY	0	0	0	0	0	0	0	0	0	0	0	0	1	1	0	1	1	0	0	0
OTHER EUROPE	6	4	0	1	1	5	3	0	1	1	0	0	0	1	0	1	1	0	2	1
EUROPE EX. U.K.	115	63	31	10	11	72	41	18	6	7	21	13	2	2	4	22	9	11	2	1
SOUTHERN DOMINIONS	38	27	8	2	1	22	15	4	2	1	13	10	3	0	0	3	2	1	1	0
S. AFRICA +RHOD.	10	6	3	1	1	6	3	2	1	0	3	3	3	0	0	1	1	0	1	0
AUSTRALIA + N.Z.	28	21	5	1	1	16	12	2	1	1	10	7	3	0	0	2	2	0	0	0
ASIA + OTHER AFRICA	20	7	6	4	2	7	5	0	0	1	10	2	5	2	1	2	1	0	1	0
JAPAN	5	0	1	3	2	1	0	0	0	1	2	0	1	1	0	1	0	1	1	0
OTHER ASIA+AFR.	15	7	5	1	2	6	5	0	0	0	8	2	4	1	2	1	1	0	0	0
BLACK AFRICA	0	0	0	0	0	0	0	0	0	0	0	0	0	0	0	0	0	0	0	0
ARAB WORLD	0	0	0	0	0	0	0	0	0	0	0	0	0	0	0	0	0	0	0	0
INDIA	5	4	0	1	0	3	3	0	0	0	2	1	0	1	0	0	0	0	0	0
PHILIPPINES	1	1	0	1	0	1	1	0	1	0	2	0	1	1	0	2	0	1	1	0
OTHER E. ASIA	1	1	1	0	1	1	1	1	1	0	0	1	0	0	0	0	0	0	0	0
OTHER ASIA	9	2	4	1	2	2	1	0	1	1	6	1	3	1	1	1	1	1	0	0

CHAPTER 5- PATTERNS OF OWNERSHIP
SECTION 5- THE FLOW OF MANUFACTURING BY CHARACTERISTIC OF SUBSIDIARY
TABLE A2- MANUFACTURING SUBSIDIARIES WHICH WERE AMONG
THE 4TH - 10TH FOREIGN MANUFACTURING SUBSIDIARIES IN THEIR PARENT SYSTEM,
CLASSIFIED BY COUNTRY, PERIOD MANUFACTURE BEGAN, AND SYSTEM OWNERSHIP %

PERIOD AND OWNERSHIP PERCENTAGE
(WHL=95-100%, MAJ=50-94%, MIN=5-49%, UNK=UNKNOWN)

COUNTRY OR REGION	TOTAL PRE 1968					PRE 1946					1946-1957					1958-1967				
	ALL	WHL	MAJ	MIN	UNK	ALL	WHL	MAJ	MIN	UNK	ALL	WHL	MAJ	MIN	UNK	ALL	WHL	MAJ	MIN	UNK
OUTSIDE U.S.	1279	747	276	161	95	403	254	67	35	47	390	242	82	48	18	486	251	127	78	30
OUT. U.S. + CANADA	1053	571	249	152	81	319	185	62	32	40	302	177	65	46	14	432	209	122	74	27
OUT. WEST. HEMIS.	694	372	172	89	61	222	129	47	12	34	222	101	33	28	8	302	142	92	49	19
OUT. WHITE CWEALTH	788	408	203	121	56	232	129	50	26	27	223	126	53	33	11	333	153	100	62	18
OUT. DEVLPED WORLD	416	223	96	71	26	111	64	16	20	11	150	86	37	20	7	155	73	43	31	8
CANADA	226	176	27	9	14	84	69	5	3	7	88	65	17	2	4	54	42	5	4	3
LATIN AMERICA	359	199	77	63	20	97	56	15	20	6	132	76	32	18	6	130	67	30	25	8
C. AMER.+CARIB.	153	93	27	24	9	38	21	4	11	2	56	40	9	4	3	59	32	14	9	4
CUBA	21	10	4	6	1	11	5	2	4	0	8	3	2	2	1	2	2	0	0	0
MEXICO	104	71	14	12	7	17	12	1	3	1	44	35	5	2	2	43	24	8	7	4
OTHER	28	12	9	6	1	10	4	1	4	1	4	2	2	0	0	14	6	6	2	0
S. AMERICA	206	106	50	39	11	59	35	11	9	4	76	36	23	14	3	71	35	16	16	4
ARGENTINA	49	28	10	10	1	16	13	2	1	0	15	8	4	3	0	18	7	4	7	0
BRAZIL	65	36	10	15	4	22	14	2	4	2	24	11	7	6	0	19	11	4	5	1
PERU	14	5	6	2	1	6	3	0	3	0	5	1	2	2	0	3	1	1	0	2
COLOMBIA	29	15	10	2	2	3	0	1	2	0	12	7	2	2	1	14	8	5	0	1
VENEZUELA	34	16	11	5	2	3	2	0	1	0	16	7	4	5	0	15	7	5	3	0
OTHER	15	6	3	5	1	9	3	3	2	1	4	2	1	1	0	2	1	0	1	0
EUROPE	484	262	122	53	47	167	95	35	8	29	107	64	19	18	6	210	103	68	27	12
EFTA	176	103	32	17	24	70	42	10	2	16	44	28	6	8	2	62	33	16	7	6
U.K.	131	76	24	13	18	49	29	5	3	13	37	23	6	7	1	45	24	13	4	4
SCANDINAVIA	23	15	5	2	1	10	7	3	0	0	4	3	0	1	0	5	5	2	1	1
SWITZERLAND	10	6	1	1	3	3	2	2	0	1	2	0	0	1	1	5	2	1	1	1
OTHER EFTA	12	6	2	1	3	8	4	2	0	2	1	0	0	0	1	3	2	0	1	0
EUROP. COMMUNITY	276	148	77	32	19	89	49	23	6	11	52	32	11	7	2	135	67	43	19	6
FRANCE	95	50	23	13	9	34	16	8	4	6	17	13	2	1	1	44	21	13	8	2
GERMANY	73	39	26	5	3	23	15	7	0	1	16	10	2	0	0	34	14	13	5	2
ITALY	52	28	16	5	3	12	8	3	0	1	9	4	2	2	1	31	16	11	3	1
BELGIUM + LUX	29	16	5	4	4	10	6	3	1	0	6	3	1	2	0	13	9	1	3	0
NETHERLANDS	27	15	7	5	0	10	6	3	1	0	4	2	1	2	0	13	7	4	2	0
SPAIN	19	4	11	1	3	4	0	2	0	2	4	1	0	2	0	11	4	8	1	0
GREECE + TURKEY	3	1	1	1	0	0	0	0	0	0	3	1	1	1	0	0	0	0	0	0
OTHER EUROPE	10	6	1	0	3	4	3	0	0	1	4	2	1	1	0	2	1	1	0	0
EUROPE EX. U.K.	353	186	98	40	29	118	66	30	6	16	70	41	13	11	5	165	79	55	23	8
SOUTHERN DOMINIONS	127	83	21	18	5	37	26	7	4	0	38	26	6	6	0	52	31	8	8	5
S. AFRICA +RHOD.	42	31	7	4	0	12	11	1	0	0	13	10	2	1	0	17	10	4	3	0
AUSTRALIA + N.Z.	85	52	14	14	5	25	15	6	4	0	25	16	4	5	0	35	21	4	5	5
ASIA + OTHER AFRICA	83	27	29	18	9	18	8	5	0	5	25	11	8	4	2	40	8	16	14	2
JAPAN	26	3	10	10	3	4	0	4	0	0	7	1	1	5	1	15	2	3	8	2
OTHER ASIA+AFR.	57	24	19	8	6	14	8	0	0	5	18	10	5	2	1	25	6	13	6	0
BLACK AFRICA	1	0	0	1	0	0	0	0	0	0	1	1	0	0	0	0	0	0	0	0
ARAB WORLD	5	2	2	1	0	0	0	0	0	0	1	1	0	0	0	4	0	2	1	1
INDIA	16	6	6	4	0	2	2	0	0	0	4	4	0	0	0	10	3	0	4	0
PHILIPPINES	12	5	2	2	3	3	3	0	0	0	5	3	1	1	0	4	1	2	1	0
OTHER E. ASIA	5	1	1	2	0	3	0	0	0	3	3	0	1	1	0	1	3	1	0	0
OTHER ASIA	18	6	9	0	3	6	3	1	0	2	6	2	3	1	0	6	1	5	0	0

CHAPTER 5- PATTERNS OF OWNERSHIP
SECTION 5- THE FLOW OF MANUFACTURING BY CHARACTERISTIC OF SUBSIDIARY
TABLE A3- MANUFACTURING SUBSIDIARIES WHICH WERE AMONG
THE 11TH - 25TH FOREIGN MANUFACTURING SUBSIDIARIES IN THR PARENT SYSTEM,
CLASSIFIED BY COUNTRY, PERIOD MANUFACTURE BEGAN, AND SYSTEM OWNERSHIP %

PERIOD AND OWNERSHIP PERCENTAGE
(WHL=95-100%, MAJ=50-94%, MIN=5-49%, UNK=UNKNOWN)

COUNTRY OR REGION	TOTAL PRE 1968					PRE 1946					1946-1957					1958-1967				
	ALL	WHL	MAJ	MIN	UNK	ALL	WHL	MAJ	MIN	UNK	ALL	WHL	MAJ	MIN	UNK	ALL	WHL	MAJ	MIN	UNK
OUTSIDE U.S.	1896	1030	475	242	126	205	148	22	9	26	382	225	93	45	19	1286	657	360	188	81
OUT. U.S. + CANADA	1661	844	449	236	115	175	125	20	9	21	323	176	87	43	17	1146	543	342	184	77
OUT. WEST. HEMIS.	1147	590	307	157	80	122	90	13	4	15	182	101	47	24	10	830	399	247	129	55
OUT. WHITE CWEALTH	1294	614	367	212	91	120	82	14	8	16	264	140	74	36	14	900	392	279	168	61
OUT. DEVLPED WORLD	663	318	181	119	40	60	41	7	5	7	164	91	46	20	7	434	186	128	94	26
CANADA	235	186	26	6	11	30	23	2	0	5	59	49	6	2	2	140	114	18	4	4
LATIN AMERICA	514	254	142	79	35	53	35	7	5	6	141	75	40	19	7	316	144	95	55	22
C. AMER.+CARIB.	209	97	55	37	18	14	10	0	2	2	47	29	12	3	3	146	58	43	32	13
CUBA	12	6	2	2	2	1	0	0	0	1	7	4	2	1	0	1	0	0	0	1
MEXICO	130	60	34	26	10	10	8	0	1	1	26	14	9	1	2	94	38	25	24	7
OTHER	67	31	19	11	6	2	2	0	0	0	14	11	1	2	0	51	20	18	8	5
S. AMERICA	305	157	87	42	19	39	25	7	3	4	94	46	28	16	4	170	86	52	23	9
ARGENTINA	68	34	19	11	4	15	11	3	1	0	16	6	5	4	1	37	17	10	7	3
BRAZIL	77	44	23	5	5	9	6	1	0	2	30	15	12	3	0	38	23	10	3	2
PERU	21	13	4	4	0	2	0	0	1	1	9	5	1	3	0	10	7	3	0	0
COLOMBIA	47	21	15	8	3	6	4	1	1	0	12	6	2	3	1	29	11	12	4	2
VENEZUELA	58	26	19	8	5	6	4	1	1	0	14	7	6	3	1	38	18	12	6	2
OTHER	34	19	7	6	2	4	2	0	0	2	12	7	2	2	1	18	10	5	3	0
EUROPE	756	404	196	82	63	83	57	10	3	13	121	66	27	20	8	541	281	159	59	42
EFTA	252	156	52	16	22	39	28	5	1	5	43	23	11	6	3	164	105	36	9	14
U.K.	187	117	35	12	17	25	17	4	0	4	33	17	7	6	3	123	83	24	6	10
SCANDINAVIA	37	23	9	3	2	8	7	0	0	1	8	6	2	0	0	21	10	7	3	1
SWITZERLAND	13	8	4	0	1	1	1	0	0	0	1	0	1	0	0	11	7	3	0	1
OTHER EFTA	15	8	4	1	2	1	1	0	0	0	5	4	1	0	0	9	3	3	2	1
EUROP. COMMUNITY	402	211	108	42	36	34	23	5	5	1	62	35	13	9	5	301	153	90	32	26
FRANCE	120	48	41	19	9	9	6	1	1	1	11	4	4	2	1	97	38	36	16	7
GERMANY	116	65	28	10	13	14	8	3	0	3	24	13	5	4	2	78	44	20	8	6
ITALY	95	51	28	8	6	4	3	0	0	1	16	11	3	2	0	73	37	25	6	5
BELGIUM + LUX	32	22	5	3	2	2	1	1	0	0	3	2	0	0	1	27	19	4	3	1
NETHERLANDS	39	25	6	2	6	5	5	0	0	0	8	5	1	2	0	26	15	5	5	1
SPAIN	67	19	28	17	3	10	5	0	3	2	3	1	1	1	0	54	13	27	13	1
GREECE + TURKEY	17	6	6	4	1	0	0	0	0	0	3	3	0	0	0	14	3	6	4	1
OTHER EUROPE	18	12	3	3	0	4	3	0	1	0	6	5	1	0	0	8	4	2	2	0
EUROPE EX. U.K.	569	287	161	70	46	58	40	6	3	9	88	49	20	14	5	418	198	135	53	32
SOUTHERN DOMINIONS	170	105	46	11	7	28	24	2	2	0	24	16	6	1	1	118	65	38	9	6
S. AFRICA +RHOD.	46	31	8	6	1	8	7	1	0	0	8	5	2	1	0	30	19	5	4	1
AUSTRALIA + N.Z.	124	74	38	5	6	20	17	1	2	0	16	11	4	0	1	88	46	32	4	6
ASIA + OTHER AFRICA	221	81	65	64	10	11	9	0	1	1	38	19	8	9	2	171	53	50	61	7
JAPAN	72	17	26	24	5	4	1	2	1	0	15	5	7	1	2	53	11	17	22	3
OTHER ASIA+AFR.	149	64	39	40	5	7	6	0	0	1	23	16	3	4	0	118	42	33	39	4
BLACK AFRICA	16	9	3	3	0	0	0	0	0	0	4	3	0	1	0	12	6	3	3	0
ARAB WORLD	17	8	4	5	0	0	0	0	0	0	4	3	1	0	0	13	5	3	5	0
INDIA	38	8	8	19	1	1	0	0	1	0	5	2	1	2	0	32	6	7	18	1
PHILIPPINES	25	14	6	4	1	3	3	0	0	0	8	5	2	0	1	14	6	4	4	0
OTHER E. ASIA	18	9	5	3	1	0	0	0	0	0	0	0	0	0	0	18	9	5	3	1
OTHER ASIA	35	15	13	6	1	3	3	0	0	0	3	2	1	0	0	29	10	12	6	1

CHAPTER 5- PATTERNS OF OWNERSHIP
SECTION 5- THE FLOW OF MANUFACTURING BY CHARACTERISTIC OF SUBSIDIARY
TABLE A4- MANUFACTURING SUBSIDIARIES WHICH WERE AMONG
THE MORE THAN 25TH FOREIGN MANUFACTURING SUBSIDIARIES IN THEIR PARENT SYSTEM,
CLASSIFIED BY COUNTRY, PERIOD MANUFACTURE BEGAN, AND SYSTEM OWNERSHIP %

PERIOD AND OWNERSHIP PERCENTAGE
(WHL=95-100%, MAJ=50-94%, MIN=5-49%, UNK=UNKNOWN)

COUNTRY OR REGION	TOTAL PRE 1968					PRE 1946					1946-1957					1958-1967				
	ALL	WHL	MAJ	MIN	UNK	ALL	WHL	MAJ	MIN	UNK	ALL	WHL	MAJ	MIN	UNK	ALL	WHL	MAJ	MIN	UNK
OUTSIDE U.S.	1492	728	381	153	114	104	71	22	3	8	56	37	7	7	5	1216	620	352	143	101
OUT. U.S. + CANADA	1336	624	365	147	101	88	58	20	3	7	45	28	7	7	3	1104	538	338	137	91
OUT. WEST. HEMIS.	965	471	267	98	58	57	41	11	3	2	33	19	6	7	1	804	411	250	88	55
OUT. WHITE CWEALTH	1033	438	308	131	88	61	38	15	2	6	31	17	6	5	3	873	383	287	124	79
OUT. DEVLPED WORLD	517	213	139	68	57	37	21	10	0	6	15	11	2	0	2	425	181	127	68	49
CANADA	156	104	16	16	13	16	13	2	0	1	11	9	0	0	2	112	82	14	6	10
LATIN AMERICA	371	153	98	49	43	31	17	9	0	5	12	6	1	0	2	300	127	88	49	36
C. AMER.+CARIB.	156	59	41	27	14	7	6	1	0	0	7	1	1	0	0	127	47	39	27	14
CUBA	4	4	0	0	0	2	2	0	0	0	1	1	0	0	0	1	1	0	0	0
MEXICO	92	35	22	17	8	5	4	1	0	0	4	3	1	0	0	73	28	20	17	8
OTHER	60	20	19	10	6	0	0	0	0	0	2	2	0	0	0	53	18	19	10	6
S. AMERICA	215	94	57	22	29	24	11	8	0	5	5	2	0	0	2	173	80	49	22	22
ARGENTINA	30	16	7	1	3	3	0	3	0	0	2	2	0	0	0	22	14	4	1	3
BRAZIL	55	30	16	2	5	13	6	3	0	4	0	0	0	0	0	40	24	13	2	1
PERU	18	8	5	1	1	0	0	0	0	0	1	0	0	0	0	14	7	5	1	1
COLOMBIA	36	14	10	6	5	2	1	0	0	1	0	0	0	0	0	33	13	9	6	5
VENEZUELA	43	12	8	7	14	3	2	1	0	0	2	2	0	0	0	36	10	8	7	11
OTHER	33	14	11	5	1	3	2	1	0	0	0	0	0	0	0	28	12	10	5	1
EUROPE	602	315	171	48	36	37	27	7	2	1	26	13	5	2	1	507	275	159	39	34
EFTA	211	137	37	8	12	17	13	2	1	1	13	9	2	0	2	164	115	33	5	11
U.K.	134	86	19	7	7	13	9	2	1	1	10	7	1	0	1	96	70	16	4	6
SCANDINAVIA	46	29	12	0	4	3	1	0	0	0	1	0	1	0	0	41	26	11	0	4
SWITZERLAND	14	11	2	0	1	1	0	0	0	0	1	1	0	0	0	11	10	2	0	1
OTHER EFTA	17	11	4	1	0	0	0	0	0	0	1	1	0	0	0	16	10	4	1	1
EUROP. COMMUNITY	307	151	100	22	20	17	12	4	0	1	7	2	2	0	3	269	138	94	18	19
FRANCE	78	31	31	7	3	4	3	0	0	1	2	1	0	0	1	68	28	31	6	3
GERMANY	84	43	20	7	10	3	3	0	0	0	3	1	1	0	0	74	39	19	7	9
ITALY	65	31	26	3	5	7	5	2	0	0	1	0	1	0	0	56	26	23	2	5
BELGIUM + LUX	45	27	13	1	1	1	1	0	0	0	1	0	0	0	0	42	27	12	2	1
NETHERLANDS	35	19	10	3	1	2	0	1	0	0	1	0	0	1	0	29	18	9	1	1
SPAIN	44	10	23	10	2	1	0	0	1	0	0	0	0	1	0	40	8	22	9	1
GREECE + TURKEY	22	7	3	5	2	0	0	0	0	0	2	2	0	0	0	21	7	7	5	2
OTHER EUROPE	18	10	3	3	3	2	2	0	0	0	1	0	1	0	0	13	7	3	3	1
EUROPE EX. U.K.	468	229	152	41	29	24	18	5	1	0	16	6	4	2	1	411	205	143	35	28
SOUTHERN DOMINIONS	154	92	35	7	5	12	9	3	0	0	4	4	0	0	0	123	79	32	7	5
S. AFRICA +RHOD.	61	42	8	3	0	4	3	1	0	0	0	0	0	0	0	49	39	7	3	0
AUSTRALIA + N.Z.	93	50	27	4	5	8	6	2	0	0	4	4	0	0	0	74	40	25	4	5
ASIA + OTHER AFRICA	209	64	61	43	17	8	5	2	1	0	3	2	1	0	0	174	57	59	42	16
JAPAN	63	4	20	24	3	2	1	1	0	0	0	0	0	0	0	49	3	20	23	3
OTHER ASIA+AFR.	146	60	41	19	14	6	4	1	1	0	3	2	0	1	0	125	54	39	19	13
BLACK AFRICA	31	18	4	5	2	0	0	0	0	0	0	0	0	0	0	29	18	4	5	2
ARAB WORLD	17	7	7	2	1	1	0	1	0	0	2	2	0	0	0	13	6	4	2	1
INDIA	14	3	7	2	1	0	0	0	0	0	0	0	0	0	0	13	3	7	2	1
PHILIPPINES	16	6	3	2	1	2	1	0	1	0	0	0	0	0	0	13	5	6	2	0
OTHER E. ASIA	15	8	7	0	3	2	2	0	0	0	0	0	0	0	0	12	6	3	0	3
OTHER ASIA	53	18	15	8	6	1	1	0	0	0	1	1	0	0	0	45	16	15	8	6

CHAPTER 5- PATTERNS OF OWNERSHIP
SECTION 5- THE FLOW OF MANUFACTURING BY CHARACTERISTIC OF SUBSIDIARY
TABLE B1- MANUFACTURING SUBSIDIARIES WHICH ENTERED A PARENT SYSTEM
WHICH HAD LESS THAN 11 YEARS "FOREIGN MANUFACTURING EXPERIENCE",
CLASSIFIED BY COUNTRY, PERIOD MANUFACTURE BEGAN, AND SYSTEM OWNERSHIP %

PERIOD AND OWNERSHIP PERCENTAGE
(WHL=95-100%, MAJ=50-94%, MIN=5-49%, UNK=UNKNOWN)

COUNTRY OR REGION	TOTAL PRE 1968					PRE 1946					1946-1957					1958-1967				
	ALL	WHL	MAJ	MIN	UNK	ALL	WHL	MAJ	MIN	UNK	ALL	WHL	MAJ	MIN	UNK	ALL	WHL	MAJ	MIN	UNK
OUTSIDE U.S.	1154	690	270	128	66	426	304	58	28	36	242	166	41	24	11	486	220	171	76	19
OUT. U.S. + CANADA	864	445	250	113	56	262	169	45	21	27	175	107	39	19	10	427	169	166	73	19
OUT. WEST. HEMIS.	630	335	178	74	43	214	139	37	14	24	110	73	20	10	7	306	123	121	50	12
OUT. WHITE CWEALTH	613	274	201	96	42	150	86	28	17	19	124	66	34	17	7	339	122	139	62	16
OUT. DEVLPED WORLD	291	128	93	52	18	58	36	8	7	7	77	39	24	10	4	156	53	61	35	7
CANADA	290	245	20	15	10	164	135	13	7	9	67	59	2	5	1	59	51	3	3	0
LATIN AMERICA	234	110	72	39	13	48	30	8	7	3	65	34	19	9	3	121	46	45	23	7
C. AMER.+CARIB.	122	62	34	18	8	26	15	5	4	2	31	20	7	2	2	65	27	22	12	4
CUBA	16	8	3	2	3	8	4	1	1	1	7	3	1	1	1	1	1	0	0	0
MEXICO	80	47	19	9	5	16	11	3	1	1	23	17	5	1	0	41	19	11	7	4
OTHER	26	7	12	7	0	2	0	1	2	0	1	0	1	1	0	23	7	11	5	0
S. AMERICA	112	48	38	21	5	22	15	3	3	1	34	14	12	7	1	56	19	23	11	3
ARGENTINA	31	14	11	5	1	9	8	1	0	0	7	3	3	1	0	15	3	7	4	1
BRAZIL	26	17	5	3	1	5	5	0	0	0	12	7	3	3	0	9	5	3	0	1
PERU	9	5	4	0	0	2	1	1	0	0	2	0	2	0	0	5	4	0	0	1
COLOMBIA	16	5	2	6	3	1	0	1	0	0	4	0	2	2	0	11	2	6	2	1
VENEZUELA	21	6	10	7	1	1	0	0	1	0	7	3	1	3	0	13	3	6	4	1
OTHER	9	4	1	1	3	4	1	0	2	1	2	1	2	1	0	3	2	0	1	0
EUROPE	465	257	130	43	35	177	113	33	11	20	74	51	12	6	5	214	93	85	26	10
EFTA	181	125	35	7	14	93	67	16	2	8	30	25	3	0	2	58	33	16	5	4
U.K.	156	112	27	5	12	85	62	13	2	8	28	23	3	0	2	43	27	11	3	2
SCANDINAVIA	15	10	3	1	1	6	5	1	0	0	2	2	0	0	0	7	3	2	1	1
SWITZERLAND	5	2	2	1	0	0	0	0	0	0	0	0	0	0	0	5	2	2	1	0
OTHER EFTA	5	1	3	0	1	2	0	2	0	0	0	0	0	0	0	3	1	1	0	1
EUROP. COMMUNITY	244	121	73	32	18	76	42	15	8	11	37	24	7	4	2	131	55	51	20	5
FRANCE	86	37	23	16	10	31	17	8	0	6	11	7	4	0	0	44	13	16	11	4
GERMANY	66	40	21	2	3	28	17	7	0	3	14	11	2	1	0	24	12	11	1	0
ITALY	36	17	13	5	1	8	3	2	2	1	4	1	2	0	1	29	11	13	5	0
BELGIUM + LUX	33	16	11	5	1	6	2	3	0	1	4	4	0	0	0	21	12	7	2	0
NETHERLANDS	23	11	5	4	3	6	4	1	1	0	4	2	1	1	0	13	7	4	1	1
SPAIN	26	5	18	2	1	5	0	2	2	1	3	1	1	1	0	18	4	15	1	0
GREECE + TURKEY	6	2	2	1	1	0	0	0	0	0	2	0	1	0	1	4	2	1	1	0
OTHER EUROPE	8	4	2	1	1	3	2	0	1	0	2	1	0	1	0	2	1	2	0	0
EUROPE EX. U.K.	309	145	103	38	23	92	51	20	9	12	46	28	9	6	3	171	66	74	23	8
SOUTHERN DOMINIONS	90	56	21	12	1	26	20	4	2	0	21	17	2	2	0	43	19	15	8	1
S. AFRICA +RHOD.	32	19	8	5	0	11	8	2	1	0	7	7	0	0	0	14	4	6	4	0
AUSTRALIA + N.Z.	58	37	13	7	1	15	12	2	1	0	14	10	2	2	0	29	15	9	4	1
ASIA + OTHER AFRICA	75	22	27	19	7	11	6	0	0	4	15	5	6	2	2	49	11	21	16	1
JAPAN	18	4	6	6	2	1	0	0	1	0	3	0	1	1	1	14	4	5	4	1
OTHER ASIA+AFR.	57	18	21	13	5	10	6	0	0	4	12	5	5	2	1	35	7	16	12	0
BLACK AFRICA	2	2	1	0	0	0	0	0	0	0	2	2	0	0	0	0	0	1	0	0
ARAB WORLD	2	1	1	0	0	0	0	0	0	0	0	0	0	0	0	2	1	1	0	0
INDIA	11	1	4	6	0	4	4	0	0	0	2	0	1	0	1	8	1	3	4	0
PHILIPPINES	14	8	4	2	0	4	1	0	0	3	2	1	0	1	0	8	3	4	1	0
OTHER E. ASIA	5	3	0	1	1	1	1	0	0	0	2	2	0	0	0	2	0	2	0	0
OTHER ASIA	23	3	12	4	4	4	1	0	0	3	8	2	4	1	1	11	0	3	8	0

CHAPTER 5- PATTERNS OF OWNERSHIP
SECTION 5- THE FLOW OF MANUFACTURING BY CHARACTERISTIC OF SUBSIDIARY
TABLE 82- MANUFACTURING SUBSIDIARIES WHICH ENTERED A PARENT SYSTEM
WHICH HAD 11 -20 YEARS "FOREIGN MANUFACTURING EXPERIENCE",
CLASSIFIED BY COUNTRY, PERIOD MANUFACTURE BFGAN, AND SYSTEM OWNERSHIP %

PERIOD AND OWNERSHIP PERCENTAGE
(WHL=95-100%, MAJ=50-94%, MIN=5-49%, UNK=UNKNOWN)

COUNTRY OR REGION	TOTAL (PRE 1968)					PRE 1946					1946-1957					1958-1967				
	ALL	WHL	MAJ	MIN	UNK	ALL	WHL	MAJ	MIN	UNK	ALL	WHL	MAJ	MIN	UNK	ALL	WHL	MAJ	MIN	UNK
OUTSIDE U.S.	872	479	206	127	60	294	207	42	16	29	140	71	35	25	9	438	201	129	86	22
OUT. U.S. + CANADA	749	386	186	125	52	239	159	38	16	26	114	55	27	25	7	396	172	121	84	19
OUT. WEST. HEMIS.	506	268	120	80	38	171	118	27	5	21	54	23	9	18	4	281	127	84	57	13
OUT. WHITE CWEALTH	584	286	152	112	34	163	106	29	15	13	96	48	23	19	6	325	132	100	78	15
OUT. DEVLPED WORLD	312	152	82	63	15	80	53	11	11	5	70	38	20	8	4	162	61	51	44	6
CANADA	123	93	20	2	8	55	48	4	0	3	26	16	8	0	2	42	29	8	2	3
LATIN AMERICA	243	118	66	45	14	68	41	11	11	5	60	32	18	7	3	115	45	37	27	6
C. AMER.+CARIB.	106	54	23	22	7	25	14	3	5	3	28	21	3	2	2	53	19	17	15	2
CUBA	9	5	2	2	0	7	4	2	1	0	2	1	0	1	0	0	0	0	0	0
MEXICO	74	39	14	17	4	14	9	1	3	1	23	17	3	1	2	37	13	10	13	1
OTHER	23	10	7	3	3	4	1	0	1	2	3	3	0	0	0	16	6	7	2	1
S. AMERICA	137	64	43	23	7	43	27	8	6	2	32	11	15	5	1	62	26	20	12	4
ARGENTINA	36	26	7	3	0	16	15	1	0	0	6	2	2	2	0	14	9	4	1	0
BRAZIL	30	11	11	6	2	10	5	1	3	1	8	1	6	1	0	12	5	4	2	1
PERU	8	4	2	1	1	4	2	1	1	0	1	1	0	0	0	3	1	1	0	1
COLOMBIA	14	7	4	2	1	4	1	2	1	0	5	2	2	0	1	5	4	0	1	0
VENEZUELA	28	7	13	6	2	4	1	1	1	1	8	2	5	1	0	16	4	7	4	1
OTHER	21	9	6	5	1	5	3	2	0	0	4	3	0	1	0	12	3	4	4	1
EUROPE	332	176	77	46	33	121	74	22	5	20	32	12	3	14	3	179	90	52	27	10
EFTA	125	73	22	9	21	60	36	7	2	15	10	4	1	3	2	55	33	14	4	4
U.K.	82	46	13	7	16	40	22	5	1	12	7	2	3	1	1	35	22	5	5	3
SCANDINAVIA	24	16	7	0	1	12	6	5	0	1	2	1	1	0	0	10	9	1	0	0
SWITZERLAND	10	5	0	2	3	1	0	0	0	1	0	0	0	0	0	9	5	0	2	2
OTHER EFTA	9	6	0	0	3	7	5	0	0	2	1	1	0	0	0	1	0	0	0	1
EUROP. COMMUNITY	172	94	43	25	10	54	33	14	5	2	16	7	2	6	1	102	54	27	14	7
FRANCE	48	21	14	10	3	15	7	5	2	1	3	1	1	1	0	30	13	8	7	2
GERMANY	51	31	13	4	3	20	15	3	1	1	5	3	1	1	0	26	13	9	2	2
ITALY	35	21	8	5	1	9	5	1	2	1	2	1	1	0	0	24	15	6	3	0
BELGIUM + LUX	22	11	6	3	2	6	3	3	0	0	2	1	0	1	0	14	7	3	2	2
NETHERLANDS	16	10	2	3	1	4	3	0	1	0	4	2	1	0	1	8	5	1	2	0
SPAIN	25	5	9	10	1	4	3	0	0	1	4	0	4	0	0	17	2	5	10	0
GREECE + TURKEY	4	1	1	1	1	0	0	0	0	0	1	0	0	0	1	3	1	1	1	0
OTHER EUROPE	6	3	2	0	1	3	2	1	0	0	1	0	0	0	1	2	1	1	0	0
EUROPE EX. U.K.	250	130	64	39	17	81	52	17	4	8	25	10	2	11	2	144	68	45	24	7
SOUTHERN DOMINIONS	79	52	19	6	2	35	30	4	0	1	10	4	3	3	0	34	18	12	3	1
S. AFRICA +RHOD.	24	16	5	1	2	11	10	0	0	1	4	2	2	0	0	9	4	3	1	1
AUSTRALIA + N.Z.	55	36	14	5	0	24	20	4	0	0	6	2	1	3	0	25	14	9	2	0
ASIA + OTHER AFRICA	95	40	24	28	3	15	14	0	1	0	12	6	3	2	1	68	20	21	25	2
JAPAN	26	6	8	10	2	3	2	1	0	0	2	0	1	1	0	21	4	6	9	2
OTHER ASIA+AFR.	69	34	16	18	1	12	12	0	0	0	10	6	2	2	0	47	16	14	16	1
BLACK AFRICA	8	3	2	3	0	0	0	0	0	0	0	0	0	0	0	8	3	2	3	0
ARAB WORLD	8	4	3	1	0	0	0	0	0	0	1	1	0	0	0	7	3	3	1	0
INDIA	17	5	3	9	0	5	5	0	0	0	3	0	1	2	0	9	0	2	7	0
PHILIPPINES	10	6	2	2	0	2	2	0	0	0	0	0	0	0	0	8	4	2	2	0
OTHER E. ASIA	10	7	2	1	0	2	2	0	0	0	3	1	1	1	0	5	4	1	0	0
OTHER ASIA	16	9	4	2	1	3	3	0	0	0	3	1	1	1	0	10	5	3	1	1

CHAPTER 5- PATTERNS OF OWNERSHIP
SECTION 5- THE FLOW OF MANUFACTURING BY CHARACTERISTIC OF SUBSIDIARY
TABLE B3- MANUFACTURING SUBSIDIARIES WHICH ENTERED A PARENT SYSTEM
WHICH HAD 21 - 40 YEARS "FOREIGN MANUFACTURING EXPERIENCE",
CLASSIFIED BY COUNTRY, PERIOD MANUFACTURE BEGAN, AND SYSTEM OWNERSHIP %

PERIOD AND OWNERSHIP PERCENTAGE
(WHL=95-100%, MAJ=50-94%, MIN=5-49%, UNK=UNKNOWN)

COUNTRY OR REGION	TOTAL PRE 1968					PRE 1946					1946-1957					1958-1967				
	ALL	WHL	MAJ	MIN	UNK	ALL	WHL	MAJ	MIN	UNK	ALL	WHL	MAJ	MIN	UNK	ALL	WHL	MAJ	MIN	UNK
OUTSIDE U.S.	1719	992	393	208	126	244	149	45	17	33	422	265	92	42	23	1053	578	256	149	70
OUT. U.S. + CANADA	1482	810	361	202	109	203	122	40	16	25	347	209	78	41	19	932	479	243	145	65
OUT. WEST. HEMIS.	1000	555	247	124	74	141	82	31	7	21	197	120	42	26	9	662	353	174	91	44
OUT. WHITE CWEALTH	1118	572	300	165	81	144	85	29	11	19	257	153	60	28	16	717	334	211	126	91
OUT. DEVLPED WORLD	579	299	147	92	41	68	42	10	9	7	171	102	43	16	10	340	155	94	67	24
CANADA	237	182	32	6	17	41	27	5	1	8	75	56	14	1	4	121	99	13	4	5
LATIN AMERICA	482	255	114	78	35	62	40	9	9	4	150	89	36	15	10	270	126	69	54	21
C. AMER.+CARIB.	190	101	47	31	11	20	13	2	5	0	58	41	12	3	2	112	47	33	23	9
CUBA	16	10	2	2	2	4	2	0	2	0	10	7	2	0	1	2	1	0	0	1
MEXICO	110	57	28	18	7	11	8	1	2	0	34	24	8	1	1	65	25	19	15	6
OTHER	64	34	17	11	2	5	3	1	1	0	14	10	2	2	0	45	21	14	8	2
S. AMERICA	292	154	67	47	24	42	27	7	4	4	92	48	24	12	8	158	79	36	31	12
ARGENTINA	58	23	16	14	5	14	8	5	0	1	14	4	6	4	0	30	11	5	10	4
BRAZIL	87	50	19	11	7	15	10	2	1	2	32	16	10	4	2	40	24	7	8	1
PERU	15	9	2	3	1	2	2	0	0	0	8	5	1	2	0	5	2	1	1	1
COLOMBIA	53	26	14	9	4	5	3	2	0	0	12	7	1	2	2	36	16	13	5	2
VENEZUELA	54	30	13	4	7	3	2	0	2	1	20	11	6	1	2	31	17	3	4	0
OTHER	25	16	3	6	0	3	2	0	0	0	6	5	0	1	0	16	3	3	4	0
EUROPE	668	377	162	76	53	105	63	22	3	17	121	74	20	19	8	442	240	120	54	28
EFTA	236	153	44	23	16	47	30	10	1	6	59	33	11	12	3	130	90	23	10	7
U.K.	164	102	28	20	14	30	18	6	1	5	46	23	9	11	3	88	61	13	8	6
SCANDINAVIA	43	29	11	0	1	6	4	2	0	0	10	7	2	0	0	27	18	7	1	1
SWITZERLAND	11	10	1	0	0	7	4	2	0	1	2	1	0	0	0	5	4	1	0	0
OTHER EFTA	18	12	4	1	1	4	4	0	0	0	1	1	0	0	0	10	7	2	1	0
EUROP. COMMUNITY	354	195	95	33	31	44	24	12	1	7	53	35	6	7	5	257	136	77	25	19
FRANCE	110	55	36	13	12	15	8	4	2	1	16	8	3	3	2	79	39	30	9	1
GERMANY	101	55	21	13	12	14	8	6	0	0	11	8	1	2	0	76	41	14	11	10
ITALY	87	48	26	4	9	7	4	2	1	0	16	11	2	2	1	64	33	22	2	7
BELGIUM + LUX	24	18	3	2	1	3	2	1	0	0	3	3	0	0	0	18	13	2	2	1
NETHERLANDS	32	19	9	2	2	5	4	0	1	0	7	5	2	0	0	20	10	8	2	0
SPAIN	40	10	16	11	3	5	4	2	0	0	5	3	0	2	0	31	5	14	11	1
GREECE + TURKEY	16	4	7	5	0	0	0	0	0	0	1	0	1	0	0	15	4	6	5	0
OTHER EUROPE	22	9	2	8	3	10	7	0	1	2	3	1	0	1	0	9	5	0	3	1
EUROPE EX. U.K.	504	275	134	56	39	75	45	16	2	12	75	51	11	8	5	354	179	107	46	22
SOUTHERN DOMINIONS	188	127	33	15	13	27	17	5	4	1	41	30	9	2	0	120	80	19	9	12
S. AFRICA +RHOD.	66	55	5	5	1	4	3	0	1	0	13	10	2	1	0	49	42	4	3	0
AUSTRALIA + N.Z.	122	72	28	10	12	23	14	5	0	4	28	20	7	1	0	71	38	16	5	12
ASIA + OTHER AFRICA	144	51	52	33	8	9	2	3	0	3	35	16	13	5	1	100	33	35	28	4
JAPAN	47	7	19	19	2	3	3	0	0	0	14	3	6	4	1	30	4	10	15	1
OTHER ASIA+AFR.	97	44	33	14	6	6	2	2	0	3	21	13	7	1	0	70	29	25	13	3
BLACK AFRICA	14	5	3	5	1	1	0	1	0	0	5	3	1	1	0	12	4	3	5	1
ARAB WORLD	15	8	4	3	0	1	1	0	0	0	4	3	1	0	0	10	4	3	3	1
INDIA	12	7	4	1	0	1	0	1	0	0	2	2	0	0	0	8	5	4	1	0
PHILIPPINES	17	9	6	1	1	1	1	0	0	0	8	5	3	0	0	7	3	3	1	0
OTHER E. ASIA	11	4	2	2	3	2	2	0	0	0	2	1	0	1	0	7	3	2	1	1
OTHER ASIA	28	11	14	2	1	2	1	1	0	0	3	1	2	0	0	23	9	11	2	1

CHAPTER 5- PATTERNS OF OWNERSHIP
SECTION 5- THE FLOW OF MANUFACTURING BY CHARACTERISTIC OF SUBSIDIARY
TABLE B4- MANUFACTURING SUBSIDIARIES WHICH ENTERED A PARENT SYSTEM
WHICH HAD MORE THAN 40 YEARS "FOREIGN MANUFACTURING EXPERIENCE",
CLASSIFIED BY COUNTRY, PERIOD MANUFACTURE BEGAN, AND SYSTEM OWNERSHIP %

PERIOD AND OWNERSHIP PERCENTAGE
(WHL=95-100%, MAJ=50-94%, MIN=5-49%, UNK=UNKNOWN)

COUNTRY OR REGION	TOTAL PRE 1968					PRE 1946					1946-1957					1958-1967				
	ALL	WHL	MAJ	MIN	UNK	ALL	WHL	MAJ	MIN	UNK	ALL	WHL	MAJ	MIN	UNK	ALL	WHL	MAJ	MIN	UNK
OUTSIDE U.S.	1342	720	370	134	118	211	132	51	16	12	68	36	15	12	5	1063	552	304	106	101
OUT. U.S. + CANADA	1211	620	355	128	108	178	103	48	16	11	60	29	14	12	5	973	488	293	100	92
OUT. WEST. HEMIS.	859	443	262	186	68	110	66	31	6	7	29	12	8	8	1	720	365	223	72	60
OUT. WHITE CWEALTH	953	450	290	118	95	141	76	41	15	9	51	24	13	9	5	761	350	236	94	81
OUT. DEVLPED WORLD	483	236	127	65	55	80	45	19	11	5	33	18	7	4	4	370	173	101	50	46
CANADA	131	100	15	6	10	33	29	3	0	1	8	7	1	0	0	90	64	11	6	9
LATIN AMERICA	352	177	93	42	40	68	37	17	6	4	31	17	6	4	4	253	123	70	28	32
C. AMER.+CARIB.	134	61	31	23	19	15	7	2	1	2	9	6	1	1	1	110	46	28	20	16
CUBA	5	3	1	1	0	3	1	1	1	0	1	1	0	0	0	1	1	0	0	0
MEXICO	91	45	19	16	11	11	7	1	1	1	5	1	0	1	0	75	35	17	15	8
OTHER	38	13	11	6	8	1	1	0	0	0	3	2	1	0	0	34	10	11	5	8
S. AMERICA	218	116	62	19	21	53	28	15	8	2	22	11	5	3	3	143	77	42	8	16
ARGENTINA	33	25	5	2	1	6	5	1	0	0	6	5	0	1	0	21	4	4	1	1
BRAZIL	62	39	16	3	4	20	12	5	2	1	5	3	0	0	2	37	24	11	0	2
PERU	22	10	9	3	0	4	4	1	1	0	4	2	0	1	0	14	8	6	0	0
COLOMBIA	33	15	11	3	4	8	4	3	3	1	0	0	0	0	0	25	11	8	2	4
VENEZUELA	39	14	8	5	12	8	3	3	1	0	0	0	0	0	0	29	11	6	3	9
OTHER	29	13	13	3	0	7	4	3	2	0	5	1	3	0	1	17	8	7	2	0
EUROPE	550	305	167	32	46	77	47	21	4	5	22	8	6	7	1	451	250	140	21	40
EFTA	186	124	39	6	17	26	19	5	1	1	7	3	2	2	0	153	102	32	3	16
U.K.	130	90	26	4	10	20	15	3	1	1	6	3	1	2	0	104	72	22	1	9
SCANDINAVIA	31	18	7	1	5	3	3	0	0	0	1	0	1	0	0	27	15	6	1	5
SWITZERLAND	10	8	2	0	0	2	1	1	0	0	0	0	0	0	0	8	7	1	0	0
OTHER EFTA	15	8	4	1	2	1	0	1	0	0	0	0	0	0	0	14	8	3	1	2
EUROP. COMMUNITY	287	146	100	15	26	42	22	15	2	3	10	4	2	3	1	235	120	83	10	22
FRANCE	71	32	28	6	5	7	6	0	1	0	4	2	1	2	0	60	24	28	3	5
GERMANY	81	41	26	4	10	17	8	7	0	2	3	1	1	0	1	61	32	18	4	7
ITALY	62	28	27	3	4	13	7	5	1	0	1	0	0	1	0	48	21	21	2	4
BELGIUM + LUX	39	24	10	2	3	2	0	1	0	1	1	0	1	0	0	36	24	9	1	2
NETHERLANDS	34	21	9	0	4	2	1	2	0	0	1	0	0	1	0	30	19	7	0	4
SPAIN	46	18	21	7	0	4	3	0	0	1	2	1	0	0	1	40	15	20	5	0
GREECE + TURKEY	16	7	5	2	2	3	2	0	1	0	1	0	0	1	0	13	6	3	2	2
OTHER EUROPE	15	10	2	2	1	3	2	0	0	1	2	1	1	0	0	10	7	2	1	0
EUROPE EX. U.K.	420	215	141	28	36	57	32	18	3	4	16	5	5	5	1	347	178	118	20	31
SOUTHERN DOMINIONS	116	72	37	5	2	14	10	4	0	0	3	2	0	0	0	99	60	33	4	2
S. AFRICA +RHOD.	29	20	8	1	0	4	2	2	0	0	3	2	0	0	0	25	18	6	3	0
AUSTRALIA +N.Z.	87	52	29	4	2	10	8	2	0	0	3	2	0	0	2	74	42	27	3	2
ASIA + OTHER AFRICA	193	66	58	49	20	19	9	6	2	2	4	2	2	1	0	170	55	50	47	18
JAPAN	62	7	24	26	5	7	1	4	1	1	2	1	2	0	0	53	5	18	25	5
OTHER ASIA+AFR.	131	59	34	23	15	12	8	2	1	1	2	1	1	0	0	117	50	31	22	14
BLACK AFRICA	22	16	3	2	2	1	0	1	0	0	1	0	1	0	0	21	16	2	2	2
ARAB WORLD	13	3	2	2	2	1	0	0	0	0	0	0	0	1	0	11	2	2	2	2
INDIA	26	11	2	9	3	4	4	0	0	0	1	0	1	0	0	23	6	2	10	3
PHILIPPINES	16	10	3	3	0	1	1	0	0	0	0	0	0	0	0	12	6	2	2	0
OTHER E. ASIA	12	5	3	1	1	1	1	0	0	0	0	0	0	0	0	11	4	3	1	3
OTHER ASIA	42	18	12	6	6	2	2	0	0	0	1	1	0	0	0	39	15	12	6	6

CHAPTER 5- PATTERNS OF OWNERSHIP
SECTION 5- THE FLOW OF MANUFACTURING BY CHARACTERISTIC OF SUBSIDIARY
TABLE C1- MANUFACTURING SUBSIDIARIES
WHICH WERE NEWLY FORMED,
CLASSIFIED BY COUNTRY, PERIOD MANUFACTURE BEGAN, AND SYSTEM OWNERSHIP %

PERIOD AND OWNERSHIP PERCENTAGE
(WHL=95-100%, MAJ=50-94%, MIN=5-49%, UNK=UNKNOWN)

COUNTRY OR REGION	TOTAL PRE 1968					PRE 1946					1946-1957					1958-1967				
	ALL	WHL	MAJ	MIN	UNK	ALL	WHL	MAJ	MIN	UNK	ALL	WHL	MAJ	MIN	UNK	ALL	WHL	MAJ	MIN	UNK
OUTSIDE U.S.	2183	1222	572	246	115	527	392	74	30	31	465	292	113	48	12	1163	538	385	168	72
OUT. U.S. + CANADA	1937	1019	539	241	110	404	285	62	28	29	399	242	100	46	11	1106	492	377	167	70
OUT. WEST. HEMIS.	1288	670	381	150	68	276	198	43	13	22	216	129	56	25	6	777	343	282	112	40
OUT. WHITE CWEALTH	1553	776	453	212	91	279	186	49	22	22	313	187	81	36	9	940	403	323	154	60
OUT. DEVLPED WORLD	862	440	231	127	52	144	100	20	15	9	215	128	57	24	6	491	212	154	88	37
CANADA	246	203	33	5	5	123	107	12	2	2	66	50	13	2	1	57	46	8	1	2
LATIN AMERICA	649	349	158	91	42	128	87	19	15	7	183	113	44	21	5	329	149	95	55	30
C. AMER.+CARIB.	261	132	62	46	17	54	33	7	10	4	67	50	10	6	1	136	49	45	30	12
CUBA	22	12	6	3	0	8	4	2	2	0	12	7	4	1	0	1	1	0	0	0
MEXICO	159	86	31	30	11	35	24	5	3	3	47	38	4	4	1	76	24	22	23	7
OTHER	80	34	25	13	5	11	5	0	5	1	8	5	2	1	0	59	24	23	7	5
S. AMERICA	388	217	96	45	26	74	54	12	5	3	116	63	34	15	4	193	100	50	25	18
ARGENTINA	73	44	16	8	2	26	23	3	0	0	17	7	6	4	0	27	14	7	4	2
BRAZIL	100	66	22	10	2	22	19	3	0	0	37	23	11	3	0	41	24	8	7	2
PERU	30	17	7	3	1	6	3	2	1	0	11	4	3	2	0	13	10	2	0	1
COLOMBIA	55	28	17	7	3	8	6	2	0	0	14	6	5	3	0	33	16	10	4	3
VENEZUELA	91	42	23	12	14	8	3	2	1	2	28	14	7	4	3	55	25	14	7	9
OTHER	39	20	11	6	2	6	3	0	3	0	9	6	3	0	1	24	11	8	4	1
EUROPE	771	434	217	61	49	192	131	33	9	19	132	85	26	17	4	437	218	158	35	26
EFTA	251	163	50	15	19	87	65	11	3	8	51	26	7	7	2	112	66	32	5	9
U.K.	158	100	30	13	12	60	45	6	3	6	42	24	7	7	1	56	31	17	3	5
SCANDINAVIA	49	34	12	1	2	12	10	2	0	0	7	1	0	0	0	30	23	10	1	2
SWITZERLAND	14	10	2	0	1	3	3	0	0	0	1	1	0	0	0	10	6	2	0	1
OTHER EFTA	30	19	6	1	4	12	7	3	0	2	1	0	0	0	1	17	12	3	1	1
EUROP. COMMUNITY	415	227	129	30	23	90	56	19	6	9	65	43	15	6	1	254	128	95	18	13
FRANCE	112	55	36	11	7	26	14	6	6	4	18	15	3	1	0	68	30	31	4	3
GERMANY	107	55	34	7	9	35	22	10	4	3	12	15	6	1	0	58	28	18	6	2
ITALY	100	57	31	9	3	14	9	4	0	1	22	16	3	3	0	64	32	24	6	2
BELGIUM + LUX	48	30	14	1	3	6	4	1	0	1	9	6	2	1	1	35	21	11	1	2
NETHERLANDS	48	30	14	2	1	9	7	2	0	1	7	4	1	2	0	29	17	11	0	1
SPAIN	54	18	23	10	3	7	3	0	0	1	6	1	3	2	1	40	11	19	8	2
GREECE + TURKEY	30	11	13	4	2	0	0	0	0	0	6	5	0	1	0	24	10	10	2	2
OTHER EUROPE	21	15	2	2	2	7	7	0	0	1	9	6	0	3	0	7	3	2	2	0
EUROPE EX. U.K.	613	334	187	48	37	132	86	27	6	13	93	61	19	10	3	381	187	141	32	21
SOUTHERN DOMINIONS	213	133	55	15	6	63	52	7	3	3	41	26	12	3	0	105	55	36	9	5
S. AFRICA +RHOD.	72	50	14	4	1	22	19	2	0	0	18	13	4	1	0	29	18	8	3	0
AUSTRALIA + N.Z.	141	83	41	11	6	41	33	5	3	3	23	13	8	2	0	76	37	28	6	5
ASIA + OTHER AFRICA	304	103	109	74	13	21	15	3	1	2	43	18	18	5	2	235	70	88	68	9
JAPAN	91	12	36	38	3	5	2	1	1	0	11	3	5	2	1	73	7	29	35	2
OTHER ASIA+AFR.	213	91	73	36	10	16	13	2	0	2	32	15	13	3	0	162	63	59	33	7
BLACK AFRICA	25	15	5	8	1	0	0	0	0	0	3	2	1	0	0	21	13	4	8	0
ARAB WORLD	24	7	8	4	1	0	0	0	0	0	2	1	1	0	0	22	6	7	4	1
INDIA	40	14	14	13	1	5	5	0	0	0	11	4	1	1	0	28	2	13	12	1
PHILIPPINES	34	21	8	4	1	4	4	0	0	0	1	1	0	0	0	18	11	8	4	1
OTHER E. ASIA	21	11	6	2	2	0	0	0	0	0	1	0	0	0	0	19	11	6	1	1
OTHER ASIA	69	26	32	5	5	4	4	0	0	1	9	2	6	0	1	54	20	25	5	4

CHAPTER 5- PATTERNS OF OWNERSHIP
SECTION 5- THE FLOW OF MANUFACTURING BY CHARACTERISTIC OF SUBSIDIARY
TABLE C2- MANUFACTURING SUBSIDIARIES
WHICH WERE ACQUIRED,
CLASSIFIED BY COUNTRY, PERIOD MANUFACTURE BEGAN, AND SYSTEM OWNERSHIP %

PERIOD AND OWNERSHIP PERCENTAGE
(WHL=95-100%, MAJ=50-94%, MIN=5-49%, UNK=UNKNOWN)

COUNTRY OR REGION	TOTAL ALL	TOTAL WHL	PRE 1968 MAJ	TOTAL MIN	TOTAL UNK	PRE 1946 ALL	PRE 1946 WHL	PRE 1946 MAJ	PRE 1946 MIN	PRE 1946 UNK	1946-1957 ALL	1946-1957 WHL	1946-1957 MAJ	1946-1957 MIN	1946-1957 UNK	1958-1967 ALL	1958-1967 WHL	1958-1967 MAJ	1958-1967 MIN	1958-1967 UNK
OUTSIDE U.S.	2199	1234	514	304	128	304	186	47	32	39	372	227	72	51	22	1504	821	395	221	67
OUT. U.S. + CANADA	1760	889	471	282	106	207	109	40	28	30	264	136	63	47	18	1277	644	368	207	58
OUT. WEST. HEMIS.	1280	678	331	181	81	160	86	34	16	24	166	91	30	31	14	945	501	267	134	43
OUT. WHITE CWEALTH	1266	561	380	240	76	133	62	27	23	21	190	88	53	36	13	934	411	300	181	42
OUT. DEVL PED WORLD	559	239	163	124	29	51	25	6	12	8	107	52	34	17	4	397	162	123	95	17
CANADA	439	345	43	22	22	97	77	7	4	9	108	91	9	4	4	227	177	27	14	9
LATIN AMERICA	480	211	140	101	25	47	23	6	12	6	98	45	33	16	1	332	143	101	73	15
C. AMER.+CARIB.	215	99	60	45	10	14	8	1	4	1	38	24	11	2	1	162	67	48	39	8
CUBA	8	5	0			5	3	0	1	1	2	1	1	0		1	1	0	0	0
MEXICO	158	78	43	29	8	9	5	1	3	0	32	21	10	1	0	117	52	32	26	7
OTHER	49	16	17	14		0	0	0	0	0	4	2	1	1	0	44	14	16	13	1
S. AMERICA	265	112	80	56	15	33	15	5	8	5	60	21	22	14	3	170	76	53	34	7
ARGENTINA	67	32	16	15		11	8	2	0	1	13	5	5	3	0	43	19	9	12	2
BRAZIL	71	33	19	11	8	9	3	0	4	2	19	5	8	3	3	43	25	11	4	3
PERU	19	8	8	3	0	3	2	1	0	0	5	1	2	2	0	11	5	5	1	0
COLOMBIA	44	16	17	10	0	2	0	0	1	0	10	4	3	3	0	31	12	13	6	0
VENEZUELA	34	14		8	3	1	0	1	0	0	8	3	4	1	0	25	6	10	7	2
OTHER	30	14	6	9	1	7	2	1	3	1	5	3	0	2	0	18	5	5	4	0
EUROPE	955	515	247	119	67	138	75	27	14	22	115	62	18	22	13	695	378	202	83	32
EFTA	349	235	58	27	26	70	44	12	3	10	46	28	6	8	4	230	163	40	15	12
U.K.	282	193	41	23	23	59	38	9	3	9	40	25	4	7	4	180	130	28	12	10
SCANDINAVIA	41	28	9	3	1	7	4	2	1	0	5	3	1	1	0	29	21	6	1	1
SWITZERLAND	13	8	3	1	1	1	0	0	1	0	0	0	0	0	0	12	8	3	1	1
OTHER EFTA	13	6	5	1	1	3	2	1	0	0	1	0	0	0	0	9	4	3	1	0
EUROP. COMMUNITY	506	255	145	66	36	59	29	14	8	8	58	29	11	10	8	385	197	120	48	20
FRANCE	167	69	55	20	12	26	14	6	4	2	13	4	4	2	3	126	51	45	23	7
GERMANY	144	82	39	15	8	19	6	6	4	3	28	19	4	2	3	97	54	29	11	3
ITALY	100	48	34	7	0	9	3	0	5	1	10	4	3	1	2	85	43	31	5	6
BELGIUM + LUX	53	33	8	9	2	5	1	1	1	2	3	1	0	2	0	45	31	8	6	0
NETHERLANDS	42	23	8	6	5	6	4	1	1	0	4	3	0	0	1	32	18	8	3	4
SPAIN	72	13	39	18	5	6	2	1	1	2	8	3	3	2	0	58	8	37	13	0
GREECE + TURKEY	7	1	1	1	0	0	0	0	0	0	0	0	0	0	0	7	1	1	2	0
OTHER EUROPE	21	11	4	5	3	2	0	0	1	1	3	2	0	0	1	15	9	4	2	0
EUROPE EX. U.K.	673	322	206	97	44	79	37	18	11	13	75	37	14	15	9	515	248	174	71	22
SOUTHERN DOMINIONS	196	126	46	18	6	15	9	4	2	0	31	21	6	4	0	150	96	36	12	6
S. AFRICA +RHOD.	66	46	11	9	6	2	1	0	1	0	7	5	1	1	0	57	40	10	7	0
AUSTRALIA + N.Z.	130	80	35	9	6	13	8	4	1	0	24	16	5	3	0	93	56	26	5	6
ASIA + OTHER AFRICA	129	37	38	44	8	7	2	3	2	0	20	8	8	5	1	100	27	29	39	5
JAPAN	50	9	15	21	4	4	0	0	3	0	11	1	1	4	0	35	8	14	17	3
OTHER ASIA+AFR.	79	28	23	23	4	3	2	3	0	0	9	7	7	1	1	65	19	22	22	1
BLACK AFRICA	10	5	2	2	1	0	0	0	0	0	0	0	0	0	0	10	5	2	2	1
ARAB WORLD	7	5	0	2	0	0	0	0	0	0	2	2	0	0	0	5	3	0	2	0
INDIA	20	3	5	11	1	0	0	0	0	0	0	0	0	0	0	20	3	5	11	1
PHILIPPINES	15	7	3	3	2	2	2	0	0	1	2	1	2	0	0	11	3	3	3	1
OTHER E. ASIA	10	5	2	1	2	2	0	0	1	1	1	1	0	0	0	7	4	2	1	0
OTHER ASIA	17	3	7	6	0	0	0	0	0	0	4	2	1	2	0	12	1	6	5	0

CHAPTER 5- PATTERNS OF OWNERSHIP
SECTION 6- CHANGES IN STATE OF BEING, MAIN ACTIVITY AND OWNERSHIP
TABLE 1- SUBSIDIARIES, MANUFACTURING OR NON-MANUFACTURING,
WHICH WERE LIQUIDATED OR EXPROPRIATED,
CLASSIFIED BY COUNTRY, PERIOD CHANGE OCCURRED, AND SYSTEM OWNERSHIP %

PERIOD AND OWNERSHIP PERCENTAGE
(WHL=95-100%, MAJ=50-94%, MIN=5-49%, UNK=UNKNOWN)

COUNTRY OR REGION	TOTAL PRE 1968					PRE 1946					1946-1957					1958-1967				
	ALL	WHL	MAJ	MIN	UNK	ALL	WHL	MAJ	MIN	UNK	ALL	WHL	MAJ	MIN	UNK	ALL	WHL	MAJ	MIN	UNK
OUTSIDE U.S.	2497	1909	303	89	196	449	325	56	7	61	497	400	53	16	28	1551	1184	194	66	107
OUT. U.S. + CANADA	1981	1459	282	84	156	307	214	48	6	39	387	303	48	15	21	1287	942	186	63	96
OUT. WEST. HEMIS.	1361	1028	186	52	95	247	172	40	6	29	267	216	25	11	15	847	640	121	35	51
OUT. WHITE CWEALTH	1504	1078	237	73	116	241	167	40	6	28	285	209	43	14	19	978	702	154	53	69
OUT. DEVLPED WORLD	716	501	113	34	68	78	57	9	0	12	145	106	26	5	8	493	338	78	29	48
CANADA	516	450	21	5	40	142	111	8	1	22	110	97	5	1	7	264	242	8	3	11
LATIN AMERICA	620	431	96	32	61	60	42	8	0	10	120	87	23	4	6	440	302	65	28	45
C. AMER.+CARIB.	339	236	47	19	37	34	21	7	0	6	57	39	12	2	4	248	176	28	17	27
CUBA	76	53	10	5	8	8	5	2	0	1	10	8	2	0	0	58	40	6	5	7
MEXICO	183	117	29	12	25	25	15	5	0	5	35	22	8	2	3	123	80	16	10	17
OTHER	80	66	8	2	4	1	1	0	0	0	12	9	2	0	1	67	56	6	2	3
S. AMERICA	281	195	49	13	24	26	21	1	0	4	63	48	11	2	2	192	126	37	11	18
ARGENTINA	64	46	10	6	2	5	5	0	0	0	16	10	5	1	0	43	31	5	5	2
BRAZIL	60	42	11	3	4	4	3	0	0	1	9	6	3	0	0	47	33	8	3	3
PERU	19	17	2	0	0	5	5	0	0	0	4	4	0	0	0	10	8	2	0	0
COLOMBIA	39	26	10	2	1	1	1	0	0	0	12	11	1	0	0	26	14	9	2	1
VENEZUELA	64	35	13	1	15	5	2	1	0	2	10	6	2	0	2	49	27	10	1	11
OTHER	35	29	3	1	2	6	5	0	0	1	12	11	0	1	0	17	13	3	0	1
EUROPE	1047	801	140	37	69	211	143	36	6	26	200	162	19	7	12	636	496	85	24	31
EFTA	462	381	42	9	30	77	54	11	0	12	96	86	6	2	2	289	241	25	7	16
U.K.	280	232	23	3	21	53	35	8	0	10	64	59	3	1	0	163	138	12	2	9
SCANDINAVIA	81	65	11	1	3	8	7	0	0	1	14	11	3	0	0	59	46	8	2	3
SWITZERLAND	72	62	5	2	3	9	6	3	0	0	12	10	0	2	0	51	46	2	0	3
OTHER EFTA	29	22	3	0	4	7	5	0	0	2	6	6	0	0	0	16	11	3	0	2
EUROP. COMMUNITY	481	350	87	16	28	101	66	22	3	10	63	49	10	0	4	317	235	55	13	14
FRANCE	144	95	31	6	12	36	19	8	2	7	17	13	2	0	2	91	63	21	4	3
GERMANY	133	102	21	3	7	31	24	5	0	2	22	17	4	1	0	80	61	12	2	5
ITALY	94	66	18	5	5	15	8	6	0	1	11	10	1	0	0	68	48	11	5	4
BELGIUM + LUX	51	38	10	1	2	5	4	1	0	0	9	5	3	1	0	37	29	6	1	1
NETHERLANDS	59	49	8	1	1	14	11	3	0	0	4	4	0	0	0	41	34	5	1	1
SPAIN	25	14	5	3	3	7	3	0	1	3	3	2	1	0	0	15	9	4	2	0
GREECE + TURKEY	10	6	3	1	0	2	1	2	0	0	2	1	0	0	0	6	4	1	1	0
OTHER EUROPE	69	50	13	3	8	25	20	3	0	2	35	23	2	5	5	9	7	0	1	1
EUROPE EX. U.K.	767	569	117	33	48	158	108	28	8	14	136	103	16	5	12	473	358	73	20	22
SOUTHERN DOMINIONS	187	140	22	7	18	12	11	0	0	1	36	33	2	1	0	139	96	20	6	17
S. AFRICA +RHOD.	51	40	6	4	1	2	1	0	1	0	12	11	0	0	1	37	28	6	3	0
AUSTRALIA + N.Z.	136	100	16	3	17	10	10	0	0	0	24	22	2	1	0	102	68	14	3	17
ASIA + OTHER AFRICA	127	87	24	8	8	24	18	4	1	2	31	21	4	3	3	72	48	16	4	3
JAPAN	31	17	7	6	1	6	3	3	5	0	6	2	1	0	3	19	12	3	1	3
OTHER ASIA+AFR.	96	70	17	2	7	18	15	1	2	0	25	19	3	3	0	53	36	13	4	1
BLACK AFRICA	14	6	6	1	1	2	1	1	0	0	4	3	0	1	0	8	3	4	1	0
ARAB WORLD	23	16	5	1	1	4	4	0	0	0	4	3	1	0	0	15	9	4	1	1
INDIA	6	4	2	0	0	1	0	1	0	0	2	2	0	0	0	3	3	0	0	0
PHILIPPINES	13	11	0	0	2	4	3	0	1	0	4	3	0	1	0	5	5	0	0	0
OTHER E. ASIA	17	13	2	0	2	4	3	0	0	1	5	2	2	0	1	8	8	0	0	0
OTHER ASIA	23	20	2	0	1	3	3	0	0	0	6	6	0	0	0	14	11	2	0	1

CHAPTER 5- PATTERNS OF OWNERSHIP
SECTION 6- CHANGES IN STATE OF BEING, MAIN ACTIVITY AND OWNERSHIP
TABLE 2- SUBSIDIARIES, MANUFACTURING OR NON-MANUFACTURING,
WHICH WERE SOLD, PERIOD CHANGE OCCURRED, AND SYSTEM OWNERSHIP %
CLASSIFIED BY COUNTRY, PERIOD CHANGE OCCURRED, AND SYSTEM OWNERSHIP %

PERIOD AND OWNERSHIP PERCENTAGE
(WHL=95-100%, MAJ=50-94%, MIN=5-49%, UNK=UNKNOWN)

COUNTRY OR REGION	TOTAL PRE 1968					PRE 1946					1946-1957					1958-1967				
	ALL	WHL	MAJ	MIN	UNK	ALL	WHL	MAJ	MIN	UNK	ALL	WHL	MAJ	MIN	UNK	ALL	WHL	MAJ	MIN	UNK
OUTSIDE U.S.	315	164	61	60	30	42	20	8	10	4	69	37	10	5	17	204	107	43	45	9
OUT. U.S. + CANADA	271	137	51	58	25	36	17	7	9	3	54	28	8	5	13	181	92	36	44	9
OUT. WEST. HEMIS.	206	103	37	45	21	25	11	6	7	1	43	19	6	5	13	138	73	25	33	7
OUT. WHITE CWEALTH	182	91	37	43	11	23	11	4	5	3	32	22	4	4	3	127	58	29	35	5
OUT. DEVLPED WORLD	79	43	15	16	5	11	6	1	2	2	13	10	2	0	1	55	27	12	14	2
CANADA	44	27	10	2	5	6	3	1	1	1	15	9	2	2	2	23	15	7	1	0
LATIN AMERICA	65	34	14	13	4	11	6	1	2	2	11	9	2	0	0	43	19	11	11	1
C. AMER.+CARIB.	27	18	2	7	0	4	2	1	1	0	3	3	0	0	0	20	13	1	6	0
CUBA	4	4	0	0	0	4	2	1	1	0	2	2	0	0	0	2	2	0	0	0
MEXICO	18	11	2	5	0	0	0	0	0	0	1	1	0	0	0	13	8	1	4	0
OTHER	5	3	0	2	0	0	0	0	0	0	0	0	0	0	0	5	3	0	2	0
S. AMERICA	38	16	12	6	4	7	4	0	1	2	8	6	2	0	0	23	6	10	5	2
ARGENTINA	8	6	1	0	1	2	1	1	0	0	1	1	0	0	0	5	1	0	4	0
BRAZIL	9	3	4	2	0	1	0	0	0	1	6	4	2	0	0	2	2	3	0	0
PERU	3	1	2	0	0	0	0	0	0	0	0	0	0	0	0	3	0	2	0	1
COLOMBIA	4	1	2	1	0	0	0	0	0	0	1	0	0	1	0	3	1	2	0	0
VENEZUELA	8	2	2	2	2	1	1	0	0	0	0	0	0	0	0	7	2	0	1	0
OTHER	6	3	1	1	1	3	1	1	1	0	0	0	0	0	0	2	1	1	0	0
EUROPE	157	75	31	33	18	20	9	5	5	1	38	17	4	5	12	99	49	22	23	5
EFTA	66	34	12	9	11	10	4	3	3	0	20	6	2	2	10	36	24	7	4	1
U.K.	54	26	9	8	11	9	4	3	2	0	19	5	1	2	10	26	17	4	4	1
SCANDINAVIA	7	5	1	1	0	1	0	0	1	0	0	0	0	0	0	5	4	1	0	0
SWITZERLAND	4	2	2	0	0	0	0	0	0	0	0	0	0	0	0	4	2	2	0	0
OTHER EFTA	1	1	0	0	0	0	0	0	0	0	0	0	0	0	0	1	1	0	0	0
EUROP. COMMUNITY	78	37	16	20	5	8	5	1	1	1	17	11	2	3	1	53	21	13	16	3
FRANCE	18	6	3	7	2	2	2	0	0	0	3	2	1	0	0	13	7	3	2	1
GERMANY	23	14	4	3	2	4	2	0	1	1	6	6	0	0	0	17	11	3	2	1
ITALY	14	8	4	3	0	1	0	0	0	0	2	1	0	1	0	7	1	3	3	0
BELGIUM + LUX	8	2	3	3	0	1	0	1	0	0	2	0	0	1	1	6	2	2	2	0
NETHERLANDS	15	7	3	4	1	1	1	0	0	0	4	2	1	1	0	10	5	2	2	1
SPAIN	6	2	1	2	1	0	0	0	0	0	1	0	0	0	1	5	2	1	2	0
GREECE + TURKEY	1	0	0	1	0	0	0	0	0	0	0	0	0	0	0	1	0	0	1	0
OTHER EUROPE	6	2	2	1	1	2	0	0	1	1	0	0	0	0	0	4	2	2	0	1
EUROPE EX. U.K.	103	49	22	25	7	11	5	2	3	1	19	12	2	3	2	73	32	18	19	4
SOUTHERN DOMINIONS	31	18	4	7	2	4	2	0	2	0	3	1	2	0	0	24	15	5	2	2
S. AFRICA +RHOD.	10	7	1	2	0	1	1	0	0	0	2	1	2	1	0	8	7	2	1	1
AUSTRALIA + N.Z.	21	11	3	5	2	3	1	0	2	0	2	2	1	1	0	16	9	1	5	2
ASIA + OTHER AFRICA	18	10	2	2	1	3	1	0	0	1	1	0	0	0	1	15	9	1	5	0
JAPAN	4	1	1	2	0	1	0	0	1	0	0	0	0	0	0	3	1	0	2	0
OTHER ASIA+AFR.	14	9	1	3	1	1	0	0	0	0	2	1	0	1	0	12	8	3	3	0
BLACK AFRICA	3	3	0	0	0	0	0	0	0	0	0	0	0	0	0	2	2	0	0	0
ARAB WORLD	1	0	0	1	0	0	0	0	0	0	0	0	0	0	0	2	0	1	1	0
INDIA	1	0	0	1	0	0	0	0	0	0	0	0	0	0	0	1	0	0	1	0
PHILIPPINES	3	1	1	1	0	1	1	0	0	0	1	1	0	0	0	3	1	1	1	0
OTHER E. ASIA	1	1	0	0	0	1	0	0	1	0	0	0	0	0	0	0	1	0	1	0
OTHER ASIA	5	5	0	0	0	0	0	0	0	0	0	0	0	0	0	5	5	0	0	0

CHAPTER 5- PATTERNS OF OWNERSHIP
SECTION 6- CHANGES IN STATE OF BEING, MAIN ACTIVITY AND OWNERSHIP
TABLE 3- MANUFACTURING SUBSIDIARIES
WHICH WERE LIQUIDATED OR EXPROPRIATED,
CLASSIFIED BY COUNTRY, PERIOD CHANGE OCCURRED, AND SYSTEM OWNERSHIP %

PERIOD AND OWNERSHIP PERCENTAGE
(WHL=95-100%, MAJ=50-94%, MIN=5-49%, UNK=UNKNOWN)

COUNTRY OR REGION	TOTAL PRE 1968					PRE 1946					1946-1957					1958-1967				
	ALL	WHL	MAJ	MIN	UNK	ALL	WHL	MAJ	MIN	UNK	ALL	WHL	MAJ	MIN	UNK	ALL	WHL	MAJ	MIN	UNK
OUTSIDE U.S.	1127	813	179	60	75	162	123	19	2	18	205	170	22	4	9	760	520	138	54	48
OUT. U.S. + CANADA	855	570	166	57	62	96	67	13	2	14	144	113	20	4	7	615	390	133	51	41
OUT. WEST. HEMIS.	554	389	102	30	33	80	53	12	2	13	92	79	7	2	4	382	257	83	26	16
OUT. WHITE CWEALTH	637	396	141	51	49	68	47	9	2	10	97	69	18	4	6	472	280	114	45	33
OUT. DEVLPED WORLD	332	203	70	28	31	21	18	1	0	2	59	40	13	2	4	252	145	56	26	25
CANADA	272	243	13	3	13	66	56	6	0	4	61	57	2	0	2	145	130	5	3	7
LATIN AMERICA	301	181	64	27	29	16	14	1	0	1	52	34	13	2	3	233	133	50	25	25
C. AMER.+CARIB.	152	93	28	17	14	4	4	0	0	0	23	14	7	1	1	121	72	20	16	13
CUBA	39	23	6	5	5	4	4	0	0	0	3	1	2	0	0	32	18	4	5	5
MEXICO	90	56	16	11	7	0	0	0	0	0	16	11	4	0	1	70	42	11	10	7
OTHER	23	14	6	1	2	0	0	0	0	0	4	2	1	1	0	19	12	5	1	1
S. AMERICA	149	88	36	10	15	8	7	0	0	1	29	20	6	1	2	112	61	30	9	12
ARGENTINA	40	27	6	5	2	4	4	0	0	0	11	8	2	0	1	25	15	4	4	2
BRAZIL	38	26	8	2	2	1	1	0	0	0	6	4	2	0	0	31	21	6	2	2
PERU	6	5	1	0	0	1	1	0	0	0	1	1	0	0	0	4	3	1	0	0
COLOMBIA	22	10	9	2	1	0	0	0	0	0	2	2	0	0	0	20	8	9	2	1
VENEZUELA	33	12	10	1	10	1	0	0	0	1	6	2	2	0	2	26	10	8	1	7
OTHER	10	8	2	0	0	1	1	0	0	0	3	3	0	0	0	6	4	2	0	0
EUROPE	421	296	76	20	29	67	44	9	2	12	62	53	5	1	3	292	199	62	17	14
EFTA	171	131	24	4	12	28	19	4	0	5	33	30	2	0	1	110	82	18	4	6
U.K.	125	101	12	2	10	23	15	4	0	4	25	23	1	0	1	77	63	7	2	5
SCANDINAVIA	29	18	8	2	1	1	1	0	0	0	4	3	1	0	0	24	14	7	2	1
SWITZERLAND	6	5	1	0	0	1	1	0	0	0	2	2	0	0	0	3	3	0	0	0
OTHER EFTA	11	7	3	0	1	3	2	0	0	1	2	2	0	0	0	6	3	3	0	0
EUROP. COMMUNITY	218	148	46	11	13	29	20	4	1	4	22	18	2	0	2	167	110	40	10	7
FRANCE	74	47	18	4	5	11	6	1	1	3	4	4	0	0	0	59	37	17	3	2
GERMANY	56	41	9	2	4	12	10	1	0	1	9	7	2	0	0	35	24	6	2	3
ITALY	47	32	10	3	2	3	1	1	0	1	3	3	0	0	0	41	28	9	3	1
BELGIUM + LUX	22	14	6	1	1	1	1	0	0	0	3	3	0	0	0	18	10	6	1	1
NETHERLANDS	19	14	3	1	1	2	2	0	0	0	1	1	0	0	0	16	11	3	1	1
SPAIN	12	4	3	3	2	3	2	0	0	1	1	1	0	0	0	8	1	3	3	1
GREECE + TURKEY	6	3	2	1	0	0	0	0	0	0	0	0	0	0	0	6	3	2	1	0
OTHER EUROPE	14	10	1	1	2	6	5	0	0	1	5	4	1	0	0	3	1	0	1	1
EUROPE EX. U.K.	296	195	64	18	19	44	29	5	2	8	37	30	4	1	2	215	136	55	15	9
SOUTHERN DOMINIONS	88	69	13	4	2	4	4	0	0	0	21	20	1	0	0	63	45	12	4	2
S. AFRICA +RHOD.	26	19	4	3	0	0	0	0	0	0	8	8	0	0	0	18	11	4	3	0
AUSTRALIA + N.Z.	62	50	9	1	2	4	4	0	0	0	13	12	1	0	0	45	34	8	1	2
ASIA + OTHER AFRICA	45	24	13	6	2	9	5	3	0	1	9	6	3	0	0	27	13	9	5	0
JAPAN	14	7	2	5	0	4	4	0	0	0	2	2	0	0	0	8	1	2	5	0
OTHER ASIA+AFR.	31	22	6	1	2	5	4	1	0	0	7	6	1	0	0	19	12	6	1	0
BLACK AFRICA	7	4	2	1	0	0	0	0	0	0	0	0	0	0	0	6	3	1	1	0
ARAB WORLD	4	4	2	0	0	0	0	0	0	0	0	0	0	0	0	2	1	0	0	0
INDIA	4	2	2	0	0	1	1	0	0	0	2	1	0	1	0	2	0	2	0	0
PHILIPPINES	4	2	0	0	2	1	0	0	0	1	1	1	0	0	0	2	0	0	0	2
OTHER E. ASIA	7	5	0	0	2	1	0	0	0	0	2	1	1	0	1	4	2	2	0	0
OTHER ASIA	8	6	2	0	0	2	2	0	0	0	2	2	0	0	0	4	2	2	0	0

CHAPTER 5- PATTERNS OF OWNERSHIP
SECTION 6- CHANGES IN STATE OF BEING, MAIN ACTIVITY AND OWNERSHIP
TABLE 4- MANUFACTURING SUBSIDIARIES
WHICH WERE SOLD,
CLASSIFIED BY COUNTRY, PERIOD CHANGE OCCURRED, AND SYSTEM OWNERSHIP %

PERIOD AND OWNERSHIP PERCENTAGE
(WHL=95-100%, MAJ=50-94%, MIN=5-49%, UNK=UNKNOWN)

COUNTRY OR REGION	TOTAL PRE 1968					PRE 1946					1946-1957					1958-1967				
	ALL	WHL	MAJ	MIN	UNK	ALL	WHL	MAJ	MIN	UNK	ALL	WHL	MAJ	MIN	UNK	ALL	WHL	MAJ	MIN	UNK
OUTSIDE U.S.	190	90	37	41	22	24	13	3	7	1	43	20	5	3	15	123	57	29	31	6
OUT. U.S. + CANADA	157	69	28	40	20	20	11	2	6	1	31	12	3	3	13	106	46	23	31	6
OUT. WEST. HEMIS.	124	51	21	33	19	15	7	2	5	1	27	8	3	3	13	82	36	16	25	5
OUT. WHITE CWEALTH	106	47	19	33	7	12	7	0	4	1	15	9	0	3	3	79	31	19	26	3
OUT. DEVLPED WORLD	39	21	8	8	2	5	4	0	1	0	5	4	0	0	1	29	13	8	7	1
CANADA	33	21	9	1	2	4	2	1	1	0	12	8	2	0	2	17	11	6	0	0
LATIN AMERICA	33	18	7	7	1	5	4	0	1	0	4	4	0	0	0	24	10	7	6	1
C. AMER.+CARIB.	15	11	1	3	0	1	1	0	0	0	3	3	0	0	0	11	7	1	3	0
CUBA	4	4	0	0	0	0	0	0	0	0	2	2	0	0	0	2	2	0	0	0
MEXICO	10	7	1	2	0	1	1	0	0	0	1	1	0	0	0	8	5	1	2	0
OTHER	1	0	0	1	0	0	0	0	0	0	0	0	0	0	0	1	0	0	1	0
S. AMERICA	18	7	6	4	1	4	3	0	1	0	1	1	0	0	0	13	3	6	3	1
ARGENTINA	2	2	0	0	0	1	1	0	0	0	0	0	0	0	0	1	1	0	0	0
BRAZIL	6	3	2	1	0	1	1	0	0	0	1	1	0	0	0	4	1	2	1	0
PERU	2	2	0	0	0	0	0	0	0	0	0	0	0	0	0	2	2	0	0	0
COLOMBIA	2	0	1	0	1	0	0	0	0	0	1	0	0	0	1	1	0	1	0	0
VENEZUELA	4	0	0	2	1	0	0	0	0	0	0	0	0	0	0	4	0	2	2	0
OTHER	2	1	0	1	0	2	1	0	0	1	0	0	0	0	0	0	0	0	0	0
EUROPE	105	42	19	27	17	13	6	2	4	1	25	8	2	3	12	67	28	15	20	4
EFTA	41	18	7	5	11	7	3	2	2	0	15	3	2	0	10	19	12	3	3	1
U.K.	37	15	7	4	11	6	3	2	1	0	15	3	2	0	10	16	9	3	3	1
SCANDINAVIA	3	2	0	0	0	0	0	0	0	0	0	0	0	0	0	2	2	0	0	0
SWITZERLAND	0	0	0	0	0	0	0	0	0	0	0	0	0	0	0	0	0	0	0	0
OTHER EFTA	1	1	0	0	0	0	0	0	0	0	0	0	0	0	0	1	1	0	0	0
EUROP. COMMUNITY	55	22	10	19	4	5	3	0	1	1	9	5	0	3	1	41	14	10	15	2
FRANCE	14	4	2	7	1	2	2	0	0	0	1	0	0	0	1	11	2	2	7	0
GERMANY	18	10	3	3	2	3	1	0	1	1	1	1	0	0	0	14	8	3	2	1
ITALY	9	3	3	3	0	0	0	0	0	0	2	2	0	0	0	7	1	3	3	0
BELGIUM + LUX	4	1	1	2	0	0	0	0	0	0	1	0	0	0	1	3	1	1	1	0
NETHERLANDS	10	4	1	4	1	0	0	0	0	0	2	2	0	0	0	6	2	1	3	1
SPAIN	4	1	1	1	1	0	0	0	0	0	1	0	0	0	1	3	1	1	1	0
GREECE + TURKEY	1	0	0	1	0	0	0	0	0	0	0	0	0	0	0	1	0	0	1	0
OTHER EUROPE	4	1	1	1	1	1	0	0	1	0	0	0	0	0	0	3	1	1	0	1
EUROPE EX. U.K.	68	27	12	23	6	7	3	0	3	1	10	5	0	3	2	51	19	12	17	3
SOUTHERN DOMINIONS	11	6	1	3	1	2	1	0	1	0	1	1	0	0	0	8	5	0	2	1
S. AFRICA +RHOD.	2	1	0	1	0	1	1	0	0	0	0	0	0	0	0	2	1	0	0	1
AUSTRALIA + N.Z.	9	5	1	2	1	2	0	0	2	0	1	1	0	0	0	6	4	1	1	1
ASIA + OTHER AFRICA	8	3	1	3	1	2	2	0	0	0	1	1	0	0	0	7	3	1	3	0
JAPAN	2	0	1	1	0	0	0	0	0	0	0	0	0	0	0	2	0	1	1	0
OTHER ASIA+AFR.	6	3	0	2	1	0	0	0	0	0	1	1	0	0	0	5	3	0	2	0
BLACK AFRICA	0	0	0	0	0	0	0	0	0	0	0	0	0	0	0	0	0	0	0	0
ARAB WORLD	0	0	0	0	0	0	0	0	0	0	0	0	0	0	0	0	0	0	0	0
INDIA	1	1	0	0	0	0	0	0	0	0	0	0	0	0	0	1	1	0	0	0
PHILIPPINES	2	1	1	0	0	0	0	0	0	0	0	0	0	0	0	2	1	1	0	0
OTHER E. ASIA	1	0	0	1	0	0	0	0	0	0	0	0	0	0	1	2	1	1	0	0
OTHER ASIA	2	2	0	0	0	0	0	0	0	0	0	0	0	0	0	2	2	0	0	0

CHAPTER 5- PATTERNS OF OWNERSHIP
SECTION 6- CHANGES IN STATE OF BEING, MAIN ACTIVITY AND OWNERSHIP
TABLE 5- NON-MANUFACTURING SUBSIDIARIES
WHICH BEGAN MANUFACTURING,
CLASSIFIED BY COUNTRY, PERIOD CHANGE OCCURRED, AND SYSTEM OWNERSHIP %

PERIOD AND OWNERSHIP PERCENTAGE
(WHL=95-100%, MAJ=50-94%, MIN=5-49%, UNK=UNKNOWN)

COUNTRY OR REGION	TOTAL PRE 1968					PRE 1946					1946-1957					1958-1967				
	ALL	WHL	MAJ	MIN	UNK	ALL	WHL	MAJ	MIN	UNK	ALL	WHL	MAJ	MIN	UNK	ALL	WHL	MAJ	MIN	UNK
OUTSIDE U.S.	289	207	40	6	36	71	52	10	1	8	88	65	13	1	9	130	90	17	4	19
OUT. U.S. + CANADA	266	191	38	6	31	60	44	8	1	7	81	60	13	1	7	125	87	17	4	17
OUT. WEST. HEMIS.	184	126	30	6	22	51	37	6	1	7	51	37	9	1	4	82	52	15	4	11
OUT. WHITE CWEALTH	198	140	31	6	21	34	26	5	1	2	63	46	11	1	5	101	68	15	4	14
OUT. DEVLPED WORLD	109	82	14	3	10	14	11	3	0	0	37	29	4	1	3	58	42	7	2	7
CANADA	23	16	2	0	5	11	8	2	0	1	7	5	0	0	2	5	3	0	0	2
LATIN AMERICA	82	65	8	0	9	9	7	2	0	0	30	23	4	0	3	43	35	2	0	6
C. AMER.+CARIB.	38	31	2	0	5	2	1	1	0	0	13	11	1	0	1	23	19	0	0	4
CUBA	5	4	1	0	0	1	1	0	0	0	3	3	0	0	0	1	1	0	0	0
MEXICO	26	21	1	0	4	1	0	1	0	0	7	5	1	0	1	18	15	0	0	3
OTHER	7	6	0	0	1	0	0	0	0	0	3	3	0	0	0	4	3	1	0	1
S. AMERICA	44	34	6	0	4	7	6	1	0	0	17	12	3	0	2	20	16	2	0	2
ARGENTINA	9	7	0	0	2	0	0	0	0	0	5	3	2	0	0	4	2	0	0	2
BRAZIL	14	10	3	0	1	4	4	0	0	0	7	4	2	0	1	6	6	0	0	0
PERU	2	1	1	0	0	1	1	0	0	0	0	0	0	0	0	1	0	1	0	0
COLOMBIA	5	5	0	0	0	1	1	0	0	0	1	0	1	0	0	3	3	0	0	0
VENEZUELA	8	6	1	0	1	0	0	0	0	0	4	2	1	0	1	4	4	0	0	0
OTHER	6	5	1	0	0	0	0	0	0	0	4	4	0	0	0	2	1	1	0	0
EUROPE	119	80	22	0	17	38	27	5	0	6	35	25	7	0	3	46	28	10	0	8
EFTA	54	32	11	0	11	21	12	4	0	5	17	12	3	0	2	16	8	4	0	4
U.K.	36	22	6	0	8	18	11	3	0	4	11	8	1	0	2	7	3	2	0	2
SCANDINAVIA	11	5	5	0	1	1	1	0	0	0	3	1	2	0	0	7	4	2	0	1
SWITZERLAND	4	3	0	0	1	1	0	1	0	0	2	2	0	0	0	1	0	0	0	1
OTHER EFTA	3	2	0	0	1	1	0	0	0	1	1	1	0	0	0	1	1	0	0	0
EUROP. COMMUNITY	58	41	11	0	6	13	11	1	0	1	18	13	4	0	1	27	17	6	0	4
FRANCE	15	10	4	0	1	3	2	1	0	0	5	3	2	0	0	5	3	2	0	0
GERMANY	22	16	3	0	3	2	2	0	0	0	9	7	2	0	0	11	7	2	0	3
ITALY	8	5	1	0	2	3	1	1	0	1	1	1	0	0	0	5	3	1	0	1
BELGIUM + LUX	7	6	1	0	0	1	1	0	0	0	1	1	0	0	0	3	3	1	0	0
NETHERLANDS	6	4	0	0	2	3	3	0	0	0	2	1	1	0	0	3	2	1	0	0
SPAIN	3	3	0	0	0	1	1	0	0	0	0	0	0	0	0	2	2	0	0	0
GREECE + TURKEY	1	1	0	0	0	0	0	0	0	0	0	0	0	0	0	1	1	0	0	0
OTHER EUROPE	3	3	0	0	0	3	3	0	0	0	0	0	0	0	0	0	0	0	0	0
EUROPE EX. U.K.	83	58	16	0	9	20	16	2	0	2	24	17	6	0	1	39	25	8	0	6
SOUTHERN DOMINIONS	31	28	0	0	2	7	6	0	0	1	7	6	1	0	0	17	16	0	0	1
S. AFRICA +RHOD.	10	10	0	0	0	1	1	0	0	0	1	1	0	0	0	8	8	0	0	0
AUSTRALIA + N.Z.	21	18	1	0	2	6	5	1	0	0	6	5	1	0	0	9	8	0	0	1
ASIA + OTHER AFRICA	34	18	7	6	3	6	4	1	1	0	9	6	1	1	1	19	8	5	4	2
JAPAN	27	17	6	1	3	1	0	1	0	0	2	2	0	0	0	4	1	2	0	1
OTHER ASIA+AFR.	15	7	1	6	1	5	4	0	1	0	7	4	1	1	1	15	7	5	2	1
BLACK AFRICA	6	4	0	1	1	0	0	0	0	0	0	0	0	0	0	1	1	0	0	0
ARAB WORLD	6	4	1	1	0	2	1	0	1	0	2	2	0	0	0	2	2	0	0	0
INDIA	5	2	3	0	0	0	0	0	0	0	1	0	1	0	0	2	2	3	0	1
PHILIPPINES	5	5	0	0	0	0	0	0	0	0	0	0	0	0	0	6	2	0	0	0
OTHER E. ASIA	2	5	1	1	1	0	0	0	0	0	5	5	0	0	0	2	2	1	1	1
OTHER ASIA	7	5	2	0	0	3	3	0	0	0	0	0	0	0	0	4	2	2	0	0

CHAPTER 5- PATTERNS OF OWNERSHIP
SECTION 6- CHANGES IN STATE OF BEING, MAIN ACTIVITY AND OWNERSHIP
TABLE 6- MANUFACTURING JOINT VENTURES
WHICH BECAME WHOLLY OWNED BY THE PARENT SYSTEM,
CLASSIFIED BY COUNTRY, PERIOD CHANGE OCCURRED, AND SYSTEM OWNERSHIP %

PERIOD AND OWNERSHIP PERCENTAGE
(WHL=95-100%, MAJ=50-94%, MIN=5-49%, UNK=UNKNOWN)

COUNTRY OR REGION	TOTAL PRE 1968					PRE 1946					1946-1957					1958-1967				
	ALL	WHL	MAJ	MIN	UNK	ALL	WHL	MAJ	MIN	UNK	ALL	WHL	MAJ	MIN	UNK	ALL	WHL	MAJ	MIN	UNK
OUTSIDE U.S.	464	0	314	69	81	50	0	29	9	12	80	0	57	8	15	334	0	228	52	54
OUT. U.S. + CANADA	403	0	274	63	66	37	0	22	6	9	61	0	43	7	11	305	0	209	50	46
OUT. WEST. HEMIS.	269	0	185	42	42	28	0	17	4	7	42	0	28	4	10	199	0	140	34	25
OUT. WHITE CWEALTH	314	0	214	51	49	27	0	13	5	9	45	0	32	6	7	242	0	169	40	33
OUT. DEVLPED WORLD	148	0	96	21	31	10	0	5	2	3	25	0	16	3	6	113	0	75	16	22
CANADA	61	0	40	6	15	13	0	7	3	3	19	0	14	1	4	29	0	19	2	8
LATIN AMERICA	134	0	89	21	24	9	0	5	2	2	19	0	15	3	1	106	0	69	16	21
C. AMER.+CARIB.	47	0	30	9	8	3	0	2	1	0	3	0	2	1	0	41	0	26	7	8
CUBA	7	0	5	1	1	1	0	1	0	0	0	0	0	0	0	6	0	4	1	1
MEXICO	33	0	22	5	6	2	0	1	1	0	3	0	2	1	0	28	0	19	3	6
OTHER	7	0	3	3	1	0	0	0	0	0	0	0	0	0	0	7	0	3	3	1
S. AMERICA	87	0	59	12	16	6	0	3	1	2	16	0	13	2	1	65	0	43	9	13
ARGENTINA	20	0	14	3	3	3	0	3	0	0	5	0	4	1	0	12	0	7	2	3
BRAZIL	25	0	19	2	4	1	0	0	0	1	5	0	4	1	0	19	0	15	1	3
PERU	5	0	4	0	1	0	0	0	0	0	1	0	1	0	0	4	0	3	0	1
COLOMBIA	15	0	10	3	2	0	0	0	0	0	0	0	0	0	0	15	0	10	3	2
VENEZUELA	16	0	9	3	4	1	0	0	0	1	4	0	3	0	1	11	0	6	3	2
OTHER	6	0	3	1	2	1	0	0	1	0	1	0	1	0	0	4	0	2	0	2
EUROPE	206	0	146	31	29	25	0	17	4	4	26	0	16	4	6	155	0	113	23	19
EFTA	65	0	45	7	13	11	0	7	2	2	8	0	5	1	2	46	0	33	4	9
U.K.	45	0	30	5	10	9	0	7	1	1	7	0	4	1	2	29	0	19	3	7
SCANDINAVIA	12	0	8	2	2	1	0	0	1	0	1	0	1	0	0	10	0	7	1	2
SWITZERLAND	3	0	3	0	0	0	0	0	0	0	0	0	0	0	0	3	0	3	0	0
OTHER EFTA	5	0	4	0	1	1	0	0	0	1	0	0	0	0	0	4	0	4	0	0
EUROP. COMMUNITY	129	0	95	21	13	12	0	9	1	2	18	0	11	3	4	99	0	75	17	7
FRANCE	41	0	35	6	0	2	0	2	0	0	2	0	2	0	0	37	0	31	6	0
GERMANY	33	0	25	3	5	8	0	6	1	1	6	0	4	0	2	19	0	15	2	2
ITALY	27	0	18	4	5	2	0	1	0	1	1	0	0	0	1	24	0	17	4	3
BELGIUM + LUX	14	0	9	3	2	0	0	0	0	0	4	0	4	0	0	10	0	5	3	2
NETHERLANDS	14	0	8	5	1	0	0	0	0	0	5	0	1	3	1	9	0	7	2	0
SPAIN	5	0	3	2	0	0	0	0	0	0	0	0	0	0	0	5	0	3	2	0
GREECE + TURKEY	2	0	2	0	0	1	0	1	0	0	0	0	0	0	0	1	0	1	0	0
OTHER EUROPE	5	0	1	1	3	1	0	0	1	0	0	0	0	0	0	4	0	1	0	3
EUROPE EX. U.K.	161	0	116	26	19	16	0	10	3	3	19	0	12	3	4	126	0	94	20	12
SOUTHERN DOMINIONS	40	0	29	7	4	1	0	0	0	1	9	0	9	0	0	30	0	20	7	3
S. AFRICA +RHOD.	15	0	7	5	3	1	0	0	0	1	3	0	3	0	0	11	0	4	5	2
AUSTRALIA + N.Z.	25	0	22	2	1	0	0	0	0	0	6	0	6	0	0	19	0	16	2	1
ASIA + OTHER AFRICA	23	0	10	4	9	0	0	0	0	0	9	0	1	2	6	14	0	9	2	3
JAPAN	9	0	6	1	2	0	0	0	0	0	2	0	0	0	2	7	0	6	1	0
OTHER ASIA+AFR.	14	0	4	3	7	0	0	0	0	0	7	0	1	2	4	7	0	3	1	3
BLACK AFRICA	3	0	0	1	2	0	0	0	0	0	0	0	0	0	0	3	0	0	1	2
ARAB WORLD	2	0	2	0	0	0	0	0	0	0	0	0	0	0	0	2	0	2	0	0
INDIA	1	0	1	0	0	0	0	0	0	0	1	0	1	0	0	0	0	0	0	0
PHILIPPINES	1	0	1	0	0	0	0	0	0	0	0	0	0	0	0	1	0	1	0	0
OTHER E. ASIA	3	0	0	1	2	0	0	0	0	0	3	0	0	1	2	0	0	0	0	0
OTHER ASIA	4	0	0	1	3	0	0	0	0	0	3	0	0	1	2	1	0	0	0	1

CHAPTER 5- PATTERNS OF OWNERSHIP
SECTION 6- CHANGES IN STATE OF BEING, MAIN ACTIVITY AND OWNERSHIP
TABLE 7- MANUFACTURING SUBSIDIARIES IN WHICH THE PARENT SYSTEM
"SIGNIFICANTLY" INCREASED ITS OWNERSHIP PERCENTAGE,
CLASSIFIED BY COUNTRY, PERIOD CHANGE OCCURRED, AND SYSTEM OWNERSHIP %

PERIOD AND OWNERSHIP PERCENTAGE
(WHL=95-100%, MAJ=50-94%, MIN=5-49%, UNK=UNKNOWN)

COUNTRY OR REGION	TOTAL PRE 1968 ALL	WHL	MAJ	MIN	UNK	PRE 1946 ALL	WHL	MAJ	MIN	UNK	1946-1957 ALL	WHL	MAJ	MIN	UNK	1958-1967 ALL	WHL	MAJ	MIN	UNK
OUTSIDE U.S.	456	0	314	142	0	42	0	29	13	0	76	0	57	19	0	338	0	228	110	0
OUT. U.S. + CANADA	399	0	274	125	0	30	0	22	8	0	56	0	43	13	0	313	0	209	104	0
OUT. WEST. HEMIS.	263	0	185	78	0	22	0	17	5	0	35	0	28	7	0	206	0	140	66	0
OUT. WHITE CWEALTH	318	0	214	104	0	20	0	13	7	0	44	0	32	12	0	254	0	169	85	0
OUT. DEVLPED WORLD	148	0	96	52	0	8	0	5	3	0	22	0	16	6	0	118	0	75	43	0
CANADA	57	0	40	17	0	12	0	7	5	0	20	0	14	6	0	25	0	19	6	0
LATIN AMERICA	136	0	89	47	0	8	0	5	3	0	21	0	15	6	0	107	0	69	38	0
C. AMER.+CARIB.	50	0	30	20	0	3	0	2	1	0	3	0	2	1	0	44	0	26	18	0
CUBA	7	0	5	2	0	1	0	1	0	0	0	0	0	0	0	6	0	4	2	0
MEXICO	35	0	22	13	0	2	0	1	1	0	3	0	2	1	0	30	0	19	11	0
OTHER	8	0	3	5	0	0	0	0	0	0	0	0	0	0	0	8	0	3	5	0
S. AMERICA	86	0	59	27	0	5	0	3	2	0	18	0	13	5	0	63	0	43	20	0
ARGENTINA	18	0	14	4	0	3	0	3	0	0	5	0	4	1	0	10	0	7	3	0
BRAZIL	27	0	19	8	0	0	0	0	0	0	7	0	4	3	0	20	0	15	5	0
PERU	4	0	4	0	0	0	0	0	0	0	1	0	1	0	0	3	0	3	0	0
COLOMBIA	15	0	10	5	0	0	0	0	0	0	0	0	0	0	0	15	0	10	5	0
VENEZUELA	16	0	9	7	0	0	0	0	0	0	4	0	3	1	0	12	0	6	6	0
OTHER	6	0	3	3	0	2	0	0	2	0	1	0	1	0	0	3	0	2	1	0
EUROPE	202	0	146	56	0	20	0	15	5	0	24	0	18	6	0	158	0	113	45	0
EFTA	57	0	45	12	0	10	0	8	2	0	5	0	4	1	0	42	0	33	9	0
U.K.	40	0	30	10	0	9	0	8	1	0	4	0	3	1	0	27	0	19	8	0
SCANDINAVIA	10	0	8	2	0	1	0	0	1	0	1	0	1	0	0	8	0	7	1	0
SWITZERLAND	3	0	3	0	0	0	0	0	0	0	0	0	0	0	0	3	0	3	0	0
OTHER EFTA	4	0	4	0	0	0	0	0	0	0	0	0	0	0	0	4	0	4	0	0
EUROP. COMMUNITY	125	0	95	30	0	7	0	6	1	0	17	0	14	3	0	101	0	75	26	0
FRANCE	47	0	35	12	0	1	0	1	0	0	3	0	3	0	0	43	0	31	12	0
GERMANY	28	0	25	3	0	5	0	4	1	0	6	0	6	0	0	17	0	15	2	0
ITALY	25	0	18	7	0	0	0	0	0	0	1	0	1	0	0	24	0	17	7	0
BELGIUM + LUX	14	0	10	4	0	1	0	1	0	0	3	0	2	1	0	10	0	7	3	0
NETHERLANDS	11	0	7	4	0	0	0	0	0	0	4	0	2	2	0	7	0	5	2	0
SPAIN	14	0	3	11	0	1	0	1	0	0	1	0	0	1	0	12	0	2	10	0
GREECE + TURKEY	3	0	2	1	0	1	0	0	1	0	0	0	0	0	0	2	0	2	0	0
OTHER EUROPE	3	0	1	2	0	1	0	0	1	0	1	0	0	1	0	1	0	1	0	0
EUROPE EX. U.K.	162	0	116	46	0	11	0	7	4	0	20	0	15	5	0	131	0	94	37	0
SOUTHERN DOMINIONS	40	0	29	11	0	1	0	1	0	0	8	0	8	0	0	31	0	20	11	0
S. AFRICA +RHOD.	13	0	7	6	0	1	0	1	0	0	2	0	2	0	0	10	0	4	6	0
AUSTRALIA + N.Z.	27	0	22	5	0	0	0	0	0	0	6	0	6	0	0	21	0	16	5	0
ASIA + OTHER AFRICA	21	0	10	11	0	1	0	1	0	0	3	0	2	1	0	17	0	7	10	0
JAPAN	9	0	3	6	0	1	0	1	0	0	2	0	1	1	0	6	0	1	5	0
OTHER ASIA+AFR.	12	0	7	5	0	0	0	0	0	0	1	0	1	0	0	11	0	6	5	0
BLACK AFRICA	2	0	2	0	0	0	0	0	0	0	0	0	0	0	0	2	0	2	0	0
ARAB WORLD	3	0	2	1	0	0	0	0	0	0	0	0	0	0	0	3	0	2	1	0
INDIA	2	0	1	1	0	0	0	0	0	0	1	0	1	0	0	1	0	0	1	0
PHILIPPINES	4	0	1	3	0	0	0	0	0	0	0	0	0	0	0	4	0	1	3	0
OTHER E. ASIA	0	0	0	0	0	0	0	0	0	0	0	0	0	0	0	0	0	0	0	0
OTHER ASIA	1	0	1	0	0	0	0	0	0	0	0	0	0	0	0	1	0	1	0	0

CHAPTER 5- PATTERNS OF OWNERSHIP
SECTION 6- CHANGES IN STATE OF BEING, MAIN ACTIVITY AND OWNERSHIP
TABLE 8- MANUFACTURING SUBSIDIARIES IN WHICH THE PARENT SYSTEM
"SIGNIFICANTLY" DECREASED ITS OWNERSHIP PERCENTAGE,
PERIOD CHANGE OCCURRED, AND SYSTEM OWNERSHIP %
CLASSIFIED BY COUNTRY,

PERIOD AND OWNERSHIP PERCENTAGE
(WHL=95-100%, MAJ=50-94%, MIN=5-49%, UNK=UNKNOWN)

COUNTRY OR REGION	TOTAL PRE 1968					PRE 1946					1946-1957					1958-1967				
	ALL	WHL	MAJ	MIN	UNK	ALL	WHL	MAJ	MIN	UNK	ALL	WHL	MAJ	MIN	UNK	ALL	WHL	MAJ	MIN	UNK
OUTSIDE U.S.	290	259	31	0	0	33	32	1	0	0	49	46	3	0	0	208	181	27	0	0
OUT. U.S. + CANADA	243	213	30	0	0	21	20	1	0	0	37	35	2	0	0	185	158	27	0	0
OUT. WEST. HEMIS.	154	137	17	0	0	16	15	1	0	0	22	22	0	0	0	116	100	16	0	0
OUT. WHITE CWEALTH	191	165	26	0	0	16	15	1	0	0	25	23	2	0	0	150	127	23	0	0
OUT. DEVLPED WORLD	103	87	16	0	0	6	6	0	0	0	16	14	2	0	0	81	67	14	0	0
CANADA	47	46	1	0	0	12	12	0	0	0	12	11	1	0	0	23	23	0	0	0
LATIN AMERICA	89	76	13	0	0	5	5	0	0	0	15	13	2	0	0	69	58	11	0	0
C. AMER.+CARIB.	42	37	5	0	0	0	0	0	0	0	6	4	2	0	0	36	33	3	0	0
CUBA	8	8	0	0	0	0	0	0	0	0	1	1	0	0	0	7	7	0	0	0
MEXICO	27	24	3	0	0	0	0	0	0	0	3	2	1	0	0	24	22	2	0	0
OTHER	7	5	2	0	0	0	0	0	0	0	2	1	1	0	0	5	4	1	0	0
S. AMERICA	47	39	8	0	0	5	5	0	0	0	9	9	0	0	0	33	25	8	0	0
ARGENTINA	12	12	0	0	0	1	1	0	0	0	4	4	0	0	0	7	7	0	0	0
BRAZIL	14	12	2	0	0	1	1	0	0	0	3	3	0	0	0	10	8	2	0	0
PERU	2	1	1	0	0	0	0	0	0	0	1	1	0	0	0	1	0	1	0	0
COLOMBIA	7	4	3	0	0	1	1	0	0	0	0	0	0	0	0	6	3	3	0	0
VENEZUELA	9	7	2	0	0	1	1	0	0	0	1	1	0	0	0	7	5	2	0	0
OTHER	3	3	0	0	0	1	1	0	0	0	0	0	0	0	0	2	2	0	0	0
EUROPE	108	97	11	0	0	14	13	1	0	0	13	13	0	0	0	81	71	10	0	0
EFTA	35	34	1	0	0	4	4	0	0	0	5	5	0	0	0	26	25	1	0	0
U.K.	24	23	1	0	0	4	4	0	0	0	4	4	0	0	0	16	15	1	0	0
SCANDINAVIA	7	7	0	0	0	0	0	0	0	0	0	0	0	0	0	7	7	0	0	0
SWITZERLAND	1	1	0	0	0	0	0	0	0	0	0	0	0	0	0	1	1	0	0	0
OTHER EFTA	3	3	0	0	0	0	0	0	0	0	1	1	0	0	0	2	2	0	0	0
EUROP. COMMUNITY	67	58	9	0	0	9	8	1	0	0	7	7	0	0	0	51	43	8	0	0
FRANCE	22	19	3	0	0	5	4	1	0	0	1	1	0	0	0	16	14	2	0	0
GERMANY	11	10	1	0	0	2	2	0	0	0	4	4	0	0	0	5	4	1	0	0
ITALY	18	15	3	0	0	1	1	0	0	0	0	0	0	0	0	17	14	3	0	0
BELGIUM + LUX	10	9	1	0	0	0	0	0	0	0	0	0	0	0	0	10	9	1	0	0
NETHERLANDS	6	5	1	0	0	1	1	0	0	0	2	2	0	0	0	3	2	1	0	0
SPAIN	4	3	1	0	0	0	0	0	0	0	0	0	0	0	0	4	3	1	0	0
GREECE + TURKEY	0	0	0	0	0	0	0	0	0	0	0	0	0	0	0	0	0	0	0	0
OTHER EUROPE	2	2	0	0	0	1	1	0	0	0	1	1	0	0	0	0	0	0	0	0
EUROPE EX. U.K.	84	74	10	0	0	10	9	1	0	0	9	9	0	0	0	65	56	9	0	0
SOUTHERN DOMINIONS	28	25	3	0	0	1	1	0	0	0	8	8	0	0	0	19	16	3	0	0
S. AFRICA +RHOD.	5	5	0	0	0	1	1	0	0	0	1	1	0	0	0	3	3	0	0	0
AUSTRALIA + N.Z.	23	20	3	0	0	0	0	0	0	0	7	7	0	0	0	16	13	3	0	0
ASIA + OTHER AFRICA	18	15	3	0	0	1	1	0	0	0	1	1	0	0	0	16	13	3	0	0
JAPAN	4	4	0	0	0	0	0	0	0	0	0	0	0	0	0	4	4	0	0	0
OTHER ASIA+AFR.	14	11	3	0	0	1	1	0	0	0	1	1	0	0	0	12	9	3	0	0
BLACK AFRICA	1	1	0	0	0	0	0	0	0	0	0	0	0	0	0	1	1	0	0	0
ARAB WORLD	2	2	0	0	0	0	0	0	0	0	0	0	0	0	0	2	2	0	0	0
INDIA	2	1	1	0	0	1	1	0	0	0	0	0	0	0	0	1	0	1	0	0
PHILIPPINES	3	3	0	0	0	0	0	0	0	0	0	0	0	0	0	3	3	0	0	0
OTHER E. ASIA	0	0	0	0	0	0	0	0	0	0	0	0	0	0	0	0	0	0	0	0
OTHER ASIA	6	4	2	0	0	0	0	0	0	0	1	1	0	0	0	5	3	2	0	0